Third Edition

COST ACCOUNTING

Third Edition

COST ACCOUNTING

Processing, Evaluating, and Using Cost Data

Wayne J. Morse
Clarkson University

Harold P. Roth
University of Tennessee at Knoxville

ADDISON-WESLEY PUBLISHING COMPANY
Reading, Massachusetts • Menlo Park, California
Don Mills, Ontario • Wokingham, England • Amsterdam • Bonn • Sydney
Singapore • Tokyo • Madrid • Bogota • Santiago • San Juan

WORLD STUDENT SERIES EDITION

Sponsoring Editor: Frank Burns
Copy Editor: Margaret Hill
Text Designer: Catherine Johnson Dorin
Illustrator: Textbook Art Associates
Manufacturing Supervisor: Hugh Crawford

ISBN 0-201-05523-6
DEFGH-DO-8987

Preface

THE OBJECTIVES OF THIS BOOK ARE TO PROVIDE THE STUDENT WITH A thorough grounding in cost concepts, cost behavior, and costing techniques and with an understanding of the uses and limitations of cost data in planning and control and special decisions. After successfully completing this book the student will be able to:

- Assist in the development of cost accounting data for use in external and internal reports.
- Properly use accounting data in short-run decisions.
- Participate in annual and long-range budgeting activities.
- Understand the information feedback process and how accounting data are used in performance evaluation.
- Assist in the development of performance reports.
- Appreciate the issues in human behavior that are involved in budgeting and performance evaluation.

Topics discussed herein are important to users and suppliers of cost accounting information. Those who use cost accounting information must understand its characteristics; those who supply it must be familiar with its uses and limitations.

KEEPING PACE WITH A CHANGING WORLD

Although the second edition of *Cost Accounting* received wide market acceptance, the third edition is a major revision intended to keep abreast of important changes that have occurred in recent years. Four major factors influencing the third edition of *Cost Accounting* are: (1) changes in the structure of introductory accounting courses; (2) the explosive growth in the availability and use of spreadsheet software; (3) the increased emphasis by managers on product quality; and (4) the continuing trend towards a more service oriented economy.

In recent years the traditional coverage of introductory accounting courses has expanded to include more management accounting, and even some cost accounting, topics. Accounting principles textbooks have devoted increasing space to these topics, and many schools have opted for separate courses in financial and managerial accounting as an alternative to a two-course sequence in principles. The net result is some frustration with cost accounting textbooks whose early chapters appear to be an introductory level rehash of management accounting and whose cost assignment chapters do not appear to go beyond the coverage contained in popular management accounting textbooks. In response to these problems, the third edition of *Cost Accounting* has been restructured to provide an earlier and more thorough coverage of cost assignment topics, and greater flexibility in selecting the depth of coverage of management accounting topics.

The availability of personal computers (pc) and spreadsheet software is having a profound effect on accounting education. As a minimum, accounting educators must teach students how computers and spreadsheets can be used in accounting. Under ideal circumstances, accounting educators should use the computer to help teach accounting. Properly used, the computer can help students obtain a greater understanding of accounting concepts, techniques, and the impact of alternative techniques on decision models. Significantly, it may be possible to obtain this greater understanding in less time, thereby increasing the productivity of each class or study hour. To take full advantage of the pc and spreadsheet software, well designed instructional materials are needed. Instructional materials, such as exercises and problems, designed for solution with pencil and paper, may not be satisfactory pedagogical vehicles when the sudents' task is to develop a spreadsheet template that can be used for a particular type of problem. Hence the third edition of *Cost Accounting* contains a large number of exercises and problems designed to facilitate assignments involving the development of spreadsheet templates. Thirty completed spreadsheet templates are also available for the use of the instructor.

The authors' recent experiences in management development programs, consulting activities, and research activities, have led them to conclude that students need exposure to a variety of quality related topics seldom included in cost accounting texts. Accordingly, the topical coverage of the third edition has been expanded to include quality costs and a more thorough treatment of statistical process control.

Although it is not new, the trend toward a more service oriented economy is continuing. Recognizing the need to accurately determine the cost of providing services and the transferability of many product-costing concepts to service costing, the third edition of *Cost Accounting* contains additional assignment material dealing with service industries. A detailed list of new topics and topics receiving expanded attention is presented in the following section.

MAJOR CHANGES IN THE THIRD EDITION

An obvious addition to the book is a second author, Harold P. Roth of the University of Tennessee at Knoxville. It was our belief that the addition of a second author at this time allows for more knowledgeable coverage of significant topics, serves as a source of new problem material, provides a capability to thoroughly update all elements of the book, and keeps the book fresh and vigorous. Additional major changes are as follows:

- The book has been reorganized to place greater emphasis on cost assignment topics. Chapters 2 through 6 provide a thorough grounding in product-costing concepts with additional product-costing topics being covered in Chapters 14 and 20. The authors believe students have a greater appreciation of cost estimation, cost-volume-profit analysis, budgeting, and special decisions in short-range planning *after* they study product costing. Furthermore, students who have had exposure to management accounting prior to enrolling in cost accounting are capable of approaching management accounting issues in greater depth *after* a detailed study of product costing. Exposure to management accounting topics prior to a study of product costing is necessarily at a lower level.
- The book has also been reorganized to give the instructor greater flexibility in selecting the appropriate depth of coverage of quantitative topics. The instructor can choose between an awareness level of coverage or an in-depth study of how quantitative techniques are used to analyze cost data and how cost data are used in quantitative models. This flexibility has been accomplished by the generous use of appendices in chapters dealing with quantitative topics. Placing more advanced quantitative topics in appendices allows the instructor to integrate this material into the mainstream presentation or defer it to another course. Note especially the appendices to Chapters 7, 8, 15, 16, 18, and 19.
- The book has been increased from 19 to 21 chapters. This was accomplished by splitting the previous chapter on Divisional Performance Evaluation and Transfer Pricing into two chapters: Responsibility Accounting for Investment Centers (Chapter 13), and Transfer Pricing (Chapter 21). A previous chapter appendix on Payroll and Labor Distribution Accounting has been expanded into a complete chapter on Special Considerations in Payroll Accounting (Chapter 20).
- The former chapter on the Significance of Production Variances has been extensively revised into the new Chapter 19: Quality Control and Variance Analysis. The chapter now contains an introduction to statistical process control and quality costs.
- A large number of exercises and problems have been specifically prepared to support course assignments requiring students to develop or use spreadsheets. These materials are clearly identified in their topical heading with the letter T. They are also summarized in the instructor's manual.
- The following topics received significant attention in the preparation of the third edition:

  Product costing and service costing (Chapter 2)

  Costs and decision making (Chapter 2)

  When to establish departmental cost pools (Chapter 3)

  Spoilage (Chapter 4)

  Purposes of cost allocation (Chapter 6)

  Cost allocation techniques (Chapter 6)

  Data requirements and limitations (Chapter 7)

  Statistical considerations in regression analysis (Chapter 7 appendix)

  Learning curve analysis (Chapter 7 appendix)

  Extensions of the C-V-P model (Chapter 8)

Underapplied and overapplied overhead (Chapter 9)
Segment reporting (Chapter 9)
Extended budgeting example (Chapter 10 appendix)
Responsibility reports and corporate structure (Chapter 11)
Additional considerations in responsibility accounting (Chapter 11)
Production mix and yield variances (Chapter 11 appendix)
Marketing performance reports (Chapter 12)
Multiple product sales variances (Chapter 12)
Multinational companies (Chapter 13)
Agency theory (Chapter 13)
Spoilage (Chapter 14)
Prorating variances (Chapter 14)
Standard costs for joint products (Chapter 14 appendix)
Special decisions based on differential analysis (Chapter 15)
Information acquisition decisions (Chapter 15)
Product mix decisions with multiple constraints (Chapter 15 appendix)
Taxes and capital budgeting (Chapter 16)
Changing prices and capital investment models (Chapter 16 appendix)
Depreciation methods and measures of investment performance (Chapter 16 appendix)
Investment and financing decisions (Chapter 17)
Approaches to inventory planning and control (Chapter 18)
Statistical significance of variances (Chapter 19)
Quality costs (Chapter 19)
Payroll accounting (Chapter 20)
Transfer pricing (Chapter 21)

PEDAGOGICAL FEATURES

Significant pedagogical features of *Cost Accounting* include the following:

- An outline presented at the start of each chapter provides an orientation to the chapter material and its structure.
- The purpose or primary learning objective of each chapter is clearly stated and highlighted in the introduction to each chapter.
- Key terms are highlighted when first introduced, listed at the end of each chapter, and defined in a glossary at the back of the book.
- Important relationships are always expressed in words.
- A summary at the end of each chapter reiterates key points of the chapter.
- Review questions at the end of each chapter ask the student to recall basic concepts presented in the chapter. The questions are sequenced to the order in which topics are introduced in the chapter.

- Nineteen chapters contain review problems whose solutions are contained at the end of the chapter assignment material.
- The end-of-chapter exercises reinforce the student's knowledge of basic material contained in the chapter. Exercises are generally short and are sequenced in the order in which topics are introduced in the chapter.
- The end-of-chapter problems provide detailed assignments related to the material presented in the chapter. Many problems are also designed to integrate the material from several chapters or to relate cost accounting to topics covered in other courses or to illustrate the use of accounting information in the kinds of unstructured decision situations managers and professional accountants are likely to encounter.
- The topical coverage of each exercise and problem is clearly identified in a boldface heading.
- The book contains over 850 questions, exercises, and problems, including almost 150 representative exercises and problems adapted from professional examinations.
- Problems designed to facilitate spreadsheet assignments are clearly identified with a boldface letter T.
- Suggested readings for further study provide a starting point for a more detailed study of material introduced in the text.

SUPPLEMENTS

Supplementary materials accompanying the text include an instructor's manual, instructor's spreadsheet template disks, transparencies for selected problems and exercises, checklists of key figures, an instructor's test bank, and a student study guide. The instructor's manual contains:

- Illustrative course outlines.
- Exercises and problems classified as to level of difficulty.
- Exercises and problems classified as to estimated completion times.
- Detailed solutions to all review questions, exercises, and problems.
- Hints on computer spreadsheet assignments and a list of exercises and problems prepared to facilitate spreadsheet assignments. Naturally, these materials can also be used without a computer.
- A list of check figures for exercises and problems.

The instructor's spreadsheet template disk, prepared by Wayne J. Morse, contains 30 templates. All templates are complete with illustrative data taken from textbook examples and review problems. The templates also serve as the solutions guide to text exercises and problems designated as appropriate for spreadsheet solution. Templates are available in Lotus 1-2-3 and Microsoft Multiplan for the IBM pc, and IBM pc compatible computers. A separate manual contains printouts of all templates and offers suggestions for their use.

The instructor's test bank, prepared by Professor G. A. Swanson of Tennessee Technological University, contains true-false, matching, and objective questions, as well as short problems, organized on a chapter by chapter basis.

The student study guide, prepared by Professor Imogene Posey of the University of Tennessee at Knoxville and Harold Roth, contains separate learning units for each chapter and major chapter appendix. Each learning unit contains:

- Learning objectives.
- Review material.
- Self-test (completion, multiple choice, and exercises).
- Detailed solutions to the self-test.

ORGANIZATION

The text is divided into an introductory chapter and four parts. Instructors in a single semester course will likely cover Chapter 1 (Introduction), all materials in Part I (Processing Cost Data With Actual and Normal Cost Systems), all but the appendix materials in Part II (Evaluating and Using Cost Data for Planning), and selected materials from Parts III (Evaluating and Using Cost Data for Performance Evaluation), and IV (Selected Topics for Further Study). The most likely chapters to be covered from Part III are Chapters 11 (Responsibility Accounting for Cost Centers) and 14 (Standard Cost Systems). The structure of the book is such that Chapter 14 should not be covered before Chapters 4 and 11.

In programs where students have not had previous exposure to management accounting topics, instructors may desire earlier coverage of Part II. It is possible to assign materials from Part II anytime after Chapter 3 is assigned. The structure of the book is such that an earlier assignment of these chapters is not recommended. In graduate programs or programs where students have had previous exposure to management accounting topics, instructors may obtain a more in-depth coverage of Part II topics by assigning the appendix materials accompanying Part II chapters and selecting appropriate topics from Part IV.

While there is considerable flexibility in the assignment of Part IV topics, Chapter 8 should normally be covered before Chapters 15 (Special Decisions in Short Range Planning), 16 (Capital Budgeting I), 17 (Capital Budgeting II), or 18 (Inventory Planning and Control Systems). It is also recommended that Chapter 11 be covered before Chapter 19 (Quality Control and Variance Analysis), Chapter 3 be covered before Chapter 20 (Special Considerations in Payroll Accounting), and Chapter 13 be covered before Chapter 21 (Transfer Pricing). A number of suggested course outlines are contained in the instructor's manual.

ACKNOWLEDGMENTS

Cost Accounting could not have been completed without the generous cooperation, assistance, and support of numerous individuals and organizations. We are indebted to the following professors who offered helpful comments on the second edition of the textbook or the manuscript for the third:

Earl Anderson (University of Nebraska at Omaha)

Yezdi K. Bhada (Georgia State University)

Robert Campbell (Miami University of Ohio)

Robert Capettini (San Diego State University)

C. Margaret Briscall (British Columbia Institute of Technology)

Norm Dittrich (University of Tennessee at Knoxville)

Gary A. Fox (Miami University of Ohio)

Jeff Gillespie (University of Delaware)

Michael J. Gift (Indiana University at Bloomington)

Song K. Kim (University of Illinois at Urbana-Champaign)

S. Laimon (University of Saskatchewan)

Wallace R. Lease (California State University at Chico)

Pat McKenzie (Arizona State University)

Alfred Nanni (Boston University)

Imogene A. Posey (University of Tennessee at Knoxville)

Howard Rockness (University of North Carolina at Chapel Hill)

Peter Silhan (University of Illinois at Urbana-Champaign)

Howard R. Toole (San Diego State University)

A special note of thanks goes to our students at Clarkson University and the University of Tennessee. We are indebted to them both for their comments on the second edition and for their feedback on material new to the third.

Materials from Uniform CPA Examinations, Copyright 1965 through 1983 by the American Institute of Certified Public Accountants, Inc., are adapted with permission. They are identified as "CPA adapted."

Materials from CMA Examinations, Copyright 1972 through 1983 by the (USA) National Association of Accountants, are adapted with permission. They are identified as "CMA adapted."

Materials from CGA Examinations, Copyright 1977 through 1982 by the Canadian Certified General Accountants Association, are adapted with permission. They are identified as "CGA adapted."

Material from the Certified Internal Auditor Examination, Copyright 1983 by the Institute of Internal Auditors, is adapted with permission. It is identified as "CIA adapted."

Material from the CICA Examination, Copyright 1977, by the Canadian Institute of Chartered Accountants, is adapted with permission. It is identified as "CICA adapted."

We are grateful to the Literary Executor of the Late Sir Ronald A. Fisher, F.R.S., to Dr. Frank Yates, F.R.S., and to Longman Group Ltd., London, for permission to reprint Table II from their book *Statistical Tables for Biological, Agricultural and Medical Research* (6th edition, 1975).

Comments or suggestions from readers are most welcome.

Potsdam, New York W.J.M.
Knoxville, Tennessee H.P.R.

Brief Table of Contents

1 Introduction 1

PART I: PROCESSING COST DATA WITH ACTUAL AND NORMAL COST SYSTEMS

2 Product Costing Concepts 19
3 Actual and Normal Job-Order Costing 55
4 Actual and Normal Process Cost Systems 102
5 Costing Joint Products and By-Products 147
6 Allocating Service Department and Other Indirect Costs 180

PART II: EVALUATING AND USING COST DATA FOR PLANNING

7 Estimating Costs From Accounting Data 229
8 Cost-Volume-Profit Analysis 288
9 The Contribution Income Statement and Variable Costing 340
10 The Master Budget 387

PART III: EVALUATING AND USING COST DATA FOR PERFORMANCE EVALUATION

11 Responsibility Accounting for Cost Centers 449
12 Responsibility Accounting for Revenue and Profit Centers 503
13 Responsibility Accounting for Investment Centers 545
14 Standard Cost Systems 588

PART IV: SELECTED TOPICS FOR FURTHER STUDY

15 Special Decisions in Short-Range Planning 643
16 Capital Budgeting I 704
17 Capital Budgeting II 758
18 Inventory Planning and Control Systems 798
19 Quality Control and Variance Investigation 840
20 Special Considerations in Payroll Accounting 881
21 Transfer Pricing 913

Appendix A: An Introduction to the Time Value of Money 954

Appendix B: Tables 962

Glossary 969

Index 981

Detailed Table of Contents

1 Introduction

INTRODUCTION 1

FINANCIAL AND MANAGEMENT ACCOUNTING 1
The accounting model of the firm 2
Uses of historical cost data 3

COST ACCOUNTING 3

DIFFERENT COSTS FOR DIFFERENT PURPOSES 5
External reporting 5
Planning and control 5
Special decisions 6

ACCOUNTING IS A STAFF FUNCTION 7

LEARNING COST ACCOUNTING 9
Motivation 10
Inadequate effort 10
Overemphasis on memorization 11
Inadequate accounting background 11

ACCOUNT ACTIVITY AND INTERRELATIONSHIPS 11

SUMMARY 12

KEY TERMS 12

SELECTED REFERENCES 13

GENERAL REFERENCES 13

REVIEW QUESTIONS 13

EXERCISES 14

Part One PROCESSING COST DATA WITH ACTUAL AND NORMAL COST SYSTEMS

2 Product Costing Concepts

INTRODUCTION 19

BASIC COST BEHAVIOR PATTERNS 19
- Variable costs 20
- Fixed costs 20
- Mixed (semivariable) costs 21
- Step costs 22
- Total cost behavior pattern 22
- Average unit costs 23

ECONOMIC AND ACCOUNTING COST PATTERNS 24
- Differences 24
- Relevant range 26

PRODUCT COSTING CONCEPTS 26
- Matching concept 26
- Product costs and period costs 28
- Three product costs 29
- Prime and conversion costs 30
- Statement of cost of goods manufactured 30
- Product costing and service costing 33

COSTS AND DECISION MAKING 35
- Sunk costs are never relevant 35
- Outlay costs may be relevant 35
- Opportunity costs 36
- Imputed opportunity cost 37

SUMMARY 37

KEY TERMS 38

SELECTED REFERENCES 39

REVIEW QUESTIONS 39

REVIEW PROBLEM 39

EXERCISES 40

PROBLEMS 49

SOLUTION TO REVIEW PROBLEM 53

3 Actual and Normal Job-Order Costing

INTRODUCTION 55

JOB-ORDER COSTING 56
- Job-cost sheet 57
- Direct materials 58
- Direct labor 59
- Factory overhead 61

ACTUAL JOB-ORDER COST SYSTEMS 61
- Limitations of actual overhead rates 65

NORMAL JOB-ORDER COST SYSTEMS, 68
Developing a predetermined overhead rate 69
Treatment of overapplied and underapplied overhead 71

OVERHEAD APPLICATIONS WITH MULTIPLE PRODUCTION DEPARTMENTS 74
Plant-wide overhead rate 75
Departmental overhead rates 76
When to establish departmental cost pools 77

SUMMARY 77

KEY TERMS 78

SELECTED REFERENCES 78

REVIEW QUESTIONS 79

REVIEW PROBLEM 79

EXERCISES 80

PROBLEMS 91

SOLUTION TO REVIEW PROBLEM 100

4 Actual and Normal Process Cost Systems

INTRODUCTION 102

JOB-ORDER AND PROCESS COSTING 102

EQUIVALENT UNITS 104

COST PER EQUIVALENT UNIT 105

COST OF PRODUCTION REPORTS 106

BEGINNING INVENTORIES 107
Weighted average 108
FIFO 109
LIFO? 112

SUBSEQUENT DEPARTMENTS 112

SPOILAGE 115
Spoilage as a loss 115
Spoilage as a product cost 117
Normal and abnormal spoilage 120
Point of spoilage detection 122
Disposal value for spoiled goods 122

SUMMARY 123

KEY TERMS 124

REVIEW QUESTIONS 124

REVIEW PROBLEM 125

EXERCISES 125

PROBLEMS 132

SOLUTION TO REVIEW PROBLEM 145

5 Costing Joint Products and By-Products

INTRODUCTION 147

SPLIT-OFF POINT AND JOINT COSTS 147

COSTING JOINT PRODUCTS 149
Physical measures 149
Sales value 150
Net realizable value 151

COSTING BY-PRODUCTS AND SCRAP 157
Miscellaneous income 157
Net realizable value 158

JOINT PRODUCTS AND SPECIAL DECISIONS 159
Sell or process further 159
Total production decisions 160
Other considerations 161

SUMMARY 161

KEY TERMS 162

SELECTED REFERENCES 162

REVIEW QUESTIONS 162

REVIEW PROBLEM 163

EXERCISES 164

PROBLEMS 169

SOLUTION TO REVIEW PROBLEM 177

6 Allocating Service Department and Other Indirect Costs

INTRODUCTION 180

COST POOLS AND COST OBJECTIVES 180

PURPOSES OF COST ALLOCATION 182

SERVICE DEPARTMENT COST ALLOCATION 183
Basis of service department cost allocation 184
Cost allocation techniques 185
Cost per unit of service 197

PREDETERMINED ALLOCATION RATES FOR SERVICE DEPARTMENTS 197

ALLOCATION OF NONMANUFACTURING COSTS 198
Cost Accounting Standards Board 198

SUMMARY 200

APPENDIX: BASIC ELEMENTS OF MATRIX ALGEBRA 200
Matrix addition and subtraction 201
Matrix multiplication 202
Matrix inversion 203
Solving a series of linear equations

KEY TERMS 205

APPENDIX KEY TERMS 206

SELECTED REFERENCES 206

REVIEW QUESTIONS 206

REVIEW PROBLEM 207

EXERCISES 208

PROBLEMS 212

SOLUTION TO REVIEW PROBLEM 225

Part Two EVALUATING AND USING COST DATA FOR PLANNING

7 Estimating Costs from Accounting Data

INTRODUCTION 229

APPROACHES TO COST ESTIMATION AND PREDICTION 229
- Account classification 230
- High-low 232
- Scatter diagrams 234
- Simple linear regression 235
- Multiple linear regression 237
- Longitudinal and cross-sectional analysis 239

DATA REQUIREMENTS AND LIMITATIONS 240
- Areas of concern 240
- Adjusting for price changes 241

SELECTING A COST-ESTIMATING EQUATION 244
- Selection of activity base 244
- Statistical considerations 244

SUMMARY 245

APPENDIX A: BASIC STATISTICAL CONCEPTS 246
- Measures of central tendency 246
- Measures of dispersion 249
- The normal distribution and tables 250
- The t-distribution and tables 253
- The cost-estimating problem 254

APPENDIX B: STATISTICAL CONSIDERATIONS IN REGRESSION ANALYSIS 254
- Statistical data and tests 254
- Statistical assumptions 262

APPENDIX C: LEARNING CURVE ANALYSIS 263
- Learning curve cost patterns 263
- Learning curve model 263
- Estimating learning curve percentage 265
- Estimating learning curve costs 265

KEY TERMS 266

APPENDICES KEY TERMS 266

SELECTED REFERENCES 266

REVIEW QUESTIONS 267

REVIEW PROBLEM 268

EXERCISES 268

PROBLEMS 274

SOLUTION TO REVIEW PROBLEM 286

8 Cost-Volume-Profit Analysis

INTRODUCTION 288

ECONOMIC AND ACCOUNTING COST-VOLUME-PROFIT MODELS 289
- Sources of data 290
- Basic relationships 290

ASSUMPTIONS UNDERLYING COST-VOLUME-PROFIT ANALYSIS 300

EXTENSIONS OF THE BASIC MODEL 302
Cash break-even point 302
Income taxes and cost behavior 303
Cash break-even point with taxes 303
Multiple break-even points 304
Average unit contribution margin 305
Product mix decisions 307

SUMMARY 308

APPENDIX: THE ANALYSIS OF UNCERTAINTY IN SHORT-RANGE PLANNING 308
Sensitivity analysis 309
Statistical analysis 310
Probability trees 312
Stochastic simulation 313
Utility 315

KEY TERMS 317

APPENDIX KEY TERMS 317

SELECTED REFERENCES 317

REVIEW QUESTIONS 318

REVIEW PROBLEM 319

EXERCISES 319

PROBLEMS 326

SOLUTION TO REVIEW PROBLEM 339

9 The Contribution Income Statement and Variable Costing

INTRODUCTION 340

FUNCTIONAL AND CONTRIBUTION INCOME STATEMENTS 341

ABSORPTION AND VARIABLE COSTING 343
Production equals sales 344
Production exceeds sales 344
Sales exceeds production 345
A matter of timing 347

UNDERAPPLIED AND OVERAPPLIED OVERHEAD ARE ABSORPTION COSTING PROBLEMS 349
Planned underapplied or overapplied fixed overhead 352
Selecting a denominator activity level for fixed overhead application 354

THE VARIABLE COSTING CONTROVERSY 356

THE USE OF CONTRIBUTION INCOME STATEMENTS FOR SEGMENT REPORTING 357

SUMMARY 360

KEY TERMS 361

SELECTED REFERENCES 361

REVIEW QUESTIONS 362

REVIEW PROBLEM 362

EXERCISES 363
PROBLEMS 371
SOLUTION TO REVIEW PROBLEM 385

10 The Master Budget

INTRODUCTION 387
TYPES OF PLANNING 388
OBJECTIVES OF BUDGETING 389
Compels planning 389
Promotes communication and coordination 389
Provides a guide to action 390
Provides a basis for performance evaluation 390
APPROACHES TO BUDGETING 390
REQUIREMENTS FOR AN EFFECTIVE BUDGET 391
Overall goals 391
Goal decomposition 391
Goal congruence 392
Acceptance 392
Feedback 392
BUILDING BLOCKS 393
Standard costs 393
ASSEMBLING THE MASTER BUDGET 394
Sales budget 396
Production budget 396
Manufacturing cost budget 397
Purchases budget 398
Selling and administrative expense budget 398
Budgeted income statement 399
Budgeted changes in retained earnings 400
Cash budget 400
Budgeted balance sheet 401
Budgeting in nonmanufacturing organizations 402
ADDITIONAL CONSIDERATIONS 403
Feasibility and acceptability 404
Use of computers 404
SUMMARY 405
APPENDIX: EXTENDED EXAMPLE 405
KEY TERMS 410
SELECTED REFERENCES 411
REVIEW QUESTIONS 412
REVIEW PROBLEM 412
EXERCISES 413
PROBLEMS 418
SOLUTION TO REVIEW PROBLEM 444

Part Three EVALUATING AND USING COST DATA FOR PERFORMANCE EVALUATION

11 Responsibility Accounting for Cost Centers

INTRODUCTION 449
CHARACTERISTICS OF EFFECTIVE PERFORMANCE REPORTS 449
Behaviorally sound 449
Relevant 450
Timely 450
Accurate and cost effective 451
RESPONSIBILITY ACCOUNTING 451
PERFORMANCE REPORTS AND CORPORATE STRUCTURE 451
Types of responsibility centers 453
RESPONSIBILITY ACCOUNTING FOR MANUFACTURING COSTS 454
Flexible budgets as a basis of performance evaluation 455
Materials variances 456
Timing of materials price variance 459
Labor variances 460
Variable overhead variances 461
Fixed overhead budget variance 462
Fixed overhead volume variance 463
Alternative approaches to overhead variances 464
Additional considerations 466
SUMMARY 470
APPENDIX: PRODUCTION MIX AND YIELD VARIANCES 471
Interpreting mix and yield variances 474
Labor mix and yield variances 475
KEY TERMS 475
APPENDIX KEY TERMS 476
SELECTED REFERENCES 476
REVIEW QUESTIONS 477
REVIEW PROBLEM 477
EXERCISES 478
PROBLEMS 486
SOLUTION TO REVIEW PROBLEMS 502

12 Responsibility Accounting for Revenue and Profit Centers

INTRODUCTION 503
REVENUE AND PROFIT CENTERS 503
Marketing and manufacturing reports compared 504
Marketing performance reports 505
Performance reports and special decisions 507
Other marketing performance data 507
PERFORMANCE REPORTS FOR DISCRETIONARY COST CENTERS 508

SALES VARIANCES 510
Single product sales price and volume variances 510
Multiple product sales price, mix, and volume variances 514
SUMMARY 518
APPENDIX: SALES CONTRIBUTION AND SALES REVENUE VARIANCES 519
KEY TERMS 520
SELECTED REFERENCES 520
REVIEW QUESTIONS 520
REVIEW PROBLEM 521
EXERCISES 522
PROBLEMS 527
SOLUTION TO REVIEW PROLEM 543

13 Responsibility Accounting for Investment Centers

INTRODUCTION 545
DECENTRALIZATION 545
Divisional organization structure 545
The divisional controller 547
Advantages of decentralization 547
Problems of decentralization 548
EVALUATING INVESTMENT CENTER PERFORMANCE 548
Return on investment (ROI) 548
Residual income (RI) 551
PROBLEMS IN MEASURING INVESTMENT CENTER PERFORMANCE 551
Defining investment 551
Measuring investment 552
Price-level changes and undervalued assets affect divisional comparisons 554
Price-level changes and undervalued assets affect investment decisions 556
Leased assets 558
Other unrecorded assets 558
Interest expense 559
Allocated indirect costs 559
Depreciation methods 560
MULTINATIONAL COMPANIES 562
AGENCY THEORY 563
Agency relationships 563
Agency problem 563
Agency costs 563
SUMMARY 564
KEY TERMS 564
SELECTED REFERENCES 565
REVIEW QUESTIONS 565
REVIEW PROBLEM 566
EXERCISES 567

PROBLEMS 571
SOLUTION TO REVIEW PROBLEM 587

14 Standard Cost Systems

INTRODUCTION 588
CHARACTERISTICS OF STANDARD COST SYSTEMS 589
Inventory valuation 589
Cost flows and variance analysis 590
Disposition of variances 593
STANDARD PROCESS COSTING 594
SPOILAGE 598
Abnormal spoilage in other variance accounts 598
Abnormal spoilage variance account 599
Normal spoilage: Summary of alternative treatments 603
Disposal value for spoiled units 604
REWORK 607
STANDARD JOB-ORDER COSTING 607
PRORATING VARIANCES 608
Theoretically correct method 609
Total cost method 610
Subsequent periods 612
SUMMARY 612
APPENDIX: STANDARD COSTS FOR JOINT PRODUCTS 613
KEY TERMS 613
SELECTED REFERENCES 614
REVIEW QUESTIONS 614
REVIEW PROBLEM 615
EXERCISES 616
PROBLEMS 621
SOLUTION TO REVIEW PROBLEM 638

Part Four SELECTED TOPICS FOR FURTHER STUDY

15 Special Decisions in Short-Range Planning

INTRODUCTION 643
SPECIAL DECISIONS BASED ON DIFFERENTIAL ANALYSIS 643
Special order 644
Make or buy 644
Service department decisions 645
Segment decisions 646
Product-mix decisions 646
Input-mix decisions 647

INFORMATION ACQUISITION DECISIONS 648
Payoff table 648
Expected value 649
Conditional loss 649
Expected payoff with perfect information 650
Expected value of perfect information 651
Revising probabilities using sample information 651
Expected value of sample information 655

PRICING DECISIONS 656
Pricing policies and pricing decisions 656
Economic approaches 656
Cost-based approaches 659
Cost-plus pricing 660
The role of costs in pricing 661
Legal forces increase the role of costs 662

SUMMARY 662

APPENDIX: PRODUCT MIX DECISIONS WITH TWO PRODUCTS AND MULTIPLE CONSTRAINTS **662**
Graphic analysis 663
Simplex method 666
Sensitivity analysis and uncertainty 667
Multiple constraints and multiple products 669
The role of the cost accountant 670
Income taxes 671

KEY TERMS 671

APPENDIX KEY TERMS 672

SELECTED REFERENCES 672

REVIEW QUESTIONS 673

REVIEW PROBLEM 673

EXERCISES 674

PROBLEMS 678

SOLUTION TO REVIEW PROBLEM 702

16 Capital Budgeting I

INTRODUCTION 704

CAPITAL-BUDGETING POLICY 704

CAPITAL-BUDGETING MODELS 705
Nondiscounting models 706
Discounting models 710

USAGE OF CAPITAL-BUDGETING MODELS 715

COST OF CAPITAL AS A CUTOFF OR DISCOUNT RATE 716
After-tax cost of debt 717
Cost of preferred stock 717
Cost of equity capital 718

ESTIMATING PROJECT CASH FLOWS 718
Initial investment 718
Operations 720
Disinvestment 723

SUBSEQUENT CONTROL AND PERFORMANCE EVALUATION 725
SUMMARY 725
APPENDIX A: IMPACT OF CHANGING PRICES ON CAPITAL-BUDGETING MODELS **726**
Price-level changes and cash flows 726
Nominal and constant dollars 729
Adjusting capital-budgeting models for inflation 729
APPENDIX B: IMPACT OF DEPRECIATION METHODS ON MEASURES OF INVESTMENT PERFORMANCE **732**
Impact of depreciation methods on ROI 732
Compound interest depreciation 733
KEY TERMS 735
APPENDICES KEY TERMS 735
SELECTED REFERENCES 735
REVIEW QUESTIONS 736
REVIEW PROBLEM 737
EXERCISES 737
PROBLEMS 743
SOLUTION TO REVIEW PROBLEM 756

17 Capital Budgeting II

INTRODUCTION 758
INCREMENTAL ANALYSIS 758
Cost reduction proposals 758
Variable investment size 762
MUTUALLY EXCLUSIVE INVESTMENTS 764
Initial investment 764
Investment life 766
Timing and amount of cash flows 766
CAPITAL RATIONING 767
Ranking 767
Trial and error 769
Mathematical programming 770
INVESTMENT AND FINANCING DECISIONS 771
LEASE-PURCHASE DECISIONS 773
UNCERTAINTY OR RISK 776
Decision trees 777
SUMMARY 778
KEY TERMS 779
SELECTED REFERENCES 779
REVIEW QUESTIONS 780
REVIEW PROBLEM 780
EXERCISES 781
PROBLEMS 786
SOLUTION TO REVIEW PROBLEM 796

18 Inventory Planning and Control Systems

INTRODUCTION 798
PURPOSE OF INVENTORY MODELS 798
INVENTORY COSTS 799
ECONOMIC ORDER QUANTITY (EOQ) 800
RELEVANT COSTS 802
Unit cost 803
Carrying costs 805
Ordering costs 806
ASSUMPTIONS UNDERLYING EOQ MODEL 806
ACCURACY OF COST PREDICTIONS 807
REORDER POINT (ROP) 807
ROP with certainty 808
ROP with uncertainty 808
Signaling need for reorders 811
OTHER APPROACHES TO INVENTORY PLANNING AND CONTROL 812
A-B-C approach 812
Just-in-time scheduling 812
Material requirements planning 813
SUMMARY 814
APPENDIX: PLANNING AND CONTROL WITH PERT 815
PERT/Time 815
PERT/Cost 818
PERT/Cost resource allocation supplement 818
PERT for time and cost control 820
Problem areas 820
KEY TERMS 820
APPENDIX KEY TERMS 821
SELECTED REFERENCES 821
REVIEW QUESTIONS 822
REVIEW PROBLEM 822
EXERCISES 823
PROBLEMS 826
SOLUTION TO REVIEW PROBLEM 839

19 Quality Control and Variance Investigation

INTRODUCTION 840
SOURCES OF VARIANCES 841
Random fluctuations 841
Measurement errors 841
Inappropriate standards 842
Operating errors 842
DECISION SIGNIFICANCE OF VARIANCES 842
No decision signifiance 842
Planning significance 843
Control significance 843

THE DECISION TO INVESTIGATE 843
Materiality 844
Statistical significance 844
Expected costs 854

RESPONSIBILITY FOR VARIANCES 856

QUALITY COSTS 856
Types of quality costs 857
Economics of quality costs 859

SUMMARY 860

APPENDIX: ESTIMATING THE PROBABILITY A PROCESS IS IN CONTROL 860

KEY TERMS 863

SELECTED REFERENCES 863

REVIEW QUESTIONS 864

REVIEW PROBLEM 864

EXERCISES 865

PROBLEMS 869

SOLUTION TO REVIEW PROBLEM 879

20 Special Considerations in Payroll Accounting

INTRODUCTION 881

THE GENERAL TREATMENT OF LABOR COSTS 881

PAYROLL AND LABOR DISTRIBUTION ACCOUNTING 883
Federal income taxes 883
Federal Insurance Contribution Act 883
Unemployment taxes 885
Compensation insurance 885
Voluntary items affecting labor costs 885

PAYROLL PROCEDURES 887

PAYROLL ACCOUNTING PROBLEMS 891
Magnitude of additional labor costs 891
Volume of payroll transactions 892
Transaction dates and comprehensive illustration 896

SUMMARY 899

KEY TERMS 900

REVIEW QUESTIONS 900

EXERCISES 901

PROBLEMS 906

21 Transfer Pricing

INTRODUCTION 913

CORPORATE VIEWPOINT 914

ECONOMICS OF TRANSFER PRICING 915
Competitive intermediate market 916
No intermediate market 917

DETERMINING TRANSFER PRICES 919
Market price 919
Variable cost 919
Variable cost plus opportunity cost 920
Full cost or full cost plus 920
Negotiated prices 921
Other transfer prices 921
TRANSFER-PRICING PRACTICES 921
THE TRANSFER-PRICING PROBLEM 922
INTERNATIONAL TRANSFER PRICING 924
ACCOUNTING ENTRIES 926
SUMMARY 926
KEY TERMS 926
SELECTED REFERENCES 927
REVIEW QUESTIONS 927
REVIEW PROBLEM 928
EXERCISES 929
PROBLEMS 935
SOLUTION TO REVIEW PROBLEM 952

Appendix A: An Introduction to the Time Value of Money

FUTURE AMOUNT 954
PRESENT VALUE 957
PRESENT VALUE OF AN ANNUITY IN ARREARS 958
DEFERRED ANNUITIES 959
FINDING AN INTEREST RATE 960

Appendix B: Tables

TABLE A: AREAS UNDER THE NORMAL CURVE 963
TABLE B: ORDINATE VALUES FOR THE NORMAL CURVE 964
TABLE C: CRITICAL POINTS FOR THE *t*-DISTRIBUTION 965
TABLE D: AMOUNT OF $1 966
TABLE E: PRESENT VALUE OF $1 967
TABLE F: PRESENT VALUE OF AN ANNUITY OF $1 IN ARREARS 968

Glossary **969**
Index **981**

1 Introduction

INTRODUCTION
FINANCIAL AND MANAGEMENT ACCOUNTING
COST ACCOUNTING
DIFFERENT COSTS FOR DIFFERENT PURPOSES
ACCOUNTING IS A STAFF FUNCTION
LEARNING COST ACCOUNTING
ACCOUNT ACTIVITY AND INTERRELATIONSHIPS
SUMMARY

INTRODUCTION

THE MANAGERS OF SUCCESSFUL ORGANIZATIONS ROUTINELY USE ACCOUNTING data to help plan for the future, determine whether or not operations are going according to previously developed plans, and make a myriad of important decisions pertaining to specific activities. One very important decision that often determines the profitability, and perhaps even the survival, of a business is the pricing decision. Managers of businesses as simple as the local supermarket or as complex as International Business Machines make thousands of decisions about product pricing. Although competition and salability must be taken into consideration in determining a final price, the starting point in developing a selling price is most often cost plus a markup to provide for a profit. When prices are based on cost, the accurate determination of the cost of producing a product or providing a service becomes crucial, and an organization's cost accounting system is called on to provide the necessary information.

The purpose of this chapter is to introduce cost accounting. To provide an overall framework, we begin by defining accounting and noting similarities and differences between financial accounting and management accounting. Next we define cost accounting, review its historical development, and indicate the major uses of cost accounting data. After studying the job assignments of various accountants within an organization, we conclude the chapter by stating the objectives of this textbook, identifying certain problems encountered in learning cost accounting, and reviewing basic notions that underlie cost accounting.

FINANCIAL AND MANAGEMENT ACCOUNTING

Accounting is a specialized information system. Its purpose is to provide economic information concerning the past, current, or expected future activities of an organization to such diverse groups as managers, investors, creditors, taxing authorities, regulatory agencies, labor unions, and the general public. Accounting is traditionally divided into financial accounting and management accounting on the basis of the relationship between the organization and the user group to whom information is supplied.

Financial accounting is concerned with the development of *general-purpose* financial statements (such as the statement of financial position and income statement) that are intended for the primary use of persons *external* to the organization. Organizations whose securities are issued to the general public are *required by law* to issue financial statements that disclose the organization's current financial condition and report on management's handling of the affairs of the organization in the *past*. These financial statements are *highly aggregated* and provide only a broad overview of the organization. General-purpose financial statements are prepared in accordance with *external standards* imposed by the public accounting profession (in the form of generally accepted accounting principles) and by regulatory agencies, such as the Securities and Exchange Commission. A significant feature of externally imposed standards is their emphasis on *objectivity*. General-purpose financial statements should not be influenced by emotion, surmise, or personal prejudice. They should be based on objective, verifiable economic transactions that two trained accountants would interpret in a similar manner.

Management accounting is concerned with providing *special-purpose* financial statements and reports to managers and other persons *inside* the organization. The accountant cannot know the specific use to be made of financial accounting reports, and accordingly prepares general-purpose financial statements for external users, but the management accountant can communicate directly with internal users of accounting information. Consequently, after carefully considering the potential benefits that can be derived from accounting information and the related costs of developing the information, management accountants design reports to serve the specific needs of individual or group decision makers. These reports should emphasize factors under the decision maker's control.

Because management accounting reports are not required by law, they should only be *prepared when deemed useful* to management. Because internal decision makers are primarily concerned with the impact of their decisions on the future performance of the organization, management accounting reports are *future oriented*. Past and current activities are reported to the extent that such information helps management plan for the future. Management accounting reports are only as aggregated as management desires. If a manager requests information for a specific decision, the report should be *very specific*. Because *no external standards* are imposed on information provided to internal users, management accounting reports may be quite *subjective*. The primary criterion in developing management accounting information is *relevance*. The key question is: "Is this information relevant to the decision being considered?" The significant differences between financial and managerial accounting are summarized in Exhibit 1–1.

The Accounting Model of the Firm

Despite their differences, the similarities that exist within financial and managerial accounting are so significant that a thorough grounding in financial accounting concepts is usually regarded as a prerequisite to the study of management

EXHIBIT 1–1 Differences Between Financial and Managerial Accounting

Financial Accounting	*Managerial Accounting*
General-purpose financial statements	Special-purpose statements and reports
External orientation	Internal orientation
Required by law	Prepared as deemed useful
Reports on past	Future oriented
Highly aggregated (broad)	May be very specific (narrow)
Must conform to external standards	Has no external standards
Emphasis on objective data	Emphasis on relevant data, even if subjective

accounting. Because the double-entry accounting system, which is used to accumulate and classify data reported in general-purpose financial statements, touches every area of activity within an organization, this system and the general-purpose financial statements based on it serve as a model of the entire organization.

A **model** is a simplified representation of some real-world phenomenon. A model is useful to management because the variables in it can be quickly and inexpensively manipulated to study the impact of a proposed action. Hence, the financial accounting model of the firm is a useful planning tool, which is used extensively in management accounting. A manager who is familiar with the income statement, for example, can use this portion of the financial model to predict the probable impact of a proposed action on net income.

Uses of Historical Cost Data

Financial and management accounting both use historical cost data; however, their perspectives are different. Financial accounting is primarily concerned with summarizing and reporting historical costs in general-purpose financial statements, whereas management accounting uses information about historical cost relationships as a starting point in predicting future costs. This common interest in historical costs leads to common interests in cost concepts, cost behavior, and costing techniques. The financial accountant's interest is motivated by a desire to better report on past operations, whereas the management accountant's interest is motivated by a desire to better plan for the future. This textbook contains cost concepts, cost behavior, and costing techniques that are useful for external and internal purposes. The material contained herein serves the needs of both financial and management accounting.

COST ACCOUNTING

A **cost** is a measure of economic sacrifice. **Cost accounting** is the accumulation, assignment, and analysis of production and activity cost data to provide information for external reporting, internal planning and control of ongoing operations, and special decisions. As illustrated in Exhibit 1–2, cost accounting is concerned with providing information for financial accounting and management accounting purposes. Cost accounting provides the product cost data needed for inventory valuation in the statement of financial position and for income determination (the deduction for cost of goods sold) in the income statement. It also provides the

EXHIBIT 1–2 Uses of Cost Accounting Data

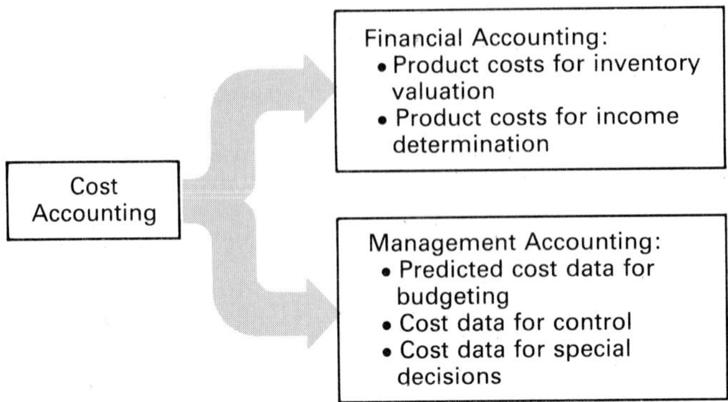

cost data needed for budgeting, the control of operations, and special decisions (such as pricing).

In recent years the distinction between management accounting and cost accounting has become somewhat hazy. We have reached a point where no sharp line can be drawn between them. To the extent that a difference exists, it is a matter of relative emphasis. Cost accounting emphasizes the accumulation, assignment, and analysis of cost data. Management accounting emphasizes the use of cost data in internal planning and control and in special decisions. Because interrelationships exist between the accumulation, assignment, analysis, and use of cost data, most cost accounting textbooks give considerable attention to management accounting issues, and most management accounting textbooks include at least a rudimentary discussion of the accumulation, assignment, and analysis of cost data.

The original financial accounting model was developed for *retail* establishments. In such organizations, it is relatively easy to determine inventory costs. There is only one major category—merchandise purchased for sale. The only costs assigned to merchandise inventories are the purchase price and, sometimes, transportation-in. These costs remain in the Merchandise Inventory or Purchases account until the related goods are sold. At that time they are transferred to the expense account, Cost of Goods Sold.

The early development of cost accounting paralleled the development of *manufacturing* firms and increases in business size. Its origins are in engineering and financial accounting. Manufacturing organizations differ from retail organizations by having three major inventory categories: finished goods available for sale, materials in the process of being transformed into finished goods (**work-in-process**), and raw materials purchased for use in future production. The cost of raw materials is readily determined by their purchase price, but it is difficult to establish costs for work-in-process and finished goods inventories. Accountants concluded that the costs assigned to work-in-process and finished goods inventories should include the cost of raw materials and the cost of all other factors used to transform raw materials into finished goods. Determining proper inventory cost assignments required studies of engineering relationships and input costs. The discipline of cost accounting grew out of such studies.

In its early days, cost accounting was an adjunct to financial accounting, used primarily to determine the periodic profit and inventory values of manufacturing firms. However, the combination of cost information, engineering relationships, and the financial accounting model of the firm provided managers who were not directly involved in day-to-day operations with an opportunity to study firm-wide interrelationships and develop firm-wide planning and control models. In developing plans for the future, management was interested in past costs only to the extent they assisted in predicting future costs. Hence, the cost accountant became concerned with future as well as historical costs.

DIFFERENT COSTS FOR DIFFERENT PURPOSES

Cost accounting is now used in for-profit and not-for-profit sectors of the economy by retail, service, and manufacturing organizations. It is used to aid in external reporting, the planning and control of ongoing operations, and special decisions. A basic premise of cost accounting that allows it to be used in such diverse tasks is that *costs are a means to an end.* The cost accountant must determine the use to be made of cost data in order to supply the most appropriate cost data. *Different costs are used for different purposes.*

External Reporting

As previously stated, cost accounting provides information on the historical cost of manufacturing products intended for sale. This information is used in general-purpose financial statements to value inventories and determine the cost of goods sold. Cost accounting also supplies information used in filings with the Internal Revenue Service and in filings with other regulatory agencies such as state and local utility commissions, which use cost accounting information in establishing utility rates. Insurance companies and government agencies have also placed pressure on hospitals to justify reimbursement claims. The Federal Trade Commission can require companies to justify differences in prices charged customers. Agencies of the federal government frequently require suppliers to justify prices charged on negotiated contracts.

Large businesses often keep three sets of books: one for the annual financial statements provided to shareholders and the general public, another for the Internal Revenue Service, and a third for a regulatory commission. They do this not to be devious, but because it is necessary to comply with legal requirements. Fortunately the increasing availability of computer-based accounting data facilitates the speedy preparation of the necessary reports. The problems of determining what information is needed for each report and selecting the accounting techniques to provide the needed information will remain with us, however, throughout the computer age.

Planning and Control

In planning, management is interested in future costs. To supply the appropriate information, the cost accountant might start by analyzing the cost of past operations. But the cost accountant must adjust historical costs to reflect changes in products, technology, volume, production efficiency, and input costs. These adjustments require consultation with engineers, salespeople, suppliers, production supervisors, economists, and others. Subsequent to these consultations, the cost accountant must coordinate the development of standards for the costs of various activities. In the final stage of the planning process, management determines the activities to be undertaken during some subsequent time period, and a formal plan of action expressed in monetary terms, called a **budget**, is adopted.

During the budget period, cost accounting assists in controlling operations by comparing actual results with plans. If significant deviations from plans occur, management is notified so appropriate action can be taken. The appropriate action might be to correct some inefficient aspect of operations, or to adjust the organization's plans because some environmental factor, such as the cost of inputs or the demand for the product, has changed.

Planning and control is an ongoing cycle, illustrated in Exhibit 1–3. Assume the cycle starts with the current budget. **Performance reports**, containing a comparison of actual and budgeted data, are prepared on a regular basis. Operating management receives these reports and other explanatory information from various functional areas of the business such as production or marketing. Based on this information, management attempts to improve current operations and plans for the future, which are summarized in the new budget. With time, the new budget becomes the current budget and the cycle continues.

Special Decisions

Management uses cost data in making a large number of decisions on a nonscheduled basis. Examples include the decision to accept or reject a customer's request for a special order of goods at a predetermined price, the determination of whether it is less expensive to make or buy a product or service, the decision to continue or discontinue a product, and the determination of whether to repair an old machine or to purchase a new one. To help management make the appropriate selection, the cost accountant provides information illustrating how future revenues, or costs, or both, will differ under each alternative.

EXHIBIT 1–3 The Planning and Control Cycle

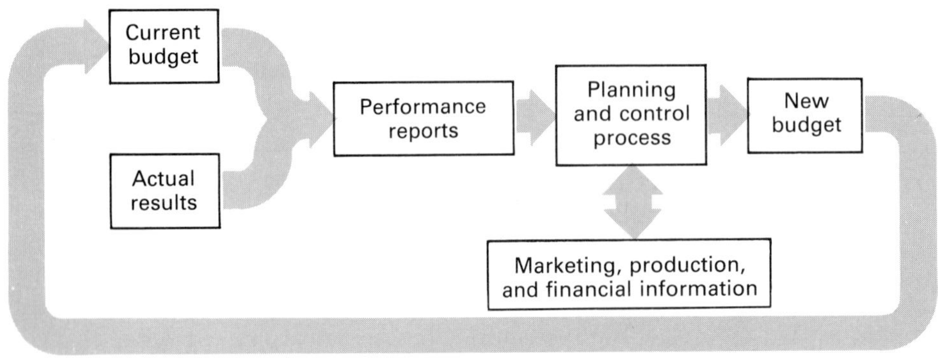

EXHIBIT 1–4 **Line and Staff Relationships in a Centralized Manufacturing Organization**

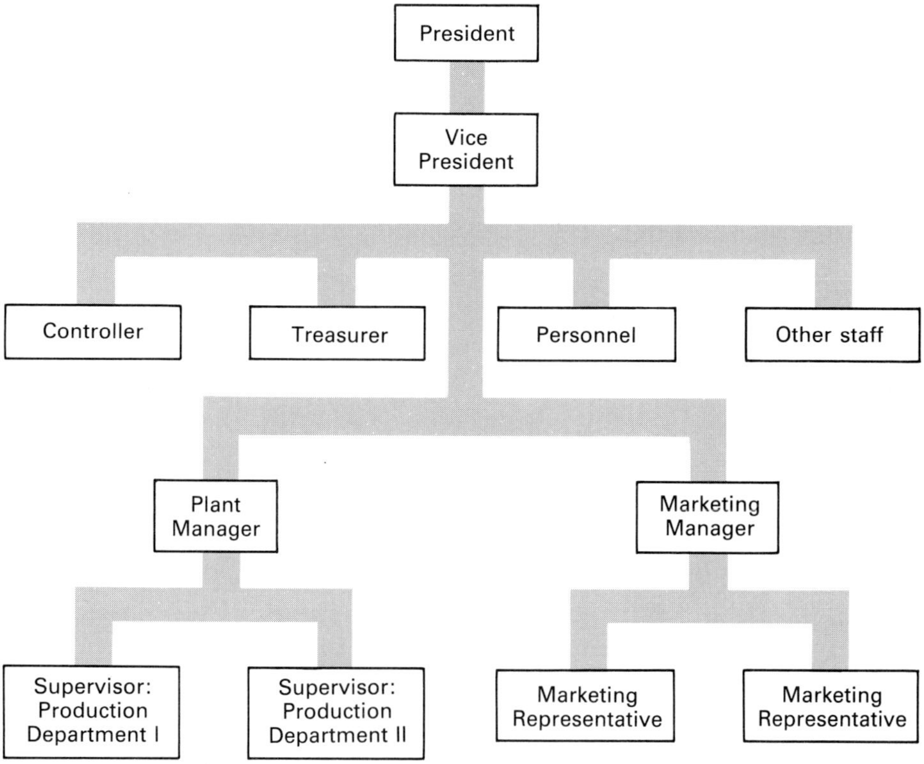

ACCOUNTING IS A STAFF FUNCTION

A simplified organization chart for a manufacturing firm is presented in Exhibit 1–4. The firm is under the overall direction of a president and a vice president. Reporting directly to the vice president are the plant manager and the marketing manager. The plant manager is responsible for manufacturing activities that take place in two production departments, each of which has its own supervisor. The marketing manager is responsible for selling products produced in the firm's factory. Two marketing representatives report directly to the marketing manager.

An uninterrupted line can be traced from the president to the production supervisors and marketing representatives, who are directly responsible for production and sales. Managers on this line, who can trace their authority and responsibility directly to production and/or sales activities, are called **line managers**. Managers who cannot trace their authority and responsibility directly to production or sales activities are called **staff managers**. Staff members assist line members by performing a variety of services that help the organization accomplish its goals.

The **controller** is the organization's chief accountant. Although the controller reports directly to top management and the position is near the top of most organization charts, controllers are staff managers and do not have line authority over the activities of any person or group except their staff. Sometimes controllers are perceived as having line authority, especially in budgeting. But, they are acting on behalf of top management in these activities by following directives or approved procedures. Duties frequently assigned to the controller include:

- Designing, installing, and maintaining the cost accounting system
- Predicting future costs
- Coordinating the development of the budget
- Accumulating and analyzing actual costs
- Preparing and analyzing performance reports
- Consulting with management as to the meaning of cost information
- Providing information for special decisions
- Planning and reporting taxes
- Internal auditing
- Designing, installing, and maintaining computer-based information systems
- Preparing reports for external users

In all but the smallest organizations, a staff assists the controller in performing these duties. One possible way of organizing the controller's department is illustrated in Exhibit 1–5.

EXHIBIT 1–5 **Organization Chart of the Controller's Department**

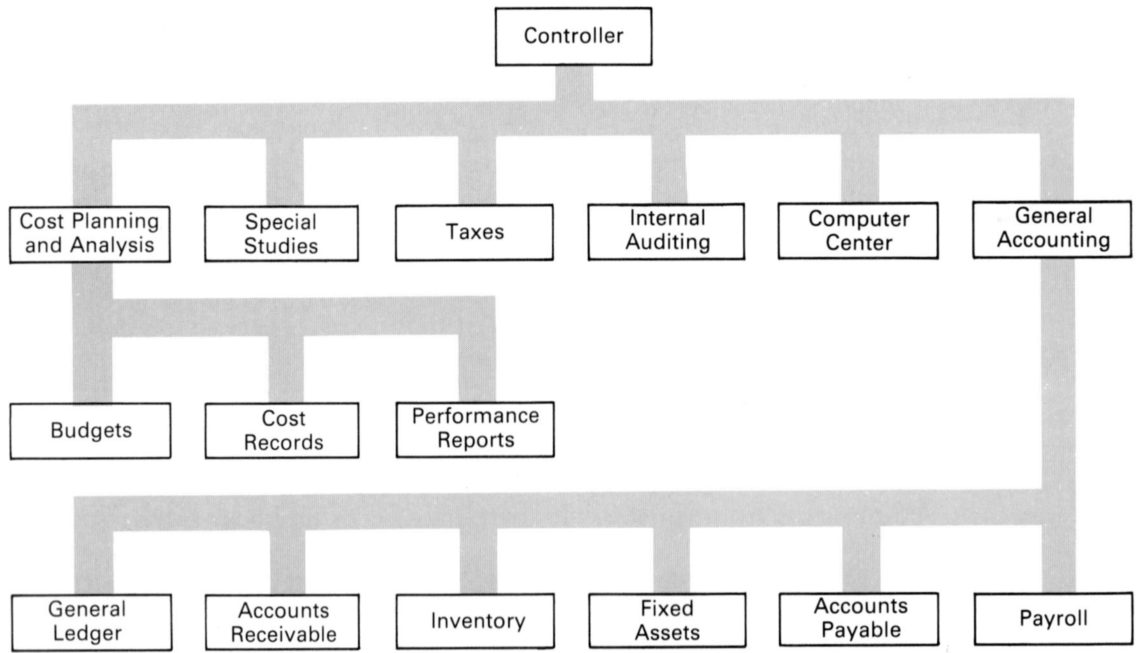

The duties just listed and the organization chart in Exhibit 1–5 are quite extensive. It is unlikely that the controller's office would be assigned responsibility for all of the listed duties. To help ensure independence, the internal auditors might report directly to the board of directors or an audit committee consisting of selected board members. Designing, installing, and maintaining computer-based management systems might be placed in a separate staff department, and accounting data would be one of many types of data handled by the computer center. Even if the computer center is independent of the controller's department, the controller would remain interested in the content, accuracy, timeliness, and integrity of accounting data.

To perform their duties, the controller and appropriate members of the controller's staff must be well versed in financial and cost accounting, auditing, corporate taxation, information systems, planning models used by management, quantitative techniques, and the pronouncements of appropriate regulatory agencies. It is equally important that the controller and members of the controller's staff understand human behavior. Organizations achieve their goals through people, and the manner in which planning and control systems operate influences the actions of people. It is possible to destroy the long-run profitability of a business by blindly holding to established rules and insisting on current profit maximization. The controller's office must maintain the confidence of line managers and not be perceived as threatening.

Somewhat related to the controller's function is that of the treasurer. The **treasurer** is the officer responsible for money management and serves chiefly as custodian of the organization's funds. Typical duties of the treasurer include:

- Receiving, maintaining custody of, and disbursing monies and securities
- Investing the organization's funds
- Directing the granting of credit
- Maintaining sources of short-term borrowing
- Establishing and maintaining a market for the organization's debt and equity securities

The positions of controller and treasurer are sometimes combined into the single position of **chief financial executive**. Other titles of this position include "chief financial officer," and "vice president of finance."

LEARNING COST ACCOUNTING

The objectives of this book are to provide you with a thorough grounding in cost concepts, cost behavior, and costing techniques; and with an understanding of the uses and limitations of cost data in planning and control and special decisions. After completing this book, you should be able to:

- Assist in the development of cost accounting data for use in external and internal reports.
- Properly use accounting data in short-run decisions.

- Participate in annual and long-range budgeting activities.
- Understand the information feedback process and how accounting data are used in performance evaluation.
- Assist in the development of performance reports.
- Appreciate the issues in human behavior that are involved in budgeting and performance evaluation.

The topics discussed herein are important to users and suppliers of cost accounting information. To perform their functions, users of cost accounting information must understand the characteristics of that information. To provide the most appropriate information, cost accountants must be familiar with the uses and limitations of cost data.

For a variety of reasons students, including some who have done well in other subjects, occasionally have difficulty learning cost accounting. In teaching, the authors have often encountered the following sources of learning difficulty: motivation, inadequate effort, overemphasis on memorization, and inadequate accounting background.

Motivation

Many students who do not have a primary interest in accounting fail to appreciate the relevance of the subject. Yet, the authors have taught this material in management development programs to enthusiastic audiences of nonaccountants who have incurred considerable personal and economic sacrifice to attend. Typically these people have been successful in entry-level positions and, because of promotions to management positions, they have found it essential to learn more about accounting in order to participate in budgeting and performance evaluating activities and to properly use accounting data in a variety of important decisions.

Occupational titles of program participants include sales manager, labor relations manager, branch manager, process engineer, production supervisor, program administrator, plant superintendent, pastor, vice president, and president. All these people were motivated to learn cost accounting because they had to work with costs, budgets, and performance reports. In their chosen careers each learned that, regardless of the nature of a business, accounting terms are an important part of the language of business.

Inadequate Effort

Some students believe studying involves only reading a textbook and listening in class. Although this minimal activity will provide some familiarity with cost accounting, it will not result in a working knowledge of the subject. Accounting is a detailed subject that builds from lesson to lesson. Consequently, mere familiarity is not enough. To obtain a working knowledge of cost accounting, students must read critically, verify significant classroom and textbook examples with pencil and paper, commit significant terms and concepts to memory, and encounter the frustration of following an inappropriate tack on a problem assignment. These wrong turns and blind alleys are an essential part of the learning process. They motivate questions and, as answers are found, help develop an ability to properly accumulate, allocate, and analyze cost data.

Overemphasis on Memorization

Some hard-working students attempt to memorize textbook and classroom examples and the solutions to homework problems. Because these students perceive everything they encounter as unique, they become overwhelmed and complain about the volume of material. They are especially frustrated when examinations do not contain exact replicas of previously studied material.

The problem is one of not being able to see the forest for the trees. One way to help overcome this problem in cost accounting is to recall the key phrase "different costs for different purposes." Determining the purpose for which cost information is being accumulated, allocated, or analyzed helps determine the best approach to the problem. It also helps keep costing techniques in perspective.

The authors recommend that, after completing a homework assignment, you close the book and think generally about the readings and homework problems. A useful study technique is to use the table of contents as an outline to help review the material in your mind. Use the list of key terms and review questions found at the end of most chapters to help structure a review of conceptual material. Finally, solve the review problems found at the end of most chapters to review technical material. The solutions to review problems are included in the textbook.

Inadequate Accounting Background

Because the financial accounting model of the firm provides the basic framework within which cost accounting systems operate, this text assumes you have had previous exposure to financial accounting principles (one course). You may at times find it useful to refer back to your basic accounting textbook to review some portion of the accounting cycle or the content of general-purpose financial statements. If it has been more than a year since you studied financial accounting, we recommend you review these materials before proceeding.

ACCOUNT ACTIVITY AND INTERRELATIONSHIPS

Two simple notions about the accounting model of the firm are extremely important in product costing and in budgeting. The first concerns the activity within an account. The second concerns the relationships between accounts.

First, during any time period, the activity in any account can be broken down into four parts:

1. Beginning balance
2. +Increases
3. −Decreases
4. =Ending balance

If we know three of these items, we can always find the fourth. Typical accounts and their activity include:

Cash	*Accounts Receivable*	*Inventory (Merchandising firm)*
Beginning balance +Cash receipts −Cash disbursements	Beginning balance +Sales on account −Collections and write-offs	Beginning balance +Purchases −Cost of goods sold
=Ending balance	=Ending balance	=Ending balance

Second, activity in one account always affects at least one other account. A payment on account reduces Cash and Accounts Payable. A purchase of inventory on account increases Inventory and Accounts Payable. Being aware of the typical interrelationships that exist among accounts assists in planning and controlling the activities of an organization.

SUMMARY

Cost accounting is the accumulation, assignment, and analysis of production and activity cost data to provide information for external reporting, for internal planning and control of ongoing operations, and for special decisions. A basic premise of cost accounting is that costs are a means to an end. Different costs are used for different purposes. External reporting requires historical cost data. Planning requires predictions of future costs. Performance evaluation requires a comparison of prior cost predictions and actual results. Special decisions require an analysis of cost and revenue differences.

To perform their functions, users of cost accounting information must understand the characteristics of that information. To provide advice and the most appropriate information, cost accountants must be familiar with the uses and limitations of cost accounting information. In recognition of the needs of these two groups, this book is intended to provide the reader with a thorough grounding in cost accounting concepts and an understanding of the uses and limitations of cost data.

KEY TERMS

Accounting
Budget
Chief financial executive
Controller
Cost
Cost accounting
Financial accounting
Line manager
Management accounting
Model
Performance report
Staff manager
Treasurer
Work-in-process

SELECTED REFERENCES

Edwards, James B., and Julie A. Heard, "Is Cost Accounting the No. 1 Enemy of Productivity?" *Management Accounting* **65,** No. 12 (June 1984): 44–49.

Hartman, Bart P., Vincent G. Brenner, Richard A. Lydecker, and Jeffrey M. Wilkinson, "Mission Control Starts in the Controller's Department," *Management Accounting* **63,** No. 3 (September 1981): 27–31.

Johnson, H. Thomas, "Toward a New Understanding of Nineteenth-Century Cost Accounting," *Accounting Review* **56,** No. 3 (July 1981): 510–518.

Lander, Gerald H., James R. Holmes, Manuel A. Tipgos, and Marc J. Wallace, Jr., *Profile of the Management Accountant,* New York: National Association of Accountants, 1983.

National Association of Accountants, *Statement on Management Accounting, No. 1A, Objectives: Definition of Management Accounting,* New York: National Association of Accountants, 1981.

——, *Statement on Management Accounting, No. 1B, Objectives: Objectives of Management Accounting,* New York: National Association of Accountants, 1982.

——, *Statement on Management Accounting, No. 1C, Objectives: Standards of Ethical Conduct for Management Accountants,* New York: National Association of Accountants, 1983.

——, *Statement on Management Accounting, No. 2, Management Accounting Terminology,* New York: National Association of Accountants, 1983.

Tipgos, Manuel A., James R. Holmes, and Gerald H. Lander, "The Management Accountant Today: A Status Report," *Management Accounting* **65,** No. 5 (November 1983): 53–57.

GENERAL REFERENCES

The following references are applicable not so much to specific chapters as to the book in general.

Belkaoui, Ahmed, *Conceptual Foundations of Management Accounting,* Reading, Mass.: Addison-Wesley, 1980.

Davidson, Sidney, and Roman L. Weil, eds., *Handbook of Cost Accounting,* New York: McGraw-Hill Book Company, 1978.

Goodman, Sam R., and James S. Reece, *Controller's Handbook,* Homewood, Ill.: Dow Jones-Irwin, 1978.

Seed, Allen H., III, *The Impact of Inflation on Internal Planning and Control,* New York: National Association of Accountants, 1981.

REVIEW QUESTIONS

1–1 What is the purpose of accounting?

1–2 On what basis is accounting divided into financial and management accounting?

1–3 Why is relevance a more important criterion for the development of management accounting information than for the development of financial accounting information?

1–4 Why does the double-entry bookkeeping system used in financial accounting serve as a model of the firm?

1–5 Why are management accountants interested in historical cost data?

1–6 Define cost accounting.

1–7 What type of information does cost accounting supply to financial accounting? To management accounting?

1–8 In manufacturing firms, what types of costs should be assigned to work-in-process and finished goods inventories?

1–9 What basic premise of cost accounting allows it to be used for a variety of external and internal purposes?

1–10 How does cost accounting assist in controlling operations?

1–11 What type of information does the cost accountant supply in special decisions, such as the decision to continue or discontinue a product?

1–12 Distinguish between line and staff managers.

1–13 Identify several duties often assigned to the controller.

1–14 Why is it important that members of the controller's department understand human behavior?

1–15 Identify several skills you should have after completing a thorough study of cost accounting.

EXERCISES

1–1 Financial and Management Accounting

Distinguish between financial and management accounting on the basis of each of the following criteria:

- Purpose of statements and reports
- User orientation
- Relative emphasis on legal requirements
- Time orientation
- Level of aggregation
- Objectivity of data

1–2 Usefulness of Cost Accounting Information

Briefly respond to each of the following comments. Indicate how cost accounting information can assist managers in doing their job.

a) Plant manager: "Our accountants do a good job in keeping the stockholders informed about how our company has done in the past, but I don't see how they can help me run this plant."

b) Restaurant owner: "There is no question that cost accounting is useful in a manufacturing firm, but I run a restaurant. How can it help me?"

c) City recreation director: "Cost accounting may be important in a for-profit organization, but my job is to provide social services, not a profit. I shouldn't be concerned with costs."

d) Production supervisor: "I take a careful look at my department's performance report whenever we spend too much money and really chew out my men for not doing a better job."

e) Sales manager: "Product pricing is a shot in the dark. You make an educated guess and then hope the product will sell, and, if it does, that the company will make a profit."

f) Civil engineering student: "My goal is to supervise the construction of highways, bridges, and dams. I don't see why I should take a cost accounting course."

1–3 Account Activity and Account Interrelationships

For each of the following independent cases, find the required information.

1. *Merchandise Inventory*

Ending balance	$ 20,000
Beginning balance	10,000
Purchases	150,000

Find: Cost of goods sold

2. *Accounts Payable to Suppliers*

Beginning balance	$100,000
Purchases on account	480,000
Payments on account	520,000

Find: Ending balance

3. *Retained Earnings*

Dividends	$ 20,000
Beginning balance	340,000
Ending balance	360,000

Find: Net income

4. *Accounts Receivable*

Beginning balance	$ 10,000
Sales on account	100,000
Ending balance	15,000

Find: The total of collections and write-offs

5. *Accounts Payable to Suppliers*

Beginning balance	$ 40,000
Payments on account	160,000
Ending balance	70,000

Merchandise Inventory

Beginning balance	$100,000
Ending balance	20,000

All purchases are on account.
Find: Cost of goods sold

6. *Merchandise Inventory*

Beginning balance	$ 25,000
Purchases	40,000
Ending balance	10,000

Accounts Receivable

Beginning balance	$ 5,000
Ending balance	15,000

Find: Collections*

* All sales are on account. There are no uncollectable accounts. Markup is 100 percent of cost (sales = 2 × cost of goods sold).

1–4 Account Activity and Account Interrelationships

For each of the following independent cases, find the required information.

1. *Raw Materials Inventory*

Ending balance	$ 15,000
Issued to factory	145,000
Purchases	143,000

Find: Beginning balance

2. *Accounts Payable to Suppliers*

Beginning balance	$ 75,000
Purchases on account	350,000
Ending balance	105,000

Find: Payments on account

3. *Salaries Payable*

Salaries paid	$420,000
Beginning balance	260,000
Ending balance	180,000

Find: Salaries expense

4. *Accounts Receivable*

Sales on account	$580,000
Ending balance	210,000
Beginning balance	125,000

Find: The total of collections and write-offs

5. *Merchandise Inventory*

Beginning balance	$ 35,000
Ending balance	80,000
Cost of goods sold	240,000

Accounts Payable to Suppliers

Beginning balance	$ 65,000
Ending balance	50,000

All purchases are on account.
Find: Payments on account

6. *Accounts Receivable from Sales*

Beginning balance	$ 50,000
Collections on account	370,000
Ending balance	40,000

Merchandise Inventory

Beginning balance	$105,000
Ending balance	86,000

Find: Purchases*

* All sales are on account. There are no uncollectable accounts. Markup is 80 percent of cost (sales = 1.80 × cost of goods sold).

1–5 Analysis of Account Interrelationships

Presented is recent information taken from the records of the Izard Company.

Balance Sheet	*12/31/x3*	*12/31/x4*
Cash	$100,000	$ 92,000
Accounts receivable, from customers	80,000	60,000
Merchandise inventory	20,000	100,000
Fixed assets, net of depreciation	400,000	200,000
Accounts payable to suppliers	50,000	?
Notes payable, long-term	200,000	200,000
Retained earnings	?	120,000

Income Statement	*19x4*
Sales	$400,000
Cost of goods sold	220,000
Depreciation on fixed assets	100,000
Net income	40,000

ADDITIONAL INFORMATION

19x4 Payments to suppliers	$200,000
19x4 Dividends declared	$ 20,000

REQUIREMENTS

Determine each of the following:

a) Collections on account during 19x4. Assume all sales are on account and there are no bad debts or sales returns and allowances.

b) The purchases of merchandise inventory during 19x4.

c) The 12/31/x4 balance in Accounts Payable. Assume all purchases are on account.

d) The 12/31/x3 balance in Retained Earnings.

Part One

PROCESSING COST DATA WITH ACTUAL AND NORMAL COST SYSTEMS

2 Product Costing Concepts

INTRODUCTION
BASIC COST BEHAVIOR PATTERNS
ECONOMIC AND ACCOUNTING COST PATTERNS
PRODUCT COSTING CONCEPTS
COSTS AND DECISION MAKING
SUMMARY

INTRODUCTION

SEVERAL IMPORTANT CONCEPTS WERE INTRODUCED IN CHAPTER 1. COST WAS defined as a measure of economic sacrifice. **Cost accounting** was defined as the accumulation, assignment, and analysis of production and activity cost data to provide information for external reporting, internal planning and control of ongoing operations, and special decisions. A **cost accounting system** is a set of procedures for accumulating costs and assigning them to cost objectives. Most cost accounting systems are used for **product costing**, that is, the assignment of costs to inventories as they are converted from raw materials to finished goods. This information is used for external reporting in general-purpose financial statements.

The details of a specific product costing system depend on the nature of the product, the complexity of the production procedures, and management's willingness to pay for a system that can also provide information that will serve internal needs on an ongoing basis. Indeed, there may be as many different product costing systems as there are firms. Despite this diversity, all product costing systems share a number of common concepts.

The purpose of this chapter is to examine the common concepts that form the foundation of all product costing systems. In the process of examining these concepts, we will introduce a number of important cost terms and consider some of the ways costs respond to changes in the level of activity. We will focus on how product costs flow through inventory accounts and how this flow is summarized in the Statement of Cost of Goods Manufactured. The chapter concludes by contrasting the use of cost data in product costing and in decision making.

BASIC COST BEHAVIOR PATTERNS

In predicting future costs and in evaluating past performance, cost accountants make extensive use of four basic cost behavior patterns: variable, fixed, mixed, and step costs. These cost behavior patterns are discussed and illustrated in the first section of this chapter. In each, activity is the independent variable and total cost is the dependent variable. When graphed, activity is plotted on the horizontal axis and total cost is plotted on the vertical axis. Depending on the particular situation under consideration, activity may refer to total production, total sales, total clients served, or another variable of interest. By convention, activity is most often called "volume." Volume increases to the right from the origin and cost increases up from the origin.

Variable Costs

A **variable cost** is a cost whose total amount changes in direct proportion to changes in the volume of activity. The relationship between an organization's volume of activity and its total variable costs is illustrated in Exhibit 2–1(a). Here, the slope of the total variable cost line represents the variable cost of one unit. The greater the variable costs associated with each unit of activity, the steeper the slope. Typical variable costs include the cost of food served in a restaurant, the cost of postage for a magazine publisher, sales commissions, the cost of materials and parts used in production, and wages paid to production employees.

Fixed Costs

A **fixed cost** is a cost that does not respond to changes in the volume of activity within a given period. The relationship between an organization's volume of activity and its total fixed costs is illustrated in Exhibit 2–1(b). Total fixed costs do not increase as the volume of activity increases; hence, they plot as a straight line with a slope of zero. Typical fixed costs include rent, depreciation, property taxes, insurance, and salaries.[1]

Although fixed costs do not respond to changes in volume within a given time period, they often increase with the passage of time. An organization's cumulative total rent expense increases on a month-by-month basis throughout an organization's fiscal year. Fixed costs can also differ from month to month and from year to year.

Fixed costs are sometimes identified as "committed" or "discretionary," depending on their immediate impact on the organization if they are reduced. **Committed fixed costs** are required to maintain the current production or service capacity. Consider, for example, depreciation on a bus fleet. Because depreciation is usually incurred on the basis of time (so much per month or year), this cost does not vary with the volume of activity. It can only be reduced by reducing the size of the bus fleet. But, reducing the size of the fleet also reduces the capacity to serve as measured by the maximum number of passenger miles. Thus depreciation on the bus fleet is a committed fixed cost. Committed fixed costs are frequently called **capacity costs** because an organization must incur them to maintain its current capacity to render a service or to manufacture a product.

Discretionary fixed costs are set at a fixed amount each year at the discretion of management. These costs are not required to maintain current production or service capacity in the near term. Typical discretionary fixed costs include

---

[1] The term "wages" refers to an hourly rate of pay, whereas the term "salary" refers to a weekly, monthly, or yearly rate of pay. Total wages vary with the number of hours worked, whereas total salaries do not vary with the total number of hours worked.

EXHIBIT 2–1 Four Basic Total Cost Behavior Patterns

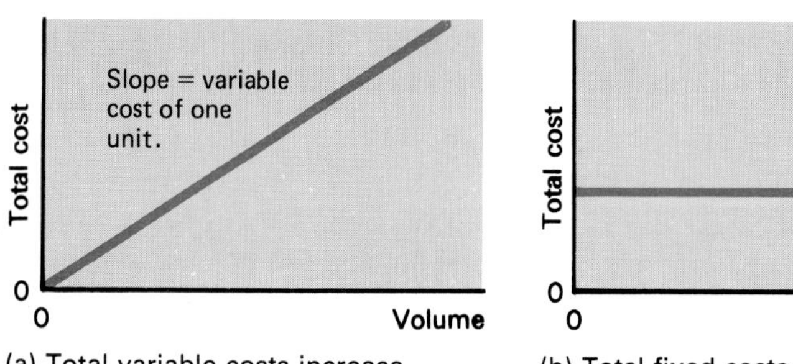

(a) Total variable costs increase as volume increases.

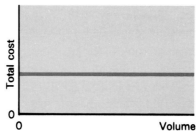

(b) Total fixed costs do not increase as volume increases within a period.

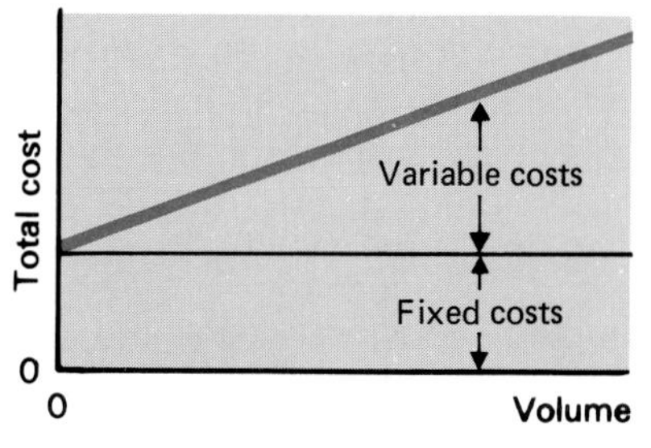

(c) Mixed costs contain a fixed and a variable cost element.

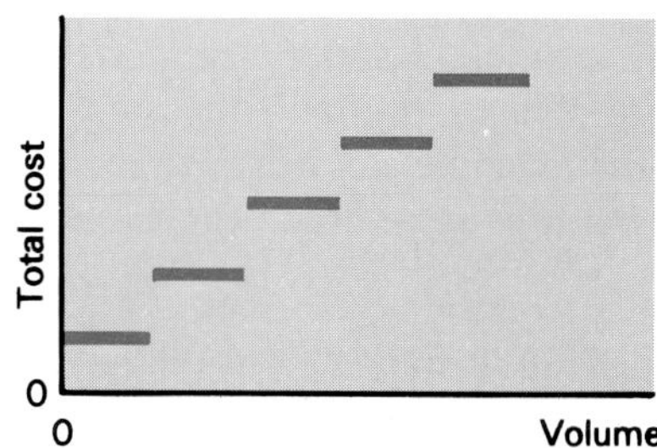

(d) Step costs remain constant over a range of activity.

advertising, executive salaries, charitable contributions, and research and development. As an alternative, management may budget certain discretionary costs, such as advertising, on the basis of volume. In that event they behave as variable costs.

Expenditures on discretionary costs are frequently regarded as investments in the future. During periods of financial well-being, organizations often make large expenditures on discretionary cost items. Conversely, during periods of financial stress, organizations tend to reduce their discretionary expenditures before reducing their committed fixed costs (and their production or service capacity). Unfortunately the potential benefit of such long-run programs as research and development can be greatly reduced or even destroyed by arbitrary reductions in funding. Smooth funding levels and long-term commitments to selected discretionary programs tend to be most productive.

Mixed (Semivariable) Costs

Mixed costs, sometimes called **semivariable costs**, contain a fixed and a variable cost element. As illustrated in Exhibit 2–1(c), mixed costs are positive, like fixed costs, when volume is zero, and they increase linearly, like variable costs, as volume increases. Typical semivarible costs include electricity, maintenance, and salespeople's compensation. Some electricity is necessary to provide basic lighting; additional electricity is required to operate machinery as production increases. Some maintenance is required to prevent equipment from deteriorating; additional maintenance is required to keep equipment in good repair as production increases. Salespeople, especially new salespeople, are often paid a basic salary plus a commission stated as a percentage of total sales dollars.

Step Costs

Step costs are constant within a range of activity, but different between ranges of activity. As shown in Exhibit 2–1(d), a graph of step costs appears to be a series of steps that reach higher levels at higher volumes. Step costs are caused by indivisibilities in inputs. One production supervisor may be able to supervise a given number of employees. Beyond this number it is necessary to hire a second supervisor, then a third, and so on. The salaries of case workers in a welfare agency also follow a step function, as do the basic charges for equipment rentals. However, the size (length) of the steps is not rigid. For example, for certain time periods, a supervisor may be able to oversee one more employee. It is also possible to "soften" the steps. Instead of hiring an additional quality inspector, for example, an organization may pay current inspectors time-and-a-half to work a few extra hours each week.

Total Cost Behavior Pattern

Combining an organization's variable, fixed, mixed, and step costs into one representative cost behavior pattern results in something that looks very much like the mixed pattern in Exhibit 2–1(c). It should be obvious that adding the variable, fixed, and mixed costs yields a mixed pattern (see Exhibit 2–2), but what about the step costs? The answer depends on the width of the steps relative to the total potential range of activity.

If there are many steps of equal width in the range of potential activity, step costs may be treated as variable costs, as in Exhibit 2–3. When a variable cost function is used to predict step costs, the prediction is usually too high or too low. However, if the error is not significant enough to affect decisions based on the prediction, it can be ignored.

If the steps are very large and one step encompasses the range of normal operations, the step costs can be treated as fixed costs. When neither the variable nor the fixed cost approximations are reasonable, step costs must be explicitly

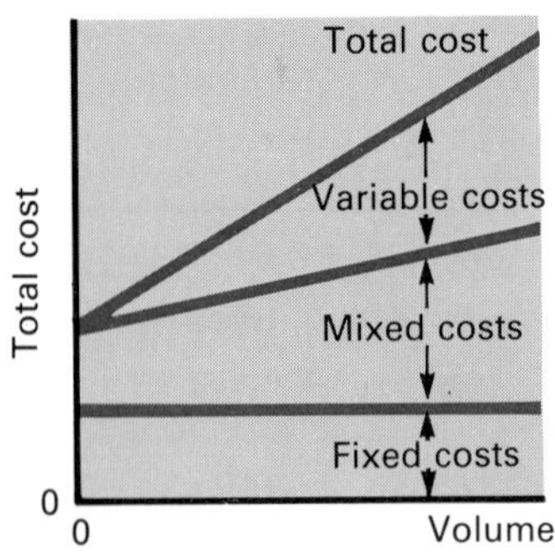

EXHIBIT 2–2 The Behavior of Total Costs (Mixed costs are layered on top of the fixed costs, and, in turn, the variable costs are layered on top of the mixed costs.)

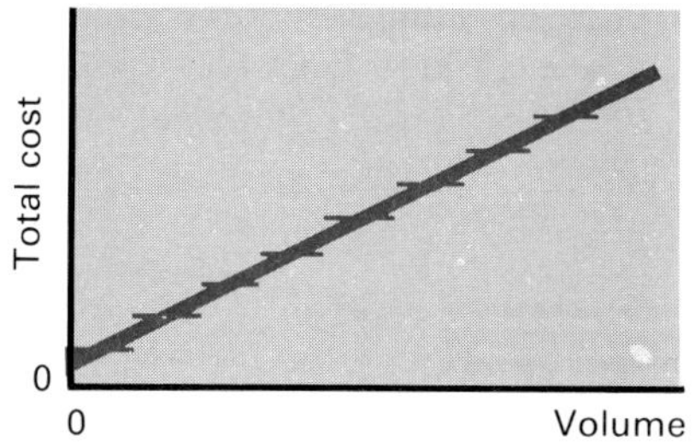

EXHIBIT 2–3 Variable Cost Approximation on Step Costs (If the steps are narrow, relative to total volume, a variable cost behavior pattern may be used to approximate a step cost.)

incorporated into the total cost behavior pattern. Note that the step cost function is discontinuous. This makes developing an equation for step costs difficult. Unless specified otherwise, we will assume that step costs are represented by fixed costs in the relevant range.

In words, the total cost equation for an organization is:

Total costs = Fixed costs + (Variable costs per unit × Volume in units).

This text frequently uses the following equation for total costs:

$$T = a + bX \tag{2–1}$$

where

T = total costs,
a = fixed costs (including the fixed portion of mixed costs),
b = variable costs per unit,
X = volume in units of the independent variable.

This formula is simply the equation for the top line in Exhibit 2–2. All costs are assumed to be classified as either fixed or variable.

Average Unit Costs

For external reporting purposes, accountants are frequently interested in determining the **average cost** per unit of service or product. The average cost is simply the total costs divided by the volume in units. Alternatively, the average cost is the sum of (1) the variable costs per unit, and (2) the total fixed costs divided by the volume in units. The average cost per unit declines as volume increases because the fixed costs are being spread over a larger number of units.

Example 2–1

Fixed costs are $1,000 per period and variable costs are $100 per unit. The total and average unit costs at production levels of 1, 2, and 10 units are as follows:

Volume in units (X)	*Total fixed costs*	*Total variable costs ($100X)*	*Total cost (T = $1,000 + $100X)*	*Average unit cost (T/X)*
1	$1,000	$ 100	$1,100	$1,100
2	1,000	200	1,200	600
10	1,000	1,000	2,000	200

EXHIBIT 2–4 Total and Average Costs

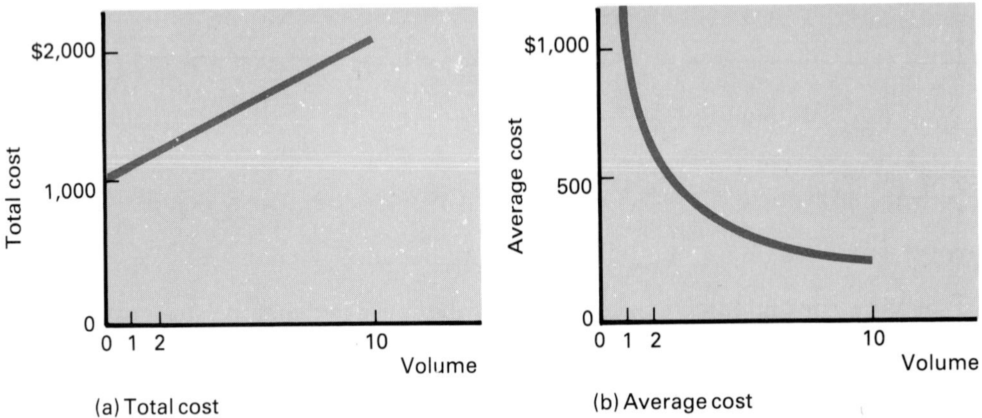

(a) Total cost

(b) Average cost

The increase in total costs and the decline in average unit costs for this situation are illustrated in Exhibit 2–4, parts (a) and (b). Because division by zero is not possible, the average unit cost is undefined at zero units.

ECONOMIC AND ACCOUNTING COST PATTERNS

Because the cost behavior patterns used in most accounting models differ from those presented in economic models, it is desirable to compare them and determine the circumstances in which accounting models are reasonable approximations of economic models and of the underlying cost behavior patterns that the economic models represent.

Differences

Given the existence of productive capacity during a specific time period, economic models indicate a curvilinear relationship between the volume of production and unit costs. The varying increment in total costs required to produce and sell one additional unit, called the **marginal cost**, is illustrated in Exhibit 2–5(a). Initially, marginal costs decline as production becomes more efficient. Then they level off for a range of activity before they start to rise due to capacity constraints (less efficient machinery may have to be put into use) and increases in input costs (extra high wages may have to be paid for extra hours worked).[2]

The economist's short-run total cost function is illustrated in Exhibit 2–5(b). The vertical axis intercept represents capacity costs. Note the influence that marginal costs have on the slope of the total cost function. Initially the slope is quite steep where the marginal costs are high. The slope levels off in the range

---

[2] To be technically correct we might also note that economic models include opportunity costs in their cost functions, whereas accounting models do not.

EXHIBIT 2–5 Economic and Accounting Cost Behavior Patterns

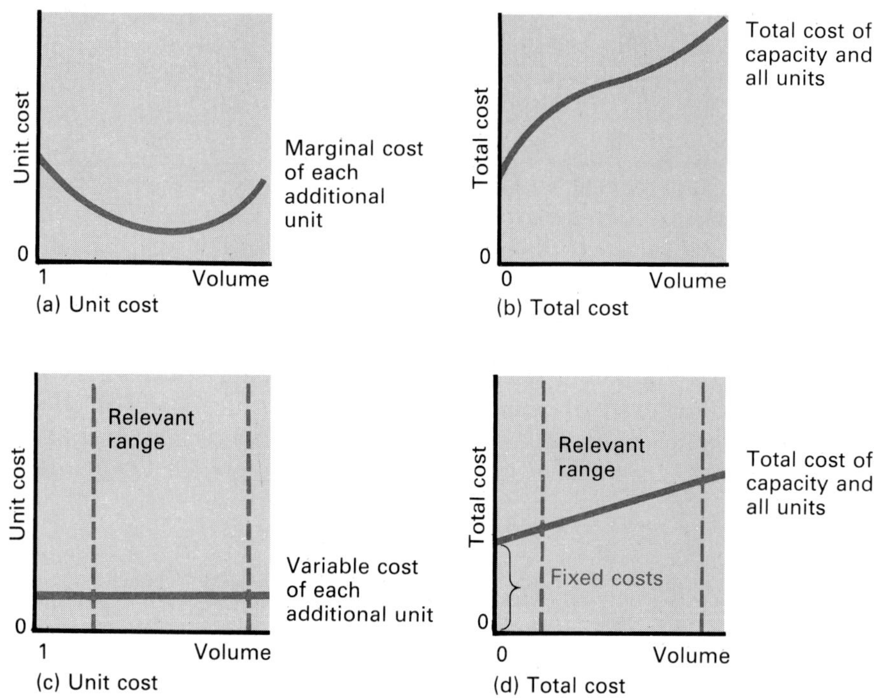

where marginal costs are relatively low, and then increases again as marginal costs increase.[3]

Accounting models assume that the marginal or incremental cost of producing each additional unit during a specific time period is constant. In accounting models this constant incremental unit cost was previously identified as a variable

---

[3] The economist's total cost function in Exhibit 2–5(b) is based on an equation similar to:

$$T = 3X^3 - 30X^2 + 100X + 300$$

The slope of the total cost function at any given value of X is the marginal cost of the Xth unit. The slope of the total cost function at a given value of X can be found by taking the first derivative of the total cost function and solving for X. The marginal cost function for the preceding total cost equation is:

$$\text{Marginal cost} = 9X^2 - 60X + 100$$

Using this equation, the marginal cost of the second unit, found by setting X equal to 2, is 16.

In taking the first derivative, use was made of the following rule:

$$d/dx(aX^n) = naX^{n-1}$$

where a is a constant and n is an exponent. This rule was applied to each part of the total cost equation:

$$\begin{aligned} d/dx(3X^3) &= 9X^2 \\ d/dx(-30X^2) &= -60X \\ d/dx(100X) &= 100 \\ d/dx(300) &= 0 \end{aligned}$$

cost. The relationship between volume and *total* variable cost was illustrated in Exhibit 2–1(a). The relationship between volume and *unit* variable costs is illustrated in Exhibit 2–5(c). The accountant's total cost function, which was discussed previously, is illustrated again in Exhibit 2–5(d). The constant slope results from the assumption of constant incremental unit costs.

Relevant Range

Whereas the accountant's linear cost behavior pattern may be a poor representation of the economist's curvilinear cost behavior pattern over the entire range of possible activity, the accountant's pattern is often a reasonable approximation within the range of normal operations. Because organizations attempt to adjust their size in order to operate at peak efficiency, the range of normal operations frequently occurs in the area where the economist's marginal cost curve is relatively flat. The area of normal operations within which a linear cost function is a good approximation of the economist's curvilinear cost function is called the **relevant range**. The relevant range is marked by vertical dashed lines in Exhibit 2–5, parts (c) and (d). Accounting estimates of cost behavior are valid only within the relevant range.

PRODUCT COSTING CONCEPTS

If we understand cost behavior patterns, we can develop a conceptual framework to accumulate manufacturing costs and to assign these costs to inventories. The concepts developed here are expanded in subsequent chapters to include more complex production situations. Once we understand the product costing model used for external reporting, we will examine the characteristics of the data it produces and determine the modifications necessary to make that data more useful for internal planning and control. In subsequent chapters we will also use the relationships between the various components of the product costing model to assist in budgeting.

In Chapter 1 we noted some important differences between accounting for merchandising and manufacturing operations:

- A merchandising establishment has one major inventory category: merchandise purchased for resale. A manufacturing establishment has three major inventory categories: finished goods available for sale, materials that are in the process of being transformed into finished goods (work-in-process), and raw materials purchased for use in future production.
- In merchandising establishments, the only costs associated with inventories are the purchase price and, sometimes, transportation-in. In manufacturing establishments, the cost of raw materials and all manufacturing costs incurred to transform them into finished goods are placed in inventory accounts. These include such costs as production employees' wages, depreciation on plant and equipment, and utilities used in production operations.

Matching Concept

The flow of costs in merchandising and manufacturing organizations is illustrated, in T-account form, in Exhibit 2–6. Both types of organizations incur costs to obtain inventory suitable for sale. However, manufacturers incur many more types of costs, and the flow of these costs is more complex. A primary cause of

EXHIBIT 2–6 Flow of Inventory Costs

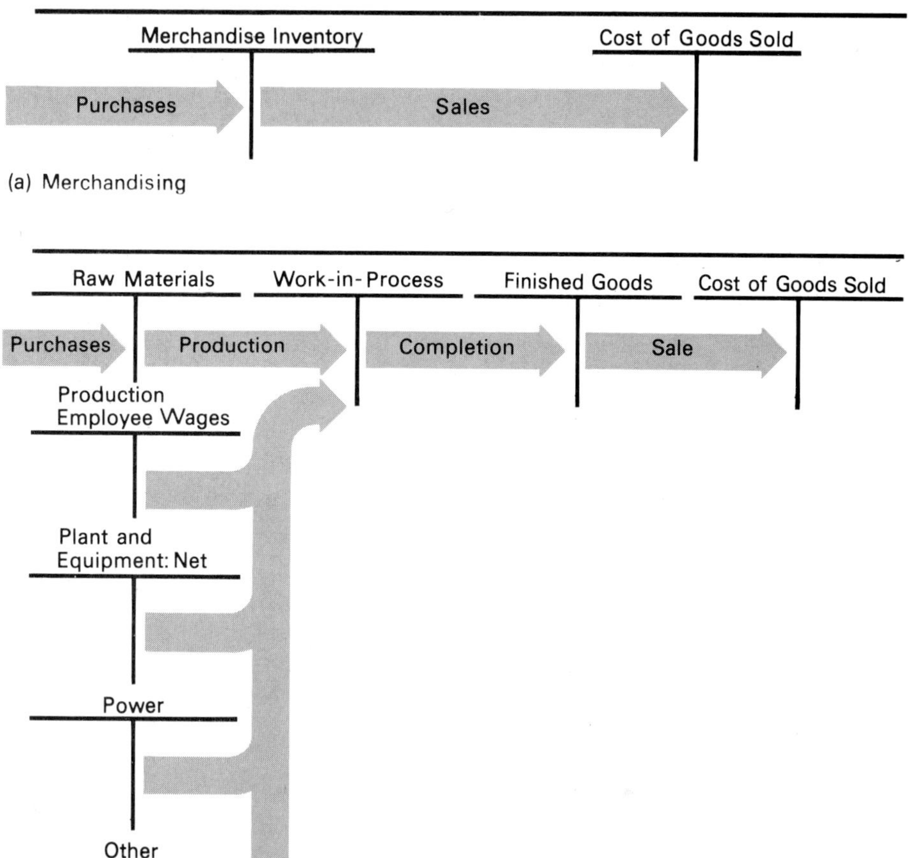

this complexity is found in the matching concept that influences asset valuation and income determination in financial accounting. According to the **matching concept**, when the relationship between costs and revenues is clear, costs incurred to generate future revenues should not be expensed until the revenues are recognized.[4] To implement this concept, we must clearly establish the relationship

[4] Note that the terms "cost" and "expense" are not synonymous. A *cost* is a measure of economic sacrifice. If the economic sacrifice has future value, because it can be used to generate future revenues (inventory, for example) or because it can reduce future costs (prepaid insurance, for example), the cost should be assigned to an asset account on the statement of financial position. If the economic sacrifice does not have a future value, it is an expense and should be deducted from revenues on the income statement. It follows that an *expense* is an expired cost, that is, a cost that can no longer be used to generate future revenues (inventory that was sold, for example) or to reduce future costs (expired insurance premiums, for example).

between costs and revenues. Such relationships are easily established when manufactured products are intended for sale.

To implement the matching concept in a merchandising organization, the cost of inventory purchased for sale is initially recorded as an asset, and it is deducted from revenues as an expense only when the inventory is sold. To implement the matching concept in a manufacturing organization, the cost of raw materials and all other costs incurred to transform raw materials into finished goods are assigned to asset accounts, and they are expensed only when the finished goods inventory is sold.

Product Costs and Period Costs

Expenditures that have future value to an organization are recorded as assets. If the futue value of an asset expires, the cost of the asset is expensed. If, however, the asset is used to produce a second asset that has a future value, the cost of the first asset becomes part of the cost of the second. Consider the cost of office and factory buildings. An office is not used to manufacture a product intended for future sale. As the value of an office building expires with the passage of time, the related cost of the office building is assigned to depreciation expense and is deducted from revenues on the income statement. However, a factory building is used to manufacture products intended for future sale. Consequently, the value of the factory building is transformed into the value of the goods manufactured and the expired cost of the factory building is assigned to an inventory account, remaining an asset until the inventory is sold.

All costs assigned to inventory accounts as products are produced are **product costs**. Product costs are sometimes said to "attach to" or be "absorbed by" the units produced. Product costs are transformed into the cost of the finished goods inventory and, in financial statements, they are treated as an asset until the goods they are assigned to are sold. At that time they become the expense, cost of goods sold.

Product costs ⟶ Asset (inventory) ⟶ Expense (cost of goods sold)

All expired costs that are not necessary for production are called **period costs**. In financial statements period costs are always an expense.

Period costs ⟶ Expense

The following are examples of product and period costs:

Product costs (an asset then an expense)	*Period costs (always an expense)*
Raw materials used	Office supplies used
Production employees' wages	Sales' salaries
Depreciation on plant	Depreciation on showroom
Plant manager's salary	President's salary
Plant maintenance	Maintenance of retail store
Plant utilities	Travel expenses

Three Product Costs

Product costs are traditionally classified into three categories: direct materials, direct labor, and factory overhead. **Direct materials** are the cost of the primary raw materials converted into finished goods. Examples of direct materials include crude oil to a refinery, cattle to a slaughterhouse, and lumber to a builder. At the time of their purchase, the cost of raw materials is placed in a special inventory account. When an organization has many types of raw materials, this account is more apt to be titled Stores Control than Raw Materials. The former title indicates that this account has a subsidiary ledger with one subsidiary account established for each type of raw material. As raw materials are placed in production, their costs are moved from Stores Control, and the appropriate subsidiary accounts, to Work-in-Process. Because the use of raw materials varies directly with production volume, *direct materials displays a variable cost behavior pattern*.

Wages earned by production employees for the time they actually spend working on a particular product or process are called **direct labor**. As employees earn wages, direct labor is debited to Work-in-Process and credited to a liability account, such as Payroll Payable. Because the time employees actually spend working on production varies directly with production volume, *direct labor displays a variable cost behavior pattern*. Note that the definition of direct labor, by restricting this term to wages earned for the time actually spent working on the product, results in the variable cost pattern. In reality, the total wages earned by production employees are more apt to display a fixed cost behavior pattern. Any excess of total wages earned by production employees over the wages classified as direct labor and assigned to Work-in-Process is classified as factory overhead and is assigned to Factory Overhead Control.

All manufacturing costs other than direct materials and direct labor are collectively identified as **factory overhead**.[5] Included in factory overhead are such costs as depreciation on plant and equipment, insurance on plant and equipment, property taxes on plant and equipment, repairs and maintenance, plant utilities, production supervisors' salaries, operating costs of the factory personnel office, and manufacturing supplies. Manufacturing supplies are sometimes identified as **indirect materials**. They include low-cost items that are difficult to associate with specific units of product, such as lubricants, nails, glue, and small tools.

For product costing purposes, factory overhead costs are accumulated in the account Factory Overhead Control before being assigned to Work-in-Process. To better plan and control factory overhead, each specific factory overhead cost is also recorded in a separate subsidiary record. Unlike the Stores Control subsidiary accounts, the Factory Overhead Control subsidiary records are not individually reduced as factory overhead is assigned to Work-in-Process. Instead, a cumulative total is kept in each factory overhead subsidiary record throughout the period. The subsidiary records begin each year with a zero balance. The information in the factory overhead subsidiary records is used to analyze the behavior of overhead costs and to assist in their planning and control.

---

[5] Factory overhead is sometimes called *burden, manufacturing burden*, or *manufacturing overhead*.

Each factory overhead cost displays its own unique cost behavior pattern. When all factory overhead costs are combined, however, they are most apt to display a mixed cost behavior pattern.

Prime and Conversion Costs

Raw materials are easily traced to the units produced, and production employees can be observed working on products. Because of this direct association between products and direct materials and direct labor, these two costs are collectively identified as **prime product costs**. Product costs are then grouped into prime product costs and factory overhead.

Factory overhead refers to a pool of costs that are incurred to facilitate production. Because factory overhead costs are applied to products as a group, rather than individually, and because it is difficult to trace each overhead cost to the production of specific products, factory overhead costs are sometimes referred to as **indirect product costs**, whereas direct materials and direct labor are identified as **direct product costs**.

Reference is frequently made to the costs incurred to convert raw materials into finished goods. These costs, which include direct labor and factory overhead, are collectively identified as **conversion costs**. Note that direct labor is both a prime cost and a conversion cost.

These classifications of the three product costs are summarized as follows:

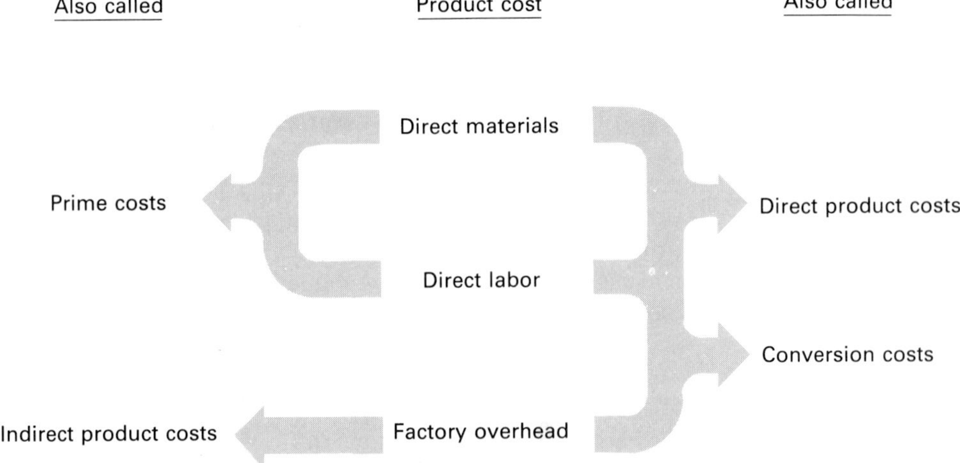

Statement of Cost of Goods Manufactured

Our discussion of product costing concepts is best reviewed by an example of the flow of product costs through the inventory accounts of a manufacturing organization. We then examine the **statement of cost of goods manufactured**, which is a financial summary of the activity in the Work-in-Process inventory account.

Example 2–2

On October 1, 19x2, the Concord Manufacturing Company had beginning inventories of $4,000, $2,000, and $6,000, respectively, in Stores Control, Work-in-Process, and Finished Goods Inventory. There were no receivables or payables on that date. During the month of October the following events occurred:

- Raw materials costing $10,000 were purchased on account.
- Raw materials costing $12,000 were placed in production.
- Wages earned by production employees for direct labor totaled $30,000.
- Other salaries and wages earned by factory personnel totaled $20,000.
- Depreciation on plant and equipment amounted to $10,000.
- Electricity and water costing $30,000 were used in production operations. This amount is payable to the local utility company.
- Products costing $95,000 were completed and transferred to finished goods.

The journal entries necessitated by October activities are presented in Exhibit 2–7(a). The flow of product costs through the various inventory accounts is illustrated in Exhibit 2–7(b). To emphasize manufacturing cost relationships, references to sales, nonmanufacturing costs, and the payment of liabilities are intentionally omitted. These items would be handled in the manner discussed in introduction to financial accounting or principles of accounting textbooks.

The flow of product costs is formally presented in a statement of cost of goods manufactured, which summarizes the activity in an organization's Work-in-Process account. It discloses the beginning balance, additions, deductions for goods transferred to Finished Goods Inventory, and the ending balance. The total additions to Work-in-Process during a given period are identified as **current manufacturing costs**. In this section of the statement, the details of current direct materials, direct labor, and factory overhead are presented. The total costs assigned to products completed during a given period are collectively identified as the **cost of goods manufactured**. Occasionally the statement is expanded to disclose the changes in Stores Control or Finished Goods Inventory or both. When the changes in Finished Goods Inventory are included, the statement is identified as a **statement of cost of goods manufactured and sold**

Example 2–3

Continuing the Concord Manufacturing Company example, assume that goods costing $90,000 were sold for $200,000 during the month of October and that general and administrative expenses for the month amounted to $60,000. Further assume that the cost of goods sold and general and administrative expenses were Concord's only expenses.

A statement of cost of goods manufactured and an accompanying income statement for the month of October are presented in Exhibit 2–8. Note that the changes in the Stores Control account are shown on the Statement of Cost of Goods Manufactured in this example. A statement of cost of goods manufactured and sold and an accompanying income statement are presented in Exhibit 2–9. In both exhibits note the ultimate disposition of product costs as the expense, cost of goods sold. In studying these statements, reflect on the flow of product

EXHIBIT 2–7 Flow of Product Costs

(a) Journal entries

1. Stores Control	$10,000	
Accounts Payable		$10,000
2. Work-in-Process	12,000	
Stores Control		12,000
3. Work-in-Process	30,000	
Factory Overhead Control	20,000	
Payroll Payable		50,000
4. Factory Overhead Control	40,000	
Accumulated Depreciation: Plant and Equipment		10,000
Utilities Payable		30,000
5. Work-in-Process	60,000	
Factory Overhead Control		60,000
6. Finished Goods Inventory	95,000	
Work-in-Process		95,000

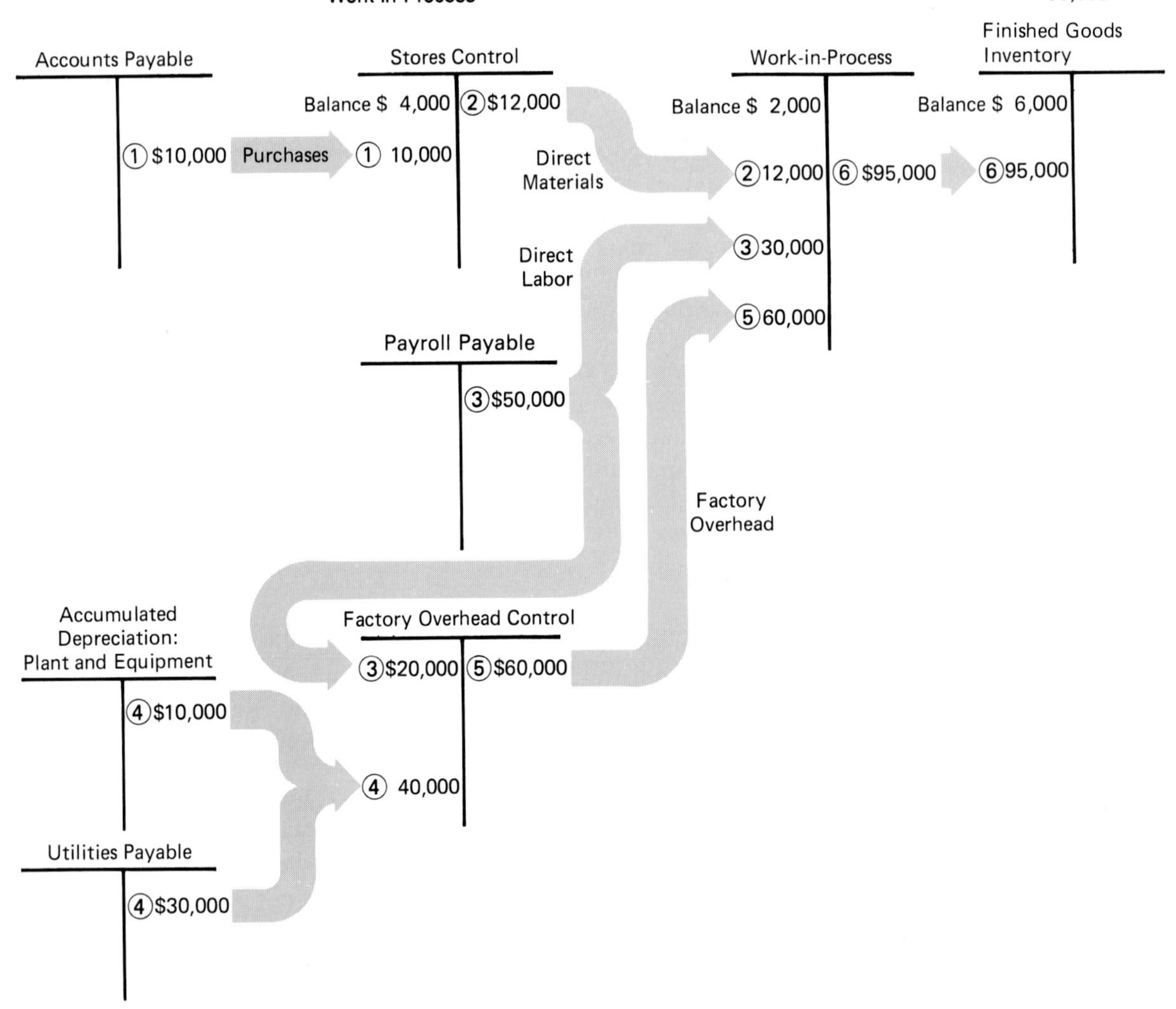

(b) Inventory account relationships

EXHIBIT 2–8 Statement of Cost of Goods Manufactured

Concord Manufacturing Company
Statement of Cost of Goods Manufactured
For the Month Ending October 31, 19x2

Current manufacturing costs:			
Cost of materials placed in production:			
Stores Control, 10/1/x2	$ 4,000		
Purchases	10,000		
Total raw materials available	$14,000		
Stores Control, 10/31/x2	−2,000	$12,000	
Direct labor		30,000	
Factory overhead:			
Indirect labor	$20,000		
Depreciation on plant and equipment	10,000		
Utilities	30,000	60,000	$102,000
Work-in-Process, 10/1/x2			2,000
Total costs in process			$104,000
Work-in-Process, 10/31/x2			−9,000
Cost of goods manufactured			$ 95,000

Concord Manufacturing Company
Income Statement
For the Month Ending October 31, 19x2

Sales		$200,000
Cost of goods sold:		
Finished Goods Inventory, 10/1/x2	$ 6,000	
Cost of goods manufactured:	95,000	
Total goods available for sale	$101,100	
Finished Goods Inventory, 10/31/x2	−11,000	−90,000
Gross profit		$110,000
Selling and administrative expenses		−60,000
Net income		$ 50,000

costs, the three basic product costs, and the concepts of account activity and account interrelationships (discussed in Chapter 1).

Product Costing and Service Costing

In this chapter we have been primarily concerned with product costing, that is, the assignment of costs to inventories as they are converted from raw materials to finished goods. This is the traditional focus of cost accounting textbooks because product costing topics must be mastered in order to prepare general-purpose financial statements for external reporting. Additionally, product costing concepts are well developed and most significant product costing issues have been identified by cost accountants.

In recent years cost accountants have become increasingly involved in **service costing**, that is, the assignment of costs to units of service. Examples of service costing include determining the cost of: flying a passenger from New York to

EXHIBIT 2–9 Statement of Cost of Goods Manufactured and Sold

Concord Manufacturing Company
Statement of Cost of Goods Manufactured and Sold
For the Month Ending October 31, 19x2

Current manufacturing costs:			
Cost of materials placed in production:			
Stores Control, 10/1/x2	$ 4,000		
Purchases	10,000		
Total raw materials available	$14,000		
Stores Control, 10/31/x2	−2,000	$12,000	
Direct labor		30,000	
Factory overhead:			
Indirect labor	$20,000		
Depreciation on plant and equipment	10,000		
Utilities	30,000	60,000	$102,000
Work-in-Process, 10/1/x2			2,000
Total costs in process			$104,000
Work-in-Process, 10/31/x2			−9,000
Cost of goods manufactured			$ 95,000
Finished Goods Inventory, 10/1/x2			6,000
Total goods available for sale			$101,000
Finished Goods Inventory, 10/31/x2			−11,000
Cost of goods sold			$ 90,000

Concord Manufacturing Company
Income Statement
For the Month Ending October 31, 19x2

Sales	$200,000
Cost of goods sold	−90,000
Gross profit	$110,000
Selling and administrative expenses	−60,000
Net income	$ 50,000

Atlanta, transporting a ton of coal from West Virginia to Illinois, processing a check, offering a section of a cost accounting course, serving a hamburger, and responding to a fire alarm. As the service sector of our economy becomes more significant, we need to plan and control service costs more closely. Consequently service costing is a new frontier for cost accounting. The exciting aspect of this emerging area is that service costing concepts can be developed primarily for the needs of management, rather than for the needs of external reporting, because inventory accounting principles apply only to physical products. Additionally, persons charged with implementing a new service costing system are less likely to run into the resistance to change that is often faced when attempts are made to revamp an in-place, but out-of-date product costing system.

Although we will focus most of our attention on the more developed product costing issues, we will frequently draw examples, exercises, and problems from service industries. We will find that many product costing procedures and concepts can be directly applied to service costing.

COSTS AND DECISION MAKING

Anyone who has studied financial accounting should know to be careful making decisions based on historical cost data. The current publicity given such topics as replacement cost, exit prices, and price level adjusted financial statements is one indication of dissatisfaction with historical cost numbers. Indeed, in management accounting, historical costs are frequently referred to disdainfully as "sunk costs."

Sunk Costs Are Never Relevant

Sunk costs are historical costs that result from past decisions over which management no longer has control. They are irrelevant for making decisions about the future. For example, the cost of mineral rights purchased in 1905 is not relevant in deciding whether to mine, sell the rights, or hold the rights. What is important is how much cash could be gained in the future from operations, from sale, or from appreciation if the rights are held for an additional period of time.

Even though historical costs, in and of themselves, are irrelevant for making decisions, they are frequently analyzed in detail before decisions about the future are made. There are at least two reasons for this:

1. Future tax payments, which are relevant because they involve cash outflows, may be based on historical costs.
2. An analysis of historical costs may provide information about how future costs will differ under alternative courses of action.

Regardless of the relevance of historical costs, records must be maintained of historical costs because historical cost information is required for external reporting and determining income taxes. Additionally, historical costs are often used by regulatory agencies as a basis for rate setting and cost reimbursement.

Outlay Costs May Be Relevant

Outlay costs are costs that require future expenditures of cash or other resources. Outlay costs are sometimes called **out-of-pocket costs** because they will require a future outflow of resources. Outlay costs may be, but are not necessarily, relevant to a particular decision. Their relevance depends on whether or not they will differ with the alternative selected.

Example 2–4

The Mountain View Restaurant had the following costs and revenues during March, 19x9:

Sales	$175,000
Cost of food used	75,000
Salaries and wages	25,000
Utilities	2,500
Rent on building	12,000
Depreciation on equipment	3,000
Laundry	450
Sales taxes	3,000

March is a typical month and similar costs and revenues are expected in future months.

Management is concerned about the monthly laundry bill of $450 and is considering the alternative of leasing a commercial washer and dryer to do their own laundry. The commercial washer and dryer will lease for $120 per month. It is expected that the additional water and electricity used to run the washer and dryer will increase the utilities bill by $140 per month. A local college student would also be hired to work two afternoons a week doing the laundry, increasing salaries and wages $75 per month. Management wishes to know whether it is more desirable to continue to have the laundry professionally cleaned or to clean the laundry at the restaurant.

The best way to approach such situations is first to identify which costs will be affected by the alternatives under consideration, and then to determine the amount by which each item will differ. In Example 2–4, because the depreciation represents an allocation of a historical cost, it will not be affected by the decision alternatives. All other costs will likely require future cash outlays at some level in future months. Consequently they are outlay or out-of-pocket costs. But not all of these outlay costs will be affected by the decision. Cost of food used, rent on building, and sales taxes are not affected by the decision. Items affected by the decision include salaries and wages, utilities, laundry, and rent on the commercial washer and dryer. Only these costs should be analyzed because only they are relevant to the decision at hand.

Relevant costs are costs that differ between competing alternatives. Analyzing the relevant costs, we can see that the advantage of doing the laundry at the restaurant is $115 per month:

	Professional laundry	*Cleaning at restaurant*	*Difference*
Salaries and wages	$25,000	$25,075	$ (75)
Utilities	2,500	2,640	(140)
Rent on washer and dryer		120	(120)
Laundry	450		450
Total	$27,950	$27,835	$ 115
Advantage of cleaning at restaurant	$ 115		

Relevant costs are future costs that differ among competing alternatives. Historical costs that result from a past decision are never relevant. Future costs may be relevant depending on whether or not they are affected by the decision at hand. The determination of the difference between the cash flows of competing actions that management is considering is called **differential analysis.** In Example 2–4 we prepared a differential analysis of relevant costs.

Opportunity Costs

The **opportunity cost** of using a resource in one manner is the expected net cash inflow that could be obtained if the resource were used in the most desirable other alternative action. Opportunity costs are not recorded in the accounting records, but they should be considered in evaluating a proposed course of action.

Assume a firm has a raw material recorded at its historical cost of $10. Management is evaluating the desirability of incurring additional cash expenses of $23 to transform this material into a product that can be sold for $50. This is a profitable use of resources that would result in a net cash inflow of $27 ($50 − $23). However, this may or may not be the most profitable use of resources. If the raw material could be sold for $20, the opportunity cost of using the raw material in this product is $20. Comparing the $20 cash inflow that would result from selling the raw material with the net cash inflow of $27 that would result from further production and sale reveals that production and sale has a net advantage of $7.

It is important to understand that opportunity costs are defined in relation to a particular action that management is considering. In the previous example, management was considering the use of a material in production. The alternative use of the material, selling it, provided the opportunity cost of $20. If management were contemplating the sale of the raw material for $20, the opportunity cost would be $27, the net cash inflow from production and sale. In this case the opportunity cost exceeds the net cash inflow of the proposed action by $7. The net disadvantage of a proposed action when compared to the best available alternative is called an **opportunity loss**. The opportunity loss from selling the material is $7.

Imputed Opportunity Cost

Sometimes we cannot identify and evaluate all alternative courses of action. When this happens, we should try to impute an opportunity cost. For example, if action A requires an investment of $1,000,000, it may not be desirable to evaluate all possible alternative investments of $1,000,000. Indeed, clear-cut alternatives may not be available. However, management may impute interest on the $1,000,000 and use this as the opportunity cost of selecting action A. If money can be invested in a certificate of deposit earning 11 percent interest, the imputed opportunity cost of using the $1,000,000 might be computed to be $110,000 ($1,000,000 × 0.11). An **imputed opportunity cost** is the interest that could be earned if the cash invested in one activity were invested in another.

SUMMARY

In predicting future costs and in evaluating past costs, cost accountants extensively use four basic cost behavior patterns: variable costs that increase in direct proportion to changes in the volume of activity, fixed costs that do not respond to changes in the volume of activity within a given time period, mixed costs that contain a fixed and a variable cost element, and step costs that are constant within a range of activity, but different between ranges of activity. For external reporting purposes accountants are often interested in the average cost of a unit of product or service. The average cost is simply the total costs divided by the volume in units.

According to the matching concept, when a clear relationship exists between costs and revenues, the costs incurred to generate future revenues should not be expensed until the revenues are recognized. When the matching concept is implemented in manufacturing organizations, the cost of raw materials and all other costs incurred to transform raw materials into finished goods are assigned to inventory accounts, and transferred to expenses only when the goods are sold.

Three types of costs are assigned to manufactured products: direct materials, direct labor, and factory overhead. Because of their immediate association with the product, direct materials and direct labor are often referred to as prime or direct product costs. Because they are incurred to convert raw materials into finished goods, direct labor and factory overhead are collectively identified as conversion costs.

Except for the information they provide about the wisdom of past decisions and the behavior of costs as volume changes, historical costs are not useful in decision making. The costs that are relevant to decision making are future costs that differ between alternative actions. The determination of the difference between the cash flows of alternative actions is called differential analysis.

KEY TERMS

Average cost
Capacity cost
Committed fixed cost
Conversion cost
Cost
Cost accounting
Cost accounting system
Cost of goods manufactured
Current manufacturing costs
Differential analysis
Direct labor
Direct materials
Direct product cost
Discretionary fixed cost
Factory overhead
Fixed cost
Imputed opportunity cost
Indirect materials
Indirect product cost
Marginal cost
Matching concept
Mixed cost
Opportunity cost
Opportunity loss
Out-of-pocket cost
Outlay cost
Period cost
Prime product cost
Product cost
Product costing
Relevant cost
Relevant range
Semivariable cost
Service costing
Statement of cost of goods manufactured
Statement of cost of goods manufactured and sold
Step cost
Sunk cost
Variable cost

SELECTED REFERENCES

Herman, Michael P., "Uniform Cost Accounting Standards: Are They Necessary," *Management Accounting* **53,** No. 10 (April 1972): 15–19.

Horngren, Charles T., "Choosing Accounting Practices for Reporting to Management," *N.A.A. Bulletin* **44,** No. 1 (September 1962): 3–15.

Janell, Paul A., and Raymond M. Kinnunen, "Portrait of the Divisional Controller," *Management Accounting* **61,** No. 12 (June 1980): 15–19, 24.

Kaplan, Robert S., "The Evolution of Management Accounting," *Accounting Review* **59,** No. 3 (July 1984): 390–418.

McRay, T. W., "Opportunity and Incremental Costs: An Attempt to Define in Systems Terms," *Accounting Review* **45,** No. 2 (April 1970): 315–321.

REVIEW QUESTIONS

2–1 Identify the four basic cost behavior patterns used in accounting models. For each pattern, indicate how total costs respond to changes in volume.

2–2 Distinguish between committed and discretionary fixed costs.

2–3 How do average costs respond to increases in volume? Why?

2–4 What is the relevant range? Why is it important to specify a relevant range for accounting cost functions?

2–5 What are the three major types of inventories found in manufacturing organizations?

2–6 What is the significance of the matching concept for manufacturing organizations?

2–7 Distinguish between product costs and period costs. Indicate when each becomes an expense.

2–8 Identify the three basic types of product costs.

2–9 Distinguish between prime costs and conversion costs. What basic product cost is both a prime cost and a conversion cost?

2–10 Identify the basic components of current manufacturing costs and distinguish between current manufacturing costs and the cost of goods manufactured.

2–11 Distinguish between product costing and service costing.

2–12 "Even though historical costs, in and of themselves, are irrelevant for making decisions, they are frequently analyzed in detail before decisions about the future are made." Why?

2–13 For the purpose of making future-oriented decisions, distinguish between relevant and irrelevant outlay costs.

2–14 In what way does an imputed opportunity cost differ from other types of opportunity costs?

REVIEW PROBLEM

Journal Entries for Cost Flows and Statement Preparation

On August 1, 19w3, the Mistic River Boat Company had inventories of $8,000, $50,000, and $90,000 in Stores Control, Work-in-Process, and Finished Goods

Inventory, respectively. During the month of August the following events occurred:

- Materials costing $30,000 were purchased on account.
- Materials costing $25,000 were placed in production.
- Salaries and wages earned by factory employees, including direct labor of $80,000, totaled $102,000.
- Factory overhead included:

Depreciation on plant and equipment	$20,000
Utilities	18,000
Amortization of prepaid insurance	1,000

August 31, 19w3, inventories amounted to $13,000, $40,000, and $75,000 in Stores Control, Work-in-Process, and Finished Goods Inventory, respectively.

REQUIREMENTS

a) Prepare journal entries for all August activities affecting Factory Overhead Control or any inventory account.

b) Prepare a formal statement of cost of goods manufactured and sold for August.

The solution to this problem is given at the end of the Chapter 2 problems and exercises.

EXERCISES

2–1 Cost Terminology: Matching

Presented are a number of terms frequently encountered in cost accounting. For each numbered statement or phrase, select the most appropriate term. Each term is used only once.

COST TERMS

a) Variable costs	f) Historical cost
b) Prime costs	g) Period costs
c) Marginal cost	h) Conversion costs
d) Fixed costs	i) Relevant costs
e) Relevant range	j) Opportunity costs

STATEMENTS

1. Volumes over which cost relationships are valid.
2. Direct materials and direct labor.
3. Change in direct proportion to changes in the volume of activity.
4. Future costs that differ under two alternatives.

5. The varying increment in total costs required to produce and sell one additional unit.
6. Do not respond to changes in volume within a given period.
7. Except for possible tax considerations, this cost should not be considered in evaluating alternative courses of action.
8. Costs that are not necessary for production.
9. Overhead and direct labor.
10. Costs that are important to decision makers, but are not recorded in the accounting records.

2–2 Multiple Classification of Costs

For each item listed, indicate its cost behavior pattern (fixed, variable, and so on); specify whether it is a product or period cost; and if it is a product cost, indicate whether it is a prime cost and/or a conversion cost and/or an overhead cost

Item	*Cost behavior pattern*	*Product/ period cost*	*Prime/ conversion/ overhead cost*
a) Raw materials used in production			
b) Coal used in generating electricity to support production in plant			
c) Depreciation on delivery equipment owned by the company			
d) Salaries of inspection personnel			
e) President's salary			
f) Property taxes on production plant			
g) Production supervisor's salary			
h) Income taxes			
i) Depreciation on generating equipment used to support production in plant			
j) Depletion on mine			
k) Production employees' wages			
l) Auditor's fee			
m) Advertising fees			

2–3 Cost Behavior Patterns

For each situation presented, select the most appropriate cost or revenue pattern. The dots represent actual cost data. The horizontal axis represents volume starting at zero.

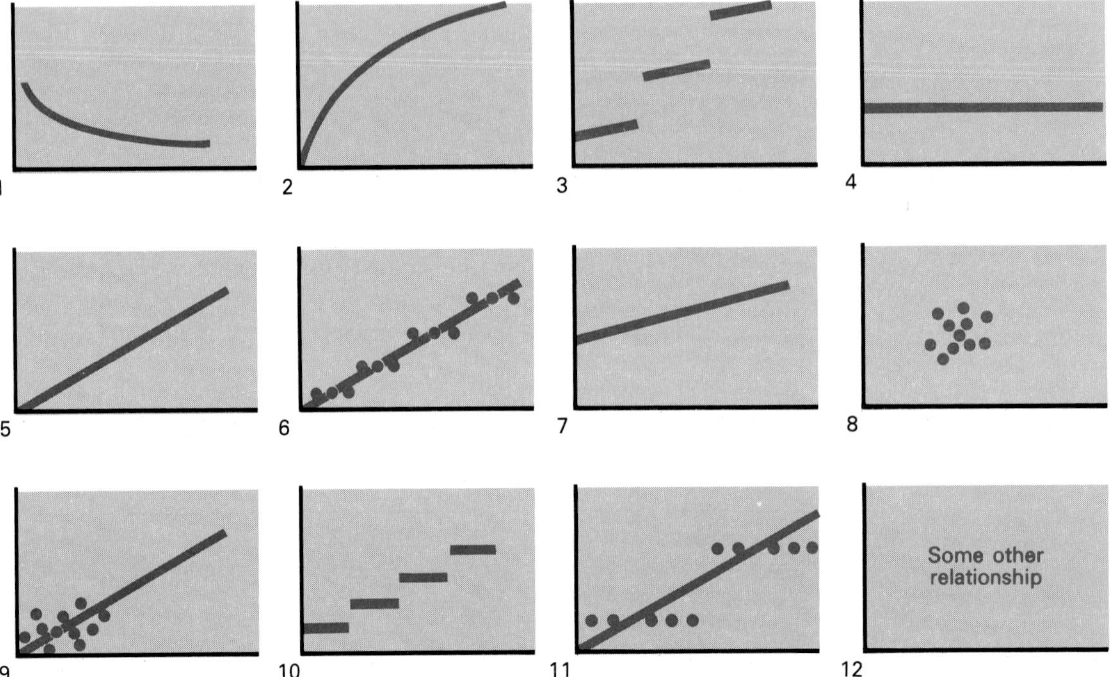

a) Total revenue as sales increase in a perfectly competitive market.

b) Total variable cost line properly used to estimate step costs.

c) Total variable cost line improperly used to estimate step costs.

d) Unit variable cost line.

e) Average fixed cost per unit of production.

f) A linear extrapolation of total variable costs beyond the relevant range.

g) Total salaries of quality inspection personnel in a small organization.

h) Total salaries of quality inspection personnel in a large organization.

i) The total cost of renting delivery trucks in a local wholesale operation when the rent is based on the number of trucks used and miles driven.

j) The total cost of renting delivery trucks in a regional wholesale operation when the rent is based on the number of trucks used and miles driven.

k) The total cost of operating a laundry.

l) The total cost of operating a drugstore.

m) Total revenue as sales increase in a monopolistic market.

n) The total cost of renting photocopying equipment when the rent is based on a fixed fee plus usage.

2–4 T-Account Cost Flows

The following T-accounts were taken from the records of Massachusetts Manufacturing Co. However, the junior accountant spilled her coffee and made some figures illegible.

Raw Materials Inventory

Debit		Credit
12/1 Balance	$12,000	? → (to Direct materials)
→ Purchases	?	
12/31 Balance	15,000	

Work-in-Process

Debit		Credit
12/1 Balance	$14,000	
→ Direct materials	?	
Direct labor	?	? Cost of goods manufactured →
Factory overhead	90,000	
12/31 Balance	18,000	

Conversion costs are ⅔ of total current manufacturing costs. Factory Overhead is 150 percent of direct labor cost.

REQUIREMENT

Calculate the following:

a) Direct labor
b) Direct materials used
c) Purchases
d) Cost of goods manufactured
e) Prime product costs
f) Conversion costs

2–5 T-Account Cost Flows

The following T-accounts were taken from the records of Georgia Products Co. However, the junior accountant spilled her cola and made some figures illegible.

Raw Materials Inventory

Debit		Credit
12/1 Balance	$8,000	
		? → (to Direct materials)
→ Purchases	?	
12/31 Balance	10,000	

Work-in-Process

Debit		Credit
12/1 Balance	$9,000	
→ Direct materials	?	
Direct labor	?	$105,000 Cost of goods manufactured →
Factory overhead	?	
12/31 Balance	$4,000	

Material costs are 40 percent of total current manufacturing costs. Factory Overhead is 200 percent of direct labor cost.

REQUIREMENT

Calculate the following:

a) Direct materials used
b) Direct labor
c) Factory overhead
d) Purchases
e) Prime product costs
f) Conversion costs

2–6 T-Account Cost Flows

Presented is information pertaining to the 19x2 manufacturing operation of the Ezy Company:

Stores Control			Work-in-Process			Finished Goods Inventory	
1/1 Balance	$5,000	1/1 Balance	?	1/1 Balance	$15,000	$40,000 Cost of→ goods sold	
		?——→Direct materials	?*	$35,000——→Cost of goods manufactured	35,000		
——→Purchases	?	Direct labor	20,000				
		Factory overhead	10,000				
12/31 Balance	2,000	12/31 Balance	15,000	12/31 Balance	?		

* Materials constituted one-third of the current manufacturing costs.

REQUIREMENTS

a) Determine 19x2 purchases of raw materials.

b) Determine the 1/1 balance of Work-in-Process.

c) Determine the cost of materials used.

d) Determine the 12/31 balance in Finished Goods Inventory.

2–7 Cost Flows

The following inventory data relate to the Shirley Company:

	Inventories	
	Beginning	*Ending*
Finished Goods	$110,000	$95,000
Work-in-Process	70,000	80,000
Stores Control	90,000	95,000

ADDITIONAL INFORMATION

o Cost of goods available for sale	$684,000
o Total costs in process during period	654,000
o Factory overhead	167,000
o Direct materials used	193,000

REQUIREMENTS

a) Determine raw materials purchases.

b) Determine the direct labor costs incurred.

c) Determine the cost of goods sold. (CPA Adapted)

2–8 T Statement of Cost of Goods Manufactured, Statement of Cost of Goods Manufactured and Sold[6]

Presented is information pertaining to the October, 19x2, operations of the Delaney Company:

	Beginning Inventory	*Ending Inventory*
Stores Control	$ 2,500	$3,200
Work-in-Process	1,700	1,350
Finished Goods	9,500	8,500
Purchases of raw materials	$27,000	
Direct labor	30,000	
Factory overhead:		
Indirect labor	5,000	
Depreciation	8,000	
Utilities	4,680	
Manufacturing supplies	560	

REQUIREMENTS

a) Prepare a statement of cost of goods manufactured for the month ending October 31, 19x2.

b) Prepare a statement of cost of goods manufactured and sold for the month ending October 31, 19x2.

2–9 T Statement of Cost of Goods Manufactured, Statement of Cost of Goods Manufactured and Sold

Presented is information pertaining to the January 31, 19y1, operations of the Wyoming Job Shop:

	Beginning Inventory	*Ending Inventory*
Stores Control	$ 6,000	$3,500
Work-in-Process	3,900	5,400
Finished Goods	2,100	950
Purchases of raw materials	$ 4,600	
Direct labor	16,000	
Factory overhead:		
Indirect labor	3,200	
Depreciation	900	
Utilities	1,700	
Repairs	280	
Miscellaneous	370	

[6] Exercises and problems identified with a T are designed in a manner that makes them suitable for solution using spreadsheet computer software.

REQUIREMENTS

a) Prepare a statement of cost of goods manufactured for the month ending January 31, 19y1.

b) Prepare a statement of cost of goods manufactured and sold for the month ending January 31, 19y1.

2–10 Statement of Cost of Goods Manufactured: Algebra

Mat Company's cost of goods sold for the month ending March 31, 19x4, was $345,000. Ending work-in-process inventory was 90 percent of beginning work-in-process inventory. Factory overhead was 50 percent of direct labor cost. Other information pertaining to Mat Company's inventories and production for the month of March is as follows:

Beginning inventories—March 1:	
Direct materials	$ 20,000
Work-in-process	40,000
Finished goods	102,000
Purchases of direct materials during March	110,000
Ending inventories—March 31:	
Direct materials	26,000
Work-in-process	?
Finished goods	105,000

REQUIREMENTS

a) Prepare a statement of cost of goods manufactured for the month of March.

b) Determine the prime costs incurred during March.

c) Determine the conversion costs charged to Work-in-Process during March.

(CPA Adapted)

2–11 Statement of Cost of Goods Manufactured: Algebra

The Helper Corporation manufactures one product. You have obtained the following information for the year ended December 31, 19x3, from the corporation's books and records:

- Total current manufacturing costs were $1,000,000.
- The 19x3 cost of goods manufactured was $970,000.
- Current factory overhead costs were 75 percent of current direct-labor costs and 27 percent of total current manufacturing costs.
- Beginning Work-in-Process, January 1, was 80 percent of ending Work-in-Process, December 31.

REQUIREMENT

Prepare a formal statement of cost of goods manufactured for the year ended December 31, 19x3.

(CPA Adapted)

2–12 Account Analysis and Journal Entries for Cost Flows

The following information pertains to the Valley Company:

	Inventories	
	Beginning	*Ending*
Stores Control	$15,000	$25,000
Work-in-Process	25,000	20,000
Finished Goods	40,000	20,000

ADDITIONAL INFORMATION

- Direct materials used $ 30,000
- Factory overhead 15,000
- Cost of goods available for sale 100,000

REQUIREMENTS

a) Prepare journal entries for the activity in *all* inventory accounts. Assume all purchases are on account.

b) Determine the following:

1. Total prime costs.
2. Total conversion costs.

2–13 Account Analysis and Journal Entries for Cost Flows

The following information is taken from the records of the Boston Tea Company:

	Inventories	
	Beginning	*Ending*
Stores Control	$19,000	$13,000
Work-in-Process	8,000	5,000
Finished Goods	21,000	27,000

ADDITIONAL INFORMATION

- Purchase of raw materials $ 24,000
- Direct labor 60,000
- Cost of goods sold 220,000

REQUIREMENTS

a) Prepare journal entries for the activity in all inventory accounts. Assume all purchases are on account. (*Hint:* Set up the entries and then compute the amounts.)

b) Determine the following:

1. Total prime costs.
2. Total conversion costs.

2–14 Account Analysis and Journal Entries for Cost Flows

The following information is taken from the records of the Fast Clock Company:

	Inventories	
	Beginning	*Ending*
Stores Control	$15,000	$17,000
Work-in-Process	4,000	9,000
Finished Goods	25,000	22,000

ADDITIONAL INFORMATION

o Direct materials used	$42,000
o Factory overhead	30,000
o Cost of goods manufactured	120,000

REQUIREMENTS

a) Prepare journal entries for the activity in all inventory accounts. Assume all purchases are on account.

b) Determine the following:

1. Total prime costs.
2. Total conversion costs.

2–15 Sunk Costs

Gandy Company has 5,000 obsolete desk lamps that are carried in inventory at a manufacturing cost of $50,000. If the lamps are reworked for $20,000, they could be sold for $35,000. Alternatively, the lamps could be sold for $8,000 to a jobber located in a distant city.

REQUIREMENT

Determine the sunk cost for a decision model analyzing these alternatives.

(CPA Adapted)

2–16 Sunk vs. Relevant Costs

The Slippery Step General Hospital keeps its cardiograph machines in a central storage area under the supervision of an administrative intern. A recently hired RN, John C., was returning one of the machines when he slipped on a freshly waxed floor and shoved the machine into a nearby stairwell as he fell. The resulting crash brought the intern, Dr. Jane E., to the scene of the disaster. Observing the RN, who had a broken arm, and the inoperable parts of the decimated machine she mumbled, "(Expletive deleted) . . . if only we used accelerated depreciation!"

REQUIREMENT

Distinguish between the sunk cost (about which the intern was concerned) and the relevant cost (about which the intern did not appear to be concerned).

2–17 Relevant Costs

The Living Stones, a well-known hard-rock group, are thinking about starting their own record company. They believe this will require an investment of $500,000 and require them to devote two weeks each year to administrative duties. Mr. F. B. (Fly By) Knight, who would be the operating manager of the firm, has estimated that yearly operating revenues and expenses would total $450,000 and $300,000, respectively, not including salaries paid the Stones. Mr. Knight has assured the Stones that they could recover their $500,000 investment at any time by selling the company.

ADDITIONAL INFORMATION

- The Stones have over $1,000,000 available in a time deposit that is earning interest of 10 percent per year.
- The administrative duties associated with the company would require the Stones to cancel three concerts. Each concert has a guaranteed contract of $50,000. Travel expenses, and so forth average $15,000 per concert. The Stones will have to pay penalties totaling $3,000 if they cancel all three concerts.

REQUIREMENTS

a) Assuming the Stones can recover their $500,000 investment in one year if they decide to sell, determine the outlay and opportunity costs associated with the proposed action.

b) Determine the net advantage or disadvantage of the proposed course of action.

PROBLEMS

2–18 T Journal Entries for Cost Flows and Statement Preparation

On November 1, 19w6, the Oconee River Canoe Company had inventories of $1,000, $4,000, and $2,000 in Stores Control, Work-in-Process, and Finished Goods, respectively.

During the month of November the following activities occurred:

- Materials costing $2,000 were purchased on account.
- Materials costing $2,500 were placed in production.
- Salaries and wages earned by factory employees including direct labor of $6,000, totaled $7,200.
- Factory overhead included:

Depreciation on plant and equipment	$500
Utilities	425
Supplies, purchased on account as used	360

On November 30, 19w6, inventories amounted to $500, $3,200, and $4,200 in Stores Control, Work-in-Process, and Finished Goods, respectively.

REQUIREMENTS

a) Prepare journal entries for all activities affecting Factory Overhead Control or any inventory account.

b) Prepare a formal statement of cost of goods manufactured and sold for the month of November, 19w6.

2–19 T Journal Entries for Cost Flows and Statement Preparation

Presented is information pertaining to the September, 19x8, activities of the Muddy River Production Company:

- Purchases of raw materials, $60,000. All on account.
- Wages *paid* production employees, $78,000.
- Salaries *paid* production supervisors, $6,500.
- Unpaid utilities for electricity and water used in the factory amounted to $2,000.

ADDITIONAL INFORMATION

- Monthly depreciation on production facilities is $5,000.
- Selected beginning and ending balances in relevant accounts are:

	Beginning	*Ending*
Stores Control	$10,000	$20,000
Work-in-Process	25,000	28,000
Accounts Payable	8,000 cr.	8,000 cr.
Payroll Payable (wages)	3,000 cr.	5,000 cr.
Payroll Payable (salaries)	1,000 cr.	500 cr.

- All factory overhead costs are summarized in a single control account and then assigned to Work-in-Process at the end of the month.

REQUIREMENTS

a) Prepare journal entries summarizing the flow of costs in Stores Control and Work-in-Process inventory accounts. Do not prepare journal entries for any cash disbursements.

b) Prepare a formal statement of cost of goods manufactured for the month of September.

2–20 Statement of Cost of Goods Manufactured and Income Statement

Presented is information taken from the records of the Marrow Company:

Cash Receipts and Disbursements for 19x4:	
Sales	$400,000
Purchases of raw materials	60,000
Purchases of manufacturing supplies	1,500
Purchases of office supplies	400
Dividends	20,000
Utilities:	
Manufacturing	3,300
Offices	1,200
Wages paid production employees	60,000
Salaries paid production supervisors	15,000
Salaries paid administrative and sales personnel	50,000
Income taxes	50,500

Inventory Account Balances:	*1/1/x4*	*12/31/x4*
Raw Materials	$10,000	$25,000
Manufacturing Supplies	500	300
Office Supplies	200	300
Finished Goods Inventory	20,000	10,000
Work-in-Process	30,000	13,000

ADDITIONAL INFORMATION

- Marrow had no receivables or payables on 1/1/x4 or 12/31/x4.
- Depreciation on manufacturing facilities for 19x4 was $8,000.
- Depreciation on office facilities for 19x4 was $1,000.

REQUIREMENTS

a) Prepare a statement of cost of goods manufactured and sold for 19x4.

b) Prepare an income statement for 19x4.

2–21 T Statement of Cost of Goods Manufactured and Sold

The following information is taken from the accounts of the Apex Manufacturing Company:

Account Balances:	*1/1/x4*	*12/31/x4*
Stores Control	$ 20,000	$ 10,000
Supplies (manufacturing)	5,000	6,000
Work-in-Process	50,000	80,000
Finished Goods Inventory	80,000	100,000
Accounts Payable, to suppliers of raw materials	30,000	20,000
Payroll Payable, to production employees	25,000	15,000
Income Taxes Payable	8,000	5,000
Dividends Payable	10,000	0
Plant and Equipment	500,000	600,000
Accumulated Depreciation—Plant and Equipment	70,000	120,000

Cash Payments During 19x4:	
To suppliers of raw materials	$110,000
For manufacturing supplies	10,000
To production employees	250,000
For income taxes	45,000
To purchase new equipment	100,000
Salesperson's commissions	75,000
Dividends	20,000
Repairs and maintenance of plant and equipment	5,000
Administrative salaries	50,000
Rent for administrative and sales offices	10,000
Property taxes on plant	4,000
Utilities:	
Plant	20,000
Office	2,000

REQUIREMENT

Prepare a statement of cost of goods manufactured and sold for 19x4.

2–22 Determining Inventory Balances: A Gross Profit Approach

On September 1, 19x3, an early morning brush fire ignited the Bushey Mountain plant of the Southern California Wood Company. Plant, property, and equipment with a total estimated value of $650,000 were destroyed in the subsequent fire. At high personal risk the firm's chief accountant entered the burning office and saved many of the firm's accounting records. The information is as follows:

Stores Control, 1/1/x3	$ 20,000
Work-in-Process, 1/1/x3	50,000
Finished Goods Inventory, 1/1/x3	40,000
Purchases of raw materials, 1/1/x3 to 9/1/x3	35,000
Direct labor, 1/1/x3 to 9/1/x3	80,000
Factory overhead, 1/1/x3 to 9/1/x3	40,000
Selling expenses, 1/1/x3 to 9/1/x3	30,000
Depreciation on administrative offices, 1/1/x3 to 9/1/x3	5,000
Officers salaries, 1/1/x3 to 9/1/x3	20,000
Sales, 1/1/x3 to 9/1/x3	250,000

The firm is under a periodic inventory system. Hence, they do not have information on the cost of the inventories destroyed by the fire. Before filing an insurance claim they must estimate the cost of such inventories.

ADDITIONAL INFORMATION

- The firm's gross profit percentage has averaged 20 percent of sales in recent years.
- Direct materials have averaged 25 percent of product costs in recent years.
- The firm normally maintains sufficient finished goods inventory for one month's sales. Sales occur evenly throughout the year.

REQUIREMENT

Estimate the cost of all inventories destroyed by the fire.

2–23 Determining Work-in-Process: A Gross Profit Approach

On June 30, 19x8, a flash flood damaged the warehouse and factory of Padway Corporation, completely destroying the work-in-process inventory. There was no damage to either the raw materials or finished goods inventories. A physical inventory taken after the flood revealed the following valuations:

Raw materials	$ 62,000
Work-in-process	0
Finished goods	119,000

The inventory on January 1, 19x8, consisted of the following:

Raw materials	$ 30,000
Work-in-process	100,000
Finished goods	140,000
Total	$270,000

A review of the books and records disclosed that the gross profit margin historically approximated 25 percent of sales. The sales for the first six months of 19x8 were $340,000. Raw materials purchases were $115,000 for the six months. Direct labor costs for this period were $80,000, and factory overhead has historically been 50 percent of direct labor.

REQUIREMENT

Compute the cost of the work-in-process inventory lost on June 30, 19x8.

(CPA Adapted)

SOLUTION TO REVIEW PROBLEM

	Debit	Credit
a) Stores Control	$ 30,000	
Accounts Payable		$ 30,000
Work-in-Process	25,000	
Stores Control		25,000
Work-in Process	80,000	
Factory Overhead Control	22,000	
Payroll Payable		102,000
(*Note:* Indirect labor must be $102,000 − $80,000.)		
Factory Overhead Control	39,000	
Accumulated Depreciation—Plant and Equipment		20,000
Utilities Payable		18,000
Prepaid Insurance		1,000
Work-in-Process	61,000	
Factory Overhead Control		61,000
Finished Goods Inventory	176,000	
Work-in-Process		176,000
[See the solution to (b) for supporting computations.]		
Cost of Goods Sold	191,000	
Finished Goods Inventory		191,000
[See the solution to (b) for supporting computations.]		

b) **Mistic River Boat Company**
Statement of Cost of Goods Manufactured and Sold
For the Month Ending August 31, 19w3

Current manufacturing costs:			
Cost of materials placed in production:			
Stores Control, 8/1/w3	$ 8,000		
Purchases	30,000		
Total raw materials available	$38,000		
Stores Control, 8/31/w3	– 13,000	$25,000	
Direct labor		80,000	
Factory overhead:			
Indirect labor	$22,000		
Depreciation on plant and equipment	20,000		
Utilities	18,000		
Insurance	1,000	61,000	$166,000
Work-in-Process, 8/1/w3			50,000
Total costs in process			$216,000
Work-in-Process, 8/30/w3			– 40,000
Cost of goods manufactured			$176,000
Finished Goods Inventory, 8/1/w3			90,000
Total goods available for sale			$266,000
Finished Goods Inventory, 8/30/w3			– 75,000
Cost of goods sold			$191,000

3 Actual and Normal Job-Order Costing

INTRODUCTION
JOB-ORDER COSTING
ACTUAL JOB-ORDER COST SYSTEMS
NORMAL JOB-ORDER COST SYSTEMS
OVERHEAD APPLICATIONS WITH MULTIPLE PRODUCTION DEPARTMENTS
SUMMARY

INTRODUCTION

PRODUCT COSTING IS THE ASSIGNMENT OF COSTS TO INVENTORIES AS THEY are converted from raw materials to finished goods. We examined common concepts that form the foundation of all product costing systems in Chapter 2. We distinguished between product costs, which are assigned to products as they are produced and expensed when products are sold, and period costs, which are expired costs that are not necessary for production and are expensed immediately in financial statements. We also examined the characteristics of the three major categories of product costs: direct materials, direct labor, and factory overhead.

The purpose of this chapter is to examine job-order costing, a widely used product costing system. Another widely used product costing systems, process costing, is examined in Chapter 4. Assigning costs to joint products simultaneously produced from a single raw material is examined in Chapter 5. The allocation of service department costs to production departments, for the purpose of product costing, is examined in Chapter 6.

Product costing topics may be studied in their own right by students interested in financial reporting or price justification, or they may be studied as background information before embarking on a study of cost estimation techniques, short-range planning, and performance evaluation. Although students whose primary interest is cost estimation and short-range planning may defer the study of process costing or service department cost allocation, they are urged to read Chapter 3 with care. In addition to helping students understand the data base used in many cost-estimating techniques, the study of job-order costing provides a framework or model that can be used for budgeting.

The placement of cost accumulation and assignment topics early in this book reflects the increasing importance of costs in setting and justifying prices. Prices in an expanding sector of our economy are often based, by government regulation or third-party agreement, on full cost allocation. Professor Robert Anthony has observed that this is the case for public utility rates, railroad and truck freight rates, telephone rates, public construction contracts, the health care industry, and the tens of billions of dollars of contracts let annually by the U.S. Department of Defense.[1]

Even in industries that are not normally regulated, costs are sometimes critical for justifying prices. In the early 1970s, the U.S. government established a price commission to help control inflation. One of the principles the commission used was that increases in selling prices must be justified by increases in costs. In a similar vein, "voluntary" wage-price guidelines in the late 1970s attempted to limit price increases to a fixed percent unless companies could demonstrate that cost increases were reducing profit margins below a specified level. In this environment, all managers must be familiar with cost accumulation and assignment concepts and procedures.

JOB-ORDER COSTING

To determine the cost of goods manufactured during a period, production costs must be assigned to units completed during the period and to units in process at the end of the period. How this is accomplished depends, in part, on the cost system used. A **job-order cost system** assigns costs to specifically identifiable batches of goods or to a specifically identifiable project. Under a job-order cost system, all costs associated with a job are placed in the Work-in-Process account as work progresses, and the costs remain in Work-in-Process until the entire job is complete. When the job is completed, all costs assigned to the job are transferred from Work-in-Process to Finished Goods Inventory. As the units contained in the job are sold, costs are transferred from Finished Goods Inventory to Cost of Goods Sold.

Job-order costing is used for work performed pursuant to an order or contract with an outside entity and for speculative work such as replenishing inventories or internal construction. Job-order costing is appropriate in the following situations:

- A contractor building a ship for the navy
- A hospital billing a patient for services rendered
- A print shop printing 5,000 copies of a college newspaper
- A tool company producing 50 lathes for inventory
- A foundry manufacturing a special part to order
- A manufacturer using its own labor force to build a warehouse

The distinguishing feature of job-order costing is not the origin of the work order, but rather the ability to identify costs with a specific project or group of units.

In operation, job-order cost systems vary widely. Factors such as the size and nature of jobs, the size of the organization, external and internal data requirements, whether manual or mechanical or computer facilities are used for

---

[1] Robert N. Anthony, "The Rebirth of Cost Accounting," *Management Accounting* **57**, No. 4 (October 1975): 13.

data processing, and the preferences of management affect the design and operation of the system. Nevertheless the essential elements are always present in some form.

Job-Cost Sheet

The backbone of job-order systems is a **job-cost sheet**, a record used to accumulate the costs for specific jobs. Every job has a separate job-cost sheet such as the one illustrated in Exhibit 3–1(a). On the job-cost sheet, costs are recorded in three basic categories: direct materials, direct labor, and factory overhead. Depending on data requirements for performance evaluation, planning, or pricing, additional information (for example, departments in which work was performed, type and quantity of materials used, labor classifications and hours of employees working on the job, and machine types and hours used on the job) may also be recorded. For very large jobs such as a contract to build an office building, the job-cost sheet is expanded to become an entire set of accounting records.

EXHIBIT 3–1 **Cost System Records**

Job Number *201*
Item *DIRECTORY* Number of Units *500*
Date Started *10/21/x9* Completed *11/15/x9*

Date	Direct Materials	Direct Labor	Overhead	Total
10/21/x9	*$180*			*$180*
10/30/x9		*$150*	*$180*	*510*
11/15/x9		*50*		*560*
11/30/x9			*65*	*625*

TOTAL *$625*

(a) Job cost sheet

Inventory Number ____
Description ____

Date	Units: Received	Units: Issued	Units: Balance	Unit Cost	Balance

(b) Materials inventory record

Inventory Number ____ Date ____
Job Number ____

Quantity	Unit Cost	Total Cost

Received by ____
Issued by ____

(c) Materials requisition record

Job Number ____ Date ____
Employee Name ____ Badge No. ____
Time Started ____ Time Completed ____

Office Use

Hours ____ Rate ____ Charge ____

(d) Direct labor ticket

In a job-order system, Work-in-Process is a control account and each job-cost sheet is a subsidiary account. As a unit, the job-cost sheets of all jobs in process constitute a subsidiary ledger and the sum of the balances of all costs for jobs in process is equal to the balance in Work-in-Process. As costs are assigned to job-cost sheets, a like amount is also debited to Work-in-Process. As jobs are completed, the job-cost sheet is removed from the work-in-process file and is placed in the finished goods file. Simultaneously, Work-in-Process is credited and Finished Goods Inventory is debited.

Example 3–1

On September 1, 19x9, the Kingsport Machine Shop had three jobs, 674, 678, and 679, in process. Total costs assigned to these jobs as of September 1 are as follows:

Job	*Total costs on job-cost sheets*
674	$8,500
678	5,000
679	1,000

The September 1 balance in Work-in-Process is $14,500 ($8,500 + $5,000 + $1,000).

Direct Materials

Each type of raw material held by the organization is accounted for in a separate **materials inventory record** such as the one illustrated in Exhibit 3–1(b). Although the materials inventory records may be separate cards or pages in a ledger, they are just as likely to be recorded on a computer disk. As a unit, the materials inventory records constitute a subsidiary ledger whose related control account is frequently titled Stores Control.

When raw materials are purchased, the transaction is posted both to the control account and to the appropriate subsidiary records. If, for example, 500 units of Material Q are purchased at a total cost of $950, this amount is debited to Stores Control and credited to Accounts Payable. The same amount is recorded on Material Q's inventory record and in the appropriate Accounts Payable subsidiary ledger account.

When materials are issued for use on a job, a **materials requisition record** is used to record the transfer of direct materials costs from Stores Control to Work-in-Process. The materials requisition record may be a physically existing paper or card such as the one illustrated in Exhibit 3–1(c), or it may be a computerized record. In any case, the dollar amount recorded on the materials requisition record is the basis for reducing the balance in Stores Control and on the appropriate materials inventory record. The dollar amount on the materials requisition record also is the basis for increasing the balance in the control account, Work-in-Process, and assigning the materials costs to a particular job-cost sheet.[2]

---

[2] Besides the number of units, the costs transferred also depend on the inventory-costing techniques used (LIFO, FIFO, moving average, etc.).

Note that the raw materials of one firm may be the finished product of another. Two-by-fours are a finished product of a sawmill, but they are a raw material of a housing contractor.

Direct Labor

As work progresses, employees fill out a **direct-labor ticket** such as the one in Exhibit 3–1(d), indicating the time they started and completed working on each job. The time spent working on a job is determined by taking the difference between the starting and finishing time. The direct-labor cost assigned to a job is computed as the time spent working on the job multiplied by the employee's wage rate. This amount is debited to Work-in-Process and assigned to the appropriate job-cost sheet. The corresponding credit is made to a liability account, such as Payroll Payable. The Payroll Payable account is a control account, supported by a number of subsidiary accounts, indicating the amount payable to each employee.

The actual amount employees earn usually exceeds the direct-labor costs charged to Work-in-Process and individual job-cost sheets. This difference is the result of such factors as **idle time** (that is, nonproductive time caused by a lack of work), nonchargeable personal time (such as a coffee break during working hours), nonchargeable time spent receiving instructions, and overtime premiums. **Overtime premiums** are bonus wages, in excess of the regular hourly rate, paid production employees working more than the regular number of hours. The difference between the actual amount employees earn and the direct-labor costs charged to job-cost sheets is usually assigned to factory overhead.

Example 3–2

Sandy Jones is paid $8 per hour for a normal 40-hour work-week and an overtime premium of 50 percent of her regular wage rate for working more than 40 hours in a given week. Last week Sandy worked 45 hours. A breakdown of her time is as follows:

Job 2301	21 hours
Job 2307	9 hours
Job 2308	12 hours
Idle and nonchargeable time	3 hours
Total	45 hours

Ms Jones' total earnings are $380:

Regular earnings (45 hours × $8)	$360
Overtime premium [(45 − 40) × $8 × 0.50]	20
Total earnings	$380

The $380 would be credited to Payroll Payable. The portion of it assignable to specific jobs, $336, would be debited to Work-in-Process, and the balance, $44, would be debited to Factory Overhead Control:

Total earnings		$380
Assigned to specific jobs and Work-in-Process:		
Job 2301 (21 hours × $8)	$168	
Job 2307 (9 hours × $8)	72	
Job 2308 (12 hours × $8)	96	−336
Assigned to Factory Overhead Control		$ 44

To the extent that idle and nonchargeable time is necessary for efficient operations, its cost should be treated as factory overhead. However, if idle or nonchargeable time becomes excessive due to poor planning and control, it should be written off as a period cost. Including such excessive costs in overhead overstates income for the period and inventory at the end of the period. Additionally, including the cost of idle time in factory overhead reduces the usefulness of accounting information for predicting future costs because inefficiencies are incorporated into it. If excessive nonchargeable time were included in the records, an adjustment would be required before the data could be used for cost estimation purposes.

Overtime premium is usually treated as overhead even if the overtime hours are identified with a particular job. Overtime is the result of the overall level of activity. If the overall level of activity were lower, the job(s) worked on during overtime hours would be worked on during regular hours. Accordingly, overtime premiums are allocated to all jobs through the factory overhead account.[3]

For an accounting system to provide information useful for controlling current operations and predicting future costs, it is critical that direct-labor tickets and other cost system records be completed promptly and accurately. Unfortunately the required speed and accuracy are not always attained. Busy workers may regard filling out forms as a bothersome waste of time and may delay completing them. This results in less timely information that is only as accurate as employees' memories.

Other behavioral factors may also reduce the accuracy of direct labor tickets.

- If pressure is placed on employees to avoid nonassigned time, they may arbitrarily assign all working hours to jobs.
- Under a piece rate system, where workers are paid on the basis of predetermined rates for individual jobs, employees may save work tickets for extended periods of time to smooth their income or avoid changes in favorable rates.
- If there is pressure to complete individual jobs in the planned time, the supervisor may urge employees to assign excess labor hours to jobs completed in less than the planned time.

---

[3] A different treatment should be accorded overtime premium when it results from a "rush" order where the purchaser wants a shorter than normal delivery time. In this case it seems appropriate to assign the overhead to a specific job. If overtime is for a very large job such as a new building, it also seems appropriate to assign the overtime premium to the specific job, rather than to treat it as overhead.

Factory Overhead

The Achilles' heel of product costing in general and of job-order costing in particular is overhead. The relationship between the product and direct materials or labor is apparent. The physical flow of raw materials may be traced. The time employees spend working on a job can be observed. But what about factory overhead? It is difficult, if not impossible, to relate the production supervisor's salary, property taxes, nonchargeable time, electricity, and depreciation to specific jobs.

Factory overhead includes fixed costs that relate to productive capacity as well as variable costs that increase with production. Clearly the fixed costs are not caused by individual jobs. Although the incurrence of variable overhead costs is caused by the work performed, these costs vary with many different elements of each job. Power to run machines and repairs and maintenance relate to the hours different machines are operated. Occupancy costs relate to the number and size of units produced. Some nonchargeable time and supply costs relate to direct-labor hours. Because of the interactive effect of these and other factors, the allocation of overhead to specific jobs is imprecise and sometimes arbitrary.

Typically, a single basis that is common to all jobs is used to allocate overhead costs. Although this single basis cannot reflect all dimensions of overhead, it should have some logically causal relationship, as well as a high correlation, with overhead. It should also be easy to implement. Kilograms of scrap might have a logically causal relationship and a high correlation with overhead, and be common to all jobs, but not be used as a basis of overhead application because of the difficulty in measuring the scrap of each job. Because direct-labor hours and costs are identified with jobs for product-costing purposes, labor bases are frequently used to allocate overhead costs. Unfortunately this ease of application sometimes has led organizations to misapply overhead on the basis of labor. If the overhead of a machine-intensive operation has a high correlation with machine hours and a low correlation with labor hours, machine hours rather than labor hours should be used for overhead allocation.

The imprecise nature of overhead allocation has implications for cost estimation. An analysis of the behavior of overhead costs should not be based on overhead costs allocated to jobs in the past; such an analysis should be based on total overhead costs for several periods. A study of total overhead costs will likely show that several factors—the number of jobs started, raw materials used, direct-labor hours, direct-labor dollars, machine hours, depreciation methods, and the season of the year—affect overhead. Predictions of future overhead should be based on one or more of the factors.

ACTUAL JOB-ORDER COST SYSTEMS

Job-order costing has several variations. Actual and normal job-order cost systems are discussed in this chapter. Standard job-order cost systems are discussed in Chapter 14. An **actual cost system** assigns actual direct materials, actual direct labor, and actual factory overhead to products. Factory overhead is applied using an **actual factory overhead rate** determined *after the end of each month* within a year as:

$$\text{Actual overhead rate} = \frac{\text{Actual factory overhead for month}}{\text{Actual units of activity for month}} \quad (3\text{–}1)$$

A **normal cost system** assigns actual direct materials and actual direct labor to products. Factory overhead is applied to products using a **predetermined overhead rate** established *before the start of each year* as:

$$\text{Predetermined overhead rate} = \frac{\text{Predicted factory overhead for year}}{\text{Predicted units of activity for year}} \quad (3\text{–}2)$$

Predetermined overhead rates have numerous advantages over actual overhead rates, but these advantages are better understood after examining a cost system that uses actual overhead rates.

Example 3–3

On November 1, 19x9, the Hendrix Print Shop had one job (201) in process. This job was started on October 21 and had the following costs assigned to it during October:

Direct materials	$180
Direct labor	150
Factory overhead	180
Total	$510

During November, four more jobs (205, 206, 207, and 208) were started, and three jobs (201, 205, and 206) were completed. Raw materials costing $1,980 were purchased on account. Direct-material costs of $1,780 and direct-labor costs of $1,100 were assigned to individual jobs as shown on the abbreviated job-cost sheets in Exhibit 3–2. November factory overhead costs were as follows:

Indirect labor	$ 500
Supplies	30
Depreciation	400
Utilities	300
Property taxes	200
Total	$1,430

Hendrix assigns actual factory overhead to jobs on the basis of direct-labor dollars. The November overhead rate is 130 percent ($1,430/$1,100) of direct-labor dollars. The assignment of overhead to jobs is shown in Exhibit 3–2. The final cost of job 201 is $625:

	Job 201		
	October	*November*	*Total*
Direct materials	$180	$ 0	$180
Direct labor	150	50	200
Factory overhead	180	65	245
Total	$510	$115	$625

EXHIBIT 3–2 Hendrix Print Shop Assignment of November 19x9 Costs: Actual Cost System

		Job				
	Total	*201*	*205*	*206*	*207*	*208*
Prime:						
Direct materials	$1,780	$ 0	$ 500	$180	$ 700	$ 400
Direct labor	1,100	50	300	200	250	300
Overhead*	1,430	65	390	260	325	390
Total	$4,310	$115	$1,190	$640	$1,275	$1,090

* 130 percent of direct labor

Job 201's costs are recorded on a job-cost sheet in Exhibit 3–1(a). Note that overhead costs could not be assigned until November 30 even though job 201 was completed on November 15. The overhead and labor costs for the entire month must be known before the actual overhead rate can be determined.

Using the job-cost sheets, the total costs assigned to jobs completed during November amount to $2,455:

Job	*Cost*
201	$ 625
205	1,190
206	640
Total	$2,455

The costs in ending Work-in-Process total $2,365:

Job	*Cost*
207	$1,275
208	1,090
Total	$2,365

A flowchart of Hendrix's costs during November is presented in Exhibit 3–3, and the related control account journal entries are presented in Exhibit 3–4. The explanation accompanying each journal entry indicates the subsidiary records that are also affected by the cost assignment. Finally, a formal statement of the cost of goods manufactured is presented in Exhibit 3–5.

In reviewing Exhibits 3–3 and 3–4, note the importance of the job-cost sheets. To operate a job-cost system, detailed records must be kept for each job. The total costs assigned to each completed job must be determined before the entry transferring costs from Work-in-Process to Finished Goods Inventory can be made.

EXHIBIT 3–3 Flow of Costs in an Actual Job-Order Cost System

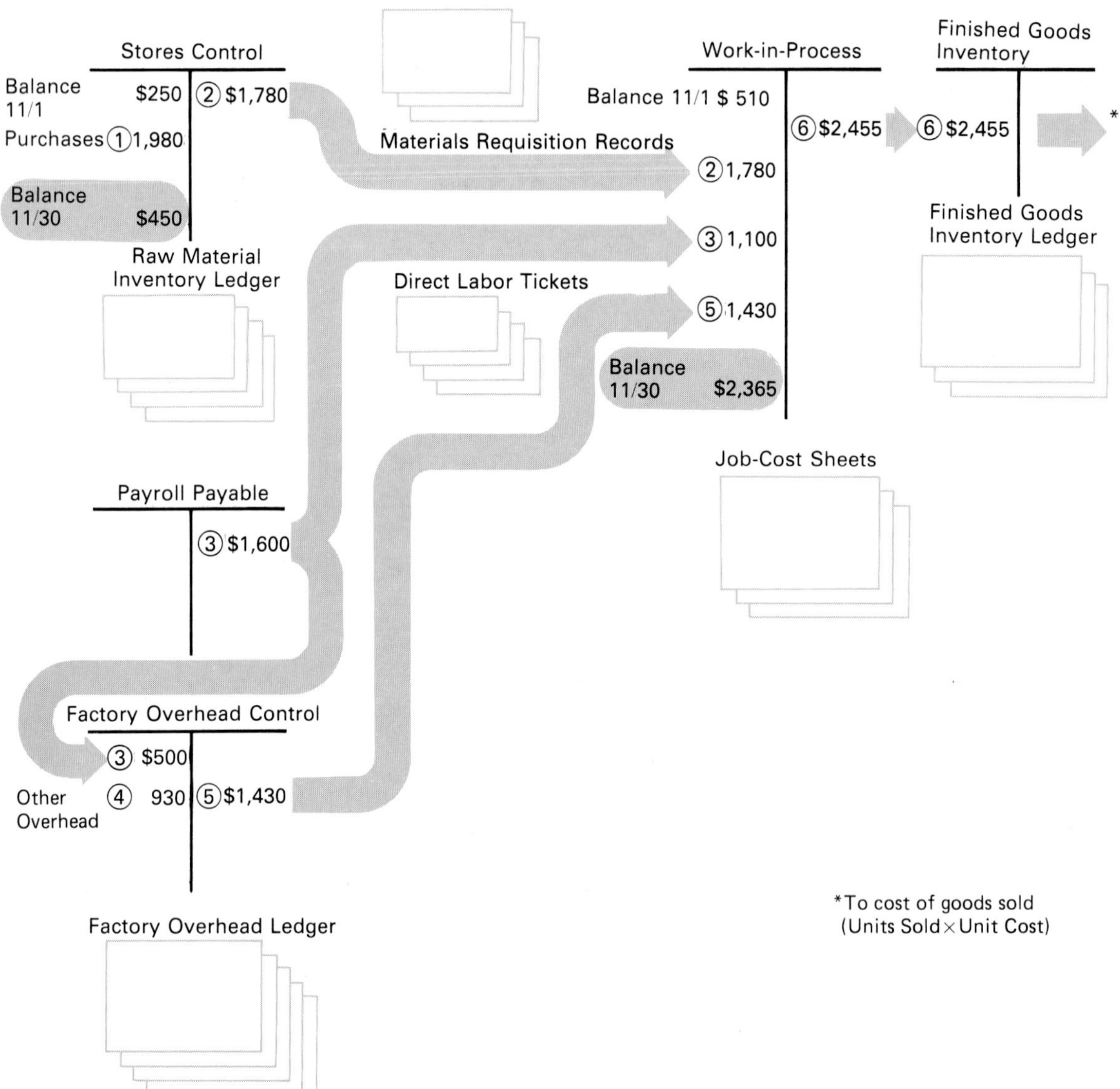

*To cost of goods sold (Units Sold × Unit Cost)

EXHIBIT 3–4 Control Account Journal Entries for an Actual Job-Order Cost System

	Debit	Credit
1. Stores Control	1,980	
Accounts Payable		1,980
The costs of specific raw materials are assigned to the appropriate raw materials inventory ledger accounts and credits are made to the appropriate accounts payable subsidiary ledger accounts.		
2. Work-in-Process	1,780	
Stores Control		1,780
Direct materials costs assigned to specific jobs are recorded on the appropriate job-cost sheets and credited to the appropriate raw materials inventory ledger accounts.		
3. Work-in-Process	1,100	
Factory Overhead Control	500	
Payroll Payable		1,600
Direct-labor costs assigned to specific jobs are recorded on the appropriate job-cost sheets. Specific factory overhead costs are recorded in factory overhead ledger accounts. The payroll payable to each employee is recorded in a subsidiary ledger for Payroll Payable.		
4. Factory Overhead Control	930	
Supplies Inventory*		30
Accumulated Depreciation†		400
Accounts Payable		300
Taxes Payable†		200
Specific factory overhead costs are recorded in the factory overhead ledger accounts. Credits are made to subsidiary ledger accounts for supplies inventory and accounts payable.		
5. Work-in-Process	1,430	
Factory Overhead Control		1,430
Factory overhead costs assigned to specific jobs are recorded on appropriate job-cost sheets.		
6. Finished Goods Inventory	2,455	
Work-in-Process		2,455
Job-cost sheets of completed jobs are removed from the work-in-process subsidiary ledger and placed in the finished goods inventory subsidiary ledger.		

* Hendrix maintains separate inventory accounts for direct materials and supplies. The journal entry for the purchase of supplies is not shown.

† One-twelfth of the yearly depreciation and property taxes are allocated to each month.

Limitations of Actual Overhead Rates

The use of actual factory overhead rates has two major deficiencies:

1. Overhead costs cannot be applied until the end of the period.
2. The overhead costs applied to identical jobs may vary widely from month to month.

Consider the first deficiency. Job 201 was completed on November 15. Recall, however, that overhead costs could not be assigned until the end of the month

EXHIBIT 3–5 Statement of Cost of Goods Manufactured

Hendrix Print Shop
Statement of Cost of Goods Manufactured
For the Month Ending November 30, 19x9

Current manufacturing costs:		
Cost of materials placed in process:		
Stores Control, 11/1/x9	$ 250	
Purchases	1,980	
Available	$2,230	
Stores Control, 11/30/x9	450	$1,780
Direct labor		1,100
Overhead:		
Indirect labor	$ 500	
Supplies	30	
Depreciation	400	
Utilities	300	
Property taxes	200	1,430
Total		$4,310
Work-in-Process, 11/1/x9		510
Total costs in process		$4,820
Work-in-Process, 11/30/x9		−2,365
Cost of goods manufactured		$2,455

when total overhead and direct-labor costs were known. This kind of delay necessitates the processing of a large volume of cost data at the end of each period and reduces the timeliness of product cost information. Additional delays result if some overhead costs are still not known at the end of the period. If prices are based on costs, this delay creates a problem in determining the price to charge for products.

The second deficiency can be illustrated with two simple examples. If jobs 201 and 205 were the only jobs worked on during November, their final costs would be much larger than the $625 and $1,190 previously indicated because all overhead costs, fixed and variable, would be assigned to them.

Example 3–4

Assume the November overhead costs include fixed costs of $990 and variable costs of $0.40 per direct-labor dollar. In Example 3–3 five jobs were worked on during November with total direct-labor costs of $1,100. Under these circumstances, total overhead is verified to be $1,430:

Fixed factory overhead	$ 990
Variable factory overhead ($1,100 × 0.40)	440
Total	$1,430

But what if jobs 201 and 205 were the only ones in process during November. Under this assumption, total overhead costs are $1,130:

Fixed factory overhead		$ 990
Variable factory overhead:		
Job 201 ($50 × 0.40)	$ 20	
Job 205 ($300 × 0.40)	120	140
Total		$1,130

With overhead allocated on the basis of direct-labor dollars, the November overhead rate is 323 percent ($1,130/$350) of direct-labor dollars, and the following overhead costs are assigned to individual jobs:

Job 201 ($50 × 3.23)	$ 161.50
Job 205 ($300 × 3.23)	969.00
Total[4]	$1,130.50

There is no physical change in either job, but there is a dramatic increase in the overhead costs assigned to them, from $65 to $161.50 for job 201, and from $390 to $969 for job 205. If management makes decisions to accept or reject jobs on the basis of predicted cost assignments during the production period, they may reject jobs during periods of low activity that would otherwise be accepted.

Example 3–5

On November 1, Hendrix received the order for job 205 at a selling price of $1,500. If management includes jobs 201, 205, 206, 207, and 208 in their cost estimates, they would project a profit on job 205 and accept it:

Selling price	$1,500
Costs (see Exhibit 3–2)	−1,190
Profit	$ 310

If management includes only jobs 201 and 205 in the analysis, they might reject job 205 as unprofitable:

Selling price		$1,500
Costs:		
Direct materials	$ 500	
Direct labor	300	
Factory overhead	969	−1,769
Loss		$(269)

[4] A $0.50 error is the result of rounding. To eliminate this discrepancy, the overhead assigned to job 201 might be reduced to $161. The difference, because it is a small percentage of total job cost, is immaterial.

But note what happens to job 201 if job 205 is rejected. Job 201 might then appear unprofitable because all fixed overhead costs would be assigned to it. Fortunately most managers are aware of the difficulty illustrated in Example 3–5 and use normal cost systems with predetermined overhead rates, as explained in the next section, to avoid this problem.

Also note that the analysis used in Example 3–5, to make the decision to accept or reject the order, is incorrect in any event. The decision to accept or reject job 205 might better be based on a differential analysis of costs and revenues. The differential revenues are $1,500. The differential costs are: direct materials, $500; direct labor, $300; and variable overhead, $120 ($300 × 0.40). Profits would increase $580 if job 205 is accepted:

Selling price		$1,500
Variable costs:		
Direct materials	$500	
Direct labor	300	
Factory overhead	120	−920
Advantage of accepting job 205		$580

If excess capacity exists, job 205 will contribute $580 to fixed expenses and profits. However, for their long-run policy, most managers insist that all jobs bear a share of fixed overhead. Perhaps they take this action to hold the line in pricing for fear that accepting jobs on the basis of short-run differential costs and revenues will result in lower prices on all jobs.

Seasonal variations in operating costs also cause variations in the overhead applied to identical jobs. Summer cooling and winter heating increase power consumption and utility bills. Businesses with seasonal variations in demand may experience month-to-month fluctuations in idle time and overtime costs. Repair and maintenance costs are likely to have large monthly variations. Should these costs be assigned to jobs worked on during the month they are incurred, or should they be spread over all jobs worked on throughout the year? Using an actual overhead rate, the first alternative is taken. Using a normal cost system, the second alternative is taken.

NORMAL JOB-ORDER COST SYSTEMS

Regardless of whether an actual or a normal cost system is used, actual direct materials and actual direct labor are applied to jobs. The difference between actual and normal cost systems is in the treatment of overhead.

Under an actual cost system, actual overhead application rates are developed at or after the end of each period. These rates are based on the actual overhead costs and the actual activity of each period. Because overhead costs cannot be applied until the end of the period when actual costs and activity are known, a fiscal year is normally broken down into twelve monthly periods. Each month is likely to have a different overhead application rate.

Under a normal cost system, a predetermined rate is established before the start of each fiscal year. The rate is developed by predicting total overhead costs for the coming year and dividing them by the predicted total activity for the coming year.

Predetermined overhead rates are generally believed to be superior to actual overhead rates because they provide for more rapid product costing and avoid fluctuations in overhead costs applied to identical jobs manufactured during different months of the year. Using a predetermined overhead rate makes it possible for individual jobs to be costed as soon as they are completed; providing more rapid cost information to management and avoiding a backlog of paperwork at the end of each month. The monthly fluctuations in overhead rates under an actual cost system are caused by variations in actual overhead costs and variations in actual activity. Smoothing out these two sources of rate fluctuations are said to be the ''numerator'' and ''denominator'' reasons for using a normal cost system and a predetermined overhead rate.

Implementing a normal cost system requires the solution to two problems. The first is the development of a predetermined overhead rate before the start of the year; the second is the treatment of overapplied or underapplied overhead.

Developing a Predetermined Overhead Rate

As we stated previously in Eq. 3–2, a predetermined overhead rate is determined before the start of the year as:

$$\text{Predetermined overhead rate} = \frac{\text{Predicted factory overhead for year}}{\text{Predicted units of activity for year}}$$

Developing a predetermined overhead rate involves at least four steps:

1. Determining the relationship between total factory overhead and total activity.
2. Predicting the coming year's activity.
3. Predicting total factory overhead for the coming year.
4. Dividing predicted factory overhead by the predicted activity.

The first step—determining the relationship between total factory overhead and total activity—is frequently accomplished by analyzing historical cost data to determine past relationships and then adjusting for anticipated changes in prices and technology. Out of this analysis may come an equation of the following form:

$$\begin{matrix}\text{Total}\\ \text{factory}\\ \text{overhead}\end{matrix} = \begin{matrix}\text{Fixed}\\ \text{factory}\\ \text{overhead}\end{matrix} + \left(\begin{matrix}\text{Variable}\\ \text{factory}\\ \text{overhead}\\ \text{per unit}\end{matrix} \times \begin{matrix}\text{Predicted}\\ \text{units of}\\ \text{activity}\end{matrix}\right) \qquad (3\text{–}3)$$

The activity measure used in Eqs. 3–2 and 3–3 must be a factor that is common to all jobs, has a high correlation with the incurrence of overhead costs, and is easy to measure. Frequently used measures include direct-labor hours, direct-labor dollars, and machine hours.

The second step in developing a predetermined overhead rate is to predict the coming year's activity. One possible way to do this is to adjust last year's activity on the basis of management's expectations for the coming year. Hence, if the management of a job shop anticipates a 5 percent increase in the number of jobs to be completed next year, with no change in the mix of jobs, they could also anticipate a 5 percent increase in direct-labor hours.

The third step is to use the equation for total factory overhead to predict total factory overhead for the coming year. Finally, Eq. 3–2 is used to develop the predetermined overhead rate.

Example 3–6

Assume that in early January, 19x9 (the year referred to in Examples 3–3 through 3–5), Hendrix's cost accountant analyzed and adjusted historical cost data to develop the following equation:

$$\text{Total factory overhead} = \$10{,}800 + \left(0.30 \times \text{Total direct-labor dollars}\right)$$

In 19x8 Hendrix had direct-labor costs of \$9,000. For 19x9 management anticipated a one-third increase in the total number of jobs worked on. They did not expect an increase in the hourly wage rate or any change in the size or mix of jobs. Hence the predicted activity for 19x9 was \$12,000 direct-labor dollars [\$9,000 + (⅓ × \$9,000)].

Using this information the cost accountant predicted 19x9 overhead at \$14,400:

$$\$10{,}800 + (0.30 \times \$12{,}000) = \underline{\underline{\$14{,}400}}$$

and the predetermined overhead rate for 19x9 was set at 120 percent of direct-labor costs:

$$\frac{\$14{,}400}{\$12{,}000} = \underline{\underline{1.2}}$$

If Hendrix uses a normal job-order cost system, the journal entries for November are the same as in Exhibit 3–4, except for entries 5 and 6. With a predetermined overhead rate of 120 percent of direct-labor dollars, the journal entry to apply overhead is:

Work-in-Process	1,320	
Factory Overhead Control		1,320

The journal entry to transfer the cost of the jobs completed to Finished Goods Inventory would then be:

Finished Goods Inventory	2,400	
Work-in-Process		2,400

The cost of the jobs completed was determined as follows:

		Job		
	Total	*201*	*205*	*206*
Costs from previous period	$ 510	$ 510	$ 0	$ 0
Current manufacturing costs:				
Direct materials	680	0	500	180
Direct labor	550	50	300	200
Applied overhead	660	60	360	240
Total	$2,400	$ 620	$1,160	$ 620

Treatment of Overapplied and Underapplied Overhead

When predetermined overhead rates are used, the total overhead applied to jobs during a given month is seldom equal to the actual overhead costs of the month. Consider, for example, the situation Hendrix might face in November 19x9. In Example 3–3 total overhead costs were $1,430 and total direct-labor costs were $1,100. Under a normal cost system, with a predetermined overhead rate of 120 percent of direct-labor dollars, November applied overhead would only amount to $1,320 [$1,100 × 1.2]. Overhead is underapplied by $110 [$1,430 − $1,320], and there is a debit balance in Factory Overhead Control at the end of November.

	Factory Overhead Control[5]			*Work-in-Process*	
Actual ⟶	$1,430	$1,320	⟵ Applied ⟶	$1,320	
Balance	$ 110				

Because external reporting practices require a full accounting of all overhead costs, any overapplied or underapplied overhead is usually treated as a deduction from or an addition to inventory on interim financial statements. Net overapplied overhead (a credit balance in Factory Overhead Control) is deducted from total inventory (which has a debit balance). Net underapplied overhead (a debit balance in Factory Overhead Control) is added to total inventory.[6] At the end of November, assuming the use of a normal cost system and no ending inventory of finished goods, the inventory section of Hendrix's Statement of Financial Position might appear as follows:

Inventory:		
Stores Control	$ 450	
Work-in-Process	2,310	
Factory Overhead Control	110	$2,870

[5] The name and number of overhead control accounts used in conjunction with predetermined overhead rates vary widely. Some firms use three accounts: Factory Overhead Control, Applied Factory Overhead, and Underapplied or Overapplied Factory Overhead. Actual costs are recorded in the first, applied costs are recorded in the second, and monthly differences are closed to the third.

[6] It is also possible to carry underapplied overhead as an "other asset" and overapplied overhead as an "other liability" on interim financial statements.

The detailed job-cost information supporting the $2,310 balance in Work-in-Process is as follows:

	Job		
Product cost	*207*	*208*	*Total*
Direct materials	$ 700	$ 400	$1,100
Direct labor	250	300	550
Applied overhead*	300	360	660
Total	$1,250	$1,060	$2,310

*120 percent of direct-labor costs.

Comparing the preceding cost information for jobs 207 and 208 with that previously developed in Exhibit 3–2, we can see that, although the direct-materials and the direct-labor costs are the same, the overhead costs differ. Exhibit 3–2 was developed using an actual overhead rate of 130 percent of direct-labor dollars; the preceding job-cost information was developed using a predetermined overhead rate of 120 percent of direct labor dollars.

At the end of the year the preclosing balance in Factory Overhead Control should be close to zero. If the final amount of overapplied or underapplied overhead is small compared to the balance in Cost of Goods Sold, it may be treated expediently and closed to this account. Closing underapplied overhead increases the balance in Cost of Goods Sold:

Cost of Goods Sold	XXXX	
Factory Overhead Control		XXXX

Closing overapplied overhead decreases the balance in Cost of Goods Sold:

Factory Overhead Control	XXXX	
Cost of Goods Sold		XXXX

The treatment of a relatively large preclosing balance in Factory Overhead Control is complicated by generally accepted accounting principles which specify that

1. The use of anything but actual costs is acceptable only if the resulting cost assignments closely approximate those that would result if actual costs were used.
2. Inventories should not be valued at more than selling price less costs to complete and sell.

Based on these external reporting requirements it appears that:

- A large underapplied balance in Factory Overhead Control that resulted from unusual events of the current period should be disposed of as a loss. This will not affect inventory accounts or the Cost of Goods Sold.
- A large underapplied balance in Factory Overhead Control that resulted from cost prediction errors or fundamental changes in cost structure should be prorated over Work-in-Process, Finished Goods Inventory, and Cost of Goods Sold. This will increase the balance in each account.

- A large overapplied balance in Factory Overhead Control should be prorated over Work-in-Process, Finished Goods Inventory, and Cost of Goods Sold. This will reduce the balance in each account.

To **prorate** a cost is to distribute it proportionately. Prorating underapplied or overapplied overhead is done to try to change the balances in inventory accounts and Cost of Goods Sold to what they would have been if an actual rather than a predetermined overhead rate had been used. To prorate underapplied or overapplied overhead, we can use one of two methods:

1. The **cost element method of prorating**, which bases the prorating on the percent of a cost element (applied factory overhead in this case) in each affected account.
2. The **total cost method of prorating**, which bases the prorating on the percent of total cost in each affected account.

Example 3–7

At the end of 19x2 Birmingham, Limited, had overapplied overhead of $10,000. Detailed information regarding inventories and the Cost of Goods Sold is presented in Exhibit 3–6. Also presented is information on the amount in dollars that would be allocated to each account using the cost element and the total cost methods of prorating. Because Factory Overhead Control has a credit balance from overapplied overhead, the journal entry accompanying either method would involve credits to Work-in-Process, Finished Goods Inventory, and Cost of Goods Sold. Using the cost element method, the prorating journal entry is:

Factory Overhead Control	10,000	
Work-in-Process		3,000
Finished Goods Inventory		2,000
Cost of Goods Sold		5,000

Using the total cost method, the prorating journal entry is:

Factory Overhead Control	10,000	
Work-in-Process		2,000
Finished Goods Inventory		2,000
Cost of Goods Sold		6,000

EXHIBIT 3–6 Prorating Overapplied and Underapplied Overhead

	Account			
	Work-in-Process	*Finished Goods*	*Cost of Goods Sold*	*Total*
Direct materials	$100,000	$ 80,000	$350,000	$ 530,000
Direct labor	70,000	100,000	200,000	370,000
Applied overhead	30,000	20,000	50,000	100,000
Total	$200,000	$200,000	$600,000	$1,000,000
Percentage of applied overhead	30	20	50	100
Cost element prorating	$ 3,000	$ 2,000	$ 5,000	$ (10,000)
Percentage of total cost	20	20	60	100
Total cost prorating	$ 2,000	$ 2,000	$ 6,000	$ (10,000)

If overhead were underapplied by $10,000, Factory Overhead Control would have a debit balance, and the debits and credits in the preceding journal entries would be reversed.

When the relative portion of the materials, labor, and overhead costs assigned to each job varies, the cost element method results in more accurate cost assignments. Unfortunately the cost element method requires detailed information on the factory overhead costs in each account while the total cost method only requires information on the total costs in each account. Consequently it is much easier to prorate variances using the total cost method. If a decision is made to prorate, care should be taken to ensure that final inventory values do not exceed net realizable value, that is, selling price less costs to complete and sell.

Regardless of the preceding comments regarding prorating, if the ending inventories are an insignificant portion of the total goods manufactured during the year, prorating will not have a significant effect on the firm's end-of-year financial statements (because almost all underapplied or overapplied overhead would be prorated to the Cost of Goods Sold). Under these circumstances, it seems appropriate to follow the expedient procedure of writing the underapplied or overapplied overhead off to Cost of Goods Sold. Note that the determination of what is and what is not significant is a matter of professional judgment.

OVERHEAD APPLICATIONS WITH MULTIPLE PRODUCTION DEPARTMENTS

The Hendrix Print Shop had a single production department and all overhead costs were summarized in a single overhead control account before being assigned to products. Many organizations have two or more production departments.

An organization that has two or more production departments can assign overhead costs to products in two basic ways. The first way is to place all overhead costs in a single factory overhead control account and assign them to products on the basis of a plant-wide overhead rate. A **plant-wide overhead rate** is computed by dividing total plant-wide factory overhead by an activity basis that is common to all products worked on in all departments.

$$\text{Plant-wide overhead rate} = \frac{\text{Total factory overhead}}{\text{Total units of activity in factory}} \tag{3–4}$$

The second way to assign overhead costs is to develop a separate departmental overhead rate for each production department. A **departmental overhead rate** is computed by dividing total departmental factory overhead by an activity basis that is common to all products worked on in the department.

$$\text{Departmental overhead rate} = \frac{\text{Total departmental overhead}}{\text{Total units of activity in department}} \tag{3–5}$$

A machine-intensive department may use machine hours and a labor-intensive department may use labor hours or direct-labor dollars. When departmental rates are used, each production department has its own departmental overhead control account. Although plant-wide overhead rates are easier to develop and use than departmental overhead rates, plant-wide rates are inappropriate if the size and nature of overhead costs vary greatly between production departments, and if jobs spend varying percents of their total time in each production department.

Example 3–8

The Piedmont Wood Products Company has two production departments and no service departments. In Department P_1, wood is cut to specifications. In Department P_2, the cut wood is assembled and finished. Department P_1 is highly automated. Employees control up to five machines with programmed cutting instructions. Department P_2 is labor intensive. Skilled craftsmen sand, assemble, stain, and polish the final product. For October 19x1 the following information is available about actual P_1 and P_2 activities and costs:

	P_1	P_2	*Total*
Departmental overhead	\$35,000	\$25,000	\$60,000
Labor hours	1,000	5,000	6,000
Machine hours	5,000	0	5,000

Plant-Wide Overhead Rate

If Piedmont elects to use a plant-wide rate, an activity factor that is common to both departments must be used. Machine hours cannot be used because P_2 does not have any machine hours. Using labor hours, the actual plant-wide overhead rate is \$10 per direct-labor hour.

$$\text{Plant-wide overhead rate} = \frac{\$60{,}000}{6{,}000} = \$10 \text{ per direct-labor hour}$$

Using this plant-wide overhead rate, factory overhead costs are assigned primarily to products worked on in P_2, the labor-intensive department, even though most of the overhead costs were incurred in P_1, the machine-intensive department:

	P_1	P_2	*Total*
Labor hours	1,000	5,000	6,000
Plant-wide rate	× \$10	× \$10	× \$10
Overhead assignment	\$10,000	\$50,000	\$60,000

Comparing the actual overhead incurred in each department with the overhead costs assigned to products worked on in each department, we can see that \$25,000 of overhead costs were shifted from products worked on in P_1 to products worked on in P_2:

	P_1	P_2	*Total*
Actual overhead	\$35,000	\$25,000	\$70,000
Overhead assignment	−10,000	−50,000	−70,000
Overhead shift	\$25,000	\$(25,000)	\$ 0

Assigning costs in this manner can lead to assigning too few costs to products worked on primarily in P_1 and too many costs to products worked on primarily in P_2. This error in cost assignment may subsequently lead to errors in evaluating product profitability and uneconomical pricing decisions.

Example 3–9

Extending Example 3–8, the following information is available about two jobs, 403 and 405, that were started and completed during October.

	P_1 hours		P_2 hours	Total labor
Job	*Labor*	*Machine*	*Labor*	*hours*
403	4	20	10	14
405	1	4	26	27

With a plant-wide rate based on labor hours, the following overhead cost assignments are made:

Job 403 (14 labor hours × \$10) = \$140
Job 405 (27 labor hours × \$10) = \$270

Departmental Overhead Rates

Departmental overhead rates are based on activity variables that reflect the incurrence of overhead in each department. For P_1 this is machine hours. For P_2 this is labor hours. Using these bases, the departmental overhead rates are \$7 in P_1 and \$5 in P_2.

	P_1	P_2
Departmental overhead	\$35,000	\$25,000
Activity measure		
P_1: Machine hours	÷5,000	
P_2: Labor hours		÷5,000
Departmental overhead rate	\$ 7.00	\$ 5.00

Using departmental rates, the overhead costs assigned to jobs 403 and 405 are as follows:

	P_1 assignment		P_2 assignment		Total assignment
Job 403	(20 × \$7)	+	(10 × \$5)	=	\$190
Job 405	(4 × \$7)	+	(26 × \$5)	=	\$158

The difference in the overhead costs assigned to these two jobs using plant-wide and departmental overhead rates is as follows:

	Job 403	Job 405
Plant-wide	\$140	\$270
Departmental	−190	−158
Difference	\$(50)	\$112

If prices were based on cost and a plant-wide rate were used, management might overprice labor-intensive jobs (such as job 405), and underprice machine-intensive jobs (such as job 403).

When to Establish Departmental Cost Pools

A **cost pool** is a group of related costs, such as factory overhead costs, that are allocated together to cost objectives. **Cost objectives** are objects (such as jobs or products) to which costs are assigned. One of the most difficult problems in establishing or revising a product costing system is to determine the optimal number of overhead cost pools. We have seen that in multiple-department organizations the decision to establish a single plant-wide or to establish departmental overhead cost pools can significantly influence the cost assigned to jobs. But, the question remains as to when departmental pools are preferred to a plant-wide pool.

The cost accountant might initially turn to financial reporting requirements for guidance in this matter. Unfortunately (or fortunately, depending on your point of view) the only guidance in the financial accounting literature is that all product costs must be accounted for in a consistent, systematic manner, and that the final product costs should not exceed net realizable value, that is, selling price less selling costs. At the other extreme, companies that do significant amounts of business with the government or are in regulated industries may have detailed guidelines as to how their cost accounting system should be set up and operated.

For the majority of businesses, the operation of their cost accounting system is an internal decision that depends on the perceived costs and benefits associated with the system. Although departmental overhead cost pools and rates provide more accurate cost data and better information for planning and controlling costs, they are more expensive to operate than a plant-wide overhead cost pool and rate. Unfortunately no rules can be formulated to tell when a departmental approach is superior to a plant-wide approach, or to tell the number of departmental cost pools that should be established.

Also, to establish or revise a cost accounting system, we must look beyond the formal organization structure. An organization may have several production departments, but it may only need one overhead cost pool because of the nature of its products or production procedures. Alternatively, an organization may have only one production department, which, because of its size and diversity, should be broken down into several cost centers for product-costing purposes.

SUMMARY

Job-order costing is used both for work performed pursuant to a special order or contract with outside parties and for speculative work such as replenishing inventories or internal plant construction. The distinguishing feature of job-order costing is the ability to identify costs with specific batches or projects.

Job-cost sheets are the backbone of job-order costing. Direct-material, direct-labor, and factory overhead costs assigned to specific jobs are recorded on these sheets. Although it is easy to trace the physical flow of raw materials and observe employees working on jobs, it is difficult to associate overhead costs with specific jobs. Both actual and normal cost systems apply factory overhead on the basis of some activity measure that is common to all jobs, has a high correlation with the incurrence of overhead, and is easy to apply. In actual cost systems, the application rate is typically developed at the end of each month. In normal cost systems, a predetermined rate is typically developed before the start of each year.

Normal cost systems are superior to actual cost systems because they provide for more rapid product costing and avoid fluctuations in the overhead costs applied to identical jobs manufactured during different months of a year. Normal cost systems do, however, require the development of a predetermined overhead rate, and they may require the prorating of underapplied or overapplied overhead at the end of the year.

When an organization contains two or more production departments, overhead costs may be applied to individual jobs using either a single plant-wide overhead rate or separate rates for each production department. Departmental overhead rates provide more accurate product costs if there are differences in the size or nature of the overhead costs associated with individual production departments and if jobs spend varying percentages of their total time in each production department.

KEY TERMS

Actual cost system
Actual factory overhead rate
Cost element method of prorating
Cost objective
Cost pool
Departmental overhead rate
Direct-labor ticket
Idle time
Job-cost sheet
Job-order cost system
Materials inventory record
Materials requisition record
Normal cost system
Overtime premium
Plant-wide overhead rate
Predetermined overhead rate
Prorate
Total cost method of prorating

SELECTED REFERENCES

Anthony, Robert N., "The Rebirth of Cost Accounting," *Management Accounting* **57,** No. 4 (October 1975): 13–16.

Carbone, Frank J., "Automated Job Costing Helps Mulach Steel Stay Competitive," *Management Accounting* **61,** No. 12 (June 1980): 29–31.

Curtin, Frank T., "New Costing Methods Needed for Manufacturing Technology," *Management Review* **73,** No. 4 (April 1984): 29, 33–34.

Dilts, David, and Grant W. Russell, "Accounting for the Factory of the Future," *Management Accounting* **66,** No. 10 (April 1985): 34–40.

Hunt, Rick, Linda Garrett, and C. Mike Merz, "Direct Labor Cost Not Always Relevant at H-P," *Management Accounting* **66,** No. 8 (February 1985): 58–62.

Littrel, Earl K., "The High Tech Challenge to Managerial Accounting," *Management Accounting* **66,** No. 4 (October 1984): 33–36.

Seed, Allen H., III, "Cost Accounting in the Age of Robotics," *Management Accounting* **66,** No. 4 (October 1984): 39–43.

REVIEW QUESTIONS

3–1 What is the distinguishing feature of job-order costing?

3–2 What three basic categories of costs are found on a job-cost sheet?

3–3 The balances in two accounts are affected by the dollar amount recorded on a materials requisition record. Name these accounts.

3–4 Why is it important that direct-labor tickets be completed promptly and accurately? Suggest some behavioral factors that may influence the accuracy of direct-labor tickets.

3–5 Why is overhead cost assignment more difficult than direct-materials or direct-labor cost assignments?

3–6 What are some desirable characteristics of a basis used to allocate overhead costs to individual jobs?

3–7 Are there any differences in the treatment of direct-materials costs and direct-labor costs under actual and normal cost systems?

3–8 Why is it possible to cost jobs sooner under a normal cost system than under an actual cost system?

3–9 What are the "numerator" and "denominator" reasons for implementing a normal cost system?

3–10 Subsequent to predicting total overhead and total activity, how is a predetermined overhead rate computed?

3–11 Briefly outline the procedures required to predict total overhead.

3–12 How is overapplied or underapplied overhead usually treated on interim financial statements?

3–13 What are the alternative end-of-year treatments of overapplied and underapplied overhead? When is each appropriate?

3–14 Identify two methods that can be used to prorate underapplied or overapplied overhead.

3–15 Distinguish between plant-wide and departmental overhead rates.

REVIEW PROBLEM

Actual and Normal Job-Order Costing: Journal Entries

The Redwood Furniture Company manufactures heavy-duty outdoor furniture to order. The January 1, 19x5, work-in-process inventory consisted of one job, 875, with assigned costs totaling $8,000. Presented is summary information regarding January activities:

- Raw materials costing $35,000 and factory supplies costing $6,000 were purchased on account. A single inventory control account is used for raw materials and supplies.
- Materials and supplies were requisitioned as follows:

Job 875	$ 2,000
Job 876	15,000
Job 877	12,000
Total direct materials	$29,000
Factory supplies	3,000
Total	$32,000

- Liabilities were incurred for the following labor-related costs:

Job 875	$ 5,000
Job 876	10,000
Job 877	6,000
Total direct labor	$21,000
Indirect labor and factory supervision	7,000
Total payroll	$28,000

- Other factory overhead costs for January were as follows:

Depreciation on plant and equipment	$ 1,000
Utilities	5,000
Miscellaneous	800
Total	$ 6,800

- Jobs 875 and 876 were completed and transferred to finished goods inventory.

REQUIREMENTS

a) Assume an actual cost system is used with factory overhead applied on the basis of direct-labor dollars. Prepare summary journal entries for January activities affecting inventory accounts and Factory Overhead Control.

b) Assume a normal cost system is used. On an annual basis estimated total factory overhead is equal to $80,000 + (0.5 × direct-labor dollars). Estimated 19x5 direct labor is $320,000.

1. Determine the 19x5 predetermined factory overhead rate per direct-labor dollar.
2. Prepare summary journal entries for January activities affecting inventory accounts and Factory Overhead Control.
3. Determine the amount of over- or underapplied overhead for January.

The solution to this problem is found at the end of the Chapter 3 problems and exercises.

EXERCISES

3–1 Job-Order Costing and Unit Cost Information

During July, the Duncan Company started and completed three jobs, 704, 705, and 706. The following costs were assigned to these jobs:

	Job		
	704	*705*	*706*
Direct materials	$10,000	$ 5,000	$ 8,000
Direct labor	6,000	4,000	4,000
Factory overhead	9,000	6,000	6,000
Total costs	$25,000	$15,000	$18,000
Units	1,000	2,000	6,000

REQUIREMENTS

a) Determine the unit cost for each job to be used in external financial reports.

b) Assuming 50 percent of the factory overhead assigned to each job represents fixed costs, determine the variable unit manufacturing costs for each job.

c) How much would total manufacturing costs increase if job 705 were for 3,000 units rather than 2,000 units?

3–2 Job-Order Costing and Unit Cost Information

The Eldron Corporation started and completed three jobs, 809, 810, and 811, during September. The following costs were assigned to these jobs:

	Job		
	809	*810*	*811*
Direct material	$ 7,000	$ 4,000	$ 3,000
Direct labor	4,000	5,000	4,500
Factory overhead	10,000	15,000	12,500
Total costs	$21,000	$24,000	$20,000
Units	3,000	6,000	2,000

REQUIREMENTS

a) Determine the unit cost for each job to be used in external financial reports.

b) Assuming 75 percent of the factory overhead assigned to each job represents fixed costs, determine the variable unit manufacturing costs for each job.

c) How much would total manufacturing costs increase if job 809 were for 5,000 units rather than 3,000 units?

3–3 Job-Order Costing: Cost Sheet Relationships

Blackwood uses a job-order cost system and applies factory overhead to production orders on the basis of direct-labor costs. The overhead rates for 19x2 are 200 percent for Department A and 50 percent for Department B. Job 123, started and completed during 19x2, was charged with the following costs:

	Department	
	A	*B*
Direct materials	$25,000	$ 5,000
Direct labor	?	30,000
Factory overhead	40,000	?

REQUIREMENT

Determine the total manufacturing costs assigned to job 123. (CPA Adapted)

3–4 Job-Order Costing: Cost Sheet Relationships

Woodstock uses a job-order cost system and applies factory overhead to jobs on the basis of direct-labor dollars. The 19x5 overhead rates are 75 percent for Department I and 300 percent for Department II. Job 456, started and completed during 19x5, was assigned the following costs:

	Department	
	I	*II*
Direct materials	$ 7,000	$15,000
Direct labor	20,000	?
Factory overhead	?	45,000

REQUIREMENT

Determine the total manufacturing costs assigned to job 456.

3–5 Job-Order Costing: Account and Cost Sheet Relationships

Worrell Corporation has a job-order cost system. The following items appeared in the account Work-in-Process for the month of March 19x2:

March 1, balance	$ 12,000
Direct materials	40,000
Direct labor	30,000
Factory overhead	27,000
Cost of goods manufactured	100,000

Worrell applies overhead to production using a rate based on the direct-labor dollars. Job 232, the only job still in process at the end of March 19x2, has been charged with factory overhead of $2,250.

REQUIREMENTS

a) Prepare a T-account for Work-in-Process showing the March beginning and ending balances and all transactions affecting the account during March.

b) Determine the direct materials charged to job 232. (CPA Adapted)

3–6 Job-Order Costing: Account and Cost Sheet Relationships

Heyward Corporation has a job-order cost system. The following items appeared in the account Work-in-Process for the month of June 19x7:

June 1, balance	$ 20,000
Direct materials	?
Direct labor	?
Factory overhead	60,000
Cost of goods manufactured	160,000
June 30, balance	7,400

Heyward applied overhead to products at a rate of 120 percent of direct-labor costs. Job 487, the only job in process at the end of June, has been assigned direct materials costs of $3,000.

REQUIREMENTS

a) Prepare a T-account for Work-in-Process showing the June beginning and ending balances and all transactions affecting the account during June.

b) Determine the factory overhead assigned to job 487.

3–7 Costing Identical Jobs with Actual and Predetermined Overhead Rates

The Northern Pine Wood Company manufactures a variety of household furniture items in batches. One particular item, a TV table, is manufactured in batches of 50 units. Batches of this item were manufactured in January, May, July, September, and November of 19x5. The prime costs assigned to each batch were identical as follows:

Direct materials	$150
Direct labor	300
Total prime costs	$450

Total direct-labor costs and total factory overhead costs for each month of 19x5 were as follows:

Month	*Direct labor*	*Factory overhead*
January	$ 8,000	$10,000
February	6,000	9,000
March	4,000	9,000
April	4,000	8,000
May	8,000	8,000
June	10,000	6,000
July	20,000	7,000
August	14,000	5,000
September	14,000	7,000
October	12,000	6,000
November	10,000	7,000
December	10,000	8,000
Total	$120,000	$90,000

Overhead is applied on the basis of direct-labor dollars.

REQUIREMENTS

a) Determine the total and unit cost of each batch of TV tables, assuming an actual monthly overhead rate is used.

b) Determine the total and unit cost of each batch of TV tables, assuming a predetermined overhead rate, based on an accurate prediction of 19x5 direct-labor costs and factory overhead costs, is used.

c) Assuming Northern Pine Wood bases selling prices on unit manufacturing costs, comment on the solutions to parts (a) and (b).

3–8 Costing Identical Jobs with Actual and Predetermined Overhead Rates

The Montana Stove Company manufactures several models of wood-burning stoves in batches. One particular stove, the Heat Saver, is manufactured in batches of 10 units. Batches of this item were manufactured in January, February, June, July, and September of 19x8. The prime costs assigned to each batch were identical as follows:

Direct materials	$1,500
Direct labor	2,000
Total prime costs	$3,500

The direct-labor costs and total factory overhead costs for each month of 19x8 were as follows:

Month	*Direct labor*	*Factory overhead*
January	$ 20,000	$ 16,000
February	20,000	18,000
March	14,000	12,400
April	10,000	9,000
May	5,000	6,000
June	5,000	6,000
July	14,000	14,000
August	20,000	19,000
September	30,000	21,000
October	40,000	24,000
November	25,000	17,000
December	30,000	24,000
Total	$233,000	$186,400

Overhead is applied on the basis of direct-labor dollars.

REQUIREMENTS

a) Determine the total and unit cost of each batch of Heat Savers, assuming an actual monthly overhead rate is used.

b) Determine the total and unit cost of each batch of Heat Savers, assuming a predetermined overhead rate, based on an accurate prediction of 19x8 direct-labor costs and factory overhead costs, is used.

c) Assuming Montana Stove bases selling prices on unit manufacturing costs, comment on the solutions to parts (a) and (b).

3–9 Account Relationships: Actual Cost System

Data relating to the manufacturing activities of Weldco Ltd. for December 19y7 are as follows:

Inventories		
Raw Materials, December 1		$ 9,000
Raw Materials, December 31		4,500
Work-in-Process:		
December 1 (3,000 units)		
December 31 (2,000 units)		
The December 1 and 31 unit costs are identical and include direct materials of $2.40 per unit and direct labor of $0.80 per unit.		
Finished Goods, December 1		12,000
Finished Goods, December 31 includes:		
Direct materials	$5,000	
Direct labor	3,000	
Other Accounts		
Raw materials purchased		84,000
Freight-in on raw materials purchased		1,500

Current manufacturing costs were $180,000. The December overhead rate was 200 percent of direct-labor dollars. Weldco assigns freight-in costs to raw materials inventory.

REQUIREMENTS

Compute each of the following:

a) Raw materials used during December 19y7.
b) Work-in-Process, December 31, 19y7.
c) Cost of goods manufactured during December 19y7.
d) Finished Goods Inventory, December 31, 19y7.
e) Cost of goods sold during December 19y7. (CPA Adapted)

3–10 Account Relationships: Normal Cost System

The Brighton Company had the following account balances on January 1, 19x8:

Stores Control		$15,000
Work-in-Process:		
Materials	$ 5,000	
Labor	10,000	
Applied overhead	15,000	30,000
Finished Goods		10,000

During January, the following data were recorded:

Materials purchased	$45,000
Direct-labor costs	40,000
Actual overhead	57,000
Cost of goods sold	30,000

Ending balances on January 31 included:

Stores Control	$10,000
Finished Goods	85,000

Overhead is applied on the basis of direct-labor costs.

REQUIREMENTS

a) Determine the January 31 balance in Work-in-Process.

b) Determine the amount of the overapplied or underapplied overhead for January. Assume the overhead rate is the same during January as in the previous period.

c) How should this overapplied or underapplied overhead be treated on 1/31/x8 financial reports if it is the result of seasonal factors and represents a normal variation in production costs?

3–11 Account Relationships: Normal Cost System

The Toronto Co. Ltd. operates under a job-cost system and applies overhead at a predetermined rate of 50 percent of direct-labor cost. At the beginning of March 19y8, balances in factory-related accounts were as follows:

Stores Control	$12,000
Work-in-Process	6,000
Finished Goods Inventory	34,000
Accounts Payable (used for materials purchases only)	25,000
Payroll Payable	14,000
Accumulated Depreciation—Factory	95,000
Prepaid Insurance—Factory	3,000

The following information is available regarding March activities:

Direct materials used in production	$ 20,000
Direct-labor cost	160,000
Cost of goods sold	320,000
Payment of factory payroll	206,000
Miscellaneous overhead	11,000
Stores purchases	100,000

One job was still in process on March 31. Materials of $500 and direct labor of $2,000 were charged to this job. Relevant account balances at March 31 were as follows:

Finished Goods Inventory	$26,500
Accounts Payable	36,000
Wages Payable	8,000
Accumulated Depreciation—Factory	105,000
Prepaid Insurance—Factory	2,000

REQUIREMENTS

Using T-accounts, determine the following:

a) Applied overhead

b) Ending balance of Work-in-Process

c) Cost of goods manufactured
d) Materials used
e) Ending balance of Stores Control
f) Payment of accounts payable
g) Under- or overapplied overhead (CGA Adapted)

3–12 Account Relationships: Normal Job-Order Costing

Hamilton Company uses job-order costing. Factory overhead is applied to production at a predetermined rate of 150 percent of direct-labor cost.

ADDITIONAL INFORMATION

- Job 101 was the only job in process at January 31, 19x2, with accumulated costs as follows:

Direct materials	$4,000
Direct labor	2,000
Applied factory overhead	3,000
Total	$9,000

- Jobs 102, 103, and 104 were started during February.
- Direct materials requisitions for February totaled $26,000.
- Direct-labor costing $20,000 was incurred for February.
- Actual factory overhead was $32,000 for February.
- The only job still in process at February 28, 19x2, was job 104, with costs of $2,800 for direct materials and $1,800 for direct labor.

REQUIREMENT

With the aid of T-accounts for Work-in-Process and Factory Overhead Control, determine: (1) the cost of goods manufactured for February, and (2) over- or underapplied overhead for February. (CPA Adapted)

3–13 Account Relationships: Normal Job Order Cost System

Baehr Company is a manufacturing company with a fiscal year that runs from July 1 to June 30. The company uses a normal job-order accounting system for its production costs.

A predetermined overhead rate based on direct-labor hours is used to apply overhead to individual jobs. For the 19y7–y8 fiscal year, the predetermined overhead rate is based on an expected level of activity of 120,000 direct-labor hours and the following cost-estimating equation:

$$T = \$216{,}000 + \$3.25X$$

where: T = estimated total overhead
X = direct-labor hours

The information presented is for November 19y7. Jobs 87-50 and 87-51 were completed during November.

Inventories November 1, 19y7:		
Raw materials and supplies		$ 10,500
Work-in-process (Job 87-50)		54,000
Finished goods		112,500
Purchases of raw materials and supplies:		
Raw materials		$135,000
Supplies		15,000
Materials and supplies requisitioned for production:		
Job 87-50		$ 45,000
Job 87-51		37,500
Job 87-52		25,500
Supplies		12,000
Total		$120,000
Factory direct-labor hours:		
Job 87-50	3,500 DLH	
Job 87-51	3,000 DLH	
Job 87-52	2,000 DLH	
Labor costs:		
Direct-labor wages		$ 51,000
Indirect-labor wages (4,000 hours)		15,000
Supervisory salaries, factory		6,000
Building occupancy costs (heat, light, depreciation, etc.):		
Factory facilities		$ 6,500
Sales offices		1,500
Administrative offices		1,000
Total		$ 9,000
Factory equipment costs:		
Power		$ 4,000
Repairs and maintenance		1,500
Depreciation		1,500
Other		1,000
Total		$ 8,000

REQUIREMENTS

a) Determine the predetermined overhead rate to be used to apply overhead to individual jobs during the 19y7–y8 fiscal year.

b) Determine the total cost of job 87-50.

c) Determine the over- or underapplied overhead for November 19y7.

(CMA Adapted)

3–14 Selecting A Basis of Overhead Application

The Stein Company is going to use a predetermined annual factory overhead rate to charge factory overhead to products. In conjunction with this, Stein Company must decide whether to use direct-labor hours or machine hours as the overhead rate base.

REQUIREMENT

Discuss the objectives and criteria that Stein Company should use in selecting the base for its predetermined annual factory overhead rate. (CPA Adapted)

3–15 Predetermined Overhead Rate

The Forcast Company has the following formula for predicting factory overhead costs.

$$\text{TC} = \$250{,}000 + \$3.25X$$

where

TC = total overhead costs
X = direct-labor hours

REQUIREMENTS

a) Determine the 19x2 predetermined factory overhead rate if Forcast Company estimates 100,000 hours of direct labor will be used in 19x2.

b) Determine the over- or underapplied overhead if costs behave as expected for 19x2 and 110,000 hours are actually worked.

3–16 Predetermined Overhead Rate

The Estimation Company has the following formula for estimated factory overhead costs.

$$\text{TC} = \$175{,}000 + \$4.50X$$

where

TC = total overhead costs
X = direct-labor hours

REQUIREMENTS

a) Determine the 19x2 predetermined factory overhead rate if Estimation Company estimates 200,000 direct-labor hours will be used in 19x2.

b) Determine the over- or underapplied overhead if costs behave as expected for 19x2 and 190,000 hours are actually worked.

3–17 Prorating Underapplied Overhead

Hawkeye, Inc., began operations on January 2, 19x7. On December 31, 19x7, after all overhead allocations were completed using a predetermined overhead rate, a $45,000 debit balance remained in Factory Overhead Control. A comparison of predicted volume and actual volume has convinced the controller that the underapplied overhead was the result of significantly overestimating the first year's volume of activity. Accordingly, the $45,000 is to be prorated. The following information is available about the composition of various accounts on December 31, 19x7:

	Work-in process	*Finished goods*	*Cost of goods sold*
Direct materials	$50,000	$ 60,000	$ 90,000
Direct labor	20,000	160,000	220,000
Applied overhead	10,000	80,000	110,000
Total	$80,000	$300,000	$420,000

REQUIREMENTS

a) Suggest two ways of prorating the underapplied overhead and prepare a prorating schedule for each method.

b) Prepare the journal entries necessary to prorate the underapplied overhead for the answers developed in part (a).

c) If volume is the only factor causing the underapplied overhead, what type of costs were not properly allowed for in the predetermined rate?

3–18 Prorating Overapplied Overhead

At the end of 19x1 Foresight Limited had overapplied overhead of $40,000 that resulted from a significant underestimation of 19x1 production and sales volume. The following information is available concerning the composition of various accounts on December 31, 19x1.

	Work-in process	*Finished goods*	*Cost of goods sold*
Direct materials	$30,000	$25,000	$200,000
Direct labor	20,000	25,000	100,000
Applied overhead	10,000	40,000	150,000
Total	$60,000	$90,000	$450,000

REQUIREMENTS

a) Suggest two ways of prorating the overapplied overhead and prepare a prorating schedule for each method.

b) Prepare the journal entries necessary to prorate the overapplied overhead for the answers developed in part (a).

c) If volume is the only factor causing the overapplied overhead, what type of costs were not properly allowed for in the predetermined rate?

3–19 Predetermined Overhead Rate: Multiple Products

The following equation was developed to predict the Reston Company's annual factory overhead costs:

$$\text{Factory overhead} = \$270{,}000 + \$1.25X$$

where

X = machine hours

Planned yearly production includes 4,000 units of product Z1 and 10,000 units of product Z2. Each Z1 requires 5 machine hours and each Z2 requires 2 machine hours.

REQUIREMENTS

a) Calculate Reston's predetermined overhead rate per machine hour. Round calculations to two decimal places.

b) Determine the expected amount of over- or underapplied overhead when production consists of 6,000 units of product Z1 and 8,000 units of product Z2.

3–20 Predetermined Overhead Rate: Multiple Products

The following equation was developed to predict the Norton Company's annual factory overhead costs:

$$\text{Factory overhead} = \$150{,}000 + \$5X$$

where

$$X = \text{direct-labor hours}$$

Planned yearly production includes 5,000 units of product A1 and 5,000 units of product A2. Each A1 requires 10 labor hours and each A2 requires 5 labor hours.

REQUIREMENTS

a) Calculate Norton's predetermined overhead rate per direct-labor hour. Round calculations to two decimal places.

b) Determine the expected amount of over- or underapplied overhead when production consists of 4,000 units of product A1 and 6,000 units of product A2.

PROBLEMS

3–21 Actual Job-Order Costing: Journal Entries

John's Job Shop started operations on August 1, 19x7. During the month the following events occured:

- Materials costing $10,000 were purchased on account.
- Materials costing $8,000 were placed in process.
- A total of 500 direct-labor hours were charged to individual jobs at a rate of $5/hour.
- The fixed manufacturing overhead totaled $4,000.
- Variable manufacturing overhead totaled $1,000.
- Only job 631, with material charges of $200, direct-labor charges of $400, and applied overhead, was in process at the end of the period.

ADDITIONAL INFORMATION

- John's Job Shop uses an actual job-order cost system.
- Variable manufacturing overhead is a function of direct-labor hours.
- All overhead is allocated to individual jobs with the use of a single rate based on direct-labor hours.

REQUIREMENTS

a) Prepare summary journal entries for August.

b) Job 617 was one of those completed during August. It consisted of 100 units produced for inventory. Costs assigned to job 617 were as follows:

Direct materials	$1,000
Direct labor	500
Applied overhead	1,000
Total	$2,500

The units produced in job 617 have a normal selling price of $35 each. Determine the total costs charged to job 617 under each of the following circumstances:

1. A $2,000 seasonal decrease in monthly fixed manufacturing overhead. Total direct labor remains 500 hours.
2. Total monthly direct labor declines to 200 hours. Variable and fixed monthly overhead are $400 and $4,000, respectively.

3–22 Actual Job-Order Costing: Journal Entries

The Dolan Company manufactures special-purpose machines to order. On 1/1/x4, two jobs were in process, 405 and 406. The following costs were applied to them in 19x3:

	Job	
	405	*406*
Direct materials	$ 5,000	$ 8,000
Direct labor	4,000	3,000
Overhead	4,440	3,330
Total	$13,440	$14,330

During January 19x4, the following transactions took place:

- Raw materials costing $40,000 were purchased on account.
- Supplies costing $8,000 were purchased for cash.
- Jobs 407, 408, and 409 were started and the following costs incurred:

	Job		
	407	*408*	*409*
Direct materials	$3,000	$10,000	$7,000
Direct labor	5,000	6,000	4,000

- Jobs 405 and 406 were completed after incurring additional direct-labor costs of $2,000 and $4,000, respectively.
- Wages paid to production employees during January totaled $25,000, of which $5,000 was for wages payable on 1/1/x4. Wages payable on 1/31/x4 totaled $4,000.

- Depreciation on factory equipment for the month totaled $10,000.
- Utilities bills totaling $12,000 were received for January operations.
- Supplies costing $2,000 were used.
- Miscellaneous overhead totaled $2,400 for January.

Actual overhead is applied to individual jobs at the end of each month using a rate based on actual direct-labor costs.

REQUIREMENTS

a) Determine the January 19x4 overhead rate.

b) Prepare journal entries for each of the transactions that took place during January. Indicate the name of any subsidiary records affected by each transaction.

c) Prepare a statement of cost of goods manufactured.

3–23 Normal Job-Order Costing: Journal Entries

The Colorado Corp. uses a job-order cost system with normal overhead application. The rate estimated for 19x3 was 150 percent of direct-labor dollars. There was no over- or underapplied overhead on December 1. The inventory accounts had the following balances on December 1:

Manufacturing Supplies	$1,500
Stores Control	3,000
Work-in-Process (Job 101)	5,200
Finished Goods (Job 99)	3,000

During December the following events occurred:

- Materials costing $12,000 were purchased on account.
- Materials were issued to work-in-process to start three new orders:

Job 102	$ 4,000
Job 103	3,500
Job 104	5,000
Total	$12,500

- The December labor summary for salaries and wages incurred was as follows:

Job 101	$ 2,000
Job 102	3,700
Job 103	4,500
Job 104	1,200
Total direct labor	$11,400
Supervision and indirect labor	4,000
Total	$15,400

- Supplies that cost $1,500 were issued to the production department.

- Other overhead costs incurred during December were:

Utilities	$5,000
Depreciation of plant and equipment	7,000
Repairs and maintenance	1,000

- Jobs 101, 102, and 103 were completed and transferred to Finished Goods.
- Jobs 99 and 101 were sold on account for 125 percent of cost.

REQUIREMENTS

a) Prepare journal entries to record the December events.

b) Prepare T-accounts for all inventory accounts and Factory Overhead Control. Post the journal entries prepared for part (a) and determine all ending balances.

3–24 Normal Job-Order Costing: Journal Entries

The Montana Corp. uses a job-order cost system with normal overhead application. The rate estimated for 19x4 was $8 per labor hour. There was no over- or underapplied overhead on December 1. The inventory accounts had the following balances on December 1:

Manufacturing Supplies	$3,000
Stores Control	4,000
Work-in-Process (Job 210)	6,500
Finished Goods (Job 209)	7,000

During December the following events occurred:

- Materials costing $18,000 were purchased on account.
- Materials and supplies were issued as follows:

Job 211	$ 4,500
Job 212	5,300
Job 213	6,200
Supplies	1,800
Total	$17,800

- The December direct-labor costs were as follows:

Job 210	150 hrs. @ $6	$ 900
Job 211	400 hrs. @ $6	2,400
Job 212	350 hrs. @ $6	2,100
Job 213	100 hrs. @ $6	600
Total		$6,000

- Factory indirect labor for December was $2,400.
- Other overhead costs incurred during December were:

Utilities	$2,500
Depreciation of plant and equipment	1,000
Repairs and maintenance	500

- Jobs 210, 211, and 212 were completed and transferred to Finished Goods.
- Jobs 209 and 210 were sold on account for 120 percent of cost.

REQUIREMENTS

a) Prepare journal entries to record the December events.

b) Prepare T-accounts for all inventory accounts and Factory Overhead Control. Post the journal entries prepared for part (a) and determine all ending balances.

3–25 Normal Job-Order Costing: Journal Entries[5]

The Can-Do Mfg. Company uses a job-order cost system. The beginning balances and operations for May 19x8 for their office furniture plant are given as:

- Beginning balances for the inventories:

Stores Control	$12,000
Work-in-Process, Job 1004	20,000
Finished Goods, Job 1002	45,000

- Can-Do uses a single inventory account for raw materials and supplies. Purchases of raw materials and supplies totaled $65,000 during May.
- The following summary of materials and supplies requisitions is available:

	Sheet metal parts	*Formica*	*Total*
Job 1005	$11,000	$4,000	$15,000
Job 1006	13,000	5,000	18,000
Job 1007	10,000	6,000	16,000
Job 1008	5,000	1,000	6,000
Total			$55,000
Supplies for office furniture production			4,500
Total			$59,500

- The payroll summary for May is as follows:

	Hours	*Cost*
Job 1004	250	$ 1,500
Job 1005	2,500	15,000
Job 1006	2,000	11,500
Job 1007	1,800	9,000
Job 1008	400	2,200
Total direct labor	6,950	$39,200
Indirect labor and factory supervision	1,000	6,000
Selling and administrative		12,000
Total May payroll		$57,200

[5] Adapted from a problem prepared by Professor Imogene Posey.

- The budget for 19x8 was prepared in early December 19x7 after a study of past records and forecasts for future costs. Total factory overhead for the furniture plant for 19x8 was budgeted at $600,000. A predetermined rate based on direct-labor hours is used to apply overhead. The 19x8 forecast for total direct-labor hours of work was 75,000.
- Other factory overhead costs for May were:

Depreciation of plant and equipment	$14,000
Energy and other utilities	20,000
Expired insurance	2,000
Property taxes	3,000
Miscellaneous	2,000

- Jobs 1004, 1005, 1006, and 1007 were completed and transferred to Finished Goods.
- Jobs 1002, 1004, and 1005 were sold for $155,000 and shipped to customers.
- Other selling and administrative expenses were $10,000.

REQUIREMENTS

a) Prepare journal entries to record all information needed for May operations.

b) Show T-accounts for all inventory accounts with ending balances calculated.

c) Determine the amount of over- or underapplied factory overhead.

3–26 Actual and Normal Job-Order Costing: Journal Entries

Linhurst Motor Company produces custom race cars. On April 1, 19w9, work-in-process consisted of three jobs:

Job 153	$28,000
Job 154	35,000
Job 155	15,000
Total	$78,000

The following information is available regarding April activities:

- Raw materials costing $25,000 and factory supplies costing $3,000 were purchased on account. A single inventory account is used for raw materials and supplies.
- Materials and supplies were requisitioned as follows:

Job 153	$ 2,000
Job 154	0
Job 155	8,000
Job 156	15,000
Total direct materials	$25,000
Factory supplies	3,500
Total	$28,500

- Liabilities were incurred for the following labor-related costs:

Job 153	$ 5,000
Job 154	1,500
Job 155	15,000
Job 156	6,000
Total direct labor	$27,500
Indirect labor and factory supervision	4,000
Total payroll	$31,500

- Other factory overhead costs equal $9,000.
- Jobs 153, 154, and 155 were completed.

REQUIREMENTS

a) Assume an actual cost system is in use with overhead applied on the basis of direct-labor dollars. Prepare summary journal entries for April.

b) Assume a normal cost system is used. On an annual basis, estimated total overhead is equal to $18,000 + 0.55 (direct-labor dollars). Estimated 19w9 direct labor is $180,000.

1. Determine the 19w9 predetermined overhead rate per direct-labor dollar.
2. Prepare summary journal entries for April.
3. Determine the amount of the April over- or underapplied overhead.

3–27 Plant-Wide and Departmental Overhead Rates

Cornhusker Products has two production departments, P1 and P2. The amount of time a job spends in P1 and P2 depends on the job's specifications. For November 19y1 the following information is available about P1 and P2:

	P1	*P2*	*Total*
Departmental overhead	$24,000	$75,000	$99,000
Direct labor	20,000	30,000	50,000

REQUIREMENTS

a) Determine the plant-wide overhead rate per direct-labor dollar.

b) Determine the departmental overhead rates per direct-labor dollar.

c) Using the rates developed in parts (a) and (b), determine the overhead cost assigned to the following jobs which were started and completed during November:

	Job			
	906	*907*	*908*	*Total*
Direct labor:				
P1	$10,000	$10,000	$ 0	$20,000
P2	0	15,000	15,000	30,000
Total	$10,000	$25,000	$15,000	$50,000

d) If prices are based on product costs, evaluate the impact of a decision to use a plant-wide overhead rate rather than departmental overhead rates.

3–28 Plant-Wide and Departmental Overhead Rates

Spartan Institute has two academic departments, Computer Science and Office Science. The number of courses a student takes in each department depends on whether they are a Computer Science or an Office Science major. For the fall 19x2 term the following information is available about each department.

	Computer Science	*Office Science*	*Institute Total*
Operating costs	$120,000	$60,000	$180,000
Student credit hours (SCHs)	800	1,200	2,000

REQUIREMENTS

a) Determine the institute-wide operating cost per student credit hour.

b) Determine the departmental operating cost per student credit hour.

c) In a typical one-year certificate program, the credit hour distribution of Computer Science and Office Science majors is as follows:

	Major	
	Computer Science	*Office Science*
Credits taken in:		
Computer Science	15	3
Office Science	3	15
Total	18	18

Using the credit hour operating cost rates developed in parts (a) and (b), determine the cost of educating a Computer Science major and an Office Science major.

d) If tuition is based on costs, evaluate the impact of using an institute-wide operating cost rate rather than departmental operating cost rates.

3–29 Normal Job-Order Costing: Journal Entries and all Statements (Comprehensive Problem)

The Bridgeport Tool Company operates a normal job-order cost system. Manufacturing overhead is applied to jobs at the rate of $5 per direct-labor hour. Over- or underapplied overhead is treated as an inventory adjustment on interim financial statements.

Bridgeport's March 1, 19x6, statement of financial position is presented as follows:

Bridgeport Tool Company
Statement of Financial Position
As of March 1, 19x6

Assets:		
Cash		$23,000
Inventories:		
Stores control	$ 8,000	
Work-in-process	4,000	
Add: Underapplied overhead	500	12,500
Plant and equipment	$250,000	
Less accumulated depreciation	−50,000	200,000
Total assets		$235,500
Liabilities:		
Payroll payable (wages)	$ 2,000	
Payroll payable (salaries)	500	$ 2,500
Shareholders' Equity:		
Common stock, par value $5	$ 50,000	
Paid in capital in excess of par	150,000	
Retained earnings	33,000	233,000
Total liabilities and shareholders' equity		$235,500

The March 1 work-in-process inventory consisted of one job, 904. During March the following events occurred:

- Paid two months' rent on administrative facilities, $2,000.
- Purchased raw materials costing $7,000 for cash.
- The following assignments were made to job 904 and to two new jobs:

	Job			
	904	*905*	*906*	*Total*
Direct materials	$ 0	$ 8,000	$4,000	$12,000
Direct labor	$500	$10,000	$3,000	$13,500
Direct-labor hours	80	2,000	900	2,980

- Jobs 904 and 905 were completed and sold for $50,000 in cash.
- Wages earned by production employees totaled $15,000.
- Wages paid production employees totaled $16,000.
- Salaries earned by the production supervisor totaled $2,000.
- Salaries paid the production supervisor totaled $2,400.
- Depreciation on plant and equipment amounted to $5,000.

- Other current manufacturing overhead costs in the amount of $5,000 were paid in cash.
- Other selling and administrative expenses totaling $8,000 were paid in cash.

REQUIREMENTS

a) Prepare all journal entries (except those required to close temporary accounts) for the month of March.

b) Prepare the March 19x6 statement of cost of goods manufactured and sold.

c) Prepare the March 19x6 income statement. You need not show the details involved in computing the cost of goods sold.

d) Prepare the March 31, 19x6, statement of financial position.

SOLUTION TO REVIEW PROBLEM

a)

Account	Debit	Credit
Stores Control	$41,000	
Accounts Payable		$41,000
Work-in-Process	29,000	
Factory Overhead Control	3,000	
Stores Control		32,000
Work-in-Process	21,000	
Factory Overhead Control	7,000	
Payroll Payable		28,000
Factory Overhead Control	6,800	
Accumulated Depreciation—Plant and Equipment		1,000
Utilities Payable		5,000
Sundry Accounts		800
Work-in-Process	16,800	
Factory Overhead Control ($4,000 + $8,000 + $4,800)		16,800
Finished Goods Inventory	52,000	
Work-in-Process		52,000

Job 875	$19,000	(see job-cost sheets)
Job 876	33,000	
Total	$52,000	

	Job 875	*Job 876*	*Job 877*
Beginning balance	$ 8,000	$ 0	$ 0
Direct materials	2,000	15,000	12,000
Direct labor	5,000	10,000	6,000
Overhead*	4,000	8,000	4,800
Total	$19,000	$33,000	$22,800

* Overhead rate = ($16,800/$21,000) = 0.80 direct-labor dollar.

b) 1. Estimated 19x5 overhead = \$80,000 + 0.5 (\$320,000) = \$240,000
Predetermined overhead rate = \$240,000/\$320,000 = 0.75

2.

Stores Control	\$41,000	
Accounts Payable		\$41,000
Work-in-Process	29,000	
Factory Overhead Control	3,000	
Stores Control		32,000
Work-in-Process	21,000	
Factory Overhead Control	7,000	
Payroll Payable		28,000
Factory Overhead Control	6,800	
Accumulated Depreciation—Plant and Equipment		1,000
Utilities Payable		5,000
Sundry Accounts		800
Work-in-Process	15,750	
Factory Overhead Control (\$21,000 × 0.75)		15,750
Finished Goods Inventory	51,250	
Work-in-Process		51,250

Job 875	\$18,750 (see job-cost sheets)
Job 876	32,500
Total	\$51,250

	Job 875	Job 876	Job 877
Beginning balance	\$ 8,000	\$ 0	\$ 0
Direct materials	2,000	15,000	12,000
Direct labor	5,000	10,000	6,000
Overhead*	3,750	7,500	4,500
Total	\$18,750	\$32,500	\$22,500

* Applied at 0.75 direct-labor dollars.

3.

Actual overhead	\$16,800
Applied overhead	−15,750
Underapplied overhead	\$ 1,050

4 Actual and Normal Process Cost Systems

INTRODUCTION
JOB-ORDER AND PROCESS COSTING
EQUIVALENT UNITS
COST PER EQUIVALENT UNIT
COST OF PRODUCTION REPORTS
BEGINNING INVENTORIES
SUBSEQUENT DEPARTMENTS
SPOILAGE
SUMMARY

INTRODUCTION

THIS IS THE THIRD CHAPTER OF A FIVE-CHAPTER SEQUENCE DEVOTED TO product costing, the assignment of costs to inventories as they are converted from raw materials to finished goods. Our focus once again is on *product costs* that are assigned to products as they are produced and expensed when products are sold. Chapter 3 was devoted to *job-order costing,* where costs were assigned to specifically identifiable batches of goods or to a specifically identifiable project.

The purpose of this chapter is to examine another widely used product costing system, namely, process costing. In studying this chapter keep in mind that many of the issues raised in our examination of job-order costing are equally applicable to process costing. A process cost system, for example, can be operated using either an actual or a predetermined overhead rate, and, if a predetermined overhead rate is used, management is faced with the problem of determining how to treat overapplied or underapplied overhead.

JOB-ORDER AND PROCESS COSTING

In job-order costing, production costs are identified with each batch of units. As work on an individual job progresses, costs are assigned to the general ledger account Work-in-Process and the appropriate job-cost sheet in the detailed cost system records. When a job is completed, all costs accumulated on its job-cost sheet are transferred from Work-in-Process to Finished Goods Inventory and the job-cost sheet is removed from the Work-in-Process subsidiary records. In multiunit jobs, unit costs are the total job costs divided by the number of units produced.

Job-order costing is appropriate when many different products are produced in batches that receive varying degrees of attention in each production department or operation. If, however, a product is produced on a continuous basis and all units of the product passing through a particular department or production operation are homogeneous (alike in all respects), a process cost system, rather than a job-order cost system, should be used.

In the context of product costing, a **process** is a standardized operation, or a series of standardized operations, used in the continuous production of units of a homogeneous product. A **process costing system** assigns costs to units of a homogeneous product as the units pass through one or more production processes. Process cost systems are appropriate for such industries as canning, chemical processing, food processing, glass, metal manufacturing, paper making, and petroleum refining.

The differences between job-order and process costing are subtle, but important. Essentially a job-order system identifies costs with specific *batches of product* and then averages them over the units in the batch, whereas a process cost system identifies costs with a *specific department* and then averages them over *units of work* performed in the department during a *period of time*. Some of the units of work were performed on products completed during the period; others represent effort applied to the ending inventory of work-in-process.

Individual cost sheets for each job constitute the backbone of a job-cost system, whereas cost of production reports for each production department or operation are the backbone of a process cost system. A **cost of production report** is a summary of the unit and cost data of a department in a process cost system. It includes a summary of the units worked on, the costs assigned to the department, a computation of unit costs, and the costs transferred out of the department or assigned to ending inventories in the department. The differences between job-order and process cost systems are presented in Exhibit 4–1.

After discussing the differences between job-order and process cost systems, we should also mention their similarities. These include the relationships between inventory accounts, the distinction between actual and normal costing, and all issues pertaining to the use of plant-wide or departmental overhead rates.

In Chapter 3 we mentioned that departmental overhead rates should be used when jobs spend varying amounts of time in each production department. This discussion is also applicable to process costing. A chemical company, for example, may produce several different chemicals on a continuous basis in several different departments. To ensure proper cost assignments, each department should have its own overhead rate.

EXHIBIT 4–1 Differences Between Job-Order and Process Cost Systems

Job-order cost system	*Process cost system*
○ Many different products produced in batches.	○ A single product produced on a continuous basis.
○ Batches receive varying degrees of attention in each production department or operation.	○ Units receive identical attention in each production department or operation.
○ Costs are assigned to jobs and averaged over units in job.	○ Costs are assigned to departments and averaged over units of work performed during a given time period.
○ Job-cost sheets for each job are the backbone of the system.	○ Cost of production reports for each production department or operation are the backbone of the system.

EQUIVALENT UNITS

Equivalent units are the basic building blocks of all applications of process costing. Equivalent units are used to measure work performed or in process. An **equivalent unit** represents the amount of direct materials, direct labor, or factory overhead required to produce one unit of finished product. In process cost systems, the beginning or ending work-in-process inventories of production departments are restated in terms of equivalent units. If the ending inventory consists of 900 units of work-in-process, containing an average of 20 percent of the direct materials they will have when completed, the ending inventory contains 180 (900 × 0.20) equivalent units of direct materials.

In equivalent unit computations, the categories of direct labor and factory overhead are often combined into a single category labeled "conversion." This simplification is often used when factory overhead is applied on the basis of direct-labor hours or dollars. If the ending inventory of 900 units contains an average of three hours of direct labor and it is estimated that the units will be completed with an average of one additional hour each, the ending inventory is 75 percent (3/(3 + 1)) complete as to conversion and it contains 675 (900 × 0.75) equivalent units of conversion.

To simplify textbook examples, we will use the categories of materials and conversion for equivalent unit computations. Some problems contain the more detailed categories of materials, labor, and overhead.

Example 4–1

The Watson Company started producing a new product on August 1, 19x8. Of the 1,000 units started, 600 units were completed and 400 units were in process on August 31. Because all materials were added at the start of the production process, the units in the ending inventory were complete as to materials. However, on the average, they were only one-half of the way through the manufacturing process. How many equivalent units were in process?

Because the units in the ending inventory are in different stages of completion as to materials and conversion, we must compute equivalent units for each of them.

	Materials	*Conversion*
Units completed	600	600
Equivalent units in ending inventory	+400*	+200*
Equivalent units in process	1,000	800

* 400 units, complete as to materials, one-half complete as to conversion.

In Example 4–1, the 600 units that were completed obviously had 600 equivalent units of materials and conversion contained in them. Otherwise, they would not be complete. There were 400 units in the ending inventory, but they were the equivalent of only 200 whole units of conversion because they were only one-half complete as to conversion. If all efforts had been directed toward completing the maximum number of units in process, 800 units would have been complete and there would be sufficient materials for 200 units in the ending work-in-process inventory.

An important part of equivalent unit computations is the estimation of the ending inventory's percentage of completion. These estimates are normally based on engineering estimates or visual observation. Consider the case of an assembly line where materials are added at the start of the process and conversion takes place evenly throughout the process. If the assembly line is fully operative, all units in process are complete as to materials and, on the average, one-half complete as to conversion.

To facilitate more rapid product costing, in situations where the ending inventory is always small in comparison with the volume of completed units, it may be acceptable to develop assumptions about the stage of the ending inventory's completion. The cost accountant, for example, might assume the ending inventory is 60 percent complete as to materials and 50 percent complete as to conversion. Under certain circumstances, involving a very stable rate of production, it might even be acceptable to make assumptions regarding the number of units in the ending inventory. This would further reduce the time and effort required for product costing.

COST PER EQUIVALENT UNIT

Having overcome the major hurdle of computing the number of equivalent units of materials and conversion, we must still calculate the cost per equivalent unit before we can determine the costs transferred out and in ending Work-in-Process.

Example 4–2

Continuing Example 4–1, assume Watson purchased raw materials costing $40,000 during August, and that August manufacturing costs included direct materials of $30,000, direct labor of $7,000, and factory overhead of $9,000. Watson uses an actual cost system with factory overhead applied on the basis of direct-labor dollars. Prepare August journal entries pertaining to overhead and inventory accounts.

Based on the given information, the following journal entries are prepared:

Stores Control	40,000	
Accounts Payable		40,000
Work-in-Process	37,000	
Stores Control		30,000
Payroll Payable		7,000
Factory Overhead Control	9,000	
Sundry Accounts[1]		9,000
Work-in-Process	9,000	
Factory Overhead Control		9,000

Before the journal entry transferring the cost of goods manufactured to Finished Goods Inventory can be prepared, we must determine the cost per equivalent unit. To simplify computations, we combine direct labor and factory overhead into a single cost category, namely, conversion.

---

[1] The title **Sundry Accounts** is used when the specific name(s) of the account(s) involved is (are) unknown.

	Materials	*Conversion*	*Total*
Current and total costs	$30,000	$16,000	$46,000
Equivalent units in process	÷1,000	÷800	
Cost per equivalent unit	$30	$20	$50

Because there are a different number of equivalent units of materials and conversion, the total cost per equivalent unit can only be computed by adding the equivalent unit costs for each cost element. The $50 cost per equivalent unit consists of equivalent unit materials costs of $30 and equivalent unit conversion costs of $20. If we had broken the conversion costs into subcategories, direct labor would be $8.75 ($7,000/800) and factory overhead would be $11.25 ($9,000/800).

The cost of goods manufactured is $30,000 (600 × $50). This amount is transferred from Work-in-Process to Finished Goods Inventory. The final August journal entry affecting inventory accounts is as follows:

Finished Goods Inventory	30,000	
Work-in-Process		30,000

The ending balance in Work-in-Process is $16,000 ($46,000 − $30,000), verified as follows:

Materials (400 × $30)	$12,000
Conversion (200 × $20)	4,000
Total	$16,000

COST OF PRODUCTION REPORTS

Cost of production reports, used to summarize unit and cost data for each department or operation, are an essential part of a process cost system. A cost of production report contains five elements:

1. A summary of the flow of whole or partial units, regardless of their stage of completion.
2. A computation of equivalent units of materials and conversion.
3. A determination of the total costs to be accounted for, computed as the beginning balance in Work-in-Process plus current manufacturing costs assigned to Work-in-Process.
4. A computation of the cost per equivalent unit.
5. An accounting for total costs in process.

A formal cost of production report for Watson's August operations is presented in Exhibit 4–2. The five elements of the report are identified in capital letters. The last element of the report indicates the costs transferred to Finished Goods Inventory and the costs remaining in Work-in-Process at the end of the period. In preparing a cost of production report, always verify the equality of the total costs to be accounted for and the total costs accounted for.

EXHIBIT 4–2 Process Costing Without Beginning Inventories

Watson Company
Cost of Production Report
For the Month of August, 19x8

FLOW OF WHOLE OR PARTIAL UNITS	
Beginning	0
Started	1,000
In process	1,000
Completed	– 600
Ending	400

	Materials	*Conversion*	*Total*
EQUIVALENT UNITS IN PROCESS			
Units completed	600	600	
Equivalent units in ending inventory	400	200*	
Equivalent units in process	1,000	800	
TOTAL COSTS TO BE ACCOUNTED FOR			
COST PER EQUIVALENT UNIT IN PROCESS			
Current and total costs	$30,000	$16,000	$46,000
Equivalent units in process	÷ 1,000	÷ 800	
Cost per equivalent unit	$30	$20	$50
ACCOUNTING FOR TOTAL COSTS			
Transferred out (600 × $50)			$30,000
Work-in-Process, ending:			
Materials (400 × $30)		$12,000	
Conversion (200 × $20)		4,000	16,000
Total costs accounted for			$46,000

* 400 units, one-half complete.

BEGINNING INVENTORIES

In Examples 4–1 and 4–2 there were no beginning inventories, and all units completed or in ending inventory were started during the period. In a process cost system, when there are no beginning inventories, it is not necessary to make a cost flow assumption. When there are beginning inventories, the cost accountant must decide whether to use a weighted-average or a first-in, first-out (FIFO) cost flow assumption. In the absence of beginning inventories or changes in input prices, weighted-average and FIFO inventory costing give identical results. However, if there are beginning inventories and if costs increase during the period, the FIFO method results in fewer costs being transferred out and a higher ending work-in-process inventory value than does the weighted-average method. The weighted-average method pools the lower beginning inventory costs with the current costs, whereas the FIFO method separates the beginning costs from the higher current costs, transferring the beginning costs out first.

Weighted Average

In the weighted-average method, *total costs in process* are divided by *equivalent units in process* to determine the *cost per equivalent unit in process*. **Total costs in process** are determined by adding current manufacturing costs to the costs in Work-in-Process at the beginning of the period. **Equivalent units in process** are computed by adding equivalent units in ending inventory to the units completed (which consist of the equivalent units in the beginning inventory, the equivalent units necessary to complete the beginning inventory, and the units started and completed during the period).

Example 4–3

Continuing Example 4–2, on September 1, 19x8, Watson Company had a beginning work-in-process inventory of 400 units that was complete as to materials and one-half complete as to conversion. Related costs were $12,000 and $4,000, respectively. During September, 1,100 units were started and 1,300 units were completed. The September 30 inventory of 200 units was estimated to be complete as to materials and three-fourths complete as to conversion. During September, raw materials costing $20,000 were purchased. September manufacturing costs include direct materials of $22,550, direct labor of $7,875, and factory overhead of $8,100. However, *Watson instituted a normal cost system for overhead* on September 1 and the cost accountant, after analyzing predicted overhead costs and predicted direct-labor costs, developed a predetermined overhead rate of 100 percent of direct-labor dollars.

Watson's September cost of production report is presented in Exhibit 4–3. Note that the current conversion costs, with a normal cost system, are the total of direct labor and overhead applied at 100 percent of direct labor, or $15,750 [($7,875 + ($7,875 × 1.00)]. If an actual cost system were used, the current conversion costs would have been the total of direct labor and actual overhead, or $15,975 ($7,875 + $8,100). With a normal cost system, September factory overhead is underapplied by $225 ($8,100 actual − $7,875 applied). This amount would be shown as an adjustment to inventories if interim financial statements were prepared on September 30.

Using the given information and the September cost of production report in Exhibit 4–3, the September journal entries are:

Account	Debit	Credit
Stores Control	20,000.00	
Accounts Payable		20,000.00
Work-in-Process	38,300.00	
Stores Control		22,550.00
Payroll Payable		7,875.00
Factory Overhead Control		7,875.00
Factory Overhead Control	8,100.00	
Sundry Accounts		8,100.00
Finished Goods Inventory	47,650.20	
Work-in-Process		47,650.20

The last journal entry, transferring costs from Work-in-Process to Finished Goods Inventory, could not have been completed without the information in the cost of production report. Note the similarity in the use of cost of production

EXHIBIT 4–3 Weighted-Average Process Costing with Beginning Inventories

Watson Company
Cost of Production Report
For the Month of September, 19x8

FLOW OF WHOLE OR PARTIAL UNITS	
Beginning	400
Started	1,100
In process	1,500
Completed	−1,300
Ending	200

	Materials	*Conversion*	*Total*
EQUIVALENT UNITS IN PROCESS			
Units completed	1,300	1,300	
Equivalent units in ending inventory	200	150*	
Equivalent units in process	1,500	1,450	
TOTAL COSTS TO BE ACCOUNTED FOR			
COST PER EQUIVALENT UNIT IN PROCESS			
Work-in-Process, beginning	$12,000	$ 4,000	$16,000
Current manufacturing costs	22,550	15,750†	38,300
Total costs in process	$34,550	$19,750	$54,300
Equivalent units in process	÷1,500	÷1,450	
Cost per equivalent unit in process	$23.033	$13.621	$36.654
ACCOUNTING FOR TOTAL COSTS			
Transferred out (1,300 × $36.654)			$47,650.20
Work-in-Process, ending:			
Materials (200 × $23.033)		$4,606.60	
Conversion (150 × $13.621)		2,043.15	6,649.75
Total costs accounted for			$54,299.95‡

* 200 units, three-quarters complete.
† Includes direct labor of $7,875 and applied overhead of $7,875.
‡ Answer reflects $0.05 rounding error. Because all costs must be accounted for in the Watson Company's records we will assume the $0.05 could be left in Work-in-Process, as a conversion cost, at the end of September, making the ending balance in Work-in-Process $6,649.80.

reports and job-cost sheets. In a job-order cost system, the entry transferring costs from Work-in-Process to Finished Goods Inventory cannot be prepared without the use of information contained in job-cost sheets.

FIFO

The FIFO method used in process costing is, in reality, a modified FIFO method. Regardless of the number of input price changes that take place during a period, only two price categories are used, one for the beginning inventory and one for current production. Additionally, to the extent necessary to complete beginning inventories, current production costs are pooled with beginning inventory costs.

In the weighted-average method, beginning inventories were pooled with current production to compute *equivalent units in process,* and the beginning balance in Work-in-Process was pooled with current manufacturing costs to compute *total costs in process*. Under FIFO, beginning inventories and costs are separated from current production and current manufacturing costs; and current manufacturing costs are divided by *equivalent units manufactured* this period to compute the *cost per equivalent unit manufactured* this period. **Equivalent units manufactured** is a measure of the amount of work performed during the current period. It is often computed as the equivalent units in process minus the equivalent units in the beginning inventory.

Note the subtle difference in terminology. Weighted-average terminology includes "total costs in process," "equivalent units in process," and "cost per equivalent unit in process." All production and costs are pooled or averaged. FIFO terminology includes "current manufacturing costs," "equivalent units manufactured," and "cost per equivalent unit manufactured." Beginning inventories and costs are separated from current production and costs.

Using FIFO process costing, Watson's September 19x8 cost of production report is presented in Exhibit 4–4. Comparing Exhibits 4–3 and 4–4 note the following:

- Under FIFO, the equivalent units in the beginning inventory are subtracted from the *equivalent units in process* (the endpoint in the weighted-average computation) to determine the *equivalent units manufactured*. The equivalent units manufactured can also be computed by adding the equivalent units for the work performed during the current period to (1) complete the beginning inventory; (2) complete units started during the current period; and (3) get the ending inventory to its current stage of completion. Using this approach, Watson Company's September 19x8 equivalent units manufactured are computed as follows:

	Materials	*Conversion*
Equivalent units needed to complete beginning inventory	0	200*
Units started and completed (1,300 − 400)	900	900
Equivalent units in ending inventory	200	150†
Equivalent units manufactured	1,100	1,250

* 400 units, one-half complete
† 200 units, three-quarters complete

Although this presentation is occasionally encountered, the authors prefer the one used in Exhibit 4–4 because it emphasizes the difference between FIFO and weighted average, namely, the separate treatment of beginning inventory.

- Under FIFO, only the current manufacturing costs (rather than the total costs in process) are divided by the equivalent units manufactured this period to obtain the cost per equivalent unit manufactured.
- Under FIFO, transferred-out costs are presented in two parts (rather than the one part used under weighted average). The first part consists of the beginning inventory plus the current costs necessary to complete the beginning inventory. The second part consists of the cost of the units started and completed this period.

EXHIBIT 4–4 FIFO Process Costing with Beginning Inventories

Watson Company
Cost of Production Report
For the Month of September, 19x8

FLOW OF WHOLE OR PARTIAL UNITS	
Beginning	400
Started	1,100
In process	1,500
Completed	−1,300
Ending	200

	Materials	*Conversion*	*Total*
EQUIVALENT UNITS MANUFACTURED			
Units completed	1,300	1,300	
Equivalent units in ending inventory	200	150*	
Equivalent units in process	1,500	1,450	
Less equivalent units in beginning inventory	−400	−200†	
Equivalent units manufactured	1,100	1,250	
TOTAL COSTS TO BE ACCOUNTED FOR			
COST PER EQUIVALENT UNIT IN PROCESS			
Work-in-Process, beginning	omit‡	omit‡	$16,000
Current manufacturing costs	22,550	15,750	38,300
Total costs in process	omit‡	omit‡	$54,300
Equivalent units manufactured	÷1,100	÷1,250	
Cost per equivalent unit manufactured	$20.50	$12.60	$33.10
ACCOUNTING FOR TOTAL COSTS			
Transferred out:			
First batch:			
Work-in-Process, beginning	$16,000		
Cost to complete:			
Conversion (200§ × $12.60)	2,520	$18,520	
Second batch, started and completed this period (900** × $33.10)		29,790	$48,310
Work-in-Process, ending:			
Materials (200 × $20.50)		$ 4,100	
Conversion (150 × $12.60)		1,890	5,990
Total costs accounted for			$54,300

* 200 units, three-quarters complete.
† 400 units, one-half complete.
‡ Cost per equivalent unit manufactured is based on current costs only.
§ Additional equivalent units required to complete beginning inventory.
** 1,300 units completed less 400 units in the beginning inventory.

- Under FIFO, the costs transferred out of Work-in-Process to Finished Goods Inventory will differ from those transferred out under weighted-average process costing, if there have been changes in input costs during the period. During September Watson's input costs actually fell. Following a FIFO procedure, a greater portion of the previously higher costs are transferred to Finished Goods Inventory. This would result in the following journal entry:

Finished Goods Inventory	48,310	
Work-in-Process		48,310

- Under FIFO, all other entries are the same as those previously illustrated for weighted average.

LIFO?

Last-in, first-out (LIFO) is not used as a mechanical procedure for costing work-in-process inventories. The layering aspects of this technique would make its process costing applications extremely difficult. Raw materials and finished goods inventories could be valued on a LIFO basis if management desired. It is also possible to convert inventories, including work-in-process, to a LIFO basis for external reporting using techniques such as dollar value LIFO. Readers interested in this topic should consult an intermediate accounting textbook.

SUBSEQUENT DEPARTMENTS

No major complications are introduced when the output of one department is an input to a subsequent one. All that is necessary is to treat the transferred-out costs from the previous department as a current input cost to the second. Typically these costs are accounted for separately from other materials added in the second department. Additionally, under FIFO process costing, all transferred-in costs are lumped together into one group of current input costs. If this were not done, FIFO process costing with multiple departments would become unwieldy. With these minor modifications, all calculations in subsequent departments are identical to those illustrated.

The flow of costs in a process cost system with multiple production departments is illustrated in Exhibit 4–5. Note the use of two work-in-process and two factory overhead control accounts.

Example 4–4

Assume the same information given in Example 4–3, except that Watson now has two departments, an Assembly Department and a Finishing Department. The information in Example 4–3 pertains to the Assembly Department. The Finishing Department started operations on September 1, 19x8. Prior to that time, assembled units were sold to other businesses for finishing. After September 1, all assembled units were transferred to the Finishing Department.

The Finishing Department has no September beginning inventory. Of the 1,300 units transferred in from the Assembly Department, 1,000 were completed and 300 were in work-in-process on September 30. The only additional materials added in the Finishing Department are added at the end of the finishing operation. Consequently no additional materials have been added to the 300 units in ending work-in-process; they are zero percent complete as to additional materials. The ending inventory is estimated to be two-thirds complete as to conversion.

EXHIBIT 4–5 Flow of Costs in a Process Cost System with Multiple Departments

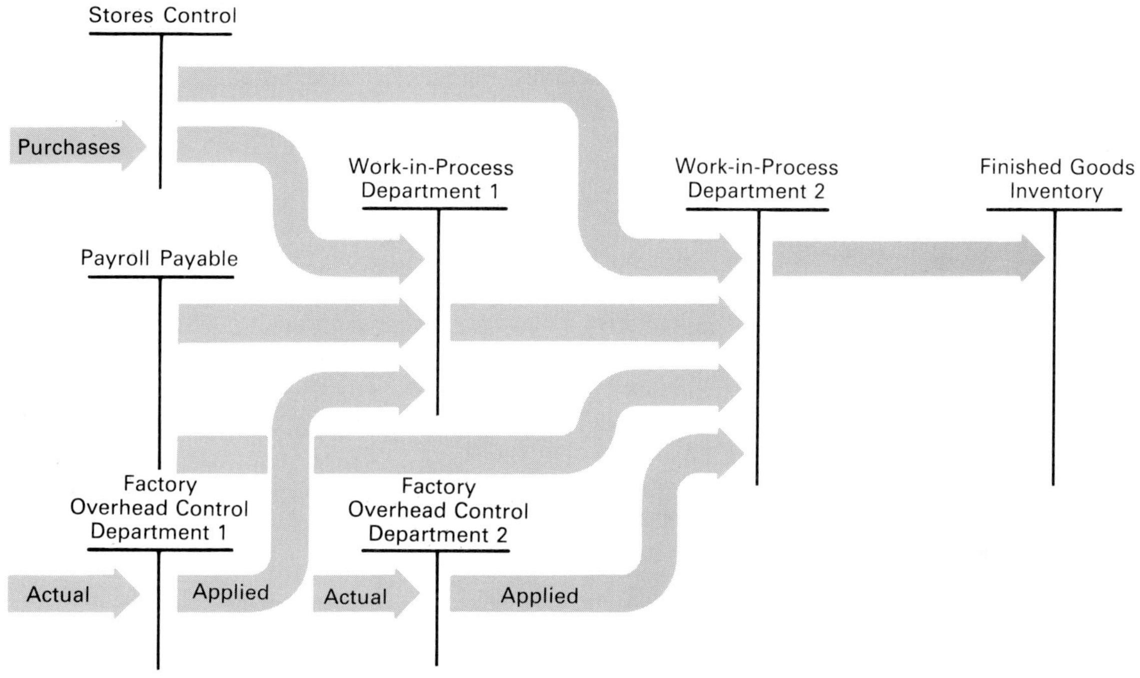

Costs assigned the Finishing Department in September include transferred-in of $48,310 (see Exhibit 4–4), direct materials of $2,000, direct labor of $3,000, and factory overhead of $2,000. Overhead is applied at a predetermined rate of 60 percent of direct labor. Hence, total conversion costs assigned to Work-in-Process: Finishing Department are $4,800 [$3,000 + 0.6($3,000)].

Watson uses FIFO costing in the Assembly Department (Exhibit 4–4) and weighted-average costing in the Finishing Department. A cost of production report for September Finishing Department operations is presented in Exhibit 4–6. Note that the units are always 100 percent complete as to their transferred-in element. Because there were no beginning inventories in the Finishing Department, the report would be the same, given the transferred-in costs, regardless of whether weighted-average or FIFO process costing were used. In the absence of beginning inventories, current manufacturing costs are the same as total costs in process, and equivalent units in process are the same as equivalent units manufactured. Journal entries summarizing September activities of the Finishing Department are as follows:

Work-in-Process: Finishing Department	48,310	
Work-in-Process: Assembly Department		48,310
Work-in-Process: Finishing Department	6,800	
Stores Control		2,000
Payroll Payable		3,000
Factory Overhead Control: Finishing Department		1,800

EXHIBIT 4–6 Weighted Average Process Costing in Subsequent Departments

Watson Company—Finishing Department
Cost of Production Report
For the Month of September, 19x8

FLOW OF WHOLE OR PARTIAL UNITS	
Beginning	0
Transferred in	1,300
In process	1,300
Completed	−1,000
Ending	300

	Transferred-in	*Materials*	*Conversion*	*Total*
EQUIVALENT UNITS IN PROCESS				
Units completed	1,000	1,000	1,000	
Equivalent units in ending inventory	300	0*	200†	
Equivalent units in process	1,300	1,000	1,200	
TOTAL COSTS TO BE ACCOUNTED FOR				
COST PER EQUIVALENT UNIT IN PROCESS				
Current and total manufacturing costs	$48,310	$2,000	$4,800	$55,110
Equivalent units in process	÷1,300	÷1,000	÷1,200	
Cost per equivalent unit in process	$37.162	$2.000	$4.000	$43.162
ACCOUNTING FOR TOTAL COSTS				
Transferred out (1,000 × $43.162)				$43,162.00
Work-in-Process, ending:				
Transferred in (300 × $37.162)			$11,148.60	
Conversion (200 × $4.00)			800.00	11,948.60
Total costs accounted for				$55,110.60‡

* 300 units, 0% complete.
† 300 units, two-thirds complete.
‡ Answer reflects $0.60 rounding error.

Factory Overhead Control: Finishing Department	2,000	
Sundry Accounts		2,000
Finished Goods Inventory	43,162	
Work-in-Process: Finishing Department		43,162

The first entry replaces the previous transfer from Work-in-Process to Finished Goods Inventory. Because a predetermined overhead rate is used, overhead can be applied before actual overhead costs are known. Any September 30 balance in Factory Overhead Control: Finishing Department is treated as an adjustment to total inventories on interim financial statements. The cost of production report, presented in Exhibit 4–6 is needed to prepare the last entry transferring costs from Work-in-Process: Finishing Department to Finished Goods Inventory.

SPOILAGE

Spoiled units (sometimes called **defective units**) are units that do not meet quality standards and must be junked, sold as seconds, or reworked. Examples of spoilage include cracked or scratched dishes, floppy disks with bad sectors, ink blots on books, off-color paint, and bruised produce. The central accounting issue is determining what to do with the cost of spoiled units. The proper approach depends on whether or not spoilage is an expected or normal occurrence in the production of good units.

1. If spoilage is not expected to occur, the cost of the equivalent units spoiled should be written off as a loss.
2. In some production operations, the additional cost required to completely eliminate the occasional production of defective units has led management to accept the production of some spoiled goods. Under these circumstances, the costs associated with the spoiled units are an expected cost of producing good units and are assigned to the good units.
3. When some spoilage is expected to occur, but spoilage rates are higher than expected, the cost of the expected or normal spoilage should be assigned to the good units and the cost of the excessive or abnormal spoilage should be treated as a loss.

Regardless of the treatment of spoilage *costs,* careful records should be kept of spoiled *units*. Failure to keep such records, or to maintain physical controls over spoiled units, is evidence of poor internal control. Without spoilage records management may not be aware of the magnitude of spoilage and, therefore, could be less likely to institute procedures for reducing spoilage. Additionally, alleged spoiled units can be diverted for the personal use or gain of employees.

Spoilage as a Loss

When spoilage costs are treated as a loss, the costs assigned to spoiled units are transferred out of Work-in-Process to a spoilage loss account, and the costs assigned to good units are transferred to Finished Goods Inventory or the work-in-process account of a subsequent department. To do this, it is necessary to include the equivalent units spoiled in all equivalent unit computations. Estimating the equivalent units spoiled requires knowledge of when spoiled units are identified and separated from good units. If, for example, 150 units are identified as spoiled and separated from good units when they are two-thirds converted, there are 100 [$150 \times \frac{2}{3}$] spoiled equivalent units of conversion. If all materials were added at the start of production, there would be 150 spoiled equivalent units of materials.

Example 4–5

On October 1, 19x8, the Assembly Department of the Watson Company had a beginning inventory of 200 units that were complete as to materials and three-fourths complete as to conversion. Related costs were $4,606.60 and $2,043.15, respectively. During October, 1,500 units were started and 1,400 good units were completed. A freak accident resulted in the destruction of 100 units that were complete as to materials and 80 percent complete as to conversion. The October 31 inventory of 200 units was complete as to materials and one-half complete as to conversion. Costs assigned to Work-in-Process included direct materials of

$30,000 and conversion of $18,000. Because of the unusual nature of the accident, the cost of spoiled units is to be treated as a loss of the period.

Using weighted-average process costing, the Assembly Department's October cost of production report is presented in Exhibit 4–7. (Exhibit 4–7 is a continuation of Exhibit 4–3, September's weighted-average cost of production report.) Note that equivalent units spoiled were included in the computation of equivalent units

EXHIBIT 4–7 Weighted Average Process Costing with Spoilage Loss

Watson Company—Assembly Department
Cost of Production Report
For the Month of October, 19x8

FLOW OF WHOLE OR PARTIAL UNITS		
Beginning		200
Started		1,500
In process		1,700
Spoiled	100	
Good units completed	1,400	− 1,500
Ending		200

	Materials	*Conversion*	*Total*
EQUIVALENT UNITS IN PROCESS			
Good units completed	1,400	1,400	
Equivalent units spoiled	100	80*	
Equivalent units in ending inventory	200	100†	
Equivalent units in process	1,700	1,580	
TOTAL COSTS TO BE ACCOUNTED FOR			
COST PER EQUIVALENT UNIT IN PROCESS			
Work-in-Process, beginning	$ 4,606.60	$ 2,043.15	$ 6,649.75
Current manufacturing costs	30,000.00	18,000.00	48,000.00
Total costs in process	$34,606.60	$20,043.15	$54,649.75
Equivalent units in process	÷ 1,700	÷ 1,580	
Cost per equivalent unit in process	$ 20.357	$ 12.686	$ 33.043
ACCOUNTING FOR TOTAL COSTS			
Transferred out:			
Good units (1,400 × $33.043)		$46,260.20	
Spoiled units			
Materials (100 × $20.357)	$ 2,035.70		
Conversion (80 × $12.686)	1,014.88	3,050.58	$49,310.78
Work-in-Process, ending:			
Materials (200 × $20.357)		$ 4,071.40	
Conversion (100 × $12.686)		1,268.60	5,340.00
Total costs accounted for			$54,650.78‡

* 100 units, 80 percent converted.
† 200 units, one-half complete.
‡ Answer reflects $1.03 rounding error.

in process and the cost per equivalent unit. Also note the separation of spoilage costs in the last section of the report. Assuming the good units are processed further in the Finishing Department, the final Assembly Department journal entry is:

Spoilage Loss	3,050.58	
Work-in-Process: Finishing Department	46,260.20	
Work-in-Process: Assembly Department		49,310.78

Using a FIFO cost flow assumption would add only one complication. As noted previously, the equivalent units in the beginning inventory would be deducted from the equivalent units in process to compute the equivalent units manufactured, and the current manufacturing costs would be divided by the equivalent units manufactured to obtain the cost per equivalent unit manufactured. However, *three sets of costs would be transferred out in the final section of the report*. These include:

1. The cost of the spoiled units.
2. The costs in the beginning inventory plus the current costs to complete the beginning inventory.
3. The cost of units started and completed during the current period.

With FIFO process costing, all spoilage is assumed to be from units started during the current period. It is assumed that no units in the beginning inventory are spoiled. Although this assumption is often incorrect, the additional costs of further refining cost accounting systems to eliminate the need for this assumption are seldom warranted.

Spoilage as a Product Cost

If it is determined that spoilage is expected using current production procedures, the cost of spoiled units should be assigned to the good units. Two alternative procedures for accomplishing this objective are as follows:

1. Omit spoiled units from equivalent unit computations and average the cost of spoiled units in with the cost of good (unspoiled) units.
2. Include spoiled units in all equivalent unit computations and assign spoilage costs to Factory Overhead Control.

The first approach is easy to implement. When spoiled units are omitted from equivalent unit computations, spoilage merely reduces the number of equivalent units used in computing unit costs. In the weighted-average method, total materials and conversion costs are divided by the equivalent good units of materials and conversion in process. With FIFO, current manufacturing costs for materials and conversion are divided by the equivalent good units of materials and conversion manufactured. In either case, the cost of spoiled units is spread over the good units completed and the units in ending work-in-process inventory, including units that have not yet reached the point where spoilage can be detected.

Omitting spoiled units from equivalent unit computations provides satisfactory results if spoilage rates are constant and ending work-in-process inventory levels are stable. If expected spoilage rates fluctuate or if ending work-in-process inventory levels vary, the cost of spoiled units should be separately accounted for and spread over all good units by assigning these costs to Factory Overhead Control. Under a normal cost system, spoilage costs would then be allowed for in the predetermined overhead rate. This procedure ensures that all units bear their "fair share" of spoilage costs.

Example 4–6

Assume the situation is the same as presented in Example 4–5 except that spoilage is expected and that equivalent units spoiled are omitted from equivalent unit computations. Using weighted-average process costing, the Assembly Department's October cost of production report is presented in Exhibit 4–8. Comparing Exhibits 4–7 and 4–8, note that the effect of omitting equivalent units spoiled is to increase the cost per equivalent unit and, consequently, the costs transferred to Finished Goods Inventory and the ending balance in Work-in-Process.

Omitting equivalent units spoiled and assuming good units are processed further in the Finishing Department, the final Assembly Department journal entry is as follows:

Work-in-Process: Finishing Department	48,987.40	
Work-in-Process: Assembly Department		48,987.40

A FIFO cost of production report that is prepared omitting equivalent units spoiled contains no new complications. The equivalent units in the beginning inventory are deducted from the equivalent *good units in process* to compute the equivalent *good units manufactured.* Current manufacturing costs for direct materials and conversion are divided by equivalent *good units manufactured* to compute the *cost per equivalent good unit manufactured.* Two sets of costs that are transferred out in the final section of the report are:

1. The costs in the beginning inventory plus the current costs to complete the beginning inventory.
2. The cost of good units started and completed this period.

Because FIFO process costing identifies all spoilage with current operations, the units started and completed this period are reduced by the number of whole or partial units spoiled.

Despite the simplicity of ignoring equivalent units spoiled when spoilage costs are to be assigned to good units, we do not recommend this procedure. When there are fluctuations in spoilage rates or in ending work-in-process inventory levels, this procedure will result in month-to-month variations in the costs assigned identical units. Of more fundamental concern is that this procedure fails to identify spoilage costs on a routine basis. Failing to see spoilage cost information, management may not be as aggressive in reducing spoilage and increasing product quality as they should be. With spoilage costs information readily available, management is better able to evaluate the costs and benefits involved in programs to improve product quality.

EXHIBIT 4–8 **Weighted-Average Process Costing Without Identifying Spoilage**

Watson Company—Assembly Department
Cost of Production Report
For the Month of October, 19x8

FLOW OF WHOLE OR PARTIAL UNITS		
Beginning		200
Started		1,500
In process		1,700
Spoiled	100	
Good units completed	1,400	−1,500
Ending		200

	Materials	*Conversion*	*Total*
EQUIVALENT GOOD UNITS IN PROCESS			
Good units completed	1,400	1,400	
Equivalent units in ending inventory	200	100*	
Equivalent good units in process	1,600	1,500	
TOTAL COSTS TO BE ACCOUNTED FOR			
COST PER EQUIVALENT GOOD UNIT IN PROCESS			
Work-in-Process, beginning	$ 4,606.60	$ 2,043.15	$ 6,649.75
Current manufacturing costs	30,000.00	18,000.00	48,000.00
Total costs in process	$34,606.60	$20,043.15	$54,649.75
Equivalent units in process	÷ 1,600	÷ 1,500	
Cost per equivalent good unit in process	$ 21.629	$ 13.362	$ 34.991
ACCOUNTING FOR TOTAL COSTS			
Transferred out (1,400 × $34.991)			$48,987.40
Work-in-Process, ending:			
Materials (200 × $21.629)		$ 4,325.80	
Conversion (100 × $13.362)		1,336.20	5,662.00
Total costs accounted for			$54,649.40†

* 200 units one-half complete.
† Answer reflects $0.35 rounding error.

Including equivalent units spoiled in equivalent unit computations and assigning spoilage costs to Factory Overhead Control when they are an expected part of normal operations provides useful information to management. If a normal cost system is used and the predetermined overhead rate is adjusted to allow for spoilage, the cost of spoiled units will be spread, in a consistent manner, over all good units. The form of the cost of production report when the costs of spoiled units are assigned to Factory Overhead Control is identical to the form of the cost of production report when spoilage is treated as a loss. The only difference in the two procedures is that Factory Overhead Control, rather than Spoilage Loss, is debited for the spoilage costs.

Normal and Abnormal Spoilage

Normal spoilage is expected and occurs under efficient operating conditions. The costs of normal spoilage are regarded as product costs assignable to products directly or by way of the factory overhead control account. **Abnormal spoilage** is not expected and should not occur under efficient operating conditions. The costs of abnormal spoilage are not regarded as a product cost and should be assigned to a loss account.

When some spoilage is expected, but the spoilage that occurs during a particular period exceeds this amount, the cost of normal spoilage should be assigned to the good units or factory overhead, and the cost of abnormal spoilage should be treated as a loss. To do this it is necessary to include spoiled units in all computations and clearly distinguish between normal and abnormal spoilage costs in accounting for the total costs in process.

Example 4–7

The Michigan Manufacturing Company uses a weighted-average process costing system with a predetermined overhead rate of 100 percent of direct labor. At the start of November 19x3, 1,000 units were in process. They were complete as to materials and 60 percent complete as to conversion. During the period, 20,000 additional units were started and 15,000 good units were completed and transferred to finished goods inventory. A total of 2,000 units were spoiled. The November 30 ending inventory of 4,000 units was complete as to materials and one-half complete as to conversion.

Spoilage is detected at the end of the production process when units are 100 percent complete. Normal spoilage, up to 10 percent of the good units completed, is treated as an addition to the cost of the good units at the time they are transferred to finished goods inventory. Any spoilage in excess of 10 percent is regarded as abnormal and treated as a loss.

On November 1, 19x3, Work-in-Process had a balance of $11,000, including direct materials of $5,000 and conversion of $6,000. Additional November manufacturing costs include direct materials of $100,000 and direct labor of $92,000.

A cost of production report for the Michigan Manufacturing Company is presented in Exhibit 4–9. Note the breakdown of spoiled units into normal spoilage and abnormal spoilage. The final journal entry transferring costs out of Work-in-Process at the end of November is as follows:

Finished Goods Inventory	247,500	
Spoilage Loss	7,500	
Work-in-Process		255,000

In Example 4–7 the cost of normal spoilage is assigned directly to the good units completed, increasing the cost per good unit completed from $15 to $16.50 ($247,500 total costs assigned to good units ÷ 15,000 good units completed). It is also possible to assign the cost of normal spoilage to Factory Overhead Control and make an appropriate increase in the predetermined overhead rate. This procedure, which is not illustrated, would be preferable to the direct assignment of normal spoilage costs to good units if normal spoilage fluctuated within a wide range.

EXHIBIT 4–9 **Weighted-Average Process Costing With Normal and Abnormal Spoilage**

Michigan Manufacturing Company
Cost of Production Report
For the Month of November, 19x3

FLOW OF WHOLE OR PARTIAL UNITS		
Beginning		1,000
Started		20,000
In process		21,000
Completed:		
Good units	15,000	
Normal spoilage	1,500*	
Abnormal spoilage	500†	−17,000
Ending		4,000

	Materials	*Conversion*	*Total*
EQUIVALENT UNITS IN PROCESS			
Good units completed	15,000	15,000	
Normal spoilage	1,500	1,500	
Abnormal spoilage	500	500	
Equivalent units in ending inventory	4,000	2,000‡	
Equivalent units in process	21,000	19,000	
TOTAL COSTS TO BE ACCOUNTED FOR			
COST PER EQUIVALENT UNIT IN PROCESS			
Work-in-Process, beginning	$ 5,000	$ 6,000	$ 11,000
Current manufacturing costs	100,000	184,000§	284,000
Total costs in process	$105,000	$190,000	$295,000
Equivalent units in process	÷21,000	÷19,000	
Cost per equivalent unit in process	$ 5.00	$ 10.00	$ 15.00
ACCOUNTING FOR TOTAL COSTS			
Transferred out:			
To finished goods inventory:			
Good units (15,000 × $15)		$225,000	
Normal spoilage (1,500 × $15)		22,500	$247,500
Abnormal spoilage loss (500 × $15)			7,500
Total			$255,000
Work-in-Process, ending:			
Materials (4,000 × $5)		$ 20,000	
Conversion (2,000 × $10)		20,000	40,000
Total costs accounted for			$295,000

* 15,000 × 0.10 normal spoilage rate.
† 2,000 − 1,500 normal spoilage.
‡ 4,000 units one-half complete as to conversion.
§ Direct labor of $92,000 plus factory overhead applied at a rate of 100 percent of direct labor.

Point of Spoilage Detection

Most textbook examples and problems assume that spoiled units are detected at the end of the production process when units are 100 percent complete. This assumption simplifies computations by allowing us to combine the equivalent units of materials and conversion spoiled into the single category of spoiled units. It also allows us to avoid assigning the cost of *normal spoilage* to the ending work-in-process inventory.

The spoilage in Example 4–5 was detected when goods were 80 percent converted. However, because the Watson Company did not expect any spoilage, all spoilage costs were assigned to a loss account. If spoilage was expected and it was detected when goods were 80 percent converted, spoilage costs should also be assigned to any work-in-process inventories that have passed the point of spoilage detection. This could be easily accomplished if the cost of normal or expected spoilage was assigned to Factory Overhead Control. In this case the cost assignment would be automatic through a slightly higher predetermined overhead rate. If, however, the cost of normal spoilage was being explicitly added to good units, as in Example 4–7, then these costs would have to be added both to the completed goods and to the ending inventory of work-in-process. In subsequent periods only the units passing the point of spoilage detection in that period would have normal spoilage costs assigned to them.

Product costing under these circumstances can become unnecessarily complex. It would be far easier to: (1) assign normal spoilage costs to Factory Overhead Control or (2) revamp the product costing system so that a cost of production report is prepared for segments of the production process that end with product inspection. Note that the product costing system should conform to management's needs for information and control. Hence, the cost accounting system is adjusted so that a costing segment ends with an inspection point, rather than having the inspection point moved so that it conforms with the end of a costing segment, as defined by the cost accounting system.

Disposal Value for Spoiled Goods

The preceding examples have assumed that the spoiled goods are worthless and can be disposed of at no additional cost. If additional expenditures are required to dispose of the spoiled units, these costs must also be accounted for. The proper treatment depends on whether spoilage is expected or unexpected. If spoilage is expected, the disposal costs are a product cost and should be assigned to products as part of factory overhead. If spoilage is not expected, the disposal costs increase the spoilage loss and should be assigned to the spoilage loss account.

If spoiled units can be sold as seconds, their **net realizable value** (selling price less costs to complete and sell) should be placed in a spoiled goods inventory account. This would reduce the spoilage costs assignable to other accounts.

Example 4–8

Returning to Example 4–5, assume Watson is treating the cost of the 100 units spoiled in October as a loss, and that they can be sold as seconds for $500 with costs to complete and sell totaling $150. In this case the spoilage loss is reduced by $350, the net realizable value of the spoiled goods ($500 – $150). The journal entry transferring costs out of the Assembly Department's work-in-process account would be as follows:

Spoiled Goods Inventory	350.00	
Spoilage Loss	2,700.58	
Work-in-Process: Finishing Department	46,260.20	
Work-in-Process: Assembly Department		49,310.78

No additional gain or loss would be recognized on the final sale of the spoiled goods. The costs to complete and sell would be assigned to the spoiled goods inventory account:

Spoiled Goods Inventory	150.00	
Cash		150.00

The final sale would show an exchange of spoiled goods for cash:

Cash	500.00	
Spoiled Goods Inventory		500.00

The underlying assumption for this treatment is that Watson is not in business to produce spoiled units. Consequently they do not need to report the sale of such units as a credit to a sales revenue account.

SUMMARY

Job-order costing and process costing are the two primary methods used to assign production costs to units produced. Job-order costing is used when many different products are produced in batches that receive varying degrees of attention in each production department or operation. Process costing is used for products that are produced on a continuous basis with all units receiving equal attention in each production department or operation.

Essentially process costing is an averaging technique in which costs are spread over the units in process during the period. Under the weighted-average method, all costs in process are spread over all equivalent units in process. Under the FIFO method, a distinction is made between beginning inventories and costs, and current effort and costs. Current manufacturing costs are spread over equivalent units manufactured. Costs are transferred out in two batches: beginning inventory plus costs to complete, and units started and completed this period. In subsequent departments all costs transferred in during a period are lumped together into one group even if the preceding department is using the FIFO method.

If spoilage exists, it can be accounted for in different ways. If spoilage is not expected, spoilage costs should be assigned to a loss account. If spoilage is an expected part of the production process, spoilage costs may be assigned to good units either by spreading all Work-in-Process costs over the good units in process or manufactured, or by the preferred procedure of assigning spoilage costs to Factory Overhead Control and increasing the predetermined overhead rate. If some spoilage is expected but spoilage rates are abnormally high, a distinction should be made between normal and abnormal spoilage; with the costs of normal spoilage treated as a product cost and the costs of abnormal spoilage treated as a loss.

The key to the solution of process costing problems is proper organization. This organization is provided by a five-step cost of production report consisting of:

1. Flow of whole or partial units
2. Computation of equivalent units
3. Determination of the total costs to be accounted for
4. Computation of the cost per equivalent unit
5. Accounting for total costs

KEY TERMS

Abnormal spoilage
Cost of production report
Defective units
Equivalent unit
Equivalent units in process
Equivalent units manufactured
Net realizable value
Normal spoilage
Process
Process costing system
Spoiled units
Sundry accounts
Total costs in process

REVIEW QUESTIONS

4–1 Distinguish between the production situations that are more suitable to job-order costing and those suitable to process costing.

4–2 Mention several accounting issues that are just as important in process costing as in job-order costing.

4–3 Identify the cost system record that is the backbone of a job-order cost system. Identify the accounting report that is the backbone of a process cost system.

4–4 List the five elements of a cost of production report.

4–5 What journal entry is based on information contained in a cost of production report?

4–6 Under what circumstances are identical results obtained with weighted-average and FIFO process costing?

4–7 Why is the FIFO cost flow method used in process costing in reality a modified FIFO method?

4–8 What element of work-in-process inventory included in equivalent units in process is excluded from equivalent units manufactured?

4–9 At what stage of completion are transferred-in units in a subsequent department?

4–10 Distinguish between normal and abnormal spoilage.

4–11 How should spoilage costs be disposed of when spoilage is not expected to occur?

4–12 Describe two alternative ways of assigning normal spoilage to good units when all spoilage is normal.

4–13 Describe two alternative ways of assigning normal spoilage to good units when there is both normal and abnormal spoilage.

4–14 What complication occurs when normal spoilage is detected before the end of an operation and the cost of normal spoilage is assigned directly to good units?

4–15 What accounting treatment should be given disposal costs when (1) spoilage is expected to occur and (2) spoilage is not expected to occur?

REVIEW PROBLEM

FIFO Process Costing with Spoilage Loss

The following information pertains to the October 19x8 operations of the Watson Company's Assembly Department. It is based on the ending inventory amounts in Exhibit 4–4 and the information given in Example 4–5.

	Whole or partial units	*Materials*	*Conversion*
Inventory information: Units			
Beginning	200	complete	3/4 complete
Started	1,500		
Completed:			
Good	1,400		
Spoiled	100	complete	4/5 complete
Ending	200	complete	1/2 complete
Inventory information: Costs			
Beginning		$ 4,100	$ 1,890
Current		$30,000	$18,000

REQUIREMENT

Prepare a cost of production report for the month of October using FIFO process costing with spoilage written off as a loss.

The solution to this problem is found at the end of the Chapter 4 problems and exercises.

EXERCISES

4–1 Job-Order Costing vs. Process Costing

For each of the following situations indicate whether job-order or process costing would be more appropriate and why:

a) An order is received for five identical custom-made machines. They will be shipped as a unit when all are completed.

b) An order is received for 4,000 identical custom-made refrigerators. They will be shipped as each unit is completed.

c) An order is received for 100 identical aircraft. They will be shipped as each is completed.

d) A firm manufactures mobile homes on a continuous basis for subsequent sale.

e) A firm manufactures several models of small boats in batches of ten for subsequent sale.

f) A firm processes dog food on an assembly-line basis.

4–2 Weighted Average: Basic

Texas Texturizing is a texturizer of polyester yarn. On June 1, 19y6, they had an inventory of 10,000 pounds that was complete as to materials, but only three-quarters complete as to conversion. During the period, 160,000 pounds were completed. The inventory at the end of the period consisted of 40,000 pounds that were complete as to materials but only one-quarter complete as to conversion.

Costs in process at the beginning of the period consisted of $10,000 for materials and $5,000 for conversion. Costs added during the period included materials costs of $140,000 and conversion costs of $76,600.

REQUIREMENT

Prepare a cost of production report using the weighted-average method.

4–3 Basic FIFO

Using data from the previous problem, prepare a cost of production report using the FIFO method.

4–4 Basic Weighted Average

The Alpine Watch Company manufactures the famous "Timesetter" watch on an assembly-line basis. The April 1 work-in-process inventory consisted of 1,000 watches that were complete as to materials and 50 percent complete as to labor and overhead. Costs in process on April 1 were:

Materials	$ 5,000
Conversion	13,000
Total	$18,000

During the month 10,000 units were started and 9,500 units were completed. The ending inventory was complete as to materials and one-third complete as to conversion. Costs placed in process during April were:

Materials (10,000 units)	$ 61,000
Labor (5,000 hours)	40,000
Variable overhead	2,500
Fixed overhead	94,500
Total	$198,000

REQUIREMENT

Prepare a cost of production report using the weighted-average method.

4–5 Basic FIFO

Using data from the previous problem, prepare a cost of production report using the FIFO method.

4–6 T[2] Basic Weighted Average

Presented is information pertaining to the September 19y1 production operations of the New York Company.

Beginning units	200
Units started	2,000
Units completed	1,400

	Materials	*Conversion*	*Total*
Costs:			
Beginning	$ 2,220	$ 624	$ 2,844
Current	20,000	11,502	31,502
Percent completed:			
Ending inventory	100%	40%	

REQUIREMENT

Prepare a cost of production report using the weighted-average method.

4–7 T Basic FIFO

Presented is information pertaining to the September 19y1 operations of the New York Company.

Beginning units	200
Units started	2,000
Units completed	1,400

	Materials	*Conversion*	*Total*
Costs:			
Beginning			$ 2,844
Current	$20,000	$11,502	31,502
Percent completed:			
Beginning inventory	100%	50%	
Ending inventory	100%	40%	

REQUIREMENT

Prepare a cost of production report using the FIFO method.

4–8 T Basic Weighted Average

Presented is information pertaining to the May 19y7 operations of the New Mexico Company.

---

[2] Exercises and problems identified with a T are designed in a manner that makes them suitable for solution using spreadsheet computer software.

Beginning units	2,000
Units started	8,000
Units completed	9,500

	Materials	*Conversion*	*Total*
Costs:			
Beginning	$ 11,750	$ 20,540	$ 32,290
Current	119,875	130,380	250,255
Percent completed:			
Ending inventory	50%	60%	

REQUIREMENT

Prepare a cost of production report using the weighted-average method.

4–9 T Basic FIFO

Presented is information pertaining to the May 19y7 operations of the New Mexico Company.

Beginning units	2,000
Units started	8,000
Units completed	9,500

	Materials	*Conversion*	*Total*
Costs:			
Beginning			$ 32,290
Current	$119,875	$130,380	250,255
Percent completed:			
Beginning inventory	50%	80%	
Ending inventory	50%	60%	

REQUIREMENT

Prepare a cost of production report using the FIFO method.

4–10 T Weighted Average in Subsequent Department

The North Dakota Company processes chemicals in two departments, Mixing and Packaging. Presented is information pertaining to the June 19w2 Packaging Department operations.

Beginning units	200
Units transferred in	1,000
Units completed	1,100

	Transferred in	*Materials*	*Conversion*	*Total*
Costs:				
Beginning inventory	$1,560	$ 0	$ 1,600	$ 3,160
Current	8,040	2,200	10,000	20,240
Percent completed:				
Ending inventory	100%	0%	60%	

REQUIREMENT

Prepare a cost of production report for the Packaging Department using the weighted-average method.

4–11 T Weighted Average in Subsequent Department

The West Virginia Company manufactures a product in a multistep process in three departments. Presented is information pertaining to the February 19x9 operations of the Finishing Department:

Beginning units	400
Units transferred in	5,600
Units completed	5,000

	Transferred in	*Materials*	*Conversion*	*Total*
Costs:				
Beginning inventory	$ 16,000	$ 2,000	$ 90,000	$108,000
Current	224,000	53,000	600,000	877,000
Percent completed:				
Ending inventory	100%	50%	75%	

REQUIREMENT

Prepare a cost of production report for the Finishing Department using the weighted-average method.

4–12 Weighted-Average Journal Entries

The Red River Production Company's October 1, 19x3, work-in-process inventory contained 1,200 units that were complete as to materials and one-third complete as to conversion. Costs in process on October 1 included materials of $6,000 and conversion of $4,000.

During October the following events occurred:

- Materials costing $50,000 were purchased on account.
- Materials costing $49,000 were placed in process.
- Direct-labor charges amounted to $50,500.
- Manufacturing overhead costs for October include:

Depreciation	$20,000
Utilities	28,000
Salaries	11,000
Supplies (from supplies inventory)	2,000

- Overhead was applied to Work-in-Process at a predetermined rate of 100 percent of direct-labor dollars.
- 10,000 units were completed.

ADDITIONAL INFORMATION

- Red River uses a weighted-average process costing system.
- The ending work-in-process inventory contained 1,000 units that were completed as to materials and 50 percent complete as to conversion.

REQUIREMENT

Prepare a cost of production report and summary journal entries for the purchase of materials and all activity in the production department.

4–13 Weighted-Average Journal Entries

The Ohio Valley Company did not have a work-in-process inventory on November 1, 19y7. During November, 500 units were started and 400 units were completed. The November 30 inventory was 50 percent complete as to materials and 80 percent complete as to conversion.

Materials costing $30,000 were purchased on account, and the following costs were assigned to the production department:

Direct materials	$24,750
Direct labor	24,000
Factory overhead:	
Depreciation	7,500
Utilities	4,800
Salaries	6,000
Supplies	1,300

Factory overhead is applied to products at a predetermined rate of 80 percent of direct labor.

REQUIREMENT

Prepare a cost of production report and summary journal entries for the purchase of raw materials and all activity in the production department.

4–14 Weighted-Average Journal Entries in Subsequent Departments

The Word Book Company manufactures the famous "Word" dictionary in two production departments. In the first department, large rolls of paper are run through Word's printing presses where all 2,000 pages of each dictionary are printed simultaneously in a single operation. In the second department, the printed rolls of paper are cut, collated, and bound in book covers purchased from another company. The book covers are the only material added in the second department, and once they are added the dictionaries are completed. This problem concerns the second department.

On April 1, 19x8, the Department II work-in-process inventory consisted of 800 dictionaries that were 40 percent converted as to Department II operations.

The costs associated with this inventory were as follows:

Transferred in	$3,200
Conversion	640
Total	$3,840

During April, 20,000 dictionaries were transferred into Department II and 19,000 dictionaries were completed and transferred to finished goods inventory. The Department II ending inventory was 60 percent complete as to conversion. Costs assigned to Department II during April were as follows:

Transferred in	$ 80,000
Materials	57,000
Conversion	39,520
Total	$176,520

The conversion costs include direct-labor costs of $30,100 and applied factory overhead of $9,420.

REQUIREMENTS

a) Prepare a cost of production report for Department II for the month of April. Use weighted-average process costing.

b) Prepare summary journal entries for the April activity in Department II.

4–15 Weighted-Average Journal Entries in Subsequent Departments

Hoosier Production Company manufactures a product on a continuous basis in two departments, Machining and Assembly/Finishing. This problem concerns the Assembly/Finishing Department. Production is started in the Machining Department and completed in the Assembly/Finishing Department. The last step in the latter department consists of placing the finished product in a box. These boxes are the only materials added in the second department.

During a recent period the following events occurred in the Assembly/Finishing Department:

o Units transferred in from Machining Department	8,000
o Units completed and transferred to finished goods inventory	7,500
o Costs assigned to department:	
From Machining Department	$71,000
From Stores Control	15,000
Direct labor	33,500
Supervisors' salaries	6,000
Other labor costs of departmental production employees	7,000
Utility bill for month	5,000
Depreciation on departmental machinery and equipment	8,000
Other sundry costs	4,000

ADDITIONAL INFORMATION

- Hoosier uses *weighted-average process costing and a normal cost system.* Overhead is applied to Work-in-Process at 100 percent of direct-labor dollars.
- The ending inventory in the Assembly/Finishing Department consists of 1,500 units that are one-third complete as to conversion.
- The beginning inventory in the Assembly/Finishing Department contained 1,000 units that were half complete as to conversion.
- Costs assigned to the beginning inventory were:

Transferred in	$10,000
Conversion	5,000

REQUIREMENT

Prepare a cost of production report and all journal entries affecting the accounts "Work-in-Process: Assembly/Finishing" and "Factory Overhead Control: Assembly/Finishing."

PROBLEMS

4–16 Weighted-Average Error Correction

The Tar Heel Manufacturing Company began operations on December 1, 19x1. At December 31, 19x1, an inexperienced staff accountant was assigned the task of calculating ending inventories.

The staff accountant estimated that the ending work-in-process inventory was 40 percent complete as to both materials and conversion costs. She calculated 2,000 equivalent units in the ending work-in-process inventory. This inventory was valued at $80,000, with materials and conversion costs each contributing 50 percent of the total cost.

A review of the inexperienced accountant's work revealed that she had erroneously assumed that both materials and conversion costs were incurred evenly throughout the process. Materials in the ending work-in-process inventory were correctly estimated to be 40 percent complete, but the units were actually only 20 percent complete as to conversion.

REQUIREMENTS

a) How many unfinished units were in the ending work-in-process inventory?

b) If the units were only 20 percent complete as to conversion, rather than 40 percent, how many equivalent units of conversion were in the ending work-in-process inventory?

c) What cost per unit did the staff accountant calculate for conversion?

d) Assume 9,000 units were completed during the month of December. Calculate the correct cost per equivalent unit of conversion. (*Hint:* Evaluate the total conversion costs in process.)

e) Calculate the correct cost of the ending work-in-process inventory. Assume the staff accountant correctly valued materials.

f) By how much was the cost of goods manufactured misstated as a result of the staff accountant's error? Indicate whether the cost of goods manufactured was overstated or understated.

4–17 Weighted-Average Error Correction
You are engaged in the audit of the December 31, 19x8, financial statements of Spirit Corporation, a manufacturer of a digital watch. You are attempting to verify the cost of goods sold and the costing of the ending inventory of work-in-process and finished goods, which were recorded in Spirit's books as follows:

	Units	*Cost*
Cost of goods sold	700,000	$3,525,240
Work-in-process (50% complete as to labor and overhead)	300,000	660,960
Finished goods	200,000	1,009,800

Materials are added to production at the beginning of the manufacturing process and overhead is applied to each product at the rate of 60 percent of direct-labor costs. *There was no finished goods inventory on January 1, 19x8.* A review of Spirit's inventory cost records disclosed the following information:

		Costs	
	Units	*Materials*	*Labor*
Work-in-process January 1, 19x8 (80% complete as to labor and overhead)	200,000	$ 200,000	$ 315,000
Units started in production	1,000,000		
Current costs:			
Materials costs		1,300,000	
Labor costs			1,995,000
Units completed	900,000		

The beginning and current cost information has been verified.

REQUIREMENTS

a) Using weighted-average process costing, prepare a cost of production report for 19x8.

b) Determine the proper balance in Finished Goods Inventory.

c) Prepare the necessary journal entry to correctly state the inventory of finished goods and work-in-process, assuming the books have not been closed.

(CPA Adapted)

4–18 T Weighted Average with Spoilage Costs to Overhead: Journal Entries
The Big Foot Snowshoe Company manufactures cross-country snowshoes from bamboo frames and cowhide in a single production department. The November 1, 19x9, work-in-process inventory consisted of 400 units that were 80 percent complete as to materials and 50 percent complete as to conversion. During November, 1,100 units were started and 1,200 good units were completed. One hundred units were identified as defective when they were 100 percent complete as to materials and 60 percent complete as to conversion. The November 30 inventory was complete as to materials and 75 percent complete as to conversion.

November work-in-process cost information is as follows:

	Beginning	*Current*
Direct materials	$2,400	$8,850
Direct labor	900	5,210
Factory overhead*	?	?

* Applied at 50 percent of direct labor.

The cost of spoiled units is assigned to factory overhead.

REQUIREMENTS

a) Prepare a cost of production report for the month of November using weighted-average process costing.

b) Prepare summary journal entries for all November activities affecting work-in-process.

4–19 T FIFO with Spoilage Costs to Overhead: Journal Entries
This problem is based on the data for the Big Foot Snowshoe Company presented in Problem 4–18.

REQUIREMENTS

a) Prepare a cost of production report for the month of November using FIFO process costing.

b) Prepare summary journal entries for all November activities affecting work-in-process.

4–20 T Weighted Average with Spoilage Costs to Overhead: Journal Entries
The Flash Camera Company manufactures camera bags from nylon fabric in a single production department. The January 1, 19y1, work-in-process inventory consisted of 300 units that were 90 percent complete as to materials and 80 percent complete as to conversion. During January 1,400 units were started and 1,400 good units were completed. Two hundred units were identified as defective when they were 100 percent complete as to materials and 25 percent complete as to conversion. The January 31 inventory was complete as to materials and 50 percent complete as to conversion.

January work-in-process cost information is as follows:

	Beginning	*Current*
Direct materials	$1,282	$6,793
Direct labor	1,600	7,400
Factory overhead*	?	?

* Applied at 40 percent of direct labor.

The cost of spoiled units is assigned to factory overhead.

REQUIREMENTS

a) Prepare a cost of production report for the month of January using weighted-average process costing.

b) Prepare summary journal entries for all January activities affecting work-in-process.

4–21 T FIFO with Spoilage Costs to Overhead: Journal Entries

This problem is based on the data for the Flash Camera Company presented in Problem 4–20.

REQUIREMENTS

a) Prepare a cost of production report for the month of January using FIFO process costing.

b) Prepare summary journal entries for all January activities affecting work-in-process.

4–22 FIFO with Spoilage Loss: Journal Entries

The Tellico Company's February 1 work-in-process inventory consisted of 2,000 units that were 50 percent complete as to materials and 100 percent complete as to conversion. Costs in process on February 1 included materials of $5,000 and conversion of $16,000.

During February the following events occurred:

- Materials costing $30,000 were placed in process.
- Wages paid to production employees totaled $14,000. The balance in Payroll Payable (Production Employees) was $4,000 on February 1 and $2,000 on February 28.
- Manufacturing overhead costs for February totaled $10,000 (actual). They were all paid in cash.
- Overhead was applied to work-in-process at a predetermined rate equal to two-thirds of direct-labor dollars.
- Five thousand good units were completed.
- One hundred spoiled units were detected at the end of the production process.

ADDITIONAL INFORMATION

- Tellico uses a FIFO process costing system.
- Because spoilage is not expected, the cost of spoiled units is treated as a loss.
- The ending inventory of work-in-process contained 1,800 units that were half complete as to materials and half complete as to conversion.

REQUIREMENTS

a) Prepare a cost of production report for February.

b) Prepare summary journal entries for all February activity in the production department.

4–23 Subsequent Departments: Spoilage Loss

The Dexter Production Company manufactures a single product. Its operations are a continuous process carried on in two departments—Machining and Finishing. In the production process, materials are added to the product in each department *without increasing the number of units produced.*

For June 19y5, the company records indicated the following production statistics for each department:

	Machining department	*Finishing department*
Units in process, June 1, 19y5	0	0
Units transferred from preceding dept.	0	60,000
Units started in production	80,000	0
Units completed and transferred out	60,000	50,000
Units in process, June 30, 19y5*	20,000	8,000
Units spoiled in production	0	2,000
*Percent of completion of units in process at June 30, 19y5:		
Materials	100%	100%
Labor	50%	70%
Overhead	25%	70%

The units spoiled in production had no scrap value and were 50 percent complete as to material, labor, and overhead. The company's policy is to treat the cost of units spoiled in production as a loss chargeable to *the department in which the spoilage occurs.*

Cost records showed the following charges for the month of June:

	Machining department	*Finishing department*
Materials	$240,000	$ 88,500
Labor	140,000	141,500
Overhead	65,000	56,600

REQUIREMENT

Prepare a cost of production report for each department. (CPA Adapted)

4–24 T Weighted Average with Spoilage Spread Over Good Units

Presented is information pertaining to the May 19x5 operations of Megachip, Incorporated. Spoilage costs are spread over all equivalent good units.

Beginning units	5,000
Units started	70,000
Spoiled units	10,000
Good units completed	60,000

	Materials	*Conversion*	*Total*
Costs:			
Beginning	$ 1,900	$ 250	$ 2,150
Current	30,600	6,000	36,600
Percent completed:			
Ending inventory	100%	50%	

REQUIREMENT

Prepare a cost of production report for May 19x5 operations using the weighted-average method.

4–25 T FIFO with Spoilage Spread Over Good Units

Presented is information pertaining to the May 19x5 operations of Megachip, Incorporated. Spoilage costs are spread over all equivalent good units.

Beginning units	5,000
Units started	70,000
Units spoiled	10,000
Units completed	60,000

	Materials	*Conversion*	*Total*
Costs:			
Beginning			$ 2,150
Current	$30,600	$6,000	$36,600
Percent completed:			
Beginning inventory	100%	50%	
Ending inventory	100%	50%	

REQUIREMENT

Prepare a cost of production report for May 19x5 operations using the FIFO method.

4–26 T Weighted Average with Spoilage Spread Over Good Units

Presented is information pertaining to the July 19x6 operations of Nebraska Products. Spoilage costs are spread over all equivalent good units.

Beginning units	800
Units started	5,000
Spoiled units	300
Good units completed	4,500

	Materials	*Conversion*	*Total*
Costs:			
Beginning	$ 2,135	$2,302	$ 4,437
Current	11,115	22,100	33,215
Percent completed:			
Ending inventory	80%	40%	

REQUIREMENT

Prepare a cost of production report for July 19x6 operations using the weighted-average method.

4–27 T FIFO with Spoilage Spread Over Good Units

Presented is information pertaining to the July 19x6 operations of Nebraska Products. Spoilage costs are spread over all equivalent good units.

Beginning units	800
Units started	5,000
Units spoiled	300
Units completed	4,500

	Materials	*Conversion*	*Total*
Costs:			
Beginning			$ 4,437
Current	$11,115	$22,100	33,215
Percent completed:			
Beginning inventory	100%	60%	
Ending inventory	80%	40%	

REQUIREMENT

Prepare a cost of production report for July 19x6 operations using the FIFO method.

4–28 Weighted Average with Subsequent Departments: Spoilage Spread Over Good Units

Carolina Cotton Company uses a two-step process to produce cotton yarn. Each step is performed in a separate department. All raw materials are entered in the first department. One-half of the conversion process takes place in each department. Waste equal to 10 percent of the poundage of good cotton produced occurs in the second department. All beginning or ending work-in-process is in temporary storage between departments one and two.

The work-in-process at the start of a recent week consisted of 500 pounds. During the week, twenty 100-pound bales of cotton were started in Department 1 and 250 cones of spun yarn were transferred out of Department 2. Each cone contains 8 pounds of cotton yarn. The work-in-process at the end of the week consisted of 300 pounds.

The materials and conversion costs at the start of the period were each $1,000. Current costs included $4,060 for materials and $8,245 for conversion. Detailed cost information is not available for Departments 1 and 2.

REQUIREMENT

Determine the costs transferred out of Department 2 and the costs in the ending work-in-process inventory. Ignore spoilage and use weighted-average process costing. (*Hint:* Use pounds as equivalent units.)

4–29 T Weighted Average with Normal and Abnormal Spoilage

Presented is information pertaining to the March 19y5 operations of Arizona Products:

Beginning units	3,500
Units started	30,000
Units spoiled	800
Good units completed	25,000

	Materials	*Conversion*	*Total*
Costs:			
Beginning	$ 11,125	$ 30,000	$ 41,125
Current	106,125	189,410	295,535
Percent completed:			
Spoiled units	100%	100%	
Ending inventory	100%	50%	
Normal spoilage rate	2% of good units completed		

The normal spoilage costs are assigned to the good units transferred out. Abnormal spoilage costs are treated as a loss.

REQUIREMENT

Prepare a cost of production report for March 19y5 operations using the weighted-average method.

4–30 Weighted Average with Normal and Abnormal Spoilage

A manufacturer uses a weighted-average process cost system for its only product. For each unit of finished product, 2 pounds of Material A are introduced at the start of the process, and 1 pound of Material B is added when the process is 60 percent complete. Labor and overhead costs are incurred uniformly throughout the process.

Inspection occurs at the 50 percent stage of completion and any spoiled units are scrapped. Normal spoilage at that stage is expected to be 3 percent of the units processed up to that point. *Normal spoilage costs are added to the cost of the good units completed and abnormal spoilage costs are treated as an expense of the period.*

The following information applies to November operations:

	Number of units	*Percent complete*	*Costs*
Work-in-process, November 1	2,000	80	
Work-in-Process, November 30	1,000	20	
Total units spoiled, including abnormal spoilage	800		
Good units completed	21,200		
Unit costs incurred:			
Material A, per pound			$4.00
Material B, per pound			$2.00
Conversion costs per equivalent unit			$5.00

REQUIREMENTS

a) How many pounds of Material A and of Material B were put into production in November?

b) How much should be charged to November expense for abnormal spoilage costs?

c) Compute the total cost of the good units completed during November.

d) Management has become aware of a material which, if added at the 75 percent stage of completion, would extend the life of the product. If this material had been added during November's production run, what would be the direct effect on:

1. Work-in-process at November 1?
2. Work-in-process at November 30?
3. Spoilage costs for the month?

State your reasoning. (CPA Adapted)

4–31 Weighted Average with Normal and Abnormal Spoilage

The Browning Co. Ltd. uses a weighted-average process costing system in accounting for costs in its one production department. Material A is added at the beginning of the process and Material B is added when the units are 90 percent complete.

Conversion costs are incurred uniformly throughout the process. Inspection takes place at the end of the process, and spoilage is expected to be 5 percent of good output. Normal spoilage is added to the cost of the good units completed. Abnormal spoilage is treated as a loss. The following information pertains to the month of April 19x7:

Beginning Inventory:		
3,000 units, one-third complete		
Material A	$13,000	
Labor	5,500	
Variable overhead	1,700	
Fixed overhead	3,500	
	$23,700	
Current Period:		
11,000 units were started		
8,000 good units were finished		
5,000 units were still in process at the end of the period and were 40 percent complete		
Material A		$ 50,000
Material B		13,500
Labor		61,200
Variable overhead		20,100
Fixed overhead		40,000
		$184,800

REQUIREMENT

Prepare a cost of production report for April 19x7. (CGA Adapted)

4–32 Weighted Average with Normal and Abnormal Spoilage

Ranka Company manufactures high-quality leather products. The company's profits have declined during the past nine months. In planning and controlling its operations, Ranka has used unit cost data that were developed eighteen months ago. To try to isolate the causes of poor profit performance, management is investigating the manufacturing operations of each of its products.

One of Ranka's main products is fine leather belts. The belts are produced in a single, continuous process in the Bluett Plant. During the process, leather strips are sewn, punched, and dyed. Buckles are attached by rivets when the belts are 70 percent complete as to direct labor and overhead (conversion costs). The belts then enter a final finishing stage to conclude the process. Labor and overhead are applied continuously during the process.

The leather belts are inspected twice during the process: (1) just before the buckles are attached (70 percent point in the process) and (2) at the conclusion of the finishing stage (100 percent point in the process). Ranka uses the weighted-average method to calculate its unit costs.

The leather belts produced at the Bluett Plant wholesale for \$9.95 each. Management wants to compare the current manufacturing costs per unit with the prices that exist on the market for leather belts. Top management has asked the Bluett Plant to submit data on the cost of manufacturing the leather belts in the month of October. These cost data will be used to evaluate whether modifications in the production process should be initiated or whether an increase in the selling price of the belts is justified. The cost per equivalent unit that management is using for planning and controlling purposes is \$5.35 per unit.

The October 1 work-in-process inventory consisted of 400 partially completed units. The belts were 25 percent complete as to conversion costs. The costs included in the inventory on October 1 were as follows:

Leather strips	\$1,000
Conversion costs	300
	\$1,300

During October, 7,600 leather strips were placed in production. A total of 6,800 good leather belts were completed. A total of 300 belts were identified as defective at the two inspection points—100 at the first inspection point (before buckle is attached) and 200 at the final inspection point (after finishing). This quantity of defective belts was considered normal.

In addition, 200 belts were removed from the production line when the process was 40 percent complete as to conversion costs because they had been damaged as a result of a malfunction during the sewing operation. This malfunction was considered an unusual occurrence, and consequently the spoilage was classified as abnormal. Defective (spoiled) units are not reprocessed and have zero salvage value. The cost of normal spoilage is assigned to the good units. The cost of abnormal spoilage is treated as a loss. The work-in-process inventory on October 31 consisted of 700 belts that were 50 percent complete as to conversion costs.

The costs charged to production during October were as follows:

Leather strips	\$20,600
Buckles	4,550
Conversion costs	20,700
	\$45,850

REQUIREMENTS

a) To provide cost data regarding the manufacture of leather belts in the Bluett Plant to the top management of the Ranka Company, prepare a cost of production report for October. (*Hint:* There are two materials.)

b) If the Ranka Company decided to repair (rework) the 300 defective belts that were considered normal spoilage, explain how the company could account for the rework costs. (CMA Adapted)

4–33 Process Costing Overview[3]

The Itsosimple Process Co. has two departments for producing a single product on a continuous basis. All spoilage occurs in Department 1 where all costs are assigned to good units.

Materials are added at the beginning of the process in Department 1 and at the *50 percent* stage in Department 2. Itsosimple uses *weighted-average costing* in Department 1 and *modified FIFO costing* in Department 2. Overhead is applied at 200 percent of direct-labor cost in Department 1 and at $8 per direct-labor hour in Department 2.

The following data are available for October 19x8:

	Department 1	*Department 2*
Beginning inventory	6,000 units, all 25% complete	5,000 units, all 70% complete
Ending inventory	5,000 units, all 60% complete	4,000 units, all 25% complete
Units started (transferred in)	20,000 units	19,000 units
Good units completed	19,000 units	20,000 units

	Department 1	*Department 2*
Beginning inventory costs:		
Material	$ 30,608	$ 10,000
Transferred in		205,000
Direct labor	7,502	14,000
Applied overhead	15,004	15,000
	$ 53,114	$244,000
Current costs:		
Materials	$100,000	$ 29,400
Direct labor	68,200	70,115 (10,000 hours)

REQUIREMENT

Prepare a cost of production report for both Department 1 and Department 2. Round all calculations to three decimal places.

4–34 Process Costing Challenge Problem

Nostrum Pharmaceuticals, Inc., manufactures an antihistamine on a continuous basis. Secret ingredients are blended in Department 1 and then transferred to

[3] Adapted from a problem prepared by Professor Imogene Posey.

Department 3. Patented "Snuffers" are assembled in Department 2 and placed in temporary storage until they are requisitioned for use in Department 3. In Department 3 the secret ingredients are placed in the Snuffers. In a schematic form these operations are represented as:

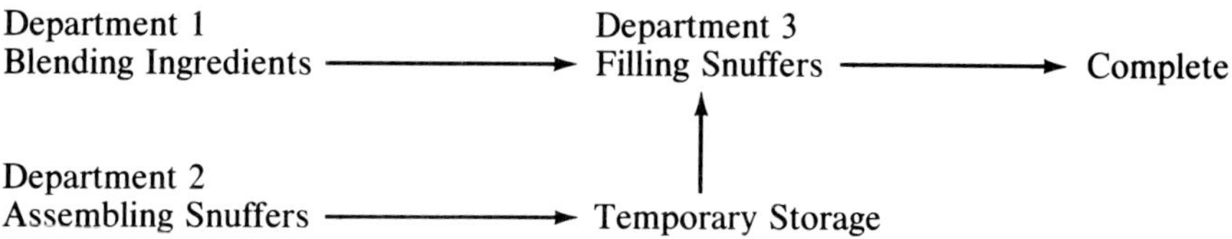

The output of Department 1 is measured in terms of liters (one liter = 1.0567 liquid quarts), and the outputs of Departments 2 and 3 are measured in terms of cases of Snuffers. A case contains 100 Snuffers, and one liter of blended ingredients is sufficient to fill 200 Snuffers. *All measurements in Department 3, including equivalent unit computations, are in terms of cases.*

In Department 1, inventories are valued on a first-in, first-out basis. In Departments 2 and 3, and in the temporary storage facilities, inventories are valued on a weighted-average basis.

Information pertaining to a recent period is as follows:

Department 1:		
Transferred out:		
First batch:		
Beginning inventories (500 liters)	$8,000	
Cost to complete	4,000	$12,000
Second batch (4,000 liters)		78,000
Total		$90,000
Department 2:		
Transferred out (7,000 cases)		$15,000
Temporary storage:		
Beginning inventory (1,300 cases)		$ 1,600
Department 3:		
Beginning inventory of work-in-process:		
From Department 1 (100 cases)		$ 1,000
From Temporary Storage (50 cases)		100
Conversion costs		500
Total		$ 1,600
Completed (7,000 cases)		$?
Current conversion costs		$22,000
Ending inventory of work-in-process:		
From Department 1 (? cases)		
Sufficient Snuffers are in process to package one-half of the secret ingredients from Department 1.		
Equivalent units of conversion (500 cases)		

REQUIREMENTS

a) Determine the flow of whole or partial units (in terms of cases) in Department 3.

b) Determine the equivalent units in process in Department 3 for each of the following categories: Transferred in from Department 1, Transferred in from Temporary Storage, and Conversion.

c) Determine the cost per equivalent unit in process in Department 3. Organize your work using four columns: one for each item mentioned in part (b) and one for totals.

d) Determine the costs transferred out of Department 3 and the costs in the ending work-in-process inventory of Department 3.

4–35 Process Costing Challenge Problem

The Killer Chemical Company produces a widely distributed insect spray. Production takes place in two departments. In the first department, the insect-killing chemicals are blended. In the second department, the insect killer is placed in an aerosol can and an inert chemical propellant is added. After the propellant is added, the production process is complete. It is estimated that both steps that take place in the second department require equal amounts of conversion and material. There is no spoilage.

Selected production information for a recent week is as follows:

Department 1

Ending Inventory of 2,000 units:
1/2 complete as to materials.
1/2 complete as to conversion.

10,000 units were started this period.

Completed units transferred to Department 2 include conversion costs of $0.07 each.

Department 2

Ending Inventory of 3,000 units:
1,000 are 0% converted.
2,000 are 50% converted.

Beginning Inventory of 4,000 units:
$100 in conversion costs.
$1,640 in transferred-in-costs.
$100 in materials costs.

Completed 9,000 units.

Unit cost data:
Cost per equivalent unit in process is $0.60.
Cost per equivalent unit of conversion in process is $0.05.
Cost per equivalent unit of material in process is $0.10.

REQUIREMENTS

Using the weighted-average method, determine the following:

a) Complete or partial units in Department 1 at the beginning of the week.

b) Total costs in process in Department 2.

c) Total costs transferred to Department 2 during the week.

d) The cost per equivalent unit in process in Department 1.

e) Total costs in process in Department 1.

f) Total costs in the ending inventory of Department 2.

g) Total costs in the ending inventory of Department 1.

4–36 Process Costing Challenge Problem

Post-Renaissance Reproductions produces hand-painted copies of Rembrandt originals on an assembly-line basis. Reproductions' accounting system assigns the net cost (actual less disposal valuc) of normal spoilage to the actual cost of good paintings *at the time spoilage is detected.* The net cost of abnormal spoilage is treated as an expense. The disposal value of spoiled paintings is removed from Work-in-Process and placed in Spoiled Paintings Inventory.

Spoilage is detected just before the good paintings go into the drying room. At that time, they are complete as to materials and labor, but only 50 percent complete as to overhead. Normal spoilage is 10 percent of the good paintings placed in the drying room. Spoiled paintings are sold as seconds for $10 each.

On July 1, 19x7, 1,000 paintings were in the drying room. They were 90 percent complete as to overhead. During July, 10,000 paintings were removed from the drying room and 1,000 paintings were placed in spoiled paintings inventory. The ending inventory on July 31 consisted of 500 paintings. All were 80 percent complete as to overhead.

The July 1, 19x7, inventory was recorded on the books at $74,500. The actual costs of July operations include:

Direct materials	$210,000
Direct labor (2,100 labor-hours)	420,000
Variable overhead (4,200 room-hours)	42,000
Fixed overhead (4,200 room-hours)	58,000

Only the good paintings are placed in the drying room. Spoiled paintings are transferred to a warehouse prior to sale.

REQUIREMENTS

a) Prepare a cost of production report using FIFO process costing. (*Hint:* The beginning and ending inventories are past the point of spoilage detection.)

b) Prepare all journal entries affecting Work-in-Process.

SOLUTION TO REVIEW PROBLEM

Watson Company
Cost of Production Report
For the Month of October, 19x8

FLOW OF WHOLE OR PARTIAL UNITS		
Beginning		200
Started		1,500
In process		1,700
Spoiled	100	
Good units completed	1,400	− 1,500
Ending		200

(*continued*)

	Materials	*Conversion*	*Total*
EQUIVALENT UNITS MANUFACTURED			
Good units completed	1,400	1,400	
Equivalent units spoiled	100	80*	
Equivalent units in ending inventory	200	100†	
Equivalent units in process	1,700	1,580	
Less equivalent units in beginning inventory	−200	−150‡	
Equivalent units manufactured	1,500	1,430	
TOTAL COSTS TO BE ACCOUNTED FOR			
COST PER EQUIVALENT UNIT MANUFACTURED			
Work-in-Process, beginning	—	—	$ 5,990
Current manufacturing costs	$30,000	$18,000	48,000
Total costs in process	—	—	$53,990
Equivalent units manufactured	÷1,500	÷1,430	
Cost per equivalent unit manufactured	$ 20.00	$ 12.59	$ 32.59
ACCOUNTING FOR TOTAL COSTS			
Transferred out:			
Good units:			
First batch:			
Work-in-Process, beginning	$5,990.00		
Costs to complete:			
Conversion (50§ × $12.59)	629.50	$ 6,619.50	
Second batch, started and completed this period (1,200 × $32.59)		39,108.00	$45,727.50
Spoiled units:			
Materials (100 × $20)		$ 2,000.00	
Conversion (80 × $12.59)		1,007.20	3,007.20
Total costs transferred out			$48,734.70
Work-in-Process, ending:			
Materials (200 × $20.00)		$ 4,000.00	
Conversion (100 × $12.59)		1,259.00	5,259.00
Total costs accounted for			$53,993.70**

* 100 units, four-fifths complete
† 200 units, half complete
‡ 200 units, three-quarters complete
§ Additional equivalent units required to complete beginning inventory.
** Answer reflects $3.70 rounding error.

5 Costing Joint Products and By-Products

INTRODUCTION
SPLIT-OFF POINT AND JOINT COSTS
COSTING JOINT PRODUCTS
COSTING BY-PRODUCTS AND SCRAP
JOINT PRODUCTS AND SPECIAL DECISIONS
SUMMARY

INTRODUCTION

TWO OR MORE PRODUCTS SIMULTANEOUSLY PRODUCED FROM A SINGLE SET of inputs are called **joint products.** Joint products are frequently found in basic industries that process raw materials. Examples include dairy products, chemicals, meat products, petroleum, and wood products. In the petroleum industry, crude oil is refined into fuel oil, gasoline, kerosene, lubricating oil, and other products.

The simultaneous production of joint products presents the cost accountant with a difficult problem, namely, the assignment of production costs incurred up to the point each product is separately identifiable. Because these costs are incurred for the purpose of producing the joint products, for financial reporting purposes they must be treated as product costs and allocated to the joint products.

The purpose of this chapter is to present and evaluate several widely used procedures for costing joint products. This is the fourth of a five-chapter series on product costing. Although our primary focus, once again, is on developing information needed for external reporting, we also evaluate the usefulness of joint product costs for management decision making. Attention is also given to special decisions involving joint products.

SPLIT-OFF POINT AND JOINT COSTS

The point at which joint products become separately identifiable is called the **split-off point.** Production costs incurred prior to the split-off point are called **joint costs.** For financial reporting, joint costs incurred prior to the split-off point must be allocated to the joint products.

Example 5–1

In March 19x3 the Lemke Chemical Company began processing Chemical A into two joint products, B and C, in the ratio of 4:1 by a complex cracking process. During March, to convert 10,000 liters of A into 8,000 liters of B and 2,000 liters of C, Lemke incurred the following costs:

Direct materials	$110,000
Direct labor	40,000
Factory overhead	40,000
Total	$190,000

The March production relationships are illustrated in Exhibit 5–1(a).

EXHIBIT 5–1 Joint Products and Joint Cost Allocations

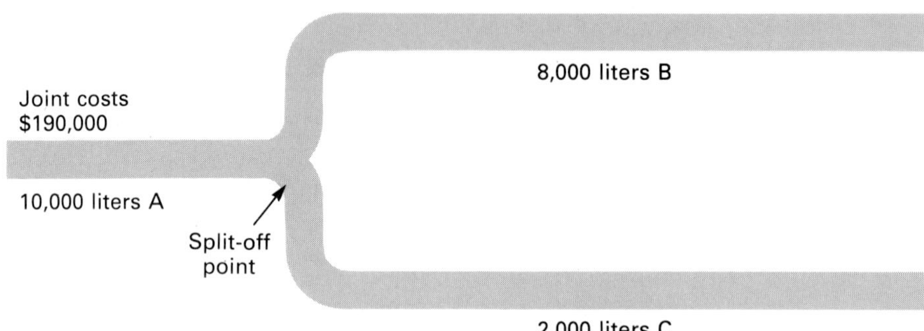

(a) Diagram of relationships

Lemke Company
Partial Income Statement
For the Month of March, 19x3

	Total	*Product B*	*Product C*
Unit sales	10,000	8,000	2,000
Sales	$200,000	$180,000	$ 20,000
Cost of goods sold	– 190,000	– 152,000	– 38,000
Gross profit	$ 10,000	$ 28,000	$ (18,000)

(b) Partial product line income statements: Joint costs allocated using physical measures.

Lemke Company
Partial Income Statement
For the Month of March, 19x3

	Total	*Product B*	*Product C*
Unit sales	10,000	8,000	2,000
Sales	$200,000	$180,000	$ 20,000
Cost of goods sold	– 190,000	– 171,000	– 19,000
Gross profit	$ 10,000	$ 9,000	$ 1,000

(c) Partial product line income statements: Joint costs allocated using sales values.

The problem is how to allocate the joint costs, \$190,000, to each of the joint products. There are similarities between this situation and that of allocating factory overhead. Because both types of costs are common to several products, it is difficult to relate them to specific products. If anything, it is more difficult to find a rational basis for joint cost allocation than it is to find a rational basis for the allocation of factory overhead. In Chapters 3 and 4, factory overhead was allocated to specific products on the basis of such factors as direct-labor hours, direct-labor dollars, or machine hours. But note that only one product utilized either a labor hour or a machine hour at a particular time. When joint products are being produced, two or more products *simultaneously* utilize the same labor hour or machine hour.

In the final analysis, joint costs must be allocated to joint products on some arbitrary, but systematic, basis. Because joint cost allocations are necessarily arbitrary, allocated joint costs normally should not be considered in decisions affecting individual joint products. Nevertheless joint cost allocations are required for external reporting, taxation, and pricing in regulated industries. Realizing the necessity for, and the arbitrary nature of, joint cost allocation, cost accountants have attempted to develop procedures that, although not useful for management decision making, will not cause individual joint products to appear unprofitable when all joint products are making a positive contribution to fixed costs and profits.

COSTING JOINT PRODUCTS

Among the many procedures for allocating joint costs to joint products, the most frequently used methods involve the use of physical measures, sales values, or net realizable values (also called net sales values).

Physical Measures

Methods based on physical measures use some physical attribute common to all joint products as a basis for joint cost allocation. Units produced, weight, volume, surface area, and potential heat content are frequently used. Using physical measures as a basis for joint cost allocation,

1. The common physical attribute selected as a basis for allocation is summed across all joint products.
2. Joint costs are allocated on the basis of each joint product's relative portion of the common physical attribute.

Example 5–2

Assuming Lemke has selected volume in liters as the common basis of joint cost allocation, the following results are obtained:

Product	*Volume*	*Relative volume*		*Joint costs*		*Allocation*
B	8,000	0.80	×	\$190,000	=	\$152,000
C	2,000	0.20	×	\$190,000	=	38,000
	10,000	1.00				\$190,000

Each product has a cost of $19 per liter ($152,000/8,000 for B and $38,000/2,000 for C).

Allocating joint costs on the basis of a physical measure is satisfactory when a close relationship exists between the physical measure and the selling price of individual products. When this is not the case, the use of physical measures may be misleading.

Consider what would happen if all March production was sold, B for $22.50 per liter and A for $10.00 per liter. As shown in Exhibit 5–1(b), product-line income statements would report a positive gross profit for B and a negative gross profit for C. Yet, if B is produced, C must also be produced. Because C does not have any additional processing costs, Lemke is better off by $10 for every liter of C sold[1]. In more complex situations, Lemke's management might erroneously conclude that profits could be increased by $18,000 if C were discontinued. If the sale of C were discontinued, all $190,000 would be assigned to B, producing a negative gross profit of $10,000 ($180,000 sales revenue − $190,000 cost of goods sold). Note that the decline in total gross profit, from a positive $10,000 to a negative $10,000, is exactly equal to C's sales revenue.

If the selling price of a product or service is determined by regulatory or legal forces, a close relationship between physical measures and selling prices is likely. When selling prices are set by market forces, the existence of such a relationship is less likely.

Sales Value

Using the sales-value method, joint costs are allocated on the basis of relative sales values. This method assumes a pro rata recovery of joint costs is obtained from each sales dollar without distinction among the different products. If no costs are incurred beyond the split-off point, the use of relative sales values as a basis for joint cost allocation avoids misleading inferences regarding the profitability of individual joint products.

Example 5–3

Assuming selling prices for B and C are $22.50 and $10.00, respectively, the sales value method produces the following allocations:

	Sales value		*Relative sales*		*Joint*		
Product	*Computation*	*Amount*	*value*		*cost*		*Allocation*
B	8,000 × $22.50 =	$180,000	0.90	×	$190,000	=	$171,000
C	2,000 × $10.00 =	20,000	0.10	×	$190,000	=	19,000
		$200,000	1.00				$190,000

Product B costs $21.375 per liter ($171,000/8,000 liters) and Product C costs $9.50 per liter ($19,000/2,000 liters).

---

[1] Generally accepted accounting principles, used for external reporting, require end-of-period inventories to be valued at the lower of cost or market. In the absence of selling costs, the inventory costs assigned to C in external reports cannot exceed C's $10 unit selling price.

As is illustrated in Exhibit 5–1(c), both products have positive gross profits when joint costs are allocated on the basis of relative sales values. In the absence of separate costs beyond the split-off point, the sales-value method results in a positive gross profit for each product if the joint product group has sufficient revenues to cover all joint costs. In this example, each product's gross profit as a percentage of sales is 0.05 [($22.50 − $21.375)/$22.50 for B and ($10.00 − $9.50)/$10.00 for C].

Although allocation on the basis of relative sales values avoids the major drawbacks of physical-measure allocations, the use of sales values does have some problems. Because this method is based on selling prices, allocated costs cannot be used as an input to pricing decisions. In Examples 5–2 and 5–3 all products were sold in the period they were produced. When goods are produced for inventory, the expected or budgeted selling price of each product must be used as a basis of joint cost allocation.

Net Realizable Value

To make products salable, additional processing may be necessary. Although separate production costs incurred after the split-off point are easier to identify with individual products, the existence of separate costs requires us to modify the sales-value method. When separate production costs exist, joint costs are allocated on the basis of relative net realizable values. A product's **net realizable value,** sometimes called its **net sales value,** is the product's final selling price less additional processing and selling costs.

Example 5–4

Even though Product B can be sold at the split-off point for a total sales value of $180,000, assume Product C does not have a market. Accordingly Lemke processes C further into salable Product D, which has a selling price of $40 per liter. In March, to convert 2,000 liters of C into 2,000 liters of D, Lemke incurred the following separate processing costs:

Direct labor	$10,000
Factory overhead	10,000
Total	$20,000

These relationships are illustrated in Exhibit 5–2.

At the split-off point, the net realizable value of Product C is $60,000, the final selling price of Product D less the costs to process C into D:

Sales value of D (2,000 units × $40)	$80,000
Less separate costs	−20,000
Net realizable value of C	$60,000

Using relative net realizable value as a basis of allocation, the allocated joint costs are:

EXHIBIT 5–2 **Allocating Joint Costs Using Net Realizable Values**

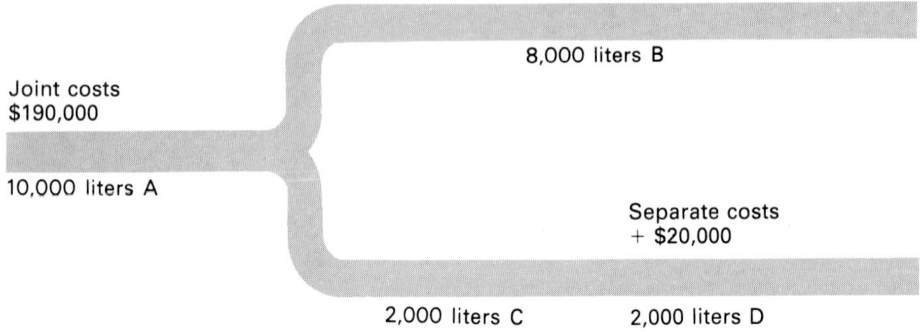

(a) Diagram of relationships

Lemke Company
Partial Income Statement
For the Month of March, 19x3

	Total	*Product B*	*Product D*
Unit sales	10,000	8,000	2,000
Sales	$260,000	$180,000	$ 80,000
Cost of goods sold	−210,000	−142,500	−67,500
Gross profit	$ 50,000	$ 37,500	$ 12,500

(b) Partial product line income statements

Product	*Net realizable value*	*Relative net realizable value*		*Joint cost*		*Allocation*
B	$180,000	0.75	×	$190,000	=	$142,500
C	60,000	0.25	×	$190,000	=	47,500
	$240,000	1.00				$190,000

For the purposes of inventory valuation and income determination in external financial statements, Product B costs $17.8125 per liter ($142,500/8,000 liters), intermediate Product C costs $23.75 per liter ($47,500/2,000 liters) and Product D costs $33.75 per liter (($47,500 allocated to C + $20,000 of separate processing costs)/2,000 liters). Note that the final cost of Product D includes both the joint costs allocated to Product C and the separate costs required to convert Product C into Product D.

Assuming all C is converted into D and sold, partial product-line income statements are presented in Exhibit 5–2(b). Observe that, although the joint costs, production of B, and sales values of B are identical in Examples 5–3 and 5–4, the costs allocated to B differ between Examples 5–3 and 5–4 because of the difference in C's relative value at the split-off point.

Assuming that B and C are joint products produced in Department 1 and that C is processed into D in Department 2, summary journal entries for March manufacturing activities, with costs allocated on the basis of relative net realizable values, are as follows:

Work-in-Process: Department 1	190,000	
Stores Control		110,000
Payroll Payable		40,000
Factory Overhead Control: Department 1		40,000
Finished Goods Inventory (for B)	142,500	
Work-in-Process: Department 2 (for C)	47,500	
Work-in-Process: Department 1		190,000
Work-in-Process: Department 2	20,000	
Payroll Payable		10,000
Factory Overhead Control: Department 2		10,000
Finished Goods Inventory (for D)	67,500	
Work-in-Process: Department 2		67,500

The allocation of the joint costs in Department 1 was necessary to prepare the second journal entry.

Multiple Split-Off Points When multiple products exist, product-costing relationships can become quite complex. The authors recommend a three-step approach to the solution of problems containing two or more split-off points:

1. Diagram the physical relationships, clearly noting the physical flow of products and the point of incurrence of all joint and separate costs.
2. Determine the total sales value of all salable products and then work *backwards*, starting with the last split-off point(s), subtracting separate and additional joint costs to determine the net realizable values and the relative net realizable values of joint products at each split-off point.
3. Work *forwards*, starting with the first split-off point, allocating joint costs at each split-off point on the basis of relative net realizable values. As you work forward be sure to add previously allocated costs to those incurred subsequently.

Example 5–5 Instead of converting unsalable intermediate Product C into Product D, management elects to convert C into Products E and F. During April 19x3, 10,000 liters of A are converted into 8,000 liters of B and 2,000 liters of C in Department 1. The 2,000 liters of C are processed further in Department 2, where 6,000 liters of material W are added, to produce 2,000 liters of Product E, 4,000 liters of Product F, and 2,000 liters of waste. Before Product E could be sold, it was processed further in Department 3. April production costs were as follows:

	Department		
	1	*2*	*3*
Direct materials	$110,000	$ 20,000	$ 0
Direct labor	40,000	15,000	10,000
Factory overhead	40,000	5,000	10,000
Total	$190,000	$ 40,000	$ 20,000

Unit selling prices per liter of final product are as follows:

Product	*Unit selling price per liter*
B	$22.50
E	$50.00
F	$20.00

The physical relationships among products and the points of cost incurrence are illustrated in Exhibit 5–3(a). The computation of net realizable values and relative net realizable values at each split-off point is presented in Exhibit 5–3(b). Here the total of the net realizable values of Products E and F at the second split-off point, $160,000, is also the net realizable value of Product C at the end of processing in Department 2. Hence the $160,000 value at the second split carries down as the "sales" value of Product C, from which we subtract the Department 2 processing costs of $40,000 to obtain the net realizable value of Product C at the first split-off point, $120,000.

A schedule allocating the joint costs is presented in Exhibit 5–3(c). Here we work forwards from the first split-off point, allocating joint costs on the basis of relative net realizable values. The costs allocated at the second split-off point include the $76,000 allocated to Product C at the first split-off point and the $40,000 additional processing costs incurred in Department 2.

The final cost assigned to Product E includes the $58,000 allocated at the second split-off point plus $20,000 of separate processing costs, for a total of $78,000. The final costs per liter are as follows:

Product	*Total cost*		*Liters*		*Cost per liter*
B	$114,000	÷	8,000	=	$14.25
E	78,000	÷	2,000	=	39.00
F	58,000	÷	4,000	=	14.50

Once again, a change in the net realizable value of Product C has affected the costs allocated to Product B. If the waste material had a disposal cost, this would be added to the joint processing costs of Products E and F.

The journal entries affecting Work-in-Process for April 19x3 production activities under an actual cost system are presented in Exhibit 5–4. Entries accumulating costs in Factory Overhead Control have been omitted. Once again, the previous discussions concerning the use of actual or predetermined overhead rates, the selection of a basis for overhead application, and the use of departmental or plant-wide overhead rates are pertinent.

Sales Values for Intermediate Products As is apparent from Example 5–5, the allocation of joint costs can become unwieldy when there are multiple split-off points. Fortunately an important convention of the net-realizable-value and sales-value methods specifies that *if a joint product can be either sold at a split-off point or processed further, the sales value at the split-off point is used in determining relative values, even if the product is processed further.* Because many intermediate products have market values, this greatly reduces the complexity of product costing.

EXHIBIT 5–3 **Allocating Joint Costs Using Net Realizable Values with Multiple Split-off Points**

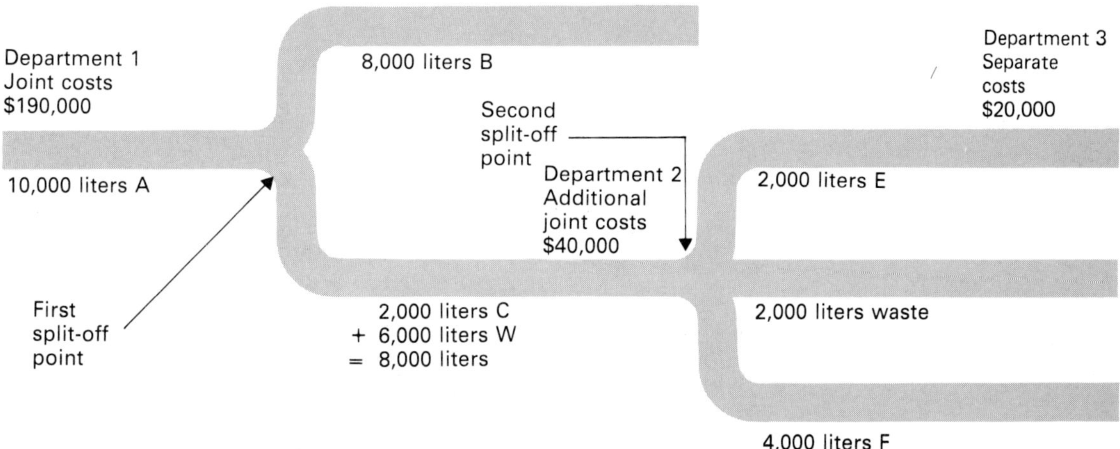

(a) Diagram of relationships

Relative net realizable value

	Sales value		*Separate costs*		*Net realizable value*	*Relative net realizable values*
Second split:						
E	(2,000 × $50.00)	–	$20,000	=	$ 80,000	0.50
F	(4,000 × $20.00)	–	0	=	80,000	0.50
					$160,000	1.00
First split:						
B	(8,000 × $22.50)	–	$ 0	=	$180,000	0.60
C	$160,000	–	40,000	=	120,000	0.40
					$300,000	1.00

(b) Computation of relative net realizable values

Allocation of joint costs

	Allocated joint cost		*Additional joint costs*		*Total*	*Relative net realizable value*		*Allocation*
First split:								
B	$0	+	$190,000	=	$190,000	× 0.60	=	$114,000
C						× 0.40	=	76,000
								$190,000
Second split:								
E	$76,000	+	$ 40,000	=	$116,000	× 0.50	=	$ 58,000
F						× 0.50	=	58,000
								$116,000

(c) Schedule of joint cost allocations

EXHIBIT 5–4 Joint Product Journal Entries for Example 5–5

	Debit	Credit
Work-in-Process: Department 1	190,000	
Stores Control		110,000
Payroll Payable		40,000
Factory Overhead Control: Department 1		40,000
Finished Goods Inventory (for B)	114,000	
Work-in-Process: Department 2 (for C)	76,000	
Work-in-Process: Department 1		190,000
Work-in-Process: Department 2	40,000	
Stores Control		20,000
Payroll Payable		15,000
Factory Overhead Control: Department 2		5,000
Finished Goods Inventory (for F)	58,000	
Work-in-Process: Department 3 (for E)	58,000	
Work-in-Process: Department 2		116,000
Work-in-Process: Department 3	20,000	
Payroll Payable		10,000
Factory Overhead Control: Department 3		10,000
Finished Goods Inventory (for E)	78,000	
Work-in-Process: Department 3		78,000

Example 5–6

Assume Lemke can either sell Product C at the first split-off point for $10 per liter or process it further into Products E and F.

In this case the joint costs incurred in Department 1, $190,000, are allocated to Products B and C on the basis of each product's relative sales value, regardless of whether or not Product C is processed further. The allocation of the joint costs would be as given in Example 5–3, $171,000 to Product B and $19,000 to Product C. If Product C is processed further in Department 2, the joint costs allocated to Products E and F would be $59,000:

	Department 2 Costs
Allocated from Department 1	$ 19,000
Direct materials	20,000
Direct labor	15,000
Factory overhead	5,000
Total	$ 59,000

The relative net realizable values of Products E and F at the second split-off point were computed as 0.50 and 0.50, respectively, in Exhibit 5–3(b). Using these relative values, $29,500 of Department 2 costs are allocated to each. The total costs assigned to Product E total $49,500 ($29,500 from Department 2 and separate processing costs of $20,000 from Department 3). The final costs per liter are as follows:

Product	*Total cost*		*Liters*		*Cost per liter*
B	$171,000	÷	8,000	=	$21.375
E	49,500	÷	2,000	=	24.750
F	29,500	÷	4,000	=	7.375

Compared with costs in Example 5–5, the cost of Product B is higher and the costs of Products E and F are lower.[2]

COSTING BY-PRODUCTS AND SCRAP

The type of joint products considered to this point are often referred to as "major" or "co-products" to differentiate them from "by-products," "scrap," and "waste." No hard and fast rules are available regarding distinctions among major products, by-products, scrap, and waste, but the following statements typify the flavor of their differences:

- When compared with each other, **major products** have "high" relative total sales values.
- When compared with major products, **by-products** have "low" relative total sales values. This can be due to a small output or to low unit selling prices or to both.
- By-products are incidental items that accompany the production of major products. The process would not be carried on to produce the by-products alone.
- **Scrap** is left-over bits and pieces from raw materials used in the production process; by-products are residues resulting when the physical characteristics of the original material are changed.
- By-products may undergo additional processing to place them in salable form. Scrap is sold "as is."
- A by-product has a positive value, but scrap or **waste** products have no value and additional costs may be incurred to dispose of them.

These distinctions leave much room for professional judgment. An item regarded as a by-product by one firm may be regarded as a major product by another. The distinction between by-products and scrap with a positive sales value is so fine that both are accorded similar accounting treatment. The distinction between spoilage and scrap and waste is also worth mentioning. Spoilage refers to units of major products that contain imperfections. Scrap or waste refers to discarded raw materials or outputs that were never intended to be major products. In this text, the unmodified use of the term "joint products" refers to major products.

Miscellaneous Income

Considerable variation exists in accounting for by-products and scrap. The two most frequently cited procedures are (1) not assigning a value to by-product or scrap inventory and recording by-product or scrap sales as miscellaneous income, and (2) costing the by-product or scrap inventory at its net realizable value and deducting this amount from the costs to be assigned major products.

---

[2] Note that the use of sales values for intermediate product costing ensures that financial accounting's lower-of-cost-or-market rule is not violated. In published financial statements Product C inventories must be assigned an inventory cost no higher than their $10 selling price. In Example 5–5, where costs were allocated to Product C on the basis of the relative net realizable values of Products B, E, and F, the lower-of-cost-or-market rule was violated. Here, with allocated costs of $76,000 (see Exhibit 5–3), each unit of C had a cost $38 ($76,000/2,000). In Example 5–6, where costs were allocated to Product C on the basis of the relative sales values of Products B and C, the lower-of-cost-or-market rule was not violated. Here, with allocated costs of $19,000, each unit of C has a cost of $9.50 ($19,000/2,000).

The miscellaneous income approach is regarded as appropriate when the value of by-products or scrap is uncertain or so small that it does not have a noticeable effect on inventory or profit. Under these circumstances, the short-cut accounting treatment of debiting Cash or Accounts Receivable and crediting Miscellaneous Income at the time of sale is justified. The by-product or scrap inventory is not assigned a value and all joint costs are assigned to the major product(s). This method is modified slightly if the by-product requires additional processing after the split-off point. Then these separate costs are assigned to the by-products. But if the firm is willing to process a by-product further, its sales value is likely to be sufficiently large to render the miscellaneous income treatment inappropriate.

Net Realizable Value

If the net realizable value of a by-product is large enough to have a noticeable effect on inventory or profits, the by-product should be costed at its net realizable value. This reduces the cost assigned major products and usually results in no revenue recognition on by-product sales. If the by-product is not processed further in a subsequent department, the appropriate journal entries are:

By-Product Inventory	XXX	
Work-in-Process		XXX

at the time of split-off, and

Cash or Accounts Receivable	XXX	
By-Product Inventory		XXX

at the time of sale. Any differences between actual selling prices and prices used in by-product costing are treated as a gain or loss.

Example 5–7

Extending Example 5–6, assume the waste material can be processed into by-product K. Product K sells for $5.00 per liter and requires additional processing costs of $3.00 per liter in Department 4.

At the split-off point the 2,000 liters of K have a net realizable value of $4,000 [2,000($5 – $3)]. Accordingly, K is costed at this amount and $4,000 is deducted from the joint costs allocated to Products E and F, whose joint costs are now $55,000 ($19,000 allocated from Department 1 to Department 2, plus $40,000 of additional Department 2 costs, less $4,000 assigned to by-product K). The $55,000 is assigned to Products E and F on the basis of their relative net realizable values (0.50 and 0.50 in Exhibit 5–3), $27,500 to each. Additional Department 3 costs of $20,000 are also assigned to Product E, giving it a final total cost of $47,500. The final per liter cost of each product is as follows:

Product	*Total cost*		*Liters*		*Cost per liter*
B	$171,000	÷	8,000	=	$21.375
E	47,500	÷	2,000	=	23.750
F	27,500	÷	4,000	=	6.875
K					5.000*

* $2.00 allocated plus $3.00 to complete.

Because of the joint costs allocated to by-product K, the costs of E and F are slightly lower than in Example 5–6.

With Product C salable at the first split-off point and the waste material treated as by-product K, using the net realizable value method of costing by-products, the journal entry transferring costs out of Department 2 is as follows:

Finished Goods Inventory (for F)	27,500	
Work-in-Process: Department 3 (for E)	27,500	
Work-in-Process: Department 4 (for K)	4,000	
Work-in-Process: Department 2		59,000

The entries to record the completion and sale of by-product K at $5.00 per liter are:

Work-in-Process: Department 4	6,000	
Payroll Payable Factory Overhead Control: Department 4		6,000
By-Product Inventory	10,000	
Work-in-Process: Department 4		10,000
Cash or Accounts Receivable	10,000	
By-Product Inventory		10,000

If by-product K was sold for $6, rather than the $5 used for product costing, Lemke would realize a gain of $2,000 [2,000($6 − $5)] on the sale, and the journal entry to record the sale would be:

Cash or Accounts Receivable	12,000	
By-Product Inventory		10,000
Gain on Sale of By-Product Inventory		2,000

Many by-products start as scrap or waste. Later a use is found for them and they become valuable. Wood chips were initially regarded as waste by forest products companies. They were not assigned any inventory value. Today power plants are being constructed to burn wood chips. As more such plants are constructed, it is likely that wood chips will become a valuable by-product. Conceivably, if the demand for wood chips as a source of fuel becomes large enough, wood chips may become a major product. The cost accountant should regularly review the status of all joint products to determine whether they should be accounted for as major products, by-products, scrap, or waste. Changed circumstances necessitate a change in an organization's cost accounting system to prevent it from becoming obsolete.

JOINT PRODUCTS AND SPECIAL DECISIONS

Sell or Process Further

Decisions involving joint products should be made on the basis of future costs and revenues that will differ under each alternative. If the decision has already been made to process joint products to the split-off point, joint costs are not relevant to the evaluation of individual products. Each of the products will appear at the split-off point regardless of any additional decision management may make. Management must now decide how best to use each joint product. Typical alternatives are to either sell at the split-off point or process further into one or more products. To arrive at a decision, the net cash flows from each alternative are considered. The alternative with the largest positive net cash inflow is usually preferred.

Example 5–8

At the first split-off point Lemke has three alternative uses of Product C: (1) sell as is, (2) process into Product D, or (3) process into Products E and F and by-product K.

For a monthly production volume of 2,000 liters of C, the cash flows of each alternative are shown in Exhibit 5–5. Assuming that all additional processing costs are variable, and ignoring interest on any additional investments required for alternatives 2 and 3, the most profitable action is to process C further into Products E and F, and by-product K, to obtain net cash inflows of $124,000.

Total Production Decisions

As just demonstrated, if Product C is produced, it should be processed further into E, F, and K, since the net cash inflows of this action exceed the net cash inflows of either alternative. But the analysis is not complete. Once the optimal use of each joint product is known, the entire product group should be evaluated to determine if the group makes a positive contribution to fixed costs and profits. This is done by deducting the joint outlay costs from the sum of the net cash inflows produced by each joint product to determine if the product group has a positive net cash inflow.

Example 5–9

Assume that $165,000 of the $190,000 in monthly costs associated with the production of Products B and C in Department 1 are outlay costs that can be eliminated if these products are discontinued. Assuming there is no alternative

EXHIBIT 5–5 Alternative Uses of By-Product C

		Process further	
	Sell as is	*Into D*	*Into E, F, & K*
Cash inflow	$20,000	$80,000	$190,000†
Cash expenditures	−0	−20,000*	−66,000‡
Net cash inflow	$20,000	$60,000	$124,000

* Separate costs in Example 5–4.

† Sales values:

E = (2,000 × $50) =	$100,000	
F = (4,000 × $20) =	80,000	
K = (2,000 × $5) =	10,000	$190,000

‡ Separate costs:

To second split-off	$40,000	
E = (2,000 × $10) =	20,000	
K = (2,000 × $3) =	6,000	$ 66,000

use of the production facilities, the net advantage of processing 10,000 liters of chemical A per month is $139,000:

Sales of Product B	$180,000	
Net cash inflows from E, F, and K (see Exhibit 5–5)	124,000	$304,000
Joint outlay costs		– 165,000
Net advantage of continued production		$139,000

It appears that the production of this joint product group should be continued.

Other Considerations

Joint product situations sometimes involve several split-off points with multiple alternative uses and sources of materials at each split-off point. In these complex situations, decision makers quickly become overwhelmed with alternatives to analyze, and with production and market constraints to consider. Fortunately techniques such as linear programming provide a systematic approach to these situations.

In this chapter, it is assumed that all joint products are produced in fixed proportions (for example, 5 liters of Chemical A always yields 4 liters of Product B and 1 liter of Product C). It is sometimes possible to vary the proportions in which products are produced. By incurring additional processing costs, for example, Lemke might be able to vary the yield of Products B and C between the ratios of 4:1 and 2:3. Linear programming is also helpful in determining the optimal yield for variable proportions. However, a discussion of these issues is beyond the scope of this book.

SUMMARY

Joint products are simultaneously produced from a common set of inputs by a single process. Joint products are classified as major products, by-products, scrap, or waste on the basis of such factors as their relative sales value or disposal costs and the amount of physical transformation they have undergone. Although allocated joint costs are not useful for management decision making, joint cost allocations are required for external reporting, taxation, and price setting in regulated industries.

When a close relationship exists between some physical characteristic of joint products and their selling price at the split-off point, the two major methods of joint cost allocation (relative physical measures and relative sales value) give similar results. When this is not the case, the sales-value method is preferred. When additional costs are incurred beyond the split-off point and products are not salable at the split-off point, the preferred allocation is based on relative net realizable value (also called relative net sales value).

By-products and scrap may be assigned a cost of zero and the proceeds of their sale recorded as miscellaneous income if their value is so small it does not have a noticeable effect on inventory or profit. Otherwise by-products should be costed at their net realizable value and this amount should be deducted from the cost of the main product.

In making decisions involving individual joint products and product groups, the emphasis should be on future costs and revenues that differ under alternative actions. Costs incurred prior to the point at which a product is separately identifiable are not relevant to the evaluation of alternative uses of that product.

KEY TERMS

By-products
Joint costs
Joint products
Major products
Net realizable value
Net sales value
Scrap
Split-off point
Waste

SELECTED REFERENCES

Balachandran, Bala V., and Ram T. S. Ramakrishnan, "Joint Cost Allocation: A Unified Approach," *Accounting Review* **56,** No. 1 (January 1981): 85–96.

Bierman, Harold Jr., "Inventory Valuation: The Use of Market Price," *Accounting Review* **42,** No. 4 (October 1967): 731–737.

Billera, Louis J., David C. Heath, and Robert E. Verrecchia, "A Unique Procedure for Allocating Common Costs from a Production Process," *Journal of Accounting Research* **19,** No. 1 (Spring 1981): 185–196.

Gangolly, Jagdish D., "On Joint Cost Allocation: Independent Cost Proportional Scheme (ICPS) and Its Properties," *Journal of Accounting Research* **19,** No. 2 (Autumn 1981): 299–311.

Hamlen, Susan S., William A. Hamlen, Jr., and John Tschirhart, "The Use of the Generalized Shapley Allocation in Joint Cost Allocation," *Accounting Review* **55,** No. 2 (April 1980): 269–287.

Hughes, John S., and James H. Scheiner, "Efficient Properties of Mutually Satisfactory Cost Allocations," *Accounting Review* **55,** No. 1 (January 1980): 85–95.

Jensen, Daniel L., "The Role of Cost in Pricing Joint Products: A Case of Production in Fixed Proportions," *Accounting Review* **49,** No. 3 (July 1974): 465–476.

Moriarity, Shane, ed., *Joint Cost Allocations, Proceedings of the University of Oklahoma Conference on Cost Allocations,* Norman, Okla.: Center for Economic and Management Research, University of Oklahoma, 1981.

Williams, David J., and John O. S. Kennedy, "A Unique Procedure for Allocating Joint Costs from a Production Process?" *Journal of Accounting Research* **21,** No. 2 (Autumn 1983): 644–645.

REVIEW QUESTIONS

5–1 Mention several industries where joint products are frequently found.

5–2 For what purpose are production costs incurred up to the point each product is separately identifiable assigned to joint products?

5–3 In what way are joint costs similar to overhead?

5–4 Under what conditions will the physical measures method of joint cost allocation provide satisfactory results?

5–5 What assumption forms the basis of the sales-value method of joint cost allocation?

5–6 Why can't the sales-value method of joint cost allocation be used as a basis for price setting?

5–7 In what way is the sales-value method modified if there are separate production costs after the split-off point and joint products are not salable at the split-off point?

5–8 Briefly describe the three-step approach to allocating joint costs using the net-realizable-value method when there are multiple split-off points.

5–9 How is the three-step approach modified if an intermediate product has a sales value at the split-off point? Why is this modification necessary for inventory costing in general-purpose financial statements?

5–10 Distinguish between major products, by-products, and scrap.

5–11 Describe two alternative accounting treatments of by-products and indicate the circumstances under which each might be used.

5–12 Why are allocated joint costs irrelevant in the evaluation of alternative uses of a joint product?

5–13 For what type of decisions are joint production costs relevant?

REVIEW PROBLEM

Joint Products, By-Products, Scrap, and Waste

The following information pertains to the Brooks Company:

- During February 19x4, Department 1 produced 1,000 units of major product MP1, 1,000 units of major product MP2, 500 units of by-product BP, 100 units of scrap, and 1,000 pounds of solid waste. MP1 was sold immediately. MP2 and BP underwent further processing in Departments 2 and 3, respectively. Brooks paid an outside contractor to dispose of the waste. There were no beginning or ending inventories of work-in-process.
- February 19x4 cost data:

	Department		
	1	*2*	*3*
Direct materials	$10,000	$ 0	$ 0
Direct labor	6,000	2,000	1,000
Factory overhead	8,500*	6,000	1,000
Total	$24,500	$ 8,000	$ 2,000

* Including $200 for disposal of waste.

- Selling prices:

MP1	$100 per unit
MP2	$ 58 per unit
BP	$ 10 per unit
Scrap	$ 5 per unit

- Brooks uses an actual cost system and allocates joint costs to major products on the basis of their relative net realizable values at the split-off point. By-products and scrap are costed at their net realizable value.

REQUIREMENT

Prepare journal entries for February activities in Departments 1, 2, and 3.

The solution to this problem is found at the end of the Chapter 5 problems and exercises.

EXERCISES

5–1 T Fundamentals of Joint Cost Allocation: No Separate Costs

Charlie's Longhorn Restaurant purchases bulk sirloin on the hook. After the meat is aged for an appropriate period of time, a meat cutter divides the bulk sirloin into the several portions and styles of meat served in the restaurant. During a recent week 2,000 pounds of meat that cost $2.10 per pound were cut into 2,685 individual servings. Information about these servings is as follows:

Item	*Servings*	*Total weight (oz)*	*Unit sales value*	*Total sales value*
6 oz. sirloin	10	60	$1.50	$ 15
8 oz. sirloin	1,550	12,400	1.70	2,635
12 oz. sirloin	800	9,600	2.00	1,600
16 oz. sirloin	60	960	3.00	180
Hamburger (8 oz.)	140	1,120	1.00	140
Kabob (8 oz.)	125	1,000	3.44	430
Total	2,685			$5,000

REQUIREMENTS

a) Determine the cost per serving of each joint product using:

1. Physical measures that allocate an equal cost to all units produced.
2. Physical measures based on weight.
3. Relative sales values.

Round calculations to three decimal places.

b) Evaluate the costs per serving developed in part (a). Are any of them likely to give management misleading signals about individual products?

5–2 T Fundamentals of Joint Cost Allocation: No Separate Costs

Presented is information pertaining to the July 19x0 operations of the Moody Company.

	Product		
	AAA	*BBB*	*CCC*
Physical measures:			
Units produced	4,000	3,000	3,000
Total weight	5,000 lbs	5,000 lbs	10,000 lbs
Final unit selling price	$40.00	$20.00	$10.00
Total joint costs	$90,000		

REQUIREMENT

Determine the unit cost of each product when joint costs are allocated on the basis of:

1. Units produced.
2. Weight.
3. Relative net realizable value.

5–3 T Fundamentals of Joint Cost Allocation: Separate Costs

Presented is information pertaining to the July 19y3 operations of the Sheldon Company.

	Product			
	X1	*X2*	*X3*	*X4*
Physical measures:				
Units produced	5,000	4,000	8,000	3,000
Total volume	15,000 gal	15,000 gal	20,000 gal	10,000 gal
Final unit selling price	$5.00	$8.00	$4.00	$9.00
Separate processing costs	$20,000	$0	$16,000	$0
Total joint costs	$180,000			

REQUIREMENT

Determine the final unit cost of each product when joint costs are allocated on the basis of:

1. Units produced.
2. Volume.
3. Relative net realizable value.

5–4 T Fundamentals of Joint Cost Allocation: Separate Costs

The Daffodil Co. Ltd. manufactures three products—D, F, and L. The first part of the manufacturing process is joint, and for the current period joint materials cost $60,000 and joint processing costs $40,000. Other current information is as follows:

	Separate processing costs	*Number of units produced*	*Number of units sold*	*Sales price*
D	$ 60,000	5,000	4,000	$20
F	40,000	2,000	1,500	30
L	140,000	7,000	6,300	40

REQUIREMENTS

a) Determine, by product and in total, the costs to be assigned the finished goods inventory for financial reporting purposes when joint costs are allocated using:

1. Physical measures that allocate an equal cost to all units produced.
2. Relative net realizable value.

Round calculations to two decimal places.

b) Daffodil now discovers that it would be possible to sell products D and F at the split-off point. Prices would be $10 for D and $8 for F. Should they sell these products at the split-off point or process them further? (CGA Adapted)

5–5 Costing Joint Products and By-Products

The Athens Supply Company manufactures three joint products from a single process in batches that contain 40 units of Alpha, 100 units of Beta, and 100 units of Gamma. Unit weight and selling prices at the split-off point are:

Product	*Weight (kg)*	*Selling price*
Alpha	10	$ 50
Beta	15	120
Gamma	21	360

Processing costs total $30,000/batch.

REQUIREMENTS

a) Determine the unit cost of each joint product using:

1. Physical measures that allocate an equal cost to all units produced.
2. Physical measures based on weight.
3. Relative sales values.

b) Evaluate the unit costs developed in part (a). Are any of these likely to give management misleading signals about individual products? Are they acceptable for external reporting?

c) Assuming Alpha is regarded as a by-product, use the sales-value method to determine the unit cost of each major product when:

1. All by-product revenue is recorded as miscellaneous income.
2. By-products are costed at their net realizable value.

5–6 Costing Joint Products and By-Products

The Vertex Company manufactures two major products, MP1 and MP2, and one by-product, BP. All products are produced from a single input in Department 1. However, MP1 must undergo additional processing in Department 2 before it can be sold. Planned production for next month includes 20,000 units of MP1, 2,000 units of MP2, and 4,000 units of BP. Budgeted manufacturing costs are $300,000 in Department 1 and $80,000 in Department 2. Current unit selling prices of MP1 and MP2 are $20 and $40, respectively.

Management is concerned about the appropriate method of accounting for by-product BP. The selling price of BP has recently increased to $25/unit. In the past all by-product revenue was treated as miscellaneous income. The manager of MP1 argues that this procedure understates MP1 income; accordingly, she argues that BP should be treated as a full joint product rather than a by-product.

REQUIREMENTS

a) Determine the final per unit cost of MP1 when BP is treated as a joint product.

b) Determine the final per unit cost of MP1 when BP is treated as a by-product using the miscellaneous income approach.

c) Determine the final per unit cost of MP1 when BP is treated as a by-product using the net realizable value approach.

d) Briefly explain the differences in the preceding cost assignments.

5–7 Joint Cost Allocation: Multiple Split-Off Points

The Green Mountains Supply Company manufactures three final products, F, G, and H, and one intermediate product, R. During a recent month, the joint cost of producing 1,000 units of F and 2,000 units of R was $15,000. Product R was processed further into 1,000 units of G and 1,000 units of H at a cost of $12,000. Additional costs to complete G and H were $5,000 and $10,000, respectively. The unit selling prices of F, G, and H are $17, $10, and $20, respectively.

REQUIREMENTS

a) Determine the total production cost of each final product when joint costs are allocated on the basis of relative net realizable value.

b) Assuming that F, G, and H have no sales value before they are completed, what action should be taken if the selling price of H falls to $4/unit?

5–8 Joint Cost Allocation: Multiple Split-Off Points

In Department 1 the Cosmic Chemical Company utilizes 10 cubic meters of sea water to produce 1 unit of A and 2 units of B. Product A is sold immediately for $6/unit. Product B does not have a ready market and is processed further in Department 2. *Each unit* of B is converted into 1 unit of C *and* 1 unit of D. The selling price of products C and D are $5 and $3, respectively.

During May, Cosmic processed 50,000 cubic meters of sea water to obtain 5,000 units of A, 10,000 units of C, and 10,000 units of D. May operating costs were:

Department 1	$40,000 (all fixed)
Department 2	$60,000 (all variable at a rate of $6 per unit of B processed)

There are no separate costs of A, C, or D. The sea water is costless.

REQUIREMENTS

a) Use the relative net realizable value method to determine the total costs allocated to products A, C, and D.

b) *Describe* how your answer to part (a) would differ if Product B could be sold at the split-off point.

c) *Describe* how your answer to part (a) would differ if Product D were regarded as a by-product.

d) If the market price of Product C fell to $0.50/unit, what action would you recommend? Assume the plant is operating at capacity. Support your answer with computations.

5–9 Sell or Process Further

The Los Alamos Chemical Company manufactures two products, X1 and X2, from a single input X. During a recent month 100,000 units of X were processed into 60,000 units of X1 and 40,000 units of unfinished X2 at a cost of $180,000. All units of X2 were completed at an additional cost of $20,000. The unit selling prices of X1 and X2 are $2.00 and $3.50, respectively.

REQUIREMENTS

a) Determine the final unit costs of X1 and X2 when joint costs are allocated on the basis of relative net realizable value.

b) Assuming that X2 could be sold at the split-off point or processed further, describe how the joint costs should be allocated when relative net realizable value is used.

c) If X2 can be sold for $1.75 at the split-off point, should management sell it then or process it further?

5–10 Sell or Process Further

From a particular process, the Acme Chemical Company produces three grades of Ultradine in the ratio of 1:1:1. The selling prices for each grade of Ultradine are:

Grade 1: $15/liter   Grade 2: $10/liter   Grade 3: $4/liter

Grades 2 and 3 may be processed further into grades 1 and 2, respectively, if additional costs are incurred. Because of high demand for the top grades of Ultradine, the Acme Chemical Company performed this additional processing in 19x8. They also allocated joint-processing costs of $60,000 to all units produced on the basis of liters. The 19x8 cost of goods manufactured for grades 1 and 2 are:

Grade	*Liters produced*	*Cost of goods manufactured*
1	40,000	$120,000
2	20,000	160,000

REQUIREMENT

Determine the net advantage or disadvantage of further processing of grades 2 and 3.

5–11 Profitability Analysis of Joint Products

Linda Jones, the Vice President of Central Industries, is evaluating the profitability of one of the firm's joint products. A partial product-line income statement for that product is as follows:

Central Industries
Product T, Partial Income Statement
For the Year Ending June 30, 19x1

Sales (16,000 units)		$288,000
Cost of goods sold:		
Materials	$128,000	
Conversion (all variable)	144,000	−272,000
Gross profit		$ 16,000

ADDITIONAL INFORMATION

- Product T is produced from the intermediate Product H.
- H can be sold for $8/unit and purchased for $10/unit.
- Joint costs allocated to the intermediate Product H, on the basis of relative net realizable values, amount to $6/unit.
- Central Industries produces 8,000 units of H each year.

REQUIREMENT

Prepare a report evaluating the current profitability of Product T. Make any appropriate suggestions that would enable Central Industries to increase its earnings.

PROBLEMS

5–12 Journal Entries for Joint Products

The ACE Company manufactures Products A and B in Department 1. Neither product has a sales value. Product A is processed into salable Products C and D in Department 2. Product B is processed into salable Products E and F in Department 3. On November 1, 19x9, there was no work-in-process in any department.

November production cost information is as follows:

	Department		
	1	*2*	*3*
Transferred-in	$ 0	$?	$?
Direct materials	10,000	0	1,000
Direct labor	5,000	10,000	4,000
Factory overhead	5,000	10,000	5,000

There was no November 30, 19x9, work-in-process in any department.

Joint costs are allocated on the basis of relative net realizable value. The sales value of November production is:

Product	*Sales value*
A	$ 0
B	0
C	10,000
D	30,000
E	15,000
F	15,000
	$70,000

REQUIREMENTS

a) Prepare a diagram of relationships, a schedule of relative net realizable values, and a schedule allocating all joint costs to joint products.

b) Prepare journal entries for all November activities affecting work-in-process accounts.

c) If November's production of Product B could be sold for $5,000 should it have been processed further? Why or why not?

d) Assume that Product B is processed into E and F even though it is salable for $5,000 at the split-off point. Determine the allocation of Department 1 costs to Products A and B.

5–13 Journal Entries for Joint Products and By-Products

Lares Confectioners, Inc., makes a candy bar called Rey, which sells for $0.50 per pound. The manufacturing process also yields a product known as Nagu. Without further processing, Nagu sells for $0.10 per pound. With further processing, Nagu sells for $0.30 per pound. During April, total joint manufacturing costs up to the point of separation consisted of the following charges to Work-in-Process:

Raw materials	$150,000
Direct labor	120,000
Factory overhead	30,000

Production for the month aggregated 394,000 pounds of Rey and 30,000 pounds of Nagu. To complete Nagu during April and obtain a selling price of $0.30 per pound, further processing of Nagu during April would entail the following additional costs:

Raw materials	$2,000
Direct labor	1,500
Factory overhead	500

REQUIREMENTS

Prepare the April journal entries of Nagu, if Nagu is:

a) Transferred as a by-product at sales value to the warehouse without further processing, with a corresponding reduction of Rey's manufacturing costs.

b) Further processed as a by-product and transferred to the warehouse at net realizable value, with a corresponding reduction of Rey's manufacturing costs.

c) Further processed and transferred to finished goods, with joint costs being allocated between Rey and Nagu based on relative sales value at the split-off point

(CGA Adapted)

5–14 Journal Entries for Joint Products and By-Products

The Davis Company produces two major products, X and Y, and one by-product, Z, in two production departments. Joint costs are allocated to major products on the basis of relative net realizable value. The by-product is recorded at its net realizable value at the time of production. Unit selling prices are stable at $10, $25, and $2 for X, Y, and Z, respectively.

During January the following events occurred:

- In Department I:

Production of X	1,000 units
Production of intermediate Y	2,000 units
Direct materials cost	$ 8,000
Direct labor cost	$10,000
Overhead applied	$ 8,000
Actual overhead	$ 8,500

- In Department II:

Production of final Y	2,000 units
Production of Z	500 units
Direct labor costs	$15,000
Overhead applied	$ 6,000
Actual overhead	$ 6,100

ADDITIONAL INFORMATION

- Davis uses a normal cost system with separate work-in-process and overhead control accounts for Departments I and II.
- There are no beginning or ending inventories of work-in-process.

REQUIREMENTS

a) Prepare a schedule allocating the joint costs of Department I to Product X and intermediate Product Y.

b) Prepare journal entries to record all January activities in Departments I and II.

5–15 Costing Joint Products and By-Products with Shrinkage: Multiple Departments

The Harrison Corporation produces three products—Alpha, Beta, and Gamma. Alpha and Gamma are joint products, whereas Beta is a by-product of Alpha. No joint cost is to be allocated to the by-product. The production processes for a given year are as follows:

- In Department I, 110,000 units of raw material, Rho, are processed at a total cost of $120,000. After processing in Department I, 60 percent of the units are transferred to Department II and 40 percent of the units (now Gamma) are transferred to Department III.

- In Department II, the material is further processed at a total additional cost of \$38,000. Seventy percent of the units (now Alpha) are transferred to Department IV and 30 percent emerge as Beta, the by-product, to be sold at \$1.20 per unit. Selling expenses related to disposing of Beta are \$8,100.
- In Department III, Gamma is processed at a total additional cost of \$165,000. In this department, a normal loss of units of Gamma occurs which equals 10 percent of the good output of Gamma. The remaining good output of Gamma is then sold for \$12 per unit.
- In Department IV, Alpha is processed at a total additional cost of \$23,660. After this processing, Alpha is ready for sale at \$5 per unit.

REQUIREMENT

Prepare a schedule showing the allocation of the \$120,000 joint cost between Alpha and Gamma using the relative net sales value approach. The net realizable value of Beta should be treated as an addition to the sales value of Alpha. You should diagram the physical relationships before starting, clearly indicating the final outputs in pounds. (CPA Adapted)

5–16 Joint Products and By-Products with Shrinkage: Multiple Departments[3] Oscar's Meat Shop processes slaughtered cattle into several by-products and cuts of meat. Oscar has three departments: Killing, Chilling, and Processing. In the Killing Department steers are slaughtered and by-products such as cowhide are separated from the main products. In this department a 1,000-pound steer normally yields a 600-pound carcass. The carcass is then sent to the Chilling Department where it is aged for a minimum of two weeks. From the Chilling Department the carcass is transferred to the Processing Department where it is carved into the cuts required by retail outlets. In this department a 600-pound carcass normally yields 24 pounds of scrap and 576 pounds of the following final joint products:

Product	*Weight in lbs.*	*Selling price/lb.*	*Total selling price*
Chuck	164	\$1.50	\$246
Brisket	25	0.80	20
Shank	18	1.50	27
Short plate	48	1.25	60
Flank	30	1.20	36
Rib	63	2.00	126
Loin	100	2.25	225
Round	128	1.75	224
	576		\$964

By-products and scrap are recorded at their net realizable value. The by-products of a 1,000-pound steer normally sell for \$70 at the end of processing in

[3] Adapted from "The High Price of Beef: How One Company Accounts for It," by Kailas J. Rao, *Management Accounting*, **61,** No. 2 (August 1979): 37–40: 48, with permission.

the Killing Department. The scrap accumulated in the Processing Department has a selling price of $0.25/pound.

The average *cost per pound of input* in each department is as follows:

	Department		
	Killing	*Chilling*	*Processing*
Transferred-in	$ 0	$?	$?
Direct materials	0.50	0	0.02
Direct labor	0.06	0.02	0.10
Factory overhead	0.05	0.02	0.20

REQUIREMENTS

a) Determine the average cost per pound of final product at the end of the processing operation.

b) Assuming joint costs are allocated to joint products on the basis of relative sales value, determine the cost per pound of each final product: (*Hint:* Determine the final joint cost for 576 pounds of joint product as a percent of the total selling price of 576 pounds of joint product.) Round calculations to three decimal places.

5–17 Process Costing and Joint Cost Allocation

The Gulf States Processing Company produces two products, A and B, in two production departments. In Department I, raw material Y is processed into A and B. Product A is sold immediately. Product B undergoes further processing in Department II. On April 1, 19x7, there were no beginning inventories of work-in-process. During April, the following events occurred:

- In Department I:

Production of A	2,000 units
Production of intermediate B	4,000 units
Total production costs	$10,000

- In Department II:

Production of final B	3,000 units
Conversion costs	$10,500

ADDITIONAL INFORMATION

- The unit selling prices of A and B are $4 and $6, respectively.
- There is no ending inventory in Department I.
- The ending inventory in Department II is 50 percent complete as to conversion.
- Joint costs are allocated on the basis of relative net realizable value.

REQUIREMENT

Prepare a cost of production report for Department II.

5–18 FIFO Process Costing of Joint Products with Scrap: Journal Entries

Lehigh Manufacturing, Inc., produces two intermediate products, Z25 and Z95, and two final products, Z26 and Z96, from a single input. All production is started in Department I where two joint products, Z25 and Z95, are produced. In Department II Product Z25 is processed further into the salable Product Z26. In Department III Product Z95 is processed further into the salable Product Z96. The production of Z96 from Z95 results in certain amounts of scrap.

Lehigh uses a FIFO process costing system. Scrap is inventoried at its expected net realizable value. Joint costs are allocated on the basis of expected relative net realizable value.

Presented is selected production, cost, price, and inventory information for November 19x7.

Production Information:

Department I	8,000 units Z25, 2,000 units Z95
Department II	8,000 units Z26
Department III	2,000 units Z96, 500 kilograms scrap

Cost Information:	*Direct materials*	*Direct labor*	*Manufacturing overhead*
Department I	$28,000	$40,000	$12,000
Department II	0	20,000	7,500*
Department III	0	15,000	16,000

Price Information:

Z26	$11.50/unit
Z96	30.00/unit
Scrap	2.00/kilogram

Inventory Information:	*November 1*		*November 30*
Department I	0 units	$ 0	0
Department II	5,000 units†	$10,000	5,000 units‡
Department III	0 units	$ 0	0

* All variable.
† 40 percent complete as to conversion.
‡ 80 percent complete as to conversion.

REQUIREMENTS

a) Determine the cost per equivalent unit of conversion manufactured this period in Department II.

b) Allocate the Department I production costs to Z25 and Z95.

c) For November 19x7 prepare *all* journal entries affecting all work-in-process accounts.

5–19 Joint Cost Allocation and Decision Analysis

The following is taken from the August 28, 1981, *Wall Street Journal.*

> The hen has an awesome job keeping people in omelets and fried chicken. It's an important, if thankless calling.
>
> The chicken farmer has a big job, too, cleaning up after his birds. "That is and always has been our No. 1 problem," says Russ Dugan, Vice President of Farmegg Products Inc. in Humboldt, Iowa.

> Mr. Dugan speaks with authority. Farmegg's 750,000 layers, as hens in the egg trade are called, produce 650 tons of this problem each week. Of course, as farmers know, animal droppings have their uses.
>
> Indeed, Joseph Brill, a 60-year-old part-time inventor and former poultry-farm manager from Snover, Michigan, has designed a machine that in just 48 hours can turn 10 tons of chicken excrement into five tons of dry, odorless flakes for use as a fertilizer and cattle-feed supplement.

Assume Clucker Products has 500,000 layers. Clucker incurs monthly operating costs of \$2,000,000 to produce \$3,750,000 in monthly revenue from egg sales and \$200,000 in monthly revenue from chicken sales. Prior to June 1, 19x7, Clucker paid a sanitation company an additional \$20,000 each month to dispose of chicken excrement. On June 1, 19x7, Clucker leased several Brill Digesters which can process Clucker's monthly chicken excrement into chicken flakes which can be sold for \$60,000. The monthly cost of leasing and operating the digesters is \$10,000.

REQUIREMENTS

a) Assuming the eggs, flakes, and chicken sales are all treated as joint products, allocate the \$2,000,000 in monthly operating costs to each on the basis of relative net realizable value. Round calculations to four decimal places.

b) In your opinion, should the eggs, flakes, and chicken sales all be regarded as joint products? Why or why not?

c) How much have Clucker Products monthly profits increased as a result of the use of the Brill Digesters?

5–20 Joint Cost Allocation and Decision Analysis

Talor Chemical Company is a highly diversified chemical processing company. The company manufactures swimming pool chemicals, chemicals for metal processing companies, specialized chemical compounds for other companies, and a full line of pesticides and insecticides.

Currently the Norwood plant is producing two derivatives, RNA-1 and RNA-2, from the chemical compound VDB developed by Talor's research labs. Each week 1,200,000 pounds of VDB are processed at a cost of \$246,000 into 800,000 pounds of RNA-1 and 400,000 pounds of RNA-2. The proportion of these two outputs is fixed and cannot be altered because this is a joint process. RNA-1 has no market value until it is converted into a product with the trade name Fastkil. The cost to process RNA-1 into Fastkil is \$240,000. Fastkil wholesales at \$50 per 100 pounds.

RNA-2 is sold as is for \$80 per hundred pounds. However, Talor has discovered that RNA-2 can be converted into two new products through further processing. The further processing would require the addition of 400,000 pounds of compound LST to the 400,000 pounds of RNA-2. The joint process would yield 400,000 pounds each of DMZ-3 and Pestrol—the two new products. The additional raw material and related processing costs of this joint process would be \$120,000. DMZ-3 and Pestrol would each be sold for \$57.50 per 100 pounds. Talor's management has decided not to process RNA-2 further based on the analysis presented in the following schedule. Talor uses the physical method to allocate the common costs arising from joint processing.

		Process Further		
	RNA-2	*DMZ-3*	*Pestrol*	*Total*
Production in pounds	400,000	400,000	400,000	
Revenue	$320,000	$230,000	$230,000	$460,000
Costs:				
VDB costs	$ 82,000	$ 61,500	$ 61,500	$123,000
Additional raw materials (LST) and processing of RNA-2	0	60,000	60,000	120,000
Total costs	−82,000	−121,500	−121,500	−243,000
Weekly gross profit	$238,000	$108,500	$108,500	$217,000

A new staff accountant who was to review the preceding analysis commented that it should be revised and stated, "Product costing of products such as these should be done on a net relative sales value basis not a physical volume basis."

REQUIREMENTS

a) Discuss whether the use of the net relative sales value method would provide data more relevant for the decision to market DMZ-3 and Pestrol.

b) Critique the Talor Company's analysis and make any revisions that are necessary. Your critique and analysis should indicate:

1. Whether Talor Chemical Company made the correct decision.
2. The gross savings (loss) per week of Talor's decision not to process RNA-2 further, if different from the company prepared analysis. (CMA Adapted)

5–21 Costing Joint Products with Shrinkage and Intermediate Inventories: Challenge Problem

Amaco Chemical Company manufacturers several products:

- In Department 1, the two materials amanic acid and bonyl hydroxide are used to produce Amanyl, Bonanyl, and Am-Salt. Amanyl is sold to others who use it as a raw material in the manufacture of stimulants. Bonanyl is not salable without further processing. Although Am-Salt is a commercial product for which there is a ready market, Amaco does not sell this product, preferring to submit it to further processing.
- In Department 2, Bonanyl is processed into the marketable product, Bonanyl-X. The relationship between Bonanyl used and Bonanyl-X produced has remained constant for several months.
- In Department 3, Am-Salt and the raw material colb are used to produce Colbanyl, a liquid propellant which is in great demand. As an inevitable part of this process, Demanyl is also produced. Demanyl was discarded as scrap until discovery of its

usefulness as a catalyst in the manufacture of glue; for two years Amaco has been able to sell all of its production of Demanyl.

In its financial statements, Amaco states inventory at the lower of cost (on the first-in, first-out basis) or market. Unit costs of the items most recently produced must therefore be computed. Costs allocated to Demanyl are computed so that, after allowing for packaging and selling costs of $0.04/pound, no profit or loss will be recognized on sales of this product.

Certain data for October 19x2 follow:

Raw materials	*Pounds used*	*Total cost*
Amanic acid	6,300	$5,670
Bonyl hydroxide	9,100	6,370
Colb	5,600	2,240

Conversion costs (labor and overhead)	*Total cost*
Department 1	$33,600
Department 2	3,306
Department 3	22,400

Products	*Pounds produced*	*Inventories (pounds)*		*Sales price per pound*
		Sept. 30	*Oct. 31*	
Amanyl	3,600			$ 6.65
Bonanyl	2,800	210	110	
Am-Salt	7,600	400	600	6.30
Bonanyl-X	2,755			4.20
Colbanyl	1,400			43.00
Demanyl	9,800			0.54

There are no beginning or ending work-in-process inventories in Departments 1, 2, or 3.

REQUIREMENTS

Prepare for October 19x2 the following schedules. Supporting computations should be prepared in good form. Round answers to the nearest cent.

a) Cost per pound of Amanyl, Bonanyl, and Am-Salt produced using the relative net sales value method.

b) Cost per pound of Amanyl, Bonanyl, and Am-Salt produced using the average unit cost method.

c) Cost per pound of Colbanyl produced. Assume that the cost per pound of Am-Salt produced was $3.40 in September 19x2 and $3.50 in October 19x2. (CPA Adapted)

SOLUTION TO REVIEW PROBLEM

Prior to preparing journal entries for February activities in Departments 1, 2, and 3, a schedule allocating the joint costs of Department 1 must be prepared.

The physical relationships and points of cost incurrence are as follows:

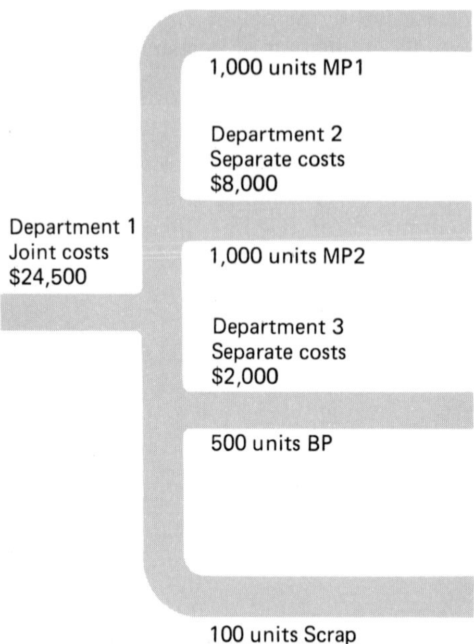

The net realizable value of the scrap and by-product are deducted from the joint costs of Department 1. The remaining Department 1 costs are then allocated to MP1 and MP2 on the basis of their relative net realizable values.

Dept. 1 costs			$24,500
Less:			
Net realizable value of BP:			
Sales value (500 × $10)	$5,000		
Dept. 3 costs	−2,000	$3,000	
Net realizable value of scrap:			
Sales value (100 × $5)		500	−3,500
Dept. 1 costs allocated to MP1 and MP2			$21,000

Product	*Sales value*		*Separate costs*		*Net realizable value*	*Relative net realizable value*
MP1	(1,000 × $100)	−	0	=	$100,000	⅔
MP2	(1,000 × $ 58)	−	$8,000	=	50,000	⅓
					$150,000	1.00

Product	*Joint costs*	*Relative net realizable value*	*Allocation*
MP1	$21,000	× ⅔	$14,000
MP2		× ⅓	7,000
			$21,000

Journal Entries (Order May Vary Slightly)

Account	Debit	Credit
Work-in-Process: Department 1	$24,500	
Stores Control		$10,000
Payroll Payable		6,000
Factory Overhead Control: Department 1		8,500
Finished Goods Inventory (for MP1)	14,000	
Scrap Inventory	500	
Work-in-Process: Department 2 (for MP2)	7,000	
Work-in-Process: Department 3 (for BP)	3,000	
Work-in-Process: Department 1		24,500
Work-in-Process: Department 2	8,000	
Payroll Payable		2,000
Factory Overhead Control: Department 2		6,000
Work-in-Process: Department 3	2,000	
Payroll Payable		1,000
Factory Overhead Control: Department 3		1,000
Finished Goods Inventory (for MP2)	15,000	
Work-in-Process: Department 2		15,000
By-Product Inventory (for BP)	5,000	
Work-in-Process: Department 3		5,000

6 Allocating Service Department and Other Indirect Costs

INTRODUCTION
COST POOLS AND COST OBJECTIVES
PURPOSES OF COST ALLOCATION
SERVICE DEPARTMENT COST ALLOCATION
PREDETERMINED ALLOCATION RATES FOR SERVICE DEPARTMENTS
ALLOCATION OF NONMANUFACTURING COSTS
SUMMARY
APPENDIX: BASIC ELEMENTS OF MATRIX ALGEBRA

INTRODUCTION

THE PRIMARY ACTIVITIES OF MANUFACTURING PLANTS TAKE PLACE IN **PRODUCTION DEPARTMENTS** where raw materials are physically transformed into finished goods. To help facilitate the operation of production departments many manufacturing organizations establish **service departments.** Service departments are not directly engaged in production activities; instead, they provide services to production departments. Typical service departments include Security, Work Scheduling, Maintenance, Power Generation, Personnel, and Factory Supervision.

Because service departments exist to facilitate the manufacture of products intended for future sale, service department costs are product costs that should be assigned to products as they are produced and should be expensed when products are sold. If a factory places all overhead costs in a single plant-wide overhead cost pool and assigns all factory overhead costs to products with a plant-wide overhead rate, service department costs should be placed in this cost pool. Most factories containing two or more production departments can achieve better cost assignments by using separate overhead rates for each production department. If, however, separate departmental overhead rates are used, service department costs must be allocated to the factory overhead control accounts of individual production departments, where they are combined with other overhead costs before being reassigned to products.

The primary purpose of this chapter is to introduce, illustrate, and evaluate techniques used to allocate service department costs to production departments. We will also study the development of predetermined departmental overhead rates. Although our initial focus is on product costing for the purpose of external reporting, we will also consider other purposes for which service department costs are allocated and the allocation of nonmanufacturing costs.

COST POOLS AND COST OBJECTIVES

A **cost pool** was defined in Chapter 3 as a group of related costs allocated together to cost objectives. **Cost objectives** were in turn defined as objects to which costs are assigned. Factory Overhead Control was presented as an example of a cost pool, and jobs were presented as examples of cost objectives. In product costing, factory overhead costs are accumulated in cost pools before being assigned to cost objectives.

When departmental overhead rates are used, each service department's operating costs are accumulated in a separate cost pool before being allocated to production departments. Once service department costs are allocated to production departments, they are pooled with other factory overhead costs and reallocated to products. These allocations and reallocations produce a hierarchy of cost pools and cost objectives, as illustrated in Exhibit 6–1.

Exhibit 6–1 illustrates the hierarchy of cost pools and cost objectives in a factory containing one service department, Power, and two production departments, P1 and P2. All the costs of operating the power department are accumulated in Power Department Control, which is supported by a subsidiary ledger indicating the exact nature of each Power Department cost, such as salaries and wages, fuel, maintenance, depreciation, and so forth. Power Department Control is a *cost pool;* the costs in this pool are allocated to Factory Overhead Control: P1 and Factory Overhead Control: P2. From the perspective of the Power Department Control account, Factory Overhead Control: P1 and Factory Overhead Control: P2 are *cost objectives*.

EXHIBIT 6–1 Cost Allocation Terminology

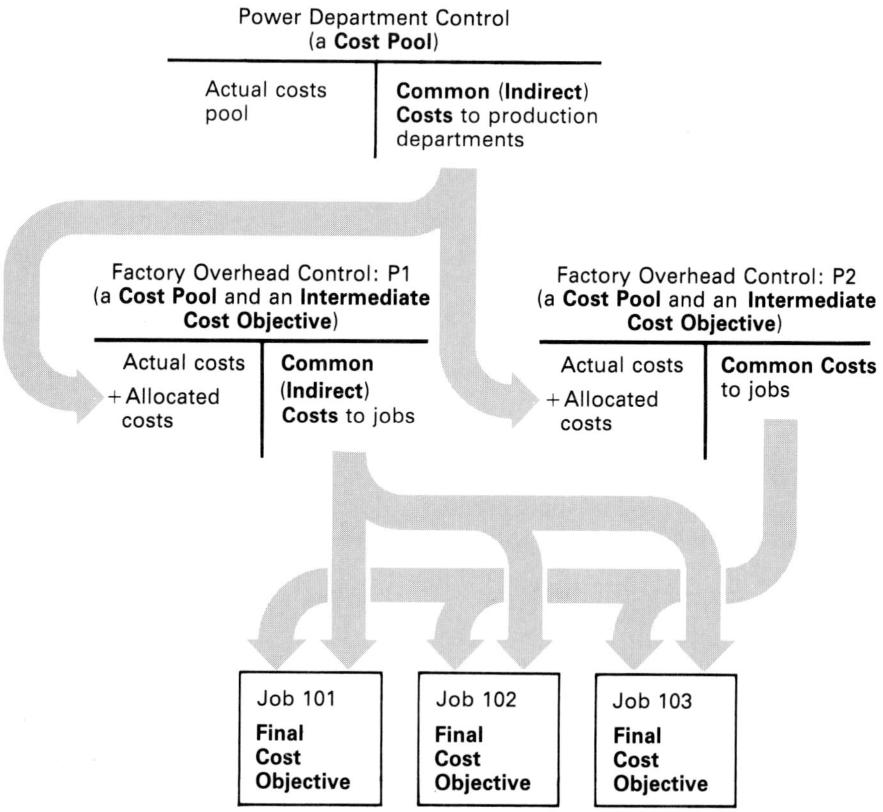

But the costs allocated to the departmental factory overhead control accounts plus all other overhead costs of each production department are subsequently reallocated to individual jobs. Consequently each departmental overhead control account is also an **intermediate cost objective,** that is, a cost objective to which costs are allocated and from which costs are reallocated to other cost objectives. Once costs are assigned to individual jobs they follow the job to which they are assigned through the inventory accounts and eventually to Cost of Goods Sold. Thus each individual job is best described as a **final cost objective,** that is, an objective from which costs are not reassigned to other cost objectives.

The costs accumulated in cost pools are often identified as **common costs,** that is, costs incurred for the benefit of two or more cost objectives. One of the most significant planning problems with which cost accountants are asked to assist is the determination of the impact of activity changes in cost objectives on the incurrence of common costs. Some common costs may vary with activity, but many will not. Additionally the relationship between cost objective activities and the incurrence of common costs is often difficult to determine. This is especially true as we move farther away from final cost objectives and toward common costs incurred in service departments.

From the perspective of a cost objective, allocated common costs are often identified as **indirect costs**, that is, costs allocated to a cost objective from a cost pool. In Chapter 2 factory overhead costs assigned to individual products from the Factory Overhead Control cost pool were identified as *indirect product costs*. Direct materials and direct labor, which are not accumulated in a cost pool before being assigned to products, were identified as *direct product costs*. In a similar manner, the costs allocated to departments from service department cost pools are identified as **indirect departmental costs,** whereas other departmental costs that are not allocated from a cost pool are called **direct departmental costs.**

PURPOSES OF COST ALLOCATION

One of the major problems facing an organization is the determination of the optimal number of cost pools. We were introduced to this problem in Chapter 3 when we analyzed the product-costing implications of plant-wide and departmental overhead rates. Using a plant-wide rate allows us to pool all overhead costs in a single factory overhead control account. Using departmental rates requires us to establish separate overhead cost pools for each production department. There we concluded that, when the size and nature of the overhead costs associated with individual production departments differ and jobs spend varying portions of their total time in each production department, departmental overhead rates (and cost pools) provide more accurate product costs than a plant-wide overhead rate (and a single cost pool).

In theory, the costs accumulated in a cost pool should have as homogeneous (common) a relationship to the cost objective as possible. Because of the expense involved in establishing and operating cost pools, the practical test for determining the optimal number of cost pools is: "Do the benefits of more accurate cost assignments outweigh the related costs?" The answer to this question depends to a large extent on the intended use of the resulting cost information. Professors

Fremgen and Liao, in a study prepared for the National Association of Accountants, identified four distinct uses of allocated cost information:

1. *Financial reporting,* in which cost allocations are used to value assets and to determine income.
2. *Planning and decision analysis,* in which cost allocations are used to predict the financial effects of future actions.
3. *Pricing,* in which cost allocations are used to establish appropriate selling prices.
4. *Performance evaluation and control,* in which cost allocations are used to influence managers' behavior with respect to costs."[1]

Unfortunately the cost accounting systems found in many, if not most, organizations were established for the sole purpose of external reporting; and cost allocation practices that are used for external financial reporting may not be good enough for other purposes. Precise allocations are not required for financial reporting purposes. The cost allocation procedures need only be consistent, systematic in assigning product costs to products, and reasonable in allocating costs on the basis of benefit; and they must not result in product costs that exceed product selling prices. Clearly these criteria leave much leeway in establishing cost pools and selecting cost allocation procedures. It is likely that management will desire more accurate cost allocations for planning and decision analysis, pricing, and performance evaluation and control. Care should be taken to ensure that cost data developed primarily for the purpose of external reporting are not inadvertently used for other purposes.

If the cost accounting system is not designed for internal management uses, it will be a hindrance to decision making rather than an aid. Imprecise cost allocation can result in errors in predicting the need for financial resources, overpriced products that are not competitive, underpriced products that provide an inadequate profit or no profit, and performance measurements that injure employee morale or motivate them to take actions that are not in the best interests of the organization. We provide illustrations of these problems throughout this chapter, in subsequent chapters, and in end-of-chapter assignment material.

SERVICE DEPARTMENT COST ALLOCATION

In allocating service department costs to production departments, the cost accountant faces three significant problems:

1. Establishing the optimal number of cost pools and determining the costs that should go in each.
2. Selecting a basis for service department cost allocation.
3. Selecting a service department cost allocation technique.

In this chapter we sidestep the first problem and assume the organization has the optimal number of cost pools and that the proper costs are being assigned

---

[1] James M. Fremgen, and Shu S. Liao, *The Allocation of Corporate Indirect Costs* (New York: National Association of Accountants, 1981), p. 3.

to each pool. This issue is perhaps the most complex one facing cost accountants. Unfortunately little research has been done on this topic. In most organizations, the determination of the number of cost pools and the costs to go in each is a matter of professional judgment. Typically the cost accountant accepts the departmental organization structure as a given and establishes one overhead cost pool for each department. For now we will accept the convention of one overhead cost pool per department and move on to selecting a basis for service department cost allocation.

Basis of Service Department Cost Allocation

Service department costs should be allocated to other departments on a basis that reflects the type of activity in which the service department is engaged. The ideal basis should be logical, have a high correlation with the incurrence of service department costs, and be easy to implement. Following this rule, the costs of a personnel department might be allocated on the basis of the number of employees, the costs of a building and grounds department might be allocated on the basis of floorspace, and so forth. A list of some service departments and possible bases for allocating their costs is presented in Exhibit 6–2.

Self-Service Self-service refers to a department's consumption of its own service. Examples of self-service include electricity used by an electric power department and food consumed by cafeteria employees. Because all costs of operating a service department must be assigned to other departments, self-service must be ignored in service department cost allocation.

Example 6–1

Plastic Product's Plant Number 7 contains a cafeteria and three production departments. Information on the exact number of employees in each department is presented in the first row of Exhibit 6–3.

To encourage employees to remain at the plant during their lunch hour, the cafeteria serves meals at less than cost. The cafeteria's operating loss is allocated on the basis of the number of employees in each department. Self-service is ignored. Hence, as shown in the second row of Exhibit 6–3, the cafeteria's operating loss is allocated on the basis of the 240 employees in the other departments serviced rather than on the basis of the 250 plant employees. If the cafeteria had a monthly operating loss of $7,200, the loss would be allocated at

EXHIBIT 6–2 **Basis for Allocating Service Department Costs**

Buildings and Grounds—Square or cubic meters
Personnel—Number of employees or placements
Power—Kilowatt-hours used or capacity
Repairs and Maintenance—Number of calls or time
Cafeteria—Number of employees
Purchasing—Number of orders or cost of orders
Employee Health Services—Number of employees or calls
Warehouse (for raw materials)—Cost of materials used, number of requisitions

EXHIBIT 6–3 Basis for Allocating Cafeteria Department Costs

	Department receiving service				
		Other departments serviced			
	Self-service to cafeteria	*Production Department 1*	*Production Department 2*	*Production Department 3*	*Total*
Employees in all departments	10	120	60	60	250
Employees in other departments serviced		120	60	60	240
Percent distribution of services		50%	25%	25%	100%

the rate of $30 ($7,200/240) per employee. The journal entry allocating this loss is as follows:

Factory Overhead Control: Production Department 1	3,600	
Factory Overhead Control: Production Department 2	1,800	
Factory Overhead Control: Production Department 3	1,800	
Cafeteria Department Control		7,200

As a matter of convenience, we will frequently allocate service department costs on a percentage or proportional basis rather than on a unit basis. The appropriate percentages for Example 6–1 are shown in the last row of Exhibit 6–3. Using these percentages, the allocation of the cafeteria's operating loss is computed as follows:

Production Department 1 ($7,200 × 0.50)	$3,600
Production Department 2 ($7,200 × 0.25)	1,800
Production Department 3 ($7,200 × 0.25)	1,800
Total	$7,200

Cost Allocation Techniques

If service departments only served production departments, as in Example 6–1, the task of service department cost allocation would be hard enough, but service departments also serve other service departments. This leads to a complicated set of relationships between cost pools and cost objectives.

Example 6–2

The Jones Company's factory has three service departments, S1, S2, and S3, and two production departments, P1 and P2. Information about each of the service departments and cost data for July 19x0 are as follows:

Dept.	*Function*	*Basis of cost allocation*	*Direct operating cost*
S1	Personnel & employee services	Number of employees	$ 8,000
S2	Factory power	Kilowatt hours used (kwh)	18,000
S3	Maintenance & tool room	Time	5,000

The direct overhead costs of P1 and P2 for July 19x0 were $20,000 and $40,000, respectively.

EXHIBIT 6–4 Distribution of Services

	Department receiving service					
Department providing service	*S1*	*S2*	*S3*	*P1*	*P2*	*Total*
PART I ALL DEPARTMENTS						
S1	3	5	5	20	20	53 employees
S2	0	40,000	60,000	60,000	480,000	640,000 KWH
S3	60	240	60	180	120	660 hours
PART II OTHER SERVICED DEPARTMENTS						
S1	0	5	5	20	20	50 employees
S2	0	0	60,000	60,000	480,000	600,000 KWH
S3	60	240	0	180	120	600 hours
PART III PERCENTAGE DISTRIBUTION OF SERVICES						
S1	0	10%	10%	40%	40%	100%
S2	0	0	10%	10%	80%	100%
S3	10%	40%	0	30%	20%	100%

Information on the actual distribution of services during July is presented in Exhibit 6–4, part I. Eliminating self-service, the distribution of services to other departments receiving services is presented in Exhibit 6–4, part II. Finally, the percentage distribution of services to other departments receiving services is presented in Exhibit 6–4, part III.

Even though the Jones Company's factory service departments provide services to each other, all service department costs must be assigned to production departments. There are three basic techniques for service department cost allocation:

1. The direct method
2. The step (or step-down) method
3. The linear algebra method

The primary difference among them is in the amount of recognition each gives to services rendered other service departments.

Direct Method The **direct method** of service department cost allocation gives *no recognition* to services provided other service departments. The costs of each service department are allocated directly to production departments on the basis of the relative portion of services rendered each production department. For Example 6–2, the cost allocation pattern followed when the direct method is used is illustrated in Exhibit 6–5.

Although we could base the cost allocations on the information in Exhibit 6–4, part II, we will use the percentage distributions in Exhibit 6–4, part III.[2] The allocations using the direct method are shown in Exhibit 6–6. To perform these allocations, the *relative* percent of services rendered each production

[2] The linear algebra method, discussed later, requires information in percentage form.

EXHIBIT 6–5 Illustration of Service Department Cost Allocation Relationships: Direct Method

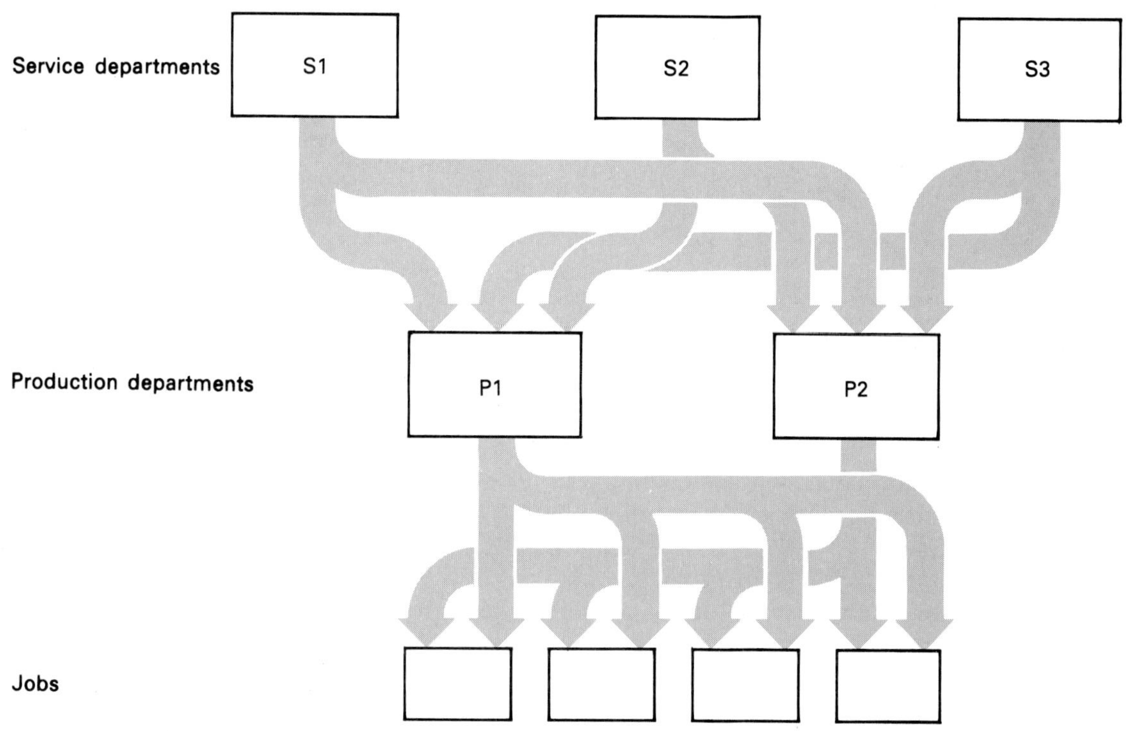

department was determined. Service Department S1 only provided 80 of its services to production departments (40 percent to P1 and 40 percent to P2), but the production departments are to receive 100 percent of S1's costs. The relative proportion of services S1 rendered each production department and the related cost allocations are as follows:

	S1	
Services provided to	*Computation of relative proportion*	*Allocation*
P1	40/(40 + 40) = 0.50	\$8,000 × 0.50 = \$4,000
P2	40/(40 + 40) = 0.50	\$8,000 × 0.50 = \$4,000

EXHIBIT 6–6 Service Department Cost Allocation: Direct Method

	Department					
	S1	*S2*	*S3*	*P1*	*P2*	*Total*
Direct department costs	\$ 8,000	\$ 18,000	\$ 5,000	\$20,000	\$40,000	\$91,000
S1 distribution	(8,000)			4,000	4,000	
S2 distribution		(18,000)		2,000	16,000	
S3 distribution			(5,000)	3,000	2,000	
Total production departmental overhead				\$29,000	\$62,000	\$91,000

Similar computations are made prior to the allocation of S2 and S3 costs. You are encouraged to verify the remaining allocations in Exhibit 6–6.

For product-costing purposes, the cost accountant would use the information contained in Exhibit 6–6 as the basis for a journal entry crediting control accounts for S1, S2, and S3, and debiting the overhead control accounts of P1 and P2:

Factory Overhead Control: Department P1	9,000	
Factory Overhead Control: Department P2	22,000	
Department S1 Control		8,000
Department S2 Control		18,000
Department S3 Control		5,000

Step Method The **step method** of service department cost allocation (sometimes identified as the **step-down method**) gives *some recognition* to services provided other service departments. The service departments are listed in decreasing order on the basis of the percentage of services they render other service departments.[3] Then, the costs of the service department listed first are allocated to other service and production departments. The process continues through the service department that provides the smallest portion of its services to other service departments. However, *once a service department's costs are allocated, no costs are subsequently reallocated to it.*

In each step of the allocation process, the allocation is based on the relative portion of services rendered departments that are to receive the allocation. If two service departments should happen to provide an equal relative portion of their services to other eligible service departments, the costs of the department that serves the greatest number of eligible service departments, or has the highest total costs (direct and indirect), should be allocated first. Care must be taken in each step of the allocation process to verify that the initial ordering of service departments has not changed. Because reallocations are not permitted in the step method, the sequence of service department allocations should be verified before each step on the basis of the portion of services rendered service departments eligible to receive cost allocations.

For Example 6–2, the cost allocation pattern followed using the step method is illustrated in Exhibit 6–7. Here S3 provides the greatest portion of its services to other service departments and S2 provides the smallest portion of its services to other service departments.

The allocation of the Jones Company's service department costs to production departments using the step method is shown in Exhibit 6–8. The costs of S3 are allocated first because S3 provides 50 percent of its services to other service departments, whereas S1 and S2 provide only 20 percent and 10 percent, respectively. Because S3 costs are allocated first, the relative portion of S3 services rendered departments receiving the allocation is the same as the percentage distribution of S3 services listed in Exhibit 6–4. The allocation of S3

---

[3] Other rules for ordering are possible. Ordering on the basis of total cost or the number of other service departments served are encountered in practice.

costs is as follows:

	S3	
Services provided to	*Relative percentage*	*Allocation*
S1	10	\$5,000 × 0.10 = \$ 500
S2	40	5,000 × 0.40 = 2,000
P1	30	5,000 × 0.30 = 1,500
P2	20	5,000 × 0.20 = 1,000

EXHIBIT 6–7 Illustration of Service Department Cost Allocation Relationships: Step Method

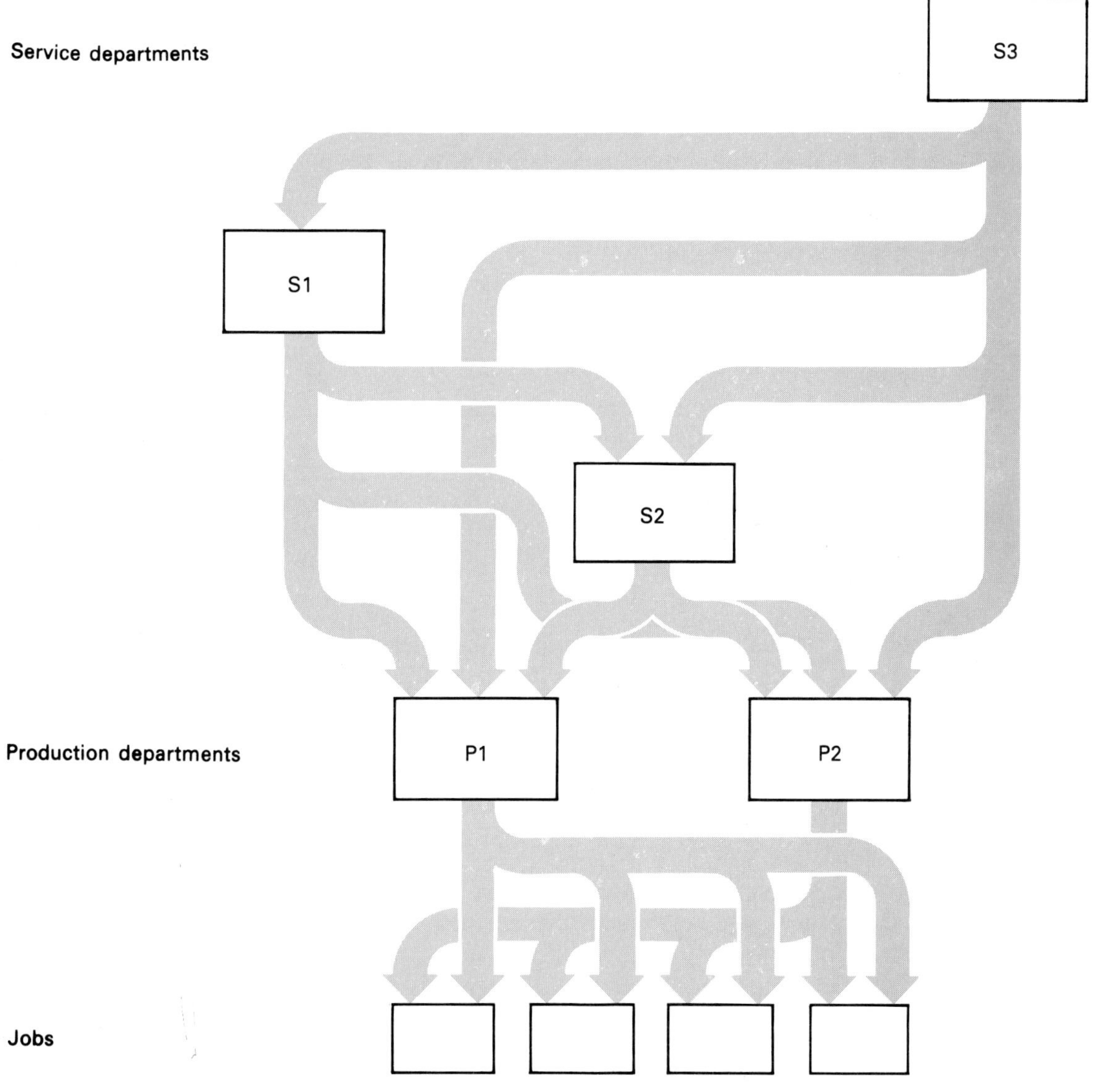

EXHIBIT 6–8 Service Department Cost Allocation: Step Method

	Department					
	S1	*S2*	*S3*	*P1*	*P2*	*Total*
Direct department costs	$ 8,000	$ 18,000	$ 5,000	$20,000	$40,000	$91,000
S3 distribution	500	2,000	(5,000)	1,500	1,000	
S1 distribution	(8,500)	944		3,778	3,778	
S2 distribution		(20,944)		2,327	18,617	
Total production departmental overhead				$27,605	$63,395	$91,000

At this point the ordering of the remaining service departments should be verified. Because S3 is ineligible to receive an allocation, the ordering of S1 and S2 should be verified on the basis of the relative portion of services they provide each other. In this case, S1 serves S2, whereas S2 does not serve S1. Consequently the initial ordering is not changed and S1 costs are allocated next.

Service Department S1 now has $8,500 to distribute, including direct departmental costs of $8,000 and indirect departmental costs of $500. Because no costs can be allocated to S3 after its costs have been allocated, the total costs of S1 must be assigned to the remaining departments on the basis of the relative proportion of services rendered each. The relative proportion of services S1 provides S2, P1, and P2, and the subsequent allocation, is:

	S1	
Services provided to	*Computation of relative percentage*	*Allocation*
S2	10/(10 + 40 + 40) = 0.1111	$8,500 × 0.1111 = $ 944*
P1	40/(10 + 40 + 40) = 0.4444	8,500 × 0.4444 = 3,778*
P2	40/(10 + 40 + 40) = 0.4444	8,500 × 0.4444 = 3,778*

* Rounded

Similar calculations are made prior to the allocation of S2's costs, which are only allocated to P1 and P2 because the costs of all other service departments were previously allocated. You are encouraged to verify the remaining allocations in Exhibit 6–8.

Correctly used, the step method usually provides more accurate cost allocations than the direct method. Yet, it is subject to some inaccuracy because it does not give complete recognition to reciprocal services. Of more serious concern in large organizations is the time required to determine the steps and perform the necessary computations (or to prepare a computer program). Additionally the step method may yield results that are less accurate than the direct method if the steps are improperly ordered.[4] If S2's costs are allocated first and S3's costs are

[4] The order in which service department costs are allocated under the step method is so important that Medicare reimbursement rules specify a standard sequence for the allocation of service department costs to revenue-producing centers.

EXHIBIT 6–9 Illustration of Service Department Cost Allocation Relationships: Linear Algebra Method

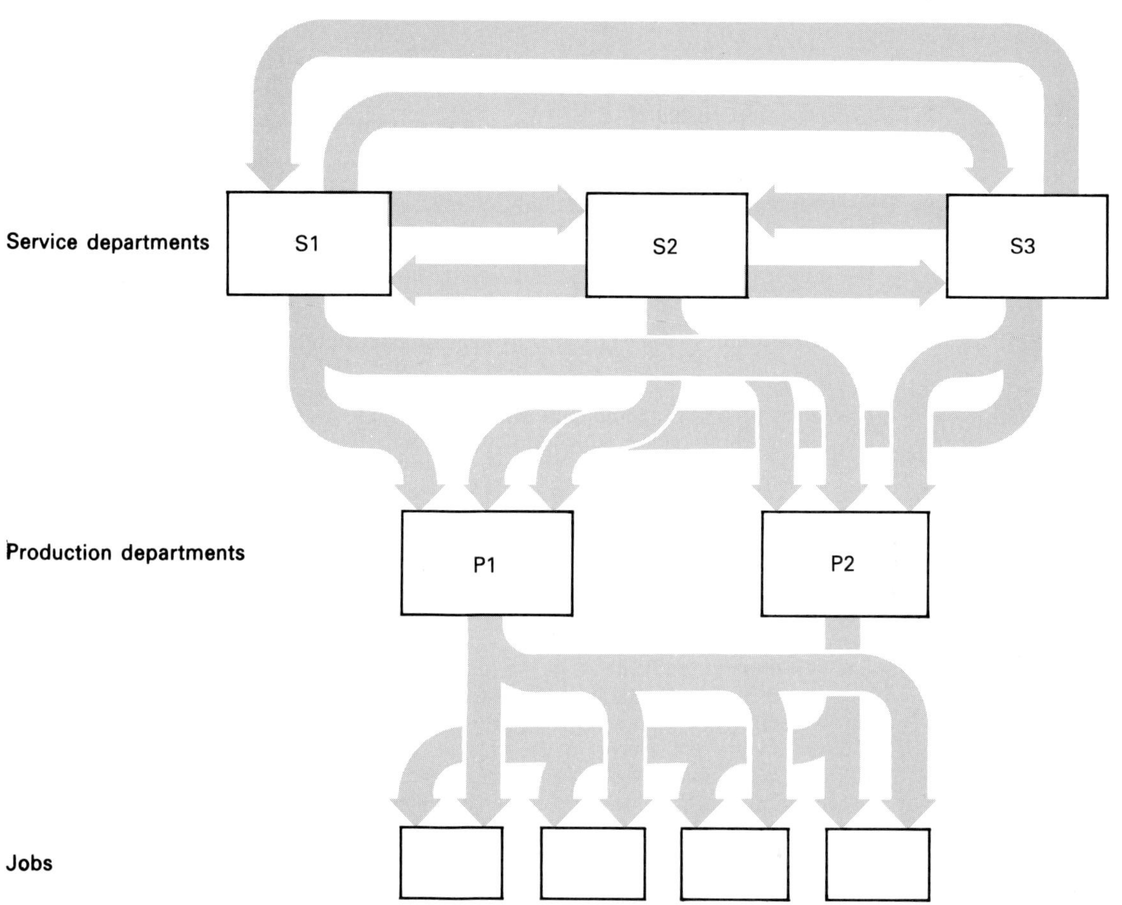

allocated last, total overhead costs for P1 and P2 are $29,969 and $61,032, respectively. A disproportionate share of S1 and S2 costs are allocated to P1 through S3.

Linear Algebra Method[5] The **linear algebra method** of service department cost allocation gives *complete recognition* to reciprocal services. A series of linear equations recognizing the services each department receives from all other departments is formulated and solved with the use of matrix algebra. Exhibit 6–9 contains an illustration of the cost allocation pattern followed when the linear algebra method is used. If computational facilities are available to perform matrix

[5] Students who need an introduction to or a review of matrix algebra should study the appendix to this chapter.

manipulations, the linear algebra method of service department cost allocation should be used. This method is an improvement over the step method because:

- The complete recognition of reciprocal services gives more accurate cost allocations.
- There is no danger of allocating costs in the wrong sequence.
- No time is required to determine a sequence of service department cost allocations.
- When applied to variable costs only, the linear algebra method provides data useful in estimating the internal cost of providing services.

We can formulate and solve service department cost allocation problems by matrix manipulations in several ways, but the most straightforward way to become familiar with the concepts is by following this sequence:

1. Develop a series of equations in which the variables represent the total overhead costs assigned to each production department or the total costs that flow through each service department:

$$
\begin{aligned}
P1 &= \$20{,}000 + 0P2 + 0.4S1 + 0.1S2 + 0.3S3\\
P2 &= \$40{,}000 + 0P1 + 0.4S1 + 0.8S2 + 0.2S3\\
S1 &= \$8{,}000 + 0P1 + 0P2 + 0.0S2 + 0.1S3\\
S2 &= \$18{,}000 + 0P1 + 0P2 + 0.1S1 + 0.4S3\\
S3 &= \$5{,}000 + 0P1 + 0P2 + 0.1S1 + 0.1S2
\end{aligned}
$$

   The first equation indicates that the total overhead costs assigned to P1 are equal to P1's direct overhead costs of $20,000 plus indirect overhead assigned from other departments. Overhead assigned to P1 includes 0 percent of P2's costs, and 40, 10, and 30 percent of the costs of S1, S2, and S3, respectively. These coefficients are taken from Exhibit 6–4. You are encouraged to state the meaning of the remaining equations in words. Note that on the right-hand side of all equations the production departments always have a coefficient of zero. This is because production department overhead costs are assigned to jobs rather than to other departmental overhead accounts.

2. Reformulate the equations so that all known dollar amounts are on the right and all variables and coefficients are on the left. When reformulating the equations, line up the variables in columns and always state the coefficient 1:

$$
\begin{aligned}
1P1 - 0P1 - 0.4S1 - 0.1S2 - 0.3S3 &= \$20{,}000\\
-0P1 + 1P2 - 0.4S1 - 0.8S2 - 0.2S3 &= \$40{,}000\\
-0P1 - 0P2 + 1.0S1 - 0.0S2 - 0.1S3 &= \$\ 8{,}000\\
-0P1 - 0P2 - 0.1S1 + 1.0S2 - 0.4S3 &= \$18{,}000\\
-0P1 - 0P2 - 0.1S1 - 0.1S2 + 1.0S3 &= \$\ 5{,}000
\end{aligned}
$$

3. Reformulate the equations in matrix notation as a coefficients matrix, a vector of unknowns, and a vector of knowns:

$$
\begin{bmatrix}
1 & 0 & -0.4 & -0.1 & -0.3\\
0 & 1 & -0.4 & -0.8 & -0.2\\
0 & 0 & 1.0 & 0.0 & -0.1\\
0 & 0 & -0.1 & 1.0 & -0.4\\
0 & 0 & -0.1 & -0.1 & 1.0
\end{bmatrix}
\cdot
\begin{bmatrix} P1\\ P2\\ S1\\ S2\\ S3 \end{bmatrix}
=
\begin{bmatrix} 20{,}000\\ 40{,}000\\ 8{,}000\\ 18{,}000\\ 5{,}000 \end{bmatrix}
$$

4. Solve for the unknowns by matrix manipulation:[6]

$$\begin{bmatrix} P1 \\ P2 \\ S1 \\ S2 \\ S3 \end{bmatrix} = \begin{bmatrix} 1 & 0 & -0.4 & -0.1 & -0.3 \\ 0 & 1 & -0.4 & -0.8 & -0.2 \\ 0 & 0 & 1.0 & 0.0 & -0.1 \\ 0 & 0 & -0.1 & 1.0 & -0.4 \\ 0 & 0 & -0.1 & -0.1 & 1.0 \end{bmatrix}^{-1} \cdot \begin{bmatrix} 20{,}000 \\ 40{,}000 \\ 8{,}000 \\ 18{,}000 \\ 5{,}000 \end{bmatrix}$$

$$\begin{bmatrix} P1 \\ P2 \\ S1 \\ S2 \\ S3 \end{bmatrix} = \begin{bmatrix} 1 & 0 & 0.4542 & 0.1402 & 0.4015 \\ 0 & 1 & 0.5458 & 0.8598 & 0.5985 \\ 0 & 0 & 1.0116 & 0.0105 & 0.1054 \\ 0 & 0 & 0.1475 & 1.0432 & 0.4320 \\ 0 & 0 & 0.1159 & 0.1054 & 1.0537 \end{bmatrix} \cdot \begin{bmatrix} 20{,}000 \\ 40{,}000 \\ 8{,}000 \\ 18{,}000 \\ 5{,}000 \end{bmatrix}$$

$$\begin{bmatrix} P1 \\ P2 \\ S1 \\ S2 \\ S3 \end{bmatrix} = \begin{bmatrix} 28{,}164.7 \\ 62{,}835.3 \\ 8{,}808.8 \\ 22{,}117.6 \\ 8{,}092.9 \end{bmatrix}$$

The total overhead costs of P1 and P2 are \$28,164.70 and \$62,835.30, respectively, including direct and indirect departmental overhead. For product-costing purposes, the cost accountant would use this information as the basis for a journal entry transferring costs from S1, S2, and S3 to P1 and P2:

Factory Overhead Control: P1	8,164.70	
Factory Overhead Control: P2	22,835.30	
S1 Department Control		8,000.00
S2 Department Control		18,000.00
S3 Department Control		5,000.00

The debits to Factory Overhead Control: P1 and Factory Overhead Control: P2 are less than their total overhead costs because the direct costs of \$20,000 and \$40,000 were assigned to these accounts from other sources. Because the objective is to allocate service department costs to production departments, the allocations could have been made without any knowledge of direct production department costs. Using the linear algebra method, the unknown direct costs of P1 and P2 could be set equal to zero; then, the values of P1 and P2 in Step 4 would be \$8,164.70 and \$22,835.30, respectively, the indirect costs allocated to these departments.

The credits to the service department control accounts are for the direct costs of each service department. The final amounts of S1, S2, and S3 in the linear algebra solution represent the total flow of costs through variables S1, S2, and S3. Because of allocations and reallocations involved in the solution techniques, the total flow of costs through S1, S2, and S3 exceeds the direct

---

[6] In general $\mathbf{A} \cdot \mathbf{X} = \mathbf{B}$, where **A** is the coefficient matrix, **X** is the vector of unknowns, and **B** is the vector of knowns. Solving for the vector of unknowns, $\mathbf{X} = \mathbf{A}^{-1} \cdot \mathbf{B}$. For an introduction to matrix algebra and a discussion of accounting applications of matrix algebra, see John K. Shank, *Matrix Methods in Accounting* (Reading, Mass.: Addison-Wesley, 1972).

costs of the service departments. However, once a cost is allocated to a production department, there are no subsequent reallocations.

Successive Allocation to Approximate the Linear Algebra Method The successive allocation of direct and indirect service department costs provides results that are very close to those obtained with the linear algebra method of service department cost allocation. The primary advantages of this approach are its relative simplicity and the accuracy of the final results. The primary disadvantage is the time required to perform the successive allocations or to develop an appropriate computer program.

The successive allocation approximation, like the linear algebra method, bases allocations on the original percentage distribution of services. Unlike the step method, successive allocation allows us to rank the service departments in any convenient order and it allows us to reallocate costs to service departments whose costs have been previously allocated. Unlike the other methods, successive allocation may require us to allocate costs from a service department several times. In each allocation, the total remaining costs assigned to a service department are allocated on the basis of the original percentage distribution of services. You must use professional judgment to determine when to stop the successive allocation process. Once this decision is made, the remaining service departments costs are allocated to production departments using the direct method.

The successive allocation approximation is illustrated, for the Jones Company, in Exhibit 6–10. The original percentage distribution of services in Exhibit 6–4, part III, is used in each allocation. In this particular case, the remaining service department costs are deemed insignificant after the third allocation; accordingly, they are allocated to production departments using the direct method.

Observe that with successive allocations, the costs assigned to P1 and P2 become closer and closer to those obtained by using the linear algebra method:

	P1	*P2*
Successive approximation:		
First allocation	$27,384.00	$59,776.00
Second allocation	28,123.58	62,680.58
Third allocation	28,161.30	62,828.72
Final result	28,163.19	62,836.82
Linear algebra method	$28,164.70	$62,835.30

If the successive allocations were repeated many times, the results would be the same as those obtained by using the linear algebra method.

In this example, the sequence of allocation was selected for convenience. Similar results would be obtained if another sequence, such as S2, S1, S3, were used.

Single and Dual Rate Methods The direct, step, or linear algebra methods can be used with either single or dual rates. The **single rate methods** do not distinguish between fixed and variable service department costs and allocate them together using some common basis. The **dual rate methods** distinguish between fixed and

EXHIBIT 6–10 **Successive Allocation to Approximate the Linear Algebra Method**

	Department					
	S1	*S2*	*S3*	*R1*	*R2*	*Total*
Direct overhead costs	$ 8,000.00	$ 18,000.00	$ 5,000.00	$20,000.00	$40,000.00	$91,000.00
First allocation:						
S1	(8,000.00)	800.00	800.00	3,200.00	3,200.00	
S2		(18,800.00)	1,880.00	1,880.00	15,040.00	
S3	768.00	3,072.00	(7,680.00)	2,304.00	1,536.00	
Intermediate results	$ 768.00	$ 3,072.00	$ 0.00	$27,384.00	$59,776.00	$91,000.00
Second allocation:						
S1	(768.00)	76.80	76.80	307.20	307.20	
S2		(3,148.80)	314.88	314.88	2,519.04	
S3	39.17	156.67	(391.68)	117.50	78.34	
Intermediate results	$ 39.17	$ 156.67	$ 0.00	$28,123.58	$62,680.58	$91,000.00
Third allocation:						
S1	(39.17)	3.92	3.92	15.67	15.67*	
S2		(160.59)	16.06	16.06	128.47*	
S3	2.00	7.99	(19.98)	5.99	4.00*	
Intermediate results	$ 2.00	$ 7.99	$ 0.00	$28,161.30	$62,828.72	$91,000.01
Direct allocation:						
S1	(2.00)			1.00	1.00	
S2		(7.99)		0.89	7.10*	
Final results				$28,163.19	$62,836.82	$91,000.01

* Computations reflect rounding to two decimal places.

variable service department costs and allocate them on separate bases. All the preceding examples used a single rate. If enough information were available, we could have developed dual rates for each and allocated variable and fixed costs separately.

The rationale underlying the dual rate methods is that fixed costs relate to the capacity to serve, whereas variable costs relate to the actual use of services. Consequently, if a service department's fixed costs are high because of the high potential service needs of a particular production department, that production department should be assigned its share of these capacity costs regardless of whether or not the capacity was actually used. The following example illustrates both the mechanics of the dual rate method and the significance of the decision to use a single or dual rate in a simple situation involving one service department and two production departments.

Example 6–3

During May 19x3, the Power Department incurred direct operating costs of $90,000, including fixed costs of $50,000 and variable costs of $40,000. The Power Department serves two production departments, P1 and P2, and has sufficient capacity to fill the maximum power needs of these production departments. Information on maximum potential monthly power consumption and actual May power consumption is as follows:

Use (kilowatt-hours)	*P1*	*P2*	*Total*
Maximum	400,000	1,600,000	2,000,000
Actual	400,000	400,000	800,000

The allocation of Power Department costs to P1 and P2 using single and dual rates is shown in Exhibit 6–11. The cost allocations to the production departments differ by $15,000 under the two methods, illustrating that the decision to use single or dual rates can have a significant impact on the assignment of service department costs to production departments and, ultimately, to products. In this example, most of the capacity of the Power Department is designed to serve the maximum needs of P2. Because P2 did not use this capacity in May, a single rate based on actual use shifts a disproportionate share of the Power Department's capacity costs to P1. If these costs were inappropriately used for management decision making, products produced in P1 might be overpriced or the supervisor of P1 might be asked to explain excessive costs over which he or she had no control.

By separating capacity and activity costs, the dual rate method provides more accurate cost assignments. In Example 6–3, P1 is not burdened with extra indirect costs merely because P2 did not operate at capacity. Furthermore, whenever it is possible to do so, it is desirable to separate costs on the basis of cost behavior. Management is often interested in knowing the variable and fixed costs of an activity or product. This information can only be provided if fixed and variable costs are separated throughout the cost accounting records.

EXHIBIT 6–11 Direct Method With Single and Dual Rates

a) Direct Method With Single Rate

	P1	*P2*	*Total*
Actual use (kilowatt-hours)	400,000	400,000	800,000
Percent of actual use	50	50	100
Allocation:			
Single rate	$ 45,000	$ 45,000	$ 90,000

b) Direct Method With Dual Rates

	P1	*P2*	*Total*
Maximum use (kilowatt-hours)	400,000	1,600,000	2,000,000
Actual use (kilowatt-hours)	400,000	400,000	800,000
Percent of maximum use	20	80	100
Percent of actual use	50	50	100
Allocation:			
Fixed costs	$ 10,000	$ 40,000	$ 50,000
Variable costs	20,000	20,000	40,000
Total	$ 30,000	$ 60,000	$ 90,000

Cost per Unit of Service

In the previous section, costs were allocated using percentage distributions of services. We could also have developed a cost per unit of service or a cost per unit of service capacity and allocated costs using these unit rates. In Example 6–3, the single rate allocation might have been stated as $0.1125 ($90,000/800,000) per kilowatt-hour and the dual rates might have been stated as $0.025 ($50,000/2,000,000) per kilowatt-hour and $0.05 ($40,000/800,000) per kilowatt-hour for fixed and variable Power Department costs, respectively. These rates per unit would produce the same allocations shown in Exhibit 6–11. It might be useful to verify this as an exercise.

PREDETERMINED ALLOCATION RATES FOR SERVICE DEPARTMENTS

To provide for more rapid cost allocations and to reduce the variability in cost allocations that might occur because of variations in the demand for services, many organizations develop predetermined cost allocation rates for service departments as well as predetermined overhead rates for production departments.

Predetermined cost allocation rates are often developed by reviewing the total costs and total activity of each service department during recent years. The predetermined rate is then set equal to or close to the actual rate of these previous periods. If experience subsequently proves the rate is too low, it is increased; and if experience subsequently proves the rate is too high, it is lowered.

Predetermined cost allocation rates can also be developed using information on service department cost behavior and the predicted demand for services. The necessary procedures are similar to those used to develop predetermined overhead rates for production departments. The four steps are as follows:

1. Determine the relationship between total costs and total activity.
2. Predict the coming year's activity. This requires information on the predicted demand for services by production and other service departments.
3. Use the cost estimating equation and the prediction of activity to predict total service department costs for the coming year.
4. Compute the predetermined cost allocation rate per unit of activity as predicted total service department costs divided by predicted activity.

When a predetermined cost allocation rate is used, service department costs probably will be overapplied or underapplied. These costs can be treated in a manner similar to overapplied or underapplied production department overhead. Leave the accounts open and treat the overapplied or underapplied service department costs as an adjustment to inventories on interim financial statements. At the end of the year any remaining balance is either prorated to the inventory accounts and the Cost of Goods Sold or written off. A remaining balance would be written off if it is small or if it is due to some unusual event of the current period. A remaining balance would be prorated if it is large and occurs because of an inappropriate allocation rate.

As service department cost allocations become a larger portion of total production costs, using predetermined overhead rates for service and production departments becomes increasingly desirable. This provides for rapid product costing, smooths out the bookkeeping workload, and ensures that similar units produced in different months have similar product costs.

ALLOCATION OF NONMANUFACTURING COSTS

The previous discussion was set in the context of a manufacturing firm that was primarily concerned with the financial reporting objective of product costing. When cost is an important factor in product pricing, or price justification, the allocation of service department costs takes on added significance. Indeed, for the purpose of product pricing or price justification, organizations frequently allocate what are normally regarded as period costs to final cost objectives.[7] In a manufacturing firm the final cost objective is a product, in a restaurant it is a meal, in a college it is a student credit hour, and in a hospital it might be an operating room minute or a bed-day.

Although the techniques used to allocate period costs to cost objectives are similar to those used for allocating product costs, the allocation process becomes increasingly complex as the number of cost pools increases. Some organizations have hundreds of cost pools. Additionally, because many period costs have little or no correlation with the current volume of activity, their allocation is likely to be quite arbitrary. Nevertheless, because all costs must be recovered if a business is to survive in the long run, managers have a craving for **full cost** data that includes direct materials, direct labor, manufacturing overhead, distribution costs, and selling and administrative costs.

Cost Accounting Standards Board

In an effort to standardize the procedures for determining "cost" in negotiated cost-plus government contracts, the **Cost Accounting Standards Board** (CASB) was established in 1970 as an agent of the U.S. Congress. The mission of the CASB was to narrow the cost accounting options available to defense contractors and subcontractors by issuing cost accounting standards to be followed in predicting, accumulating, and reporting costs of defense contracts and subcontracts. Between 1970 and 1980, when it ceased operations and the task of interpreting CASB standards was transferred to the General Accounting Office, the CASB issued 19 cost accounting standards. The applicability of these standards has been extended to include virtually all negotiated contracts in excess of $100,000 let by the U.S. government.

Because CASB standards concern both manufacturing and nonmanufacturing costs they are of interest to anyone wishing to justify prices on the basis of cost data. Furthermore, the standards, rules, and regulations issued by the CASB are similar in nature to those issued by many other government and nongovernment

---

[7] For external reporting purposes, general and administrative expenses are normally considered period costs. The only exception is the **completed-contract method of accounting,** where all income and expenses related to a contract are recognized on completion of the contract. To achieve a better matching of costs and revenues, especially when multiyear contracts are involved, generally accepted accounting principles permit the allocation of general and administrative costs to the contract (job) when the completed-contract method is used.

organizations. A list of CASB standards is presented in Exhibit 6–12. The standards are classified into the following categories:

1. Standards addressing overall cost accounting matters
2. Standards addressing classes, categories, or elements of cost
3. Standards addressing pools of indirect costs

Although a detailed discussion of CASB standards is beyond the scope of this text, a cursory review of their titles is enlightening. Standards 403, 410, and 418, dealing with pools of indirect costs, are of particular interest in this section of Chapter 6.

- Standard 403, *Allocation of Home Office Expenses to Segments*. This standard classifies home office expenses into three cost pools and specifies preferred bases for allocating each pool to divisions, branches, and plants.
- Standard 410, *Allocation of Business Unit General and Administrative Expenses to Final Cost Objectives*. Standard 410 is a continuation of Standard 403. It provides criteria for the allocation of business unit general and administrative expenses (including any assigned to the business unit from a home office) to final cost objectives.
- Standard 418, *Allocation of Direct and Indirect Costs*. Standard 418 provides criteria for the accumulation of indirect costs in cost pools, such as those established for service departments, and offers guidance for the selection of allocation bases. The standard states that indirect costs are to be accumulated in

EXHIBIT 6–12 **Titles of CASB Standards***

Standards addressing overall cost accounting matters:
401 Consistency in Estimating, Accumulating, and Reporting Costs
402 Consistency in Allocating Costs Incurred for the Same Purpose
405 Accounting for Unallowable Costs
406 Cost Accounting Period

Standards addressing classes, categories, or elements of cost:
404 Capitalization of Tangible Assets
407 Uses of Standard Cost for Direct Material and Direct Labor
408 Accounting for Costs of Compensated Personal Absences
409 Depreciation of Tangible Capital Assets
411 Accounting for Acquisition Costs of Material
412 Compensation and Measurement of Pension Cost
413 Adjustment and Allocation of Pension Cost
414 Cost of Money as an Element of the Cost of Capital
415 Accounting for the Cost of Deferred Compensation
416 Accounting for Insurance Costs
417 Cost of Money as an Element of the Cost of Capital Assets Under Construction

Standards addressing pools of indirect costs:
403 Allocation of Home Office Expenses to Segments
410 Allocation of Business Unit General and Administrative Expenses to Final Cost Objectives
418 Allocation of Direct and Indirect Costs†
420 Accounting for Independent Research and Development Costs and Bid and Proposal Costs

*Copies of CASB standards, rules, and regulations are available for sale from the Superintendent of Documents, U.S. Government Printing Office, Washington, D.C., 20402.
† Proposed Standard 419 was combined with Standard 418.

homogeneous cost pools. An indirect cost pool is homogeneous if all the activities included in the pool have a similar relationship to cost objectives or if the resulting allocation is substantially the same as it would be if the costs of the activities were allocated separately.

Standard 418 also provides a hierarchy of allocation bases. The preferred allocation basis is a *resource consumption measure,* such as labor hours, machine hours, or kilowatt-hours. The second order of preference is an *output measure* such as the number of orders processed by a purchasing department. The third order of preference is a *surrogate measure of output,* such as the number of employees served by a personnel department or the number of square meters served by the building and grounds department.

SUMMARY

To the extent that service departments serve production departments, service department operating costs, or deficits, should be assigned to production departments and, ultimately, to products. Such allocations are required for external reporting. A number of techniques may be used to accomplish this.

Service department costs and the direct overhead costs of all production departments can be placed in a single cost pool and assigned to final cost objectives using a single plant-wide rate. Alternatively separate cost pools and overhead application rates can be established for each production department. Departmental overhead rates are preferred if there are differences in the size or nature of the overhead costs associated with individual production departments and if products spend varying percentages of their total time in each production department.

When departmental overhead rates are used, service department costs must be assigned to production departments. This can be done with the direct, step, or linear algebra method, using single or dual rates. The direct method gives no recognition to services provided other service departments. The step method gives some recognition to services provided other service departments. The linear algebra method gives complete recognition to reciprocal services. The successive allocation approach approximates the allocations obtained with the linear algebra method. Dual rates distinguish between the capacity costs and the variable costs of service departments and allocate them on separate bases.

When cost is an important factor in pricing or price justification, it might also be necessary to develop special reports allocating what are normally regarded as period costs to final cost objectives. Because period costs often have little or no correlation with the current volume of activity, such allocations are likely to be quite arbitrary.

APPENDIX Basic Elements of Matrix Algebra

This appendix serves as an introduction or review of matrix algebra. You must understand the concepts presented here before studying the linear algebra method of service department cost allocation.

A **matrix** is an array of numbers. It is represented by a boldface capital letter. We are only concerned with two-dimensional arrays, such as the following:

$$\mathbf{A} = \begin{bmatrix} 1 & 2 & 4 \\ 2 & 5 & 1 \\ 3 & 6 & 8 \end{bmatrix}$$

$$\mathbf{B} = \begin{bmatrix} 5 & -8 & 6 \\ 0 & 1 & 1 \\ 3 & 0 & 0 \end{bmatrix}$$

$$\mathbf{C} = [0 \quad 0 \quad 5]$$

$$\mathbf{D} = \begin{bmatrix} 100 \\ 50 \\ 1{,}000 \end{bmatrix}$$

$$\mathbf{E} = \begin{bmatrix} 5 & 6 & 99 & 40 & -50 \\ 50 & 66 & 80 & 0 & 5 \end{bmatrix}$$

The brackets emphasize that the array of numbers is a matrix. The size of a matrix is determined by the number of rows and columns it contains. A matrix that has m rows and n columns is of dimension m by n. For example, **A** and **B** are 3×3 matrices; **C** is a 1×3 matrix; **D** is a 3×1 matrix; and **E** is a 2×5 matrix. A matrix that has only a single row, such as **C**, or a single column, such as **D**, is called a **vector**.

Any element within a matrix can be referred to by its row and column location. When referring to a particular element within a matrix, lower-case letters and subscripts are used. A complete enumeration of all elements within matrix **A** is as follows:

$$\begin{array}{lll} a_{1,1} = 1 & a_{1,2} = 2 & a_{1,3} = 4 \\ a_{2,1} = 2 & a_{2,2} = 5 & a_{2,3} = 1 \\ a_{3,1} = 3 & a_{3,2} = 6 & a_{3,3} = 8 \end{array}$$

An **identity matrix**, identified by a boldfaced **I**, is a square matrix containing ones along the upper-left to lower-right diagonal and zeros everywhere else. Here is an example of a 4×4 identity matrix:

$$\mathbf{I} = \begin{bmatrix} 1 & 0 & 0 & 0 \\ 0 & 1 & 0 & 0 \\ 0 & 0 & 1 & 0 \\ 0 & 0 & 0 & 1 \end{bmatrix}$$

An identity matrix is the matrix algebra equivalent of the number one. Any matrix multiplied by an identity matrix of proper dimension is equal to the original matrix. If, for example, **I** is a 3×3 identity matrix, then $\mathbf{I} \cdot \mathbf{A} = \mathbf{A}$ and $\mathbf{I} \cdot \mathbf{B} = \mathbf{B}$.

MATRIX ADDITION AND SUBTRACTION

Two matrices of the same dimension can be added or subtracted from each other to form a third matrix. This is done by adding or subtracting the corresponding elements in each matrix. Assume $\mathbf{A} + \mathbf{B} = \mathbf{F}$ and $\mathbf{A} - \mathbf{B} = \mathbf{G}$:

$$\begin{matrix} \mathbf{A} & + & \mathbf{B} & = & \mathbf{F} \\ \begin{bmatrix} 1 & 2 & 4 \\ 2 & 5 & 1 \\ 3 & 6 & 8 \end{bmatrix} & + & \begin{bmatrix} 5 & -8 & 6 \\ 0 & 1 & 1 \\ 3 & 0 & 0 \end{bmatrix} & = & \begin{bmatrix} 6 & -6 & 10 \\ 2 & 6 & 2 \\ 6 & 6 & 8 \end{bmatrix} \end{matrix}$$

$$\underset{\mathbf{A}}{\begin{bmatrix}1 & 2 & 4\\2 & 5 & 1\\3 & 6 & 8\end{bmatrix}} - \underset{\mathbf{B}}{\begin{bmatrix}5 & -8 & 6\\0 & 1 & 1\\3 & 0 & 0\end{bmatrix}} = \underset{\mathbf{G}}{\begin{bmatrix}-4 & 10 & -2\\2 & 4 & 0\\0 & 6 & 8\end{bmatrix}}$$

Note that matrices can be added or subtracted only if they have the same dimensions. Matrices **B** and **C**, for example, cannot be added or subtracted because they do not have the same dimensions.

MATRIX MULTIPLICATION

Two matrices can be multiplied if the number of columns in the first equals the number of rows in the second ($n = m$). Each element in the product matrix is obtained by multiplying each element in the ith row of the first by the corresponding element in the jth column of the second and summing the products. If $\mathbf{A} \cdot \mathbf{B} = \mathbf{H}$, **H** is computed as follows:

$$\underset{\mathbf{A}}{\begin{bmatrix}1 & 2 & 4\\2 & 5 & 1\\3 & 6 & 8\end{bmatrix}} \cdot \underset{\mathbf{B}}{\begin{bmatrix}5 & -8 & 6\\0 & 1 & 1\\3 & 0 & 0\end{bmatrix}} =$$

$$\mathbf{H}$$

$$\begin{bmatrix}(1 \times 5) + (2 \times 0) + (4 \times 3) & (1 \times -8) + (2 \times 1) + (4 \times 0) & (1 \times 6) + (2 \times 1) + (4 \times 0)\\(2 \times 5) + (5 \times 0) + (1 \times 3) & (2 \times -8) + (5 \times 1) + (1 \times 0) & (2 \times 6) + (5 \times 1) + (1 \times 0)\\(3 \times 5) + (6 \times 0) + (8 \times 3) & (3 \times -8) + (6 \times 1) + (8 \times 0) & (3 \times 6) + (6 \times 1) + (8 \times 0)\end{bmatrix}$$

Note the row-times-column computation procedure. The first row of **H** is computed by multiplying the first row of **A** and each column of **B**; the second row of **H** is computed by multiplying the second row of **A** and each column of **B**. The process is continued until each row of **A** is multiplied by each column of **B**. Completing the multiplication and addition, the following matrix is obtained:

$$\mathbf{H} = \begin{bmatrix}17 & -6 & 8\\13 & -11 & 17\\39 & -18 & 24\end{bmatrix}$$

Matrices **A** and **E** cannot be multiplied together because **A** has three columns whereas **E** only has two rows. It is possible to multiply **A** by **D**. It is also possible to multiply **C** by **D**. Let $\mathbf{A} \cdot \mathbf{D} = \mathbf{P}$ and $\mathbf{C} \cdot \mathbf{D} = \mathbf{R}$.

$$\underset{\mathbf{A}}{\begin{bmatrix}1 & 2 & 4\\2 & 5 & 1\\3 & 6 & 8\end{bmatrix}} \cdot \underset{\mathbf{D}}{\begin{bmatrix}100\\50\\1{,}000\end{bmatrix}} = \underset{\mathbf{P}}{\begin{bmatrix}(1 \times 100) + (2 \times 50) + (4 \times 1{,}000)\\(2 \times 100) + (5 \times 50) + (1 \times 1{,}000)\\(3 \times 100) + (6 \times 50) + (8 \times 1{,}000)\end{bmatrix}}$$

$$\mathbf{P} = \begin{bmatrix}4{,}200\\1{,}450\\8{,}600\end{bmatrix}$$

$$\underset{\mathbf{C}}{[0 \quad 0 \quad 5]} \cdot \underset{\mathbf{D}}{\begin{bmatrix}100\\50\\1{,}000\end{bmatrix}} = \underset{\mathbf{R}}{[5{,}000]}$$

In this case **R** is a **scalar**, that is, a 1×1 matrix. All the elements of a matrix of any size can be multiplied by a scalar without regard to restrictions on the number of rows and columns. Let $\mathbf{S} = 4\mathbf{A}$:

$$\mathbf{S} = 4 \cdot \begin{bmatrix} 1 & 2 & 4 \\ 2 & 5 & 1 \\ 3 & 6 & 8 \end{bmatrix} = \begin{bmatrix} 4 & 8 & 16 \\ 8 & 20 & 4 \\ 12 & 24 & 32 \end{bmatrix}$$

MATRIX INVERSION

In algebra the following equation is solved for X by division:

$$aX = b \qquad (6\text{–}1)$$

$$X = b/a \qquad (6\text{–}2)$$

The solution can also be found by multiplying the inverse of a by b:

$$X = (1/a)b \qquad (6\text{–}3)$$

The inverse of a is frequently represented by a^{-1}, giving the following presentation of Eq. 6–3:

$$X = a^{-1}b \qquad (6\text{–}4)$$

The product of a and a^{-1} is 1:

$$a^{-1} \cdot a = 1 \qquad (6\text{–}5)$$

Division is not permitted in matrix algebra; however, the same objective is accomplished by matrix inversion followed by matrix multiplication. The inverse of **A** is represented by $\mathbf{A}^{-1}$ and the product of **A** and $\mathbf{A}^{-1}$ is an identity matrix:

$$\mathbf{A}^{-1} \cdot \mathbf{A} = \mathbf{I} \qquad (6\text{–}6)$$

Eq. 6–6 assists in verifying the computation of the matrix inverse.

There are several alternative computational procedures for determining the inverse of a matrix. They all have one thing in common: they are too unwieldy for hand computations in any realistic application. Hence most applications of matrix algebra use computer facilities. For the purposes of illustration, one technique for finding the inverse of a matrix is shown in conjunction with an illustrative application of matrix algebra.

SOLVING A SERIES OF LINEAR EQUATIONS

Assume we want to solve the following series of linear equations for P and S:

$$5P + 2S = 62 \qquad (6\text{–}7)$$

$$2P + 4S = 44 \qquad (6\text{–}8)$$

In this relatively simple situation we would probably solve by substitution and/or elimination rather than by matrix algebra.

Solution by Substitution or Elimination

Using elimination, we multiply Eq. 6–8 by 0.5 and subtract the product from Eq. 6–7:

$$\begin{array}{rcr} 5P + 2S &=& 62 \\ -1P - 2S &=& -22 \\ \hline 4P \qquad &=& 40 \end{array}$$

In this case P equals 10. Next we solve for S by substituting the value of P in either Eq. 6–7 or 6–8. Here S equals 6.

For two equations and two unknowns, solution by elimination is straightforward; however, as the number of variables and equations increase, solution by substitution and/or elimination becomes awkward. Ultimately we must resort to matrix algebra and the use of a computer.

Solution by Matrix Algebra

Prior to solving for P and S by matrix algebra, Eqs. 6–7 and 6–8 must be placed in matrix notation:

$$\begin{bmatrix} 5 & 2 \\ 2 & 4 \end{bmatrix} \cdot \begin{bmatrix} P \\ S \end{bmatrix} = \begin{bmatrix} 62 \\ 44 \end{bmatrix} \qquad (6\text{–}9)$$

Use matrix multiplication to verify that Eq. 6–9 is equivalent to Eqs. 6–7 and 6–8.

The first matrix in Eq. 6–9, containing the coefficients of P and S, is called the **coefficients matrix**, **A**; the second, which contains the unknown values of P and S, is called the **vector of unknowns**, **X**; and the third, which contains the results of the computations for each equation, is called the **vector of knowns**, **B**. In matrix notation, Eq. 6–9 is shown as $\mathbf{A} \cdot \mathbf{X} = \mathbf{B}$. Solving for **X**, the vector of unknowns:

$$\mathbf{X} = \mathbf{A}^{-1} \cdot \mathbf{B} \qquad (6\text{–}10)$$

or

$$\begin{bmatrix} P \\ S \end{bmatrix} = \begin{bmatrix} 5 & 2 \\ 2 & 4 \end{bmatrix}^{-1} \cdot \begin{bmatrix} 62 \\ 44 \end{bmatrix} \qquad (6\text{–}11)$$

The inverse of the coefficients matrix, **A,** must be determined before we can solve for P and S. One approach to determining the inverse of a matrix is to form an **augmented matrix**, which consists of the matrix we want to invert and an identity matrix of the same dimension. For the coefficients matrix in Eq. 6–11, the augmented matrix is:

$$\left[\begin{array}{cc|cc} 5 & 2 & 1 & 0 \\ 2 & 4 & 0 & 1 \end{array}\right]$$

Once the augmented matrix is formed, row operations are performed on it until the portion of the augmented matrix representing the original matrix is reduced to an identity matrix. The other portion of the augmented matrix is then the inverse of the original matrix. We will only use two of the many possible row operations we could perform on this matrix:

1. Multiply each element in a row by a constant and substitute for the previous row.
2. Multiply each element in a row by a constant and add the product to another row.

In performing these operations, our objective is to replace the original matrix by an identity matrix. When this is accomplished, the other portion of the augmented matrix will be the inverse of the original matrix. Row operations are continued in any order until our objective is accomplished.

1. Multiply row 2 by 0.25 to change element 2,2 to a 1. Replace the previous row.

$$\left[\begin{array}{cc|cc} 5 & 2 & 1 & 0.00 \\ 0.5 & 1 & 0 & 0.25 \end{array}\right]$$

2. Multiply row 2 by -2 and add the product to row 1 to change element 1,2 to a zero.

$$\left[\begin{array}{cc|cc} 4 & 0 & 1 & -0.50 \\ 0.5 & 1 & 0 & 0.25 \end{array}\right]$$

3. Multiply row 1 by 0.25 to change element 1,1 to a 1. Replace the previous row.

$$\left[\begin{array}{cc|cc} 1 & 0 & 0.25 & -0.125 \\ 0.5 & 1 & 0.00 & 0.250 \end{array}\right]$$

4. Multiply row 1 by -0.5 and add the product to row 2 to change element 2,1 to a 0.

$$\left[\begin{array}{cc|cc} 1 & 0 & 0.2500 & -0.1250 \\ 0 & 1 & -0.1250 & 0.3125 \end{array}\right]$$

The original matrix has been reduced to an identity matrix. Hence $\mathbf{A}^{-1}$ is given on the right-hand side of the last augmented matrix. This solution is verified using Eq. 6–6:

$$\begin{bmatrix} 0.2500 & -0.1250 \\ -0.1250 & 0.3125 \end{bmatrix} \cdot \begin{bmatrix} 5 & 2 \\ 2 & 4 \end{bmatrix} = \begin{bmatrix} 1 & 0 \\ 0 & 1 \end{bmatrix}$$

Solving for P and S:

$$\begin{bmatrix} P \\ S \end{bmatrix} = \begin{bmatrix} 0.2500 & -0.1250 \\ -0.1250 & 0.3125 \end{bmatrix} \cdot \begin{bmatrix} 62 \\ 44 \end{bmatrix} = \begin{bmatrix} 10 \\ 6 \end{bmatrix}$$

The final solution is P equals 10 and S equals 6, the same as the solution obtained by substitution and elimination.[8]

---

[8] A brief computer program can solve this and longer problems quickly. The following Extended BASIC program will solve the preceding problem:

```
100 DIM A(2, 2),B(2,1)
110 MAT READ A (2,2),B(2,1)
120 MAT PRINT A
130 MAT PRINT B
140 MAT C = INV(A)
150 MAT X = C*B
160 PRINT "THE INVERSE IS AS FOLLOWS"
170 MAT PRINT C
180 PRINT "THE SOLUTION IS AS FOLLOWS"
190 MAT PRINT X
200 DATA 5,2
210 DATA 2,4
220 DATA 62
230 DATA 44
999 END
RUN
```

In this program, C is the inverse of the coefficients matrix, **A**; B is the vector of knowns, **B**; and X is the solution for the vector of unknowns, **X**. If computer facilities containing extended BASIC software are available, you are encouraged to run this program as an exercise. Note that by changing the dimensions in statements 100 and 110 and by inserting the proper data statements, it is possible to solve problems of varying size.

KEY TERMS

Common costs
Completed-contract method of accounting
Cost Accounting Standards Board
Cost objective
Cost pool
Direct departmental costs

Direct method
Dual rate methods
Final cost objective
Full cost
Indirect costs
Indirect departmental costs
Intermediate cost objective
Linear algebra method
Production department
Self-service
Service department
Single rate methods
Step-down method
Step method

APPENDIX KEY TERMS

Augmented matrix
Coefficients matrix
Identity matrix
Matrix
Scalar
Vector
Vector of knowns
Vector of unknowns

SELECTED REFERENCES

Chen, Joyce T., "Cost Allocation and External Acquisition of Services When Self-Services Exist," *Accounting Review* **68,** No. 3 (July 1983): 600–605.

Ching, Donald F., "How to Isolate Medicare Costs," *Management Accounting* **61,** No. 1 (July 1979): 27–30.

Fremgen, James M., and Shu S. Liao, *The Allocation of Corporate Indirect Costs,* New York: National Association of Accountants, 1981.

Kaplan, Robert S., "Variable and Self-Service Costs in Reciprocal Allocation Models," *Accouning Review* **48,** No. 4 (October 1973): 738–748.

Manes, Rene P., Soong H. Park, and Robert Jensen, "Relevant Costs of Intermediate Goods and Services," *Accounting Review* **57,** No. 3 (July 1982): 594–606.

Minch, R., and E. Petri, "Matrix Models of Reciprocal Service Cost Allocation," *Accounting Review* **47,** No. 3 (July 1972): 576–580.

Shank, J. K., *Matrix Methods in Accounting,* Reading, Mass.: Addison-Wesley, 1972.

Sunder, Shyam, "Simpson's Reversal Paradox and Cost Allocation," *Journal of Accounting Research* **21,** No. 1 (Spring 1983): 222–233.

Verrecchia, Robert E., "An Analysis of Two Cost Allocation Cases," *Accounting Review* **57,** No. 3 (July 1982): 579–593.

REVIEW QUESTIONS

6–1 Distinguish between production departments and service departments.

6–2 In the cost allocation process, what is the relationship between cost pools and cost objectives?

6–3 Distinguish between intermediate and final cost objectives.

6–4 Distinguish between indirect and direct departmental costs.

6–5 Identify four distinct uses of allocated cost information.

6–6 What can happen if cost data developed primarily for external reporting are used for internal management purposes?

6–7 Mention three significant problems that the cost accountant faces in allocating service department costs to production departments.

6–8 What is self-service? Why is it ignored in service department cost allocation?

6–9 Distinguish between the three basic service department cost allocation techniques on the basis of the amount of recognition they give to services rendered other service departments.

6–10 Why is the linear algebra method preferred to the step method?

6–11 What rationale underlies the dual rate methods of service department cost allocation?

6–12 Why do some organizations develop predetermined overhead rates for service departments?

6–13 Mention two approaches to developing predetermined allocation rates for service departments.

6–14 What was the mission of the Cost Accounting Standards Board?

REVIEW PROBLEM

Service Department Cost Allocation: Three Methods and Successive Approximation

Peninsula Hospital has five departments, three are classified as service centers and two are classified as revenue centers. All service center costs are allocated to the revenue centers. The percentage distribution of actual services during a recent period is as follows:

From \ To	*S1*	*S2*	*S3*	*R1*	*R2*
S1	0%	20%	20%	30%	30%
S2	20%	0%	30%	40%	10%
S3	15%	15%	0%	35%	35%

The operating costs of the departments are as follows:

S1	$10,000
S2	20,000
S3	5,000
R1	20,000
R2	30,000

REQUIREMENTS

a) Using the direct method, prepare a schedule allocating the service department costs to the revenue departments.

b) Using the step method, prepare a schedule allocating the service department costs to the revenue departments.

c) Set up equations for the linear algebra method of allocating service department costs to revenue departments and place them in matrix notation.

d) Assume the inverse of the coefficients matrix is as follows:

$$\begin{bmatrix} 1 & 0 & 0.5397 & 0.6672 & 0.5310 \\ 0 & 1 & 0.4603 & 0.3328 & 0.4690 \\ 0 & 0 & 1.0977 & 0.2816 & 0.2069 \\ 0 & 0 & 0.2644 & 1.1149 & 0.2069 \\ 0 & 0 & 0.2989 & 0.3908 & 1.1035 \end{bmatrix}$$

Determine the final allocation of service department costs to R1 and R2.

e) Use successive allocation to approximate the results of the linear algebra method. Use three allocations before allocating any remaining amounts with the direct method.

The solution to this problem is found at the end of the Chapter 6 problems and exercises.

EXERCISES

6–1 T Direct and Step Service Department Allocation

Presented is information regarding the May 19y4 operations of Steinfatt Communications, Inc. The proportional distribution of services is as follows

From \ To	S1	S2	P1	P2
S1	0.0	0.4	0.2	0.4
S2	0.2	0.0	0.6	0.2

Direct service department costs and production department overhead are as follows:

S1	S2	P1	P2
$36,000	$20,000	$50,000	$45,000

REQUIREMENTS

a) Prepare a schedule allocating the service department costs to the production departments using the direct method.

b) Prepare a schedule allocating the service department costs to the production departments using the step method.

6–2 T Successive Allocation to Approximate the Linear Algebra Method

Based on the information in Exercise 6–1, use successive allocation to approximate the linear algebra method. Use three allocations before allocating any remaining amounts with the direct method.

6–3 T Direct and Step Service Department Allocation

Presented is information pertaining to the 19x2 operations of Manitoba Limited. The proportional distribution of services is as follows:

From \ To	S1	S2	P1	P2	P3
S1	0.0	0.5	0.2	0.1	0.2
S2	0.2	0.0	0.3	0.2	0.3

Direct service department costs and production department overhead are as follows:

S1	S2	P1	P2	P3
$40,000	$20,000	$70,000	$60,000	$130,000

REQUIREMENTS

a) Prepare a schedule allocating the service department costs to the production departments using the direct method.

b) Prepare a schedule allocating the service department costs to the production departments using the step method.

6–4 T Successive Allocation to Approximate the Linear Algebra Method

Based on the information in Exercise 6–3, use successive allocation to approximate the linear algebra method. Use three allocations before allocating any remaining amounts with the direct method.

6–5 T Plant-Wide and Departmental Overhead Rates with Service Departments: Direct Department Allocation

Thames Products Ltd. has two production departments, P1 and P2, and two service departments, S1 and S2. S1 is the employee services department (personnel, first aid, cafeteria, and so on). S2 is the maintenance department. For December 19x2, the following information is available:

	S1	*S2*	*P1*	*P2*	*Total*
Employees	5	20	126	14	165
Machine-hours	0	0	1,000	9,000	10,000
Direct-labor hours	0	0	13,000	3,000	16,000

Direct service department costs and production department overhead are as follows:

S1	*S2*	*P1*	*P2*	*Total*
$8,000	$10,000	$39,000	$15,000	$72,000

REQUIREMENTS

a) Determine the plant-wide overhead rate per direct-labor hour.

b) Determine the departmental overhead rates per direct-labor hour. Using the direct method of service department cost allocation, allocate S1 costs on the basis of the number of employees and S2 costs on the basis of machine hours.

6–6 T Departmental Overhead Rates with Step Service Department Allocation

Based on the information presented in Exercise 6–5, prepare a schedule allocating the service department costs to the production departments using the step method of service department cost allocation. Allocate S1 costs on the basis of the number of employees and S2 costs on the basis of machine hours. Determine the resulting overhead rates per labor hour in each production department.

6–7 T Plant-Wide and Departmental Overhead Rates with Service Departments: Step Allocation

The Larch Co. Ltd. uses the step method in allocating service department costs to producing departments. Buildings and Grounds is allocated first using square feet as a base. The number of employees is used as a base for allocating factory administration.

	Buildings and Grounds	*Factory administration*	*Machining*	*Assembly*	*Total*
Overhead budget	$40,000	$25,000	$360,000	$420,000	$ 845,000
Square feet	1,500	1,000	9,000	10,000	21,500
Number of employees	50	30	440	460	980
Direct-labor hours			452,000	567,250	1,019,250
Machine hours			195,600	23,000	218,600

REQUIREMENTS

a) Compute the plant-wide overhead rate using direct-labor hours as a base.

b) Compute the overhead rate for machining using machine hours as a base.

c) Compute the overhead rate for assembly using direct-labor hours as a base.

(CGA Adapted)

6–8 Single and Dual Overhead Rates

During July 19y6 the maintenance department incurred fixed costs of $4,500 and variable costs of $9,000. The maintenance department serves three production departments, P1, P2, and P3; information on their actual use during July and estimated maximum monthly use is as follows:

	P1	*P2*	*P3*	*Total*
Actual use (hours)	300	200	400	900
Estimated maximum use (hours)	500	600	400	1,500

REQUIREMENTS

a) Determine costs allocated to P1, P2, and P3 when a single rate, based on actual use, is used to allocate total maintenance costs.

b) Determine the costs allocated to P1, P2, and P3 when dual rates are used to allocate maintenance costs.

6–9 Single and Dual Overhead Rates

During August 19x9 the Collections Department of Xcellent Stores incurred fixed costs of $50,000 and variable costs of $20,000. The Collections Department serves four stores, Uptown, Downtown, Westside, and Eastside. Information on each store's actual number of credit sales for August and predicted maximum monthly credit sales is as follows:

	Uptown	*Downtown*	*Westside*	*Eastside*
Actual number of credit sales	20,000	100,000	40,000	40,000
Maximum number of credit sales	75,000	120,000	60,000	45,000

REQUIREMENTS

a) Determine the costs allocated to each store when a single rate, based on actual credit sales, is used to allocate total Collections Department costs.

b) Determine the costs allocated to each store when dual rates are used to allocate Collections Department costs.

6–10 T Service Department Cost Allocation: Three Methods

The Inverse Corporation has two service departments, S1 and S2, and two production departments, P1 and P2. The percent distribution of the service departments' costs are as follows:

From \ *To*	*S1*	*S2*	*P1*	*P2*
S1	0	80%	10%	10%
S2	20%	0	20%	60%

The direct operating costs of the service departments and the direct overhead costs of the production departments are as follows:

S1	$10,000
S2	5,000
P1	20,000
P2	20,000

REQUIREMENTS

a) Determine the total overhead costs of P1 and P2 using the direct method to allocate service department costs.

b) Determine the total overhead costs of P1 and P2 using the step method of allocating overhead costs.

c) Develop the linear equations necessary to determine the total overhead costs of P1 and P2 when the linear algebra method is used and place these equations in matrix format.

d) Assume that the inverse of the coefficient matrix is:

$$\begin{bmatrix} 1 & 0 & 0.3092 & 0.2619 \\ 0 & 1 & 0.6908 & 0.7381 \\ 0 & 0 & 1.1905 & 0.2381 \\ 0 & 0 & 0.9528 & 1.1905 \end{bmatrix}$$

Determine the total overhead costs of P1 and P2 using the linear algebra method.

6–11 T Successive Allocation to Approximate Linear Algebra Method

Based on the information in Exercise 6–10, use successive allocation to approximate the linear algebra method. Use three allocations before allocating any remaining amounts with the direct method.

6–12 T Service Department Cost Allocation: Three Methods

Fisher Rod and Reel manufactures fishing rods and reels in two production departments, P1 and P2. The production departments receive services from three service departments, S1, S2, and S3, which also provide some services to each other. The 19x3 operating costs of S1, S2, and S3 were $12,000, $6,000, and $10,000, respectively. The proportional distribution of each department's services are as follows:

From \ *To*	*S1*	*S2*	*S3*	*P1*	*P2*
S1	0.0	0.5	0.0	0.3	0.2
S2	0.4	0.0	0.0	0.1	0.5
S3	0.2	0.2	0.0	0.3	0.3

REQUIREMENTS

a) Use the direct method to allocate service department costs to P1 and P2.

b) Use the step method to allocate service department costs to P1 and P2.

c) Develop the linear equations necessary to allocate service department costs using the linear algebra method

d) Assume that the inverse of the coefficient matrix is:

$$\begin{bmatrix} 1 & 0 & 0.4375 & 0.2750 & 0.4425 \\ 0 & 1 & 0.5625 & 0.7250 & 0.5575 \\ 0 & 0 & 1.2500 & 0.5000 & 0.3500 \\ 0 & 0 & 0.6250 & 1.2500 & 0.3750 \\ 0 & 0 & 0.0000 & 0.0000 & 1.0000 \end{bmatrix}$$

Determine the final allocation of service department costs to each production department using the linear algebra method.

6–13 T Successive Allocation to Approximate Linear Algebra Method

Based on the information in Exercise 6–12, use successive allocation to approximate the linear algebra method. Use three allocations before allocating any remaining amounts with the direct method.

PROBLEMS

6–14 T Plant-Wide and Departmental Overhead Rates with Service Departments: Step Service Department Allocation: Journal Entries

The Suspended File Company manufactures a variety of metal file cabinets in three production departments. Sheet metal purchased from outside vendors is cut and stamped into the necessary shapes in the Stamping Department. The shaped metal is then assembled into cabinets in the Assembly Department. Finally, the assembled cabinets are painted in the Painting Department.

Two departments, Employee Services and Building Services, facilitate the operations of the production departments. The following information is available regarding January 19x7 operations:

	Stamping	*Assembly*	*Painting*	*Employee Services*	*Building Services*	*Total*
Direct production department overhead	$80,000	$20,000	$40,000			$140,000
Direct service department costs				$10,000	$40,000	$ 50,000
Employees	10	50	20	10	20	110
Floor space (sq. ft.)	30,000	60,000	30,000	2,000	3,000	125,000
Direct-labor hours	1,200	7,000	2,800			11,000

All service department costs and all direct production department overhead costs are assigned to units produced using an actual overhead rate.

REQUIREMENTS

a) Determine the *plant-wide overhead* rate per direct-labor hour.

b) Use the step method to prepare a schedule allocating the service department costs to the production departments. Employee Services costs should be allocated on the basis of the number of employees and Building Services costs should be allocated on the basis of square feet of floorspace. The schedule should also disclose the resulting *departmental overhead rate* per direct-labor hour.

c) Based on the schedule prepared in part (b), prepare a journal entry to assign the service department costs to the production departments.

d) Under what circumstances would the use of a plant-wide rate be adequate? Under what circumstances would the use of departmental overhead rates be preferred?

6–15 T Determining Percent Distributions for Services and Step Method

The Lewistown General Hospital contains several revenue and nonrevenue cost centers. The step method is used to allocate the direct costs of the nonrevenue cost centers. The names of the nonrevenue cost centers, their prescribed order of cost allocation, and the basis of cost allocation are as follows:

Nonrevenue cost center	*Order of allocation*	*Basis of allocation*
Depreciation	1	Square meters
Employee services	2	Salaries
Maintenance	3	Square meters
Laundry	4	Kilograms used

The following information is available for February 19x7:

	Total direct cost	*Square meters*	*Salaries*	*Kilograms of laundry*
Nonrevenue cost centers:				
Depreciation	$100,000			
Employee services	4,000	2,000	$2,000	50
Maintenance	8,000	3,000	4,000	200
Laundry	6,000	1,500	2,000	40
Revenue cost centers:				
Operating room	50,000*	3,000	6,000*	800
Radiology	40,000*	3,000	10,000*	100
Laboratory	30,000	1,500	3,000	400
Patient rooms	90,000*	66,000	25,000*	1,200

*Excludes cost of professional services that are billed directly to the patient.

REQUIREMENT

Using the step method allocate the costs of the nonrevenue cost centers to the revenue cost centers.

6–16 Developing Predetermined Overhead Rates with Service Department Costs

The East Tennessee manufacturing facility of the Jacobs Company contains two production departments, P1 and P2, and one service department, S.

Operating costs of S:

Fixed costs	$40,000 per year
Variable costs	$4 per service unit

Direct overhead costs of P1 and P2:

	P1	*P2*
Fixed costs per year	$20,000	$40,000
Variable costs per direct-labor hour	$2	$4

Budgeted direct-labor hours for 19w7 are 8,000 in P1 and 2,000 in P2. Each direct-labor hour in P1 requires two service units. Each direct-labor hour in P2 requires six service units.

REQUIREMENTS

a) Prepare a budget for 19w7 service department costs.

b) Assume East Tennessee uses a single plant-wide rate to apply overhead costs to individual jobs. Determine the 19w7 *rate* per direct-labor hour.

c) Assume East Tennessee uses separate overhead application rates in P1 and P2. Determine the 19w7 *rates* per direct-labor hour. The allocation from S to P1 and P2 is based on use only.

6–17 Predetermined Plant-wide and Departmental Overhead Rates: Direct Method: Single and Dual Rates

MumsDay Corporation manufactures a complete line of fiberglass attaché cases and suitcases. MumsDay has three manufacturing departments—Molding, Component, and Assembly—and two service departments—Power and Maintenance.

The sides of the cases are manufactured in the Molding Department. The frames, hinges, locks, and so on are manufactured in the Component Department. The cases are completed in the Assembly Department. Varying amounts of materials, time, and effort are required for each of the various cases. The Power Department and Maintenance Department provide services to the three manufacturing departments.

MumsDay has always used a plant-wide overhead rate. Direct-labor hours are used to assign the overhead to its product. The predetermined rate is calculated by dividing the company's total predicted overhead by the total predicted direct-labor hours to be worked in the three manufacturing departments.

Whit Portlock, Manager of Cost Accounting, has recommended that MumsDay use departmental overhead rates. The planned operating costs and expected levels of activity for the coming year have been developed by Portlock and are presented by department in the following schedules (000 omitted):

	Manufacturing departments		
	Molding	*Component*	*Assembly*
Departmental activity measures:			
Direct-labor hours	500	2,000	1,500
Machine hours	875	125	–0–
Departmental costs:			
Raw materials	$12,400	$30,000	$ 1,250
Direct labor	3,500	20,000	12,000
Variable overhead	3,500	10,000	16,500
Fixed overhead	17,500	6,200	6,100
Total departmental costs	$36,900	$66,200	$35,850
Use of service departments:			
Maintenance:			
Predicted usage in labor hours for coming year	90	25	10
Power (in kilowatt-hours):			
Predicted usage for coming year	360	320	120
Maximum allotted capacity	500	350	150

	Service departments	
	Power	*Maintenance*
Departmental activity measures:		
Maximum capacity	1,000 KWH	Adjustable
Predicted usage in coming year	800 KWH	125 hours
Departmental costs:		
Materials and supplies	$ 5,000	$ 1,500
Variable labor and overhead	1,400	2,250
Fixed overhead	12,000	250
Total service department costs	$18,400	$ 4,000

REQUIREMENTS

a) Calculate the plant-wide overhead rate for MumsDay Corporation for the coming year using the same method as used in the past.

b) Whit Portlock has been asked to develop departmental overhead rates for comparison with the plant-wide rate. The following steps are to be used to develop the departmental rates.

1. The Maintenance Department costs should be allocated to the three manufacturing departments using the direct method on the basis of predicted usage in direct-labor hours.
2. The Power Department costs should be allocated to the three manufacturing departments using the dual method, that is, the fixed costs allocated according to long-term capacity and the variable costs according to planned usage.
3. Calculate departmental overhead rates for the three manufacturing departments using a machine hour base for the Molding Department and a direct labor-hour base for the Component and Assembly Departments.

c) Should MumsDay Corporation use a plant-wide rate or departmental rates to assign overhead to its products? Explain your answer. (CMA Adpated)

6–18 Developing Predetermined Overhead Rates with Service Departments: A Special Decision

The steam-generating department of the Collins Company provides the power necessary to run the machines in two production departments, P1 and P2. Based on past experience, it has been determined that the total costs of operating the steam-generating department contain a fixed element of $30,000 per year and a variable element of $2.00 per 1,000 cubic meters of steam.

In addition to any allocated overhead costs, P1 has direct fixed overhead of $20,000 per year and P2 has direct fixed overhead of $10,000 per year. Direct variable overhead in P1 is $1 per machine hour. Direct variable overhead in P2 is $2 per machine hour.

Each machine hour in P1 requires the use of 1,000 cubic meters of steam. Each machine hour in P2 requires the use of 250 cubic meters of steam. Maximum yearly machine hours in P1 and P2 are 20,000 and 30,000, respectively.

Under current economic conditions, management expects to use 10,000 machine hours in P1 and 30,000 machine hours in P2 during 19x0.

REQUIREMENTS

a) Determine the expected 19x0 operating costs of the steam-generating department. Round computations to three decimals places in all parts.

b) Develop predetermined overhead rates for each department, assuming dual rates are to be used in allocating steam costs.

c) Develop predetermined overhead rates for each department, assuming a single rate based on use is used to allocate steam costs.

d) Develop a single predetermined plant-wide rate for allocating all overhead costs.

e) Indicate the effect of each of the preceding rates on the costing of two jobs:

	Machine hours		
	P1	*P2*	*Total*
Job 607	50	20	70
Job 301	20	50	70

f) Which rate do you prefer? Why?

g) The Collins Company has just received an order to manufacture 100 Liebos for a total price of $6,200. Each Liebo will require direct materials costing $20, direct labor costing $25, and will use one machine hour in P1 and four machine hours in P2. Should Collins accept the order if they have excess capacity?

6–19 Overhead Allocation and Product Pricing

The Upstate Appliance Company was founded in 19x4 to manufacture two products, Whambos and Gisbos. Whambos had been manufactured for a number of years by the Downstate Appliance Company. Gisbos were a new product, and only Upstate manufactured them.

Mr. Stomer, Upstate's President, set the price of Whambos and Gisbos at 110 percent of full manufacturing costs in 19x4 and, thanks to the absence of inflation, there have been no changes in costs or prices. Mr. Stomer's pricing calculations are as follows:

	Whambos	*Gisbos*
Direct materials	$ 40.00	$20.00
Direct labor	25.00	25.00
Overhead	27.50	27.50
Total	$ 92.50	$72.50
Markup, 10 percent	9.25	7.25
Selling price	$101.75	$79.25

Upstate prospered for a number of years as the sales of both products increased. Gisbos' rapid sales growth was expected, but Whambos' increase in sales was the result of Downstate's maintaining a $109/unit selling price.

In June 19x9 Downstate's president announced that the firm would cease production of Whambos and start producing Gisbos to sell for $72 each. Mr. Stomer was pleased that Upstate would now have the Whambos market to itself, but dismayed that Downstate's selling price for Gisbos was less than Upstate's full cost. He felt they could not maintain that price indefinitely because Downstate's plant and operating costs were similar to Upstate's. In July, when he learned that Downstate reported a large profit for June with the $72 price, he ran to the controller's office for an explanation.

The controller obtained the following information:

- Upstate has two production departments, P1 and P2. P1 has fixed operating expenses of $50,000 per year and variable overhead of $3 per direct-labor hour. P2 has fixed operating expenses of $20,000 per year and variable overhead of $1 per direct-labor hour.

- Whambos require four labor hours in P1 and one labor hour in P2.
- Gisbos require one labor hour in P1 and four labor hours in P2.
- Annual direct-labor hours are 10,000 in each department.

REQUIREMENTS

a) Evaluate Upstate's cost allocation and pricing policies.

b) Based on your analysis in part (a), indicate why Downstate decided to discontinue the production of Whambos and to start producing Gisbos?

c) What will probably happen to Upstate's sales and profits if they do not change their prices on Whambos and Gisbos?

d) What is the lowest price Upstate can charge for a Gisbos and still have incremental revenues greater than incremental costs?

6–20 Cost Finding in a Hospital

Over the years, a hospital operating as a not-for-profit corporation, has followed the policy of first allocating the central administrative costs to all functional departments and then allocating all service department costs to the revenue-producing departments. The following table reflects last year's allocations:

	Functional departments					
	Service departments			*Revenue-producing departments*		
	Hematology	*Physical therapy*	*X-ray*	*Out-patient emergency*	*In-patient*	*Maternity*
Costs incurred in department	$70,000	$100,000	$150,000	$300,000	$2,000,000	$400,000
Central administration	10,000	20,000	50,000	200,000	1,000,000	400,000
	$80,000			10,000	40,000	30,000
		$120,000		15,000	60,000	45,000
			$200,000	25,000	100,000	75,000
				$550,000	$3,200,000	$950,000

The central administrative costs were allocated on the basis of square footage used in each department, whereas service department costs were allocated on the basis of the number of patients treated in each revenue department during the year. The service departments provide service only to the revenue-producing departments.

REQUIREMENTS

Ignore reimbursement implications.

a) In general, what are the purposes of cost allocations?

b) Evaluate the process by which the hospital allocates its costs and discuss the advantages and disadvantages of this approach.

c) Would the numbers generated for the maternity revenue-producing departments be useful for planning a new maternity wing? If so, why; if not, why?

d) Assuming costs are unchanged, what would be the general effect on the proportion of costs allocated to the out-patient emergency revenue department if the number of maternity patients increased (that is, would the amount decrease, increase, or remain unchanged)? What effect would this have on the use of the cost data?

(CIA Adapted)

6–21 Cost Finding in a University

Regional University is a state-supported university with a total enrollment of 5,000 full-time students and faculty of 350. State appropriations are the sole source of operating funds as all tuition and fees collected from students are required to be remitted to the state treasurer. The 19x6 operating appropriation was $12.5 million, which represents an average cost of $2,500 per student.

The basic product of the university is the granting of degrees to students who complete degree requirements in a particular program. The departments granting degrees are somewhat analogous to production departments and the various support departments (for example, facilities services, academic support services, and administrative services) are similar to overhead departments in a manufacturing environment.

The administration has implemented a model used by a nearby university to analyze operating costs. The university's central administration believes that the new cost model will provide information that will be helpful in assessing the effectiveness of internal resource utilization, in assisting budget preparation and the related budget justification before the legislature, and in providing data for examining options for allocating funds based on current program costs and projected university enrollments. The cost model is designed to provide information about the traceable direct costs incurred by academic departments and allocated support costs charged to academic departments; the sum of the traceable direct and allocated support costs are considered to be the total costs of an academic department. Various cost measures are calculated for each academic department and for the student degree programs (majors) offered by each department.

The following schedules for the Electrical Engineering Department of Regional University's College of Engineering have been prepared according to the new cost model. These are examples of schedules that are prepared for academic departments and degree programs in the university. The following definitions for student activity measures should help you interpret the cost data:

1. Student Credit Hour (SCH)—the standard measure of instructional activity equivalent to one student enrolled in an academic course for which one credit hour is granted; for example, a three-credit-hour course with 20 students equals 60 SCH of instructional activity.
2. Full-Time Student—a student enrolled for 30 credit hours in an academic year.
3. Equivalent Full-Time Students—the number of credit hours taken by students divided by 30 credit hours.

Schedule 1 presents the total instructional costs (traceable direct and allocated support) and the instructional costs per SCH taught by the Electrical Engineering Department. Schedule 2 presents the traceable direct and total costs of the electrical engineering degree program (major); the cost per SCH taken and per student major is also presented there.

SCHEDULE 1

Regional University—College of Engineering
Instructional Costs for the Electrical Engineering Department
For the 19x6–x7 Academic Year

Traceable direct costs	*Total cost (000 omitted)*	*Cost per SCH taught**
Salaries and benefits	$ 600	$ 73.20
Travel expenses	25	3.00
Printing and advertising	3	0.40
Supplies	29	3.50
Equipment	16	1.90
Rentals	12	1.50
Total direct costs	$ 685	$ 83.50
Allocated support costs		
Facilities services (utilities, building and grounds, etc.)†	$ 180	$ 22.00
Academic support services (library, computer, etc.)‡	206	25.10
Administrative services (admissions, placement, etc.)‡	103	12.60
Office of Engineering Dean†	15	1.80
Total allocated support costs	504	61.50
Total department instruction costs	$1,189	$145.00

* 8,200 student credit hours (SCH) were taught in the electrical engineering department.
† Cost allocated on the basis of square feet occupied.
‡ Cost allocated on the basis of the number of student majors.

SCHEDULE 2

Regional University—College of Engineering
Program Costs of Students Majoring in Electrical Engineering
For the 19x6–x7 Academic Year

Department providing instruction	*Traceable direct costs**		*Total costs**	
Chemical	($92.90 × 200)	$ 18,580	($169.60 × 200)	$ 33,920
Civil	($69.80 × 100)	6,980	($147.30 × 100)	14,730
Electrical	($83.50 × 6,500)	542,750	($145.00 × 6,500)	942,500
Mechanical	($74.80 × 1,150)	86,020	($126.50 × 1,150)	145,475
All nonengineering†		112,500		202,500

Costs associated with students enrolled as electrical engineering majors	$766,830	$1,339,125
Electrical engineering degree program costs per SCH taken‡	$ 49.63	$ 86.67
Electrical engineering degree program costs per student major§	$ 1,489	$ 2,600

* The costs of each academic department used by students majoring in electrical engineering are determined by multiplying the cost per SCH taught in that department by the number of SCH taken by students enrolled in the electrical engineering degree program from that department.

† Students majoring in electrical engineering were enrolled in 7,500 SCH from various nonengineering departments. Each nonengineering department has its own traceable direct and total cost per SCH and the cost to the electrical engineering program is charged according to these rates. However, the detail of these charges has been omitted from this schedule.

‡ A total of 15,450 SCH were taken by students in the electrical engineering degree program.

§ The electrical engineering degree program has 515 full-time equivalent student majors.

REQUIREMENTS

a) The total traceable direct costs per SCH taught in the Electrical Engineering Department is $83.50 (Schedule 1). Is this an approximation of the variable costs per SCH taught in that department? Explain your answer.

b) The annual traceable direct cost per student majoring in electrical engineering is $1,489 (Schedule 2). Is this an approximation of the annual variable cost per student major in electrical engineering? Explain your answer.

c) The allocated support costs per SCH taught are $61.50 for the Electrical Engineering Department and $76.70 for the Chemical Engineering Department. Does this mean that more support costs were allocated to the Chemical Engineering Department? Explain your answer.

d) Should the Electrical Engineering Department use traceable direct and total department instructional cost per SCH taught (as presented in Schedule 1) in preparing its budget for presentation to the university administration? Explain your answer. (CMA Adpated)

6–22 Step Service Department Cost Allocation and FIFO Process Costing: Review Problem

The Panhandle Supply Company manufactures two products, X and Y, on a continuous basis in two separate departments, Px and Py. Px and Py receive services from two service departments, S1 and S2. S1 allocates its actual operating costs to all other departments on the basis of number of employees. S2 allocates its direct and indirect costs to P1 and P2 on the basis of direct-labor costs.

Px and Py apply overhead with the use of predetermined overhead rates. In Px, the overhead rate is $0.25/direct-labor dollar. In Py, the overhead rate is

$0.60/direct-labor dollar. The following information is available about January 19x1 operations:

	S1	*S2*	*Px*	*Py*
Number of employees	10	20	50	30
Units in process, beginning			2,000*	0
Units completed			8,000	6,000
Units in process, ending			5,000†	0
Work-in-Process, beginning			$14,000	0
Current costs:				
Direct materials			$24,000	$ 7,000
Direct labor			$90,000	$22,500
Direct department overhead	$10,000	$8,000	$20,000	$40,000

* 50 percent complete as to materials and conversion.
† 100 percent complete as to materials; 40 percent complete as to conversion.

REQUIREMENTS

a) Develop a schedule allocating S1 and S2 operating costs to Px and Py.

b) For Department Px only:

1. Determine the normal cost per equivalent unit manufactured.
2. Compute the underapplied or overapplied overhead in Department Px Overhead Control.
3. Prepare a statement of cost of goods manufactured.

6–23 Normal Job-Order Costing with Service Departments: Journal Entries: Review Problem

The Ziegler Company, which uses predetermined departmental overhead rates for product costing, contains two service departments, S1 and S2, and two production departments, P1 and P2. The service departments provide services only to production departments. They use dual rates to allocate their fixed and variable operating costs. The fixed costs of S1 and S2 are allocated as follows:

From \ To	*P1*	*P2*
S1	40%	60%
S2	50%	50%

The variable costs of S1 are allocated on the basis of direct-labor hours, and the variable costs of S2 are allocated on the basis of machine hours.

The predetermined overhead rate in P1 is $20 per direct-labor hour and the predetermined overhead rate in P2 is $13 per machine hour. All jobs are started in P1 and transferred to P2 for completion.

On December 1, 19x9, there was no work-in-process in P1. One Job, 607, was in process in P2. Total costs assigned to job 607 through November 30, 19x9, included direct materials of $8,000; direct labor of $4,000; and overhead of $10,000. The December 1 balances in the departmental overhead control accounts for P1 and P2 were $200 credit and $4,900 debit, respectively.

During December, the following events took place:

- S1 incurred fixed costs of \$8,000 and variable costs of \$12,500.
- S2 incurred fixed costs of \$15,000 and variable costs of \$6,000.
- Three new jobs, 608, 609, and 610, were started and two jobs, 607 and 608, were completed and sold.
- P1 and P2 incurred the following direct overhead costs:

	P1	*P2*
Supervision	\$4,000	\$2,000
Depreciation	800	1,800
Supplies	500	900
Indirect labor	200	300
Overtime premium	300	–0–

- The following materials cost information was recorded on job-cost sheets:

	Job			
	607	*608*	*609*	*610*
P1	\$ –0–	\$2,500	\$1,800	\$2,000
P2	2,000	2,100	1,900	800

- The following information was recorded on job work tickets:

	Job			
	607	*608*	*609*	*610*
P1 Labor hour	—	600	350	250
P1 Machine hours	—	200	100	100
P2 Labor hours	500	300	400	100
P2 Machine hours	600	1,000	700	300

- Production employees were paid \$5 per hour.

REQUIREMENTS

a) Prepare summary journal entries for the incurrence of costs in all departments and for their transfer to other departments or to the Cost of Goods Sold.

b) Prepare a schedule of changes in the P1 and P2 Departmental Overhead Control accounts.

c) How should the ending balances in the Departmental Overhead Control accounts be disposed of? Why?

6–24 Basics of Matrix Algebra (Appendix)

Presented are four matrices:

$$\mathbf{A} = \begin{bmatrix} 17 & 4 \\ 8 & 2 \end{bmatrix} \qquad \mathbf{C} = \begin{bmatrix} 10 \\ 2 \end{bmatrix}$$

$$\mathbf{B} = \begin{bmatrix} 20 & -5 \\ -10 & 2 \end{bmatrix} \qquad \mathbf{D} = [3 \quad 5]$$

REQUIREMENTS

Compute each of the following:

a) $\mathbf{A} + \mathbf{B}$

b) $\mathbf{A} - \mathbf{B}$

c) 5**A**

d) **AB**

e) **AC**

f) **DC**

g) $\mathbf{A}^{-1}$ (Verify your answer).

6–25 Basics of Matrix Algebra (Appendix)

Presented are four matrices:

$$\mathbf{A} = \begin{bmatrix} 5 & 4 & 4 \\ 4 & 2 & 0 \\ 0 & 2 & 2 \end{bmatrix} \qquad \mathbf{C} = \begin{bmatrix} -2 \\ 4 \\ 5 \end{bmatrix}$$

$$\mathbf{B} = \begin{bmatrix} 8 & 0 & 0 \\ 4 & 1 & 0 \\ -5 & 0 & -2 \end{bmatrix} \qquad \mathbf{D} = [3 \quad -4 \quad 10]$$

REQUIREMENTS

Compute each of the following:

a) $\mathbf{A} + \mathbf{B}$

b) $\mathbf{A} - \mathbf{B}$

c) 3**A**

d) **AB**

e) **AC**

f) **DC**

g) $\mathbf{A}^{-1}$ (Verify your answer).

6–26 Matrix Algebra and Simultaneous Equations (Appendix)

Solve the following series of simultaneous equations for X and Y:

$$-0.5X + 10Y = 39$$

$$-1X + 4Y = 14$$

6–27 Matrix Algebra and Simultaneous Equations (Appendix)

Solve the following series of simultaneous equations for P, S, and N:

$$-3P + 0S + 4N = -3$$

$$-1P + 2S + 1N = 2$$

$$-2P + 0S + 2N = -4$$

SOLUTION TO REVIEW PROBLEM

a) Direct method of service department cost allocation.

	Department					
	S1	*S2*	*S3*	*R1*	*R2*	*Total*
Direct overhead costs	$10,000	$20,000	$5,000	$20,000	$30,000	$85,000
Distribution:						
S1	(10,000)			5,000	5,000	
S2		(20,000)		16,000	4,000	
S3			(5,000)	2,500	2,500	
Total revenue department overhead				$43,500	$41,500	$85,000

b) Step method of service department cost allocation.

	Department					
	S1	*S2*	*S3*	*R1*	*R2*	*Total*
Direct overhead costs	$10,000	$20,000	$5,000	$20,000	$30,000	$85,000
Distribution:						
S2	4,000	(20,000)	6,000	8,000	2,000	
S1	(14,000)		3,500	5,250	5,250	
S3			(14,500)	7,250	7,250	
Total revenue department overhead				$40,500	$44,500	$85,000

c) Equations for linear algebra method.

$$\begin{array}{rrrrrcr}
+1R1 & -0R2 & -0.30S1 & -0.40S2 & -0.35S3 & = & 20{,}000 \\
-0R1 & +1R2 & -0.30S1 & -0.10S2 & -0.35S3 & = & 30{,}000 \\
-0R1 & -0R2 & +1.00S1 & -0.20S2 & -0.15S3 & = & 10{,}000 \\
-0R1 & -0R2 & -0.20S1 & +1.00S2 & -0.15S3 & = & 20{,}000 \\
-0R1 & -0R2 & -0.20S1 & -0.30S2 & +1.00S3 & = & 5{,}000
\end{array}$$

$$\begin{bmatrix} 1 & 0 & -0.30 & -0.40 & -0.35 \\ 0 & 1 & -0.30 & -0.10 & -0.35 \\ 0 & 0 & 1.00 & -0.20 & -0.15 \\ 0 & 0 & -0.20 & 1.00 & -0.15 \\ 0 & 0 & -0.20 & -0.30 & 1.00 \end{bmatrix} \cdot \begin{bmatrix} R1 \\ R2 \\ S1 \\ S2 \\ S3 \end{bmatrix} = \begin{bmatrix} 20{,}000 \\ 30{,}000 \\ 10{,}000 \\ 20{,}000 \\ 5{,}000 \end{bmatrix}$$

$$\begin{bmatrix} R1 \\ R2 \\ S1 \\ S2 \\ S3 \end{bmatrix} = \begin{bmatrix} 1 & 0 & -0.30 & -0.40 & -0.35 \\ 0 & 1 & -0.30 & -0.10 & -0.35 \\ 0 & 0 & 1.00 & -0.20 & -0.15 \\ 0 & 0 & -0.20 & 1.00 & -0.15 \\ 0 & 0 & -0.20 & -0.30 & 1.00 \end{bmatrix}^{-1} \cdot \begin{bmatrix} 20{,}000 \\ 30{,}000 \\ 10{,}000 \\ 20{,}000 \\ 5{,}000 \end{bmatrix}$$

d) Final allocation using linear algebra method

$$\begin{bmatrix} R1 \\ R2 \\ S1 \\ S2 \\ S3 \end{bmatrix} = \begin{bmatrix} 1 & 0 & 0.5397 & 0.6672 & 0.5310 \\ 0 & 1 & 0.4603 & 0.3328 & 0.4690 \\ 0 & 0 & 1.0977 & 0.2816 & 0.2069 \\ 0 & 0 & 0.2644 & 1.1149 & 0.2069 \\ 0 & 0 & 0.2989 & 0.3908 & 1.1035 \end{bmatrix} \cdot \begin{bmatrix} 20{,}000 \\ 30{,}000 \\ 10{,}000 \\ 20{,}000 \\ 5{,}000 \end{bmatrix}$$

$$\begin{bmatrix} R1 \\ R2 \\ S1 \\ S2 \\ S3 \end{bmatrix} = \begin{bmatrix} 41{,}396 \\ 43{,}604 \\ 17{,}643.5 \\ 25{,}976.5 \\ 16{,}322.5 \end{bmatrix}$$

The indirect revenue department overhead costs are:

	R1	*R2*	*Total*
Total revenue department overhead	$41,396	$43,604	$85,000
Direct revenue department overhead	– 20,000	– 30,000	– 50,000
Indirect revenue department overhead	$21,396	$13,604	$35,000

e) Successive allocation approximation

	Department					
	S1	*S2*	*S3*	*R1*	*R2*	*Total*
Direct overhead costs	$ 10,000.00	$ 20,000.00	$ 5,000.00	$20,000.00	$30,000.00	$85,000.00
First allocation:						
S1	(10,000.00)	2,000.00	2,000.00	3,000.00	3,000.00	
S2	4,400.00	(22,000.00)	6,600.00	8,800.00	2,200.00	
S3	2,040.00	2,040.00	(13,600.00)	4,760.00	4,760.00	
Intermediate results	$ 6,440.00	$ 2,040.00	$ 0.00	$36,560.00	$39,960.00	$85,000.00
Second allocation:						
S1	(6,440.00)	1,288.00	1,288.00	1,932.00	1,932.00	
S2	665.60	(3,328.00)	998.40	1,331.20	332.80	
S3	342.96	342.96	(2,286.40)	800.24	800.24	
Intermediate results	$ 1,008.56	$ 342.96	$ 0.00	$40,623.44	$43,025.04	$85,000.00
Third allocation:						
S1	(1,008.56)	201.71	201.71	302.57	302.57	
S2	108.93	(544.67)	163.40	217.87	54.47	
S3	54.77	54.77	(365.11)	127.79	127.79*	
Intermediate results	$ 163.70	$ 54.77	$ 0.00	$41,271.67	$43,509.87	$85,000.01
Direct allocation:						
S1	(163.70)			81.85	81.85	
S2		(54.77)		43.82	10.95	
Final results				$41,397.34	$43,602.67	$85,000.01

* Answer reflects rounding to two decimal places.

Part Two

EVALUATING AND USING COST DATA FOR PLANNING

7 Estimating Costs from Accounting Data

INTRODUCTION
APPROACHES TO COST ESTIMATION AND PREDICTION
DATA REQUIREMENTS AND LIMITATIONS
SELECTING A COST ESTIMATING EQUATION
SUMMARY
APPENDIX A: BASIC STATISTICAL CONCEPTS
APPENDIX B: STATISTICAL CONSIDERATIONS IN REGRESSION ANALYSIS
APPENDIX C: LEARNING CURVE ANALYSIS

INTRODUCTION

IN AND OF THEMSELVES, THE HISTORICAL COSTS USED IN JOB ORDER AND process costing are not relevant to decisions about the future. However, in limited circumstances, an analysis of them provides information that is useful in planning and controlling ongoing operations and in making special decisions. Assuming operations continue as they have in the past, cost estimates based on historical cost data may be used in developing standards and budgets. Likewise, probability intervals based on historical cost data may be used in controlling operations. Historical cost data may also be analyzed to obtain the coefficients needed in linear programming models and to estimate the potential cost savings from investing in new facilities. These applications are discussed in later chapters.

The purpose of this chapter is to present how cost estimates are developed from accounting data. Our ultimate objective is to use cost estimates as a basis for predicting future costs and controlling future operations.

APPROACHES TO COST ESTIMATION AND PREDICTION

A variety of methods are used for analyzing cost behavior and predicting future costs. These methods range from simple procedures such as account classification and high-low to sophisticated procedures such as multiple linear regression. The procedure that should be used depends on the costs and benefits of the particular method. A good rule of thumb is "don't use a more complex procedure when a simpler one will do." A more sophisticated procedure is justified only if it has a greater ratio of benefits to costs than a simpler procedure. This may occur if the results suggest a different course of action or if the information is provided on a more timely basis.

In many cases, cost behavior is summarized in an equation of the following form:

$$\hat{T} = a + bX \tag{7-1}$$

where

$\hat{T}$ = estimated total costs
a = estimated fixed costs
b = estimated variable unit costs
X = units of activity

The "cap" or "caret" is inserted over the variable T to indicate that the equation is used to *estimate* total costs. $\hat{T}$ is referred to as the **dependent variable** because changes in it are explained by changes in one or more independent variables, and X is referred to as the **independent variable** used to explain changes in the dependent variable. Note that since $\hat{T}$ is an estimate, an actual value of T may not equal the estimate $\hat{T}$.

Starting with the lowest level of mathematical sophistication, the following methods of analyzing costs are examined in this chapter:

- Account classification
- High-low method
- Scatter diagram
- Simple linear regression
- Multiple linear regression

In addition to these methods for analyzing historical costs, engineering methods are sometimes used to set production standards and estimate the costs of special projects. **Engineering methods** of cost estimation are based on the resources that should be used and the cost that should be incurred to produce a product under efficient operating conditions. Unfortunately engineering methods are complex, job specific, and expensive. Because it is difficult to generalize the procedures involved, a detailed discussion of them is beyond the scope of this book.

Account Classification

The most traditional accounting method of cost estimation is the **account classification method,** which uses the cost accountant's professional judgment to analyze costs recorded in each account and determine whether they are fixed, variable, or mixed (semivariable) costs. Professional judgment is then used to break mixed costs into fixed and variable elements. Because of the subjectivity involved in classifying the costs and determining the fixed and variable elements of mixed costs, this method relies heavily on the cost accountant's professional judgment.

Once the accountant has classified all costs as either fixed or variable, the costs in each category are totaled. The total fixed costs are then used as an estimate of a in Eq. 7–1, and the estimated variable unit costs, b, are equal to total variable costs divided by the number of units produced.

Example 7–1

The Dickens Company began manufacturing kitchen and dining room tables in June 19x0. At the end of December 19x1 management requested the controller to develop a cost-estimating equation to assist in planning future operations.

The controller obtained the December production and cost data presented in Exhibit 7–1 and classified all costs as fixed or variable. It was necessary to use professional judgment to break the mixed indirect-labor and utilities costs into their fixed and variable elements. After analyzing these costs, the following cost-estimating equation was developed:

$$\hat{T} = \$3{,}930 + \$130X$$

If no changes are expected in prices or technology, Dickens can use this equation to predict total costs at a given level of production. For example, if production in January 19x2 is expected to be 240 units, the predicted total production cost is \$35,130 [\$3,930 + (\$130 × 240)].

The primary strengths of account classification are limited data requirements and formal reliance on professional judgment. Because only one period's operating results are required, this method is ideal for new products or situations involving rapid changes in prices and/or technology. Additionally, account classification usually provides the best estimate of capacity costs of all techniques considered in this chapter because it is based on analyzing the behavior of each cost. **Capacity costs** are fixed costs incurred to provide the current level of manufacturing facilities.

The primary weaknesses of account classification are its total lack of a range of observations and subjectivity. Because the data used in the analysis are from only one period, they may reflect unusual circumstances or inefficient operations (as is likely with new products). When this occurs, predictions of future costs based on these conditions will be misleading. Subjectivity is a weakness because different analysts may classify costs differently or split mixed costs into different fixed or variable elements. This leads to different cost-estimating equations depending on who does the analysis.

EXHIBIT 7–1 Account Classification Analysis of Dickens Company Costs

	Actual production costs	*Estimated fixed costs*	*Estimated variable costs*
Direct materials	\$ 7,400		\$ 7,400
Direct labor	10,500		10,500
Departmental overhead:			
Indirect labor	1,750	\$1,000	750
Supplies	1,000		1,000
Utilities	2,380	580	1,800
Depreciation*	2,000	2,000	
Miscellaneous	350	350	
Total	\$25,380	\$3,930	\$21,450

Actual production = 165 tables

Variable costs per unit = \$21,450/165 = \$130

* Straight-line depreciation

High-Low

The high-low method can be used to derive a cost-estimating equation when two or more observations are available. The **high-low method** uses data from two observations, the observations containing the highest and lowest activity (values of X), to estimate fixed and variable costs. Assuming identical fixed costs in the observations of highest and lowest activity, the difference in costs between these two observations is due entirely to the difference in total variable costs. This difference, in turn, is due entirely to the difference in activity. Hence,

$$\text{Variable cost per unit} = \frac{\text{Difference in total costs}}{\text{Difference in total activity}} \tag{7–2}$$

The relationships underlying Eq. 7–2 are illustrated in Exhibit 7–2. The estimated variable cost per unit, b, is the slope of the total cost line in Exhibit 7–2. Once this slope is determined, we can find the fixed costs by using total costs and activity for *either* the observation of highest or lowest activity. The fixed costs are equal to the total costs minus the variable costs. In equation form,

$$a = T - bX \tag{7–3}$$

Example 7–2

Over 19 months of operations, the Dickens Company experienced the operating results summarized in Exhibit 7–3. The observations of highest and lowest activity are in April and December of 19x1. Using Eqs. 7–2 and 7–3, the following cost estimates are obtained:

$$b = \frac{\$59{,}000 - \$25{,}380}{350 - 165} = \underline{\underline{\$181.73}}$$

$$a = \$59{,}000 - (\$181.73 \times 350) = \underline{\underline{-\$4{,}605.50}}$$

EXHIBIT 7–2 High-Low Cost Estimation

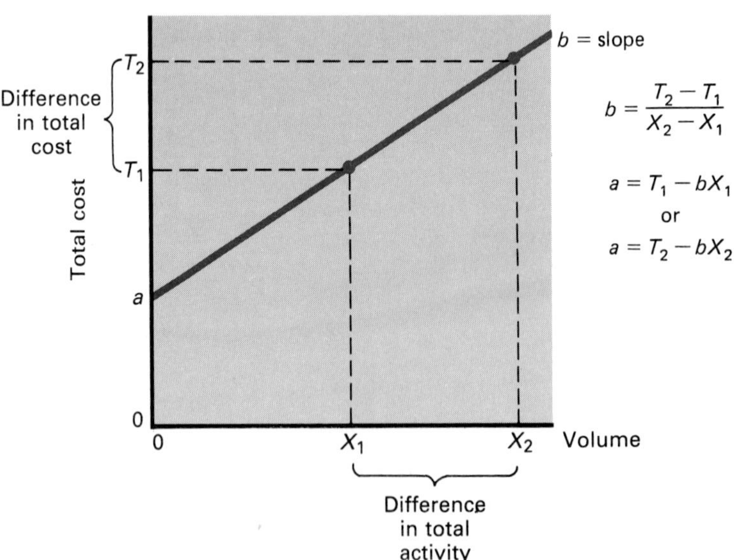

EXHIBIT 7–3 Operating Results of Dickens Company

Period	*Total production costs*	*Total units produced*
June, 19x0	$31,100	250
July	33,925	205
August	40,420	285
September	26,495	210
October	28,080	175
November	35,050	210
December	35,345	245
January, 19x1	31,550	250
February	31,490	220
March	29,650	180
April	59,000	350
May	39,955	280
June	34,695	255
July	36,920	235
August	30,815	195
September	40,290	260
October	35,805	250
November	38,400	270
December	25,380	165

The cost-estimating equation is:

$$\hat{T} = -\$4,605.50 + \$181.73X$$

and the predicted cost of 240 units is $39,009.70 [−$4,605.50 + ($181.73 × 240)], which compares with $35,130 using the account classification method.

Note that the cost-estimating equation in Example 7–2 includes a negative "fixed" cost. Two possible explanations are:

1. A linear function is used to represent a nonlinear function.
2. The zero-output level is beyond the relevant range.

Consequently the negative "fixed" cost is not an estimate of capacity costs. The −$4,605.50 is merely a number that is useful in fitting a cost-estimating line through the observed data within the range of observations. This is true of all fixed cost estimates that fall outside the relevant range. If management wants an estimate of capacity costs at the zero-production level, account classification is usually the best method to use. Although the value of a in the cost-estimating equation may not represent fixed costs, b is an estimate of variable unit costs within the relevant range because it is based on incremental costs and activity in this area.

Because of the nature of the high-low method, at least two periods of data are required rather than just one period as with account classification. The high-low method is more objective than the account-classification method. Because judgments are not required to classify costs as fixed or variable, two analysts will arrive at the same cost-estimating equation if they base their estimates on the same data. Unfortunately the high-low method is, almost by definition, based on unusual events. If the observations of highest and lowest activity are not representative of normal operations, they are not a good basis for predicting costs under normal circumstances. In Example 7–2, the slope of the cost-estimating line b is influenced by the unusually high costs of April 19x1. To overcome this problem, we might use data from the observations of second or third highest and/or lowest activity. But these may also reflect unusual circumstances. Additionally, when adjustments of this type are made, the high-low method becomes less objective.

Scatter Diagrams

The **scatter-diagram method** is a cost-estimating method in which observations of costs and activity are plotted on graph paper and professional judgment is used to draw a cost-estimating line with an equal number of observations on either side. The horizontal axis on the graph represents the independent variable X, and the vertical axis represents the dependent variable T.

Example 7–3

The 19x0 and 19x1 operating results of the Dickens Company are plotted in Exhibit 7–4, and two possible lines are fitted to them.

The scatter-diagram method is frequently used in preliminary analysis of cost data before using more sophisticated techniques. It is a rough-and-ready technique that is easily applied to determine possible relationships between two variables. Plotting the data helps us to determine if a linear cost function is appropriate, to spot "outlier" observations that result from unusual circumstances, and to determine if statistical problems exist. In Exhibit 7–4, the April 19x1 observation is far removed from normal operating levels and above both fitted lines. Consequently it may be **desirable to exclude** this observation in further analysis.

When used by itself, the scatter diagram is limited by the judgment of the analyst. The two lines in Exhibit 7–4 are far apart, although each appears reasonable. Interestingly, most possible lines will converge near the center of the range of normal operations. This means that the scatter-diagram method may be a useful way of estimating total costs in this area. However, the slope of the line and, consequently, variable cost estimates are subject to large errors.

EXHIBIT 7–4 **Scatter Diagram of Dickens Company Operating Results**

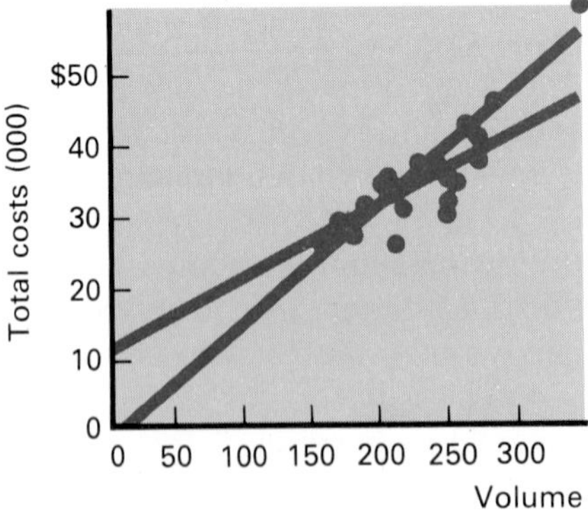

EXHIBIT 7–5 The Least-Squares Criterion

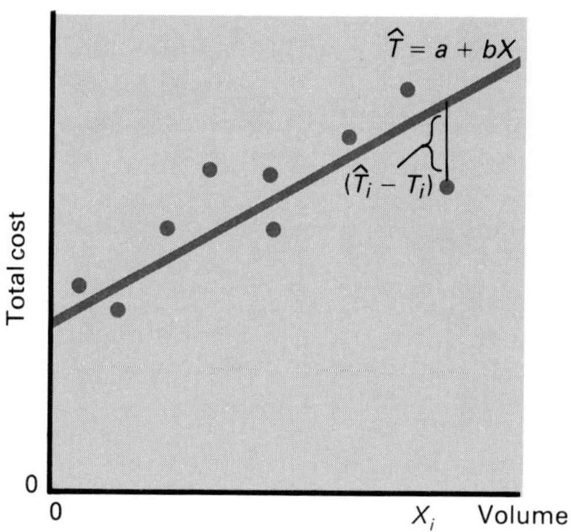

Dots represent actual observations of T_i at X_i.
Line represents estimate of T_i at X_i.
Estimate error at X_i is $\hat{T}_i - T_i$.
Criterion is to minimize sum of squared errors (vertical differences).

Simple Linear Regression[1]

Linear regression is conceptually similar to the scatter-diagram method. In **linear regression** the mathematical criterion of least squares is used to fit an equation for a straight line through a series of observations of activity and costs. The **least-squares criterion** is a mathematical criterion specifying that the sum of the squared vertical differences between observed data and a line representing an equation be minimized. In mathematical notation, the least-squares criterion is:

$$\text{minimize} \sum_{i=1}^{n} (\hat{T}_i - T_i)^2 \tag{7–4}$$

where

Σ = summation symbol
T_i = actual total cost of observation i
$\hat{T}_i$ = estimate of total cost for observation i
i = particular observation
n = number of observations

The least-squares criterion is illustrated in Exhibit 7–5. In Exhibit 7–5, $\hat{T}_i$ is a point on the total cost line and T_i is the corresponding actual total cost.

Regression analysis can be used with any number of independent variables. When only one independent variable is used to estimate costs, the procedure is called **simple linear regression.** If two or more independent variables are used, the procedure is called **multiple linear regression.**

---

[1] Students who need to review basic statistical concepts are referred to Appendix A of this chapter.

Although regression analysis is usually performed by computer, the calculations for simple linear regression are not difficult. For simple linear regression, the values for a and b are determined using the following equations:

$$b = \frac{\Sigma XT - \overline{X}\Sigma T}{\Sigma X^2 - \overline{X}\Sigma X} \tag{7–5}$$

$$a = \overline{T} - b\overline{X} \tag{7–6}$$

where

T = actual total cost (value of dependent variable)
X = actual units produced (value of independent variable)
$\overline{T}$ = average (mean) of actual costs
$\overline{X}$ = average (mean) of actual units produced

Example 7–4

The computations involved in using simple linear regression to fit a straight line to the 19x0 and 19x1 operating results of Dickens Company are shown in Exhibit 7–6. The resulting total cost-estimating equation is

$$\hat{T} = \$722.50 + \$144.908X$$

For a volume of 240 units, estimated total costs are $35,500.42 [$722.50 + ($144.908 × 240)]. This compares with the account-classification estimate of $35,130 and the high-low estimate of $39,009.70.

Simple linear regression analysis is an objective procedure that you can use to estimate average total costs at activity levels within the range of observations when there is only one independent variable. When you use this method, you can determine the degree to which the independent and dependent variables move together, how well the estimating equation fits the past data, how statistically significant the estimating equation is, and how large a variation can be expected between actual and estimated costs. These concepts are discussed in Appendix B to this chapter. Unfortunately regression analysis may give misleading results if a number of very stringent statistical assumptions are not satisfied.

The criterion used to derive the least-squares estimate (Eq. 7–4) corresponds to what is called a "quadratic loss function." Large errors are to be avoided because their significance increases with the square of their size. To avoid one large error, the quadratic loss function permits numerous smaller ones. (The reason why this criterion is used is discussed in books on regression analysis.) The impact of this criterion is to pull the estimating line toward "outlier" observations. Hence, outlier observations that are not the result of normal operations should be removed from the analysis. The April 19x1 observation appears to be an outlier.

Example 7–5

After eliminating the April 19x1 observation, the estimating equation is

$$T = \$9{,}534.749 + \$104.768X$$

For a volume of 240 units, estimated costs are $34,679.069 [$9,534.749 + ($104.768 × 240)].

EXHIBIT 7–6 Simple Linear Regression Computations

Period	*Total production costs (T)*	*Total units produced (X)*	*(X)(T)*	X^2
June, 19x0	31,100	250	7,775,000	62,500
July	33,925	205	6,954,625	42,025
August	40,420	285	11,519,700	81,225
September	26,495	210	5,563,950	44,100
October	28,080	175	4,914,000	30,625
November	35,050	210	7,360,500	44,100
December	35,345	245	8,659,525	60,025
January, 19x1	31,550	250	7,887,500	62,500
February	31,490	220	6,927,800	48,400
March	29,650	180	5,337,000	32,400
April	59,000	350	20,650,000	122,500
May	39,955	280	11,187,400	78,400
June	34,695	255	8,847,225	65,025
July	36,920	235	8,676,200	55,225
August	30,815	195	6,008,925	38,025
September	40,290	260	10,475,400	67,600
October	35,805	250	8,951,250	62,500
November	38,400	270	10,368,000	72,900
December	25,380	165	4,187,700	27,225
Totals	664,365	4,490	162,251,700	1,097,300

$$\bar{T} = \frac{664{,}365}{19} = 34{,}966.579$$

$$\bar{X} = \frac{4{,}490}{19} = 236.316$$

$$b = \frac{162{,}251{,}700 - (236.316 \times 664{,}365)}{1{,}097{,}300 - (236.316 \times 4{,}490)} = \frac{5{,}251{,}620.66}{36{,}241.16} = 144.908$$

$$a = 34{,}966.579 - (144.908 \times 236.316) = 722.50$$

Deleting the outlier observation had a significant effect on the computed values of a and b. Estimated total costs at 240 units are not significantly affected because this is near the center of the relevant range.

Multiple Linear Regression

Multiple linear regression analysis is an extension of simple linear regression. The only difference is in the number of independent variables. Simple linear regression has one independent variable, whereas multiple linear regression analysis contains two or more independent variables. Multiple linear regression analysis is a useful cost-estimating technique when an organization produces two or more products, or when factors other than volume affect costs. Because the computations are complex, multiple regression analysis is usually performed by computer programs.

The accountant uses multiple linear regression analysis to estimate the amount by which each of the cost-causing factors (that is, independent variables) affects costs. This is accomplished by measuring the effect on costs of changing one independent variable while holding the other independent variables constant. The cost-estimating equation takes the following form:

$$\hat{T} = a + b_1X_1 + b_2X_2 + \cdots + b_nX_n \qquad (7\text{–}7)$$

where

$\hat{T}$ = an estimate of total costs
a = vertical axis intercept
b_n = coefficient of independent variable n
X_n = value of observation for independent variable n
n = number of independent variables

Example 7–6

Although the Dickens Company produces both kitchen and dining room tables, it has made no attempt to keep separate cost records. Before submitting a bid to sell dining room tables to a large hotel, management wants to obtain data on the variable cost of producing dining room tables. Exhibit 7–7 contains total cost and production data by type of table for 19x0 and 19x1 except for the April 19x1 observation, which has been omitted because it is an outlier. Using these data and multiple linear regression, the following cost-estimating equation is developed:

$$\hat{T} = \$5{,}471.79 + \$196.254X_1 + \$79.607X_2$$

where

X_1 = number of dining room tables produced
X_2 = number of kitchen tables produced

EXHIBIT 7–7 Total Cost and Production Data by Type of Tables

Period	*Total production costs*	*Dining room tables produced*	*Kitchen tables produced*
June, 19x0	$31,100	50	200
July	33,925	105	100
August	40,420	105	180
September	26,495	40	170
October	28,080	75	100
November	35,050	110	100
December	35,345	90	155
January, 19x1	31,550	50	200
February	31,490	70	150
March	29,650	80	100
May	39,955	105	175
June	34,695	75	180
July	36,920	110	125
August	30,815	85	110
September	40,290	120	140
October	35,805	90	160
November	38,400	100	170
December	25,380	60	105

An estimate of the variable cost of producing a dining room table is \$196.254. Note that the variable cost estimate of producing a table was \$104.768 in Example 7–5. If Dickens' management based a bid on this amount, it is unlikely that the resulting contract would have been profitable.

A **dummy variable** is an independent variable that takes on the value of one or zero, depending on whether or not some specified condition exists. These conditions may relate to seasonal factors, the direction of a change in production, the percentage of capacity used, or a host of other things. When special conditions exist, dummy variables may sometimes be used to improve the accuracy of cost-estimating equations developed with multiple regression analysis.

Example 7–7

Assume that in January, February, and March the Dickens Company incurs seasonally high utilities costs. The cost-estimating equation when a dummy variable for these months is used in the regression analysis is:

$$\hat{T} = \$5{,}056.37 + \$199.499X_1 + \$79.950X_2 + \$547.917X_3$$

where X_3 = a dummy variable that takes on the value of one in January, February, and March, and zero in all other months.

In January, February, and March the fixed costs are estimated to be \$5,604.287 (\$5,056.37 + \$547.917). In all other months they are estimated at \$5,056.37.

Multiple linear regression analysis can provide very accurate cost estimates if a number of statistical assumptions are met. (These assumptions are discussed in Appendix B of this chapter.) Its major weakness is the high probability of inappropriate use. Because of the wide availability of statistical packages for computers, multiple linear regression analysis may be used to determine a cost-estimating equation because it is easy to input the values for a large number of observations and obtain results that appear to be precise. However, the results may be very misleading unless the data used in the analysis conform to the assumptions underlying the procedure.

Longitudinal and Cross-Sectional Analysis

The data used in regression analysis may consist of observations taken over a number of periods at a single facility or observations taken at a number of different facilities during a single period. An analysis of observations taken over a period of time at a single facility is called **longitudinal analysis**. An analysis of observations taken during a single period at a number of different facilities is called **cross-sectional analysis**. The data used in the Dickens Company example is longitudinal.

Organizations that operate a large number of similar facilities (for example, governments and chain stores) may be able to use cross-sectional analysis to overcome some of the data base problems mentioned in the next section. If a large number of observations can be obtained from a single recent period, the problems associated with changes in prices and technology may be reduced. Of course, the facilities being compared must be similar.

DATA REQUIREMENTS AND LIMITATIONS

Cost estimates based on historical cost data are only as good as the data base used to derive them. Cost accountants frequently supply the data used in statistical analysis and participate in the design of data processing and accumulation systems. To supply the best data possible, cost accountants should be familiar with the problems that arise in cost estimation that can be attributed to the data that were used.

Areas of Concern

Range of Observations Little confidence can be placed in statements about cost behavior beyond the range of activity used in developing cost estimates. Accordingly, the range of production levels included in the analysis should be as wide as possible.

Number of Observations Statistical models require a large number of observations in order to measure accurately and to make probability statements about costs.

Matching Costs and Production Costs and production must be matched within each observation. Accuracy will be reduced if costs are recorded in the wrong period, as sometimes happens at the end or beginning of a period, or if costs are applied to the wrong job, as sometimes happens when employees work on a number of different jobs.

Overhead Costs In a normal cost system, overhead is applied at a predetermined rate on the basis of units produced, labor hours, or some other factor. This has the effect of making all overhead costs appear as variable costs in cost estimates. To overcome this difficulty, actual rather than applied overhead costs must be used in cost analysis.

Length of Time Periods The longer the time period included in each observation, the more likely it is that periods of high and low activity will be averaged together. With long time periods, it is also difficult to obtain a large number, and a wide range, of observations. Conversely, if the time period is very short, it is difficult to match costs and production within observations. To solve this dilemma you must consider the benefits and costs of trading long for short time periods, but a working rule is that you should not use a long time period if accurate data are available for a shorter time.

Depreciation of Plant and Equipment When you have accelerated depreciation, including depreciation in the analysis creates a source of error. When accelerated depreciation methods are used, you should exclude depreciation from the cost data when you are using the high-low method or regression analysis. If you are using the account-classification method, you should include the depreciation for the future period as a separate cost element in the cost-predicting equation. Unfortunately it may be very difficult to factor out the depreciation included in indirect department costs.

Changes in Technology If major changes in technology have occurred in the past, only observations made under current production procedures should be included in the analysis.

Unusual Operating Conditions Observations of production under unusual circumstances should not be included in an analysis that attempts to determine what costs are expected in usual circumstances.

Inefficient Operating Conditions If operations were performed inefficiently in the past, cost estimates based on past observations will incorporate the inefficiencies. Under these conditions, the more expensive engineering methods of cost estimation may prove cost effective because of their higher accuracy.

Changes in Prices All observations included in the analysis should be based on constant input prices. If different observed costs are at different price levels, errors will be introduced into the analysis.

Adjusting for Price Changes

If product costs have changed during the time period covered by the observations, you should adjust the historical cost data for price changes before using a cost-estimating equation to predict future costs. The adjustment is made to restate the historical costs to what they would have been if the current prices had been in effect at the time the costs were incurred.

Example 7–8

Assume Dickens Company experienced a 15 percent increase in the costs of direct materials on March 1, 19x1, and a 10 percent increase in the cost of direct labor on July 1, 19x1. Factory overhead costs have not changed since production started in June 19x0.

Exhibit 7–8(a) shows the historical costs incurred by Dickens Company and the break down of the total into direct materials, direct labor, and factory overhead. Since the direct materials costs for June 19x0 through February 19x1 were incurred before the price increase, they should be adjusted to reflect the price at the end of 19x1. In Exhibit 7–8(b), the materials costs for those months have been multiplied by 1.15 (that is, cost + 15 percent increase) to adjust for the price change. Likewise, the direct-labor costs incurred from June 19x0 to June 19x1 should be multiplied by 1.10 (that is, cost + 10 percent increase) to reflect the increase in labor costs experienced on July 1, 19x1. This adjustment is also reflected in Exhibit 7–8(b). Because no price changes were related to overhead costs, the overhead costs in Exhibit 7–8(b) are the same as the costs in Exhibit 7–8(a). The total cost in Exhibit 7–8(b) is the sum of the adjusted materials, labor, and overhead costs.

If a cost-estimating equation is developed using simple linear regression from the total cost data in Exhibit 7–8(b) and the total units produced in Exhibit 7–3, the resulting equation is

$$\hat{T} = \$10{,}561.557 + \$107.284X$$

EXHIBIT 7–8 Adjusting Costs for Price Changes

(a) Unadjusted Historical Costs:

Period	*Direct materials*	*Direct labor*	*Factory overhead*	*Total production costs*
June, 19x0	$ 9,300	$12,400	$ 9,400	$31,100
July	10,200	13,600	10,125	33,925
August	12,000	16,300	12,120	40,420
September	8,000	10,600	7,895	26,495
October	8,400	11,300	8,380	28,080
November	10,300	14,000	10,750	35,050
December	10,500	14,100	10,745	35,345
January, 19x1	9,200	12,600	9,750	31,550
February	9,500	12,500	9,490	31,490
March	9,100	11,700	8,850	29,650
May	12,200	15,600	12,155	39,955
June	10,400	13,200	11,095	34,695
July	11,500	14,800	10,620	36,920
August	9,400	12,500	8,915	30,815
September	12,100	16,200	11,990	40,290
October	10,750	14,320	10,735	35,805
November	11,520	15,360	11,520	38,400
December	7,400	10,500	7,480	25,380

(b) *Historical Costs Adjusted for Price Changes* (15 percent increase in direct materials cost on March 1, 19x1, and 10 percent increase in direct-labor cost on July 1, 19x1):

Period	*Direct materials*	*Direct labor*	*Factory overhead*	*Total production costs*
June, 19x0	$10,695	$13,640	$ 9,400	$33,735
July	11,730	14,960	10,125	36,815
August	13,800	17,930	12,120	43,850
September	9,200	11,660	7,895	28,755
October	9,660	12,430	8,380	30,470
November	11,845	15,400	10,750	37,995
December	12,075	15,510	10,745	38,330
January, 10x1	10,580	13,860	9,750	34,190
February	10,925	13,750	9,490	34,165
March	9,100	12,870	8,850	30,820
May	12,200	17,160	12,155	41,515
June	10,400	14,520	11,095	36,015
July	11,500	14,800	10,620	36,920
August	9,400	12,500	8,915	30,815
September	12,100	16,200	11,990	40,290
October	10,750	14,320	10,735	35,805
November	11,520	15,360	11,520	38,400
December	7,400	10,500	7,480	25,380

Comparing this with the results in Example 7–5 shows that the fixed cost term has increased from \$9,534.749 to \$10,561.557, and the unit variable cost has increased from \$104.768 to \$107.284. For a volume of 240 units, predicted total costs are \$36,309.72 [\$10,561.557 + (\$107.284 × 240)]. This compares with a predicted cost of \$34,679.069 when unadjusted historical costs are used in the analysis.

Unfortunately adjustments for price changes are seldom this simple, with only one increase in materials costs, one increase in labor costs, and no increase in overhead costs. In reality, the prices of various cost elements are likely to change frequently, and past data are likely to contain several different price levels. Another approach to adjusting for changing prices under these circumstances is to adjust all costs using a general price index. A **price index** is a standardized measure of the amount of money needed to purchase a standardized package or basket of goods and services. General price indices are available for segments of the economy. Examples of general price indices include the Gross National Product Implicit Price Deflator, the Wholesale Price Index, and the Consumer Price Index.

To adjust costs for general price-level changes, we must know the price index at the time the costs were incurred and the price index for the time to which the costs are being adjusted. Then, to determine the price-level adjusted costs, we multiply the historical costs by a fraction representing the change in the price level. The numerator of the fraction is the price index at the time to which the costs are being adjusted and the denominator is the price index at the time the costs were incurred. In equation form, this is:

$$\text{Price-level adjusted historical cost} = \text{Historical cost} \times \frac{\text{Price index at the time to which costs are being adjusted}}{\text{Price index at the time when costs were incurred}} \qquad (7\text{–}8)$$

Example 7–9

The general price index was 120 in June 19x0 and 135 at December 31, 19x1. Dickens Company can adjust the June 19x0 costs of \$31,100 to December 31, 19x1, dollars by multiplying the historical costs by the fraction, 135/120. The price-level adjusted cost is \$34,987.50 [\$31,100 × (135/120)].

To develop an equation for predicting costs, Dickens Company would convert each month's cost to the December 31, 19x1, price level. The company would then use these price-level adjusted costs as the dependent variable in developing the cost-estimating equation. General price-level adjustments do not provide the accuracy of specific price-level adjustments, but, when determining which type of adjustment to use, you must weigh the additional costs of adjusting each specific cost element against the additional benefits. Regardless of how adjustments are made, only data reflecting a single price level should be used in developing a cost-estimating equation. As an analyst, you should be suspicious when using an equation derived from unadjusted historical cost data to predict future costs, especially when the historical data are from different years.

SELECTING A COST-ESTIMATING EQUATION

It should be obvious from the preceding discussion of cost estimation and prediction that various cost-estimating equations can be derived from the same data. As noted previously, the appropriate cost-estimating technique should be determined by comparing the benefits and costs of the various procedures. If a sophisticated technique has a higher ratio of benefits to costs than a simpler technique, the sophisticated technique should be used to determine the cost-estimating equation.

In addition to selecting the appropriate technique, the analyst must also select the activity base before deriving the cost-estimating equation. Because the objective of cost estimation is to determine how costs respond to changes in activity, selecting the appropriate activity measure is a major decision.

Selection of Activity Base

The most appropriate activity measure depends on the cost being studied. The activity measure should have a logical relationship to the cost and it should be easy to measure. Thus, units produced is a logical activity measure when we are trying to estimate total production costs. However, units produced would be inappropriate if we were trying to estimate selling expenses because selling expenses are related to the units sold rather than to the units produced.

If factory overhead costs are being estimated, the appropriate activity measure depends on whether production is labor intensive or machine intensive. For labor-intensive operations, activity might be measured by the number of employees, direct-labor hours, or direct-labor costs. Each of these measures has a logical relationship to overhead costs. For machine-intensive operations, machine hours may be the best activity measure. However, if no records are kept of machine hours, we may have to use another activity measure such as days worked during the period.

In selecting an activity measure, it is important to determine if the activity causes the incurrence of the cost being analyzed. Professional judgment is very important when making this determination. Statistical measures such as the correlation coefficient are often used to assist in selecting the best activity base.

Statistical Considerations

The computer programs used for regression analysis produce statistics that are useful in evaluating the relationship between the independent and dependent variables. One of these statistics is the correlation coefficient.

The **correlation coefficient,** R, is a standardized measure of the relationship between two variables. It can take on any value between $+1$ and -1. A value close to $+1$ indicates that the variables move simultaneously in the same direction; they become larger or smaller at the same time. A value close to -1 indicates that the variables move simultaneously in the opposite direction; as one becomes larger the other becomes smaller. A value close to zero indicates the absence of a relationship. Possible relationships between variables X and Y are illustrated as follows.

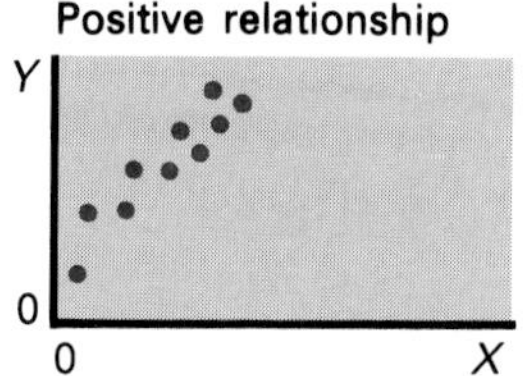

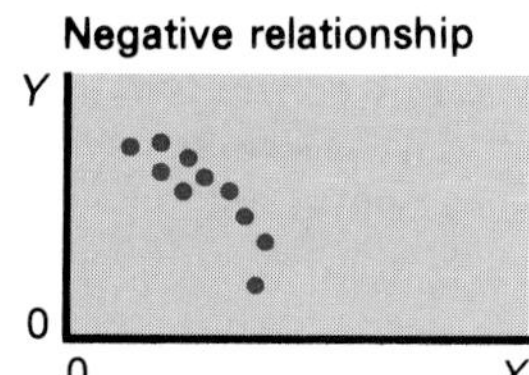

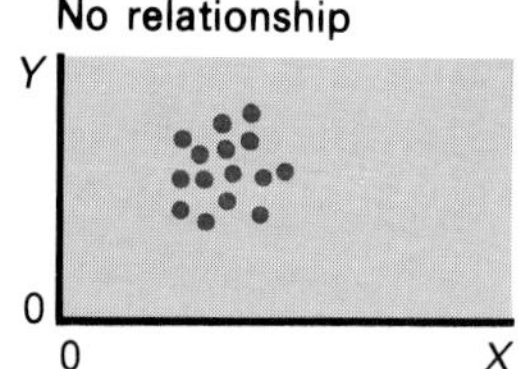

In evaluating two alternative cost-estimating equations, if other factors are equal, the one with the higher correlation coefficient is preferred. However, a high correlation (positive or negative) between the independent and dependent variables does not necessarily imply that the size of the latter is *caused* by the size of the former. Changes in both variables may be caused by a third variable, or the correlation between the variables may occur solely by chance. Direct materials and direct-labor costs may be highly correlated, but both are caused by a third variable, the units produced.

Although the correlation coefficient measures the relationship between two variables, you must still use professional judgment to determine the independent and dependent variables. A high positive correlation may exist when the independent and dependent variables are illogical. For example, if tables were specified as the dependent variable and costs as the independent variable in Example 7–4, a positive correlation would be obtained. Obviously this does not mean that all Dickens Company must do to obtain tables is to spend money.

SUMMARY

When used properly, the cost-estimating techniques presented in this chapter are a valuable management tool. They can be used in planning and controlling ongoing operations, and they provide data that are useful in making special decisions. When we use these models, we encounter two major types of problems: those concerning the data and those concerning statistical considerations. Data problems are related to the range of observations, the number of observations, the proper matching of costs and production, the treatment of overhead costs, the length of time periods, depreciation, changes in technology, unusual operating conditions, the efficiency of past operations, and changes in prices. One approach to the problem caused by changing prices is to adjust for specific or general price-level changes. Major statistical considerations are discussed in Appendix B to this chapter.

Although sophisticated procedures can provide more accurate information when used properly, they may also provide misleading information when used improperly. Unless the statistical assumptions underlying the sophisticated procedures are valid, we must avoid placing too much faith in their apparent precision. Misleading information can result if a linear cost function is used to represent a nonlinear function, or if the equation is used to estimate costs outside the relevant range. One type of nonlinear function is discussed in Appendix C to this chapter.

APPENDIX A Basic Statistical Concepts

The purpose of this appendix is to review the basic statistical concepts that are used in the analysis of data. These concepts form the foundation of cost estimation, the analysis of uncertainty in short-range planning, and variance investigation decisions.[2] Specifically this appendix reviews the following:

- Measures of central tendency
- Measures of dispersion
- The normal distribution
- The *t*-distribution

Example 7–10

Assume that the Newark Company produced 23 widgets last week. If Newark had an unusually detailed and accurate cost accounting system, they might accumulate variable unit production cost information for each widget. Assuming they did keep such records, the 23 observations of production costs might be as follows:

Widget number	*Variable cost*	*Widget number*	*Variable cost*	*Widget number*	*Variable cost*
1	$25	9	$22	17	$26
2	27	10	23	18	21
3	22	11	28	19	20
4	23	12	29	20	25
5	30	13	25	21	27
6	26	14	25	22	28
7	24	15	26	23	24
8	25	16	24		

Newark's management could use these data as a starting point for predicting future variable widget production costs. Unfortunately the present unsummarized form of the data might confuse as much as it enlightens. To improve its usefulness, these data must be summarized in a manner that emphasizes their significant features. One way to do this is to construct a frequency distribution. One type of **frequency distribution** is a bar graph that shows the number of observations in each group. For Example 7–10, a frequency distribution showing the number of widgets produced with each variable cost is presented in Exhibit 7–9. In Exhibit 7–9 the variable widget production costs are organized on the horizontal axis in order of increasing dollar amount. The height of each bar above each dollar amount indicates its frequency.

MEASURES OF CENTRAL TENDENCY

Instead of, or in addition to, the frequency distribution, summary statistics might be developed to describe variable widget production costs. Two important types of summary statistics concern themselves with measures of central tendency and measures of dispersion. A measure of **central tendency** indicates the location of the center of a distribution. A measure of **dispersion** indicates the spread of the distribution. The most frequently used measures of central tendency are the mean, median, and mode.

The **mode** is the most frequent value. As can be seen in Exhibit 7–9, $25 is the most frequent variable widget production cost.

The **median** is the value of the observation that splits the observations when arrayed from highest to lowest into two equal parts. Arranging the 23 observations of widget production costs in this manner, the twelfth observation splits the data into two equal

[2] The analysis of uncertainty in short-range planning is discussed in the appendix of Chapter 8. Variance investigation decisions are discussed in Chapter 19.

EXHIBIT 7–9 **Frequency Distribution of Variable Widget Production Costs: Symmetric Distribution**

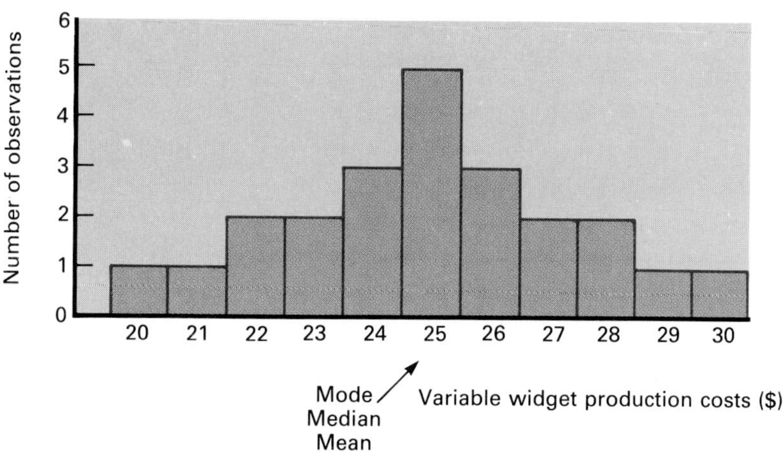

parts;[3] there are 11 higher and 11 lower observations. As can be seen in Exhibit 7–9, \$25 is the median variable widget production cost.

The **mean** is the average value computed by summing the value of all observations and dividing by the number of observations. In statistical notation a distinction is made between the mean of a population and the mean of a sample. A population mean is represented by the Greek letter mu, μ. This symbol might be used to describe the average widget production cost if widget production had ceased and the costs of all widgets were included in the computation. In most cases we do not have information on an entire population. This is especially true when production has not ceased. We have some past production cost data and we are interested in summarizing them as a starting point in predicting future production costs. The available data represent a sample taken from the entire population. The mean of a sample is represented by X with a line over the top of it, $\overline{X}$. It is referred to as "X-bar." The computation of $\overline{X}$ is represented as:

$$\overline{X} = \frac{1}{n} \sum_{i=1}^{n} X_i \tag{7–9}$$

where

$\overline{X}$ = sample mean
n = number of observations
X_i = value of observation i
Σ = summation sign

In Eq. 7–9 we are summing n observations of X and then multiplying this sum by the inverse of n (this is equivalent to dividing by n, which we can also do). Last week's average variable widget production cost was \$25:

$$\begin{aligned}\overline{X} &= \frac{1}{23}(\$25 + \$27 + \$22 + \$23 + \$30 + \$26 + \$24 + \$25 + \$22 + \$23 + \$28 \\ &\quad + \$29 + \$25 + \$25 + \$26 + \$24 + \$26 + \$21 + \$20 + \$25 + \$27 + \$28 \\ &\quad + \$24) \\ &= \underline{\underline{\$25}}\end{aligned}$$

[3] When there are an even number of observations, the median is computed as the average of the two middle observations.

We are assuming that last week's variable widget production cost data represent a sample taken from the population of all widget production costs. If we defined last week's widget production cost data as the population, we would use the symbol μ to represent the average.

Equation 7–9 is sometimes expressed as:

$$\overline{X} = \sum_{i=1}^{k} X_i (f_i / n) \tag{7–10}$$

where

f_i = number of observations of X with a particular value
X_i = a particular value of X
n = total number of observations
k = number of different values of X_i.

Using Eq. 7–10, last week's average variable widget production cost of \$25 is computed as follows:

$$\begin{aligned}\overline{X} &= \$20(1/23) + \$21(1/23) + \$22(2/23) + \$23(2/23) + \$24(3/23) + \$25(5/23) + \\ &\quad \$26(3/23) + \$27(2/23) + \$28(2/23) + \$29(1/23) + \$30(1/23) \\ &= \underline{\underline{\$25}}\end{aligned}$$

For Example 7–10 the mean, median, and mode all equal \$25. This occurs because the distribution of variable widget production costs is symmetric. When the distribution is not symmetric, as in Exhibit 7–10, the mean, median, and mode are not equal. In Exhibit 7–10 the mean is to the right of the other measures of central tendency because, as an average value, it is affected by extremes. Under these circumstances statisticians disagree as to the best measure of central tendency. However, if predictions of future costs are to be based on the sample summarized in Exhibit 7–10, the most likely cost is the mode of \$55 rather than the mean of \$57.

EXHIBIT 7–10 **Nonsymmetric Distribution***

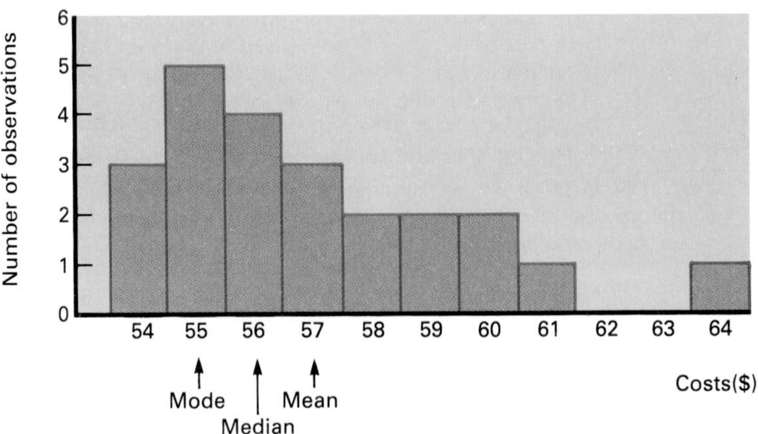

* This particular distribution is skewed to the right.

MEASURES OF DISPERSION

Although all measures of central tendency for Example 7–10 indicate variable widget production costs of \$25, it is unlikely that the actual variable cost of the next widget produced will equal this amount. Last week's variable widget production costs ranged from \$20 to \$30 per unit. If last week was indicative of normal operations, a similar variability in future costs can be expected. Hence, to provide a better basis for predicting future costs, management should obtain information on the dispersion, or spread of the distribution, as well as the central tendency of past costs. The two most frequently used statistical measures of dispersion are the variance and the standard deviation.

The **variance** of a population is computed as the average squared deviation of individual observations, X_i, from the population mean, μ. In symbolic notation the computation of the variance of a population is:

$$\sigma_X^2 = \frac{1}{N}\sum_{i=1}^{N}(X_i - \mu)^2 \tag{7–11}$$

where

N = number of items in the population
σ_X^2 = population variance (small Greek letter sigma, frequently identified as "sigma-squared"). The X indicates that this is the variance of variable X.

In most cost accounting applications we are trying to infer something about a population from sample data. Hence we use sample data to estimate μ and σ_X^2. $\overline{X}$ is regarded as an estimate of μ. Sigma-caret squared sub-X, $\hat{\sigma}_X^2$, represents an estimate of σ_X^2 based on sample data. It is computed as

$$\hat{\sigma}_X^2 = \frac{1}{n-1}\sum_{i=1}^{n}(X_i - \overline{X})^2 \tag{7–12}$$

Note that the sum of the squared deviations from the sample mean is multiplied by the inverse of (or divided by) $n - 1$ rather than N. Whenever inferences about population parameters are made from sample data, an adjustment is made for something called degrees of freedom. For a specific statistic, **degrees of freedom** refer to the number of observations in the sample minus the number of previously computed statistics used in computing the statistic of interest.

Before any inferences are made about a population from sample data, there are n degrees of freedom in the sample, one for each observation. One degree of freedom is used for each statistic computed and used in the computation of a subsequent statistic. In Eq. 7–12 we have $n - 1$ degrees of freedom because the previously computed value of $\overline{X}$ is used in the computation of $\hat{\sigma}_X^2$. If we now continued to determine the value of a third sample statistic, the computation of which used previously determined values of $\overline{X}$ and $\hat{\sigma}_X^2$, that sample statistic would have $n - 2$ degrees of freedom when it is used as a basis for inferring something about the population from which the sample is drawn.

The **standard deviation** is the square root of the variance. Hence the standard deviation of a population is:

$$\sigma_X = \sqrt{\frac{1}{N}\sum_{i=1}^{N}(X_i - \mu)^2} \tag{7–13}$$

An estimate of the population standard deviation from sample data is:

$$\hat{\sigma}_X = \sqrt{\frac{1}{n-1}\sum_{i=1}^{n}(X_i - \overline{X})^2} \tag{7–14}$$

Assuming last week's variable widget production cost data represent a sample drawn from the population of all variable production costs, the estimate of the population variance is 6.36:

$$\hat{\sigma}_X{}^2 = \frac{1}{23 - 1}[(\$25 - \$25)^2 + (\$27 - \$25)^2 + \cdots + (\$24 - \$25)^2]$$

$$= \underline{\underline{6.36}}$$

The estimate of the population standard deviation is 2.52:

$$\hat{\sigma}_X = \sqrt{6.36}$$

$$= \underline{\underline{2.52}}$$

THE NORMAL DISTRIBUTION AND TABLES

In reality the actual distribution of cost or other data varies widely. If, however, the data are distributed in accordance with one of several theoretical probability distributions, the data can be completely summarized in terms of statistical parameters such as the mean and the standard deviation. In this appendix attention is focused on the widely discussed and used standard normal distribution.

The **standard normal distribution** is a theoretical probability distribution having a mean of zero and a standard deviation of one. A standard normal distribution is illustrated in Exhibit 7–11. By definition, the area under the standard normal distribution curve sums to 1.0 or 100 percent. Of this total, 68.26 percent lies between plus or minus 1 standard deviation of the mean, 95.44 percent lies between plus or minus 2 standard deviations of the mean, and 99.73 percent lies between plus or minus 3 standard deviations of the mean.

If the population of interest is normally distributed, very precise statistical statements can be made about it. This is done by treating the population of interest as a linear transformation of a population with a mean of zero and a standard deviation of one. Assuming variable widget production costs are normally distributed, we can say that 99.73 percent of them are within 3 standard deviations of the mean variable widget production cost. With a standard deviation of \$2.52, this interval is shown in Exhibit 7–12 to be \$17.44 to \$32.56 [\$25 ± (3 × \$2.52), or 25 ± \$7.56].

EXHIBIT 7–11 **Areas Under the Normal Curve**

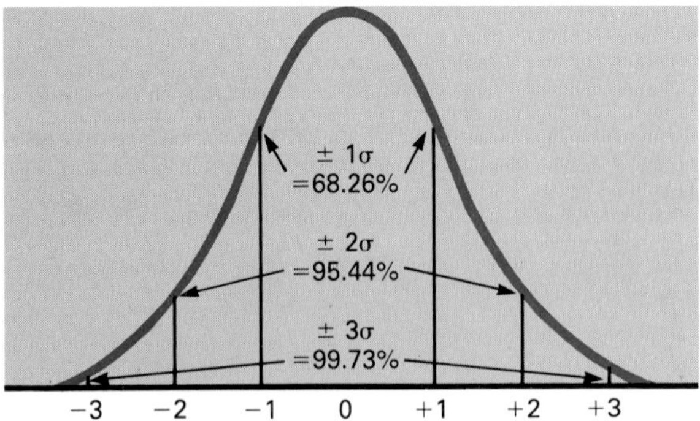

EXHIBIT 7–12 **Linear Transformation of a Standard Normal Distribution**

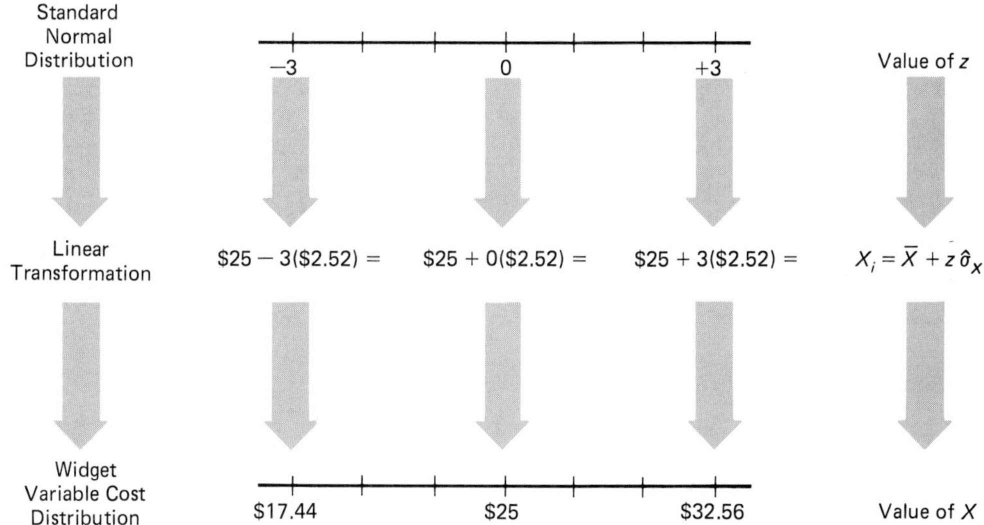

where
z = number of standard normal deviations from zero
X_i = a widget production cost

Table A in the appendix to this book presents the areas under one-half of the standard normal distribution. Because the normal curve is symmetric, the tabled values can be used for either side of the distribution. Using Table A we can calculate the answer to a large number of questions about the distribution of variable widget production costs.

Example 7–11 Determine the probability that Newark Company's variable cost of a widget will be more than $30.04.

This problem is illustrated in Exhibit 7–13(a). To solve it, we must find the percentage of the total area under the curve represented by the shaded area. To find this percentage, we restate $30.04 in terms of the standard normal distribution by using the following formula:

$$z = \frac{X_i - \overline{X}}{\hat{\sigma}_X} \tag{7–15}$$

where

z = the number of standard normal deviations X_i is from $\overline{X}$
X_i = the value of interest

For Example 7–11,

$$z = \frac{\$30.04 - \$25.00}{\$2.52} = \underline{\underline{2.00}}$$

Hence, $30.04 is 2 standard deviations from the mean of $25.00.

This standardization procedure is illustrated in Exhibit 7–13(b). Table A indicates that 2.28 percent of the area is to the right of $z = 2.00$. We conclude that there is a 2.28 percent probability that the variable costs of a widget will amount to more than $30.04.

Example 7–12

Determine the 95 percent probability interval for variable widget production costs.

The 95 percent probability interval will leave 2.5 percent of the area in the extreme tail on each side of the distribution of variable widget production costs. In Table A the value of z that leaves 2.5 percent of the area in one tail under the curve is 1.96. Hence, in the standard normal distribution, 95 percent of the area is in the interval 0 ± 1.96. These facts are illustrated in Exhibit 7–14(a).

A standard normal distribution has a mean of zero and a standard deviation of one. The distribution of variable widget production costs has a mean of $25 and a standard

EXHIBIT 7–13 Widget Production Costs Related to Standard Normal Distribution: Example 7–11

(a) Distribution of Variable Widget Production Costs

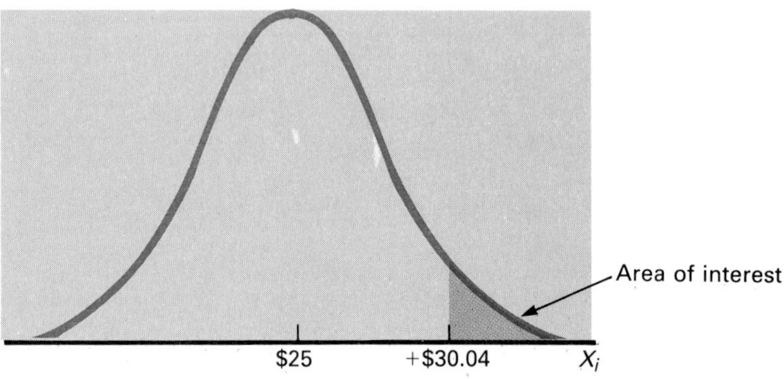

(b) Standardization of Variable Widget Production Cost Distribution*

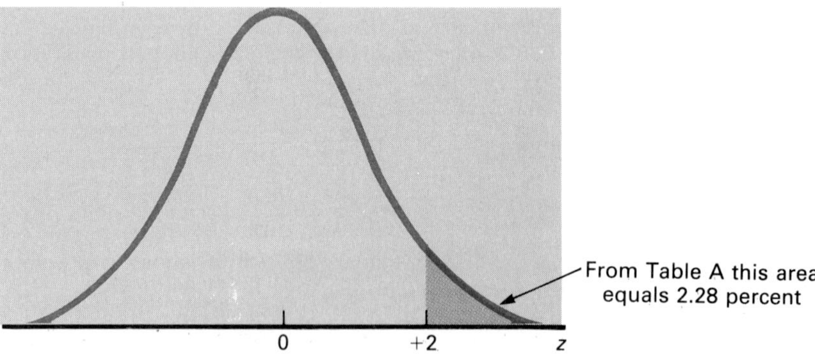

*Using the formula $z = \dfrac{X_i - \bar{X}}{\hat{\sigma}_X}$

EXHIBIT 7–14 Widget Production Costs Related to the Standard Normal Distribution: Example 7–12

(a) Ninety-five Percent Probability Interval for Standard Normal Distribution.

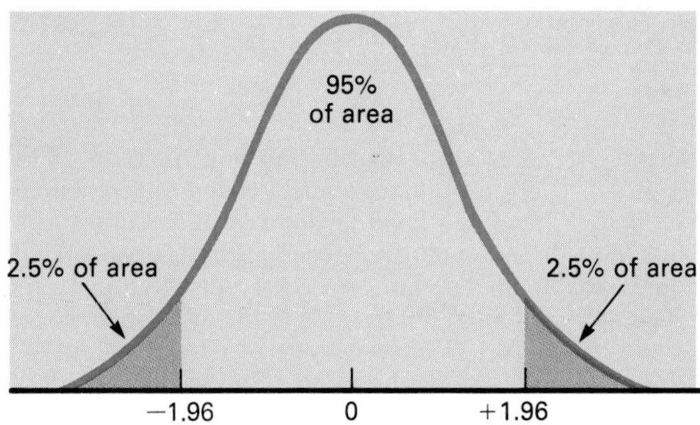

(b) Ninety-five Percent Probability Interval for Variable Widget Production Costs*.

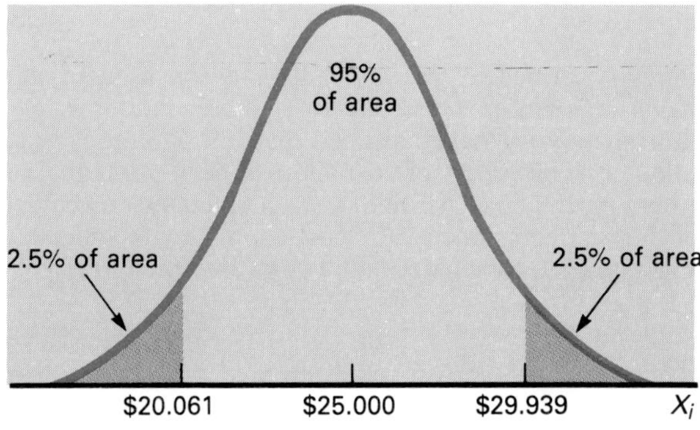

*Using the formula $X_i = \overline{X} + z\hat{\sigma}_X$

deviation of \$2.52. Reversing the normalization procedure, the 95 percent probability interval for widget production costs is \$20.061 to \$29.939 [\$25 ± 1.96(\$2.52)]. This is illustrated in Exhibit 7–14(b).

THE *t*-DISTRIBUTION AND TABLES

When making inferences about the distribution of a population from a sample of size 30 or less, it is more appropriate to use a *t*-distribution than it is to use a standard normal, or *z*, distribution. A ***t*-distribution** is a theoretical probability distribution similar in shape to the standard normal distribution except that its dispersion varies with the size of the sample and the resulting degrees of freedom. As the number of degrees of freedom increases, the *t*-distribution converges on the standard normal distribution. For a distribution that has a mean of zero and a standard deviation of one, the effect of degrees of freedom on a 95 percent probability interval is as follows:

Degrees of freedom	*Probability interval*
5	0 ± 2.571
10	0 ± 2.228
15	0 ± 2.131
20	0 ± 2.086
25	0 ± 2.060
∞	0 ± 1.960

Because the spread of the t-distribution is a function of the degrees of freedom, a complete set of t-distribution tables requires many pages. There are tables, each similar to Appendix Table A, for each level of degrees of freedom. To conserve space, t-values (which are analogous to z-values) are presented in Appendix Table C for specified degrees of freedom and areas under one tail of several t-distributions. The values listed here were taken from the column labeled 0.025. This is the area under the extremity of a *single tail.*

Because we only have 23 observations of widget production costs, we should have used a t-distribution to determine the 95 percent probability interval. This will give a wider interval than that computed previously. With 23 observations and $\overline{X}$ based on sample data, there are 22 degrees of freedom $(23 - 1)$. In Table C the value of t for 22 degrees of freedom that leaves 2.5 percent of the area in the extreme of each tail is 2.074. Hence the 95 percent probability interval for widget production costs is $\$25 \pm 2.074(\$2.52)$ rather than previously computed $\$25 \pm 1.96(\$2.52)$. This decline in accuracy is the "price" we pay for basing an inference about the population on a sample of less than 30.

THE COST-ESTIMATING PROBLEM

The procedures described in this appendix may be used to summarize unit production cost data and/or make inferences concerning a population on the basis of a sample drawn from it. Unfortunately we have assumed that information is readily available concerning unit production costs. Because of cost and technical problems, this is seldom the case. In most situations, production cost data are accumulated for batches of units or periods of time. Under these circumstances, the cost-estimating techniques discussed in the body of Chapter 7 must be used to separate total costs into their variable and fixed cost elements.

APPENDIX B Statistical considerations in regression analysis

When statistical methods are used to analyze data, various statistics can be computed to determine the relationship between variables and the significance of the estimated parameters. The purpose of this appendix is to provide an overview of statistical considerations in regression analysis. These considerations involve the statistical data and tests that can be computed when using regression analysis and the assumptions underlying regression analysis.

STATISTICAL DATA AND TESTS

Although we will illustrate the computation of various statistical data and tests in this appendix, most computer software packages that are used for regression analysis provide the data and tests as part of the output. Many calculators are also programmed to produce these data as part of their statistical functions. The statistical data and tests considered in this appendix are as follows:

- Correlation coefficient
- Coefficient of determination
- Standard error of the estimate
- Standard error of the coefficient

Correlation Coefficient

As noted earlier in this chapter, the **correlation coefficient** (identified as R) is a standardized measure of the relationship between two variables. The relationship may vary from minus one to plus one. A correlation coefficient close to minus one indicates a strong negative correlation. In that event the variables move simultaneously in opposite directions. A correlation coefficient of zero indicates that there is no relationship between the variables. A correlation coefficient close to plus one indicates a strong positive correlation. In that event, the variables move simultaneously in the same direction.

The correlation coefficient between two variables is computed using the following equation:

$$R = \frac{\sum_{i=1}^{n} X_i T_i - n\overline{X}\overline{T}}{(n - 1)\,\hat{\sigma}_X \hat{\sigma}_T} \qquad (7\text{–}16)$$

where

R = correlation coefficient
X_i = value of observation i for variable X
T_i = value of observation i for variable T
n = number of observations
$\overline{X}$ = mean of variable X observations
$\overline{T}$ = mean of variable T observations
$\hat{\sigma}_X$ = estimated standard deviation of variable X
$\hat{\sigma}_T$ = estimated standard deviation of variable T

Example 7–13

The Starger Company has collected the following data related to factory overhead costs and direct-labor hours for the past fifteen weeks of operations:

Week	*Direct-labor hours*	*Factory overhead costs*
1	2,000	$6,500
2	2,500	7,200
3	1,500	5,200
4	1,800	5,000
5	2,000	6,200
6	2,900	8,700
7	2,400	7,000
8	3,000	8,500
9	2,400	8,400
10	2,700	7,000
11	2,100	6,000
12	2,500	7,700
13	1,600	5,100
14	2,300	6,400
15	2,800	8,000

Determine the correlation coefficient between direct-labor hours and factory overhead costs.

The computations for determining the correlation coefficient are presented in Exhibit 7–15. The correlation coefficient of 0.910 shows that there is a high positive correlation between the two variables. Thus a knowledge of direct-labor hours may be useful in estimating factory overhead costs.

EXHIBIT 7–15 Calculation of Correlation Coefficient

Week	X_i	T_i	X_iT_i	$X_i - \bar{X}$	$(X_i - \bar{X})^2$	$T_i - \bar{T}$	$(T_i - \bar{T})^2$
1	2,000	6,500	13,000,000	−300	90,000	−360	129,600
2	2,500	7,200	18,000,000	200	40,000	340	115,600
3	1,500	5,200	7,800,000	−800	640,000	−1,660	2,755,600
4	1,800	5,000	9,000,000	−500	250,000	−1,860	3,459,600
5	2,000	6,200	12,400,000	−300	90,000	−660	435,600
6	2,900	8,700	25,230,000	600	360,000	1,840	3,385,600
7	2,400	7,000	16,800,000	100	10,000	140	19,600
8	3,000	8,500	25,500,000	700	490,000	1,640	2,689,600
9	2,400	8,400	20,160,000	100	10,000	1,540	2,371,600
10	2,700	7,000	18,900,000	400	160,000	140	19,600
11	2,100	6,000	12,600,000	−200	40,000	−860	739,600
12	2,500	7,700	19,250,000	200	40,000	840	705,600
13	1,600	5,100	8,160,000	−700	490,000	−1,760	3,097,600
14	2,300	6,400	14,720,000	0	0	−460	211,600
15	2,800	8,000	22,400,000	500	250,000	1,140	1,299,600
Totals	34,500	102,900	243,920,000	0	2,960,000	0	21,436,000

$\bar{X} = 34{,}500 \div 15 = \underline{\underline{2{,}300}}$

$\bar{T} = 102{,}900 \div 15 = \underline{\underline{6{,}860}}$

$\hat{\sigma}_X = \sqrt{(1 \div (15 - 1)) \times 2{,}960{,}000} = \underline{\underline{459.81}}$

$\hat{\sigma}_T = \sqrt{(1 \div (15 - 1)) \times 21{,}436{,}000} = \underline{\underline{1{,}237.39}}$

$$R = \frac{243{,}920{,}000 - 15(2{,}300)(6{,}860)}{(15 - 1)(459.81)(1{,}237.97)} = \frac{7{,}250{,}000}{7{,}969{,}233.8} = \underline{\underline{0.910}}$$

Coefficient of Determination

The **coefficient of determination** (identified as R squared or R^2) is a measure of the proportion of the total variation in the dependent variable explained by the regression. It can take on any value between 0 and +1. If we look at how R squared is computed, we can gain some insight into how regression analysis works and why it is used.

If we had just the factory overhead costs for several recent weeks, the best objective estimate of overhead costs we could develop for any given week (assuming a normal distribution) would be the average overhead cost:

$$\bar{T} = \frac{1}{n}\sum_{i=1}^{n} T_i \tag{7–17}$$

where

$\bar{T}$ = average overhead cost
n = number of observations
T_i = value of observation i of overhead cost

If direct-labor hours were an important determinant of overhead cost, Eq. 7–17 would be of limited usefulness. The total squared variation of T_i around $\bar{T}$ would be:

$$\text{Total squared variation} = \Sigma(T_i - \bar{T})^2 \tag{7–18}$$

By pairing observations of T_i and X_i regression analysis develops an equation to estimate overhead cost at any given value of X. Although this equation probably cannot completely explain the past variability in total cost, it should do better than Eq. 7–17. The remaining unexplained squared variations of T_i around $\hat{T}_i$ would be:

$$\text{Unexplained squared variation} = \Sigma(T_i - \hat{T}_i)^2 \qquad (7\text{–}19)$$

where $\hat{T}_i$ = estimated value of T given the regression equation

Note that minimizing Eq. 7–19 is the least-squares criterion.

The squared variation of $\hat{T}_i$ about $\overline{T}$ that is explained by the regression equation is:

$$\text{Explained squared variation} = \Sigma(\hat{T}_i - \overline{T})^2 \qquad (7\text{–}20)$$

and the total squared variation is composed of two parts:

$$\begin{matrix}\text{Total} & & \text{Unexplained} & & \text{Explained} \\ \text{squared} & = & \text{squared} & + & \text{squared} \\ \text{variation} & & \text{variation} & & \text{variation}\end{matrix}$$

$$\Sigma(T_i - \overline{T})^2 = \Sigma(T_i - \hat{T}_i)^2 + \Sigma(\hat{T}_i - \overline{T})^2 \qquad (7\text{–}21)$$

The proportion of the variation in the dependent variable that is explained by regression analysis, the coefficient of determination, is:

$$R^2 = \frac{\text{Explained squared variation}}{\text{Total squared variation}}$$

In symbolic notation,

$$R^2 = \frac{\Sigma(\hat{T}_i - \overline{T})^2}{\Sigma(T_i - \overline{T})^2} \qquad (7\text{–}22)$$

R squared tells us how much better off we are using the regression equation to estimate T_i than we would be by simply using the past average value of T as an estimate.

Example 7–14

Using direct-labor hours as the independent variable X and overhead costs as the dependent variable T, the regression equation for the data in Example 7–13 is:

$$\hat{T} = \$1{,}226.554 + \$2.449X$$

The calculations needed for computing the coefficient of determination are presented in Exhibit 7–16. R squared is 0.828. Hence 82.8 percent of the squared variation in the observations of factory overhead costs is explained by the regression equation.[4] The concepts underlying the computation of the coefficient of determination are illustrated in Exhibit 7–17.

---

[4] When the fitted line is based on a small number of observations, great care should be taken in interpreting the meaning of a high R squared. An R squared based on two observations that have differing values will always be 1.0. Yet, few people would be willing to make a very positive statement about the significance of a line fitted to two observations. To provide additional information on the significance of a fitted line, most regression software packages automatically compute an F-statistic. The value of this statistic is used in evaluating the significance of the fitted line. A detailed discussion of the F-statistic and appropriate test tables are found in most elementary statistics books.

EXHIBIT 7–16 Calculation of Coefficient of Determination

Week	X_i	T_i	$\hat{T}_i = 1{,}226.554 + 2.449X_i$	$(\hat{T}_i - \bar{T})^2$	$(T_i - \bar{T})^2$
1	2,000	6,500	6,124.554	540,880.819	129,600
2	2,500	7,200	7,349.054	239,173.815	115,600
3	1,500	5,200	4,900.054	3,841,388.323	2,755,600
4	1,800	5,000	5,634.754	1,501,227.761	3,459,600
5	2,000	6,200	6,124.554	540,880.819	435,600
6	2,900	8,700	8,328.654	2,156,944.572	3,385,600
7	2,400	7,000	7,104.154	59,611.175	19,600
8	3,000	8,500	8,573.554	2,936,267.311	2,689,600
9	2,400	8,400	7,104.154	59,611.175	2,371,600
10	2,700	7,000	7,838.854	958,155.153	19,600
11	2,100	6,000	6,369.454	240,635.378	739,600
12	2,500	7,700	7,349.054	239,173.815	705,600
13	1,600	5,100	5,144.954	2,941,382.782	3,097,600
14	2,300	6,400	6,859.254	0.557	211,600
15	2,800	8,000	8,083.754	1,497,573.853	1,299,600
Totals				17,752,907.318	21,436,000

$$R^2 = \frac{17{,}752{,}907.318}{21{,}436{,}000} = \underline{\underline{0.828}}$$

EXHIBIT 7–17 The Value of Regression in Explaining Variation at X_i

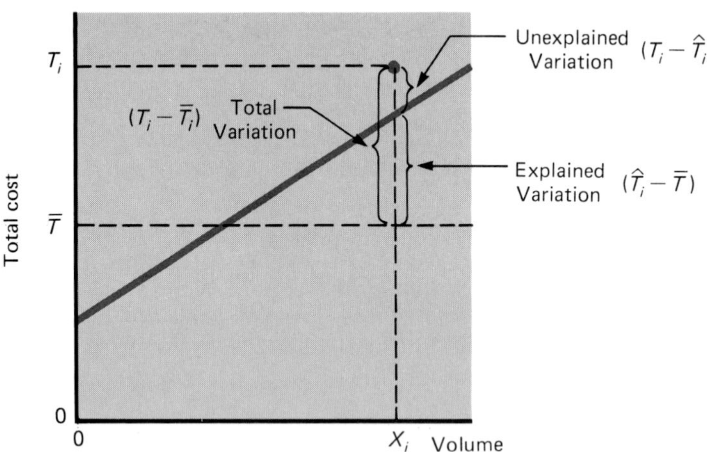

Squared values are used in computing the coefficient of determination.

$$R\text{-squared} = \frac{\text{Explained squared variation}}{\text{Total squared variation}}$$

$$R\text{-squared} = \frac{\Sigma(\hat{T}_i - \bar{T})^2}{\Sigma(T_i - \bar{T})^2}$$

Standard Error of the Estimate

Regression analysis is based on the assumption that if all possible observations of the dependent and independent variables were known in advance, they would fall in a normally distributed pattern around an underlying linear trend. The **standard error of the estimate,** σ_e, is a measure of the dispersion of dependent variable observations around an equation. The standard error of the estimate is conceptually similar to a standard deviation, σ, and it is used to make statements about the percentage of observations included in some specified interval around a known linear trend. For example, 95 percent of the observations around a known linear trend should fall between the upper and lower limits illustrated in Exhibit 7–18(b).

The value 1.96 comes from Appendix Table A. It is the number of standard deviations that leaves 2.5 percent of a normal probability distribution in a single tail. The interval determined by ± 1.96 standard deviations encloses 95 percent of a two-tailed distribution. See Exhibit 7–18(a).

Because the actual value of σ_e cannot be determined before all observations are known, it is estimated from the available observations. For simple regression analysis, the estimated value of the population standard error of the estimate is symbolized by $\hat{\sigma}_e$ and computed as follows:

$$\hat{\sigma}_e = \sqrt{\frac{\Sigma(T_i - \hat{T}_i)^2}{n - 2}} \qquad (7\text{–}23)$$

where

T_i = value of observation i of variable T
$\hat{T}_i$ = estimated value of observation i of variable T
n = number of observations

The computations for determining the standard error of the estimate for the data in Example 7–13 are shown in Exhibit 7–19. The standard error of the estimate is 531.935.

$$\hat{\sigma}_e = \sqrt{\frac{3{,}678{,}407.310}{15 - 2}} = \underline{\underline{531.935}}$$

The higher the standard error of the estimate, the greater the likelihood of estimating error through the use of the regression equation. In evaluating two alternative equations, other things being equal, the one with the lower standard error of the estimate is preferred.

EXHIBIT 7–18 Standard Deviation and Standard Error of the Estimate Used for 95 Percent Probability Intervals

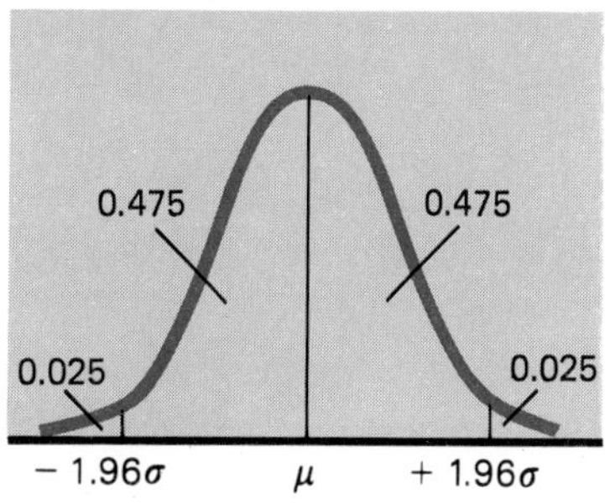

(a) Standard deviation measures dispersion around mean of single variable. Area totals to 1.0.

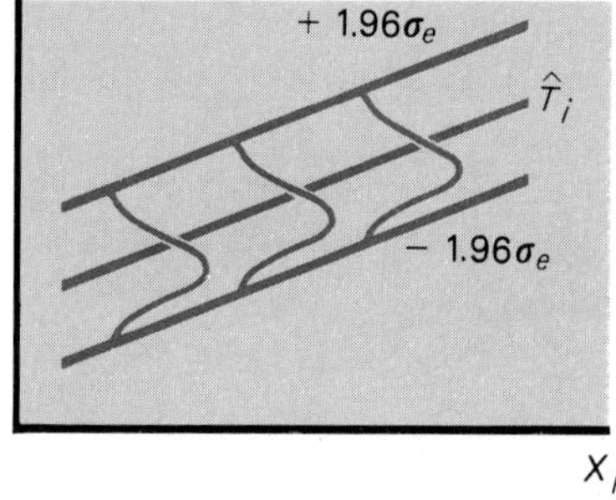

(b) Standard error of estimate measures dispersion around linear trend. Area, at a given X_i, also totals to 1.0.

EXHIBIT 7–19 **Computation of Standard Error of the Estimate**

Week	X_i	T_i	$\hat{T}_i = 1{,}226.554 + 2.449X_i$	$(T_i - \hat{T}_i)$	$(T_i - \hat{T}_i)^2$
1	2,000	6,500	6,124.554	375.446	140,959.699
2	2,500	7,200	7,349.054	−149.054	22,217.095
3	1,500	5,200	4,900.054	299.946	89,967.603
4	1,800	5,000	5,634.754	−634.754	402,912.641
5	2,000	6,200	6,124.554	75.446	5,692.099
6	2,900	8,700	8,328.654	371.346	137,897.852
7	2,400	7,000	7,104.154	−104.154	10,848.056
8	3,000	8,500	8,573.554	−73.554	5,410.191
9	2,400	8,400	7,104.154	1,295.846	1,679,216.856
10	2,700	7,000	7,838.854	−838.854	703,676.033
11	2,100	6,000	6,369.454	−369.454	136,496.258
12	2,500	7,700	7,349.054	350.946	123,163.095
13	1,600	5,100	5,144.954	−44.954	2,020.862
14	2,300	6,400	6,859.254	−459.254	210,914.237
15	2,800	8,000	8,083.754	−83.754	7,014.733
Total					3,678,407.310

$\sigma_e = \sqrt{3{,}678{,}407.310 \div (15 - 2)} = 531.935$

The standard error of the estimate, or the conceptually related standard error of the forecast, can also be used in conjunction with a regression equation to develop probability intervals for predicted future costs that fall within the relevant range. Because a rather complicated set of adjustments is required to develop these probability intervals, the interested reader is referred to books on regression analysis and/or econometrics.[5]

---

[5] Near the center of the range of observations the 95 percent probability interval for the dependent variable is occasionally estimated as follows:

$$\hat{T}_i = a + bX_i \pm 1.96\,\sigma_e$$

The z-value, 1.96 is used if the regression equation is based on a sample size of 30 or more observations. For sample sizes of less than 30, t-tables must be used. With two previously computed values (a and b), there are $n - 2$ degrees of freedom.

An adjustment should be made to increase the probability interval as we move away from the center of the range of observations. The following diagram, with probability intervals developed using the standard error of the forecast, illustrates this increase:

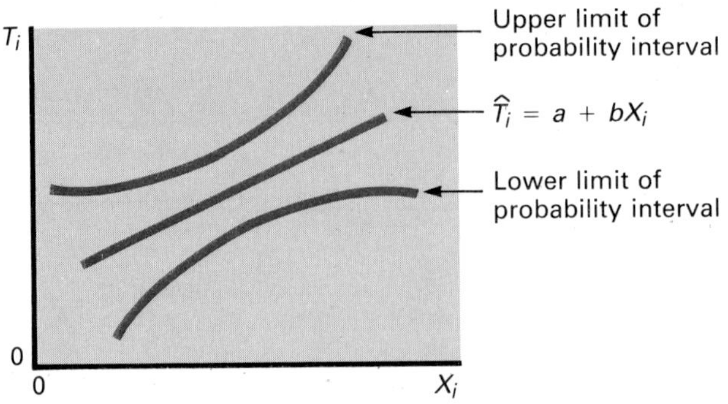

Standard Error of the Coefficient

Until all possible observations occur, it is not possible to know the "true" slope and vertical axis intercept of the regression equation. Values for a and b are based on sample data. They are regarded as estimates of the true population values of α and β, respectively.

Because the vertical axis intercept, α, is usually beyond the relevant range, management is seldom interested in how good a is as an estimator of α. Management may, however, be very interested in knowing how good b is as an estimator of the true variable cost, β. They may, for example, wish to know the probability of variable cost exceeding some critical value given its estimate from the regression.

The **standard error of the coefficient,** $\hat{\sigma}_b$, is a measure of how accurate the estimated value of a coefficient is as an estimator of the true value of the coefficient. The standard error of the coefficient is conceptually similar to the standard deviation, and it is used to make statements concerning the probability that the true slope of the regression equation is within some specified interval around b.

For simple regression analysis, the standard error of the coefficient is calculated using the following formula:

$$\hat{\sigma}_b = \frac{\hat{\sigma}_e}{\sqrt{\Sigma(X_i - \overline{X})^2}} \tag{7–24}$$

where

$\hat{\sigma}_b$ = standard error of the coefficient
$\hat{\sigma}_e$ = standard error of the estimate
X_i = value of observation i of variable X
$\overline{X}$ = mean of variable X

Example 7–15

For Example 7–14, $\hat{\sigma}_b = 0.309$.

$$\hat{\sigma}_b = \frac{531.935}{\sqrt{2{,}960{,}000}} = \underline{\underline{0.309}}$$

Determine the 95 percent probability interval for β.

Because of the small sample size (15 observations), tables for the t-distribution are used rather than the z-table. With 15 observations and two previously computed statistics (a and b) there are 13 (15 observations − 2) degrees of freedom. For 13 degrees of freedom, the corresponding t-value for a 95 percent probability interval is 2.160. The 95 percent probability interval for the true value of β is:

$$\beta = 2.449 \pm 2.160(0.309)$$

There is a 95 percent probability that the true variable overhead cost per direct-labor hour is between \$1.781 and \$3.116. This information might be useful in pricing to avoid setting a price that may be less than variable costs.

When b is used as an estimate of variable costs it is important to verify that the computed value is not due to chance. The normal test for the significance of b is to test the null hypothesis that $\beta = 0$, given computed values of b and $\hat{\sigma}_b$. For Example 7–15, the computed value of b, 2.449, is 7.926 [(2.449 − 0)/0.309] standard errors of the coefficient from zero. Using t-tables, the null hypothesis is rejected. Most regression software packages compute the number of standard errors of the estimate that the estimated value of a coefficient is from zero. It is called the ***T*-statistic**. As a rule of thumb, the coefficient is regarded as significantly different from zero if the T-statistic is greater than or equal to two. The validity of the coefficient is questioned when the T-statistic is less than two.

STATISTICAL ASSUMPTIONS

Cost estimates developed with the aid of regression analysis may be in error if the following four statistical assumptions are not met:

1. Normal distribution of variances
2. Equal variance
3. No autocorrelation
4. No multicollinearity

Normal Distribution of Variances

If the equation developed from linear regression analysis is to be used to estimate costs, the observations must be normally distributed at each output level. If they are not, the estimating equation will be influenced by extreme values and probability intervals will be subject to error. Although it will still be possible to predict expected values, the expected value may not be the most likely value.

Equal Variance

To develop probability intervals based on the standard error of the estimate, the distribution of the dependent variable must be the same at all values of the independent variable. The presence of this condition is called **homoscedasticity**. Its absence is called **heteroscedasticity**. When heteroscedasticity exists, expected values can still be predicted, but probability statements about these expected values cannot be made.

Heteroscedasticity is likely to be present in cost data because larger output levels are usually accompanied by larger variances. It can be detected by computing and comparing the variances at different output levels using a standard statistical test. Plotting the data may reveal the presence of heteroscedasticity. When this condition exists, homoscedasticity may sometimes be obtained by transforming the data into logarithmic or other forms. Homoscedasticity and heteroscedasticity are illustrated as follows:

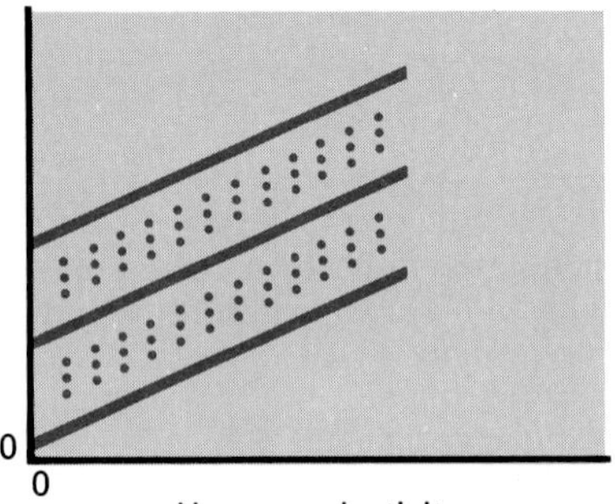

Homoscedasticity

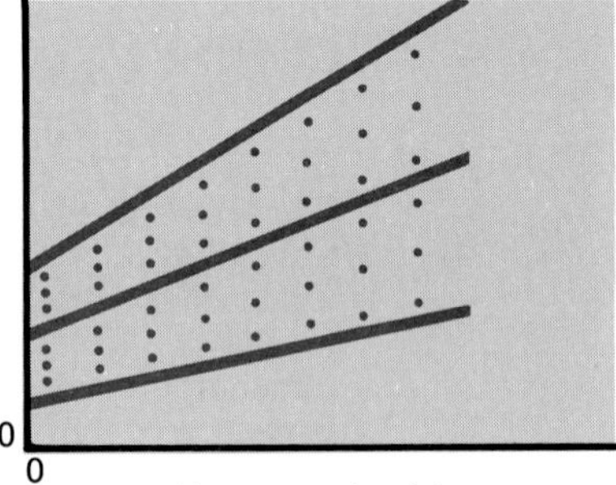

Heteroscedasticity

Autocorrelation

Autocorrelation is present when the estimating error at time t is affected by the value of a previous observation. The problem of "sticky" costs frequently causes autocorrelation in accounting data. During a period of expanding volume, organizations may hire additional personnel to fill their needs. However, as volume declines, there is usually a delay in contracting capacity. This causes costs to be sticky on the downside and influences the size and direction of estimating errors as production declines. When autocorrelation is caused by sticky costs, use of a dummy variable might help adjust for it. The dummy variable would be assigned the value one in periods of declining volume and the value zero in other periods.[6]

---

[6] Autocorrelation may be detected by statistical tests developed by Durban and Watson or Theil and Nager. Plotting successive estimating errors is also useful in detecting this condition. The interested reader is referred to a book on regression analysis.

Multicollinearity Multicollinearity is a potential problem only in multiple regression analysis. **Multicollinearity** exists when two independent variables are highly correlated with each other (that is, they move together). When this condition exists, it may not be possible to compute the coefficient of each independent variable. If coefficients can be computed, little confidence can be placed in them.

Multicollinearity can be detected by computing the correlation coefficient between the independent variables or by plotting the independent variables on a graph. Although correlation probably will always exist, a frequently suggested rule of thumb states that it should be regarded as a serious problem if the correlation coefficient between two independent variables is greater than 0.80. In that event, the independent variables displaying multicollinearity should be combined in the regression analysis. Alternatively, if it makes sense, the independent variable that shows the weakest relationship to the dependent variable may be eliminated.

APPENDIX C Learning curve analysis

Although most cost relationships used in accounting models are linear, accountants occasionally will use a nonlinear cost function for planning and controlling operations if the assumption of linearity within the relevant range is not valid. Occasionally, if the cost pattern is sufficiently well documented and verifiable, such a cost pattern is even used for product costing.

The purpose of this appendix is to discuss the accounting implications of a particular nonlinear cost pattern described by the learning curve phenomenon. The **learning curve phenomenon** exists when unit or average costs decline in a systematic manner as cumulative production increases. It is most likely to exist in complex operations and it is caused both by management becoming more skillful in organizing the factors of production and by skilled labor becoming more adept at executing their assigned tasks. Models based on the learning curve phenomenon have been used for such diverse purposes as contract bidding and termination settlements, production scheduling, developing standards and variance analysis, and financial planning. They also form the bases of the percentage of completion inventory valuation procedure used in the aircraft industry.

LEARNING CURVE COST PATTERNS

There are two widely used learning curve models. One model describes the decline in the incremental costs as production continues and the other model describes the decline in the average unit cost as production continues. The authors prefer the learning curve model that is based on average costs because it has computational advantages. This model states that whenever the total quantity of units produced doubles, the cumulative average unit cost declines by a constant percentage. The relationship between cumulative production and average unit cost is illustrated in Exhibit 7–20(a). The effect of this decline of average unit cost on cumulative total costs is illustrated in Exhibit 7–20(b).

Consider the example presented in Exhibit 7–21. It costs $100 to produce the first unit, $80 to produce the second unit, and $144 to produce both the third and fourth units. Every time the total quantity of units produced doubled, the cumulative average unit cost declined by 10 percent, from $100 to $90 to $81. It could also be said that every time the total quantity of units produced doubled, the cumulative average cost was 90 percent of its previous amount. This 90 percent is used to identify this particular learning curve.

LEARNING CURVE MODEL

The equation that fits the learning curve presented in Exhibit 7–20(a) is:

$$\hat{Y} = a/X^b \qquad (7\text{–}25)$$

where

$\hat{Y}$ = an estimate of cumulative average variable costs that are subject to the learning curve phenomenon
a = an estimate of the variable costs (subject to the learning curve) of the first unit
b = exponent for the slope of the learning curve
X = cumulative units produced

The exponent for the slope of the learning curve, b, is equal to minus 1 multiplied by the log of the learning curve percentage divided by the log of 2.00. The 2.00 is used in the denominator because the model describes the change in the cumulative average variable costs when production doubles or increases 200 percent. In equation form,

$$b = -\frac{\text{log of learning curve percentage}}{\log 2.00} \tag{7–26}$$

For a 90 percent learning curve, $b = 0.152$.

$$b = -\frac{\log 0.90}{\log 2.00} = -\frac{-0.0457}{0.3010} = \underline{\underline{0.152}}$$

Equation 7–25 may be transformed into a linear relationship by the use of logarithms and standard simple regression analysis procedures used to calculate a and b:

$$\log \hat{Y} = \log a - b \log X \tag{7–27}$$

Using regression analysis on the logs of the data in Exhibit 7–21, the values of a and b are determined to be 100 and 0.152, respectively. This value for b agrees with the previous calculation using the known learning curve percentage.

EXHIBIT 7–20 Learning-Curve Cost Patterns

(a) Average unit cost

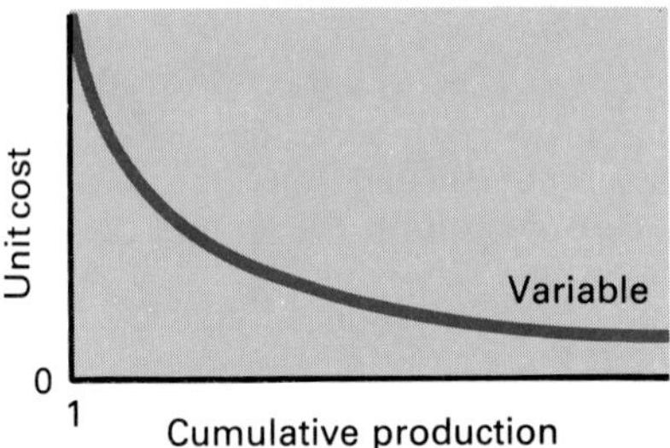

(b) Total cost

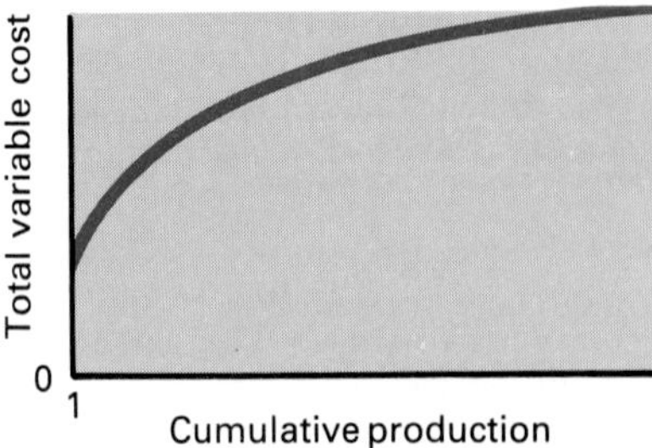

EXHIBIT 7–21 Ninety Percent Learning Curve

Doubling points	*Units produced*	*Group cost*	*Total cost*	*Cumulative average unit cost*	*Percent decline*
0	1	$100.00	$ 100.00	$100.00	—
1	2	80.00	180.00	90.00	10*
2	3–4	144.00	324.00	81.00	10
3	5–8	259.20	583.20	72.90	10
4	9–16	466.40	1,049.60	65.60	10

*Sample computation: ($100 − $90)/$100

ESTIMATING LEARNING CURVE PERCENTAGE

If the learning curve percentage is unknown, it can be estimated by using regression analysis procedures on the logs of the data to determine b and then solving for the learning curve percentage using Eq. 7–26. Assuming the learning curve percentage for the data in Exhibit 7–21 was unknown and a b value of 0.152 was found from regression analysis, the learning curve percentage is determined as follows:

$$b = -\frac{\text{log of learning curve percentage}}{\log 2.00}$$

$$0.152 = -\frac{\text{log of learning curve percentage}}{0.3010}$$

$$\text{log of learning curve percentage} = -(0.152 \times 0.3010) = -0.0458$$

$$\text{learning curve percentage} = \underline{\underline{0.90}} \text{ or } \underline{\underline{90}} \text{ percent}$$

ESTIMATING LEARNING CURVE COSTS

Once a and b are determined, the total variable cost of X units is estimated by multiplying the estimated cumulative average variable cost of X units by X:

$$T = Xa/X^b \qquad (7\text{–}28)$$

Equation 7–28 can be reduced to:

$$T = XaX^{-b} = aX^{1-b} \qquad (7\text{–}29)$$

Example 7–15

Using the data in Exhibit 7–21, estimate the total variable cost of producing the first 32 units.

Because the 32 units represent a doubling of production from 16 units, a simple extension of the data in Exhibit 7–21 provides the answer. The cumulative average variable cost for 32 units should be $59.04 (0.90 × $65.60). This gives a total cost for 32 units of $1,889.28 (32 × $59.04). Total cost for 32 units can also be determined using Eq. 7–29:

$$T = \$100(32)^{1-0.152} = \$100(32)^{0.848} = \$100(18.896) = \underline{\underline{\$1{,}889.60}}$$

The difference between the $1,889.28 and $1,889.60 is due to rounding.

To determine the incremental cost of a particular unit, X, we must solve Eq. 7–29 for total costs at X and $X - 1$ units, and subtract the total cost at $X - 1$ units from the total cost at X units.

Example 7–16 For the situation presented in Exhibit 7–21, b is 0.152 and the cost of producing the seventeenth unit is computed by subtracting the total cost of producing 16 units, known to be \$1,049.60, from the total cost of producing 17 units. For 17 units:

$$T = \$100(17)^{0.848} = \underline{\underline{\$1,105.15}}$$

Hence the incremental cost of the seventeenth unit is \$55.55 (\$1,105.15 − \$1,049.60).

The learning curve phenomenon is a form of time-series analysis. Consequently it cannot be used for cross-sectional data or applied to situations that do not involve a continuous increase in production. Although normal tests can be used to determine how good the estimating equation fits the historical data, it is difficult to set probability intervals on cost projections because they are beyond the range of observations. The use of learning curve models to project costs is based on the assumption that the systematic decline in variable costs that occurred in the past will continue in the future.

KEY TERMS

Account classification method (of cost estimation)
Capacity costs
Correlation coefficient
Cross-sectional analysis
Dependent variable
Dummy variable
Engineering method (of cost estimation)
High-low method (of cost estimation)
Independent variable
Least-squares criterion
Linear regression
Longitudinal analysis
Multiple linear regression
Price index
Scatter-diagram method (of cost estimation)
Simple linear regression

APPENDICES KEY TERMS

Autocorrelation
Central tendency (measure)
Coefficient of determination
Correlation coefficient
Degrees of freedom
Dispersion (measure)
Frequency distribution
Heteroscedasticity
Homoscedasticity
Learning curve phenomenon
Mean
Median
Mode
Multicollinearity
Standard deviation
Standard error of the coefficient
Standard error of the estimate
Standard normal distribution
t-distribution
T-statistic
Variance

SELECTED REFERENCES

Benston, George, "Multiple Regression Analysis of Cost Behavior," *Accounting Review* **41,** No. 4 (October 1964): 657–672.

Chen, Joyce T., "Modeling Learning Curve and Learning Complementarity for Resource Allocation and Production Scheduling," *Decision Sciences* **14,** No. 2 (April 1983): 170–186.

Jensen, Robert, "Multiple Regression Models for Cost Control—Assumptions and Limitations," *Accounting Review* **42,** No. 2 (April 1967): 265–272.

Johnson, J., *Statistical Cost Analysis,* New York: McGraw-Hill, 1960.

———, *Econometric Methods,* 3rd ed., New York: McGraw-Hill, 1984.

Kaplan, Robert S., *Advanced Management Accounting,* Englewood Cliffs, N.J.: Prentice-Hall, 1982.

Leininger, Wayne E., *Quantitative Methods in Accounting,* New York: Van Nostrand, 1980.

McClenon, Paul R., "Cost Finding Through Multiple Correlation Analysis," *Accounting Review* **38,** No. 3 (July 1963): 540–547.

Yelle, Louis, "The Learning Curve: Historical Review and Comprehensive Survey," *Decision Sciences* **10,** No. 2 (April 1979): 302–328.

REVIEW QUESTIONS

7–1 Before the advent of high-speed computers, almost all accounting cost estimates were based on either account classification, the high-low method, or scatter diagrams. What are the primary strengths and weaknesses of each of these methods?

7–2 What assumption does the high-low method make about fixed costs in the periods of highest and lowest activity? Given this assumption, what causes the difference in total costs?

7–3 Why is a scatter diagram frequently used in the preliminary analysis of historical data?

7–4 In words, what is the primary difference between the scatter diagram and the simple linear regression approaches to cost estimation?

7–5 What is the difference between simple linear regression analysis and multiple linear regression analysis?

7–6 Why are dummy variables used in regression analysis?

7–7 Distinguish between longitudinal and cross-sectional studies. Which type of study is better able to avoid the data base problems associated with changes in prices and technology?

7–8 What is the relationship between the range of observations and the relevant range?

7–9 Why is it very important to ensure that costs are recorded in the proper time period? During what parts of each period should extra care be exerted to ensure that costs are properly recorded?

7–10 Why is there frequently a tradeoff between obtaining a large number of observations and problems related to matching costs with production?

7–11 What bias is likely to be introduced into cost projections when accelerated depreciation charges are included in the data used in developing cost projections?

7–12 Why should production cost data obtained during unusual operating conditions be excluded in developing cost estimates?

7–13 How can cost data used in regression analysis be adjusted for price changes?

7–14 What does the correlation coefficient measure? What range of values can it take on?

7–15 Does a high correlation between the independent and dependent variables necessarily prove that a change in the independent variable causes a change in the dependent variable? Why or why not?

REVIEW PROBLEM

High-Low and Simple Linear Regression Cost Estimation

Lucarelli Company has collected data on direct-labor hours and factory overhead costs for the past 15 weeks of operations. These data are as follows:

Week	*Direct-labor hours*	*Factory overhead costs*
1	800	$4,300
2	750	3,900
3	675	3,650
4	775	4,200
5	600	3,400
6	945	4,500
7	850	4,100
8	650	3,500
9	825	4,300
10	980	4,700
11	1,050	4,750
12	1,000	4,550
13	875	4,400
14	740	4,050
15	680	3,800

REQUIREMENTS

a) Using the high-low method, develop an equation to estimate overhead costs from direct-labor hours.

b) Using simple linear regression, develop an equation to estimate overhead costs from direct-labor hours.

c) Using the cost-estimating equation developed in part (a), estimate factory overhead costs for a week when 900 direct-labor hours are worked.

d) Using the cost-estimating equation developed in part (b), estimate factory overhead costs for a week when 900 direct-labor hours are worked.

The solution to this problem is found at the end of the Chapter 7 problems and exercises.

EXERCISES

7–1 Account Classification

Eskey Corporation expects to produce 4,000 units of Product X during 19x4 and incur the following manufacturing costs:

Direct materials	$140,000
Direct labor	200,000

Variable factory overhead	100,000
Fixed factory overhead	150,000

REQUIREMENT

Use the account classification method to develop a cost-estimating equation for yearly manufacturing costs.

7–2 Account Classification

During 19x5, Bunker Corporation produced 50,000 units of Product Y and incurred the following manufacturing costs:

Direct materials	$220,000
Direct labor	360,000
Variable factory overhead	180,000
Fixed factory overhead	225,000

REQUIREMENT

Use the account classification method to develop a cost-estimating equation for total yearly manufacturing costs.

7–3 High-Low Cost Estimation

An examination of monthly maintenance expenses and machine hours reveals the following:

	Highest	*Lowest*
Maintenance expense	$45,000	$36,000
Machine hours	22,000	16,000

REQUIREMENT

Use the high-low method to develop a cost-estimating equation for monthly maintenance expenses.

7–4 High-Low Cost Estimation

The Milan Company has requested your help in developing a cost-estimating equation for overhead. During July and August overhead costs were $1,200,000 and $800,000, respectively. July direct-labor costs amounted to $400,000. August direct-labor costs amounted to $200,000.

REQUIREMENT

Use the high-low method to develop a cost-estimating equation for monthly overhead. Direct-labor dollars is the independent variable.

7–5 High-Low Cost Estimation

Presented is production and cost information from five recent months:

Month	*Units produced*	*Total overhead*
October	90,000	$145,000
November	100,000	170,000
December	20,000	50,000
January	40,000	80,000
February	80,000	140,000

REQUIREMENTS

a) Use the high-low method to develop a cost-estimating equation for monthly total overhead.

b) Mention several strengths and weaknesses of the high-low method of cost estimation.

7–6 Scatter Diagrams

The Southport Tool Company is trying to determine the most appropriate basis for allocating factory overhead. Possible bases include direct-labor hours, direct-labor costs, and direct-machine hours. Data have been accumulated for each of these bases and for actual factory overhead for each of the past six months.

Month	*Actual factory overhead*	*Direct-labor hours*	*Direct-labor costs*	*Direct-machine hours*
	(000)	(000)	(000)	(000)
April	$ 60	2	$ 11	3
May	80	4	15	5
June	90	3.5	14	2
July	110	4.5	20	3
August	70	2.5	11	4.5
September	110	4.5	18	6

REQUIREMENTS

a) Prepare a scatter diagram using actual factory overhead as the dependent variable and direct-labor hours as the independent variable.

b) Prepare a scatter diagram using actual factory overhead as the dependent variable and direct-labor costs as the independent variable.

c) Prepare a scatter diagram using actual factory overhead as the dependent variable and direct-machine hours as the independent variable.

d) Which basis appears to be the best for allocating overhead?

7–7 T Simple Linear Regression

The Ace Co. Ltd. produces one product, M. Management has plotted a scatter diagram and found that a linear relationship exists between the total costs of a batch of units and the number of machine hours used in producing the batch. The following observations and computations are available.

	Observations		Computations		
Batch	Machine hours (X)	Total costs (T)	X^2	T^2	$X \times T$
1	23	$25	529	625	575
2	21	20	441	400	420
3	27	30	729	900	810
4	29	32	841	1,024	928
5	29	33	841	1,089	957
6	26	31	676	961	806
7	19	32	361	1,024	608
8	20	24	400	576	480
9	21	24	441	576	504
10	27	34	729	1,156	918
11	19	26	361	676	494
12	30	38	900	1,444	1,140
	291	$349	7,249	10,451	8,640

REQUIREMENTS

a) Use simple regression analysis to develop an equation for the total cost of a batch.

b) Determine the estimated costs for a batch run 24 machine hours long.

(CICA Adapted)

7–8 T Simple Linear Regression

The Blue Corporation produces one product and management has found from preparing a scatter diagram that a linear relationship exists between total manufacturing costs and number of units produced during a week. The following observations and computations are available:

	Observations		Computations		
Week	Number of units (X)	Total manufacturing costs (T)	X^2	T^2	$X \times T$
1	40	$12,000	1,600	144,000,000	480,000
2	60	16,000	3,600	256,000,000	960,000
3	75	18,500	5,625	342,250,000	1,387,500
4	80	22,000	6,400	484,000,000	1,760,000
5	50	15,000	2,500	225,000,000	750,000
6	30	10,000	900	100,000,000	300,000
7	25	9,500	625	90,250,000	237,500
8	55	17,000	3,025	289,000,000	935,000
9	70	19,000	4,900	361,000,000	1,330,000
10	80	24,000	6,400	576,000,000	1,920,000
	565	$163,000	35,575	2,867,500,000	10,060,000

REQUIREMENTS

a) Develop an equation for total weekly manufacturing costs using simple linear regression analysis.

b) Determine the estimated costs for a week when 65 units are produced.

7–9 High-Low Cost Estimation and Price Changes

Artex Corporation has accumulated the following 19x5 production cost data.

Month	*Units produced*	*Direct materials*	*Direct labor*	*Factory overhead*	*Total manufacturing costs*
February	2,000	$4,000	$8,000	$5,000	$17,000
December	8,000	17,600	33,600	14,000	65,200

Artex experienced a 10 percent increase in direct materials costs on June 1, 19x5, and a 5 percent increase in direct-labor costs on October 1, 19x5. No price increases related to overhead costs occurred during 19x5.

REQUIREMENTS

a) Restate the February direct materials and direct-labor costs in terms of the December price level.

b) Based on the answer to part (a), use the high-low method to develop a cost-estimating equation for total monthly manufacturing costs.

c) Assuming there are no further price changes, determine the expected manufacturing costs for a month when Artex produces 6,000 units?

7–10 High-Low Cost Estimation and Price Changes

Dexter Company has analyzed production cost data for 19x1 and obtained the following data for May and October, the months with the highest and lowest levels of production.

	Units produced	*Manufacturing costs*
May	13,000	$80,000
October	3,000	31,500

During 19x1, Dexter experienced several price increases related to manufacturing costs. Management did not keep track of each increase, however, they believe the changes in the general price level are indicative of the changes in costs experienced by Dexter. The general price-level indices during the two months and at the end of the year were as follows:

Period	*Price level index*
Average for May 19x1	200
Average for October 19x1	210
December 31, 19x1	215

REQUIREMENTS

a) Adjust the May and October costs to December 31, 19x1, dollars using the general price-level index.

b) Using the high-low method and your answer to part (a), develop a cost-estimating equation for total monthly manufacturing costs.

7–11 Analyzing Cost-Estimating Equations

K & M Company produces one product and has developed the following cost-estimating equations for total annual costs:

Total factory overhead = \$100,000 + \$4X

Total manufacturing costs = \$100,000 + \$20X

Total costs = \$200,000 + \$25X

where

X = units produced and sold

Each unit requires direct materials costing \$3 and 2 direct-labor hours.

REQUIREMENTS

a) Determine the cost of a direct-labor hour.

b) Assuming all costs are classified as either (1) manufacturing or (2) selling, general, and administrative, develop a cost-estimating equation for total annual selling, general, and administrative costs.

c) If K & M Company produces and sells 20,000 units during 19x8 and incurs costs at the same rate as in 19x7, estimate the (1) total factory overhead and (2) total manufacturing costs.

7–12 Analyzing Cost-Estimating Equations

The Frost Corporation has developed the following cost-estimating equations for total annual costs.

Total factory overhead = \$300,000 + \$4X

Total manufacturing costs = \$300,000 + \$40Y

Total costs = \$500,000 + \$50Y

where

X = direct-labor hours
Y = units produced and sold

Each unit of output requires direct materials costing \$7 and 3 direct-labor hours.

REQUIREMENTS

a) Determine the cost of a direct-labor hour.

b) Assuming all costs are classified as either (1) manufacturing or (2) selling, general, and administrative, develop a cost-estimating equation for total annual selling, general, and administrative costs.

c) If Frost Corporation produces and sells 10,000 units during 19x3 and incurs costs at the same rate as in 19x2, estimate the (1) total factory overhead and (2) total manufacturing costs.

PROBLEMS

7–13 Negative Fixed Costs

"This is crazy!" exclaimed the senior cost accountant as he reviewed the work of his new assistant. "You and that dumb computer are telling me that my fixed costs are negative! According to your calculations we will make more money if we don't do anything that we do now! Tell me, 'genius,' how did you get these negative fixed costs? What am I supposed to do with them?"

REQUIREMENT

Respond.

7–14 High-Low Cost Estimation and Dual Rates for Service Departments

Presented is information pertaining to the volume and cost of services provided by a particular service department during 19x3 and 19x4.

	19x3	*19x4*
Service department operating costs	$540,000	$690,000
Units of service provided to:		
Production Department I	10,000 units	20,000 units
Production Department II	40,000 units	40,000 units
Production Department III	25,000 units	40,000 units
Maximum possible demand for services:		
Production Department I	30,000 units	
Production Department II	45,000 units	
Production Department III	75,000 units	

REQUIREMENTS

a) Using the high-low method, develop a cost-estimating equation for annual service department costs.

b) Using the dual rate method of service department cost allocation, prepare a schedule allocating the 19x4 service department costs to each of the production departments.

7–15 Developing High-Low Cost Estimates from Job-Order Cost Data

The Hang High Drapery Company manufactures custom-made draperies for leading department stores. The company uses a single type of fabric to maintain an even quality and manufactures the draperies in a standard mix of sizes. The only difference in jobs pertains to the size of the order and the drapery pattern used.

You have been asked to develop a cost-estimating equation for total monthly production costs. The following information is available:

Factory overhead control

6/x9 Actual	$3,750	$1,000	Balance	6/1/x9
		3,500	Applied	6/x9
7/x9 Actual	$3,250	$ 750	Balance	7/1/x9
		2,500	Applied	7/x9
		$ 0	Balance	8/1/x9

Only four jobs were in process during June and July of 19x9. Their job-cost sheets are as follows.

Job 475: 6,000 square yards, completed June 15

Date	*Materials*	*Labor*	*Applied overhead*	*Total*
5/28	$6,300	$ 500	$ 500	$7,300
6/15		1,000	1,000	2,000
				$9,300

Job 501: 10,000 square yards, completed June 30

Date	*Materials*	*Labor*	*Applied overhead*	*Total*
6/2	$9,500	$2,000	$2,000	$13,500
6/30		500	500	1,000
				$14,500

Job 522: 8,000 square yards, completed July 28

Date	*Materials*	*Labor*	*Applied overhead*	*Total*
7/1	$8,200	$1,000	$1,000	$10,200
7/28		1,000	1,000	2,000
				$12,200

Job 524: 3,000 square yards, in process

Date	*Materials*	*Labor*	*Applied overhead*	*Total*
7/29	$3,000	$ 500	$ 500	$4,000

ADDITIONAL INFORMATION

- All materials are added at the start of production.
- Variable overhead is a function of direct-labor dollars.
- All overhead is applied on the basis of direct-labor dollars.

REQUIREMENT

Develop a cost-estimating equation for monthly production in square yards.

7–16 Use of Process Costing Data in Cost Estimation

T. Buckman recently accepted a position as senior cost accountant for the Snowshoe Ski Company. Snowshoe manufactures a number of brands of skis, including the famous "Foot" ski. Because of the popularity of the Foot brand, a new factory is being constructed to manufacture it on a continuous basis.

Mr. Buckman believes an actual process-costing system (as opposed to a normal process-costing system) should be used until enough operating experience is obtained to develop predetermined overhead rates. He also wishes to develop cost-estimating equations, production standards, and probability intervals for costs as soon as possible. However, he does not want to maintain separate cost accumulation systems for product costing and statistical data.

REQUIREMENT

Mr. Buckman must choose between a weighted-average and FIFO process-costing system. Which do you believe will provide information that is more useful in developing cost estimates? Why?

7–17 Process Costing and High-Low Cost Estimation

The Dudley Company manufactures a chemical on a continuous basis. The following monthly information is available about factory overhead costs and equivalent units of conversion for four consecutive months.

	January	*February*	*March*	*April*
Equivalent units:				
Beginning inventory	2,000	6,000	8,000	2,000
Completed and transferred out	20,000	14,000	18,000	18,000
Ending inventory	6,000	8,000	2,000	0
Factory overhead	$40,000	$28,000	$25,000	$30,000

REQUIREMENTS

a) Prepare a schedule of the number of equivalent units *manufactured* each month.

b) Use the high-low method to develop a cost-estimating equation for monthly factory overhead.

7–18 Account Classification and Adjusting Data for Data Base Problems

The ACE Radio Company began manufacturing small electronic calculators in a new plant on 1/1/x0. The plant cost $500,000, had an estimated life of 10 years, and an estimated salvage value of $50,000. ACE elected to use double declining balance depreciation for financial-reporting purposes. After three years of operations, ACE hired you as a consultant to help in developing cost estimates. Management realizes that it will take considerable time to obtain good cost estimates, but they need preliminary estimates as soon as possible. After much effort you obtain the following data:

ACE Radio Company, Calculator Plant
Statement of Cost of Goods Manufactured
For the Year Ending December 31, 19x2

Work-in-process, 1/1/x2		$ 0
Current costs placed in process:		
Direct materials	$ 49,000	
Direct labor	210,000	
Applied factory overhead	136,000	395,000
Total costs in process		$395,000
Work-in-process, 12/31/x2		– 0
Cost of goods manufactured		$395,000

ADDITIONAL INFORMATION

- Production takes place evenly throughout the year.
- The current replacement cost of the direct materials used in 19x2 is $58,000.
- All ACE employees received a 10 percent increase in wages on 7/1/x2.
- The local utilities company announced a 25 percent rate increase effective 1/1/x3.
- Actual overhead costs for 19x2 are as follows:

Depreciation on plant	$ 64,000
Indirect labor	16,800
Utilities	20,000
Total	$100,800

- Management estimates that 25 percent of the 19x2 indirect-labor and utilities are fixed.
- Management believes it can reduce the variable use of utilities by 10 percent in 19x3.
- Production totaled 50,000 calculators in 19x2. This is also the activity level used in developing ACE's predetermined overhead rate.

REQUIREMENTS

a) Use the account classification method to develop a cost-estimating equation for use in 19x3.

b) What is the likely cause of the overapplied 19x2 overhead?

c) Develop a predetermined overhead rate, based on a 50,000 unit production volume, for 19x3.

d) State any major assumptions that underlie your analysis in parts (a) and (c).

e) If ACE had completed 49,000 calculators in 19x2 and had an ending work-in-process inventory of 1,000 units, what additional information would be needed to develop a cost-estimating equation for 19x3?

7–19 Evaluating Historical Cost Data: Simple Regression

In an attempt to develop production cost standards, the controller of a rug company has compiled the following production cost information. The company uses absorption costing and allocates all costs except administrative and selling expenses to the units produced.

(All in 000's)

Year	*Applied fixed overhead**	*Actual variable overhead*	*Actual direct materials*	*Actual direct labor*	*Actual production (sq. yards)*
19x5	$ 900	$ 720	$1,215	$1,125	4,500
19x6	1,000	750	1,250	1,250	5,000
19x7	800	640	1,000	4,040	4,000
19x8	900	765	1,260	1,305	4,500
19x9	1,000	1,000	1,500	1,500	5,000
19x0	1,200	1,320	1,980	1,920	6,000
19x1	1,000	1,250	1,750	1,750	5,000
19x2	1,600	2,160	2,960	2,880	8,000
19x3	1,700	2,380	3,230	3,060	8,500
19x4	1,400	2,100	2,800	2,800	7,000

* Fixed overhead is applied at the rate of $0.20 per square yard. Any difference between actual and applied overhead at the end of each year is disposed of as an adjustment to the cost of goods sold.

REQUIREMENT

Evaluate the usefulness of the cost data provided by the controller. What weaknesses exist in the data that may make the data inappropriate to use in trying to determine what current operating costs should be? What historical data might be more useful and why?

7–20 Estimating Machine Repair Costs

In an attempt to determine a basis for estimating repair and maintenance costs and allocating them to units produced, the assistant controller accumulated daily information on these costs and on production over a one-month period. After simple regression analysis was applied to the data, the following estimating equation was obtained:

$$T = \$750 - \$2.562X$$

where

X = hundreds of units produced
T = daily repair and maintenance costs

Because of the negative relationship between daily costs and production, the assistant controller was somewhat skeptical of the results.

REQUIREMENTS

a) What is the most likely explanation of the negative relationship?

b) Suggest an alternate procedure for estimating repair and maintenance costs that might prove more useful.

7–21 Evaluating Historical Cost Data: Multiple Regression

The Doctors Building Laboratory in Low Point has been providing seven basic tests ($X_1, X_2, \ldots, X_7$) as an outpatient service for the past five years. Currently the physicians who own the facility as a partnership are in the process of reevaluating the prices charged for each of the lab's seven basic tests. You have been called in to analyze the lab's historical cost data to determine if regression analysis is an appropriate technique to use in estimating fixed and variable costs in the range of normal activity. After much digging and questioning, you have come up with the following information:

- The organization has detailed records on the number of tests performed each year.
- The organization has no information about the costs of performing each test. The bookkeeper can provide you with only the total cost of operating the lab each period.
- The bookkeeper is very accurate and always records costs in the proper period.
- Building overhead is allocated to the pharmacy, to the laboratory, and to the individual physicians who maintain offices in the building on the basis of a predetermined rate for each service unit that is provided for patients or customers. For a physician, one service unit is one office visit by a patient. For the pharmacy, one unit is filling a prescription. For the laboratory, one service unit is performing a basic test.
- Cost data:

		Number of tests						
Year	*Total cost*	X_1	X_2	X_3	X_4	X_5	X_6	X_7
19x0	$11,060	200	400	200	1,000	50	900	22
19x1	10,615	225	400	225	500	55	700	42
19x2	12,160	300	400	300	650	60	650	35
19x3	19,461	299	400	299	700	55	500	40
19x4	28,959	250	400	250	900	57	1,000	45

REQUIREMENT

Indicate the weaknesses that exist in the data just presented that might make multiple regression analysis an inappropriate cost-estimating technique. How might data that is more appropriate for cost estimation be obtained?

7–22 T High-Low and Simple Linear Regression (Appendix B)

Armer Company is accumulating data to be used in preparing its annual profit plan for the coming year. The cost behavior pattern of the maintenance costs must be determined. The accounting staff has suggested that linear regression be employed to derive an equation in the form of $T = a + bX$ for maintenance costs. Data regarding last year's maintenance hours and costs are as follows:

	Hours of activity	*Maintenance costs*
January	480	$4,200
February	320	3,000
March	400	3,600
April	300	2,820
May	500	4,350
June	310	2,960
July	320	3,030
August	520	4,470
September	490	4,260
October	470	4,050
November	350	3,300
December	340	3,160

REQUIREMENTS

a) Using the high-low method, develop an equation for monthly maintenance costs.

b) Using simple linear regression, develop an equation for monthly maintenance costs.

c) Using the results of parts (a) and (b), develop two estimates of maintenance costs for a month where 420 maintenance hours are worked.

d) Determine the correlation coefficient for hours of activity and maintenance costs.

e) Determine the coefficient of determination for the equation developed in part (b).

(CMA Adapted)

7–23 T Simple Linear Regression (Appendix B)

Motomation Corporation plans to acquire several retail automotive parts stores as part of its expansion program. Motomation carries out an extensive review of possible acquisitions prior to making any decision to approach a specific company. Currently Motomation is conducting a preacquisition review of Atlas Auto Parts, a regional chain of retail automotive parts stores. Among the financial data to be projected for Atlas is the future rental cost for its stores. The following schedule presents the rent and revenues (in millions of dollars) for the past ten years.

Year	*Revenues*	*Annual rent expense*
1977	$22	$1.00
1978	24	1.15
1979	36	1.40
1980	27	1.10
1981	43	1.55
1982	33	1.25
1983	45	1.65
1984	48	1.60
1985	61	1.80
1986	60	1.95

The following three alternative methods have been suggested for predicting future annual rental expense.

- *Alternative A:* Develop a linear regression equation using time as the independent variable. The resultant equation will be of the form:

  Rental expense $= a + bx$

  where $x =$ actual year $-$ 1976 (For example, x for 1986 is 10.)

- *Alternative B:* Develop a linear regression equation relating rental expense to annual revenues. The resultant equation will be of the form:

  Rental expense $= a + bx$

  where $x =$ revenues $\div$ 1,000,000 (For example, x for 1986 is 60.)

- *Alternative C:* Calculate rental expense as a percentage of revenues using the arithmetic average for the ten-year period of 1977–1986 inclusive.

REQUIREMENTS

a) Use simple linear regression to develop the equation suggested under Alternative A.

b) Use simple linear regression to develop the equation suggested under Alternative B.

c) Use each alternative to estimate Atlas Auto Parts' 1987 rental expense assuming the 1987 projected revenue will be the same as the 1986 revenue, that is, $60 million.

d) Discuss the advantages and disadvantages of each alternative method.

e) Determine the correlation coefficients of the equations developed in parts (a) and (b).

f) Determine the coefficient of determination for the equations developed in parts (a) and (b).

g) Identify the one alternative, A, B, or C, that you recommend Motomation Corporation use to estimate rental expense. Explain why you selected that alternative.

h) Do you believe a statistical technique is an appropriate method in this situation for estimating rental expense? Why or why not? (CMA Adapted)

7–24 Using and Evaluating Simple and Multiple Regression Equations (Appendix B)

John Wood, a financial analyst for a major automobile corporation, has been monitoring the funds used in advertising campaigns and the funds used for automobile factory rebates. Financial data have been accumulated for the last 24 months along with customer sales, that is, automobiles sold. Wood contends that there may be a relationship between the level of automobile sales and funds expended on advertising and/or factory rebates. If such a relationship between the level of automobile sales and funds expended can be determined, the company may be able to estimate sales demand based on various levels of funding commitments for one or both types of expenditures.

The following regression equations and supporting statistical values were developed for the various relationships between variables:

Equation 1:	
Equation	$D = 2.455 + 0.188A$
Coefficient of determination	0.414
Standard error of the estimate	1.325
Equation 2:	
Equation	$D = 2.491 + 0.44R$
Coefficient of determination	0.314
Standard error of the estimate	1.434
Equation 3:	
Equation	$R = 6.052 + 0.005A$
Coefficient of determination	0.0002
Standard error of the estimate	2.202
Equation 4:	
Equation	$D = -0.184 + 0.186A + 0.437R$
Coefficient of determination	0.703
Standard error of the estimate	0.922

The meanings of the notations used in the equations are as follows:

A = advertising funds in \$100,000.

R = funds for factory rebates in \$1,000,000.

D = automobiles sold in 10,000 units.

The appropriate t-values for use in determining probability intervals are as follows:

- 50 percent $+0.69$
- 95 percent $+2.07$

REQUIREMENTS

a) If the corporation is projecting advertising expenditures amounting to \$1,500,000 and factory rebate expenditures amounting to \$12,000,000 for the next time period, calculate expected unit sales using

1. Equation 1.
2. Equation 4.

b) Assume that Equation 4 is used to predict total sales of 104,160 automobiles for a time period. Develop a 50 percent probability interval for the range of automobile sales that could occur during the time period.

c) Select the regression equation that would be most advantageous to predict sales and explain why it is the best.

d) Each of the regression equations included a constant.

1. Discuss the meaning of the constant term included in regression Equation 2.
2. What is the significance of the negative constant in regression Equation 4? Explain your answer. (CMA Adapted)

7–25 Using and Evaluating Simple and Multiple Regression Equations (Appendix B)

The Lockit Company manufactures door knobs for residential homes and apartments. Lockit is considering the use of simple and multiple linear regression analysis to forecast annual sales because previous forecasts have been inaccurate. The sales forecast will be used to initiate the budgeting process and to better identify the underlying process that generates sales.

Larry Husky, the controller of Lockit, has considered many possible independent variables and equations to predict sales and has narrowed his choices to four equations. Husky used annual observations from 20 prior years to estimate each of the four equations.

A statistical summary of these four equations and definitions of the variables used are as follows:

Equation 1:

Dependent variable	S_t
Independent variable	S_{t-1}
Intercept	\$ 500,000
Coefficient of independent variable	\$ 1.10
T-statistic	5.50
Standard error of the estimate	\$ 500,000
Coefficient of determination	0.94

Equation 2:

Dependent variable	S_t
Independent variable	G_t
Intercept	\$ 1,000,000
Coefficient of independent variable	\$ 0.00001
T-statistic	10.00
Standard error of the estimate	\$ 510,000
Coefficient of determination	0.90

Equation 3:

Dependent variable	S_t
Independent variable	G_{t-1}
Intercept	\$ 900,000
Coefficient of independent variable	\$ 0.000012
T-statistic	5.00
Standard error of the estimate	\$ 520,000
Coefficient of determination	0.81

Equation 4:

Dependent variable	S_t
Independent variables	N_{t-1}, G_t, G_{t-1}
Intercept	\$ 600,000

Coefficients of independent variables:

Variable	*Coefficient*	*T-statistic*
N_{t-1}	\$ 10.00	4.00
G_t	\$ 0.000002	1.50
G_{t-1}	\$ 0.000003	3.00

Standard error of the estimate	\$ 490,000
Coefficient of determination	0.96

where

S_t = forecasted sales (in dollars) for Lockit in time period t
S_{t-1} = actual sales (in dollars) for Lockit in time period $t - 1$
G_t = forecasted U.S. gross national product in time period t
G_{t-1} = actual U.S. gross national product in time period $t - 1$
N_{t-1} = Lockit's net income in time period $t - 1$

REQUIREMENTS

a) Write equations 2 and 4 in the form $T = a + bx$.

b) If actual sales are $1,500,000 in 19x1, what would be the forecasted sales for Lockit in 19x2?

c) Explain the meaning and significance of the coefficient of determination.

d) Why might Larry Husky prefer equation 3 to equation 2?

e) Explain the advantages and disadvantages of using equation 4 to forecast annual sales. (CMA Adapted)

7–26 Learning Curves: Basics (Appendix C)

Mr. Chips was delighted. His firm, Home Computers, Inc., had achieved a significant technological and cost breakthrough with the new Model X home computer. Mr. Chips was also pleased to learn that Computer House, Inc., had agreed to test market Model X at their Fifth Avenue and Sheffield Point stores.

Computer House wanted a minimum of 16 units on hand prior to commencing newspaper, radio, and television advertising. A suggested selling price also had to be determined. The selling price to Computer House would be based on the average cost of the 16 units plus a 50 percent markup.

Even though only four units had been produced to date, Mr. Chips, who was quite familiar with the learning curve phenomenon, was confident that the total and average cost of 16 units could be accurately predicted. The following information is available about the first four units:

Unit	*Unit cost*
1	$400
2	280
3	247
4	229

REQUIREMENTS

a) Assuming the preceding process follows the learning curve phenomenon, predict the total cost of producing 16 units. Round all calculations to two decimal places.

b) What selling price should Mr. Chips charge Computer House for 16 Model X home computers?

7–27 Learning Curves: Basics (Appendix C)

The Kelly Company plans to manufacture a product called Electrocal, which requires a substantial amount of direct labor. Based on the company's experience with other products, management believes there is a learning factor in the production process used to manufacture Electrocal.

Each unit of Electrocal requires 50 square feet of raw material at a cost of $30 per square foot for a total material cost of $1,500. The direct-labor rate is $25 per direct-labor hour. Variable factory overhead is assigned to products at a rate of $40 per direct-labor hour. The company adds a markup of 30 percent on variable manufacturing cost in determining an initial bid price for all products.

Data on the production of the first two lots (16 units) of Electrocal are as follows:

- The first lot of 8 units required a total of 3,200 direct-labor hours.
- The second lot of 8 units required a total of 2,240 direct-labor hours.

REQUIREMENTS

a) What is the basic premise of the learning curve?

b) Based on the data presented for the first 16 units, what learning rate appears to be applicable to the direct labor required to produce Electrocal? Support your answer with appropriate calculations.

c) Determine the total variable manufacturing costs of producing 32 units.

(CMA Adapted)

7–28 Learning Curves (Appendix C)

Catonic, Inc., recently developed a new product that includes a rather complex printed circuit board as a component (Catonic's part number PCB-31). Although Catonic has the capability to manufacture the PCB-31 internally, the circuit board is purchased from an independent supplier because the company's printed circuit line has been operating at capacity for some time.

The first contract for 50 units of the PCB-31 was awarded to Rex Engineering Company in September 19x2 on the basis of a competitive bid. Rex was significantly lower than other bidders. Additional orders for 50 units each were placed with Rex as shown in the following purchase history schedule. Rex has proved to be a reliable supplier of other component parts over a period of several years.

Date ordered	*Quantity*	*Unit price*	*Total price*
September 15, 19x2	50	$374	$18,700
November 15, 19x2	50	374	18,700
January 1, 19x3	50	374	18,700
February 1, 19x3	50	374	18,700

Mark Polmik, a buyer for Catonic, has determined that the next order for PCB-31 should be for 600 units. He has contacted Kathy Wentz, a Rex salesperson. Polmik indicated that the next PCB-31 order would be for 600 units and that he believed that Catonic should receive a lower unit price because of the increased quantity. Wentz provided a proposal of $355 per unit for the 600-unit contract a few days later.

Polmik has scheduled a meeting with Wentz for next week for the purpose of negotiating the 600-unit contract. He has asked Catonic's cost accounting department for assistance in evaluating the $355 unit price for the PCB-31 circuit board.

The price bid on the original contract for 50 units was estimated to be a "full cost" price because, at that time, Catonic was not sure if there would be future contracts for the PCB-31 board. The cost of materials included in the PCB-31 is estimated to be $180 per unit. Cost accounting is fairly sure that Rex applies overhead at 100 percent of direct labor and employee benefit cost. The labor and fringe benefit costs at Rex are known to be approximately $20 per hour. The printed circuit line at Rex is very similar to the one at Catonic, and Rex's overhead is believed to be approximately 50 percent variable and 50 percent fixed. Similar work at Catonic evidences a 90 percent learning curve effect.

Using the foregoing data, the price of the initial 50-unit order was estimated to be composed of the following cost components:

Materials	$ 180
Labor and employee benefits (4 labor hours × $20)	80
Overhead (100 percent of labor and employee benefits)	80
Full cost of PCB-31 component	$ 340
Profit contribution (10 percent of full cost)	34
Unit price	$ 374
Units purchased	× 50
Total contract price	$18,700

REQUIREMENTS

a) Prepare a schedule that Mark Polmik can use at his meeting with Kathy Wentz next week. This schedule should incorporate the learning curve effect that Rex would have experienced on the first 200 units produced and should be of use to Polmik in negotiating a contract with Rex Engineering. (*Hint:* Use lot sizes of 50 as the basic unit and determine the cumulative average time per unit when production doubles.)

b) The learning curve (also known as a progress function or an experience curve) was first formally recognized in the 1920's. Since that time the learning effect has been observed in a number of different industries.

1. What are the implications of an 80 percent learning curve as opposed to a 90 percent learning curve?
2. Identify factors that would tend to reduce the degree of learning that takes place in an industrial operation.

(CMA Adapted)

SOLUTION TO REVIEW PROBLEM

a) $b = \dfrac{\$4{,}750 - \$3{,}400}{1{,}050 - 600} = \dfrac{\$1{,}350}{450} = \underline{\underline{\$3.00}}$

$a = \$4{,}750 - \$3.00(1{,}050) = \$4{,}750 - \$3{,}150 = \underline{\underline{\$1{,}600}}$

or

$a = \$3{,}400 - \$3.00(600) = \$3{,}400 - \$1{,}800 = \underline{\underline{\$1{,}600}}$

Equation: $\hat{T} = \$1{,}600 + \$3.00X$

b)

Week	Factory overhead costs (T)	Direct labor hours (X)	X × T	X^2
1	$4,300	800	3,440,000	640,000
2	3,900	750	2,925,000	562,500
3	3,650	675	2,463,750	455,625
4	4,200	775	3,255,000	600,625
5	3,400	600	2,040,000	360,000
6	4,500	945	4,252,500	893,025
7	4,100	850	3,485,000	722,500
8	3,500	650	2,275,000	422,500
9	4,300	825	3,547,500	680,625
10	4,700	980	4,606,000	960,400
11	4,750	1,050	4,987,500	1,102,500
12	4,550	1,000	4,550,000	1,000,000
13	4,400	875	3,850,000	765,625
14	4,050	740	2,997,000	547,600
15	3,800	680	2,584,000	462,400
Totals	62,100	12,195	51,258,250	10,175,925

$$\overline{T} = \frac{\$62,100}{15} = \underline{\underline{\$4,140}}$$

$$\overline{X} = \frac{12,195}{15} = \underline{\underline{813}}$$

$$b = \frac{51,258,250 - 813(62,100)}{10,175,925 - 813(12,195)} = \frac{770,950}{261,390} = \underline{\underline{2.949}}$$

$$a = 4,140 - 2.949(813) = \underline{\underline{1,742.463}}$$

Equation: $\hat{T} = \$1,742.463 + \$2.949X$

c) $\hat{T} = \$1,600 + \$3.00(900) = \underline{\underline{\$4,300}}$

d) $\hat{T} = \$1,742.463 + \$2.949(900) = \underline{\underline{\$4,396.563}}$

8 Cost-Volume-Profit Analysis

INTRODUCTION

ECONOMIC AND ACCOUNTING COST-VOLUME-PROFIT MODELS

ASSUMPTIONS UNDERLYING COST-VOLUME-PROFIT ANALYSIS

EXTENSIONS OF THE BASIC MODEL

SUMMARY

APPENDIX: THE ANALYSIS OF UNCERTAINTY IN SHORT-RANGE PLANNING

INTRODUCTION

COST-VOLUME-PROFIT ANALYSIS IS A TECHNIQUE USED TO ANALYZE THE IMpact of changes in volume on costs, revenues, and profits. It is used extensively in planning because it helps answer such questions as: At what volume of operations are revenues and costs equal? What profit will be earned if there is a 10 percent increase in sales volume? What volume is needed to earn a profit of $50,000?

The differential analysis that underlies cost-volume-profit relationships is also useful in making many types of managerial decisions, including accepting or rejecting a special order, making or buying a part used in production, and adding or dropping a product line. Chapter 15 considers these decisions.

The purpose of this chapter is to introduce the relationships and assumptions that underlie the cost-volume-profit model and to consider some extensions of the basic model. The usefulness of the model is not limited to manufacturing firms. It can also be used by retailing, service, and not-for-profit organizations. For example, a university might use cost-volume-profit relationships to determine how much tuition to charge students in order to have enough revenues to cover costs. A city could use cost-volume-profit analysis to determine the impact of an increase in bus fares on profits if riders are not expected to change.

Before examining the cost-volume-profit model, an explanation of the term "cost" is needed. In cost-volume-profit analysis, the word "cost" is restricted to costs that are deducted from revenues to determine profit. Normally these deductions are called "expenses." An important assumption of the cost-volume-profit model is that inventories either do not exist or are the same at the end of the period as at the beginning of the period. Consequently all product costs are charged against revenues in the period they are incurred. Thus the term "cost" as used in this chapter includes both product and period costs.

EXHIBIT 8–1 Economic and Accounting Cost-Volume-Profit Models

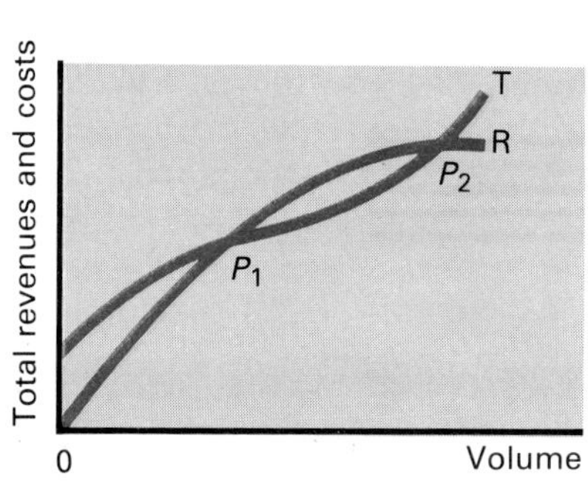

(a) Economic model

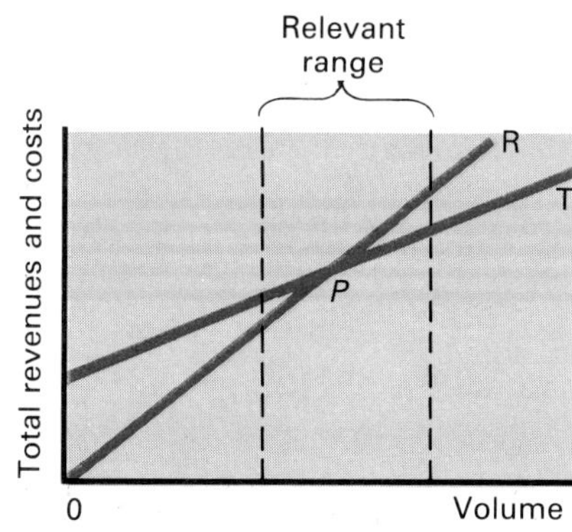

(b) Accounting model

ECONOMIC AND ACCOUNTING COST-VOLUME-PROFIT MODELS

Differences between the cost patterns used in economic and accounting models were considered in Chapter 2. Given the existence of productive capacity during a specified time period, the economic model displays a curvilinear cost function and covers the entire range of possible production, whereas the accounting model displays a linear cost function within the range of normal operations. As noted in Chapter 2, this range of normal operations within which the accountant's cost function approximates the economist's cost function is called the relevant range. The economist's cost pattern is labeled T in Exhibit 8–1(a), and the accountant's cost pattern is labeled T in Exhibit 8–1(b).

As might be expected, the economist's and the accountant's revenue patterns also differ. In most situations, the economist's revenue pattern, labeled R in Exhibit 8–1(a), has a decreasing slope as volume increases because additional sales can only be attained by a price reduction. The basic accounting model has a constant unit selling price regardless of the sales volume. Hence the accountant's revenue pattern, labeled R in Exhibit 8–1(b), is represented by a straight line. Although the accountant's revenue assumption is only valid across the entire range of possible production in a purely competitive market, it is assumed to reasonably approximate the economist's revenue pattern within the range of normal operations.

The different formulations of the economist's and accountant's models lead to two major differences in cost-volume-profit analysis. (1) The economist's model has two points at which revenues and costs are equal, P_1 and P_2, in Exhibit 8–1(a), whereas the accountant's model has only one such point, P, in Exhibit 8–1(b). (2) The economist's model has a profit-maximizing (equilibrium) volume

[1] A calculus approach to the determination of the optimal sales volume is illustrated in Chapter 15, footnote 4.

that can be determined by differential calculus,[1] whereas the accountant's model does not have an equilibrium volume. In the accountant's model the difference between R and T appears to increase without limit as volume increases.

Sources of Data

The cost functions used in cost-volume-profit analysis may be specified with the aid of engineering methods or the cost-estimating techniques discussed in Chapter 7. When the cost function is determined from an analysis of historical cost data, all of the caveats discussed in Chapter 7 apply to cost-volume-profit analysis.

The development of a revenue function, even in purely competitive markets such as farm products, is extremely difficult. The development of pricing policies is a top management decision. The determination of optimal prices requires the close cooperation of accountants, economists, and marketing personnel. In this chapter, we assume that selling prices have been set by top management. Pricing decisions are considered in Chapter 15.

Assuming that the pricing decision has been made, sales volume estimates are subject to more rigorous analysis. Economists and marketing personnel have developed numerous techniques to predict sales volume under differing economic situations. Many of these techniques are analogous to those presented in Chapter 7 for cost estimation. Using multiple regression analysis, sales volume may be specified as the dependent variable, and population, income and gross national product may be specified as independent variables. Dummy variables can be used for such factors as the previous period's sales, and exponential models can be used to allow for trends or product life-cycles.

Basic Relationships

The basic relationships underlying cost-volume-profit analysis include a linear revenue function and a linear cost function. Because the cost-volume-profit model assumes a constant selling price per unit, total revenues are equal to the number of units produced and sold multiplied by the unit selling price. In equation form:

$$R = pX, \qquad (8\text{–}1)$$

where

R = total revenues
p = unit selling price
X = number of units produced and sold

In the case of a service organization, X would refer to the number of units of service produced, such as meals served or insurance policies sold.

The total cost for a firm was previously shown to be the sum of the fixed and variable costs:

$$T = a + bX \qquad (8\text{–}2)$$

where

T = total costs
a = fixed costs
b = variable costs per unit
X = number of units produced and sold

Profit is the difference between total revenues and total costs:

$$\pi = R - T \tag{8–3}$$

where

π = profits
R and T are as previously defined

Contribution Margin If Eq. 8–1 and Eq. 8–2 are substituted into Eq. 8–3 and the terms rearranged, another profit equation can be developed:

$$\begin{aligned} \pi &= pX - a - bX \\ &= (p - b)X - a \end{aligned} \tag{8–4}$$

The difference between the unit selling price p and the unit variable cost b is the **unit contribution margin**. In manufacturing organizations, the unit contribution margin is the amount that each unit produced and sold contributes toward covering fixed costs and providing a profit. In Eq. 8–4, profit is the amount by which the total contribution margin exceeds the fixed costs. Total contribution margin is computed as the unit contribution margin multiplied by the number of units produced and sold. Total contribution margin can also be calculated as the difference between total revenues and total variable costs.

Example 8–1

The Sneider Radio Company manufactured and sold 20,000 units of a standard model radio during 19x1. The unit selling price was \$60. Variable manufacturing costs of \$40 consisted of direct materials, direct labor, and variable factory overhead of \$20, \$15, and \$5, respectively. Fixed factory overhead was \$250,000. Selling and administrative costs included a variable element of \$5 per unit manufactured and sold and a fixed element of \$50,000.

To determine Sneider Radio's unit contribution margin, all variable costs must be added together and deducted from the unit selling price.

Unit variable costs	
Direct materials	\$20
Direct labor	15
Variable factory overhead	5
Variable selling and administrative	5
Total	\$45

The unit contribution margin is \$60 − \$45, or \$15. Note that variable selling and administrative costs as well as the variable manufacturing costs were included in the computation.

The total contribution margin at 19x1 volume is the unit contribution margin multiplied by the number of units produced and sold or \$300,000 (\$15 × 20,000 units). The total contribution margin can also be computed by deducting the total variable costs from the total sales:

Total sales (20,000 × $60)		$1,200,000
Total variable costs:		
Direct materials (20,000 × $20)	$400,000	
Direct labor (20,000 × $15)	300,000	
Variable factory overhead (20,000 × $5)	100,000	
Variable selling and administrative (20,000 × $5)	100,000	−900,000
Total contribution margin		$ 300,000

Contribution Margin Percent The contribution margin concept is sometimes expressed as a percentage of sales. The **contribution margin percent** (CM%), also called the **contribution margin ratio,** is the portion of each sales dollar that goes to covering fixed costs and to profits. This percentage can be calculated using either (1) unit contribution margin and unit selling price or (2) total contribution margin and total sales. If unit data are used, the contribution margin percentage is equal to the unit contribution margin divided by the unit sales price:

$$\text{CM\%} = \frac{\text{Unit contribution margin}}{\text{Unit sales price}}$$

$$\text{CM\%} = \frac{(p - b)}{p} \tag{8–5}$$

If total sales and variable costs are used, the contribution margin percentage is equal to total contribution margin divided by total sales:

$$\text{CM\%} = \frac{\text{Total sales} - \text{Total variable costs}}{\text{Total sales}}$$

$$\text{CM\%} = \frac{(pX - bX)}{pX} \tag{8–6}$$

Example 8–2 Sneider Radio Company has a 25 percent contribution margin. Using unit data:

$$\text{CM\%} = \frac{(\$60 - \$45)}{\$60} = \frac{\$15}{\$60} = \underline{\underline{0.25}}$$

Using total data:

$$\text{CM\%} = \frac{(\$1{,}200{,}000 - \$900{,}000)}{\$1{,}200{,}000} = \frac{\$300{,}000}{\$1{,}200{,}000} = \underline{\underline{0.25}}$$

From each dollar of sales, 25 cents went to covering fixed costs and to profits. Note that the percentage is the same regardless of whether unit data or total sales and variable costs are used.

Break-Even Point The **break-even point** is the unit or dollar sales volume at which total revenues equal total costs. The break-even unit sales volume can be determined from Eq. 8–4 by setting π equal to zero and solving for X:

$$(p - b)X_{BE} - a = 0$$

$$X_{BE} = \frac{a}{(p - b)} \tag{8–7}$$

where

X_{BE} = break-even unit sales volume
a, b, and p are as defined in Eqs. 8–1 and 8–2

In words, Eq. 8–7 is:

$$\text{Break-even unit sales volume} = \frac{\text{Fixed costs}}{\text{Unit contribution margin}}$$

Note the importance of the unit contribution margin. The break-even point is where the total contribution margin of all units produced and sold equals the fixed costs. The break-even unit sales volume tells us the number of units that are required to cover the fixed costs.

Example 8–3 The 19x1 break-even unit sales volume for Sneider Radio Company was 20,000 units.

$$X_{BE} = \frac{\$300{,}000}{(\$60 - \$45)} = \frac{\$300{,}000}{\$15} = \underline{\underline{20{,}000}} \text{ units}$$

We can determine the break-even dollar sales volume by multiplying the unit selling price by the break-even unit sales volume, $p(X_{BE})$. It can also be determined as the fixed costs divided by the contribution margin percentage:[2]

$$pX_{BE} = \frac{a}{(p - b)/p} \tag{8–8}$$

In words,

$$\text{Break-even dollar sales volume} = \frac{\text{Fixed costs}}{\text{Contribution margin percentage}}$$

Example 8–4 In 19x1, \$1,200,000 of sales were required for Sneider Radio Company to break-even:

$$pX_{BE} = \frac{\$300{,}000}{(\$60 - \$45)/\$60} = \frac{\$300{,}000}{0.25} = \underline{\underline{\$1{,}200{,}000}}$$

---

[2] We can verify the relationship in Eq. 8–8 by multiplying both sides of Eq. 8–7 by $1/(1/p)$:

$$\frac{1}{1/p} X_{BE} = \frac{1}{1/p} \cdot \frac{a}{p - b}$$

$$\frac{X_{BE}}{1/p} = \frac{a}{(p - b)/p}$$

Then, because

$$\frac{1}{1/p} = \frac{1p}{1} = p$$

we can write:

$$pX_{BE} = \frac{a}{(p - b)/p}$$

Note that with sales of 20,000 units, or $1,200,000, Sneider Radio Company merely broke even in 19x1.

Since the contribution margin percentage is the same regardless of whether unit sales price and unit variable costs or total sales and total variable costs are used, the break-even dollar sales volume can be calculated even if per unit data are not available. This becomes important for multiple product firms such as department stores and restaurants. Multiple product firms sell different products with different unit contribution margins. The break-even unit sales volume for multiple product firms is expressed in terms of a mix of products. This unit volume may be difficult to compute if many products are produced and sold. However, we can easily calculate the break-even dollar sales volume using total amounts without having data on individual products of the product mix.

Example 8–5 Assume that Sneider began producing two additional radios, a clock radio and a portable radio, in 19x2. Further assume that sales of the standard radio and total fixed costs of $300,000 remain the same as in 19x1. The 19x2 sales and variable costs of each model were:

Model	*Sales*	*Total variable costs*
Standard	$1,200,000	$ 900,000
Clock	500,000	300,000
Portable	300,000	200,000
Total	$2,000,000	$1,400,000

Sneider now has a 30 percent contribution margin:

$$\text{CM\%} = \frac{\$2{,}000{,}000 - \$1{,}400{,}000}{\$2{,}000{,}000} = \frac{\$600{,}000}{\$2{,}000{,}000} = \underline{\underline{0.30}}$$

and their break-even sales volume is $1,000,000:

$$pX_{\text{BE}} = \frac{\$300{,}000}{0.30} = \underline{\underline{\$1{,}000{,}000}}$$

Given the level of fixed costs and the 19x2 mix of products, sales of at least $1,000,000 are needed to break even. The 19x2 break-even point is lower than the 19x1 break-even point of $1,200,000 because the 19x2 contribution margin percentage is greater than the 19x1 contribution margin percentage (0.30 versus 0.25). The addition of the new models increased Sneider's overall contribution margin percentage.

Cost-Volume-Profit Graphs Cost-volume-profit relationships are frequently presented in a **cost-volume-profit graph** illustrating revenues, costs, and profits or losses at various sales volumes. In a cost-volume-profit graph, the revenue line has a vertical-axis intercept equal to zero and a slope equal to the unit selling price. The total cost line has a vertical-axis intercept equal to the fixed costs and a slope equal to the unit variable costs. The difference between the slope of the revenue line and the slope of the total cost line is the unit contribution margin.

Example 8–6

Sneider's cost-volume-profit graph for 19x1, when only standard radios were produced and sold, is presented in Exhibit 8–2. The revenue line intersects the vertical-axis at $0 and increases at a rate of $60 per unit. The total cost line intersects the vertical axis at $300,000 and increases at a rate of $45 per unit. Note that fixed costs are layered on top of variable costs allowing us to see how the total contribution margin, the difference between total revenues and total variable costs, goes first to cover fixed costs and then to provide a profit. The break-even point of 20,000 units is the level where the total revenue and total cost lines intersect.

Another way of showing cost-volume profit relationships is to layer the variable costs on top of the fixed costs as is done in Exhibit 8–3 for Sneider's 19x1 data. Although Exhibit 8–3 illustrates the same data as Exhibit 8–2, it does not show the total contribution margin at all volumes. In Exhibit 8–2, the vertical difference between the total revenue line and the total variable costs line represents the total contribution margin. This information is not readily available from Exhibit 8–3.

A **profit-volume graph** illustrating profits or losses for various sales volumes is sometimes used as an alternative to a cost-volume-profit graph. A profit-volume graph for the Sneider Radio Company is presented in Exhibit 8–4.

The profit line in Exhibit 8–4 has a vertical-axis intercept of $ – 300,000. This is the loss at zero volume and is equal to the fixed costs. At zero volume, nothing

EXHIBIT 8–2 **Graph of Cost-Volume-Profit Relationships**

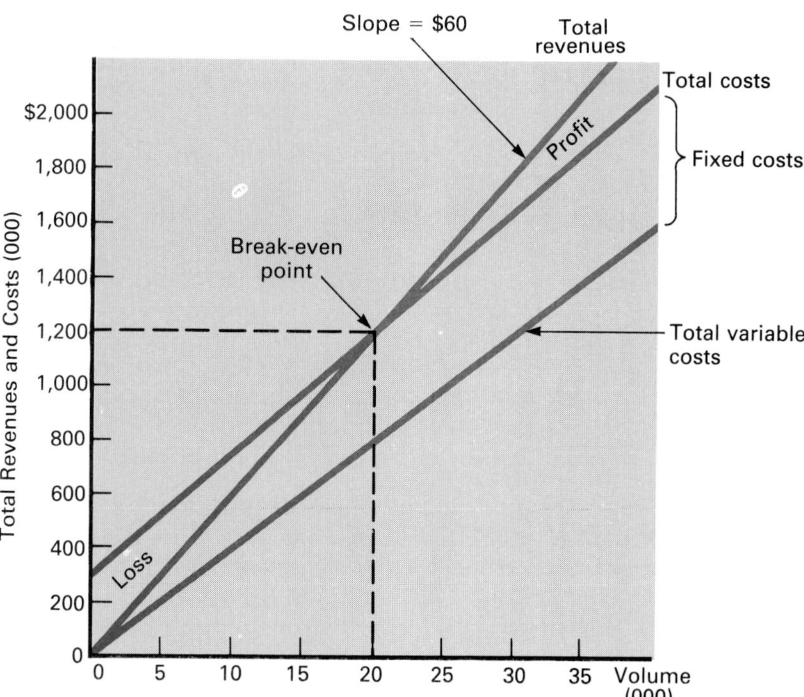

is being contributed to cover fixed costs. The slope of the profit line is the unit contribution margin of $15 ($60 sales price per unit minus $45 variable costs per unit). Break-even volume occurs where the profit line intersects the horizontal axis. One advantage of a profit-volume graph is that we can determine profits or losses at any volume directly from the graph without having to subtract total costs from total revenues. A disadvantage is that the dollar sales volume and total costs required to produce the profit or loss are not disclosed.

Margin of Safety The **margin of safety** is the excess of actual or budgeted sales over break-even sales. The margin of safety can be expressed in units or sales dollars. Management may want to know the margin of safety in actual or planned activity because it indicates the amount by which sales could decrease before losses occur.

Example 8–7

As previously illustrated, Sneider's 19x1 break-even unit sales volume was 20,000 units. Assume Sneider's management was contemplating a return to the exclusive production of standard radios in 19x3 with an expected sales volume of 25,000 units. This planned sales volume would provide a margin of safety of 5,000 units or $300,000.

EXHIBIT 8–3 **Alternative Graph of Cost-Volume Profit Relationships**

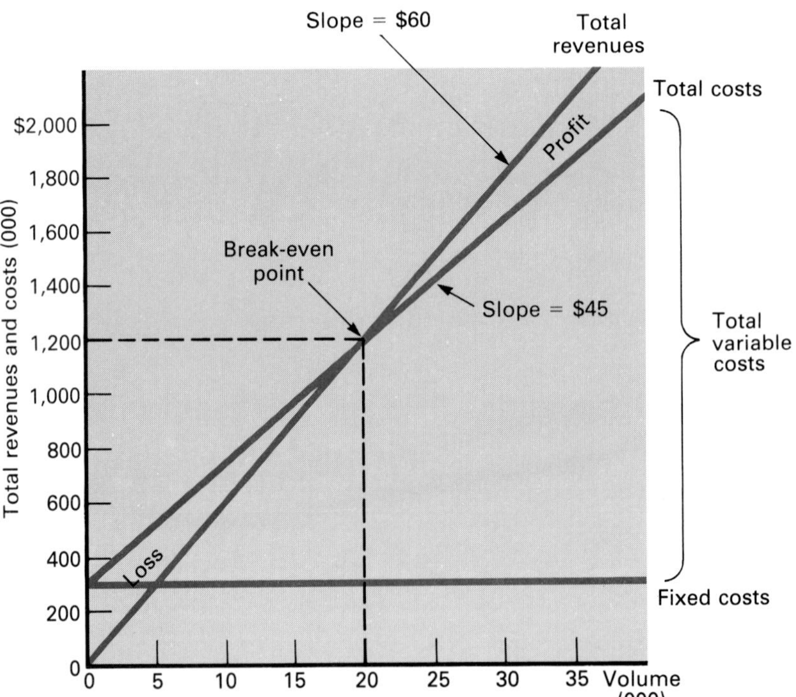

EXHIBIT 8–4 Graph of Profit-Volume Relationships

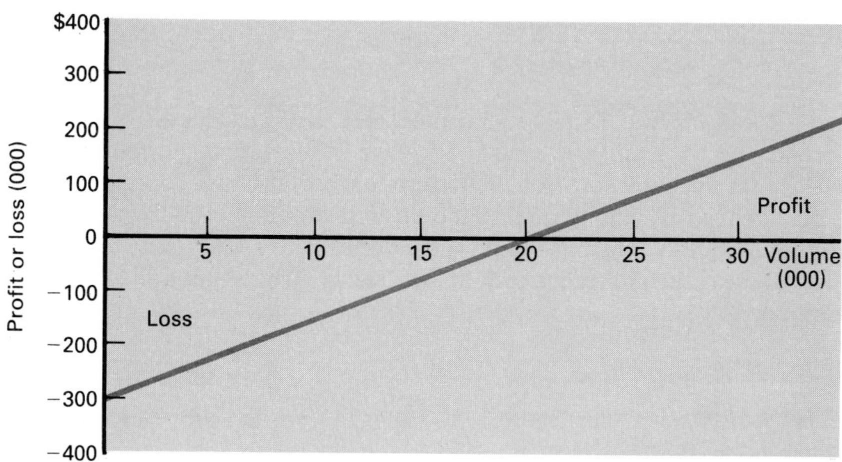

	Units	*Sales dollars*
Expected sales	25,000	$1,500,000
Break-even sales	−20,000	−1,200,000
Margin of safety	5,000	$ 300,000

Profit Planning The unit sales volume that will cover all fixed expenses and provide a desired profit can be determined from Eq. 8–4 by setting π equal to the desired profit and solving for X:

$$\pi = (p - b)X - a$$

$$X = \frac{a + \pi}{p - b} \tag{8–9}$$

where

X = volume required to earn a profit of π
a, b, and p are as previously defined

In words,

$$\text{Unit sales volume for desired profits} = \frac{\text{Fixed costs + Desired profit}}{\text{Unit contribution margin}}$$

The unit sales volume for desired profit tells us the number of unit contributions required to cover the fixed costs and provide the desired profit.

Example 8–8 Sneider's management desires to know the 19x3 unit sales volume necessary to earn a profit of $150,000 from the standard model radio. Recall that fixed costs are $300,000; the unit selling price is $60; and the unit variable costs are $45.

Using Eq. 8–9, the required volume is 30,000 units:

$$X = \frac{\$300{,}000 + \$150{,}000}{(\$60 - \$45)} = \frac{\$450{,}000}{\$15} = \underline{\underline{30{,}000}} \text{ units}$$

Profit Planning with Income Taxes If income taxes are considered in planning after-tax profits, Eq. 8–9 must be modified to take into account the reduction in profits that occurs because some of the before-tax profits must be paid out for income taxes. Instead of simply adding the desired profits to the fixed costs in the numerator of Eq. 8–9, we must convert the desired after-tax profits to before-tax profits. After-tax profits are equal to before-tax profits multiplied by one minus the tax rate:

$$\pi_{AT} = (1 - t)\pi \tag{8–10}$$

where

π_{AT} = after-tax profits
π = before-tax profits
t = income tax rate

Solving Eq. 8–10 for π, before-tax profits are equal to after-tax profits divided by one minus the tax rate:

$$\pi = \frac{\pi_{AT}}{1 - t} \tag{8–11}$$

Example 8–9 If Sneider desires after-tax profits of $150,000 in 19x3 and is subject to a 40 percent tax rate, the before-tax profits must total $250,000:

$$\pi = \frac{\$150{,}000}{1 - 0.40} = \frac{\$150{,}000}{0.60} = \underline{\underline{\$250{,}000}}$$

This number is verified by calculating the after-tax profits when the before-tax profits are $250,000.

Before-tax profits	$250,000
Income taxes (0.40 × $250,000)	– 100,000
After-tax profits	$150,000

Income taxes do not affect break-even computations because no income taxes are paid if a firm has zero profits. They do, however, affect the sales volume needed to reach a certain level of after-tax profits. If Eq. 8–11 is substituted into Eq. 8–9, the sales volume needed to obtain a certain level of after-tax profits is:

$$X_{\pi_{AT}} = \frac{a + [\pi_{AT}/(1 - t)]}{(p - b)} \tag{8–12}$$

Example 8–10 The sales volume needed to provide Sneider with 19x3 after-tax profits of $150,000 if they produce and sell only standard radios is 36,667 units.

$$X_{\pi_{AT}} = \frac{\$300{,}000 + [\$150{,}000/(1 - 0.40)]}{\$60 - \$45} = \underline{\underline{36{,}667}} \text{ units}$$

Structure of Costs The structure of the costs in an organization has an impact on profit planning. **Cost structure** refers to the relationship between an organization's fixed and variable costs. Consider two firms with the same sales but different cost structures:

	Firm A	*Firm B*
Sales in units	10,000	10,000
Sales in dollars	$200,000	$200,000
Total variable costs	$ 80,000	$150,000
Fixed costs	100,000	30,000
Total costs	−180,000	−180,000
Profits	$ 20,000	$ 20,000

Although these two firms have the same level of sales and the same total costs and profits, Firm A has relatively higher fixed and lower variable costs than Firm B. This difference in cost structure has an impact on the break-even point of the firms.

The break-even points are calculated as follows:

	Firm A	*Firm B*
Selling price per unit	$20	$20
Variable costs per unit	−8	−15
Unit contribution margin	$12	$ 5

$$\text{Break-even units} \quad \frac{\$100{,}000}{\$12} = \underline{\underline{8{,}333}} \qquad \frac{\$30{,}000}{\$5} = \underline{\underline{6{,}000}}$$

Exhibit 8–5 shows cost-volume-profit relationships for these firms. Part (a) is a graph for Firm A and part (b) is a graph for Firm B. Firm B has a lower break-even volume than Firm A because fewer units are required to cover the fixed costs. However, the total contribution margin for Firm A increases at a faster rate than for Firm B. Although profits are equal at 10,000 units, if sales increase, Firm A will show greater profits.

Example 8–11 What are the profits for Firms A and B if sales increase to 12,000 units?

	Firm A	*Firm B*
Sales	$240,000	$240,000
Variable costs	$ 96,000	$180,000
Fixed costs	100,000	30,000
Total costs	−196,000	−210,000
Profits	$ 44,000	$ 30,000

EXHIBIT 8–5 Cost-Volume-Profit Graphs: Different Cost Structures

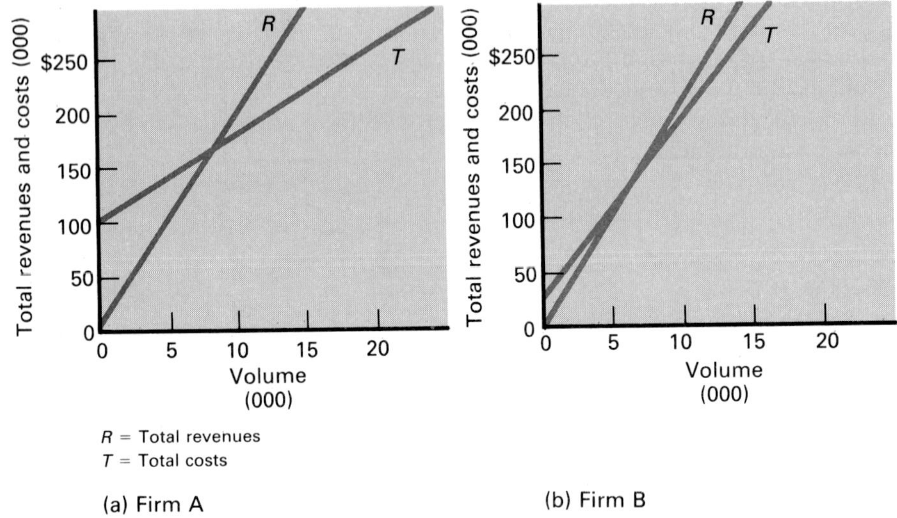

(a) Firm A (b) Firm B

The impact of cost structure on profits means that firms with higher unit contribution margins can increase profits at a faster rate than firms with lower contribution margins, once the fixed costs are covered. However, if operations are below the break-even point, the firm with a higher contribution margin will incur greater losses. The trend in most firms is toward higher fixed costs as they invest more heavily in automated operations. These firms are likely to have higher profits in times of economic prosperity but lower profits when economic conditions turn down.

ASSUMPTIONS UNDERLYING COST-VOLUME-PROFIT ANALYSIS

The basic cost-volume-profit model is subject to a number of limiting assumptions. Among the more important are the following:

All costs are classified as fixed or variable. Mixed costs must be broken down into their fixed and variable elements. The techniques discussed in Chapter 7 are used to do this.

Total costs change at a linear rate. This is the traditional assumption underlying accounting cost models. We assume that input costs are constant and production efficiency does not change. However, if a nonlinear cost function can be specified, the model can still be useful in analyzing cost-volume-profit relationships.

One example of a nonlinear cost function occurs when costs follow the learning curve phenomenon (discussed in Appendix C to Chapter 7). The learning curve phenomenon describes the systematic decrease in the time required to perform certain repetitive activities. Since less time is required to produce a unit of output as learning or experience occurs, the direct-labor costs and certain overhead costs associated with each additional unit of output decrease. If the learning rate is known or can be estimated, cost-volume-profit relationships can be determined by taking this relationship into account.

Fixed costs do not change in the relevant range. Although the basic model assumes there are no step costs, such costs should be included in cost estimates if they are significant. When step costs are included in the model, there may be more than one break-even point.

Selling prices do not change as sales volume increases. Although an analysis can be made of the effect of changes in selling prices on the model, the basic model assumes constant selling prices. This assumption could be relaxed if we could specify a curvilinear revenue function.[3] Unfortunately this is usually not possible.

There is only one product or a constant mix of products. This assumption is examined later in this chapter.

Inventories do not change. A synchronization between production and sales is assumed to exist with inventories kept constant or at zero. If this were not the case, the basic model would understate costs during periods in which inventories increase and overstate costs during periods in which inventories decline. Remember that production *costs* are not the same as the *expense* "cost of goods sold." The former is related to the expenditure of resources necessary for production, whereas the latter is related to the transformation of a cost into an expense. This assumption is given additional attention in Chapter 9.

Volume is the only factor affecting costs. This assumption can be relaxed when a model is being used for a number of periods by including dummy variables for seasonal factors, "sticky costs," etc. However, these costs are treated as a fixed element when the model is used for a single period.

Periods are short enough that the time value of money is not important. This assumption is relaxed in Chapters 16 and 17.

There is a relevant range for all underlying relationships. The concept of relevant range is very important in cost-volume-profit analysis. Very often the break-even point will be outside the relevant range. In that event, even though we can still compute a break-even point, we cannot make statistical inferences regarding the probability of breaking even. In some circumstances we may not be able to compute a break-even point. If regression analysis is used to estimate the total cost line and it has a negative vertical-axis intercept, the revenue line may not intercept the total cost line; hence, there is no accounting break-even point. As illustrated in Exhibit 8–6, this happens because the underlying economic relationships change beyond the range of observations used in computing the cost-estimating equation.

EXTENSIONS OF THE BASIC MODEL

The basic cost-volume-profit model is easily modified to incorporate a large number of important considerations such as cash flows, income taxes for a division of a profitable firm, and muiltiple products.

---

[3] Refer to Chapter 15, footnote 4.

EXHIBIT 8–6 Cost-Volume-Profit Analysis with Negative Vertical-Axis Intercept for Total Costs

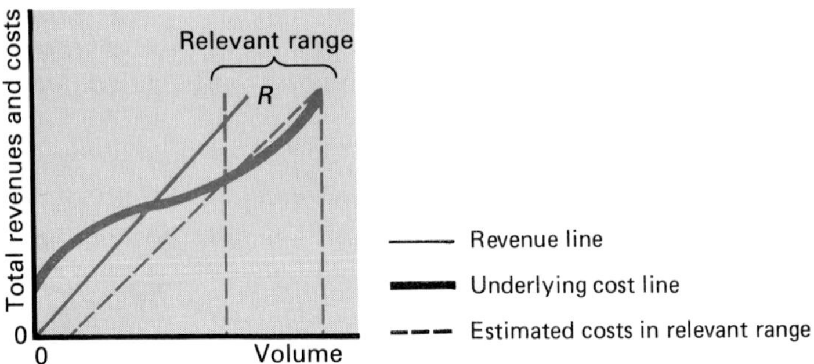

Cash Break-Even Point

If an organization has a minimum of available cash, or the opportunity cost of holding excess cash is high, management may want to know the **cash break-even point**, that is, the unit or dollar sales volume at which operating cash receipts equal operating cash disbursements. Due to the existence of noncash expenses such as depreciation and amortization, the cash break-even point is lower than the break-even point calculated for profits. Ignoring taxes, the cash break-even point may be calculated as follows:

$$X_{CBE} = \frac{a - n}{p - b} \tag{8–13}$$

where

X_{CBE} = cash break-even volume
n = noncash expenses included in fixed costs
a, b, and p are as previously defined.

In words,

$$\text{Cash break-even point} = \frac{\text{Fixed costs} - \text{Noncash fixed expenses}}{\text{Unit contribution margin}}$$

Example 8–12

Alpha Corporation produces and sells a product that has a selling price of \$60 per unit and variable costs of \$35 per unit. Total fixed costs are \$200,000, including \$50,000 for depreciation and amortization. With a \$25 unit contribution, Alpha's break-even point for profits is 8,000 units:

$$X_{BE} = \frac{\$200,000}{\$25} = \underline{\underline{8,000}} \text{ units,}$$

and Alpha's cash break-even point is 6,000 units:

$$X_{CBE} = \frac{\$200,000 - \$50,000}{\$25} = \underline{\underline{6,000}} \text{ units}$$

Alpha needs to sell 2,000 fewer units to break-even with cash flows than they do to break-even with profits.

Income Taxes and Cost Behavior

Income taxes do not affect the break-even point of the basic model, but they have an impact on profit planning and may have an impact on cost behavior. For a division of a profitable firm or a firm that can take advantage of operating-loss carrybacks or carryforwards, income taxes have an impact on the cost function.[4] Recall that the cost function used in the derivation of the basic model is

$$T = a + bX$$

If income taxes are taken into account, the effective cost function is:[5]

$$T = (1 - \text{Tax rate})a + [b + \text{Tax rate}\ (p - b)]X \quad (8\text{–}14)$$

Example 8–13

Assume Alpha is organized as a division of a profitable firm. Alpha's after-tax cost function is:

$$T = (1 - 0.40)\$200{,}000 + [\$35 + 0.40(\$60 - \$35)]X$$

$$T = \$120{,}000 + \$45X$$

At a volume of zero, Alpha's effective fixed costs are reduced to $120,000 because fixed costs of $200,000 reduce taxes by $80,000 (0.40 × $200,000) for net after-tax fixed costs of $120,000. The $45 of variable costs per unit is the sum of the before-tax variable costs ($35) plus the income taxes of $10 that must be paid on the increase in profits from the sale of each unit [0.40($60 − $35)]. This cost function can be used to calculate the break-even point for Alpha.

$$X_{\text{BE}} = \frac{\$120{,}000}{\$60 - \$45} = \underline{\underline{8{,}000}}\ \text{units}$$

The break-even volume is the same as calculated in Example 8–12. Because no taxes are paid at the break-even sales volume, the inclusion of income taxes did not affect the computation.

Cash Break-Even Point with Taxes

Although the traditional accounting break-even point for a division of a profitable firm or a firm with operating loss carrybacks is not affected by income taxes, taxes do have an impact on the cash break-even point. This occurs because a

---

[4] The income tax law allows businesses to offset a portion of one year's losses against another year's income. If a loss occurs in a particular tax year, the loss can offset income of the three preceding years. If the loss exceeds the income of the three preceding years or if the firm elects not to carry the loss back, it can be carried forward and offset against income for up to 15 subsequent years.

[5] With income taxes, this equation is derived as follows:

$$T = a + bX + \text{Income taxes}$$

If we let t equal the income tax rate, then

$$\begin{aligned}\text{Income taxes} &= t\ (\text{Net income before taxes})\\ &= t[(p - b)X - a]\end{aligned}$$

Substituting for income taxes gives

$$T = a + bX + t[(p - b)X - a]$$

$$T = a + bX + t(p - b)X - t(a)$$

$$T = (1 - t)a + [b + t(p - b)]X$$

firm that has had profitable operations in the past may carry the loss back and file for a refund of taxes paid in prior periods. This additional cash flow, when a loss occurs, will further reduce the cash break-even point. A similar situation occurs when a firm has other profitable operations against which to offset losses.[6]

The cash break-even point occurs when cash receipts equal cash disbursements. In the presence of a tax loss that generates a tax refund or offset, there are two sources of cash, sales receipts and tax refunds or offsets, and two uses of cash, variable and fixed costs. The tax refund or offset is equal to the tax rate times the amount of the loss. In equation form, the equality of cash receipts and disbursements is represented as follows:

$$\text{Cash receipts} = \text{Cash disbursements}$$

$$\text{Sales} + \text{Tax refund or offset} = \text{Cash outflow for variable and fixed costs}$$

$$pX + \text{Tax rate}\,[a - (p - b)X] = bX + a - \text{Noncash fixed expenses}$$

Solving for X gives:

$$X_{\text{Cash}} = \frac{(1 - \text{Tax rate})a - \text{Noncash expenses}}{(1 - \text{Tax rate})\,(p - b)} \tag{8–15}$$

where X_{Cash} = cash break-even point

Example 8–14

Using Eq. 8–15, Alpha's cash break-even point, with the ability to file for a tax refund, is 4,667 units, and its profit break-even point is 8,000 units, as shown in Example 8–12.

$$X_{\text{Cash}} = \frac{(1 - 0.40)(\$200{,}000) - \$50{,}000}{(1 - 0.40)(\$60 - \$35)} = \underline{\underline{4{,}667}} \text{ units}$$

The cash break-even point is verified as follows:

Sales (4,667 units × $60)		$280,020
Expenses:		
Variable (4,667 × $35)	$163,345	
Fixed	200,000	−363,345
Income (Loss) before taxes		$ (83,325)
Tax refund ($83,325 × 0.40)		33,330
Net income (loss) after taxes		$ (49,995)
Add: Noncash expense		50,000
Increase (Decrease) in cash		$ (5)*

* Answer reflects rounding.

Multiple Break-Even Points

One of the assumptions underlying cost-volume-profit analysis is that there is one product or a constant mix of products. If the mix of products can vary, an organization will have as many possible break-even points as it has possible sales

[6] For a further discussion see W. J. Morse, and I. A. Posey, "Income Taxes Do Make a Difference in C-V-P Analysis," *Management Accounting* **61,** No. 6 (December 1979):20–24.

mixes, unless the contribution margin is the same for all products. Profit-volume graphs can be used to illustrate the range of possible break-even sales volumes by graphing the break-even points for the products with the highest and lowest contribution margins.

Example 8–15

Karson Company produces three types of microwave ovens: Space-saver, Deluxe, and Standard. Information pertaining to the unit selling price, unit variable costs, and unit contribution margins of each model are as follows:

	Space-saver	*Deluxe*	*Standard*
Selling price	\$700	\$500	\$400
Variable costs	−400	−300	−250
Contribution margin	\$300	\$200	\$150

The manufacturing facilities can be used to produce any type of oven. Annual fixed costs of operating the plant are \$6,000,000.

The break-even sales volumes for the exclusive production of each model are:

Space-saver $\frac{\$6{,}000{,}000}{\$300} = \underline{\underline{20{,}000}}$ units

Deluxe $\frac{\$6{,}000{,}000}{\$200} = \underline{\underline{30{,}000}}$ units

Standard $\frac{\$6{,}000{,}000}{\$150} = \underline{\underline{40{,}000}}$ units

Exhibit 8–7 is a profit-volume graph showing the break-even unit sales volumes for the Space-saver and the Standard models. Depending on the sales mix, Karson Company can break even by selling between 20,000 and 40,000 microwave ovens. The break-even volume of a specific sales mix is computed as total fixed costs divided by an average unit contribution margin.

Average Unit Contribution Margin

The average unit contribution margin at a given mix is the sum of the individual product contribution margins multiplied by their proportion of the total sales. In equation form:

$$\text{Avg. CM} = p_1X_1 + p_2X_2 + \cdots + p_iX_i \tag{8–16}$$

where

Avg. CM = average unit contribution margin
p_i = proportion of sales mix of product X_i
X_i = unit contribution margin of product X_i

Example 8–16

Assume Karson Company sells the three models of microwave ovens in a 1:1:1 mix, that is, for each Space-saver oven sold, one Deluxe and one Standard model

EXHIBIT 8–7 Range of Break-even Unit Sales Volumes: Multiple Products

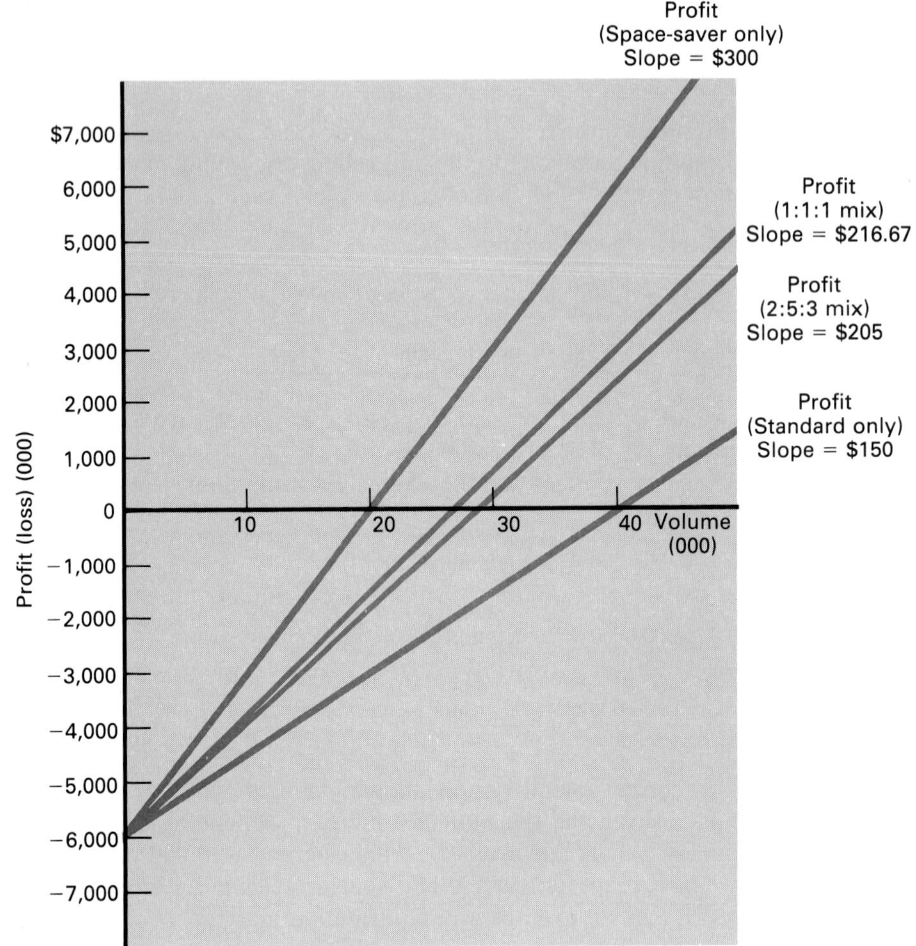

are also sold. Using Eq. 8–16, the average unit contribution margin is $216.67, determined as follows:

$$\text{Avg. CM} = \tfrac{1}{3}(\$300) + \tfrac{1}{3}(\$200) + \tfrac{1}{3}(\$150) = \underline{\underline{\$216.67}}$$

(*Note:* With a 1:1:1 mix, each product is $\frac{1}{3}$ of the total mix, that is, $p_1 = p_2 = p_3 = \frac{1}{3}$.)

The break-even sales volume at this mix is 27,692 units ($6,000,000/$216.67). Karson Company would need to sell 9,231 units (27,692 × $\frac{1}{3}$) of each model to break even.

Example 8–17

Karson's break-even sales volume will change if the sales mix changes to the following proportions:

	Percent of total sales
Space-saver	20%
Deluxe	50
Standard	30

The average contribution margin at this mix is $205 [0.20($300) + 0.50($200) + 0.30($150)], and Karson's break-even sales volume is now 29,268 units ($6,000,000/$205), consisting of 5,854 (29,268 × 0.20) Space-saver ovens, 14,634 (29,268 × 0.50) Deluxe ovens, and 8,780 (29,268 × 0.30) Standard ovens. These quantities can be verified as follows:

Total contribution margin:	
Space-savers (5,854 units × $300)	$1,756,200
Deluxe (14,634 units × $200)	2,926,800
Standard (8,780 units × $150)	1,317,000
Total	$6,000,000
Fixed costs	−6,000,000
Net income	$ 0

Product Mix Decisions

If an organization can produce two or more profitable products, management may have to decide which products they should produce. If the organization has excess capacity, they should produce as many of each product as they can sell. Many organizations, however, face capacity constraints which prevent them from producing as many units of each product as they desire. *When a single factor, such as labor hours or machine hours, limits production, management should maximize the contribution per unit of the constraining factor in determining which product to produce and sell.*

Example 8–18

With current facilities, Karson Company has a maximum capacity of 20,000 machine hours per month. It requires 10 machine hours to produce a Space-saver oven, 6 machine hours to produce a Deluxe oven, and 5 machine hours to produce a Standard oven. Given this machine hours constraint, the maximum number of ovens for each model that can be produced are:

Space-saver	20,000 hrs./10 hrs. per unit	= 2,000 units
Deluxe	20,000 hrs./6 hrs. per unit	= 3,333 units
Standard	20,000 hrs./5 hrs. per unit	= 4,000 units

The contribution margin per machine hour for each model is:

Space-saver	$300/10 hrs.	= $30.000
Deluxe	$200/6 hrs.	= $33.333
Standard	$150/5 hrs.	= $30.000

Although the Space-saver model has the highest unit selling price and the highest unit contribution margin, total contribution margin and profits are maximized if only the Deluxe model is produced and sold. This is illustrated as follows:

	Space-saver	*Deluxe*	*Standard*
Maximum production	2,000	3,333	4,000
Total contribution margin	$600,000	$666,600	$600,000
Fixed costs*	−500,000	−500,000	−500,000
Profit	$100,000	$166,600	$100,000

* Monthly fixed costs are equal to 1/12 of the annual fixed costs of $6,000,000

Producing the Deluxe model is most profitable because it provides the highest contribution per machine hour. Despite this analysis, management may decide to produce some of each model because of nonquantifiable long-run factors. However, they are making a short-run economic sacrifice to do so.

This type of analysis becomes unwieldy when there are several constraints. It may take considerable time to determine what the limiting factors are, and it will take even longer to determine the optimal production volume and mix. Linear programming is used in the appendix to Chapter 15 to solve these types of problems.

SUMMARY

The basic cost-volume-profit model is a fundamental, but exceedingly useful, technique for analyzing the impact of changes in revenues, costs, or volume on profits. The model is used extensively in budgeting and the concepts underlying it are used in making special decisions.

Despite the model's usefulness, cost-volume-profit analysis is limited by a number of underlying assumptions. The primary assumptions relate to the classification of costs as fixed or variable, the absence of step costs, the requirement of linear revenue and cost functions, the synchronization between production and sales, the absence of factors other than volume affecting cost, the length of time considered in the analysis, and the relevant range.

The model has been extended to include such factors as income taxes, cash flows, and multiple products. In recent years, considerable attention has been given to the importance of uncertainty in cost-volume-profit analysis. The appendix to this chapter introduces this topic.

APPENDIX The Analysis of Uncertainty in Short-Range Planning

Cost-volume-profit models are frequently used for short-range planning. In such models, profit is a function of the selling price; the variable costs of manufacturing, selling, and administration; the sales volume; and the fixed costs. The unit selling price minus the unit variable costs is identified as the unit contribution margin. In equation form, profit is expressed as follows:

$$\pi = (p - b)X - a$$

where

π = profit
p = selling price per unit
b = variable cost per unit
a = fixed costs
X = number of units produced and sold

If one or more of the variables that enter into the determination of profit is subject to uncertainty, management should analyze the potential impact of this uncertainty. This additional analysis is useful in evaluating alternative courses of action and in developing contingency plans. If a company must choose to produce one of two mutually exclusive products, expected profitability and risk[7] should be considered before a choice is made. If both products have the same expected profits, but one has a higher probability of sustaining a loss, risk-averse management will select the less risky project. An analysis of uncertainty will also help management develop contingency plans such as lines of credit and alternative sources of materials.

The accounting and finance literature is replete with discussions of alternative approaches to summarizing uncertainty. Frequently mentioned approaches include sensitivity analysis, statistical analysis, probability trees, and stochastic simulation. We will consider each of these approaches.

SENSITIVITY ANALYSIS

Sensitivity analysis is the study of the responsiveness of a model's dependent variable(s) to changes in one or more of the model's independent variables. In the accounting model of the firm, frequently studied dependent variables include income and cash flow. Although sensitivity analysis was not identified as such, extensive use was made of this technique in Chapter 8. Sensitivity analysis is a technique used to answer "what if" type questions. Using expected profits as the dependent variable, typical questions include:

What will happen to profits if . . .

- Selling price increases by $4 per unit?
- Direct labor increases by 10 percent?
- Sales volume increases by 20 percent and selling price decreases by $2 per unit?

By determining the answers to such questions, management becomes aware of the potential impact of uncertainty. This helps in determining whether to accept or reject a proposed project or to obtain additional information before making a decision. If a project is undertaken, sensitivity analysis assists management in determining those aspects of a project that should be closely monitored; namely, those that have the greatest potential impact on one or more important dependent variables such as profit or cash flow.

Although sensitivity analysis is a powerful management tool, it has limitations. These limitations center around the fact that sensitivity analysis is performed without giving any consideration to the probabilities of the various scenarios occurring. Additionally systematic procedures are not used to select scenarios. One way of overcoming the latter problem is to develop most likely, pessimistic, and optimistic estimates for each of the model's independent variables (for example, variable costs per unit, selling price per unit, sales

[7] In this text "risk" and "uncertainty" have similar meanings. Some writers use "risk" to identify a situation in which possible outcomes and their probabilities can be specified in advance. Those writers then use "uncertainty" to identify situations in which possible outcomes and/or their probabilities cannot be specified in advance.

volume, and fixed costs). Using all the pessimistic forecasts and then all the optimistic forecasts will give management information on the range of possible operating results. Even if this is done, we are still left without information on the likelihood of specific outcomes.

STATISTICAL ANALYSIS

In a classic paper, Professors Jaedicke and Robichek[8] demonstrated that when a *single, normally distributed* variable (such as sales volume) is subject to uncertainty and the degree of uncertainty can be specified in advance, standard statistical procedures may be used to summarize the effect of this uncertainty on a dependent variable such as profit.

Any uncertainty in sales volume affects the total contribution and profits. The expected contribution is the unit contribution margin multiplied by the expected volume. In equation form,

$$E(C) = (p - b)E(X) \tag{8–17}$$

where

$E(C)$ = expected contribution
$p - b$ = unit contribution margin
$E(X)$ = expected sales volume

The expected profit is the expected contribution minus the fixed costs. In equation form,

$$E(\pi) = E(C) - a = (p - b)E(X) - a \tag{8–18}$$

where

$E(\pi)$ = expected profits
a = fixed costs

Because of the uncertainty in the sales volume, the expected contribution and profits are also uncertain. The standard deviation of the expected contribution and profits is equal to the unit contribution margin multiplied by the standard deviation of the sales volume. In equation form,

$$S_{\pi} = (p - b)\, S_{v} \tag{8–19}$$

where

S_{π} = standard deviation of expected profits
S_{v} = standard deviation of sales volume

Example 8–19

The Manhattan Company has monthly fixed costs of $24,000 and variable costs of $300 per unit. The selling price per unit is known to be stable at $350, but the monthly sales volume is uncertain. During the past year, monthly sales have averaged 600 units with a standard deviation of 100 units. Management expects this pattern to continue in the future.

Determine the expected contribution, expected profits, and the standard deviation of the expected contribution and profits for Manhattan Company.

---

[8] R. K. Jaedicke, and A. Robichek, "Cost-Volume-Profit Analysis Under Conditions of Uncertainty," *Accounting Review* **39**, No. 4 (October 1964): 917–926.

The expected contribution is $30,000:

$$E(C) = (\$350 - \$300)600 \text{ units} = \underline{\underline{\$30,000}}$$

The expected profits are $6,000:

$$E(\pi) = \$30,000 - \$24,000 = \underline{\underline{\$6,000}}$$

The standard deviation of the expected contribution and profits is $5,000.

$$S_\pi = (\$350 - \$300)100 \text{ units} = \underline{\underline{\$5,000}}$$

Using information on the expected profits and the standard deviation of the expected profits, management can determine other amounts of interest such as the probability of at least breaking even in any single month, or the probability of obtaining a profit of $15,000 or more in any single month. The distribution of profits is illustrated in Exhibit 8–8.

Example 8–20 For the data in Example 8–19, determine the probability of at least breaking even and the probability of obtaining a profit of $15,000 or more in any month.

To find the probability of at least breaking even, we first determine the number of standard deviations zero profit is from the expected profit:

$$z = \frac{\$0 - \$6,000}{\$5,000} = \underline{\underline{-1.200}}$$

In Appendix Table A, the probability of obtaining a z value of -1.200 or less is 0.1151. Hence the probability of at least breaking even in any month is 0.8849 (1.000 − 0.1151).

To find the probability of obtaining a monthly profit of $15,000 or more, we first determine the number of standard deviations $15,000 is from the expected profit:

$$z = \frac{\$15,000 - \$6,000}{\$5,000} = \underline{\underline{1.800}}$$

In Appendix Table A, the probability of obtaining a z value of 1.8 or more is 0.0359. This is the probability of obtaining a monthly profit of $15,000 or more.

EXHIBIT 8–8 Probability Distribution of Profits

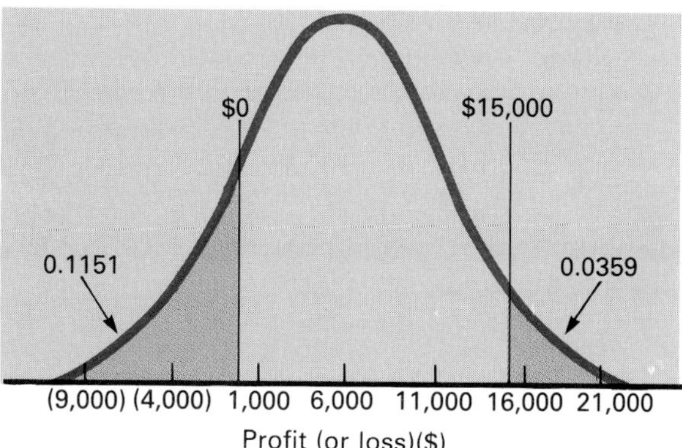

Although basic statistical analysis is useful when applied to a single, normally distributed variable, *it becomes complex and may give misleading results when a number of variables are subject to uncertainty.*[9]

PROBABILITY TREES

When a small number of items are subject to uncertainty and each of them has a limited number of possible states, probability trees may be used to enumerate all possible outcomes and the joint probabilities of each. A **probability tree** is a diagram showing the possible values of the independent and dependent variables and the probabilities of each possible outcome. After this enumeration is complete, expected values and probability information for important dependent variables (such as profit) are easily developed.

Example 8–21

The Shannon Company is evaluating the desirability of undertaking production of a novelty product that has a marketing life of one year. Although the fixed costs associated with the project are known to be $450,000, the sales volume and the unit contribution margin are uncertain. After talking with management, the following outcomes and subjective probabilities were developed:

Sales Volume		*Contribution margin*	
Units	*Probability*	*(Price – variable costs)*	*Probability*
150,000	0.3	$5.00	0.4
100,000	0.5	$4.50	0.6
60,000	0.2		

The probability tree for profits is presented in Exhibit 8–9. The probability of each final profit is the joint probability of each of the events leading to that profit. For example, the 0.12 probability of obtaining a profit of $300,000 is equal to the joint probability of sales of 150,000 units (0.30) and a unit contribution of $5.00 (0.40). It is computed this way because a profit of $300,000 will occur only if both of these events occur. Note that the joint probabilities sum to 1.00 or 100 percent, indicating that one of the final profit outcomes will occur if the project is undertaken.

Shannon's expected profit on this project is $52,900. Referring directly to Exhibit 8–9 we can see that the range of possible profit is $300,000 to $(180,000). Adding up the joint probabilities associated with profit and loss outcomes, there is a 50 percent probability the project will be profitable, a 30 percent probability it will exactly break even, and a 20 percent probability it will be unprofitable.

As the number of independent variables subject to uncertainty increases, the development of probability trees becomes more and more complex until a point is reached where further analysis is not feasible. In Example 8–21 there were six possible profit outcomes. The number of possible outcomes is the number of possible sales volumes multiplied by the number of possible contribution margins. Consider just the slightly more complicated situation where there are five sales volumes, two selling prices, three variable manufacturing costs, two variable selling and administrative costs, and three fixed manufacturing cost states. There would be 180 ($5 \times 2 \times 3 \times 2 \times 3$) possible outcomes! A computer program might be written to determine expected profit, but the development of a probability tree would be quite tedious.

---

[9] William L. Ferrara, Jack C. Hayya, and D. A. Nachman, "Normalcy of Profit in the Jaedicke-Robichek Model," *Accounting Review* **47**, No. 2 (April 1972): 299–307.

EXHIBIT 8–9 Probability Tree Analysis of Uncertainty

Sales volume (units) (probability)	Contribution margin (dollars per unit) (probability)	Total contribution margin	Fixed costs		Profit (loss)	Joint probability	Profit × joint probability
150,000 (0.30)	$5.00 (0.40)	$750,000	−450,000	=	$300,000	0.12	$36,000
	$4.50 (0.60)	$675,000	−450,000	=	$225,000	0.18	40,500
100,000 (0.50)	$5.00 (0.40)	$500,000	−450,000	=	$ 50,000	0.20	10,000
	$4.50 (0.60)	$450,000	−450,000	=	$ 0	0.30	0
60,000 (0.20)	$5.00 (0.40)	$300,000	−450,000	=	$(150,000)	0.08	(12,000)
	$4.50 (0.60)	$270,000	−450,000	=	$(180,000)	0.12	(21,600)
							$ 52,900

Expected profit $[E(\pi)] = \Sigma\, \pi P(\pi)$
where π = a particular profit,
$E(\pi)$ = expected profit, and
$P(\pi)$ = probability of a particular profit.

STOCHASTIC SIMULATION

A **model** is an abstract representation of a real-world phenomenon. When the model's independent variables are assigned specific values and the values of the model's dependent variables are computed, the model is said to simulate the corresponding real-world phenomenon. **Stochastic simulation** is the repeated random assignment of values to a model's independent variables and the subsequent computation of the values of the model's dependent variable(s). This provides a probability distribution for the dependent variables.

Stochastic simulation is used to summarize uncertainty information when the relationships between a model's independent and dependent variables become so complex that probability distributions for dependent variables cannot be determined by analytic methods. It is an approach to the analysis of uncertainty that we use as a last resort. Because the development and operation of stochastic simulation models are quite complex, most applications are computer based. Only a brief example of their potential use in short-range planning is presented here.

Example 8–22

In addition to unit sales volume and unit contribution margin, Shannon's monthly fixed costs are also subject to uncertainty. The possible fixed cost states and associated probabilities are as follows:

Monthly Fixed Costs	*Probability*
$400,000	0.2
450,000	0.5
480,000	0.3

There are now three independent variables (sales volume, unit contribution margin, and monthly fixed costs) with 3, 2, and 3 possible states. With only 18 (3 × 2 × 3) possible outcomes, this situation is still simple enough to analyze with a probability tree. Stochastic simulation is used for illustrative purposes.

Under stochastic simulation, hypothetical profit distributions are developed by repeated use of Shannon's profit model. On each trial, values are randomly selected for each independent variable and the resultant profit is computed. The selection of values is based on the relative probabilities of each. If a large number of trials were made, 20 percent of them should have monthly fixed costs of $400,000, 30 percent of them should have monthly sales of 150,000 units, and so on. The results of each trial are recorded. After a large number of trials are performed, the expected profit is computed.

Because a random process, such as the spinning of a roulette wheel, is used to determine the value of each independent variable on each trial, this technique is frequently identified as "Monte Carlo simulation." In practice, random numbers generated by a computer or obtained from published tables are used to determine the value of the independent variables. Regardless of their source, the use of random numbers requires the development of a link between the probability distribution and possible random numbers. For Example 8–22, one possible link is presented in Exhibit 8–10.

Note that the assignment of random numbers is based on the assumption that each random number has an equal probability of occurring. Hence the greater the probability of an event, the more random numbers are assigned to it.

Once the random numbers have been assigned to the possible states of each independent variable, the number of trials to be run and a series of random numbers must be determined. Although several hundred trials are normally run, for illustrative purposes we will only perform 10 trials. Because each trial requires one random number for each variable, performing 10 trials with three independent variables requires 30 random numbers. Assume the following random numbers were selected from a random number table:

4, 3, 9, 4, 9, 5, 1, 2, 7, 8, 6, 4, 5, 6, 8
4, 3, 8, 9, 5, 6, 1, 0, 6, 0, 1, 7, 2, 9, 1

EXHIBIT 8–10 Assignment of Random Numbers

Unit sales	*Probability*	*Random numbers*	*Unit contribution margin*	*Probability*	*Random numbers*	*Monthly fixed cost*	*Probability*	*Random numbers*
150,000	0.30	1–3	$5.00	0.40	1–4	$400,000	0.20	1–2
100,000	0.50	4–8	4.50	0.60	5–0	450,000	0.50	3–7
60,000	0.20	9–0				480,000	0.30	8–0

EXHIBIT 8–11 Stochastic Simulation of Shannon's Profit Model

Trial	*RN**	*Unit sales*	*RN*	*Unit contribution*	*Total contribution margin*	*RN*	*Fixed costs*	*Profit*
1	4	100,000	3	$5.00	$500,000	9	$480,000	$ 20,000
2	4	100,000	9	4.50	450,000	5	450,000	0
3	1	150,000	2	5.00	750,000	7	450,000	300,000
4	8	100,000	6	4.50	450,000	4	450,000	0
5	5	100,000	6	4.50	450,000	8	480,000	(30,000)
6	4	100,000	3	5.00	500,000	8	480,000	20,000
7	9	60,000	5	4.50	270,000	6	450,000	(180,000)
8	1	150,000	0	4.50	675,000	6	450,000	225,000
9	0	60,000	1	5.00	300,000	7	450,000	(150,000)
10	2	150,000	9	4.50	675,000	1	400,000	275,000

$$E(\pi) = \frac{\Sigma\pi}{n} = \$48{,}000$$

*RN = random number

The results of these trials are presented in Exhibit 8–11. The probability of each outcome is equal to $1/n$, where n is the number of trials. Based on the 10 trials shown in Exhibit 8–10, Shannon's expected monthly profit is $48,000. Adding up the number of profit and loss outcomes and dividing by the number of trials gives a 70 percent probability that the project will break even or be profitable and a 30 percent probability it will be unprofitable.

The analysis of uncertainty in short-range planning is an extremely complex topic to which this appendix serves as a brief introduction. In recent years a number of articles have dealt with the use of stochastic simulation in short- and long-range planning. These articles have dealt with cost-volume-profit analysis, cash management, inventory order levels, and investments in new plant and equipment. The interested reader is referred to the suggested readings for Chapter 8, 10, 17, and 18.

UTILITY

Although sensitivity analysis, statistical analysis, probability trees, and stochastic simulation can help provide a decision maker with information regarding the impact of uncertainty on dependent variables, these techniques do not make the decision to accept or reject a project. This is a management decision and it must be made in the light of management's attitudes regarding risk. Consider the project analyzed with the use of a probability tree in Example 8–21. Even though the project has an expected profit of $52,900, many business people might hesitate to accept the project because of the risk of sustaining a loss. There is a 20 percent probability that the project will not break even and losses may be as high as $180,000. If a loss of this size might cause the firm to go bankrupt, management may reject the project.

Utility theory is a systematic attempt to explain a manager's decision preferences under conditions involving risk. In an early paper, Swalm described utility theory as follows:

> . . . each individual has a measurable preference among various choices available in risk situations. This preference is called his utility. Utility is measured in arbitrary units which we will call "utiles." By suitable questioning we can determine for each individual a relationship between utility and dollars which is called his utility function. This plot offers a picture of his attitude toward taking risks.

EXHIBIT 8–12 Utility Function of a Risk-Averse Decision Maker

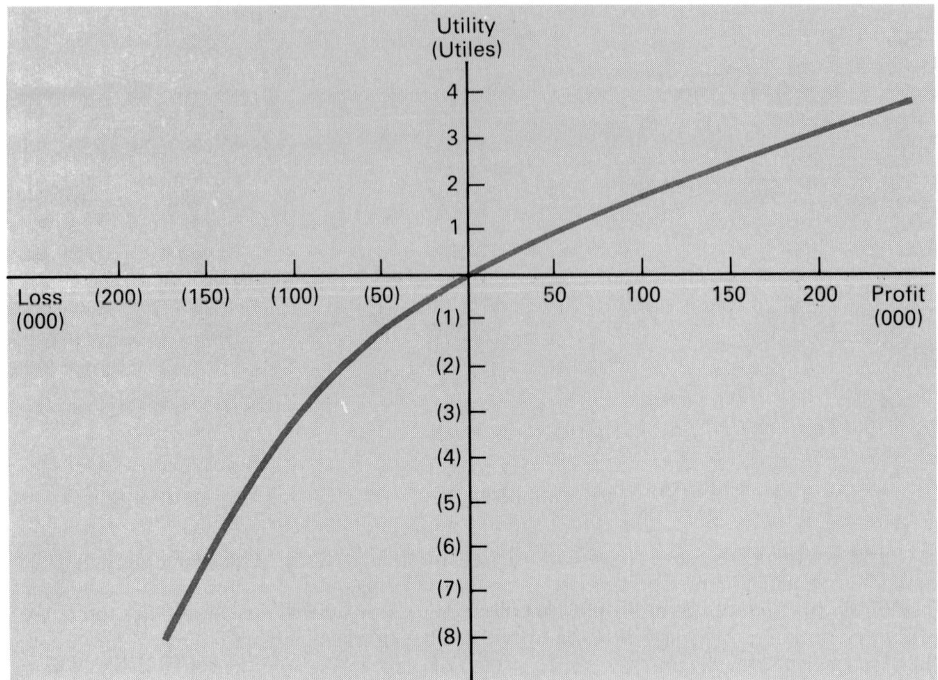

In any decisions involving a risk, a man will choose that alternative which maximizes his utility function. Once we know this utility function, the odds he assigns to events in a decision-making situation, and the consequences of each possible outcome, we should be able to predict his choice in that situation, since he will attempt to maximize his utility.[10]

A typical utility function for a risk-averse decision maker is presented in Exhibit 8–12. The utility function has a decreasing positive slope.[11] Out typical decision maker is favorably disposed toward profits; however, he or she receives decreasing amounts of incremental utility from them as profits increase. On the other hand, our typical decision maker is quite averse to losses and his or her aversion increases dramatically as the amount of the loss increases. He or she would not be indifferent to a 50-50 chance of winning or losing $100,000. Although a $100,000 gain has a positive utility of 1.76, a $100,000 loss has a negative utility of −3. The expected utiliy is negative:

$$E(U) = 0.5(1.76) + 0.5(-3) = \underline{\underline{-0.62}}$$

---

[10] R. O. Swalm, "Utility Theory—Insights into Risk Taking," *The Harvard Business Review* **44**, No. 6 (November-December 1966): 124.

[11] For the purpose of developing the utility function illustrated in Exhibit 8–12 the following equation was used:

$$\text{Utility} = 10 \log \left(\frac{\pi + \$200{,}000}{\$200{,}000} \right)$$

Although this utility function was selected arbitrarily, it is representative of typical utility functions.

EXHIBIT 8–13 Computation of Expected Utility of Proposed Project

*Profit (loss)**	*Utility†*	*Probability**	*Utility × Probability*
$300,000	3.979	0.12	0.477
225,000	3.273	0.18	0.589
50,000	0.969	0.20	0.194
0	0	0.30	0.000
(150,000)	−6.021	0.08	−0.482
(180,000)	−10.000	0.12	−1.200
		Expected utility	−0.422

*From Exhibit 8–9
† Read from Exhibit 8–12 or computed using the formula in footnote 11.

Returning to Example 8–21, if we know the decision maker's utility function, the desirability of the proposed project can be evaluated by (1) determining the utility of each possible outcome and (2) computing the expected utility of the proposal. Assuming the owner-manager's utility function is as shown in Exhibit 8–12, the expected utility of the proposal is determined in Exhibit 8–13.

As one might expect, the project has a negative expected utility. In this case, the decision maker's aversion to losses overcame his or her favorable attitudes toward larger, and more probable, gains. The project would be rejected despite its positive expected value.

The determination of the expected utility of a project depends on management's overall attitudes toward risk as reflected in their utility function, the amount of the expected profits of other projects, and the risk associated with these other projects. Many corporate finance books extend the analysis of risk to consider a portfolio of projects. A discussion of these topics is beyond the scope of this book.

KEY TERMS

Break-even point
Cash break-even point
Contribution margin percent
Contribution margin ratio
Cost structure
Cost-volume-profit analysis
Cost-volume-profit graph
Margin of safety
Profit-volume graph
Unit contribution margin

APPENDIX KEY TERMS

Model
Probability tree
Sensitivity analysis
Stochastic simulation
Utility theory

SELECTED REFERENCES

Adar, Z., A. Barnea, and B. Lev, "A Comprehensive Cost-Volume-Profit Analysis Under Uncertainty," *Accounting Review* **52,** No. 1 (January 1977): 137–149.

Buzby, Stephen L., "Extending the Applicability of Probabilistic Management Planning and Control Models," *Accounting Review* **49,** No. 1 (January 1974): 42–49.

Cantrell, R. Stephen, and Louis P. Ramsay, "Some Statistical Issues in the Estimation of a Simple Cost-Volume-Profit Model," *Decision Sciences* **15,** No. 4 (Fall 1984): 507–521.

Dillon, Ray D., and J. F. Nash, "The True Relevance of Relevant Costs," *Accounting Review* **53,** No. 1 (January 1978): 11–17.

Ferrara, William L., and Jack C. Hayya, "Towards Probabilistic Profit Budgets," *Management Accounting* **52,** No. 4 (October 1970): 23–28.

Ferrara, William L., Jack C. Hayya, and D. A. Nachman, "Normalcy of Profit in the Jaedicke-Robichek Model," *Accounting Review* **47,** No. 2 (April 1972): 299–307.

Helmkamp, John G., "Simulating a Stochastic Proforma Income Statement," *Managerial Planning* **21,** No. 4 (January-February 1973): 35–40.

Ismail, Badr E., and Joseph G. Lauderback, "Optimizing and Satisficing in Stochastic Cost-Volume-Profit Analysis," *Decision Sciences* **10,** No. 2 (April 1979): 205–217.

Jaedicke, R. K., and A. Robichek, "Cost-Volume-Profit Analysis Under Conditions of Uncertainty," *Accounting Review* **39,** No. 4 (October 1964): 917–926.

Johnson, Glenn L., and S. Stephen Simik, II, "Multiproduct C-V-P Analysis Under Uncertainty," *Journal of Accounting Research* **9,** No. 2 (Autumn 1971): 278–286.

Karnani, Aneel, "Stochastic Cost-Volume-Profit Analysis in a Competitive Oligopoly," *Decision Sciences* **14,** No. 2 (April 1983): 187–193.

Liao, Mawsen, "Model Sampling: A Stochastic Cost-Volume-Profit Analysis," *Accounting Review* **50,** No. 4 (October 1975): 780–790.

Liao, Woody M., "The Effects of Learning on Cost-Volume-Profit Analysis," *Cost and Management* **57,** No. 6 (November-December 1983): 38–40.

Morse, Wayne J., and Imogene A. Posey, "Taxes Do Make a Difference in Cost-Volume-Profit Analysis," *Management Accounting* **61,** No. 6 (December 1979): 20–24.

Shih, Wei, "A General Decision Model for Cost-Volume-Profit Analysis Under Uncertainty," *Accounting Review* **54,** No. 4 (October 1979): 687–706.

Swalm, R. O., "Utility Theory—Insights into Risk Taking," *The Harvard Business Review* **44,** No. 6 (November-December 1966): 123–138.

REVIEW QUESTIONS

8–1 What is the unit contribution margin? How is it computed?

8–2 What is the contribution margin percentage? How is it computed?

8–3 What is the break-even unit sales volume? How is it computed?

8–4 What is the margin of safety?

8–5 Mention several assumptions that underlie basic cost-volume-profit analysis.

8–6 What is the impact of income taxes on the break-even point? What is their impact on the sales volume required to obtain a desired profit?

8–7 What is the effect of income taxes on the slope and vertical-axis intercept of a firm's total cost line?

8–8 What factor(s) cause the cash break-even point to be lower than the profit break-even point?

8–9 Mention three ways in which profit-volume graphs differ from cost-volume-profit graphs.

8–10 With linear cost and revenue functions, how can an organization have multiple break-even points?

8–11 How does the cost structure of a firm affect its profits?

8–12 With multiple break-even points, which product will have the lowest unit break-even sales volume? Which product will have the highest unit break-even sales volume?

8–13 When might a multiproduct firm decide not to maximize production of the product with the greatest unit contribution margin?

REVIEW PROBLEM

Basic Cost-Volume-Profit

The Premier Watch Company manufactures high-quality quartz watches. Anticipated 19y1 sales are 30,000 watches at $60 each. Information on manufacturing and selling and administrative expenses is as follows:

Manufacturing costs:		
Direct material	$20	per watch
Direct labor	$15	per watch
Variable overhead	$10	per watch
Fixed overhead	$100,000	per year including noncash expenses of $30,000
Selling and administrative expenses:		
Variable	$5	per watch
Fixed	$100,000	per year including noncash expenses of $20,000

REQUIREMENTS

a) In the absence of income taxes determine:
   1. The unit contribution margin
   2. The contribution margin percentage
   3. The annual break-even sales volume in units and dollars
   4. The margin of safety in units
   5. The cash break-even point in units

b) Assuming an income tax rate of 40 percent, determine:
   1. The annual break-even unit sales volume
   2. Estimated 19y1 after-tax profit
   3. The cash break-even point in units (Assume Premier can file for a refund of prior taxes.)

The solution to this problem is found at the end of the Chapter 8 problems and exercises.

EXERCISES

8–1 Unit Contribution Margin

The estimated monthly sales of a product priced at $10 is 10,000 units. Variable costs include manufacturing costs of $6 and distribution costs of $2. Fixed costs are $16,000 per month.

REQUIREMENTS

Determine each of the following:

a) Unit contribution margin
b) Total contribution margin
c) Contribution margin percentage
d) Monthly break-even unit sales volume
e) Monthly break-even dollar sales volume
f) Monthly profit (Ignore taxes.)
g) Monthly margin of safety in units
h) Monthly margin of safety in dollars

8–2 Unit Contribution Margin

The estimated annual sales of a product priced at $30 is 60,000 units. Variable costs include manufacturing costs of $21 and selling and administrative costs of $3. Fixed costs are $240,000 per year.

REQUIREMENTS

Determine each of the following:

a) Unit contribution margin
b) Total contribution margin
c) Contribution margin percentage
d) Annual break-even unit sales volume
e) Annual break-even dollar sales volume
f) Annual profit (Ignore taxes.)
g) Annual margin of safety in units
h) Annual margin of safety in dollars

8–3 Contribution Margin Percentage

At a monthly sales volume of $30,000 the Rider Shop incurs variable costs of $21,000 and fixed costs of $6,000.

REQUIREMENTS

a) Determine each of the following:
   1. Contribution margin percentage
   2. Monthly break-even dollar sales volume
   3. Monthly margin of safety in dollars
b) Assume the unit contribution margin is $6. Determine each of the following:
   1. Unit sales price
   2. Monthly break-even unit sales volume
   3. Monthly margin of safety in units

8–4 Contribution Margin Percentage

At an annual sales volume of $500,000, Tucker Company incurs variable costs of $200,000 and fixed costs of $240,000.

REQUIREMENTS

a) Determine each of the following:
   1. Contribution margin percentage
   2. Annual break-even dollar sales volume
   3. Annual margin of safety in dollars

b) Assume the unit selling price is $20. Determine each of the following:
   1. Unit contribution margin
   2. Annual break-even unit sales volume
   3. Annual margin of safety in units

8–5 Cost-Volume-Profit Graph

Presented is a typical cost-volume-profit graph:

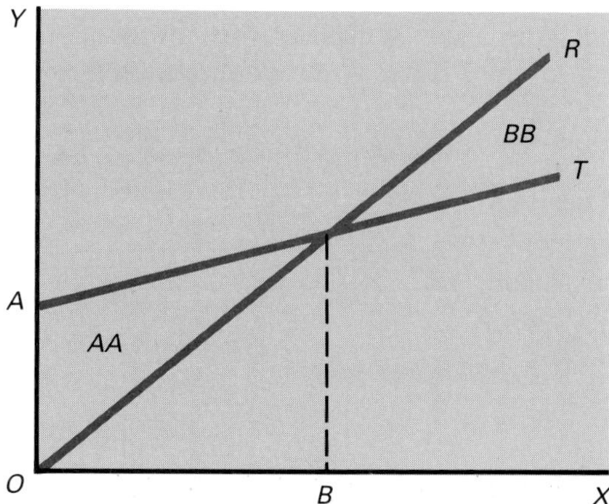

REQUIREMENTS

a) Identify each of the following:
   1. Line *OX*
   2. Line *OY*
   3. Line *OR*
   4. Line *AT*
   5. Point *A*
   6. Point *B*
   7. Difference between lines *AT* and *OR* in area *AA*
   8. Difference between lines *AT* and *OR* in area *BB*

9. The slope of line *OR*
10. The slope of line *AT*

b) Indicate the effect of each of the following independent events on line *AT*, line *OR*, and the break-even sales volume:

1. An increase in the unit selling price
2. A decrease in fixed costs
3. A decrease in fixed costs and unit variable costs
4. A decrease in fixed costs and an increase in the unit selling price
5. An increase in unit variable costs and an increase in the unit selling price

c) Which of the following would cause the greatest increase in the unit contribution margin?

1. A 10 percent decrease in fixed costs
2. A 10 percent increase in selling price
3. A 10 percent decrease in variable costs

8–6 Profit-Volume-Graph

The following profit-volume graph pertains to the Ace Company, which sells two products, A and B, in a constant sales mix. Product A has a unit contribution margin of $2 and Product B has a unit contribution margin of $1.

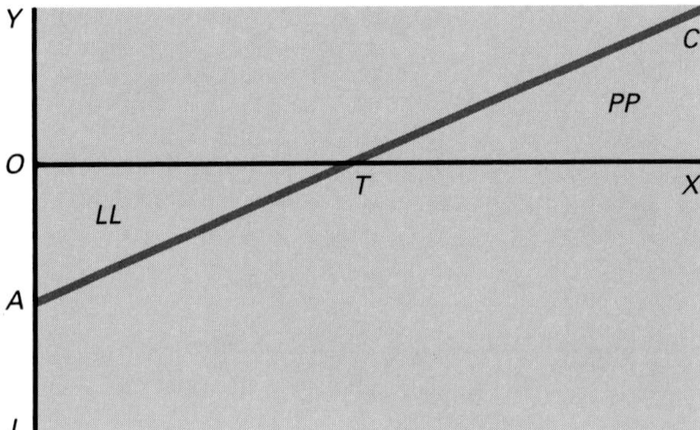

REQUIREMENTS

a) Identify each of the following elements of the profit-volume graph:

1. Line *OX*
2. Line *LY*
3. Point *T*
4. Point *A*
5. Line *AC*
6. Area *LL*

7. Area *PP*
8. Slope of line *AC*

b) Indicate the effect of each of the following on line *AC*:

1. An increase in the selling price of Product A
2. A decrease in the variable costs of Product B
3. An increase in fixed costs
4. A shift in the product mix toward more of Product B and less of Product A
5. An increase in the variable costs of Product B and a decrease in the selling price of Product A
6. An increase in the variable costs of Product B and an increase in the selling price of Product A

8–7 Cost-Volume-Profit Graphs

The North Company had the following revenue and cost functions for 19y3:

$$\text{Total revenues} = \$30X$$
$$\text{Total costs} = \$150{,}000 + \$20X$$

REQUIREMENTS

a) Prepare a cost-volume-profit graph for North Company. Label the vertical axis in $50,000 increments and the horizontal axis in 5,000 unit increments.

b) Prepare a profit-volume graph for North Company.

c) What is the break-even point in units and dollars? Prove your answer by calculating profits at the break-even level.

8–8 Profit Planning

Flame Corporation sells a product with a unit selling price of $200 and unit variable costs of $150. Annual fixed costs are $300,000 and the corporation is subject to an income tax rate of 30 percent.

REQUIREMENTS

Determine each of the following:

a) Break-even unit sales volume
b) Unit sales volume needed to provide after-tax profits of $140,000
c) Dollar sales volume needed to provide after-tax profits of $105,000
d) After-tax profits if sales are 8,000 units

8–9 Profit Planning

Sarah Company sells a product with a unit selling price of $80 and unit variable costs of $60. Annual fixed costs are $400,000 and the company is subject to an income tax rate of 40 percent.

REQUIREMENTS

Determine each of the following:

a) Break-even dollar sales volume

b) Volume of sales in units needed to provide after-tax profits of $90,000

c) Volume of sales in dollars needed to provide after-tax profits of $45,000

d) After-tax profits if sales are 30,000 units

8–10 T Multiple Products

The Fireside Book Shop sells Adventure Series, Mystery Series, and Classics Series books. Unit selling prices and variable costs per series are as follows:

	Adventure Series	*Mystery Series*	*Classics Series*
Selling price	$50	$35	$100
Variable cost	30	25	50

Fireside incurs fixed costs of $90,000 per year and is subject to an income tax rate of 0.40. The company would like to earn after-tax profits of $27,000 per year. The current unit sales mix is as follows:

	Percentage of total
Adventure Series	40
Mystery Series	50
Classics Series	10

REQUIREMENTS

a) Determine each of the following for the current sales mix.

1. The range of break-even points in units
2. The average unit contribution margin
3. The break-even unit sales volume
4. The unit sales volume needed to attain the desired after-tax profits

b) Assume Fireside can change the unit sales mix to 10 percent Adventure Series, 50 percent Mystery Series, and 40 percent Classics Series. Determine each of the following:

1. The average unit contribution margin
2. The break-even unit sales volume
3. The unit sales volume needed to attain the desired after-tax profits

8–11 T Multiple Products

The Bavarian Ice Cream Shop sells cones, sundaes, and floats. During the past year, fixed costs totaled $27.500 and unit selling price and variable costs were as follows:

	Selling price	*Variable costs*
Cones	$1.50	$0.50
Sundaes	4.00	2.00
Floats	2.50	1.00

Current unit sales mix and proposed sales mix for next year are as follows:

	Current mix	*Proposed mix*
Cones	0.50	0.10
Sundaes	0.25	0.40
Floats	0.25	0.50

Bavarian is subject to an income tax rate of 40 percent and would like to have after-tax profits of $8,250 per year.

REQUIREMENTS

a) Determine each of the following for the current sales mix:
   1. The range of break-even points in units
   2. The average unit contribution margin
   3. The break-even unit sales volume
   4. The unit sales volume needed to attain the desired after-tax profits

b) Determine each of the following for the proposed sales mix:
   1. The average unit contribution margin
   2. The break-even unit sales volume
   3. The unit sales volume needed to attain the desired after-tax profits

8–12 Contribution Margin With Constraining Resource

Sunrise Corporation produces products A, B, and C with the following unit selling prices and variable costs.

	Product A	*Product B*	*Product C*
Selling price	$15	$20	$30
Variable costs	10	12	18

All products use the same manufacturing facilities. The maximum machine hours available for production are 20,000 hours per month. Each unit of Product A requires 1 machine hour, each unit of Product B requires 1.5 machine hours, and each unit of Product C requires 2 machine hours.

REQUIREMENTS

a) Determine the unit contribution margin for each product.

b) Determine the contribution margin per machine hour for each product.

c) If demand for each product exceeds the maximum possible production, which product(s) should Sunrise Company produce?

8–13 Cost-Volume-Profit Concepts and Limitations

Bard Company has determined the number of units of Product Y that it would have to sell in order to break even. However, Bard would like to attain a 20 percent profit on sales of Product Y.

REQUIREMENTS

a) Explain how break-even analysis can be used to determine the number of units of Product Y that Bard would have to sell to attain a 20 percent profit on sales.

b) If variable cost per unit increases as a percentage of the sales price, how would that affect the number of units of Product Y that Bard would have to sell in order to break even and why?

c) Identify the limitations of break-even analysis in managerial decision-making.

(CPA Adapted)

PROBLEMS

8–14 Basic Cost-Volume-Profit

The Lake Ski Company manufactures water skis. Anticipated sales for 19y4 are 50,000 pair at $40 each. Information on manufacturing costs and selling and administrative expenses is as follows:

Manufacturing costs:	
Direct material	$14 per pair
Direct labor	$10 per pair
Variable overhead	$4 per pair
Fixed overhead	$150,000 per year including noncash expenses of $20,000
Selling and administrative expenses:	
Variable	$6 per pair
Fixed	$90,000 per year including noncash expenses of $10,000

REQUIREMENTS

a) In the absence of income taxes determine:

1. The unit contribution margin
2. The contribution margin percentage
3. The annual break-even unit sales volume
4. Estimated 19y4 profit
5. The margin of safety in units and dollars
6. The cash break-even point in units

b) Assuming an income tax rate of 40 percent determine:

1. The annual break-even unit sales volume
2. Estimated 19y4 after-tax profit
3. The cash break-even point in units (Assume Lake can file for a refund of prior taxes.)

8–15 Cost-Volume-Profit and Profit Planning with Taxes

The following income statement for Davann Company represents the operating results for the fiscal year just ended. Davann had sales of 1,800 tons of product during the year. The manufacturing capacity of Davann's facilities is 3,000 tons of product.

Davann Co.
Statement of Income
For the Year Ended December 31, 19x4

Sales	$900,000
Variable costs:	
Manufacturing	$315,000
Selling costs	180,000
Total variable costs	−495,000
Contribution margin	$405,000
Fixed costs:	
Manufacturing	$ 90,000
Selling	112,500
Administration	45,000
Total fixed costs	−247,500
Net income before income taxes	$157,500
Income taxes (40%)	−63,000
Net income after income taxes	$ 94,500

REQUIREMENTS

a) Determine the break-even volume in tons of product for 19x4.

b) Determine the after-tax net income that Davann can expect for 19x5 if the sales volume is 2,100 tons and prices and costs remain as in 19x4.

c) Davann has a potential foreign customer who has offered to buy 1,500 tons at $450 per ton. Assume that all of Davann's costs would remain as in 19x4. What net income after taxes would Davann make if it took this order and rejected some business from regular customers so as not to exceed capacity.

d) Davann plans to market its product in a new territory. Davann estimates that an advertising and promotion program costing $61,500 annually would need to be undertaken for the next two or three years. In addition, a $25 per ton sales commission over and above the current commission to the sales force in the new territory would be required. How many tons would have to be sold in the new territory to maintain Davann's current after-tax income of $94,500?

e) Davann is considering replacing a highly labor-intensive process with a machine. This would result in an increase of $58,500 annually in fixed manufacturing costs. The variable manufacturing costs would decrease $25 per ton. Determine the new break-even volume in tons.

f) Ignore the facts presented in part (e) and now assume that Davann estimates that the per-ton selling price would decline 10 percent next year. Variable costs would increase $40 per ton and the fixed costs would not change. What dollar sales volume would be required to earn an after-tax net income of $94,500 next year?

(CMA Adapted)

8–16 Cost-Volume-Profit with Taxes

Lang Company produces a single product. Last year the company produced and sold 30,000 units with the following results:

Lang Company
Statement of Income
For the Year Ended December 31, 19x5

Sales		$750,000
Variable costs	$450,000	
Fixed costs	180,000	−630,000
Net income before taxes		$120,000
Income taxes (45%)		−54,000
Net income		$ 66,000

In an attempt to improve its product, Lang is considering replacing a component part that cost $3.00 a unit with a new and better part costing $5.00 per unit. A new machine would also be needed to increase plant capacity. The machine would cost $20,000 with a useful life of five years and no salvage value. The company uses straight-line depreciation on all plant assets.

REQUIREMENTS

a) What was Lang Company's unit break-even point in 19x5?

b) How many units of product would Lang Company have had to sell in 19x5 to earn $110,000 after taxes?

c) If Lang Company holds the sales price constant and makes the suggested changes, how many units of product must be sold in 19x6 to break even?

d) If Lang Company holds the sales price constant and makes the suggested changes, how many units of product will the company have to sell in 19x6 to make the same after-tax income as in 19x5?

e) If Lang Company wishes to maintain the same after-tax contribution margin percentage, what selling price per unit of product must it charge in 19x6 to cover the increased material cost? (CMA Adapted)

8–17 Account Classification and Cost-Volume-Profit Analysis

In 19y5, Interstate Company had the following experience:

Interstate Company
Statement of Income
For the Year Ended December 31, 19y5

Sales (20,000 units at $300)			$6,000,000
Costs:	*Fixed*	*Variable*	
Direct material		$1,200,000	
Direct labor		1,600,000	
Manufacturing overhead	$1,200,000	800,000	
Selling and administrative	400,000	400,000	
Total costs	$1,600,000	$4,000,000	−5,600,000
Net income before taxes			$ 400,000
Income taxes @ 0.40			−160,000
Net income after taxes			$ 240,000

REQUIREMENTS

a) Use the account classification method to develop a before-tax cost-estimating equation for Interstate Company.

b) Calculate the break-even point in units.

c) What was Interstate's margin of safety, in sales dollars, for 19y5?

d) What is the break-even point in units if management makes a decision that increases fixed costs by $200,000 and unit sales price and variable cost remain the same?

e) What unit sales volume is required to provide an after-tax net income of $360,000 assuming there is no change in the current cost structure?

f) Management is contemplating the addition of a second product. This product appears to be desirable. However, the addition of the second product will require Interstate to produce 2,000 fewer units of its current product than would otherwise be the case. Determine the after-tax opportunity cost of the proposed action.

8–18 High-Low Cost Estimation and Cost-Volume-Profit Analysis

The following is selected information taken from the records of Clarkson Company:

	April	*May*	*June*	*July*
Production-units	1,000	800	500	1,250
Sales-units	750	500	1,000	800
Sales revenue	$60,000	$40,000	$80,000	$64,000
Cost of goods sold:				
Beginning inventory	$ 0	$15,000	$34,375	$ 3,500
Cost of goods manufactured	60,000	50,000	35,000	72,500
Available for sale	$60,000	$65,000	$69,375	$76,000
Ending inventory	−15,000	−34,375	−3,500	−29,000
Cost of goods sold	−45,000	−30,625	−65,875	−47,000
Gross profit	$15,000	$ 9,375	$14,125	$17,000
Selling and administrative expenses	−12,500	−10,000	−15,000	−13,000
Net income (loss)	$ 2,500	$ (625)	$ (875)	$ 4,000

ADDITIONAL INFORMATION

- There are no changes in prices or technology.
- The beginning and ending work-in-process inventories are zero for all months.
- Clarkson values its finished goods inventory using an actual FIFO cost flow assumption.

REQUIREMENTS

a) If all beginning and ending inventories are constant at zero, with current production equaling current sales, determine Clarkson's monthly break-even sales volume in units.

b) Explain why Clarkson's largest loss occurred in June, the month of the highest sales volume.

8–19 Cost Structure

Candice Company has decided to introduce a new product. The new product can be manufactured by either a capital-intensive method or a labor-intensive method. The manufacturing method will not affect the quality of the product. The estimated unit manufacturing costs of the two methods are as follows:

	Capital intensive		*Labor intensive*	
Raw materials		$5.00		$5.60
Direct labor	0.5DLH @ $12 =	6.00	0.8DLH @ $9 =	7.20
Variable overhead	0.5DLH @ $ 6 =	3.00	0.8DLH @ $6 =	4.80
Directly traceable incremental fixed manufacturing costs		$2,440,000		$1,320,000

Candice's market research department has recommended an introductory unit sales price of $30. The incremental selling expenses are estimated to be $500,000 annually plus $2 for each unit sold regardless of manufacturing method.

REQUIREMENTS

a) Calculate the estimated break-even point in annual unit sales of the new product if Candice Company uses the following methods:
   1. Capital intensive manufacturing method.
   2. Labor intensive manufacturing method.

b) Determine the annual unit sales volume at which Candice Company would be indifferent between the two manufacturing methods.

c) Candice's management must decide which manufacturing method to employ. One factor it must consider is cost structure.
   1. Explain cost structure and the relationship between cost structure and business risk.
   2. Explain the circumstances under which Candice should employ each of the two manufacturing methods.

d) Identify the business factors other than cost structure that Candice must consider before selecting the capital-intensive or labor-intensive manufacturing method.

(CMA Adapted)

8–20 Cost Estimation and Profit Planning with Changes in Costs

Quinn Company had the following costs during 19y6 when 50,000 units of Product Z were produced and sold.

	Fixed	*Variable*
Direct materials		$200,000
Direct labor		250,000
Factory overhead	$400,000	300,000
Selling and administrative	300,000	140,000
Total	$700,000	$890,000

ADDITIONAL INFORMATION

- Quinn's break-even volume for 19y6 was 35,000 units of Product Z.
- On January 1, 19y7, direct-labor costs increased by 10 percent.
- On January 1, 19y7, direct materials costs increased by 15 percent.
- All other costs are expected to be the same in 19y7 as 19y6.

REQUIREMENTS

a) Determine the selling price per unit for Product Z in 19y6.

b) Determine the before-tax profits for 19y6.

c) Using the account classification method, develop a cost-estimating equation for total costs for 19y7.

d) If the selling price remains the same in 19y7 as 19y6, determine the 19y7 break-even point in units.

e) If Quinn wishes to maintain the same contribution margin percentage in 19y7 as 19y6, what selling price should they charge?

f) If Quinn produces and sells 55,000 units in 19y7 at a sales price of $40 per unit, what is the expected before-tax profit?

8–21 Cost-Volume-Profit Analysis for Hospitals

Melford Hospital operates a general hospital, but rents space and beds to separately owned entities rendering specialized services such as pediatrics and psychiatric. Melford charges each separate entity for common services such as patients' meals and laundry, and for administrative services such as billings and collections. Space and bed rentals are fixed charges for the year, based on bed capacity rented to each entity.

Melford charged the following costs to pediatrics for the year ended June 30, 19x5:

	Patient days (variable)	*Bed capacity (fixed)*
Dietary	$ 600,000	
Janitorial		$ 70,000
Laundry	300,000	
Laboratory	450,000	
Pharmacy	350,000	
Repairs and maintenance		30,000
General and administrative		1,300,000
Rent		1,500,000
Billings and collections	300,000	
Totals	$2,000,000	$2,900,000

During the year ended June 30, 19x5, pediatrics charged each patient an average of $300 per day, had a capacity of 60 beds, and had revenue of $6,000,000 for 365 days.

In addition, pediatrics directly employed the following personnel:

	Annual salary per employee
Supervising nurses	$25,000
Nurses	20,000
Aides	9,000

Melford has the following minimum departmental personnel requirements based on total annual patient days:

Annual patient-days	*Aides*	*Nurses*	*Supervising nurses*
Up to 21,900	20	10	4
21,901 to 26,000	26	13	4
26,001 to 29,200	30	15	4

These staffing levels represent full-time equivalents. Pediatrics always employs only the minimum number of required full-time equivalent personnel. Salaries of supervising nurses, nurses, and aides are therefore fixed within ranges of annual patient-days.

Pediatrics operated at 100 percent of capacity on 90 days during the year ended June 30, 19x5. It is estimated that during these 90 days the demand exceeded capacity by more than 20 patients. Melford has an additional 20 beds available for rent for the year ending June 30, 19x6. Such additional rental would increase pediatrics' fixed charges based on bed capacity.

REQUIREMENTS

a) Calculate pediatrics' break-even patient days for the year ending June 30, 19x6, if the additional 20 beds are not rented. Assume that revenue per patient-day, cost per patient-day, cost per bed, and salary rates will remain the same as for the year ended June 30, 19x5.

b) Assume that patient demand, revenue per patient-day, cost per patient-day, cost per bed, and salary rates for the year ending June 30, 19x6, remain the same as for the year ended June 30, 19x5. Determine the net increase or decrease in earnings from the additional 20 beds if pediatrics rent this extra capacity from Melford. (*Hint:* Prepare a schedule showing differential revenues and costs for the year ending June 30, 19x6.) (CPA Adapted)

8–22 Nonlinear Cost Function

The Briar Pipe Company manufactures high-quality briar pipes by hand. The company employs seven experienced pipe carvers and produces 28,000 pipes during 14,000 regular working hours for a production rate of 2 pipes per hour. The carvers are members of the Pipemakers Union and their most recent contract with the Briar Pipe Company contains the following terms:

1. Total regular compensation, including fringe benefits, shall be $15 per hour.
2. In the event employees work more than the regular number of yearly working hours, they shall be paid an overtime premium of $7.50 per hour.
3. In no event shall an employee be compensated for less than 1,000 hours of work per year. All members of the union shall earn a minimum of $15,000 per year even if they are not employed 1,000 hours.

Other manufacturing costs include direct materials of $4 per pipe, variable factory overhead of $3.00 per direct-labor hour, and fixed factory overhead of $10,000 per year. Administrative expenses total $30,000 per year. Briar Pipes are sold to retail stores at a price of $15 each.

REQUIREMENTS

a) Prepare a schedule showing revenues, expenses, and profits at yearly volumes of 10,500, 24,500, and 35,000 pipes.

b) Determine the break-even point(s) in units and sales dollars.

c) Prepare a graph of the yearly cost-volume-profit relationships.

d) Is there a profit maximizing volume? If so, what is it?

8–23 Cost-Volume-Profit Analysis: Multiple Products

The Oak Shop manufactures a line of oak office furniture including desks, bookcases, and file cabinets. The Oak Shop's income statement for July broken down on a product line basis is as follows:

	Total	*Desks*	*Bookcases*	*File cabinets*
Unit selling price		$ 600	$ 200	$ 300
Sales volume	100	20	50	30
Sales revenues	$31,000	$12,000	$10,000	$ 9,000
Cost of goods sold:				
Direct materials	$ 8,400	$ 4,000	$ 2,000	$ 2,400
Direct labor	7,000	3,500	1,400	2,100
Factory overhead	3,500	1,750	700	1,050
Total	−18,900	−9,250	−4,100	−5,550
Gross profit	$12,100	$ 2,750	$ 5,900	$ 3,450
Other expenses:				
Distribution	$ 3,000	$ 600	$ 1,500	$ 900
Administrative	5,000	1,000	2,500	1,500
Total	−8,000	−1,600	−4,000	−2,400
Income before taxes	$ 4,100	$ 1,150	$ 1,900	$ 1,050

ADDITIONAL INFORMATION

- Employees are paid at a rate of $7 per hour.
- Average monthly fixed manufacturing costs are $1,500. Fixed overhead is applied at a constant rate per direct-labor hour.
- Distribution expenses are completely variable and identical on a per-unit basis.
- Administrative expenses are fixed. They are allocated to each product line on the basis of sales volume.

REQUIREMENTS

a) Determine the unit contribution margin for each product and the average unit contribution margin of the current production mix.

b) Determine the Oak Shop's break-even unit sales volume for the current product mix and the number of units of each product in this break-even volume.

c) Plot the current profit-volume relationship assuming a constant sales mix.

d) Use a profit-volume graph to illustrate the range of possible break-even points.

e) Assume that unit selling price, unit variable costs, and total fixed costs are the same in August as in July, but the sales volume for August is as follows:

	Number of units
Desks	30
Bookcases	72
File cabinets	28
Total	130

Determine the average unit contribution margin and the break-even sales volume in units for August.

8–24 Multiple Products with Constraining Resource

JCA Company manufactures three models of garden roto-tillers called Super, Standard, and Mini. Relevant data for each model for 19y8 are as follows:

	Super	*Standard*	*Mini*
Sales volume — units	15,000	30,000	10,000
Selling price per unit	$1,000	$ 800	$ 600
Variable manufacturing costs per unit	$ 830	$ 650	$ 420
Variable selling and admin. costs per unit	$ 50	$ 50	$ 40
Machine hours required per unit	6	4	4

ADDITIONAL INFORMATION

- Each model requires the use of the same production machinery. The total machine hours available are 250,000 hours per year.
- Annual fixed manufacturing costs are $3,500,000 and annual fixed selling and administrative costs are $1,700,000.

REQUIREMENTS

a) Determine the average unit contribution margin for the current product mix.

b) Determine the contribution margin per machine hour for each product. Which product should be produced if demand for each product exceeds maximum possible production?

c) Determine how much higher 19x8 before-tax profits would have been if JCA had used its limited machine hours to produce only the product suggested in part (b).

d) What other factors should JCA consider before changing to the product mix that maximizes before-tax profits?

8–25 Statistical Analysis of Uncertainty in C-V-P Analysis (Appendix)

Gamma Corporation produces Product Beta, which has the following unit selling price and costs:

Selling price per unit	$4,000
Variable costs per unit	$3,000
Fixed costs	$8,000,000

The selling price and costs are certain; however, demand is uncertain and normally distributed with an expected value of 10,000 units and a standard deviation of 1,000 units.

REQUIREMENTS

Determine each of the following for Product Beta:

a) Expected profit

b) Standard deviation of expected profit

c) The probability of at least breaking even

d) The probability of making less than $500,000 profit

e) The probability of making at least $1,000,000 profit

8–26 Statistical Analysis of Uncertainty in C-V-P Analysis (Appendix)

Tim Fan is considering becoming a vendor at Central State University's football games this fall. He has two alternatives available: (1) selling program booklets, and (2) selling soft drinks.

The unit selling price and amount Tim must pay for each product are as follows:

	Program booklets	*Soft drinks*
Selling price	$3.00	$1.00
Cost	2.25	0.75

The demand for each product depends on various factors including attendance and weather. Tim estimates that his sales for each product per game will be normally distributed with the following expected value and standard deviation.

	Program booklets	*Soft drinks*
Expected sales in units	50	150
Standard deviation of unit sales	15	50

Since all equipment is furnished by the Athletic Department of Central State University, Tim will not incur any costs other than for the booklets or soft drinks under either alternative.

REQUIREMENTS

a) Determine the following for each alternative:

   1. Expected profits
   2. Standard deviation of expected profits
   3. Probability of making less than $30 profit per game
   4. Probability of making more than $40 profit per game

b) Which alternative should Tim prefer? State your reason(s).

8–27 Alternative Production Procedures and Uncertain Sales (Appendix)
Annual sales for a new product that sells for \$8 per unit are estimated to be 50,000 units with a standard deviation of 20,000 units. The new product may be manufactured by labor-intensive or machine-intensive operations. If it is manufactured by labor-intensive operations, variable costs will total \$6 per unit and fixed costs will total \$20,000 per year. If it is manufactured by machine-intensive operations, variable costs will total \$3 per unit and fixed costs will total \$170,000 per year.

REQUIREMENTS

a) Determine the expected profit using each production method.

b) Determine the break-even unit sales volume using each production method and the probability of at least breaking even.

c) Which production procedure do you prefer and why?

d) Would your answer differ if the expected sales volume were estimated to be 100,000 units? Why or why not?

8–28 Statistical Analysis of Uncertainty in Cash Budgets (Appendix)
Jackson Co. is experiencing cash management problems. In particular, they have been unable to determine their temporary cash needs on a timely basis. This has increased the cost of borrowing because they have often been unable to obtain desirable terms. Borrowing in advance would give them better terms at a lower cost. A review of the cash flows indicates that all factors can be adequately predicted except the expenditures for hourly payroll and certain other expenditures. The cash receipts can be accurately determined because Jackson's customers are all reliable and pay on an identifiable schedule within two calendar months following the sale. The payments for raw materials are similarly predictable because they are all paid in the calendar month subsequent to purchase. Disbursements for monthly fixed obligations, such as lease payments, salaried personnel, and so on, are known well in advance of the payment dates.

In an attempt to better forecast cash changes for the next month, the company conducted a statistical analysis of many possible variables that might be suitable as a basis for forecasting the expenditure for payroll and other items. This analysis revealed a high correlation between the advance sales orders received in a month and expenditures in the next month. The following relationships have been identified:

N = the forecast month
S = sales in dollars
R = raw material purchases in dollars
A = advance sales orders in dollars
Collections on accounts: $C_N = 0.9S_{N-1} + 0.1S_{N-2}$
Disbursements for raw material purchases: $D_N = R_{N-1}$
Monthly fixed obligations: $F_N = \$400,000$
Payroll and other expenditures: $P_N = 0.25A_{N-1} + \$70,000$

The following data relate to the equation for payroll and other expenditures:

Coefficient of correlation	= 0.96
Standard error of the estimate	= 10,000
Standard error of the regression coefficient of the independent variable	= 0.0013
t-statistic for 95% probability interval	= 2.07

REQUIREMENTS

a) Estimate the change in the cash balance for July 19x5 using the relationship previously specified and the following data:

	Sales (S)	*Raw material purchases (R)*	*Advance sales orders (A)*
April	$1,300,000	$300,000	$1,225,000
May	1,200,000	400,000	1,050,000
June	1,000,000	350,000	1,400,000

b) Establish a 95 percent probability interval for the change in cash to recognize the uncertainty associated with the payroll and other expenditures.

c) How could management use this information to study alternative plans to reduce the short-term borrowing costs? (CMA Adapted)

8–29 Probability Tree Analysis of Uncertainty in Budgets (Appendix)
The Empire Novelty Company is considering the desirability of introducing a novelty scrub board called the "Wishey Washer." Based on preliminary estimates, projected product line before-tax net income is:

Sales (30,000 units @ $10)		$300,000
Variable costs:		
Manufacturing (30,000 @ $3)	$90,000	
Distribution (30,000 @ $2)	60,000	− 150,000
Contribution margin		$150,000
Fixed costs		− 100,000
Net income before taxes		$ 50,000

To achieve economies of scale and meet anticipated demand, a minimum of 20,000 Wishey Washers must be produced before any are sold. Unfortunately there is some uncertainty about consumer demand. Although there is a 30 percent probability that demand will support the budgeted sales volume and price, there is also a 30 percent probability of a higher demand. In this event, Empire will produce 40,000 units and sell them at $15. There is also a 30 percent probability that the budgeted sales volume can be achieved only by lowering the selling price to $8. Finally, there is a 10 percent probability that the product will be a real loser. In that event, the first 20,000 units will be sold at $4 and no additional production will take place.

Empire also faces uncertainty in its distribution costs. There is a 50 percent probability that distribution costs will remain at $2 and a 50 percent probability that they will increase to $3.

REQUIREMENTS

a) Develop a probability tree to show the possible outcomes from the sale of Wishey Washers.

b) Determine the expected profits and the probability of at least breaking even.

8–30 Budget Simulation (Appendix)

From the information in Problem 8-29, determine the expected profits and the probability of breaking even by simulation. In approaching this problem, assign single-digit random numbers to possible levels of demand and possible distribution costs. Then obtain sufficient random numbers for five trials either from a random-number table or by selecting a series of telephone numbers from a city telephone directory. If you use a telephone directory, to help ensure that all numbers have an equal probability of occurring, use only the last digit of each telephone number. For simplicity, perform your analysis on the basis of only five trials.

8–31 Probability Trees: Different Cost Structures (Appendix)

Canton Corporation can produce a product using either labor-intensive or machine-intensive operations. Costs of each method are as follows:

	Labor intensive	*Machine intensive*
Variable costs per unit	$15	$5
Fixed costs	$900,000	$2,400,000

Demand for the product and unit selling price are uncertain. The following possible outcomes and associated probabilities have been estimated by management:

Demand		*Unit selling price*	
Number of units	*Probability*	*Price*	*Probability*
150,000	0.30	$20	0.40
200,000	0.40	23	0.40
250,000	0.20	25	0.20
300,000	0.10		

REQUIREMENTS

a) Develop probability trees to show the possible profits from labor-intensive and machine-intensive production.

b) Determine the following for each production method:

1. Expected profits
2. Probability of at least breaking even
3. Probability of profits of at least $1,000,000

c) Which production method do you prefer and why?

d) Discuss other factors that Canton Corporation's management should consider before deciding on the production method.

8–32 Simulation (Appendix)

Based on the information in Problem 8–31 for the labor-intensive method of production, determine the expected profits and the probability of at least breaking even by simulation. In approaching this problem, assign single-digit random numbers to possible levels of demand and selling price. Then obtain sufficient random numbers for five trials from a random number table or by selecting a series of telephone numbers from a city telephone directory. If you use a telephone directory, use only the last digit of each number to help ensure that all numbers have an equal probability of occurring.

SOLUTION TO REVIEW PROBLEM

a) 1.

Unit selling price	\$60
Unit variable costs (\$20 + \$15 + \$10 + \$5)	−50
Unit contribution margin	\$10

2. Contribution margin percentage $= \dfrac{\$10}{\$60} = 0.1667$

3. Break-even unit sales $= \dfrac{\$200{,}000}{\$10} = 20{,}000$ units

Break-even dollar sales = 20,000 units × \$60 = \$1,200,000

4.

Planned sales	30,000 units
Break-even unit sales	−20,000 units
Margin of safety	10,000 units

5. Cash break-even point $= \dfrac{\$200{,}000 - \$50{,}000}{\$10} = 15{,}000$ units

b) 1. Break-even unit sales $= \dfrac{\$200{,}000}{\$10} = 20{,}000$ units

2.

Total contribution	(30,000 units × \$10)	\$ 300,000
Fixed costs	(\$100,000 + \$100,000)	−200,000
Before-tax income		100,000
Income taxes	(0.40 × \$100,000)	−40,000
After-tax income		\$ 60,000

3. Cash break-even point $= \dfrac{(1 - 0.40)(\$200{,}000) - \$50{,}000}{(1 - 0.40)(\$10)}$

$= \dfrac{\$120{,}000 - \$50{,}000}{\$6} = 11{,}667$ units

9 The Contribution Income Statement and Variable Costing

INTRODUCTION

FUNCTIONAL AND CONTRIBUTION INCOME STATEMENTS

ABSORPTION AND VARIABLE COSTING

UNDERAPPLIED AND OVERAPPLIED OVERHEAD ARE ABSORPTION COSTING PROBLEMS

THE VARIABLE COSTING CONTROVERSY

THE USE OF CONTRIBUTION INCOME STATEMENTS FOR SEGMENT REPORTING

SUMMARY

INTRODUCTION

IN CHAPTER 8 WE STUDIED COST-VOLUME-PROFIT ANALYSIS, A PLANNING technique used to analyze the impact of changes in volume on costs, revenues, and profits. We saw that cost-volume-profit relationships are often studied with the aid of graphs that contain separate lines for total revenues, total variable costs, and total fixed costs. The break-even point occurs at that volume where total revenues equal total costs. Alternatively, the break-even point occurs at that volume where the total contribution, computed as total revenues minus total variable costs, equals the fixed costs.

Although cost-volume-profit analysis is widely used for planning, the cost relationships used in cost-volume-profit models are seldom emphasized in income statements. The format of the traditional income statement necessitates special studies to determine a firm's variable and fixed costs before managers use cost-volume-profit models for planning. Furthermore the format of the traditional income statement prevents a direct comparison of cost-volume-profit plans (where costs are classified as fixed and variable) with the reported results of operations (where costs are classified by functional categories such as cost of goods sold, and selling and administrative expenses).

The cost-volume-profit model's assumption that inventories are constant also prevents a direct comparison of actual and planned profits. This assumption requires all current manufacturing costs, fixed and variable, to become part of the cost of goods sold. Unfortunately the constant inventory assumption is not realistic, and when it does not hold, the income of a manufacturing firm reported using conventional accounting procedures seldom agrees with the income predicted in cost-volume-profit graphs. Indeed, reported profits may go down, while sales go up due to changes in inventory. This divergence sometimes leads to heated discussions between accountants and managers and gives managers innumerable problems explaining financial reports to stockholders.

The purposes of this chapter are to introduce the contribution income statement, where costs are classified by cost behavior, and to introduce variable costing, a procedure that eliminates the need for the constant inventory assumption. The use of contribution income statements and variable costing produces income statements that facilitate the development of cost-volume-profit relationships and the comparison of cost-volume-profit plans with actual results. We will also illustrate the use of contribution income statements in evaluating the profitability of business segments, such as products, territories, or classes of customers.

FUNCTIONAL AND CONTRIBUTION INCOME STATEMENTS

The income statement traditionally used for external reporting is often referred to as a **functional income statement** because costs are classified according to function, such as manufacturing or selling and administrative. Variable and fixed costs are included within each functional category. The cost of goods sold includes variable and fixed manufacturing costs; likewise, the selling and administrative expenses include variable and fixed costs.

Example 9–1

In 19x3 the Keller Company began producing a product that has the following unit selling price, variable costs, and contribution margin:

Selling price		$25 per unit
Variable costs:		
Direct materials	$ 4	
Direct labor	7	
Factory overhead	2	
Selling and administrative	2	− 15 per unit
Contribution margin		$10 per unit

Quarterly fixed costs include manufacturing, $120,000, and selling and administrative, $80,000.

A functional income statement for the first quarter of 19x3, when production and sales equaled 30,000 units, is presented in Exhibit 9–1. For the purpose of exposition, detailed computations of the cost of goods sold and selling and administrative expenses are shown. In reality, it is unlikely that each functional category would be further classified by cost behavior.

One immediate problem with this functional income statement is the difficulty of relating it to the cost-volume-profit model where costs are classified by behavior rather than by function. The cost and profit consequences of changes in sales volume are not readily apparent in a functional income statement, especially when cost information is presented at an aggregate level. For planning and control purposes, costs should be classified by behavior. This facilitates a determination of how costs respond to changes in volume and a comparison of planned with actual results.

In a **contribution income statement,** costs are classified according to behavior. Variable manufacturing costs and variable selling and administrative costs are grouped together and subtracted from revenues. The difference between revenues and variable costs, the **contribution margin,** is the amount of money contributed to cover fixed costs and to provide a profit. Fixed manufacturing costs and fixed

EXHIBIT 9–1 Functional and Contribution Income Statements

Keller Company
Functional Income Statement
For the First Quarter of 19x3

Sales ($25 × 30,000)		$750,000
Cost of goods sold:		
Direct materials ($4 × 30,000)	$120,000	
Direct labor ($7 × 30,000)	210,000	
Variable factory overhead ($2 × 30,000)	60,000	
Fixed factory overhead	120,000	−510,000
Gross profit		$240,000
Selling and administrative expenses:		
Variable ($2 × 30,000)	$ 60,000	
Fixed	80,000	−140,000
Net income		$100,000

Keller Company
Contribution Income Statement
For the First Quarter of 19x3

Sales ($25 × 30,000)			$750,000
Variable expenses:			
Cost of goods sold:			
Direct materials ($4 × 30,000)	$120,000		
Direct labor ($7 × 30,000)	210,000		
Factory overhead ($2 × 30,000)	60,000	$390,000	
Selling and administrative ($2 × 30,000)		60,000	−450,000
Contribution margin			$300,000
Fixed expenses:			
Factory overhead		$120,000	
Selling and administrative		80,000	−200,000
Net income			$100,000

selling and administrative costs are also grouped together and subtracted from the contribution margin to obtain net income. A contribution income statement for the first quarter of 19x3 is also presented in Exhibit 9–1.

When production equals sales and inventories are constant, we will obtain the same net income with either type of income statement. However, the gross profit in a functional income statement will seldom equal the contribution margin in a contribution income statement. This is because the computation of gross profit includes a deduction for fixed manufacturing costs and excludes a deduction for variable selling and administrative costs. If we mix fixed and variable costs when computing a manufacturing firm's gross profit, it will be difficult to determine how gross profit responds to changes in sales volume. Note, however, that a merchandising firm's costs of goods sold includes only the variable cost of goods purchased and sold; hence, the gross profit of a merchandising firm represents a contribution that is available to cover selling and administrative costs and to provide a profit. It should increase in direct proportion to changes in sales volume.

ABSORPTION AND VARIABLE COSTING

When production does not equal sales, income figures obtained with functional income statements are unlikely to be the same as income figures obtained with contribution income statements. This is because functional income statements are based on an inventory costing concept known as absorption costing, whereas contribution income statements are based on an inventory costing concept known as variable costing.

Under **absorption costing** all manufacturing costs, including direct materials, direct labor, variable factory overhead, and fixed factory overhead, are assigned to products. Use of absorption costing in general-purpose financial statements prepared for persons external to the organization is a generally accepted accounting principle. Because the product-costing procedures discussed in Chapters 2 through 6 were primarily concerned with the development of inventory cost data for use in external financial statements, they followed the absorption costing convention.

Under **variable costing** (also called **direct costing**) only variable manufacturing costs are assigned to products. All other costs, including fixed factory overhead, variable selling and administrative, and fixed selling and administrative, are treated as period costs.

Recall that fixed manufacturing costs are related to providing productive capacity. Under absorption costing, the assignment of fixed factory overhead to products is based on the belief that costs incurred to provide productive capacity should be assigned to the products produced with the use of that capacity. Because it looks to past costs and the use of productive capacity that was available in the past, absorption costing has a historical cost orientation.

Under variable costing, fixed overhead costs are not assigned to products because of a belief that once a decision is made to provide productive capacity, capacity costs are no longer relevant to the determination of how best to use that capacity. Variable costing tends to be future oriented in its approach to inventory cost assignment. Because fixed factory overhead does not change with a decision to produce each additional unit, variable costing treats fixed factory overhead as having no association with individual units and concludes that these costs should not be assigned to individual units. Some variable costing advocates also argue that only the variable costs of a product has a future value because the firm would only have to incur the variable costs to produce additional units. A cost that does not have a future value should be written off as a period cost. Therefore variable costing treats fixed factory overhead as a period cost.

Example 9–2

Information about the Keller Company's cost structure and the company's operations for the first quarter of 19x3 were presented in Example 9–1. First quarter functional and contribution income statements were presented in Exhibit 9–1. Continuing Example 9–1, Keller Company's unit product costs under absorption and variable costing are as follows:

Absorption cost per unit:	
Direct materials	$ 4
Direct labor	7
Variable factory overhead	2
Fixed factory overhead ($120,000/30,000)	4
Total	$17
Variable cost per unit:	
Direct materials	$ 4
Direct labor	7
Variable factory overhead	2
Total	$13

Note that the only difference between the two unit costs is the treatment of fixed factory overhead. With quarterly fixed costs of $120,000 and a production volume of 30,000 units, the fixed factory overhead is $4 per unit.

Production Equals Sales

The functional and contribution income statements for the first quarter of 19x3, when production equaled sales, are presented again in a more condensed form in Exhibit 9–2(a). The differences in inventory costs under absorption and variable costing are illustrated in Exhibit 9–2(b). In this example there are no beginning or ending inventories and all current manufacturing costs become part of the cost of goods manufactured and then part of the cost of goods sold. Note that the cost of goods sold under absorption costing exceeds the cost of goods sold under variable costing by $120,000 ($510,000 – $390,000), the amount of the fixed manufacturing costs included in the absorption cost of goods sold.

Production Exceeds Sales

The income results under absorption and variable costing will only be identical when production equals sales. *If production exceeds sales, absorption costing net income will exceed variable costing net income.* This is because absorption costing assigns some current fixed manufacturing costs to the ending inventory, whereas variable costing treats all current fixed manufacturing costs as a period cost. This differing treatment of fixed manufacturing costs will also lead to higher inventory values under absorption costing than under variable costing.

Example 9–3

During the second quarter of 19x3, Keller produced 30,000 units and sold 20,000 units. Variable and fixed cost behavior patterns are the same as in the first quarter of 19x3. Resulting absorption and variable costing income statements are presented in Exhibit 9–3(a). Note that absorption costing income exceeds variable costing by $40,000, an amount entirely explained by the alternative treatments of fixed manufacturing costs.

Under absorption costing, fixed manufacturing costs of $80,000 (20,000 × $4) were included in cost of goods sold and fixed manufacturing costs of $40,000 (10,000 × $4) were assigned to ending inventory. Under variable costing, the entire $120,000 was treated as a period cost. A reconciliation of absorption and

EXHIBIT 9–2 Variable- and Absorption-Costing Income: Production Equals Sales

Keller Company
First Quarter of 19x3

A. COMPARATIVE INCOME STATEMENTS

Functional Income Statement: Absorption Costing

Sales (30,000 × $25)		$750,000
Cost of goods sold (30,000 × $17)		−510,000
Gross profit		$240,000
Selling and administrative expenses:		
Variable (30,000 × $2)	$ 60,000	
Fixed	80,000	−140,000
Net income		$100,000

Contribution Income Statement: Variable Costing

Sales (30,000 × $25)		$750,000
Variable expenses:		
Cost of goods sold (30,000 × $13)	$390,000	
Selling and administrative (30,000 × $2)	60,000	−450,000
Contribution margin		$300,000
Fixed expenses:		
Manufacturing	$120,000	
Selling and administrative	80,000	−200,000
Net income		$100,000

B. INVENTORY COSTS

	Absorption costing		*Variable costing*	
Beginning balance		$ 0		$ 0
Cost of goods manufactured:				
Direct materials (30,000 × $4)	$120,000		$120,000	
Direct labor (30,000 × $7)	210,000		210,000	
Variable overhead (30,000 × $2)	60,000		60,000	
Fixed overhead	120,000	510,000	0	390,000
Total available for sale		$510,000		$390,000
Cost of goods sold:				
(30,000 × $17)		−510,000		
(30,000 × $13)				−390,000
Ending balance		$ 0		$ 0

variable costing income is presented in Exhibit 9–3(b). Inventory cost information for the second quarter of 19x3 is presented in Exhibit 9–3(c).

Sales Exceeds Production

If sales exceeds production, absorption costing net income will be less than variable costing net income. This is because absorption costing includes all current and some previously deferred fixed manufacturing costs in the cost of goods sold, whereas variable costing only expenses current fixed manufacturing

EXHIBIT 9–3 Variable- and Absorption-Costing Income: Production Exceeds Sales

Keller Company
Second Quarter of 19x3

A. COMPARATIVE INCOME STATEMENTS

Functional Income Statement: Absorption Costing

Sales (20,000 × $25)		$500,000
Cost of goods sold (20,000 × $17)		−340,000
Gross profit		$160,000
Selling and administrative expenses:		
Variable (20,000 × $2)	$ 40,000	
Fixed	80,000	−120,000
Net income		$ 40,000

Contribution Income Statement: Variable Costing

Sales (20,000 × $25)		$500,000
Variable expenses:		
Cost of goods sold (20,000 × $13)	$260,000	
Selling and administrative (20,000 × $2)	40,000	−300,000
Contribution margin		$200,000
Fixed expenses:		
Manufacturing	$120,000	
Selling and administrative	80,000	−200,000
Net income		$ 0

B. RECONCILIATION OF VARIABLE AND ABSORPTION-COSTING NET INCOME

Variable-costing net income	$ 0
Add: Increase in fixed costs deferred in inventory (20,000 × $4)	40,000
Absorption-costing net income	$40,000

C. INVENTORY COSTS

	Absorption costing		Variable costing	
Beginning balance		$ 0		$ 0
Cost of goods manufactured:				
Direct materials (30,000 × $4)	$120,000		$120,000	
Direct labor (30,000 × $7)	210,000		210,000	
Variable overhead (30,000 × $2)	60,000		60,000	
Fixed overhead	120,000	510,000	0	390,000
Total available for sale		$510,000		$390,000
Cost of goods sold:				
(20,000 × $17)		−340,000		
(20,000 × $13)				−260,000
Ending balance		$170,000*		$130,000†

* Including variable manufacturing costs of $130,000 [10,000 × $13] and fixed manufacturing costs of $40,000 [10,000 × $4].
† Variable manufacturing costs of $130,000 [10,000 × $13].

costs. Previously deferred fixed manufacturing costs were included in the absorption cost of the beginning finished goods inventory.

Example 9–4

During the third quarter of 19x3, Keller produced 30,000 units and sold 40,000 units. Cost behavior patterns were unchanged. Absorption and variable costing income statements for the third quarter of 19x3 are presented in Exhibit 9–4(a). Once again, the difference between absorption and variable costing income is entirely explained by the alternative treatment of fixed manufacturing costs.

Under absorption costing, the beginning inventory of 10,000 units included variable manufacturing costs of $130,000 (10,000 × $13) and fixed manufacturing costs of $40,000 (10,000 × $4). Under variable costing, the beginning inventory included only variable manufacturing costs. Inventory reductions resulted in previously deferred costs being expensed in the third quarter. A reconciliation of absorption and variable costing income is presented in Exhibit 9–4(b). Inventory cost information for the third quarter of 19x3 is presented in Exhibit 9–4(c).

A Matter of Timing

In Examples 9–3 and 9–4 differences between absorption and variable costing income are entirely due to differences in the treatment of fixed manufacturing costs.

- When production exceeds sales, absorption costing income is greater than variable costing income because of an increase in fixed manufacturing costs deferred in absorption costing ending inventory. Current fixed manufacturing costs are an expense under variable costing.
- When sales exceed production, absorption costing income is less than variable costing income because of a decrease in fixed manufacturing costs deferred in absorption costing inventory. These fixed manufacturing costs were previously expensed under variable costing.
- When sales and production are equal, absorption and variable costing income are equal.[1]

In the long run, production and sales tend to be equal and absorption and variable costing provide similar results. For the first three quarters of 19x3, Keller's production and sales totaled 90,000 units and absorption and variable costing income both totaled $300,000. However, planning and performance evaluation periods consist of a series of short runs in which decisions based on cost data must be made. For this reason many managers prefer variable costing and contribution income statements; they tie in with cost-volume-profit analysis.

---

[1] There are two exceptions, both of which assume the existence of beginning and ending inventories, a change in period fixed costs, and FIFO inventory valuation. If current fixed manufacturing costs increase under these circumstances, absorption costing income will be greater than variable costing income. In this case, the higher current fixed costs are deferred, and the previously lower fixed costs are included in the Cost of Goods Sold. If current fixed manufacturing costs decrease under the previously specified assumptions, absorption costing net income will be less than variable costing net income. Here, the lower fixed costs are deferred, and the previously higher fixed costs are included in the Cost of Goods Sold.

EXHIBIT 9–4 Variable- and Absorption-Costing Income: Sales Exceed Production

Keller Company
Third Quarter of 19x3

A. COMPARATIVE INCOME STATEMENTS

Functional Income Statement: Absorption Costing		
Sales (40,000 × $25)		$1,000,000
Cost of goods sold (40,000 × $17)		−680,000
Gross profit		$ 320,000
Selling and administrative expenses:		
Variable (40,000 × $2)	$ 80,000	
Fixed	80,000	−160,000
Net income		$ 160,000

Contribution Income Statement: Variable Costing		
Sales (40,000 × $25)		$1,000,000
Variable expenses:		
Cost of goods sold (40,000 × $13)	$520,000	
Selling and administrative (40,000 × $2)	80,000	−600,000
Contribution margin		$ 400,000
Fixed expenses:		
Manufacturing	$120,000	
Selling and administrative	80,000	−200,000
Net income		$ 200,000

B. RECONCILIATION OF VARIABLE- AND ABSORPTION-COSTING NET INCOME

Variable-costing net income	$ 200,000
Less: Decrease in fixed costs deferred in inventory (10,000 × $4)	−40,000
Absorption-costing net income	$160,000

C. INVENTORY COSTS

	Absorption costing		Variable costing	
Beginning balance		$170,000*		$ 130,000†
Cost of goods manufactured:				
Direct materials (30,000 × $4)	$120,000		$120,000	
Direct labor (30,000 × $7)	210,000		210,000	
Variable overhead (30,000 × $2)	60,000		60,000	
Fixed overhead	120,000	510,000		390,000
Total available for sale		$680,000		$ 520,000
Cost of goods sold:				
(40,000 × $17)		−680,000		
(40,000 × $13)				−520,000
Ending balance		$ 0		$ 0

* Including variable manufacturing costs of $130,000 [10,000 × $13] and fixed manufacturing costs of $40,000 [10,000 × $4].
† Variable manufacturing costs of $130,000 [10,000 × $13].

UNDERAPPLIED AND OVERAPPLIED OVERHEAD ARE ABSORPTION COSTING PROBLEMS

An example in Chapter 3 demonstrated that the absorption cost of identical products may vary from month to month under actual job-order costing due to changes in the volume of activity or variations in monthly fixed manufacturing costs. Normal job-order costing was presented as an improvement over actual job-order costing because it allows faster cost assignment and provides insulation from short-term fluctuations in activity or fixed costs. Recall that normal costing uses a predetermined overhead rate to assign overhead costs to products. This overhead rate is developed from predictions of fixed overhead costs, variable overhead per unit of activity, and total activity:

$$\text{Predetermined overhead rate} = \frac{\text{Predicted total overhead}}{\text{Predicted total activity}}$$

Although the use of a single overhead rate and a single overhead control account fulfills the absorption costing requirement of a normal job-order cost system, it does not adequately fulfill management's needs for planning and control information. Using a single account and a single rate mixes two very different types of costs. To obtain better information for determining how costs vary with volume and/or the passage of time, we could use separate variable and fixed overhead control accounts, Variable Factory Overhead Control and Fixed Factory Overhead Control.[2] Variable and fixed factory overhead are then applied using separate rates:

$$\text{Variable overhead rate} = \text{Variable overhead per unit of activity}$$

$$\text{Fixed overhead rate} = \frac{\text{Predicted fixed overhead}}{\text{Predicted total activity}}$$

Attempting to average fixed factory overhead over activity, the fixed overhead rate varies inversely with denominator activity level, as illustrated in Exhibit 9–5(a).

This distinction between fixed and variable overhead is important for planning and control. Variable factory overhead, along with prime costs, are a function of the number of units produced. A budget for total variable factory overhead is computed as planned production multiplied by the variable overhead per unit of activity. An end of period comparison of actual and applied variable factory overhead provides information for performance evaluation and reformulating plans. The actual and applied amounts should equal. If they do not, management may request an investigation to determine the cause of the difference. Probable causes of overapplied or underapplied variable factory overhead include errors in predicting unit costs, changes in the production process and inefficient operations.

Fixed factory overhead costs are not a function of short-run changes in production volume. Given the current production capacity, fixed factory overhead

---

[2] Although it is almost always possible to develop separate rates for variable and fixed factory overhead, it may be very difficult to break the actual overhead costs of a single period into these two categories. In this case actual overhead is accumulated in a single control account and separate credits are made to this account for variable and fixed overhead costs applied to products.

EXHIBIT 9–5 Predetermined Fixed Overhead Rate and Applied Fixed Overhead

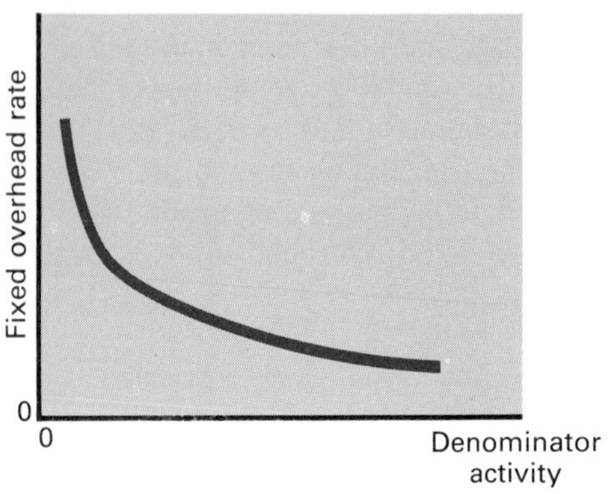

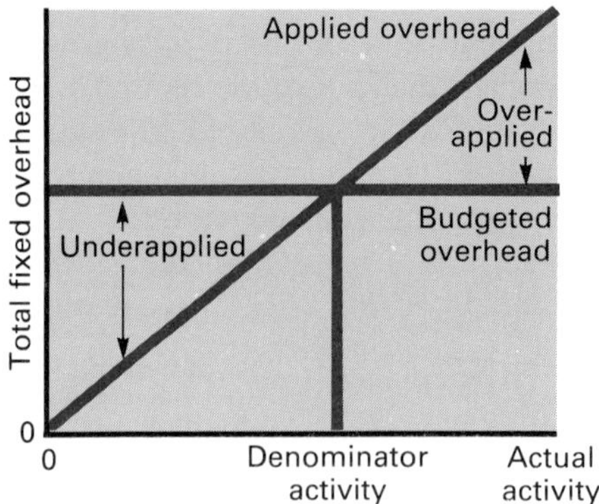

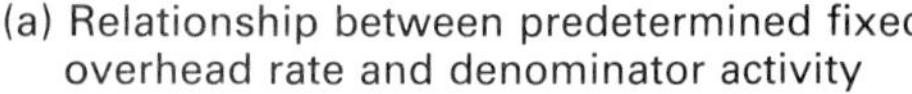
(a) Relationship between predetermined fixed overhead rate and denominator activity

(b) Relationship between volume and applied fixed overhead

costs are a function of time and their total yearly amount increases from month to month with the passage of time. Yet, *although fixed factory overhead costs are a function of time, absorption costing applies them to products using a predetermined overhead rate based on some denominator level of activity. A graph of applied fixed factory overhead displays a variable cost behavior pattern.* (See Exhibit 9–5(b).) If actual activity is at any level other than the denominator level used in developing the predetermined fixed overhead rate, applied fixed factory overhead will not equal predicted fixed factory overhead.

Assume that actual fixed factory overhead equals predicted fixed factory overhead. Then, in Exhibit 9–5(b) when actual activity is less than the denominator activity used in developing the fixed overhead rate, fixed factory overhead is underapplied. When the actual activity equals the denominator activity, actual and applied fixed factory overhead are equal. Finally, when actual activity is greater than the denominator activity, fixed factory overhead is overapplied.

Overapplied or underapplied fixed factory overhead can also be computed as:

$$\text{Overapplied or underapplied fixed factory overhead} = \text{Actual fixed factory overhead} - \left(\text{Predetermined fixed factory overhead rate} \times \text{Actual total activity}\right)$$

Procedures for disposing of overapplied or underapplied overhead were discussed in Chapter 3. When overhead is overapplied, its disposition as an adjustment to Cost of Goods Sold decreases the balance in this account and increases income. When overhead is underapplied, its disposition to Cost of Goods Sold increases the balance in this account and decreases income.

Example 9–5 The Keller Company uses a normal cost system with separate accounts and predetermined rates for variable and fixed factory overhead. All rate and cost information is as given in Example 9–2. During the fourth quarter of 19x3, Keller produced 25,000 units and sold 20,000 units.

The flow of production costs during the fourth quarter is illustrated in Exhibit 9–6. The budgeted fixed manufacturing costs are $120,000. The current manufacturing costs assigned to Work-in-Process are determined as follows:

Direct materials (25,000 × $4)	$100,000
Direct labor (25,000 × $7)	175,000
Variable factory overhead (25,000 × $2)	50,000
Fixed factory overhead (25,000 × $4)	100,000
Total	$425,000

EXHIBIT 9–6 Flow of Absorption Costs With Separate Control Accounts for Fixed and Variable Factory Overhead

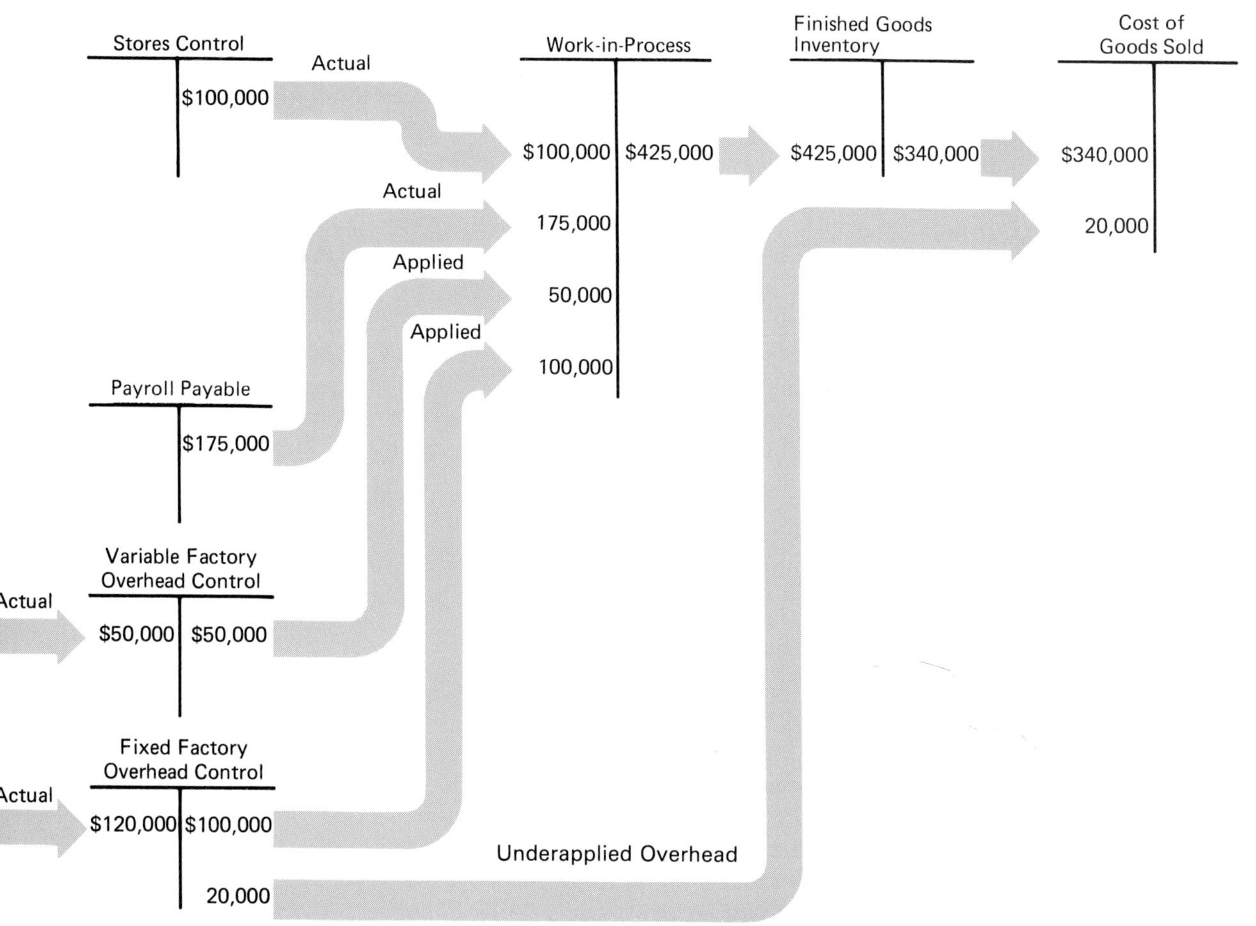

Because the predetermined fixed overhead rate is based on a quarterly production volume of 30,000 units, while actual production was only 25,000, management can expect underapplied fixed factory overhead of $20,000:

Predicted fixed factory overhead	$120,000
Applied fixed factory overhead	– 100,000
Underapplied fixed factory overhead	$ 20,000

Assuming underapplied or overapplied overhead is closed to Cost of Goods Sold at the end of each quarter, Keller's fourth quarter functional income statement using absorption costing is presented in Exhibit 9–7(a). Also presented in Exhibit 9–7(a) is a contribution income statement using variable costing. A reconciliation of absorption costing and variable costing income is presented in Exhibit 9–7(b). Inventory cost information for the fourth quarter of 19x3 is presented in Exhibit 9–7(c).

Planned Underapplied or Overapplied Fixed Overhead

Users of accounting information are sometimes surprised to learn that overapplied and underapplied fixed factory overhead are frequently incorporated into company plans. When expected annual activity is used in developing the predetermined fixed overhead rate, planned underapplied or overapplied fixed overhead results from expected monthly or quarterly fluctuations in production volume.

Example 9–6

In developing plans for 19x4, Keller's management anticipates fixed manufacturing costs of $120,000 per quarter, or $480,000 for the year. Production is expected to average 30,000 units per quarter, or 120,000 units for the year. The predetermined fixed factory overhead rate is $4 per unit ($480,000/120,000).

If the average quarterly production volume of 30,000 units is based on production of 40,000 units in the first quarter, 20,000 units in the second quarter, and 30,000 units in each of the last two quarters, planned overapplied and underapplied overhead for each of the first two quarters would be as follows:

	First quarter	*Second quarter*
Predicted fixed overhead	$ 120,000	$120,000
Applied fixed overhead:		
First quarter (40,000 × $4)	– 160,000	
Second quarter (20,000 × $4)		– 80,000
Underapplied (overapplied) fixed factory overhead	$ (40,000)	$ 40,000

Expected overapplied or underapplied overhead should be treated as an adjustment to inventories on interim financial statements, with any remaining balance disposed of by prorating or direct write-off to Cost of Goods Sold at the end of the year. As a matter of convenience, some firms may write off underapplied or overapplied overhead on a monthly or quarterly basis. This treatment is acceptable unless there are wide fluctuations in expected overapplied or underapplied overhead between months or quarters.

EXHIBIT 9–7 Variable- and Absorption-Costing Income: Production Exceeds Sales Under a Normal Cost System

Keller Company
Fourth Quarter of 19x3

A. COMPARATIVE INCOME STATEMENTS

Functional Income Statement: Absorption Costing

Sales (20,000 × $25)		$500,000
Cost of goods sold (20,000 × $17)	$340,000	
Add: Underapplied overhead [$120,000 − ($4 × 25,000)]	20,000	−360,000
Gross profit		$140,000
Selling and administrative expenses:		
Variable (20,000 × $2)	$ 40,000	
Fixed	80,000	−120,000
Net income		$ 20,000

Contribution Income Statement: Variable Costing

Sales (20,000 × $25)		$500,000
Variable expenses:		
Cost of goods sold (20,000 × $13)	$260,000	
Selling and administrative (20,000 × $2)	40,000	−300,000
Contribution margin		$200,000
Fixed expenses:		
Manufacturing	$120,000	
Selling and administrative	80,000	−200,000
Net income		$ 0

B. RECONCILIATION OF VARIABLE- AND ABSORPTION-COSTING NET INCOME

Variable-costing net income	$ 0
Add: Increase in fixed costs deferred in inventory* (5,000 × $4)	20,000
Absorption-costing net income	$20,000

C. INVENTORY COSTS

	Absorption costing		Variable costing	
Beginning balance		$ 0		$ 0
Cost of goods manufactured:				
Direct materials (25,000 × $4)	$100,000		$100,000	
Direct labor (25,000 × $7)	175,000		175,000	
Variable overhead (25,000 × $2)	50,000		50,000	
Applied fixed overhead (25,000 × $4)	100,000	425,000	0	325,000
Total available for sale		$425,000		$325,000
Cost of goods sold:				
(20,000 × $17)		−340,000		
(20,000 × $13)				−260,000
Ending balance		$ 85,000†		$ 65,000‡

* If the underapplied overhead was left in the overhead account and treated as an adjustment to inventory, absorption-costing net income would amount to $40,000 and the reconciliation would also include an element for the $20,000 increase in the underapplied fixed overhead.

† Including variable manufacturing costs of $65,000 [5,000 × $13] and fixed manufacturing costs of $20,000 [5,000 × $4].

‡ Variable manufacturing costs of $65,000 [5,000 × $13].

Selecting a Denominator Activity Level for Fixed Overhead Application

So far, only expected annual activity has been used as the denominator in developing predetermined fixed overhead rates. Accordingly, in the absence of planning errors, overapplied or underapplied overhead should be zero at the end of the year. However, when something other than expected annual activity is used in developing predetermined rates, it is unlikely that overapplied or underapplied overhead will be close to zero at the end of the year. Denominator activity levels that are often suggested as a basis for developing predetermined overhead rates include:

- Theoretical capacity
- Practical capacity
- Average annual activity
- Expected activity for the coming year

Theoretical capacity is the maximum level of activity possible if production took place at maximum speed, with 100 percent efficiency, and without interruptions. In terms of available hours, the theoretical capacity of a machine is 8,760 hours per year (365 days × 24 hours per day). If the predicted fixed overhead was $200,000 per year, the predetermined fixed overhead rate using theoretical capacity would be $22.83 per machine hour ($200,000/8,760).

Practical capacity is the maximum level of activity possible, allowing for routine repairs and maintenance, nonworking hours, and plant shutdowns for vacations. If a plant only operates eight hours per day, five days per week, fifty weeks per year, with routine repairs and maintenance requiring one hour per day, the practical capacity of the machine would be 1,750 hours per year [(8 work hours − 1 repair hour) × 5 days per week × 50 weeks per year]. With fixed overhead of $200,000, the predetermined fixed overhead rate using practical capacity would be $114.29 per machine hour ($200,000/1,750).

Average annual activity, sometimes called **normal annual activity,** is the activity level required to satisfy customer demand over a number of years. Average annual activity may be based on an arbitrarily selected time span, such as five years, or it may be selected as the length of the business cycle, encompassing both an upturn and a downturn in the economy. The average annual activity level required to satisfy customer demand for the products produced with a particular machine might be 1,300 hours. With $200,000 of annual fixed costs, the predetermined fixed overhead rate is $153.85 per machine hour ($200,000/1,300).

Expected activity for the coming year, as its name implies, is the planned activity level for the coming year. It is developed giving full recognition to machine capabilities, the need for repairs and maintenance, nonworking hours, and production requirements for current sales and inventory. With $200,000 of annual fixed costs and 1,600 machine hours of expected activity, the predetermined fixed overhead rate is $125 per machine hour ($200,000/1,600).

It is apparent that the selection of a denominator activity level has an impact on the absorption cost per unit and on overapplied or underapplied overhead. If actual fixed factory overhead and machine hours were $200,000 and 1,600, respectively, the following results would be obtained using each of the preceding denominator activity levels:

Denominator activity	*Applied overhead*	*Underapplied (overapplied) overhead**
Theoretical capacity	$22.83 × 1,600 = $ 36,528	$163,472
Practical capacity	$114.29 × 1,600 = 182,864	17,136
Average annual activity	$153.85 × 1,600 = 246,160	(46,160)
Expected activity for the coming year	$125.00 × 1,600 = 200,000	0

* $200,000 minus applied overhead.

The selection of any activity level other than expected activity for the coming year is likely to produce overapplied or underapplied overhead. Nevertheless, arguments are often made for the use of another denominator activity level. Proponents of theoretical and practical capacity argue that the resultant underapplied overhead indicates the cost of wasted or excess capacity that must be absorbed by products and that the resultant per-unit costs provide useful management goals. Practical capacity is said to be superior to theoretical capacity because it allows for normal downtime. Because a significant amount of underapplied overhead is expected with either activity level, their use in overhead rate development is likely to necessitate the prorating of underapplied overhead.

Average annual activity is sometimes used in an attempt to insulate absorption costs from yearly fluctuations in activity in the same way that expected annual activity insulates absorption costs from monthly fluctuations in activity. Proponents of this base argue it provides better information for product pricing, especially if the base is large enough to encompass a business cycle. Some proponents also suggest that any resulting underapplied or overapplied overhead should be carried forward from year to year throughout the business cycle rather than being closed at the end of each year.

Proponents of expected annual activity argue that this base provides the best measure of product costs during the year in question, while it also reduces the need to prorate or carry forward overapplied or underapplied overhead. In an age where computational costs are falling, the authors believe the best response to these arguments is to provide different information for different purposes. We no longer need to try and make do with a single measure. Instead, we can use expected annual activity for product costing, average annual activity for product pricing, and variable costing for short-range profit planning and performance evaluation. Information on unused capacity should also be provided when requested for special purposes. This information might be stated in physical quantities, such as theoretical versus actual machine hours, or it might be expressed in terms of extra dollars that must be absorbed by product selling prices because unused capacity is available.

THE VARIABLE COSTING CONTROVERSY

Although variable costing has attained the status of an accepted technique for internal reporting, controversy still surrounds discussions of variable costing. Most of the arguments have been between proponents of variable and absorption costing. However, in recent years, proponents of replacement costs, who believe inventory should be recorded at reproduction cost, and proponents of exit values, who believe inventory should be recorded at net realizable value, have argued that both variable and absorption costing are faulty because they are based on historical costs.

Proponents of absorption costing argue against the use of variable costing by stating that it:

- Fails to recognize the importance of capacity costs. Pricing decisions based on variable costing may result in prices that do not cover all costs.
- Understates inventory values. (This argument assumes that current practice is correct.)
- May mislead investors in their analysis of financial reports. In the long run, all costs are variable. Absorption costing gives better recognition to long-run variable costs.
- Is not acceptable for income tax determination; hence, its use requires costly adjustments. (But, as noted, computational costs are declining rapidly.)

Proponents of variable costing cite a long list of internal uses of variable cost information and attack the notion that fixed costs in ending inventory are a measure of value. They stress that variable costing:

- Facilitates differential analysis and short-run pricing decisions by separating fixed and variable costs.[3]
- Eliminates the confusion surrounding overapplied and underapplied fixed overhead.
- Facilitates the development of cost-volume-profit models.
- Facilitates the evaluation of plans based on cost-volume-profit models.
- Removes from income the effect of inventory changes. Under absorption costing, profits are a function of both sales volume and changes in inventory levels.

Proponents of variable costing have also questioned the propriety of including fixed costs in inventory by developing a cost-avoidance concept of the service potential of past cost. According to the **cost avoidance concept,** ending inventories have value only to the extent that they avert the necessity of incurring costs in the future. Variable manufacturing costs meet this test, but the past incurrence of fixed manufacturing costs does not avoid the reincurrence of similar costs in the future. Professor Fremgen has stated this position as follows:

> The production of goods for inventory in one period enables the firm to realize some revenue in a subsequent period without reincurring the variable costs of producing the inventory. But the availability of inventory completed in one period

---

[3] Differential analysis and pricing decisions are considered in Chapter 15.

> does not forestall the incurrence of any fixed costs in a subsequent period. Hence the variable costs are relevant to future periods but the fixed costs are not.[4]

Professors Sorter and Horngren refined the concept of cost avoidance by arguing for the inclusion of some fixed costs in inventory when future sales would be lost due to inventory shortages if current production does not exceed current sales or when variable costs are expected to rise in the future.[5] Although this refinement may be desirable for management decision making because it gives some recognition to opportunity costs, it is not objective enough for external reporting.

After reviewing the arguments presented by participants in the variable-costing controversy, the authors conclude that, although absorption costing is required for external reporting and income tax determination, variable costing provides management with better information to use in evaluating the consequences of decision alternatives and in ongoing planning and control activities. Thus contribution income statements using variable costing should be routinely generated for management's use while functional income statements using absorption costing are routinely prepared for external reporting.

THE USE OF CONTRIBUTION INCOME STATEMENTS FOR SEGMENT REPORTING

Businesses that produce several products, operate two or more plants, serve distinct groups of customers, or serve customers in different geographic regions often use segment reports to evaluate the profitability of their diverse operations. **Segment reports** are simply income statements that show operating results for portions or segments of a business. Common types of segment reports include:

- Income statements for products
- Income statements for plants
- Income statements for major classes of customers
- Income statements for sales territories

Segment reports can be prepared at any level of detail desired, for example, by product within a specific sales territory or by sales territory for a specific type of customer (government versus nongovernment or commercial versus residential).

Regardless of the type of segment for which management desires information, the segment report should be designed so that it emphasizes the segment's contribution toward covering costs that are common to two or more segments. **Common segment costs,** also called **indirect segment costs,** are related to more than one segment and are not directly identified with the operations of a particular segment. By contrast, **direct segment costs,** are immediately identified with the

---

[4] James M. Fremgen, "The Direct Costing Controversy—An Identification of the Issues," *Accounting Review* **39**, No. 1 (January 1964): 43–51.

[5] George H. Sorter, and Charles T. Horngren, "Asset Recognition and Economic Attributes—The Relevant Costing Approach," *Accounting Review* **37**, No. 3 (July 1962): 391–399.

operations of a specific segment. Examples of common segment costs include the president's salary, corporate image advertising, and the fixed cost of operating a warehouse used by several segments. These costs are sometimes called indirect segment costs because they are allocated to the segments for the purpose of measuring segment income.

However, common segment costs should not be allocated to segments in reports intended to assist management in making major decisions related to the segment, such as the decision to continue or discontinue segment operations. Common cost allocations are likely to give a misleading impression of the segment's contribution to corporate profits and the effect on corporate profits of discontinuing segment operations. Consider the following example.

Example 9–7

Sharp Razor Company sells three separate products: razors, blades, and shaving cream. Using a functional income statement format, with common costs allocated to segments, Sharp's 19x8 operating results are presented in total and on a product line basis in Exhibit 9–8.

At first glance it appears that the production and sale of razors should be discontinued because they showed a 19x8 loss of $15,000. Further investigation reveals that:

- Production takes place in *common* facilities that do not have any alternative use and fixed manufacturing costs of $9,000 were allocated equally to razors, blades, and cream, $3,000 each. All other product manufacturing costs are *direct* and variable.
- Product selling and administrative expenses are *direct* segment costs. They include variable costs equal to 10 percent of product dollar sales. All other product selling and administrative expenses are fixed.
- Central selling and administrative expenses are *common* to all three products and allocated to products on the basis of sales revenue. Management believes these costs cannot be reduced from their current level.

A properly structured contribution income statement for each segment provides a clear indication of the contribution made by the sales of each product to (1) cover the direct fixed costs of the segment and (2) cover the common segment costs and provide for a profit. The Sharp Razor Company's product line contribution income statement is also presented in Exhibit 9–8. Note that the variable costs of each product are subtracted from sales to determine the product's contribution margin. Subsequently the product's direct fixed costs are subtracted from the contribution margin to compute the **product margin**, that is, the contribution each product makes toward covering common costs and providing for a profit.

If we were analyzing sales territories, rather than products, we would compute the **territory margin**, the contribution each territory makes toward covering common costs and providing for a profit. If we were analyzing classes of customers, we would compute the **customer margin**, the contribution each class of customers makes toward covering common costs and providing for a profit. A similar approach could be made to the analysis of any other segment of

EXHIBIT 9–8 **Functional and Contribution Segment Income Statements**

Sharp Razor Company
Functional Income Statement by Product Line
For the Year Ending December 31, 19x8

	Product			
	Razors	*Blades*	*Shaving cream*	*Company totals*
Sales	$20,000	$60,000	$80,000	$160,000
Cost of goods sold	−5,000	−10,000	−15,000	−30,000
Gross profit	$15,000	$50,000	$65,000	$130,000
Product selling and adm. expenses	$25,000	$20,000	$10,000	$ 55,000
Central selling and adm. expenses	5,000	15,000	20,000	40,000
Total selling and adm. expenses	−30,000	−35,000	−30,000	−95,000
Net income (loss)	$(15,000)	$15,000	$35,000	$ 35,000

Sharp Razor Company
Contribution Income Statement by Product Line
For the Year Ending December 31, 19x8

	Product			
	Razors	*Blades*	*Shaving cream*	*Company totals*
Sales	$20,000	$60,000	$80,000	$160,000
Variable expenses:				
Cost of goods sold	$ 2,000	$ 7,000	$12,000	$ 21,000
Product selling and adm.	2,000	6,000	8,000	16,000
Total	−4,000	−13,000	−20,000	−37,000
Contribution margin	$16,000	$47,000	$60,000	$123,000
Direct fixed expenses:				
Product selling and adm.	−23,000	−14,000	−2,000	−39,000
Product margin	$ (7,000)	$33,000	$58,000	$ 84,000
Common fixed expenses:				
Manufacturing				$ 9,000
Central selling and adm.				40,000
Total				−49,000
Net income				$ 35,000

interest. In general, the **segment margin** represents the segment's contribution toward covering common costs and providing a profit.

In this particular example, razors have a negative product margin of $7,000. Accordingly, dropping razors might increase company profits by $7,000. However, management must also consider interdependencies that are likely to exist between products. A decline in the sale of razors will likely be followed by a decline in the sale of blades and cream. If the blades fit only Sharp razors, sales of blades will ultimately fall to zero. This will leave Sharp with cream producing a product margin of \$58,000 and absorbing all fixed manufacturing costs and all central selling and administrative expenses, totaling \$49,000, for a possible profit of \$9,000 (\$58,000 − \$49,000). Profits might even decline further if the sale of cream is affected by the advertising of Sharp razors and blades.

SUMMARY

The income statement traditionally used for external reporting is often referred to as a functional income statement; it classifies costs according to function, such as manufacturing, and selling and administration. Absorption costing, where all manufacturing costs (fixed and variable) are assigned to products, is used in conjunction with functional income statements.

A contribution income statement, where costs are classified according to behavior, provides more useful information to management. Variable costing, where only variable manufacturing costs are assigned to products, is used in conjunction with contribution income statements. A primary advantage of contribution income statements and variable costing stems from their articulation with cost-volume-profit models.

EXHIBIT 9–9 A Comparison of Variable and Absorption Costing

	Variable Costing	Absorption Costing
Primary purpose	Internal planning and control	External reporting
Product costs	Variable manufacturing costs	Variable and fixed manufacturing costs
Period costs	Current fixed manufacturing costs Variable selling and administrative costs Fixed selling and administrative costs	Variable selling and administrative costs Fixed selling and administrative costs
Form of income statement	Emphasis on cost behavior: Revenue − Variable costs = Contribution margin − Fixed costs = Net income	Emphasis of cost function: Revenue − Cost of goods sold = Gross profit − Selling and adm. costs = Net income
Normal net income relationships:		
Production > Sales	Smaller	Larger
Production = Sales	Equal	Equal
Production < Sales	Larger	Smaller
Long-run	Equal	Equal
Net income reconciliation	Variable-costing net income + Deferred fixed costs at end of period − Deferred fixed costs at start of period = Absorption-costing net income	Absorption-costing net income + Deferred fixed costs at start of period − Deferred fixed costs at end of period = Variable-costing net income

When production and sales are equal, absorption costing and variable costing produce identical income figures. If production exceeds sales, absorption costing income exceeds variable costing income, and if production is less than sales, absorption costing income is less than variable costing income. In either case, the difference between the two income figures can be entirely explained by changes in fixed manufacturing costs assigned to inventory under absorption costing. A summary of variable and absorption costing is presented in Exhibit 9–9.

Properly structured contribution income statements can also assist managers of multiple-segment businesses in evaluating the profitability of individual segments. In this case the income statement should clearly indicate the contribution margin produced by each segment's sales revenues and the segment margin. The segment margin is computed as the contribution margin minus fixed direct segment costs. It indicates the total contribution of the segment toward common fixed costs and providing a profit.

KEY TERMS

Absorption costing
Average annual activity
Common segment costs
Contribution income statement
Contribution margin
Cost avoidance concept
Customer margin
Direct costing
Direct segment costs
Expected activity for the coming year
Functional income statement
Indirect segment costs
Normal annual activity
Practical capacity
Product margin
Segment margin
Segment reports
Territory margin
Theoretical capacity
Variable costing

SELECTED REFERENCES

Fremgen, James M., "The Direct Costing Controversy—An Identification of Issues," *Accounting Review* **39,** No. 1 (January 1964): 43–51.

Green, David, Jr., "A Moral to the Direct Costing Controversy?" *Journal of Business* **33,** No. 3 (July 1960): 218–226.

Greenball, Melvin N., "The Accuracy of Different Methods of Accounting for Earnings—A Simulation Approach," *Journal of Accounting Research* **6,** No. 1 (Spring 1968): 114–129.

Marple, Raymond P., ed., *National Association of Accountants on Direct Costing,* New York: Ronald Press, 1965. This is a collection of early articles dating from 1936, and *N.A.A. Research Report 23: Direct Costing.*

National Association of Accountants, *N.A.A. Research Report 37: Current Applications of Direct Costing,* New York: National Association of Accountants, 1961.

Sorter, George H., and Charles T. Horngren, "Asset Recognition and Economic Attributes—The Relevant Costing Approach," *Accounting Review* **37,** No. 3 (July 1962): 391–399.

REVIEW QUESTIONS

9–1 Distinguish between the format of functional and contribution income statements.

9–2 How do variable and absorption costing differ in their treatment of fixed manufacturing costs?

9–3 Indicate the direction of the difference, if any, between variable and absorption costing income when (1) production equals sales, (2) production exceeds sales, and (3) production is less than sales.

9–4 Why are absorption costing inventory costs greater than variable costing inventory costs?

9–5 How are variable and absorption costing income reconciled?

9–6 Over an extended period of time, what is the relationship between total absorption and total variable costing income?

9–7 What is the relationship between the size of the denominator used to develop the fixed overhead rate and the resulting fixed overhead rate?

9–8 What type of a cost behavior pattern does a graph of applied fixed factory overhead display?

9–9 Indicate the likely balance in Fixed Factory Overhead Control when (1) actual activity exceeds the denominator activity used in developing the fixed overhead rate, and (2) actual activity is less than the denominator activity used in developing the fixed overhead rate.

9–10 Identify four denominator activity levels often suggested for use in developing fixed overhead rates.

9–11 What are the primary arguments for and against the use of variable costing?

9–12 In what type of businesses are segment reports likely to be used?

9–13 Distinguish between common and direct segment costs.

9–14 Identify two monetary amounts that should be clearly identified in segment reports.

REVIEW PROBLEM

Variable and Absorption Costing: Actual Cost System

The Greco Corporation uses an actual cost system. On January, 1, 19y8, Greco had no work-in-process or finished goods inventories. Unit production and sales information for the first three months of 19y8 is as follows:

	January	*February*	*March*
Production (units)	50,000	50,000	50,000
Sales (units)	30,000	50,000	70,000

Monthly fixed costs include manufacturing costs of $100,000 and selling and administration costs of $40,000. Variable costs are as follows:

Direct materials	$ 5 per unit
Direct labor	5 per unit
Factory overhead	10 per unit
Selling and administration	3 per unit sold

Each unit sells for $30.

REQUIREMENTS

a) Prepare functional income statements using absorption costing for January, February, and March.

b) Prepare contribution income statements using variable costing for January, February, and March.

c) Reconcile all differences between variable- and absorption-costing net income.

The solution to this problem is found at the end of the Chapter 9 problems and exercises.

EXERCISES

9–1 Variable and Absorption Costing: Actual Cost System

Wiles Manufacturing uses an actual cost system. In 19x8 they produced 10,000 units of a new product and sold 8,000. Revenue and cost information for 19x8 is as follows:

Sales	$140,000
Manufacturing costs:	
Direct materials	25,000
Direct labor	40,000
Variable manufacturing overhead	20,000
Fixed manufacturing overhead	35,000
Selling and administrative costs:	
Variable	10,000
Fixed	40,000

REQUIREMENTS

a) Prepare an absorption-costing income statement for 19x8.

b) Prepare a variable-costing income statement for 19x8.

c) Prepare a reconciliation of variable- and absorption-costing income.

9–2 Variable and Absorption Costing: Actual Cost System

Relevant production, cost, and sales data for the Norton Company are as follows:

Direct materials	$4.00 per unit
Direct labor	8.00 per unit
Variable overhead	3.00 per unit
Fixed overhead	300,000 per month
Selling expenses:	
Variable	2.00 per unit sold
Fixed	20,000 per month

During January of 19y3, Norton produced 200,000 units and sold 150,000 units at $20 each. Norton uses an actual cost system.

REQUIREMENTS

a) Use variable costing to prepare a contribution income statement for January.

b) Use absorption costing to prepare a functional income statement for January.

c) Reconcile the difference between the contribution and the functional income statements.

d) Would the income computed using absorption costing differ from the amount computed in part (b) if 300,000 units were produced and 150,000 were sold? Why or why not?

9–3 T Variable and Absorption Costing: Actual Cost System: Constant Production Level

The Arrow-Highway Manufacturing Corporation uses an actual cost system. On January 1, 19w5, Arrow had no work-in-process or finished goods inventories. Unit production and sales information for the first three months of 19w5 are as follows:

	January	*February*	*March*
Production (units)	100,000	100,000	100,000
Sales (units)	20,000	100,000	180,000

Monthy fixed costs include manufacturing costs of $100,000 and selling and administration costs of $60,000. Variable costs are as follows:

Direct materials	$ 2 per unit
Direct labor	1 per unit
Factory overhead	3 per unit
Selling and administration	0.50 per unit sold

Each unit sells for $10.

REQUIREMENTS

a) Prepare absorption-costing income statements for each month.

b) Prepare variable-costing income statements for each month.

c) Reconcile monthly differences between variable- and absorption-costing net income.

9–4 T Variable and Absorption Costing: Actual Cost System: Constant Production Level

Stern Production uses an actual cost system. On January 1, 19x5, Stern had no work-in-process or finished goods inventories. Information pertaining to the first three months of 19x5 is as follows:

	January	*February*	*March*
Production (units)	120,000	120,000	120,000
Sales (units)	80,000	160,000	120,000
Unit selling price	$8.00		
Variable costs per unit:			
Direct materials	$1.50		
Direct labor	2.75		
Factory overhead	0.50		
Selling and administration	0.25		

Fixed costs per month:	
Factory overhead	$180,000
Selling and administration	30,000

REQUIREMENTS

a) Prepare an absorption-costing income statement for each month.

b) Prepare a variable-costing income statement for each month.

c) Reconcile monthly differences between variable- and absorption-costing income.

9–5 T Variable and Absorption Costing: Actual Cost System: Constant Sales Level

Presented is information pertaining to the July, August, and September 19x2 operations of Mouse products:

	July	*August*	*September*
Production (units)	20,000	15,000	10,000
Sales (units)	15,000	15,000	15,000
Unit selling price	$12.00		
Variable costs per unit:			
Direct materials	$4.00		
Direct labor	2.00		
Factory overhead	1.00		
Selling and administration	0.50		
Fixed costs per month:			
Factory overhead	$50,000		
Selling and administration	10,000		

ADDITIONAL INFORMATION

- There were no July 1 inventories.
- An actual cost system with a weighted-average cost flow assumption is used.

REQUIREMENTS

a) Prepare an absorption-costing income statement for each month.

b) Prepare a variable-costing income statement for each product.

c) Reconcile monthly differences between variable- and absorption-costing net income.

9–6 T Variable and Absorption Costing: Actual Cost System: Constant Sales Level

Presented is information pertaining to the July, August, and September 19x4 operations of the Chipmunk Nut Company:

	July	*August*	*September*
Production (pounds)	30,000	50,000	10,000
Sales (pounds)	30,000	30,000	30,000
Selling price per pound	$3.00		
Variable costs per pound:			
Direct materials	$0.25		
Direct labor	0.75		
Factory overhead	0.25		
Selling and administration	0.65		
Fixed costs per month:			
Factory overhead	$27,000		
Selling and administration	4,000		

ADDITIONAL INFORMATION

- There were no July 1 inventories.
- An actual cost system with a weighted-average cost flow assumption is used.

REQUIREMENTS

a) Prepare an absorption-costing income statement for each month.

b) Prepare a variable-costing income statement for each month.

c) Reconcile monthly differences between variable- and absorption-costing net income.

9–7 Variable and Absorption Costing: Normal Cost System With Under- or Overapplied Overhead Written Off

The following data are taken from the 19w2 yearly budget of the Great Lakes Manufacturing Company:

	Units
Beginning inventory	20,000
Production	240,000
Available	260,000
Sales	−210,000
Ending inventory	50,000
Selling price	$6 per unit
Variable manufacturing costs	3 per unit
Variable selling and administrative costs	2 per unit sold
Fixed manufacturing costs at an average annual activity of 200,000 units	0.30 per unit
Fixed selling and administrative costs	80,000 per year

Over- and underapplied overhead is written off at the end of each year.

REQUIREMENTS

a) Determine the break-even sales volume in units.

b) Prepare a pro forma variable-costing income statement for 19w2.

c) Prepare a pro forma absorption-costing income statement for 19w2.

d) Reconcile the income differences in parts (b) and (c).

e) Determine the 12/31/w2 balance in Finished Goods Inventory under variable and absorption costing.

9–8 Variable and Absorption Costing: Normal Cost System With Under- or Overapplied Overhead Written Off

The Green Co. Ltd. is reviewing its accounting methods and considering a number of alternatives. As a basis for their analysis they are using the following data from the accounting records for 19x2:

Actual sales	14,000 units
Production	15,000 units
Practical capacity	20,000 units
Average annual activity	18,000 units
Inventory, January 1, 19x2	1,000 units
Sales price per unit	$20
Variable manufacturing costs per unit	8
Variable selling expenses per unit	2
Fixed overhead	54,000
Fixed selling and administrative expense	30,000

All under- or overapplied overhead is treated as a period cost.

REQUIREMENTS

a) Compute the net income under variable (direct) costing.

b) Compute the net income using absorption costing with average annual activity as the denominator level of activity.

c) Would the use of practical capacity as the denominator make a difference to your answer to part (b)? If so, how much? (CGA Adapted)

9–9 T Variable and Absorption Costing: Normal Cost System With Under- or Overapplied Overhead Written Off

Presented is information pertaining to the January, February, and March 19x6 operations of the Wilson Company:

	January	*February*	*March*
Production (units)	150,000	100,000	50,000
Sales (units)	100,000	100,000	100,000
Unit selling price	$5.00		
Variable costs per unit:			
Direct materials	$1.00		
Direct labor	0.75		
Factory overhead	0.75		
Selling and administration	0.25		
Fixed costs per month:			
Factory overhead	$100,000		
Selling and administration	50,000		
Activity level for fixed overhead rate (units)	100,000		

ADDITIONAL INFORMATION

- There were no January 1 inventories.
- Wilson uses a normal cost system with variable and fixed overhead each applied at a constant rate per unit manufactured.
- Any monthly under- or overapplied overhead is written off as an adjustment to the cost of goods sold.

REQUIREMENTS

a) Prepare an absorption-costing income statement for each month.

b) Prepare a variable-costing income statement for each month.

c) Reconcile monthly differences between variable- and absorption-costing net income.

9–10 T Variable and Absorption Costing: Normal Cost System With Under- or Overapplied Overhead Written Off

Presented is information pertaining to the April, May, and June 19x6 operations of Casper's Products:

	April	*May*	*June*
Production (units)	5,000	8,000	3,000
Sales (units)	3,000	2,000	2,000
Unit selling price	$35.00		
Variable costs per unit:			
Direct materials	$8.00		
Direct labor	4.00		
Factory overhead	2.00		
Selling and administration	1.50		
Fixed costs per month:			
Factory overhead	$66,000		
Selling and administration	8,000		
Activity level for fixed overhead rate (units)	6,000		

ADDITIONAL INFORMATION

- There were no April 1 inventories.
- Casper's uses a normal cost system with variable and fixed overhead each applied at a constant rate per unit manufactured.
- Any monthly under- or overapplied overhead is written off as an adjustment of the cost of goods sold.

REQUIREMENTS

a) Prepare an absorption-costing income statement for each month.

b) Prepare a variable-costing income statement for each month.

c) Reconcile monthly differences between variable- and absorption-costing net income.

9–11 Variable and Absorption Costing: Normal Cost System With Over- or Underapplied Overhead Deferred

Relevant production, cost, and sales data for the Nanton Co. Ltd. follow:

Direct labor	$2.00 per unit
Materials	4.00 per unit
Overhead:	
Variable	3.00 per unit
Fixed	1.20 per unit
Selling expenses	210,000 per month
Administrative expenses	220,000 per month
Sales price	15.00 per unit

During February, Nanton experienced the following:

Beginning inventory	20,000 units
Production	190,000 units
Sales	205,000 units

ADDITIONAL INFORMATION

- The denominator used in arriving at the fixed overhead rate was 200,000 units per month.
- Under- or overapplied overhead is treated as an adjustment to inventories on interim financial statements.

REQUIREMENTS

a) Prepare a variable-costing income statement for February.

b) Determine the absorption-costing net income for February. (CGA Adapted)

9–12 T Variable and Absorption Costing: Normal Cost System With Under- or Overapplied Overhead Deferred

Presented is information pertaining to the April, May, and June 19y2 operations of the Duce Company:

	April	*May*	*June*
Production (units)	40,000	25,000	20,000
Sales (units)	30,000	30,000	25,000
Unit selling price	$18.00		
Variable costs per unit:			
Direct materials	$6.00		
Direct labor	3.00		
Factory overhead	2.00		
Selling and administration	1.00		
Fixed costs per month:			
Factory overhead	$90,000		
Selling and administration	20,000		
Activity level for fixed overhead rate (units)	40,000		

ADDITIONAL INFORMATION

- There were no April 1 inventories.
- Duce uses a normal cost system with variable and fixed overhead each applied at a constant rate per unit manufactured.
- Any monthly under- or overapplied overhead is deferred as an adjustment to inventories.
- There was no under- or overapplied overhead on April 1.

REQUIREMENTS

a) Prepare an absorption-costing income statement for each month.

b) Prepare a variable-costing income statement for each month.

c) Reconcile monthly differences between variable- and absorption-costing net income.

9–13 T Variable and Absorption Costing: Normal Cost System With Under- or Overapplied Overhead Deferred

Presented is information pertaining to the October, November, and December 19x7 operations of the Ace Company:

	October	*November*	*December*
Production (units)	3,000	5,000	7,000
Sales (units)	2,000	3,000	10,000
Unit selling price	$20.00		
Variable costs per unit:			
Direct materials	$4.00		
Direct labor	5.00		
Factory overhead	5.00		
Selling and administration	1.00		
Fixed costs per month:			
Factory overhead	$12,000		
Selling and administration	6,000		
Activity level for fixed overhead rate (units)	4,000		

ADDITIONAL INFORMATION

- There were no October 1 inventories.
- Ace uses a normal cost system with variable and fixed overhead each applied at a constant rate per unit manufactured.
- Any monthly under- or overapplied overhead is deferred as an adjustment to inventories.
- Cumulative underapplied overhead was $4,000 on October 1.

REQUIREMENTS

a) Prepare an absorption-costing income statement for each month.

b) Prepare a variable-costing income statement for each month.

c) Reconcile monthly differences between variable- and absorption-costing net income.

9–14 Direct (Variable) Costing for Internal Use

Grisp Company, a manufacturer with heavy investments in property, plant, and equipment, is presently using absorption costing for both external and internal reporting. The management of Grisp Company is considering using the direct-(variable-) costing method for internal reporting only.

REQUIREMENTS

a) What would be the rationale for using the direct-costing method for internal reporting?

b) Assuming that the quantity of ending inventory is higher than the quantity of beginning inventory, would operating income using direct costing be different from operating income using absorption costing? If so, specify if it would be higher or lower. Discuss the rationale for your answer. (CPA Adapted)

PROBLEMS

9–15 Journal Entries for Separate Overhead Accounts: Absorption Costing

The Midwest Processing Company operates a normal cost accounting system with separate control accounts for fixed and variable overhead. During 19x7, the overhead rates for variable and fixed overhead were $2/direct-labor hour and $1/direct-labor hour, respectively. On January 1, Work-in-Process had a balance of $5,000. On December 31, the balance in Work-in-Process was $6,000. Actual costs incurred during 19x7 were:

Purchases of raw materials	$120,000
Raw materials placed in process	90,000
Direct labor	200,000
Supplies*	10,000
Utilities*	30,000
Indirect labor*	50,000
Supervision	30,000
Depreciation	20,000

* All variable.

ADDITIONAL INFORMATION

- Production employees are paid $5/hour.
- Budgeted and actual fixed costs are equal.

REQUIREMENTS

a) Prepare journal entries to record the 19x7 transactions.

b) Determine the amount of over- or underapplied balances in the overhead control accounts.

c) Suggest some possible causes of over- or underapplied overhead.

d) Prepare a Statement of Cost of Goods Manufactured.

9–16 Variable and Absorption Costing: Under- or Overapplied Overhead Written Off

BBG Corporation is a manufacturer of a synthetic element. Gary Voss, President of the company, has been eager to get the operating results for the just completed fiscal year. He was surprised when the income statement revealed that income before taxes had dropped to $885,000 from $900,000 even though sales volume had increased 100,000 kg. This drop in net income had occurred even though Voss had implemented the following changes during the past 12 months to improve the profitability of the company.

- In response to a 10 percent increase in production costs, the sales price of the company's product was increased by 12 percent. This action took place on December 1, 19x1.
- The managements of the selling and administrative departments were given strict instructions to spend no more in fiscal 19x2 than in fiscal 19x1.

BBG's Accounting Department prepared and distributed to top management the following comparative income statements.

BBG Corporation
Statements of Operating Income
For the Years Ended November 30, 19x1 and 19x2
($000 omitted)

	19x1	*19x2*
Sales revenue	$9,000	$11,200
Cost of goods sold	$7,200	$ 8,320
Under- (over-) applied overhead	(600)	495
Adjusted cost of goods sold	−6,600	−8,815
Gross profit	$2,400	$ 2,385
Selling and administrative expenses	−1,500	−1,500
Income before taxes	$ 900	$ 885

The accounting staff also prepared related financial information that is presented in the following schedule to help management evaluate the company's performance. BBG uses the FIFO inventory method for finished goods. Fixed manufacturing overhead is applied on the basis of a production volume of 1,000,000 kg.

BBG Corporation
Selected Operating and Financial Data
For the Years Ended November 30, 19x1 and 19x2

	19x1	*19x2*
Sales price	$10.00/kg.	$11.20/kg.
Material cost	$ 1.50/kg.	$ 1.65/kg.
Direct labor cost	$ 2.50/kg.	$ 2.75/kg.
Variable overhead cost	$ 1.00/kg.	$ 1.10/kg.
Fixed overhead cost	$ 3.00/kg.	$ 3.30/kg.
Total fixed overhead costs	$3,000,000	$3,300,000
Selling and administrative (all fixed)	$1,500,000	$1,500,000
Sales volume	900,000 kg.	1,000,000 kg.
Beginning inventory	300,000 kg.	600,000 kg.

REQUIREMENTS

a) Explain to Gary Voss why BBG Corporation's net income decreased in the current fiscal year despite the sales price and sales volume increases.

b) A member of BBG's Accounting Department has suggested that the company adopt variable (direct) costing for internal reporting purposes.

1. Prepare an operating income statement through income before taxes for the year ended November 30, 19x2, for BBG Corporation using the variable- (direct-) costing method.
2. Present a numerical reconciliation of the difference in income before taxes using the absorption-costing method as currently employed by BBG and the variable- (direct-) costing method as proposed.

c) Identify and discuss the advantages and disadvantages of using the variable- (direct-) costing method for internal reporting purposes. (CMA Adapted)

9–17 Review of High-Low Cost Estimation, CVP Analysis, and Variable and Absorption Costing

Presented are the Ides of March Company's income statements for January and February of 19x3 using a functional format.

Ides of March Company
Income Statements
For the Months of January and February 19x3

	January	*February*
Production and sales (units)	40,000	50,000
Sales revenue	$1,000,000	$1,250,000
Cost of goods manufactured and sold	−525,000	−625,000
Gross profit	$ 475,000	$ 625,000
General and administrative expenses	−235,000	−235,000
Net income before taxes	$ 240,000	$ 390,000
Income taxes at 0.40	−96,000	−156,000
Net income	$ 144,000	$ 234,000

ADDITIONAL INFORMATION

- Ides of March uses an actual cost system.
- General and administrative expenses are all fixed.

REQUIREMENTS

a) Using the high-low method, develop a cost estimating equation for total monthly manufacturing costs.

b) Determine the unit break-even point.

c) Determine the unit sales volume required to earn an after-tax income of $150,000.

d) Prepare a contribution income statement using variable (direct) costing for the month of January.

e) If the January income in the given information differs from that in the solution to part (d), explain why. If they are identical, explain why.

9–18 Alternative Activity Bases for Overhead: Process Costing

Control Standards, Incorporated, manufactures thermostats for residential use on a continuous basis. In the past, they have applied actual overhead costs to the equivalent units manufactured at the end of each month. This procedure has proven satisfactory for product-costing purposes, but management has found the wide fluctuation in unit costs to be confusing, especially when the full cost of units exceeds their selling price. To obtain more accurate information for planning and controlling operations and to avoid the wide fluctuations in unit costs, the controller has agreed to set up a normal cost system with separate overhead rates and control accounts for fixed and variable overhead.

Unfortunately the controller does not have time to perform a detailed analysis of costs because management requires fixed and variable cost estimates in time for a meeting that is scheduled for this afternoon. At the meeting management intends to review its full cost pricing policy and discuss the budget for the coming year, 19x9.

The following summary information is available about two previous years, 19x6 and 19x7:

	19x6	*19x7*
Manufacturing costs:		
Direct materials	$50,000	$90,000
Direct labor	36,000	76,000
Factory overhead	69,000	79,000
Work-in-process (units):		
Beginning	0	2,000*
Started	10,000	18,000
Completed	8,000	20,000
Ending	2,000*	0

* Complete as to materials, 50 percent complete as to conversion.

ADDITIONAL INFORMATION

- Practical capacity is 25,000 units/year.
- Average annual activity is 15,000 units/year.
- Expected activity for 19x9 is 18,000 units.

REQUIREMENTS

a) Prepare a report containing unit cost information that will be useful to management in setting long-run prices and in accepting special orders.

b) Develop the fixed and variable overhead rates that should be used for product costing during the coming year.

c) Suggest two alternative procedures for measuring capacity utilization.

9–19 Variable and Absorption Costing with Tax Considerations

The Roman Wheel Company manufactures a little-known auto, the Centurion. Normal production volume is 100 Centurions per month. For a recent month, when 80 Centurions were manufactured and 110 were sold, the following operating results were reported using absorption costing.

Roman Wheel Company
Income Statement
For the Month Ending 10/31, 19x8

Sales	$1,100,000
Cost of goods sold	−550,000
Gross profit	$ 550,000
Less selling and adm. expenses	−155,000
Net income before taxes	$ 395,000
Less income taxes @ 40%	−158,000
Net income after taxes	$ 237,000

ADDITIONAL INFORMATION

- October overhead was underapplied by $40,000. It is being carried as an asset.
- Variable selling and administrative expenses are $500 per unit.
- Per-unit variable costs are not subject to change.
- Monthly fixed costs are not subject to change.
- There is no beginning or ending work-in-process.

REQUIREMENTS

a) Determine the dollar change between beginning and ending Finished Goods Inventory under absorption costing.

b) Determine the dollar change between beginning and ending Finished Goods Inventory under variable costing.

c) Prepare a variable-costing income statement for the month ending 10/31/x8. The Internal Revenue Service requires the use of absorption costing for determining tax payments. In this part of the problem assume that variable-costing income taxes are $158,000.

d) Reconcile the variable- and absorption-costing net income after taxes.

e) For variable-costing income statements to articulate with cost-volume-profit models that incorporate income taxes, the variable-costing income taxes must be based on variable-costing income before taxes. Any resulting differences between income taxes under absorption costing and income taxes under variable costing are treated as a timing difference and as Deferred Income Tax Expense or Deferred Income Tax Liability until the situation is reversed. The resulting change in these accounts will also have to be analyzed in reconciling the difference between absorption- and variable-costing net income after taxes. Prepare a variable-costing income statement for the month ending 10/31/x8. Base income tax computations on net income before taxes.

f) Reconcile the variable-costing net income after taxes in part (e) with the absorption-costing net income after taxes.

9–20 Cost of Goods Sold Under Variable and Absorption Costing: Process Costing

Norwood Corporation is considering changing its method of inventory valuation from absorption costing to variable costing and engages you to determine the effect of the proposed change on the 19x8 financial statements.

The corporation manufactures Gink, which is sold for $20 per unit. Marsh is added before processing starts, and labor and overhead are added evenly during the manufacturing process. Production capacity is budgeted at 110,000 units of Gink annually. The predetermined overhead rates for 19x8 are:

Variable manufacturing overhead	$1.00 per unit
Fixed manufacturing overhead	1.10 per unit

Each unit of Gink requires four kilograms of Marsh and one direct-labor hour. The price of Marsh has been stable at $0.75/kilogram. Estimated direct-labor costs are $6/hour. Inventory data for 19x8 follow:

	Units	
	January 1	*December 31*
Marsh (kilograms)	200,000	160,000
Work-in-process:		
⅖ processed	10,000	
⅓ processed		15,000
Finished goods	20,000	12,000

During 19x8, 420,000 kilograms of Marsh were purchased and 460,000 kilograms were transferred to work-in-process. Also, 110,000 units of Gink were transferred to finished goods. Actual fixed manufacturing overhead during the year was $121,000. Any under- or overapplied overhead is charged or credited to the Cost of Goods Sold.

REQUIREMENTS

a) Prepare schedules that present the computation of:
   1. Equivalent units of production for material and conversion
   2. Number of units sold
   3. Amount, if any, of over- or underapplied fixed manufacturing overhead
b) Prepare a comparative statement of Cost of Goods Sold using variable costing and absorption costing. (CPA Adapted)

9–21 Multiple Product Profit-Volume Graphs With Variable and Absorption Costing

The Extant Glove Company manufactures a high-quality dishwashing glove called the Super Glove. The glove is well known, but its relatively high retail price provides definite market limits. Extant currently manufactures and sells 30,000 pairs of Super Gloves per month at an f.o.b. factory price of $1/pair. The current absorption cost per pair is:

Material	$0.20
Labor	0.20
Variable overhead	0.10
Fixed overhead	0.30
Total	$0.80

Extant also incurs selling costs of $0.10/pair sold.

To broaden its market appeal, Extant wants to introduce a new lower-priced glove, called "Hand Jive." Management anticipates that the f.o.b. factory price of a pair of Hand Jives will be $0.75. Variable manufacturing costs are expected to be $0.45/pair and selling costs will be $0.10/pair. The monthly fixed costs of manufacturing Hand Jives are estimated to be $5,000. This will increase total fixed manufacturing costs by $5,000, but it will not affect the absorption cost of Super Gloves.

Management is concerned that the products will be regarded as substitutes in the market and they have requested you to analyze the impact of product substitutions on Extant's monthly profits.

REQUIREMENTS

a) Develop a profit-volume graph to indicate Extant's monthly range of break-even unit sales volumes assuming they produce both Super Gloves and Hand Jive gloves.

b) Assuming that management expects to sell 30,000 pairs of Hand Jives, determine the number of pairs of Super Gloves they must sell to obtain their previous monthly profits.

c) During the first month of Hand Jives production, 30,000 Super Gloves were produced and 20,000 Super Gloves were sold. For Super Gloves only:

1. Determine absorption-costing net income when under- or overapplied overhead is deferred.
2. Determine absorption-costing net income when under- or overapplied overhead is written off against the related product line revenues.
3. Determine variable-costing net income.

9–22 Absorption Costing and Performance Evaluation

On July 2, 19x6, Go Go Incorporated acquired 90 percent of the outstanding stock of Medioker Industries in exchange for 2,000 shares of its own stock. Go Go Incorporated has a reputation as a "high flier." (Its stock has a high price/earnings ratio and its management team "works wonders" in improving the performance of ailing companies.)

At the time of the acquisition, Medioker was producing and selling at an annual rate of 100,000 units/year. This is in line with the firm's average annual activity. Fifty thousand units were produced during the first half of 19x6.

Immediately after the takeover, Go Go installed its own management team and increased production to practical capacity. One hundred thousand units were produced during the second half of 19x6.

At the end of the year, the new management declared another dramatic turn around and a $500,000 cash dividend when the following set of income statements were issued:

Medioker Industries
Income Statement
For the First and Second Six Months of 19x6

	First	*Second*	*Total*
Sales	$1,500,000	$1,500,000	$3,000,000
Cost of goods sold*	−1,200,000	− 700,000	−1,900,000
Gross profit	$ 300,000	$ 800,000	$1,100,000
Other expenses	− 200,000	− 400,000	− 600,000
Net income	$ 100,000	$ 400,000	$ 500,000

* Medioker Industries accounting reports now follow their parent company's practice of writing off all under- or overapplied overhead as an adjustment to the Cost of Goods Sold.

REQUIREMENT

As the only representative of the minority interest on the board of directors, evaluate the performance of the new management team.

9–23 Relevant and Absorption Costing for Performance Evaluation[6]

The B. E. Company uses an actual cost system for applying all production costs incurred during, or allocated to, a period to the units produced. Although the plant has a maximum production capacity of 40,000,000 units, only 17,000,000 units were produced and sold during 19x1. There were no beginning or ending inventories.

The B. E. Company income statement for 19x1 is as follows:

B. E. Company
Income Statement
For the Year Ending December 31, 19x1

Sales (17,000,000 units × $2.00)		$34,000,000
Cost of goods sold:		
Variable (17,000,000 × $1.00)	$17,000,000	
Fixed	8,400,000	−25,400,000
Gross profit		$ 8,600,000
Selling and administrative expenses:		
Variable (17,000,000 × $0.50)	$ 8,500,000	
Fixed	600,000	−9,100,000
Net income (loss)		$ (500,000)

[6] Adapted from "Asset Recognition and Economic Attributes—The Relevant Costing Approach," by George H. Sorter and Charles T. Horngren, *Accounting Review* **38,** No. 3 (July 1962): 391–399, with permission.

The board of directors has approached an outside executive to take over the company. He is an optimistic soul, and so he agrees to become president for a token salary plus a year-end bonus amounting to 10 percent of net income (before considering the bonus).

The new president promptly raised the advertising budget by $3,500,000 and stepped up production to an annual rate of 30,000,000 units. Sales for 19x2 increased to 25,000,000 units. The resulting B. E. Company income statement for 19x2 is as follows:

B. E. Company
Income Statement
For the Year Ending December 31, 19x2

Sales (25,000,000 × $2.00)			$50,000,000
Cost of goods sold:			
Cost of goods manufactured:			
Variable (30,000,000 × $1)	$30,000,000		
Fixed	8,400,000	$38,400,000	
Less ending inventory			
((5,000,000/30,000,000) × $38,400,000)		−6,400,000	−32,000,000
Gross profit			$18,000,000
Selling and administrative expenses:			
Variable (25,000,000 × $0.50)		$12,500,000	
Fixed ($600,000 + $3,500,000)		4,100,000	−16,600,000
Net income before bonus			$ 1,400,000
Bonus			− 140,000
Net income			$ 1,260,000

The day after the statement was verified, the president took his check for $140,000 and resigned to take a job with another corporation. The president remarked, "I enjoy challenges. Now that B. E. Company is in the black, I'd prefer tackling another knotty situation." (His contract with his new employer is similar to the one he had with B. E. Company.)

REQUIREMENTS

a) As a member of the board of directors, comment on the 19x2 income statement.

b) Professors Sorter and Horngren argue that fixed costs should only be inventoried if they will favorably affect future income. This may occur under two circumstances:

  - Variable production costs are expected to rise in the future. In this case, production now avoids higher variable costs later and current fixed costs may be inventoried up to the amount of the expected increase in variable production costs times the number of unsold units produced in this period.
  - Future sales will exceed productive capacity. In this case, current fixed costs may be inventoried up to the amount of the future unit sales that would be lost if the current ending inventory was not available times the unit contribution margin.

  Following these rules, determine B. E.'s 19x2 ending inventory and net income before bonus in each of the following independent situations:

1. Expected sales for 19x3 equal 30,000,000 units.
2. Expected sales for 19x3 equal 45,000,000 units.
3. Expected sales for 19x3 equal 20,000,000 units. Variable production costs are expected to increase to $1.10.

c) Evaluate the propriety of using the rules stated in part (b) for performance evaluation and external reporting.

9–24 Product Line Reporting and Special Decisions

Olat Corporation produces three gauges. These gauges measure density, permeability, and thickness and are known as D-gauges, P-gauges, and T-gauges, respectively. For many years the company has been profitable and has operated at capacity. However, in the last two years, prices on all gauges were reduced and selling expenses increased to meet competition and keep the plant operating at full capacity. The following third-quarter results are representative of recent experiences.

Olat Corporation
Income Statement
Third Quarter 19x3
($000 omitted)

	D-Gauge	*P-Gauge*	*T-Gauge*	*Total*
Sales	$900	$1,600	$900	$3,400
Cost of goods sold	−770	−1,048	−950	−2,768
Gross profit	$130	$ 552	$ (50)	$ 632
Selling and administrative expenses	−185	− 370	−135	− 690
Income before income taxes	$ (55)	$ 182	$(185)	$ (58)

Mel Carlo, President, is very concerned about the results of the pricing, selling, and production policies. After reviewing the third-quarter results he announced that he would ask his management staff to consider a course of action that includes the following three suggestions.

- Discontinue the T-gauge line immediately. T-gauges would not be returned to the line of products unless the problems with the gauge can be identified and resolved.
- Increase quarterly sales promotion by $100,000 on the P-gauge product line in order to increase sales volume 15 percent.
- Cut production on the D-gauge line by 50 percent, a quantity sufficient to meet the demand of customers who purchase P-gauges. In addition, the direct advertising and promotion for this line would be cut to $20,000 each quarter.

George Sperry, Controller, suggested that a more careful study of the financial relationships be made to determine the possible effect on the company's operating results as a consequence of the president's proposed course of action. The president agreed and JoAnn Brower, Assistant Controller, was assigned to prepare an analysis. To do so, she gathered the following information.

- All three gauges are manufactured with common equipment and facilities.
- The quarterly general selling and administrative expenses of $170,000 are allocated to the three gauge lines in proportion to their dollar sales volume.
- Special selling expenses (primarily advertising, promotion, and shipping) are incurred for each gauge as follows.

	Quarterly advertising and promotion	Shipping expense
D-gauge	$100,000	$ 4 per unit
P-gauge	210,000	10 per unit
T-gauge	40,000	10 per unit

- The unit manufacturing costs for the three products are as follows:

	D-gauge	*P-gauge*	*T-gauge*
Direct materials	$17	$ 31	$ 50
Direct labor	20	40	60
Variable manufacturing overhead	30	45	60
Fixed manufacturing overhead	10	15	20
Total	$77	$131	$190

- The unit sales prices for the three products are as follows.

D-gauge	$ 90
P-gauge	200
T-gauge	180

- The company is manufacturing at capacity and is selling all the gauges it produces.

REQUIREMENTS

a) JoAnn Brower has suggested that the Olat Corporation's product-line income statement as presented for the third quarter of 19x3 is not suitable for analyzing proposals and making decisions such as the ones suggested by Mel Carlo.

1. Explain why the product-line income statement as presented is not suitable for analysis and decision making.
2. Describe an alternative income statement format that would be more suitable for analysis and decision making, and explain why it is better.

b) Use the operating data presented for Olat Corporation and assume that President Mel Carlo's proposed course of action had been implemented at the beginning of the third quarter of 19x3. Then evaluate the president's proposed course of action by specifically responding to the following points:

1. Are each of the three suggestions cost effective? Support your discussion by a differential analysis that shows the net impact on income before taxes for each of the three suggestions.
2. Was the president correct to eliminate the T-gauge line? Explain your answer.
3. Was the president correct to promote the P-gauge line rather than the D-gauge line? Explain your answer.

4. Does the proposed course of action make effective use of Olat's capacity? Explain your answer.

c) Are there any nonquantitative factors that Olat Corporation should consider before it drops the T-gauge line? Explain your answer. (CMA Adapted)

9–25 Product Line Reporting and Special Decisions

Pralina Products Company has three major product lines: cereals, breakfast bars, and dog food. The income statement for the year ended April 30, 19x8, is as follows (the statement was prepared by product line using absorption [full] costing):

Pralina Products Company
Income Statement
For the Year Ended April 30, 19x8
(000 omitted)

	Cereals	*Breakfast bars*	*Dog food*	*Total*
Sales in pounds	2,000	500	500	3,000
Revenue from sales	$1,000	$400	$200	$1,600
Cost of sales:				
Direct materials	$ 330	$160	$100	$ 590
Direct labor	90	40	20	150
Factory overhead	108	48	24	180
Total cost of sales	− 528	− 248	− 144	− 920
Gross profit	$ 472	$152	$ 56	$ 680
Operating expenses:				
Selling expenses:				
Advertising	$ 50	$ 30	$ 20	$ 100
Commissions	50	40	20	110
Salaries and related benefits	30	20	10	60
Total selling expenses:	$ 130	$ 90	$ 50	$ 270
General and administrative expenses:				
Licenses	$ 50	$ 20	$ 15	$ 85
Salaries and related benefits	60	25	15	100
Total general and administrative expenses	110	45	30	185
Total operating expenses	− 240	− 135	− 80	− 455
Operating income before taxes	$ 232	$ 17	$ (24)	$ 225

ADDITIONAL INFORMATION

- *Cost of sales.* All three products are produced with common facilities. The company's inventories of raw materials and finished products do not vary significantly from year to year. The inventories at April 30, 19x8, were essentially identical to those at April 30, 19x7.

Factory overhead was applied to products at 120 percent of direct-labor dollars. The factory overhead costs for the 19x7–x8 fiscal year were as follows:

Variable indirect labor and supplies	$ 15,000
Variable employee benefits on factory labor	30,000
Supervisory salaries and related benefits	35,000
Plant occupancy costs	100,000
Total	$180,000

There was no overapplied or underapplied overhead at year end.

- *Advertising*. The company has been unable to determine any direct causal relationship between the level of sales volume and the level of advertising expenditures. However, because management believes advertising is necessary, an annual advertising program is implemented for each product line. Each product line is advertised independently of the others.
- *Commissions*. Sales commissions are paid to the sales force at the rates of 5 percent on the cereals and 10 percent on the breakfast bars and dog food.
- *Licenses*. Various licenses are required for each product line. These are renewed annually for each product line.
- *Salaries and related benefits*. Sales and general and administrative personnel devote time and effort to each product line and the company as a whole. Salaries and wages are allocated on the basis of management's estimates of the relative time spent on each product line. These costs are related to the company's overall activities rather than to any product line.

REQUIREMENT

The controller of Pralina Products Company has recommended the company do a cost-volume-profit analysis of its operations. The controller has requested that you first prepare a revised income statement for Pralina Products Company that employs a product contribution margin format that will be useful in cost-volume-profit analysis. The statement should show the profit contribution for each product line and the net income before taxes for the company as a whole.

(CMA Adapted)

9–26 Product Line Reporting and Special Decisions

The Scio Division of Georgetown, Inc., manufactures and sells four related product lines. Presented is a product-line profitability statement for the year ended December 31, 19x7, which shows a loss for the baseball equipment line. A similar loss is projected for 19x8.

The management of Georgetown, Inc., has requested a profitability study of the baseball equipment line to determine if the line should be discontinued. The marketing department of the Scio Division and the accounting department at the plant, where all Scio Division products are manufactured, have developed the following additional data to be used in the study:

1. If the baseball equipment line is discontinued, the company will lose approximately 10 percent of its sales in each of the other lines.

2. The equipment now used in the manufacture of baseball equipment is quite specialized. Although the annual depreciation on the baseball equipment is $115,000, the equipment has a current salvage value of only $105,000 and a remaining useful life of five years. This equipment cannot be used elsewhere in the company.
3. The company has been able to invest excess funds at 10 percent per annum. If the baseball equipment is sold, any proceeds will be invested at 10 percent.
4. The plant space now occupied by the baseball equipment line could be closed off from the rest of the plant and rented for $175,000 per year.
5. If the line is discontinued, the supervisor of the baseball equipment line, whose $30,000 salary is included in the baseball lines fixed overhead, will be released.
6. All fixed manufacturing costs except salaries of the line supevisors and depreciation are common to all four product lines.
7. The fixed selling expenses are common to all products.

Scio Division
Product Line Profitability
For the Year Ending December 31, 19x7
(000 omitted)

	Football equipment	*Baseball equipment*	*Hockey equipment*	*Miscellaneous sports items*	*Total*
Sales	$2,200	$1,000	$1,500	$ 500	$5,200
Cost of goods sold:					
Material	$ 400	$ 175	$ 300	$ 90	$ 965
Labor and variable overhead	800	400	600	60	1,860
Fixed overhead	350	275	100	50	775
Total	−1,550	− 850	−1,000	− 200	−3,600
Gross profit	$ 650	$ 150	$ 500	$ 300	$1,600
Selling expenses:					
Variable	$ 440	$ 200	$ 300	$ 100	$1,040
Fixed	100	50	100	50	300
Corporate administration expenses	48	24	36	12	120
Total selling and administration	− 588	− 274	− 436	− 162	−1,460
Product contribution	$ 62	$ (124)	$ 64	$ 138	$ 140

REQUIREMENTS

a) Should Georgetown, Inc., discontinue the baseball equipment line? Support your answer with appropriate calculations and qualitative arguments.

b) A member of the board of directors of Georgetown, Inc., has inquired whether the information regarding the discontinuance of product lines should be included in the financial statements on a regular monthly basis for all product lines. Draft a memorandum in response to the board member's inquiry. Your memorandum should:

1. State why or why not this information should be included in the regular monthly financial statements distributed to the board.
2. Detail the reasons for your response.

(CMA Adapted)

SOLUTION TO REVIEW PROBLEM

At a monthly production volume of 50,000 units the absorption cost is $22 per unit:

Direct materials	$ 5
Direct labor	5
Variable factory overhead	10
Fixed factory overhead ($100,000/50,000)	2
Absorption cost/unit	$22

Regardless of the monthly production volume the variable cost is $20 per unit:

Direct materials	$ 5
Direct labor	5
Variable factory overhead	10
Variable cost/unit	$20

a) **Greco Corporation**
Functional Income Statements: Absorption Costing
For the First Three Months of 19y8

	January	*February*	*March*
Sales (@ $30)	$900,000	$1,500,000	$2,100,000
Cost of goods sold (@ $22)	−660,000	−1,100,000	−1,540,000
Gross profit	$240,000	$ 400,000	$ 560,000
Selling and admin. expenses:			
Variable (@ $3)	$ 90,000	$ 150,000	$ 210,000
Fixed	40,000	40,000	40,000
Total	−130,000	−190,000	−250,000
Net income	$110,000	$ 210,000	$ 310,000

b) **Greco Corporation**
Contribution Income Statements: Variable Costing
For the First Three Months of 19y8

	January	*February*	*March*
Sales (@ $30)	$900,000	$1,500,000	$2,100,000
Variable expenses:			
Cost of goods sold (@ $20)	$600,000	$1,000,000	$1,400,000
Selling and admin. (@ $3)	90,000	150,000	210,000
Total	−690,000	−1,150,000	−1,610,000
Contribution margin	$210,000	$ 350,000	$ 490,000
Fixed expenses:			
Manufacturing	$100,000	$ 100,000	$ 100,000
Selling and admin.	40,000	40,000	40,000
Total	−140,000	−140,000	−140,000
Net income	$ 70,000	$ 210,000	$ 350,000

c) **Greco Corporation**
Reconciliation of Variable- and Absorption-Costing Net Income
For the First Three Months of 19y8

	January	*February*	*March*
Variable-costing net income	$ 70,000	$210,000	$350,000
January increase in deferred fixed costs (20,000 × $2)	40,000		
February		0	
March decrease in deferred fixed costs (20,000 × $2)			(40,000)
Absorption-costing net income	$110,000	$210,000	$310,000

10 The Master Budget

INTRODUCTION
TYPES OF PLANNING
OBJECTIVES OF BUDGETING
APPROACHES TO BUDGETING
REQUIREMENTS FOR AN EFFECTIVE BUDGET
BUILDING BLOCKS
ASSEMBLING THE MASTER BUDGET
ADDITIONAL CONSIDERATIONS
SUMMARY
APPENDIX: EXTENDED EXAMPLE

INTRODUCTION

A BUDGET IS A FORMAL PLAN OF ACTION EXPRESSED IN MONETARY TERMS. A budget can be drawn up for an entire organization, any segment of the organization such as a department or sales territory or division, or for a significant activity such as the production and sale of a specific product. A budget developed for an entire organization is called a **master budget**. Because master budgets must consider all interrelationships that exist between organizational subunits, they are considerably more complex than budgets developed for business segments or specific activities.

The purpose of this chapter is to examine the concepts, relationships, and procedures used in developing an organization's master budget. This chapter, like the budgeting process itself, is a pivot point in studying the ongoing planning and control activities of an organization. The accounting model of the firm, as represented by general-purpose financial statements, provides an overall framework for studying planning and control activities. This framework was introduced in a previous course. In previous chapters of this book we continued by studying how costs behave and flow through an organization's accounting records, by studying procedures for estimating how costs respond to changing conditions, by examining short-run planning models, and by noting fundamental differences between the behavior of fixed costs and the way they are reported in general-purpose financial statements. We are now ready to put all this knowledge together as we develop a single, coordinated plan of action for an entire organization, the master budget. In subsequent chapters the master budget will serve as a basis of performance evaluation in order to (1) ensure that operations, to the extent desirable, proceed according to plan; and (2) alert management to changes that should be incorporated into future plans.

A significant difference between the product-costing topics studied in previous chapters and the development of an annual budget is that the former is oriented to reporting the financial consequences of past activities, whereas the latter is

EXHIBIT 10–1 The Use of Product Costing Relationships in Budgeting

(a) Product costing follows the actual sequence of production activities.

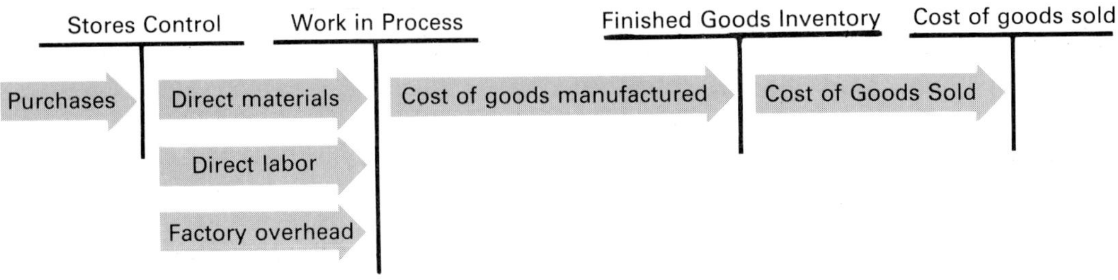

(b) Budgeting starts with forecasted sales and determines needed resources.

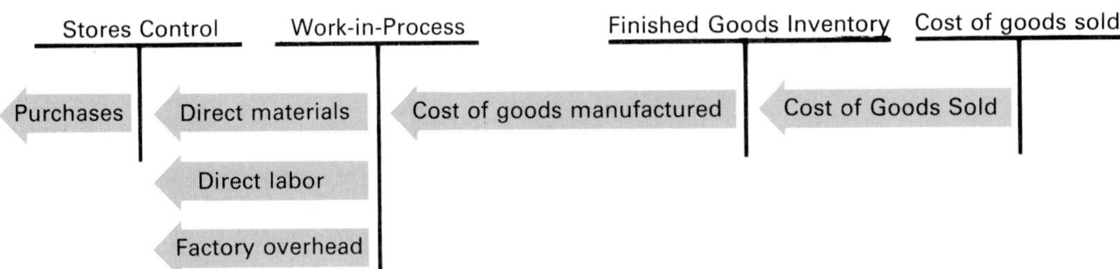

oriented to predicting the financial consequences of proposed future activities. However, the account relationships underlying product costing are used to budget manufacturing costs. The use of account relationships in product costing and budgeting activities is illustrated in Exhibit 10–1. In product costing, the starting point is the acquisition of raw materials and the ending point is the determination of the cost of goods sold. When we budget manufacturing costs, our starting point is the prediction of the cost of sales required for the budgeted sales volume and our ending point is the budgeting of manufacturing resources needed to support production.

TYPES OF PLANNING

Successful organizations engage in different types of planning at various levels of management. The broadest and most pervasive type of planning, called **strategic planning,** deals with such fundamental issues as the long-range goals and characteristics of the organization. It attempts to answer such questions as: Why does the organization exist? What is our product or service? Who are our customers? How large do we want to be? Strategic planning is performed on an irregular basis by the highest levels of management. This is a job for the president and the board of directors. Lower levels of management do not have time to engage in strategic planning; they accept the organization's strategic plan as a constraint. Courses in business policy and entrepreneurship typically deal with strategic planning issues.

Within the framework of the organization's strategic plan, **long-range planning** is concerned with the identification and selection of major courses of action that will achieve the strategic plan. The evaluation of socioeconomic data, forecasting long-range demand, evaluating major investment proposals for new plant and equipment, and planning to introduce or discontinue major products are all part of long-range planning. Tentative budget projections for several years may also be included in the plan. Long-range planning is performed by upper management and by the corporate staff. It may be done annually or on an irregular basis every few years. Courses in economics, finance, marketing, and cost accounting typically deal with long-range planning.

The master budget is the organization's formal plan of action for the coming year. It encompasses all areas of responsibility within the organization. Included within the master budget are separate budgets for each area of responsibility within the organization. Because it is developed within the framework of the long-range plan, the master budget accepts such variables as the organization's objectives, customers, products, plant, equipment, and agreed upon plans for new investments or major product line changes as given. Although the controller often coordinates the development of the master budget, the budget belongs to the operating managers who develop it and must implement it. Courses in cost accounting and management accounting deal with budgeting.

After the master budget is adopted, first line managers engage in **operations scheduling**, the weekly and daily (perhaps hourly) assignment of salespersonnel to potential customers, assignment of jobs to specific machines and workers, and procurement of resources. Production, management science, and operations research courses traditionally deal with operations scheduling.

OBJECTIVES OF BUDGETING

Operating managers frequently regard budgeting as a time-consuming task that diverts attention from current problems. Indeed, the development of an effective budget is a hard job. It is also a necessary one. Organizations that do not plan ahead are likely to wander aimlessly and ultimately succumb to the swirl of current events. To help ensure both survival and success, the formal development of a budget (1) compels planning, (2) promotes communication and coordination, (3) provides a guide to action, and (4) provides a basis for performance evaluation.

Compels Planning

Formal budgeting procedures compel people to think about the future. Without formal procedures, many busy operating managers would not find time to plan. Immediate needs would consume all available time. Formal budgeting procedures, with specified deadlines, force managers to plan for the future by making the completion of the budget another immediate need.

Promotes Communication and Coordination

When operating responsibilities are divided, it is difficult to synchronize activities. Production must know what marketing intends to sell. Purchasing and personnel must know the factory's material and labor requirements. The treasurer must plan to ensure the availability of the cash required to support receivables, inventories, and capital expenditures. Budgeting forces the managers of these diverse functions to communicate their plans and coordinate their activities. It helps ensure that plans are feasible (for example, production can produce the quantities and types of products marketing intends to sell), and that they are synchronized (for example, inventory is produced in advance of an advertising campaign).

Provides a Guide to Action

Once the budget is approved, the various operating managers know what is expected of them and they can set about doing it. If employees do not have a guide to action, their efforts may be wasted on unproductive or even counter-productive activities. If management expects nothing, it will get nothing.

Provides a Basis for Performance Evaluation

Once employees know what the budget is and accept it as a guide to action, they should be held responsible for their portion of the budget. When results do not conform to plans, managers attempt to determine the cause of the divergence. This is an important part of **management by exception**, whereby management directs attention to only those activities not proceeding according to plan. Significantly, management does not seek an explanation of performance that is in line with plans. Without the budget as a basis of performance evaluation, management may spend an inordinate amount of time seeking an explanation of past activities and telling employees what they should have done.

APPROACHES TO BUDGETING

The budgeting process is characterized as authoritative, consultative, or participative, on the basis of the amount and type of employee involvement. Following the **authoritative** (or **autocratic**) **approach to budgeting**, top management develops the final budget without consulting employees at lower management levels. This approach is usually found in organizations that have centralized decision making and well-defined lines of authority and responsibility. The authoritative approach is based on the **Theory X** view of motivation which assumes that work is inherently distasteful and people avoid work, lack creativity, and must be motivated to work by economic rewards.

The authoritative approach may be adequate in organizations with established and stable products, technology, and markets, but it is inefficient in organizations where top management is not completely familiar with all aspects of current operations. Additionally, under the authoritative approach, there is no assurance that employees, especially those whose basic economic needs have been satisfied, will accept the budget as their guide to action. Indeed, employees may fight the budget's implementation by claiming it is an unrealistic, top management dream.

Under the **consultative approach to budgeting**, top management develops the final budget after consulting employees regarding important aspects of current operations and their projections for the future. Although this consultation may be extensive, the final budget is set by top management without the formal agreement of employees who must implement it.

Under the **participative** (or **democratic**) **approach to budgeting** all levels of management actively participate in the development of the budget and the budgeting process continues until everyone accepts the final budget. The objectives of the participative approach are to obtain a realistic budget and an environment in which all managers have a better understanding of each other and the organization. The participative approach is based on the **Theory Y** view of motivation which assumes that work is natural, people are creative, and people are motivated to work by a variety of needs. By embodying employees' personal goals in organizational goals, participative budgeting is said to satisfy the personal needs of employees, develop organizational loyalty, and promote organizational vitality.

The participative approach may be well suited to changing environments, but it is time consuming and it can result in consensus management and dissipated responsibility as employees attempt to reconcile widely divergent views. However, the participative approach can lead to excessive politicking and empire building within the organization.

There is no single correct approach to budgeting. The best approach will vary from organization to organization; what's more, the best approach within a single organization may change over time.

REQUIREMENTS FOR AN EFFECTIVE BUDGET

As can be gleaned from the preceding paragraphs, the budgeting process is fraught with behavioral implications. Although a complete discussion of these implications is beyond the scope of this book, the topic cannot be avoided in discussions of budgeting or performance evaluation. Accordingly, some behavioral topics will be mentioned in the discussion of the requirements for an **effective budget**, that is, a budget with a high probability of successful implementation that will move the organization toward its long-run goals. A number of conditions must be met for a budget to be effective:

- The organization must have a set of overall goals.
- The organization's goal(s) must be decomposed into meaningful subgoals.
- The subgoals must be congruent with the organization's overall goal(s) and with each other.
- Employees must accept the subgoals and not feel threatened by them.
- The budget must be tied to some feedback or performance evaluation procedure.

Overall Goals

The basic requirement for an effective budget is that the organization (really its dominant members) have an overall goal or set of overall goals for the budget period. These overall goals must be quantifiable and they must be based on the organization's strategic and long-range plans. Possible overall goals include the attainment of a market share, sales volume, or net income.

Goal Decomposition

To provide meaningful guidelines for action, the organization's overall goal(s) must be broken down into subgoals. Stating that the organization's overall goal is a 5 percent increase in after-tax income provides little guidance to a salesperson or production supervisor. As we descend the organization chart, the goals of each level must become more specific. Typical subgoals might include sales quotas by product for a marketing territory and production quotas for a factory. Where possible, subgoals should also be stated in terms of **standard costs**, that is, allowable costs per unit of work. In a factory, a standard cost can be viewed as a budget for a single unit. Standard costs are discussed in the next section of this chapter.

Goal Congruence

Subgoals must be specified in a manner that helps the organization attain its overall goals. It would, for example, be undesirable to specify the output of a foundry in terms of tons of nails. The result might be hundreds of tons of unsold spikes while the demand for finishing nails went unfilled.

The subgoals must also be congruent with each other. An effective budget must coordinate the activities of the organization and not cause unnecessary internal conflicts. The marketing department's desire to fill a rush order (to increase sales volume) may conflict with the production department's desire to manufacture units in long production runs (to reduce setup costs). Rush orders that interrupt the normal scheduling of work may cause actual manufacturing costs to exceed standard costs. The net result is that production resists rush orders and marketing seeks them. A solution to this particular problem is sometimes found by charging the marketing department for extra production costs resulting from the acceptance of a rush order.

In developing subgoals, management must also consider the long-run objectives of the organization. Excessive pressure to meet current goals may lead to actions that prevent the organization from achieving its long-run goals. If, for example, excessive pressure is placed on the production department to meet current production volumes at current standard costs, product quality may suffer. The long-run effect may be a decline in sales.

Acceptance

Employees who do not accept the subgoals or feel threatened by the budgeting process may react in a manner that negates much of the value of budgeting. Such employees may argue that cost overruns are meaningless or they may attempt to develop a loose budget that makes the attainment of their subgoals relatively easy. This latter tack is accomplished by intentionally understating expected sales volume or overstating expected costs. The result is **budgetary slack.** The desire to maintain budgetary slack, in departments with many discretionary fixed costs, occasionally leads to a spending spree near the end of the budget period. Managers of departments with discretionary fixed costs often fear that a failure to spend their budget will result in a smaller budget for the next period.

Acceptance of the budget requires that employees regard the procedures used to establish the budget as legitimate. Employees must also believe the budget reflects actual capabilities. This argues against the use of excessively tight standards or application of the **ratchet principle**, whereby any increase in productivity automatically results in a new standard.

Feedback

Feedback in the form of performance reports is essential if the budgeting process is to be effective over an extended period of time. Employees need to know how current results compare with plans in order to make appropriate adjustments during the current period and to improve plans for the future. Employees will regard the budgeting process as irrelevant if they are not provided with feedback and held accountable for deviations from the budget. The implication of not providing feedback or not inquiring as to the cause of deviations is that top management does not really care about the budget or the budgeting process.

BUILDING BLOCKS

The building blocks used in constructing a budget consist of a number of statements or assumptions about revenues, input/output relationships, capacity constraints, costs, inventory policy, and cash flows. The revenue assumptions deal with expected unit sales and selling prices. The input/output relationships consider the materials, labor, overhead, and other resources required to produce and distribute a unit of product or service. The capacity constraints recognize the maximum production capacity of the plant and other resources expected to be available during the budget period. The costs include those associated with manufacturing, selling, administration, and other activities, such as research and development. The cash flow assumptions deal with the length of time between sales and cash receipts and between the acquisition of resources and payments.

Standard Costs

The most basic building block in a manufacturing firm is the standard cost per unit of work performed. As previously stated, a standard cost is a budget for one unit. The standard cost for each unit of finished goods is determined by multiplying and summing standard quantities and standard costs for direct materials, direct labor, and factory overhead. For the example presented later in this chapter, the standard cost per unit of finished goods is as follows:

	Standard quantity of inputs		*Standard cost per unit of input*	*Total*
Direct materials	5 square meters	×	\$3.00	\$15.00
Direct labor	0.5 direct-labor hours	×	\$10.00	5.00
Variable factory overhead	0.5 direct-labor hours	×	\$18.00	9.00
Fixed factory overhead	0.5 direct-labor hours	×	\$12.00	6.00
Standard cost per unit of finished goods				\$35.00

The fixed factory overhead rate was computed as predicted annual fixed factory overhead, \$720,000, divided by predicted annual direct-labor hours, 60,000. While the resulting fixed factory overhead rate of \$12 per direct-labor hour should not be used for budgeting manufacturing costs, the fixed factory overhead rate is used to construct budgeted absorption-costing income statements and balance sheets.

Development Unit standard costs for direct materials, direct labor, and variable factory overhead should be the same as the predicted unit costs used in Chapters 7 through 9. They are developed on the basis of engineering estimates or from an analysis of historical cost data adjusted for expected changes in the product, production technology, and costs. Because of the manner of their development, some uncertainty surrounds their use. Even though standard costs represent the expected value of future costs, management knows that even under normal operating conditions it is unlikely that actual costs will exactly equal standard costs. The budgeting implications of this uncertainty were explored in the context of cost-volume-profit analysis in the appendix to Chapter 8. The implications of this uncertainty for performance evaluation are explored in Chapter 19.

Uses Standard costs have three uses:

1. Standard costs aid in budgeting.
2. Standard costs aid in performance evaluation.
3. Standard costs reduce the complexity of product costing and inventory valuation.

In this chapter we will use standard costs in budgeting. We will consider how standard costs can be used for performance evaluation in Chapters 11, 12, and 19. Finally, we will consider the use of standard costs for product costing in Chapter 14.

To obtain the full benefit of standard costs, the standards must be based on realistic expectations. Managers occasionally set "tight" standards in an effort to motivate employees toward higher levels of productivity. If this is done, these "tight" or "motivating" standards should not be used to budget input requirements and cash flows—management expects to use more units of resources than the standards allow. If cash flows are forecast on the basis of tight standards, management may underestimate the organization's cash needs. The use of tight standards may also have undesirable behavioral effects if employees find that another set of standards is used in the "real" budget, or if they are constantly subjected to unfavorable performance reports.

ASSEMBLING THE MASTER BUDGET

The standard sequence of assembling the annual budget is as follows:

1. Obtain a sales budget for the period.
2. Develop a production budget to meet the sales budget.
3. Develop a manufacturing cost budget with separate categories for direct materials, direct labor, and factory overhead.
4. Develop a purchases budget to meet the needs of the factory.
5. Develop a selling and administrative expense budget.
6. Develop a budgeted income statement.
7. Develop a budgeted statement of changes in retained earnings.
8. Develop a cash budget, including an analysis of receivables and payables.
9. Develop a budgeted statement of financial position as of the end of the budget period.

The interrelationships between these steps are illustrated in Exhibit 10–2. They are explained as we develop a budget for McDonald Products Company.

EXHIBIT 10–2 Assembling the Master Budget: Manufacturing Organization

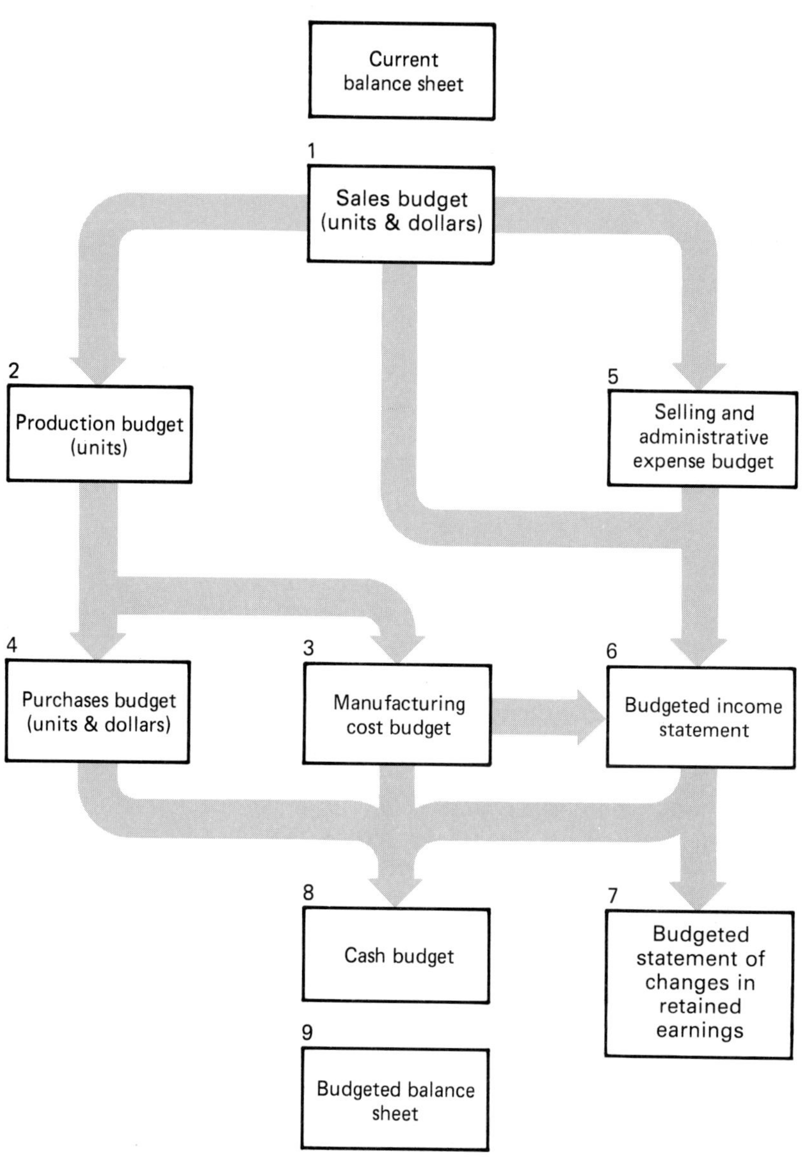

Throughout the remainder of this chapter we will be developing a January 19x2 budget for the McDonald Products Company, which produces a single product whose standard cost was presented previously. Before we start to plan where we are going, we must know where we are. Much information on the current status of an organization is contained in its statement of financial position (balance sheet) at the start of the budget period. McDonald's December 31, 19x1, statement of financial position is presented in Exhibit 10–3.

EXHIBIT 10–3 McDonald's Statement of Financial Position

McDonald Products Company
Statement of Financial Position
December 31, 19x1

ASSETS		
Cash		$ 300,000
Accounts receivable (all from December sales)		250,000
Inventories:		
Raw materials (9,600 units × $3)	$ 28,800	
Finished goods (1,800 units × $35)	63,000	91,800
Fixed assets:		
Cost	$2,000,000	
Less: Accumulated depreciation	– 450,000	1,550,000
Total assets		$2,191,800
EQUITIES		
Accounts payable (all for December purchases)		$ 40,000
Taxes payable (all for December income)		25,000
Capital stock ($10 par)		500,000
Paid-in-capital in excess of par		600,000
Retained earnings		1,026,800
Total equities		$2,191,800

Sales Budget

For-profit organizations achieve their goals by producing a product or providing a service that is salable to customers. Because for-profit organizations are market oriented, the first step in developing a for-profit organization's annual budget is to develop a **sales budget** outlining planned unit and dollar sales for the budget period. All other elements in the budget depend on the sales forecast because they either exist to support sales or they result from sales. Assume that McDonald's marketing personnel have developed the following sales budget for the first quarter of 19x2 with a unit selling price of $50:

SALES BUDGET (SCHEDULE 1)

	January	*February*	*March*
Unit sales	9,000	12,000	16,000
Dollar sales (@ $50)	$450,000	$600,000	$800,000

Production Budget

The **production budget** is used to determine the number of units of finished goods that must be produced to meet budgeted sales and ending inventory requirements. The production requirements of a period are computed as the budgeted unit sales plus the desired units in ending inventory less the units available at the start of the period.

On December 31, 19x1, McDonald has 1,800 units of finished goods. Assuming management desires ending inventory equal to 20 percent of the following month's budgeted sales, McDonald's production budget for January and February is as follows:

PRODUCTION BUDGET (SCHEDULE 2)

	January	*February*	*March*
Budgeted unit sales	9,000	12,000	16,000
Desired ending inventory	+2,400*	+3,200*	
Finished goods requirements	11,400	15,200	
Beginning inventory	−1,800	−2,400	
Production requirements	9,600	12,800	

* 20 percent of the following month's budgeted unit sales.

The arrows indicate that the desired ending inventory is based on the following month's budgeted unit sales and that the ending inventory in one month is the beginning inventory in the next month. It is not possible to develop a production budget for March without obtaining an April sales budget or setting the March desired ending inventory at some arbitrary quantity.

Manufacturing Cost Budget

A **manufacturing cost budget** contains a detailed forecast of the direct materials, direct labor, and factory overhead costs that should be incurred by the production department in producing the number of units called for in the production budget. With multiple service and production departments, the development of a manufacturing cost budget can become quite complex—a separate budget would be developed for each department. To keep our illustration as simple as possible, in this chapter we will only consider organizations with a single production department.

Standard cost information is used to budget direct materials, direct labor, and variable factory overhead. Fixed manufacturing costs are included in the manufacturing cost budget at a set amount. If a firm wants to prepare absorption-costing income statements, planned overapplied and underapplied overhead may also be included in the manufacturing cost budget. Using the previously developed standard cost information and assuming fixed manufacturing costs are incurred uniformly throughout the year, McDonald's manufacturing cost budget for January is as follows:

MANUFACTURING COST BUDGET (SCHEDULE 3)

		January
Variable costs:		
Direct materials (9,600 units × \$15)	\$144,000	
Direct labor (9,600 units × \$5)	48,000	
Factory overhead (9,600 units × \$9)	86,400	\$278,400
Fixed factory overhead (\$720,000/12 months)		60,000
Budgeted manufacturing costs		\$338,400

Budgeted fixed manufacturing costs	$ 60,000
Planned application of fixed manufacturing overhead (9,600 units × $6)	−57,600
Planned underapplied fixed factory overhead	$ 2,400

Note that the January budget for fixed factory overhead is one-twelfth of the annual fixed factory overhead budget. However, based on a planned January production volume of 9,600 units, only $57,600 of fixed factory overhead will be applied to production. The resulting planned underapplied overhead is treated as an adjustment to inventory on interim financial statements. A manufacturing cost budget could also be prepared for February if we desired.

Purchases Budget

A **purchases budget** is used to determine the number of units of raw materials that must be purchased to meet production and ending inventory requirements. In developing a purchases budget, consideration is given to the number of units of raw material available at the start of the period. The final purchases budget is stated in units and dollars.

Continuing our McDonald Products Company example, recall that the standard requires 5 square meters of raw materials for each unit of final product. On December 31, 19x1, McDonald had 9,600 square meters of raw materials. Assuming management desires an ending raw materials inventory equal to 20 percent of the following month's raw materials required for production, McDonald's January purchases budget is as follows:

PURCHASES BUDGET (SCHEDULE 4)

	January	*February*
Production requirements (Schedule 2)	9,600	12,800
Raw materials required for production	48,000*	64,000*
Desired ending inventory	+12,800†	
Raw materials requirements	60,800	
Beginning inventory	−9,600	
Purchase requirements (sq. meters)	51,200	
Purchase requirements (dollars, @ $3)	$153,600	

* 5 square meters per unit of final product times budgeted production.
† 20 percent of the following month's raw materials required for production.

The arrow indicates that the desired ending inventory is based on the following month's raw materials required for production. It is not possible to develop a purchases budget for February without obtaining a March production budget or setting the desired February ending inventory equal to some arbitrary quantity.

Selling and Administrative Expense Budget

The **selling and administrative expense budget** contains a detailed forecast of planned selling and administrative costs for the budget period. In a large organization, separate budgets are developed for each selling or administrative department. For the purpose of exposition, we will only present a single selling and administrative expense budget. Although some selling costs, such as sales commissions and transportation-out, vary with sales volume, many of them are discretionary fixed costs. The existence of discretionary fixed costs, such as research and development, advertising, and administrative salaries, makes this an extremely difficult budget to develop. In the absence of input/output relationships, budgets for these items are apt to be set in an arbitrary manner.

For simplicity, assume that McDonald has fixed selling and administrative expenses of $20,000 per month and variable selling and administrative expenses of $5 per unit sold. Although a separate selling and administrative expense budget is not necessary for this simple situation, we present it for illustrative purposes.

SELLING AND ADMINISTRATIVE EXPENSE BUDGET (SCHEDULE 5)

	January
Unit sales (Schedule 1)	9,000
Variable costs ($5 per unit sold)	$45,000
Fixed costs	20,000
Total selling and administrative expenses	$65,000

We could also develop selling and administrative expense budgets for February and March, if we wanted. If McDonald Products had bad debts, the bad debts expense would also be included in this budget.

Budgeted Income Statement

The **budgeted income statement** contains a forecast of sales revenues, expenses, and income for the budget period. It is based on the sales budget, the standard cost per unit of final product, the selling and administrative expense budget, and estimated income taxes. Consideration must also be given to any revenues and expenses not included in other budgets, such as sales or purchase discounts, interest income, and interest expense. Because absorption costing is required for external reporting and income tax purposes, we will develop McDonald's income statement in a functional format using absorption costing. Some managers prefer contribution income statements with variable costing for internal budgeting purposes. A budgeted income statement in a contribution format using variable costing is presented in the appendix to this chapter.

McDonald's sales budget, unit standard costs, and selling and administrative expense budget have been previously developed. In preparing the budgeted income statement, we assume the following additional information:

- All sales are on account. Payments received within ten days of the date of sale are subject to a 2 percent discount. Experience indicates that 60 percent of the accounts receivable are collected during the month of sale and 40 percent are collected during the following month. Of the receivables collected during the month of sale, 50 percent are collected during the discount period. None of the receivables collected after the month of sale are collected during the discount period. Accounts receivable are recorded at their gross amount and sales discounts are treated as a reduction in arriving at net sales during the month they are taken.

- There are no purchase discounts.
- McDonald is subject to a 40 percent income tax rate.

McDonald's budgeted January 19x2 income statement is as follows:

BUDGETED INCOME STATEMENT (SCHEDULE 6)

	January
Gross sales (Schedule 1)	$450,000
Less sales discounts ($450,000 × 0.6 × 0.5 × 0.02)*	−2,700
Net sales	$447,300
Cost of goods sold (9,000 units × $35)	−315,000
Gross profit	$132,300
Selling and administrative expenses (Schedule 5)	−65,000
Income before income taxes	$ 67,300
Income taxes ($67,300 × 0.40)	−26,920
Net income	$ 40,380

* All sales are on account. Sixty percent are collected during the month of sale. Fifty percent of the collections during the month of sale are subject to a 2 percent discount.

Budgeted Changes in Retained Earnings

With information regarding the retained earnings balance at the start of the budget period, budgeted net income, and planned dividends, the development of the budgeted changes in retained earnings is straightforward. Assuming McDonald does not plan to declare any dividends, the January budgeted statement of changes in retained earnings is as follows:

BUDGETED STATEMENT OF CHANGES IN RETAINED EARNINGS (SCHEDULE 7)

	January
Beginning balance (Exhibit 10–3)	$1,026,800
Add: Net income (Schedule 6)	40,380
Ending balance	$1,067,180

Cash Budget

The **cash budget**, which contains a detailed listing of budgeted cash receipts and disbursements, is the most critical budget in short-range planning. A business can operate with an accounting loss, but it cannot operate without cash. Cash management, an extremely important finance topic, is concerned with ways to speed up the inflow of cash, ways to delay the outflow of cash, sources of cash, and temporary uses of excess cash.

In developing a cash budget consideration is given to the beginning cash balance and operating and nonoperating sources and uses of cash. Operating sources include cash sales and collections on account. Operating uses include payments for the purchase of materials, other manufacturing costs, selling and administrative expenses, and taxes. Nonoperating sources and uses of cash include those related to debt, investments, and dividends.

In developing McDonald's January cash budget, we make the following additional assumptions:

- All purchases of raw materials are on account. Two-thirds are paid for in the month of purchase and one-third are paid for in the following month. There are no discounts for early payment.
- Fixed manufacturing costs include depreciation of $20,000 per month.
- All other product and period costs require cash expenditures and are paid in the month incurred.
- Taxes are paid in the following month.
- There are no nonoperating sources or uses of cash.

McDonald Products Company's January 19x2 cash budget is as follows:

CASH BUDGET (SCHEDULE 8)

			January
Beginning balance (Exhibit 10–3)			$300,000
Receipts:			
Collections from December sales (Exhibit 10–3)		$250,000	
Collections from January sales:			
Gross ($450,000 × 0.6)	$270,000		
Less sales discounts ($270,000 × 0.5 × 0.02)	−2,700	267,300	517,300
Total cash available			$817,300
Disbursements:			
Purchases:			
December (Exhibit 10–3)	$ 40,000		
January ($153,600* × 2/3)	102,400	$142,400	
Direct labor (Schedule 3)		48,000	
Variable factory overhead (Schedule 3)		86,400	
Fixed factory overhead:			
Total (Schedule 3)	$ 60,000		
Less depreciation (noncash)	−20,000	40,000	
Variable selling and administrative expenses (Schedule 5)		45,000	
Fixed selling and administrative expenses (Schedule 5)		20,000	
Income taxes (December, Exhibit 10–3)		25,000	−406,800
Ending balance			$410,500

* Schedule 4.

In reviewing the cash budget, note the absence of a monthly relationship between the cost of goods sold and disbursements for direct materials, direct labor, and factory overhead. This is so because the purchase of raw materials precedes production and production precedes sales.

Budgeted Balance Sheet

Given the beginning balance and the budgeted increases and decreases in each account, a budgeted statement of financial position at the end of the budget period can be prepared. McDonald's budgeted statement of financial position as of January 31, 19x2, is presented in Exhibit 10–4. Verify the ending balance in each account by referring to Exhibit 10–3 and Schedules 1 through 8.

Budgeting in Nonmanufacturing Organizations

The McDonald Products Company is a manufacturing organization and, as such, purchases raw materials and converts them into finished goods sold to other organizations or persons. These activities necessitate the development of production, manufacturing cost, and purchases budgets. Nonmanufacturing organizations do not need to prepare production and manufacturing cost budgets. Because nonmanufacturing organizations do not transform raw materials into finished goods, the purchases budget for a nonmanufacturing organization is directly tied to the sales budget rather than to a production budget.

The steps required to develop a master budget for a nonmanufacturing organization are illustrated in Exhibit 10–5. Because there are fewer steps in Exhibit 10–5 than in Exhibit 10–2, it might appear easier to develop a budget for a nonmanufacturing organization than for a manufacturing organization. This may be true for a small merchandising or service organization, but it is not necessarily true for large nonmanufacturing organizations.

Consider the situation faced by a municipal government. It does not produce a physical product; however, it does provide a wide range of services, possibly including police and fire protection, road maintenance, health services, public education, and public recreation. Because funds are limited and clear input/output relationships do not exist for any of these services, the budgeting process

EXHIBIT 10–4 **McDonald's Budgeted Statement of Financial Position**

McDonald Products Company
Budgeted Statement of Financial Position
As of January 31, 19x2

ASSETS		
Cash (Schedule 8)		$ 410,500
Accounts receivable (January sales $450,000 × 0.4)		180,000
Inventories:		
Raw materials [12,800 square meters (Schedule 4) × $3]	$38,400	
Finished goods [2,400 units (Schedule 2) × $35]	84,000	
Underapplied fixed factory overhead (Schedule 3)	2,400	124,800
Fixed assets:		
Cost	$2,000,000	
Less: Accumulated depreciation ($450,000 + $20,000)	−470,000	1,530,000
Total assets		$2,245,300
EQUITIES		
Accounts payable ($40,000 + $153,600 − $142,400)		$ 51,200
Taxes payable ($25,000 + $26,920 − $25,000)		26,920
Capital stock ($10 par)		500,000
Paid-in-capital in excess of par		600,000
Retained earnings (Schedule 7)		1,067,180
Total equities		$2,245,300

EXHIBIT 10–5 Assembling the Master Budget: Nonmanufacturing Organization

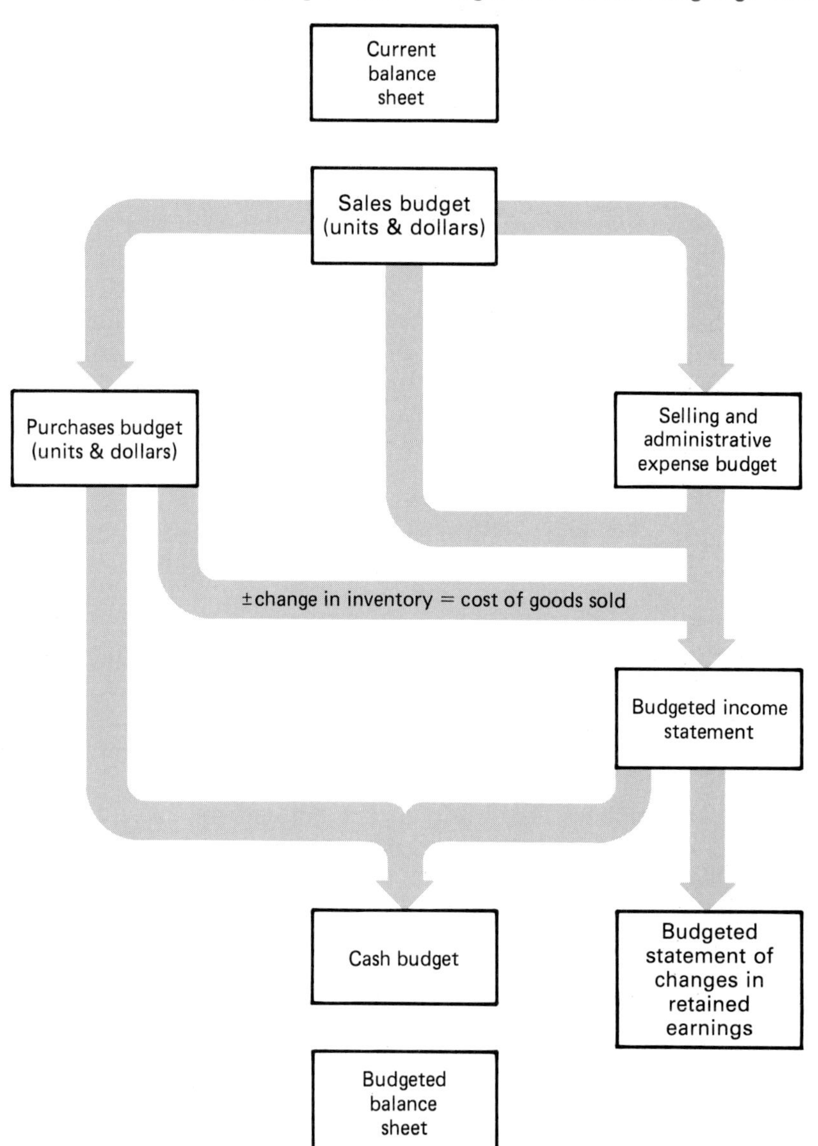

will likely center around the determination of how to allocate the available resources. Even though the final budget assembly may be straightforward, the development of the budget will be complex and political.

ADDITIONAL CONSIDERATIONS

Despite the complexity of the preceding example, it is an oversimplification. It is unlikely that McDonald's budget could be developed without disputes regarding standards, forecasted sales, discretionary fixed costs, or the adequacy of budgeted net income. Instead of just developing a budget for January, McDonald's management would, in practice, develop a budget for all of 19x2 and each quarter, month, or week thereof. The budgeting process for 19x2 might start in March of 19x1 with final acceptance of the 19x2 budget scheduled for early December of 19x1. Developing the 19x2 budget would likely require several iterations of the budgeting sequence illustrated in Exhibit 10–2 and many man-weeks of work.

Feasibility and Acceptability

At the end of each iteration, the feasibility and acceptability of the proposed budget would be evaluated. Cash or capacity constraints might make the budget infeasible. The desire for a higher cash flow or profit might make the budget unacceptable. Either of these occurrences would require another iteration of the budgeting process with possible changes in sales forecasts, products, standard costs, production processes, production facilities, channels of distribution, discretionary fixed costs, and financing. In the final analysis, top management may also have to change its profit objectives.

Use of Computers

Until recent years only the largest organizations used computers for budget preparation. Today, with the low cost of personal computers and the availability of easy-to-use spreadsheet software, even the smallest organizations have begun to use computers to aid in the budgeting process. Using spreadsheet software with a personal computer, budget schedules and pro forma financial statements can be programmed as a series of templates. Each template consists of column headings and row labels for a particular budget schedule as well as formulas for all computations required to complete the schedule from given information. Formulas linking budget schedules together are also programmed into the spreadsheet. Once the templates are developed and data pertaining to cost and revenue projections are entered into the template, the computer automatically prepares the schedules.

Although the initial development of budgeting templates is time consuming, most spreadsheet users believe the benefits of spreadsheet development far outweigh the costs. Primary benefits include the faster preparation of budget schedules in subsequent periods and an increased ability to evaluate the consequences of alternative actions. Spreadsheets provide an ability to perform sensitivity analysis on a wide range of issues that could not be considered if manual computations were required.

The extended example contained in the appendix to this chapter was developed using a spreadsheet software package on a personal computer. If appropriate computer facilities and software are available, you are encouraged to try to duplicate the budget templates and then study the impact of changes in various budgeting parameters.

Finally, it is important to remember that the computer is just a tool to help *managers* make decisions. The output of a computer program is limited by the quality of the program and the data. Budget schedules developed with the aid of a computer should always be evaluated on the basis of reasonableness, feasibility, and acceptability. Managers should not accept the computer output unless, on the basis of their professional judgment, it makes sense to them. Even in this computerized age, managers, not computers, are responsible for the success or failure of business activities.

SUMMARY

The master budget is the primary management tool for planning and controlling ongoing operations. The usefulness of the budgeting process is derived from its ability to compel planning, promote communication and coordination, provide a guide to action, and provide a basis of performance evaluation. If the budget is to have a high probability of moving the organization toward its long-run objectives, it must be based on a clear set of management goals for the coming period. These overall goals must also be decomposed into subgoals that are meaningful to operating personnel. Care must be taken to ensure these subgoals are congruent with each other and with the overall goals and objectives of the organization.

The formal development of a master budget is a complex task that takes place over an extended period of time and considers all interrelationships existing within an organization. The process begins with the development of a sales budget and proceeds through a number of steps that ultimately lead to the all-important cash budget and the budgeted balance sheet. In recent years a number of the mechanical aspects of budgeting have been computerized in an effort to speed up the budgeting process and allow management to easily determine how sensitive the budget is to changes in budget assumptions. The programming has not eliminated the final stage of budget development, the evaluation of the budget on the basis of feasibility and acceptability.

APPENDIX Extended Example

An extended example of the steps required to assemble a reasonably complex budget is presented in Exhibit 10–6. You should have a thorough understanding of the example presented in the body of Chapter 10 before studying this appendix. Significant differences between the example presented in the text and in this appendix are as follows:

- The budget is for a one-year period broken down into four quarters.
- There are two raw materials.
- There are bad debts and a provision for bad debts is made at the time of sale.
- The budget uses variable costing and contribution income statements.
- There is a minimum end-of-quarter cash balance and provisions are made for borrowing and repayment.

Because the focus is on operations rather than financial reporting, the statement of changes in retained earnings and the statement of financial position are omitted from the example. The example is presented in the same manner as it was developed on a computer spreadsheet. The first portion, called the parameters area, includes all given information and budgeting assumptions. The second portion, called the solutions area, includes the detailed budget schedules. The schedules are presented in the order suggested in Exhibit 10–2 and used in the Chapter 10 example. If you have difficulty following the extended example, you should refer back to Exhibit 10–2.

EXHIBIT 10–6 Extended Budgeting Example for Tracy's Toygel, Inc.

PARAMETERS AREA

Name of company:	Tracy's Toygel Incorporated
Budget year ending:	December 31, 19x7

Beginning of year balances:	
Cash	$20,000
Accounts receivable (net)	$15,000
Raw materials:	
Material 101	300 units
Material 102	250 units
Finished goods	400 units
Accounts payable	$9,000
Borrowed funds	$4,000
Desired end-of-year inventory balances:	
Raw materials:	
Material 101	150 units
Material 102	80 units
Finished goods	1,000 units
Desired end-of-quarter balances:	
Cash	$10,000
Raw materials as a portion of following quarter's production needs	0.2
Finished goods as a portion of following quarter's sales	0.3
Unit selling price	$200

Manufacturing costs:

Standard variable cost per unit

	Units	*Unit price*	*Total*
Material 101	3	$5.00	$15.00
Material 102	2	$4.00	8.00
Direct labor	2.5 hours	$8.00	20.00
Variable overhead	2.5 hours	$5.00	12.50
Total			$55.50

Fixed overhead per quarter:	
Cash	$50,000
Noncash	30,000
Total	$80,000
Selling and administrative expenses:	
Variable costs per unit sold	$2.00
Fixed costs per quarter:	
Cash	$ 8,000
Noncash	2,000
Total	$10,000
Other costs:	
Interest rate per quarter	0.04
Income tax rate	0.4

EXHIBIT 10–6 Extended Budgeting Example for Tracy's Toygel, Inc. (*Continued*)

Portion of sales collected:	
Quarter of sale	0.4
Subsequent quarter	0.55
Bad debts	0.05
Portion of purchases paid:	
Quarter of purchase	0.75
Subsequent quarter	0.25

Sales forecast:

Quarter	*First*	*Second*	*Third*	*Fourth*	*Total*
Units	5,000	2,000	3,000	2,500	12,500

ADDITIONAL INFORMATION

- All cash payments except purchases are made quarterly as incurred.
- All repayments and borrowings occur at the end of the quarter.
- Interest on borrowed funds is paid at the end of each quarter.
- Borrowings and repayments may be made in any amount.

SOLUTIONS AREA

Tracy's Toygel, Inc.
Sales Budget
For the Budget Year Ending December 31, 19x7

	First	*Second*	*Third*	*Fourth*	*Total*
Unit sales	5,000	2,000	3,000	2,500	12,500
Sales revenue	$1,000,000	$400,000	$600,000	$500,000	$2,500,000

Tracy's Toygel, Inc.
Production Budget
For the Budget Year Ending December 31, 19x7

	First	*Second*	*Third*	*Fourth*	*Total*
Unit sales	5,000	2,000	3,000	2,500	12,500
Desired ending inventory	600	900	750	1,000	1,000
Finished goods requirements	5,600	2,900	3,750	3,500	13,500
Less beginning inventory	−400	−600	−900	−750	−400
Production requirements	5,200	2,300	2,850	2,750	13,100

EXHIBIT 10–6 Extended Budgeting Example for Tracy's Toygel, Inc. (*Continued*)

Tracy's Toygel, Inc.
Manufacturing Cost Budget
For the Budget Year Ending December 31, 19x7

	First	*Second*	*Third*	*Fourth*	*Total*
Production requirements	5,200	2,300	2,850	2,750	13,100
Manufacturing resource requirements:					
Direct materials (units):					
Material 101	15,600	6,900	8,550	8,250	39,300
Material 102	10,400	4,600	5,700	5,500	26,200
Direct-labor hours	13,000	5,750	7,125	6,875	32,750
Variable manufacturing costs:					
Direct materials:					
Material 101	$ 78,000	$ 34,500	$ 42,750	$ 41,250	$ 196,500
Material 102	41,600	18,400	22,800	22,000	104,800
Direct labor	104,000	46,000	57,000	55,000	262,000
Factory overhead	65,000	28,750	35,625	34,375	163,750
Total variable costs	$288,600	$127,650	$158,175	$152,625	$ 727,050
Fixed manufacturing costs	80,000	80,000	80,000	80,000	320,000
Total manufacturing costs	$368,600	$207,650	$238,175	$232,625	$1,047,050

Tracy's Toygel, Inc.
Purchases Budget
For the Budget Year Ending December 31, 19x7

	First	*Second*	*Third*	*Fourth*	*Total*
Material 101:					
Required for production	15,600	6,900	8,550	8,250	39,300
Desired ending inventory	1,380	1,710	1,650	150	150
Total requirements	16,980	8,610	10,200	8,400	39,450
Less beginning inventory	−300	−1,380	−1,710	−1,650	−300
Purchase requirements (units)	16,680	7,230	8,490	6,750	39,150
Material 102:					
Required for production	10,400	4,600	5,700	5,500	26,200
Desired ending inventory	920	1,140	1,100	80	80
Total requirements	11,320	5,740	6,800	5,580	26,280
Less beginning inventory	−250	−920	−1,140	−1,100	−250
Purchase requirements (units)	11,070	4,820	5,660	4,480	26,030
Dollar purchases:					
Material 101	$ 83,400	$ 36,150	$ 42,450	$ 33,750	$195,750
Material 101	44,280	19,280	22,640	17,920	104,120
Total	$127,680	$ 55,430	$ 65,090	$ 51,670	$299,870

EXHIBIT 10–6 **Extended Budgeting Example for Tracy's Toygel, Inc. (*Continued*)**

Tracy's Toygel, Inc.
Selling and Administrative Expense Budget
For the Budget Year Ending December 31, 19x7

	First	*Second*	*Third*	*Fourth*	*Total*
Unit sales	5,000	2,000	3,000	2,500	12,500
Sales revenue	$1,000,000	$400,000	$600,000	$500,000	$2,500,000
Variable costs:					
Bad debts	$ 50,000	$ 20,000	$ 30,000	$ 25,000	$ 125,000
Other	10,000	4,000	6,000	5,000	25,000
Total	$ 60,000	$ 24,000	$ 36,000	$ 30,000	$ 150,000
Fixed costs	10,000	10,000	10,000	10,000	40,000
Total selling and administrative	$ 70,000	$ 34,000	$ 46,000	$ 40,000	$ 190,000

Tracy's Toygel, Inc.
Budgeted Contribution Income Statement
For the Year Ending December 31, 19x7

	First	*Second*	*Third*	*Fourth*	*Total*
Sales revenue	$1,000,000.00	$400,000.00	$600,000.00	$500,000.00	$2,500,000.00
Less variable costs:					
Cost of goods sold	$ 277,500.00	$111,000.00	$166,500.00	$138,750.00	$ 693,750.00
Selling and admin.	60,000.00	24,000.00	36,000.00	30,000.00	150,000.00
Total variable costs	−337,500.00	−135,000.00	−202,500.00	−168,750.00	−843,750.00
Contribution margin	$ 662,500.00	$265,000.00	$397,500.00	$331,250.00	$1,656,250.00
Less fixed costs:					
Factory overhead	$ 80,000.00	$ 80,000.00	$ 80,000.00	$ 80,000.00	$ 320.000.00
Selling and admin.	10,000.00	10,000.00	10,000.00	10,000.00	40,000.00
Total fixed costs	−90,000.00	−90,000.00	−90,000.00	−90,000.00	−360,000.00
Operating income	$ 572,500.00	$175,000.00	$307,500.00	$241,250.00	$1,296,250.00
Less interest expense*	−160.00	−5,994.24	−0.00	−0.00	−6,154.24
Net income before taxes	$ 572,340.00	$169,005.76	$307,500.00	$241,250.00	$1,290,095.76
Less income taxes	−228,963.00	−67,602.30	−123,000.00	−96,500.00	−516,038.30
Net income (loss)	$ 343,404.00	$101,403.46	$184,500.00	$144,750.00	$ 774,057.46
*Principal at start of quarter	$4,000.00	$149,856.00	$0.00	$0.00	

EXHIBIT 10–6 Extended Budgeting Example for Tracy's Toygel, Inc. (*Continued*)

Tracy's Toygel, Inc.
Cash Budget
For the Year Ending December 31, 19x7

	First	*Second*	*Third*	*Fourth*	*Total*
Operating cash receipts:					
Current quarter's sales	$ 400,000.00	$ 160,000.00	$ 240,000.00	$ 200,000.00	$1,000,000.00
Previous quarter's sales	15,000.00	550,000.00	220,000.00	330,000.00	1,115,000.00
Total operating receipts	$ 415,000.00	$ 710,000.00	$ 460,000.00	$ 530,000.00	$2,115,000.00
Operating cash disbursements:					
Purchases:					
Current quarter	$ 95,760.00	$ 41,572.50	$ 48,817.50	$ 38,752.50	$ 224,902.50
Previous quarter	9,000.00	31,920.00	13,857.50	16,272.50	71,050.00
Direct labor	104,000.00	46,000.00	57,000.00	55,000.00	262,000.00
Variable factory overhead	65,000.00	28,750.00	35,625.00	34,375.00	163,750.00
Fixed factory overhead	50,000.00	50,000.00	50,000.00	50,000.00	200,000.00
Variable selling and admin.	10,000.00	4,000.00	6,000.00	5,000.00	25,000.00
Fixed selling and admin.	8,000.00	8,000.00	8,000.00	8,000.00	32,000.00
Total operating disbursements	−341,760.00	−210,242.50	−219,300.00	−207,400.00	−978,702.50
Net operating cash receipts	$ 73,240.00	$ 499,757.50	$ 240,700.00	$ 322,600.00	$1,136,297.50
Income taxes	(228,936.00)	(67,602.30)	(123,000.00)	(96,500.00)	(516,038.30)
Beginning balance	20,000.00	10,000.00	286,304.96	404,004.96	20,000.00
Interest	(160.00)	(5,994.24)	0.00	0.00	(6,154.24)
Available before borrowing or repayment	$ (135,856.00)	$ 436,160.96	$ 404,004.96	$ 630,104.96	$ 634,104.96
Borrowing	145,856.00	0.00	0.00	0.00	145,856.00
Repayment	0.00	(149,856.00)	0.00	0.00	(149,856.00)
Ending balance	$ 10,000.00	$ 286,304.96	$ 404,004.96	$ 630,104.96	$ 630,104.96

Although a personal computer and spreadsheet software were used to develop the extended example, familiarity with spreadsheet software is not required to follow the presentation. If you are an experienced spreadsheet user, a thorough understanding of the usefulness of such software can be gained by developing a spreadsheet for this example. Specifically identified problems accompanying this chapter are designed to be solved with this template, thereby illustrating the power of spreadsheets for repetitive applications.

KEY TERMS

Authoritative approach to budgeting
Autocratic approach to budgeting
Budget
Budgetary slack
Budgeted income statement
Cash budget
Consultative approach to budgeting
Democratic approach to budgeting

Effective budget
Long-range planning
Management by exception
Manufacturing cost budget
Master budget
Operations scheduling
Participative approach to budgeting
Production budget
Purchases budget
Ratchet principle
Sales budget
Selling and administrative expense budget
Standard costs
Strategic planning
Theory X
Theory Y

SELECTED REFERENCES

Andersen, Anker V., *Budgeting for Data Processing,* New York: National Association of Accountants, 1983.

Becker, Selwyn, and David Green, Jr., "Budgeting and Employee Behavior," *Journal of Business* **35,** No. 4 (October 1962): 392–402.

Brownell, Peter, "A Field Study Examination of Budgetary Participation and Locus of Control," *Accounting Review* **57,** No. 4 (October 1982): 766–777.

_____, "Participation in Budgeting, Locus of Control and Organizational Effectiveness," *Accounting Review* **56,** No. 4 (October 1981): 844–860.

_____, "The Motivational Impact of Management-by-Exception in a Budgetary Context," *Journal of Accounting Research* **21,** No. 2 (Autumn 1983): 456–472.

_____, "The Role of Accounting Data in Performance Evaluation, Budgetary Participation, and Organization Effectiveness," *Journal of Accounting Research* **20,** No. 1 (Spring 1982): 12–27.

Caplan, Edwin H., *Management Accounting and Behavioral Science,* 2nd ed., Reading, Mass.: Addison-Wesley, 1981.

Chandler, John S., and Thomas N. Trone, " 'Bottom-Up' Budgeting and Control," *Management Accounting* **63,** No. 8 (February 1982): 37–40.

Charnes A., W. W. Cooper, and Y. Ijiri, "Breakeven Budgeting and Programming to Goals," *Journal of Accounting Research* **1,** No. 1 (Spring 1963): 16–43.

Cheng, Thomas T., "Financial Forecasting: Throw Away the Crystal Ball," *Management Accounting* **64,** No. 11 (May 1983): 50–52.

Gershefski, George W., "Building a Corporate Financial Model," *Harvard Business Review* **47,** No. 4 (July-August 1969): 61–72.

Ijiri, Y, F. Levy, and R. Lyon, "A Linear Programming Model for Budgeting and Financial Planning," *Journal of Accounting Research* **1,** No. 2 (Autumn 1963): 198–212.

Merchant, Kenneth A., "The Design of the Corporate Budgeting System: Influences on Managerial Behavior and Performance," *Accounting Review* **56,** No. 4 (October 1981): 813–829.

Naylor, Thomas H., "The Future of Corporate Planning Models," *Managerial Planning* **24,** No. 5 (March-April 1976): 1–9.

_____, *Corporate Planning Models,* Reading, Mass.: Addison-Wesley, 1979.

Parker, Lee D., "Goal Congruence: A Misguided Accounting Concept," *Abacus* **12,** No. 1 (June 1976): 3–13.

Scheff, Michael, and Arie Y. Lewin, "The Impact of People on Budgets," *Accounting Review* **45,** No. 2 (April 1970): 259–268.

Tiller, Mikel G., "The Dissonance Model of Participative Budgeting: An Empirical Exploration," *Journal of Accounting Research* **21,** No. 2 (Autumn 1983): 581–595.

Trapani, Cosmo S., "Six Critical Areas in the Budgeting Process," *Management Accounting* **64,** No. 5 (November 1982): 52–56.

Williams, John J., "Environmental and Systems Characteristics: Influences on Designing a Budgeting System," *Cost and Management* **57,** No. 6 (November-December 1983): 20–25.

REVIEW QUESTIONS

10–1 Briefly describe four types of planning and distinguish between them on two dimensions: (1) the management level responsible for its development, and (2) its timeframe.

10–2 Mention four objectives of developing a master budget.

10–3 Distinguish between the authoritative, consultative, and participative approaches to budgeting.

10–4 Why is it necessary to decompose an organization's overall goals into subgoals?

10–5 What is the problem of goal congruence?

10–6 What is budgetary slack?

10–7 Why is performance evaluation an important part of the budgeting process?

10–8 What are standard costs? Mention three uses of standard costs.

10–9 What problems may result from the use of "tight" or "motivating" standards?

10–10 What is the first step in assembling a master budget?

10–11 Why might someone conclude it is easier to develop a budget for a nonmanufacturing organization than for a manufacturing organization? Is this necessarily true?

10–12 Before a budget is accepted, what overall criteria should be used to evaluate it?

10–13 What are the primary benefits of developing a computer spreadsheet for budgeting?

10–14 Who is responsible for the success or failure of budgets developed with the aid of computers?

REVIEW PROBLEM

Budgeting Income and Cash: Normal Cost System

In conjunction with its budgeting activities for the coming year, the Hassan Corporation developed the following information for 19x6:

- Sales (actual and budgeted):

	April (actual)	*May (estimate)*	*June (estimate)*	*July (estimate)*
Unit sales	10,000	15,000	18,000	12,000
Dollar sales	$200,000	$300,000	$360,000	$240,000

- All sales are on account. Forty percent are collected in the month of sale. Fifty-eight percent are collected the following month. A 2 percent allowance for bad debts is established at the time of sale. There are no discounts for early payment.

- At a monthly production volume of 15,000 units the standard cost is $12 per unit of final product:

Direct materials (1 unit of item number 123 × $4)	$ 4
Direct labor (0.2 direct-labor hours × $10)	2
Variable factory overhead (0.2 direct-labor hours × $5)	1
Fixed factory overhead ($75,000 per month ÷ 3,000 monthly direct-labor hours × 0.2 direct-labor hours per unit)	5
Total	$12

- Selling and administrative expenses:

Variable, excluding estimated bad debts	$2 per unit sold
Fixed	$20,000 per month

- Purchases are paid for at the time of acquisition. There are no purchase discounts.
- Noncash fixed expenses total $25,000 per month, including $20,000 for manufacturing and $5,000 for selling and administrative. All other manufacturing costs and selling and administrative expenses are paid as incurred.
- The May 1 cash balance is $15,000.
- Hassan desires to have ending finished goods equal to 20 percent of the following month's sales and ending raw materials equal to 50 percent of the following month's production requirements. The May 1 inventories are in line with this policy.
- There are no beginning or ending work-in-process inventories.
- Any overapplied or underapplied overhead is treated as an adjustment to total inventories on interim financial statements.
- Ignore income taxes.

REQUIREMENTS

a) Prepare a production budget for May and June.

b) Prepare a manufacturing cost budget for May. Also indicate the amount of any planned underapplied or overapplied fixed factory overhead.

c) Prepare a purchases budget in units and dollars for May.

d) Prepare a budgeted income statement for May.

e) Prepare a cash budget for May.

The solution to this problem is found at the end of the Chapter 10 problems and exercises.

EXERCISES

10–1 T Budgeting Production and Purchases: Manufacturing

At the beginning of August 19x2 the Wooley Rug Company had 100,000 square yards of rugs and 400,000 pounds of raw materials on hand. Budgeted sales for the next three months are as follows:

August	200,000 sq. yds.
September	180,000 sq. yds.
October	150,000 sq. yds.

The Wooley Rug Company wants to have sufficient raw materials on hand at the end of each month to meet 50 percent of the following month's production requirements and sufficient square yards of finished product on hand at the end of each month to meet 40 percent of the following month's budgeted sales. Five pounds of raw materials are required to produce one square yard of carpeting. The standard cost per pound of raw materials is $1.50.

REQUIREMENTS

a) Prepare a production budget for August and September.

b) Prepare a purchases budget in units and dollars for August.

10–2 T Budgeting Production and Purchases: Manufacturing

At the beginning of October, the Cumfort Cushion Company had 2,400 cushions and 7,740 pounds of raw materials on hand. Budgeted unit sales for the next three months are:

October	8,000 cushions
November	10,000 cushions
December	12,000 cushions

The Cumfort Cushion Company wants to have sufficient raw materials on hand at the end of each month to meet 25 percent of the following month's production requirements and sufficient cushions on hand at the end of each month to meet 30 percent of the following month's budgeted sales. Three pounds of raw materials are required to produce each cushion. The standard cost per pound of raw materials is $0.60.

REQUIREMENTS

a) Prepare a production budget for October and November.

b) Prepare a purchases budget in units and dollars for October.

10–3 Budgeting Cash Receipts: From Credit Sales

The Fresh Company is preparing its cash budget for May. The following information is available concerning its accounts receivable:

Estimated credit sales for May	$200,000
Actual credit sales for April	$150,000
Estimated collections in May for credit sales in May	20%
Estimated collections in May for credit sales in April	70%
Estimated collections in May for credit sales prior to April	$ 12,000
Estimated write-offs in May for uncollectable credit sales	$ 8,000
Estimated provision for bad debts in May for credit sales in May	$ 7,000

REQUIREMENT

Determine the estimated cash receipts from accounts receivable in May. (CPA Adapted)

10–4 Budgeted Cash Receipts from Credit Sales

All sales of the Bunny Co. Ltd. are made on account. A 3 percent discount is offered to customers who pay by the tenth of the next month. Sixty percent of the sales are collected during the discount period. Accounts are due by the end of the month after sale. Twenty-five percent of the sales are collected by the due date. A further 12 percent of the sales are collected in the second month after sale, and 3 percent are never collected. Part of the sales budget is as follows:

January	$35,000
February	40,000
March	70,000
April	25,000
May	20,000

REQUIREMENT

Compute the budgeted cash receipts for April from collection of Accounts Receivable. (CGA Adapted)

10–5 Budgeted Cash Disbursements: Merchandising

Serven Wholesalers, Limited, estimated its activity for June 19x9. Selected data from these estimated amounts are as follows:

- Sales $700,000
- Gross profit (based on sales) 30%
- Increase in trade accounts receivable during month $ 20,000
- Change in accounts payable during month $ 0
- Increase in inventory during month $ 10,000
- Variable selling, general, and administrative expenses (S, G & A) includes a charge for uncollectable accounts of 1 percent of sales.
- Total S, G & A is $71,000 per month plus 15 percent of sales.
- Depreciation expense of $40,000 per month is included in fixed S, G & A.

REQUIREMENT

Determine the estimated operating cash disbursements for June. (CPA Adpated)

10–6 Budgeted Cash Disbursements for Purchases: Merchandising

The Saskatoon Co. Ltd. manufactures a product for which the following sales forecast has been prepared.

	Number of units
January	12,000
February	10,000
March	13,000
April	11,000

Saskatoon has a policy of producing enough units so that there will be a beginning inventory each month equal to 20 percent of the month's predicted sales. The standard cost per unit is as follows:

Materials (3 lbs. × $5.00)	$15.00
Direct labor (1 hr. × $6.00)	6.00
Variable overhead	2.00
Fixed overhead	7.00
Total	$30.00

Materials inventories at the beginning of each month are to be equal to 40 percent of that month's production requirements.

All materials are purchased on account with terms of 2/10, net/30. *Purchases are made evenly throughout the month.* For convenience, assume that all months have 30 days and that payment is always made at the end of the discount period.

REQUIREMENT

Compute the amount of cash required in February for payment of accounts payable related to the purchase of materials. (CGA Adapted)

10–7 Budgeted Cash Disbursements for Purchases: Manufacturing

The Partee Co. Ltd. manufactures a product called Par. Each unit of Par takes 3 pieces of a material called Tee whose standard price is $5.00 per piece.

Budgeted inventory levels are as follows:

	Par	*Tee*
June 1	5,000	20,000
July 1	3,000	14,000
August 1	3,000	11,000

Budgeted sales of Par are 50,000 for June and 30,000 for July.

The Partee Co. Ltd. intends to take advantage of a 2/10, n/30 discount. Assume one-third of the purchases of any month due for discount are paid in the following month.

REQUIREMENT

How much cash will be required in July for purchases of Tee? (CGA Adapted)

10–8 Budgeting Cash Receipts and Disbursements: Merchandising

The following information was available from Montero Corporation's books:

19x2	*Purchases*	*Sales*
January	$42,000	$72,000
February	48,000	66,000
March	36,000	60,000
April	54,000	78,000

Collections from customers are normally 70 percent in the month of sale, 20 percent in the month following the sale, and 9 percent in the second month following the sale. The balance is expected to be uncollectable. Montero takes full advantage of the 2 percent discount allowed on purchases paid for by the tenth of the following month. Purchases for May are budgeted at $60,000, and sales for May are budgeted at $66,000. Cash disbursements for expenses are expected to be $14,400 for May. Montero's cash balance at May 1 was $22,000.

REQUIREMENT

Prepare the following schedules:

1. Budgeted cash collections during May.
2. Budgeted cash disbursements during May.
3. Budgeted cash balance at May 31. (CPA Adapted)

10–9 Budgeted Cash Receipts and Disbursements: Merchandising

The Delta Company anticipates the following sales for the first quarter of 19x6:

	January	*February*	*March*
Units	10,000	12,000	15,000
Dollars	$100,000	$120,000	$150,000

Delta has 3,000 units on January 1 and desires to maintain an ending inventory equal to 30 percent of the following month's sales.

Purchases are made on terms of 2/10, net/30. Purchase discounts are always taken and they are recorded as other income. Eighty percent of the purchases are paid for in the month they are received and 20 percent are paid for in the following month.

The units are priced to sell at 125 percent of cost and they are sold on account only. Terms are 2/10, net/30. In the past, 60 percent of the billings are collected in the month of sale and 40 percent are collected in the following month. One hundred percent of the collections during the month of sale are made during the discount period. Fifty percent of the collections during the subsequent month are made during the discount period. There are no uncollectable accounts.

REQUIREMENTS

a) Prepare a purchases budget for January and February.
b) Prepare a February cash disbursements budget.
c) Prepare a February cash receipts budget for collections from customers.

10–10 Budgeting Income: Merchandising

Eriksen Company, a merchandising firm, has budgeted its activity for October 19x2 based on the following information:

- Sales are budgeted at $300,000. All sales are credit sales and a provision for doubtful accounts is made monthly at the rate of 3 percent of sales.

- Merchandise inventory was $70,000 at September 30, 19x2, and an increase of $10,000 is planned for the month.
- All merchandise is marked up to sell at invoice cost plus 50 percent.
- Estimated cash disbursements for selling and administrative expenses for the month are $40,000.
- Depreciation for the month is projected at $5,000.

REQUIREMENT

Prepare a budgeted income statement for October 19x2. (CPA Adapted)

PROBLEMS

10–11 Budgeting Absorption-Costing Income and Cash: Manufacturing With a Normal Cost System

The Contemporary Production Company is widely known for the Purple Psychic Light Generator, which is distributed through gift shops located in major shopping centers across the country. Contemporary Production anticipates selling 100,000 generators in April, 120,000 in May, and 140,000 in June. The generator sells for $20 and has the following standard unit production costs at a monthly volume of 100,000 units:

Raw materials	$5.00
Direct labor	8.00
Variable overhead	2.00
Fixed overhead	0.50

The budgeted fixed production costs include noncash expenses of $20,000. Under- or overapplied overhead is closed to the Cost of Goods Sold each month. Other monthly expenses include distribution expenses of 10 percent of sales and administrative expenses of $5,000.

The company currently has 40,000 light generators on hand and sufficient raw materials to produce 100,000 additional units. Contemporary desires to have sufficient quantities of the finished product on hand at the end of each month to supply 50 percent of the following month's sales and sufficient raw materials to supply 80 percent of the following month's production.

The company believes in "cash on the barrel head." It pays all debts immediately and it does not sell on account. The current March 30 cash balance is $10,000.

REQUIREMENTS

a) Prepare a production budget for April and May.

b) Prepare a budgeted income statement for April. Use absorption costing.

c) Prepare a purchases budget for April.

d) Prepare a budgeted statement of cash receipts and disbursements for April.

e) What advice do you have for management?

10–12 Budgeting Absorption-Costing Income and Cash: Manufacturing With an Actual Cost System

Fiesta, Inc., manufactures a product that sells for $50 per unit. Monthly and unit cost data are as follows:

Variable:	
Selling and administrative	$ 5 per unit sold
Direct materials	10 per unit manufactured
Direct labor	10 per unit manufactured
Variable overhead	5 per unit manufactured
Fixed:	
Selling and administrative	$20,000 per month
Manufacturing (including depreciation of $10,000)	30,000 per month

Fiesta pays all bills in the month they are incurred. All sales are on account. Fifty percent of the sales are collected during the month of sale. The balance is collected during the following month. There are no sales discounts or bad debts.

The company desires to maintain a finished goods inventory equal to 20 percent of the following month's sales and a raw materials inventory sufficient for 10 percent of the following month's production. January 1 inventories are in line with these policies.

Actual sales for December and projected sales for January, February, and March are as follows:

December	*January*	*February*	*March*
6,250 units	5,000 units	10,000 units	8,000 units

ADDITIONAL INFORMATION

- Fiesta uses an *actual* cost system with monthly fixed manufacturing overhead spread over the units actually produced during the month.
- All units in the January 1 inventory of finished goods are costed at $40 each.
- Because the absorption cost of units manufactured varies from month to month (due to the use of an actual cost system), a FIFO cost flow assumption is used in inventory valuation.

REQUIREMENTS

a) Prepare a production budget for January and February.

b) Prepare a budgeted income statement for January. Use absorption costing.

c) Prepare a purchases budget for January.

d) Prepare a budgeted statement of cash receipts and disbursements for January.

e) Assuming that it is not possible to change the budgeted sales volume, prices, or costs, how might the January net income be increased?

10–13 Budgeting Absorption-Costing Income and Cash: Manufacturing With an Actual Cost System

The Big Orange Company is about to introduce a new, noncarbonated beverage called "Mellow Orange." Mellow Orange is to be introduced in July 19x8. Projected sales, in cases, for the first three months are:

	July	*August*	*September*
Sales in cases	200,000	150,000	150,000

Mellow Orange will wholesale for $20 per case. Due to heavy promotion, July selling and distribution costs will be $1 per case. Subsequent selling and distribution costs will be $0.50 per case.

Manufacturing costs include bottles at $4.00 per case and mix at $5.00 per liter. *Each case of Mellow Orange requires 2 liters of mix*. Due to the nature of the production process, all other manufacturing costs are fixed. Labor and overhead costs total $215,000 per month. Overhead costs include noncash expenses of $105,000 per month. *Big Orange uses an actual cost system.*

Big Orange has no inventory on July 1. Effective July 31 management desires to have ending inventories of raw materials equal to 10 percent of the following month's anticipated use and ending inventories of finished goods equal to 10 percent of the following month's sales. Administrative expenses (all cash) are $20,000 per month.

It is anticipated that all sales will be on account. One-half of the sales will be collected during the month of the sale and one-half will be collected during the following month. One-half of the collections during the month of sale (25 percent of total sales) will receive a 2 percent sales discount. Sales discounts are treated as a deduction from sales revenues during the month they are taken.

Big Orange pays all debts immediately. The projected July 1, 19x8, cash balance is $600,000. The desired August 1 cash balance is $50,000. Big Orange has a $1,200,000 line of credit. Interest on borrowed money is 1 percent per month or any portion thereof, payable on the first day of the following month.

REQUIREMENTS

a) Prepare a production budget in cases for July and August.

b) Prepare a manufacturing cost budget for July.

c) Prepare a purchases budget in units and total dollars for July.

d) Prepare a cash budget for July. Clearly indicate the amount of any borrowings.

e) Prepare a budgeted income statement for the month of July.

10–14 Budgeting Production, Purchases, and Absorption-Costing Income: Manufacturing with an Actual Cost System[1]

The budget department of the Easy-Way Manufacturing Company prepared these estimates for the year beginning July 1, 19w2.

- Inventories:

	Beginning	*Ending*
Raw materials:		
Units	5,000	6,000
LIFO cost	$ 6,250	$?
Finished goods:		
Units	10,000	12,000
LIFO cost	$60,000	$?

[1] Adapted from a problem prepared by Professor Imogene Posey.

- Sales at an average sales price of $10 per unit — $1,000,000
- Production costs:

Raw materials (2 units of material for each unit of finished goods @ $1.50)	$3.00
Direct labor, per unit of finished product	$2.00
Factory overhead:	
Variable, per unit of finished product	$1.00
Fixed overhead per year	$51,000.00

- Marketing and administrative expenses are $50,000 fixed per year plus 5 percent of dollar sales.
- The income tax rate is 40 percent.

REQUIREMENTS

a) Prepare a production budget (annual basis) indicating units to be produced.

b) Prepare a purchases budget (annual basis) indicating units and dollars of purchases.

c) Prepare a budgeted income statement in detail and in good form. Show cost of goods manufactured. Assume finished goods and cost of goods sold are at actual costs, using a LIFO flow. There are no beginning or ending inventories of work-in-process.

10–15 Budgeting Variable-Costing Income and Cash: Manufacturing

Old Forge Valve Company manufactures water flow regulators. Presented is information pertaining to actual May sales and certain assumptions needed to prepare the July budget.

	Actual	*Forecast*		
Sales:	*May*	*June*	*July*	*August*
Units	8,000	7,000	7,000	10,000
Dollars	$800,000	$700,000	$700,000	$1,000,000

Inventories:

Old Forge does not maintain raw materials inventories; instead, materials are purchased from suppliers as needed. The company maintains monthly ending inventories of finished goods equal to 50 percent of the following month's forecasted sales. The June 1 inventories are in line with company policies.

Manufacturing Costs:

Direct materials (1 component set)	$ 19.60	per valve
Direct labor (3 hours at $6 per hour)	18.00	per valve
Variable overhead	20.00	per valve
Fixed overhead (including depreciation of $30,000)	100,000.00	per month

Selling and Administrative Costs:

Variable	$ 5	per valve sold
Fixed	50,000	per month

Cash Receipts:

All sales are on account and are billed to customers on the first day of the month following the sale. Sixty percent of the receivables are collected during the month billed. They receive a 2 percent sales discount. Thirty-eight percent of the receivables are collected during the following month. They do not receive a sales discount. Two percent of the receivables are never collected.

Sales discounts are deducted from sales revenue in the month the related collections are made. Uncollectable accounts are estimated and deducted from sales revenue in the month of sale. Sales revenue minus these amounts is identified as "Net Sales."

Cash Disbursements:

Raw materials are purchased on terms of 2/10, net/30. The discount is always taken and the materials cost of $19.60 is the net cost, computed as $20 × 0.98. Fifty percent of the purchases are paid for in the month of purchase, with the remainder paid in the following month.

Eighty percent of the variable selling and administrative costs are paid in the month incurred, with the remainder paid in the following month. All other costs requiring a cash expenditure are paid in the month incurred.

REQUIREMENTS

a) Prepare production budgets for June and July.

b) Prepare a contribution income statement (based on variable costing) for July.

c) Prepare a detailed cash budget for July. The budgeted July 1 cash balance is $25,000.

10–16 T Budgeting Variable-Costing Income and Cash: Manufacturing

Presented is information pertaining to the Christmas Company's budget for the year ending December 25, 19x4:

Beginning of year balances:			
Cash	$100,000		
Accounts receivable	20,000 (from previous quarter sales)		
Raw materials in units:			
Material A	100		
Finished goods in units	50		
Desired end-of-quarter balances:			
Raw materials as portion of following quarter's production needs	0.1		
Finished goods as portion of following quarter's sales	0.4		
Unit selling price:	$ 50		
Manufacturing costs:	*Units*	*Unit price*	*Total*
Standard variable cost per unit:			
Material A units at price	2.0	$4.50	$ 9.00
Direct-labor hours at rate	1.5	5.00	7.50
Variable overhead/labor hr.	1.5	2.00	3.00
Total standard variable cost			$19.50

Fixed overhead per quarter:	
Cash	$10,000
Noncash	5,000
Total	$15,000
Selling and administrative costs:	
Variable cost per unit	$2.00
Fixed costs per quarter:	
Cash	$2,000
Noncash	1,000
Total	$3,000
Portion of sales collected:	
Quarter of sale	0.4
Subsequent quarter	0.6

Sales forecast:

Quarter	*First*	*Second*	*Third*	*Fourth*	*Total*
Unit sales	0	2,000	6,000	10,000	18,000

ADDITIONAL INFORMATION

- All purchases are paid for in the quarter purchased.
- All other costs are paid as incurred.

REQUIREMENTS

a) Prepare a production budget in units for each quarter of 19x4.

b) Prepare a raw materials purchases budget in units and dollars for the first two quarters of 19x4.

c) Prepare a manufacturing cost budget for the first quarter of 19x4.

d) Prepare a budgeted contribution income statement for the first quarter of 19x4. Use variable (direct) costing.

e) Prepare a cash budget for the first quarter of 19x4.

10–17 T Budgeting Variable-Costing Income and Cash: Manufacturing

Presented is information pertaining to the Main Blanket Company's budget for the year ending December 31, 19x6:

Beginning of year balances:	
Cash	$ 4,500
Accounts receivable	$30,000
Raw materials in units:	
Wool yarn (lbs.)	500
Finished goods in units	100
Accounts payable	$400
Desired end-of-year inventory balances:	
Raw materials in units:	
Wool yarn (lbs.)	500
Finished goods in units	120

Desired end-of-quarter balances:				
Cash				$ 2,000
Raw materials as portion of following quarter's production needs				0.1
Finished goods as portion of following quarter's sales				0.2
Unit selling price				$40

Manufacturing costs:

	Units	Unit price	Total
Standard variable cost per unit:			
Wool yarn (lbs.)	3	$2.00	$ 6.00
Direct-labor hours at rate	2	$4.00	8.00
Variable overhead/labor hr.	2	$0.50	1.00
Total standard variable cost			$15.00

Fixed overhead per quarter:	
Cash	$3,000
Noncash	500
Total	$3,500
Selling and administrative costs:	
Variable cost per unit	$2.00
Fixed costs per quarter:	
Cash	$10,000
Noncash	600
Total	$10,600
Income tax rate	0.4
Portion of sales collected:	
Quarter of sale	0.6
Subsequent quarter	0.4
Portion of purchases paid:	
Quarter of purchase	0.9
Subsequent quarter	0.1

Sales forecast:

Quarter	*First*	*Second*	*Third*	*Fourth*	*Total*
Units sales	7,000	1,000	5,000	12,000	25,000

ADDITIONAL INFORMATION

- All cash payments except purchases are made monthly as incurred.
- The beginning accounts receivable is from the previous quarter's sales.
- The beginning accounts payable is from the previous quarter's purchases.

REQUIREMENTS

a) Prepare a production budget in units for each quarter of 19x6.

b) Prepare a purchases budget in units and dollars for the first two quarters of 19x6.

c) Prepare a manufacturing cost budget for the first quarter of 19x6.

d) Prepare a budgeted contribution income statement for the first quarter of 19x6. Use variable costing.

e) Prepare a cash budget for the first quarter of 19x6.

10–18 Budgeting Multiple Product Absorption-Costing Income and Cash: Manufacturing with a Normal Cost System

The Scarborough Corporation manufactures and sells two products, Thingone and Thingtwo. In July 19x7, Scarborough's budget department gathered the following data to project sales and budget requirements for 19x8.

19x8 Projected Sales

Product	*Units*	*Price*
Thingone	60,000	$ 70
Thingtwo	40,000	100

19x8 Inventories (in units)

	Expected	*Desired*
Product	*January 1, 19x8*	*December 31, 19x8*
Thingone	20,000	25,000
Thingtwo	8,000	9,000

To produce one unit of Thingone and Thingtwo, the following raw materials are used:

		Amount used per unit	
Raw material	*Unit*	*Thingone*	*Thingtwo*
A	lbs.	4	5
B	lbs.	2	3
C	each	0	1

Projected data for 19x8 with respect to raw materials are as follows:

Material	*Standard purchase price*	*Expected inventories January 1, 19x8*	*Desired inventories December 31, 19x8*
A	$8/lb.	32,000 lbs.	36,000 lbs.
B	$5/lb.	29,000 lbs.	32,000 lbs.
C	$3/unit	6,000 units	7,000 units

Projected direct-labor requirements for 19x8 and rates are as follows:

Product	*Standard hours per unit*	*Standard rate per hour*
Thingone	2	$6
Thingtwo	3	$8

Variable and fixed overhead are each applied at the rate of $1 per direct-labor hour. The fixed overhead rate is based on an activity level of 250,000 direct-labor hours per year.

Selling and administrative expenses are:

Variable	$2 per unit of either product
Fixed	$100,000 per year

REQUIREMENTS

a) Determine the standard costs for Thingone and Thingtwo.

b) Prepare a 19x8 production budget for Thingone and Thingtwo (in units).

c) Prepare a 19x8 raw materials purchases budget for all raw materials (in units).

d) Prepare a 19x8 manufacturing cost budget (in dollars).

e) Prepare a 19x8 budgeted absorption-costing income statement. Any under- or overapplied overhead is written off as an adjustment to the Cost of Goods Sold.

f) Determine the 19x8 budgeted variable-costing net income. (You need not prepare a complete statement.) (CPA Adapted)

10–19 Budgeting Income and Cash: Service Organization

The Big Apple Typing Service prepares legal and other documents for professional organizations. Big Apple uses high-quality word processing machines that are rented for $400 per month. Assuming an 8-hour work day and a 20-work-day month, each machine is capable of processing up to 800 pages of manuscript per month. Because Big Apple rents word processors by the month as they are needed, the *machine rental costs follow a step pattern.*

To provide additional flexibility, all typists are hired on an as-needed basis and paid a piece rate of $2.50 per accurately processed page. Big Apple's other monthly costs include $20,000 fixed ($15,000 cash and $5,000 building depreciation) and $0.10 per page.

Information on the timing of cash payments is as follows:

- Machine rental fees are paid during the month following the month incurred.
- Typists wages are paid 75 percent during the month incurred and 25 percent during the following month.
- All other costs are paid during the month incurred.

Big Apple charges customers $5 per processed page. Fifty percent of the revenues are collected during the month the processing is performed and 50 percent are collected during the following month. Because of the quality of Big Apple's clients, there are no bad debts. Actual and projected sales are as follows:

	Actual	*Budgeted*		
	April	*May*	*June*	*July*
Pages	10,400	8,200	9,000	10,000

REQUIREMENTS

a) Prepare a budgeted income statement for May.

b) Prepare a budgeted schedule of changes in cash for May. The schedule should clearly identify cash receipts, cash disbursements, and the increase or decrease in cash.

c) Management is quite concerned about Big Apple's performance and its prospects for the immediate future. Consequently you are asked to determine Big Apple's monthly break-even unit sales volume. You should also indicate the number of word processors Big Apple will need to rent at the break-even unit volume. (*Hint:* As an *initial* approach to determining the break-even point, treat the step cost as a mixed cost.)

10–20 Budgeting Revenues, Expenses, and Cash: Service Organization

The Silver Lake Medical Center is located in a summer resort community. During the summer months the center operates an outpatient clinic for the treatment of minor injuries and illnesses. The clinic is administered as a separate department within the hospital. It has its own budget and maintains its own records. It refers all patients in need of extensive or intensive care to other hospital departments.

An analysis of past monthly operating data reveals the following:

- *Staff:* Five base employees with monthly salaries totaling $20,000. One additional staff member is hired for every 500 patient visits, in excess of 3,000, at a cost of $2,000/month.
- *Facilities:* Monthly maintenance costs total $1,000. Monthly depreciation totals $500 on the clinic facilities.
- *Supplies:* The supplies expense averages $3 per patient. The center likes to keep a supplies inventory equal to 10 percent of the following month's needs on hand at the end of each month. Supplies are purchased at cost from the hospital.
- *Payments:* All staff and maintenance expenses are paid in the month the services are received. Supplies are paid for when received.
- *Collections:* The average bill for services rendered is $20. Of the total bills, 50 percent are paid in cash at the time services are rendered, 10 percent are never paid, and the remaining 40 percent are covered by insurance. In the past, insurance companies have disallowed 10 percent of the claims filed and paid the balance two months after services are rendered.

It is anticipated that the clinic will have 2,000 patients in June, 3,000 in July, and 4,000 in August of 19x5. As of May 30, the clinic has $8,000 in cash and $1,200 in supplies.

REQUIREMENTS

a) Prepare a revenue and expense budget for June.

b) Prepare cash budgets for June and July.

10–21 Budgeting Income and Incremental Analysis: Manufacturing

The Barr Food Manufacturing Company is a medium-sized publicly held corporation, producing a variety of consumer food and specialty products. The following data was prepared for the salad dressing product line using five months of actual expenses and a seven-month projection. These data were prepared for a preliminary 19x9 budget meeting between the Specialty Products Division president, marketing vice president, production vice president, and the controller. The 19x8 projection was accepted as being accurate, but it was agreed that the projected income was not at a satisfactory level.

Barr Food Manufacturing Company: Salad Dressing Product Line
Projected Income Statement
For the Year Ending December 31, 19x8
(5 months actual; 7 months projected)
(000 omitted)

Volume in gallons	5,000
Gross sales	$30,000
Freights, allowances, discounts	−3,000
Net sales	$27,000
Less manufacturing costs:	
Variable	$13,500
Fixed	2,100
Depreciation	700
Total manufacturing costs	−16,300
Gross profit	$10,700
Less other expenses:	
Marketing	$ 4,000
Brokerage	1,650
General and administrative	2,100
Research and development	500
Total expenses	−8,250
Income before taxes	$ 2,450

The division president stated she wanted at least a 15 percent increase in gross sales dollars and a before-tax profit of 10 percent of sales for 19x9. She also stated that she would be responsible for a $200,000 reduction in the general and administrative expenses to help achieve the profit goal.

Both the marketing vice president and the production vice president felt that the president's objectives would be difficult to achieve. However they offered the following suggestions to reach the objectives:

1. *Sales volume*—The current share of the salad dressing market is 15 percent and the total salad dressing market is expected to grow 5 percent for 19x9. Barr's current market share can be maintained by a marketing expenditure of $4,200,000. The two vice presidents estimated that the market share could be increased by additional expenditures for advertising and sales promotion. For each additional expenditure of $525,000, the market share can be raised by one percentage point until the market share reaches 17 percent. To get further market penetration, an additional $875,000 must be spent for each percentage point until the market share reaches 20 percent. Any advertising and promotion expenditures beyond this level are not likely to increase the market share to more than 20 percent.
2. *Selling price*—The selling price will remain at $6.00 per gallon. The selling price is very closely related to the costs of the ingredients, which are not expected to change in 19x9 from the costs experienced in 19x8.
3. *Variable manufacturing costs*—Variable manufacturing costs are projected at 50 percent of the net sales dollar (gross sales less freight, allowances, and discounts).
4. *Fixed manufacturing costs*—An increase of $100,000 is projected for 19x9.

5. *Depreciation*—A projected increase in equipment will increase depreciation by $25,000 over the 19x8 projection.
6. *Freight, allowances, and discounts*—The current rate of 10 percent of gross sales dollars is expected to continue in 19x9.
7. *Brokerage expense*—A rate of 5 percent of gross sales dollars is projected for 19x9.
8. *General and administrative expense*—A $200,000 decrease in general and administrative expense from the 19x8 forecast is projected; this is consistent with the president's commitment.
9. *Research and development expense*—A 5 percent increase from the absolute dollars in the 19x8 forecast will be necessary to meet divisional research targets.

REQUIREMENTS

a) The controller must put together a preliminary profit plan from the facts given. Can the president's objectives be achieved? If so, present the profit plan that best achieves them. If not, present the profit plan that most nearly meets the president's objectives. (*Hint:* Prepare budgeted income statements for each possible market share.)

b) The president's objectives, as described in the case, were stated in terms of a percentage increase in gross sales and a percentage return on sales.

1. What other measures of performance (other than sales dollars and return on sales percentage) could be used in setting objectives?
2. Discuss the advantages or disadvantages of the measures you present in relation to those in the case. (CMA Adapted)

10–22 Budgeted Income and Cash Flows: Construction

David Construction, Inc., builds heavy construction equipment for commercial and government purposes. Because of two new contracts and the anticipated purchase of new equipment, management needs certain projections for the next three years. You have been requested to prepare these projections.

You have acquired the following information from the company's records and personnel:

- David Construction uses the completed-contract method of accounting whereby construction costs are capitalized until the contract is completed. Since all general and administrative expenses can be identified with a particular contract, they also are capitalized until the contract is completed.
- David's December 31, 19y3, balance sheet follows:

David Construction, Inc.
Balance Sheet
As of December 31, 19y3

Assets:		
Cash		$ 72,000
Due on contracts		0
Costs of uncompleted contracts in excess of billings		0
Plant and equipment	$2,800,000	
Less accumulated depreciation	– 129,600	2,670,400
Total		$2,742,400

Liabilities and stockholders' equity:	
Loans payable	$ 0
Accrued construction costs	612,400
Accrued income tax payable	65,000
Common stock ($10 par value)	500,000
Paid-in-capital	100,000
Retained earnings	1,465,000
Total	$2,742,400

- Two contracts will be started in 19y4—Contract A and Contract B. Contract A and Contract B are expected to be completed in December 19y5 and December 19y6, respectively. No other contracts will be started until after Contracts A and B are completed. All other outstanding contracts had been completed in 19y3.

- Total estimated revenue for Contract A is $2,000,000 and for Contract B it is $1,500,000. The estimated cash collections per year follow:

	19y4	*19y5*	*19y6*
Contract A	$ 800,000	$1,200,000	$ 0
Contract B	300,000	450,000	750,000
Total	$1,100,000	$1,650,000	$750,000

- Estimated construction costs to be incurred per contract per year follow:

	Contract A	*Contract B*
19y4	$ 720,000	$ 250,000
19y5	1,000,000	400,000
19y6	0	650,000
Total	$1,720,000	$1,300,000

- Depreciation expense is included in these estimated construction costs. For 19y4, 10 percent of the estimated construction costs represents depreciation expense. For 19y5 and 19y6, 15 percent of the estimated construction costs represents depreciation expense. The cash portion of these estimated construction costs is paid as follows: 70 percent in the year incurred and 30 percent in the following year.

- Total general and administrative expenses (not included in construction costs) consist of a fixed portion each year for each contract and a varible portion which is a function of cash collected each year. For the two prior years, cash collected and total general and administrative expenses (based on one contract each year) were as follows:

	Cash collected	*Total general and administrative expenses*
19y3	$1,350,000	$27,250
19y2	1,180,000	24,700

All these general and administrative expenses represent cash expenses and are paid in the year incurred.

- Dividends are expected to be distributed as follows:

Year	*Distribution*
19y4	Stock: 10% of common shares outstanding (estimated fair market value is $15 per share).
19y5	Stock split: 2 for 1 (par value to be reduced to $5 per share).
19y6	Cash: $1.00 per share.

- David will acquire a new asset in 19y5 for $700,000 and plans to pay for it that year.
- When the cash balance falls below $70,000, David obtains short-term loans in multiples of $10,000. (For purposes of this problem, ignore interest on short-term loans and ignore any repayments on these loans.)
- Assume income taxes are paid in full the following year.

REQUIREMENTS

a) Prepare projected income statements for each of the calendar years 19y5 and 19y6 (when contracts are to be completed). The income tax rate is 40 percent, and the company uses the same methods for accounting and tax purposes.

b) Prepare cash budgets for each of the calendar years 19y4, 19y5, and 19y6. The budgets should follow this format:

Cash (beginning of year)	$
Plus: collections	
Less: disbursements (enumerated)	
Plus: borrowing (if any)	______
Cash (end of year)	$

(CPA Adapted)

10–23 Comprehensive Cash Budget: Service Organization

Prime Time Court Club (PTCC) has been in business for five years. The club has experienced cash flow problems each year, especially in the summer when court use is quite low and new membership sales are insignificant. The club has obtained temporary loans from the local bank to cover the summer shortages. The owners have also invested additional permanent capital.

The owners and the bank have decided that some action needs to be taken now to improve PTCC's net cash flow position. They would like to review a quarterly cash budget based on a revised fee structure that they hope would increase club revenues. The purpose of the cash budget would be to better anticipate both the timing and amounts of the probable cash flow of the club and to determine if the club can survive.

John Harper, Club Manager, recommended that the membership dues be increased and that the hourly court time fees be replaced with a monthly charge for unlimited court use. He believes that this plan will increase membership and reduce the cash flow and timing problem. In his opinion, the proportions of the different membership categories should not change, but the total number of members will increase by 10 percent. Court use will also increase an estimated 20 percent as a result of this new program. The pattern of use throughout the year is not expected to change. The proposed fee schedule, which is consistent with rates at other clubs, follows.

PROPOSED FEE SCHEDULE

Membership category	*Annual membership fees*	*Monthly court charges*
Individual	$ 75	$10
Youth	45	8
Family	150	18

The present fee structure, the distribution among membership categories, and the projected 19x3 operating data including membership status, court usage, and estimated operating costs are presented below. The projected operating data presented in the table were based on the present fee structure before Harper's proposed fee schedule was recommended.

PRESENT FEE STRUCTURE

Annual membership dues	
Individual	$ 45
Youth	30
Family	100

Court time fees	
Prime	$ 10 per hour
Regular	6 per hour

MEMBERSHIP DISTRIBUTION

Individual	50%
Youth	20
Family	30
	100%

PROJECTED OPERATING DATA

		Court time in hours		Costs	
Quarter	*Membership renewal or new memberships*	*Prime*	*Regular*	*Fixed**	*Variable*
1	600	5,500	6,000	$ 56,500	$ 57,500
2	200	2,000	4,000	56,500	30,000
3	200	1,000	2,000	56,500	15,000
4	600	5,500	6,000	56,500	57,500
	1,600			$226,000	$160,000

*Includes a quarterly depreciation charge of $12,500.

REQUIREMENTS

a) Construct a quarterly cash budget for one year for PTCC assuming the new fee structure is adopted and John Harper's estimates of increases in membership and court use occur. Assume also that the transition from the old to the new fee structure is immediate and complete when preparing the budget.

b) Will John Harper's proposal solve the summer cash shortfall problem? Explain your answer.

c) Will John Harper's proposal support a conclusion that the club can become profitable and survive in the long run? Explain your answer. (CMA Adapted)

10–24 Pro Forma Statement of Financial Position: Manufacturing
Einhard Enterprises has a comprehensive budgeting program. Pro forma statements of earnings and financial position are prepared as the final step in the budget program. Einhard's projected financial position as of June 30, 19x2, is presented here. Various 19x2–x3 master budget schedules based on the plans for the fiscal year ending June 30, 19x3, are also presented.

All sales are made on account. Raw material, direct labor, factory overhead, and selling and administrative expenses are credited to vouchers payable. Federal income tax expense is credited to income taxes payable. The federal income tax rate is 40 percent.

Einhard Enterprises
Pro Forma Statement of Financial Position
As of June 30, 19x2
(000 omitted)

Assets:	
Cash	$ 800
Accounts receivable	750
Direct material inventory	506
Finished goods inventory	648
Total current assets	$ 2,704
Land	$ 1,500
Property, plant, & equipment	11,400
Less accumulated depreciation	(2,250)
Total long-term assets	10,650
Total assets	$13,354
Liabilities and Equity:	
Vouchers payable	$ 1,230
Income taxes payable	135
Notes payable (due 12/30/x2)	1,000
Total liabilities	$ 2,365
Common stock	$10,200
Retained earnings	789
Total equity	10,989
Total liabilities and equity	$13,354

Sales Schedule in Units and Dollars

Unit sales	*Selling price per unit*	*Total sales revenue*
2,100,000	$16	$33,600,000

Production Schedule in Units and Dollars

Production (in units)	*Cost per unit*	*Total manufacturing cost*
2,110,000	$12.00	$25,320,000

Raw Material Purchases Schedule in Units and Dollars

*Purchases (in pounds)**	*Cost per pound*	*Total purchase cost*
4,320,000	$2.75	$11,880,000

* Two pounds of raw material are needed to make one unit of finished product.

Direct-Labor Schedule in Units and Dollars

*Production (in units)**	*Direct-labor cost per hour*	*Total direct-labor cost*
2,110,000	$8	$8,440,000

*Each unit requires one-half hour of direct-labor time.

Manufacturing Overhead Schedule in Dollars
(Expected activity level: 1,055,000 direct-labor hours)

Variable expenses	$2,954,000*
Depreciation	600,000
Other fixed expenses	1,721,000*
Total manufacturing overhead	$5,275,000

*All require cash expenditures. The manufacturing overhead rate is $5.00 per direct-labor hour ($5,275,000/1,055,000).

Selling and Administrative Expense Schedule in Dollars

Selling expenses	$2,525,000
Administrative expenses	2,615,000
Total*	$5,140,000

*All selling and administrative expenses require the expenditure of cash.

Beginning Inventory Schedule in Units and Dollars

	Quantity	*Cost per unit*	*Total cost*
Direct material	184,000 lbs.	$ 2.75 per lb.	$506,000
Finished goods	54,000 units	$12.00 per unit	$648,000

Cash Receipts and Disbursements Schedule
($000 omitted)

Cash balance 7/1/x2 (estimated)		$ 800
Cash receipts: Collection of accounts receivable		33,450
Total cash available		$34,250
Cash disbursements:		
Payment of vouchers payable:		
Direct material	$11,900	
Direct labor	8,400	
Manufacturing overhead	4,650	
Selling and administrative expenses	5,200	
Total	$30,150	
Income taxes	1,100	
Purchase of equipment	400	
Cash dividends	820	
Total cash disbursements		−32,470
Excess cash		$ 1,780
Financing costs		
Repayment of note payable 12/30/x2	$ 1,000	
Interest expense	50	−1,050
Projected cash balance 6/30/x3		$ 730

REQUIREMENT

Construct a Pro Forma Statement of Financial Position for Einhard Enterprises as of June 30, 19x3. (CMA Adapted)

10–25 Hospital Revenues and Costs

The administrator of Wright Hospital has presented you with a number of service projections for the year ending June 30, 19x2. Estimated room requirements for in-patients by type of service are:

Type of operation	*Total patients expected*	*Average number of days in hospital*		*Percent of regular patients selecting types of service*		
		Regular	*Medicare*	*Private*	*Semiprivate*	*Ward*
Medical	2,100	7	17	10%	60%	30%
Surgical	2,400	10	15	15	75	10

Of the patients served by the hospital 10 percent are expected to be Medicare patients, all of whom are expected to select semiprivate rooms. Both the number and proportion of Medicare patients have increased over the past five years. Daily rentals per patient are $120 for a private room, $100 for a semiprivate room, and $80 for a ward.

Operating room charges are based on "man-minutes" (number of minutes the operating room is in use multiplied by number of personnel assisting in the operation). The per man-minute charges are $0.25 for in-patients and $0.50 for out-patients. Studies for the current year show that operations on in-patients are divided as follows:

Type of operation	*Number of operations*	*Average number of minutes per operation*	*Average number of personnel required*
A	800	30	4
B	700	45	5
C	300	90	6
D	200	120	8
	2,000		

The same proportion of in-patient operations is expected for the next fiscal year and 180 out-patients are expected to use the operating room. Out-patient operations average 20 minutes and require the assistance of three persons.

The budgeted expenses for the year ending June 30, 19x2, by departments, are:

General services:	
Maintenance of plant	$ 100,000
Operation of plant	55,000
Administration	195,000
All others	384,000
Revenue producing services:	
Operating room	136,880
All others	1,400,000
Total	$2,270,880

The following information is provided for cost allocation purposes:

	Square feet	*Salaries*
General services:		
Maintenance of plant	12,000	$ 80,000
Operation of plant	28,000	50,000
Administration	10,000	110,000
All others	36,250	205,000
Revenue producing services:		
Operating room	17,500	30,000
All others	86,250	605,000
Total	190,000	$1,080,000

Basis of allocations:
Maintenance of plant—salaries
Operation of plant—square feet
Administration—salaries
All others—8% to operating room, 92% of all other revenue-producing services.

REQUIREMENTS

Prepare schedules showing the computation of:

a) The number of "patient-days" (number of patients multiplied by average stay in hospital) expected by type of patient (medical and surgical) and service (private, semiprivate, and ward).

b) The total number of man-minutes expected for operating room services for in-patients and out-patients. For in-patients, show the breakdown of total operating room man-minutes by type of operation.

c) Expected gross revenue from room rentals.

d) Expected gross revenue from operating room services.

e) Cost per man-minute for operating room services, assuming that the total man-minutes computed in part (b) is 800,000 and that the step method of cost allocation is used. (*Hint: All* budgeted expenses are to be allocated to revenue producing activities.) (CPA Adapted)

10–26 Educational Revenues and Expenditures

The Board of Education of the Victoria School District is developing a budget for the school year ending June 30, 19x7. The budgeted expenditures follow:

Victoria School District
Budgeted Expenditures
For the Year Ending June 30, 19x7

Current operating expenditures:			
Instruction:			
General	$1,401,600		
Vocational training	112,000	$1,513,600	
Pupil service:			
Bus transportation	$ 36,300		
School lunches	51,700	88,000	
Attendance and health service		14,000	
Administration		46,000	
Operation and maintenance of plant		208,000	
Pensions, insurance, etc.		154,000	$2,023,600
Other expenditures:			
Capital outlays from revenues		$ 75,000	
Debt service (annual installment and interest on long-term debt)		150,000	225,000
Total budgeted expenditures			$2,248,600

The following data are available:

- The estimated average daily school enrollment of the school district is 5,000 pupils including 4,800 regular pupils and 200 pupils enrolled in a vocational training program.
- Estimated revenues include equalizing grants-in-aid from the state of $150 per pupil. The grants were established by state law under a plan intended to encourage raising the level of education.

- The federal government matches 60 percent of state grants-in-aid for pupils enrolled in a vocational training program. In addition, the federal government contributes toward the costs of bus transportation and school lunches: a maximum of $12 per pupil based on total enrollment within the school district but not to exceed 6⅔ percent of the state per-pupil equalization grants-in-aid.
- Interest on temporary investment of school tax receipts and rents of school facilities are expected to be $75,000 and are earmarked for special equipment acquisitions listed as "Capital outlays from revenues" in the budgeted expenditures. Cost of the special equipment acquisitions will be limited to the amount derived from these miscellaneous receipts.
- The remaining funds needed to finance the budgeted expenditures of the school district are to be raised from local taxation. An allowance of 9 percent of the local tax levy is necessary for possible tax abatements and losses. The assessed valuation of the property located within the school district is $80,000,000.

REQUIREMENTS

a) Prepare a schedule computing the estimated total funds required from local taxation for the school year ending June 30, 19x7, for the Victoria School District.

b) Prepare a schedule computing the estimated current operating cost per regular pupil and per vocational pupil to be met by local tax funds. Assume that costs other than instructional costs are assignable on a per capita basis to regular and vocational students.

c) Without prejudice to your solution to part (a), assume that the estimated total tax levy for the ensuing school year ending June 30, 19x7, is $1,092,000. Prepare a schedule computing the estimated tax rate per $100 of assessed valuation of the property within the Victoria School District. (CPA Adapted)

10–27 Budget Pressure

The Noton Company has operated a comprehensive budgeting system for many years. This system is a major component of the company's program to control operations and costs at its widely scattered plants. Periodically the plants' general managers gather to discuss the overall company control system with the top management.

At this year's meeting, one of the most senior plant managers severely criticized the budgetary system. He said that the system discriminated unfairly against the older, well-run, and established plants in favor of the newer plants. The impact was lower year-end bonuses and poor performance ratings. In addition, there were psychological consequences in the form of lower employee morale. In his judgment, revisions were needed to make the system more effective. The basic factors of Noton's budget include:

1. Announcement of an annual improvement percentage target established by top management
2. Plant submission of budgets implementing the annual improvement target
3. Management review and revision of the proposed budget
4. Establishment and distribution of the final budget

To support his arguments, the plant manager compared the budget revisions and performance results. The older plants were expected to achieve the improvement target but often were unable to meet it. On the other hand, the newer plants were often excused from meeting a portion of this target in their budgets. However, their performance was usually better than the final budget.

He further argued that the company did not recognize the operating differences that made attainment of the annual improvement factor difficult, if not impossible. His plant has been producing essentially the same product for its twenty years of existence. The machinery and equipment, which underwent many modifications in the first five years, have had no major changes in recent years. Because the machines are old, repair and maintenance costs have increased each year and the machines are less reliable. The plant management team has been together for the last ten years and works well together. The labor force is mature, with many employees having the highest seniority in the company. In his judgment, the significant improvements have been "wrung out" of the plant over the years and that merely keeping even is difficult.

For comparison the plant manager noted that one plant, opened within the past four years, could more easily meet the company's expectations. The plant is new and contains modern equipment that is in some cases still experimental. Major modifications in equipment and operating systems have been made each year as plant management's understanding of the operations improves. Plant management, although experienced, has been together only since its opening. The plant is located in a previously nonindustrial area and therefore has a relatively inexperienced work force.

REQUIREMENTS

a) Evaluate the plant manager's views.

b) Equitable application of a budget system requires the ability of corporate management to remove "budgetary slack" in plant budgets. Discuss how each plant could conceal slack in its budget. (CMA Adapted)

10–28 Goal Congruence

Duval, Inc., is a large, publicly held corporation that is well known throughout the United States for its product. The corporation has always had good profit margins and excellent earnings. However, in the past two years, Duval has experienced a leveling of sales and a reduced market share, resulting in a stabilization of profits rather than growth. Despite these trends, the firm has maintained an excellent cash and short-term investment position. The president has called a meeting of the treasurer and the vice presidents for sales and production to develop alternative strategies for improving Duval's performance. The four individuals form the nucleus of a well-organized management team that has worked together for several years to bring success to Duval, Inc.

The vice president of sales suggests that sales levels can be improved by presenting the company's product in a more attractive and appealing package. She also recommends that advertising be increased and that the current price be maintained. This latter step would have the effect of a price decrease because the prices of most other competing products are rising.

The treasurer is skeptical of maintaining the present price when other corporations are increasing prices because this holding action will curtail revenues—unless this policy provides a competitive advantage. He also points out that the repackaging will increase costs in the near future, at least, because of the start-up costs of a new packing process. He does not favor increasing advertising outright because he is doubtful of the short-run benefit.

The vice president of sales replies that increased, or at least redirected, advertising is necessary to promote the price stability and to take advantage of the new packaging; the combination would provide the company with a competitive advantage. The president adds that they should study advertising closely to determine what type of advertising—television, radio, newspaper, or magazine—to use. In addition, if television is used, they must decide what type of programs—children's, family, sporting events, or news specials—to sponsor.

The vice president of production suggests several possible production improvements. A systems study of the manufacturing process could identify changes in the work flow that would cut costs. Operating costs could be further reduced by the purchase of new equipment. The product could be improved by employing a better grade of raw materials and by engineering changes in the fabrication of the product. When queried by the president on the impact of the proposed changes, the vice president indicated that the primary benefit would be product performance, but that appearance and safety would also be improved. The vice president of sales and the treasurer commented that this would result in increased sales.

The treasurer notes that all the production proposals would increase immediate costs and this could result in lower profits. If profit performance is going to be improved, the price structure should be examined closely. He recommends that the current level of capital expenditures be maintained unless substantial cost savings can be obtained.

The treasurer further believes that expenditures for research and development should be decreased since previous outlays have not prevented a decrease in Duval's share of the market. The vice president of production agrees that the research and development activities have not proven profitable, but thinks that this is because the research effort was applied in the wrong area. The vice president of sales cautions against any drastic reductions because the packaging change will provide only a temporary advantage in the market; consequently, more effort will have to be devoted to product development.

Focusing on the use of liquid assets and the present high yields on securities, the treasurer suggests that the firm's profitability can be improved by shifting funds from the presently held short-term marketable securities to longer term, higher yield securities. He further states that cost reductions would provide more funds for investments. He recognizes that the restructuring of the investments from short-term to long-term would hamper flexibility.

In his summarizing comments, the president observes that the team has a good start and the ideas provide some excellent alternatives. He states, "I think we ought to develop these ideas further and consider other ramifications. For instance, what effect would new equipment and the systems study have on the labor force? Shouldn't we also consider the environmental impact of any plant and product change? We want to appear as a leader in our industry—not a follower."

"I note that none of you considered increased community involvement through such groups as the Chamber of Commerce and the United Fund."

"The factors you mentioned plus these additional points should all be considered as we reach a decision on the final course of action we will follow."

REQUIREMENTS

a) State explicitly the implied corporate goals being expressed by each of the following.
   1. Treasurer
   2. Vice president of sales
   3. Vice president of production
   4. President

b) Compare these types of goals with the corporate goal(s) postulated by the economic theory of the firm. (CMA Adapted)

10–29 T Budgeting Variable-Costing Income and Cash: Manufacturing Challenge Problem (Appendix)

Presented is information pertaining to Complex Products' budget for the budget year ending December 31, 19x3.

Beginning-of-year balances:		
Cash	$40,000	
Accounts receivable (net)	$18,000	(previous quarter sales)
Raw materials in units:		
Material 1	200	
Material 2	160	
Finished goods in units	500	
Accounts payable	$10,000	(previous quarter purchases)
Borrowed funds	$25,000	
Desired end-of-year inventory balances:		
Raw materials in units:		
Material 1	600	
Material 2	400	
Finished goods in units	800	
Desired end-of-quarter balances:		
Cash	$20,000	
Raw materials as portion of following quarter's production needs	0.2	
Finished goods as portion of following quarter's sales	0.25	
Unit selling price	$ 130	

Manufacturing costs:			
Standard cost per unit:	*Units*	*Unit price*	*Total*
Material 1 lbs. at price	2	$ 4.00	$ 8.00
Material 2 lbs. at price	1.5	6.00	9.00
Direct-labor hours at rate	0.5	16.00	8.00
Variable overhead/labor hr.	0.5	7.00	3.50
Total std. variable cost			$28.50
Fixed overhead per quarter:			
Cash	$140,000		
Noncash	40,000		
Total	$180,000		
Selling and administrative costs:			
Variable cost per unit	$ 3.00		
Fixed costs per quarter:			
Cash	$30,000		
Noncash	10,000		
Total	$40,000		
Other costs:			
Interest rate per quarter	0.04		
Income tax rate	0.4		
Portion of sales collected:			
Quarter of sale	0.4		
Subsequent quarter	0.55		
Bad debts	0.05		
Portion of purchases paid:			
Quarter of purchase	0.8		
Subsequent quarter	0.2		

Sales forecast:

Quarter	*First*	*Second*	*Third*	*Fourth*	*Total*
Unit sales	4,000	8,000	2,000	1,000	15,000

ADDITIONAL INFORMATION

- All cash payments except purchases are made quarterly as incurred.
- All repayments and borrowings occur at the end of the quarter.
- All interest on borrowed funds is paid at the end of each quarter.
- Borrowings and repayments may be made in any amount.

REQUIREMENT

For each quarter of 19x3 and the year in total, prepare the following budgets:

1. Sales
2. Production
3. Manufacturing costs
4. Purchases
5. Selling and administrative expenses

6. Contribution income statement (Use variable costing.)
7. Cash

10–30 T Budgeting Variable-Costing Income and Cash: Manufacturing Challenge Problem (Appendix)

Presented is information pertaining to Big Bear Incorporated's budget for the budget year ending December 31, 19x5.

Beginning-of-year balances:			
Cash	$ 30,000		
Accounts receivable (net)	$ 18,000 (previous quarter sales)		
Raw materials in units:			
Material A	260		
Material B	240		
Finished goods in units	1,200		
Accounts payable	$ 25,000 (previous quarter purchases)		
Borrowed funds	$120,000		
Desired end-of-year inventory balances:			
Raw materials in units:			
Material A	400		
Material B	600		
Finished goods in units	1,200		
Desired end-of-quarter balances:			
Cash	$ 30,000		
Raw materials as portion of following quarter's production needs	0.4		
Finished goods as portion of following quarter's sales	0.5		
Unit selling price:	$ 60		
Manufacturing costs:			

Standard cost per unit:	*Units*	*Unit price*	*Total*
Material A lbs. at price	1.5	$ 2.00	$ 3.00
Material B lbs. at price	4.0	3.00	12.00
Direct-labor hours at rate	0.05	20.00	1.00
Variable overhead/labor hr.	0.05	30.00	1.50
Total std. variable cost			$17.50

Fixed overhead per quarter:	
Cash	$180,000
Noncash	70,000
Total	$250,000

Selling and administrative costs:	
Variable cost per unit	$ 2.00
Fixed costs per quarter:	
Cash	$ 40,000
Noncash	10,000
Total	$ 50,000

Other costs:	
Interest rate per quarter	0.04
Income tax rate	0.45
Portion of sales collected:	
Quarter of sale	0.3
Subsequent quarter	0.68
Bad debts	0.02
Portion of purchases paid:	
Quarter of purchase	0.75
Subsequent quarter	0.25

Sales forecast:

Quarter	*First*	*Second*	*Third*	*Fourth*	*Total*
Unit sales	6,000	12,000	10,000	5,000	33,000

ADDITIONAL INFORMATION

- All cash payments except purchases are made quarterly as incurred.
- All repayments and borrowings occur at the end of the quarter.
- All interest on borrowed funds is paid at the end of each quarter.
- Borrowings and repayments may be made in any amount.

REQUIREMENT

For each quarter of 19x3 and the year in total, prepare the following budgets:

1. Sales
2. Production
3. Manufacturing cost
4. Purchases
5. Selling and administrative expense
6. Contribution income statement (Use variable costing.)
7. Cash

SOLUTION TO REVIEW PROBLEM

a) **Hassan Corporation**
Production Budget
For the Months of May and June, 19x6

	May	*June*	*July*
Unit sales	15,000	18,000	12,000
Desired ending inventory	+3,600*	+2,400*	
Finished goods requirements	18,600	20,400	
Less beginning inventory	−3,000†	−3,600	
Production requirements	15,600	16,800	

* 20 percent of the following month's unit sales.
† 15,000 × 0.20

b) **Hassan Corporation**
Manufacturing Cost Budget
For the Month of May, 19x6

	May
Variable costs:	
Direct materials (15,600 units × 1 × $4)	$ 62,400
Direct labor (15,600 units × 0.2 × $10)	31,200
Factory overhead (15,600 × 0.2 × $5)	15,600
Total variable costs	$109,200
Fixed factory overhead	75,000
Total manufacturing costs	$184,200
Budgeted fixed factory overhead	$75,000
Planned application of fixed factory overhead (15,600 × $5)	−78,000
Planned overapplied fixed factory overhead	$(3,000)

c) **Hassan Corporation**
Purchases Budget
For the Month of May, 19x6

	May	*June*
Production requirements	15,600	16,800
Raw materials required for production	15,600	16,800
Desired ending inventory	+8,400*	
Raw materials requirements	24,000	
Beginning inventory	−7,800†	
Purchase requirements (units of material)	16,200	
Purchase requirements (dollars at $4/unit)	$64,800	

* 50 percent of the following month's requirements for production.
† 15,600 × 0.50

d) **Hassan Corporation**
Budgeted Income Statement
For the Month of May, 19x6

		May
Sales		$300,000
Cost of goods sold (15,000 × $12)		−180,000
Gross profit		$120,000
Selling and administrative expenses:		
Allowance for bad debts ($300,000 × 0.02)	$ 6,000	
Other variable (15,000 × $2)	30,000	
Fixed	20,000	−56,000
Net income		$ 64,000

e) **Hassan Corporation**
Cash Budget
For the Month of May, 19x6

		May
Beginning balance		$ 15,000
Receipts:		
Collections from April sales ($200,000 × 0.58)	$116,000	
Collections from May sales ($300,000 × 0.40)	120,000	236,000
Total cash available		$251,000
Disbursements:		
Purchases	$ 64,800	
Direct labor	31,200	
Variable factory overhead	15,600	
Fixed factory overhead ($75,000 − $20,000)	55,000	
Variable selling and administrative	30,000	
Fixed selling and administrative ($20,000 − $5,000)	15,000	−211,600
Ending balance		$ 39,400

Part Three

EVALUATING AND USING COST DATA FOR PERFORMANCE EVALUATION

11 Responsibility Accounting for Cost Centers

INTRODUCTION

CHARACTERISTICS OF EFFECTIVE PERFORMANCE REPORTS

RESPONSIBILITY ACCOUNTING

PERFORMANCE REPORTS AND CORPORATE STRUCTURE

RESPONSIBILITY ACCOUNTING FOR MANUFACTURING COSTS

SUMMARY

APPENDIX: PRODUCTION MIX AND YIELD VARIANCES

INTRODUCTION

FEEDBACK IN THE FORM OF PERFORMANCE REPORTS IS ESSENTIAL IF THE budgeting process, studied in Chapter 10, is to be effective. Employees need to know how current results compare with the budget in order to make appropriate adjustments during the current period and to improve plans for future periods. Upper management also uses accounting performance reports as one means of evaluating employees' activities. Knowing they will be held accountable for plans outlined in the master budget, employees and managers are motivated to pay more attention to the budgeting process for the benefit of the organization.

The purpose of this chapter is to examine the characteristics of effective performance reports, introduce responsibility accounting concepts used in the development of performance reports, and present the basic types of accounting variances often computed for manufacturing activities. Chapter 12 extends the application of responsibility accounting concepts to sales, distribution, and administrative activities. After studying Chapters 11 and 12 we will be able to completely reconcile the difference between budgeted and actual net income. Responsibility accounting concepts are further extended in Chapter 13 to include the evaluation of the overall performance of a semi-independent segment of a for-profit organization.

CHARACTERISTICS OF EFFECTIVE PERFORMANCE REPORTS

Performance reports assist in achieving the organization's goals by informing employees and managers of deviations from plans. To be effective, performance reports must be behaviorally sound, relevant, timely, accurate, and cost effective.

Behaviorally Sound

The vital element in the development and use of performance reports is people. Performance reports must motivate people to action. Writing in a slightly different context, Professors Miles and Vergin[1] suggested four criteria that must be filled if performance reports are to be behaviorally sound:

1. Standards must be recognized as legitimate. The people affected by the standards must understand how the standards are derived, and the standards must reflect the actual capabilities of the organizational process for which they are established.
2. Individual organization members must feel that they have some voice or influence in the establishment of their performance goals. Participation of those affected in the establishment of performance objectives helps establish legitimacy of these standards.
3. Standards must convey "freedom to fail." Individuals need assurance that they will not be unfairly censured for an occasional mistake or for variations that are beyond their control.
4. Performance data must flow not only upward for analysis by higher echelons, but they must also be fed back to those directly involved in the process.

The preceding criteria reveal a substantial overlap between the behavioral considerations involved in budgeting and in performance evaluation. This is expected because the budgeting-performance evaluation process is a continuous cycle.

Relevant

Performance reports should emphasize factors over which the report user has control. The appropriate question to ask in designing performance reports is "Is this information relevant to decisions made by the person or group to whom the report is addressed?" The data processing capabilities of computers provide a temptation to generate long lists of detailed data on every aspect of operations. Unfortunately such lists may obscure relevant information. In fact, performance reports should be as terse as possible. They need only direct attention to potential problems and opportunities.

When performance reports are used for performance evaluation, it is particularly important they they be limited to controllable factors. The notion of limiting performance reports to factors controllable by the report user is the essence of responsibility accounting, which we will discuss later in detail.

Timely

Performance reports for an entire year may assist in developing plans and evaluating personnel, but they are of limited use in adjusting operations during the year. To achieve their full benefits, performance reports must be received in time to adjust activities during the budget period. This leads to the tentative conclusion that earlier and more frequent feedback is preferable to later and less frequent feedback. Although this is true within limits, if the speed and frequency of feedback were carried to an extreme, all members of an organization would spend all their time reviewing their own and their subordinates' performance.

Fortunately this dilemma has several solutions. One is to use exception reports that include only deviations from plans. Another is to recognize that

[1] Raymond E. Miles, and Roger C. Vergin, "Behavioral Properties of Variance Controls," *California Management Review* **9**, No. 3 (Spring 1966): 57–65.

different levels of management and different personnel at each level have differing needs for feedback. A production supervisor may require daily, hourly, or continuous information regarding operations under his or her control, whereas the supervisor's superior, the plant superintendent, may need only weekly reports from each supervisor. Similarly, the vice president of manufacturing may require only monthly performance reports from each plant. As we move further from actual operations, the need for rapid and frequent feedback decreases. Higher levels of management spend more time planning and motivating personnel to execute plans, and lower levels of management spend more time executing plans. Hence the latter has greater need for frequent and rapid feedback.

Accurate and Cost Effective

Tradeoffs exist among timeliness, accuracy, and cost. In general, it is desirable to have relevant data available on a timely basis even if the data are somewhat inaccurate. Precisely accurate irrelevant data arriving three months after the end of a budget period is of little value to management. However, accuracy should be strived for and many organizations have internal auditing staffs to help ensure the accuracy of accounting data.

RESPONSIBILITY ACCOUNTING

Responsibility accounting is the structuring of performance reports addressed to individual or group members of an organization in a manner that emphasizes factors over which they have control. Because responsibility-accounting reports are based on an organization's structure, they must be tailor-made for each organization. Although organization charts and other documents may provide clues to the organization's structure, many instances of misunderstanding, overlapping duties, authority not commensurate with responsibility, and expenditures for which no one appears responsible, come to light when an attempt is made to implement a responsibility-accounting system. These circumstances make the development of a responsibility-accounting system difficult, but their resolution is a benefit of successful implementation.

Even though we can develop performance reports for areas as small as a single worker, the basic responsibility unit in most organizations is the department. In a manufacturing plant, separate responsibility centers are established for each production and service department. When a large department performs a number of diverse and significant activities, responsibility accounting may be further refined so that a single department contains several cost centers with performance reports prepared for each.

PERFORMANCE REPORTS AND CORPORATE STRUCTURE

Because effective performance reports are based on an organization's structure, the first task in designing them is to look at the organization chart. Exhibit 11–1 presents a partial organization chart for a manufacturing firm. The president and executive vice president are responsible for overall operations and profitability; the vice president of manufacturing is responsible for production; and the vice president of marketing is responsible for sales and distribution.

EXHIBIT 11–1 **Partial Organization Chart of a Manufacturing Firm**

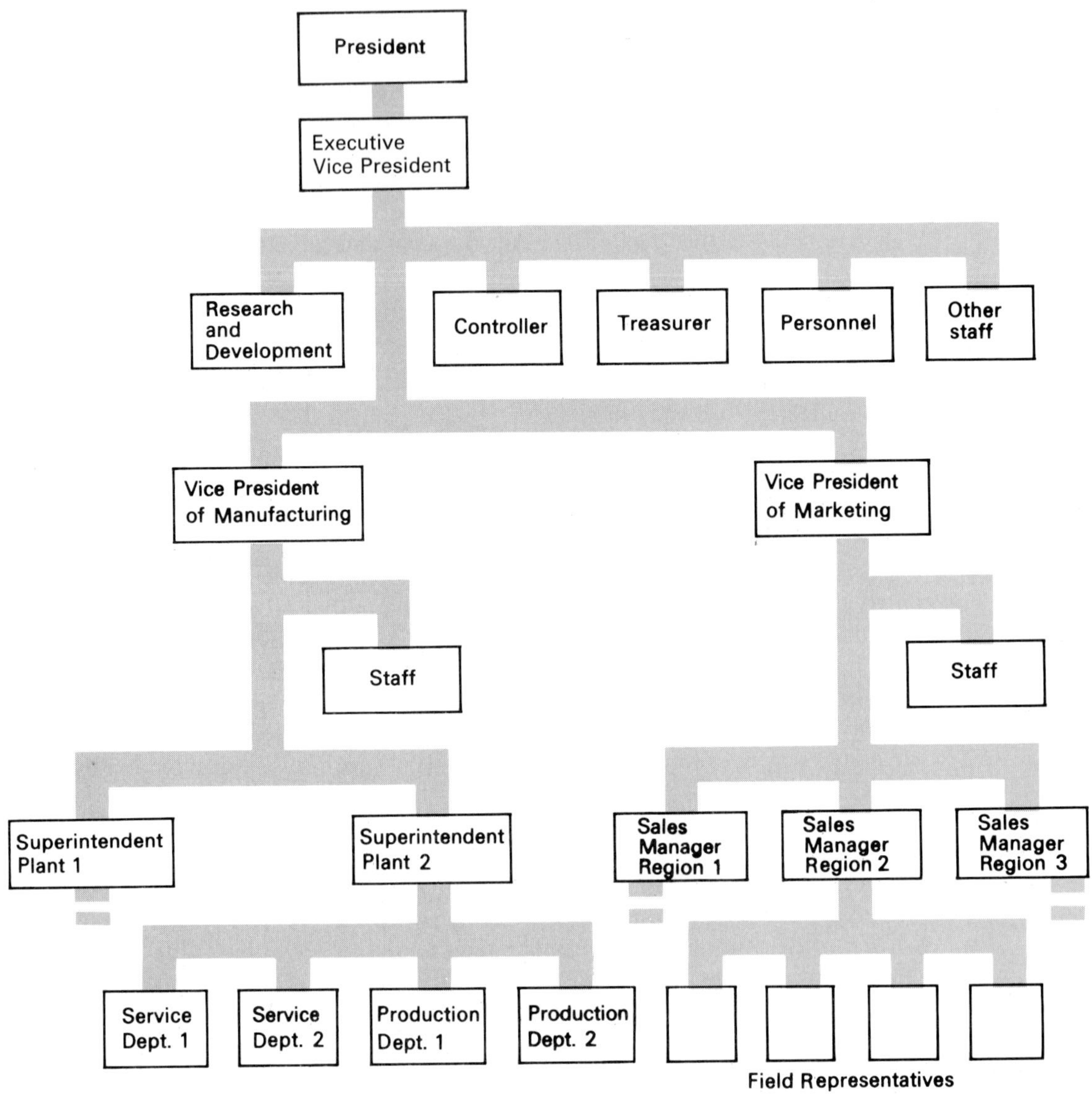

The vice president of manufacturing is in charge of the operation of two plants and a supporting staff. Each plant is under the overall direction of a superintendent who is responsible for the activities of service and production departments. Finally, each production and service department is under the direct control of a supervisor. In Exhibit 11–1 marketing activities are broken down into three regions, each under the supervision of a regional sales manager who reports directly to the vice president of marketing. Several field representatives report to each regional sales manager.

Types of Responsibility Centers

Under responsibility accounting, performance reports are prepared for segments of an organization that operate under the control and authority of a responsible manager. Each organizational unit for which performance reports are prepared is identified as a **responsibility center**. Depending on the nature of their activities, responsibility centers are classified as investment centers, profit centers, revenue centers, or cost centers.

An **investment center** is responsible for the relationship between its profits and the total assets invested in the center. In general, the management of an investment center is expected to earn a target profit per dollar invested. Investment center managers are evaluated on the basis of how well they use the total resources entrusted to their care to earn a profit. An investment center is the broadest and most inclusive type of responsibility center. The entire organization depicted in Exhibit 11–1 is an investment center.

A **profit center** is responsible for the difference between revenues and costs. Although a profit center may be an entire organization, it is more frequently a segment of an organization, such as a product line, marketing territory, or store. In the context of performance evaluation, the word "profit" refers to the profit center's contribution to common costs and profit. The segment reports in Exhibit 9–8 prepared using contribution income statements are examples of profit center performance reports.

A **revenue center** is responsible for the generation of sales revenues. In Exhibit 11–1 there are four revenue centers: Region 1, Region 2, and Region 3, and the entire marketing organization. Even though the basic performance reports of revenue centers emphasize revenues, revenue centers are likely to be assigned responsibility for the costs they incur in generating revenues. If revenues and costs are evaluated separately, the center has dual responsibility as a revenue center and as a cost center. If costs are deducted from revenues to obtain some bottom-line contribution, the center is, in fact, being treated as a profit center.

A **cost center** is only responsible for the incurrence of costs; it does not have a revenue responsibility. In Exhibit 11–1, each production and service department is a separate cost center, as is each production plant and all manufacturing operations. Each staff function, such as the Controller's Office or the Treasurer's Office, is also treated as a cost center.

A distinction is often made between standard and discretionary cost centers. A **standard cost center** is a cost center that has clearly defined relationships between effort and accomplishment. A **discretionary cost center** is a cost center that does not have clearly defined relationships between effort and accomplishment. Examples of discretionary cost centers include research and development, advertising, and general administration. Because it is difficult to develop predetermined relationships between resources used and accomplishments, evaluating the performance of discretionary cost centers is often difficult and judgmental.

A production department is the most obvious example of a standard cost center. Here, the standard costs for each product specify the materials and hours (effort) required to produce each unit of finished product (accomplishment). As accomplishments (measured in terms of production volume) increase, the allowed effort (measured in terms of unit standard costs times units of production) also increases. The remainder of this chapter is devoted to responsibility accounting for standard cost centers, especially in manufacturing organizations.

RESPONSIBILITY ACCOUNTING FOR MANUFACTURING COSTS

The manufacturing cost budget (studied in Chapter 10) serves as a guide to action and a basis of performance evaluation for manufacturing personnel. The starting point in the development of this budget is a sales forecast. Information from the sales forecast is combined with information on desired ending inventories of finished goods to determine current production requirements. The information on current production requirements is then combined with information on standard variable costs for materials, labor, and overhead, and information on budgeted fixed overhead to develop the manufacturing cost budget.

Because manufacturing managers should be encouraged to adjust production volumes to correspond with changes in sales volumes, the original manufacturing cost budget must be adjusted to the actual production volume before it is used for performance evaluation. If such an adjustment is not made, manufacturing managers are likely to be reluctant to increase production volumes above the budgeted levels if sales increase unexpectedly. Consider the following example.

Example 11–1

The Wild River Production Company has the following standard costs at a quarterly production volume of 2,500 units:

Direct materials (5 kilograms @ $2.00)	$10.00
Direct labor (3 hours @ $5.00)	15.00
Factory overhead:	
Variable (3 labor hours @ $2.00)	6.00
Fixed (3 labor hours @ $4.00)	12.00
Total standard cost	$43.00

The $4-per-labor-hour fixed factory overhead rate is based on budgeted quarterly fixed factory overhead of $30,000 divided by 7,500 labor hours at a quarterly volume of 2,500 units (each unit requires 3 labor hours). Although this $4 rate is used for product costing on an absorption cost basis, the manufacturing cost budget is based on quarterly fixed factory overhead of $30,000.

Assume Wild River's budget for the first quarter of 19x6 called for the production of 2,500 units; however, because of an unanticipated increase in sales volume, the actual first-quarter production was 3,000 units. Wild River incurred the following production costs at this volume:

Direct materials (18,000 kilograms @ $2.10)	$37,800
Direct labor (8,900 hours @ $5.20)	46,280

Factory overhead:	
Variable	17,000
Fixed	31,000
Total manufacturing costs	$132,080

A comparison of actual costs with costs in the original budget is presented in Exhibit 11–2(a). Actual costs were far in excess of budgeted costs, resulting in large unfavorable (U) cost variances for all items. In his or her own defense, the production supervisor might rightfully observe that the excess costs resulted from the need to increase production to help the company take advantage of the sales increase. A better analysis of manufacturing performance would attempt to determine if costs were higher than expected for the actual level of production.

Flexible Budgets as a Basis of Performance Evaluation

What is needed is a **flexible budget**, based on cost-volume relationships and drawn up for the actual level of production. A flexible budget is used to determine what costs should be at the actual level of production. A comparison of actual first-quarter manufacturing costs with costs allowed in a flexible budget is presented in Exhibit 11–2(b). Here the results are mixed with some cost variances being favorable (F) because actual costs are less than allowed and some being unfavorable (U) because actual costs are more than allowed. Significantly, this budget cannot be criticized as being for the wrong activity level.

A comparison of actual manufacturing costs with costs allowed in a flexible budget is a useful starting point in the evaluation of manufacturing costs or any other costs based on clearly defined input/output relationships. However, we can analyze variable cost variances further. The standards for variable cost items

EXHIBIT 11–2 Flexible Budgets and Performance Evaluation

Wild River Production Company
Manufacturing Cost Performance Report
For the First Quarter of 19x6

	Part A: Based on original budget			*Part B: Based on flexible budget*		
	Actual	*Original budget*	*Variance favorable (F) unfavorable (U)*	*Actual*	*Flexible budget*	*Variance favorable (F) unfavorable (U)*
Volume	3,000	2,500		3,000	3,000	
Variable costs:						
Direct materials	$ 37,800	$ 25,000	$12,800U	$ 37,800	$ 30,000	$ 7,800U
Direct labor	46,280	37,500	8,780U	46,280	45,000	1,280U
Factory overhead	17,000	15,000	2,000U	17,000	18,000	(1,000)F
Fixed costs:						
Factory overhead	31,000	30,000	1,000U	31,000	30,000	1,000U
Total	$132,080	$107,500	$24,580U	$132,080	$123,000	$ 9,080U

contain two elements: a standard input quantity per unit manufactured and a standard price or rate per unit of input. The variances in Exhibit 11–2 indicate only the net effect of variations between (1) actual and allowed input quantities, and (2) actual and standard prices or rates per unit of input. Additional information is obtained by decomposing the direct materials, direct labor, and variable factory overhead variances into two or more parts.

Materials Variances

The total materials variance is determined by comparing actual materials costs with costs allowed in the flexible budget:

$$\text{Total materials variance} = \underset{\text{Actual costs}}{(AQ_U \times AP)} - \underset{\text{Flexible budget}}{(SQ_A \times SP)} \qquad (11\text{–}1)$$

where

AQ_U = Actual quantity of materials used
AP = Actual unit price of materials used
SQ_A = Standard quantity of materials allowed for units manufactured
SP = Standard unit price of materials

As shown in Exhibit 11–2, when the actual costs exceed those allowed in the flexible budget, the variance is unfavorable (U). Using Eq. 11–1 the total materials variance for the Wild River Production Company is:

$$(18{,}000 \times \$2.10) - (15{,}000 \times \$2) = \underline{\underline{\$7{,}800\text{U}}}$$

This variance is represented graphically in Exhibit 11–3. The standard quantity and price is represented by the unlined area. Note that additional computations are required to determine the standard quantity of materials allowed. The standard quantity of materials allowed is equal to the actual production multiplied by the standard quantity per unit produced (3,000 units × 5 kilograms).

To obtain additional information, the total materials variance is decomposed into materials price and materials quantity variances.

$$\text{Materials price variance} = \underset{\text{Actual costs}}{(AQ_U \times AP)} - \underset{\text{Actual quantity at standard cost}}{(AQ_U \times SP)} \qquad (11\text{–}2)$$

EXHIBIT 11–3 Graphic Analysis of Total Materials Variances

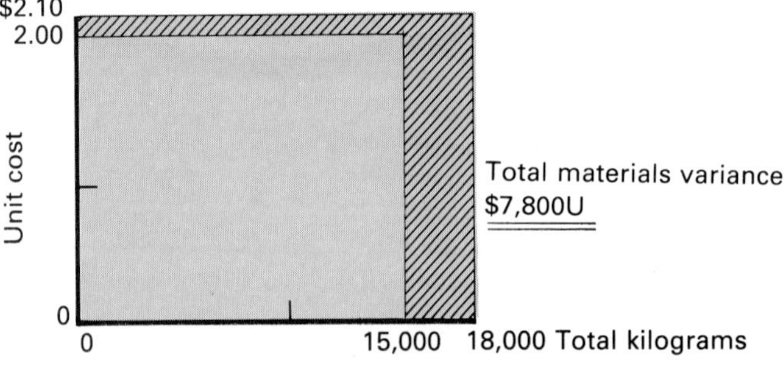

		Actual quantity at standard cost		Flexible budget	
Materials quantity variance	=	$(AQ_U \times SP)$	−	$(SQ_A \times SP)$	(11–3)

The **materials price variance** indicates the impact on costs of changes in the price of direct materials when the quantity of direct materials is held constant. The **materials quantity variance** indicates the impact of deviations between the actual and allowed use of direct materials when the price of direct materials is held constant at standard.

The difference between the actual cost of materials used and the flexible budget is reconciled as follows:

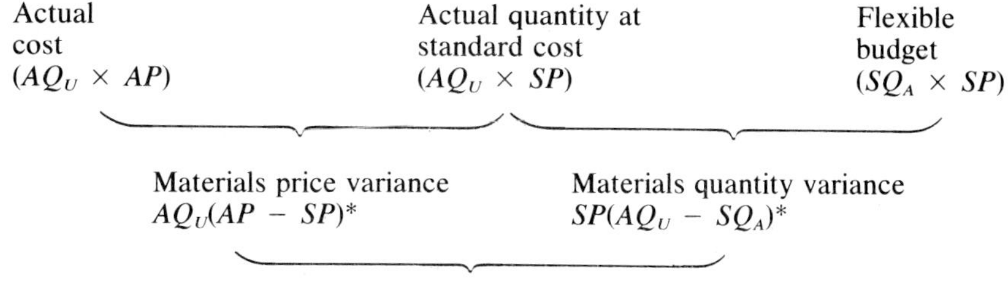

* Short computational formula.

The materials price and materials quantity variances for Wild River are:

Materials price variance	=	(18,000 × \$2.10) − (18,000 × \$2.00)	=	\$1,800U
Materials quantity variance	=	(18,000 × \$2.00) − (15,000 × \$2.00)	=	\$6,000U
Total materials variance	=	\$1,800U + \$6,000U	=	\$7,800U

The reconciliation between actual costs and the flexible budget is:

Actual costs	Actual quantity at standard cost	Flexible budget
(18,000 × \$2.10) = \$37,800	(18,000 × \$2.00) = \$36,000	(15,000 × \$2.00) = \$30,000

18,000(\$2.10 − \$2.00) = \$1,800U

\$2.00(18,000 − 15,000) = \$6,000U

\$7,800U

These variances are represented graphically in Exhibit 11–4.

A portion of the materials price variance is the result of the joint effect of increases in materials price and increases in materials use. This is illustrated in Exhibit 11–5. Some authors advocate the computation of three materials variances to isolate the effect of this joint variation. They compute a "pure materials price

EXHIBIT 11–4 Graphic Analysis of Materials Price and Quantity Variances

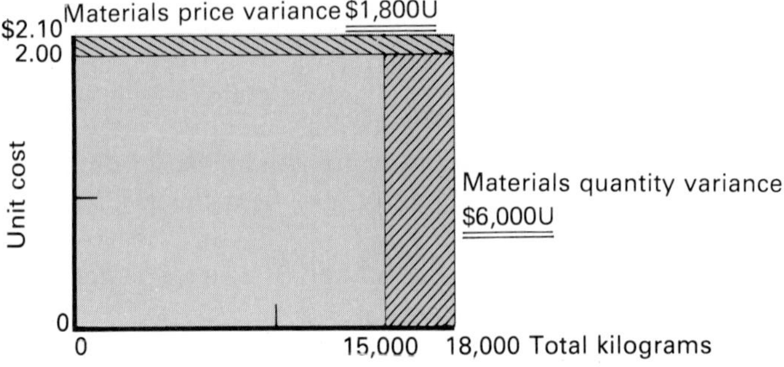

variance," a "pure materials quantity variance," and a "joint materials price-quantity variance" as follows:

$$\text{Pure materials price variance} = SQ_A(AP - SP) \quad (11\text{–}4)$$

$$\text{Pure materials quantity variance} = SP(AQ_U - SQ_A) \quad (11\text{–}5)$$

$$\text{Joint materials price-quantity variance} = (AQ_U - SQ_A)(AP - SP) \quad (11\text{–}6)$$

The "pure" and joint materials variances for Wild River are:

Pure materials price variance = 15,000($2.10 − $2.00) = $1,500U

Pure materials quantity variance = $2.00(18,000 − 15,000) = $6,000U

Joint materials price-quantity variance
= (18,000 − 15,000)($2.10 − $2.00) = $ 300U

Total materials variance = $1,500U + $6,000U + $300U = $7,800U

The authors do not recommend this three-way analysis of variances because of an unusual characteristic of the joint materials price-quantity variance. If both the pure price and the pure quantity variance are unfavorable, the joint variance is unfavorable. If one is unfavorable and the other is favorable, the joint variance

EXHIBIT 11–5 Graphic Analysis of Pure and Joint Materials Variances

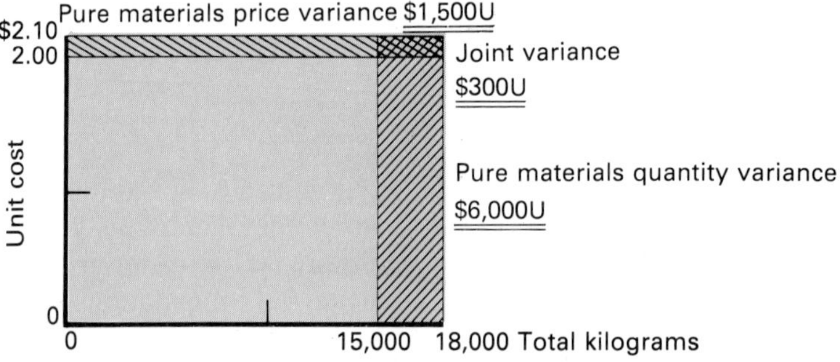

is also favorable. But, if the pure price and the pure quantity variances are both favorable, the joint variance is unfavorable! (Try this by drawing diagrams similar to Exhibit 11–5 with the requirement that the sum of all three variances equal the total variance.) Imagine the plant superintendent speaking to a production supervisor: "I am glad to see that your pure materials price variance and pure materials quantity variance are favorable, but what about this unfavorable joint variance?" Clearly this is ludicrous, but it can happen.

Timing of Materials Price Variance

In large organizations the responsibilities for the purchase and use of materials are divided between a purchasing agent and the production supervisors. Under these circumstances only materials quantity variances appear on production department performance reports; materials price variances appear on the purchasing department's performance report.

Organizations frequently purchase materials well in advance of their use on the basis of inventory models, such as those presented in Chapter 18. To obtain timely performance information, materials price variances should be computed and reported when materials are purchased rather than when materials are used. Following this approach, the materials price variance is based on quantities purchased and the materials quantity variance is based on quantities used:

$$\text{Materials price variance} = (AQ_P \times AP) - (AQ_P \times SP) \qquad (11\text{–}7)$$

$$\text{Materials quantity variance} = (AQ_U \times SP) - (SQ_A \times SP) \qquad (11\text{–}8)$$

where AQ_P = Actual quantity of materials purchased.

The computation of materials price variances at the time of purchase causes a discontinuity between the materials price and materials quantity variances that makes it impossible to reconcile the difference between the actual cost of materials purchased and the flexible budget without considering the impact of inventory changes (if any):

Actual cost $(AQ_P \times AP)$	Actual quantity purchased at standard cost $(AQ_P \times SP)$	Actual quantity used at standard cost $(AQ_U \times SP)$	Flexible budget $(SQ_A \times SP)$

Materials price variance $AQ_P(AP - SP)$	Inventory change at standard $SP(AQ_P - AQ_U)$	Materials quantity variance $SP(AQ_U - SQ_A)$

Example 11–2

Wild River purchased 20,000 kilograms of raw materials at $1.90 per kilogram. They used 18,000 kilograms to produce 3,000 units. The materials price variance, based on purchases, amounts to $2,000F:

Materials price variance = (20,000 × $1.90) − (20,000 × $2.00) =	$(2,000)F
Materials quantity variance = (18,000 × $2.00) − (15,000 × $2.00) =	$ 6,000U
Total materials variance = $(2,000)F + $6,000U =	$ 4,000U

The actual cost of materials purchased and the flexible budget are reconciled as follows:

Flexible budget (15,000 × \$2.00)		\$30,000
Add:		
Unfavorable materials variances	\$4,000	
Standard cost of increase in inventory [\$2.00(20,000 − 18,000)]	4,000	8,000
Actual cost of materials purchased (20,000 × \$1.90)		\$38,000

Labor Variances

The total labor variance is determined by comparing the actual labor costs with those allowed in the flexible budget:

$$\text{Total labor variance} = \underset{\text{Actual costs}}{(AH \times AR)} - \underset{\text{Flexible budget}}{(SH_A \times SR)} \qquad (11\text{–}9)$$

where

AH = Actual direct-labor hours
AR = Actual rate of pay per direct-labor hour
SH_A = Standard direct-labor hours allowed for the units manufactured
SR = Standard rate of pay per direct-labor hour

The total labor variance is also decomposed into two variances: "labor rate variance" and "labor efficiency variance."

$$\text{Labor rate variance} = \underset{\text{Actual costs}}{(AH \times AR)} - \underset{\text{Actual hours at standard cost}}{(AH \times SR)} \qquad (11\text{–}10)$$

$$\text{Labor efficiency variance} = \underset{\text{Actual hours at standard cost}}{(AH \times SR)} - \underset{\text{Flexible budget}}{(SH_A \times SR)} \qquad (11\text{–}11)$$

The **labor rate variance** indicates the impact on costs of changes in the labor rate when the quantity of direct labor is held constant at actual. The **labor efficiency variance** indicates the impact on costs of deviations between the actual and the allowed use of direct labor when the labor rate is held constant at standard.

The reconciliation of actual costs and those allowed in the flexible budget is:

Actual costs $(AH \times AR)$	Actual hours at standard cost $(AH \times SR)$	Flexible budget $(SH_A \times SR)$
Labor rate variance $AH(AR - SR)$*		Labor efficiency variance $SR(AH - SH_A)$*
Total labor variance		

* Short computational formula.

Example 11–3

In producing 3,000 units during the first quarter of 19x8, Wild River used 8,900 direct-labor hours at \$5.20 per direct-labor hour. The direct-labor standard is 3 hours per unit manufactured at \$5 per hour.

Labor rate variance = (8,900 × \$5.20) − (8,900 × \$5.00) =	\$1,780U
Labor efficiency variance = (8,900 × \$5.00) − (9,000 × \$5.00) =	\$ (500)F
Total labor variance = \$1,780U + \$(500)F =	\$1,280U

Although the production supervisor may be held accountable for a labor-efficiency variance resulting from a failure to adequately supervise employees, a labor rate variance resulting from a wage increase negotiated by someone else is beyond the supervisor's control. Of course, the supervisor is responsible if the labor rate variance results from the assignment of highly skilled and highly paid employees to jobs rated for employees of lower skill and pay. Sometimes a supervisor will assign "overskilled" employees in an effort to expedite a job and/or obtain favorable materials quantity variances and labor efficiency variances. When this is done, the net effect may be favorable even though the labor rate variance is unfavorable.

Variable Overhead Variances

The total variable overhead variance is computed by comparing the actual variable overhead costs with those allowed in the flexible budget:

$$\text{Total variable overhead variance} = \underset{\text{Actual costs}}{(AH \times AR)} - \underset{\text{Flexible budget}}{(SH_A \times SR)} \qquad (11\text{–}12)$$

where

AH = Actual direct-labor hours (or other activity base)
AR = Actual rate per direct-labor hour (or other activity base)
SH_A = Standard direct-labor hours (or other activity base) allowed for units manufactured
SR = Standard rate per direct-labor hour (or other activity base)

While the variable overhead variance in Eq. 11–12 uses direct-labor hours as an activity base, direct-labor dollars or machine hours may also be used. If direct-labor dollars are used, the flexible budget for variable overhead is determined by multiplying the standard variable overhead rate by the flexible budget for direct-labor dollars. Once again, the total variance is decomposed into two variances: "variable overhead spending variance" and "variable overhead efficiency variance."

$$\text{Variable overhead spending variance} = \underset{\text{Actual costs}}{(AH \times AR)} - \underset{\text{Actual hours at standard cost}}{(AH \times SR)} \qquad (11\text{–}13)$$

$$\text{Variable overhead efficiency variance} = \underset{\text{Actual hours at standard cost}}{(AH \times SR)} - \underset{\text{Flexible budget}}{(SH_A \times SR)} \qquad (11\text{–}14)$$

The **variable overhead spending variance** indicates the difference between actual variable overhead costs and the variable overhead costs allowed for the actual labor hours (or other activity base). The **variable overhead efficiency variance** indicates the difference between the standard variable overhead cost for the actual labor hours (or other activity base) and the standard variable overhead cost for the allowed labor hours (or other activity base).

The reconciliation of actual costs and the flexible budget is:[2]

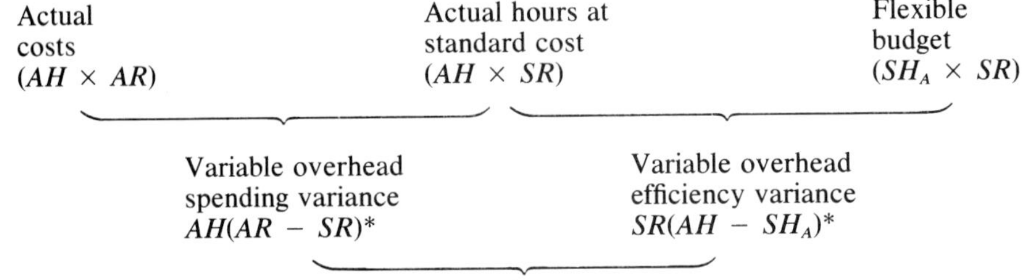

Total variable overhead variance

* Short computational formula.

Example 11–4

During the first quarter of 19x8, Wild River's variable overhead costs totaled \$17,000 when 3,000 units were produced using 8,900 direct-labor hours. The variable overhead standard is \$2 per direct-labor hour and 3 direct-labor hours are allowed per unit.

Variable overhead spending variance = \$17,000 − (8,900 × \$2) =	\$ (800)F
Variable overhead efficiency variance = (8,900 × \$2) − (9,000 × \$2) =	\$ (200)F
Total variable overhead variance = \$(800)F + \$(200)F =	\$(1,000)F

Note that the actual variable overhead rate per direct-labor hour is not given in Example 11–4. To determine the variable overhead spending variance, the actual variable overhead costs are substituted for $AH \times AR$ in Eq. 11–13. Many students who memorize formulas waste exam time determining the actual variable overhead rate by dividing \$17,000 by 8,900, and then multiplying the result by 8,900 to obtain \$17,000.

Fixed Overhead Budget Variance

Unlike the flexible budget for variable cost items, the flexible budget for fixed cost items is not adjusted for changes in the level of activity. This is because there are no input/output relationships for fixed costs. Hence the difference between actual and budgeted fixed costs cannot be decomposed into input cost and input use variances. The **fixed overhead budget variance** indicates the difference between actual and budgeted fixed factory overhead.

[2] When variable overhead is applied on the basis of direct-labor dollars, the actual direct-labor hours times the standard labor cost per direct-labor hour is used in place of actual direct-labor hours in Eqs. 11–12, 13 and 14. If actual direct-labor costs were used, the direct-labor rate variance would affect the size of the variable overhead spending and efficiency variances.

		Actual costs		Flexible budget	
Fixed overhead budget variance	=	(Actual fixed overhead costs)	−	(Budgeted fixed overhead costs)	(11–15)

The reconciliation of actual costs and the flexible budget is simply:

Actual costs	Flexible budget
Fixed overhead budget variance	

Example 11–5 During the first quarter of 19x8, Wild River's actual fixed overhead totaled $31,000 and the budgeted fixed overhead for the first quarter was $30,000.

Fixed overhead budget variance = $31,000 − $30,000 = $1,000U

Fixed Overhead Volume Variance When standard absorption costing is used, a fixed overhead volume variance results whenever there is a difference between the activity level used in developing the fixed overhead rate and the activity level allowed for actual production. The **fixed overhead volume variance** is the difference between budgeted fixed factory overhead and the fixed factory overhead costs assigned to products. For standard absorption costing,

		Flexible budget		Applied fixed overhead	
Fixed overhead volume variance	=	(Budgeted fixed overhead costs)	−	$(SH_A \times SR)$	(11–16)

where SR = Fixed overhead rate per direct-labor hour (or other activity base) used to assign fixed overhead to products.

Although the volume variance has little or no control significance, it is included in the analysis of fixed overhead costs because of its importance in income determination and asset valuation under absorption costing. When we consider the volume variance, the total fixed overhead variance equals the sum of the fixed overhead budget variance and the fixed overhead volume variance. The reconciliation between actual and applied fixed overhead under standard absorption costing is:

Actual costs (Actual fixed overhead costs)	Flexible budget (Budgeted fixed overhead costs)	Applied fixed overhead $(SH_A \times SR)$
Fixed overhead budget variance		Fixed overhead volume variance
	Total fixed overhead variance	

Note that the fixed overhead volume variance appears as a supplement to performance evaluation variances that reconcile actual costs to the flexible budget. It exists solely because of the absorption costing requirements of external reporting and taxation. The unusual nature of the volume variance causes problems for many students as they study cost accounting.

Example 11–6

Wild River's fixed overhead rate is $4 per labor hour and 9,000 labor hours are allowed for the work done.

Fixed overhead volume variance = $30,000 – ($4 × 9,000) = $(6,000)F

Total fixed overhead variance = $1,000U budget + $(6,000)F volume = $(5,000)F

Because Wild River produces only one product, the fixed overhead rate could be stated on a per unit basis as $12 per unit. When two or more products are manufactured, the fixed overhead rate must be expressed in terms of a factor that is common to all of them and representative of their proportionate use of available capacity. Typical bases include direct-labor hours, direct-labor dollars, and machine hours. Finally, note that the hours or dollars *allowed* for the work done rather than the *actual* hours or dollars is used in Eq. 11–16.

Alternative Approaches to Overhead Variances

Four-Way Analysis The separate computation of variances for fixed and variable overhead is identified as a ''four-way analysis'' of overhead variances. Using a four-way analysis, we computed the following variances:

- Variable overhead spending variance
- Variable overhead efficiency variance
- Fixed overhead budget variance
- Fixed overhead volume variance

EXHIBIT 11–6 Alternative Approaches to Overhead Variances (Amounts refer to Wild River overhead computations.)

Four-way	*Three-way*	*Two-way*
Variable overhead spending variance $(800)F	Overhead spending variance $200U (variable overhead spending + fixed overhead budget)	Overhead budget variance $0 (overhead spending + overhead efficiency)
Fixed overhead budget variance $1,000U		
Variable overhead efficiency variance $(200)F	Overhead efficiency variance $(200)F	
Fixed overhead volume variance $(6,000)F	Overhead volume variance $(6,000)F	Overhead volume variance $(6,000)F

The four-way analysis requires the identification of actual variable and actual fixed overhead. Unfortunately we cannot always separately identify the actual variable and actual fixed portions of semivariable costs such as power and maintenance. Without such a separation, we cannot perform a four-way analysis.

Three-Way Analysis When an analysis of historical costs permits the prediction of fixed and variable overhead, but the accounting records do not allow the separation of actual overhead costs into their fixed and variable elements, a three-way analysis of overhead variance is used. In the cost-estimating equation for total overhead costs, $T = a + bX$, b is the variable overhead rate and (a/budgeted X) is the fixed overhead rate. The three-way analysis provides the following reconciliation between actual and applied overhead:

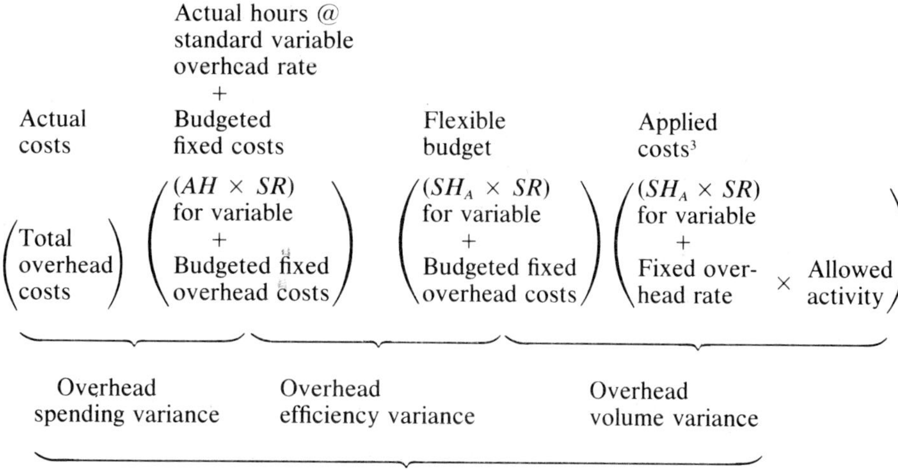

This may appear complex, but Exhibit 11–6 illustrates that the only change is the combining of the variable overhead spending variance and the fixed overhead budget variance into a single overhead spending variance. In computing the efficiency variance, the fixed overhead is held constant at the budgeted amount. In computing the volume variance, the variable overhead is held constant at the flexible budget amount.

Example 11–7

Wild River bases its standard costs for overhead on a quarterly activity level of 2,500 units and the following cost-estimating equation:

Total overhead = \$30,000 + \$2 (direct-labor hours)

During the first quarter of 19x8, overhead costs totaled \$48,000, direct-labor hours totaled 8,900, and 3,000 units were produced.

---

[3] If overhead is applied using a single rate based on allowed activity, the applied costs may be expressed as Overhead rate × Allowed activity. The single overhead rate includes the standard rate for variable overhead and the fixed overhead rate.

Overhead spending variance = \$48,000 − [(8,900 × \$2) + \$30,000] = \$ 200 U

Overhead efficiency variance = [(8,900 × \$2) + \$30,000] − [(9,000 × \$2) + \$30,000] = \$ (200)F

Overhead volume variance = [(9,000 × \$2) + \$30,000] − [(9,000 × \$2) + (\$4 × 9,000)] = \$(6,000)F

Total overhead variance = \$200U + \$(200)F + \$(6,000)F = \$(6,000)F

Two-Way Analysis The two-way analysis of overhead variances also assumes that no attempt is made to separate fixed and variable overhead in the accounting records and requires the determination of fixed and variable overhead rates. Yet, although sufficient information is available to perform a three-way analysis, the two-way analysis combines the overhead spending and efficiency variances into a single overhead budget variance. This leaves only a budget variance and the volume variance.

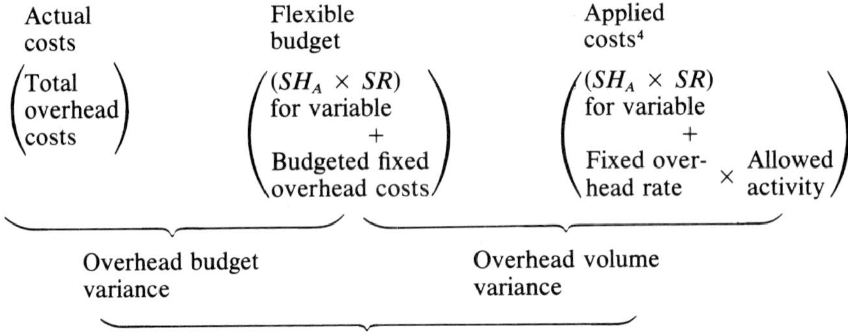

The relationships among the two-, three-, and four-way analysis of overhead variances are illustrated in Exhibit 11–6. The two-way analysis of Wild River's overhead is as follows:

Overhead budget variance = \$48,000 − [(9,000 × \$2) + \$30,000)] = \$ 0

Overhead volume variance = [(9,000 × \$2) + \$30,000] − [(9,000 × \$2) + (\$4 × 9,000)] = \$(6,000)F

Total overhead variance = \$0 + \$(6,000)F = \$(6,000)F

Additional Considerations

Under responsibility accounting, we must ensure that supervisors are evaluated on the basis of costs that they can control or influence. The general rule in responsibility accounting is to assign initial responsibility for cost control to the manager who most immediately authorizes the acquisition or use of a resource. Following this rule, the purchasing agent is assigned responsibility for materials price variances, whereas the production supervisor is assigned responsibility for

---

[4] See footnote 3.

materials quantity variances. Because responsibility expands at higher levels of management, all managers above the one assigned initial responsibility for a cost are also held responsible for that cost. Hence the plant superintendent is responsible for materials price variances and materials quantity variances. The department supervisor normally does not control certain overhead costs such as depreciation and a department supervisor's salary. Therefore the plant superintendent, who authorizes equipment purchases and has some control over the identity and pay of his or her immediate subordinates, is responsible for these costs.

Manufacturing Performance Reports and Corporate Structure To gain a further understanding of responsibility accounting and the expanding responsibility for cost control at higher levels in an organization, examine the hypothetical manufacturing performance reports presented in Exhibit 11–7 for the company whose organization chart is presented in Exhibit 11–1. At the bottom of the exhibit is a flexible budget performance report for the supervisor of Production Department 1 in Plant 2. The supervisor likely would have more detailed cost information available on request.

A flexible budget performance report for the superintendent of Plant 2 is presented in the center section of Exhibit 11–7. Note that the cost totals for Production Department 1 are summarized on one line of the plant superintendent's report, which also includes one line summaries for all other departments in the plant. Again, more detailed information would normally be available on request.

Finally, a flexible budget performance report for the vice president of manufacturing is presented at the top of Exhibit 11–7. Because the vice president of manufacturing has responsibility for all manufacturing costs, this report contains summary information on production costs in all plants as well as cost information for the vice president's office and any supporting staff.

Although the actual content and format of performance reports vary considerably, those presented in Exhibit 11–7 illustrate a number of important points:

- Manufacturing performance reports are based on a flexible budget drawn up for the actual level of activity.
- As we move up the organization chart, performance reports become more condensed.
- Performance reports normally emphasize factors controllable by each manager. The report of the vice president of manufacturing, who has authority over all manufacturing operations, contains costs that are not controllable by subordinate managers.
- An interesting aspect of the performance reports in Exhibit 11–7 is the treatment of service department costs. Service departments presumably provide services to production departments on request. To prevent the production department supervisors from treating services as a free good and consuming them without regard to cost, the production supervisors' performance reports include service department costs. However, the actual cost of operating service departments should not be included in the users' performance reports. If this were done, the cost assignment rates would fluctuate with changes in actual costs and the total volume of services (due to the existence of fixed service department costs), and

EXHIBIT 11–7 Responsibility Accounting Reports for Manufacturing

Vice President of Manufacturing

	Actual	*Flexible budget*	*(Favorable) unfavorable variance*
Vice President's office	$ 11,000	$ 10,000	$ 1,000 U
Manufacturing office staff	8,000	8,000	0
Plant 1	96,000	90,000	6,000 U
Plant 2	116,000	115,000	1,000 U
Other	20,000	20,000	0 U
Controllable costs	$251,000	$243,000	$ 8,000 U

Superintendent—Plant 2

	Actual	*Flexible budget*	*(Favorable) unfavorable variance*
Superintendent's office	$ 8,000	$ 8,000	$ 0
Service Department 1	10,000	10,000	0
Service Department 2	9,000	8,000	1,000 U
Production Department 1	41,000	43,000	(2,000)F
Production Department 2	52,000	50,000	2,000 U
Other	9,000	9,000	0
Total	$129,000	$128,000	$ 1,000 U
Less service dept costs included in production dept. reports at standard:			
Production Department 1	$ 4,000	$ 5,000	$(1,000)F
Production Department 2	9,000	8,000	1,000 U
Total	−13,000	−13,000	0
Total controllable costs	$116,000	$115,000	$ 1,000 U

Supervisor—Production Department 1, Plant 2

	Actual	*Flexible budget*	*(Favorable) unfavorable variance*
Direct materials	$ 11,000	$ 12,000	$(1,000)F
Direct labor	20,000	18,000	2,000 U
Factory overhead:			
Direct overhead	6,000	8,000	(2,000)F
Indirect overhead:			
Service Department 1	3,000*	3,000†	0
Service Department 2	1,000*	2,000†	(1,000)F
Total controllable costs	$ 41,000	$ 43,000	$(2,000)F

*Actual use at standard cost.
† Allowed use at standard cost.

inefficiencies of service department operations would be passed on to production departments. Accordingly, service department costs are assigned to production departments at a predetermined rate per actual unit of service provided. Knowing in advance the charge per unit of service facilitates planning. This treatment is somewhat analogous to not assigning the materials price variance to the production supervisor.

- Note that any double counting of service department costs must be eliminated in the plant superintendent's performance report. Service Departments 1 and 2 had actual operating costs of \$10,000 and \$9,000, respectively. Based on actual use, Production Departments 1 and 2 were assigned service department costs of \$4,000 (\$3,000 + \$1,000) and \$9,000, respectively, in their performance reports. For the plant as a whole the only real service department costs are those incurred in the service departments. Accordingly, the service department costs included in production department reports are deducted in computing the total controllable costs of the plant superintendent.

Full-Cost Performance Reports In some organizations, departmental performance reports do include costs that the department supervisor cannot control. This information gives department supervisors some comprehension of the total costs of operating and supporting their departments. Such costs should be clearly separated and distinguished from controllable costs. An abbreviated full-cost performance report is illustrated in Exhibit 11–8. Note that variances are not

EXHIBIT 11–8 Full-Cost Performance Report

Williams Company
Production Department Performance Report
For the Week Ending February 21, 19y6

	Actual	*Flexible budget*	*(Favorable) unfavorable variance*
Direct materials	\$11,050	\$10,000	\$ 1,050 U
Direct labor	16,000	17,800	(1,800)F
Factory overhead:			
Supplies	475	400	75 U
Utilities	1,200	1,040	160 U
Other	200	300	(100)F
Total controllable costs	\$28,925	\$29,540	\$ (615)F
Other costs:			
Share of Superintendent's office	2,500		
Share of General Administration	3,000		
Other	1,800		
Total	\$36,225		

EXHIBIT 11–9 Additional Measures of Manufacturing Performance

Labor hours available	Actual production in units
Labor hours used	Units produced per square meter
Idle time	Units spoiled to good units
Overtime	Machine hours available
Budgeted production in units	Machine hours used

computed for noncontrollable items; such computations would serve no useful purpose and might detract from the attention given controllable items.

Other Performance Data The performance reports in this chapter are presented in terms of dollars because of the advantages dollar performance measures have over nondollar performance measures. They can be summarized and reported for several organizational units, thereby facilitating more concise reports to upper management. Furthermore, the impact of a variance stated in dollars on profits is easily understood. However, dollars should not be used to the exclusion of nondollar performance measures. Especially at lower management levels, information on materials used, direct-labor hours, and machine hours is quite useful. Exhibit 11–9 lists several additional performance measures that may be included in performance reports.

SUMMARY

Performance evaluation is essential if the budgeting process is to be effective. Performance reports provide employees with information on how their current activities compare with the goals of the organization as expressed by the master budget and standard costs. This information helps employees adjust activities during the budget period and improve plans for future periods.

Because performance reports, like budgets, must motivate people to action, their development and use have many behavioral implications. Effective performance reports must be behaviorally sound as well as relevant, timely, accurate, and cost effective.

Responsibility accounting involves the structuring of performance reports addressed to individual members of an organization in a manner that emphasizes the factors they control. Under responsibility accounting, performance reports are prepared for segments of an organization that operate under the control and authority of an individual manager. Depending on the nature of their activities, responsibility centers are classified as investment centers, profit centers, revenue centers, and cost centers. Cost centers are further classified into standard cost centers and discretionary cost centers.

This chapter focused on standard cost centers in manufacturing organizations. Here, performance reports are based on a flexible budget drawn up for the actual level of production. For variable cost items, variances between actual manufacturing costs and costs allowed in the flexible budget can be further divided into those related to the cost of resources and those related to the use of resources. The only meaningful variance for fixed manufacturing costs is the fixed overhead budget variance. However, when fixed costs are applied to products on the basis of allowed activity, a volume variance is often caused by differences between budgeted and applied fixed factory overhead.

Although variances stated in terms of dollars are useful and necessary in determining the financial implications of deviations from the budget, nondollar performance measures are also informative. A topic not addressed in this chapter is the significance of variances. Variances merely act as attention directors. They point out potential problems and opportunities. Managerial judgment is required to determine their ultimate significance.

APPENDIX Production Mix and Yield Variances

In many production processes, such as the manufacture of food, chemicals, petroleum products, and metals, a number of raw materials are blended to obtain an acceptable output. When it is possible to vary the proportions in which raw materials are combined, the production supervisor is held responsible for ensuring that materials are mixed in a cost-efficient manner. To determine how efficiently mixing operations are performed, two additional manufacturing variances, the materials mix variance and the materials yield variance, are computed. These variances are introduced using an example developed by Professors Wolk and Hillman.[5]

Example 11–8

The W & H Feed Company produces cattle feed with various combinations of four raw materials, all of which need not be utilized in any given production run. Assumptions and constraints relative to production are:

1. The feed is produced in ten-ton batches.
2. Each batch must contain at least 18 percent protein.
3. Each batch must contain a maximum of 20 percent of raw materials 2 and/or 3.
4. Other factor costs are independent of the raw materials mix.

The following materials information is available:

Raw material	*Percent protein*	*Standard cost per ton*
1	50	$90
2	10	60
3	15	50
4	35	80

[5] Harry I. Wolk and Douglas A. Hillman, "Materials Mix and Yield Variances: A Suggested Improvement," *Accounting Review* **47,** no. 3 (July 1972): 549–555.

Using linear programming,[6] the following standards are developed for each 10-ton batch of output:

Raw material	*Standard quantity (in tons)*	*Standard price per ton*	*Standard cost per batch*
1	0.0	$90	$ 0
2	0.0	60	0
3	2.0	50	100
4	8.0	80	640
Total			$740

The standard mix is 20 percent of material 3 and 80 percent of material 4:

Material	*Portion*	*Percentage*
1	0/10	0
2	0/10	0
3	2/10	20
4	8/10	80

During a recent period, the following materials were used to produce 10 tons of feed:

Material	*Actual quantity*	*Actual price per ton*	*Actual cost of batch*
1	0.0	$90	$ 0.00
2	2.1	50	105.00
3	0.0	56	0.00
4	8.2	64	524.80
Total			$629.80

The total materials variance, assuming the price variance is computed at the time materials are used is $(110.20)F ($740 standard cost per batch − $629.80 actual cost per batch). This total materials variance is broken down into materials price and quantity variances in Exhibit 11–10(a). In studying Exhibit 11–10(a), observe that the materials

---

[6] To determine the standard mix and cost per 10-ton batch, the following cost-minimizing linear programming model is used:

Objective function:

$$\text{Minimize} \quad 90X_1 + 60X_2 + 50X_3 + 80X_4$$

Constraints:

$$\begin{array}{lrcrcrcrcl}
(1) & X_1 & + & X_2 & + & X_3 & + & X_4 & = & 10.0 \\
(2) & 0.50X_1 & + & 0.10X_2 & + & 0.15X_3 & + & 0.35X_4 & \geq & 1.8 \\
(3) & & & X_2 & + & X_3 & & & \leq & 2.0 \\
(4) & X_1, & & X_2, & & X_3, & & X_4 & \geq & 0.0
\end{array}$$

Constraint (1) limits production to 10-ton batches; constraint (2) covers the 18 percent protein minimum; constraint (3) represents the 20 percent maximum weight content for raw materials 2 and 3; constraint (4) indicates the use of each material must be greater than or equal to zero.

EXHIBIT 11–10 Production Mix and Yield Variances

(a) Materials Price and Quantity Variances

Material	*Actual costs* — *Actual quantity at actual mix and actual price*	*Actual quantity at actual mix and standard price*	*Flexible budget* — *Standard quantity allowed at standard mix and standard price*
1	0.0 × $90.00 = $ 0.00	0.0 × $90.00 = $ 0.00	0.0 × $90.00 = $ 0.00
2	2.1 × 50.00 = 105.00	2.1 × 60.00 = 126.00	0.0 × 60.00 = 0.00
3	0.0 × 56.00 = 0.00	0.0 × 50.00 = 0.00	2.0 × 50.00 = 100.00
4	8.2 × 64.00 = 524.80	8.2 × 80.00 = 656.00	8.0 × 80.00 = 640.00
	$629.80	$782.00	$740.00

$(152.20)F Materials price variance

$42.00U Materials quantity variance

($110.20)F Total materials variance

(b) Materials Mix and Yield Variances

Material	*Actual quantity at actual mix and standard price*	*Actual quantity at standard mix and standard price*	*Flexible budget* — *Standard quantity allowed at standard mix and standard price*
1	0.0 × $90.00 = $ 0.00	(10.3 × 0.00) × $90.00 = $ 0.00	0.0 × $90.00 = $ 0.00
2	2.1 × 60.00 = 126.00	(10.3 × 0.00) × 60.00 = 0.00	0.0 × 60.00 = 0.00
3	0.0 × 50.00 = 0.00	(10.3 × 0.20) × 50.00 = 103.00	2.0 × 50.00 = 100.00
4	8.2 × 80.00 = 656.00	(10.3 × 0.80) × 80.00 = 659.20	8.0 × 80.00 = 640.00
	10.3 $782.00	762.20	$740.00

$19.80U Materials mix variance

$22.20U Materials yield variance

$42.00U Materials quantity variance

quantity variance results from variations in the mix of raw materials as well as from variations in the total quantity of raw materials. The standard input allowed for the work done consists of 2 tons of raw material 3 and 8 tons of raw material 4, a total of 10 tons. The actual input included 2.1 tons of raw material 2 and 8.2 tons of raw material 4, a total of 10.3 tons. To separate these two elements, the materials quantity variance is further decomposed into a materials mix variance and a materials yield variance.

The **materials mix variance** indicates the impact on materials costs of deviations between the actual and the standard mix. It is computed using standard costs and holding the total quantity of materials used constant at their actual amount while allowing the mix to vary between actual and standard. The **materials yield variance** indicates the impact on materials costs of deviations from the total standard materials allowed for the work done. It is computed using standard costs and holding the mix constant at standard while allowing total quantities to vary between actual and the standard quantity allowed for the work done.

W & H's materials quantity variance is decomposed into materials mix and yield variances in Exhibit 11–10(b). The only change in the computation of the quantity variance between Exhibit 11–10(a) and Exhibit 11–10(b) is the addition of the column labeled "actual quantity at standard mix and standard price." In Exhibit 11–10(b), the materials yield variance could be called the "pure materials quantity variance;" it is purified by removing the impact of changes in the input mix.

INTERPRETING MIX AND YIELD VARIANCES

The variances in Exhibit 11–10(b), indicate that a shift was made to a mix that had higher standard costs than the standard mix, and that an excess quantity of materials was used. Yet, in Exhibit 11–10(a), the total materials variance was favorable due to price changes. It is interesting to ask if total costs would have been higher if the mix had not been changed. The answer is no. At the actual prices, the standard mix would have cost $624 [(2 tons of material 3 × $56 per ton) + (8 tons of material 4 × $64 per ton)]. It appears that, by changing the mix, the production supervisor incurred additional costs of $5.80U ($629.80 − $624). Yet, the analysis in Exhibit 11–10(a), clearly suggests that the overall impact was favorable.

The problem is that the standard mix is appropriate for only a particular set of materials prices. If there are price changes, there can also be changes in the optimal mix. The advent of computers and linear programming software packages allows production supervisors to constantly change the input mix in an effort to produce an acceptable product at the lowest possible cost. If a production supervisor is assigned responsibility for changing the materials mix in response to changes in materials costs, his or her performance should not be evaluated on the basis of the "old" standard mix. It should be evaluated using the low-cost mix appropriate for the actual prices at the time production took place. Adjusting the linear programming model used to develop W & H's original standard mix for the materials price changes, the following standards are developed:

Raw material	*Standard quantity (in tons)*	*Standard price per ton*	*Standard cost per batch*
1	0	$90	$ 0
2	2	50	100
3	0	56	0
4	8	64	512
Total			$612

These standards are called **ex post standards,** meaning they were developed after production took place. Ex post standards should not be used to evaluate the performance

EXHIBIT 11–11 Ex Post Analysis of Mix and Yield Variances

Material	Actual quantity at actual mix and standard price	Actual quantity at standard mix and standard price	Flexible budget: Standard quantity allowed at standard mix and standard price
1	0.0 × $90.00 = $ 0.00	(10.3 × 0.00) × $90.00 = $ 0.00	0.0 × $90.00 = $ 0.00
2	2.1 × 50.00 = 105.00	(10.3 × 0.20) × 50.00 = 103.00	2.0 × 50.00 = 100.00
3	0.0 × 56.00 = 0.00	(10.3 × 0.00) × 56.00 = 0.00	0.0 × 56.00 = 0.00
4	8.2 × 64.00 = 524.80	(10.3 × 0.80) × 64.00 = 527.36	8.0 × 64.00 = 512.00
	10.3 $629.80	630.36	$612.00

$(0.56)F Material mix variance

$18.36U Materials yield variance

$17.80U Materials quantity variance

of a production supervisor unless he or she has the responsibility, authority, and ability to change the mix in response to changing circumstances. Furthermore, the supervisor must be constantly informed of the changed circumstances. Using these ex post standards, the final materials mix and yield variances are computed in Exhibit 11–11.

LABOR MIX AND YIELD VARIANCES

Many organizations have standard mixes for the skills of employees assigned to certain tasks. Under these circumstances the total labor efficiency variance reflects changes in the labor mix as well as deviations in the total quantity of labor used. To isolate these two factors, the labor efficiency variance can be decomposed into labor mix and labor yield (or pure labor efficiency) variances. The **labor mix variance** indicates the impact on labor costs of deviations between the actual and the standard mix. It is computed using standard labor rates and holding the total labor hours constant at their actual amount while allowing the mix to vary between actual and standard. The **labor yield variance** (also called the **pure labor efficiency variance**) indicates the impact on labor costs of deviations from the total standard labor hours allowed for the work done. It is computed holding the labor mix constant at standard while allowing the total labor hours to vary between actual and the standard quantity allowed for the work done. Because the computations are similar to those for the materials mix and yield variances, they are omitted.

KEY TERMS

Cost center
Discretionary cost center
Fixed overhead budget variance
Fixed overhead volume variance
Flexible budget
Investment center

Labor efficiency variance
Labor rate variance
Materials price variance
Materials quantity variance
Profit center
Responsibility accounting
Responsibility center
Revenue center
Standard cost center
Variable overhead efficiency variance
Variable overhead spending variance

APPENDIX KEY TERMS

Ex post standards
Labor mix variance
Labor yield variance
Materials mix variance
Materials yield variance
Pure labor efficiency variance

SELECTED REFERENCES

Barnes, John L., "How to Tell if Standard Costs Are Really Standard," *Management Accounting* **64,** No. 12 (June 1983): 50–54.

Bruns, William J., Jr., and John H. Waterhouse, "Budgetary Control and Organization Structure," *Journal of Accounting Research* **13,** No. 2 (Autumn 1975): 177–203.

Ferrara, William L., "Responsibility Accounting—A Basic Control Concept," *N.A.A. Bulletin* **46,** No. 1 (September 1964): 11–19.

Gillespie, Jackson F., "An Application of Learning Curves to Standard Costing," *Management Accounting* **63,** No. 3 (September 1981): 63–65.

Goodman, Richard A., "A Systems Diagram of the Functions of a Manager," *California Management Review* **10,** No. 4 (Summer 1968): 27–31.

Hicks, James O., "The Application of Exponential Smoothing to Standard Cost Systems," *Management Accounting* **60,** No. 3 (September 1978): 28–32, 53.

McIntyre, Edward V., "A Note on the Joint Variance," *Accounting Review* **51,** No. 1 (January 1976): 151–155.

_____, "The Joint Variance: A Reply," *Accounting Review* **53,** No. 2 (April 1978): 534–537.

Mensah, Yaw M., "A Dynamic Approach to the Evaluation of Input-Variable Cost Center Performance," *Accounting Review* **57,** No. 4 (October 1982): 681–700.

Miles, Raymond E., and Roger C. Vergin, "Behavioral Properties of Variance Controls," *California Management Review* **9,** No. 3 (Spring 1966): 57–65.

Mullett, Matthew, "Benefits From Standard Costing in the Restaurant Industry," *Management Accounting* **60,** No. 3 (September 1978): 47–53.

Owens, Robert W., "Cash Flow Variance Analysis," *Accounting Review* **55,** No. 1 (January 1980): 111–116.

Piper, R. M., "The Joint Variance: A Comment," *Accounting Review* **52,** No. 2 (April 1977): 527–533.

Talbott, John C., and James S. H. Chin, "Factory Overhead Variance Analysis," *Managerial Planning* **27,** No. 1 (July-August 1978): 36–39.

Wolf, Warren, "Developing a Cost System for Today's Decision Making," *Management Accounting* **64,** No. 6 (December 1982): 19–23.

Wolk, Harry I., and Douglas A. Hillman, "Material Mix and Yield Variances: A Suggested Improvement," *Accounting Review* **47,** No. 3 (July 1972): 549–555.

REVIEW QUESTIONS

11–1 Mention five characteristics of effective performance reports.

11–2 What is responsibility accounting?

11–3 Identify four types of responsibility centers.

11–4 Distinguish between standard and discretionary cost centers.

11–5 For what purpose is a flexible budget developed?

11–6 What activity level is used in a flexible budget?

11–7 What factor is held constant in the computation of the materials price variance?

11–8 What factor is held constant in the computation of the materials quantity variance?

11–9 Why is it desirable to compute the materials price variance at the time materials are purchased?

11–10 Indicate the factor that is held constant in the computation of the labor efficiency and the variable overhead efficiency variances.

11–11 What is the only meaningful fixed overhead variance? How is it computed? Why does the computation of this variance differ from the computation of variances for variable costs?

11–12 What is the cause of a fixed overhead volume variance? How is this variance computed?

11–13 Why is it not always possible to prepare a four-way analysis of overhead variances? What two variances are combined into the overhead spending variance when a three-way analysis of overhead variances is prepared?

11–14 Why is it desirable to include service department costs in the performance reports of departments receiving services? Why is it undesirable to include the actual costs of operating service departments in the performance reports of departments receiving services?

REVIEW PROBLEM

Flexible Budget and Overview of Variance Computation

The Burque Furniture Company has the following standard cost per unit of furniture:

Direct material (50 board-feet of lumber @ $400 per 1,000 board-feet)	$20.00
Direct labor (3 hours @ $10 per hour)	30.00
Variable factory overhead (3 direct-labor hours @ $5 per direct-labor hour)	15.00
Fixed factory overhead ($30,000 per month ÷ 3,000 monthly direct-labor hours × 3 direct-labor hours)	30.00
Total	$95.00

For July 19w2, when 1,100 units of furniture were produced, the following information is available:

Lumber purchased: 50,000 board-feet at $390 per 1,000 board-feet
Lumber used: 56,000 board-feet
Direct labor: 3,100 hours at $10.50 per hour
Variable overhead: $15,500
Fixed overhead: $29,000

Any materials price variance is computed at the time materials are purchased and assigned to the Purchasing Department.

REQUIREMENTS

a) Prepare a flexible budget for the actual level of activity. In the flexible budget indicate the total variance of each production cost assigned to the Production Department.

b) Prepare a complete analysis of all variances, including a four-way analysis of overhead variances.

c) Prepare a three-way analysis of overhead variances.

d) Prepare a two-way analysis of overhead variances.

The solution to this problem is found at the end of the Chapter 11 problems and exercises.

EXERCISES

11–1 Behavioral Considerations in Performance Evaluation

Briefly comment on each of the following statements:

a) "Our company is a firm believer in management by exception. In the evaluation of our supervisors we look only at unfavorable variances."

b) "Our organization is a firm believer in budgeting. Budgeting forces employees to plan and it helps us coordinate activities. However, because we are a professional organization, we do not develop performance reports. Our employees are self-motivated and would react poorly to accounting variances and their implicit attempt to place blame."

c) "In developing our standards for the coming year, we take past performance and subtract a 10 percent improvement factor. This keeps our employees on their toes and gives them something to strive for."

d) "A great benefit of performance reports based on responsibility accounting is that it is easy to tell who is to blame. The report spells it out in black and white and no supervisor can refute it."

e) "There is just no way to deal with those people in production. We finally get a chance to get our foot in the door as a supplier to Mammoth Motors and we lose the business because they refuse to expedite the order. They should put that in their performance report!"

f) "Of course, I have an unfavorable materials price variance. Demand is up so much I had to send in two special orders. I should be rewarded for being able to get sufficient materials under these circumstances."

11–2 Dysfunctional Consequences of Selected Performance Measures

Suggest dysfunctional consequences that may result from each of the following performance measures:

a) In an employment agency, employment interviewers are evaluated on the basis of the number of interviews they conduct.

b) In a federal agency, case workers have a quota for the number of cases they must investigate each month.

c) The supervisor of a job shop is evaluated on the basis of the number of jobs completed each month.

d) A large trucking firm pays drivers on the basis of the number of miles driven.

e) A processing company pays a bonus of $500 to supervisors every time their departments' net variances are favorable. Standards are set on the basis of the previous period's performance less a 5 percent improvement factor.

11–3 Original Budgets and Performance Evaluation

The Aldrich Company's manufacturing cost budget for June 19x1 called for labor costs totaling $114,000. Because the actual labor costs were equal to precisely this amount, management concluded there were no labor variances. Comment.

11–4 Materials Variances: Time of Recognition

At a normal monthly volume of 200,000 square meters, the Albany Rug Company has the following standard cost per square meter for materials:

Direct materials (2 kilograms @ $2.50)	$5

The July 1 raw materials inventory consisted of 350,000 kilograms of material purchased at $2.60 per kilogram. During July, 500,000 kilograms were purchased at $2.30 per kilogram and 420,000 kilograms were issued to the factory. July production totaled 205,000 square meters.

REQUIREMENTS

a) Prepare an analysis of July materials variances assuming price variances are isolated when materials are placed in production and FIFO inventory valuation is used.

b) Prepare an analysis of July materials variances assuming price variances are isolated when materials are purchased.

c) Evaluate the usefulness of the variance information contained in parts (a) and (b).

11–5 Materials Variances: Time of Recognition

The Stilwater Company has the following materials standard per unit produced:

Direct materials (2.5 liters @ $3)	$7.50

The August 1 raw materials inventory consisted of 10,000 liters of raw materials purchased at $2.50 per liter. During August, 20,000 liters of raw materials were purchased at $3.10 per liter and 15,000 liters of raw materials were issued to the factory. August production totaled 5,000 units.

REQUIREMENTS

a) Prepare an analysis of August materials variances assuming price variances are isolated when materials are placed in production and FIFO inventory valuation is used.

b) Prepare an analysis of August materials variances assuming price variances are isolated when materials are purchased.

11–6 "Pure" and Joint Materials Variances

For a certain process the direct materials standard per unit manufactured is 4 pounds at $5 per pound.

REQUIREMENT

Determine the pure materials price variance, the pure materials quantity variance, and the joint materials price-quantity variance for each of the following cases:

	Case			
	1	*2*	*3*	*4*
Units produced	1,000	500	800	600
Pounds of materials purchased and used	4,100	2,200	3,000	2,200
Actual cost of purchases	$21,320	$10,560	$14,100	$11,550

11–7 "Pure" and Joint Materials Variances

For a certain process the direct materials standard per unit manufactured is 2 gallons at $4 per gallon.

REQUIREMENT

Determine the pure materials price variance, the pure materials quantity variance, and the joint materials price-quantity variance for each of the following cases.

	Case			
	1	*2*	*3*	*4*
Units produced	1,000	1,000	1,000	1,000
Pounds of materials purchased and used	2,200	2,200	1,800	1,800
Purchase price per pound	$4.50	$3.50	$3.50	$4.50

11–8 T Basic Manufacturing Variances: Four-Way Overhead

Presented is information on the Northern Furniture Company's standard costs and the actual results of December 19x4 operations.

	Direct materials	*Direct labor*	*Variable factory overhead*	*Fixed factory overhead*
Standard quantity	4 units	2 hours	2 direct-labor hours	2 direct-labor hours
Standard price or rate	$5.00	$8.00	$10.00	$10.00
Total	$20.00	$16.00	$20.00	$20.00

Budgeted fixed costs per period	$100,000
Units manufactured	5,000
Purchases of raw materials:	
Units	22,000
Cost per unit	$5.10
Total	$112,200.00
Use of raw materials in units	21,000
Direct labor:	
Actual hours	11,000
Actual rate	$8.00
Total	$88,000.00
Actual factory overhead:	
Variable	$99,000.00
Fixed	$105,000.00

REQUIREMENTS

a) Prepare a flexible budget performance report comparing actual and allowed costs.

b) Determine each of the following variances:

1. Materials price (at purchase) and quantity
2. Labor rate and efficiency
3. Variable overhead spending and efficiency
4. Fixed overhead budget and volume

11–9 T Three- and Two-Way Overhead

For the situation presented in Exercise 11–8, prepare both a three-way and a two-way analysis of overhead variances.

11–10 T Basic Manufacturing Variances: Four-Way Overhead

Presented is information pertaining to the Westcott Company's standard costs and the actual results of January 19y2 operations.

	Direct materials	*Direct labor*	*Variable factory overhead*	*Fixed factory overhead*
Standard quantity	3 units	1.5 hours	1.5 direct-labor hours	1.5 direct-labor hours
Standard price or rate	$4.00	$10.00	$6.00	$4.00
Total	$12.00	$15.00	$9.00	$6.00

	Variable factory overhead
Budgeted fixed costs per period	$40,000
Units manufactured	6,000
Purchases of raw materials:	
Units	20,000
Cost per unit	$4.80
Total	$96,000.00
Use of raw materials in units	19,000
Direct labor:	
Actual hours	9,500
Actual rate	$10.00
Total	$95,000.00
Actual factory overhead:	
Variable	$54,000.00
Fixed	$39,000.00

REQUIREMENTS

a) Prepare a flexible budget performance report comparing actual and allowed costs.

b) Determine each of the following variances:

1. Materials price (at purchase) and quantity
2. Labor rate and efficiency
3. Variable overhead spending and efficiency
4. Fixed overhead budget and volume

11–11 T Three- and Two-Way Overhead

For the situation presented in Exercise 11–10, prepare both a three-way and a two-way analysis of overhead variances.

11–12 Basic Manufacturing Variances: Four-Way Overhead

Molded Chairs manufactures molded plastic chairs. Information on budgeted and actual manufacturing activity and costs is presented in this performance report:

	Actual	*Original budget*	*(Favorable) unfavorable variance*
Production (chairs)	25,000	20,000	
Direct materials:			
Budget (100,000 lbs. × $2)		$200,000	$250,000U
Actual (150,000 lbs. × $3)	$ 450,000		
Direct labor:			
Budget (10,000 hrs. × $20)		200,000	20,000U
Actual (11,000 hrs. × $20)	220,000		
Variable factory overhead:			
Budget (20,000 machine hrs. × $5)		100,000	26,000U
Actual (26,000 machine hrs.)	126,000		
Fixed factory overhead:			
Budget		250,000	0
Actual	250,000		
Total	$1,046,000	$750,000	$296,000U

ADDITIONAL INFORMATION

- There were no beginning or ending inventories.
- A purchasing agent is responsible for purchases of raw materials.
- For product costing, fixed factory overhead is applied at the rate of $12.50 per chair.
- The production supervisor was fired for failing to control costs shortly after the preceding performance report was presented to her supervisor.

REQUIREMENTS

a) Prepare a flexible budget performance report comparing actual and allowed costs.

b) Determine the following variances:

1. Materials price and materials quantity
2. Labor rate and labor efficiency
3. Variable overhead spending and variable overhead efficiency
4. Fixed overhead budget and fixed overhead volume

c) Evaluate the original performance report. Should the production supervisor have been fired? Why or why not?

11–13 Basic Manufacturing Variances: Four-Way Overhead

Eastern Company manufactures special electrical equipment and parts. Eastern uses standard costs with separate standards established for each product. A special transformer is manufactured in the Transformer Department. Production volume is measured by direct-labor hours in this department and a flexible budget system is used to plan and control department overhead.

Standard costs for the special transformer are determined annually in September for the coming year. The standard cost of a transformer for 19y7 was $67.00:

Direct materials:		
Iron	5 sheets @ $2.00 =	$10.00
Copper	3 spools @ $3.00 =	9.00
Direct labor	4 hours @ $7.00 =	28.00
Variable overhead	4 hours @ $3.00 =	12.00
Fixed overhead	4 hours @ $2.00 =	8.00
Total		$67.00

Overhead rates were based on normal and expected monthly capacity for 19y7, both of which were 4,000 direct-labor hours. Practical capacity for this department is 5,000 direct-labor hours per month. Variable overhead costs are expected to vary with the number of direct-labor hours actually used.

During October 19y7, 800 transformers were produced. This was below expectations because a work stoppage occurred during contract negotiations with the labor force. Once the contract was settled, the department scheduled overtime in an attempt to catch up to expected production levels. Actual costs incurred in October 19y7 were as follows:

	Purchased:	Used:
Direct materials:		
Iron	5,000 sheets @ $2.00 per sheet	3,900 sheets
Copper	2,200 spools @ $3.10 per spool	2,600 spools
Direct labor:		
Regular time—	2,000 hours @ $7.00	
	1,400 hours @ $7.20	
Overtime—	600 of the 1,400 hours were subject to overtime premium. The total overtime premium of $2,160 is included in variable overhead in accordance with company accounting practices.	
Variable overhead	$10,000	
Fixed overhead	$ 8,800	

REQUIREMENT

Prepare a complete analysis of all production variances. Use a four-way analysis for overhead. Materials price variances are isolated at the time of purchase.

(CMA Adapted)

11–14 Basic Variances: Delivery Company: Four-Way Overhead

The Metropolitan Delivering Company operates a fleet of five trucks to deliver small packages in a major metropolitan area. Based on past experience, the Company has developed the following standard costs per delivery:

Direct labor (3 minutes @ $6 per hour)	$0.30
Material (gasoline) (10 deliveries per gallon @ $1.60 per gallon)	0.16
Variable overhead (20 deliveries per direct-labor hour @ $2 per direct-labor hour)	0.10
Fixed overhead (budgeted at $1,000 and 4,000 deliveries per week)	0.25
Total	$0.81

The actual results for a recent week, when 3,800 deliveries were made, are:

Labor (200 hours at $6.00)	$1,200
Materials purchased and used (360 gallons at $1.60 per gallon)	576
Variable overhead	380
Fixed overhead	1,000

REQUIREMENTS

a) Prepare an analysis of each of the following variances:

1. Materials variances
2. Labor variances
3. Variable overhead variances
4. Fixed overhead variances

b) After studying the information given in the problem and the pattern of favorable and unfavorable variances, can you draw any conclusions as to a likely cause?

11–15 Basic Manufacturing Variances: Three-Way Overhead

The Terry Company manufactures a commercial solvent that is used for industrial maintenance. This solvent is sold by the drum and generally has a stable selling price. In December 19x6, due to a decrease in demand for this product, Terry produced and sold 60,000 drums, which is 50 percent of normal capacity.

The following information is available regarding Terry's operations for December 19x6:

1. Standard costs per drum of product manufactured were as follows:

Materials:	
10 gallons of raw material	$20
1 empty drum	1
Total materials	$21
Direct labor:	
1 hour	$ 7
Factory overhead (fixed):	
Per direct-labor hour	$ 4
Factory overhead (variable):	
Per direct-labor hour	$ 6

2. Costs incurred during December 19x6 were as follows:

Raw materials:
600,000 gallons were purchased at a cost of $1,150,000.
700,000 gallons were used.
Empty drums:
85,000 drums were purchased at a cost of $85,000.
60,000 drums were used.
Direct labor:
65,000 hours were worked at a cost of $470,000.
Factory overhead:

Depreciation of building and machinery (fixed)	$230,000
Supervision and indirect labor (semivariable)	360,000
Other factory overhead (variable)	76,500
Total factory overhead	$666,500

3. The fixed overhead budget for the December level of production was $275,000.

REQUIREMENT

Prepare a complete analysis of all manufacturing variances. The materials price variance is computed at the time of purchase. If a four-way analysis of overhead variances cannot be prepared, indicate why and prepare a three-way analysis.

(CPA Adapted)

11–16 Basic Manufacturing Variances: Three-Way Overhead

At the beginning of 19x4, Beal Company adopted the following standards:

Direct materials (3 lbs. @ $2.50 per lb.)	$ 7.50
Direct labor (5 hrs. @ $7.50 per hr.)	37.50
Factory overhead:	
Variable ($3.00 per direct-labor hour)	15.00
Fixed ($4.00 per direct-labor hour)	20.00
Standard cost per unit	$80.00

Normal volume per month is 40,000 direct labor hours. Beal's January 19x4 budget was based on normal volume. During January Beal produced 7,800 units, with records indicating the following:

Direct materials purchased	25,000 lbs. @ $2.60
Direct materials used	23,100 lbs.
Direct labor	40,100 hrs. @ $7.30
Factory overhead	$300,000

REQUIREMENTS

a) Prepare a flexible budget for January 19x4 production costs, based on actual production of 7,800 units.

b) For the month of January 19x4, compute the following variances, indicating whether each is favorable or unfavorable:

1. Direct materials price variance, based on purchases
2. Direct materials usage variance
3. Direct labor rate variance
4. Direct labor efficiency variance
5. Factory overhead spending variance
6. Variable factory overhead efficiency variance
7. Factory overhead volume variance (CPA Adapted)

PROBLEMS

11–17 Overview of Variance Computations Including Four-, Three-, and Two-Way Overhead

The Brown Manufacturing Company uses a flexible budget and standard costs to develop variances. Selected data concerning three of Brown's products are presented as follows:

	Product A	*Product B*	*Product C*
Standard cost information/unit:			
Raw materials/unit	3 lbs. @ $2.00 per lb.	2 meters @ $3.00 per meter	1.5 liters @ $2.00 per liter
Direct labor/unit	3 hrs. @ $5.00 per hr.	1.5 hrs. @ $6.00 per hr.	2 hrs. @ $8.00 per hr.

	Product A	*Product B*	*Product C*
Variable factory overhead/unit	$4.00 per direct-labor hour	$1.50 per direct-labor dollar	4 machine hours at $2.00 per machine hour
Fixed factory overhead/month	$27,000	$60,000	$20,000
Normal activity/month	6,000 direct-labor hours	$30,000 direct-labor dollars	20,000 machine hours
November production information:			
Units produced	2,000	2,500	5,000
Raw materials purchased and used	5,500 lbs. @ $2.10 per lb.	6,000 meters @ $3.00 per meter	7,500 liters @ $2.10 per liter
Direct labor	6,300 hrs. @ $5.00 per hr.	3,500 hrs. @ $6.50 per hr.	12,000 hrs. @ $6.00 per hr.
Variable factory overhead	$25,000	$31,000	$41,000
Fixed factory overhead	$26,500	$62,000	$23,000
Machine hours	—	—	21,000

REQUIREMENTS

a) For each product prepare a complete analysis of materials, labor, and overhead (four-way analysis) variances.

b) For each product prepare a three-way analysis of overhead variances. Indicate why it is not always possible to prepare a four-way analysis.

c) For each product prepare a two-way analysis of overhead variances.

11–18 Behavioral Consequences of Cost Reduction Program

Olim Corporation is a large manufacturing company in a heavily industrialized region of the northeast United States. Top management has indicated the need for production economy in its manufacturing processes because of declining profits. To encourage employees to work toward this goal, cost consciousness has been emphasized. A monetary incentive scheme has been developed to reward production managers who produce cost reductions that will be reflected immediately in the company's financial results.

The production managers have responded to this pressure in several ways. The rate at which products are being manufactured has been increased. Production managers are now rejecting greater quantities of raw materials and parts as they are received from the storeroom. They have postponed repair and maintenance work on machines where possible and have specified quick emergency repairs to avoid imminent breakdowns or to get machines back into production.

Each of these actions has increased friction among personnel in the plant. For example, the production managers' actions with respect to repair and maintenance have caused serious conflict between themselves and the maintenance department. The maintenance managers argue that the postponement of certain repairs in the short term and the use of emergency repair techniques will result in increased costs later and, in some instances, will reduce the life of the machine. They further argue that these practices reduce machine safety.

An even more serious matter is the growing bitterness among the production managers themselves. The production managers who are more aggressive, check up on the progress of the repair work in their department, have close friends in the maintenance department, or intimidate the maintenance department to have their repair work completed promptly. In several instances production departments whose production has been halted due to machine breakdowns have had to wait while another production department, with an aggressive manager, has received repair service on machines not needed in the current production run. Consequently such managers are not popular with the other production managers.

The maintenance managers are upset at being subjected to the pressure and intimidation. They claim this makes it hard to determine which jobs are the most important. Further, the production departments' demands for immediate return to service of machines results in substandard repair work.

The production departments are charged with the actual costs of the repairs. A record of the repair work conducted in individual production departments is prepared by maintenance managers. This record, when completed in the accounting department, shows the repair hours, the rate of the maintenance worker who did the work, the maintenance overhead charge, and the cost of any parts. The record serves as the basis for the charges to the production department.

Production managers have complained about this charging system. They claim the charges to them depend on which maintenance worker does the work (the hourly rate and efficiency), when the work is done (the production department is charged for the overtime premium), and how careful the worker is in recording the time on the job.

REQUIREMENTS

a) Identify and briefly explain the motivational factors that may promote friction between the production and maintenance managers of Olim Corporation.

b) Revise the Olim's system to charge production departments for repair costs so as to eliminate or reduce the production departments' complaints. (CMA Adapted)

11–19 Job-Order Costing and Overhead Variance Analysis

Department 203 uses a normal cost system with a single overhead control account. The following information is available regarding 19x7 costs assigned to Department 203:

DEPARTMENT 203—WORK IN PROCESS—BEGINNING OF PERIOD

Job	*Material*	*Labor*	*Overhead*	*Total*
1376	$17,500	$22,000	$33,000	$72,500

DEPARTMENT 203 COSTS FOR 19x7

Incurred by jobs: Job:	*Material*	*Labor*	*Other*	*Total*
1376	$ 1,000	$ 7,000	$ —	$ 8,000
1377	26,000	53,000	—	79,000
1378	12,000	9,000	—	21,000
1379	4,000	1,000	—	5,000
Not incurred by jobs: Item:				
Indirect materials & supplies	15,000	—	—	15,000
Indirect labor	—	53,000	—	53,000
Employee benefits	—	—	23,000	23,000
Depreciation	—	—	12,000	12,000
Supervision	—	20,000	—	20,000
Total	$58,000	$143,000	$35,000	$236,000

DEPARTMENT 203 OVERHEAD RATE FOR 19x7

Budgeted overhead:	
Variable:	
Indirect materials and supplies	$ 16,000
Indirect labor	56,000
Employee benefits	24,000
Fixed:	
Supervision	20,000
Depreciation	12,000
Total	$128,000
Budgeted direct-labor dollars	$ 80,000
Rate per direct-labor dollar ($128,000 ÷ $80,000)	160%

REQUIREMENTS

a) Determine the actual 19x7 overhead.

b) Determine the amount by which 19x7 overhead was over- or underapplied.

c) Determine the 19x7 volume variance.

d) Determine the 19x7 overhead spending variance.

e) Job number 1376 was the only job completed and sold in 19x7. Determine the final cost of this job.

f) Determine the Work-in-Process balance at the end of 19x7. Assume overapplied or underapplied overhead is closed to Cost of Goods Sold. (CMA Adapted)

11–20 Flexible Budget Performance Evaluation: Process Costing
Williams Company produces a single product on a continuous basis. On January 1, 400 units, 75 percent complete as to materials and 50 percent complete as to conversion, were in process. During January, 1,000 units were started and 1,200 units were completed and transferred to finished goods inventory. The January

31 ending work-in-process inventory consisted to 200 units, 50 percent complete as to materials and 25 percent complete as to conversion.

Actual costs assigned to the production department during January are as follows:

Direct materials	$20,800
Direct labor	31,400
Factory overhead	11,250

Williams uses standard costs for planning and control. The following standard costs are based on a monthly volume of 800 units with fixed costs budgeted at $6,000 per month:

Direct materials	2 sq. m @ $8 per square meter
Direct labor	1.5 hrs. @ $20 per hr.
Factory overhead	1.5 labor hours @ $10 per hr.

REQUIREMENTS

a) Determine the equivalent units of materials and conversion manufactured during January.

b) Prepare a flexible budget for January manufacturing costs and determine the *total* variances for materials, labor, and overhead.

11–21 Process Costing and Variance Analysis: Four-Way Overhead

The Blow Hard Fan Company began manufacturing attic ventilators on May 1, 19x0. To assist in budgeting, record keeping, and performance evaluation, Mr. Rednose (the company controller) instituted a standard cost system. Based on normal monthly activity of 5,000 direct-labor hours and budgeted monthly fixed costs of $25,000, the standard cost per ventilator is as follows:

Direct materials (10 sq. m @ $1)	$10
Direct labor (2 hrs. @ $5)	10
Factory overhead (2 direct-labor hours @ $10)	20
Total	$40

During May, 1,900 ventilators were completed and 1,500 were sold. The ending inventory of work-in-process consists of 600 units that are complete as to materials and ⅙ complete as to conversion. Actual costs for May are as follows:

Cost of materials placed in production	$30,000
Direct labor	22,000
Variable overhead	18,000
Fixed overhead	24,000

REQUIREMENTS

a) Determine the equivalent units of materials and conversion manufactured during May.

b) Prepare a *flexible budget* for the equivalent units manufactured.

c) Determine all variances for each of the following:

1. Direct materials
2. Direct labor
3. Variable factory overhead
4. Fixed factory overhead

d) Would your analysis differ if there had been a beginning inventory of work-in-process? Why or why not?

11–22 Process Costing and Variance Analysis: Three-Way Overhead

The Hartwell Company manufactures a product that has the following standard costs per unit:

Direct materials (5 lbs. @ \$10)	\$ 50
Direct labor (2 hrs. @ \$10)	20
Factory overhead (2 direct-labor hours @ \$15)	30
Total	\$100

The standard for overhead is based on a monthly activity level of 80,000 direct-labor hours. Variable overhead costs are estimated to be \$5 per direct-labor hour.

During October 160,000 pounds of raw materials were purchased and used at a total cost of \$1,650,000. The company also used 70,000 direct-labor hours at a total direct-labor cost of \$770,000. October overhead costs totaled \$1,200,000.

The October 1 work-in-process inventory consisted of 7,000 units that were complete as to materials and 2/7 complete as to conversion. The October 31 work-in-process inventory contained 3,000 units that were complete as to materials and 1/3 complete as to conversion. During October 34,000 units were transferred to finished goods inventory.

REQUIREMENTS

a) Determine the equivalent units of materials and conversion manufactured during October.

b) Prepare an analysis of all variances. Use a three-way analysis for overhead.

11–23 Process Costing and Variance Analysis: Two-Way Overhead

Melody Corporation is a manufacturing company that produces a single product known as "Jupiter." Melody uses the first-in, first-out (FIFO) process costing method for both financial statement and internal management reporting.

In analyzing production results, standard costs are used, whereas actual costs are used for financial statement reporting. The standards, which are based on equivalent units of production, are as follows:

Raw materials per unit	1 lb. at \$10 per lb.
Direct labor per unit	2 hrs. at \$4 per hr.
Factory overhead per unit	2 direct-labor hours at \$1.25 per hr.

The factory overhead flexible budget for standard hours allowed for April production is $30,000. Data for April 19x7 are as follows:

- The beginning inventory consisted of 2,500 units, which were 100 percent complete as to raw material and 40 percent complete as to direct labor and factory overhead.
- An additional 10,000 units were started during the month.
- The ending inventory consisted of 2,000 units, which were 100 percent complete as to raw material and 40 percent complete as to direct labor and factory overhead.
- Actual costs applicable to April production are as follows:

Raw materials purchased and used (11,000 lbs.)	$121,000
Direct labor (25,000 hrs. actually worked)	105,575
Factory overhead	31,930

REQUIREMENTS

a) Determine the equivalent units of materials and conversion manufactured during April.

b) Prepare a complete analysis of all materials and labor variances and a two-way analysis of overhead variances. (CPA Adapted)

11–24 Evaluation of Materials Variance Computations

Maidwell Company manufactures washers and dryers on a single assembly line in its main factory. The market has deteriorated over the last five years and competition has made cost control very important. Management has been concerned about the materials cost of both washers and dryers. There have been no model changes in the past two years and economic conditions have allowed the company to negotiate price reductions in many key parts.

Maidwell uses a standard cost system in accounting for materials. Purchases are charged to inventory at a standard price with purchase discounts considered an administrative cost reduction. Production is charged at the standard price of the materials used. Thus the price variance is isolated at time of purchase as the difference between gross contract price and standard price multiplied by the quantity purchased. When a substitute part is used in production rather than the regular part, a price variance equal to the difference in the standard prices of the materials is recognized at the time of substitution in the production process. The quantity variance is the actual quantity used compared to the standard quantity allowed with the difference multiplied by the standard price.

The materials variances for several of the parts Maidwell uses are unfavorable. Part No. 4121 is one of the items that has an unfavorable variance. Maidwell knows that some of these parts will be defective and fail. The failure is discovered during production. The normal defective rate is 5 percent of normal input. The original contract price of this part was $0.285 per unit; thus, Maidwell set the standard unit price at $0.285. The unit contract purchase price of Part No. 4121 was increased $0.04 to $0.325 from the original $0.285 due to a parts specification change. Maidwell chose not to change the standard, but to treat the increase in price as a price variance. In addition, the contract terms were changed from n/30 to 4/10, n/30 as a consequence of negotiations resulting from changes in the economy.

Data regarding the usage of Part No. 4121 during December are as follows.

○ Purchases of Part No. 4121	150,000 units
○ Unit price paid for purchases of Part No. 4121	$0.325
○ Requisitions of Part No. 4121 from stores for use in products	134,000 units
○ Substitution of Part No. 5125 for Part No. 4121 to use obsolete stock (standard unit price of Part No. 5125 is $0.35)	24,000 units
○ Units of Part No. 4121 and its substitute (Part No. 5125) identified as being defective	9,665 units
○ Standard allowed usage (including normal defective units) of Part No. 4121 and its substitute based on output for the month	153,300 units

Maidwell's materials variances related to Part No. 4121 for December were reported as follows.

Price variance	$7,560.00U
Quantity variance	1,339.50U
Total materials variance for Part No. 4121	$8,899.50U

Bob Speck, the Purchasing Director, claims the unfavorable price variance is misleading. Speck says that his department has worked hard to obtain price concessions and purchase discounts from suppliers. In addition, Speck has indicated that engineering changes have been made in several parts increasing their price even though the part identification has not changed. These price increases are not his department's responsibility. Speck declares that price variances simply no longer measure the purchasing department's performance.

Jim Buddle, the Manufacturing Manager, thinks that responsibility for the quantity variance should be shared. Buddle states that manufacturing cannot control quality arising from less expensive parts, substitutions of material to use up otherwise obsolete stock, or engineering changes that increased the quantity of materials used.

The Accounting Manager, Mike Kohl, has suggested that the computation of variances be changed to identify variations from standard with the causes and functional areas responsible for the variances. The following system of materials variances and the method of computation for each of them was recommended by Kohl.

Variance	*Method of calculation*
Economics variance	Quantity purchased times the changes made after setting standards that were the result of negotiations based on changes in the general economy.
Engineering change variance	Quantity purchased times change in price due to part specifications changes.

Purchase price variance	Quantity purchased times change in contract price due to changes other than parts specifications or the general economy.
Substitutions variance	Quantity substituted times the difference in standard price between parts substituted.
Excess usage variance	Standard price times the difference between the standard quantity allowed for production minus actual parts used (reduced for abnormal scrap).
Abnormal failure rate variance	Abnormal scrap times standard price.

REQUIREMENTS

a) Discuss the appropriateness of Maidwell Company's current method of variance analysis for materials and indicate whether the claims of Bob Speck and Jim Buddle are valid.

b) Compute the materials variances for Part No. 4121 for December using the system recommended by Mike Kohl.

c) Indicate who would be responsible for each of the variances in Mike Kohl's system of variance analysis for materials. (CMA Adapted)

11–25 Service Department Costs in Performance Reports

The Independent Underwriters Insurance Co. (IUI) established a Systems Department two years ago to implement and operate its own data processing systems. IUI believed that its own system would be more cost effective than the service bureau it had been using.

IUI's three departments—Claims, Records, and Finance—have different requirements with respect to hardware and other capacity related resources and operating resources. The system was designed to recognize these differing needs. In addition, the system was designed to meet IUI's long-term capacity needs. The excess capacity designed into the system would be sold to outside users until needed by IUI. The estimated resource requirements used to design and implement the system are shown in the following schedule.

	Hardware and other capacity related resources	*Operating resources*
Records	30%	60%
Claims	50	20
Finance	15	15
Expansion (outside use)	5	5
Total	100%	100%

IUI currently sells the equivalent of its expansion capacity to a few outside clients.

At the time the system became operational, management decided to redistribute total expenses of the Systems Department to the user departments based on actual computer time used. The actual costs for the first quarter of the current fiscal year were distributed to the user departments as follows:

Department	*Percentage utilization*	*Amount*
Records	60%	$330,000
Claims	20	110,000
Finance	15	82,500
Outside	5	27,500
Total	100%	$550,000

The three user departments have complained about the cost distribution method since the Systems Department was established. The Records Department's monthly costs have been as much as three times the costs experienced with the service bureau. The Finance Department is concerned about the costs distributed to the outside user category because these allocated costs form the basis for the fees billed to the outside clients.

James Dale, IUI's Controller, decided to review the distribution method by which the Systems Department's costs have been allocated for the past two years. The additional information he gathered for his review is reported in the three schedules that follow.

Dale has concluded that the method of cost distribution should be changed to reflect more directly the actual benefits received by the departments. He believes that the hardware and capacity related costs should be allocated to the user departments in proportion to the planned, long-term needs. Any difference between actual and budgeted hardware costs would not be allocated to the departments, but remain with the Systems Department.

The remaining costs for software development and operations would be charged to the user departments based on actual hours used. A predetermined hourly rate based on the annual budget data would be used. The hourly rates that would be used for the current fiscal year are as follows.

Function	*Hourly rate*
Software development	$ 30
Operations:	
Computer related	$200
Input/output related	$ 10

Dale plans to use first-quarter activity and cost data to illustrate his recommendations. The recommendations will be presented to the Systems Department and the user departments for their comments and reactions. He then expects to present his recommendations to management for approval.

SYSTEMS DEPARTMENT COSTS AND ACTIVITY LEVELS (SCHEDULE 1)

	Annual budget		*First quarter*			
			Budget		*Actual*	
	Hours	*Dollars*	*Hours*	*Dollars*	*Hours*	*Dollars*
Hardware and other capacity related costs	—	$ 600,000	—	$150,000	—	$155,000
Software development	18,750	562,500	4,725	141,750	4,250	130,000
Operations:						
Computer related	3,750	750,000	945	189,000	920	187,000
Input/output related	30,000	300,000	7,560	75,600	7,900	78,000
Total		$2,212,500		$556,350		$550,000

HISTORICAL UTILIZATION OF USERS (SCHEDULE 2)

	Hardware and other capacity needs	*Software development*		*Operations*			
				Computer		*Input/output*	
		Range	*Average*	*Range*	*Average*	*Range*	*Average*
Records	30%	0–30%	12%	55–65%	60%	10–30%	20%
Claims	50	15–60	35	10–25	20	60–80	70
Finance	15	25–75	45	10–25	15	3–10	6
Outside	5	0–25	8	3–8	5	3–10	4
Total	100%		100%		100%		100%

UTILIZATION OF SYSTEMS DEPARTMENT'S SERVICES IN HOURS (SCHEDULE 3)

	Software development	*Operations*	
		Computer related	*Input/output*
Records	425	552	1,580
Claims	1,700	184	5,530
Finance	1,700	138	395
Outside	425	46	395
Total	4,250	920	7,900

REQUIREMENTS

a) Calculate the amount of data processing costs that would be included in the Claims Department's first-quarter budget according to the method James Dale has recommended.

b) Prepare a schedule to show how the actual first-quarter costs of the Systems Department would be charged to the users if James Dale's recommended method is adopted.

c) Explain whether James Dale's recommended system for charging costs to the user departments will:

1. Improve cost control in the Systems Department.
2. Improve planning and cost control in the user departments.
3. Be a more equitable basis for charging costs to user departments.

(CMA Adapted)

11–26 T Materials Price, Mix, and Yield Variances (Appendix)

Presented are the standard input and costs per ton of output:

Material	*Amount (in tons)*	*Cost per ton*	*Total cost*
A	0.2	$80	$16
B	0.4	50	20
C	0.4	60	24
Total standard cost per ton of output			$60

The actual materials use and cost during a period in which 100 tons of output was produced are as follows:

Material	*Amount (in tons)*	*Cost per ton*	*Total cost*
A	10	$100	$1,000
B	50	60	3,000
C	50	50	2,500
			$6,500

REQUIREMENT

Determine the materials price, mix, and yield variances.

11–27 T Materials Price, Mix, and Yield Variances (Appendix)

Energy Products Company produces a gasoline additive, "Gas Gain." This product increases engine efficiency and improves gasoline mileage by creating a more complete burn in the combustion process.

Careful controls are required during the production process to ensure that the proper mix of input chemicals is achieved and that evaporation is controlled. If the controls are not effective, there can be loss of output and efficiency.

The standard cost of producing a 500-liter batch of Gas Gain is $135. The standard materials mix and related standard cost of each chemical used in a 500-liter batch are as follow.

Chemical	*Standard input quantity (in liters)*	*Standard cost per liter*	*Total cost*
Echol	200	$0.200	$ 40.00
Protex	100	0.425	42.50
Benz	250	0.150	37.50
CT-40	50	0.300	15.00
Total	600		$135.00

The quantities of chemicals purchased and used during the current production period are shown in the schedule below. A total of 140 batches of Gas Gain were manufactured during the current production period. Energy Products determines its cost and chemical usage variations at the end of each production period.

Chemical	*Quantity purchased (in liters)*	*Total purchase price*	*Quantity used (in liters)*
Echol	25,000	$ 5,365	26,600
Protex	13,000	6,240	12,880
Benz	40,000	5,840	37,800
CT-40	7,500	2,220	7,140
Total	85,500	$19,665	84,420

REQUIREMENTS

a) Calculate the purchase price variances for Energy Products Company.

b) Calculate the total material quantity variance related to Gas Gain for Energy Products Company and then analyze this total quantity variance into the following two components:

1. Total mix variance
2. Total yield variance

(CMA Adapted)

11–28 T Materials Mix and Yield Variances (Appendix)

The Dante Chemical Processing Company, located in south-central Michigan, manufactures "Liquid Inferno," a fuel oil additive that helps home heating systems burn hotter and cleaner.

The production standards for Liquid Inferno call for the following inputs per cubic meter produced:

Material	*Quantity (in liters)*	*Price per liter*	*Total*
A	480	$0.05	$ 24.00
B	600	0.20	120.00
C	120	0.30	36.00
	1,200		$180.00

The shrinkage is due to evaporation and waste that is inherent in the production process.

During a recent week, the production of 100 cubic meters required the following inputs:

Material	*Quantity (in cubic meters)*	*Price per cubic meter*	*Total*
A	44.0	$ 60	$ 2,640
B	49.5	200	9,900
C	16.5	250	4,125
	110.0		$16,665

REQUIREMENTS

a) Determine the materials price, mix, and yield variances for Dante's Liquid Inferno. (*Hint:* 1,000 liters = 1 cubic meter.)

b) Evaluate these variances. Should the production supervisor be held responsible for the mix variance and given credit for the yield variance?

11–29 T Materials Price, Mix, and Yield Variances (Appendix)

The Superior Steel Company purchases large quantities of coal, which is then converted into coke, for use in Superior's blast furnaces. In the conversion process, nut and slack coal are mixed with coals of a lower quality. The conversion process has a yield rate of 70 percent of input. Information on the materials budget for a typical monthly output of 140,000 tons of coke follows:

Material	*Cost per ton*	*Total input (in tons)*	*Total cost*
Nut & slack coal	$70	120,000	$ 8,400,000
Other coals	50	80,000	4,000,000
			$12,400,000

During a recent month the following materials were used to produce 108,000 tons of coke:

Material	*Cost per ton*	*Total input (in tons)*	*Total cost*
Nut & slack coal	$80	90,000	$ 7,200,000
Other coals	50	90,000	4,500,000
			$11,700,000

REQUIREMENTS

a) Determine the materials price, mix, and yield variances.

b) What sequence of events was the most likely cause of the mix and then the yield variances?

c) Do you believe the person in charge of the coke operation should be held accountable for the mix and yield variances as they are computed in part (a)? Why or why not?

11–30 Labor Rate, Mix, and Yield Variances (Appendix)

Presented are the labor standards per 1,000 liters of final product:

Grade	*Hours*	*Rate*	*Total*
A	10	$12	$120
B	0	10	0
C	50	8	400
D	40	6	240
			$760

During a recent period, when 100,000 liters were produced, actual labor inputs and costs were as follows:

Grade	*Hours*	*Rate*	*Total*
A	0	$15	$ 0
B	200	11	2,200
C	6,000	9	54,000
D	4,000	7	28,000
			$84,200

REQUIREMENT

Determine the labor rate, mix, and yield variances.

11–31 Labor Rate, Mix, and Yield Variances (Appendix)

Landeau Manufacturing Company has a process cost accounting system. An analysis, which compares the actual results with both a monthly plan and a flexible budget, is prepared monthly. The standard direct-labor rates used in the flexible budget are established each year at the time the annual plan is formulated and held constant for the entire year.

The standard direct-labor rates in effect for the fiscal year ending June 30, 19x8, and the standard hours allowed for the output for April are shown in the following schedule:

	Standard direct-labor rate per hour	*Standard direct-labor hours allowed for output*
Labor class III	$8.00	500
Labor class II	7.00	500
Labor class I	5.00	500

The wage rate for each labor class increased on January 1, 19x8, under the terms of a new union contract negotiated in December 19x7. The standard wage rates were not revised to reflect the new contract.

The actual direct-labor hours (DLH) worked and the actual direct-labor rates per hour experienced for April were as follows:

	Actual direct-labor rate per hour	*Actual direct-labor hours*
Labor class III	$8.50	550
Labor class II	7.50	650
Labor class I	5.40	375

REQUIREMENT

Calculate the dollar amount of the total direct-labor variance for April for the Landeau Manufacturing Company and analyze the total variance into the following components:

1. Direct-labor rate variance

2. Direct-labor mix variance
3. Direct-labor performance (yield) variance (CMA Adapted)

11–32 Labor Mix and Yield Variances (Appendix)

The Smalltown General Hospital serves a 2,500-square-mile area of a rural western state. Although the hospital has 50 beds, an emergency room, a radiology department, a delivery room, and an operating room, the hospital transfers all patients needing extensive care or major surgery to State Hospital in Capital City. As a result of its location and facilities, most of the hospital's services are routine. Due to the lack of other facilities in the area, convalescence care is important to the hospital.

Smalltown General recently instituted performance standards for its nursing services. On the basis of training and experience, the nurses have been divided into two categories, A and B, and on the basis of complexity, all nursing services have been related to something called a "service unit." Administering an injection is one service unit, checking blood pressure is two service units, performing an EKG is five service units, and so on. The standard daily compensation of A and B nurses is $72 and $40, respectively. Because a portion of an A nurse's job is to ensure the quality of a B nurse's work, the hospital wants to have a 50:50 mix of A and B nurses. This translates into a 60:40 mix of service units at a standard cost of $1.20 for A nurse units and $1.00 for B nurse units. During a recent week, A nurses worked a total of 100 days and B nurses worked a total of 200 days. A total of 12,000 service units were provided during the week.

REQUIREMENTS

a) Determine the mix and yield variances associated with nursing services. State your answer in terms of dollars and provide calculations. (*Hint:* How many A and B nurse-days should have been used to provide 12,000 service units?)

b) What factors should be considered in evaluating these variances?

11–33 Learning Curves and Labor Variances (Chapter 7, Appendix C)

The Rocky Mount Job Shop manufactures complex aircraft parts with the use of skilled labor. In the past the labor hours required to produce successive units have followed an 80 percent learning curve (that is, every time cumulative production doubled, the cumulative average time required to produce a unit was 80 percent of its previous amount.)

The first ten parts of a new unit, the B477, required 1,000 labor hours at a cost of $10 per hour.

REQUIREMENTS

a) Use the learning-curve model to determine the standard labor cost of an additional 150 units.

b) Assuming that 5,700 hours actually were required to complete the 150 additional units, determine the labor efficiency variance.

SOLUTION TO REVIEW PROBLEM

a) **Burque Furniture Company**
Flexible Budget
For the Month of July, 19w2

	Actual	*Flexible budget*	*Variance*
Volume	1,100	1,100	
Variable manufacturing costs:			
Direct materials (1,100 × $20)	$22,400*	$ 22,000	$ 400U
Direct labor (1,100 × $30)	32,550†	33,000	(450)F
Variable factory overhead (1,100 × $15)	15,500	16,500	(1,000)F
Total	$70,450	$ 71,500	$(1,050)F
Fixed factory overhead	29,000	30,000	(1,000)F
Total manufacturing costs	$99,450	$101,500	$(2,050)F

* Only the standard cost of materials used is assigned to the production department [56 thousand board-feet × ($400/1,000)].
† (3,100 × $10.50)

b) Materials price variance
[50($390 − $400)] = $ (500)F

Materials quantity variance
[$0.40*(56,000 − (50 × 1,100))] = $ 400U

Labor rate variance
[3,100($10.50 − $10.00)] = $ 1,550U

Labor efficiency variance
[$10(3,100 − (1,100 × 3))] = $(2,000)F

Variable overhead spending variance
[$15,500 − (3,100 × $5)] = $ 0

Variable overhead efficiency variance
[$5(3,100 − (1,100 × 3))] = $(1,000)F

Fixed overhead budget variance
($29,000 − $30,000) = $(1,000)F

Fixed overhead volume variance
[$30,000 − $10(1,100 × 3)] = $(3,000)F

*Price per board-foot ($400/1,000).

c) Overhead spending variance
[($15,500 + $29,000) − ((3,100 × $5) + $30,000)] = $(1,000)F

Overhead efficiency variance
[((3,100 × $5) + $30,000) − ((1,100 × 3 × $5) + $30,000)] = $(1,000)F

Volume variance
[((1,100 × 3 × $5) + $30,000) − ((1,100 × 3 × $5) + (1,100 × 3 × $10))] = $(3,000)F

d) Overhead budget variance
[($15,500 + $29,000) − ((1,100 × 3 × $5) + $30,000)] = $(2,000)F

Volume variance
[((1,100 × 3 × $5) + $30,000) − ((1,100 × 3 × $5) + (1,100 × 3 × $10))] = $(3,000)F

12 Responsibility Accounting for Revenue and Profit Centers

INTRODUCTION

REVENUE AND PROFIT CENTERS

PERFORMANCE REPORTS FOR DISCRETIONARY COST CENTERS

SALES VARIANCES

SUMMARY

APPENDIX: SALES CONTRIBUTION AND SALES REVENUE VARIANCES

INTRODUCTION

UNDER **RESPONSIBILITY ACCOUNTING**, PERFORMANCE REPORTS ADDRESSED TO individual members of an organization are structured to emphasize the factors under their control. Each organizational unit for which performance reports are prepared is identified as a **responsibility center.** Depending on the nature of their activities, responsibility centers are classified as investment centers, profit centers, revenue centers, or cost centers. Cost centers can be further classified as standard or discretionary cost centers. The development of performance reports for standard cost centers was examined in Chapter 11. Responsibility accounting for investment centers will be examined in Chapter 13.

The primary purpose of this chapter is to examine the development of performance reports for revenue and profit centers. Performance reports for discretionary cost centers will also be considered. After all variances presented in Chapters 11 and 12 are understood, we will be able to develop a complete reconciliation of budgeted and actual income.

REVENUE AND PROFIT CENTERS

A **revenue center** is responsible for generating sales revenue. Referring to Exhibit 11–1, the firm has four revenue centers: Region 1, Region 2, Region 3, and the entire marketing organization. Performance reports, comparing actual and budgeted sales, could be developed for each. In such reports the **sales revenue variance** indicates the difference between actual and budgeted sales revenue. If actual sales revenue exceeds budgeted sales revenue, the variance is favorable; and if actual sales revenue is less than budgeted sales revenue, the variance is unfavorable.

An immediate problem with this approach is its failure to encourage revenue center managers to control costs incurred in generating sales revenue. Managers evaluated solely on the basis of sales revenue might incur excessive costs to obtain sales that do not contribute to corporate profits. To increase sales revenues through volume sales, managers might even reduce selling prices to such an extent that incremental sales have a negative contribution margin.

To avoid these motivational problems, marketing activities are likely to be assigned dual responsibility as a revenue center and a cost center. Alternatively they can be evaluated as a **profit center**, responsible for the difference between revenues and controllable costs.

Marketing and Manufacturing Reports Compared

Two major differences between properly designed responsibility accounting reports for marketing as opposed to manufacturing activities are:

1. Marketing responsibility includes revenues and controllable costs, whereas manufacturing responsibility includes only costs.
2. Marketing performance reports are based on the original (master) budget, whereas manufacturing performance reports are based on a flexible budget.

As just mentioned, controllable costs are included in marketing performance reports to encourage marketing personnel to avoid (1) the incurrence of excessive costs, and (2) unprofitable price reductions. Controllable marketing costs include selling or distribution costs and the standard variable cost of goods sold. Two major types of selling or distribution costs are: **order getting costs**, such as salaries and commissions, telephone, entertainment, and travel, incurred to obtain sales orders; and **order filling costs**, such as storage, packaging, and transportation, incurred to place ordered goods in the possession of purchasers.

The standard variable cost of goods sold should also be among the costs included in marketing performance reports. Having information on variable order getting and order filling costs and the standard variable cost of goods sold, marketing personnel are aware of the minimum selling price needed for a positive unit contribution margin. With all of these costs included in marketing performance reports, there is no incentive to sell at an unprofitable price to obtain high volume sales. Note that the standard variable cost of goods sold is used rather than the actual variable cost of goods sold or an absorption cost amount. A standard cost of goods sold is used to avoid having marketing performance reports affected by manufacturing efficiencies or inefficiencies that marketing personnel cannot control. A variable cost of goods sold is used to make marketing personnel more aware of the organization's cost structure and the minimum price needed to obtain a positive unit contribution margin.

The inclusion of revenues and costs in marketing performance reports results in a bottom-line figure that represents marketing's contribution to fixed manufacturing costs, administrative costs, and company net income. If the organization is to reach its profit goal, marketing must meet its budgeted contribution. Accordingly, marketing performance reports are based on the original budget rather than on a flexible budget. It is the marketing staff that interacts with the external environment and establishes the original sales forecast. Meeting that forecast is the responsibility of marketing, not the responsibility of manufacturing, which must respond to changes in sales during the budget period. Because manufacturing responds to marketing, manufacturing activities are based on a flexible budget.

Marketing Performance Reports

In Exhibit 11–1, the vice president of marketing is responsible for sales and distribution. Reporting to the vice president of marketing are a staff and three regional sales managers. Each regional sales manager directs the activities of a number of salespeople or field representatives. Although performance reports are developed for each field representative, we will consider only those for a regional sales manager and for the vice president of marketing. Such a set of reports is presented in Exhibit 12–1.[1]

Even though the actual content and format of marketing performance reports vary considerably, those in Exhibit 12–1 illustrate a number of important points and problems:

- The overall format of the reports focuses on marketing's contribution to common corporate costs and profits. In this respect, marketing performance reports are similar to the segment reports presented in Chapter 9.
- The bottom line in each regional performance report indicates the region's contribution to common marketing costs, fixed manufacturing costs, administrative costs, and profits.
- In Exhibit 12–1, the reports for each region are reported as a single line in the performance report for the vice president of marketing.
- Additional costs that are controllable by the vice president of marketing, but not controllable by regional managers are included in the vice president's report.
- The bottom line in the vice president's report indicates marketing's contribution to common corporate costs and profits.
- Marketing performance reports are based on the original budget.
- To avoid passing on manufacturing efficiencies and inefficiencies, the cost of goods sold is included at standard.
- To provide the most useful information to marketing personnel, variable rather than absorption costing is used.
- Variable and fixed selling and distribution costs are placed in separate categories.
- Basing the performance reports on the original budget leads to difficulty in the interpretation of sales and variable cost variances. Note that a favorable sales revenue variance may not be favorable if the resulting increase in costs more than offset the increase in sales revenue. Also note that *any increase in unit sales volume will lead to an unfavorable variance for the standard variable cost of goods sold. Likewise, any decrease in unit sales volume will lead to a favorable variance for the standard variable cost of goods sold.* This does not mean, however, that the cost of goods sold was high or low for the actual sales volume.
- The first meaningful variance is for the contribution margin, which shows the net effect of changes in sales volume, sales price, and variable costs.

---

[1] In Exhibit 12–1 parentheses enclose unfavorable variances for sales and contribution. In Chapter 11 parentheses were used to enclose favorable cost variances. This is also the case in Exhibit 12–1. The reason for this treatment is the accounting convention of using parentheses to indicate a reduction in an account's normal balance. Cost accounts normally have a debit balance and a reduction in a cost is regarded as favorable; hence, favorable cost variances have parentheses. Revenue accounts normally have a credit balance and a reduction in a revenue or a contribution is regarded as unfavorable; hence, unfavorable revenue or contribution variances have parentheses. If this convention appears confusing, the identification of a variance as favorable or unfavorable can be determined by asking if the variance tends to increase (F) or decrease (U) net income.

EXHIBIT 12–1 Responsibility Accounting Reports for Marketing

Sales Manager—Region I

	Actual	*Budget*	*Favorable unfavorable variance**
Sales	$ 99,000	$104,000	$(5,000)U
Variable costs assigned to region:			
Standard cost of goods sold†	$ 29,000	$ 30,000	$(1,000)F
Distribution:			
Order getting	4,950	5,200	(250)F
Order filling	6,050	6,800	(750)F
Controllable variable costs	−40,000	−42,000	−(2,000)F
Contribution margin	$ 59,000	$ 62,000	$(3,000)U
Regional fixed costs:‡			
Field representatives' base salaries	$ 8,000	$ 8,000	$ 0
Wide area telephone service	5,000	6,000	(1,000)F
Regional advertising	3,000	3,000	0
Entertainment	1,000	2,000	(1,000)F
Total	−17,000	−19,000	−(2,000)F
Regional contribution	$ 42,000	$ 43,000	$(1,000)U

Vice President of Marketing

	Actual	*Budget*	*Favorable unfavorable variance*
Regional contributions:			
Region I	$ 42,000	$ 43,000	$(1,000)U
Region II	38,000	37,000	1,000 F
Region III	57,000	53,000	4,000 F
Total	$137,000	$133,000	$ 4,000 F
Common marketing costs:§			
Vice president's office	$ 9,000	$ 8,000	$ 1,000 U
Staff	4,000	4,000	0
National advertising	21,000	20,000	1,000 U
Total	−34,000	−32,000	−2,000 U
Marketing contribution	$103,000	$101,000	$ 2,000 F

* See footnote 1 for explanation of use of parentheses.

† To avoid passing production variances on to marketing performance reports, only the standard variable cost of goods sold is included.

‡ The regional fixed costs are direct costs of the region. Their deduction at this point is analogous to the deduction of direct fixed costs in segment income statements.

§ The common marketing costs are direct costs of marketing activities. Their deduction at this point is analogous to the deduction of direct fixed costs in segment income statements.

As is true in developing segment reports, the most difficult problems encountered in the development of marketing performance reports are caused by common costs related to more than one marketing territory. This problem may not be too severe in regional reports, but it becomes an increasing problem as more detailed reports are developed for smaller marketing segments. Costs that cannot be directly attributed to a particular marketing segment should normally be omitted from performance reports prepared for that segment.[2]

Performance Reports and Special Decisions

The purpose of performance reports is to provide feedback helpful in controlling current operations and planning future operations. Special decisions such as continuing or discontinuing the manufacture or sale of a product, operations in a particular region, or sales through a particular channel of distribution should not be based on routine performance reports. Performance reports identify potential problems and opportunities; they do not provide answers. They summarize the results of recent operations and compare them with plans; they do not predict the future.

The decision to continue or discontinue a product line or some other aspect of operations should be based on a special study of future costs and revenues that will differ under alternative actions. Because studies of this type are expensive and time consuming, they should only be made when routine performance reports identify a potential problem or opportunity. How much will costs and revenues change if an operation is discontinued? The answer may not be obvious.

Example 12–1

The USC Company manufactures and sells five products. A separate marketing group is responsible for each product. To help make the sales staff aware of USC's total cost structure and to encourage them to avoid excessive use of such services as USC's wide area telephone service, common costs are included in the performance reports for each marketing group. The marketing performance reports for a recent period suggested that, although USC's income position was positive, three of the five products were losing money. Yet, on the basis of a special study, management elected to continue all five products.

It was determined that the common costs could not be reduced by the elimination of one or more products. After these costs were removed from the reports, all but one product showed a positive contribution to common costs and profits. The one product was a new computer software line that showed significant market potential.

Other Marketing Performance Data

Marketing is an extremely complex function and the basic performance reports presented in Exhibit 12–1 do not provide sufficient information for effective planning and control. The following examples indicate two separate problems

---

[2] Some researchers have presented strong arguments for the inclusion of some common costs in performance reports in order to prevent the overconsumption of resources that display a step cost function, such as wide area telephone services or central computer processing time. The allocated cost reminds users that these resources are not free to the organization and it causes users to demand that the departments providing the resource operate efficiently. See Jerold L. Zimmerman, "The Costs and Benefits of Cost Allocation," *Accounting Review* **54,** No. 3 (July 1979): 504–521.

EXHIBIT 12–2 Additional Measures of Marketing Performance

Market share
Sales/gross national product
Change in retailer's inventories
Average contribution per order
Total orders/number of customers
Average distribution expense per order
Average order size
Number of new customers
Number of backorders
Average time between receipt and shipment of order
Miles traveled/total visits to customers

with performance reports based only on a comparison of budgeted and actual financial amounts: (1) performance reports based on the original budget may indicate favorable variances while the company is losing its market share, and (2) performance reports may not provide information on a timely basis.

Example 12–2 The President of MacDavis was pleased to see a 10 percent favorable sales volume variance until he learned that the entire market for MacDavis products was running 20 percent ahead of marketing forecasts. While MacDavis was reporting a 10 percent favorable sales volume variance, competitors were reporting favorable sales volume variances in excess of 20 percent.

Example 12–3 The Finger Lakes Supply Company distributes its products through wholesalers who resell them to retailers. The retailers, in turn, sell to consumers. Because of a three-month lag between production and sale to ultimate consumers, Finger Lakes cannot make timely adjustments in its plans by comparing actual sales against budgeted sales to wholesalers. Instead, management monitors retail inventories of its products. If they reach excessive levels, Finger Lakes reduces production in anticipation of unfavorable sales variances while they start an immediate consumer advertising campaign. By doing so they avoid large investments in unsold inventories and demonstrate support of their retail outlets.

Both of the preceding examples illustrate the need to obtain nonfinancial as well as financial measures of marketing performance. Some additional measures of marketing performance are identified in Exhibit 12–2.

PERFORMANCE REPORTS FOR DISCRETIONARY COST CENTERS

Recall that **discretionary fixed costs** are set at a fixed amount each year at the discretion of management. These costs are not required to maintain current production or service capacity. Typical discretionary fixed costs include advertising, administrative expenses, charitable contributions, and research and development. A segment of the organization that does not have any revenue responsibility and whose costs are primarily classified as discretionary is identified as a **discretionary cost center,** that is, a cost center that does not have clearly defined relationships between effort and accomplishment.

Even though the marketing function contains many discretionary fixed costs, these costs are subtracted from revenues when marketing is evaluated as a profit center. In for-profit organizations, administration is the principal functional area evaluated as a discretionary cost center.

Because discretionary cost centers do not have clearly defined relationships between effort and accomplishment, the only accounting control over them is **budgetary control,** where actual and budgeted costs are compared. The resulting **budget variance,** the difference between the actual and budgeted costs of a discretionary cost center, is computed in a manner similar to the fixed overhead budget variance for standard cost centers:

$$\text{Budget variance} = \text{Actual costs} - \text{Budgeted costs}$$

Each executive is held responsible for expenditures in his or her area of responsibility and is not allowed to spend more than a specified amount without prior approval. It is very difficult to attach the words "favorable" or "unfavorable" to discretionary cost center budget variances. A favorable variance brought about by the cancellation of a program vital to the long-run success of the organization should not be rewarded. The words "over budget" and "under budget" seem much more appropriate.

Nonmonetary performance measures are important in evaluating discretionary cost centers. A program results review is one possible nonmonetary approach to performance evaluation. Basically, a **program results review** attempts to determine if a particular program is accomplishing its objective. For example, the objective of an automobile inspection program might be to reduce the number of unsafe vehicles on the highways. One possible way to measure the program's effectiveness is to monitor the number of traffic accidents resulting from preventable mechanical failures. An objective of all police and fire departments is to minimize the response time to emergency calls. One way to measure effectiveness on this dimension would be to compare response times for these services in similar communities.

Although program results reviews do not use monetary measures (at least, not directly), accountants are becoming involved in them and similar evaluative procedures. Additionally, many organizations have changed their organization structure to try to change discretionary cost centers into standard cost centers or even into profit centers. They do this in a belief that other types of responsibility centers provide a greater incentive to control costs. A typing pool could, for example, be changed from a discretionary cost center to a profit center by charging departments requesting typing services on a per-page basis. The typing profit center's employees might then be given a bonus based on their "profits." Besides the obvious behavioral considerations, the costs of establishing a typing profit center must also be considered. Perhaps such centers were not established in the past because the potential benefits did not compare favorably with the related costs. However, significant recent declines in data processing costs are allowing many organizations to make such changes.

SALES VARIANCES

In the balance of this chapter we examine sales variances and illustrate a reconciliation of budgeted and actual income. To simplify our analysis and the accompanying examples, we use contribution income statements with variable costing as the basis of inventory valuation. This eliminates the need to deal with fixed factory overhead volume variances.

To supplement marketing performance reports, such as those presented in Exhibit 12–1, additional variances are computed for sales, variable distribution costs, and fixed distribution costs. The sales variances are based on a comparison of actual and budgeted sales. When marketing is evaluated as a profit center, the focus of the sales variances is on their impact on the budgeted contribution margin. In a multiple product firm, sales variances are computed to determine the effect of changes in selling prices, sales mix, and sales volume on the budgeted contribution margin. In computing sales variances, the variable cost of goods sold and the variable distribution costs are held constant at standard.

The variable distribution cost variances are based on a flexible budget drawn up for the actual sales volume. Their computation is similar to that of variable factory overhead. The fixed distribution cost variance is based on a comparison of actual and budgeted fixed distribution costs. Because all distribution costs are period costs, there is never a fixed distribution cost volume variance.

Single Product Sales Price and Volume Variances

Managers of for-profit firms are seldom interested in sales revenue for its own sake. They are interested in sales that make a positive contribution toward covering common fixed costs and providing for a profit. Accordingly, in analyzing sales variances, we focus on the impact of such variances on the budgeted contribution margin. To do this we must deduct variable costs from selling prices to arrive at a unit contribution margin. To avoid mixing cost and sales variances, standard variable costs are used in all sales variance computations.

The **total sales variance** indicates the impact of variations in the selling prices and unit sales volume on the contribution margin. It is computed by allowing selling prices and unit sales volume to vary between budget and actual while holding per unit variable costs constant at standard:

		Actual volume at actual prices and standard costs		Budgeted volume at budgeted prices and standard costs	
Total sales variance	=	$AQ_S(AP - SC)$	−	$BQ_S(BP - SC)$	(12–1)

where

AQ_S = Actual unit sales
AP = Actual unit selling price
SC = Standard variable unit costs of manufacturing *and* distribution
BQ_S = Budgeted unit sales
BP = Budgeted unit selling price

The total sales variance is decomposed into two variances, a "sales price variance" and a "sales volume variance."

		Actual volume at actual prices and standard costs		Actual volume at budgeted prices and standard costs	
Sales price variance	=	$AQ_S(AP - SC)$	−	$AQ_S(BP - SC)$	(12–2)

		Actual volume at budgeted prices and standard costs		Budgeted volume at budgeted prices and standard costs	
Sales volume variance	=	$AQ_S(BP - SC)$	−	$BQ_S(BP - SC)$	(12–3)

The **sales price variance** indicates the impact on the contribution margin of a change in selling price, given the actual sales volume. The **sales volume variance** indicates the impact on the contribution margin of a change in the sales volume, assuming no changes in selling prices or variable costs. The difference between the actual contribution margin at standard costs and the budgeted contribution margin is explained by the sales price and sales volume variances.

Actual volume at actual prices and standard costs	Actual volume at budgeted prices and standard costs	*Original budget* Budgeted volume at budgeted prices and standard costs
$AQ_S(AP - SC)$	$AQ_S(BP - SC)$	$BQ_S(BP - SC)$

Sales price variance $AQ_S(AP - BP)$*

Sales volume variance $(AQ_S - BQ_S)(BP - SC)$*

Total sales variance

* Short computational formula.

Example 12–4

Novelty Productions has a simple organization consisting of only three departments, Administration, Production, and Sales. Novelty's single product, Thingamabobs, has a budgeted unit selling price of $8. Budgeted variable costs of $3 per unit include the following:

Variable manufacturing costs	$2.50
Variable selling costs	0.50
Total	$3.00

Budgeted monthly fixed costs totaling $35,000 consist of the following:

Fixed manufacturing costs	$20,000
Fixed selling expenses	5,000
Fixed administrative expenses	10,000
Total	$35,000

Novelty's budgeted March 19x6 contribution income statement, when budgeted production and sales of 10,000 units was planned, follows:

Novelty Productions
Budgeted Contribution Income Statement
For the Month of March 19x6

Sales (10,000 units × $8)		$80,000
Variable costs:		
Cost of goods sold (10,000 units × $2.50)	$25,000	
Selling (10,000 units × $0.50)	5,000	−30,000
Contribution margin		$50,000
Fixed costs:		
Manufacturing	$20,000	
Sales	5,000	
Administrative	10,000	−35,000
Net income		$15,000

Actual results for the month were as follows:

Novelty Productions
Actual Contribution Income Statement
For the Month of March 19x6

Sales (8,000 units × $9)		$72,000
Variable costs:		
Cost of goods sold (8,000 units × $2.25)	$18,000	
Selling (8,000 units × $0.50)	4,000	−22,000
Contribution margin		$50,000
Fixed costs:		
Manufacturing	$21,000	
Sales	5,500	
Administrative	12,000	−38,500
Net income		$11,500

For performance evaluation purposes, Novelty treats the Administration Department as a discretionary cost center, the Production Department as a standard cost center, and the Sales Department as a profit center. Variances for each area of responsibility, computed in as much detail as possible, are as follows:

ADMINISTRATION:

Administration budget variance	=	Actual costs	−	Budgeted costs
	=	$12,000	−	$10,000
	=	$2,000U (over budget)		

PRODUCTION:

Variable mfg. costs variance	=	Actual costs	−	Flexible budget
	=	(8,000 × \$2.25)	−	(8,000 × \$2.25)
	=	\$18,000	−	\$20,000
	=	\$(2,000)F		
Fixed mfg. costs variance	=	Actual costs	−	Flexible budget
	=	\$21,000	−	\$20,000
	=	\$1,000U		

SALES:

Sales price variance	=	$AQ_S(AP - BP)$		
	=	8,000 (\$9 − \$8)		
	=	\$8,000F[3]		
Sales volume variance	=	$(AQ_S - BQ_S)(BP - SC)$		
	=	(8,000 − 10,000)(\$8 − \$3)		
		\$(10,000)U		
Variable selling costs variance	=	Actual costs	−	Flexible budget
	=	(8,000 × \$0.50)	−	(8,000 × \$0.50)
	=	\$4,000	−	\$4,000
	=	\$ 0.00		
Fixed selling costs budget variance	=	Actual costs	−	Budgeted costs
	=	\$5,500	−	\$5,000
	=	\$500U		

The difference between Novelty Production's budgeted and actual income can be reconciled by summing all variances, as is done in Exhibit 12–3(a). Alternatively, the difference can be reconciled by summing the variances for each responsibility center, as is done in Exhibit 12–3(b).

A marketing performance report for Novelty Productions is presented in Exhibit 12–4(a). It is similar to the regional sales manager's report in Exhibit 12–1. Note that the net variance for marketing contribution in Exhibit 12–4(a) is

---

[3] See footnote 1.

EXHIBIT 12–3 Reconciliation of Budgeted and Actual Variable Costing Income

(a) Based on a Detailed Listing of Variances

Budgeted income		$15,000
Add favorable variances:		
Variable mfg. cost variance	2,000	
Sales price variance	8,000	10,000
Less unfavorable variances:		
Administrative budget variance	$ 2,000	
Fixed mfg. cost variance	1,000	
Sales volume variance	10,000	
Fixed selling cost budget variance	500	(13,500)
Actual income		$11,500

(b) Based on a Summary of Responsibility Center Variances

Budgeted income		$15,000
Administration Department (A discretionary cost center):		
Administration budget variance		2,000 U
Production Department (A standard cost center):		
Variable mfg. cost variance	$ 2,000 F	
Fixed mfg. cost variance	1,000 U	1,000 F
Sales Department (A profit center):		
Sales price variance	$ 8,000 F	
Sales volume variance	10,000 U	
Variable selling cost variance	0	
Fixed selling cost budget variance	500 U	2,500 U
Actual income		$11,500

the same as the net Sales Department variance in Exhibit 12–3(b). Although the marketing performance report in Exhibit 12–4(a) presents an overview of marketing performance, the meaning of the variances for sales and variable cost items is, as discussed previously, questionable. The authors recommend a variation in the marketing performance report that does not display variances for sales and variable costs. Such a report is presented in Exhibit 12–4(b). Here, the contribution margin variance is a summary measure that is further explained by the sales variances and the variable selling expense variance. The report in Exhibit 12–4(b) performs a function similar to that performed by a manufacturing performance report based on a flexible budget; it provides an overview that can be further analyzed into a number of component variances.

Multiple Product Sales Price, Mix, and Volume Variances

When an organization sells two or more products that have differing budgeted or actual contribution margins, the sales volume variance represents the joint effect of (1) changes in the total number of units sold and (2) changes in the product mix. In analyzing the sales variances of the firm as a whole, these changes should be separately identified. To do this, the sales volume variance is further decomposed into a sales mix variance and a pure sales volume variance.

Sales volume variance

Sales mix variance — Pure sales volume variance

The **sales mix variance** indicates the impact on the budgeted contribution margin of deviations between the actual and the budgeted mix of total unit sales. It is computed using budgeted selling prices, budgeted costs, and actual unit sales, while allowing the sales mix to vary between actual and standard. The **pure sales volume variance** indicates the impact on the contribution margin of deviations between the actual and budgeted total unit sales. It is computed using

EXHIBIT 12–4 Novelty Production's Marketing Performance Report

(a) Traditional Marketing Performance Report Displaying Variances for all Items

	Actual	*Budget*	*Favorable unfavorable variance*
Sales	$72,000	$80,000	$(8,000)U
Variable costs:			
Standard cost of goods sold	$20,000	$25,000	$(5,000)F
Selling	4,000	5,000	(1,000)F
Controllable variable costs	−24,000	−30,000	−(6,000)F
Contribution margin	$48,000	$50,000	$(2,000)U
Fixed costs:			
Selling	−5,500	−5,000	−500 U
Marketing contribution	$42,500	$45,000	$(2,500)U

(b) Recommended Marketing Performance Report Displaying Variances for the Contribution Margin and Fixed Costs

	Actual	*Budget*	*Favorable unfavorable variance*
Sales	$72,000	$80,000	
Variable costs:			
Standard cost of goods sold	$20,000	$25,000	
Selling	4,000	5,000	
Controllable variable costs	−24,000	−30,000	
Contribution margin	$48,000	$50,000	$(2,000)U
Fixed costs:			
Selling	−5,500	−5,000	−500 U
Marketing contribution	$42,500	$45,000	$(2,500)U

budgeted selling prices, budgeted costs, and the budgeted mix, while allowing total unit sales to vary between actual and budget.

Example 12–6

Novelty Productions began selling a second product, Thingamajigs, in May 19x6. Thingamajigs have a budgeted unit selling price of $20 and standard variable manufacturing costs of $10. There are no changes in the selling prices or standard variable costs of Thingamabobs. The standard variable selling expenses and the budgeted fixed costs for selling and administration remain unchanged. With budgeted sales of 10,000 Thingamabobs and 10,000 Thingamajigs, Novelty Production's budgeted May 19x6 income statement is as follows:

Novelty Productions
Budgeted Contribution Income Statement
For the Month of May 19x6

Sales:		
"Bobs" (10,000 units × $8)	$ 80,000	
"Jigs" (10,000 units × $20)	200,000	$280,000
Variable costs:		
Cost of goods sold:		
"Bobs" (10,000 units × $2.50)	$ 25,000	
"Jigs" (10,000 units × $10)	100,000	
Selling (20,000 units × $0.50)	10,000	−135,000
Contribution margin		$145,000
Fixed costs:		
Manufacturing	$20,000	
Sales	5,000	
Administrative	10,000	−35,000
Net income		$110,000

Actual results for the month are as follows:

Novelty Productions
Actual Contribution Income Statement
For the Month of May 19x6

Sales:		
"Bobs" (12,000 units × $9)	$108,000	
"Jigs" (20,000 units × $18)	360,000	$468,000
Variable costs:		
Cost of goods sold:		
"Bobs" (12,000 units × $2.50)	$ 30,000	
"Jigs" (20,000 units × $10)	200,000	
Selling (32,000 units × $0.50)	16,000	−246,000
Contribution margin		$222,000
Fixed costs:		
Manufacturing	$ 20,000	
Sales	5,000	
Administrative	10,000	−35,000
Net income		$187,000

The $77,000 increase in income ($187,000 − $110,000) is due entirely to sales variances. The separate variances for Thingamabobs and Thingamajigs are:

Thingamabobs:		
Sales price variance 12,000($9 − $8)	$12,000F	
Sales volume variance (12,000 − 10,000)($8 − $3)	10,000F	$22,000F
Thingamajigs:		
Sales price variance 20,000($18 − $20)	$(40,000)U	
Sales volume variance (20,000 − 10,000)($20 − $10.50*)	95,000F	55,000F
Net sales variances		$77,000F

* ($10.00 + $0.50)

Novelty Productions' overall sales price and volume variances are computed in Exhibit 12–5(a). The sales volume variance is decomposed into sales mix and pure sales volume variances in Exhibit 12–5(b). Note that the budgeted mix was

EXHIBIT 12–5 Sales Variances for Multiple Product Firms

(a) Sales Price and Volume Variances

Product	*Actual volume at actual mix, actual prices, and standard costs*	*Actual volume at actual mix, budgeted prices, and standard costs*	*Original budget: Budgeted volume at budgeted mix, budgeted prices, and standard costs*
Bobs	12,000($9 − $3) = $ 72,000	12,000($8 − $3) = $ 60,000	10,000($8 − $3) = $ 50,000
Jigs	20,000($18 − $10.50) = 150,000	20,000($20 − $10.50) = 190,000	10,000($20 − $10.50) = 95,000
	32,000 $222,000	$250,000	$145,000

$(28,000)U Sales price variance

$105,000F Sales volume variance

(b) Sales Mix and Pure Sales Volume Variances

Product	*Actual volume at actual mix, budgeted prices, and standard costs*	*Actual volume at budgeted mix, budgeted prices, and standard costs*	*Original budget: Budgeted volume at budgeted mix, budgeted prices, and standard costs*
Bobs	12,000($8 − $3) = $ 60,000	(32,000 × 0.50)($8 − $3) = $ 80,000	10,000($8 − $3) = $ 50,000
Jigs	20,000($20 − $10.50) = 190,000	(32,000 × 0.50)($20 − $10.50) = 152,000	10,000($20 − $10.50) = 95,000
	$250,000	$232,000	$145,000

$18,000F Sales mix variance

$87,000F Pure sales volume variance

50 percent for each product:

Product	*Budgeted unit sales*	*Budgeted mix*
Thingamabobs	10,000	0.50
Thingamajigs	10,000	0.50
Total	20,000	

To compute the sales mix and pure sales volume variances, the actual sales of 32,000 units, consisting of 12,000 Thingamabobs and 20,000 Thingamajigs, is restated in the budgeted mix, consisting of 16,000 Thingamabobs (32,000 × 0.50) and 16,000 Thingamajigs (32,000 × 0.50)

In Example 12–6 we properly used sales price and sales volume variances to evaluate individual products, and the sales mix and pure sales volume variances to examine overall performance. Although the sales mix and the pure sales volume variances are useful in explaining overall sales performance, they should not be used to evaluate individual products. If we tried to determine the mix variance of individual products, Thingamabobs would have an unfavorable mix variance because their budgeted portion of sales was 0.50 (10,000/20,000), whereas their actual portion of sales was 0.375 (12,000/32,000). This decline in Thingamabob sales mix occurred when actual Thingamabob sales exceeded budgeted sales by 2,000 units (12,000 − 10,000). Assigning such an unfavorable mix variance to the Thingamabob product manager would likely lead to behavioral problems.

SUMMARY

A revenue center is responsible for the generation of sales revenue. Marketing departments could be evaluated as revenue centers, but this approach does not encourage marketing managers to control selling expenses, nor does it encourage them to avoid unprofitable price concessions. To avoid these motivational problems, marketing departments are likely to be assigned dual responsibility as a revenue center and a cost center. Alternatively, they are evaluated as profit centers, responsible for the difference between revenues and controllable costs.

The marketing performance reports presented in this chapter emphasize marketing's contribution to fixed manufacturing costs, administrative expenses, and profits. In a typical report, the standard variable cost of goods sold and the variable selling expenses are subtracted from sales revenue to compute a contribution margin. Fixed selling expenses are subtracted from this amount to arrive at the bottom-line, marketing contribution. If the organization is to reach its profit goal, marketing must meet its budgeted contribution. Accordingly, marketing performance reports are based on the original budget rather than on a flexible budget.

Comparing actual marketing performance with the original budget and taking care to include the cost of goods sold at standard in both, we can compute variances for each item in the report. The first meaningful variance, for the contribution margin, can be decomposed into variances for sales price, sales volume, and variable selling costs. In multiple product firms, the sales volume variance can be further decomposed into a sales mix variance and a pure sales volume variance.

APPENDIX Sales Contribution and Sales Revenue Variances

The sales variances computed in Chapter 12 emphasize the impact of changes in selling price and sales volume on *contribution margin*. Hence they might be called "sales contribution variances." Using the sales contribution approach, we computed the following sales variances for Example 12–4:

Sales contribution approach

Sales price variance [8,000($9 − $8)]	$ 8,000 F
Sales volume variance [(8,000 − 10,000)($8 − $3)]	(10,000)U
Total sales variance	$(2,000)U

Sales variances can also be computed to emphasize *sales revenue,* that is, the impact of changes in selling prices and sales volume on sales revenue. Such variances might be called "sales revenue variances." The computation of variances under the sales revenue approach is similar to the computation under the sales contribution approach, except that costs are excluded. Following the sales revenue approach, we would obtain the following sales variances for Example 12–4:

Sales revenue approach

Sales price variance [8,000($9 − $8)]	$ 8,000 F
Sales volume variance [$8(8,000 − 10,000)]	(16,000)U
Total sales revenue variance	$(8,000)U

The difference between the sales variances under these two approaches is due to the difference between the budgeted variable costs for the budgeted sales volume and the allowed variable costs for the actual sales. For Example 12–4, this difference amounts to $6,000 [$3(8,000 − 10,000)].

The sales revenue approach does provide a reconciliation of budgeted and actual sales revenue. However, by omitting any consideration of variable costs it (1) does not give a clear picture of the bottom-line impact of the sales volume variance and (2) increases the difficulty of reconciling budgeted and actual variable-costing net income. A complete listing of all variances to reconcile budgeted and actual variable-costing net income, following the sales revenue approach, is presented in Exhibit 12–6. Exhibit 12–6 should be compared to Exhibit 12–3(a) where the sales contribution approach is used. The sales

EXHIBIT 12–6 Reconciliation of Budgeted and Actual Variable-Costing Income: Detailed Listing Based on Sales Revenue Approach

Budgeted income			$15,000
Add favorable variances:			
Variable mfg. cost variance		$ 2,000	
Sales price variance		8,000	10,000
Less unfavorable variances:			
Administrative budget variance		$ 2,000	
Fixed mfg. cost variance		1,000	
Sales volume variance	$16,000		
Less cost savings at std.	−6,000	10,000	
Fixed selling cost budget variance		500	(13,500)
Actual income			$11,500

revenue approach in Exhibit 12–6 requires a disclosure of the cost savings, at standard, that resulted from the unfavorable sales volume variance.

Although the authors prefer the sales contribution approach because of its bottom-line significance, both approaches are encountered in practice. Unfortunately they are not labeled as the "sales contribution approach" or the "sales revenue approach." The treatment of variable costs is the key to determining which approach is being used.

KEY TERMS

Budget variance
Budgetary control
Discretionary cost center
Discretionary fixed costs
Order filling costs
Order getting costs
Profit center
Program results review
Pure sales volume variance
Responsibility accounting
Responsibility center
Revenue center
Sales mix variance
Sales price variance
Sales revenue variance
Sales volume variance
Total sales variance

SELECTED REFERENCES

Bhatia, Manohar L., "Motivational Value of Profit Centres," *Cost and Management* **57,** No. 6 (November-December 1983): 31–35.

Brown, Russell S., "Measuring Manufacturing Performance: A Targeting Approach," *Management Accounting* **61,** No. 12 (June 1980): 25–28, 31.

Demski, Joel S., "Analyzing the Effectiveness of the Traditional Standard Cost Variance Model," *Management Accounting* **49,** No. 2 (October 1967): 9–19.

Hasseldine, C. R., "Mix and Yield Variances," *Accounting Review* **42,** No. 3 (July 1967): 497–515.

Hobbs, James B., "Volume-Mix-Price/Cost Budget Variance Analysis: A Proper Approach," *Accounting Review* **39,** No. 4 (October 1964): 905–913.

Manes, Rene P., "Demand Elasticities: Supplements to Sales Budget Variance Reports," *Accounting Review* **58,** No. 1 (January 1983): 143–156.

_____, "In a Seminar on Budget Mix Variances," *Accounting Review* **43,** No. 4 (October 1968): 784–787.

Zimmerman, Jerold, "The Costs and Benefits of Cost Allocations," *Accounting Review* **54,** No. 3 (July 1979): 504–521.

REVIEW QUESTIONS

12–1 Identify two motivational problems associated with evaluating marketing as a revenue center.

12–2 Assuming marketing is evaluated as a profit center, identify two major differences between responsibility accounting reports for marketing and manufacturing.

12–3 Distinguish between order getting and order filling costs.

12–4 At what amount should the cost of goods sold be stated in marketing performance reports? Why?

12–5 What label is attached to the bottom line in a marketing performance report when marketing is evaluated as a profit center?

12–6 Should special decisions concerning the continuance or dicontinuance of some aspect of operations be based on marketing performance reports? Why or why not?

12–7 Why might a program results review be used to evaluate a discretionary cost center?

12–8 Why is it difficult to identify a discretionary cost center's variances as favorable or unfavorable?

12–9 What two variances are contained in the sales volume variance of a multiple product firm?

12–10 What does the sales mix variance indicate?

12–11 What does the pure sales volume variance indicate?

12–12 Why is it not advisable to compute sales mix variances for individual products?

REVIEW PROBLEM

Multiple Product Sales Variances and Reconciliation of Budgeted and Actual Net Income

The College Clipper operates two hairstyling shops on University Avenue. The College Clipper offers precision haircuts and hairstyling in two price categories, regular and pacesetter. Employees are paid on a commission basis. Presented is revenue and cost information for May 19w1 and May 19w2.

The College Clipper
Comparative Income Statements
For May 19w1 and May 19w2

	May 19w1			*May 19w2*		
	Regular	*Pacesetter*	*Total*	*Regular*	*Pacesetter*	*Total*
Number	4,000	1,000	5,000	2,000	2,000	4,000
Unit price	$5.00	$15.00		$7.50	$15.00	
Unit commission	$2.50	$10.00		$3.00	$10.00	
Sales revenue	$20,000	$15,000	$35,000	$15,000	$30,000	$45,000
Commissions	– 10,000	– 10,000	– 20,000	– 6,000	– 20,000	– 26,000
Contribution margin	$10,000	$ 5,000	$15,000	$ 9,000	$10,000	$19,000
Fixed costs			– 10,000			– 12,000
Net income			$ 5,000			$ 7,000

Accepting the May 19w1 performance as the standard, management is interested in studying the factors causing the $2,000 increase in May 19w2 income.

REQUIREMENTS

a) Determine the sales price and the sales volume variance for each service.

b) Determine the sales price, the sales mix, and the pure sales volume variance for the company as a whole.

c) Determine the labor rate variance for regular haircuts and the fixed cost budget variance.

d) Prepare a reconciliation of May 19w1 and May 19w2 net income.

The solution to this problem is found at the end of the Chapter 12 problems and exercises.

EXERCISES

12–1 Significance of Sales Variances

Two product sales managers of the same company were overheard in conversation recently. A part of the conversation was as follows:

Mgr. X: You know, comparison of my product's performance against the budget shows my group falling further and further behind each month. I'm really depressed. Conditions in our markets have changed so much since the budget was established that there is no way I can achieve those figures. In fact, our product's performance is worse and worse by comparison with the budget for the balance of the year.

Mgr. A: Yes, I know what you mean and sympathize with you. I had that problem last year. But this year I'm in the opposite situation! Our actual performance vis-à-vis the budget just gets better and better. It's nothing we're doing—conditions in our markets have changed for the good since the budget was established. We are, in a sense, just along for the ride, but it sure makes me look good at the head office.

REQUIREMENT

Briefly discuss what (if anything) is apparently wrong with this company's performance evaluation procedures. (CGA Adapted)

12–2 Salespeople's Compensation and Motivation

The president of Taylor School Supply Company, a wholesaler, presents you with a comparison of distribution costs for two salespeople and wants to know if you think the salespeople's compensation plan is working to the detriment of the company. The president supplies you with the following data:

	Salespeople	
	McKinney	*Sim*
Gross sales	$247,000	$142,000
Sales returns	17,000	2,000
Cost of goods sold	180,000	85,000
Reimbursed expenses (e.g., entertainment)	5,500	2,100
Other direct charges (e.g., samples distributed)	4,000	450
Commission rate on gross sales dollars	5%	5%

REQUIREMENTS

a) A salesperson's compensation plan encourages him to work to increase the measure of performance to which his compensation is related. List a salesperson's questionable sales practices that might be encouraged by basing commissions on gross sales.

b) 1. What evidence that the compensation plan may be working to the detriment of the company can be found in the data?

2. What other information should the president obtain before reaching definite conclusions about this particular situation? Why? (CPA Adapted)

12–3 T Multiple Product Sales Variances

Presented is information pertaining to the June 19x3 operations of the Quebec Carte Co.

Product	*Est*	*Quest*
Budgeted sales volume	16,000	24,000
Budgeted unit selling price	$4.25	$4.00
Standard variable cost per unit	$2.00	$2.00
Actual sales volume	12,000	36,000
Actual unit selling price	$3.75	$4.25

REQUIREMENTS

a) Determine the sales price and sales volume variances of each product.

b) Determine the sales price, sales mix, and pure sales volume variances of the company as a whole.

12–4 T Multiple Product Sales Variances

Presented is information pertaining to the August 19x7 operations of the Wood Company.

Product	*Oak tables*	*Maple rockers*
Budgeted sales volume	550	450
Budgeted unit selling price	$15.00	$30.00
Standard variable cost per unit	$8.00	$18.00
Actual sales volume	600	900
Actual unit selling price	$15.00	$25.00

REQUIREMENTS

a) Determine the sales price and sales volume variances of each product.

b) Determine the sales price, sales mix, and pure sales volume variances of the company as a whole.

12–5 T Multiple Product Sales Variances

Presented is information pertaining to the 19y2 operations of the Xerbert Co. (000s omitted)

BUDGET

	Xenox	*Xeon*	*Total*
Unit sales	150	100	250
Sales revenue	$ 900	$1,000	$1,900
Variable expenses	−450	−750	−1,200
Contribution margin	$ 450	$ 250	$ 700

ACTUAL

	Xenox	*Xeon*	*Total*
Unit sales	130	130	260
Sales revenue	$ 780	$1,235	$2,015
Variable expenses	−390	−975	−1,365
Contribution margin	$ 390	$ 260	$ 650

REQUIREMENTS

a) Determine the sales price and sales volume variances of each product.

b) Determine the sales price, sales mix, and pure sales volume variances of the company as a whole. (CMA Adapted)

12–6 T Multiple Product Sales Variances

The Mesa Verde Auto Company is a dealer for a maker of off-road recreational vehicles. The budgeted unit contribution for each model Mesa Verde sells is presented as follows:

Model	*Selling price*	*Dealer cost*	*Dealer preparation*	*Contribution margin*
Dune Leveler	$2,100	$1,400	$200	$ 500
High Country	3,000	2,000	300	700
Earth & Water	4,500	2,500	500	1,500

Budgeted sales for 19x8 were:

Model	*Sales*
Dune Leveler	300
High Country	200
Earth & Water	50

Actual results for 19x8 are as follows:

Model	*Sales*	*Average selling price*
Dune Leveler	350	$2,300
High Country	150	3,000
Earth & Water	100	3,500*

* The model was discontinued by the factory.

REQUIREMENTS

a) Determine the sales price and sales volume variances of each model.

b) Determine the sales price, pure sales volume, and sales mix variances of the dealership as a whole.

12–7 T Multiple Product Sales Variances in a Service Industry

After an extensive analysis of all anticipated expenses and revenues, the Southwood Municipal Hospital has received a federal grant to establish a Highway Intensive Treatment (HIT) unit. The HIT unit represents a new concept in the treatment of traumatic injury as a result of an automobile accident. Rather than have the police or ambulance service transport the casualties to a hospital emergency room, a mobile intensive treatment unit is dispatched to administer immediate care at the scene of the accident. Additionally, the HIT unit can provide heart attack victims with emergency care before they are brought to the hospital. It is estimated that major insurance companies will pay $50.00 per response to an accident and $90.00 per response to a heart attack, and that the marginal cost of a response is $75.00 regardless of its purpose. It is further estimated that the yearly responses will total 500 and be divided equally between accidents and heart attacks.

REQUIREMENTS

a) If the service operates according to plan, what is the average contribution margin per response?

b) If during the first year of operations all cost and revenue estimates are correct and the HIT unit makes 300 accident responses and 100 heart attack responses, what are the dollar amounts of the pure sales volume and sales mix variances?

c) Can any generalizable conclusions be drawn from this analysis?

12–8 Single Product Sales Variances and Reconciliation of Budgeted and Actual Income

Presented is the budgeted 19x0 income statement of Rodman, Inc.

Rodman, Inc.
Budgeted Contribution Income Statement
For the Year Ending December 31, 19x0

Sales (20,000 units × $3)		$60,000
Variable costs:		
Manufacturing (20,000 × $1.00)	$20,000	
Distribution (20,000 × $0.50)	10,000	−30,000
Contribution margin		$30,000
Fixed costs:		
Manufacturing	$12,000	
Selling and administration	15,000	−27,000
Net income		$ 3,000

Rodman's actual contribution income statement was as follows:

Rodman, Inc.
Actual Contribution Income Statement
For the Year Ending December 31, 19x0

Sales (25,000 units × $4)		$100,000
Variable costs:		
Manufacturing (25,000 × $2.00)	$50,000	
Distribution (25,000 × $0.75)	18,750	−68,750
Contribution margin		$ 31,250
Fixed costs:		
Manufacturing	$15,000	
Selling and administration	17,000	−32,000
Net income		$ (750)

REQUIREMENT

Prepare a report reconciling budgeted and actual variable-costing income. The report should contain as detailed a listing of as many sales and cost variances as possible.

12–9 Single Product Sales Variances and Reconciliation of Budgeted and Actual Income

Presented is the budgeted 19x1 income statement of the Geiser Company.

Geiser Company
Budgeted Contribution Income Statement
For the Year Ending December 31, 19x1

Sales (12,000 units × $5)		$60,000
Variable costs:		
Manufacturing (12,000 × $2)	$24,000	
Selling (12,000 × $1.25)	15,000	−39,000
Contribution margin		$21,000
Fixed costs:		
Manufacturing	$ 6,000	
Administration	10,000	−16,000
Net income		$ 5,000

Geiser's actual 19x1 contribution income statement was as follows:

Geiser Company
Actual Contribution Income Statement
For the Year Ending December 31, 19x1

Sales (11,000 units × $6)		$66,000
Variable costs:		
Manufacturing (11,000 × $2.50)	$27,500	
Selling (11,000 × $1.50)	16,500	−44,000
Contribution margin		$22,000

Fixed costs:		
Manufacturing	$ 5,500	
Administration	10,000	−15,500
Net income		$ 6,500

REQUIREMENT

Prepare a report reconciling budgeted and actual variable-costing net income. The report should contain as detailed a listing of as many sales and cost variances as possible.

PROBLEMS

12–10 Flexible Budgets for Selling Expenses

Wielson Company employs flexible budgeting techniques to evaluate the performance of several of its activities. The selling expense flexible budgets for three representative monthly activity levels are as follows:

Representative Monthly Flexible Budgets for Selling Expenses:			
Activity measures:			
Unit sales volume	400,000	425,000	450,000
Dollar sales volume	$10,000,000	$10,625,000	$11,250,000
Number of orders	4,000	4,250	4,500
Number of salespeople	75	75	75
Monthly expenses:			
Advertising and promotion	$1,200,000	$1,200,000	$1,200,000
Administrative salaries	57,000	57,000	57,000
Sales salaries	75,000	75,000	75,000
Sales commissions	200,000	212,500	225,000
Salesforce travel	170,000	175,000	180,000
Sales office expense	490,000	498,750	507,500
Shipping expense	675,000	712,500	750,000
Total selling expenses	$2,867,000	$2,930,750	$2,994,500

The following assumptions were used to develop the selling expense flexible budgets.

- The average size of Wielson's sales force during the year was planned to be 75 people.
- Salespeople are paid a monthly salary plus commissions on gross dollar sales.
- The travel costs are best characterized as a step variable cost. The fixed portion is related to the number of salespeople, and the variable portion tends to fluctuate with gross dollar sales.
- Sales office expense is a mixed cost with the variable portion related to the number of orders processed.

- Shipping expense is a mixed cost with the variable portion related to the number of units sold.

A sales force of 80 people generated a total of 4,300 orders resulting in a sales volume of 420,000 units during November. The gross dollar sales amounted to $10.9 mllion. The selling expenses incurred for November 19x4 were as follows:

Advertising and promotion	$1,350,000
Administrative salaries	57,000
Sales salaries	80,000
Sales commissions	218,000
Salesforce travel	185,000
Sales office expense	497,200
Shipping expense	730,000
Total selling expenses	$3,117,200

REQUIREMENTS

a) Explain why flexible budgeting is a useful management tool.

b) Explain why the selling expense flexible budgets just presented would not be appropriate for evaluating Wielson Company's November selling expenses, and indicate how the flexible budget would have to be revised.

c) Prepare a selling expense report for November that Wielson Company can use to evaluate its control over selling expenses. The report should have a line for each selling expense item showing the appropriate budgeted amount, the actual selling expense, and the monthly dollar variation. (CMA Adapted)

12–11 Analysis of Selling Expenses

The Scent Company sells men's toiletries to retail stores throughout the United States. For planning and control purposes, the Scent Company is organized into twelve geographic regions with from two to six territories within each region. One salesperson is assigned to each territory and has exclusive rights to all sales made in that territory. Merchandise is shipped from the manufacturing plant to the twelve regional warehouses, and the sales in each territory are shipped from the regional warehouse. National headquarters allocates a specific amount at the beginning of the year for regional advertising.

The net sales for the Scent Company for the year ended September 30, 19x4, totaled $10 million. Costs incurred by national headquarters for national administration, advertising, and warehousing are summarized as follows:

National administration	$250,000
National advertising	125,000
National warehousing	175,000
Total	$550,000

The results of operations for the South Atlantic Region for the year ended September 30, 19x4, are as follows:

Scent Company
Statement of Operations for South Atlantic Region
For the Year Ended September 30, 19x4

Net sales		$900,000
Costs and expenses:		
Advertising fees	$ 54,700	
Bad debt expense	3,600	
Cost of sales	460,000	
Freight-out	22,600	
Insurance	10,000	
Salaries and employee benefits	81,600	
Sales commissions	36,000	
Supplies	12,000	
Travel and entertainment	14,100	
Wages and employee benefits	36,000	
Warehouse depreciation	8,000	
Warehouse operating costs	15,000	−753,600
Territory contribution		$146,400

The salaries and employee benefits consist of the following items:

Regional vice president	$24,000
Regional marketing manager	15,000
Regional warehouse manager	13,400
Salespeople (one for each territory with all receiving the same salary base)	15,600
Other employee benefits (20% of salaries only)	13,600
Total	$81,600

The salespeople receive a base salary plus a 4 percent commission on all items sold in their territory. Bad Debt Expense has averaged 0.4 percent of net sales in the past. Travel and entertainment costs are incurred by the salespeople calling on their customers. Freight-out is a function of the quantity of goods shipped and the distance shipped. Thirty percent of the insurance is expended for protection of the inventory while it is in the regional warehouse, and the remainder is incurred for the protection of the warehouse. Supplies are used in the warehouse for packing the merchandise that is shipped. Wages relate to the hourly paid employees who fill orders in the warehouse. The Warehouse Operating Costs account contains such costs as heat, light, and maintenance.

The South Atlantic Region consists of two territories, Green and Purple. The following cost analyses and statistics by territory for the current year are representative of past experience and are representative of expected future operations:

	Green	*Purple*	*Total*
Sales	$300,000	$600,000	$900,000
Cost of sales	$184,000	$276,000	$460,000
Advertising fees	$ 21,800	$ 32,900	$ 54,700
Travel & entertainment	$ 6,300	$ 7,800	$ 14,100
Freight-out	$ 9,000	$ 13,600	$ 22,600
Units sold	150,000	350,000	500,000
Pounds shipped	210,000	390,000	600,000
Salesperson miles traveled	21,600	38,400	60,000

REQUIREMENTS

a) The top management of Scent Company wants the regional vice presidents to present their operating data in a more meaningful manner. Therefore, management has requested that the regions separate their operating costs into the fixed and variable components of order-getting, order-filling, and administration. The data are to be presented in the following format:

	Territory costs		*Regional*	*Total*
	Green	*Purple*	*costs*	*costs*
Order-getting				
Order-filling				
Administration				

Using management's suggested format, prepare a schedule that presents the costs for the region by territory with the costs separated into variable and fixed categories by order-getting, order-filling, and administrative functions.

b) Suppose the top management of Scent Company is considering splitting the Purple Territory into two separate territories (Red and Blue). From the data that have been presented, identify what data would be relevant to this decision (either for or against) and indicate what other data you would collect to aid top management in its decision. (CMA Adapted)

12–12 T Multiple Product Sales Variances and Reconciliation of Budgeted and Actual Net Income

Handler Company distributes two home-use power tools to hardware stores, a heavy-duty ½″ hand drill and a table saw. The tools are purchased from a manufacturer that attaches the Handler private label on the tools. The wholesale selling prices to the hardware stores are $60 each for the drill and $120 each for the table saw.

The 19x2 budget and actual results are presented. The budget was adopted in late 19x1 and was based on Handler's estimated share of the market for the two tools.

During the first quarter of 19x2, Handler's management estimated that the total market for these tools would actually be 10 percent below its original estimates. In an attempt to prevent Handler's unit sales from declining as much as industry projections, management developed and implemented a marketing program. Included in the program were dealer discounts and increased direct advertising. The table saw line was emphasized in this program.

Handler Company
Income Statement
For the Year Ended December 31, 19x2
(000s omitted)

	Hand drill		*Table saw*		*Total*		
	Actual	*Budget*	*Actual*	*Budget*	*Actual*	*Budget*	*Variance*
Sales in units	86	120	74	80	160	200	40
Revenue	$5,074	$7,200	$8,510	$9,600	$13,584	$16,800	$(3,216)U
Cost of goods sold	−4,300	−6,000	−6,068	−6,400	−10,368	−12,400	−(2,032)F
Gross profit	$ 774	$1,200	$2,442	$3,200	$ 3,216	$ 4,400	$(1,184)U
Unallocated costs:							
Selling					$ 1,000	$ 1,000	$ 0
Advertising					1,060	1,000	60U
Administration					406	400	6U
Total unallocated costs					−2,466	−2,400	−66U
Income before taxes					$ 750	$ 2,000	$ 1,250U

REQUIREMENTS

a) Determine the sales price, the sales mix, and the pure sales volume variances.

b) Provide a complete reconciliation of budgeted and actual income before taxes. The report should contain the sales variances determined for part (a) and as many cost variances as possible.

c) Discuss the apparent effect of the Handler Company's special marketing program (that is, dealer discounts and additional advertising) on 19x2 operating results. Support your comments with numerical data where appropriate. (CMA Adapted)

12–13 T Multiple Product Sales Variances and Reconciliation of Budgeted and Actual Net Income

Bill White, President of Nosanra Electronics Limited (NEL), was reviewing NEL's 19x2 operating results (Schedule I). Bill was pleased that the revenue budget had been exceeded, but was trying to reconcile the results with his impression that industry sales in 19x2 had actually declined. In response to a request from Bill for additional information, the accountant, Bob Raduk, produced Schedule II. In exasperation Bill asked Bob Raduk to analyze the differences for him.

SCHEDULE I

NEL 19x2 Operating Results
(1,000s)

	Budget	*Actual*
Sales	$65,000	$73,100
Cost of goods sold*	−45,000	−54,400
Gross profit	$20,000	$18,700
Selling and Administration Expenses (all fixed)	−10,000	−11,700
Income before taxes	$10,000	$ 7,000

SCHEDULE II

NEL 19x2 Supplemental Budget Data

	Radios		*Calculators*	
Per Unit	*Budget*	*Actual*	*Budget*	*Actual*
Selling price	$20	$19	$30	$28
Manufacturing costs*	−15	−16	−20	−20
Gross profit	$ 5	$ 3	$10	$ 8
Unit Sales				
NEL	1,000,000	900,000	1,500,000	2,000,000

* Fixed manufacturing overhead allocated on the basis of $1 per unit for radios and $1 per unit for calculators. There was not a fixed overhead budget variance, only a volume variance, which was deferred as an adjustment to inventories.

REQUIREMENTS

a) Prepare budgeted and actual variable costing income statements for 19x2.

b) Determine the sales price, sales mix, and pure sales volume variances.

c) Provide a complete reconciliation of budgeted and actual income before taxes. The report should contain the sales revenue variances determined in part (b) and as many cost variances as possible. (CGA Adapted)

12–14 Multiple Product Sales Variances and Reconciliation of Budgeted and Actual Net Income: Comprehensive Review

The Schroeder Music Company manufactures recordings of Beethoven's sonatas and symphonies. The sonatas and symphonies are each sold as complete sets and each requires identical amounts of input to produce. The following budget for 19x5 was based on a normal volume of 4,000 direct-labor hours.

Schroeder Music Company
Budgeted Income Statement
For the Year Ending December 31, 19x5

Sales:		
Sonatas (8,000 sets × $15)		$120,000
Symphonies (8,000 sets × $10)		80,000
Total sales		$200,000
Cost of goods manufactured and sold:		
Direct materials	$20,000	
Direct labor (4,000 hours)	40,000	
Variable manufacturing overhead*	10,000	
Fixed manufacturing overhead*	6,000	−76,000
Gross profit		$124,000
Other expenses (all fixed):		
Selling	$40,000	
Administrative	60,000	−100,000
Net income		$ 24,000

* Applied on the basis of direct-labor hours.

At the end of 19x5, Mr. C. Brown, who dropped out of college after his first cost accounting exam, prepared the following income statement and production performance report.

Schroeder Music Company
Income Statement
For the Year Ending December 31, 19x5

Sales:		
Sonatas (3,400 sets × $10)		$ 34,000
Symphonies (10,200 sets × $10)		102,000
Total sales		$136,000
Cost of goods manufactured and sold:*		
Direct materials	$20,000	
Direct labor (3,600 hours)	41,100	
Variable factory overhead	8,800	
Fixed factory overhead	6,100	−76,000
Gross profit		$ 60,000
Other expenses (all fixed):		
Selling	$40,000	
Administrative	55,000	−95,000
Net income (loss)		$ (35,000)

* Actual. There are no beginning or ending inventories.

Schroeder Music Company
Production Performance Report
For the Year Ending December 31, 19x5

	Actual	*Budget*	*Variance*
Materials	$20,000	$20,000	$ 0
Labor	41,100	40,000	1,100 U
Overhead	14,900	16,000	(1,100)F
Total	$76,000	$76,000	$ 0

Upon seeing the reports prepared by C. Brown, his boss, Ms. L. Vanpelt, exclaimed, "You blockhead! Good grief, you struck out again!"

REQUIREMENTS

a) Reformulate the budgeted and actual income statements in a contribution format using variable costing.

b) Determine all sales variances (price, sales mix, and pure sales volume). Assume sonatas and symphonies have identical costs of manufacture and sale.

c) Prepare a complete analysis of all manufacturing variances. If some variances cannot be computed, indicate why. In this section, treat the production of 3,400 sets of sonatas and 10,200 sets of symphonies as a single product, that is, 13,600 sets of records. Remember, the budget was based on a normal volume of 4,000 direct-labor hours and it called for the production of 16,000 sets of records.

d) Prepare a detailed reconciliation of budgeted and actual direct-costing net income.

e) Comment on the performance report prepared by C. Brown.

12–15 Multiple Product Sales Variances and Reconciliation of Budgeted and Actual Net Income: Comprehensive Review

The Gamma Company manufactures two products, A and B. Although of differing quality, A and B are regarded as partial substitutes for each other. The Gamma Company uses a normal costing system under which budgeted yearly overhead costs of $240,000 are applied to each product at the rate of $10 per direct-labor hour.

To assist in budgeting, the following unit production cost estimates have been developed for a normal level of activity of 24,000 direct-labor hours.

	A	*B*
Direct materials:		
5 lbs. of Z @ $4 per lb.	$20	
5 lbs. of W @ $2 per lb.		$10
Direct labor:		
2 hours @ $5	10	
2 hours @ $5		10
Overhead:		
2 hours @ $10	20	
2 hours @ $10		20
Total	$50	$40

Gamma's budgeted income statement for 19x6 is as follows:

Gamma Company
Budgeted Income Statement
For the Year Ending December 31, 19x6

Sales:		
A (8,000 × $70)	$560,000	
B (4,000 × $50)	200,000	$760,000
Cost of goods sold:		
A (8,000 × $50)	$400,000	
B (4,000 × $40)	160,000	– 560,000
Gross profit		$200,000
Other expenses:		
Fixed administrative	$ 50,000	
Variable distribution ($5 per unit of A or B)	60,000	– 110,000
Net income		$ 90,000

Using a *normal* costing system, with no beginning or ending inventories, Gamma's actual results for 19x6 were as follows:

Gamma Company
Actual Income Statement
For the Year Ending December 31, 19x6

Sales:		
A (12,000 × $60)	$720,000	
B (3,000 × $50)	150,000	$870,000
Cost of goods sold:		
A (12,000 × $55)	$660,000	
B (3,000 × $40)	120,000	
Less overapplied overhead	(20,000)	– 760,000
Gross profit		$110,000
Other expenses:		
Fixed administrative	$ 50,000	
Variable distribution	75,000	– 125,000
Net income		$(15,000)

ADDITIONAL INFORMATION

- The overapplied overhead is entirely due to the difference between the original budgeted labor hours and 28,000 actual labor hours.
- There were no efficiency variances associated with the production of B.
- There were no labor rate variances for either product.
- 66,000 pounds of Z were purchased and used at a total cost of $330,000.
- 15,000 pounds of W were purchased and used at a total cost of $30,000.

Perplexed by these results, management has requested an explanation of the difference between the budgeted net income of $90,000 and the actual loss of $15,000.

REQUIREMENTS

a) Determine the variable and fixed portion of the predetermined overhead rate.

b) Reformulate the budgeted income statement into a contribution format using variable costing.

c) Determine all sales variances at the company level (that is, price, mix, and pure volume).

d) Determine the Product A materials variances.

e) Determine the Product A labor efficiency variance.

f) Determine the Product A variable overhead efficiency variance.

g) Based on your analysis, reconcile the difference between budgeted and actual variable-costing net income.

12–16 Single Product Sales Variances and Reconciliation of Budgeted and Actual Net Income: Materials Mix and Yield Variances

Mid-Continent Aviation Supply Company manufactures cleaning solvents that are used to remove grease and other substances from aircraft engines, wings, and fuselage. Presented is Mid-Continent's budgeted income statement for 19w5 in a contribution format using variable costing:

Mid-Continent Aviation Supply Company
Budgeted Contribution Income Statement
For the Year Ending December 31, 19w5

Sales (40,000 containers × $20)		$800,000
Variable costs:		
Manufacturing*	$560,000	
Selling	40,000	− 600,000
Contribution margin		$200,000
Fixed costs:		
Manufacturing	$100,000	
Administration	50,000	− 150,000
Net income		$ 50,000

* Budgeted variable manufacturing costs per container are:

Materials:		
(2 liters of A × $1)	$2	
(3 liters of B × $2)	6	$ 8
Direct labor (0.2 hrs. × $10)		2
Variable overhead (0.2 direct-labor hours × $20)		4
Total		$14

During 19w5 Mid-Continent actually sold 50,000 containers at $22 and incurred the following costs:

Material A (200,000 liters)	$ 200,000
Material B (100,000 liters)	300,000
Direct labor (10,000 hours)	120,000
Variable overhead	200,000
Variable selling	56,000
Fixed manufacturing	110,000
Fixed administrative	50,000
Total	$1,036,000

There were no beginning or ending inventories.

REQUIREMENTS

a) Determine Mid-Continent's actual variable-costing net income for 19w5. It is not necessary to prepare a formal statement.

b) Compute the following variances:

1. Sales price and volume
2. Materials price and quantity
3. Materials mix and yield
4. Labor rate and efficiency

c) Prepare a detailed reconciliation of budgeted and actual variable-costing net income.

12–17 Performance Reports for Marketing Territories

The Justa Corporation produces and sells three products. The three products, A, B, and C, are sold in a local market and in a regional market. At the end of the first quarter of the current year, the following income statement has been prepared:

	Total	*Local*	*Regional*
Sales	$1,300,000	$1,000,000	$300,000
Cost of goods sold	−1,010,000	−775,000	−235,000
Gross profit	$ 290,000	$ 225,000	$ 65,000
Selling expenses	$ 105,000	$ 60,000	$ 45,000
Administrative expenses	52,000	40,000	12,000
Total expenses	−157,000	−100,000	−57,000
Net income	$ 133,000	$ 125,000	$ 8,000

Management has expressed special concern with the regional market because of the extremely poor return on sales. This market was entered a year ago because of excess capacity. It was originally believed that the return on sales would improve with time, but after a year no noticeable improvement can be seen from the results as reported in the quarterly statement.

In attempting to decide whether to eliminate the regional market, management has gathered the following information:

	Products		
	A	*B*	*C*
Sales	$500,000	$400,000	$400,000
Variable manufacturing expenses as a percentage of sales	60%	70%	60%
Variable selling expenses as a percentage of sales	3%	2%	3%

	Sales by markets	
Product	*Local*	*Regional*
A	$400,000	$100,000
B	300,000	100,000
C	300,000	100,000

All administrative expenses and fixed manufacturing expenses are common to the three products and the two markets and are fixed for the period. Remaining selling expenses are fixed for the period and separable by market.

REQUIREMENTS

a) Reformulate the income statement to show each market's contribution to corporate fixed costs and profits. Do not allocate costs that cannot be avoided.

b) Assuming there are no alternative uses for the Justa Corporation's present capacity, would you recommend dropping the regional market? Why or why not?

(CMA Adapted)

12–18 Special Decision Related to a Marketing Territory

You have been engaged to assist the management of the Arcadia Corporation in arriving at certain decisions. Arcadia has its home office in Ohio and leases factory buildings in Texas, Montana, and Maine, all of which produce the same product. The management of Arcadia has provided you with a projection of operations for 19x7, the forthcoming year, as follows:

	Total	*Texas*	*Montana*	*Maine*
Sales*	$4,400,000	$2,200,000	$1,400,000	$800,000
Fixed costs:				
Factory	$1,100,000	$ 560,000	$ 280,000	$260,000
Administration	350,000	210,000	110,000	30,000
Variable costs	1,450,000	665,000	425,000	360,000
Allocated home office costs	500,000	225,000	175,000	100,000
Total costs	−3,400,000	−1,660,000	−990,000	−750,000
Net profit from operations	$1,000,000	$ 540,000	$ 410,000	$ 50,000

* The sales price per unit is $25.

Due to the marginal projections for the factory in Maine, Arcadia has decided to cease operations and sell that factory's machinery and equipment by the end of 19x6. Arcadia expects that the proceeds from the sale of these assets would be greater than their book value and would cover all termination costs.

Arcadia, however, would like to continue serving its customers in that area if it is economically feasible and is considering one of the following three alternatives:

1. Close the Maine factory and cease serving customers served by it.
2. Serve some of the Maine factory customers by expanding operations at the Montana factory. This move would result in the following changes in that factory's operations:

	Percent increase over factory's current operation
Sales	50%
Fixed costs:	
Factory	20%
Administration	10%

   Under this proposal the variable costs of the additional units would be $8 per unit sold.
3. Enter into a long-term contract with a competitor who will serve the Maine factory's customers. This competitor would pay Arcadia a royalty of $4 per unit based on an estimate of 30,000 units being sold.

REQUIREMENT

To help Arcadia's management determine which alternative is more economically feasible, prepare a schedule computing Arcadia's estimated net profit from total operations that would result from each of the following methods:

1. Shutdown of Maine operations with no expansion at other locations.
2. Expansion of the Montana factory.
3. Negotiation of long-term contract on a royalty basis.

(*Note:* Total home office costs of $500,000 will remain the same under each situation.) (CPA Adapted)

12–19 Performance Measures for Government Services

In late 19x1, Mr. Sootsman, the official in charge of the State Department of Automobile Regulation, established a system of performance measurement for the department's branch offices. He was convinced that management by objectives could help the department reach its objective of better service to citizens at a lower cost. The first steps were to define the activities of the branch offices, to assign point values to the services performed, and to establish performance targets. Point values, rather than revenue targets, were used because the department is a regulatory agency, not a revenue-producing agency. Further, the specific revenue for a service did not adequately reflect the differences in effort required. The analysis was compiled at the state office, and the results were distributed to the branch offices.

The system has been in operation since 19x2. The state office has revised the performance targets for the branches each year. The revisions were designed to encourage better performance by increasing the target or reducing resources to achieve targets. The revisions incorporated noncontrollable events, such as population shifts, new branches, and changes in procedures.

Mr. Sootsman has been disappointed in the performances of branch offices because performance targets or budgets have not been met. He is especially concerned because the points earned from citizen's comments are declining.

The Barry County branch is typical of many branch offices. A summary displaying the budgeted and actual performance for three years is presented below.

Barry County Branch
Performance Report
For the Years 19x2, 19x3, and 19x4

	19x2		*19x3*		*19x4*	
Population served	38,000		38,500		38,700	
	*Budget**	*Actual*	*Budget**	*Actual*	*Budget**	*Actual*
Number of employees:						
Administrative	1	1	1	1	1	1
Professional	1	1	1	1	1	1
Clerical	3	3	2	3	1½	3
Performance points:						
Services	19,500	14,500	16,000	14,600	15,500	15,600
Citizen comments	500	200	600	900	700	200
Total	20,000	14,700	16,600	15,500	16,200	15,800
Detail of actual performance†						
Services:						
New driver's license:						
Examination & road test (3 pts.)		3,000		3,150		3,030
Road test repeat—failed prior test (2 pts.)		600		750		1,650
Renew driver's license (1 pt.)		3,000		3,120		3,060
Issue license plates (0.5 pt.)		4,200		4,150		4,100
Issue titles:						
Dealer transaction (0.5 pt.)		2,000		1,900		2,100
Individual transaction (1 pt.)		1,700		1,530		1,660
Total		14,500		14,600		15,600

	19x2		19x3		19x4	
	*Budget**	*Actual*	*Budget**	*Actual*	*Budget**	*Actual*
Citizens comments:						
Favorable (+0.5 pt.)		300		1,100		800
Unfavorable (−0.5 pt.)		− 100		− 200		− 600
Total		200		900		200

* The budget performance points for services are calculated using 3 points per available hour. One-half of the administrative employee's time is devoted to administration and one-half to regular service. The calculations for the services point budget are as follows:
19x2: 4.5 people × 8 hours × 240 days × 3 pts. × 75% productive time = 19,440 rounded to 19,500
19x3: 3.5 people × 8 hours × 240 days × 3 pts. × 80% productive time = 16,128 rounded to 16,000
19x4: 3 people × 8 hours × 240 days × 3 pts. × 90% productive time = 15,552 rounded to 15,500
The comments targets are based on rough estimates by department officials.

† The actual point totals for the branch are calculated by multiplying the weights, shown in the report in parentheses, by the number of such services performed or comments received.

REQUIREMENTS

a) Does the method of performance measurement properly capture the objectives of this operation? Justify your answer.

b) The Barry County branch office came close to its target for 19x4. Does this constitute improved performance compared to 19x3? Justify your answer.

12–20 Profit Centers, Standard Cost Centers, Discretionary Cost Centers: Comprehensive Review

The Beta Company manufactures "The Tennis Partner," an automatic tennis ball thrower that helps players develop forehand, backhand, and lob strokes. Beta (see the following organization chart) is divided into a profit center (marketing), a standard cost center (manufacturing), and a discretionary cost center (administration). Manufacturing is further divided into three standard cost centers, consisting of two service departments and one production department. Because of Beta's small size, the Production Department supervisor purchases raw materials as needed. Furthermore, the service departments only provide services to the Production Department.

Presented are Beta's budgeted and actual 19x8 income statements in a contribution format using variable costing. During 19x8 the Production Department supervisor requested and received 14,000 units of service from Service Department 1 and 12,000 units of service from Service Department 2. There were no beginning or ending inventories.

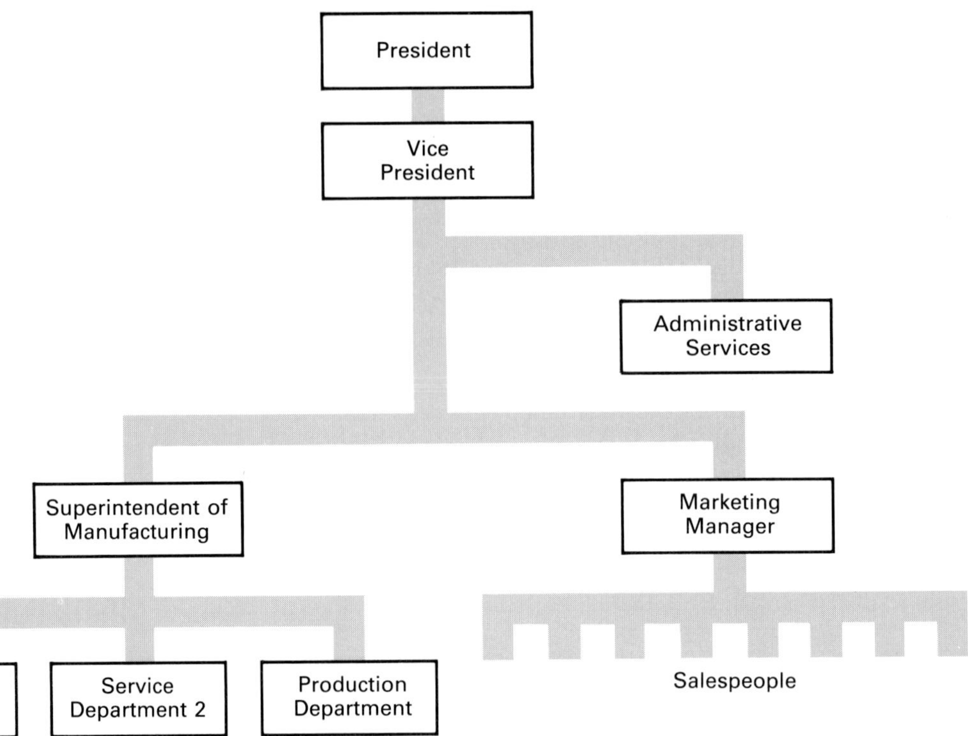

Beta Company
Budgeted and Actual Contribution Income Statements
For the Year Ending December 31, 19x8

		Budget		*Actual*
Unit sales		10,000		12,000
Sales revenue		$2,000,000		$2,640,000
Less variable costs:				
Direct materials	$400,000		$576,000	
Direct labor	300,000		432,000	
Service Dept. 1	50,000		77,000	
Service Dept. 2	50,000		66,000	
Sales commissions	200,000		264,000	
Freight-out	100,000	−1,100,000	132,000	−1,547,000
Contribution margin		$ 900,000		$1,093,000
Less fixed costs:				
Service Dept. 1	$ 30,000		$ 36,000	
Service Dept. 2	50,000		60,000	
Factory depreciation	100,000		100,000	
Mfg. div. salaries	90,000		101,000	
Advertising	250,000		250,000	
Mkt. salaries	100,000		120,000	
Administration	210,000	−830,000	270,000	−937,000
Net income		$ 70,000		$ 156,000

REQUIREMENTS

a) Prepare a responsibility accounting performance report for marketing displaying variances for the contribution margin, fixed costs, and marketing contribution. See Exhibit 12–4(b).

b) Prepare a responsibility accounting performance report for the Production Department, comparing actual costs with costs allowed in a flexible budget. See Exhibit 11–7.

c) Prepare a performance report for the Superintendent of Manufacturing, comparing actual costs with costs allowed in a flexible budget. See Exhibit 11–7.

d) Prepare a summary of responsibility center variances, reconciling budgeted and actual variable costing net income. Include only one net variance for each major responsibility center: manufacturing, marketing, and administration.

SOLUTION TO REVIEW PROBLEM

a) Regular:

Sales price variance 2,000($7.50 – $5)	$ 5,000F
Sales volume variance ($5 – $2.50)(2,000 – 4,000)	$(5,000)U

Pacesetter:

Sales price variance 2,000($15 – $15)	$ 0
Sales volume variance ($15 – $10)(2,000 – 1,000)	$ 5,000F

b)

Product	*Actual volume at actual mix, actual prices, and standard costs*		*Actual volume at actual mix, budgeted prices, and standard costs*		*Original budget: Budgeted volume at budgeted mix, budgeted prices, and standard costs*	
Regular	2,000($7.50 – $2.50) =	$10,000	2,000($5 – $2.50) =	$ 5,000	4,000($5 – $2.50) =	$10,000
Pacesetter	2,000($15 – $10) =	10,000	2,000($15 – $10) =	10,000	1,000($15 – $10) =	5,000
	4,000	$20,000		$15,000		$15,000

$5,000F Sales price variance

$ 0 Sales volume variance

Product	*Actual volume at actual mix, budgeted prices, and standard costs*		*Actual volume at budgeted mix, budgeted prices, and standard costs*		*Original budget: Budgeted volume at budgeted mix, budgeted prices, and standard costs*	
Regular	2,000($5 – $2.50) =	$ 5,000	(4,000 × 0.80)($5 – $2.50) =	$ 8,000	4,000($5 – $2.50) =	$10,000
Pacesetter	2,000($15 – $10) =	10,000	(4,000 × 0.20)($15 – $10) =	4,000	1,000($15 – $10) =	5,000
	4,000	$15,000		$12,000		$15,000

$ 3,000F Sales mix variance

$(3,000)U Pure sales volume variance

c) Labor rate variance (Regular):

2,000($3.00 − $2.50)	$1,000U

Fixed cost budget variance:

$12,000 − $10,000	$2,000U

d) **The College Clipper**
Reconciliation of Net Income
For May 19w1 and May 19w2

May 19w1 net income		$ 5,000
Add favorable variances:		
Sales price	$ 5,000	
Sales mix	3,000	8,000
Less unfavorable variances:		
Pure sales volume	$ 3,000	
Labor rate	1,000	
Fixed cost budget	2,000	(6,000)
May 19w2 net income		$ 7,000

13 Responsibility Accounting for Investment Centers

INTRODUCTION

DECENTRALIZATION

EVALUATING INVESTMENT CENTER PERFORMANCE

PROBLEMS IN MEASURING INVESTMENT CENTER PERFORMANCE

MULTINATIONAL COMPANIES

AGENCY THEORY

SUMMARY

INTRODUCTION

RESPONSIBILITY ACCOUNTING FOR COST, REVENUE, AND PROFIT CENTERS was considered in Chapters 11 and 12. When responsibility centers have considerable control over the nature and size of their investment base, they are often evaluated as investment centers. In this case, investment is included in performance measures.

The purpose of this chapter is to examine measures used to evaluate the performance of investment centers. To set the stage, we begin with a discussion of the organizational structure of a decentralized firm and consider the role of the controller in a decentralized unit.

DECENTRALIZATION

As organizations grow or their activities become more diverse, centralized planning and control through the use of master budgets, flexible budgets, and marketing performance reports becomes more and more difficult. In response to the problems of size and/or diversity, many organizations attempt to decentralize operations as much as possible. They do this by restructuring the organization into several quasi-independent segments, called **divisions.**[1] Each division might contain all of the production, marketing, and administrative functions required for an independent business.

Divisional Organization Structure

When a firm contains several plants that produce distinctive products (or service distinct geographic areas) and the manufacturing and marketing activities can be logically combined on a product-line or regional basis, administrative and motivational advantages may be obtained by establishing divisions. Such an

[1] Terminology differs between authors and organizations. The important thing is not the name "division," "department," or "subsidiary"; it is the nature and amount of authority and responsibility delegated.

organization structure is illustrated in Exhibit 13–1. In a multiproduct firm, Divisions I, II, and III might represent jet engines, home appliances, and electric generators. In a multinational corporation, they might represent North America, Europe, and South America.

Each division is given considerable freedom to develop its own plans and adapt most advantageously to its environment. Although divisions develop their

EXHIBIT 13–1 Partial Organization Chart of a Divisionalized Manufacturing Firm

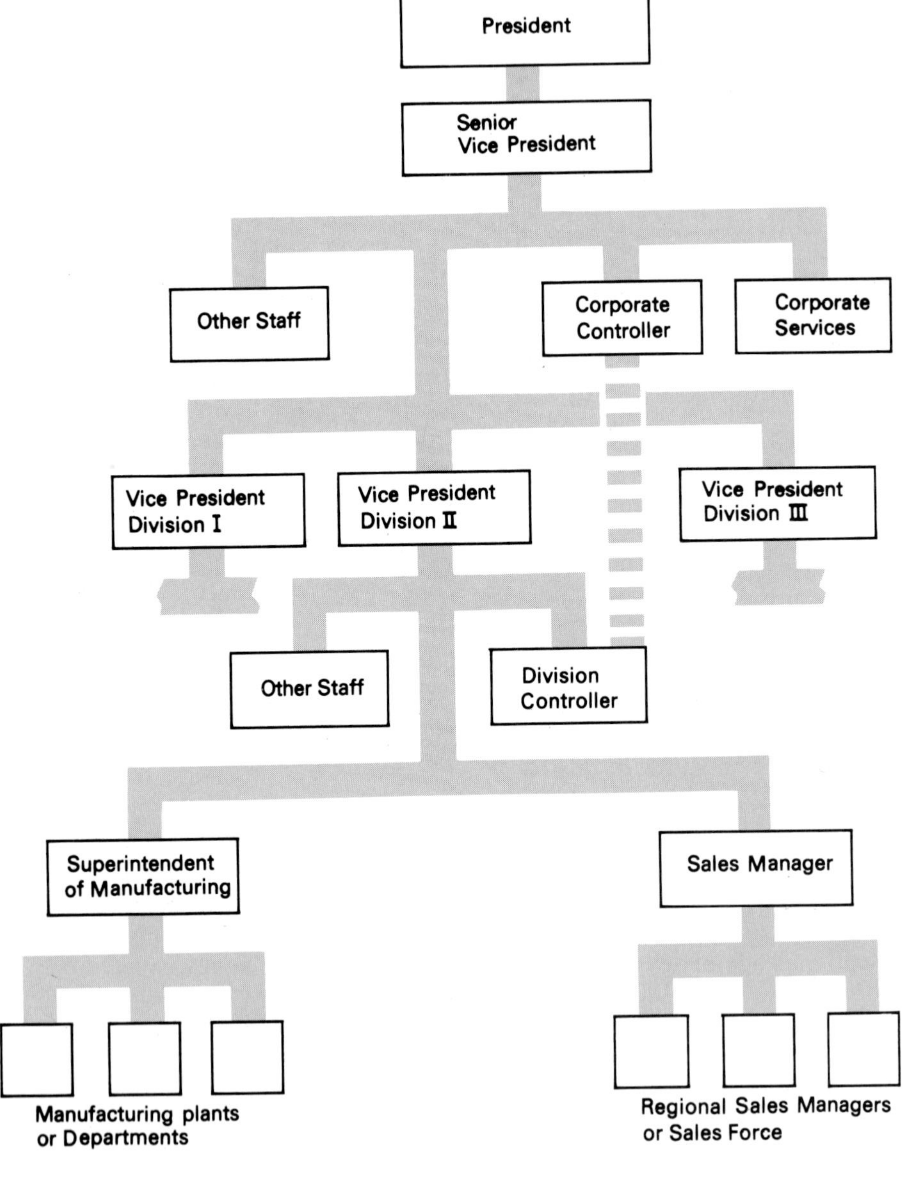

own budgets and performance reports, they may not be required to forward them to corporate headquarters. Corporate headquarters regards divisions as investment centers and evaluates them as such. Divisions may even have authority to introduce and discontinue products and to make capital expenditures for asset replacement and improvement. Most companies do, however, require corporate level approval of major capital expenditures for new fixed assets or the introduction of new products. This is done because these expenditures involve the commitment of resources over an extended period of time in a manner that may limit flexibility.

The Divisional Controller

In Exhibit 13–1 there is a solid line between the divisional controller and the divisional vice president. There is also a dashed line between the divisional controller and the corporate controller. These lines indicate that the divisional controller has a dual responsibility; (1) responsibility to the divisional vice president who exercises line authority, and (2) responsibility to the corporate controller who exercises functional authority.

The divisional controller, as a member of the division's top management team, performs at the division level most of the controllership tasks outlined in Chapter 1. A particularly important duty is to act as a consultant. In performing assignments, the divisional controller must follow certain firm-wide accounting procedures specified by the corporate controller. The relationship between the divisional controller and corporate controller is a delicate one. Although the corporate controller exercises functional authority, the divisional controller is primarily responsible to the divisional vice president. This places the divisional controller in the position of having two bosses, a situation that may present ethical problems. Sometimes the divisional controller is perceived as being an extension of the corporate controller and regarded as a "front-office spy." In this case, the divisional controller's ability to act as a consultant will be severely diminished. On the other hand, the divisional controller has a professional responsibility to report activities contrary to corporate policy or business ethics.

Advantages of Decentralization

The advantages of decentralization may be placed in two broad categories, administrative and motivational. Administrative advantages include:

- Permitting personnel more thoroughly acquainted with the local aspects of the business to make decisions concerning it.
- A more rapid response to environmental changes and opportunities by eliminating administrative bottlenecks.
- Freeing up the time of top management and the corporate staff to engage in strategic planning, policy formulation, and providing overall direction to the company.
- The ability to evaluate the performance of a division using a limited number of broad performance measures similar to those used to evaluate an independent firm.

Alleged motivational advantages include:

- The belief that creative talent and morale are more easily developed in an organization that provides greater freedom of action and does not have long chains of command.

- The belief that quasi-independent divisions provide a better training ground for corporate leaders than cost or revenue centers.

Problems of Decentralization

The primary problems associated with decentralization include:

- Competent division managers and staff must be obtained.
- It is often difficult to measure the performance of division managers.
- Division managers must be motivated to act in a manner that is consistent with the goals of the entire organization.

The measurement and motivational problems are highly interrelated. Weaknesses in performance measurement may motivate managers to act in a manner that is incongruent with the goals of the organization.

It is important to keep in mind that the establishment of quasi-independent divisions is not appropriate for all businesses. If the affairs of a proposed or existing division cannot be disentangled from the affairs of another part of the business, the division should be organized as a cost or revenue center rather than as an investment center. For example, if the transmission assembly division of an automobile manufacturer transfers all its output to the automobile production division, the assembly division cannot earn revenues from external transactions and it should be evaluated as a cost center rather than as an investment center.

EVALUATING INVESTMENT CENTER PERFORMANCE

As noted in Chapter 12, an **investment center** has responsibility for the relationship between its profits or contribution and the total assets invested in the center. Hence an investment center has a responsibility for the relationship between profits and investment as well as a responsibility for profits. In most organizations, managers of investment centers have more authority than managers of profit centers. The manager of a profit center may have authority over the use of a specific set of assets, but the manager of an investment center may also be responsible for determining the investment center's assets. Managers of investment centers may make decisions relating to plant and equipment as well as current assets.

By establishing divisions as investment centers, corporate management frees itself from the burden of evaluating detailed revenue center and cost center performance reports. Instead corporate management attempts to evaluate the effectiveness with which division managers use the assets placed in their care. The test of effectiveness is not the absolute size of divisional income. Rather, it is the relationship between divisional income and the corporation's investment in a division.

Return on Investment

Return on investment (ROI) is a measure of the relationship between income and investment. For the purpose of evaluating the performance of a division, ROI is calculated as divisional income divided by the investment in the division. In equation form,

$$\text{ROI} = \frac{\text{Divisional income}}{\text{Divisional investment}} \tag{13–1}$$

The divisional investment may refer to the investment at the beginning or at the end of the period, or to the average investment during the period. Average investment is sometimes preferred on the basis that the income from the assets is earned continuously throughout the period. We will use average investment in all examples in this chapter unless otherwise noted.

Sometimes ROI is broken down into two parts, investment turnover and income as a percentage of sales.[2] **Investment turnover** is computed as sales divided by investment. ROI is the product of the investment turnover and income as a percentage of sales. For divisional performance evaluation:

$$\text{Return on investment} = \text{Investment turnover} \times \begin{array}{c}\text{Income as a}\\ \text{percentage of sales}\end{array}$$

$$\frac{\text{Divisional income}}{\text{Divisional investment}} = \frac{\text{Divisional sales}}{\text{Divisional investment}} \times \frac{\text{Divisional income}}{\text{Divisional sales}} \tag{13–2}$$

The relationships between the factors affecting return on investment are illustrated in Exhibit 13–2. Using these relationships in Eq. 13–2 or Exhibit 13–2, management is better able to evaluate divisional performance and analyze alternative ways of improving it. ROI can be improved by increasing the investment turnover while maintaining the same income as a percentage of sales, increasing income as a percentage of sales while maintaining the same investment turnover, or changing both investment turnover and income as a percentage of sales. Possible ways of changing these factors include reducing investment, reducing expenses, and increasing sales while maintaining the same income as a percentage of sales.

Example 13–1

Presented is information pertaining to Division A of Parsons, Inc.:

Sales, 19x7	$1,000,000
Income, 19x7	60,000
Investment, average 19x7	500,000

This division currently earns a return of 12 percent ($60,000/$500,000) on average investment. Further analysis reveals that the 12 percent return is the joint result of an investment turnover of 2.0 and an income of 6 percent of sales.

$$\text{ROI} = \frac{\$1{,}000{,}000}{\$500{,}000} \times \frac{\$60{,}000}{\$1{,}000{,}000}$$

$$\text{ROI} = 2.0 \times 0.06$$

$$\text{ROI} = \underline{\underline{0.12}}$$

---

[2] The phrase "margin percent on sales" is sometimes used in place of the phrase "income as a percentage of sales." This phrase is not used here because students frequently confuse it with gross margin as a percentage of sales.

EXHIBIT 13–2 Factors Affecting Return on Investment

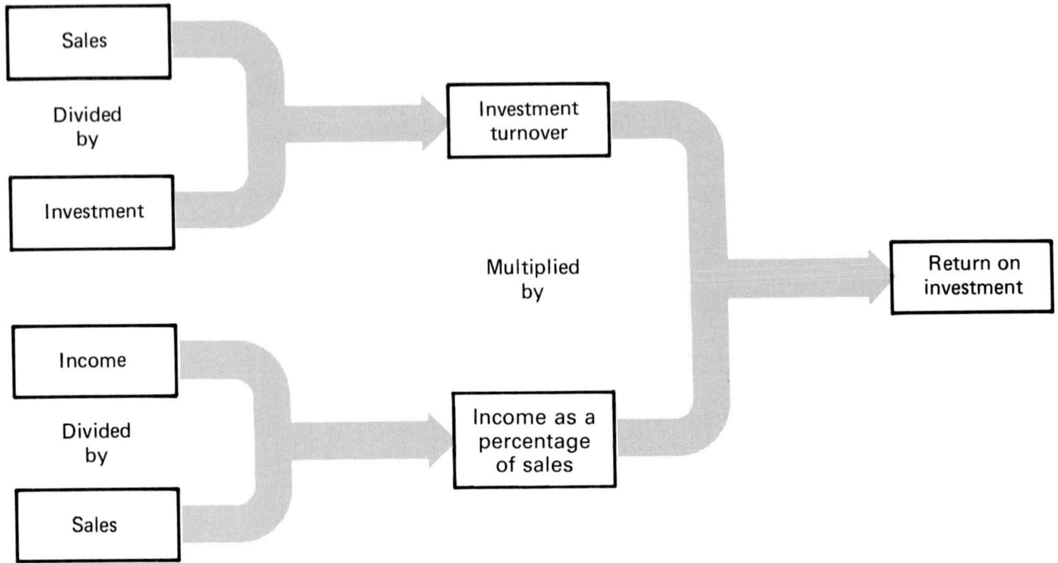

Parsons can achieve a 15 percent return on divisional investment in numerous ways. Possibilities include:

- *Reducing investment* to $400,000:

$$\text{ROI} = \frac{\$1{,}000{,}000}{\$400{,}000} \times \frac{\$60{,}000}{\$1{,}000{,}000} = \underline{\underline{0.15}}$$

- *Reducing expenses* by $15,000:

$$\text{ROI} = \frac{\$1{,}000{,}000}{\$500{,}000} \times \frac{\$75{,}000^*}{\$1{,}000{,}000} = \underline{\underline{0.15}}$$

*($60,000 + $15,000)

- *Increasing sales* to $1,250,000 while maintaining the current percentage of income to sales:

$$\text{ROI} = \frac{\$1{,}250{,}000}{\$500{,}000} \times \frac{\$75{,}000^*}{\$1{,}250{,}000} = \underline{\underline{0.15}}$$

*($1,250,000 × 0.06)

Note that the last of these three possibilities assumes that the income percentage will remain constant at 6 percent when sales are increased to $1,250,000. It is likely that the income percentage will increase if sales increase because fixed costs will represent a smaller portion of total sales.

Managers are always interested in the evaluation of statistics such as ROI, investment turnover, and income as a percentage of sales. Unfortunately statistics mean little by themselves. They take on meaning only when compared with a budget, a trend, another division, a competitor, or an industry average.

Residual Income

Residual income is a popular alternative performance measure to ROI. **Residual income** (RI) is equal to income minus a charge for invested capital. For a division,

$$\text{Residual income} = \text{Divisional income} - \left(\text{Required return on investment} \times \text{Divisional investment}\right) \quad (13\text{–}3)$$

Example 13–2

If Parsons charges Division A 10 percent for their investment in divisional assets, the residual income for Division A in Example 13–1 is $10,000 [$60,000 – 0.10($500,000)].

Before calculating RI, we must determine the appropriate rate to use to charge divisions for their investment. The rate may be based on a minimum return on investment, cost of capital,[3] or an imputed interest charge. Although an organization's cost of capital is theoretically preferred for determining the minimum rate of return that new investments should earn, it may not be appropriate to use it for divisional performance evaluation. An organization's cost of capital is based on the risk of the company as a whole, and different divisions may have different degrees of risk. Under these circumstances, the rate used for charging divisions for their investment should be adjusted for risk, that is, divisions with higher risk should be charged a higher rate than divisions with lower risk.

RI is sometimes preferred over ROI as a performance measure because it encourages managers to accept investment opportunities that have rates of return greater than the charge for invested capital. As shown later in this chapter, managers being evaluated using ROI may be reluctant to accept new investments that lower their current ROI although the investments would be desirable for the organization.

PROBLEMS IN MEASURING INVESTMENT CENTER PERFORMANCE

Despite the relevance and conceptual simplicity of ROI and RI, we must resolve many issues before we agree how to determine divisional investment and income. These issues include definition of the investment base, measurement of the investment, treatment of interest expense, allocated indirect costs, and depreciation methods. The issues are more complex than they appear at first glance, and they are fraught with behavioral implications.[4]

Defining Investment

When the primary purpose of performance measurement is to evaluate how effectively a division's operating management is using the assets entrusted to them, investment is often operationally defined as the total assets of a division

---

[3] Cost of capital is discussed in Chapter 16.

[4] For a more thorough discussion see *N.A.A. Research Report 35: Return on Capital as a Guide to Managerial Decisions* (New York: National Association of Accountants, 1959), Chapters 2 and 3, and David Solomons, *Divisional Performance: Measurement and Control* (Homewood, Ill.: Irwin, 1965), Chapters II and V.

(including cash, receivables, inventories, plant, property, and equipment). Other measures, such as shareholder's equity in the division (total assets of the division less liabilities associated with the division), include the impact of capital structure in the analysis. This may be appropriate for evaluating the operating and financial management of an independent firm, but it is not appropriate for evaluating the operating management of a division.

Corporate headquarters may hold all corporate cash and receivables. This permits more efficiency in billings and collections. It also enables the corporation to hold a smaller total amount of cash than than would otherwise be required. Although it is relatively easy to assign receivables to divisions (on the basis of their origin), the assignment of cash presents some problems. Because of operating economies, the total cash requirements of all divisions acting as independent units exceed the cash requirements of the total organization. However, assigning cash on the basis of the divisions' independent cash needs is likely to raise objections. Even though the best approach seems to be to determine the amount of incremental cash needed to support each division as part of the company as a whole and then allocate that amount, cash allocations are most frequently based on relative sales or cash expenditures. Reflecting a belief that performance measures should only contain items that managers can control, many organizations do not allocate centrally controlled cash or receivables.

The cost of physical assets used by corporate headquarters should not be included in divisional investment if the objective of calculating ROI and RI is to measure division managements' performance. Although the divisions might need additional administrative facilities if they were truly independent, divisional management has no control over the current headquarters facilities. Additionally, the joint nature and use of these facilities makes any allocation arbitrary.

Not allocating all corporate assets to divisions causes the weighted-average ROI of the divisions to exceed the ROI of the company as a whole. This should not be particularly disturbing when the objective of divisional ROI or RI computations is to motivate and measure the performance of division managers.

Measuring Investment

Even after we determine the assets that are to be assigned to divisions for performance evaluation, we still must determine how divisional investment should be measured. Net book value of assets and historical cost are two possibilities. The **net book value** of a division's assets is equal to the historical cost of the assets less accumulated depreciation and other valuation adjustments recorded in the accounting records. **Historical cost** is the original cost of an asset recorded in the accounting records.

Example 13–3

In Example 13–1, Division A's ROI for 19x7 was computed as 12 percent ($60,000/ $500,000). The investment in Division A consists of current assets of $200,000 and plant and equipment costing $1,600,000 acquired at the beginning of 19x1. The plant and equipment is being depreciated over eight years using the straight-line depreciation method with no salvage. For Example 13–1, the average net book value of Division A's assets was calculated as follows:

	Beginning of year 19x7		End of year 19x7	
Current assets		$200,000		$200,000
Plant and equipment-cost	$1,600,000		$1,600,000	
Accumulated depreciation	−1,200,000		−1,400,000	
Book value of plant and equipment		400,000		200,000
Total assets		$600,000		$400,000

$$\text{Average net book value} = \frac{\$600{,}000 + \$400{,}000}{2} = \$500{,}000$$

If Parsons, Inc., used historical cost as the denominator, Division A's ROI would be 3.33 percent:

$$\text{ROI} = \frac{\$60{,}000}{\$200{,}000 + \$1{,}600{,}000} = 0.0333.$$

One advantage of using historical cost as the denominator is that it helps make the ROI of different divisions more comparable when the assets of the different divisions were acquired at different times.

Example 13–4

In addition to Division A, Parsons, Inc., also has Division B which is identical to Division A except that Division B's plant and equipment was acquired at the beginning of 19x6 for $1,600,000. Division B's plant and equipment is also being depreciated over eight years using the straight-line method with no salvage value.

For 19x7, the average net book value of Division B's assets is $1,500,000, calculated as follows:

	Beginning of year 19x7		End of year 19x7	
Current assets		$200,000		$200,000
Plant and equipment-cost	$1,600,000		$1,600,000	
Accumulated depreciation	−200,000		−400,000	
Book value of plant and equipment		1,400,000		1,200,000
Total assets		$1,600,000		$1,400,000

$$\text{Average net book value} = \frac{\$1{,}600{,}000 + \$1{,}400{,}000}{2} = \$1{,}500{,}000$$

With divisional income of $60,000, Division B's return on average net book value is 4 percent:

$$\text{ROI} = \frac{\$60{,}000}{\$1{,}500{,}000} = 0.04.$$

A comparison of Division B's 4 percent ROI with Division A's 12 percent ROI suggests that the manager of Division B was less effective than the manager of Division A. The difference in ROI's, however, was caused by using net book value for the denominator. If historical cost were used, Division B's ROI would be 3.33 percent ($60,000/$1,800,000), exactly the same as Division A's.

The reader might insightfully ask how two divisions could acquire identical assets for the same prices at different times. Although it is true that inflation has caused the cost of most assets to increase over time, including price-level changes in Example 13–4 would have clouded the historical cost versus net book value issue. Inflation affects ROI and RI calculations because divisional assets acquired in earlier years are undervalued when compared with similar assets acquired in later years.

Price-Level Changes and Undervalued Assets Affect Divisional Comparisons

Return on investment and residual income for divisions with old assets may be overstated because inflation causes an undervaluation of the inventory and fixed assets. This problem is particularly acute if inventories are valued at LIFO and fixed assets were acquired years ago. Price-level changes causes divisions with similar assets acquired at different times to have different ROI's and RI's.

Example 13–5

Division C of Parsons, Inc., has assets and operating results identical to those of Division A in Example 13–1 except that the plant and equipment were acquired at the beginning of year 19x6 for $1,800,000. Division C's plant and equipment is being depreciated over eight years using the straight-line method with zero salvage value. Incomes for Divisions A and C for 19x7 were as follows:

	Division A	*Division C*
Income before depreciation	$260,000	$260,000
Straight-line depreciation	–200,000*	–225,000†
Divisional income	$ 60,000	$ 35,000

* From Example 13–3.
† ($1,800,000 – 0)/8 years = $225,000

Using average net book value as the investment base, the ROI of Division A is 12 percent (as shown in Example 13–1) and Division C's ROI is 2.11 percent:

Net book value:	*Beginning of year 19x7*		*End of year 19x7*	
Current assets		$200,000		$200,000
Plant and equipment-cost	$1,800,000		$1,800,000	
Accumulated depreciation	–225,000		–450,000	
Book value of plant and equipment		1,575,000		1,350,000
Total		$1,775,000		$1,550,000

$$\text{Average net book value} = \frac{\$1{,}775{,}000 + \$1{,}550{,}000}{2} = \underline{\underline{\$1{,}662{,}500}}$$

$$\text{ROI} = \frac{\$35{,}000}{\$1{,}662{,}500} = \underline{\underline{0.0211}}$$

Using historical cost as the investment base, the ROI of Division A is 3.33 percent (as shown in Example 13–3) and Division C's ROI is 1.75 percent:

$$\text{ROI} = \frac{\$35{,}000}{\$2{,}000{,}000^{*}} = \underline{\underline{0.0175}}$$

*(Current assets + historical cost of plant and equipment) = ($200,000 + $1,800,000) = $2,000,000.

Comparing either set of ROI numbers (0.12 versus 0.0211, or 0.0333 versus 0.0175), we might conclude that Division A performed better than Division C, when, in fact, the performance of each was identical. The difference is caused by the difference in the cost of the assets and the use of depreciation based on historical cost.

As shown in Chapter 7, historical cost data can be adjusted for price-level changes by multiplying the historical cost amount by a fraction representing the change in the price level since the asset was acquired. The numerator of the fraction is the price-level index at the time to which the costs are being adjusted and the denominator is the price-level index at the time the costs were incurred. In equation form,

$$\text{Price-level adjusted historical cost} = \text{Historical cost} \times \frac{\text{Price-level index at the time to which costs are being adjusted}}{\text{Price-level index at the time when costs were incurred}} \qquad (13\text{–}4)$$

Example 13–6 The price-level index was 160 at the beginning of 19x1 when Division A's plant and equipment were acquired and 180 at the beginning of 19x6 when Division C's plant and equipment were acquired. The average price-level index during all of 19x7 was 190.

The historical cost data for a division can be converted into dollars at the price level in effect when the assets of the other division were acquired or into current-year dollars. Because assets of different divisions may have been acquired at many different times, we may prefer to convert all amounts into current year dollars. If the historical costs of Division A's plant and equipment are converted into 19x7 dollars, the price-level adjusted historical costs is $1,900,000 [$1,600,000 × (190/160)]. The depreciation of $200,000 is also converted to 19x7 dollars since it is stated in dollars at a price level of 160. The price-level adjusted depreciation for Division A is $237,500 [$200,000 × (190/160)]. Likewise, Division C's price-level adjusted plant and equipment cost and depreciation are $1,900,000 [$1,800,000 × (190/180)] and $237,500 [$225,000 × (190/180)], respectively.

If price-level adjusted historical costs are used, the ROI of both divisions is shown in Exhibit 13–3(a) to be 1.07 percent.

Note that historical cost must be used as the denominator to arrive at comparable percentages for the two divisions. If net book value were used, the problem illustrated in Example 13–4 still exists even with the price-level adjustments. For example, if ROIs of Divisions A and C are calculated using net book value adjusted for price-level changes, Division A's ROI is 4.04 percent and Division C's ROI is 1.29 percent. See Exhibit 13–3(b).

Adjusting for inflation becomes important when comparing performance with a predetermined standard or the performance of another division. If the assets of two divisions were acquired at different times, a manager might prefer to operate an older, well-maintained division rather than a newer one. If all other revenues and costs are equal, the older division may be preferred because its ROI will be higher than the ROI of the newer division simply because the historical costs of the investment and related depreciation of the older division are less.

Price-Level Changes and Undervalued Assets Affect Investment Decisions

As we have shown, ROI will likely be overstated when unadjusted historical costs are used for performance measurement during inflationary periods. This overstatement of current ROI may cause managers to reject desirable new investments that would decrease the division's ROI.[5]

Example 13–7

At the beginning of 19x7 the manager of Division A is evaluating a project costing $200,000 that is expected to generate income before depreciation of $40,000 per year for eight years. The investment would be depreciated using the straight-line method with no salvage value.

If Division A invests in this project, the ROI for 19x7 using average net book value for the computation would be 10.9 percent:

Divisional income:		
Income without investment		$ 60,000
Income from investment:		
Income before depreciation	$ 40,000	
Straight-line depreciation	−25,000	15,000
Divisional income with investment		$ 75,000
Average net book value:		
Average book value without investment		$500,000
Average book value of investment [($200,000 + $175,000)/2]		187,500
Average net book value		$687,500

$$\text{ROI} = \frac{\$75{,}000}{\$687{,}500} = 0.109$$

[5] Methods for evaluating capital investment proposals are presented in Chapter 16.

EXHIBIT 13–3 **ROI with Adjustment for Price-Level Changes**

a) Historical cost used as investment base

	Division A			Division C		
	Historical cost (000)	*Fraction*	*Price-level adjusted cost (000)*	*Historical cost (000)*	*Fraction*	*Price-level adjusted cost (000)*
Plant & equip.	$1,600	190/160	$1,900	$1,800	190/180	$1,900
Depreciation	$ 200	190/160	$237.5	$ 225	190/180	$237.5

	Division A	Division C
Divisional income:		
Income before depreciation	$260,000	$260,000
Depreciation	−237,500	−237,500
Divisional income	$ 22,500	$ 22,500
Historical cost:		
Current assets	$ 200,000	$ 200,000
Plant and equipment—adjusted for price-level changes	1,900,000	1,900,000
Total historical cost	$2,100,000	$2,100,000
Return on Investment (ROI)	0.0107	0.0107

b) Net book value used as investment base

	Division A			Division C		
	Book value (000)	*Fraction*	*Price-level adjusted book value (000)*	*Book value (000)*	*Fraction*	*Price-level adjusted book value (000)*
Plant & equip.	$300*	190/160	$356.25	$1,462.5†	190/180	$1,543.75
Depreciation	$200	190/160	$237.50	$ 225.0	190/180	$ 237.50

	Division A	Division C
Divisional income:		
Income before depreciation	$260,000	$260,000
Depreciation	−237,500	−237,500
Divisional income	$ 22,500	$ 22,500
Net book value:		
Current assets	$ 200,000	$ 200,000
Plant and equipment—adjusted for price-level changes	356,250	1,543,750
Net book value	$ 556,250	$1,743,750
Return on Investment (ROI)	0.0404	0.0129

* ($400 + $200)/2
† ($1,575 + $1,350)/2

The 10.9 percent ROI with the investment is less than the 12 percent ROI that Division A would earn in 19x7 without this investment. Thus the manager of Division A may reject the proposed project because it would decrease his or her performance measure even though it would be desirable if another performance measure were used.[6] For example, if historical cost were used for the denominator in the ROI computation, ROI would have increased from 3.33 percent without the project to 3.75 percent [$75,000/($1,800,000 + $200,000)] with it.

Another solution to the problem caused by inflation is to value the assets at their replacement costs. However, obtaining accurate replacement cost data may be difficult or at least costly, and there is no assurance that assets would be replaced in kind at today's prices.

Leased Assets

Divisions may acquire the use of assets by leasing rather than purchasing. A lease is a contract between two parties where the lessor grants the use of an asset to the lessee for a specified period of time in exchange for rent. When assets leased for an extended period of time are not recorded on a division's financial statements, they should be capitalized before ROI and RI computations are made. If this is not done, operating and financial considerations will be intermixed and the measures will reflect the effect of financing decisions as well as operating decisions. Failure to capitalize long-term leases may lead division managers to accept projects that increase divisional ROI but are not in the best interest of the company. (Issues involved in the evaluation of leased assets are considered in Chapter 17.)

Other Unrecorded Assets

In addition to leased assets, many intangible assets such as patents, research and development, advertising, customer goodwill, and the value of employees to the organization are not recorded on a division's accounting records. Yet these assets are very valuable to the organization. Indeed, in the long run they may be more valuable than an organization's tangible assets. If the value of these assets is not included in ROI computations, division managers may be maximizing current performance measures at a considerable long-run cost to the organization. The following actions can improve current performance measures but have undesirable long-run effects:

- Cutting back on research and development or reducing advertising near the end of a period leads to an immediate increase in income and ROI. The long-run effect may be decreased sales and income.
- Reducing inventory levels or lowering the quality of a product by using less expensive, inferior materials may give ROI a short-term boost. However, customer goodwill may be adversely affected to the long-term loss of the business.

---

[6] The project may also have been desirable using the discounted cash flow methods in Chapter 16 for evaluating investments.

- Placing employees under severe pressure to increase output and reduce costs may increase short-run performance. In the long run, however, this may lead to dissatisfaction, increased employee turnover, and work stoppages.[7]

Recognizing the existence of unrecorded assets, whose precise value is difficult to measure, some organizations attempt to supplement ROI with other performance measures such as market position, product leadership, personnel development, employee attitudes, and public responsibility. This approach has two problems:

1. The problems of performance evaluation are greatly increased.
2. When there are conflicts among these measures, managers are placed in a "satisficing" rather than a maximizing position. If the conflicts cannot be resolved, ROI is likely to be the dominant performance measure.

One solution is to use ROI on a regular basis and employ other measures as supplements whenever there is a change in division management. This approach helps prevent an upwardly mobile manager from taking actions in anticipation of a promotion that increases current ROI at the expense of future profitability.

Interest Expense

In ROI and RI calculations, divisional income is set equal to divisional revenues less divisional operating expenses. When ROI and RI are used to evaluate operating management, interest on debts associated with the financing of divisional operations should be excluded from the computation of divisional income. If interest expense is deducted in calculating divisional income, the results of financing decisions are mixed in with the results of operating decisions. If financing decisions are usually made by corporate headquarters, divisional operating management should not be evaluated on the results of these decisions.

Allocated Indirect Costs

Theoretically corporate indirect costs should be excluded in determining divisional income for performance evaluation because divisional management has no direct control over the incurrence of these costs. Nevertheless some companies allocate corporate indirect costs. Two general types of corporate indirect costs have been identified: administrative costs and service costs.[8]

Corporate administrative costs are the costs of operating a central headquarters and maintaining the corporation as a legal entity. **Corporate service costs** are the costs of providing services to the divisions. Many corporate services could be provided separately at the divisional level; however, for economies of scale and efficiency, the activities are often consolidated at corporate headquarters. For

---

[7] For a further discussion of this point see Rensis Likert, *The Human Organization: Its Management and Value* (New York: McGraw-Hill, 1967), Chapters 8 and 9; and Rensis Likert, and William C. Pyle, "A Human Organization Measurement Approach," *Financial Analysts Journal* **27,** No. 1 (January-February 1971): 75–84.

[8] Some of the material in this section is based on a study by James M. Fremgen and Shu S. Liao, *The Allocation of Corporate Indirect Costs* (New York: National Association of Accountants, 1981).

example, the accounting function could be carried out mainly at the divisional level, with only a corporate staff needed to consolidate the financial data of all divisions for external reporting purposes.

Except for corporate service costs that can be clearly identified with the activities of individual divisions, the expenses of operating corporate headquarters should not, theoretically, be allocated for management performance evaluation. This is true even if the absence of corporate headquarters would cause the divisions to incur additional expenses. Most headquarters expenses are uncontrollable by division management and their joint nature makes any allocation arbitrary. Failure to allocate corporate expenses increases the amount by which the weighted-average ROI of the divisions exceeds the ROI of the company as a whole.

Although corporate indirect costs theoretically should not be allocated for performance evaluation, 84 percent of the companies responding to a survey by Professors Fremgen and Liao indicated they allocate at least part of corporate indirect costs to divisions. In addition, 80 percent used the allocated costs for performance evaluation. Managers gave a number of reasons for including allocated indirect costs in performance measures including:

- To remind managers that indirect costs exist and that divisional earnings must be adequate to cover some share of those costs.
- To relate divisional earnings to total company earnings so that the total of the divisional earnings equals earnings for the company as a whole.
- To show each division's usage of the essential common service since the allocation methods used fairly reflect such usage.
- To stimulate divisional managers to put pressure on central management to control service costs.
- To encourage use of central services that would otherwise be underutilized.
- To minimize state and local taxes.

Professors Fremgen and Liao concluded from their study that the main reason for allocating corporate indirect costs, that is, *to remind managers that indirect costs exist and that divisional earnings must be adequate to cover some share of those costs,* is behavioral in nature. Through the allocation process, central management tries to influence divisional managers so they will operate to produce satisfactory corporate profits. From the corporation's viewpoint, the *process* of allocation may be more important than the *amount* of the allocation. If divisional managers accept the idea that they should be charged with some portion of the indirect costs, it may not be important exactly how much is charged to them, as long as it is a reasonable amount.

Depreciation Methods

If depreciation is deducted in computing divisional income, the resulting ROI and RI numbers are affected by the depreciation method. Straight-line depreciation, for example, gives a smaller depreciation amount in the first year of an asset's life than either sum-of-the-years'-digits or double-declining balance depreciation. This affects income and the subsequent net book value of the asset.

Example 13–8

The manager of Division A is evaluating the desirability of purchasing a new asset that costs $22,500 and will provide annual income before depreciation of $10,000 for three years. The asset will have no salvage value.

As shown in Exhibit 13–4, the ROI of this investment depends on the depreciation method used. When straight-line depreciation is used, year 1 ROI on beginning of year book value is 0.111. If sum-of-the years'-digits depreciation is used, year 1 ROI is negative 0.056. If double-declining balance depreciation is used, year 1 ROI is negative 0.222. Note that ROI increases in later years because of the decline in net book value, and that the increase in ROI is most dramatic when accelerated depreciation is used.

EXHIBIT 13–4 ROI with Alternative Depreciation Procedures

A. STRAIGHT-LINE DEPRECIATION

	Year 1	*Year 2*	*Year 3*
Income before depreciation	$10,000	$10,000	$10,000
Depeciation	−7,500	−7,500	−7,500
Net income	$ 2,500	$ 2,500	$ 2,500
Net book value at start of year	$22,500	$15,000	$ 7,500
Return on investment	0.111	0.167	0.333

B. SUM-OF-THE-YEARS'-DIGITS DEPRECIATION

	Year 1	*Year 2*	*Year 3*
Income before depreciation	$ 10,000	$10,000	$10,000
Depeciation	−11,250	−7,500	−3,750
Net income (loss)	$ (1,250)	$ 2,500	$ 6,250
Net book value at start of year	$ 22,500	$11,250	$ 3,750
Return on investment	(0.056)	0.222	1.667

C. DOUBLE-DECLINING BALANCE DEPRECIATION

	Year 1	*Year 2*	*Year 3*
Income before depreciation	$ 10,000	$10,000	$10,000
Depeciation	−15,000	−5,000	−2,500*
Net income (loss)	$ (5,000)	$ 5,000	$ 7,500
Net book value at start of year	$ 22,500	$ 7,500	$ 2,500
Return on investment	(0.222)	0.667	3.000

* Adjusted to fully depreciate the asset

Although division managers should be interested in the long-run welfare of the organization, most of them are acutely aware of their need to survive in the short run in order to enjoy the benefits of the long run. This is an example of how the goals of individual managers and the goals of the organization may differ. An investment may be desirable from the organization's viewpoint, but the ROI for the first year might cause the managers to reject the asset. This would be especially likely if an accelerated depreciation method is used. Compound interest depreciation, discussed in Appendix B of Chapter 16, has been suggested as a solution to this particular problem.

MULTINATIONAL COMPANIES

Multinational companies are organizations that have established divisions or subsidiaries in two or more countries. When the decentralized units are treated as investment centers, all the problems just noted are encountered in measuring and evaluating performance. In addition, we may encounter other problems when comparing the performance of one investment center with another because divisional investment and income are stated in a foreign currency.[9]

The ROI for a division of a multinational company can be calculated using the division's income and investment stated in the foreign currency. ROIs computed in terms of the foreign currency are comparable because ROI is a percentage rather than an absolute amount. However, no meaningful comparison can be made if the residual incomes for two or more divisions are calculated in units of the foreign currency. Consider a division located in France with residual income of 100,000 francs and a division located in Mexico with residual income of 100,000 pesos. These amounts cannot be compared because they are stated in different measuring units.

We might attempt to solve the problem caused by different currencies by translating the investment and income of the divisions to a common currency, such as U.S. dollars. Translation creates other problems, however, because the appropriate exchange rates must be determined and fluctuations in exchange rates are outside the control of the local manager whose performance is being evaluated. These fluctuations cause a violation of the basic tenet of responsibility accounting that performance evaluation should be based on controllability. Thus translating foreign currency financial statements of a division does not solve the performance evaluation problem.[10]

Unfortunately no agreement has been reached on the best way to evaluate the performance of foreign divisions. At the present time, ROI calculated in terms of the foreign currency appears to present the fewest problems. However, all the problems in measuring ROI noted previously and the dysfunctional behavior they can cause apply to foreign as well as domestic investment centers.

---

[9] For a discussion of the performance evaluation problems in multinational companies see Elwood L. Miller, *Responsibility Accounting and Performance Evaluations* (New York: Van Nostrand Reinhold Company, 1982), Chapter 4.

[10] Exchange rate fluctuations also create similar problems if translated amounts are used in calculating ROI.

AGENCY THEORY

In recent years, accounting researchers have studied agency theory to find out why managers of decentralized units may not act in ways that are in the best interest of the organization. **Agency theory** is a structured attempt to explain the actions of agents. Researchers applying agency theory to large organizations believe that:

1. Managers maximize their utility.
2. It is costly for corporate headquarters to monitor or audit all the activities of division managers.

Agency Relationships

Agency relationships exist in many forms in an organization. An**agency relationship** occurs when one party hires another party to perform a service. The employer is known as the **principal** and the employee is known as the **agent.** In an organization, one agency relationship exists between stockholders (the principal) and corporate officers (the agents). Agency relationships also occur between corporate management and division managers hired to operate a division in the best interest of corporate management and the stockholders.

Agency Problem

The agency problem occurs whenever an agent takes actions to maximize his or her utility and those actions result in additional costs to the principal. The agency problem occurs in decentralized organizations because corporate management delegates decision-making authority to division managers. Since information is a costly resource, central management may find it too costly to constantly monitor or audit all the decisions made by the division managers. In fact, one advantage of decentralization is that corporate management does not need to evaluate all of the division managers' decisions, but instead can rely on a single measure to evaluate performance.

Because decisions are not constantly monitored or audited by corporate headquarters, division managers may try to maximize their performance evaluation measure or consume excessive amounts of perquisites. A **perquisite** is something of value obtained from an employer in addition to monetary compensation. For example, a divisional manager may buy an expensive automobile for company use when a less costly one would suffice. This expenditure reduces the division's ROI, but the manager may prefer the expensive automobile to the increase in the performance measure. By consuming perquisites, the divisional manager has maximized his or her utility at the expense of the organization as a whole.

Agency costs

Agency costs are the additional costs an organization incurs because local managers maximize their utility at the expense of the organization as a whole. These costs may occur because a manger is attempting to maximize a short-term performance measure such as ROI or because he or she is consuming an excessive amount of perquisities. Since it is costly for the principal to monitor or audit all the agent's activities, agency costs are likely to exist in decentralized organizations.

Agency theory helps explain why division managers sometimes behave in a manner that is not in the best interest of the organization. This theory may eventually explain many of the behavioral problems caused by using ROI as a performance measure. Agency theory may also help explain why certain noncontrollable costs are allocated to divisions in performance reports.[11]

SUMMARY

As organizations grow or their activities become more complex, they may attempt to decentralize decision making as much as possible. They do this by restructuring the organization into several divisions and treating each as a quasi-independent business. The managers of these divisions are then evaluated on the basis of the effectiveness with which they use the resources entrusted to them. The test of effectiveness is not the absolute size of divisional income. Rather it is the relationship between divisional income and divisional investment.

The most frequently used test of effectiveness is return on investment. As an overall measure of performance, return on investment has a number of problems. Some relate to the definition of divisional investment and income. Others relate to accounting procedures for asset valuation, accounting criteria for asset recognition, and the potentially depressing effect of new asset acquisitions on divisional return on investment. Although the use of residual income as a performance measure can overcome some of these problems, others, such as inflation and unrecorded assets, remain. Another problem encountered in measuring performance of investment centers, transfer pricing, is considered in Chapter 21.

Current accounting researchers are attempting to explain the behavior of divisional managers with agency theory. This theory is based on the notion that managers maximize their utility and it is costly for corporate management to monitor or audit all the activities of division managers. Division managers may, therefore, act in a manner that is not congruent with corporate goals, causing the organization to incur additional costs.

KEY TERMS

Agency costs
Agency relationship
Agency theory
Agent
Corporate administrative costs
Corporate service costs
Division
Historical cost
Investment center
Investment turnover
Multinational companies
Net book value
Perquisite
Principal
Residual income
Return on investment

[11] For an expanded discussion see Jerold L. Zimmerman, "The Costs and Benefits of Cost Allocations," *The Accounting Review* **54,** No. 3 (July 1979): 504–521.

SELECTED REFERENCES

Baiman, Stanley, and John H. Evans, III, "Pre-Decision Information and Participative Management Control Systems," *Journal of Accounting Research* **21,** No. 2 (Autumn 1983): 371–395.

Blanchard, Garth A., and Chee W. Chow, "Allocating Indirect Costs for Improved Management Performance," *Management Accounting* **64,** No. 9 (March 1983): 38–41.

Cohen, Susan I., and Martin Loeb, "Public Goods, Common Inputs, and the Efficiency of Full Cost Allocations," *Accounting Review* **57,** No. 2 (April 1982): 336–347.

Fedrock, John J., "Crisis in Conscience at Quasar," *Harvard Business Review* **46,** No. 2 (March-April 1968): 112–120. A case dealing with ethics, loyalty to superiors, and loyalty to company.

——, "Sequel to Quasar Stellar," *Harvard Business Review* **46,** No. 5 (September-October 1968): 14–24, 175–178.

Fremgen, James M., and Shu S. Liao, *The Allocation of Corporate Indirect Costs,* New York: National Association of Accountants, 1981.

Godfrey, James T., "Short-Run Planning in a Decentralized Firm," *Accounting Review* **46,** No. 2 (April 1971): 286–297.

Jannell, Paul A., and Raymond M. Kinnunen, "Portrait of the Divisional Controller," *Management Accounting* **61,** No. 12 (June 1980): 15–19, 24.

Magee, Robert P. "Equilibria in Budget Participation," *Journal of Accounting Research* **18,** No. 2 (Autumn 1980): 551–573.

Miller, Elwood L., *Responsibility Accounting and Performance Evaluations,* New York: Van Nostrand Reinhold, 1982.

Scapens, Robert W., and J. Timothy Sale, "An International Study of Accounting Practices in Divisionalized Companies and Their Associations with Organizational Variables," *Accounting Review* **60,** No. 2 (April 1985): 231–247.

Schiff, Michael, Roger M. Campbell, Leslie E. Halprin, and Judith P. Murphy, "How a Division's Reports Can Reflect Inflation," *Management Accounting* **64,** No. 4 (October 1982): 32–34.

Shwayder, Keith, "A Proposed Modification to Residual Income—Interest Adjusted Income," *Accounting Review* **46,** No. 2 (April 1970): 299–307.

Solomons, David, *Divisional Performance: Measurement and Control,* Homewood, Ill.: Irwin, 1965.

Virgil, Robert L., Walter R. Nord, and Sterling H. Schoen, "A Classroom Experience in the Behavioral Implications of Accounting Performance Evaluation Measurements," *Accounting Review* **48,** No. 2 (April 1973): 410–418.

Zimmerman, Jerold L., "The Costs and Benefits of Cost Allocations," *The Accounting Review* **54,** No. 3 (July 1979): 504–521.

REVIEW QUESTIONS

13–1 What is the relationship between the divisional and corporate controller? Why is this relationship a delicate one?

13–2 Mention several administrative and motivational advantages of decentralization.

13–3 What is return on investment? Into what two parts is it frequently broken?

13–4 What is residual income? Why is RI superior to ROI as a measure of relative performance when the size of divisional investment varies?

13–5 Why should debt and any related interest expense be excluded from the calculation of a division's return on investment?

13–6 What objections can be raised to allocating the cost of physical assets used by corporate headquarters to divisions before divisional ROI computations are made?

13–7 Why might a division manager reject an investment in new assets preferring instead to retain inefficient old assets?

13–8 How do price-level changes affect the ROI of different divisions whose assets were acquired at different times?

13–9 Mention several reasons why companies actually use allocated corporate indirect costs for performance evaluation.

13–10 How do traditional depreciation procedures affect ROI?

13–11 How might a manager improve a current performance measure such as ROI at the expense of the organization?

13–12 What problems are encountered in performance evaluation in multinational companies that would not occur in domestic organizations?

13–13 What types of agency relationships occur in an organization?

13–14 What is the agency problem encountered in organizations? What causes the agency problem to occur?

REVIEW PROBLEM

ROI and RI with Alternative Investment Bases

The Fiberglass Products Division of Clark Manufacturing Company reported divisional income for 19x5 of $150,000. Divisional assets consisted of the following:

	1/1/19x5	*12/31/19x5*
Current assets	$ 400,000	$ 600,000
Plant and equipment:		
Cost	$2,000,000	$2,200,000
Accumulated depreciation	– 1,200,000	– 1,500,000
Net plant and equipment	800,000	700,000
Total assets	$1,200,000	$1,300,000

REQUIREMENTS

a) Determine the ROI for the Fiberglass Products Division for 19x5 using:

1. Average assets at net book value for the investment base
2. Average historical cost of assets for the investment base
3. End-of-the-period historical cost for the investment base

b) Determine the residual income for the Fiberglass Products Division for 19x5 using:

1. Average assets at net book value for the investment base (Assume a required return on investment of 10 percent.)
2. Average historical cost of assets for the investment base (Assume a required return on investment of 5 percent.)

The solution to this problem is found at the end of the Chapter 13 problems and exercises.

EXERCISES

13–1 Calculating ROI

The Plastics Division of Tempo Company reported the following results for 19x1:

Sales	$1,600,000
Income	120,000
Average investment	800,000

REQUIREMENTS

a) Determine the 19x1 investment turnover.

b) Determine the 19x1 income to sales percentage.

c) Determine the 19x1 return on investment.

13–2 Calculating ROI

The Eastern Division of National Metals Company had an average investment of $3,000,000, divisional income of $600,000, and sales of $5,400,000 during 19x3.

REQUIREMENTS

a) Determine the 19x3 investment turnover.

b) Determine the 19x3 percentage of income to sales.

c) Determine the 19x3 return on investment.

13–3 Calculating ROI and RI

The Metro Division of Intrastate Corporation reported the following data for 19x5:

Average net book value of assets	$ 400,000
Average historical cost of assets	1,200,000
Income	60,000
Sales	1,500,000

For calculating residual income, each division is charged 10 percent of the average net book value of its assets.

REQUIREMENTS

a) Determine 19x5 ROI using net book value as the investment base.

b) Determine 19x5 ROI using historical cost as the investment base.

c) Determine 19x5 residual income.

13–4 Calculating Residual Income

Division C of Alpha Company reported the following for 19x6:

Average net book value of assets	$2,000,000
Income	200,000
Sales	1,500,000

For calculating residual income, each division is charged 12 percent of the average net book value of its assets.

REQUIREMENT

Determine the residual income for Division C.

13–5 ROI, Investment Turnover, and Income/Sales Percentage

During 19x4, the Toy Division of National Plastics Corporation had a 15 percent ROI and income of $60,000, which was equal to 12 percent of sales.

REQUIREMENTS

a) Determine the 19x4 sales of the Toy Division.

b) Determine the 19x4 investment turnover of the Toy Division.

c) Determine the 19x4 investment of the Toy Division.

13–6 Changes in ROI Components

The Tool Division of Locke Equipment Company reported the following data for 19x6:

Sales	$ 600,000
Income	75,000
Average investment	1,000,000

REQUIREMENTS

a) Determine the *change* in investment turnover, income as a percentage of sales, and ROI if each of the following independent events occurs in 19x7 and all other data are the same as in 19x6.

1. Average investment decreases to $800,000.
2. Expenses decrease by $25,000.
3. Sales increase to $700,000 while maintaining the same income to sales percentage.

b) If all other factors remain the same as for 19x6, how much would expenses have to decrease in 19x7 for the ROI of the Tool Division to be 12 percent?

13–7 Calculating ROI and RI for Different Divisions

The Maple Company has three divisions: West, Central, and East. Data for each division for 19x8 are as follows:

	West	*Central*	*East*
Sales	$3,000,000	$2,000,000	$3,000,000
Income	600,000	400,000	600,000
Average net book value of assets	4,000,000	3,000,000	2,000,000

REQUIREMENTS

a) Use ROI to rank the 19x8 performance of the divisions.

b) Use RI to rank the 19x8 performance of the divisions. Assume a required returned on investment of 10 percent.

c) Explain why the West and East Divisions had different ROIs although their income and sales were the same. What factor could have caused the difference if the divisions have similar assets?

13–8 Impact of Price-Level Changes

The Microchip Division of Transcomputer Company was organized in January 19x1. At that time, the Microchip Division acquired depreciable fixed assets costing $1,500,000. These assets are being depreciated over five years using the straight-line method with no salvage value.

During 19x3, the Microchip Division reported income before depreciation of $500,000. Average current assets of the Microchip Division during 19x3 were $400,000. Fixed assets have not changed since the division was established.

REQUIREMENTS

a) Determine the 19x3 ROI using historical cost as the investment base.

b) Determine the 19x3 ROI using average net book value as the investment base.

c) Assume the price level was 125 at the beginning of 19x1 and 140 during all of 19x3. Repeat parts (a) and (b) using price-level adjusted data. Assume that all revenues and expenses except depreciation are recorded at the 19x3 price level and that current assets are valued at the 19x3 price level.

13–9 Price-Level Changes and ROI

Townville Company organized their operations into two divisions, X and Y. Divisional data for 19x7 are as follows:

	Division X	*Division Y*
Sales	$2,000,000	$2,000,000
Income before depreciation	400,000	400,000
Average investment:		
Current assets	200,000	200,000
Plant and equipment—historical cost	1,000,000	1,100,000

Division X's plant and equipment was acquired in January 19x5 when the price level was 100. Division Y's plant and equipment was acquired in January 19x6 when the price level was 110. The price level was 115 during all of 19x7. Both divisions depreciate their assets over five years using the straight-line method with no salvage value.

REQUIREMENTS

a) Determine the 19x7 ROI of each division using historical cost as the investment base.

b) Determine the 19x7 ROI for each division using average net book value as the investment base.

c) Repeat parts (a) and (b) using price-level adjusted data. Assume that all revenues and expenses except depreciation are recorded at the 19x7 price level and that current assets are valued at the 19x7 price level.

13–10 Depreciation Methods and ROI

The manager of Division A of Cook Company is considering investing in a new asset that costs $200,000 and is expected to last four years with no salvage value. The asset is expected to generate annual income before depreciation and taxes of $80,000.

REQUIREMENTS

a) Ignoring income taxes and using beginning-of-the-year net book value as the investment base, determine the expected ROI for the asset for each of the four years using:

   1. Straight-line depreciation
   2. Sum-of-the-years'-digits depreciation
   3. Double-declining balance depreciation

b) Repeat part (a) using historical cost as the investment base.

c) Discuss the impact of the depreciation method on a manager's decision to invest in new assets if the manager is evaluated using ROI on beginning-of-the-year net book value.

13–11 Depreciation Methods and ROI

Charlie Long, manager of the Nebraska Division of Midwest Company, is currently evaluating a proposed investment costing $300,000 with no salvage value that is expected to generate income before depreciation of $80,000 annually for five years. If the investment is undertaken, it will be acquired and become operational in January 19x8. Without this investment, divisional income and average net book value of assets for 19x8 are expected to be $100,000 and $1,200,000, respectively.

REQUIREMENTS

a) Determine the 19x8 divisional ROI on average net book value of assets without the proposed investment.

b) Determine the 19x8 divisional ROI on average net book value of assets if the investment is undertaken and depreciated using:

   1. Straight-line method
   2. Sum-of-the-years'-digits method
   3. Double-declining balance method

c) If Mr. Long's performance is evaluated using ROI, how might the depreciation method used affect his decision about the proposed investment?

13–12 Agency Costs and ROI

Mike Lane is Vice President of the Solar Division of Energy Resources Company. During the past year, he redecorated his office at a cost of $300,000, including new office furniture and carpeting costing $200,000 and remodeling and repainting costs of $100,000. The furniture and carpeting is being depreciated over five years using the straight-line method with no salvage value. The remodeling and repainting costs were written off as an expense in the year incurred. For the past year, the solar division reported a return on investment of 8 percent with an average investment at book value of $1,500,000.

REQUIREMENTS

a) What are the agency costs associated with the redecorating?

b) Determine the impact of the office redecorating on ROI. Assume that a full year's depreciation was taken on the furniture and carpeting and that the 8 percent ROI is after depreciation on the office furniture and carpeting and the expense deductions for the redecorating.

c) Mr. Lane could have redecorated his office by spending only $60,000 on furniture and carpeting. What would the ROI for the past year have been if the less expensive furniture and carpeting had been acquired? Assume all other costs would have been the same.

d) Why did Mr. Lane prefer the alternative he selected to the less expensive alternative even though it decreased his division's ROI?

PROBLEMS

13–13 Organizational Structure

The Hooper Co. is considering a reorganization. The company's current organizational structure is represented by chart A (next page).

The company recently hired a new Vice President for Metal Products. The new Vice President for Metal Products has an extensive background in sales which complements the Vice President for Plastic Products whose background is in production. The new Vice President for Metal Products believes that Hooper Co. would be more effective if it were organized as in chart B (next page).

REQUIREMENTS

a) Identify the two types of organizational structures depicted by the two charts.

b) Compare the two organizational structures by discussing the advantages and disadvantages of each.

c) Discuss the circumstances that would favor one form of organizational structure over the other. (CMA Adapted)

A. Current Organizational Structure

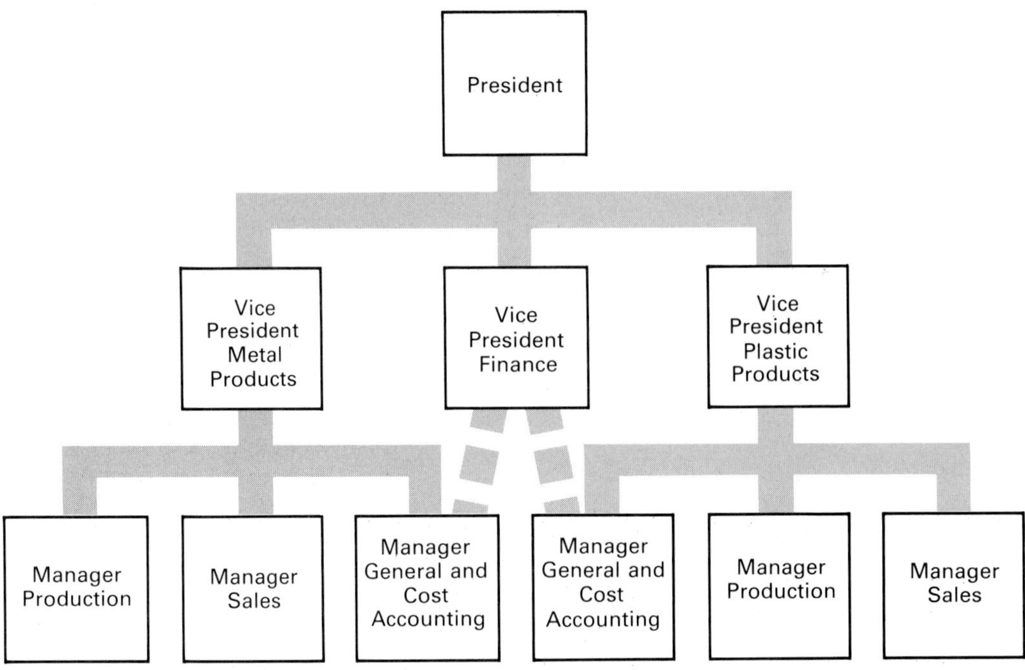

B. Proposed Organizational Structure

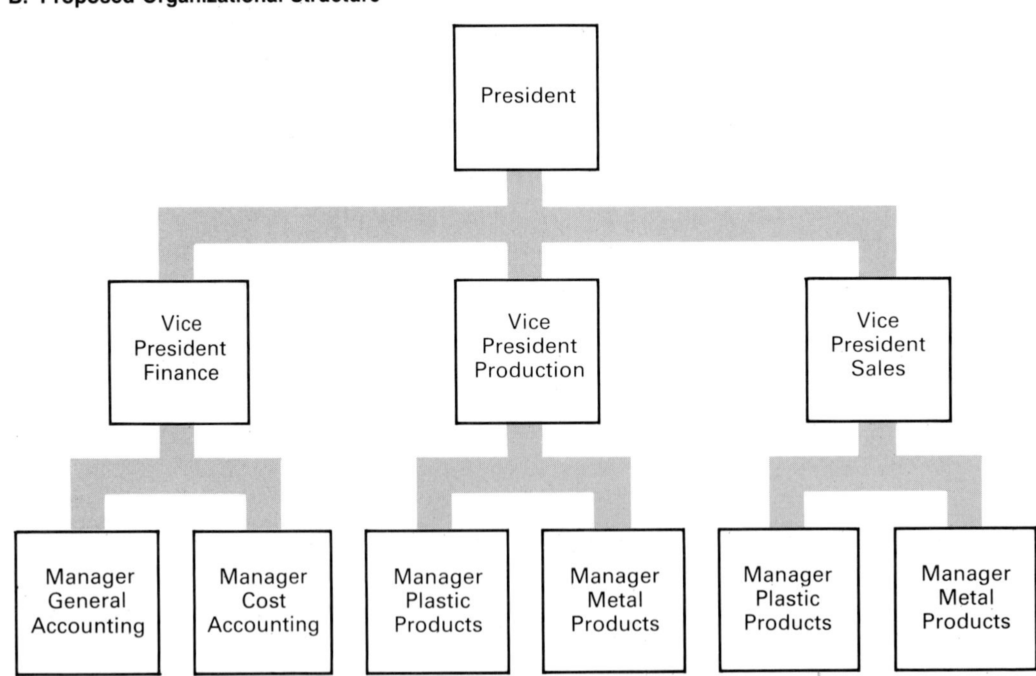

13–14 Accounting Problems in Performance Measurement

Many organizations use return on investment to motivate and evaluate the performance of division managers. Unfortunately the resulting statistic is only as accurate as the accounting numbers used in developing it and, because accounting numbers do not necessarily reflect true economic relationships, division managers are sometimes led into counterproductive actions.

REQUIREMENTS

For each of the following topics, suggest a counterproductive action (from the viewpoint of the entire organization) that a division manager may take to improve his or her current performance evaluation. Also indicate why the action is undesirable.

a) Investments in finished goods inventory

b) Employee goodwill

c) Replacement of old inefficient equipment

d) Investment in new plant and equipment

e) Research and development

f) Product quality

g) Maintenance

13–15 Limitations of ROI and Alternative Performance Measures

The Jackson Corporation is a large, divisionalized manufacturing company. Each division is viewed as an investment center and has virtually complete autonomy for product development, marketing, and production.

Performance of division managers is evaluated periodically by senior corporate management. Divisional return on investment is the sole criterion used in performance evaluation under current corporate policy. Corporate management believes return on investment is an adequate measure because it incorporates quantitative information from the divisional income statement and balance sheet in the analysis.

Some division managers complained that a single criterion for performance evaluation is insufficient and ineffective. These managers have compiled a list of criteria which they believe should be used in evaluating division managers' performance. The criteria include profitability, market position, productivity, product leadership, personnel development, employee attitudes, public responsibility, and balance between short-range and long-range goals.

REQUIREMENTS

a) Jackson management believes that return on investment is an adequate criterion to use to evaluate division management performance. Discuss the shortcomings or possible inconsistencies of using return on investment as the sole criterion to evaluate divisional management performance.

b) Discuss the advantages of using multiple criteria versus a single criterion to evaluate divisional management performance.

c) Describe the problems or disadvantages that can be associated with the implementation of the multiple performance criteria measurement system suggested to Jackson Corporation by its division managers. (CMA Adapted)

13–16 Motivational Problems Using ROI

The Notewon Corporation is a highly diversified company which grants its divisional executives a significant amount of authority in operating divisions. Each division is responsible for its own sales, pricing, production, and operating costs; the management of accounts receivable, inventories, and accounts payable; and use of existing facilities. Cash is managed by corporate headquarters; all cash in excess of normal operating needs of the divisions is transferred periodically to corporate headquarters for redistribution or investment.

The divisional executives are responsible for presenting requests to corporate management for investment projects. The proposals are analyzed and documented at corporate headquarters. The final decision to commit funds to acquire equipment, to expand existing facilities, and for other investment purposes rests with corporate management. This procedure for investment projects is necessitated by Notewon's capital allocation policy.

The corporation evaluates the performance of division executives by the return on investment (ROI) measure. The investment base is composed of fixed assets employed plus working capital exclusive of cash.

Divisional ROI is the most important appraisal factor for divisional executives' salary changes. What's more, the annual performance bonus is based on ROI with increases in ROI having a significant impact on the amount of the bonus.

The Notewon Corporation adopted the ROI performance measure and related compensation procedures about ten years ago. The corporation did so to increase the awareness of divisional management of the importance of the profit/investment relationship and to provide additional incentive to the divisional executives to seek investment opportunities.

The corporation seems to have benefited from the program. The ROI for the corporation as a whole increased during the first years of the program. Although the ROI has continued to grow in each division, the corporate ROI has declined in recent years. The corporation has accumulated a sizable amount of cash and short-term marketable securities in the past three years.

The corporation management is concerned about the increase in short-term marketable securities. A recent article in a financial publication suggested that the use of ROI was overemphasized by some companies with results similar to those experienced by Notewon.

REQUIREMENTS

a) Describe the specific actions division managers might have taken to cause the ROI to grow in each division but decline for the corporation. Illustrate your explanation with appropriate examples.

b) Explain, using the concepts of goal congruence and motivation of divisional executives, how Notewon Corporation's overemphasis on the use of the ROI measure might result in the recent decline in the corporation's return on investment and the increase in cash and short-term marketable securities.

c) What changes could be made in Notewon Corporation's compensation policy to avoid this problem? Explain your answer. (CMA Adapted)

13–17 Alternative Performance Measures

Divisional managers of SIU Incorporated have been expressing growing dissatisfaction with the current methods used to measure divisional performance. Divisional operations are evaluated every quarter by comparison with the static budget prepared during the prior year. Divisional managers claim that many factors are completely out of their control but are included in this comparison. This results in an unfair and misleading performance evaluation.

The managers have been particularly critical of the process used to establish standards and budgets. The annual budget, stated by quarters, is prepared six months prior to the beginning of the budget year. Pressure by top management to reflect increased earnings has often caused divisional managers to overstate expected revenues and/or understate expected expenses. In addition, once the budget has been established, divisions were required to "live with the budget." Frequently, external factors such as the state of the economy, changes in consumer preferences, and actions of competitors have not been adequately recognized in the budget parameters that top management supplied to the divisions.

Top management, recognizing the current problems, has agreed to establish a committee to review the situation and to make recommendations for a new performance evaluation system. The committee consists of each division manager, the Corporate Controller, and the Executive Vice President who serves as the chairperson. At the first meeting, one division manager outlined an Achievement of Objectives System (AOS). In this performance evaluation system, divisional managers would be evaluated according to three criteria:

1. Doing better than last year—Various measures would be compared to the same measures of the prior year.
2. Planning realistically—Actual performance for the current year would be compared to realistic plans and/or goals.
3. Managing current assets—Various measures would be used to evaluate the divisional management's achievements and reactions to changing business and economic conditions.

A division manager believed this system would overcome many of the inconsistencies of the current system because divisions could be evaluated from three different viewpoints. In addition, managers would have the opportunity to show how they would react and account for changes in uncontrollable external factors.

A second division manager was also in favor of the proposed AOS. However, he cautioned that the success of a new performance evaluation system would be limited unless it had the complete support of top management. Further, this support should be visible within all divisions. He believed that the committee should recommend some procedures that would enhance the motivational and competitive spirit of the divisions.

REQUIREMENTS

a) Explain whether or not the proposed AOS would be an improvement over the measure of divisional performance now used by SIU Incorporated.

b) Develop specific performance measures for each of the three criteria in the proposed AOS which could be used to evaluate divisional managers.

c) Discuss the motivational and behavioral aspects of the proposed performance system. Also recommend specific programs that could be instituted to promote morale and give incentives to divisional management. (CMA Adapted)

13–18 ROI as a Performance Measure

Lancaster Industries is a highly decentralized firm that produces a variety of products ranging from synthetic fibers to petrochemicals. Each of the company's product lines is manufactured and distributed by a separate division. The divisions are regarded as investment centers.

Until recent years division managers were evaluated solely on the basis of the size of their division's return on investment. Because Lancaster found it difficult to convince their best managers to accept assignments in divisions with poor performance records, they recently adopted a policy of evaluating managers by comparing their division's current and previous ROI. If ROI increases, managers receive a substantial bonus. If ROI decreases, they are asked to explain why.

Since the adoption of this policy, good managers have actually sought out assignments with weaker divisions. Yet, central management is not completely satisfied with the results. Although the previously weak divisions have experienced a substantial growth in investment size and ROI, the divisions with the best performance have merely maintained or only slightly improved their ROI. Additionally, these latter divisions have experienced no growth in investment size. The net result has been a decline in Lancaster's overall ROI.

REQUIREMENT

Write a brief report to management evaluating the strong and weak points of the current procedures for evaluating and rewarding division managers. Offer any suggestions that seem appropriate.

13–19 Allocating the Cost of a Service Department's Assets

The Greer Company is organized on a product-line basis. The manufacturing and distribution functions for each product line are handled by separate divisions. Divisional managers are evaluated using ROI.

As a service to the divisions, a data processing department has been established at corporate headquarters. To preserve divisional autonomy, divisions are free to use the data processing department or purchase equivalent services outside the company. Because of the company policy of billing divisions for only the variable cost of computer services, all divisions currently use this department.

To bring about a closer correspondence between the average ROI of the operating divisions and the ROI of the entire firm, corporate management is evaluating the desirability of allocating the cost of data processing facilities to the divisions that use them. The allocations would be made on the basis of billings and they would increase the investment in each affected division.

REQUIREMENT

Assume you are the manager of a division that reported an income of $400,000 and has a divisional investment of $2,000,000. During the most recent year you purchased internal data processing services at a cost of $30,000. The external cost of equivalent services is $70,000. If the new allocation plan were in effect, assets costing $300,000 would have been allocated to you last year. What will you do if the new plan is placed in effect? What action is optimal from the viewpoint of the firm?

13–20 Evaluating Performance Using ROI

Darmen Corporation is one of the major producers of prefabricated houses in the home building industry. The corporation consists of two divisions: (1) Bell Division, which acquires the raw materials to manufacture the basic house components and assembles them into kits, and (2) Cornish Division, which takes the kits and constructs the homes for final home buyers. The corporation is decentralized and the management of each division is measured by its income and return on investment.

Bell Division assembles seven separate house kits using raw materials purchased at the prevailing market prices. The seven kits are sold to Cornish for prices ranging from $45,000 to $98,000. The prices are set by corporate management of Darmen using prices paid by Cornish when it buys comparable units from outside sources. The smaller kits with the lower prices have become a larger portion of the units sold because the final house buyer is faced with prices that are increasing more rapidly than personal income. The kits are manufactured and assembled in a new plant just purchased by Bell this year. The division had been located in a leased plant for the past four years.

All kits are assembled upon receipt of an order form from the Cornish Division. When a kit is completely assembled, it is loaded immediately on a Cornish truck. Thus Bell division has no finished goods inventory.

The Bell Division's accounts and reports are prepared on an actual cost basis. There is no budget, and standards have not been developed for any product. A factory overhead rate is calculated at the beginning of each year. The rate is designed to charge all overhead to the product each year. Any under- or overapplied overhead is allocated to Cost of Goods Sold and Work-in-Process.

Bell Division's annual report, presented below, forms the basis of the evaluation of the division and its management by corporate headquarters.

ADDITIONAL INFORMATION

- Corporate headquarters does all the personnel and accounting work for each division.
- The corporate personnel costs are allocated on the basis of number of employees in each division.

- The accounting costs are allocated to the divisions on the basis of total costs excluding corporate charges.
- Divisional administration costs are included in factory overhead.
- The financing charges include a corporate imputed interest charge on divisional assets and any divisional lease payments.
- The divisional investment for the return on investment calculation includes inventory and plant and equipment at historical cost.

Bell Division
Performance Report
For the Year Ended December 31, 19x2

	19x2	19x1	Increase or (decrease) from 19x1: Amount	Increase or (decrease) from 19x1: Percent change
Production data (in units)				
Kits started	2,400	1,600	800	50.0
Kits shipped	2,000	2,100	(100)	(4.8)
Kits in process at year-end	700	300	400	133.3
Increase (decrease) in kits in process at year end	400	(500)		
Financial data ($000 omitted)				
Sales	$138,000	$162,800	$(24,800)	(15.2)
Production costs of units sold:				
Direct materials	$ 32,000	$ 40,000	$ (8,000)	(20.0)
Direct labor	41,700	53,000	(11,300)	(21.3)
Factory overhead	29,000	37,000	(8,000)	(21.6)
Cost of units sold	$102,700	$130,000	$(27,300)	(21.0)
Other costs:				
Personnel services	$ 228	$ 210	$ 18	8.6
Accounting services	425	440	(15)	(3.4)
Financing costs	300	525	(225)	(42.9)
Total other costs	953	1,175	(222)	(18.9)
Adjustments to income:				
Unreimbursed fire loss	0	$ 52	$ (52)	(100.0)
Raw material losses due to improper storage	$ 125	0	125	
Total adjustments	125	52	73	(140.4)
Total deductions	−103,778	−131,227	−(27,449)	−(20.9)
Division income	$ 34,222	$ 31,573	$ 2,649	8.4
Division investment	$ 92,000	$ 73,000	$ 19,000	26.0
Return on investment	37%	43%	(6)%	(14.0)%

REQUIREMENTS

a) Discuss the value of the annual report presented for the Bell Division in evaluating the division and its management in terms of:

1. The accounting techniques employed in the measurement of division activities

2. The manner of presentation
3. The effectiveness with which it discloses differences and similarities between years

Use the information in the problem to illustrate your discussion.

b) Present specific recommendations that would improve Darmen Corporation's accounting and financial reporting system. (CMA Adapted)

13–21 Evaluating Performance Using RI

Bio-grade Products is a multiproduct company manufacturing animal feeds and feed supplements. The need for a widely based manufacturing and distribution system has led to a highly decentralized management structure. Each divisional manager is responsible for production and distribution of corporate products in one of eight geographical areas of the country.

Residual income is used to evaluate divisional managers. The residual income for each division equals each division's contribution to corporate profits before taxes less a 20 percent investment charge on a division's investment base. The investment base for each division is the sum of its year-end balances of accounts receivable, inventories, and net plant fixed assets (cost less accumulated depreciation). Corporate policies dictate that divisions minimize their investments in receivables and inventories. Investments in plant fixed assets are a joint division/corporate decision based on proposals made by divisional plant managers, available corporate funds, and general corporate policy.

Alex Williams, Divisional Manager for the Southeastern Sector, prepared the 19x6 and preliminary 19x7 budgets in late 19x5 for his division. Final approval of the 19x7 budget took place in late 19x6 after adjustments for trends and other information developed during 19x6. Preliminary work on the 19x8 budget also took place at that time. In early October of 19x7, Williams asked the divisional controller to prepare a report that presents performance for the first nine months of 19x7. The report is as follows:

Bio-grade Products—Southeastern Sector
Performance Report
For the First Nine Months of 19x7
($000 omitted)

	19x7			*19x6*	
	Annual budget	*Nine month budget*[1]	*Nine month actual*	*Annual budget*	*Actual results*
Sales	$2,800	$2,100	$2,200	$2,500	$2,430
Divisional costs and expenses					
Direct material and labor	$1,064	$ 798	$ 995	$ 900	$ 890
Supplies	44	33	35	35	43
Maintenance and repairs	200	150	60	175	160
Plant depreciation	120	90	90	110	110
Administration	120	90	90	90	100
Total	−1,548	−1,161	−1,270	−1,310	−1,303

	19x7			19x6	
	Annual budget	*Nine month budget*[1]	*Nine month actual*	*Annual budget*	*Actual results*
Divisional margin	$1,252	$ 939	$ 930	$1,190	$1,127
Allocated corporate fixed costs	−360	−270	−240	−340	−320
Divisional contribution to corporate profits	$ 892	$ 669	$ 690	$ 850	$ 807
Imputed interest on divisional investment (20 percent)	−420	−321[2]	−300[2]	−370	−365
Divisional residual income	$ 472	$ 348	$ 390	$ 480	$ 442

	Budgeted balance 12/31/x7	*Budgeted balance 9/30/x7*	*Actual balance 9/30/x7*	*Budgeted balance 12/31/x6*	*Actual balance 12/31/x6*
Division investment:					
Accounts receivable	$ 280	$ 290	$ 250	$ 250	$ 250
Inventories	500	500	650	450	475
Plant fixed assets (net)	1,320	1,350	1,100	1,150	1,100
Total	$2,100	$2,140	$2,000	$1,850	$1,825
Imputed interest (20%)	$ 420	$ 321[2]	$ 300[2]	$ 370	$ 365

[1] Bio-grade's sales occur uniformly throughout the year.
[2] Imputed interest is calculated at only 15 percent to reflect that only nine months or three-fourths of the fiscal year has passed.

REQUIREMENTS

a) Evaluate the performance of Alex Williams for the nine months ending September 30, 19x7. Support your evaluation with pertinent facts from the problem.

b) Identify the features of Bio-grade Products' divisional performance measurement system that need to be revised if the system is to reflect effectively the responsibilities of the divisional managers. (CMA Adapted)

13–22 ROI as a Guide to Performance Betterment

Sea to Sea Discount Stores has decentralized decision making on a regional basis. Presented is information pertaining to three of Sea to Sea's retail sales divisions.

	Division		
	A	*B*	*C*
Sales, 19x3	$10,000,000	$12,000,000	$7,500,000
Investment, average 19x3	5,000,000	8,000,000	3,000,000
Income, 19x3	1,000,000	1,440,000	525,000

REQUIREMENT

Evaluate the relative performance of these divisions and suggest actions that might be taken to improve their performance.

13–23 ROI and Price-Cost Decisions

The Mammoth Automobile Company (MAC) is the largest automobile manufacturer in Mammoth. Because of its size and the quality of its product, MAC determines the selling price of its cars without regard to competitive price pressure. In arriving at the selling price for its cars, MAC considers six factors:

1. The segment of the market it is aiming for
2. Projected average annual sales
3. Variable costs to manufacture and sell
4. Average annual fixed costs of manufacturing, sales, and administration
5. Average annual investment in working capital and plant and equipment
6. A "fair" return on investment

Management is about to introduce a new, intermediate-size luxury car that contains all the normal options as standard equipment. Tentatively identified as the "Big MAC," this car is expected to sell 6,000 units annually and require variable costs of $6,000/unit. Annual fixed costs directly attributed to the Big MAC are budgeted at $14,000,000. Mammoth's investment in Big MAC working capital and depreciable assets will average $50,000,000 over the next several years.

REQUIREMENTS

a) Assuming MAC desires to earn an average before-tax ROI of 20 percent, determine the unit selling price of a Big MAC.

b) Reliable Motor Company (RMC) is considering the desirability of introducing a new car that will compete with the Big MAC in the intermediate-size luxury car market. They believe a high-quality competitively priced car could sell 4,000 units annually. The average annual investment required to produce the car would be $40,000,000. Given the answer to part (a) and assuming RMC desires to earn an average before-tax ROI of 15 percent, determine the maximum average annual costs RMC can incur to produce this car.

13–24 Ranking Divisional Performance Three Ways

The following information pertains to four divisions of the Tech Manufacturing Company.

Division	*Investment*	*Income*
A	$500,000	$120,000
B	400,000	100,000
C	200,000	60,000
D	300,000	60,000

REQUIREMENTS

a) Rank these four divisions according to their:

   1. Absolute level of income
   2. Return on investment

3. Residual income (To calculate RI, Tech uses a 20 percent cost of money.)

b) Evaluate the usefulness of these three criteria for performance evaluation.

c) Would the residual income ranking in part (a) change if the cost of money were 25 percent? 15 percent?

13–25 Alternative Depreciation Procedures and Performance Measures

The Northeastern Products Company has a cost of money of 9 percent. One of its many divisions presently has an ROI of 15 percent on average assets of $800,000. The manager of this division is currently evaluating the desirability of an investment proposal that has the following characteristics:

Initial investment	$300,000
Annual income before depreciation	$ 90,000
Life	5 years
Salvage	$ 0

Because this manager will be evaluated for promotion to a large division within the next two years, she wants to know the impact accepting this proposal may have on the division's ROI during its first year.

REQUIREMENTS

a) Determine the division's ROI for next year if the project is accepted and depreciated using:

1. Straight-line depreciation
2. Sum-of-the-years'-digits depreciation
3. Double-declining balance depreciation

Assume the return from currently held assets is the same as last year. Use historical cost as the investment base.

b) Evaluate these results from the division manager's viewpoint.

c) Determine the division's residual income for next year if the project is accepted and depreciated using:

1. Straight-line depreciation
2. Sum-of-the-years'-digits depreciation
3. Double-declining balance depreciation

Assume the return from currently held assets is the same as last year. Use historical cost as the investment base.

d) Assume the division manager is evaluated using residual income. Evaluate the results obtained in part (c) from the division manager's viewpoint.

13–26 Inflation and ROI: Different Investment Bases

Dorsey Manufacturing Company is organized on a divisional basis and treats its divisions as investment centers. The managers of the investment centers have authority to make all operating decisions and acquire and dispose of plant and equipment assets. The accounting policies used by each division, however, are determined by the corporate controller. This is done to ensure that all divisions use the same methods and procedures for determining the financial data reported to corporate headquarters. These procedures require that LIFO be used for costing inventories and that straight-line depreciation be used for plant and equipment assets.

The Home Appliance Division of Dorsey was organized early in 19x1. At that time, inventory costing $500,000 and plant and equipment costing $3,000,000 were acquired.

The Commercial Appliance Division was started in early 19x5. At that time, Dorsey invested $800,000 in inventory and $5,000,000 in plant and equipment assets for the Commercial Appliance Division.

Because of economic conditions, neither of the two appliance divisions has expanded nor reduced their operations since they were started and the inventories are costed using LIFO procedures.

For 19x7, the divisions reported the following results to corporate headquarters:

	Home Appliance Division	*Commercial Appliance Division*
Income before depreciation	$700,000	$1,000,000
Depreciation	−300,000	−500,000
Divisional income	$400,000	$ 500,000

The divisional assets of the two divisions consisted of the following:

	Home Appliance Division		*Commercial Appliance Division*	
	1/1/x7	*12/31/x7*	*1/1/x7*	*12/31/x7*
Current assets:				
Cash	$ 100,000	$ 100,000	$ 150,000	$ 150,000
Receivables	150,000	150,000	200,000	200,000
Inventories	500,000	500,000	800,000	800,000
Total	$ 750,000	$ 750,000	$1,150,000	$1,150,000
Plant and Equipment:				
Cost	$3,000,000	$3,000,000	$5,000,000	$5,000,000
Accumulated depreciation	−1,800,000	−2,100,000	−1,000,000	−1,500,000
Net	1,200,000	900,000	4,000,000	3,500,000
Total assets	$1,950,000	$1,650,000	$5,150,000	$4,650,000

REQUIREMENTS

a) Determine the 19x7 ROI for each of the divisions using average assets at net book value as the investment base.

b) Determine the 19x7 ROI for each of the divisions using average assets at historical cost as the investment base.

c) Determine the ROI for each division using average assets at net book value adjusted for price-level changes as the investment base. Assume the price-level index was as follows:

Beginning of 19x1	100
Beginning of 19x5	160
Average and end of 19x7	180

d) Using the price-level data in part (c), determine the ROI for each division using average assets at historical cost adjusted for price-level changes as the investment base.

e) If you were the manager of the Home Appliance Division, which of the methods of calculating ROI would you prefer? Why?

f) Which of the methods for calculating ROI provides better data for comparing the performances of the two divisions? Explain.

13–27 Impact of Investment on ROI and RI

At the beginning of the current year, Paul Moracco, manager of the Central Division of Sigma Products, invested in a project with the following characteristics:

Cost	$500,000
Annual income before depreciation	$200,000
Life	4 years
Salvage	$ 0

Mr. Moracco decided to invest in this project because it had a rate of return on the average investment of 30 percent. He calculated this rate as follows:

$$\text{Rate of return} = \frac{\text{Annual income}}{\text{Average investment}}$$

$$\text{Rate of return} = \frac{\$200{,}000 - \$125{,}000}{\$250{,}000} = \frac{\$75{,}000}{\$250{,}000} = \underline{\underline{0.30}}$$

The annual income was calculated as the annual income before depreciation minus straight-line depreciation. Average investment was the average of the book value of the investment when purchased and the book value at the end of its expected life [($500,000 + $0)/2].

For the year prior to investing in this project, the ROI of the Central Division was 20 percent on average assets at a historical cost of $2,000,000. Since the project's 30 percent return exceeded the division's 20 percent ROI, Mr. Moracco thought the investment would improve the division's ROI. Without the investment in the new project, the results for the current year were expected to be similar to those of the preceding year.

When the ROI for the current year was calculated, Mr. Moracco was disappointed to learn that the division's ROI had decreased to 19 percent although the income from the new project was exactly as predicted and the results from other operations were the same as the previous year.

REQUIREMENTS

a) Show how the 19 percent ROI for the current year was determined.

b) Explain why the division's ROI decreased from 20 percent to 19 percent even though the income from the new project was exactly as predicted.

c) Why is the 30 percent return calculated by Mr. Moracco not comparable with the ROI calculated for the division?

d) If the performance of Mr. Moracco is evaluated using residual income with a cost of money of 10 percent, would the new project have improved his performance measure? Support your answer with calculations.

13–28 Impact of Perquisites on Behavior and Performance

Huffco, Inc., is a large manufacturing company with three operating divisions located in Chicago, St. Louis, and Minneapolis. The corporate headquarters are also located in Chicago.

Employee perquisites are an important element of Huffco's compensation plan for its professional staff. Certain perquisites are provided to all professional employees regardless of management level. These include the following:

- Company-paid retirement benefits
- Company-paid basic medical insurance and major medical plan
- Company-paid term life insurance
- Company-paid vacation
- Company-paid holidays
- Discounts on the purchase of company products
- Reimbursement of authorized company travel

These basic perquisites vary to a certain degree among employees. For instance, the retirement benefits and term life insurance coverage are keyed to each employee's salary and the vacation time depends on management level and length of service with the company. Otherwise these benefits are the same for all professional staff.

Professional staff members classified as executive management have some additional perquisites over and above the basic plan. Those persons qualifying for executive management status are clearly identified, that is, only persons above a designated management level are entitled to this classification. The additional perquisites include the following:

- More comprehensive company-paid medical plan including dental insurance
- Company-paid disability insurance coverage
- Company-paid membership to one country or athletic club
- Access to a company car for business use
- Special executive privileges such as executive rest room and executive dining room

- Larger offices with more exquisite decor
- More liberal travel expense reimbursement

The differences in the travel expense reimbursement policy between the executive management and the other professional staff members are as follows:

	Difference in Travel Expense Policy	
	Basic	*Executive*
Air Travel	Not to exceed coach class; special reduced rates to be used when available.	First class allowed.
Rental Cars	Restricted to compact.	No restrictions on type of automobile.
Hotel	Actual amount spent up to a maximum of $75 per day unless excess authorized.	Actual amount spent.
Meal	Actual amount spent up to a maximum of $25 per day unless excess authorized.	Actual amount spent.
Reserved Lounges of Airline Clubs	None.	Payment for one membership to allow admission to reserved lounge of airline club located in terminals of major airports.

Although Huffco has a clearly defined plan for perquisites, some members of the professional staff have received special privileges. Some of the privileges have occurred several times and others have evolved over time and have tended to become accepted by top management. The following activities or special privileges have been observed:

- Several executives have memberships in two or three country/athletic clubs, and all are company paid.
- Several executives have company cars assigned to them permanently and the cars are used for all travel including to and from the office.
- The size and decor of offices does not appear to be applied consistently according to title and rank. For instance, several individuals not classified as executive management have offices as large as or larger than some executives. In addition, some offices of executives are remodeled more frequently.
- Several executives receive company products free. The dollar value of the products has never exceeded $300 annually.
- Executives' air travel is not consistent. When an executive and nonexecutive are on the same flight, most executives travel coach with the nonexecutives. However, some executives travel first class while the nonexecutives travel coach, and some executives have the nonexecutives travel first class with the company paying the additional fare.
- The travel expenses of spouses who accompany executives to meetings have been paid by the company on several occasions. This issue is not addressed in the company travel policy.

- Use of personal automobiles for company business is only allowed for short trips when company cars or common carrier service is not available. Several executives have used personal automobiles for long trips when common carrier (airlines) would have been less expensive.
- Several executives have company-paid memberships for two or more airline club lounges.

REQUIREMENTS

a) Explain the behavioral implications and the effect on employee performance of having two (or more) levels of perquisites for professional employees assuming eligibility is clearly defined and consistently applied.

b) Discuss the possible implications on (1) behavior and (2) cost control when company policy governing perquisites is not clear or is not applied consistently such as has occurred with Huffco, Inc. Use Huffco examples in your discussion when applicable. (CMA Adapted)

SOLUTION TO REVIEW PROBLEM

a) 1. Average assets at net book value $= \dfrac{\$1,200,000 + \$1,300,000}{2} = \underline{\underline{\$1,250,000}}$

$$\text{ROI} = \frac{\$150,000}{\$1,250,000} = \underline{\underline{0.12}}$$

2. Average assets at historical cost $= \dfrac{\$2,400,000 + \$2,800,000}{2} = \underline{\underline{\$2,600,000}}$

$$\text{ROI} = \frac{\$150,000}{\$2,600,000} = \underline{\underline{0.0577}}$$

3. Historical cost 12/31/19x5 $= \$600,000 + \$2,200,000$
$= \underline{\underline{\$2,800,000}}$

$$\text{ROI} = \frac{\$150,000}{\$2,800,000} = \underline{\underline{0.0536}}$$

b) 1.

Divisional income		$150,000
Interest charge	(0.10 × $1,250,000)	−125,000
Residual income		$ 25,000

2.

Divisional income		$150,000
Interest charge	(0.05 × $2,600,000)	−130,000
Residual income		$ 20,000

14 Standard Cost Systems

INTRODUCTION

CHARACTERISTICS OF STANDARD COST SYSTEMS

STANDARD PROCESS COSTING

SPOILAGE

REWORK

STANDARD JOB-ORDER COSTING

PRORATING VARIANCES

SUMMARY

APPENDIX: STANDARD COSTS FOR JOINT PRODUCTS

INTRODUCTION

A STANDARD COST IS A BUDGET FOR A SINGLE UNIT. STANDARD COSTS ARE used for:

1. Planning, where they serve as building blocks for budgets.
2. Control, where they serve as benchmarks for performance evaluation.
3. Product costing, where they simplify day-to-day recordkeeping.

The use of standard costs in planning and controlling operations was examined in Chapters 10 through 12.

The purpose of this chapter is to examine the use of standard costs for product costing and recordkeeping. When this is done, inventories are costed at standard and the computation of cost variances becomes part of the accounting cycle. However, any departure from standard costs may require prorating variances for external reporting. Prorating is also considered in this chapter.

Variance computations under actual and normal cost systems were considered in Chapter 11. We now introduce variances into the accounting record system while assigning only standard costs to products. Placing standard cost systems at the end of four chapters devoted to performance evaluation is intended to emphasize the fact that variance computations are possible under actual or normal cost systems. This chapter also completes a cycle started in Chapters 2 through 6, which dealt with product costing under actual and then normal cost systems. In those chapters and Chapter 7 we also learned how to analyze historical cost data to obtain information useful for planning and standard setting. Chapters 8 through 10 introduced short-range planning techniques and laid the foundation for the performance-evaluation issues discussed in Chapters 11 through 13. In concluding this section on performance evaluation with standard cost systems, the process begins anew; we are again studying product costing.

CHARACTERISTICS OF STANDARD COST SYSTEMS

Inventory Valuation

A variety of product-costing techniques are included in cost accounting textbooks. In addition to standard costing there are actual costing and normal costing, both of which are used with a FIFO, LIFO, or weighted-average cost-flow assumption. To complicate matters further, for internal reporting, all of these product costing techniques and cost flow assumptions may be applied using variable (direct) or absorption costing. Before delving into the mechanics of standard cost systems, you should understand the similarities and differences in the product costs that result from using each of these techniques. A summary of product costs under alternative techniques is presented in Exhibit 14–1. The emphasis in this chapter is on standard costing where each unit is assigned only its budgeted costs.

The basic idea of a standard cost system is to charge products with what it should have cost to produce them under normal, efficient operating conditions,

EXHIBIT 14–1 **Unit Inventory Values Under Various Costing Techniques**

	Variable costing	*Absorption costing*
Actual costing:		
Direct materials	$AQ_U \times AP$	$AQ_U \times AP$
Direct labor	$AH \times AR$	$AH \times AR$
Variable overhead	$AH \times AR$	$AH \times AR$
Fixed overhead	—	$AH \times AR$
Normal costing:		
Direct materials	$AQ_U \times AP$	$AQ_U \times AP$
Direct labor	$AH \times AR$	$AH \times AR$
Variable overhead	$AH \times PR$*	$AH \times PR$*
Fixed overhead	—	$AH \times PR$*
Standard costing:		
Direct materials	$SQ_A \times SP$	$SQ_A \times SP$
Direct labor	$SH_A \times SR$	$SH_A \times SR$
Variable overhead	$SH_A \times SR$	$SH_A \times SR$
Fixed overhead	—	$SH_A \times SR$

where:

AQ_U = actual quantity of materials used.
AP = actual unit price of materials used.
AH = actual direct-labor hours (or other activity base for overhead).
AR = actual rate of pay per direct-labor hour, actual overhead rate per direct-labor hour (or other activity base).
PR = predetermined overhead rate per direct-labor hour (or other activity base).
SQ_A = standard quantity of materials allowed for the units manufactured.
SP = standard unit price of materials.
SH_A = standard direct-labor hours (or other activity base for overhead) allowed for the units manufactured.
SR = standard rate per direct-labor hour (or other activity base for overhead).

* Predetermined rate = estimated total cost/estimated total hours (or other activity base). Conceptually similar to *SR*.

rather than what it did cost to produce them. The use of standard costs reduces the complexity of inventory valuation. Standard costs do not change in response to short-term fluctuations in volume, efficiency, or the cost of inputs. Under standard costing the cost of inventory equals the number of units on hand times the standard unit cost. Cost flow assumptions such as FIFO, LIFO, or weighted average are not necessary. This greatly reduces the record keeping required for product costing.

Cost Flows and Variance Analysis

The use of standard costs reduces the need to trace actual cost flows. In process costing, units transferred between departments are always valued at standard. In job-order costing, the standard cost of basic job components are recorded on job-cost sheets. When service departments serve production departments or other service departments, all cost transfers are made at standard.

Variance analysis is an integral part of standard costing. Differences between a department's actual costs and the costs allowed for the work done are assigned to one or more variance accounts. Unfavorable variances, resulting from actual costs that exceed allowed costs, are recorded as debits in variance accounts. Favorable variances, resulting from allowed costs that exceed actual costs, are recorded as credits in variance accounts.

Example 14–1

The Power Department's assigned costs for January 19x9 totaled $50,000. The standard cost of power provided other departments totaled $52,000. The Power Department's total January variances are $(2,000)F ($50,000 actual − $52,000 allowed).

The flow of the Power Department's costs is summarized, in T-account and journal entry form, in Exhibit 14–2. For simplicity it is assumed the Power Department uses a single control account with detailed cost information recorded in a subsidiary ledger. Additional information is necessary to decompose the total variance into its various components.

Journal entries in a standard cost system can be organized in many ways. Regardless of the pattern followed, the following objectives are always accomplished by the end of each accounting period:

1. All inventories are valued at standard.
2. All variances are computed.

The authors have found the cost flow pattern illustrated in Exhibit 14–3 useful in learning standard cost system fundamentals. This illustration is for a factory that contains a single production department and no service departments. Assuming all variances are unfavorable, the significant characteristics of this system are as follows:

- The materials price variance is isolated at the time of purchase and materials are recorded in Stores Control at standard:

1. Stores Control	XXX	
Materials Price Variance	XXX	
Accounts Payable		XXX

EXHIBIT 14–2 **Flow of Service Department Costs Under a Standard Cost System**

(a) T-accounts

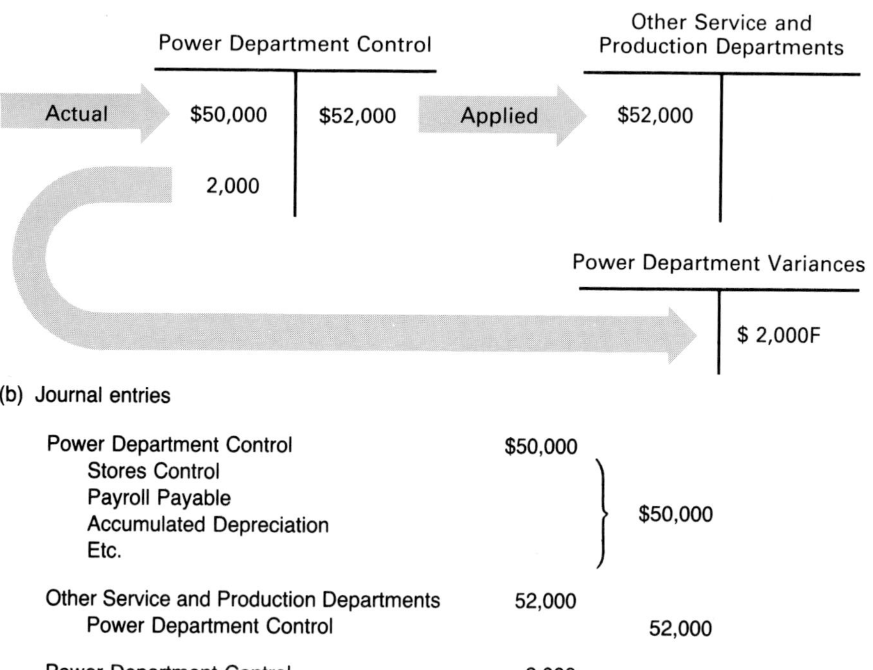

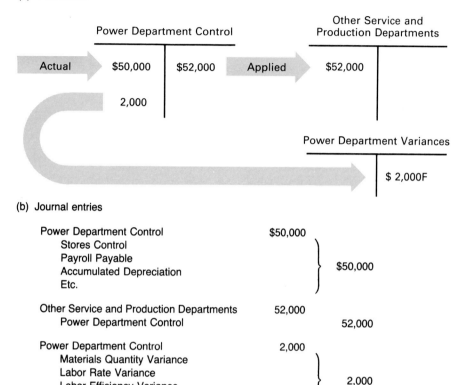

(b) Journal entries

Power Department Control	$50,000	
Stores Control Payroll Payable Accumulated Depreciation Etc.		$50,000
Other Service and Production Departments	52,000	
Power Department Control		52,000
Power Department Control	2,000	
Materials Quantity Variance Labor Rate Variance Labor Efficiency Variance Etc.		2,000

- All transfers between inventory accounts are at standard, so although variances cannot be determined until the end of the period when standard quantities allowed for the work done are known, transfers from Work-in-Process to Finished Goods Inventory can be made as units are completed. This is analogous to the use of a predetermined overhead rate in a normal cost system, where the use of a predetermined rate allows the assignment of overhead costs to Work-in-Process before the end of the period.

2. Finished Goods Inventory	XXX	
Work-in-Process		XXX

- At the end of the period, standard costs allowed for the work done are assigned to Work-in-Process, variance computations are made, and variances are assigned to appropriate variance accounts. This could have been accomplished in one large compound journal entry, but the authors recommend the use of separate entries for each product cost.

3. Work-in-Process	XXX	
Materials Quantity Variance	XXX	
Stores Control		XXX

EXHIBIT 14–3 Flow of Costs Under a Standard Cost System

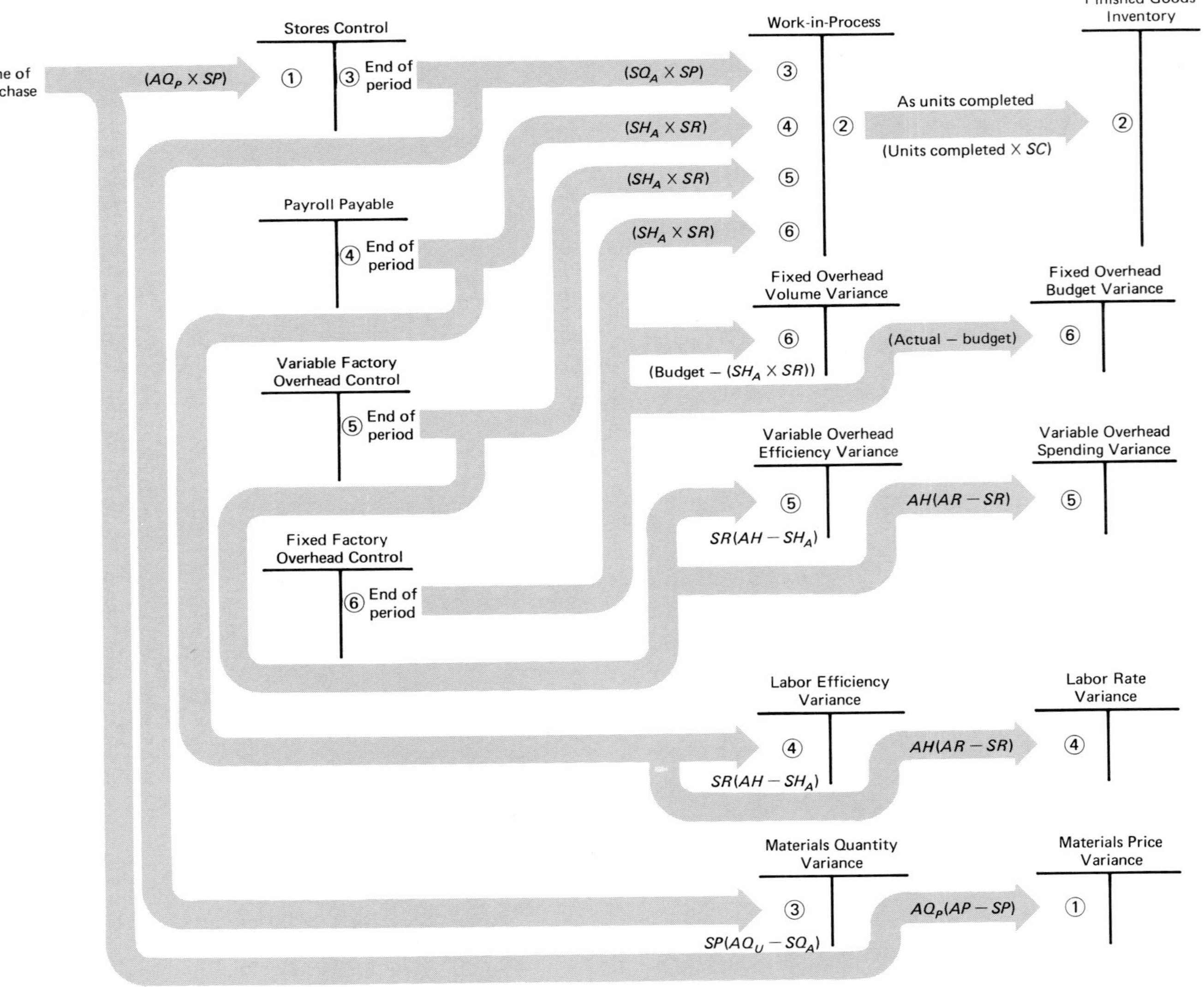

4. Work-in-Process	XXX	
Labor Rate Variance	XXX	
Labor Efficiency Variance	XXX	
Payroll Payable		XXX
5. Work-in-Process	XXX	
Variable Overhead Spending Variance	XXX	
Variable Overhead Efficiency Variance	XXX	
Variable Factory Overhead Control		XXX
6. Work-in-Process	XXX	
Fixed Overhead Budget Variance	XXX	
Fixed Overhead Volume Variance	XXX	
Fixed Factory Overhead Control		XXX

In the preceding journal entries, the credit to Stores Control is for the actual quantity times the standard price. The credits to Payroll Payable, Variable Factory Overhead Control, and Fixed Factory Overhead Control are for the actual period costs.

Disposition of Variances

On interim financial statements, production variances may be treated as an adjustment (addition or deduction) to inventory under the assumption that variances are caused by random fluctuations that will net close to zero by the end of the year. The cost accountant should, of course, monitor any buildup of variance account balances and relay this information to management with any appropriate comments.

A buildup in variance account balances can be caused by a number of factors: changed circumstances, standards that were intentionally set at a level difficult to attain, or unusual operating conditions. Management should be made aware of changed circumstances as soon as possible so they may change selling prices, change the production process, substitute raw materials, or take any other action that seems appropriate. If the standards are no longer accurate because of changed circumstances, the cost accountant should consider recommending a change in the standards. Management should also be made aware of any unusual circumstances, such as inefficient operations, as soon as possible in order to take appropriate action.

According to generally accepted accounting principles, standard costs may only be used for inventory valuation in annual financial statements if the standard product costs approximate actual product costs. Assuming this is the situation, any remaining balances in variance accounts are treated expediently and closed to Cost of Goods Sold. If large unfavorable variances are caused by unusual operating conditions, they are normally closed to the Cost of Goods Sold, rather than being prorated, to ensure that inventory is costed at less than its net realizable value. Large favorable variances and large unfavorable variances resulting from the use of standards not based on normal, efficient operating conditions (such as tight motivating standards) should be prorated to appropriate inventory accounts and the Cost of Goods Sold. The objective of prorating is to have the balances in all inventory accounts and the Cost of Goods Sold approximate the balances that would result if an actual rather than a standard cost system were used.

If large unfavorable variances result from both unusual operating conditions and the use of tight motivating standards, the variance should theoretically be split into two parts. The portion resulting from unusual operating conditions should be written off to the Cost of Goods Sold. The portion resulting from inappropriate standards should be prorated to inventory accounts and Cost of Goods Sold. It is likely, however, that the disposition of a variance will be based on its most significant cause. Hence, if the major portion of the variance were caused by unusual operating conditions, it would be written off to Cost of Goods Sold.

The authors suggest that the decision to prorate should be made on the basis of the net amount of all cost variances. When some large variances are favorable and other large variances are unfavorable, the net effect of prorating on inventory valuations may be negligible, making prorating unnecessary for external reporting. Nevertheless the existence of large variances suggests that the cost accountant should carefully evaluate the standards to determine if they reflect normal, efficient operating conditions.

Prorating is illustrated later in this chapter. Closing unfavorable variances to Cost of Goods Sold results in the following entry:

Cost of Goods Sold	XXX	
Materials Price Variance		XXX
Materials Quantity Variance		XXX
Labor Rate Variance		XXX
Labor Efficiency Variance		XXX
Variable Overhead Spending Variance		XXX
Variable Overhead Efficiency Variance		XXX
Fixed Overhead Budget Variance		XXX
Fixed Overhead Volume Variance		XXX

STANDARD PROCESS COSTING

Standard cost systems are most frequently encountered in process costing environments where identical units are produced on a continuous basis. The use of standard costs eliminates the need to compute the cost per equivalent unit. The cost per equivalent unit is the standard cost. Additionally, the costs transferred out are equal to the number of units completed times the standard cost. The equivalent units of materials and conversion in the ending inventory are also costed at standard. In subsequent departments, transferred-in costs are valued at standard.

The only complicating features of standard process costing are the additional entries required to dispose of variances and the use of the FIFO concept of equivalent units manufactured. Variances emphasize current deviations from standards. Hence they are based on a comparison of current costs assigned to production and the costs allowed for the equivalent units manufactured.

Example 14–2 The Watson Company manufactures a product that has the following standard cost:

Direct materials (2 square meters @ $10)		$20
Direct labor (1 hour @ $8)		8
Factory Overhead:		
Variable (1 direct-labor hour @ $1)	$1	
Fixed (1 direct-labor hour @ $2)	2	3
Total standard cost per equivalent unit manufactured		$31

The standard for fixed factory overhead is based on 1,300 allowed direct-labor hours per month and budgeted fixed factory overhead of $2,600 per month.

On March 1, 19y0, Watson had no inventories of raw materials or finished goods. However, the beginning inventory of work-in-process contained 400 units that were complete as to materials and ½ complete as to conversion. During the month the following events occurred:

- 2,500 square meters of raw materials were purchased at $9 per square meter.
- 1,100 new units of product were started.
- 1,300 units were completed and transferred to finished goods inventory.
- 1,350 direct-labor hours were used at $8 per hour.
- Actual variable factory overhead costs were $2,025 and actual fixed factory overhead costs were $2,925.

The ending inventory of work-in-process consisted of 200 units complete as to materials and ¾ complete as to conversion.

A cost of production report for Watson's March 19y0 activities is presented in Exhibit 14–4. Comparing this report to the cost of production reports presented in Chapter 4, we note the following similarities and differences:

- The flow of whole or partial units is the same regardless of whether an actual, normal, or standard cost system is used.
- In a standard cost system, the FIFO concept of equivalent units manufactured is used because it represents work performed during the current period.
- The total costs to be accounted for include costs in the beginning inventory (stated at standard) and current costs assigned to production. Assuming the materials price variance is isolated at purchase and is the responsibility of a purchasing agent, the actual materials used are assigned to the production department and are included in the cost of production report at standard cost. Actual direct labor and factory overhead costs are the responsibility of the production supervisor and are included in the total costs to be accounted for.
- Because all units are costed at standard, the report does not contain a computation of the cost per equivalent unit manufactured.
- The final section of the report, accounting for total costs, details the costs transferred to Finished Goods Inventory at standard, the end-of-period assignments to variance accounts, and the costs in ending Work-in-Process at standard. Because materials are assigned to the production department at standard, the materials price variance is not included in the cost of production report.

EXHIBIT 14–4 **Cost of Production Report: No Spoilage**

Watson Company
Cost of Production Report
For the Month of March 19y0

FLOW OF WHOLE OR PARTIAL UNITS

Beginning	400
Started	1,100
In process	1,500
Completed	−1,300
Ending	200

EQUIVALENT UNITS MANUFACTURED	*Materials*	*Conversion*
Units completed	1,300	1,300
Equivalent units in ending inventory	200	150*
Equivalent units in process	1,500	1,450
Less equivalent units in beginning inventory	−400	−200†
Equivalent units manufactured	1,100	1,250

* (200 units, ¾ complete)
† (400 units, ½ complete)

TOTAL COSTS TO BE ACCOUNTED FOR		
Beginning inventory at standard:		
Materials (400 × $20)	$ 8,000	
Conversion (200 × $11)	2,200	$10,200
Current costs assigned to Production Department:		
Materials (2,500 × $10)	$25,000	
Direct labor (1,350 × $8)	10,800	
Variable overhead	2,025	
Fixed overhead	2,925	40,750
Total costs to be accounted for		$50,950
ACCOUNTING FOR TOTAL COSTS		
Transferred out at standard (1,300 × $31)		$40,300
Variances:		
Materials quantity [$10(2,500 − 2,200*)]	$3,000U	
Labor rate [1,350($8 − $8)]	0	
Labor efficiency ($8(1,350 − 1,250†))	800U	
Variable overhead spending [$2,025 − $1(1,350)]	675U	
Variable overhead efficiency [$1(1,350 − 1,250)]	100U	
Fixed overhead budget ($2,925 − $2,600)	325U	
Fixed overhead volume [$2,600 − $2(1,250)]	100U	5,000
Ending inventory at standard:		
Materials (200 × $20)	$4,000	
Conversion (150 × $11)	1,650	5,650
Total costs accounted for		$50,950

* Standard square meters allowed (2 × 1,100) = 2,200

† Standard direct-labor hours allowed (1 × 1,250) = 1,250

In Exhibit 14–4, the materials quantity variance is based on the inputs allowed for 1,100 equivalent units of product. The labor efficiency and variable overhead efficiency variances are based on the labor-hours allowed for 1,250 equivalent units of product. And the fixed overhead volume variance is based on the fixed costs applied to 1,250 equivalent units of product.

Watson's standard cost journal entries, including that for the purchase of raw materials, are presented in Exhibit 14–5. Posting these journal entries, the activity in Work-in-Process appears as follows:

Work-in-Process

		Debit		Credit	
Beginning balance		$10,200	(2)	$40,300	Units completed
Direct materials	(3)	22,000			
Direct labor	(4)	10,000			
Variable overhead	(5)	1,250			
Fixed overhead	(6)	2,500			
		$45,950		$40,300	
				5,650	Ending balance
		$45,950		$45,950	
Ending balance		$ 5,650			

EXHIBIT 14–5 **Standard Costing Journal Entries**

TIME OF PURCHASE		
1. Stores Control	$25,000	
Materials Price Variance [2,500($9 – $10)]		$ 2,500
Accounts Payable		22,500
AS UNITS COMPLETED		
2. Finished Goods Inventory	40,300	
Work-in-Process		40,300
END OF PERIOD		
3. Work-in-Process	22,000	
Materials Quantity Variance	3,000	
Stores Control		25,000
4. Work-in-Process	10,000	
Labor Efficiency Variance	800	
Payroll Payable		10,800
5. Work-in-Process	1,250	
Variable Overhead Spending Variance	675	
Variable Overhead Efficiency Variance	100	
Variable Factory Overhead Control		2,025
6. Work-in-Process	2,500	
Fixed Overhead Budget Variance	325	
Fixed Overhead Volume Variance	100	
Fixed Factory Overhead Control		2,925

SPOILAGE

Spoiled units (sometimes called **defective units**) are units that do not meet quality standards and must be junked, sold as seconds, or reworked. Spoilage concepts were first introduced in Chapter 4 where we concluded that the proper treatment of spoilage depends on whether or not spoilage is an expected or normal occurrence in the production of good units. **Normal spoilage** is expected and occurs under efficient operating conditions. **Abnormal spoilage** is not expected and should not occur under efficient operating conditions. Under a standard cost system:

1. If spoilage is not expected to occur, the cost of the equivalent units spoiled should be treated as a variance.
2. If spoilage is expected to occur under efficient operating conditions, the costs associated with the spoiled units are an expected cost of producing the good units and are properly assigned to the good units.
3. When some spoilage is expected to occur, but spoilage rates are higher than expected, the cost of normal spoilage should be assigned to the good units and the costs of abnormal spoilage should be treated as a variance.

If spoilage is not expected in a standard cost system, the standard cost per unit will not include an allowance for spoilage. Assuming all variances are based on the equivalent good units manufactured, the cost of the spoiled units will be included in the following variances: materials quantity, labor efficiency, variable overhead efficiency, and fixed overhead volume. When they are caused by unexpected spoilage, these variances should be written off to the Cost of Goods Sold.

If spoilage is expected in a standard cost system, the cost of normal spoilage should be assigned to the good units and the cost of abnormal spoilage should be assigned to one or more variance accounts. Two alternative ways of accomplishing this are illustrated in this chapter:

1. An allowance for normal spoilage is *included in the standard inputs per equivalent good unit manufactured.* Following this procedure, spoiled units are omitted from equivalent unit computations, a separate variance account is not established for abnormal spoilage, and the standard cost of abnormal spoilage is included in materials quantity, labor efficiency, variable overhead efficiency, and fixed overhead volume variances.
2. An allowance for normal spoilage is *added to the standard cost per equivalent unit* to compute the standard cost per equivalent good unit. When this procedure is followed, spoiled units are included in equivalent unit computations, a separate variance account is established for abnormal spoilage, and the cost of abnormal spoilage is assigned to this account.

The first approach is illustrated in Example 14–3 and the second is illustrated in Example 14–4.

Abnormal Spoilage in Other Variance Accounts

Assume the same situation as that in Example 14–2, except that in this case the Watson Company anticipates a normal spoilage rate equal to 2 percent of the number of good units completed. In order to allow for normal spoilage, the materials, labor, and overhead inputs are increased by 2 percent from the amounts

Example 14–3

presented in Example 14–2:

Direct materials (2.04 square meters @ $10)		$20.40
Direct labor (1.02 hour @ $8)		8.16
Factory Overhead:		
Variable (1.02 direct-labor hour @ $1)	$1.02	
Fixed (1.02 direct-labor hour @ $2)	2.04	3.06
Standard cost per equivalent good unit manufactured		$31.62

Assume that the March 19y0 activity is identical to that in Example 14–2 except that 50 of the 1,300 units completed were spoiled. Spoilage is detected at the end of the production process.

A cost of production report for Example 14–3 is presented in Exhibit 14–6. Both the normal spoilage (1,250 × 0.02 = 25 units) and the abnormal spoilage (50 − 25 = 25 units) are omitted from the equivalent unit computations. Compared to Exhibit 14–4 for Example 14–2, the abnormal spoilage has increased the size of the quantity, efficiency, and volume variances. An implicit assumption that spoilage takes place throughout the production process increases the standard costs of the beginning and ending inventories (that is, the beginning and ending inventories include a proportionate allowance for normal spoilage). As a consequence of this assumption, the total costs in Exhibit 14–6 exceed the total costs in Exhibit 14–4.

Abnormal Spoilage Variance Account

Example 14–4

Assume the same situation as that in Examples 14–2 and 14–3, except that an allowance for normal spoilage is added to the standard cost per equivalent unit manufactured to compute the standard cost per equivalent good unit manufactured. Following the second approach, spoiled units are included in equivalent unit computations, a separate variance account is established for abnormal spoilage, and the cost of abnormal spoilage is assigned to this account. The standard cost per good unit manufactured is computed as follows:

Direct materials (2 square meters @ $10)		$20.00
Direct labor (1 hour @ $8)		8.00
Factory Overhead:		
Variable (1 direct-labor hour @ $1)	$1.00	
Fixed (1 direct-labor hour @ $2)	2.00	3.00
Total standard cost		$31.00
Normal spoilage allowance ($31 × 0.02)		0.62
Standard cost per equivalent good unit manufactured		$31.62

Assume that the March 19y0 activity is identical to that in Example 14–3, 1,250 good units and 50 spoiled units were completed. Spoilage is detected at the end of the production process.

A complete cost of production report for Example 14–4 is presented in Exhibit 14–7. The abnormal spoilage is 25 units [50 − (1,250 × 0.02)]. Instead of being included in other variance accounts, the cost of abnormal spoilage is assigned to a special account, Abnormal Spoilage Variance. Because the cost of

EXHIBIT 14–6 **Cost of Production Report: Abnormal Spoilage Included in Quantity, Efficiency, and Volume Variances**

Watson Company
Cost of Production Report
For the Month of March 19y0

FLOW OF WHOLE OR PARTIAL UNITS		
Beginning		400
Started		1,100
In process		1,500
Good units completed	1,250	
Spoiled	50	−1,300
Ending		200

EQUIVALENT UNITS MANUFACTURED	*Materials*	*Conversion*
Good units completed	1,250	1,250
Equivalent units in ending inventory	200	150*
Equivalent good units in process	1,450	1,400
Less equivalent units in beginning inventory	−400	−200†
Equivalent good units manufactured	1,050	1,200

* (200 units, ¾ complete)
† (400 units, ½ complete)

TOTAL COSTS TO BE ACCOUNTED FOR		
Beginning inventory at standard:		
Materials (400 × $20.40)	$ 8,160	
Conversion (200 × $11.22)	2,244	$10,404
Current costs assigned to Production Department:		
Materials (2,500 × $10)	$25,000	
Direct labor (1,350 × $8)	10,800	
Variable overhead	2,025	
Fixed overhead	2,925	40,750
Total costs to be accounted for		$51,154

ACCOUNTING FOR TOTAL COSTS		
Transferred out at standard (1,250 × $31.62)		$39,525
Variances:		
Materials quantity [$10(2,500 − 2,142*)]	$ 3,580U	
Labor rate [1,350($8 − $8)]	0	
Labor efficiency [$8(1,350 − 1,224†)]	1,008U	
Variable overhead spending [$2,025 − $1(1,350)]	675U	
Variable overhead efficiency [$1(1,350 − 1,224)]	126U	
Fixed overhead budget ($2,925 − $2,600)	325U	
Fixed overhead volume [$2,600 − $2(1,224)]	152U	5,866
Ending inventory at standard:		
Materials (200 × $20.40)	$ 4,080	
Conversion (150 × $11.22)	1,683	5,763
Total costs accounted for		$51,154

* Standard square meters allowed (2.04 × 1,050) = 2,142

† Standard direct-labor hours allowed (1.02 × 1,200) = 1,224

EXHIBIT 14–7 Cost of Production Report: Abnormal Spoilage Variance Account

Watson Company
Cost of Production Report
For the Month of March 19y0

FLOW OF WHOLE OR PARTIAL UNITS		
Beginning		400
Started		1,100
In process		1,500
Good units completed	1,250	
Normal spoilage	25	
Abnormal spoilage	25	−1,300
Ending		200

EQUIVALENT UNITS MANUFACTURED	*Materials*	*Conversion*
Good units completed	1,250	1,250
Normal spoilage	25	25
Abnormal spoilage	25	25
Equivalent units in ending inventory	200	150*
Equivalent units in process	1,500	1,450
Less equivalent units in beginning inventory	−400	−200†
Equivalent units manufactured	1,100	1,250

* (200 units, ¾ complete)
† (400 units, ½ complete)

TOTAL COSTS TO BE ACCOUNTED FOR		
Beginning inventory at standard:		
Materials (400 × $20)	$ 8,000	
Conversion (200 × $11)	2,200	$10,200
Current costs assigned to Production Department:		
Materials (2,500 × $10)	$25,000	
Direct labor (1,350 × $8)	10,800	
Variable overhead	2,025	
Fixed overhead	2,925	40,750
Total costs to be accounted for		$50,950

ACCOUNTING FOR TOTAL COSTS		
Transferred out at standard (1,250 × $31.62)		$39,525*
Variances:		
Abnormal spoilage (25 × $31)	$ 775U	
Materials quantity [$10(2,500 − 2,200)]	3,000U	
Labor rate [1,350($8 − $8)]	0	
Labor efficiency [$8(1,350 − 1,250)]	800U	
Variable overhead spending [$2,025 − $1(1,350)]	675U	
Variable overhead efficiency [$1(1,350 − 1,250)]	100U	
Fixed overhead budget ($2,925 − $2,600)	325U	
Fixed overhead volume [$2,600 − $2(1,250)]	100U	5,775

(*Continued*)

EXHIBIT 14–7 *(Cont.)*

Ending inventory at standard:		
Materials (200 × $20)	$ 4,000	
Conversion (150 × $11)	1,650	5,650
Total costs accounted for		$50,950

* An alternative presentation is

Transferred out:		
Standard cost of units manufactured (1,250 × $31)	$38,750	
Normal spoilage (25 × $31)	775	$39,525

abnormally spoiled units should not include an allowance for normal spoilage, the unit cost of each abnormally spoiled unit is the standard cost per equivalent unit manufactured rather than the standard cost per equivalent good unit manufactured. The abnormal spoilage variance is $775U ($31 × 25).

In making standard cost journal entries the debit (or credit for a favorable variance) to Abnormal Spoilage Variance is made at the end of the period. Even though the standard cost of a spoiled unit is known in advance under a standard cost system, the number of units of abnormal spoilage cannot be determined until the end of the period when normal spoilage is computed and deducted from total spoilage.

To further illustrate the operation of the abnormal spoilage variance account, standard cost journal entries for Example 14–4 are presented in Exhibit 14–8. Posting these journal entries, the activity in Work-in-Process appears as follows:

Work-in-Process

		Debit		Credit	
Beginning balance		$10,200	(2)	$39,525	Good units completed
Direct materials	(4)	22,000	(3)	775	Abnormal spoilage
Direct labor	(5)	10,000			
Variable overhead	(6)	1,250			
Fixed overhead	(7)	2,500			
		$45,950		$40,300	
				5,650	Ending balance
		$45,950		$45,950	
Ending balance		$ 5,650			

If abnormal spoilage is extremely large due to some extraordinary event such as a fire or accident, it should be disposed of as a loss. Under other circumstances, the balance in Abnormal Spoilage Variance is treated the same as the balance in any other variance account. On interim financial statements it is treated as an adjustment to inventory under the assumption that monthly variations from normal spoilage rates will net close to zero by the end of the year. At the end of the year any remaining balance is disposed of by prorating or by an adjustment to Cost of Goods Sold. If actual spoilage is less than normal spoilage, the resulting favorable variance is treated the same as any other favorable variance.

EXHIBIT 14–8 Standard Cost Journal Entries: Abnormal Spoilage Variance Account

	Debit	Credit
TIME OF PURCHASE		
1. Stores Control	$25,000	
Materials Price Variance [2,500($9 − $10)]		$ 2,500
Accounts Payable		22,500
AS GOOD UNITS COMPLETED		
2. Finished Goods Inventory	39,525	
Work-in-Process		39,525
END OF PERIOD		
3. Abnormal Spoilage Variance	775	
Work-in-Process		775
4. Work-in-Process	22,000	
Materials Quantity Variance	3,000	
Stores Control		25,000
5. Work-in-Process	10,000	
Labor Efficiency Variance	800	
Payroll Payable		10,800
6. Work-in-Process	1,250	
Variable Overhead Spending Variance	675	
Variable Overhead Efficiency Variance	100	
Variable Factory Overhead Control		2,025
7. Work-in-Process	2,500	
Fixed Overhead Budget Variance	325	
Fixed Overhead Volume Variance	100	
Fixed Factory Overhead Control		2,925

Normal Spoilage: Summary of Alternative Treatments

At this point it is useful to summarize the alternative treatments of normal spoilage under various cost systems. Under an actual or normal cost system, the cost of normal spoilage can be assigned to the good units by:

1. Omitting spoiled units from equivalent unit computations and spreading all costs over the good units.
2. Including spoiled units in equivalent unit computations and assigning their costs to Factory Overhead Control and the good units by way of the overhead rate.
3. Including spoiled units in equivalent unit computations with the cost of normal spoilage assigned to the good units completed and the costs of abnormal spoilage assigned to a loss account.

Under a standard cost system, an allowance for normal spoilage can be either:

1. Included in the standard inputs per equivalent good unit manufactured without establishing a separate abnormal spoilage variance account, or

2. Added to the standard cost per equivalent unit to compute the standard cost per equivalent good unit manufactured.

Following the first procedure, abnormal spoilage is included in the materials quantity, labor efficiency, variable overhead efficiency, and fixed overhead volume variances. When the second procedure is followed, spoiled units are included in equivalent unit computations, a separate variance account is established for abnormal spoilage, and the cost of abnormal spoilage is assigned to this account.

Disposal Value for Spoiled Units

In the previous examples it was assumed that spoiled or defective units are worthless. If they have a disposal value, the spoiled units may be accorded the same accounting treatment as scrap or by-products. Recall from Chapter 5 that the two most frequently cited practices are:

1. To not assign a cost to the by-product inventory and to record any by-product revenue as miscellaneous income at the time of sale.
2. To cost the by-product inventory at its net realizable value, deducting this amount from the cost of the main product at the time of production.

Applying these alternatives to spoiled units, the miscellaneous-income treatment is appropriate when the value of the spoiled units is uncertain or so small that it does not have a noticeable effect on inventory or profit. Under these circumstances, the short-cut accounting treatment of debiting Cash or Accounts Receivable and crediting Miscellaneous Income at the time of sale is justified. The spoiled units are not assigned an inventory cost, all costs of normal and abnormal spoilage are treated as in the previous examples.

If the sales value of the spoiled units is large enough to have a noticeable effect on inventory or profits, the net realizable value (selling price less any costs to complete and sell) of the spoiled units should be assigned to an appropriate asset account such as Spoiled Units Inventory. This reduces the net cost of the spoiled units and, consequently, the costs of normal and abnormal spoilage. In the absence of changes in the selling price of spoiled units between the time of production and sale, no profit or loss is recognized on the sale of spoiled units. At the time of their sale, Cash or Accounts Receivable is debited and Spoiled Units Inventory is credited. Costing spoiled units at their net realizable value is illustrated in the following example.

Example 14–5

Assume the same situation as the one presented in Example 14–4. The Watson Company anticipates a spoilage rate of 2 percent of the good units completed and has included an allowance for normal spoilage in its standard cost. However, for this example also assume the spoiled units can be sold for $5 each, they do not have any additional costs to complete or sell, and they are to be costed at their net realizable value.

The $5 disposal value reduces the net cost of a spoiled unit to $26 ($31 − $5), also reducing the standard cost of each equivalent good unit manufactured.

Direct materials (2 square meters @ $10)		$20.00
Direct labor (1 hour @ $8)		8.00
Factory Overhead:		
Variable (1 direct-labor hour @ $1)	$1.00	
Fixed (1 direct-labor hour @ $2)	2.00	3.00
Total standard cost		$31.00
Normal spoilage allowance [($31 − $5) × 0.02]		0.52
Standard cost per equivalent good unit manufactured		$31.52

On Watson's cost of production report and in the accompanying journal entries, Exhibits 14–9 and 14–10, costing the spoiled units at their net realizable

EXHIBIT 14–9 Cost of Production Report: Disposal Value for Spoilage

Watson Company
Cost of Production Report
For the Month of March, 19y0

FLOW OF WHOLE OR PARTIAL UNITS
Same as in Exhibit 14–7

EQUIVALENT UNITS MANUFACTURED
Same as in Exhibit 14–7

TOTAL COSTS TO BE ACCOUNTED FOR
Same as in Exhibit 14–7

ACCOUNTING FOR TOTAL COSTS		
Good units transferred out at standard (1,250 × $31.52)		$39,400*
Spoiled units transferred out at net realizable value (50 × $5)		250
Variances:		
Abnormal spoilage [($31 − $5) × 25]	$ 650U	
Materials quantity [$10(2,500 − 2,200]	3,000U	
Labor rate [1,350($8 − $8)]	0	
Labor efficiency [$8(1,350 − 1,250)]	800U	
Variable overhead spending [$2,025 − $1(1,350)]	675U	
Variable overhead efficiency [$1(1,350 − 1,250)]	100U	
Fixed overhead budget ($2,925 − $2,600)	325U	
Fixed overhead volume [$2,600 − $2(1,250)]	100U	5,650
Ending inventory at standard:		
Materials (200 × $20)	4,000	
Conversion (150 × $11)	1,650	5,650
Total costs accounted for		$50,950

* An alternative presentation is

Transferred out:

Standard cost of units manufactured (1,250 × $31)	$38,750	
Normal spoilage (25 × ($31 − $5))	650	$39,400

EXHIBIT 14–10 Standard Cost Journal Entries: Disposal Value for Spoilage

	Debit	Credit
TIME OF PURCHASE		
1. Stores Control	$25,000	
Materials Price Variance [2,500($9 − $10)]		$ 2,500
Accounts Payable		22,500
AS UNITS TRANSFERRED OUT		
2. Finished Goods Inventory	39,400	
Work-in-Process		39,400
3. Spoiled Units Inventory	250	
Work-in-Process		250
END OF PERIOD		
4. Abnormal Spoilage Variance	650	
Work-in-Process		650
5. Work-in-Process	22,000	
Materials Quantity Variance	3,000	
Stores Control		25,000
6. Work-in-Process	10,000	
Labor Efficiency Variance	800	
Payroll Payable		10,800
7. Work-in-Process	1,250	
Variable Overhead Spending Variance	675	
Variable Overhead Efficiency Variance	100	
Variable Factory Overhead Control		2,025
8. Work-in-Process	2,500	
Fixed Overhead Budget Variance	325	
Fixed Overhead Volume Variance	100	
Fixed Factory Overhead Control		2,925

value also reduces the amount of the abnormal spoilage variance. Note that the net realizable value of spoiled units is transferred out of Work-in-Process as a separate item. After posting the journal entries in Exhibit 14–10, the Work-in-Process T-account appears as follows:

Work-in-Process

		Debit		Credit	
Beginning balance		$10,200	(2)	$39,400	Good units completed
Direct materials	(5)	22,000	(3)	250	Net realizable value of spoiled units
Direct labor	(6)	10,000			
Varible overhead	(7)	1,250	(4)	650	Abnormal spoilage
Fixed overhead	(8)	2,500			
		$45,950		$40,300	
				5,650	Ending balance
		$45,950		$45,950	
Ending balance		$ 5,650			

If all 50 spoiled units were subsequently sold on account for $5 each, the following journal entry would be made:

9. Accounts Receivable	250	
Spoiled Units Inventory		250

REWORK

Rework is work performed on defective or spoiled units to make such units conform to quality standards. The treatment of rework costs, like the treatment of spoilage costs, depends on whether or not rework is expected under normal, efficient operating conditions. If spoilage and rework are not expected, rework costs might be assigned to a loss account as follows:

Spoilage Loss	XXX	
Stores Control		XXX
Payroll Payable		XXX
Factory Overhead Control		XXX

If spoilage and rework are expected, rework costs may be assigned to Factory Overhead Control and allowed for in the overhead application rate. This procedure results in all units bearing a share of rework costs. We can also establish standards for the number of units subject to rework. Use of such standards allows us to distinguish between normal and abnormal rework. To the extent that rework is normal, rework costs are assigned to Factory Overhead Control. The cost of abnormal rework is charged to a variance account such as Excessive Rework Variance or to a loss account.

STANDARD JOB-ORDER COSTING

Although standard cost systems are more frequently encountered in process-costing than in job-costing environments, standard job-order costing can be advantageously applied to a variety of production situations where standards can be developed for product components or production operations. Consider, for example, automobile assembly. Automobile dealers and buyers can order cars from the factory with various options such as a four- or a six-cylinder engine, automatic or standard transmission, heavy-duty or standard suspension, and so forth. Because the automobiles are not alike in all respects, each car built to buyer specifications is a separate job. Automobile companies are able to specify a price for each option in advance using standard production cost information developed for each option. Using standard job-order costing, the car is assigned a standard cost for each option as it moves through each operation or cost center where work is performed. Differences between the standard costs assigned to automobiles passing through a cost center and the total costs assigned to the cost center are assigned to variance accounts.

Similarly, standard job-order costing could be used by an automobile service center. Standards for materials and labor inputs and costs could be developed for various types of work such as repacking wheel bearings or installing a muffler.

This standard cost information could then be used for pricing various types of services in advance and evaluating performance.

In service industries, such as automobile service, cost information is not needed for inventory valuation. Nevertheless standard costs should be developed wherever possible to assist in bidding-for or pricing jobs, budgeting, and performance evaluation.

PRORATING VARIANCES

For external reporting purposes, standard costs are acceptable only if the resulting product costs approximate those resulting when an actual cost system is used. Companies using standard cost systems may sometimes find it necessary to adjust ending balances in inventory accounts and Cost of Goods Sold. This adjustment is accomplished by prorating the ending balances in variance accounts to inventory accounts and Cost of Goods Sold. To **prorate** a cost is to distribute it proportionally. The objective of prorating is to have the balances in all inventory accounts and Cost of Goods Sold approximate the balances that would have resulted if an actual rather than a standard cost system were used.

The steps necessary to prorate variances depend on whether the cost-element or the total cost method of prorating is used and when the materials price variance is isolated. Recall from Chapter 3 that the **cost-element method** of prorating bases the prorating on the percentage of a cost element (direct materials, direct labor, and factory overhead) in each affected account. The **total cost method** bases the prorating on the total cost in each affected account.

If the materials price variance is not isolated until the raw materials are used, the balance in Stores Control is at actual and no variances are prorated to this account. If the materials price variance is isolated at the time raw materials are purchased, the balance in Stores Control is at standard and a portion of the materials price variance must be allocated to Stores Control. Because the materials price variance is the only variance removed from the costs placed in Stores Control, the materials price variance is the only variance ever prorated to Stores Control.

To be theoretically correct, a portion of the materials price variance should also be prorated to the materials quantity variance before the materials quantity variance is prorated. Recall that the materials quantity variance is computed as $SP\ (AQ_U - SQ_A)$. If the materials actually cost more than the standard price, an unfavorable materials quantity variance, based on standard prices, understates the actual cost of the excess materials used. Conversely, if the materials used actually cost less than the standard price, an unfavorable materials quantity variance, based on standard costs, overstates the actual cost of the excess materials used. Analogous statements can be made for favorable materials quantity variances. In any case, a theoretically correct allocation of variances would have the materials price variance allocated to the materials quantity variance, affected inventory accounts, and Cost of Goods Sold. The adjusted materials quantity variance would then be allocated to affected inventory accounts and Cost of Goods Sold.

Theoretically Correct Method

The closest approximation to actual costs is obtained using the cost element method with the materials quantity variance receiving a proportionate allocation of the materials price variance. This theoretically correct method is illustrated in Example 14–6.

Example 14–6

The Kelly Company must prorate its 19x5 production variances to prepare December 31, 19x5, financial statements in accordance with generally accepted accounting principles. The following information is available concerning the standard cost of December 31 inventories, and net variances for the year:

	Stores Control	*Work-in-Process*	*Finished Goods Inv.*	*Cost of Goods Sold*
Account balances:				
Materials	$20,000	$ 3,400	$ 1,400	$ 15,200
Conversion		20,000	40,000	100,000
Total	$20,000	$23,400	$41,400	$115,200

Variances:	
Materials price (at purchase)	$ 5,000U
Materials quantity	10,000U
Labor rate	(2,000)F
Labor efficiency	0
Variable overhead spending	(1,800)F
Variable overhead efficiency	0
Fixed overhead budget	1,200U
Fixed overhead volume	3,000U

Exhibit 14–11 contains a schedule showing the theoretically correct prorating of variances. Because overhead is assumed to be applied on the basis of labor, only two cost elements are used, materials and conversion. For convenience the schedule is divided into three parts. The first part summarizes the standard costs that are to be used as a basis for prorating. The second part converts the costs into proportions. The third part contains the actual variance prorating schedule. The prorating in the third part is based on the proportional distribution of standard costs in the second.

Note that separate bases are used for allocating the materials price and the materials quantity variances. This is because the materials price variance is allocated to all inventory accounts, the materials quantity variance, and the Cost of Goods Sold, whereas the materials quantity variance is allocated only to Work-in-Process, Finished Goods Inventory, and Cost of Goods Sold. The materials quantity variance allocated to other accounts totals $11,000, including the preallocated balance of $10,000 plus $1,000 allocated from the materials price variance. Only the amount of the preallocated balance is prorated from other variance accounts.

The prorating schedule summarizes the information needed to make a journal entry assigning variances to inventory accounts and Cost of Goods Sold. For

EXHIBIT 14–11 Prorating Variances: Theoretically Correct Method

	Account					
	Stores Control	*Materials Quantity Variance*	*Work-in-Process*	*Finished Goods*	*Cost of Goods Sold*	*Total*
STANDARD COSTS						
Materials:						
All accounts	$20,000	$10,000	$ 3,400	$ 1,400	$15,200	$ 50,000
Excluding Stores Control & Materials Quantity Variance			3,400	1,400	15,200	20,000
Conversion			20,000	40,000	100,000	160,000
PORTION OF STANDARD COSTS						
Materials:						
All accounts	0.400	0.200	0.068	0.028	0.304	1
Excluding Stores Control & Materials Quantity Variance			0.170	0.070	0.760	1
Conversion			0.125	0.250	0.625	1
PRORATING OF VARIANCES						
Materials price (at purchase)	$ 2,000	$ 1,000	$ 340	$ 140	$ 1,520	$ 5,000
Materials quantity		(1,000)	1,870	770	8,360	10,000
Labor rate			(250)	(500)	(1,250)	(2,000)
Labor efficiency			0	0	0	0
Variable overhead spending			(225)	(450)	(1,125)	(1,800)
Variable overhead efficiency			0	0	0	0
Fixed overhead budget			150	300	750	1,200
Fixed overhead volume			375	750	1,875	3,000
Total	$ 2,000	$ 0	$ 2,260	$ 1,010	$ 10,130	$ 15,400

Example 14–6, the journal entry is as follows:

Stores Control	2,000	
Work-in-Process	2,260	
Finished Goods Inventory	1,010	
Cost of Goods Sold	10,130	
Labor Rate Variance	2,000	
Variable Overhead Spending Variance	1,800	
Materials Price Variance		5,000
Materials Quantity Variance		10,000
Fixed Overhead Budget Variance		1,200
Fixed Overhead Volume Variance		3,000

Total Cost Method

Many accountants think that sufficiently accurate results are obtained with the total cost method without an intermediate allocation of the materials price variance to the materials quantity variance. They argue that the increased accuracy obtained with the theoretically correct method does not justify the additional time and expense. The cost element method can be especially difficult to apply in multiple product companies.

Example 14–7

Exhibit 14–12 contains a schedule showing the total cost method of prorating variances. For convenience the schedule is again divided into three parts with the first part summarizing the standard costs used as a basis of prorating, the second converting the standard costs into proportions, and the third containing the actual prorating of variances. Because all variances are allocated on the basis of total standard cost in affected inventory accounts and Cost of Goods Sold, only total standard costs are listed.

Using the total cost method, the following journal entry is made to assign variances to inventory accounts and the Cost of Goods Sold.

Stores Control	500	
Work-in-Process	1,937	
Finished Goods Inventory	3,427	
Cost of Goods Sold	9,536	
Labor Rate Variance	2,000	
Variable Overhead Spending Variance	1,800	
Materials Price Variance		5,000
Materials Quantity Variance		10,000
Fixed Overhead Budget Variance		1,200
Fixed Overhead Volume Variance		3,000

EXHIBIT 14–12 Prorating Variances: Total Cost Method

	Account				
	Stores Control	*Work-in Process*	*Finished Goods*	*Cost of Goods Sold*	*Total*
STANDARD COSTS					
All accounts	$20,000	$23,400	$41,400	$115,200	$200,000
Excluding Stores Control		23,400	41,400	115,200	180,000
PORTION OF STANDARD COST					
All accounts	0.100	0.117	0.207	0.576	1
Excluding Stores Control		0.130	0.230	0.640	1
PRORATING OF VARIANCES					
Materials price (at purchase)	$ 500	$ 585	$ 1,035	$ 2,880	$ 5,000
Materials quantity		1,300	2,300	6,400	10,000
Labor rate		(260)	(460)	(1,280)	(2,000)
Labor efficiency		0	0	0	0
Variable overhead spending		(234)	(414)	(1,152)	(1,800)
Varaible overhead efficiency		0	0	0	0
Fixed overhead budget		156	276	768	1,200
Fixed overhead volume		390	690	1,920	3,000
Total	$ 500	$ 1,937	$ 3,427	$ 9,536	$ 15,400

Subsequent Periods

The operating characteristics of a complete standard cost system require that all transfers between inventory accounts and all beginning and ending balances in inventory accounts be stated in terms of standard costs. Accordingly, once financial statements are prepared and revenue and expense accounts closed, we must use a reversing entry to return the variances allocated to inventory accounts to their respective variance accounts. Assuming the total cost method was used to prorate Kelly Company's December 31, 19x5, variances, the appropriate reversing entry is as follows:

Materials Price Variance	2,120	
Materials Quantity Variance	3,600	
Fixed Overhead Budget Variance	432	
Fixed Overhead Volume Variance	1,080	
Labor Rate Variance		720
Variable Overhead Spending Variance		648
Stores Control		500
Work-in-Process		1,937
Finished Goods Inventory		3,427

The amount reassigned to each variance account is based on the information in Exhibit 14–12. The amount assigned to Materials Price Variance, for example, is determined by adding the amount of the materials price variance allocated to each inventory account:

Stores Control	$ 500
Work-in-Process	585
Finished Goods Inventory	1,035
Total	$2,120

Although the original price variance was $5,000U, only $2,120 is reversed to the price variance account. Variances allocated to the Cost of Goods Sold, $2,880 in this case, are not reversed because the balance in Cost of Goods Sold was reduced to zero by the end-of-the-year closing entry.

During the subsequent period, additional standard cost journal entries will be made to variance accounts and the balances in the variance accounts at the end of the year must be disposed of by closing them to the Cost of Goods Sold, writing them off as a loss, or prorating them. Assuming the 19x6 materials price variances amounted to $(500)F, the December 31, 19x6, balance in Materials Price Variance would be $1,620 [$2,120U beginning of year balance + $(500)F 19x6 year variance].

SUMMARY

Introducing standard costs into the formal accounting records simplifies record-keeping by permitting inventory and transfers between inventory accounts to be valued at standard. It also makes the computation of cost variances part of the accounting cycle. Because standard costs are acceptable for external reporting only if they approximate actual costs, it may be necessary to prorate cost variances.

Although standard cost systems are most often encountered in conjunction with process costing, they can be used in job-order systems whenever it is possible to develop standard costs for job components. Developing standard costs for job components also assists in bidding or pricing, planning, and control. Standard cost systems can also provide a significant reduction in recordkeeping costs where joint products are produced and there are beginning and ending inventories of work-in-process. Standard costs for joint products are examined in the appendix to this chapter.

APPENDIX Standard Costs for Joint Products

The examples of joint product costing presented in Chapter 5 assume that there are no beginning or ending inventories of work-in-process. When such inventories exist, the allocation of actual or normal joint product costs can become quite complex.

Example 14–8

The Ace Company manufactures joint products M and N in Department 1. Product M can be sold at the split-off point, but product N must be processed further in Department 2. During the first period of operation, 2,000 units of M and 4,000 units of N were produced in Department 1. Department 1 has no ending work-in-process inventory. However, all 4,000 units of N transferred to Department 2 are in the ending work-in-process inventory where they are one-half complete as to Department 2 conversion.

To allocate the joint costs of Department 1, using an actual or normal cost system, we must compute the relative net realizable values of 2,000 units of M and 4,000 units of N at the first split-off point. Although the value of the 2,000 units of M are easily determined, we encounter problems in determining the net realizable value of the 4,000 units of N. The net realizable value of N is not equal to the total sales value of 4,000 units less the current production costs in Department 2. These current Department 2 costs are for the manufacture of only 2,000 (4,000 × 0.5) equivalent units of conversion. The cost of completing the 4,000 units must be estimated.

To estimate the cost of completing 4,000 units of N, we multiply 4,000 by the cost per equivalent unit manufactured in Department 2 (current Department 2 conversion costs divided by 2,000 equivalent units manufactured). We then can estimate the net realizable value of 4,000 units of N at the first split-off point by subtracting the estimated cost of completing 4,000 units in Department 2 from the sales value of 4,000 units.

Example 14–8 concerned joint cost allocation with two products and a single split-off point. With several products and multiple split-off points, the complexity of joint cost allocation with beginning and ending inventories could become overwhelming if an actual or normal cost system were used.

The development of standard costs for joint products helps control costs and reduces the complexity of product costing. All transfers between inventory account are at standard, and all ending inventories are valued at standard. A useful approach to the development of standard costs for joint products is to estimate what the costs of each product would be in a hypothetical period where there were no beginning or ending inventories, operating conditions were normal, and production was efficient. Once these standards are developed, all transfers between inventory accounts can be made at standard, and any beginning or ending inventories can be valued at standard.

KEY TERMS

Abnormal spoilage
Cost-element method (of prorating)
Defective units
Normal spoilage
Prorate
Rework
Spoiled units
Standard cost
Total cost method (of prorating)

SELECTED REFERENCES

Boll, Dennis M., "How Dutch Pantry Accounts for Standard Costs," *Management Accounting* **64,** No. 6 (December 1982): 32–35.

Frank, Werner, and Rene Manes, "A Standard Cost Application of Matrix Algebra," *Accounting Review* **42,** No. 3 (July 1967): 516–525.

Livingstone, John Leslie, "Input-Output Analysis for Cost Accounting, Planning, and Control," *Accounting Review* **44,** No. 1 (January 1969): 48–64.

REVIEW QUESTIONS

14–1 Identify three uses of standard costs.

14–2 At what amount is inventory valued under a standard cost system?

14–3 At what cost are units transferred between inventory accounts under a standard cost system?

14–4 How soon can cost transfers between Work-in-Process and Finished Goods Inventory be made under a standard cost system?

14–5 Under what circumstances are standard costs acceptable for use in annual financial statements prepared in accordance with generally accepted accounting principles?

14–6 What is the appropriate theoretical treatment of a large unfavorable variance resulting from both unusual operating conditions and the use of tight standards?

14–7 Under standard process costing, why is it not necessary to compute the cost per equivalent unit?

14–8 Describe two alternative ways of assigning the cost of normal spoilage to the good units under a standard cost system.

14–9 Assuming an abnormal spoilage variance account is used, when is the entry assigning the standard cost of abnormal spoilage to this account made?

14–10 What are the alternative treatments of any end-of-year balance in Abnormal Spoilage Variance?

14–11 Describe two ways of accounting for spoiled units that have a disposal value.

14–12 Mention two alternative treatments of the cost of rework.

14–13 Identify alternative uses for standard costs in a service industry.

14–14 Following theoretically correct procedures to prorate variances, why is the materials price variance the only variance prorated to Stores Control and why does the materials quantity variance receive a portion of the materials price variance?

14–15 What argument is made in favor of the use of the total cost method of prorating variances without any intermediate allocation of the materials price variance to the materials quantity variance?

14–16 Why are variances previously prorated to inventory accounts reversed before the start of the next accounting period?

REVIEW PROBLEM

Standard Cost System: Equivalent Units: Spoilage Variance Account: Disposal Value for Spoilage

The Owen Company manufactures a product that has the following standard cost at a monthly volume of 10,000 units:

Direct materials (2 kilos @ \$15)	\$30.00
Direct labor (0.5 hours @ \$18)	9.00
Factory overhead:	
Variable (0.5 direct-labor hours @ \$12)	6.00
Fixed (0.5 direct-labor hours @ \$10)	5.00
Total standard cost	\$50.00
Normal spoilage allowance [(\$50 − \$10) × 0.25]	10.00
Standard cost per equivalent good unit manufactured	\$60.00

Owen's May 1 work-in-process inventory consisted of 3,000 units that were ⅔ complete as to materials and ⅓ complete as to conversion. Costs in process on May 1 were recorded at standard. During May the following events occurred:

- 20,000 kilos of raw materials were purchased at \$14 per kilo.
- 10,000 new units were started and 12,000 units were completed. The completed units included 10,000 good units and 2,000 spoiled units.
- 25,000 kilos of raw materials were placed in production.
- Actual May conversion costs were:

Direct labor (6,000 hours @ \$18)	\$108,000
Variable factory overhead	75,000
Fixed factory overhead	49,000
Total	\$232,000

ADDITIONAL INFORMATION

- Spoilage is detected at the end of the production process. The disposal value of spoiled units is \$10 per unit. The normal spoilage rate is 25 percent of the good units completed.
- Owen uses a standard cost system and maintains a separate abnormal spoilage variance account. The disposal value of spoiled units is assigned to Spoiled Units Inventory.
- Raw materials are costed at standard.
- The May 31 ending inventory was complete as to materials and one-half complete as to conversion.

REQUIREMENTS

a) Using standard costs, prepare a cost of production report for the month of May.

b) Prepare journal entries for all May activities affecting inventory accounts.

c) Prepare a T-account summarizing the activity in Work-in-Process.

The solution to this problem is found at the end of the Chapter 14 problems and exercises.

EXERCISES

14–1 Standard Cost System Journal Entries: No Equivalent Units or Spoilage

The Arbutus Co. Ltd. uses a standard cost system. The standard costs for its one product are as follows:

Materials (3 kilograms @ \$2.00)	\$ 6.00
Direct labor (2 hours @ \$10.50)	21.00
Variable factory overhead (2 hours @ \$3.00)	6.00
Fixed factory overhead (2 hours @ \$1.50)	3.00
Total standard cost	\$36.00

The fixed overhead rate was based on a monthly activity level of 2,000 direct-labor hours. The following information comes from the records for April 19x3:

Production	900 units
Materials purchased	5,000 kilograms @ \$1.95
Materials used	2,800 kilograms
Direct labor payroll	1,740 hours @ \$11.55
Actual factory overhead:	
Variable	\$5,500
Fixed	\$3,100

Raw materials are inventoried at standard.

REQUIREMENTS

a) Prepare journal entries for purchases and all manufacturing activities.

b) Prepare a T-account for Work-in-Process and post journal entries relevant to Work-in-Process.

c) Prepare a manufacturing performance report for April 19x3 activities. Be sure your report is based on responsibility-accounting concepts. It is not necessary to decompose variances into rate and use elements. (CGA Adapted)

14–2 Standard Cost Journal Entries: No Equivalent Units or Spoilage

The Halifax Co. Ltd. uses a standard cost system in accounting for its only product, "faxes." The standard currently in use is as follows:

Direct material (3 liters @ \$4.00)	\$12.00
Direct labor (½ hour @ \$7.00)	3.50
Variable factory overhead (½ hour @ \$6.00)	3.00
Fixed factory overhead (½ hour @ \$9.00)	4.50
Total standard cost	\$23.00

The fixed overhead budget is \$49,500 per month. Actual activity for November 19y7 was as follows:

- 40,000 liters of material were purchased for \$159,200.
- 10,000 units of faxes were produced.
- There was no inventory of work-in-process at the beginning or the end of November.

- 31,000 liters of material were issued to production.
- The direct-labor payroll was $35,616 for 4,800 hours.
- Actual overhead costs were $31,500 variable and $50,000 fixed.
- 8,000 units were sold on account at $40 per unit.
- Selling and administrative expenses of $60,000 were incurred.

REQUIREMENTS

a) Compute the level of activity used in arriving at the fixed overhead rate in terms of:
   1. Units of faxes
   2. Hours

b) Prepare all journal entries (except closing entries) required to record the described November activity using a standard cost system. Raw materials are inventoried at standard.

c) Prepare a T-account for Work-in-Process and post journal entries relevant to Work-in-Process. (CGA Adapted)

14–3 Standard Cost Journal Entries: No Equivalent Units or Spoilage

The Carberg Corporation manufactures and sells a single product. The cost system used by the company is a standard cost system. The standard cost per unit of product is given as follows:

Direct materials (one pound plastic @ $2.00)	$2.00
Direct labor (1.6 hours @ $4.00)	6.40
Variable factory overhead (1.6 direct-labor hours @ $1.875)	3.00
Fixed factory overhead	1.45
Total standard cost	$12.85

The overhead cost per unit was calculated from the following annual overhead cost budget for a 60,000 unit volume:

Variable factory overhead:	
Indirect labor (30,000 hours @ $4.00)	$120,000
Supplies—Oil (60,000 gallons @ $0.50)	30,000
Allocated variable service department costs	30,000
Total	$180,000
Fixed factory overhead cost:	
Supervision	$ 27,000
Depreciation	45,000
Other fixed costs	15,000
Total	87,000
Total budgeted annual overhead at 60,000 units	$267,000

The charges to the Manufacturing Department for November, when 5,000 units were produced, are given as follows:

Direct material (5,300 pounds @ $2.00)	$10,600
Direct labor (8,200 hours @ $4.10)	33,620
Indirect labor (2,400 hours @ $4.10)	9,840
Supplies—Oil (6,000 gallons @ $0.55)	3,300
Allocated variable service department costs	3,200
Supervision	2,475
Depreciation	3,750
Other (fixed)	1,250
Total	$68,035

ADDITIONAL INFORMATION

- The Manufacturing Department uses separate accounts for Variable Factory Overhead Control and Fixed Factory Overhead Control.
- The Purchasing Department normally buys about the same quantity of raw materials as are used for production during the month. In November, 5,200 pounds were purchased at a price of $2.10 per pound.
- Raw materials are inventoried at standard.

REQUIREMENTS

a) Prepare journal entries for purchases and all activity in the Manufacturing Department during November.

b) Prepare a T-account for Work-in-Process and post journal entries relevant to Work-in-Process.

c) Prepare a manufacturing performance report for the Manufacturing Department. Be sure your report is based on responsibility-accounting concepts. It is not necessary to decompose variances into rate and use elements. (CMA Adapted)

14–4 Spoilage and an Actual Job-Order Cost System

Harper Company's Job 501 for the manufacture of 2,200 coats was completed during August 19x2 at the following unit costs:

Direct materials	$20
Direct labor	18
Factory overhead (includes an allowance of $1 for spoiled work)	18
Total	$56

Final inspection of Job 501 disclosed 200 spoiled coats, which were sold to a jobber for $6,000.

REQUIREMENTS

a) Assume that spoilage is expected and spread over all jobs. What would be the unit cost of the good coats produced on Job 501?

b) Assume, instead, that the spoilage loss is attributable to exacting specifications of Job 501 and is charged to this specific job. What would be the unit cost of the good coats produced on Job 501? (CPA Adapted)

14–5 Rework and Disposal Value for Spoilage: Actual Job-Order Cost System

Simpson Company manufactures electric drills to the exacting specifications of various customers. During April 19x3, Job 403 for the production of 1,100 drills was completed at the following costs per unit:

Direct materials	$10
Direct labor	8
Applied factory overhead	12
Total	$30

Final inspection of Job 403 disclosed 50 defective units and 100 spoiled units. The defective drills were reworked at a total cost of $500 and the spoiled drills were sold to a jobber for $1,500.

REQUIREMENT

Determine the final unit cost of the good drills. (CPA Adapted)

14–6 Disposition of Variances

Standard costs are being used increasingly by modern manufacturing companies. Many advocates of standard costing take the position that standard costs are a proper basis for inventory valuation for external reporting purposes. Accounting Research Bulletin No. 43, however, reflects the widespread view that standard costs are not acceptable unless "adjusted at reasonable intervals to reflect current conditions so that at the balance sheet date standard costs reasonably approximate costs computed under one of the recognized (actual cost) bases."

REQUIREMENTS

a) Discuss the conceptual merits of using standard costs as the basis for inventory valuation for external reporting purposes.

b) Prepare general journal entries for three alternative dispositions of a $1,500 unfavorable variance where all goods manufactured during the period are included in the ending finished goods inventory. Assume a formal standard cost system is in operation, that $500 of the variance resulted from actual costs exceeding attainable standard cost, and that $1,000 of the variance resulted from the difference between the "ideal standard" and an attainable standard.

c) Discuss the conceptual merits of each of the three alternative methods of disposition requested in part (b). (CPA Adapted)

14–7 Prorating Underapplied Overhead: Total Cost Method

Worley Company has underapplied overhead of $45,000 for the year ended December 31, 19x2. Before disposition of the underapplied overhead, selected December 31, 19x2, balances from Worley's accounting records are as follows:

Sales	$1,200,000
Cost of goods sold	720,000
Inventories:	
Stores Control	36,000
Work-in-Process	54,000
Finished Goods Inventory	90,000

Under Worley's cost accounting system, over- or underapplied overhead is allocated to appropriate inventories and cost of goods sold based on year-end balances.

REQUIREMENT

Determine the amount Worley should report for cost of goods sold in its 19x2 income statement. (CPA Adapted)

14–8 Prorating Materials Variances: Cost Element Method: Raw Materials at Actual

You are given the following data for two independent situations:

	Situation	
	One	*Two*
Materials cost at standard:		
Stores Control	$10,000	$11,000
Work-in-Process	5,000	10,000
Finished Goods Inventory	35,000	20,000
Cost of Goods Sold	60,000	60,000
Variance:		
Materials Price	(6,000)F	$ 9,000U
Materials Quantity	2,000U	(4,500)F

The materials price variance is isolated when materials are placed in production.

REQUIREMENT

For each situation, prepare a journal entry allocating variances to the appropriate accounts. Use the cost element method.

14–9 Prorating and Reversing Variances: Total Cost Method

Presented is selected information taken from the records of the Golden Company on 12/31/y4:

At Standard:	
Stores Control	$10,000
Work-in-Process	30,000
Finished Goods Inventory	30,000
Cost of Goods Sold	90,000
Variances:	
Materials price (isolated at purchase)	$(5,000)F
Materials quantity variance	4,000U
Fixed overhead budget variance	(3,000)F

REQUIREMENTS

a) Prepare a schedule, in good form, prorating the variances. Use the total cost method. Round calculations to four decimal places.

b) Based on the preceding schedule, prepare a journal entry, recording the prorating of the variances.

c) Prepare the 1/1/y5 journal entry, reversing the 19y4 prorating of variances to inventory accounts.

PROBLEMS

14–10 T Standard Cost Journal Entries: Process Costing Without Spoilage
The Robbins Manufacturing Company has the following unit standard cost at an activity of 5,000 direct-labor hours per month:

Direct materials (2 kilograms @ $5)	$10
Direct labor (1 hour @ $6)	6
Factory overhead:	
Variable (1 direct-labor hour @ $2)	2
Fixed (1 direct-labor hour @ $5)	5
Total standard cost	$23

Budgeted monthly fixed factory overhead is $25,000.

On January 1, 19y9, work-in-process consisted of 800 units of product, 100 percent complete as to materials and 40 percent complete as to conversion with total assigned standard costs of $12,160. During January the following events occurred:

- 12,000 kilograms of raw materials were purchased on account at a net delivered cost of $58,800 and 11,000 kilograms were issued to production. Raw materials are inventoried at standard.
- 5,500 units of product were started.
- 5,700 direct-labor hours were used at a total cost of $35,340.
- 4,800 units were completed and transferred to finished goods inventory.
- Variable overhead costs incurred were $11,200; and fixed overhead costs incurred were $26,500.

The work-in-process inventory on January 31, 19y9, consisted of 1,500 units, 100 percent complete as to materials and 70 percent complete as to conversion.

REQUIREMENTS

a) Prepare a cost of production report for January. Use standard costs.
b) Prepare standard cost journal entries, isolating all variances and summarizing all activity in Work-in-Process.
c) Prepare a T-account that summarizes the activities in Work-in-Process.

14–11 T Standard Cost Journal Entries: Process Costing Without Spoilage
The Overland Manufacturing Company has the following unit standard cost at a normal monthly volume of 1,000 direct-labor hours:

Direct materials (1.5 kilograms @ $20)		$30
Direct labor (2 hours @ $5)		10
Factory overhead:		
Variable (2 direct-labor hours @ $2)	$4	
Fixed (2 direct-labor hours @ $3)	6	10
Total standard cost		$50

Budgeted monthly fixed factory overhead is $3,000.

On August 1, 19x1, work-in-process contained 200 units that were complete as to materials and ½ complete as to conversion. During August the following events occurred:

- 400 units of product were started.
- 600 kilograms of raw materials were placed in process. Raw materials are inventoried at standard.
- 1,000 direct-labor hours were used at $5 per hour.
- 500 units were completed and transferred to finished goods inventory.
- Variable overhead costs were $1,800; and fixed overhead costs were $3,000.

The work-in-process inventory on August 31, 19x1, consisted of 100 units that were complete as to materials and ⅘ complete as to conversion.

REQUIREMENTS

a) Prepare a cost of production report for August. Use standard costs.

b) Prepare standard cost journal entries summarizing all activity in Work-in-Process.

c) Prepare a T-account that summarizes the activities in Work-in-Process.

14–12 T Standard Cost Journal Entries: Process Costing and Spoilage Without Spoilage Variance Account

Addison Limited has the following unit standard cost:

Direct materials (2.4 packages @ $10)	$ 24.00
Direct labor (4.8 hours @ $5)	24.00
Factory overhead:	
Variable (4.8 direct-labor hours @ $2)	9.60
Fixed (4.8 direct-labor hours @ $20)	96.00
Total standard cost	$153.60

The standard inputs include a spoilage allowance of 20 percent. Spoilage is detected at the end of the production process. Budgeted monthly fixed factory overhead is $100,000.

On November 1, 19x3, work-in-process consisted of 100 units that were 80 percent complete as to materials and 50 percent complete as to conversion. During November the following events occurred:

- 3,000 packages of raw materials were purchased at $12 each and 2,700 packages of raw materials were issued to production. *Raw materials are inventoried at standard.*
- 1,300 units of product were started and 900 good units were completed. 180 units were spoiled.
- 4,850 direct-labor hours were used at $5 each.

- Actual variable and actual fixed factory overhead costs were $10,000 and $95,000, respectively.
- The ending work-in-process inventory was 80 percent complete as to materials and 50 percent complete as to conversion.

REQUIREMENTS

a) Prepare a cost of production report for November. Use standard costs.

b) Prepare standard cost journal entries, isolating all variances and summarizing all activity in Work-in-Process.

14–13 T Standard Cost Journal Entries: Process Costing and Spoilage Without Spoilage Variance Account

Kent Incorporated has the following unit standard cost:

Direct materials (1.1 sq. yds. @ $10)	$11.00
Direct labor (3.3 hours @ $5)	16.50
Factory overhead:	
Variable (3.3 direct-labor hours @ $4)	13.20
Fixed (3.3 direct-labor hours @ $1)	3.30
Total standard cost	$44.00

The standard inputs include a spoilage allowance of 10 percent. Spoilage is detected at the end of the production process. Budgeted monthly fixed factory overhead is $20,000. On February 1, 19w8, work-in-process consisted of 400 units that were 50 percent complete as to materials and 80 percent complete as to conversion. During February the following events occurred:

- 5,000 square yards of raw materials were purchased at $10 per square yard and 4,250 square yards were issued to production. *Raw materials are inventoried at standard.*
- 4,100 units of product were started and 3,800 good units were completed. 200 units were spoiled.
- 12,500 direct-labor hours were used at $5 each.
- Actual variable and fixed factory overhead costs were $51,216 and $21,000, respectively.
- The ending work-in-process inventory was 50 percent complete as to conversion and 80 percent complete as to materials.

REQUIREMENTS

a) Prepare a cost of production report for February. Use standard costs.

b) Prepare standard cost journal entries isolating all variances and summarizing all activity in Work-in-Process.

14–14 T Standard Cost Journal Entries: Process Costing and Spoilage with Spoilage Variance Account

The Montgomery Company manufactures a product that has the following standard cost:

Direct materials (1 square meter @ $10)	$10.00
Direct labor (1.5 hours @ $10)	15.00
Factory overhead:	
Variable (1.5 direct-labor hours @ $4)	6.00
Fixed (1.5 direct-labor hours @ $6)	9.00
Total standard cost	$40.00
Normal spoilage allowance ($40.00 × 0.05)	2.00
Standard cost per equivalent good unit manufactured	$42.00

Montgomery's April 1 work-in-process inventory consisted of 4,000 units that were 75 percent complete as to materials and 50 percent complete as to conversion. Costs in process on April 1 were recorded at standard. During April the following events occurred:

- 1,000 square meters of raw materials were purchased at a cost of $12,000.
- 6,000 new units were placed in process and 7,000 units were completed. The completed units included 6,500 good units and 500 spoiled units.
- 7,500 square meters of raw materials were placed in process.
- Actual April conversion costs were:

Direct labor (9,000 hours @ $10)	$ 90,000
Variable factory overhead	34,000
Fixed factory overhead	40,000
Total	$164,000

ADDITIONAL INFORMATION

- Spoilage is detected at the end of the production process.
- Montgomery uses a standard cost system for recordkeeping purposes. The standard is based on a production volume of 4,000 units per month. Budgeted monthly fixed factory overhead is $36,000.
- The standard cost includes an allowance for normal spoilage equal to 5 percent of the good output. The cost of normal spoilage is added to the cost of the good units. Abnormal spoilage is treated as a variance.
- Raw materials are inventoried at standard.
- The ending work-in-process inventory on April 30 contained 3,000 units that were 100 percent complete as to materials and ⅓ complete as to conversion.

REQUIREMENTS

a) Prepare a cost of production report for April. Use standard costs.

b) Prepare standard cost journal entries, isolating all variances and summarizing all activity in Work-in-Process.

14–15 T Standard Cost Journal Entries: Process Costing and Spoilage with Spoilage Variance Account

The Irwin Company manufactures a product that has the following unit standard cost:

Direct materials (2 units @ $5)	$10.00
Direct labor (1 hour @ $15)	15.00
Factory overhead:	
Variable (1 direct-labor hour @ $2)	2.00
Fixed (1 direct-labor hour @ $4)	4.00
Total standard cost	$31.00
Normal spoilage allowance ($31.00 × 0.10)	3.10
Standard cost per equivalent good unit manufactured	$34.10

Irwin's June 1, 19x2, work-in-process inventory consisted of 6,000 units that were 100 percent complete as to materials and 60 percent complete as to conversion. During June the following events occurred:

- 26,000 units of raw materials were purchased at $5.10 each.
- 20,000 new units of product were placed in process and 18,000 units of product were completed, including 15,000 good units and 3,000 spoiled units.
- 37,000 units of raw materials were placed in production.
- Actual June conversion costs were:

Direct labor (19,000 hours @ $15)	$285,000
Variable factory overhead	37,000
Fixed factory overhead	74,000
Total	$396,000

ADDITIONAL INFORMATION

- Spoilage is detected at the end of the production process.
- The standards include a normal spoilage allowance of 10 percent of good output. The cost of normal spoilage is a product cost. The cost of abnormal spoilage is treated as a variance.
- Raw materials are inventoried at standard.
- Fixed factory overhead is budgeted at $72,000 per month.
- The June 30 ending work-in-process was 80 percent complete as to materials and 50 percent complete as to conversion.

REQUIREMENTS

a) Prepare a cost of production report for June. Use standard costs.

b) Prepare standard cost journal entries, isolating all variances and summarizing all activity in Work-in-Process.

14–16 T Standard Cost Journal Entries: Process Costing and Spoilage with Spoilage Disposal Value

The Prentice Company manufactures a product that has the following unit standard cost:

Direct materials (3 lbs. @ $5)	$15.00
Direct labor (1 hour @ $10)	10.00
Factory overhead:	
Variable (1 direct-labor hour @ $2)	2.00
Fixed (1 direct-labor hour @ $5)	5.00
Total standard cost	$32.00
Normal spoilage allowance (($32 − $4) × 0.05)	1.40
Standard cost per equivalent good unit manufactured	$33.40

Prentice's April 1, 19y1, work-in-process inventory consisted of 500 units that were 100 percent complete as to materials and 80 percent complete as to conversion. During April the following events occurred:

- 4,000 pounds of raw materials were purchased at $4.90 each.
- 2,400 new units of product were placed in process and 2,110 units of product were completed, including 2,000 good units and 110 spoiled units.
- 7,200 pounds of raw materials were placed in process.
- Actual April conversion costs were:

Direct labor (2,100 hours @ $10.50)	$22,050
Variable factory overhead	4,100
Fixed factory overhead	10,750
Total	$36,900

ADDITIONAL INFORMATION

- Spoilage is detected at the end of the production process.
- Spoiled units have a disposal value of $4 each.
- The standards include a normal spoilage allowance of 5 percent of good output. The spoiled units are inventoried at their disposal value and the net cost of normal spoilage is treated as a product cost. The net cost of abnormal spoilage is treated as a variance.
- Raw materials are inventoried at standard.
- Fixed factory overhead is budgeted at $10,000 per month.
- The April 30 ending work-in-process inventory was 100 percent complete as to materials and 50 percent complete as to conversion.

REQUIREMENTS

a) Prepare a cost of production report for April. Use standard costs.

b) Prepare standard cost journal entries, isolating all variances and summarizing all activity in Work-in-Process.

14–17 T Standard Cost Journal Entries: Process Costing and Spoilage with Spoilage Disposal Value

Wesley Limited manufactures a product that has the following unit standard costs:

Direct materials (2 liters @ $5)	$10.00
Direct labor (1.5 hours @ $10)	15.00
Factory overhead:	
Variable (1.5 direct-labor hours @ $2)	3.00
Fixed (1.5 direct-labor hours @ $4)	6.00
Total standard cost	$34.00
Normal spoilage allowance (($34 − $2) × 0.02)	0.64
Standard cost per equivalent good unit manufactured	$34.64

Wesley's December 1, 19x4, work-in-process inventory consisted of 400 units that were 100 percent complete as to materials and 60 percent complete as to conversion. During December the following events occurred:

- 13,000 liters of raw materials were purchased at $4.75 each.
- 6,000 new units of product were placed in process and 5,110 units were completed, including 5,000 good units and 110 spoiled units.
- 12,500 liters of raw materials were placed in process.
- Actual December conversion costs were:

Direct labor (8,000 hours @ $10)	$ 80,000
Variable factory overhead	16,500
Fixed factory overhead	32,000
Total	$128,500

ADDITIONAL INFORMATION

- Spoilage is detected at the end of the production process.
- Spoiled units have a disposal value of $2 each.
- The standards include a normal spoilage allowance of 2 percent of good output. The spoiled units are inventoried at their disposal value and the net cost of normal spoilage is treated as a product cost. The net cost of abnormal spoilage is treated as a variance.
- Raw materials are inventoried at standard.
- Fixed factory overhead is budgeted at $30,000 per month.
- The December 31 ending work-in-process inventory was 100 percent complete as to materials and 50 percent complete as to conversion.

REQUIREMENTS

a) Prepare a cost of production report for December. Use standard costs.

b) Prepare standard cost journal entries, isolating all variances and summarizing all activity in Work-in-Process.

14–18 Cost of Production Report with Standard Costs and Spoilage Spread Over Good Units: Three-way Overhead: Journal Entries

The Bailey Company operates a standard cost system and has the following standard cost at a normal monthly volume of 2,000 direct-labor hours.

Direct materials (3 units @ $3)	$ 9
Direct labor (0.5 hours @ $6)	3
Factory overhead:	
Variable (0.5 direct-labor hours @ $4)	2
Fixed (0.5 direct-labor hours @ $10)	5
Total standard cost	$19

The April 1, 19x1, beginning work-in-process inventory consisted of 200 units that were complete as to materials and ¼ complete as to conversion. During the month, the following events occurred:

- 10,000 units of raw materials were purchased at $4 per unit.
- 5,200 units were started and 4,800 *good units* were completed. An additional 100 units were found to be spoiled at the end of the production process.
- 15,600 units of raw materials were used.
- 2,500 direct-labor hours were used at $6 per hour.
- Actual factory overhead costs totaled $32,000.

ADDITIONAL INFORMATION

- The April 30 work-in-process inventory consisted of 500 units that were complete as to materials and ½ complete as to conversion.
- Bailey does not compute an abnormal spoilage variance. An allowance for normal spoilage is incorporated into the materials, labor, and overhead standards.
- Because Bailey is unable to distinguish between actual variable and actual fixed overhead, a three-way analysis of overhead variances is used.

REQUIREMENTS

a) Prepare a cost of production report for the month of April. Use standard costs.

b) Prepare standard cost journal entries that will isolate all variances and summarize all activity in Work-in-Process.

c) Prepare a T-account summarizing the activities in Work-in-Process.

14–19 Reconstructing Standard Cost Journal Entries: Process Costing Without Spoilage

The internal auditors were due at 8 A.M. on Monday for their periodic review of the accounting records. Jim Velp, an eager new employee, was in the office Saturday morning posting summary journal entries for the previous week's work. Just as Jim completed the last transaction, a purple monkey swooped down on his desk and destroyed all but a few scraps of paper. After much effort, Jim managed to gather the following bits of information:

- Unit standard costs:

Direct materials	$ 3
Direct labor	4
Variable factory overhead (applied at 50% of direct-labor dollars)	2
Fixed factory overhead	1
Total	$10

- Work-in-Process (at standard):

Beginning (100% complete as to materials, 0% complete as to conversion)	$3,000
Ending (100% complete as to materials, 50% complete as to conversion)	1,300

- Finished Goods Inventory (at standard):

Beginning	$ 5,000
Ending	10,000

- Cost of Goods Sold (at standard) $80,000

- Variances:

Labor Efficiency	$2,500U
Variable overhead efficiency	?
Other	0

REQUIREMENT

Reconstruct all standard cost journal entries that affected Work-in-Process during the period.

14–20 Standard Job-Order Cost System

The Justin Company has recently installed a standard cost system to simplify its factory bookkeeping and to aid in cost control. The company makes standard items for inventory, but because of the many products in its line, each is manufactured periodically under a production order. Prior to the installation of the system, job-order cost sheets were maintained for each production order. Since the introduction of the standard costs system, however, they have not been kept.

The fabricating department is managed by a general supervisor who has overall responsibility for scheduling, performance, and cost control. The department consists of four machine/work centers. Each work center is staffed by a four-person work group or team and the centers are aided by a twelve-person support group. Departmental practice is to assign a job to one team and expect the team to perform most of the work necessary to complete the job, including acquisition of materials and supplies from the stores department and machining and assembling. This has been practical and satisfactory in the past and is readily accepted by the employees.

Information regarding production cost standards and products produced in March is as follows:

Unit Standard Costs	*Part* A7A	C6D	C7A
Material	$2.00	$ 3.00	$1.50
Direct labor	1.50	2.00	1.00
Factory overhead:*			
Variable	3.00	4.00	2.00
Fixed	0.75	1.00	0.50
Total	$7.25	$10.00	$5.00

* The departmental standard overhead rates are applied to the products as a percentage of direct-labor dollars. The labor base was chosen because nearly all of the variable overhead costs are caused by labor activity. The departmental overhead rates were calculated at the beginning of the year as follows:

	Variable (including indirect labor)	*Fixed*
Estimated annual cost	$360,000	$ 90,000
Estimated annual department direct-labor dollars	$180,000	$180,000
Overhead rate	200%	50%

Separate control accounts are maintained for variable and fixed factory overhead.

Analysis of the fabricating department account for March is as follows:

Costs to be accounted for:		
Materials:		
Job No. 307–11	$ 5,200	
Job No. 307–12	2,900	
Job No. 307–14	9,400	$17,500
Labor charges:		
Job No. 307–11	$ 4,000	
Job No. 307–12	2,100	
Job No. 307–14	6,200	
Indirect labor	12,200	24,500
Variable overhead costs (e.g., supplies and electricity)		18,800
Fixed overhead costs (e.g., supervisor's salary, depreciation, property tax, and insurance)		7,000
Total charges to department for March		$67,800
Accounting for costs:		
Completed jobs:		
Job No. 307–11 (2,000 units part A7A @ $7.25)	$14,500	
Job No. 307–12 (1,000 units part C6D @ $10.00)	10,000	
Job No. 307–14 (6,000 units part C7A @ $5.00)	30,000	$54,500

Variances transferred to factory variance accounts:		
Materials*	$ 1,500	
Direct labor†	1,300	
Variable overhead	9,000	
Fixed overhead	1,500	13,300
Total credits		$67,800

* Material price variances are isolated at acquisition and charged to the Stores Department.
† All direct labor was paid at the standard wage rate during March.

REQUIREMENTS

a) Justin Company assumes that its efforts to control costs in the fabricating department would be aided if variances were calculated by jobs. Management intends to add this analysis next month. Calculate all the variances by job that might contribute to cost control under this assumption.

b) Do you agree with the company's plan to initiate the calculation of job variances in addition to the currently calculated departmental variances? Explain your answer.

c) Prepare standard cost journal entries summarizing activity in the Fabricating Department. (*Hint:* There is no beginning or ending work-in-process inventory.)

(CMA Adapted)

14–21 T Prorating Variances: Total Cost Method

Presented is selected information taken from the December 31, 19x3, accounts of the Hall Company:

	Stores Control	*Work-in-Process*	*Finished Goods Inv.*	*Cost of Goods Sold*
December 31, 19x3 balances at standard	$5,000	$ 0	$15,000	$60,000
Variances:				
Materials price (at purchase)		$(2,000)F		
Materials quantity		3,000U		
Variable overhead spending		2,500U		
Fixed overhead budget		1,500U		

REQUIREMENTS

a) Prepare a schedule prorating the variances using the total cost method. Based on the schedule prepare the December 31, 19x3, prorating entry.

b) Prepare the reversing entry needed at the start of 19x4 to return the balances in the inventory accounts to standard.

14–22 T Prorating Variances: Total Cost Method

Presented is selected information taken from the December 31, 19x9, accounts of the Grit Company:

	Stores Control	*Work-in-Process*	*Finished Goods Inv.*	*Cost of Goods Sold*
December 31, 19x9 balances at standard	$5,000	$6,000	$15,000	$99,000

Variances:

Materials price (at purchase)	$ 500U
Materials quantity	(400)F
Labor rate	800U
Fixed overhead budget	200U
Fixed overhead volume	(600)F

REQUIREMENTS

a) Prepare a schedule prorating the variances using the total cost method. Based on the schedule prepare the December 31, 19x9, prorating entry.

b) Prepare the reversing entry needed at the start of 19y0 to return the balances in the inventory accounts to standard.

14–23 T Prorating Variances in Subsequent Periods: Total Cost Method

Presented is information on three groups of items for the Government Company, which has a July 1 to June 30 fiscal year:

1. June 30, 19x7, account balances at standard.
2. July 1, 19x6, variances after the beginning of the year reversing entry returning inventory accounts to standard.
3. Current year variances.

	Stores Control	*Work-in-Process*	*Finished Goods Inv.*	*Cost of Goods Sold*
June 30, 19x7 balances at standard	$100,000	$20,000	$80,000	$300,000

Variances:

	Beginning balance	*Current year*
Materials price (at purchase)	$ 6,000U	$ 40,000U
Materials quantity	20,000U	0
Labor rate	7,000U	(2,000)F
Labor efficiency	30,000U	40,000U
Variable overhead spending	(2,000)F	62,000U
Variable overhead efficiency	10,000U	2,000U
Fixed overhead budget	8,000U	22,000U
Fixed overhead volume	0	(50,000)F

REQUIREMENTS

a) Prepare a schedule prorating the June 30, 19x7, balances in the variance accounts using the total cost method. Based on the schedule, prepare the June 30, 19x7, prorating entry.

b) Prepare the reversing entry needed at the start of the 19x7–19x8 fiscal year to return the balances in the inventory accounts to standard.

14–24 T Prorating Variances in Subsequent Periods: Total Cost Method

Presented is information on three groups of items for Citizens Limited:

1. December 31, 19x6, account balances at standard.
2. January 1, 19x6, variances after the beginning of the year reversing entry returning inventory accounts to standard.
3. Current year variances.

	Stores Control	*Work-in-Process*	*Finished Goods Inv.*	*Cost of Goods Sold*
December 31, 19x6 balances at standard	$4,000	$2,800	$8,400	$16,800

Variances:

	Beginning balance	*Current year*
Materials price (at purchase)	$ 0	$ 200U
Materials quantity	(400)F	100U
Labor rate	0	(500)F
Labor efficiency	(200)F	(400)F
Variable overhead efficiency	(50)F	(100)F
Fixed overhead budget	750U	250U
Fixed overhead volume	0	300U

REQUIREMENTS

a) Prepare a schedule prorating the December 31, 19x6, balances in the variance accounts using the total cost method. Based on the schedule, prepare the December 31, 19x6, prorating entry.

b) Prepare the reversing entry needed at the start of 19x7 to return the balances in the inventory accounts to standard.

14–25 T Prorating Variances: Theoretically Correct Method

Presented is selected information taken from the December 31, 19x6, records of the Cummings Company:

	Stores Control	*Work-in-Process*	*Finished Goods Inv.*	*Cost of Goods Sold*
December 31, 19x6 balances at standard:				
Materials	$15,000	$20,000	$24,000	$ 36,000
Conversion		0	60,000	90,000
Total	$15,000	$20,000	$84,000	$126,000

Variances:	
Materials price (at purchase)	$ 4,000U
Materials quantity	5,000U
Labor rate	(2,000)F
Fixed overhead budget	1,000U

REQUIREMENTS

a) Prepare a schedule prorating the variances using the theoretically correct method. Based on the schedule, prepare the December 31, 19x6, prorating entry.

b) Prepare the reversing entry needed at the start of 19x7 to return the balances in the inventory accounts to standard.

14–26 T Prorating Variances: Theoretically Correct Method

Presented is information taken from the December 31, 19x5, records of the Wiley Company:

	Stores Control	*Work-in-Process*	*Finished Goods Inv.*	*Cost of Goods Sold*
December 31, 19x5 balances at standard:				
Materials	$5,000	$ 0	$19,800	$ 70,200
Conversion		0	30,000	130,000
Total	$5,000	$ 0	$49,800	$200,200

Variances:	
Materials price (at purchase)	$ 6,000U
Materials quantity	5,000U
Labor efficiency	(2,000)F
Variable overhead efficiency	(3,000)F

REQUIREMENTS

a) Prepare a schedule prorating the variances using the theoretically correct method. Based on the schedule prepare the December 31, 19x5, prorating entry.

b) Prepare the reversing entry needed at the start of 19x6 to return the balances in the inventory accounts to standard.

14–27 T Prorating Variances in Subsequent Periods: Theoretically Correct Method

Presented is information on three groups of items for the Boston Company:

1. December 31, 19x7, account balances at standard.
2. January 1, 19x7, variances after the beginning of the year reversing entry returning inventory account balances to standard.

3. Current year variances.

	Stores Control	*Work-in-Process*	*Finished Goods Inv.*	*Cost of Goods Sold*
December 31, 19x7 balances at standard:				
Materials	$3,000	$ 4,500	$ 0	$ 40,500
Conversion		8,000	0	92,000
Total	$3,000	$12,500	$ 0	$132,500

Variances:

	Beginning balance	*Current year*
Materials price (at purchase)	$(2,000)F	$ 6,000U
Materials quantity	6,000U	(4,000)F
Labor rate	0	2,000U
Labor efficiency	1,000U	0
Variable overhead efficiency	1,500U	0
Fixed overhead budget	0	(3,000)F
Fixed overhead volume	(2,000)F	2,000U

REQUIREMENTS

a) Prepare a schedule prorating the December 31, 19x7, balances in the variance accounts using the theoretically correct method. Based on the schedule, prepare the December 31, 19x7, prorating entry.

b) Prepare the reversing entry needed at the start of 19x8 to return the balances in the inventory accounts to standard.

14–28 T Prorating Variances in Subsequent Periods: Theoretically Correct Method

Presented is information on three groups of items for Goodyear Limited:

1. December 31, 19y3, account balances at standard.
2. January 1, 19y3, variances after the beginning of the year reversing entry returning inventory account balances to standard.
3. Current year variances.

	Stores Control	*Work-in-Process*	*Finished Goods Inv.*	*Cost of Goods Sold*
December 31, 19x3 balances at standard:				
Materials	$6,000	$ 0	$14,000	$ 56,000
Conversion		0	20,000	80,000
Total	$6,000	0	$34,000	$136,000

Variances:

	Beginning balance	*Current year*
Materials price (at purchase)	$ 4,000U	$ 2,000U
Materials quantity	(5,000)F	9,000U
Labor rate	0	(4,000)F
Labor efficiency	(2,000)F	0
Variable overhead efficiency	(3,000)F	0
Fixed overhead budget	0	1,500U
Fixed overhead volume	2,000U	0

REQUIREMENTS

a) Prepare a schedule prorating the December 31, 19y3, balances in the variance accounts using the theoretically correct method. Based on the schedule, prepare the December 31, 19y3, prorating entry.

b) Prepare the reversing entry needed at the start of 19y4 to return the balances in the inventory accounts to standard.

14–29 Alternative Inventory Costing Techniques

At a normal annual volume of 100,000 units, the Willamette Wood Company has the following unit standard costs:

Direct materials (2 square meters @ $2.50)	$ 5.00
Direct labor (½ hours @ $10.00)	5.00
Variable overhead (½ direct-labor hour @ $2.00)	1.00
Fixed overhead (½ direct-labor hour @ $2.00)	1.00
Unit standard cost	$12.00

During 19x8, 120,000 units were produced and 90,000 units were sold. There were no beginning inventories, and the only ending inventory was finished goods. Actual manufacturing costs were:

Direct materials	$ 660,000
Direct labor (62,000 hours)	580,000
Variable factory overhead	110,000
Fixed factory overhead	100,000
Total	$1,450,000

REQUIREMENTS

Determine the balance in Finished Goods Inventory under each of the following inventory valuation techniques:

a) Actual absorption costing

b) Actual variable costing

c) Normal absorption costing with variances written off

d) Normal absorption costing with variances prorated using the total cost method

e) Normal variable costing with variances written off

f) Normal variable costing with variances prorated using the total cost method

g) Standard absorption costing with variances written off

h) Standard absorption costing with variances prorated using the total cost method

i) Standard variable costing with variances written off

j) Standard variable costing with variances prorated using the total cost method

14–30 Standard Costs for Joint Products with Process Costing (Appendix) In Department I, Burton, Ltd., manufactures joint products A and B in the ratio of 2:1 from each unit of raw material X. In Department II, each unit of B is processed further into one unit of C and one unit of D.

During a normal month, 20,000 units of raw material X are processed and the following production costs are assigned to Departments I and II:

	Dept. I	*Dept. II*
Direct materials or transferred-in	$ 60,000	$?
Direct labor	40,000	80,000
Variable factory overhead	20,000	40,000
Fixed factory overhead	20,000	10,000
Total	$140,000	$?

The unit selling prices of A, C, and D are $3.00, $7.50, and $5.00, respectively.

REQUIREMENTS

a) Using relative net realizable value as a basis for joint cost allocation, develop unit standard costs of products A, C, and D.

b) Develop a standard cost for the components of each unit of B processed in Department II.

c) On July 1, the work-in-process inventory in Department II consisted of 1,200 units of B that were 50 percent complete as to conversion. During July, 15,600 units each of C and D were completed, and 500 units of B were destroyed in a freak accident when they were 50 percent converted. The July 31 inventory contained 1,600 units that were 25 percent complete. July production costs assigned to Department II were:

Transferred-in	$?
Direct labor	63,600
Variable factory overhead	31,800
Fixed factory overhead	10,500

Use the standard cost information developed in part (b) to prepare a cost of production report for the July activity in Department II. Separately account for the standard cost of units destroyed in the accident.

SOLUTION TO REVIEW PROBLEM

Budgeted fixed overhead:

10,000 units × 0.5 direct-labor hours × $10 per direct-labor hour = $50,000/month

a) **Owen Company**
Cost of Production Report
For the Month of May

FLOW OF WHOLE OR PARTIAL UNITS		
Beginning		3,000
Started		10,000
In process		13,000
Good units completed	10,000	
Normal spoilage	2,500*	
Abnormal spoilage	(500)*	– 12,000
Ending		1,000

* Normal spoilage (0.25 × 10,000)
Abnormal spoilage (2,000 – 2,500)

EQUIVALENT UNIT MANUFACTURED	*Materials*	*Conversion*
Good units completed	10,000	10,000
Normal spoilage	2,500	2,500
Abnormal spoilage	(500)	(500)
Equivalent units in ending inventory	1,000	500†
Equivalent units in process	13,000	12,500
Less equivalent units in beginning inventory	–2,000‡	–1,000§
Equivalent units manufactured	11,000	11,500

† (1,000 units, one-half complete)
‡ (3,000 units, two-thirds complete)
§ (3,000 units, one-third complete)

TOTAL COSTS TO BE ACCOUNTED FOR		
Beginning inventory at standard:		
Materials (2,000 × $30)	$ 60,000	
Conversion (1,000 × $20)	20,000	$ 80,000
Current costs assigned to Production Department:		
Materials (25,000 × $15)	$375,000	
Direct labor (6,000 × $18)	108,000	
Variable overhead	75,000	
Fixed overhead	49,000	607,000
Total costs to be accounted for		$687,000

ACCOUNTING FOR TOTAL COSTS	
Good units transferred out at standard (10,000 × $60)	$600,000
Spoiled units transferred out at net realizable value (2,000 × $10)	20,000

Variances:		
Abnormal spoilage (($50 − $10) × 500)	$(20,000)F	
Materials quantity [$15(25,000 − (2 × 11,000))]	45,000U	
Labor rate (6,000($18 − $18))	0	
Labor efficiency [$18(6,000 − (11,500 × 0.5))]	4,500U	
Variable overhead spending ($75,000 − $12(6,000))	3,000U	
Variable overhead efficiency [$12(6,000 − (11,500 × 0.5))]	3,000U	
Fixed overhead budget ($49,000 − $50,000)	(1,000)F	
Volume ($50,000 − $10(11,500 × 0.5))	(7,500)F	27,000
Ending inventory at standard:		
Materials (1,000 × $30)	$ 30,000	
Conversion (500 × $20)	10,000	40,000
Total costs accounted for		$687,000

b)

	Debit	Credit
1. Stores Control	$300,000	
Materials Price Variance [20,000($14 − $15)]		$ 20,000
Accounts Payable		280,000
2. Finished Goods Inventory	600,000	
Work-in-Process		600,000
3. Spoiled Units Inventory	20,000	
Work-in-Process		20,000
4. Work-in-Process	20,000	
Abnormal Spoilage Variance		20,000
5. Work-in-Process	330,000	
Materials Quantity Variance	45,000	
Stores Control		375,000
6. Work-in-Process	103,500	
Labor Efficiency Variance	4,500	
Payroll Payable		108,000
7. Work-in-Process	69,000	
Variable Overhead Spending Variance	3,000	
Variable Overhead Efficiency Variance	3,000	
Variable Factory Overhead Control		75,000
8. Work-in-Process	57,500	
Fixed Overhead Budget Variance		1,000
Fixed Overhead Volume Variance		7,500
Fixed Factory Overhead Control		49,000

c)

Work-in-Process

	Debit	Credit	
Beginning balance	$ 80,000	② $600,000	Finished goods
Abnormal spoilage	④ 20,000	③ 20,000	Spoiled units inventory
Direct materials	⑤ 330,000		
Direct labor	⑥ 103,500		
Variable overhead	⑦ 69,000		
Fixed overhead	⑧ 57,500		
	$660,000	$620,000	
		40,000	Ending balance
	$660,000	$660,000	
Ending balance	$ 40,000		

Part Four

SELECTED TOPICS FOR FURTHER STUDY

15

Special Decisions in Short-Range Planning

INTRODUCTION

SPECIAL DECISIONS BASED ON DIFFERENTIAL ANALYSIS

INFORMATION ACQUISITION DECISIONS

PRICING DECISIONS

SUMMARY

APPENDIX: PRODUCT MIX DECISIONS WITH TWO PRODUCTS AND MULTIPLE CONSTRAINTS

INTRODUCTION

MANAGERS ARE CONSTANTLY CONFRONTED WITH THE NEED TO MAKE DECIsions. These decisions include routine decisions such as scheduling production and special decisions such as accepting or rejecting a special order. Both quantitative and nonquantitative factors must be considered when making decisions. Accountants are often asked to provide and interpret the quantitative data needed for decision making.

The purpose of this chapter is to examine the proper use of accounting data in making special short-range planning decisions. In the process, we will consider a number of special decisions, including decisions about:

- Accepting or rejecting a special order
- Making or buying a part or service
- Continuing or discontinuing some aspect of operations
- Selecting the most profitable product mix or input mix
- Acquiring information
- Pricing products

Although we will be concerned primarily with the financial data needed for decision making, we will also consider nonquantitative aspects of decision making.

SPECIAL DECISIONS BASED ON DIFFERENTIAL ANALYSIS

In Chapter 8, the relationships that underlie cost-volume-profit analysis were considered. These relationships are also used in analyzing special decisions such as accepting or rejecting a special order and manufacturing or buying a part or component used in production. The key to these decisions is to analyze the differential effect of each of the alternatives on net cash inflows or profits. Profits are equivalent to net cash inflows if accruals and noncash expenses do not exist or are insignificant. In most special decisions, a change in the contribution margin or variable costs is analyzed. However, sometimes the fixed costs will differ between alternative courses of action. In that event, the differential fixed costs should be included in the analysis.

Special Order

Example 15–1

The National Calculator Company has developed the following predetermined unit cost estimates for its Model NC88 calculator at an annual production and sales volume of 25,000 units:

Direct materials	$15
Direct labor	10
Variable factory overhead	5
Applied fixed factory overhead	12
Variable selling and administrative	5
Fixed selling and administrative	2
Total	$49

A special order has been received from a foreign distributor to purchase 2,000 calculators at a price of $40 each. The company has sufficient excess capacity and does not currently compete in any foreign market. Accepting the special order will result in special selling and administrative expenses of $2,000. There will be no additional variable selling and administrative expenses. The alternatives are to accept or reject the order.

The relevant financial data are the differential revenues and costs associated with the order. The differential revenues are $40 per unit. The differential costs are direct materials, direct labor, and variable overhead incurred to produce the 2,000 units plus the additional selling and administrative expenses of $2,000. The direct materials, direct labor, and variable overhead total $30 ($15 + $10 + $5) per unit. Hence the unit contribution margin if the order is accepted is $10 ($40 − $30). The total contribution from the order of $20,000 ($10 × 2,000 units) far exceeds the contract's fixed costs of $2,000. Accordingly, the contract contributes $18,000 ($20,000 − $2,000) to common fixed costs and profits, and the opportunity cost of accepting the order is zero since no current sales will be lost.

The relevant costs to include in the analysis are the differential costs of the contract, not the allocated fixed costs. However, before National makes a decision to accept the order, it should consider many nonquantitative factors. A prime factor is the potential effect this order may have on the firm's long-run price structure and sales volume. Over an extended period of time, National must sell each unit for at least $49 in order to remain in business at a volume of 25,000 units with the current cost structure. Accepting the special order will increase profits and net cash inflows by $18,000 if it has no other effect on sales volume or prices. If accepting the order results in pressure to reduce all prices and/or in unhappy customers buying other products, it may not be wise to accept the special order.

Make or Buy

Example 15–2

National can reduce direct materials cost by $3 per unit and direct-labor costs by $2 per unit if it purchases component XR84 from a domestic supplier at a cost of $5.50 per unit. Accepting the order will permit National to rent one of its buildings to a local firm for $20,000 per year. Should National make or buy component XR84?

The differential cost of buying is an increase in unit costs of $0.50 [$5.50 − ($3.00 + $2.00)]. However, buying will result in additional revenues of $20,000 per year from renting the building. At a volume of 25,000 units, the additional profit from buying is $7,500 [$20,000 − ($0.50 × 25,000 units)].

Based on financial factors, it appears desirable for National to buy. But once again, other factors should be considered. How does the quality of the components compare? If National buys, is there an assured source of supply, or is the supplier merely trying to use some temporarily excess capacity? What are National's future plans? Beyond 40,000 units, it is more desirable to make component XR84, assuming our internal cost estimates hold at that volume. This is because the additional revenues of $20,000 are offset by a $20,000 increase in costs at 40,000 units ($0.50 × 40,000).

Service Department Decisions

A variation of the make-or-buy decision is the decision to *continue or discontinue* some aspect of operations, such as a service department. To make this decision, we must compare the differential costs of operating the service department with the cost of acquiring the necessary services outside the organization. This analysis is straightforward if there is only one service department or if the department does not receive services from other departments.

Example 15–3

National Calculator Company has only one service department, Cafeteria, which provides meals to production department employees. The cafeteria currently serves 20,000 meals per year. Current costs of operating the cafeteria include variable costs of $2 per meal and fixed costs of $10,000 per year. An outside firm has offered to contract for one year to provide the cafeteria service for $45,000 if no more than 22,000 meals are served. Should the offer be accepted?

The relevant costs are the variable and fixed costs that differ under alternative actions. If none of the fixed costs differs, the relevant costs of providing the service internally are $40,000 ($2 × 20,000). Since this is less than the cost of acquiring the service externally, National should reject the offer. If fixed costs can be reduced by more than $5,000, National should accept the offer. Total costs of acquiring the services externally would then be less than the costs of operating the cafeteria.

When a service department receives services from other departments, the analysis becomes more complex.

Example 15–4

Assume National has a maintenance department that provides services to the cafeteria as well as to the production department, and the offer from the outside firm specifies that these maintenance services will no longer be required. A review of maintenance work orders indicates that 10 percent of their 10,000 service hours per year are used by the cafeteria. Variable costs of the maintenance department are $6 per service hour and fixed costs are $30,000 per year. Should National now accept the offer from the outside firm to provide the cafeteria service?

Even if none of the fixed costs of the cafeteria or maintenance departments can be reduced, the offer is now attractive. The relevant costs are the variable costs of the cafeteria and the variable costs of the service hours maintenance provides the cafeteria:

Differential cafeteria variable costs	$40,000
Differential maintenance variable costs [$6 × 0.10(10,000 hours)]	6,000
Total cost savings	$46,000

Because the differential cost savings are greater than the cost of acquiring the service externally, the offer is acceptable.

Once again, nonquantitative factors such as the quality of the food and the dependability of the outside firm should also be considered. In addition, future demand for meals should be considered because this may affect future contracts if more than 22,000 meals are required in the future.

When there are more than two service departments and the departments provide reciprocal services, this type of analysis becomes impractical. We can use linear programming to analyze these decisions, but this approach is beyond the scope of this text.[1]

Segment Decisions

Product-line decisions are also based on differential analysis. The typical situation involves a decision to continue or discontinue a product, service, division, or department. The important financial data are the change in revenues and the change in costs that will occur if discontinuance takes place. Other important factors that may be difficult to quantify include the impact of discontinuance on the rest of the business and management's ability to use vacated facilities in an alternative manner. We considered these decisions in Chapter 9.

Product-Mix Decisions

When organizations produce two or more products, they may face capacity and resource constraints that prevent them from producing as many units of each product as they want. The decision as to which product to manufacture is based on differential analysis. This analysis was illustrated in Chapter 8 when a single constraint limits production. When an organization faces more than one constraint, linear programming is used to determine the optimal product mix. We present this approach in the appendix to this chapter.

---

[1] For additional information on using a linear programming approach see Robert S. Kaplan, "Variable and Self-Service Costs in Reciprocal Allocation Models," *Accounting Review* **48,** No. 4 (October 1973): 738–748; Robert Capettini, and Gerald L. Salamon, "Internal Versus External Acquisition of Services When Reciprocal Services Exist," *Accounting Review* **52,** No. 3 (July 1977): 690–696; Kenneth R. Baker, and Robert E. Taylor, "A Linear Programming Framework for Cost Allocation and External Acquisition When Reciprocal Services Exist," *Accounting Review* **54,** No. 4 (October 1979): 784–790; and René P. Manes, Soong H. Park, and Robert Jensen, "Relevant Cost of Intermediate Goods and Services," *Accounting Review* **57,** No. 3 (July 1982): 594–606.

Input-Mix Decisions

Just as organizations have to decide which products to manufacture, they may also have to decide what mix of inputs to use in manufacturing a product. In many production processes such as the manufacture of chemicals or petroleum products, a number of raw materials are mixed to obtain an acceptable product. When the proportions of each material in the mix can vary, the manager of the production process must decide which mix is most cost efficient. When only two materials can be used and there are few constraints placed on the mix, the problem is relatively simple.

Example 15–5

The Healthy Vitamin Company produces vitamins and dietary supplements. One of the products is a dietary supplement made from nuts for people who want additional potassium in their diet. The supplement is sold in one-quart cans and can be made from either almonds or pecans, but it must contain at least 2,000 milligrams (mg.) of potassium. Each cup of almonds contains 1,100 mg. of potassium, and each cup of pecans contains 600 mg. of potassium. Almonds cost $0.33 per cup and pecans cost $0.24 per cup. All other costs are independent of the mix of nuts.

Healthy Vitamin Company should produce the supplement to minimize the cost per milligram of potassium. The cost of potassium obtained from almonds is $0.0003 per mg. ($0.33/1,100 mg.), and the cost from pecans is $0.0004 per mg. ($0.24/600 mg.). To minimize costs, the supplement should be made from almonds. The cost of the almonds needed to provide 2,000 mg. of potassium is $0.60 ($0.0003 × 2,000 mg.).

If more than one constraint is imposed on the mix, the analysis becomes more complicated.

Example 15–6

In addition to the requirement that the potassium supplement contain 2,000 mg. of potassium, assume management also requires that 30 percent of the potassium be from pecans.

Since the cost of a milligram of potassium obtained from pecans is more than the cost of a milligram of potassium from almonds, Healthy Vitamin Company should use only the minimum amount of pecans. In this case, 600 mg. (0.30 × 2,000 mg.) will be obtained from pecans for a total cost for the nuts of $0.66:

Pecans	600 mg. × $0.0004 =	$0.24
Almonds	1,400 mg. × $0.0003 =	0.42
Total		$0.66

The requirement that pecans be included in the input mix has increased the cost of the nuts needed to produce a quart of supplement by $0.06 ($0.66 − $0.60).

When there are multiple possible inputs and multiple constraints placed on the mix, linear programming is used to find the optimal mix. The linear programming problem is formulated to minimize costs subject to the various constraints. We often use computers to solve linear programming problems, although we can use a graphic approach if there are only two inputs. The graphic approach is presented in the appendix to this chapter. An example of an input mix linear programming problem is presented in the appendix to Chapter 11.

INFORMATION ACQUISITION DECISIONS

It should be apparent from the preceding analyses that we need relevant information about each alternative before we can make a decision. Information, however, is a costly commodity.[2] In making a decision to acquire information that is not required for external reporting, management should carefully evaluate the potential benefits of the information and the costs of obtaining it. The potential benefits are derived from the ability to make decisions that result in greater net cash inflows and/or cost savings. The cost of information includes the cost of resources used in obtaining it and the cost of delaying a decision.

Example 15–7

Parks Manufacturing Company is considering renting one of their unoccupied buildings. A potential lessee has offered to rent the building for one year and agreed to pay for all occupancy costs such as utilities, maintenance, insurance, and property taxes. The lessee has proposed two possible rental contracts. The first contract (Contract 1) calls for an annual rental payment of $30,000 plus $50 per unit of product sold by the lessee. The other contract (Contract 2) calls for rent equal to $70 per unit sold. Both contracts specify that payment will be made at the end of the year. Assume that there are no other prospective lessees and Parks has no alternative use for the building.

Three alternatives (actions) are available to Parks: (1) rent the building and accept the first contract; (2) rent the building and accept the second contract; or (3) not rent the building. Because Parks has no other use for the building, the third alternative of not renting the building can be eliminated since there are net cash inflows under both alternatives 1 and 2 and only cash outflows for building maintenance costs under alternative 3. For this reason, the following analysis considers only alternatives 1 and 2 (Contracts 1 and 2).

Payoff Table

Parks should decide between the two possible contracts using the decision criterion of maximizing the expected cash inflows for the year. The weighted average of the possible cash inflows associated with an alternative is referred to as **expected value** (EV). The expected value of each contract, however, depends on the number of units the lessee sells. Consequently, to use this criterion, Parks must predict the demand for the lessee's product for the year.

Example 15–7 (continued)

Assume that Parks believes there is a 30 percent probability that demand for the lessee's product will be 1,200 units in the coming year, a 30 percent probability that demand will be 1,600 units, and a 40 percent probability that demand will be 2,000 units.

The possible events or outcomes that can occur for an alternative are referred to as **states of nature.** Parks' alternatives are to accept Contract 1 or accept Contract 2. The payoff Parks receives depends on both the action Parks takes and the event that occurs. If Contract 1 is accepted and demand is 1,200 units, the payoff to Parks will be $90,000 [$30,000 + $50(1,200 units)]. A **payoff table**

[2] The material and examples in this section are based on an article by Professor Robert W. Williamson, "Presenting Information Economics to Students," *The Accounting Review* **57,** No. 2 (April 1982): 414–419.

is used to enumerate the alternative actions management may take and the possible monetary outcomes of each. Exhibit 15–1 is a payoff table for Parks.

Expected Value

To determine the expected net cash inflow (expected value) for the year under each action, we multiply the possible payoffs for each action by the probability of that payoff occurring and sum those products. The probability of each payoff is the same as the probability of the event leading to that payoff. In equation form,

$$EV_A = \sum_{i=1}^{n} P_i O_i \tag{15–1}$$

where

EV_A = Expected value of action A
P_i = Probability of event i
O_i = Outcome (payoff) if event i occurs
$\Sigma P_i = 1$

Example 15–7 (continued)

Using the data in Exhibit 15–1 and Eq. 15–1, the expected value of action A1, accepting Contract 1, is $112,000:

$$EV_{A1} = 0.30(\$90{,}000) + 0.30(\$110{,}000) + 0.40(\$130{,}000) = \underline{\underline{\$112{,}000}}$$

For action A2, accepting Contract 2, the expected value is $114,800:

$$EV_{A2} = 0.30(\$84{,}000) + 0.30(\$112{,}000) + 0.40(\$140{,}000) = \underline{\underline{\$114{,}800}}$$

For convenience these amounts are placed to the right of the payoff table.

Using the decision criterion of maximizing expected value, Parks should accept Contract 2. Note that the actual payoff will not be the same as the expected value. If Contract 1 were accepted, the actual payoff will be $90,000, $110,000, or $130,000, depending on which event occurs. Likewise, under Contract 2, the actual payoff will be $84,000, $112,000, or $140,000, not the expected value of $114,800.

Conditional Loss

As shown in Exhibit 15–1, if Parks accepts Contract 2 and demand is 1,600 or 2,000 units, the payoff is greater than it would have been under Contract 1. However, if demand is only 1,200 units. Parks would have been better off

EXHIBIT 15–1 Payoff Table

	Event (Probability)			
	Demand = 1,200 (0.30)	*Demand = 1,600 (0.30)*	*Demand = 2,000 (0.40)*	*Expected value*
Actions:				
A1: Accept Contract 1	$90,000	$110,000	$130,000	$112,000
A2: Accept Contract 2	84,000	112,000	140,000	114,800

accepting Contract 1. By accepting Contract 2, Parks will not have maximized net cash inflow when demand is 1,200 units. This loss is referred to as a cost of prediction error or conditional loss. For each event a **cost of prediction error** or a **conditional loss** is determined as the difference between the payoff of the best action and the payoff of the chosen action.

Example 15–8

The conditional loss to Parks of accepting Contract 2 when demand is 1,200 units is $6,000 ($90,000 − $84,000). The conditional loss of accepting Contract 1 when demand is 1,200 units is $0 ($90,000 − $90,000). Exhibit 15–2 shows the conditional loss for each action when the specific event occurs.

As shown in Exhibit 15–2, a conditional loss can be zero but never less than zero. This occurs because it is calculated for each action and event as the difference between the payoff of the best action and the payoff of the chosen action. Since the payoff of the chosen action can be less than or equal to, but never greater than, the payoff of the best action, negative losses are not possible.

Expected Payoff With Perfect Information

The **expected payoff with perfect information** is the sum of the products of the payoffs of the best action for each event and the probability of that event. In equation form,

$$\text{Expected payoff with perfect information} = \sum_{i=1}^{n} P_i O_i \qquad (15\text{–}2)$$

where

P_i = probability of event i
O_i = outcome (payoff) of the best alternative under event i
$\Sigma P_i = 1$

Example 15–9

If Parks could predict the demand for the lessee's product perfectly, they would select Contract 1 when sales are 1,200 units and Contract 2 when sales are 1,600 or 2,000 units. This gives an expected payoff with perfect information of $116,600 [(0.30 × $90,000) + (0.30 × $112,000) + (0.40 + $140,000)].

Note that the expected payoff with perfect information, $116,600, is not the actual payoff of any action with any event. It is simply the expected value of the payoffs if Parks had perfect information. It may help you understand the concept of expected payoff with perfect information to think of what the pay-

EXHIBIT 15–2 Conditional Loss Table

	Event (Probability)			
	Demand = 1,200 (0.30)	*Demand = 1,600 (0.30)*	*Demand = 2,000 (0.40)*	*Expected value*
Actions:				
A1: Accept Contract 1	$ 0	$2,000	$10,000	$4,600
A2: Accept Contract 2	6,000	0	0	1,800

off would be over ten years with the given probabilities for each event. Over a ten-year period, demand will be 1,200 units during three years [10 years × 0.30]; 1,600 units during three years [10 years × 0.30]; and 2,000 units during four years [10 years × 0.40]. With perfect information, Parks would select Contract 1 when demand is 1,200 units and Contract 2 when demand is 1,600 or 2,000 units. This gives an average yearly payoff of $116,600 {[(3 years × $90,000) + (3 years × $112,000) + (4 years × $140,000)] ÷ 10 years}.

Expected Value of Perfect Information

The **expected value of perfect information** (EVPI) is the difference between the expected payoff with perfect information and the expected value of the best action given current information. It represents the maximum amount a manager would be willing to pay for additional information.

Example 15–10

For Parks Manufacturing Company, the expected value of perfect information (EVPI) is $1,800:

Expected payoff with perfect information	$116,600
Expected value of best action (Action A2)	−114,800
Expected value of perfect information (EVPI)	$ 1,800

Parks would be willing to pay a maximum of $1,800 to learn the actual demand of the lessee's product before selecting a contract. Although the conditional losses as shown in Exhibit 15–2 exceed this amount, we calculate the conditional losses without considering the probabilities of the various events occurring. When we consider the probabilities of the events, the expected value of the best action can only be increased by $1,800 even with perfect information. We can also calculate the EVPI from the data in Exhibit 15–2 by multiplying the conditional losses of the best action, A2, by the related probabilities and summing.

Example 15–11

For Parks, the EVPI calculated using conditional losses of Action A2 is $1,800:

$$\text{EVPI} = 0.30(\$6{,}000) + 0.30(\$0) + 0.40(\$0) = \underline{\underline{\$1{,}800}}$$

Note that the expected value or conditional losses of the best action must be used to determine the EVPI.

Revising Probabilities Using Sample Information

Although a decision maker can usually increase the expected value of a decision by obtaining perfect information, in most cases perfect information is not available. Instead, the decision maker must decide whether additional information that is less than perfect will increase the expected value and how much he or she is willing to pay for this additional information. When additional information can be obtained, but it is less than perfect, it has value if it increases expected value or, alternatively, if it reduces an expected loss. In other words, the information is valuable if it reduces the probability of a wrong decision.

Example 15–12

Parks Manufacturing Company has access to a consultant who will offer advice about the potential demand for the lessee's product. Assume Parks knows from prior experience that the consultant is correct 80 percent of the time. The consultant can provide three possible reports:

Report 1 (R1): Pessimistic report, i.e., demand = 1,200 units
Report 2 (R2): Neutral report, i.e., demand = 1,600 units
Report 3 (R3): Optimistic report, i.e., demand = 2,000 units

If the consultant is correct 80 percent of the time, he or she will issue Report 1 in 80 percent of the cases where demand is 1,200 units. Likewise, Report 2 will be issued in 80 percent of the cases where demand is 1,600 units, and Report 3 will be issued in 80 percent of the cases where demand is 2,000 units. Assume that when the consultant issues an incorrect report (20 percent of the time), it is equally likely that the report will be either of the other two. For example, when demand is 1,200 units Report 2 will be issued 10 percent of the time and Report 3 will be issued 10 percent of the time.

The probability of the occurrence of an event given that another event has occurred is a **conditional probability.** In this example, the probabilities for the various types of reports are conditional probabilities because they depend on the actual demand that will occur. For each possible report given the demand, the conditional probabilities are summarized in Exhibit 15–3.

Once the conditional probabilities are known, the joint probabilities of the outcomes for demand and type of report can be determined. A **joint probability** is the probability of the joint occurrence of two events. The joint probabilities for the outcomes of demand and the type of report are calculated as the product of the probability of demand and the conditional probability of the report given the demand. In equation form,

$$P(DR) = P(R \mid D) \times P(D) \qquad (15\text{–}3)$$

where

$P(DR)$ = Joint probability of demand and report
$P(R \mid D)$ = Conditional probability of report given demand
$P(D)$ = Probability of demand

For Parks, the probability of the joint outcome of demand of 1,200 units and report 1 is 0.24 (0.80 × 0.30). The probabilities for the joint outcomes are shown in the tree diagram in Exhibit 15–4.

EXHIBIT 15–3 Conditional Probabilities of Reports Given Events

	Event		
	Demand = 1,200	*Demand = 1,600*	*Demand = 2,000*
Report:			
R1	0.80	0.10	0.10
R2	0.10	0.80	0.10
R3	0.10	0.10	0.80

EXHIBIT 15–4 Diagram for Joint Outcomes with Probabilities

Demand	Probability	Report	Conditional Probability	Joint Probability
1,200	0.30	R1	0.80	0.24
		R2	0.10	0.03
		R3	0.10	0.03
1,600	0.30	R1	0.10	0.03
		R2	0.80	0.24
		R3	0.10	0.03
2,000	0.40	R1	0.10	0.04
		R2	0.10	0.04
		R3	0.80	0.32

After we determine the joint outcomes and probabilities, we can calculate the probability of receiving each type of report from the consultant. The probability of each type of report is the sum of the joint probabilities for each type of report given the various demand levels.

Example 15–13

For Parks, the joint probability of Report 1 and demand of 1,200 units is 0.24. (See Exhibit 15–4.) Likewise, the joint probability of Report 1 and demand of 1,600 units is 0.03, and the joint probability of Report 1 and demand of 2,000 units is 0.04. The probability of receiving Report 1 is the sum of these probabilities or 0.31 (0.24 + 0.03 + 0.04).

Exhibit 15–5 shows the probabilities for each type of report. Note that these probabilities sum to 1.00 or 100 percent because the consultant must issue one type of report.

To determine if they want to purchase the consultant's report, Parks must now revise their probabilities for each demand level given the type of report. Using a statistical concept known as Bayes' Theorem, we can state that the revised probability of demand given a specific report is equal to the product of

EXHIBIT 15–5 Probabilities for Type of Report and Level of Demand

	Type of report			
	R1	*R2*	*R3*	*Total*
Level of demand:				
1,200	0.24	0.03	0.03	0.30
1,600	0.03	0.24	0.03	0.30
2,000	0.04	0.04	0.32	0.40
Probability of report	0.31	0.31	0.38	1.00

the conditional probability of the report given the demand and the probability of demand, divided by the probability of the report. In equation form,

$$P(D_i \mid R_j) = \frac{P(R_j \mid D_i)P(D_i)}{P(R_j)} \tag{15–4}$$

where

$P(D_i \mid R_j)$ = revised probability of demand i given report j
$P(R_j \mid D_i)$ = conditional probability of report j given demand i
$P(D_i)$ = probability of demand i
$P(R_j)$ = probability of report j

Example 15–14

For Parks, the revised probabilities of each level of demand for the lessee's product given a specific report from the consultant are shown in Exhibit 15–6. The 0.774 probability of demand of 1,200 units if Report 1 is received is calculated as follows:

$$P(D = 1{,}200 \mid R1) = \frac{P(R1 \mid D = 1{,}200)P(D = 1{,}200)}{P(R1)}$$

$$P(D = 1{,}200 \mid R1) = \frac{0.80(0.30)}{0.31} = \underline{\underline{0.774}}$$

The 0.774 probability tells us that the probability is 77.4 percent that demand will be 1,200 units if Report 1 is issued. Likewise, as shown in Exhibit 15–6, the probability is 77.4 percent that demand will be 1,600 units if Report 2 is issued, and the probability is 84.2 percent that demand will be 2,000 if Report 3 is issued.

EXHIBIT 15–6 Conditional Probabilities of Events Given Reports

	Event		
	Demand = 1,200	*Demand = 1,600*	*Demand = 2,000*
Report:			
R1	0.774	0.097	0.129
R2	0.097	0.774	0.129
R3	0.079	0.079	0.842

Example 15–15 Using the payoffs in Exhibit 15–1 and the probabilities in Exhibit 15–6, Parks can now determine the expected value of each contract depending on the type of report the consultant issues. These expected values are shown in Exhibit 15–7.

When the consultant issues Report 1, the expected value of Contract 1 is \$97,100 [(0.774 × \$90,000) + (0.097 × \$110,000) + (0.129 × \$130,000)] and the expected value of Contract 2 is \$93,940 [(0.774 × \$84,000) + (0.097 × \$112,000) + (0.129 × \$140,000)]. Thus Parks will select Contract 1 if Report 1 is received from the consultant. If the consultant issues Report 2, Parks will select Contract 2 with an expected value of \$112,896, and if the consultant issues Report 3, Parks will select Contract 2 with an expected value of \$133,364. Obtaining additional information from the consultant has allowed Parks to revise the expected value of each contract.

The expected payoff with imperfect information can now be calculated by adding the products of the expected payoff of the best action for each report and the probability of each type of report. Recall that $P(R1) = 0.31$, $P(R2) = 0.31$, and $P(R3) = 0.38$. The expected payoff with imperfect information is \$115,777:

$$0.31(\$97{,}100) + 0.31(\$112{,}896) + 0.38(\$133{,}364) = \underline{\underline{\$115{,}777}}$$

Expected Value of Sample Information

The **expected value of sample information** (EVSI) is the difference between the expected payoff with imperfect information and the expected value of the best action using only current information. In equation form,

$$\text{EVSI} = \begin{array}{c}\text{Expected payoff with}\\ \text{imperfect information}\end{array} - \begin{array}{c}\text{EV with current}\\ \text{information}\end{array} \qquad (15\text{–}5)$$

EXHIBIT 15–7 Payoff Table Given a Specific Report

	Event			
	Demand = 1,200	*Demand = 1,600*	*Demand = 2,000*	*Expected value*
Conditional probability of demand given R1	0.774	0.097	0.129	
Payoff: A1	\$90,000	\$110,000	\$130,000	\$97,100
A2	84,000	112,000	140,000	93,940
Conditional probability of demand given R2	0.097	0.774	0.129	
Payoff: A1	\$90,000	\$110,000	\$130,000	110,640
A2	84,000	112,000	140,000	112,896
Conditional probability of demand given R3	0.079	0.079	0.842	
Payoff: A1	\$90,000	\$110,000	\$130,000	125,260
A2	84,000	112,000	140,000	133,364

The EVSI represents the maximum amount that would be paid to obtain additional information that is not perfect.

Example 15–16

For Parks, the EVSI is $997 [$115,777 − $114,800]. Thus the most Parks would pay a consultant who is correct only 80 percent of the time is $977, not the expected value of perfect information of $1,800.

PRICING DECISIONS

Product pricing is one of the most important and complex decisions facing management. The salability of individual products or services is directly affected by such decisions. Also affected is the profitability, and even the survival, of the organization. We cannot hope to give a thorough treatment of this topic here. We can, however, introduce some basic concepts and emphasize the important role of costs in pricing decisions.

Pricing Policies and Pricing Decisions

Before embarking on a study of pricing decisions, it is useful to distinguish between pricing policies and pricing decisions. **Pricing policies** are statements on management's attitude toward pricing products and services. Policies do not determine prices, but they do set forth the factors to be considered in setting prices.[3] In establishing a pricing policy, management must consider the overall goals of the organization. Possible goals that directly affect pricing policy include profit maximization, obtaining a target profit or a target return on investment, and increasing market share. A firm may design a pricing policy to fill a hierarchy of goals. For example, a firm may want to achieve a target rate of return while increasing its market share.

Pricing decisions are the setting of specific prices for specific products or services. These decisions are made in the light of long-run pricing policies and current economic conditions. In the short-run a firm may have to sacrifice profit objectives in order to:

- Obtain the market share necessary for long-run profitability
- Dispose of obsolete inventory
- Keep its labor force employed and intact
- Meet the price of a competitor
- Respond to social and/or legal pressures

However, each time a break in policy is made, management should carefully evaluate the impact that the break is likely to have on the organization's overall goals.

Economic Approaches

A substantial portion of microeconomic theory is devoted to product pricing. In microeconomic theory the firm has a profit maximization goal and known cost

---

[3] Arthur V. Corr, "The Role of Cost in Pricing," *Management Accounting* **56,** No. 5 (November 1974): 15–18; 32.

and revenue functions. The basic shape of the revenue function depends on whether or not the firm is operating in a purely competitive market.

A purely competitive market has many sellers, none of whom can influence the market price. Under these circumstances the firm does not have a pricing decision. Because it can sell all its output at the market price, the firm would lose profits if it charged less. On the other hand, any attempt to sell above the market price would result in sales of zero units. Profits are maximized by producing and selling until marginal costs equal the market price.

In other unregulated market situations (oligopolistic and monopolistic competition), the firm does have a pricing decision. Typically the firm faces a downward-sloping demand curve for its final product; that is, an inverse relationship exists between price and demand. Demand increases as the selling price decreases. The downward-sloping demand curve causes the decreasing slope in the economist's revenue pattern illustrated in Exhibit 15–8(a).

In Exhibit 15–8(a), profit or loss is equal to the difference between total costs and total revenues. As illustrated in Exhibit 15–8(a) and (b), there is a profit-maximizing sales volume. In microeconomics this profit-maximizing sales volume occurs where marginal costs equal marginal revenues. See Exhibit 15–8(c). The optimal selling price, which will result in the optimal sales volume, is determined by finding the value of the demand or average revenue curve at the optimal sales volume. The determination of the optimal price[4] is illustrated in Exhibit 15–8(c).

---

[4] If we know the firm's total revenue and total cost functions, we can use calculus to find the optimal sales volume X and the selling price p. Assume the demand and total cost functions are as follows: Demand function: $X = 100{,}000 - 50p$. Total cost function: $T = \$300{,}000 + \$1{,}800X$. To find the price function, solve the demand function for p: Price function: $p = 2{,}000 - 0.02X$.

We find the total revenue function by multiplying the price function by the sales volume: Total revenue function: $R = 2{,}000X - 0.02X^2$.

Taking the first derivative of the total revenue and total cost functions, we obtain the marginal revenue and marginal cost functions: Marginal revenue: $MR = 2{,}000 - 0.04X$. Marginal cost: $MC = 1{,}800$.

Setting the marginal cost equal to the marginal revenue and solving for X, we find the optimal production and sales volume, 5,000 units. Substituting this volume in the price function, the optimal selling price is \$1,900. We can then determine total revenues, total costs, and the resulting profit to be \$9,500,000, \$9,300,000, and \$200,000, respectively.

An alternative approach to determining the optimal production and sales volume is to develop an equation for total profits π, take the first derivative of this equation, set the first derivative equal to zero, and solve for X:

$$\pi = 2{,}000X - 0.02X^2 - 300{,}000 - 1{,}800X$$
$$\frac{d\pi}{dX} = 2{,}000 - 0.04X - 1{,}800$$
$$0 = 2{,}000 - 0.04X - 1{,}800$$
$$X = 5{,}000$$

When using this alternative approach, we must take the second derivative of the profit function to ensure its slope is becoming negative:

$$\frac{d\pi^2}{dX^2} = -0.04$$

If the second derivative were positive, rather than negative, we might have inadvertently found a loss-maximizing, rather than a profit-maximizing, volume.

EXHIBIT 15–8 Economic Approaches to Product Pricing

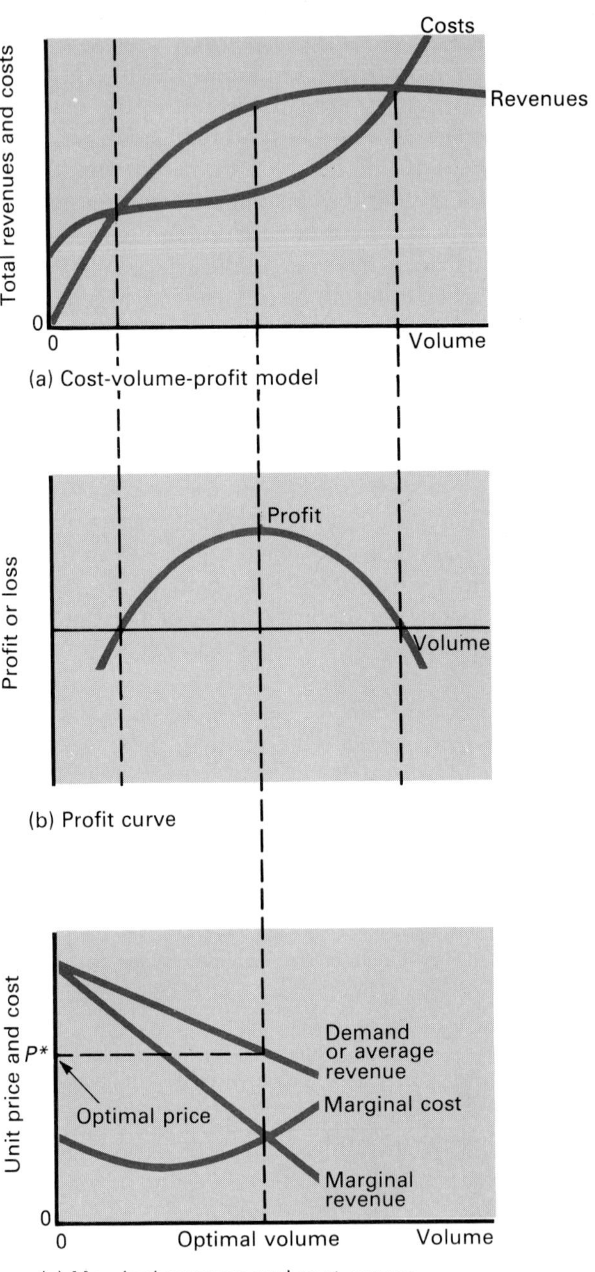

Although the economic approaches to product pricing are theoretically appealing, they are of limited practical value. Their primary weaknesses stem from the assumptions of profit maximization and known cost and revenue functions. Most for-profit firms attempt to achieve a target profit rather than maximum profit. One reason for this is an inability to determine the single set of actions out of all possible actions that will lead to profit maximization. Furthermore, management is more apt to strive to satisfy a number of goals (such as profits for owners, job security for employees, and being a "good" corporate citizen) than it is to strive for the maximization of a single profit goal. In any case, a firm must know the cost and demand functions for each and every product they sell in order to maximize profits. For most products this information either cannot be developed or it cannot be developed at a reasonable cost.

Cost-Based Approaches

Even though managers should be familiar with microeconomic pricing models, day-to-day pricing decisions are seldom derived by the direct application of such models. In practice most pricing decisions use formulas based on costs and desired profits.

The first step in the development of a pricing formula frequently is to determine a desired or target return on investment. **Return on investment** is computed by dividing income by total investment.

$$\text{Return on investment} = \frac{\text{Income}}{\text{Total investment}} \tag{15–6}$$

Example 15–17

Based on industry averages or past trends, management may decide that a particular plant or product should provide a 10 percent after-tax return on investment. If the income tax rate is 40 percent and $600,000 is invested in the plant or product, this target return on investment translates into a target before-tax profit of $100,000:

$$\text{Target after-tax profit} = 0.10(\$600{,}000) = \underline{\underline{\$60{,}000}}$$

$$\text{Target before-tax profit} = \$60{,}000/(1 - 0.40) = \underline{\underline{\$100{,}000}}$$

We can determine the unit selling price by solving the firm's profit equation for p:

$$\pi = pX - (a + bX)$$

$$p = \frac{\pi + a}{X} + b \tag{15–7}$$

where

p = Unit selling price
π = Desired or target before-tax profits
a = Fixed costs
b = Unit variable costs
X = Number of units

Example 15–18

Assume the product in Example 15–17 has annual fixed costs of $200,000, unit variable costs of $50, and an expected annual sales volume of 20,000 units. Using Eq. 15–7, the unit selling price is $65.

$$p = \frac{\$100{,}000 + \$200{,}000}{20{,}000} + \$50 = \underline{\underline{\$65}}$$

Besides basing target profit on a target return on investment, management might also base target profits on prior profits adjusted for anticipated changes in economic conditions.

Cost-Plus Pricing

In multiple-product companies, target profits are usually determined for the company as a whole. A standard markup, stated as a percentage of cost, is then determined for all products. The size of the markup percentage is determined by the cost base used in the computations. Although there are many alternative ways of determining the cost base, full cost and variable cost are frequently mentioned bases. Full cost includes all variable and fixed manufacturing, distribution, selling, and administrative costs. Variable cost includes only those costs that vary with the production and sale of a product or service.

When the markup is based on full cost it need only be large enough to provide for the desired profit. When the markup is based on variable cost, it must be large enough to provide for the desired profit and cover all fixed costs that have not been allocated to products:

$$\text{Full cost markup} = \frac{\text{Target profit}}{\text{Total predicted costs}} \tag{15–8}$$

$$\text{Variable cost markup} = \frac{\begin{matrix}\text{Target} \\ \text{profit}\end{matrix} + \begin{matrix}\text{Predicted unallocated} \\ \text{fixed costs}\end{matrix}}{\text{Predicted variable costs}} \tag{15–9}$$

Example 15–19

Winnipeg Wholesale, Ltd., has a target before-tax profit of $200,000. At the anticipated sales volume of each of its several products, the predicted variable and fixed costs for the coming year are $2,000,000 and $400,000, respectively. Assuming the fixed costs are common to all products, the markup percentage based on full cost is 8.33 percent and the markup percentage based on variable costs is 30 percent:

$$\text{Full cost markup} = \frac{\$200{,}000}{\$2{,}000{,}000 + \$400{,}000} = \underline{\underline{0.0833}}$$

$$\text{Variable cost markup} = \frac{\$200{,}000 + \$400{,}000}{\$2{,}000{,}000} = \underline{\underline{0.30}}$$

Using these markup percentages, a product with a variable cost of $10 and allocated fixed costs of $2 would be priced at $13 per unit. This selling price can be determined using either full cost or variable cost markup.

$$\text{Full cost markup price} = (1 + 0.0833) \times (\$10 + \$2) = \underline{\underline{\$13.00}}$$

$$\text{Variable cost markup price} = (1 + 0.30) \times \$10 = \underline{\underline{\$13.00}}$$

Note that the full cost markup requires the allocation of all fixed costs to total production. Unfortunately the allocation of such costs is imprecise at best. Management may, of course, modify this procedure so that certain common costs are not allocated. To the extent that this occurs, the markup percentage is increased.

Cost-plus approaches to product pricing have been widely criticized because they ignore demand, ignore the reaction of competitors, may lead to inappropriate decisions during periods of changing volume, and do not consider alternative uses of resources. The primary rationale for their use is the ease and speed of their application. When hundreds of different prices must be set in a short period of time, cost-plus pricing may be the only feasible approach. Additionally, managers threatened by legal action may feel secure using cost-plus pricing. They can argue that they are pricing all products in a similar manner in order to achieve a ''fair'' return on investment.

The Role of Costs in Pricing

The importance of costs in the pricing decision is supported by the results of a survey of Fortune 500 firms reported by Professor Gayle Rayburn.[5] Responding firms indicated that their most frequently used approaches are based on (1) cost, (2) meeting competition, or (3) a combination of cost and meeting competition.

At a minimum, costs are used to predict the profit consequences of various alternative prices. However, prices should not be based blindly on costs. Instead, costs should be used as a starting point in pricing decisions. This starting point should then be adjusted for other factors such as economic conditions and competitors' prices. Ignoring the case of a loss leader (a product whose price is set below cost to attract customers to the business), firms should always set prices high enough to cover variable costs. Except in distress situations, if a product or service cannot be marketed at its variable costs, a for-profit organization should not market it. In the long-run a firm must cover all of its costs and provide for a profit.

To make appropriate pricing decisions, management should be aware of the variable costs of a product or service and the standard markup required to provide a target profit and cover all unallocated costs. One way to do this might be to break the variable cost markup into two parts, one part to cover common fixed costs and another part to provide for a profit. For Example 15–19, this might be done as follows:

Variable cost	\$10.00
Markup to cover fixed costs (\$400,000/\$2,000,000 = 0.20)	2.00
Markup to provide a profit (\$200,000/\$2,000,000 = 0.10)	1.00
Price	\$13.00

[5] Gayle Rayburn, ''Marketing Costs—Accountants to the Rescue,'' *Management Accounting* **62** No. 7 (January 1981): 32–42.

Legal Forces Increase the Role of Costs

Legal forces such as Cost Accounting Standards Board (discussed in Chapter 6) pronouncements, governmental requirements that price increases be cost justified, and the requirements of the Robinson-Patman Act occasionally put the force of law behind cost-based approaches to product pricing. The **Robinson-Patman Act** prohibits discrimination in prices charged purchasers of commodities of like grade and quantity where the effect might be to lessen competition unless one of the following conditions holds:

1. The discriminatory lower price is in response to changing conditions in the market for or the marketability of the commodities involved (such as sales of discontinued products).
2. The discriminatory lower price is made to meet an equally low price of a competitor.
3. The discriminatory lower price makes only due allowance for specific cost differences.

Under the terms of this act, a refrigerator manufacturer could not charge different prices to a discount chain and a local appliance dealer unless one of these three conditions existed.

The Federal Trade Commission is charged with enforcing the Robinson-Patman Act. *In response to a complaint, the defendant must prove innocence.* If this cannot be done, the potential penalties include orders to cease and desist, treble damaged, fines, and jail sentences.

The cost accountant's primary responsibility under the act is determining the existence of differences in distribution and/or manufacturing costs. To ensure compliance with the act, the firm should analyze manufacturing and distribution costs before setting differential prices. Care should be taken to ensure that volume discounts reflect only the cost saving of long production runs, bulk shipments, and higher sales per invoice processed or unit of salesperson's time.

SUMMARY

Numerous decisions must be made in developing an organization's short-range plans. The criterion often used to make these decisions is to maximize expected net cash inflows or minimize expected cash outflows. We have focused on the development of relevant cost data for use in decision making, but we should also consider nonquantitative factors.

Specific decisions considered in this chapter include accepting or rejecting a special order, making or buying a part or component used in manufacturing, information acquisition, and pricing. Decisions involving the mix of products with constraining resources are considered in the appendix to this chapter.

APPENDIX
Product Mix Decisions with Two Products and Multiple Constraints

We introduced multiple-product cost-volume-profit analysis in Chapter 8 where we developed profit-volume graphs for multiple-product analysis. Examining how best to use a single resource that limits production we concluded: When a single factor, such as labor hours or machine hours, limits production, management should maximize the contribution per unit of the constraining factor in determining which product to manufacture and sell.

Although this decision criterion applies to product-mix decisions with one constraining resource, most organizations must operate with more than one constraining resource.

Under these conditions, the type of analysis presented in Chapter 8 becomes unwieldy. It may take considerable time to determine what the limiting factors are, and it will take even longer to determine the optimal production volume and mix. We can use linear programming to solve these types of problems. **Linear programming** is an optimization model used to assist managers in making decisions under constrained conditions where linear relationships can be assumed.

For two-product situations, we can graph the constraints and graphically analyze their impact. This **graphic analysis** is a form of linear programming used to determine the optimal product mix in situations involving only two products.

Example 15–20

Marion Company manufactures and sells two products, C and K. Monthly fixed costs are $18,000. The unit contribution margin of Product C is $6 and the unit contribution margin of Product K is $9. Marion's production is limited to 4,000 machine hours and 12,000 direct-labor hours per month. Each unit of Product C requires 0.5 machine hours and 2 labor hours. Each unit of Product K requires 1 machine hour and 2 labor hours.

If machine hours were the only constraining factor, Marion should maximize production of the product with the greatest contribution per machine hour. For Product C, the contribution per machine hour is $12 ($6/0.5 machine hours per unit), and for Product K, the contribution per machine hour is $9 ($9/1 machine hour per unit). Therefore, Marion would produce as many units of Product C as possible. With only the machine-hour constraint, maximum production of Product C is 8,000 units (4,000 machine hours/0.5 machine hours per unit of Product C).

A similar analysis can be made using the labor-hour constraint only. This analysis shows that Marion should produce Product K because it has a contribution per labor hour of $4.50 ($9/2 labor hours per unit), whereas the contribution per labor hour for Product C is only $3 ($6/2 labor hours per unit).

With one constraining factor, Marion can readily determine which product to manufacture to maximize profits. With more than one constraining factor, the constraints may interact in such a manner that some mix of the two products is desirable.

GRAPHIC ANALYSIS

Where there are only two products but multiple constraints, we can determine the optimal product mix from a graphic analysis. We first write the constraints as inequalities and then graph them to determine the feasible solution region.

Example 15–21

Using the symbol ≤ for "less than or equal to," the machine-hours constraint for Marion is:

$$0.5C + 1K \leq 4{,}000$$

and the labor-hours constraint is:

$$2C + 2K \leq 12{,}000$$

To be technically precise, two more constraints are added:

$$C \geq 0 \quad \text{and} \quad K \geq 0$$

The machine-hours constraint indicates any combination of Products C and K can be produced provided it does not require more than 4,000 machine hours. The labor-hours constraint indicates any combination of Products C and K can be produced provided it does not require more than 12,000 labor hours. The final set of constraints specifies that production must be greater than or equal to zero. Because these "nonnegativity" constraints are always present, they will be omitted from the presentation in this appendix.

The set of all feasible C and K values is determined by solving each constraint for its maximum C and K values and drawing lines on a graph connecting the maximum values of each variable. After all constraint lines are drawn, the universe of all production volumes is separated into feasible and infeasible regions.

Example 15–22

As noted in Example 15–20, the maximum production of Product C with the machine-hours constraint is 8,000 units. This quantity can be determined by setting K equal to zero in the equation representing the machine-hours constraint and solving for C:

$$\begin{aligned} 0.5C + 1K &= 4{,}000 \\ \text{if } K = 0\text{, then} \quad 0.5C &= 4{,}000 \\ C &= \underline{\underline{8{,}000}} \text{ units} \end{aligned}$$

Similarly, the maximum possible production of K given the machine-hours constraint is 4,000 units:

$$\begin{aligned} 0.5C + 1K &= 4{,}000 \\ \text{if } C = 0\text{, then} \quad 1K &= 4{,}000 \\ K &= \underline{\underline{4{,}000}} \text{ units} \end{aligned}$$

A similar analysis of the labor-hours constraint ($2C + 2K = 12{,}000$) gives maximum values of $C = 6{,}000$ and $K = 6{,}000$.

These maximum values for each constraint are then plotted on a graph and the points connected. See Exhibit 15–9(a). Since the constraints are "less than or equal to" some maximum, the feasible region includes all nonnegative values from the origin to the first set of enclosing lines.

Next, the set of all break-even points is illustrated by developing a total contribution equation, setting it equal to the fixed costs, solving for the extreme values of C and K, and drawing a line on the graph connecting these points.

Example 15–23

For Marion Company, the total contribution equation is:

$$\text{Total contribution} = \$6C + \$9K$$

Setting the total contribution equal to the fixed costs of $18,000 and solving for the maximum values of C and K gives $C = 3{,}000$ when $K = 0$, and $K = 2{,}000$ when $C = 0$. These points are then plotted on the graph and the points connected. See Exhibit 15–9(b).

When the extreme values for the total contribution line are calculated by setting the total contribution equal to fixed costs, the line connecting these points is the break-even isoprofit line because any point on this line yields zero profit (that is, total contribution equals fixed costs).[6] In linear programming, the contribution margin equation is called the **objective function** because the objective of the analysis is to maximize the value of this function.[7]

To determine the profit-maximizing product mix, a series of isoprofit lines must be drawn parallel to the break-even isoprofit line. Each **isoprofit line** shows mixes of the two products that yield identical profits. The optimal production of Products C and K is found where the isoprofit line farthest from the origin just touches a corner point on the lines enclosing the feasible region. In Exhibit 15–9(c) the optimal solution is 4,000 units of Product C and 2,000 units of Product K. If the labor-hours constraint did not exist, the

---

[6] An initial isoprofit line can also be plotted by selecting any arbitrary value, solving for the endpoints, and drawing a line connecting these points.

[7] In many applications, the objective of the analysis is to minimize the value of the objective function. In the typical minimization problem, the constraints represent conditions that must be filled and the coefficients of the objective function represent the variable costs of filling these conditions.

EXHIBIT 15–9 Graphic Analysis of Multiple Constraints

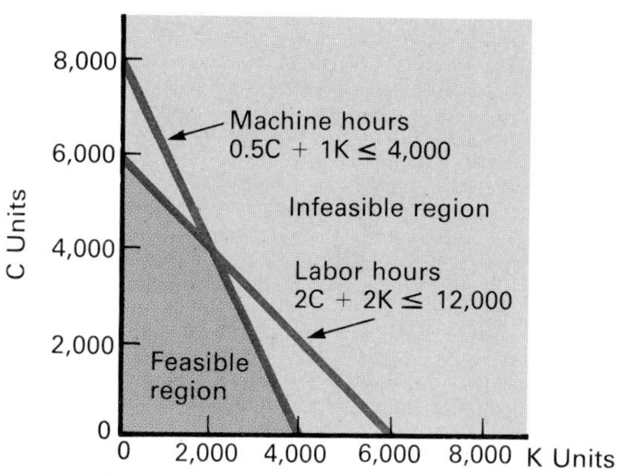

(a) Feasible and infeasible regions

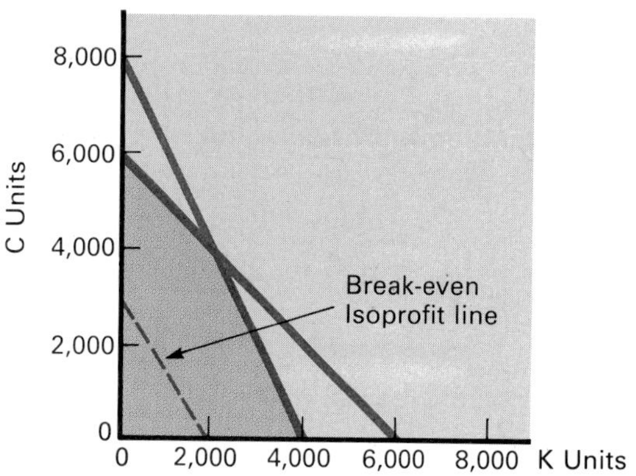

(b) Break-even Isoprofit line

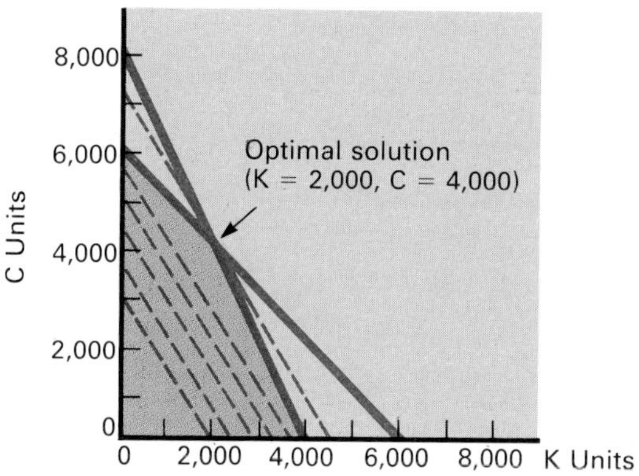

(c) Optimal solution

optimal solution would be 8,000 units of Product C and zero units of Product K, the same solution as found in Example 15–20. If the machine-hours constraint did not exist, the optimal solution would be zero units of Product C and 6,000 units of Product K.

The optimal solution results in a total contribution of $42,000 [(4,000*C* × $6) + (2,000*K* × $9)] and a profit of $24,000 ($42,000 − $18,000). This example has a unique solution. If the isoprofit lines had the same slope as one of the constraints enclosing the feasible region, there would be many solutions. For example, if the isoprofit line were parallel to the machine-hours line, all values on the machine-hours line between points (2,000; 4,000) and (4,000; 0) would provide identical profits.

If management felt they needed a minimum production of 5,000 units of Product K and specified that requirement in terms of a constraint, there would be no feasible solution. See Exhibit 15–10. One of the values of linear programming is its ability to indicate if management's plans are feasible. Conversely, if management specified that production of Product K should not exceed 5,000 units, it would not be a binding constraint. A **binding constraint** is a constraint that has an impact on the optimal solution. A **nonbinding constraint** is a constraint that does not have an impact on the optimal solution.

EXHIBIT 15–10 **No Feasible Solution (Arrows indicate direction of constraint.)**

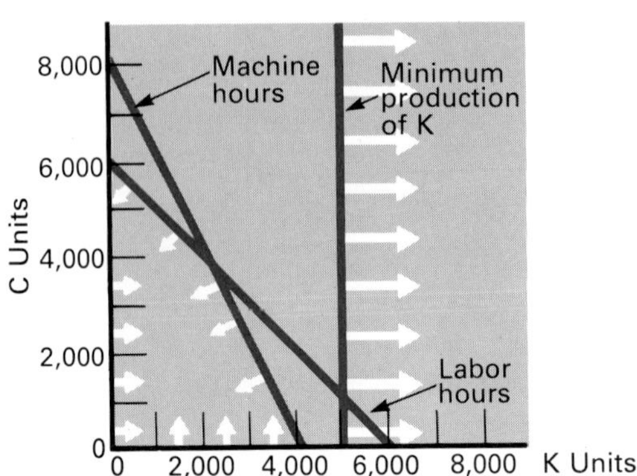

SIMPLEX METHOD

An important characteristic of linear programming problems that have a unique solution is that the solution is always found at a corner point of the feasible region. This feature allows them to be solved by a systematic mathematical procedure called the "simplex method." Although we could use the simplex method to solve simple linear programming problems by hand, most applications of linear programming techniques are solved with the aid of computer software versions of the simplex method. These software packages are readily available for both mainframes and microcomputers.

Example 15–24

The equations necessary to solve Marion's product mix problem on a computer are as follows:[8]

Objective function:
 Maximize $6C + 9K$
Constraints:
 Subject to:
 (1) $0.5C + 1K \leq 4{,}000$
 (2) $2C + 2K \leq 12{,}000$

For the optimal solution, the computer provides information on:

- The value of the objective function ($42,000)
- The product mix (C = 4,000; K = 2,000)
- The amount of each resource (constraint) used [Machine hours (1) = 4,000; Labor hours (2) = 12,000]
- Any unused capacity [Machine hours (1) = 0; Labor hours (2) = 0]
- The amount by which the value of the objective function would change if there were a one-unit change in the amount of each resource (constraint) available [Machine hours (1) = 6; Labor hours (2) = 1.50]

This last set of values is frequently referred to as "shadow prices," "the dual solution," or "opportunity costs." Their value will be zero for constraints that are not binding (that

[8] The actual formulation may vary depending on the installation and software program, but these basics are always present.

is, have excess capacity). If there is excess capacity, having one more or one less unit of capacity will not affect the optimal solution.

The **shadow price** of a resource is the amount by which total contribution (and profits) will change if there is a one-unit change in the available resource. For example, if one additional machine hour becomes available (that is, Marion can use 4,001 machine hours rather than 4,000 machine hours), the total contribution and profits will increase by \$6. As shown in Example 15–23 with 4,000 machine hours, the total contribution is \$42,000. The contribution resulted from a product mix of 4,000 units of Product C and 2,000 units of Product K. If 4,001 machine hours were available, the product mix will change because the machine-hours constraint is now

$$0.5C + 1K \leq 4{,}001$$

This causes the machine-hours constraint line on the graph to shift farther away from the origin, which changes the optimal production mix. Solving the problem with this new constraint gives a product mix of $C = 3{,}998$ units and $K = 2{,}002$ units.

This change in the solution increases the value of the objective function to \$42,006 [(3,998 × \$6) + (2,002 × \$9)], an increase of \$6 over the previous contribution.

Marion's shadow price of a labor hour is \$1.50, meaning that one additional labor hour will increase profits by \$1.50. The same type of analysis we used for machine hours will show this to be true. The new labor-hours constraint is

$$2C + 2K \leq 12{,}001$$

and the new optimal solution is $C = 4{,}001$ units and $K = 1{,}999.5$ units. This solution gives an objective function value of \$42,001.50 [(4,001 × \$6) + (1,999.5 × \$9)].

One question that might be asked now is: How much should Marion be willing to pay for an additional direct-labor hour? Since the variable costs used in calculating the objective function include the current cost of direct labor, the maximum Marion would be willing to pay for an additional hour is the current cost plus the shadow price of a direct-labor hour. If the current wage rate is \$6.00 per hour, Marion could pay up to \$7.50 (\$6.00 + \$1.50) for an additional hour. Any amount less than this maximum will increase total contribution and profits. If additional labor can be obtained only at a rate greater than \$7.50 per hour, we no longer need to consider the alternative of acquiring more of this resource.

An important limitation of shadow prices is that they are valid only for marginal analysis of binding constraints. They indicate the effect of one more or one less unit of a resource on the value of the objective function. The value of one additional labor hour may be \$1.50, but it is unlikely that the value of 6,000 additional hours will be \$9,000. Because other constraints exist, in this case machine hours, such an expansion will likely result in unused capacity.

SENSITIVITY ANALYSIS AND UNCERTAINTY

Although linear programming models are solved assuming that the objective function coefficients and technological coefficients are known with certainty, a major benefit of using such models to represent real-world phenomena is the low cost involved in determining the impact on the optimal solution of changes in these parameters. As noted in the appendix to Chapter 8, the manipulation of mathematical models to determine the impact of changes in the independent variables on the dependent variable is called **sensitivity analysis.**

In linear programming, sensitivity analysis is used to answer "what if?" questions about the effect of changes in parameters on the values of the objective function and the optimal product mix. These parameters include the objective function coefficients (including the unit selling price and unit variable costs which are used in determining the unit contribution margin), technological coefficients (such as the machine hours required to produce a unit of C and K), and changes in the value of constraints (such as the available direct-labor hours). Although this entire area is complex, you should be able to understand the major issues as they are applied to the examples in the remainder of this appendix.

Change in Constraint

Example 15–25

Marion is considering expanding its labor force so that a total of 18,000 labor hours are available each month. Because this is a permanent expansion, it will not increase unit variable costs, but it will increase fixed administrative costs by $1,000 per month.

A graphic analysis of the effect of this change is presented in Exhibit 15–11. The labor constraint is no longer binding, and the optimal solution is 8,000 units of Product C and zero units of Product K. The optimal solution results in a total contribution of $48,000 [$6 × 8,000 units of Product C] and 2,000 [18,000 − 2(8,000 units of Product C)] unused labor hours. Profits are $29,000 [$48,000 − ($18,000 + $1,000)]. The expansion results in a $5,000 [$29,000 − $24,000] increase in profits over Example 15–23. Note that although the differential fixed costs are not incorporated in the linear programming analysis, they are considered in evaluating the desirability of the proposed action. If the increase in fixed costs were greater than $6,000, the proposed expansion would not be desirable because the differential contribution would be less than the differential fixed costs.

At this new level of production in Exhibit 15–11, if one additional machine hour becomes available, it could be used to produce two units of Product C, increasing the value of the objective function by $12. Hence the shadow price for machine hours is $12. Because of excess capacity, the shadow price for labor hours is zero.

Indifference Range

Sensitivity analysis is also used to determine indifference ranges for important parameters of the linear programming model. An **indifference range** specifies the upper and lower limits between which a parameter can vary without changing the optimal solution. Frequently, indifference ranges are determined for such items as selling prices, input costs, and technological coefficients. Indifference ranges are useful in deciding whether to obtain additional information and how closely to monitor performance. If the optimal solution is not affected by large errors in cost estimation management need not use costly techniques to develop cost estimates.

Example 15–26

Based on the analysis performed in Example 15–25, the management of Marion has elected to produce 8,000 units of Product C and zero units of Product K. However, they are concerned about changes in the raw materials costs for Product C and want to know

EXHIBIT 15–11 Graph Analysis of Change in Labor Constraint

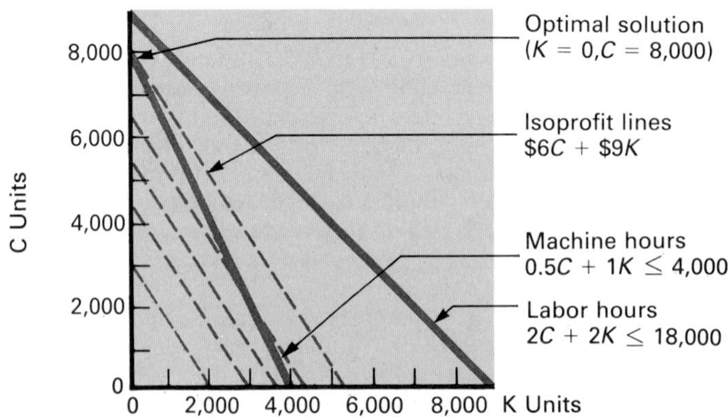

how much these costs can change before a change in the optimal product mix is indicated. The current cost of raw materials is \$5 per unit of Product C.

Any change in the cost of materials used in producing Product C changes the slope of the isoprofit lines because the unit contribution margin for Product C changes. If the cost decreases, the isoprofit lines in Exhibit 15–11 become less steep and the optimal solution does not change. If the cost of Product C materials increases, the slope of the isoprofit lines becomes steeper. When the isoprofit lines become parallel to the machine-hours constraint line, the upper boundary of the indifference range is reached.[9]

The machine-hours constraint line in Exhibit 15–11 has a slope of −2 [(0 − 8,000)/(4,000 − 0)]. The isoprofits lines have a slope of −1.50. The slope of the isoprofit lines is calculated by dividing the unit contribution margin of Product K by the unit contribution margin of Product C and multiplying by −1.

$$\text{Slope} = -1 \times \frac{\text{Unit contribution margin of Product K}}{\text{Unit contribution margin of Product C}}$$

$$\text{Slope} = -1 \times \frac{\$9}{\$6} = \underline{\underline{-1.50}}$$

The optimal solution in Exhibit 15–11 will not change until the slope of the isoprofit lines equals the slope of the machine-hours constraint, which is −2. Substituting this value into the equation for the slope and solving for the unit contribution margin of *C* gives \$4.50.

$$-2 = -1 \times \frac{\$9}{\text{Unit contribution margin of Product C}}$$

$$\text{Unit contribution margin of Product C} = -1 \times \frac{\$9}{-2} = \underline{\underline{\$4.50}}$$

This lower boundary of the indifference range for the unit contribution margin of Product C is \$1.50 [\$6.00 − \$4.50] less than the current unit contribution margin. Hence if all other variable costs and the unit selling price remain unchanged, the materials costs for Product C can increase by \$1.50 before the optimal solution changes. Given a current materials cost of \$5 for Product C, the upper boundary for the materials cost indifference range is \$6.50 (\$5 + \$1.50). If the materials cost of Product C increases by more than \$1.50, Marion should adjust its production schedule and produce only Product K. The lower boundary for the materials cost indifference range is $-\infty$. This is because any decrease in the materials cost for Product C will not change the optimal solution since no units of Product K are being produced.

MULTIPLE CONSTRAINTS AND MULTIPLE PRODUCTS

The discussion in the previous section is quite complex. Yet, it remains a simplification of an even more complex subject. Despite the pedagogical value of graphic analysis, it has limited practical significance. It cannot be used where there are more than two products, and as the number of constraints increases, it becomes unwieldy. Computers must be used for real-world applications. Fortunately this tool is readily available and linear programming technology is well developed for use by decision makers. All that is required is that decision makers be aware of computer capabilities and know what they want.

---

[9] Boundaries on the indifference ranges are usually available as part of the solution to linear programming problems when they are solved using a computer. Parametric linear programming is a more formal and systematic way of determining indifference ranges.

THE ROLE OF THE COST ACCOUNTANT

Even though the cost accountant should be familiar with the linear programming model used to determine the optimal product mix, the cost accountant seldom has primary responsibility for the development and use of such models. This responsibility rests with the operations researchers. The cost accountant is primarily concerned with determining objective function coefficients and interpreting the results.

For maximizing models, such as the one used by Marion, the cost accountant must determine each product's unit contribution margin (unit selling price minus unit variable costs of production and sales). To arrive at the unit contribution margins for Products C and K, the cost accountant may have prepared an analysis such as the following:

	C	*K*
Unit selling price	$28.00	$39.00
Unit variable costs:		
Materials	$ 5.00	$10.00
Direct labor:		
C (2 hours @ $6)	12.00	
K (2 hours @ $6)		12.00
Variable overhead:		
C (0.5 machine hours @ $6)	3.00	
K (1 machine hour @ $6)		6.00
Variable selling and administrative	2.00	2.00
Total	−22.00	−30.00
Unit contribution margin	$ 6.00	$ 9.00

The selling prices of Products C and K may have been supplied by marketing personnel, or they may have been developed using one of the cost-based approaches discussed in this chapter. The development of the variable cost data for Products C and K was probably accomplished using one or more of the cost-estimating procedures discussed in Chapter 7.

Example 15–27

Marion's engineering department determined the materials, labor hour, and machine-hour requirements of Products C and K. Multiplying the materials requirements by the current materials prices, the cost accountant determined the materials costs of Products C and K to be $5 and $10, respectively. Multiplying the labor-hour requirements by the current wage rate, the cost accountant determined the direct-labor costs of Products C and K to be $12 each.

An analysis of historical cost data was required to determine the variable overhead costs of Products C and K. As a first step, the cost accountant obtained the following data from two recent periods:

Period	*Total machine hours*	*Total factory overhead*
June 19x5	2,000	$24,000
July 19x5	4,000	36,000

Using the high-low method, the cost accountant developed the following cost-estimating equation for total factory overhead:

$$\text{Total factory overhead} = \$12{,}000 + \$6X$$

where X = Machine hours.

The variable factory overhead cost per machine hour is $6. Multiplying this cost by the machine-hour requirements of each product (0.5 hours for Product C and 1 hour for

Product K), the variable factory overhead costs of Products C and K were determined to be \$3 and \$6, respectively.

Equal amounts of effort were required to sell each unit of Products C and K; however, variable selling and administrative cost data were not readily available. As a first step in determining the variable selling and administrative expenses of Products C and K, the cost accountant obtained the following data from two recent periods:

Period	*Total units (C + K) produced and sold*	*Total selling and administrative expenses*
June 19x5	3,000	\$12,000
July 19x5	5,000	16,000

Using the high-low method, the cost accountant developed the following cost-estimating equation for total selling and administrative expenses:

Total selling and administrative expenses = \$6,000 + \$2X

where X = Units produced and sold.

Variable selling and administrative expenses are \$2 per unit of Products C and K.

Subsequent to the determination of the optimal solution, the cost accountant must determine what the organization's profit will be if the solution is implemented. The organization's profits will not equal the value of the objective function. The value of the objective function is the total contribution to covering fixed costs and providing a profit. Hence fixed costs must be deducted from the value of the objective function. In Example 15–27, Marion's fixed costs were determined to be \$18,000:

Fixed factory overhead	\$12,000
Fixed selling and administrative expenses	6,000
Total	\$18,000

INCOME TAXES

Income taxes can be included in calculating unit contribution margins by restating the unit variable costs to an after-tax basis. This procedure was illustrated in Chapter 8. However, with constant marginal tax rates for all products, including the income tax effect in calculating unit contribution margins is optional. The optimal product mix is not affected because the slope of the isoprofit lines does not change. However, profits are affected by income taxes. If management is concerned about the impact of income taxes on profit plans developed with the aid of linear programming, the contribution margin and the fixed costs might be restated on an after-tax basis. Interested readers should refer to Eq. 8–14.

KEY TERMS

Conditional loss
Conditional probability
Cost of prediction error
Expected payoff with perfect information
Expected value
Expected value of perfect information
Expected value of sample information
Joint probability
Payoff table
Pricing decisions
Pricing policies
Return on investment
Robinson-Patman Act
States of nature

APPENDIX KEY TERMS

Binding constraint
Graphic analysis
Indifference range
Isoprofit line
Linear programming
Nonbinding constraint
Objective function
Sensitivity analysis
Shadow price

SELECTED REFERENCES

Baker, Kenneth R., and Robert E. Taylor, "A Linear Programming Framework for Full Cost Allocation and External Acquisition When Reciprocal Services Exist," *Accounting Review* **54,** No. 4 (October 1979): 784–790.

Brenner, Vincent C., "An Evaluation of Product Pricing Models," *Managerial Planning* **20,** No. 1 (July-August 1971): 17–26.

Capettini, Robert, and Gerald L. Salamon, "Internal Versus External Acquisition of Services When Reciprocal Services Exist," *Accounting Review* **52,** No. 3 (July 1977): 690–696.

Corr, Arthur V., "The Role of Cost in Pricing," *Management Accounting* **56,** No. 5 (November 1974): 15–18, 32.

Demski, Joel, *Information Analysis,* 2nd ed., Reading, Mass.: Addison-Wesley, 1980.

Demski, Joel, and Gerald A. Feltham, *Cost Determination: A Conceptual Approach,* Ames, Iowa: Iowa State University Press, 1976.

Friedman, Laurence, and Bruce R. Newmann, "The Effects of Opportunity Costs on Project Investment Decisions: A Replication and Extension," *Journal of Accounting Research* **18,** No. 2 (Autumn 1980): 407–419.

Givens, Horace R., "An Application of Curvilinear Break-even Analysis," *Accounting Review* **41,** No. 1 (January 1966): 141–143.

Goggans, Travis P., "Break-even Analysis with Curvilinear Functions," *Accounting Review* **40,** No. 4 (October 1965): 867–871.

Gordon, Lawrence A., Robert Cooper, Haim Falk, and Danny Miller, *The Pricing Decision,* New York and Hamilton, Ontario: National Association of Accountants and the Society of Management Accountants of Canada, 1981 and 1980.

Govindarajan, V., and Robert N. Anthony, "How Firms Use Cost Data in Price Decisions," *Management Accounting* **65,** No. 1 (July 1983): 30–36.

Hernandez, William H., "Pricing Policies Under Inflation," *Management Accounting* **63,** No. 7 (January 1982): 51–55.

Hoskin, Robert E., "Opportunity Cost and Behavior," *Journal of Accounting Research* **21,** No. 1 (Spring 1983): 78–95.

Hye, Lee Meng, "Application of Linear Programming Analysis to Determine the Profitability of Products Involving Joint Cost—The Plywood Manufacturing Case." *The Australian Accountant* **40,** No. 11 (December 1970): 511–516.

Manes, René P., Soong H. Park, and Robert Jensen, "Relevant Cost of Intermediate Goods and Services," *Accounting Review* **57,** No. 3 (July 1982): 594–606.

Oxenfeldt, Alfred R., and William T. Baxter, "Approaches to Pricing: Economist Versus Accountant," *Business Horizons* **4,** No. 4 (Winter 1961): 77–90.

Rappaport, Alfred "Sensitivity Analysis in Decision Making," *Accounting Review* **42,** No. 3 (July 1967): 441–456.

Van Cise, Jarrold G., "The Robinson-Patman Act and the Accountant," *New York C.P.A.* **28,** No. 5 (May 1958): 351–362.

Whiting, Herbert G., "Cost Justification of Price Differences," *Management Services* **3,** No. 4 (July-August 1966): 30–38.

Williamson, Robert W., "Presenting Information Economics to Students," *Accounting Review* **57,** No. 2 (April 1982): 414–419.

REVIEW QUESTIONS

15–1 What are the relevant financial data in making a decision to accept or reject a special order?

15–2 Assuming the existence of excess capacity, what qualitative factors should be considered in a decision to accept a special order for a product at a reduced price?

15–3 What are the relevant financial data in make or buy decisions?

15–4 When different materials can be used in manufacturing a product, what criterion should be used in determining the input mix?

15–5 What is a payoff table?

15–6 How is the expected value of perfect information determined?

15–7 What is a conditional loss? Explain how a conditional loss table is developed.

15–8 How does the expected value of perfect information differ from the expected value of sample information?

15–9 Distinguish between pricing policies and pricing decisions.

15–10 What are the primary weaknesses of economic approaches to product pricing?

15–11 Distinguish between full cost and variable costs as a basis for product pricing.

15–12 How does the Robinson-Patman Act increase the role of cost in pricing decisions?

REVIEW PROBLEM

Information Acquisition Analyses

The Toyson Company currently sells a product at a sales price of $10 per unit. Last year, 200,000 units were produced and sold. The manufacturing facilities have a capacity of 250,000 units a year. Cost of manufacturing the product last year were as follows:

Direct materials	$ 400,000
Direct labor	600,000
Variable overhead	200,000
Fixed overhead	300,000
Total	$1,500,000

Toyson believes they can sell the same number of units next year with the same price and cost structure.

A foreign distributor, Wong Company, has offered to buy this product for $7 per unit. The quantity Wong will purchase, however, depends on the units they can sell. Toyson believes there is a 40 percent probability Wong will purchase 35,000 units and a 60 percent probability they will purchase 50,000 units. If Toyson sells the units to Wong, sales to regular customers will not be affected. If Toyson does not sell to Wong, the excess manufacturing capacity can be used to produce another product, X, with expected net cash inflows of $45,000 next year. Because of the space required to produce X, it can be produced only by refusing any sales to Wong.

REQUIREMENTS

a) Construct a payoff table for Toyson to use in determining whether to accept or reject Wong's order.

b) Determine the expected value of each alternative.

c) Construct a conditional loss table.

d) Determine the expected value of perfect information.

e) Assume Toyson can hire a consultant at a cost of $1,000 to predict Wong's sales. The consultant can issue two reports, a pessimistic report R1 (that is, sales = 35,000 units) or an optimistic report R2 (that is, sales = 50,000 units). The consultant is correct 70 percent of the time. Should Toyson hire the consultant?

The solution to this problem is found at the end of the Chapter 15 problems and exercises.

EXERCISES

15–1 Special Order

The Knight Restaurant specializes in a roast beef dinner selling for $5. Daily fixed costs are $1,200 and variable costs are $2.00 per meal. An average of 800 meals are served each day even though the capacity of the restaurant is 1,000 meals per day.

A bus load of 40 Boy Scouts stops by and the scoutmaster offers to bring them in if they can all be served a meal for a total of $100. The owner refuses, saying he would lose $1.00 per meal if he accepted this offer.

REQUIREMENTS

a) Determine the differential revenues and differential costs of accepting the scoutmaster's offer.

b) Should the scoutmaster's offer be accepted? Explain.

c) A local business executive on a coffee break overhears the conversation with the scoutmaster and offers the owner a one-year contract to feed 400 of his employees at a special price of $2.50 per meal. Should the restaurant owner accept? Why or why not?

15–2 Special Order

Apex Company produces a component used in the manufacture of microcomputers. Variable costs of producing and selling the component are $2 per unit. Fixed costs of providing the capacity to produce up to 100,000 units per year are

$50,000. The components are currently sold to a major computer manufacturer for $3.00 per unit and current sales are 60,000 units annually.

A manufacturer of arcade video games believes the component can be used in the production of the games and has offered to purchase 20,000 units from Apex at a price of $2.25 per unit. Since it is not known at this time if the manufacturer of the games will place additional orders, Apex considers this to be a one-time special order.

REQUIREMENTS

a) Determine the differential revenues and differential costs of accepting the order.

b) Should the special order be accepted? Explain.

c) Would your answer to part (b) be different if current capacity were only 60,000 units a year?

15–3 Make or Buy

Alexander Company currently manufactures a component they use in the production of drill presses. Each component has variable manufacturing costs of $20 and current usage is 10,000 units per year. Fixed costs directly associated with the component total $40,000 a year and will be eliminated if production of the component ceases. Main Company has offered to supply the components to Alexander for $22 a unit.

REQUIREMENTS

a) Determine the differential costs of making and buying the component.

b) Should Alexander accept the offer from Main? Explain.

c) What qualitative factors should Alexander consider in making the decision?

15–4 Make or Buy

Sanders Company currently manufactures a part they use in the production of clocks. The part has the following unit costs at an annual volume of 40,000 clocks:

Direct materials	$0.50
Direct labor	1.00
Variable overhead	0.50
Fixed overhead	2.00
Total	$4.00

A supplier has offered to provide the part to Sanders for $3.50 per unit.

REQUIREMENTS

a) If none of the fixed overhead can be reduced, should Sanders continue to make the part or buy it from the supplier? If they buy, how much will annual profits increase or decrease?

b) If all the fixed overhead can be eliminated, should Sanders make or buy the part? If they buy, by how much will annual profits increase or decrease?

c) What qualitative factors should Sanders consider in making the decision?

15–5 Input Mix Decision

The United Feed Company produces chicken feed that is made from various grains. The grains can be mixed in various proportions, but quality standards require that each ton of feed contain at least 20 percent protein. The protein can be obtained from any of three grains. Information about each of the grains is as follows:

Grain	*Percent protein*	*Cost per ton*	*Cost per pound*
1	40	$80	$0.0400
2	30	55	0.0275
3	20	45	0.0225

All other production costs are independent of the mix of grains.

REQUIREMENTS

a) Determine the cost per pound of protein for each grain.

b) Which raw material(s) should be used to minimize the cost of the feed?

15–6 Input Mix Decision

Ranch and Farm Company produces cattle feed that is made from various raw materials. The materials can be mixed in various proportions, but each ton of feed must contain at least 15 percent protein. The protein can be obtained from any of four raw materials. Information about each raw material is as follows:

Raw material	*Percent protein*	*Cost per ton*
A	30	$90
B	25	70
C	20	65
D	15	55

All other production costs are independent of the mix of raw materials.

REQUIREMENTS

a) Determine the cost per pound of protein for each raw material.

b) Which raw material(s) should be used to minimize the cost of the feed?

15–7 Payoff Table and Expected Value

Sandra Petty has a license to sell ice cream at the annual street festival in Clarksville. Her expected profits depend on the number of people who attend, which is affected by the weather and whether she sells from a tent or from an open booth "under the stars." If the weather is good, a large crowd is expected to attend. Under these conditions, Sandra expects to earn $3,000 if she sells from an open booth and $2,000 if she sells from a tent. If the weather is bad, she expects to earn $800 if she sells from an open booth and $1,500 if she sells from a tent. Assume there is a 60 percent chance of good weather.

REQUIREMENTS

a) Construct a payoff table.

b) Determine the expected value of each action.

c) Construct a conditional loss table.

d) Which alternative should Sandra prefer?

e) Determine the expected value of perfect information.

15–8 Payoff Table and Expected Value

Homestead Antiques is considering having a booth at the Eastend Antique Show and Sale. Expected profits depend on the number of people who attend and on the size of the space rented. If a large crowd attends, expected earnings are $700 from a large space and $500 from a small space. If a small crowd attends, expected earnings are $200 from a large space and $300 from a small space. The probability of a large crowd is 0.40.

REQUIREMENTS

a) Construct a payoff table.

b) Construct a conditional loss table.

c) Determine the expected value of each action.

d) Which action should Homestead prefer?

15–9 Pricing for Target Profit

The Boston Company produces one product and has annual production and sales of 100,000 units. The annual costs of producing and selling 100,000 units are as follows:

Variable manufacturing	$500,000
Fixed manufacturing	300,000
Variable selling and administrative	150,000
Fixed selling and administrative	50,000

Boston Company has an investment in plant and equipment of $2,000,000 and pays income taxes at a rate of 30 percent.

REQUIREMENTS

a) Determine the unit price Boston should charge for the product to earn a 15 percent before-tax return on the investment in plant and equipment.

b) Determine the unit price Boston should charge for the product to earn a 7 percent after-tax return on the investment.

15–10 Pricing for Target Profit

Richard Company has the following annual costs for production and sales of 50,000 units:

Variable manufacturing	$300,000
Fixed manufacturing	100,000
Variable selling and administrative	50,000
Fixed selling and administrative	200,000

Richard has an investment in plant and equipment of $1,500,000 and pays income taxes at a 40 percent rate.

REQUIREMENTS

a) Determine the price Richard should charge to obtain a 10 percent before-tax return on the investment in plant and equipment.

b) Determine the price Richard should charge to obtain a 5 percent after-tax return on the investment in plant and equipment.

15–11 Pricing for Target Profit

The Ohio Company produces one product, which they have been selling to earn a 9 percent after-tax return on their investment in plant and equipment. Last year 100,000 units were produced and sold and the costs were as follows:

Variable manufacturing	$400,000
Fixed manufacturing	300,000
Variable selling and administrative	150,000
Fixed selling and administrative	100,000

Ohio pays taxes at a 40 percent tax rate and has an investment in plant and equipment of $2,000,000. During the coming year, they expect variable unit costs to increase by 10 percent and total fixed costs to increase by 5 percent.

REQUIREMENTS

a) If sales remain at 100,000 units, what price would Ohio Company have to charge to earn their target rate of return on investment?

b) If sales increased to 120,000 units, what price would they have to charge to earn their target rate of return on investment?

PROBLEMS

15–12 Selecting from Alternatives with Different Costs

K & K Real Estate Agency is a moderately sized company serving a metropolitan area of over one million people. K & K has 20 agents, all of whom are free to list any kind of property from vacant land to commercial real estate anywhere in the greater metropolitan and surrounding three-county area. Each agent travels extensively to cover the area served by K & K.

K & K requires all agents to be willing to travel throughout the entire area. To subsidize this travel requirement, the company has a reimbursement policy of $0.25 per mile for all business-connected travel. The agents are responsible for all costs associated with the operation of their own automobiles. Last year the average mileage claimed by an agent was 50,000 miles. The number of miles driven is approximately the same each month, and the agents are reimbursed monthly. On average each agent works 25 days a month.

The agents believe that the $0.25-per-mile reimbursement is not adequate, considering the wear and tear on the car and the inconvenience of the excessive amount of travel. Many agents believe that the amount of business-related use is so great that two, and sometimes three, automobiles are required to meet their family needs. Further, the automobile used for business travel has to be traded in on an annual basis to avoid major repair costs.

Jack Kramer, the President, believes that some of the arguments are legitimate. However, he also senses that some of the agents may have been claiming excess miles during the year. Kramer is convinced that the annual mileage use would drop to 42,000 miles per year if the agents were not using their own cars. Therefore he is considering an agency fleet of automobiles.

Kramer asked both International Car Rental and a local automobile dealer, Aron Motor, to present proposals. The proposals are described as follows:

INTERNATIONAL CAR RENTAL'S PROPOSAL

1. K & K would rent 20 automobiles for an entire year at $66 per week per automobile and $0.14 per mile.
2. When one of the 20 automobiles is in for service, International would provide a replacement at $7 per day and $0.20 per mile. International would absorb all repair and maintenance costs. Normally an automobile would be out of service only one day at a time, and each automobile can be expected to be out of service 12 days per year.
3. Cost of insurance is included in the weekly rental rate.
4. K & K would be required to purchase the gasoline for the automobiles at an average cost of $1.50 per gallon. International estimates that K & K should expect to get 21 miles per gallon.
5. International has agreed to collect the rental and mileage fees on a monthly basis.

ARON MOTOR'S PROPOSAL

Aron offered a purchase–buy back arrangement with the following requirements:

1. K & K would buy 20 automobiles at $9,000 each. Aron would buy the automobiles back after one year at $4,000 each, provided that K & K subscribed to Aron's preferred customer maintenance and service plan.
2. K & K would have to bring each automobile in once every two months for preventive maintenance and service. The cost to K & K for each service visit would be $50. Aron would provide a loaner automobile at no additional cost. Aron would accept responsibility for any additional repair and maintenance charges.
3. K & K would have to purchase insurance at a cost of $200 for each automobile. This would have to be paid at the beginning of the year.
4. K & K would purchase a new set of tires after six months at $125 per set.

5. K & K also would be responsible for the purchase of gasoline at an average cost of $1.50 per gallon. Aron states that, because of proper maintenance, the automobiles will average 28 miles per gallon.
6. Aron requires that the purchase price of the automobiles be paid in full at the beginning of the year. However, the preventive maintenance service fee would be paid when service is provided.

REQUIREMENTS

a) Calculate an annual before-tax amount for:
   1. The current reimbursement practice
   2. The proposal of International Car Rental
   3. The proposal of Aron Motor

   which Jack Kramer can use to compare the three alternatives.

b) Based on the before-tax data, which alternative should Kramer accept?

(CMA Adapted)

15–13 Differential Profit

Helene's, a high fashion women's dress manufacturer, is planning to market a new cocktail dress for the coming season. Helene's supplies retailers in the East and Mid-Atlantic states.

Four yards of material are required to lay out the dress pattern. Some material remains after cutting which can be sold as remnants. The leftover material could also be used to manufacture a matching cape and handbag. However, if the leftover material is to be used for the cape and handbag, more care will be required in the cutting, which will increase the cutting costs.

The company expected to sell 1,250 dresses if no matching cape or handbag were available. Helene's market research reveals that dress sales will be 20 percent higher if a matching cape and handbag are available. The market research indicates that the cape and/or handbag will not be sold individually but only as accessories with the dress. The various combinations of dresses, capes, and handbags that are expected to be sold by retailers are as follows:

	Percent of total
Complete sets of dress, cape, and handbag	70%
Dress and cape	6
Dress and handbag	15
Dress only	9
Total	100

The material used in the dress costs $12.50 a yard or $50.00 for each dress. The cost of cutting the dress if the cape and handbag are not manufactured is estimated at $20.00 a dress, and the resulting remnants can be sold for $5.00 for each dress cut out. If the cape and handbag are to be manufactured, the cutting costs will be increased by $9.00 per dress. There will be no salable remnants if the capes and handbags are manufactured in the quantities estimated.

The selling prices and the costs to complete the three items once they are cut are as follows:

	Selling price per unit	*Unit cost to complete (excludes cost of material and cutting operation)*
Dress	$200.00	$80.00
Cape	27.50	19.50
Handbag	9.50	6.50

REQUIREMENTS

a) Calculate Helene's differential profit or loss from manufacturing the capes and handbags in conjunction with the dresses.

b) Identify any nonquantitative factors that could influence Helene's management in its decision to manufacture the matching capes and handbags. (CMA Adapted)

15–14 Special Order

The manufacturing capacity of Jordan Company's production facilities is 30,000 units of product a year. A summary of operating results for the year ended December 31, 19x5, is as follows:

Sales (18,000 units @ $100)	$1,800,000
Variable manufacturing and selling costs	−990,000
Contribution margin	$ 810,000
Fixed costs	−495,000
Operating income	$ 315,000

A foreign distributor has offered to buy 15,000 units at $90 each during 19x6. Assume that all of Jordan's costs would be at the same levels and rates in 19x6 as in 19x5. If Jordan accepts this offer, they will reject some business from regular customers so as not to exceed capacity.

REQUIREMENTS

a) Determine the differential revenues and costs of accepting the order.

b) What is the opportunity cost of accepting the order?

c) Should Jordan accept or reject the order? Why?

d) If capacity were 45,000 units rather than 30,000 units, should Jordan accept or reject the order?

e) What nonquantitative factors should Jordan consider in making the decision? (CPA Adapted)

15–15 Make or Buy

Kingwood Company needs 10,000 units of a certain part to be used in its production cycle. The following information is available:

Unit manufacturing costs:	
Direct materials	$ 6
Direct labor	24
Variable overhead	12
Fixed overhead applied	15
Total	$57
Unit cost to buy the part from Utica Company	$53

If Kingwood buys the part from Utica instead of making it, Kingwood could not use the released facilities in another manufacturing activity. Regardless of what decision is made, 60 percent of the applied fixed overhead will continue.

REQUIREMENTS

a) What are the differential costs of each alternative?

b) Should Kingwood make or buy the part? Why?

c) What nonquantitative factors should Kingwood consider in making the decision?
(CPA Adapted)

15–16 Internal vs. External Acquisition of Services

The Watson Company manufactures two products, X and Y, in two separate departments, Px and Py. Px and Py receive services from two service departments, S1 and S2. The direct costs of S1 are allocated to all other departments on the basis of number of employees. The direct and indirect costs of S2 are allocated to Px and Py on the basis of direct-labor costs.

The following information is available about January 19y1 operations:

	S1	*S2*	*Px*	*Py*
Number of employees	10	20	50	30
Current costs:				
Direct materials			$30,000	$ 7,000
Direct labor			90,000	30,000
Direct dept. overhead	$10,000	$8,000	25,000	40,000

Watson is considering an offer from Berry Company to supply the services currently rendered by S2 at a cost of $0.08 per direct-labor dollar in Px and Py.

REQUIREMENTS

a) Prepare a schedule allocating S1 and S2 operating costs to Px and Py.

b) Assuming that all service department costs are variable, determine whether Watson should accept or reject Berry's offer.

15–17 Internal vs. External Acquisition of Services

The Evert Corporation has two service departments, S1 and S2, and two production departments, P1 and P2. The percentage distribution of the service departments' costs are as follows:

From \ To	*S1*	*S2*	*P1*	*P2*
S1	0	0	50%	50%
S2	20%	0	20%	60%

The direct operating costs of the service departments and the direct overhead costs of the production departments are:

S1	$10,000
S2	5,000
P1	20,000
P2	20,000

Evert is considering external acquisition of the services provided by S1. The Reeder Company has offered to provide an equivalent amount and quality of service for $12,000. All S1 and S2 operating costs are variable.

REQUIREMENT

Determine whether Evert should accept or reject Reeder's offer.

15–18 Cost Plus Pricing and a Special Order

Prairie Dog Manufacturing produces a variety of motorized gardening tools. Management follows a pricing policy of full cost (including a fair share of selling and administrative costs) plus 15 percent markup. In response to a request from Sooner Discount Department Stores, the following price has been developed for an order of 1,000 Prairie Turners (a small tilling machine):

Manufacturing costs:	
Direct materials	$ 10,000
Direct labor	50,000
Factory overhead	20,000
Total	$ 80,000
Selling and administrative costs	8,000
Total costs	$ 88,000
Markup	13,200
Selling price	$101,200

J. P. Sooner, the president of Sooner Discount Department Stores, rejected this price as too high and offered to purchase the 1,000 Prairie Turners at a price of $80,000.

ADDITIONAL INFORMATION

- Prairie Dog has excess capacity.
- Factory overhead is applied on the basis of direct-labor dollars.
- Budgeted factory overhead is $400,000 for the current year, including $120,000 of fixed overhead.
- Budgeted production and sales for the current year total 40,000 units.
- Fixed selling and administrative costs are $160,000 for the current year. In pricing computations, these costs are applied on the basis of the total number of units sold.
- Variable selling and administrative costs are believed to be a function of the total number of units sold.

REQUIREMENTS

a) Determine the effect on before-tax income of accepting J. P. Sooner's offer.

b) Briefly explain why you omitted certain costs from your analysis in part (a).

c) How would your analysis in part (a) differ if Prairie Dog did not have excess capacity?

15–19 Expected Value of Information

Strotz Brewery produces and sells a popular premium beer and has enjoyed good profits for many years. However, in recent years its sales volume has not grown with the general market. This lack of growth is due to the increasing popularity of light beer and to the fact that Strotz has not entered the light beer market.

Strotz is now developing its own light beer and is considering potential marketing strategies. Introducing the new light beer nationally would require a large commitment of resources for a full nationwide promotion and distribution campaign. In addition, there is some risk in a nationwide introduction because Strotz is a late entry into the light beer market. Strotz's advertising agency has helped assess the market risk and has convinced the Strotz management that there are two reasonable alternative strategies to pursue.

- *Strategy 1:* Perform a test advertising and sales campaign in a limited number of states for a six-month period. Strotz would decide whether to introduce the light beer nationally on the basis of the results of the test campaign.
- *Strategy 2:* Conduct a nationwide promotion campaign and make the new light beer available in all fifty states immediately without conducting any test campaign. The nationwide promotion and distribution campaign would be allowed to run for a full two years before deciding whether to continue the light beer nationally.

Strotz management believes that if Strategy 2 is selected, there is only a 50 percent chance of it being successful. The introduction of light beer nationally will be considered a success if $40 million of revenue is generated while $30 million of variable costs are being incurred during the two-year period the nationwide promotion and distribution campaign is in effect. If the two-year nationwide campaign is unsuccessful, revenues are expected to be $16 million and variable costs will be $12 million. Total fixed costs for the two-year period will amount to $6 million regardless of the result.

The advertising agency consultants recognize that if Strategy 1 is selected, there is a chance that the test will indicate Strotz should conduct a nationwide promotion and distribution campaign when, in fact, a nationwide campaign would be unsuccessful. Also, the consultants recognize that there is a chance that the test results will indicate Strotz should not conduct a nationwide promotion and distribution campaign when, in fact, a nationwide campaign would be successful.

REQUIREMENTS

a) Calculate the expected value of Strategy 2 for Strotz Brewery.

b) Assume Strategy 1, the test campaign, could predict perfectly whether or not a nationwide campaign would be successful. Using expected value as the decision criterion, calculate the maximum dollar amount Strotz Brewery should be willing to pay for the perfect information. (CMA Adapted)

15–20 Payoff Tables and Expected Value of Perfect Information

The Campus Bookstore stocks orientation packages for incoming freshmen each fall. The packages cost $4 and sell for $6 each. Because the packages contain dated material, unsold packages are worthless, and they are burned at a fall pep rally. Because all freshmen are required to buy a package, sales are a function of fall freshmen enrollment. The Admissions Office has made the following predictions for next year's freshmen enrollment:

Freshmen Enrollment	*Probability*
2,500	0.50
3,000	0.30
3,500	0.20

Assume the Campus Bookstore wishes to maximize its profits.

REQUIREMENTS

a) Prepare a payoff table to determine the profit maximizing order size for orientation packages.

b) What is the expected value of perfect information?

c) As a student, what do you think of the Campus Bookstore's operating philosophy? Why?

15–21 Selecting the Contribution Maximizing Action

Janet Watkins recently was appointed Executive Director of a charitable foundation. The foundation raises the money for its activities in a variety of ways, but the most important source of funds is an annual mail campaign.

The annual mail campaign and accompanying public relations efforts are designed to raise the major share of the foundation's annual budget. Although large amounts of money are raised each year from the mail campaign, the year-to-year growth in the amount derived from the mail solicitation has been lower than expected by the foundation's board of directors. In addition, the board wants the mail campaign to project the image of a well-run and fiscally responsible organization in order to build a base for future contributions. Consequently the major focus of Watkins' efforts in her first year will be devoted to the mail campaign.

The campaign takes place in the spring of each year. The foundation staff makes every effort to secure newspaper, radio, and television coverage of the foundation's activities for several weeks before the mail campaign. In prior years, the foundation has mailed brochures that describe its charitable activities to a large number of people and has requested contributions from them. The addresses for the mailing are generated from the foundation's own file of past contributors and from mailing lists purchased from brokers.

The foundation staff is considering three alternative brochures for use in the upcoming campaign. All three will be 8½″ by 11″ in size. The simplest and the one sure to be ready and available on a timely basis for bulk mailing is a sheet of white paper with a printed explanation of the foundation's program and a request for funds. A more expensive brochure on colored stock would contain pictures as well as printed copy. However, this brochure may not be ready in time to take advantage of bulk postal rates, but there is no doubt that it can be ready in time for mailing at first-class postal rates. The third alternative would be an elegant, multicolored brochure printed on glossy paper with photographs as well as printed copy. The printer assures the staff that it would be ready on time to meet the first-class mailing schedule but asks for a delivery date one week later, just in case there are production problems.

The foundation staff has assembled the following costs and revenue information for mailing the three alternative brochures to 2,000,000 potential contributors. The postal rates are \$0.05 per item for bulk mail and \$0.18 per item for presorted first-class mail. First-class mail is more likely to be delivered on time than bulk mail. Outside companies who will be hired to handle the mailing charge \$0.01 per unit for the plain and colored paper brochures and \$0.02 per unit for the glossy paper one.

	Brochure costs				*Revenue potential (\$000 omitted)*		
Type of brochure	*Design*	*Type-setting*	*Unit paper cost*	*Unit printing cost*	*Bulk mail*	*First class*	*Late first class*
Plain paper	\$ 300	\$ 100	\$0.005	\$0.003	\$1,200	0	0
Colored paper	1,000	800	0.008	0.010	2,000	\$2,200	0
Glossy paper	3,000	2,000	0.018	0.040	0	2,500	\$2,200

REQUIREMENTS

a) Calculate the contribution for each brochure for each viable mailing alternative.

b) The foundation must choose one of the three brochures for the year's campaign. The criteria established by the board—net revenue raised, image of a well-run organization, and image as a fiscally responsible organization—must be considered when making the choice. Evaluate the three alternative brochures in terms of the three criteria.

(CMA Adapted)

15–22 Pricing Decision

Jenco Inc. manufactures a combination fertilizer/weed-killer under the name Fertikil. This is the only product Jenco produces at the present time. Fertikil is sold nationwide through normal marketing channels to retail nurseries and garden stores.

Taylor Nursery plans to sell a similar fertilizer/weed-killer compound through its regional nursery chain under its own private label. Taylor has asked Jenco to submit a bid for a 25,000-pound order of the private brand compound. Although the chemical composition of the Taylor compound differs from that of Fertikil, the manufacturing process is very similar.

The Taylor compound would be produced in 1,000-pound lots. Each lot would require 60 direct-labor hours and the following chemicals:

Chemicals	*Quantity (in pounds)*
CW-3	400
JX-6	300
MZ-8	200
BE-7	100

The first three chemicals (CW-3, JX-6, and MZ-8) are all used in the production of Fertikil. BE-7 was used in a compound that Jenco has discontinued. This chemical was not sold or discarded because it does not deteriorate and there have been adequate storage facilities. Jenco could sell BE-7 at the prevailing market price less $0.10 per pound for selling and handling expenses.

Jenco also has on hand a chemical called CN-5 which was manufactured to use in another product they no longer produce. CN-5, which cannot be used in Fertikil, can be substituted for CW-3 on a one-for-one basis without affecting the quality of the Taylor compound. The quantity of CN-5 in inventory has a salvage value of $500.

Inventory and cost data for the chemicals that can be used to produce the Taylor compound are as follows:

Raw material	*Pounds in inventory*	*Actual price per pound when purchased*	*Current market price per pound*
CW-3	22,000	$0.80	$0.90
JX-6	5,000	0.55	0.60
MZ-8	8,000	1.40	1.60
BE-7	4,000	0.60	0.65
CN-5	5,500	0.75	(salvage)

The current direct-labor rate is $7.00 per hour. The factory overhead rate is established at the beginning of the year and is applied consistently throughout the year on the basis of direct-labor hours (DLH). The predetermined overhead rate for the current year, based on a two-shift capacity of 400,000 total DLH with no overtime, is as follows:

Variable factory overhead	$2.25 per DLH
Fixed factory overhead	3.75 per DLH
Combined rate	$6.00 per DLH

Jenco's production manager reports that the present equipment and facilities are adequate to manufacture the Taylor compound. However, Jenco is within 800 hours of its two-shift capacity this month before it must schedule overtime. If need be, the Taylor compound could be produced on regular time by shifting a portion of Fertikil production to overtime. Jenco's rate for overtime hours is one and one-half times the regular pay rate or $10.50 per hour. There is no allowance for any overtime premium in the factory overhead rate.

Jenco's standard markup policy for new products is 25 percent of full manufacturing cost.

REQUIREMENTS

a) Assume Jenco Inc. has decided to submit a bid for a 25,000-pound order of Taylor's new compound. The order must be delivered by the end of the current month. Taylor has indicated that this is a one-time order that will not be repeated. Calculate the lowest price Jenco can bid for the order and not reduce its net income.

b) Without prejudice to your answer in part (a), assume that Taylor Nursery plans to place regular orders for 25,000-pound lots of the new compound during the coming year. Jenco expects the demand for Fertikil to remain strong again in the coming year. Therefore the recurring orders from Taylor will put Jenco over its two-shift capacity. However, production can be scheduled so that 60 percent of each Taylor order can be completed during regular hours or Fertikil production could be shifted temporarily to overtime so that the Taylor orders could be produced on regular time. Jenco's production manager has estimated that the prices of all chemicals will stabilize at the current market rates for the coming year and that all other manufacturing costs are expected to be maintained at the same rates or amounts. Calculate the price that Jenco Inc. should quote Taylor Nursery for each 25,000-pound lot of the new compound, assuming that there will be recurring orders during the coming year. (CMA Adapted)

15–23 Production and Pricing Under Pure Competition

The wholesale meat industry in a western region of the United States is characterized by a very large number of firms with no one firm dominating the market. The Perry Wholesale Meat Company is interested in expanding its production of ground beef because of available capacity and the rapid growth of franchise hamburger outlets in its market area.

The Perry management has found that it can sell all the ground beef that it can produce at $0.99 per pound. The controller's office has estimated the total costs, including a normal return on investment, for various levels of production as follows:

Company's ground beef production (in pounds)	*Company's total estimated production costs including a normal return on investment (in dollars)*
120,000	$120,000
150,000	149,000
180,000	178,200
210,000	207,900
240,000	238,000

Each production level requires a slightly larger investment than the next smaller production level.

REQUIREMENTS

a) What selling price should the Perry Wholesale Meat Company charge for the ground beef? Explain your answer.

b) What level of production will maximize total return on investment for the Perry Wholesale Meat Company? Explain your answer.

c) What pricing and output strategy would the Perry Wholesale Meat Company use if it were the exclusive distributor of ground beef in the western region of the United States? Explain your answer. (CMA Adapted)

15–24 Optimal Production Volume: Calculus

Hollis Company manufactures and markets a regulator that is used to maintain high levels of accuracy in timing clocks. The market for these regulators is limited and highly dependent on the selling price. Consequently Hollis Company employs a combination of differential calculus and economic concepts to determine the number of regulators to be produced and the selling price of each.

Based on past relationships between the selling price and the resultant demand as well as an informal survey of customers, management has derived the following demand function:

$$D = 2{,}000 - 2P$$

where

D = Annual demand in units
P = Price per unit

The predicted manufacturing and selling costs for the coming year are as follows:

Variable costs:	
Manufacturing	$100 per unit
Selling	50 per unit
Traceable fixed costs:	
Manufacturing	$30,000 per year
Selling	10,000 per year

REQUIREMENT

Determine the number of regulators Hollis should produce and the selling price it should charge per regulator in order to maximize the company's profits from the regulator line for the coming year. (CMA Adapted)

15–25 Approaches to Pricing

The president of a major railroad was once quoted as saying, "Not even God Almighty knows the cost of shipping a ton of coal from Boston to New York. . . . In pricing services we should charge what the traffic will bear."

REQUIREMENTS

a) Distinguish between the economic and accounting approaches to pricing.

b) Mention several objections to cost-plus pricing. To what problem in particular is the railroad president referring?

c) Given these objections, describe what many persons would regard as the "proper role" of costs in pricing.

15–26 Telephone Pole Rental Rates

Most utility poles carry electric and telephone lines. In areas served by cable television they also carry television cables. However, cable television companies rarely own any utility poles. Instead, they pay the utility companies a rental fee for the use of each pole on a yearly basis. The determination of the rental fee is a source of frequent disagreement between the pole owners and the cable television companies. In one situation, pole owners were arguing for a $7 annual rental fee per pole because this was the standard rate the electric and telephone companies charged each other for the use of poles.

"We object to that," stated the representative of the cable TV company. "With two users, the $7 fee represents a rental charge for one-half of a pole. This fee is too high because we only use about six inches of each 40-foot pole."

"You are forgetting federal safety regulations," responded the manager of the electric company. "They specify certain distances between different types of lines on a utility pole. Television cables must be a minimum of 40 inches below power lines and 12 inches above telephone lines. If your cable is added to the pole, the total capacity of the pole is reduced because this space cannot be used for anything else. Besides, we have an investment in the poles, you don't. We should be entitled to a fair return on this investment. Furthermore, speaking of fair, your company should pay the same rental fee that the telephone company pays us and we pay them. We do not intend to change this fee."

In response, the cable TV company representative made two points. First, any fee represents incremental income to the pole owners because the cable company would pay all costs of moving lines on existing utility poles. Second, because the electric and telephone companies both strive to own the same number of poles in a service area, their pole rental fees cancel themselves. Hence the fee they charge each other is moot.

REQUIREMENT

Evaluate the arguments presented by the cable TV and electric company representatives. What factors and costs should be considered in determining a pole rental fee?

15–27 Price Setting With Price Controls

The King of Wonderland is quite concerned with the problem of inflation. In response to increasing pressure for action to reduce inflation he declared that in the future all price increases must conform to "voluntary guidelines." These guidelines stipulate that in any given one-year period the price of a product cannot exceed 1.065 times the previous (base year) price. Realizing that this criterion would harm some organizations that have had large cost increases, the King agreed to allow organizations to use the following formula for maximum allowable profit as an alternate basis for product pricing:

$$\begin{bmatrix}\text{Allowable} \\ \text{program-year} \\ \text{profit}\end{bmatrix} = \begin{bmatrix}\text{Base} \\ \text{year} \quad \times 1.065 \\ \text{profit}\end{bmatrix} \times \begin{bmatrix} & \text{Percentage} \\ 1.0 \times & \text{volume} \\ & \text{increase}\end{bmatrix}$$

Alice Heart, Executive Vice President of the Cheshire Card Company, is quite concerned about how the King's guidelines will affect her company. After gathering the following information Alice sought out a recent business school graduate and asked, "Oh my, what shall we do?"

	Last year	*Next year (expected)*
Selling price/pack	$5.00	?
Unit variable cost	$4.00	$4.70
Fixed costs	$10,000	$11,000
Unit sales volume	20,000 packs	22,000 packs

REQUIREMENTS

a) Determine the maximum allowable price the Cheshire Card Company can charge per pack.

b) The King stipulated that if the profit-based formula were used and actual profits exceeded allowable program-year profits, an excess-profits penalty tax would be assigned using the following formula:

$$\begin{matrix}\text{Excess-profits} \\ \text{penalty} \\ \text{tax}\end{matrix} = 1.2 \begin{bmatrix}\text{Actual} & & \text{Allowable} \\ \text{program-year} & - & \text{program-year} \\ \text{profits} & & \text{profits}\end{bmatrix}$$

Assume that Cheshire charged the maximum price allowed by the profit-based formula and that all prices, revenues, and variable costs were as planned. Late in the year, Cheshire's accountant determined that fixed costs were running substantially below their estimated amount. What would you do to avoid the excess-profits penalty tax?

c) Considering your response to part (b), what may the impact of the King's guidelines be on operating efficiency and production costs, and hence prices?

15–28 Linear Programming (Appendix)

The operations of organizations and business enterprises continue to increase in size and complexity. Managers find it more difficult to capture all aspects of a problem as a consequence of the increase in size and complexity of operations. As a result, managers have had to identify, use, and rely on new tools and techniques to assist in making critical decisions. Linear programming is one tool that managers have employed in their decision-making activities.

REQUIREMENTS

a) Explain what linear programming is.

b) Identify and explain the requirements that need to be present in a decision situation to employ linear programming. (CMA Adapted)

15–29 Formulating Constraints (Appendix)

The Elon Co. manufactures two industrial products: X-10, which sells for $90 a unit, and Y-12, which sells for $85 a unit. Each product is processed through both of the company's manufacturing departments. The limited availability of labor, material, and equipment capacity has restricted the firm's ability to meet the demand for its products. The production department believes that linear programming can be used to more efficiently schedule the production of the two products.

The following data are available to the production department:

	Amount required per unit	
	X-10	*Y-12*
Direct material: weekly supply is limited to 1,800 pounds at $12.00 per pound	4 lbs.	2 lbs.
Direct labor:		
Department 1: Weekly supply limited to 10 people at 40 hours each at an hourly cost of $6.00	$\frac{2}{3}$ hour	1 hour
Department 2: Weekly supply limited to 15 people at 40 hours each at an hourly cost of $8.00	$1\frac{1}{4}$ hour	1 hour
Machine time:		
Department 1: Weekly capacity limited to 250 hours	$\frac{1}{2}$ hour	$\frac{1}{2}$ hour
Department 2: Weekly capacity limited to 300 hours	0 hours	1 hour

The overhead costs for Elon are accumulated on a plant-wide basis. Overhead is assigned to products on the basis of the number of direct-labor hours required to manufacture the product. This basis is appropriate for overhead assignment because most of the variable overhead costs vary as a function of labor time. The estimated overhead cost per direct-labor hour is:

Variable overhead cost	$ 6.00
Fixed overhead cost	6.00
Total overhead cost per direct-labor hour	$12.00

The production department formulated the following equations for the linear programming statement of the problem where

A = Number of units of X-10 to be produced
B = Number of units of Y-12 to be produced

Objective function to minimize costs:
Minimize $Z = 85A + 62B$
Constraints:

Material	$4A + 2B \leq 1{,}800$
Department 1 labor	$\frac{2}{3}A + 1B \leq 400$
Department 2 labor	$1\frac{1}{4}A + 1B \leq 600$
Nonnegativity	$A \geq 0, \quad B \geq 0$

REQUIREMENTS

a) The formulation of the linear programming equations as prepared by Elon Co.'s production department is incorrect. Explain what errors have been made in the formulation prepared by the production department.

b) Formulate and label the proper equations for the linear programming statement of Elon Co.'s production problem.

c) Explain how linear programming could help Elon Co. determine how large a change in the price of direct materials would have to be to change the optimum production mix of X-10 and Y-12. (CMA Adapted)

15–30 Formulating Constraints and Graphic Analysis (Appendix)

The Baker Company can sell as many units of X and Y as it can produce. Production information is as follows:

	Production requirements		
Process	*X*	*Y*	*Capacity*
P1	6 hours	4 hours	1,800 hours
P2	6 hours	4 hours	1,200 hours
P3	4 hours	6 hours	1,200 hours

Both products have a unit contribution margin of $40.

REQUIREMENTS

a) Formulate the objective function and the constraints necessary to determine the optimal production mix.

b) Use graphic analysis to determine the optimal solution and the value of the objective function.

c) Using the graph developed in part (b), determine the effect of each of the following independent events on the optimal solution and the value of the objective function:

1. Process P2 capacity is doubled to 2,400 hours.
2. Process P1 capacity is reduced to 1,600 hours.
3. Unit contribution margin of Y increases to $80.

4. Management requires the production of 250 units of X.
5. Unit contribution margin of X decreases to $20.

15–31 Accounting Inputs to Linear Programming (Appendix)

The TenComp Calculator Company manufactures two popular pocket calculators, the COMP1000 and the COMP2000. Recent increases in demand have pushed TenComp Calculator to the limits of their production capacity. The president is a former engineer who knows that linear programming can be used to help determine the optimal product mix. However, he needs your assistance in formulating objective function coefficients and in determining the profit implications of the optimal solution.

The following information is available from the accounting records:

	COMP1000	COMP2000
Unit selling price	$25	$35
Unit standard cost:		
Direct materials	$ 5	$10
Direct labor	10	16
Factory overhead	5	8
Total	$20	$34

The standard unit cost for factory overhead is based on an expected monthly activity level of $250,000 direct-labor dollars. Monthly fixed factory overhead costs are $50,000.

ADDITIONAL INFORMATION

- Variable selling and administrative costs are $2 per unit.
- Fixed selling and administrative costs are $40,000 per month.

REQUIREMENTS

a) Prepare a schedule that details the computation of the objective function coefficients for the COMP1000 and the COMP2000.

b) *Assuming* the optimal solution is 25,000 COMP1000s and the corresponding value of the objective function is $100,000, determine TenComp Calculator's monthly before-tax profit. (*Note:* $100,000 is an assumed value that is not necessarily correct.)

15–32 Analysis of Graph (Appendix)

Davis Company produces two products, A and B. Monthly production is limited by labor-hour and machine-hour constraints. Direct-labor hours cannot exceed 12,000 hours per month, and machine hours cannot exceed 7,000 hours per month. Monthly fixed costs of Davis Company total $40,000. The graph presented shows the constraints and break-even isoprofit line for products A and B of Davis Company.

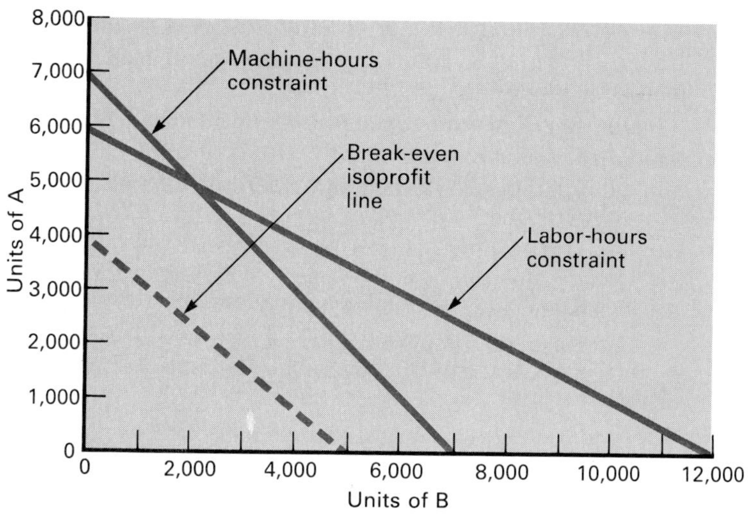

REQUIREMENTS

a) Determine the equations for the objective function and constraints.

b) Use graphic analysis to determine the optimal product mix.

c) Using your answer to part (b), determine the value of the objective function and the monthly before-tax profits.

15–33 Analysis of Constraints (Appendix)

The Sun Appliance Company manufactures both commercial and residential versions of the Sun Clothes Washer. Both models use identical motors and have similar styling. The main difference is that the commercial model has heavy-duty switches, whereas the residential version does not.

Sun purchases the component parts for both washers from a manufacturer of electric parts and from a sheet metal stamping company. Upon receipt, the parts are assembled and painted at Sun's southwest factory.

Selling and production information is as follows:

	Model	
	Commercial	*Residential*
Unit selling price	\$200	\$150
Materials cost	80	60
Variable conversion cost	40	40
Variable selling and administrative cost	20	20

The current market conditions are such that Sun could devote its entire operations to the production and sale of commercial units. However, management believes it is in the long-run interest to manufacture a minimum of 200 residential units per month.

The firm is constrained in the number of units it can produce each month by two factors, the supply of electric motors and the availability of labor hours. Under a long-term contract, Sun can purchase a maximum of 1,000 electric motors each month.

Both models require 6 direct-labor hours per unit and a total of 7,200 labor hours are available each month. Because of slack in the sheet metal industry, Sun can obtain unlimited quantities of prestamped metal.

REQUIREMENTS

a) Use graphic analysis to determine the current optimum monthly production of each model and the total monthly contribution.

b) Determine the shadow price associated with each binding constraint and the amount of slack in the nonbinding constraints. Indicate the significance of each shadow price.

c) Perform sensitivity analysis to determine the lower boundary of the indifference range for labor hours and the upper boundary of the indifference range for the selling price of residential units.

d) Determine the amount of any monthly economic sacrifice (opportunity cost) Sun is incurring to sustain its current production mix.

15–34 Single and Multiple Capacity Constraints (Appendix)

Biggest Burger Restaurants sell three types of hamburgers: Huge, Super-huge, and Colossus. All three are processed and frozen in rolls at Biggest Burger's processing plant in Beef City. The hamburgers are then shipped in refrigerated trucks to franchised outlets throughout the Southwest. Prior to serving, the hamburgers are cooked in microwave ovens.

Biggest Burger's assistant bookkeeper developed the following revenue and cost information. Information is per 1,000 hamburgers (M = 1,000).

	Per 1,000 hamburgers		
	Huge	*Super-huge*	*Colossus*
Selling price to public	$1,000	$1,800	$2,800
Less allowance for franchise costs and profits	−120	−388	−465
Revenue to Biggest Burger	$ 880	$1,412	$2,335
Less:			
Direct materials	$ 400	$ 800	$1,600
Direct labor	20	20	20
Variable factory overhead	50	80	100
Variable distribution	10	12	15
Applied fixed factory overhead	300	300	300
Total	−780	−1,212	−2,035
Unit contribution to administrative expenses and profit	$ 100	$ 200	$ 300

ADDITIONAL INFORMATION

- Direct labor is $10 per hour.
- Variable factory overhead is $20 per machine hour.
- At an annual volume of 1,000 M hamburgers, fixed factory overhead is applied at the rate of $300 per M hamburgers, regardless of the type of hamburger.
- Last year Biggest Burger sold 500 M Huge, 250 M Super-huge, and 250 M Colossus hamburgers for an average unit margin of $175 per M hamburgers.
- With annual fixed selling and administrative expenses of $100,000, Biggest Burger reported a profit of $25,000 last year.

REQUIREMENTS

(*Note:* Part (e) of this problem requires the use of a computer.)

a) At last year's sales mix determine Biggest Burger's break-even unit sales volume (in thousands).

b) Using the designations "increase," "decrease," "no change," and "can't tell," indicate the effect of each of the following independent events on Biggest Burger's break-even point:

   1. A shift in the product mix toward more Colossus and fewer Huge hamburgers.
   2. An increase in the selling price of Super-huge hamburgers and a decrease in the variable costs of distribution.
   3. An increase in the selling price of Colossus hamburgers and an increase in labor wage rates.

c) Assuming that Biggest Burger can sell 1,000 M Huge, 500 M Super-huge, and 200 M Colossus hamburgers each year, and that labor capacity is restricted to 2,000 hours per year, determine Biggest Burger's optimal product mix.

d) Assume that in addition to the labor-hour and sales-volume constraints discussed in part (c), an equipment failure limits Biggest Burger to 3,000 machine hours next year. Management wishes to determine the optimal product mix with the aid of linear programming. Formulate the objective function and constraints necessary to do this.

e) If you have computer facilities, determine Biggest Burger's optimal production and sales mix for the situation presented in part (d). What annual profit should Biggest Burger expect if the optimal mix is implemented? Assume there will be no change in fixed costs.

15–35 Four-Product Production Mix with Sensitivity Analysis: Value of Perfect Information (Appendix)[10]

The Rappaport Electric Company produces three styles of black-and-white TV sets (standard, deluxe, and super) and a color set. Because of a recent surge in demand, management believes it can sell as many sets as it can produce. Each set goes through the plant's three departments: Subassembly, Assembly, and

---

[10] Adapted from "Sensitivity Analysis in Decision Making," by Alfred Rappaport, *Accounting Review* **42,** No. 3 (July 1967): 441–456, with permission.

Testing. The number of direct-labor hours required in each department is as follows:

	Standard	*Deluxe*	*Super*	*Color*
Subassembly	12	15	15	25
Assembly	10	12	13	20
Testing	0.5	0.6	0.6	2.0

The capacity of the plant allows no more than 3,500, 3,000, and 240 daily labor hours in the Subassembly, Assembly, and Testing Departments, respectively. Due to existing contractual agreements, at least ten standard and ten deluxe models must be produced daily. The contribution margin (revenue minus variable costs) from the sale of each set is as follows:

	Standard	*Deluxe*	*Super*	*Color*
Unit contribution margin	$25	$30	$40	$100

Rappaport has daily fixed costs of $1,000.

REQUIREMENTS

(*Note:* Parts (b) through (f) require the use of computer programs.)

a) Formulate the objective function and constraints that Rappaport should use to determine the optimal daily production schedule.

b) Determine the optimal solution and the daily profits of Rappaport.

c) Perform sensitivity analysis to determine the effect of a $20 *increase* in the price of color cathode-ray picture tubes on the optimal solution and daily profits.

d) Determine the effect of a $35 *increase* in the price of color cathode-ray picture tubes on daily profits, assuming Rappaport does not change its daily product schedule.

e) Determine the optimal daily product schedule and related daily profits that can be attained with the $35 price increase.

f) If there is a 50 percent probability that prices will increase by $35, what action should management take?

g) Assuming there are 25 working days in a month, how much would Rappaport be willing to pay to obtain a one-month contract at the old price if a price increase was certain to take place without such an arrangement?

h) How much would Rappaport be willing to pay for the contract if there were a 50 percent probability of a price increase at the start of business on the first day of the month? Assume the production mix must be set for a one-month period before the start of each month.

i) How much would Rappaport be willing to pay before its production mix was set for the month to obtain perfect information on whether or not the price increase would occur?

15–36 Review of Cost Allocation, Cost Estimation and Multiple Product Linear Programming (Appendix)[11]

(*Note:* Problem 15–36 requires the use of a computer.)

---

[11] Adapted from "Report on the Committee on Measurement Methods," *Accounting Review*, supplement to vol. **46** (1971): 229–231, with permission.

In November 19x0, the Bayview Manufacturing Company was in the process of preparing its budget for 19x1. As the first step, it prepared a pro forma income statement for 19x0 based on the first 10 months of operations and revised plans for the last two months. This income statement, in condensed form, was as follows:

Sales		$3,000,000
Direct materials	$1,182,000	
Direct labor	310,000	
Factory overhead	775,000	
Selling and administrative	450,000	−2,717,000
Net income before taxes		$ 283,000

These results were better than were expected and operations were close to capacity, but Bayview's management was not convinced that demand would remain at present levels and hence had not planned any increase in plant capacity. Its equipment was specialized and made to order; over a year's lead time was necessary on all plant additions.

Bayview manufactures three products; sales have been broken down by product as follows:

100,000 of product A @ $20.00	$2,000,000
40,000 of product B @ 10.00	400,000
20,000 of product C @ 30.00	600,000
	$3,000,000

Management has ordered a profit analysis for each product and has available the following information:

	A	*B*	*C*
Direct material	$ 7.00	$ 3.75	$ 16.60
Direct labor	2.00	1.00	3.50
Factory overhead	5.00	2.50	8.75
Selling and administrative	3.00	1.50	4.50
Total costs	$17.00	$ 8.75	$ 33.35
Selling price	20.00	10.00	30.00
Profit	$ 3.00	$ 1.25	$ (3.35)

Factory overhead has been applied on the basis of direct-labor costs at a rate of 250 percent, and management asserts that approximately 20 percent of the overhead is variable and does vary with labor costs. Selling and administrative costs have been allocated on the basis of sales at the rate of 15 percent; management believes approximately one-half of this is variable and does vary with sales in dollars. All the direct-labor cost is considered to be variable.

As the first step in the planning process, the sales department has been asked to estimate what it could sell; these estimates have been reviewed by top management. They are as follows:

A	130,000 units
B	50,000 units
C	50,000 units

Production of these quantities was immediately recognized as being impossible. Estimated cost data for the three products, each of which requires activity of both departments, were based on the following production rates:

	A	*B*	*C*
Department 1	2 per hour	4 per hour	3 per hour
Department 2	4 per hour	8 per hour	$\frac{4}{3}$ per hour

Practical capacity is 67,000 labor hours in Department 1 and 63,000 labor hours in Department 2, and the industrial engineering department has concluded that this cannot be increased without the purchase of additional equipment. Thus, although last year Department 1 operated at 99 percent of its capacity and Department 2 at 71 percent of capacity, anticipated sales would require operating both Department 1 and 2 at more than 100 percent capacity.

These solutions to the limited production problem have been rejected: (1) subcontracting the production out to other firms is considered unprofitable because of problems of maintaining quality; (2) operating a second shift is impossible because of shortage of labor; (3) operating overtime would create problems because a large number of employees are "moonlighting" and would therefore refuse to work more than the normal 40-hour week. Price increases have also been rejected; although they would result in higher profits this year, the long-run competitive position of the firm would be weakened, resulting in lower profits in the future.

The treasurer then suggested that Product C has been carried at a loss too long and now is the time to eliminate it from the product line. If all facilities are used to produce Products A and B, profits would be increased.

The sales manager objected to this solution because of the need to carry a full line. In addition, he maintains that there is a group of customers who have provided, and will continue to provide, a solid base for the firm's activities and these customers' needs must be met. He listed these customers and their estimated purchases (in units) which total as follows:

A	80,000
B	32,000
C	12,000

It was impossible to verify these contentions, but they appeared to be reasonable and they served to narrow the bounds of the problem, so the president concurred.

The treasurer reluctantly acquiesced, but maintained that the remaining capacity should be used to produce Products A and B. Because Product A produced 2.4 times as much profit as Product B, he suggested that the production of Product A (in excess of the 80,000 minimum set by the sales manager) be 2.4 times that of Product B (in excess of the 32,000 minimum set by the sales manager).

The production manager made some quick calculations and said that this would result in budgeted production and sales as follows:

A	104,828
B	42,344
C	12,000

The treasurer then calculated what profits would be:

A	104,828 @ $3.00	$314,484
B	42,344 @ $1.25	52,930
C	12,000 @ $(3.35)	(40,200)
		$327,214

As this would represent an increase of almost 15 percent over the current year, there was a general feeling of self-satisfaction. Before final approval was given, however, the president said that he would like to have his new assistant check over the figures. Somewhat piqued, the treasurer agreed and at that point the group adjourned.

The next day the preceding information was submitted to you as your first assignment on your new job as the president's assistant. Prepare an analysis showing the president what he should do.

Exhibits A and B contain information that you are able to obtain from the accounting system. Assume that production costs are stable and that there are no changes in production techniques during the periods included in these data.

Exhibit A

	Direct-labor expense (000)			*Overhead expense (000)*		
Department:	*1*	*2*	*Total*	*1*	*2*	*Total*
Year						
19x0	$140	$170	$310	$341	$434	$775
19w9	135	150	285	340	421	762*
19w8	140	160	300	342	428	770
19w7	130	150	280	339	422	761
19w6	130	155	285	338	425	763
19w5	125	140	265	337	414	751
19w4	120	150	270	335	420	755
19w3	115	140	255	334	413	747
19w2	120	140	260	336	414	750
19w1	115	135	250	335	410	745

* Rounding error

Exhibit B

	Sales (000)				*Selling and administrative expense (000)*
Year	*Product A*	*Product B*	*Product C*	*Total*	
19x0	$2,000	$400	$600	$3,000	$450
19w9	1,940	430	610	2,980	445
19w8	1,950	380	630	2,960	445
19w7	1,860	460	620	2,940	438
19w6	1,820	390	640	2,850	433
19w5	1,860	440	580	2,880	437
19w4	1,880	420	570	2,870	438
19w3	1,850	380	580	2,810	434
19w2	1,810	390	580	2,780	430
19w1	1,770	290	610	2,670	425

SOLUTION TO REVIEW PROBLEM

a) Payoff Table

	Event (Probability)		
	Sales = 35,000 (0.40)	*Sales = 50,000 (0.60)*	*Expected value*
Actions:			
A1: Sell to Wong	$35,000*	$50,000*	$44,000
A2: Reject sales to Wong and produce X	$45,000	$45,000	$45,000

* The unit contribution margin from sales to Wong is $1:

Unit sales price	$7.00
Unit variable costs ($1,200,000/200,000 units)	−6.00
Unit contribution margin	$1.00

Payoffs from selling to Wrong are $1 × 35,000 units = $35,000 and $1 × 50,000 units = $50,000.

b) $EV_{A1} = 0.40(\$35{,}000) + 0.60(\$50{,}000) = \underline{\underline{\$44{,}000}}$

$EV_{A2} = 0.40(\$45{,}000) + 0.60(\$45{,}000) = \underline{\underline{\$45{,}000}}$

c) Conditional Loss Table

	Event (Probability)		
	Sales = 35,000 (0.40)	*Sales = 50,000 (0.60)*	*Expected value*
Actions:			
A1	$10,000	0	$4,000
A2	0	$5,000	$3,000

d) Using payoff table

Expected payoff with perfect information 0.40($45,000) + 0.60($50,000) =	$48,000
Expected value of best alternative (A2)	−45,000
Expected value of perfect information	$ 3,000

Using conditional loss table:

$\text{EVPI} = 0.40(\$0) + 0.60(\$5{,}000) = \underline{\underline{\$3{,}000}}$

e) The probability of each report given the event is as follows:

	Event	
	Sales = 35,000	*Sales = 50,000*
Report: R1	0.70	0.30
R2	0.30	0.70

The probability of each type of report is:

$P(\text{R1}) = 0.70(0.40) + 0.30(0.60) = \underline{\underline{0.46}}$

$P(\text{R2}) = 0.30(0.40) + 0.70(0.60) = \underline{\underline{0.54}}$

Using Bayes' Theorem to revise the probabilities of events given in the report gives:

$$P(\text{sales} = 35{,}000 \mid \text{R1}) = [0.70 \times 0.40]/0.46 = \underline{\underline{0.609}}$$
$$P(\text{sales} = 50{,}000 \mid \text{R1}) = [0.30 \times 0.60]/0.46 = \underline{\underline{0.391}}$$
$$P(\text{sales} = 35{,}000 \mid \text{R2}) = [0.30 \times 0.40]/0.54 = \underline{\underline{0.222}}$$
$$P(\text{sales} = 50{,}000 \mid \text{R2}) = [0.70 \times 0.60]/0.54 = \underline{\underline{0.778}}$$

Expected values with revised probabilities are:

Given R1: $EV_{A1} = 0.609(\$35{,}000) + 0.391(\$50{,}000) = \underline{\underline{\$40{,}865}}$

$EV_{A2} = 0.609(\$45{,}000) + 0.391(\$45{,}000) = \underline{\underline{\$45{,}000}}$

When R1 is received, Toyson should select A2.

Given R2: $EV_{A1} = 0.222(\$35{,}000) + 0.778(\$50{,}000) = \underline{\underline{\$46{,}670}}$

$EV_{A1} = 0.222(\$45{,}000) + 0.778(\$45{,}000) = \underline{\underline{\$45{,}000}}$

When R2 is received, Toyson should select A1.

This gives an expected payoff with imperfect information of $45,901.80 [0.46($45,000) + 0.54($46,670)].

The expected value of sample information is $901.80:

Expected payoff with imperfect information	$45,901.80
Expected value with current information	−45,000.00
Expected value of sample information	$ 901.80

The maximum Toyson would be willing to pay a consultant who is correct 70 percent of the time is $901.80. Thus they would not hire the consultant for $1,000.

16 Capital Budgeting I

INTRODUCTION

CAPITAL-BUDGETING POLICY

CAPITAL-BUDGETING MODELS

USAGE OF CAPITAL-BUDGETING MODELS

COST OF CAPITAL AS A CUTOFF OR DISCOUNT RATE

ESTIMATING PROJECT CASH FLOWS

SUBSEQUENT CONTROL AND PERFORMANCE EVALUATION

SUMMARY

APPENDIX A: IMPACT OF CHANGING PRICES ON CAPITAL-BUDGETING MODELS

APPENDIX B: IMPACT OF DEPRECIATION METHODS ON MEASURES OF INVESTMENT PERFORMANCE

INTRODUCTION

CAPITAL BUDGETING INVOLVES THE COMMITMENT OF RESOURCES OVER AN extended period of time in a manner that will help an organization achieve its objectives. Virtually all organizations in all sectors of our economy engage in capital budgeting. For-profit organizations may invest in tangible and intangible assets to maximize shareholders' wealth, however not-for-profit organizations and units of government make similar investments to provide services at minimum cost.

Capital budgeting is the identification of potentially desirable investments, their subsequent evaluation, and the selection of investments that meet certain criteria. Because the long-term commitments inherent in major capital expenditures affect the nature and flexibility of an organization, they should not be taken lightly. A number of models have been developed to aid in the systematic evaluation and selection of previously identified projects. The purpose of this chapter is to introduce these models and consider the role of the cost accountant during and after project evaluation and selection. A number of specialized, but important, capital-budgeting topics are discussed in Chapter 17.

Students who do not have a working knowledge of such time-value-of-money concepts as "future amount," "present value," and "annuity in arrears" should read Appendix A to this book before undertaking a study of capital budgeting.

CAPITAL-BUDGETING POLICY

In Chapter 10 we noted that the evaluation of major capital expenditures for new plant and equipment is part of an organization's long-range planning process, and that long-range planning usually takes place at the highest levels of operating management. Because long-range planning accepts the organization's strategic plan as a constraint, a basic criterion for the evaluation of proposed investments is that they conform to the organization's strategic plan. Accordingly, a company that wants to publish college-level textbooks should reject an offer to acquire a hamburger chain irrespective of the offer's inherent desirability.[1]

Following adoption, the capital budget becomes a constraint in the development of the annual master budget. During the initial investment phase, newly approved projects affect cash flows, assets, and liabilities. Subsequently they also affect capacity constraints, budgets for income, manufacturing costs, and purchases.

The size and nature of projects included in capital budgets range from the routine replacement of an old machine to the construction of a new plant or the introduction of a new product. During a single year, a large organization may commit tens of millions of dollars to thousands of projects. Formal capital-budgeting policies are needed to do this efficiently. **Capital-budgeting policies** are organizational rules specifying procedures to be followed to obtain approval for capital expenditure proposals. They may also specify the capital-budgeting models employed to evaluate projects and the criteria used to select acceptable projects as well as postselection control and project evaluation procedures.

The benefits of and the need for upper-level management review vary from project to project. Many minor capital expenditures are necessary to maintain operations to which the organization is currently committed. Unless the accounting information system signals a need to reevaluate them, these operations are assumed to be beneficial and the responsibility to select the best tools to do the job is delegated to lower level management. Under the pressure of day-to-day operations, these people may not perform a complete analysis of all alternatives. However, the risk of a nonoptimal investment is tolerated because of the relatively high cost of formal evaluation.

At the other end of the spectrum, proposals for major expenditures to extend the useful life of current plants, construct new facilities, or introduce new products typically require approval by a capital-budgeting committee composed of top operating management. To ease the burden of this committee, a full-time capital-budgeting staff may be established to assist in project evaluation, selection, postselection control, and performance evaluation.

CAPITAL-BUDGETING MODELS

Although the characteristics of some capital-budgeting models make them more desirable than others, the use of any capital-budgeting model provides certain benefits. They all require a formal projection of a project's impact on cash flows or net income so that management may objectively evaluate the project's desirability. These projections force managers to plan for the future. A formal projection also provides a basis for controlling expenditures during the investment phase and for evaluating subsequent results. The authors of investment proposals know that plans must be carefully formulated and that follow-up will occur. This awareness improves the quality of investment proposals that reach the capital-budgeting committee. Committing the projection to paper also reduces the empire-building tendency of persuasive executives who compete for funds.

---

[1] Their only other alternative is to reevaluate their strategic plan.

There are two basic types of capital-budgeting models, discounting models that consider the time value of money and nondiscounting models that do not consider the time value of money. In recent years there has been a marked increase in the number of organizations using discounting models. Nevertheless nondiscounting models remain popular. Additionally, many organizations use two or more models to evaluate different characteristics of a project. Two nondiscounting and two discounting models are considered in this chapter:

Nondiscounting:
  Payback period (bail-out factor as a variation)
  Accounting rate of return
Discounting:
  Internal rate of return (payback reciprocal as an approximation)
  Net present value

As we present each model, we discuss its uses and limitations. For the moment, we will ignore the problems involved in projecting cash receipts and disbursements.

Nondiscounting Models

Payback Period The **payback period** is the time required to recover the initial investment in a project from operational sources. With equal annual cash inflows, the payback period is the initial investment divided by the predicted annual net cash inflows.

$$\text{Payback period} = \frac{P}{S} \qquad (16\text{–}1)$$

where

P = Initial investment
S = Predicted annual net cash inflow

Example 16–1

The Odyssey Travel Agency is evaluating a proposal to purchase a new $60,000 bus. The bus has a useful life of five years and equal annual net cash inflows of $20,000 are projected. The payback period of this investment is three years ($60,000 ÷ $20,000).

If the predicted annual net cash inflows are not equal, the payback period is determined by summing the annual net cash inflows to the point where they equal the initial investment.

Example 16–2

Consider the following predicted annual net cash inflows for an Odyssey Travel Agency project costing $5,000:

Year	*Net cash inflow*	*Cumulative net cash inflow*
1	$2,000	$2,000
2	1,000	3,000
3	4,000	7,000
4	1,000	8,000

Assuming cash inflows occur evenly throughout each year, the payback period is two and one-half years. Three thousand dollars are recovered by the end of the second year. Because Year 3 cash inflows total $4,000, payback occurs when half of this amount is obtained.

To determine if a proposed investment is acceptable using the payback method, management must compare the calculated payback period with a maximum acceptable payback period. If the calculated payback period is less than or equal to this maximum, the investment is acceptable. If Odyssey Travel Agency has a maximum acceptable payback period of three years, the investments in Examples 16–1 and 16–2 meet this criterion and are acceptable.

The bail-out factor is sometimes computed as a variation of the payback period. The **bail-out factor** is the time required to recover the initial investment in a project from *any* source. The payback period recognizes only net cash inflows from operations, whereas the bail-out factor recognizes the possibility of disposing of an asset before the end of its useful life.

Example 16–3

If the Odyssey Travel Agency could sell the bus discussed in Example 16–1 for $40,000 anytime during the first two years following purchase, the bail-out factor would be one year:

Year 1 net cash inflow from operations	$20,000
Sales value of bus at end of Year 1	40,000
Initial investment	$60,000

Until recently the payback period was the most widely used model for evaluating investment proposals. It is easily understood and emphasizes liquidity. This emphasis on liquidity may be desirable in an uncertain world where a rapid payback of the initial investment is important. However, when used as the sole investment criterion, payback is subject to three major criticisms:

1. It ignores profitability.
2. It ignores the timing of cash flows within the payback period.
3. It ignores the timing of cash flows after the payback period.

Both projects presented in Exhibit 16–1(a) have payback periods of two years. Yet, the second is more profitable and, therefore, more desirable than the first because it continues to provide net cash inflows subsequent to the payback period. Similarly, both projects presented in Exhibit 16–1(b) have payback periods of three years. However, the second is more desirable than the first because it provides for an earlier payback of the bulk of the initial investment. These funds may be profitably employed in other projects or returned to investors. At a minimum, they can be invested in government securities. In Exhibit 16–1(c), both projects have payback periods of three years. Again, the second is more desirable than the first because the higher cash flows occur earlier in years after the payback period. To partially compensate for payback's failure to consider profitability, users sometimes specify criteria for payback and useful life (for

EXHIBIT 16–1 Criticism of Payback as the Sole Investment Criterion

(a) It ignores profitability.

Project	Initial investment	Net cash inflows				
		Year 1	*Year 2*	*Year 3*	*Year 4*	*Year 5*
A	$(100,000)	$50,000	$50,000	$ 0	$ 0	$ 0
B	$(100,000)	$50,000	$50,000	$50,000	$50,000	$50,000

(b) It ignores the timing of cash flows within the payback period.

Project	Initial investment	Net cash inflows				
		Year 1	*Year 2*	*Year 3*	*Year 4*	*Year 5*
A	$(200,000)	$ 40,000	$60,000	$100,000	$60,000	$40,000
B	$(200,000)	$100,000	$60,000	$ 40,000	$60,000	$40,000

(c) It ignores the timing of cash flows after the payback period.

Project	Initial investment	Net cash inflows				
		Year 1	*Year 2*	*Year 3*	*Year 4*	*Year 5*
A	$(200,000)	$100,000	$60,000	$40,000	$20,000	$60,000
B	$(200,000)	$100,000	$60,000	$40,000	$60,000	$20,000

example, acceptable projects must have a useful life greater than twice their payback period).

Accounting Rate of Return Another nondiscounting method for evaluating investment proposals, the **accounting rate of return,** is calculated as the average annual increase in net income expected to result from accepting a project divided by either the initial investment or the average investment in the project:

$$\text{Accounting rate of return} = \frac{\text{Average annual increase in net income}}{\text{Initial or average investment}} \tag{16–2}$$

In computing the accounting rate of return, remember that depreciation causes annual net income to be less than annual net cash inflows.

Example 16–4 Assuming that the investment in Example 16–1 does not have a salvage value, the average annual increase in net income is $8,000:

Average annual net cash inflow	$20,000
Less average annual depreciation ($60,000 ÷ 5 years)	– 12,000
Average annual increase in net income	$ 8,000

Accordingly, the accounting rate of return on the initial investment is 13.3 percent ($8,000 ÷ $60,000), and the accounting rate of return on average investment is 26.7 percent ($8,000 ÷ $30,000).

The average investment represents the average balance in the asset account over the life of the investment. Average investment is calculated by dividing the initial investment plus salvage value, if any, by two. In equation form,

$$\text{Average investment} = \frac{\text{Initial investment} + \text{Salvage value}}{2} \tag{16–3}$$

If the investment in Example 16–1 had a salvage value, the average annual increase in net income and the average investment would be larger.

Example 16–5

Assume the $60,000 bus in Example 16–1 has a salvage value of $10,000 at the end of its five-year life. In this case, the annual depreciation is $10,000 [($60,000 − $10,000) ÷ 5 years] and the average investment is $35,000 [($60,000 + $10,000) ÷ 2]. The accounting rate of return on initial investment is 16.7 percent ($10,000 ÷ $60,000), and the accounting rate of return on average investment is 28.6 percent ($10,000 ÷ $35,000).

If we use the accounting rate of return to evaluate proposed investments, we compare the calculated rate with a minimum rate to determine if the project is acceptable. If the minimum acceptable rate on the average investment were 20 percent, the investment in the bus meets this criterion and is acceptable.

Although the accounting rate of return does provide a measure of profitability, it does not consider the timing of cash flows. Both of the projects in Exhibit 16–2 have an accounting rate of return of 30 percent on initial investment. Yet, because of the timing of cash flows, the second is clearly preferable to the first.

The accounting rate of return continues in use primarily because it is related to the performance measures that analysts calculate from financial statements to evaluate profitability and the return on investment used to evaluate investment centers' performance. To be consistent with these calculations, managers may evaluate proposed projects using the accounting rate of return. A better approach may be to use discounted cash flow models to evaluate proposed projects and change the method of performance evaluation to be consistent with these models.

EXHIBIT 16–2 Accounting Rate of Return Ignores Timing of Cash Flows

		Net cash flows				
Project	*Initial investment*	*Year 1*	*Year 2*	*Year 3*	*Year 4*	*Total*
A	$(100,000)*	$ 55,000	$ 55,000	$55,000	$55,000	$220,000
B	$(100,000)*	$100,000	$100,000	$10,000	$10,000	$220,000

Project	*Accounting rate of return*
A	$\frac{\$55{,}000 - \$25{,}000\dagger}{\$100{,}000} = 30\%$
B	$\frac{\$55{,}000 - \$25{,}000\dagger}{\$100{,}000} = 30\%$

* No salvage value.
† The average annual depreciation is not affected by the depreciation method.

Although the accounting rate of return is a valuable tool when used by people outside the organization who do not have better information, its internal use is questionable. If yearly cash flows must be predicted to develop project proposals, the same yearly predictions can be used as a basis of performance evaluation.

Discounting Models

Internal Rate of Return (IRR) The **internal rate of return,** sometimes called **time adjusted rate of return** or **rate of return,** is the discount rate that equates the present value of a project's predicted net cash inflows with the initial investment. The internal rate of return is sometimes described as the maximum interest rate an organization could pay for the cash invested in a project without losing money. In determining a project's internal rate of return, we assume that the initial investment cash outflow occurs at the present time (referred to as time 0), and that the subsequent cash flows occur at the end of each period over the life of the investment. The problem is to determine the discount rate that equates the subsequent cash flows with the initial investment.

Eq. 16–4 or Table E (in Appendix B of this book) is used to determine the IRR if the cash flows are unequal:

$$P = \frac{S_1}{(1+r)^1} + \frac{S_2}{(1+r)^2} + \cdots + \frac{S_i}{(1+r)^i} + \cdots + \frac{S_n}{(1+r)^n} \tag{16–4}$$

where

P = Initial investment
S = Predicted net cash inflow
r = Internal rate of return
i = Time period when cash flows occur
n = Life of the investment

Eq. 16–5 or Table F (in Appendix B of this book) is used if the cash flows are equal for consecutive periods:

$$P = S\left[\frac{1}{r}\left[1 - \frac{1}{(1+r)^n}\right]\right] \tag{16–5}$$

Unfortunately IRR computations can become quite complex if done by hand. The key to using annuity tables for equal and consecutive cash flows is to determine the number of multiples of S contained in P. The resulting factor is analogous to the factor for the present value of \$1 found in Table F:

$$\frac{P}{S} = \text{Present value of an annuity of \$1 in arrears} = \text{Factor (in Table F)}$$

Once this factor is found, we enter the annuity table at the appropriate value of n and go across the corresponding row until we find the closest table factor. The corresponding value of r is the internal rate of return. In this textbook interpolations are not performed for factors listed in appropriate tables; that is, values for the internal rate of return between two tabled values are not estimated. In practice, very detailed tables, calculators with IRR functions, or computer routines are used to determine r.

Example 16–6 The internal rate of return of the investment proposal discussed in Example 16–1 is 20 percent. The basic information and computations are as follows:

$$P = \$60{,}000$$
$$S = \$20{,}000$$
$$n = 5$$
$$\text{Factor} = \frac{\$60{,}000}{\$20{,}000} = \underline{\underline{3.00}}$$

In Table F, going across the row for $n = 5$, the closest factor to 3.00 is 2.9906. The corresponding r value of 0.20 is the internal rate of return.

With unequal annual cash flows, we use a trial-and-error approach to determine the internal rate of return. We select a value of r and compute the corresponding present value of all future cash inflows.[2] If the resulting present value equals the initial investment, r is the internal rate of return. If the resulting present value is less than the initial investment, the internal rate of return is less than r. Finally, if the resulting present value is greater than the initial investment, the internal rate of return is greater than r. Both of these latter occurrences require an additional selection of r and further computations.

Example 16–7 The Ace Machine Shop is evaluating a proposal to purchase a machine that has a useful life of three years. The machine costs $18,000 to purchase and install. It will produce annual net cash inflows of $8,000, $6,000, and $10,000 in years one, two, and three, respectively.

The internal rate of return of this investment is 16 percent (see Exhibit 16–3). Note that three trials were required to determine the value of r that equates the initial investment with the subsequent cash flows. The first trial in Exhibit 16–3 resulted in a negative net present value (this indicates that the project's IRR is less than the value of r selected). The second trial resulted in a positive net present value (this indicates that the project's IRR is greater than the value of r selected).

To determine if projects are acceptable using the IRR criterion, we compare the calculated IRR with a minimum acceptable IRR. If the calculated IRR is greater than or equal to the minimum rate, the project meets the criterion and is acceptable. If Ace Machine Shop has a minimum required IRR of 14 percent, the proposal in Example 16–7 is acceptable.

In computations involving the time value of money, we assume all cash flows take place in lump sums at specific points in time, that is, time zero (the time of the initial investment) and at the end of years one, two, and so on. This assumption is made to simplify calculations. We could divide each year into a number of periods or use continuous discounting, but such refinements are unlikely to have a significant effect on the present value of future cash flows.

With equal annual cash inflows and a useful life of at least twice the payback period, the reciprocal of Eq. 16–1, called the "payback reciprocal," may be used

---

[2] A starting point might be determined by dividing the average annual cash inflows by the initial investment and looking up this factor in Table F to find an r value.

EXHIBIT 16–3 Determining the Internal Rate of Return With Unequal Cash Flows

First Trial: For r = 20 percent

	Time 0	Year 1	Year 2	Year 3
Net cash flows	$(18,000.00)	$8,000.00	$6,000.00	$10,000.00
Present value of $1 @ r = 0.20		× 0.8333	× 0.6944	× 0.5787
Present value	16,619.80	$6,666.40	$4,166.40	$ 5,787.00
Net present value	$ (1,380.20)			

Because the present value of the net cash inflows is less than the initial investment, the internal rate of return is less than 20 percent.

Second Trial: For r = 10 percent

	Time 0	Year 1	Year 2	Year 3
Net cash flows	$(18,000.00)	$8,000.00	$6,000.00	$10,000.00
Present value of $1 @ r = 0.10		× 0.9091	× 0.8264	× 0.7513
Present value	19,744.20	$7,272.80	$4,958.40	$ 7,513.00
Net present value	$ 1,744.20			

Because the present value of the net cash inflows is greater than the initial investment, the internal rate of return is greater than 10 percent.

Third Trial: For r = 16 percent

	Time 0	Year 1	Year 2	Year 3
Net cash flows	$(18,000.00)	$8,000.00	$6,000.00	$10,000.00
Present value of $1 @ r = 0.16		× 0.8621	× 0.7432	× 0.6407
Present value	17,763.00	$6,896.80	$4,459.20	$ 6,407.00
Net present value	$ (237.00)			

Although the present value of the net cash flows is slightly less than the initial investment, this is as close as we can come without interpolating.

as an estimate of the internal rate of return. The **payback reciprocal** is a project's annual net cash inflows divided by the initial investment:

$$\text{Payback reciprocal} = \frac{S}{P} \tag{16–6}$$

where S and P are as previously defined.

The relationship between the internal rate of return and the payback reciprocal of a project requiring an initial investment of $160,000 and providing yearly cash inflows of $40,000 is illustrated in Exhibit 16–4. This project has a payback period of four years ($160,000 ÷ $40,000) and a payback reciprocal of 0.25 ($40,000 ÷ $160,000). As shown in Exhibit 16–4, the payback reciprocal of 25 percent provides an upwardly biased estimate of the IRR. However, as the life of the project approaches infinity, the internal rate of return converges on the payback reciprocal. With a life of four years, the project's true IRR is zero percent. If the project's life were eight years, the true IRR would be 18 percent; and if the project's life were 15 years, the true IRR would be 24 percent.

The internal rate of return is a definite improvement over payback and the accounting rate of return. It considers profitability and the timing of cash flows. Unfortunately the IRR is not without its problems. The most obvious one is the difficulty of hand calculations if a calculator with an IRR function is not available. A project may also have two or more positive internal rates of return if periods of net cash inflow are intermixed with periods of net cash outflow. This confusing situation may occur when a major overhaul is scheduled sometime during an asset's useful life. One of the problems at the end of Chapter 16 deals with this situation. Finally, all the models discussed to date are inadequate for the evaluation of competing investment proposals because they do not consider the magnitude of investments. This problem is discussed in Chapter 17.

Net Present Value (NPV) The three investment proposal evaluation models discussed thus far do not incorporate decision criteria into their computations. Subsequent to the evaluation of a proposal, a decision maker must determine whether or not the project meets some criteria such as a payback period of less than three years, an accounting rate of return of greater than 20 percent, or an internal rate of return of greater than 10 percent. Unlike these models, the net present value method incorporates a decision criterion, in the form of a minimum discount rate, into the computation of a project's net present value. The **discount rate** is the minimum rate of return required for a project to be acceptable.

EXHIBIT 16–4 Relationship Between Payback Reciprocal and IRR

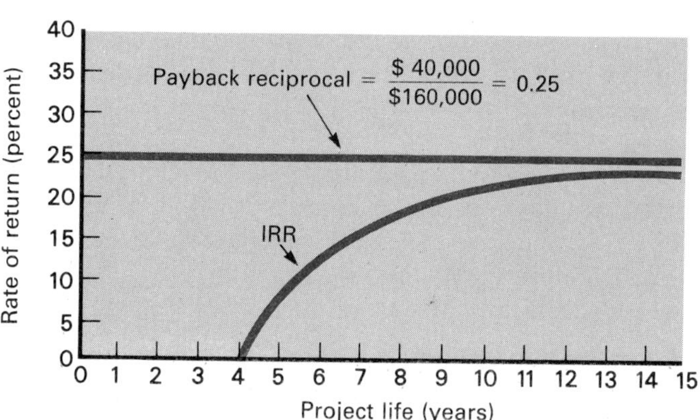

The **net present value** is the present value of a project's net cash inflows less the amount of the initial investment. The net present value is calculated using the following equation:

$$NPV = \sum_{i=1}^{n} \frac{S_i}{(1 + r)^i} - P \tag{16–7}$$

where

NPV = Net present value
r = Minimum required discount rate
i, n, S, and P are as previously defined.

Returning to Example 16–7 and Exhibit 16–3, the net present value of the investment proposal at various discount rates is:

Discount rate (r)	*NPV*
0.10	$ 1,744.20
0.16	(237.00)
0.20	(1,380.20)

If a project has a positive net present value using the minimum required discount rate, the present value of the future cash inflows exceeds the initial investment cost and the project is acceptable. Thus, if the project in Example 16–7 is evaluated using a 10 percent discount rate, it is acceptable. However, if a 16 or 20 percent discount rate is used, the project would be rejected.

The net present value and internal rate of return models are conceptually similar. Both consider the profitability of an investment and the time value of money. When used to evaluate independent projects, both give identical accept or reject signals.[3] In Example 16–7 both models give an accept signal if a 10 percent time adjusted rate of return is required and both give a reject signal if a 20 percent time adjusted rate is required. If more detailed tables were used to compute the proposal's IRR, both models would give a reject signal at 16 percent. (The true IRR is slightly less than 16 percent.) The models differ, however, in their computational form and in the amount of information they require to perform computations.

The IRR model determines the rate that equates the present value of the future cash flows to the amount of the initial investment, whereas the NPV model discounts the future cash flows at a specified discount rate and subtracts the amount of the initial investment. As a result, the NPV model has computational advantages (a trial-and-error approach is never required). Additionally, there is no possibility of obtaining multiple net present values when periods of net cash outflows are intermixed with periods of net cash inflows.

The NPV model requires that management specify the minimum acceptable return, r, before computations are performed. This should not be viewed as a disadvantage because it must be done when the IRR model is used before projects

[3] This is not always the case when competing projects are evaluated (see Chapter 17) or when a project has multiple internal rates of return.

EXHIBIT 16–5 **Usage of Capital-Budgeting Models**

	Percent of companies using model in*	
	1975	*1979*
Primary technique:		
Payback	15%	12%
Accounting rate of return	10	8
Internal rate of return	37	49
Net present value	26	19
Secondary technique:		
Payback	33	39
Accounting rate of return	3	3
Internal rate of return	7	8
Net present value/profitability index†	7	8

* The percentages total less than 100% because of survey respondents who did not indicate that they use one of these techniques.
† The profitability index is discussed in Chapter 17.
Source: Suk H. Kim, and Edward J. Farragher, "Current Capital Budgeting Practices," *Management Accounting* **62,** No. 12 (June 1981): p. 28.

can be accepted or rejected. However, if there are more acceptable projects than can be funded,[4] managers can provide a satisfactory (rather than optimal) selection of projects by ranking them on the basis of the internal rate of return and accepting the highest ranking projects. By doing this, managers avoid the selection of a minimum rate.

USAGE OF CAPITAL-BUDGETING MODELS

Although the discounting models are theoretically superior to the nondiscounting models, surveys of capital-budgeting practices show that both discounting and nondiscounting models are widely used. The results of one survey of capital-budgeting models used by Fortune 1,000 companies in 1975 and 1979 by Professors Kim and Farragher[5] are shown in Exhibit 16–5.

The data in Exhibit 16–5 show that companies may use both primary and secondary techniques to evaluate proposed investments and that discounted cash-flow models are used more than the nondiscounting models as the primary technique. In comparing the results of their survey with previous studies, Professors Kim and Farragher concluded:

> On an overall basis, there appears to be a continuing trend towards greater usage of IRR/NPV as primary evaluation techniques. Payback is still important, but mainly as a secondary evaluation technique.[6]

---

[4] This condition is known as capital rationing and is discussed further in Chapter 17.

[5] Suk H. Kim, and Edward J. Farragher, "Current Capital Budgeting Practices," *Management Accounting* **62,** No. 12 (June 1981), pp. 26–30.

[6] Kim and Farragher, p. 27.

COST OF CAPITAL AS A CUTOFF OR DISCOUNT RATE

The IRR and NPV models both require the establishment of a minimum rate of return to determine if a proposed project is acceptable. In the IRR model this number is referred to as the **cutoff rate** or **hurdle rate.** In the NPV model this number is identified as the discount rate. Unfortunately the determination of this rate is complex and controversial. Although a detailed presentation of this topic is beyond the scope of a cost accounting textbook, a brief discussion is included in this chapter to alert you to some of the important concepts in determining the proper cutoff or discount rate. Because cost accountants are more apt to use the rate than to supply it, our objectives are to show the context within which capital expenditures are made and to enable you to spot obviously erroneous rates.

The critical variables in determining the proper rate are the future cash flows investors expect to receive, the default-free interest rate (frequently specified as the interest rate on federal government securities), and investors' perceptions of the risk[7] associated with investments in a firm. As an absolute minimum, the discount or cutoff rate should equal the default-free interest rate. As risk increases this rate should be adjusted upward because investors demand a higher return as compensation for increased exposure to risk. For-profit organizations may use their weighted-average cost of capital as a cutoff or discount rate if the following circumstances exist:

1. The market for their securities is well established.
2. The relative portion of long-term debt, preferred stock, and common stock in the capital structure is reasonably constant.
3. A reasonably constant ratio is maintained between cash dividends and net operating cash inflows.
4. The acceptance of a project does not affect investors' perceptions of the risk associated with a firm.

The **weighted-average cost of capital** (WACC) is a measure of the after-tax cost of debt, preferred stock, and common stock to the organization. Thus it gives consideration to all sources of long-term financing. It is calculated as the sum of the after-tax cost of debt, preferred stock, and common equity, where each cost is given a weight equal to the portion of the firm's capital financing it provides:

$$k_c = k_d P_d + k_p P_p + k_e P_e \tag{16–8}$$

where

k_c = Weighted-average cost of capital
k_d = After-tax interest rate on long-term debt
P_d = Portion of long-term financing provided by long-term debt
k_p = Discount rate that equates future cash dividends on preferred stock with the current market price per share

[7] In this text "risk" and "uncertainty" have similar meanings. Some writers use "risk" to identify a situation in which possible outcomes and their probabilities can be specified in advance. Those writers reserve "uncertainty" to identify situations in which possible outcomes and/or their probabilities cannot be specified in advance.

P_p = Portion of long-term financing provided by preferred stock
k_e = Discount rate that equates future cash dividends on common stock with the current market price per share
P_e = Portion of long-term financing provided by common equity

The rationale underlying the use of these criteria is that the acceptance of a project that does not provide a rate of return greater than or equal to the WACC will have a depressing effect on the firm's security prices. The use of dividends rather than earnings in computing the cost of common stock is analogous to the use of cash flows rather than net income in capital-budgeting models. It is the ultimate receipt of cash that is of interest to corporations that invest in projects and to stockholders who invest in corporations.

Example 16–8

The Tanner Glove Company obtains 20 percent of its long-term financing from debt, another 20 percent from preferred stock, and 60 percent from reinvested earnings and common stock. The current before-tax interest rate on debt is 10 percent. Preferred dividends are \$6 per year. Following a "no growth" policy, common dividends are to be maintained at a constant \$4 per year. The current market prices of preferred and common stock are \$50 per share and \$25 per share, respectively. The income tax rate is 40 percent.

We must compute the costs of debt, preferred stock, and common stock before computing Tanner's weighted-average cost of capital.

After-tax Cost of Debt

The after-tax cost of debt is simply the effective interest rate multiplied by one minus the tax rate:

$$k_d = 0.10\,(1 - 0.4) = \underline{\underline{0.06}}$$

Cost of Preferred Stock

The cost of preferred stock is the discount rate that equates all future cash dividends paid to preferred shareholders with the current market price of preferred stock. When the dividends are a constant amount in perpetuity, the relationship between them and the current market price is:

$$P_0 = \frac{D}{k_p} \tag{16–9}$$

where

P_0 = Current market price per preferred share
D = Annual cash dividend per preferred share
k_p = Discount rate that equates future cash dividends on preferred stock with the current market price per share

Rearranging terms gives:

$$k_p = \frac{D}{P_0} \tag{16–10}$$

The cost of preferred stock is equal to the annual cash dividends divided by the current market price. For Tanner,

$$k_p = \frac{\$6}{\$50} = \underline{\underline{0.12}}$$

Cost of Equity Capital

The **cost of equity capital** is the discount rate that equates all future cash dividends paid to common shareholders with the current market price of common stock. If dividends are maintained at a constant amount per share, a variation of Eq. 16–10 is used to estimate k_e, the discount rate that equates future cash dividends on common stock with the current market price per share. If common shareholders expect future dividend growth, the determination of k_e must be adjusted. One possibility is to assume a constant dividend growth rate. In this case the cost of equity capital becomes:

$$k_e = \frac{D}{P_0} + g \tag{16–11}$$

where

D = Current annual cash dividends per common share
P_0 = Current market price per common share
g = Expected dividend growth rate

For Tanner,

$$k_e = \frac{\$4}{\$25} + 0.0 = \underline{\underline{0.16}}$$

Using the preceding costs for the various sources of capital, Tanner's weighted-average cost of capital is 13.2 percent:

$$k_c = 0.06(0.20) + 0.12(0.20) + 0.16(0.60) = \underline{\underline{0.132}}$$

If Tanner uses the net present value model to evaluate investment proposals, acceptable projects must have a positive present value at a discount rate of 13.2 percent. If the IRR model is used, acceptable projects must have an internal rate of return of at least 13.2 percent.

ESTIMATING PROJECT CASH FLOWS

The cash flow data used in capital-budgeting models may be placed in one of three categories:

1. Initial investment
2. Operations
3. Disinvestment

Initial Investment

The acquisition of a new production or service facility usually requires investments in land, building, and equipment (including installation). To prepare the facility for operation, additional expenditures are required to hire, train, and relocate personnel. To facilitate operations, investments must be made in inventory, and minimum cash balances must be established. Finally, if goods are sold or services are rendered on account, an investment in accounts receivable is required. (Although these expenditures or investments may extend over a number of periods, they are assumed to occur at time zero in textbook examples.) The amount used as the **initial investment** in capital-budgeting models is the total of all expenditures associated with the acquisition of new property and the preparation of the property for use.

Example 16–9

The Tanner Glove Company is evaluating a proposal to acquire equipment to produce a new type of leather glove. The equipment costs $200,000. In addition, inventories are expected to increase by $30,000 and accounts receivable by $20,000 if the new glove is produced and sold. Assuming no other cash flows are associated with starting the project, the initial investment is $250,000 ($200,000 + $30,000 + $20,000).

As this is written, the income tax code contains a provision for a reduction in income taxes in the year of acquisition[8] for qualifying personal property known as Section 38 property. This tax reduction, called the **investment tax credit,** effectively reduces the amount of the initial investment required for some projects. Qualifying **personal property,** as distinguished from real property, includes most tangible property other than inventories, buildings, and land. **Real property,** which includes buildings and land, ordinarily does not qualify for the investment tax credit.

Current investment tax credit rules were enacted by Congress in the 1981 Economic Recovery Tax Act (ERTA) and the 1982 Tax Equity and Fiscal Responsibility Act (TEFRA). These rules give a taxpayer two alternatives in determining the amount of the credit. The first alternative provides a 6 percent investment tax credit for qualifying property that can be written off (depreciated) over three years and a 10 percent investment tax credit for all other qualifying property. This alternative also specifies that the depreciation basis of the property for tax purposes be reduced by 50 percent of the investment tax credit claimed.

Example 16–10

The equipment in Example 16–9 qualifies for the investment tax credit and can be written off over five years for income tax purposes. Thus the relevant investment tax credit rate is 10 percent. Tanner can claim an income tax credit of $20,000 [$200,000 × 0.10] on its return for the year the equipment is acquired. However, the basis for depreciating the equipment for tax purposes is reduced to $190,000 [$200,000 − (0.50 × $20,000)].

The second alternative is for the taxpayer to reduce the investment tax credit rate by two percentage points and depreciate the entire cost of the qualifying property. If Tanner elects this alternative, the investment tax credit on the equipment in Example 16–9 is $16,000 [$200,000 × 0.08] and the entire $200,000

---

[8] To be technically correct, the reduction in income taxes is claimed for the year the asset is placed in service. In this book, it is assumed that the year of acquisition and the year the asset is placed in service are the same.

would be written off over five years. Ordinarily, it is better for a taxpayer to use the first alternative rather than the second. For this reason, the examples and problems in this chapter assume, unless otherwise stated, that the full investment tax credit is taken and the depreciable basis is reduced by one-half of the investment tax credit claimed.

Assuming Tanner claims an investment tax credit of $20,000, the initial investment for the project in Example 16–9 is $230,000:

Cost of Equipment	$200,000	
Less investment tax credit	−20,000	$180,000
Increase in inventories		30,000
Increase in accounts receivables		20,000
Initial investment		$230,000

The objective of the investment tax credit is to stimulate investment in qualified assets by reducing their cost. Accordingly, in all text examples, exercises, and problems, we will treat the investment tax credit as a reduction in calculating the amount of the initial investment.[9] To take advantage of the investment tax credit, the taxpayer must have taxable income. If this is not the case, the taxpayer may still be able to receive benefits from the investment tax credit through carryback and carryforward provisions of the income tax laws.

Operations

In practice, the procedures used to predict annual cash receipts and disbursements should be similar to those used to develop the cash budget. For simplicity, in the absence of statements to the contrary, we assume the following:

- Revenues and operating cash receipts are equal each year.
- Depreciation is the only noncash expense of an organization. All other operating expenses are paid as recognized.

Accordingly,

  Cash receipts from operations
− Cash expenditures for operations
= Net cash flow before income taxes and
  Income before depreciation and taxes

A year's final net cash flow is:

  Cash receipts from operations
− Cash expenditures for operations
= Net cash flow before income taxes
− Cash expenditures for income taxes
= Net cash flow

[9] For external reporting purposes, the investment tax credit may not be treated in this manner. The interested reader should consult an intermediate accounting textbook.

The predicted cash expenditures for income taxes result from the additional taxes that must be paid because taxable income is higher with the proposed investment than without it. Revenues (cash inflows from operations) increase taxable income, and expenses (cash expenditures for operations plus depreciation) decrease taxable income. Although depreciation does not involve a direct outflow of cash, it is deductible in calculating taxable income and, therefore, provides cash savings in that it reduces taxes. The reduction of income taxes that results from deducting depreciation in computing taxable income is sometimes referred to as the **depreciation tax shield.**

Under the current income tax laws, the cost of a depreciable asset may be deducted in computing taxable income over a period of time that differs from its useful life. Thus the deduction for income tax purposes may differ from the depreciation calculated using traditional depreciation methods. Although straight-line depreciation is acceptable, the method most often used for tax purposes is known as the **Accelerated Cost Recovery System** (ACRS). This system provides for the rapid depreciation of assets in the determination of taxable income. ACRS allows property to be depreciated over three, five, ten, fifteen, or nineteen years depending on the type of property. Three-year property includes primarily automobiles and light-duty trucks. Five-year property includes most other personal property such as machinery and equipment. Ten- and fifteen-year properties are restricted to specific types of assets and are not considered in this textbook. Most real property (buildings and permanent structures) has an nineteen-year ACRS life.

The depreciation deduction allowed under ACRS is calculated by multiplying the depreciable basis of the asset by a percentage that is specified in the tax regulations. The percentages for three-year and five-year properties are shown in Exhibit 16–6. These percentages were formulated using an accelerated method of cost recovery. For three-year and five-year property, the rates approximate 150 percent declining-balance depreciation rates with a switch to straight line at the optimum point. The percentages reflect the half-year convention which allows a deduction for one-half year in the first year regardless of when the asset was acquired. The accelerated rates under ACRS result in a higher present value for the depreciation tax shield than would occur with straight-line depreciation. In addition, an asset's salvage value is ignored in the computation of the ACRS

EXHIBIT 16–6 ACRS Percentages for Three-year and Five-year Properties

Year of recovery	*Three-year*	*Five-year*
1	25%	15%
2	38	22
3	37	21
4		21
5		21

deduction. Under ACRS, no deduction is allowed in the year of disposition of the asset. *The examples and problems in this textbook assume that the asset is disposed of at the start of the year following the end of its useful life and an ACRS deduction is taken in the final year of the asset's useful life.*

Example 16–11 Assume Tanner Glove Company is subject to a 46 percent tax rate and the equipment in Example 16–9 is five-year ACRS property. The computation of the annual ACRS deduction and the related tax savings is presented in Exhibit 16–7.

The depreciation tax shield presented in the last column of Exhibit 16–7 reduces the income taxes that would have to be paid if no depreciation deduction were allowed. The net cash flows used in capital-budgeting models should reflect this tax shield.

Example 16–12 Assume that the Tanner Glove Company's $200,000 investment in equipment has an expected useful life of six years. Predicted cash inflows and outflows from operations are as follows:

Year	*Operating cash inflows*	*Operating cash outflows*
1	$120,000	$70,000
2	160,000	80,000
3	180,000	90,000
4	100,000	50,000
5	80,000	50,000
6	70,000	50,000

With a tax rate of 46 percent, the computation of the expected after-tax net cash flows from the proposed investment is shown in Exhibit 16–8. Note that the cash flow for taxes in Year 5 is added to the before-tax net cash flow. This occurs because the depreciation tax shield for Year 5 of $18,354 exceeds the taxes of $13,800 that are computed on the $30,000 of before-tax cash flows. Assuming that Tanner has taxable income from other sources, the additional tax shield from depreciation of $4,554 ($18,354 – $13,800) offsets the taxes that would otherwise have to be paid and thus serves as a cash inflow in evaluating the proposed investment.

A company may elect not to adopt ACRS depreciation rates and may instead use straight-line depreciation rates based on ACRS asset lives.[10] A company might prefer this alternative if it has operating losses and receives no current benefits from using an accelerated method for calculating depreciation. If straight-line rates are adopted, the half-year convention must be used for the year the asset is acquired. The half-year convention allows a deduction for one-half year's depreciation in the first year regardless of when the asset was acquired.

---

[10] When using straight-line rates, the taxpayer may also elect a longer asset life. For three-year property, a 5- or 12-year life may be elected and for five-year property, a 12- or 25-year life may be elected.

EXHIBIT 16–7 ACRS Deduction and Related Tax Savings

Year	*Cost − 50% of investment tax credit (1)*	*ACRS rate (2)*	*ACRS deduction (3) = (1) × (2)*	*Tax rate (4)*	*Tax shield (3) × (4)*
1	$190,000	0.15	$28,500	0.46	$13,110
2	190,000	0.22	41,800	0.46	19,228
3	190,000	0.21	39,900	0.46	18,354
4	190,000	0.21	39,900	0.46	18,354
5	190,000	0.21	39,900	0.46	18,354

Disinvestment

At the end of the useful life of a project, any physical assets are sold for salvage or scrap, and the investments in operating cash balances, accounts receivable, and inventories are recovered. These cash inflows must be added to the after-tax net cash flows of the last year in evaluating capital investment proposals. Since the cash inflows from the recovery of working capital items are assumed to be equal to the initial investment in those items, they do not have an impact on income taxes for the final year.

The cash flow from the disposal of the physical asset includes the amount of cash received less any additional taxes that must be paid if the asset is sold at a gain. Under the current ACRS and investment tax credit regulations, the basis used for calculating the gain is the cost less any amounts recovered through ACRS and investment tax credit deductions.

EXHIBIT 16–8 After-Tax Cash Flows from Operations

	Year 1	*Year 2*	*Year 3*	*Year 4*	*Year 5*	*Year 6*
Cash inflows	$120,000	$160,000	$180,000	$100,000	$80,000	$70,000
Cash outflows	−70,000	−80,000	−90,000	−50,000	−50,000	−50,000
Net cash flows before income taxes	$ 50,000	$ 80,000	$ 90,000	$ 50,000	$30,000	$20,000
Cash flows for income taxes*	− 9,890	−17,572	−23,046	− 4,646	+ 4,554	− 9,200
Net cash inflows	$ 40,110	$ 62,428	$ 66,954	$ 45,354	$34,554	$10,800

* Computation of cash flow for income taxes:

	Year 1	*Year 2*	*Year 3*	*Year 4*	*Year 5*	*Year 6*
Taxes on net cash flows before income taxes @ 46%	$23,000	$36,800	$41,400	$23,000	$13,800	$9,200
Less: Tax shield from ACRS deduction (See Exhibit 16–7.)	−13,110	−19,228	−18,354	−18,354	18,354	0
Cash flows for income taxes	$ 9,890	$17,572	$23,046	$ 4,646	$(4,554)	$9,200

Example 16–13 The equipment costing $200,000 in Example 16–9 is expected to have a salvage value of $10,000 at the end of its useful life. The gain on the disposal of the equipment is $10,000:

Original cost		$200,000
Less basis reduction for:		
Investment tax credit (0.50 × $20,000)	$ 10,000	
ACRS deductions	190,000	−200,000
Adjusted basis at date of sale		0

Selling price	$ 10,000
Less: Adjusted basis at date of sale	− 0
Gain on disposal of equipment	$ 10,000

At a 46 percent tax rate, Tanner would pay additional taxes of $4,600 ($10,000 × 0.46) on the sale of the equipment and the net cash inflow from the sale is $5,400 ($10,000 − $4,600).

EXHIBIT 16–9 Comprehensive Illustration of NPV Calculation

Time	*Cash flow item*	*Amount*		*Present value factor @ 16%*		*Present value*
0	Initial investment:					
	Cost of equipment	$200,000				
	Less: Investment tax credit	(20,000)				
	Investment in inventory	30,000				
	Investment in accounts receivable	20,000				
	Total initial investment	$230,000	×	1.0000	=	$230,000
	Net cash inflows from operations:					
1		$ 40,110	×	0.8621	=	$ 34,579
2		62,428	×	0.7432	=	46,396
3		66,954	×	0.6407	=	42,897
4		45,354	×	0.5523	=	25,049
5		34,554	×	0.4761	=	16,451
6		10,800	×	0.4104	=	4,432
6	Disinvestment:					
	Sale of equipment	$ 5,400				
	Recovery of investment in inventory	30,000				
	Recovery of investment in accounts receivable	20,000				
	Total	$ 55,400	×	0.4104	=	22,736
	Total present value of future cash inflows					$192,540
	Net present value $192,540 − $230,000 =					$ (37,460)

The total predicted cash inflow from disinvestment for the Tanner Company's project is $55,400, the sum of the net cash inflow from the sale of the equipment and the recovery of the amounts invested in inventory and accounts receivable.

Net cash inflow from disposal of equipment	$ 5,400
Recovery of investment in inventory	30,000
Recovery of investment in accounts receivable	20,000
Total cash inflow from disinvestment	$55,400

Exhibit 16–9 presents an NPV analysis of the Tanner Glove Company's proposed investment, assuming a weighted-average cost of capital of 16 percent. The data in Exhibit 16–9 have been derived in previous calculations and are presented here to provide you with a comprehensive capital-budgeting example. As shown in Exhibit 16–9, the project has a negative NPV at a 16 percent discount rate and, therefore, would be rejected by Tanner.

SUBSEQUENT CONTROL AND PERFORMANCE EVALUATION

A system should be established to review actual results of approved capital expenditure proposals. Such a system:

- Helps the project manager complete the initial investment phase within the budget and on time.
- Helps identify the need to reevaluate a project if there is a significant environmental change.
- Helps improve future investment decisions by identifying past planning errors.
- Helps improve the quality of investment proposals by holding managers responsible for the outcome of projects they initiate.

During the initial investment phase such techniques as PERT (discussed in the appendix to Chapter 18) are used to evaluate progress. Comparisons are made between budgeted and actual expenditures and between the budgeted and actual times required to complete preparations for operations. Once operations begin, comparisons are made between budgeted and actual project cash flows. If a project's actual return on investment is to be compared with the project's expected internal rate of return, compound interest depreciation must be used for performance evaluation. Compound interest depreciation is discussed in Appendix B to this chapter.

SUMMARY

Capital budgeting involves the commitment of resources over an extended period of time in a manner that will help an organization achieve its objectives. The capital-budgeting process involves the identification of potentially desirable investments, their evaluation, and the selection of investments that meet certain criteria. Subsequent to the approval of investment proposals, the actual expenditure of funds and the actual operating results should be monitored.

Four capital-budgeting models were considered: payback, accounting rate of return, internal rate of return, and net present value. The internal rate of return and net present value models are superior because they consider both the profitability of a project and the timing of cash flows. However, these models require the establishment of a cutoff or discount rate. The most widely discussed cutoff or discount rate is the weighted-average cost of capital.

Of the two discounting models, net present value is preferred because it has computational advantages. Furthermore, under certain circumstances, a project may have multiple internal rates of return. Additional advantages of net present value are considered in Chapter 17.

The payback, internal rate of return, and net present value models are based on an analysis of cash flows. The cash flows result from the initial investment, operations, and disinvestment activities. Inflation may have a significant impact of these flows. The impact of changing prices on capital-budgeting models is discussed in Appendix A to this chapter.

APPENDIX A Impact of Changing Prices on Capital-Budgeting Models

The accuracy of the results obtained from capital-budgeting models depends on the accuracy of the data used in them. If the predictions of future cash flows are incorrect or the wrong discount or hurdle rate is used, the results obtained from the model are of questionable value. Failure to include price-level changes due to inflation (or deflation) in capital-budgeting analysis can result in errors in the predicting of cash flows.

PRICE-LEVEL CHANGES AND CASH FLOWS

Price-level changes affect predictions of future cash flows because the prices charged for products and the costs incurred in manufacturing and selling products depend to some extent on the price level. Under inflation, the cash flows used in capital budgeting should reflect expected increases in prices and costs.

Example 16–14

Athens Company is considering expansion into a new product line. The expansion will involve an initial investment of $100,000 for equipment. The equipment has a useful life of five years and no salvage value at the end of its life. If the investment is made, Athens expects to sell 10,000 units of the new product annually over the five years. Management believes that the product can be sold for $10 per unit during the first year. The following unit cost predictions have been developed for the first year:

Direct materials	$4.00
Direct labor	1.00
Factory overhead:	
Variable	1.50
Fixed—Depreciation	2.00
Total manufacturing	$8.50
Variable selling and administrative	$0.50

Because of inflation, management expects prices and costs to increase by 6 percent a year.

When predicting the future cash inflows from sales of the product, Athens should include the expected increase due to inflation. With expected inflation of 6 percent a year, the unit selling prices are expected to be $10.60 ($10.00 × 1.06) during the second year, $11.24 ($10.60 × 1.06) during the third year, $11.91 ($11.24 × 1.06) during the fourth year, and $12.62 ($11.91 × 1.06) during the fifth year. These expected selling prices give the following predicted cash inflows from operations for each year:

Year	*Units*	*Sales price/unit*	*Cash inflows from operations*
1	10,000	$10.00	$100,000
2	10,000	10.60	106,000
3	10,000	11.24	112,400
4	10,000	11.91	119,100
5	10,000	12.62	126,200

Predictions of cash outflows for operating costs should also include price-level changes. If all costs that involve cash flows increase at 6 percent a year, the expected unit costs for each year are as follows:

	Year 1	*Year 2*	*Year 3*	*Year 4*	*Year 5*
Direct material	$ 4.00	$ 4.24	$ 4.49	$ 4.76	$ 5.05
Direct labor	1.00	1.06	1.12	1.19	1.26
Factory overhead:					
Variable	1.50	1.59	1.69	1.79	1.90
Fixed—Depreciation	2.00	2.00	2.00	2.00	2.00
Variable selling and administrative	0.50	0.53	0.56	0.59	0.63
Total costs	$ 9.00	$ 9.42	$ 9.86	$10.33	$10.84

Note that in this case fixed overhead will not increase because it consists solely of depreciation on the equipment. The cash flow for the equipment occurs when the investment is acquired, so the depreciation is not affected by price-level changes. To the extent that fixed overhead involves a cash outflow, it should be adjusted to reflect the expected increase in cash expenditures. In addition, if different costs are subject to different price-level changes, the specific rate for each cost should be used to determine the expected costs.

Once the future unit costs have been predicted, the expected cash outflows for operations can be calculated as the unit costs that involve cash outflows multiplied by the number of units. With an annual production and sales volume of 10,000 units, the predicted cash outflows are as follows:

	Year 1	*Year 2*	*Year 3*	*Year 4*	*Year 5*
Direct material	$40,000	$42,400	$44,900	$47,600	$50,500
Direct labor	10,000	10,600	11,200	11,900	12,600
Variable factory overhead	15,000	15,900	16,900	17,900	19,000
Variable selling and administrative	5,000	5,300	5,600	5,900	6,300
Total cash outflows for operations	$70,000	$74,200	$78,600	$83,300	$88,400

The net cash inflows before income taxes are readily determined as the predicted cash inflows from operations minus the predicted cash outflows for operations. The cash outflows for income taxes are determined as the expected net cash flows before income taxes multiplied by the tax rate minus the depreciation tax shield. Assuming Athens takes the full investment tax credit of $10,000 ($100,000 × 0.10) and uses the ACRS rates in Exhibit 16–6 for five-year property, the depreciation tax shield on the equipment with an income tax rate of 46 percent is as follows:

Year	*Initial investment −50% ITC*	*ACRS rate*	*ACRS deduction*	*Income tax rate*	*Tax shield*
1	$95,000	0.15	$14,250	0.46	$6,555
2	95,000	0.22	20,900	0.46	9,614
3	95,000	0.21	19,950	0.46	9,177
4	95,000	0.21	19,950	0.46	9,177
5	95,000	0.21	19,950	0.46	9,177

The expected cash outflow for income taxes and the net cash flow for each year are shown in Exhibit 16–10.

The net cash flows shown in Exhibit 16–10 are used in the capital-budgeting analysis. With an initial investment of $90,000 ($100,000 − $10,000) and the net cash inflows presented in Exhibit 16–10, this project has an internal rate of return of 14.59 percent as determined using a hand calculator with an IRR function. Using Table E (in Appendix B of this book) for the present value of $1, you can easily verify that the project's IRR is between 14 and 16 percent. The 14.59 percent IRR would be compared to some criterion to determine if the proposed project is acceptable.

The preceding calculation of the internal rate of return uses net cash flows that are expected to occur in the future. When the cash flows reflect the predicted impact of inflation, the minimum criteria should also reflect expected inflation. Reflecting expected inflation in the discount or hurdle rate increases the rate above what it would be if inflation did not exist.

EXHIBIT 16–10 Computation of Net Cash Inflows

	Year 1	*Year 2*	*Year 3*	*Year 4*	*Year 5*
Cash inflows from operations	$100,000	$106,000	$112,400	$119,100	$126,200
Cash outflows for operations	−70,000	−74,200	−78,600	−83,300	−88,400
Net cash flows before income taxes	$ 30,000	$ 31,800	$ 33,800	$ 35,800	$ 37,800
Cash outflows for income taxes*	−7,245	−5,014	−6,371	−7,291	−8,211
Net cash inflows after income taxes	$ 22,755	$ 26,786	$ 27,429	$ 28,509	$ 29,589

* Computation of cash flow for income taxes:

	Year 1	*Year 2*	*Year 3*	*Year 4*	*Year 5*
Income taxes on net cash flow before income taxes @ 46 percent	$13,800	$14,628	$15,548	$16,468	$17,388
Tax shield from depreciation	−6,555	−9,614	−9,177	−9,177	−9,177
Cash outflows for income taxes	$ 7,245	$ 5,014	$ 6,371	$ 7,291	$ 8,211

NOMINAL AND CONSTANT DOLLARS

When future cash flows are stated in dollars expected to occur in the future, they are in nominal dollars. **Nominal dollars** are dollars that have not been adjusted for changes in purchasing power. The dollars shown in Exhibit 16–10 are nominal dollars.

Dollars that are stated in terms of uniform purchasing power are called **constant dollars.** Nominal dollars can be restated to constant dollars by multiplying the nominal dollars by a fraction representing the change in the price level. The numerator of the fraction is the price index for the time the constant dollar is being determined, and the denominator is the price index at the time the nominal dollar is measured. In equation form,

$$CD_x = ND_y \times \frac{\text{Price index at time } X}{\text{Price index at time } Y} \qquad (16\text{–}12)$$

where

CD_x = Constant dollars at time X
ND_y = Nominal dollars at time Y

Example 16–15

Athens Company is evaluating another proposed project with an initial investment of $100,000. Projected net cash inflows from the investment in nominal dollars are as follows:

Year	*Net cash inflows after taxes (nominal dollars)*
1	$40,000
2	60,000
3	50,000

Inflation is expected to be 6 percent annually.

If the price index at the time the project is being evaluated (Time 0) is 150, the expected price index at the end of Year 1 is 159.00 [150 + (0.06 × 150)]. Similarly, the expected price index at the end of Year 2 is 168.54 [159.00 + (0.06 × 159.00)], and at the end of Year 3 it is 178.65 [168.54 + (0.06 × 168.54)].

The nominal dollar cash flows in Example 16–15 can be restated to constant dollars at the time the project is being evaluated using Eq. 16–12. This restatement gives the following cash flows in constant dollars:

Time of cash flow	*Nominal dollars*		*Fraction*		*Constant dollars at time 0*
1	$40,000	×	150/159.00	=	$37,735.85
2	60,000	×	150/168.54	=	53,399.79
3	50,000	×	150/178.65	=	41,981.53

ADJUSTING CAPITAL-BUDGETING MODELS FOR INFLATION

Either nominal dollars or constant dollars may be used in capital-budgeting models. If nominal dollars are used, the discount or hurdle rate for determining whether a project is acceptable or unacceptable *should* reflect expected price-level changes. If constant dollars are used, the discount or hurdle rate *should not* reflect expected price-level changes. In the next sections, the internal rate of return and net present value models are illustrated using both nominal and constant dollars.

Internal Rate of Return (IRR)

If constant dollars are used in determining the internal rate of return for the project in Example 16–15, the IRR is 15.47 percent. Therefore, the project would be rejected if the criterion required an IRR of 16 percent or more.

If nominal dollars are used, the IRR is 22.40 percent and the project would be acceptable using a hurdle rate of 16 percent. The model has given a different accept or reject signal, depending on the type of dollars used in the analysis.

Since the IRR using nominal dollars is greater than the IRR using constant dollars, the minimum acceptable rate should be increased if nominal dollars are used in the analysis. To obtain consistent accept or reject signals, the 16 percent hurdle rate should be increased to 22.96 percent. If the inflation rate is constant for all years, the following equation is used to convert the hurdle rate in constant dollars to a hurdle rate in nominal dollars:[11]

$$IRR_{\mathrm{ND}} = r + i + (r \times i) \tag{16–14}$$

where

IRR_{ND} = Minimum required IRR in nominal dollars
r = Minimum required IRR in constant dollars
i = Expected annual inflation rate

When $r = 0.16$ and $i = 0.06$,

$$IRR_{\mathrm{ND}} = 0.16 + 0.06 + (0.16 \times 0.06) = \underline{\underline{0.2296}}$$

During a period of inflation, failure to increase the hurdle rate when nominal dollar cash flows are used may cause an organization to accept investments that do not, in fact, meet the minimum acceptable rate of return. Conversely, applying a hurdle rate that is adjusted for inflation when constant dollar cash flows are used may result in the rejection of projects that do, in fact, meet the organization's minimum acceptable rate.

It is important to note that the weighted-average cost of capital, used as the hurdle rate or discount rate in many organizations, automatically reflects investors' expectations regarding future price changes. It is a nominal dollar rate. Consequently organizations using the weighted-average cost of capital as a decision criterion should use nominal dollar cash flows. Failure to use nominal dollars may result in the rejection of projects that do, in fact, meet the organization's minimum investment criteria. It is interesting to note that during the late 1970s, a period of relatively high inflation in the United States, U.S. companies dramatically reduced their investments in new plant and equipment. Managers argued that high inflation rates made such investments unprofitable. Perhaps the problem was a failure to state predicted project cash flows in nominal dollars.

Net Present Value (NPV)

The impact of price-level changes on NPV analysis is similar to the impact of such changes on IRR analysis. If constant dollars are used for determining the NPV for the project in

---

[11] This equation is adapted from Jon W. Bartley, "A NPV Model Modified for Inflation," *Management Accounting* **62,** No. 6 (December 1980), pp. 49–52. Although Professor Bartley was writing in the context of the NPV model, his procedure for adjusting the discount rate for anticipated inflation also applies to the minimum required internal rate of return if the inflation rate is constant for all years. If the inflation rate varies significantly over time, there is no simple way of adjusting a constant dollar minimum rate to a nominal dollar minimum rate. In this situation, the internal rate of return should be calculated in constant dollars and compared with a constant dollar minimum rate.

Example 16–15 with a constant-dollar discount rate of 16 percent, the net present value is $(883.63):

Year	*Cash inflow*		*Present value factor*		*Present value of cash inflow*
1	$37,735.85	×	0.8621	=	$ 32,532.08
2	53,399.79	×	0.7432	=	39,686.72
3	41,981.53	×	0.6407	=	26,897.57
					$ 99,116.37
Less: Initial investment					– 100,000.00
Net present value					$ (883.63)

If nominal dollars are used and the discount rate is not adjusted for inflation, the NPV is $11,111:

Year	*Cash inflow*		*Present value factor*		*Present value of cash inflow*
1	$40,000	×	0.8621	=	$ 34,484
2	60,000	×	0.7432	=	44,592
3	50,000	×	0.6407	=	32,035
					$111,111
Less: Initial investment					– 100,000
Net present value					$ 11,111

As expected, different signals were given by the NPV model, depending on the type of dollars used in the analysis. To obtain results that are consistent with the constant dollar NPV, the discount rate must be increased to 22.96 percent when using nominal dollars. When inflation is constant for all years, we can use an equation similar to Eq. 16–14 to determine the nominal dollar discount rate.[12] We can verify this rate if the present value factors for 22.96 percent are used:

Year (t)	*Cash inflow*	*Present value factor* $= 1/(1 + 0.2296)^t$	*Present value of cash flows*
1	$40,000	0.8133	$ 32,532
2	60,000	0.6614	39,684
3	50,000	0.5379	26,895
			$ 99,111
Less: Initial investment			– 100,000
Net present value			$ (889)

The difference between the $(889) and the $(883.63) obtained from the NPV calculation using constant dollars is due to rounding of numbers and present value factors.

These examples show that if inflation is expected to occur in the future, capital-budgeting models should be adjusted to include the impact of price-level changes. If

[12] When the inflation rate varies significantly over time, Professor Bartley presents a method that can be used to adjust the NPV model for inflation. See the reference in footnote 11.

constant dollars are used in the analysis, the criteria for determining whether or not a project is acceptable should not reflect anticipated inflation. If nominal dollars are used in the analysis, the criteria should reflect the anticipated inflation. If managers do not recognize the impact of price-level changes in their analyses, they may accept projects that do not meet the minimum criteria required by the firm.

APPENDIX B Impact of Depreciation Methods on Measures of Investment Performance

Once a capital investment proposal has been accepted and implemented, an organization should periodically perform a **post audit,** that is, a review of the performance of the project comparing expected results with actual results. The actual return on investment (ROI) for a project is often computed as part of the post audit. An actual **return on investment** is calculated by dividing the net income from the investment by the amount of the investment. Typically the amount used as the denominator is the beginning of the period book value or average book value for the period.

If an actual ROI for an investment is compared with the internal rate of return (IRR) from the initial evaluation, differences are apt to occur because the ROI is calculated using accrual basis accounting concepts and IRR is calculated using discounted cash flows. The use of traditional depreciation methods is a major source of the differences.

IMPACT OF DEPRECIATION METHODS ON ROI

The straight-line and accelerated (for example, sum-of-the-years'-digits and double-declining balance) depreciation methods used in financial accounting will likely result in different ROIs for each year in the life of a project. Using traditional depreciation procedures, the ROI is likely to be lower than the project's IRR in early years and higher than the project's IRR in later years of the project's life.

EXHIBIT 16–11 ROI With Alternative Depreciation Procedures: Actual Cash Flows Equal Predicted Cash Flows

STRAIGHT-LINE DEPRECIATION

	Year 1	*Year 2*	*Year 3*
Operating cash flows	$10,000	$10,000	$10,000
Depreciation	− 7,487	− 7,487	− 7,486
Net income	$ 2,513	$ 2,513	$ 2,514
Net book value at beginning of year	$22,460	$14,973	$ 7,486
Return on investment	0.112	0.168	0.336

SUM-OF-THE-YEARS'-DIGITS DEPRECIATION

	Year 1	*Year 2*	*Year 3*
Operating cash flows	$10,000	$10,000	$10,000
Depreciation	−11,230	− 7,487	− 3,743
Net income	$(1,230)	$ 2,513	$ 6,257
Net book value at beginning of year	$22,460	$11,230	$ 3,743
Return on investment	(0.055)	0.224	1.672

Example 16–16

In early January 19x2, Chinook Company invested $22,460 in equipment that was predicted to provide equal net cash inflows of $10,000 annually for three years. The asset was expected to have no salvage value at the end of the three-year period. Ignoring income taxes for simplicity, the project's IRR was 16 percent. During 19x2, 19x3, and 19x4, actual cash flows were exactly as predicted.

If this project is post audited by calculating an ROI, the depreciation method affects the results. A schedule of the ROIs using straight-line and sum-of-the-years'-digits depreciation is presented in Exhibit 16–11. These rates of return are based on net book value (original cost minus accumulated depreciation) at the beginning of the year.

As shown in Exhibit 16–11, the ROI is negative in the first year using the sum-of-the-years'-digits depreciation method and it increases each year as the asset gets older. Because the actual ROI for the first year is less than the IRR, a manager might have rejected this investment proposal if he or she knew that performance was going to be measured using this method.

COMPOUND INTEREST DEPRECIATION

Compound interest depreciation has been suggested as a solution to this particular problem. **Compound interest depreciation** is a residual amount calculated by subtracting imputed interest on net book value at the beginning of each year from the predicted operating cash inflows for that year. In equation form,

Predicted operating cash inflows for year
− Imputed interest on net book value at beginning of year
= Compound interest depreciation

The imputed interest rate is the project's internal rate of return.

The internal rate of return of the investment proposal in Example 16–16 is 16 percent. Using this rate, the imputed interest on the net book value at the beginning of the first year is $3,593.60 ($0.16 × $22,460) and the compound interest depreciation for Year 1 is $6,406.40 ($10,000 − $3,593.60). Deducting this depreciation amount from the operating cash inflows gives Year 1 net income of $3,593.60 ($10,000 − $6,406.40). The ROI for Year 1 is then 16 percent ($3,593.60/$22,460). A schedule of compound interest depreciation and the resulting ROI for each year is presented in Exhibit 16–12. Note that annual depreciation increases as the asset gets older.

When actual and predicted cash flows are identical, compound interest depreciation results in a constant ROI that is equal to the project's IRR. If actual cash flows from the investment differ from predictions used in the initial evaluation, the ROI calculated with compound interest depreciation will differ from the internal rate of return. The compound interest depreciation is always calculated using predicted cash flows and the imputed interest rate. Consequently, if actual cash flows are greater than predicted cash flows, actual ROI will exceed the IRR, and if actual cash flows are less than predicted, actual ROI will be less than the IRR.

Example 16–17

Assume the same facts as in Example 16–16 except that the actual cash flows are $7,000 in Year 1, $12,000 in Year 2, and $11,000 in Year 3.

Exhibit 16–13 is a schedule showing the ROI for Example 16–17 when compound interest depreciation is used. Observe that the actual ROI is less than the IRR in Year 1 when actual cash flows are less than predicted. Likewise, the actual ROI is higher than the IRR in Years 2 and 3 when the actual cash flows exceed the predicted cash flows.

EXHIBIT 16–12 ROI With Compound Interest Depreciation: Actual Cash Flows Equal Predicted Cash Flows

	Year 1	*Year 2*	*Year 3*
Operating cash flows	$10,000.00	$10,000.00	$10,000.00
Depreciation*	−6,406.40	−7,431.42	−8,622.18†
Net income	$ 3,593.60	$ 2,568.58	$ 1,377.82
Net book value at beginning of year	$22,460.00	$16,053.60	$ 8,622.18
Return on investment	0.16	0.16	0.16

* Computation of compound interest depreciation:

	Year 1	*Year 2*	*Year 3*
Predicted operating cash flows	$10,000.00	$10,000.00	$10,000.00
Less: Imputed interest on unrecovered investment (net book value at beginning of year) @ 0.16	−3,593.60	−2,568.58	−1,379.55
Recovery of investment (depreciation)	$ 6,406.40	$ 7,431.42	$ 8,620.45†

† The discrepancy is due to rounding errors. The final year's depreciation is adjusted from $8,620.45 to $8,622.18 to reduce the asset to zero.

Although the use of compound interest depreciation results in a constant ROI when actual and predicted net cash flows are identical, the procedure is difficult to sell to management. It goes against an intuitive feeling for the pattern in which an asset's value declines. However, management's "feel" is more likely based on disposal value than on value in use. If management is going to calculate an ROI in the post audit of capital investments, compound interest depreciation must be used to obtain results that can be compared with the results of discounted cash flow models used in the initial project evaluation.

EXHIBIT 16–13 ROI With Compound Interest Depreciation: Actual Cash Flows Differ From Predicted Cash Flows

	Year 1	*Year 2*	*Year 3*
Operating cash flows	$ 7,000.00	$12,000.00	$11,000.00
Depreciation (See Exhibit 16–12 for calculation.)	−6,406.40	−7,431.42	−8,622.18
Net income	$ 593.60	$ 4,568.58	$ 2,377.82
Net book value at beginning of year	$22,460,00	$16,053.60	$ 8,622.18
Return on investment	$ 0.026	$ 0.285	$ 0.276

KEY TERMS

Accelerated Cost Recovery System
Accounting rate of return
After-tax cost of debt
Bail-out factor
Capital budgeting
Capital-budgeting policies
Cost of equity capital
Cost of preferred stock
Cutoff rate
Depreciation tax shield
Discount rate
Hurdle rate
Initial investment
Internal rate of return
Investment tax credit
Net present value
Payback period
Payback reciprocal
Personal property
Rate of return
Real property
Time adjusted rate of return
Weighted-average cost of capital

APPENDICES KEY TERMS

Compound interest depreciation
Constant dollars
Nominal dollars
Post audit
Return on investment

SELECTED REFERENCES

Accounting Principles and Practices Committee, *Management Accounting Guideline No. 1, Post Appraisal of Capital Expenditures,* Hamilton, Ontario: The Society of Management Accountants of Canada, 1984.

Bavishi, Vinod B., "Capital Budgeting Practices at Multinationals," *Management Accounting* **63,** No. 2 (August 1981): 32–35.

Bierman, Harold J., Jr., and Seymour Smidt, *The Capital Budgeting Decision,* 6th ed., New York: The Macmillian Company, 1984.

Brealey, Richard, and Stewart Myers, *Principles of Corporate Finance,* New York: McGraw-Hill, 1981.

Corr, Arthur V., *The Capital Expenditure Decision,* New York and Hamilton, Ontario: National Association of Accountants and The Society of Management Accountants of Canada, 1983.

Edge, C. Geoffrey, and V. Bruce Irvine, *A Practical Approach to the Appraisal of Capital Expenditures,* 2nd ed., Hamilton, Ont.: The Society of Management Accountants of Canada, 1981.

Hardy, John W., "How ERTA and TEFRA Affect Capital Budgeting Decisions," *Management Accounting* **64,** No. 11 (May 1983): 20–23.

Kee, Robert, and Oliver Feltus, "The Role of Abandonment Value in the Investment Decision," *Management Accounting* **64,** No. 2 (August 1982): 34–41.

Kim, Suk H., and Edward J. Farragher, "Current Capital Budgeting Practices," *Management Accounting* **62,** No. 12 (June 1981): 26–30.

Kim, Suk H., and Trevor Crick, "How Non-U.S. MNCs Practice Capital Budgeting," *Management Accounting* **65,** No. 7 (January 1984): 28–31.

Manes, René P., "A New Dimension to Breakeven Analysis," *Journal of Accounting Research* **4,** No. 1 (Spring 1966): 87–100.

McCabe, George M., and George N. Sanderson, "Abandonment Value in Capital Budgeting: Another View," *Management Accounting* **65,** No. 7 (January 1984): 32–36.

Morse, Wayne J., "The Differential Impact of Taxes on Investment Decisions of New and Established Businesses," *American Journal of Small Business* **3,** No. 3 (January 1979): 25–33.

National Association of Accountants, *Statement on Management Accounting, No. 4A, Cost of Capital,* New York: National Association of Accountants, 1984.

Pinches, George E., "Myopia, Capital Budgeting and Decision Making," *Financial Management* **11,** No. 3 (Autumn 1982): 6–19.

Rappaport, Alfred, "The Discounted Payback Period," *Management Services* **2,** No. 4 (July-August 1965): 30–36.

Roth, Harold P., and Robert M. Brown, "Post-Auditing Capital Investments Using IRR and NPV Models," *Management Accounting* **63,** No. 8 (February 1982): 29–33.

Sale, J. Timothy, and Robert W. Scapens, "The Control of Capital Investment in Divisionalized Companies," *Management Accounting* **64,** No. 4 (October 1982): 24–29.

Truitt, Jack, "Capital Budgeting: An Annualization Approach," *Cost and Management* **57,** No. 1 (January-February 1983): 47–49.

Van Breda, Michael F., "Capital Budgeting Using Terminal Values," *Management Accounting* **63,** No. 1 (July 1981): 42–48.

Van Horne, James C., *Financial Management and Policy,* 6th ed., Englewood Cliffs, N.J.: Prentice-Hall, 1983.

REVIEW QUESTIONS

16–1 In your own words, define or describe "capital budgeting" and indicate the major stages of the capital-budgeting process.

16–2 What relationship exists between capital budgeting and strategic planning?

16–3 What benefits are derived from the use of any formal capital-budgeting model?

16–4 Why do managers desire investments with low payback periods?

16–5 Mention three major deficiencies of the payback model.

16–6 What is the major deficiency of the accounting rate of return model?

16–7 What is the maximum interest rate an organization can pay for the cash invested in a project without losing money?

16–8 Under what circumstances is the payback reciprocal a reasonable approximation of a project's internal rate of return?

16–9 Define or describe "net present value."

16–10 What rationale underlies the use of a firm's weighted-average cost of capital as a cutoff or discount rate?

16–11 How are investments in working capital treated in capital-budgeting analysis?

16–12 Why does the use of Accelerated Cost Recovery System depreciation for tax purposes increase a project's net present value above what it would be if straight-line depreciation were used?

16–13 What is meant by the phrase "depreciation tax shield"?

16–14 Why should an organization follow up approved projects with a capital expenditure review?

REVIEW PROBLEM

Basic Capital Budgeting Models: No Salvage: With and Without Income Taxes

Consider the following investment proposal:

Initial investment	$42,000
Annual operating cash inflows	$14,000
Salvage	$ 0
Life	5 years

REQUIREMENTS

a) Ignoring income taxes, determine each of the following:
   1. Payback period
   2. Accounting rate of return on initial investment
   3. Accounting rate of return on average investment
   4. Internal rate of return
   5. Net present value at a 16 percent discount rate

b) Assuming a tax rate of 40 percent with ACRS depreciation for tax purposes, determine the after-tax cash flows. Assume the investment represents five-year recovery property and does not qualify for the investment tax credit.

c) Using the after-tax cash flows in part (b), determine each of the following:
   1. Payback period
   2. Internal rate of return
   3. Net present value at a 16 percent discount rate

The solution to this problem is found at the end of the Chapter 16 problems and exercises.

EXERCISES

16–1 T Basic Capital-Budgeting Models: No Salvage: No Income Taxes

Consider the following investment proposal:

Initial investment	$44,000
After-tax operating cash inflows	$16,000/year
Salvage	$ 0
Life	5 years

REQUIREMENTS

Determine each of the following:

a) Payback period
b) Accounting rate of return on initial investment
c) Accounting rate of return on average investment
d) Internal rate of return
e) Net present value at a 10 percent discount rate

16–2 T Basic Capital-Budgeting Models: No Salvage: No Income Taxes

Consider the following investment proposal:

Initial investment	$50,000
After-tax operating cash inflows:	
Year 1	$20,000
Year 2	$15,000
Year 3	$10,000
Year 4	$10,000
Year 5	$ 5,000
Salvage	$ 0
Life	5 years

REQUIREMENTS

Determine each of the following:

a) Payback period

b) Accounting rate of return on initial investment

c) Accounting rate of return on average investment

d) Internal rate of return

e) Net present value at a 12 percent discount rate

16–3 T Basic Capital-Budgeting Models: Salvage: No Income Taxes

Consider the following investment proposal:

Initial investment	$70,000
After-tax operating cash inflows	$20,000/year
Salvage	$10,000
Life	5 years

REQUIREMENTS

Determine each of the following:

a) Payback period

b) Accounting rate of return on initial investment

c) Accounting rate of return on average investment

d) Internal rate of return

e) Net present value at a 10 percent discount rate

16–4 T Basic Capital-Budgeting Models: Salvage: No Income Taxes

Consider the following investment proposal:

Initial investment	$200,000
After-tax operating cash inflows:	
Year 1	$ 30,000
Year 2	$ 50,000
Year 3	$ 60,000
Year 4	$ 50,000
Year 5	$ 50,000
Salvage	$ 20,000
Life	5 years

REQUIREMENTS

Determine each of the following:

a) Payback period

b) Accounting rate of return on initial investment

c) Accounting rate of return on average investment

d) Internal rate of return

e) Net present value at a 14 percent discount rate

16–5 T Basic Capital-Budgeting Models: No Salvage: Income Taxes

Consider the following investment proposal:

Initial investment	$40,000
Before-tax operating cash inflows	$16,000/year
Income tax rate	0.40
Salvage	$ 0
Life	5 years

The Accelerated Cost Recovery System is used for tax purposes. The initial investment represents five-year recovery property. Ignore the investment tax credit.

REQUIREMENTS

Determine each of the following:

a) Payback period

b) Accounting rate of return on initial investment

c) Accounting rate of return on average investment

d) Internal rate of return

e) Net present value at a 10 percent discount rate

16–6 T Basic Capital-Budgeting Models: No Salvage: Income Taxes

Consider the following investment proposal:

Initial investment	$50,000
Before-tax operating cash inflows:	
Year 1	$20,000
Year 2	$20,000
Year 3	$15,000
Year 4	$15,000
Year 5	$10,000
Income tax rate	0.45
Salvage	$ 0

The Accelerated Cost Recovery System is used for tax purposes and the full investment tax credit is taken. The initial investment represents five-year recovery property.

REQUIREMENTS

Determine each of the following:

a) Payback period

b) Accounting rate of return on initial investment

c) Accounting rate of return on average investment

d) Internal rate of return

e) Net present value at a 10 percent discount rate

PROBLEMS

16–7 Evaluating an Investment Using Various Models

Yipann Corporation is reviewing an investment proposal. The initial cost as well as the predictions of the book value of the investment at the end of each year, the net after-tax cash flows for each year, and the net income for each year are as follows:

Year	*Initial cost and book value*	*Annual net after-tax cash inflows*	*Annual net income*
0	$105,000		
1	70,000	$50,000	$15,000
2	42,000	45,000	17,000
3	21,000	40,000	19,000
4	7,000	35,000	21,000
5	0	30,000	23,000
			$95,000

All cash flows are assumed to occur at the end of the year for present value calculations. The salvage value of the investment at the end of each year is equal to its book value. There will be no salvage value at the end of the investment's life.

Yipann uses a 24 percent discount rate for evaluating new investment proposals.

REQUIREMENTS

a) Determine each of the following for the investment proposal.

1. Payback period
2. Bail-out payback period
3. Accounting rate of return on the initial investment
4. Net present value

b) The payback reciprocal, which is often used as an approximation of the internal rate of return, should not be used to estimate the IRR for Yipann's investment proposal. Why not? (CMA Adapted)

16–8 Capital Investment Models: Straight-line and ACRS Depreciation: Income Taxes

The Harper Company is evaluating a capital expenditure proposal requiring an initial investment of $20,000. The investment has an expected useful life of five years with no salvage value at the end of that time. Predicted annual before-tax cash inflows are $6,400. The corporate income tax rate is 40 percent. The investment does not qualify for the investment tax credit.

REQUIREMENTS

a) Assume Harper elects to use straight-line depreciation over five years for both book and tax purposes. Determine each of the following:
   1. Payback period
   2. Accounting rate of return on the initial investment
   3. Accounting rate of return on the average investment
   4. Net present value using a 14 percent discount rate

b) Assume straight-line depreciation is used for book purposes and five-year ACRS depreciation for tax purposes. Determine each of the following:
   1. Payback period
   2. Accounting rate of return on the initial investment
   3. Accounting rate of return on the average investment
   4. Net present value using a 14 percent discount rate

c) Compare the payback periods, accounting rates of return, and net present values calculated in parts (a) and (b). What caused these amounts to be different?

16–9 IRR, Payback Reciprocal, NPV: No Income Taxes

Gamma Company is evaluating the desirability of a proposed investment that requires an initial outlay of $56,000 and will provide net cash inflows of $20,000 per year for four years. At the end of four years there will be no disposal value. Gamma uses a 14 percent discount rate for evaluating investment proposals. Ignore income taxes.

REQUIREMENTS

a) Determine the project's internal rate of return.

b) Determine the payback reciprocal and indicate why it is or is not a reasonable approximation of the project's internal rate of return.

c) Determine the project's net present value at Gamma's discount rate.

d) At what annual net cash inflow will management be indifferent to accepting or rejecting this project?

16–10 Determining Annual Cash Flows: Cost and Accounting Rate of Return Given

Jarvis, Inc., purchased a new machine for $28,000 on January 1, 19x0. The machine has an estimated useful life of eight years with no salvage value and is being depreciated using the straight-line method. The accounting rate of return is expected to be 15 percent on the initial increase in required investment.

REQUIREMENT

Assuming equal annual operating cash flows, determine the annual operating cash flow. Ignore income taxes. (CPA Adapted)

16–11 Determining Initial Investment: IRR and Cash Flows Given

Hamilton Company invested in a two-year project with an internal rate of return of 12 percent. The machine is expected to produce after-tax cash flows from operations of $60,000 in the first year and $70,000 in the second year.

Determine the amount of the initial investment. (CPA Adapted)

16–12 Cost of Capital

The Tempo Company manufactures high-quality musical instruments. Prior to the evaluation of several capital expenditure proposals, the chairman of the capital-budgeting committee has requested that you determine the firm's cost of capital.

The following information is contained in the most recent balance sheet:

Bonds payable (10 percent)	$20,000,000
Preferred stock (6 percent, $100 par)	10,000,000
Common stock (1,000,000 shares)	40,000,000
Retained earnings	30,000,000

ADDITIONAL INFORMATION

- The bonds payable were recently issued at their face value.
- The preferred stock has a current market price of $96 per share.
- The common stock has a current market price of $50 per share.
- Common dividends are currently $3 per share per year. Management uses a constant dividend to earnings payment ratio and anticipates a 6 percent growth rate in annual dividends per share.
- The income tax rate is 40 percent.
- Management desires to maintain the relative portions of debt, preferred stock, and common equity found on the current balance sheet.

REQUIREMENTS

a) Determine the weighted-average cost of capital.

b) What will be the effect on common stock prices if a project with an internal rate of return of 8 percent is accepted? Why?

16–13 Cost of Capital

The following information is taken from the December 31, 19x4, Statement of Financial Position of Wyatt Company:

Bonds payable (12 percent)	$10,000,000
Preferred stock (8 percent, $100 par)	5,000,000
Common stock (500,000 shares)	15,000,000
Retained earnings	20,000,000

In January 19x5, prior to the evaluation of several capital expenditure proposals, you are asked to determine the firm's cost of capital.

ADDITIONAL INFORMATION

- The bonds payable are selling for face value.
- The preferred stock has a current market value of $80 per share.
- The common stock has a current market value of $50 a share.
- Common dividends are currently $5 per share per year. Management uses a constant dividend to earnings payment ratio and anticipates an 8 percent growth rate in annual dividends per share.
- The income tax rate is 30 percent.
- Management desires to maintain the relative portions of debt, preferred stock, and common equity found on the December 31, 19x4, Statement of Financial Position.

REQUIREMENTS

Determine each of the following:

a) After-tax cost of debt

b) Cost of preferred stock

c) Cost of equity capital

d) Weighted-average cost of capital

16–14 T Basic Capital-Budgeting Models: Salvage: Income Taxes

Consider the following investment proposal:

Initial investment	$90,000
Before-tax operating cash inflows	$40,000/year
Income tax rate	0.45
Salvage	$10,000
Life	5 years

The Accelerated Cost Recovery System is used for tax purposes. The initial investment represents five-year recovery property. Ignore the investment tax credit.

REQUIREMENTS

Determine each of the following:

a) Payback period

b) Accounting rate of return on initial investment

c) Accounting rate of return on average investment

d) Internal rate of return

e) Net present value at a 10 percent discount rate

16–15 T Basic Capital-Budgeting Models: Salvage: Income Taxes

Consider the following investment proposal:

Initial investment	$200,000
Before-tax operating cash inflows:	
Year 1	$ 50,000
Year 2	$ 50,000
Year 3	$ 60,000
Year 4	$ 60,000
Year 5	$ 40,000
Salvage	$ 20,000
Income tax rate	0.40

The Accelerated Cost Recovery System is used for tax purposes and the full investment tax credit is taken. The initial investment represents five-year recovery property.

REQUIREMENTS

Determine each of the following:

a) Payback period

b) Accounting rate of return on initial investment

c) Accounting rate of return on average investment

d) Internal rate of return

e) Net present value at a 10 percent discount rate

16–16 Rate of Return on Reduction in Credit Standards

Ayleil Corporation manufactures and sells an industrial product. All sales are on credit. The corporation has a 30-day average collection period for its accounts receivable and a 1 percent bad debt loss experience.

Ayleil's production facilities are underutilized at the present time. The Credit Manager has proposed that Ayleil relax its credit standards. This action should attract new customers, increase sales, and result in better use of manufacturing facilities. If the credit standards are relaxed, the Credit Manager believes sales will increase from the $120 million forecasted for the current year to $150 million. The current manufacturing facilities would support this larger sales level, but the average inventory would have to be increased by $5 million. As a consequence of the relaxed credit standards, the average collection period would be expected to increase to 60 days and bad debts would total 2 percent of sales.

Ayleil's product sells for $15 per unit and the variable costs to manufacture and sell the product amount to $12.30 per unit. Ayleil is subject to a 40 percent income tax rate.

Acceptable projects must have an expected after-tax rate of return greater than the corporation's after-tax cost of capital.

REQUIREMENTS

a) Calculate the after-tax rate of return that Ayleil Corporation can expect to earn on the Credit Manager's proposal to relax credit standards.

b) Without being influenced by your answer to part (a), assume that the after-tax internal rate of return on the proposal to relax credit standards is 12 percent and that Ayleil Corporation's after-tax cost of capital is 10 percent. The average after-tax internal rate of return for all of Ayleil's acceptable investment proposals is 15 percent. The corporation's after-tax return on investment earned in prior years is 17 percent. Ayleil has sufficient funds in the coming year to invest in all acceptable proposals. Can the management of Ayleil justify adopting the proposal to relax credit standards even though its after-tax return is less than the average after-tax return for all acceptable projects and less than the corporation's after-tax return on investment earned in prior years? Explain your answer. (CMA Adapted)

16–17 The Discounted Payback Period

Professor Rappaport has described the discounted payback period as the length of time it takes a project's incremental cash flows discounted at the "opportunity investment rate" to accumulate to the investment outlay.[13]

Consider a project that requires an initial investment of $55,000 and provides the following end-of-year cash inflows:

Year	*Cash inflow*
1	$15,000
2	15,000
3	20,000
4	20,000
5	15,000
6	10,000

REQUIREMENTS

a) Determine the project's payback period.

b) Assuming a discount rate of 16 percent, determine the project's net present value.

c) Determine the project's discounted payback period with a discount rate of 16 percent.

d) Evaluate the discounted payback period concept. Does it contain information not provided by the traditional payback period or the net present value? Can or should the discounted payback period be used as the sole investment criterion?

16–18 Make or Buy Decision Using Present Value Analysis

Lamb Company manufactures several lines of machine products. One unique part, a valve stem, requires specialized tools that need to be replaced. Management has decided that the only alternative to replacing these tools is to acquire the

---

[13] Alfred Rappaport, "The Discounted Payback Period," *Management Services* **2,** No. 4 (July-August 1965): 30–36.

valve stem from an outside source. A supplier is willing to provide the valve stem at a unit sales price of $20 if at least 70,000 units are ordered annually.

Lamb's average usage of valve stems over the past three years has been 80,000 units each year. Expectations are that this volume will remain constant over the next five years. Cost records indicate that unit manufacturing costs for the last several years have been as follows:

Direct material	$ 3.80
Direct labor	3.70
Variable factory overhead	1.70
Fixed factory overhead*	4.50
Total unit cost	$13.70

* Depreciation accounts for two-thirds of the fixed overhead. The balance is for other fixed overhead costs of the factory that require cash expenditures.

If the specialized tools are purchased, they will cost $2,500,000 and will have a disposal value of $100,000 after their expected economic life of five years. Straight-line depreciation is used for book purposes, but ACRS is used for tax purposes. The specialized tools are considered three-year property for ACRS purposes. The tools qualify for the investment tax credit. Lamb has elected to use the 4 percent investment tax credit and not reduce the asset basis for ACRS. The company has a 40 percent marginal tax rate, and management requires a 12 percent after-tax return on investment.

The sales representative for the manufacturer of the new tools stated, "The new tools will allow direct labor and variable factory overhead to be reduced by $1.60 per unit." Data from another manufacturer using identical tools and experiencing similar operating conditions, except that annual production generally averages 110,000 units, confirm the direct labor and variable factory overhead savings. However the manufacturer indicates that it experienced an increase in raw material cost due to the higher quality of material that had to be used with the new tools. The manufacturer indicated that its costs have been as follows:

Direct material	$ 4.50
Direct labor	3.00
Variable factory overhead	0.80
Fixed factory overhead	5.00
Total unit cost	$13.30

REQUIREMENTS

a) Present a net-present-value analysis covering the economic life of the new specialized tools to determine whether Lamb Company should replace the old tools or purchase the valve stem from an outside supplier.

b) Identify any additional factors Lamb Company should consider before deciding whether to replace the tools or purchase the valve stem from an outside supplier.

(CMA Adapted)

16–19 Cost of Capital

Yakima Electric is contemplating new projects for the next year that will require $30,000,000 of new financing. In keeping with its long-run capital structure, Yakima plans to use debt and equity financing as follows:

- Issue $10,000,000 of 20-year bonds at a price of 102½, with a coupon of 10 percent, and flotation costs of 2½ percent of par value.
- Use internal funds generated from earnings of $20,000,000.

Yakima is subject to a 40 percent income tax rate. Yakima has a price to earnings ratio of 10, a constant dividend payout ratio of 40 percent of earnings, and an expected growth rate of 12 percent.

REQUIREMENTS

a) Determine the after-tax cost of Yakima's planned debt financing.

b) Determine the after-tax cost of Yakima's planned equity financing using the expected growth rate model.

c) Without being influenced by your answers in parts (a) and (b), assume that Yakima has an after-tax cost of debt of 9 percent and an after-tax cost of equity of 15 percent. Determine Yakima's weighted-average cost of capital. (CMA Adapted)

16–20 Cost of Capital

Timel Company is in the process of determining its capital budget for 19x1. Timel's balance sheet reflects five sources of long-term funds. The current outstanding amounts from these five sources represent the company's historical sources of funds, and are as follows:

Source of funds	*Dollar amount (in millions)*	*Percent*
Mortgage bonds ($1,000 par, 7½ percent)	$135	15.0
Debentures ($1,000 par, 8 percent, due 19x5)	225	25.0
Preferred stock ($100 par, 7½ percent)	90	10.0
Common stock ($10 par)	150	16.7
Retained earnings	300	33.3
	$900	100.0

Timel will raise the funds necessary to support the selected capital investment projects so as to maintain its historical distribution among the various sources of long-term funds. Thus 15 percent will be obtained from additional mortgage bonds on new plant, 25 percent from debentures, 10 percent from preferred stock, and 50 percent from some common equity source.

Management estimates that its net income after taxes for the coming year will be $4.50 per common share. The dividend payout ratio will be 40 percent of earnings to common shareholders ($1.80 per share), the same ratio as the prior four years. The preferred stockholders will receive $6.75 million.

The capital budgeting staff, in conjunction with Timel's investment broker, has developed the following data regarding Timel's sources of funds if it were to raise funds in the current market.

Source of funds	*Par value*	*Interest or dividend rate*	*Issue price*
Mortgage bonds	$1,000	14 percent	$1,000.00
Debentures	1,000	$14\frac{1}{2}$ percent	1,000.00
Preferred stock	100	$13\frac{1}{2}$ percent	99.25
Common stock	10		67.50

The estimated interest rates on the debt instruments and the dividend rate on the preferred stock are based on the rates being experienced in the market by firms that are of the same size and quality of Timel. The investment banker believes that Timel's price to earnings ratio of 15 is consistent with the 10 percent growth rate in earnings that the market is capitalizing in arriving at a price of $67.50 for the common stock.

Timel is subject to a 40 percent income tax rate.

REQUIREMENTS

a) Calculate the after-tax cost of capital for each of the five sources of capital for Timel Company.

b) Calculate Timel Company's after-tax weighted-average cost of capital.

c) If the basic business risks are similar for all firms in the industry in which Timel Company participates, would all firms in the industry have approximately the same weighted-average cost of capital? Explain your answer. (CMA Adapted)

16–21 Dual IRR

The Eagle Ridge Mining Company is considering the desirability of starting a new open-pit mine. Site preparation, and so on will require an initial investment of $113,650. The project will provide net cash inflows of $100,000 in Years 1, 2, and 3. Because the site must be returned to a natural state when mining operations are discontinued, Year 4 will have a net cash outflow of $200,000.

REQUIREMENTS

a) Determine the project's net present value when the time value of money is 6, 14, 18, and 24 percent.

b) What is the project's internal rate of return?

c) What factors caused the results obtained in parts (a) and (b)? Would the project ever be accepted if a nondiscounting model were used?

16–22 Multiperiod Cost-Volume-Profit Analysis: No Taxes

The Gallery Candy Shop is considering the production of a new chocolate candy called the "Chocoholic's Delight." Before purchasing new equipment to manufacture Chocoholic's Delights, Sarah White, the proprietor of the Gallery Candy Shop, performed the following analysis:

Unit selling price	$2.00
Variable manufacturing and selling costs	−1.80
Unit contribution margin	$0.20
Annual fixed costs:	
Depreciation (straight-line for 3 years)	$ 8,000
Other (all cash)	16,000
Total	$24,000

Annual break-even sales volume = $24,000/$0.20 = 120,000 units.

Because the expected annual sales volume is 130,000 units, Sarah decided to start producing Chocoholic's Delights. This required an immediate investment of $24,000 in equipment that has a life of three years and no salvage value. After three years, the production of Chocoholic's Delights will be discontinued.

REQUIREMENTS

a) Evaluate Sarah's analysis.

b) If the Gallery Candy Shop has a time value of money of 14 percent, should the investment be made with projected annual sales of 130,000 units?

c) Considering the time value of money, what annual unit sales volume is required to break even?

16–23 NPV of Alternative Investments: No Taxes

Thorne Transit, Inc., has decided to inaugurate express bus service between its headquarters city and a nearby suburb (one-way fare of $0.70) and is considering the purchase of either 32- or 52-passenger buses, on which pertinent estimates are as follows:

	32-passenger bus	*52-passenger bus*
Number of each to be purchased	6	4
Useful life	8 years	8 years
Purchase price of each bus (paid on delivery)	$120,000	$150,000
Mileage per gallon	10	7.5
Salvage value per bus	$ 10,000	$ 12,000
Drivers' hourly wage	$ 9.00	$ 10.00
Price per gallon of gasoline	$ 1.20	$ 1.20
Other annual cash expenses (total)	$ 25,000	$ 20,000

During the daily rush hour (which totals 4 hours), all buses would be in service and are expected to operate at full capacity (state law prohibits standees) in both directions of the route, each bus covering the route 12 times (6 round trips) during that period. During the remainder of the 16-hour daily service period, 500 passengers would be carried and Thorn would operate 4 buses on the route.

Part-time drivers (paid at the regular rate) would be employed to drive during the rush hours. A bus traveling the route all day would go 480 miles, and one traveling only during rush hours would go 120 miles a day during the 260-day year.

REQUIREMENTS

a) Prepare a schedule showing the computation of estimated annual revenue of the new route for both alternatives.

b) Prepare a schedule showing the computation of estimated annual drivers' wages for both alternatives.

c) Prepare a schedule showing the computation of estimated annual cost of gasoline for both alternatives.

d) Assuming that a minimum rate of return of 12 percent before income taxes is desired and that all annual cash flows occur at the end of the year, prepare a schedule showing the computation of the present values of net cash flows for the eight-year period; include the cost of buses and the proceeds from their disposition under both alternatives, but disregard the effect of income taxes. Round all calculations to the nearest dollar. (CPA Adapted)

16–24 T Return on Investment and Alternative Depreciation Methods (Appendix)

An investment proposal for a new fixed asset has the following characteristics.

Initial investment	$19,214
Annual after-tax cash inflows	$ 8,000
Life	3 years
Salvage	$ 0
Internal rate of return	0.12

REQUIREMENTS

Assume actual cash flows are as expected. Determine the return on the investment for each year using book value at the beginning of the year as the investment and the following depreciation methods:

a) Straight-line

b) Sum-of-the-years'-digits

c) Compound interest

16–25 T Return on Investment and Alternative Depreciation Methods (Appendix)

An investment proposal for a new fixed asset has the following characteristics:

Initial investment	$43,486
Annual after-tax cash flows	$20,000
Life	3 years
Salvage	$ 0
Internal rate of return	0.18

REQUIREMENTS

Assume actual cash flows are as expected. Determine the return on the investment for each year using book value at the beginning of the year as the investment and the following depreciation methods:

a) Straight-line

b) Sum-of-the-years'-digits

c) Compound interest

16–26 T ROI and Alternative Depreciation Methods: Actual Results Differ from Expected (Appendix)

An investment proposal for a new fixed asset has the following characteristics:

Initial investment	$34,824
Annual after-tax cash flows	$15,000
Life	3 years
Salvage	$ 0
Internal rate of return	0.14

REQUIREMENTS

a) Prepare a schedule of compound interest depreciation for this proposed investment.

b) Assume actual after-tax cash flows are as follows:

Year 1	$16,000
Year 2	15,000
Year 3	12,000

Determine the actual return on the beginning-of-the-year investment balance using the following depreciation methods:

1. Straight-line
2. Sum-of-the-years'-digits
3. Compound interest

16–27 T ROI and Alternative Depreciation Methods: Actual Results Differ from Expected (Appendix)

An investment proposal for a new fixed asset has the following characteristics:

Initial investment	$26,951
After-tax cash flows:	
Year 1	$12,000
Year 2	$12,000
Year 3	$ 8,000
Life	3 years
Salvage	$ 4,000
Internal rate of return	0.16

REQUIREMENTS

a) Prepare a schedule of compound interest depreciation for this proposed investment.

b) Assume actual after-tax cash flows from operations are as follows:

Year 1	$10,000
Year 2	15,000
Year 3	8,000

Determine the actual return on the beginning-of-the-year investment balance using the following depreciation methods:

1. Straight-line
2. Sum-of-the-years'-digits
3. Compound interest

16–28 Performance Evaluation and Compound Interest Depreciation (Appendix)

Peterdonn Corporation made a capital investment of $100,000 in new equipment two years ago. The analysis made at that time indicated the equipment would save $36,400 in operating expenses per year over a five-year period, or a 24 percent return on capital before taxes per year based on the internal rate of return analysis.

The department manager believed that the equipment had "lived up" to its expectations. However, the departmental report showing the overall return on investment (ROI) for the first year in which this equipment was used did not reflect as much improvement as had been expected. The department manager asked the accounting section to "break out" the figures related to this investment to find out why it did not contribute more to the department's ROI.

The accounting section was able to identify the equipment and its contribution to the department's operations. The report presented to the department manager at the end of the first year is as follows:

Reduced operating expenses due to new equipment	$36,400
Less: Depreciation—20 percent of cost	−20,000
Contribution before taxes	$16,400
Investment—beginning of year	$100,000
Investment—end of year	$ 80,000
Investment—average for the year	$ 90,000
ROI ($16,400/$90,000)	0.182

The department manager was surprised that the ROI was less than 24 percent because the new equipment performed as expected. The staff analyst in the accounting section replied that the company's ROI for performance evaluation differed from that used for capital investment analysis. The analyst commented that the discrepancy could be solved if the company used the compound interest method of depreciation for its performance evaluation reports.

REQUIREMENTS

a) Discuss why the 18.2 percent return on investment for the new equipment as calculated in the department's report prepared by the accounting section differs from the 24 percent internal rate of return calculated at the time the machine was approved for purchase.

b) Will the use of the compound interest method of depreciation solve the discrepancy as the analyst claims? Explain your answer.

c) Explain how Peterdonn Corporation might restructure the data from the discounted cash flow analysis so that the expected performance of the new equipment is consistent with the operating reports received by the department manager.

(CMA Adapted)

16–29 NPV and Price-Level Changes: No Taxes (Appendix)

In December of each year, the Big Red Company evaluates investment proposals for the coming year. One of the proposals being evaluated in December 19x0 involves an initial investment of $200,000. If accepted, the investment would be placed in service in early January 19x1. The investment has a useful life of five years and is expected to have no salvage value at the end of that time. Expected cash flows in 19x0 dollars are $60,000 annually. The company has a minimum required rate of return (in constant dollars) of 12 percent and expects an inflation rate of 8 percent a year over the five years. Assume cash flows from operations occur at the end of each year. Ignore income taxes.

REQUIREMENTS

a) Determine the net present value of the proposed investment using constant dollars.

b) Determine the expected cash flows for each year in nominal dollars.

c) What discount rate should be used to determine the net present value of the proposed investment if it is evaluated using cash flows expressed in nominal dollars?

16–30 IRR and Price-Level Changes: No Taxes (Appendix)

During December 19x0, the Fitzhugh Corporation is evaluating an investment proposal with an initial investment of $500,000. If accepted, the project would be placed in service in January 19x1 and have a useful life of five years. At the end of that time, the salvage value is expected to be zero. Expected cash flows in 19x0 dollars are $150,000 annually.

The company has a minimum required rate of return (in constant dollars) of 14 percent and expects an inflation rate of 6 percent a year during the life of the investment. Assume all cash flows from operations occur at the end of the year. Ignore income taxes.

REQUIREMENTS

a) Determine the internal rate of return of the investment using constant dollars in the analysis. Should Fitzhugh invest in the project?

b) Determine the expected cash flows in nominal dollars.

c) Determine the internal rate of return of the investment using nominal dollars in the analysis.

d) What minimum internal rate of return should be used to determine whether or not the project is acceptable if nominal dollars are used in the analysis?

16–31 NPV and Price-Level Changes: Income Taxes (Appendix)

Catix Corporation is a divisionalized company, and each division has the authority to make capital expenditures up to $200,000 without corporate headquarters' approval. The corporate controller has determined that the cost of capital for Catix Corporation is 13 percent. This rate does not allow for inflation, which is expected to occur at an average annual rate of 8 percent over the next five years. Catix pays income taxes at the rate of 40 percent.

The Electronics Division of Catix is considering the purchase of an automated assembly and soldering machine to use in manufacturing its printed circuit boards. The machine would be placed in service in early 19x1. The divisional controller estimates that if the machine is purchased, two positions will be eliminated, yielding a cost savings for wages and employee benefits. However, the machine would require additional supplies and more power would be required to operate the machine. The cost savings and additional costs in 19x0 prices are as follows:

Wages and employee benefits of the two positions eliminated ($25,000 each)	$50,000
Cost of additional supplies	$ 6,000
Cost of additional power	$14,000

The new machine would be purchased and installed at the end of 19x0 at a net cost of $80,000. If purchased, the machine would be depreciated using the straight-line method for book purposes and using ACRS for tax purposes. The machine qualifies for a 10 percent investment tax credit. The machine will become technologically obsolete in five years and will have no salvage value at that time.

The Electronics Division compensates for inflation in capital expenditure analyses by adjusting the expected constant-dollar cash flows by a predicted price-level index. The adjusted after-tax cash flows are then discounted using the appropriate discount rate. The predicted year-end index values for each of the next five years are as follows:

Year	*Year-end price index*
19x0	1.00
19x1	1.08
19x2	1.17
19x3	1.26
19x4	1.36
19x5	1.47

The Plastics Division of Catix compensates for inflation in capital expenditures analyses by adding the anticipated inflation rate to the cost of capital and then using the inflation adjusted cost of capital to discount the project cash flows. The Plastics Division recently rejected a project with cash flows and economic life similar to those associated with the machine under consideration by the Electronics Division. The Plastics Division's analysis of the rejected project was as follows:

	Year 1	*Year 2*	*Year 3*	*Year 4*	*Year 5*
Net pre-tax cost savings	$30,000	$30,000	$30,000	$30,000	$30,000
Less: ACRS depreciation on $76,000 (cost less 50 percent of investment tax credit)	−11,400	−16,720	−15,960	−15,960	−15,960
Increase in taxable income	$18,600	$13,280	$14,040	$14,040	$14,040
Increase in income taxes @ 40 percent	− 7,440	− 5,312	− 5,616	− 5,616	− 5,616
Increase in after-tax income	$11,160	$ 7,968	$ 8,424	$ 8,424	$ 8,424
Add back non-cash expense (depreciation)	11,400	16,720	15,960	15,960	15,960
Net after-tax cash inflow (unadjusted for inflation)	$22,560	$24,688	$24,384	$24,384	$24,384

Present value of net cash inflows using the sum of the cost of capital (13 percent) and the inflation rate (8 percent) or a minimum required return of 21 percent:

Year	*Net after-tax cash inflow*	*Present value factor @ 21%*		*Present value of cash inflow*
19x1	$22,560	0.8264		$18,644
19x2	24,688	0.6830		16,862
19x3	24,384	0.5645		13,765
19x4	24,384	0.4665		11,375
19x5	24,384	0.3855		9,400
Total present value of cash inflows				$70,046
Less investment required:				
Cost of machine			$80,000	
Less: Investment tax credit			−8,000	−72,000
Net present value				$(1,954)

All operating revenues and expenditures occur at the end of the year.

REQUIREMENTS

a) Using the price index provided, prepare a schedule showing the net after-tax annual cash flows adjusted for inflation (that is, nominal dollars) for the automated assembly and soldering machine that the Electronics Division is considering.

b) Using the results in part (a), prepare a meaningful calculation of the net present value for the project.

c) Evaluate the methods used by the Plastics Division and the Electronics Division to compensate for expected inflation in capital expenditure analyses. (CMA Adapted)

SOLUTION TO REVIEW PROBLEM

a) 1. $\text{Payback period} = \dfrac{\$42{,}000}{\$14{,}000} = \underline{\underline{3.00}} \text{ years}$

2. $\text{Annual depreciation} = \dfrac{\$42{,}000}{5} = \$8{,}400$

$$\begin{array}{c}\text{Accounting rate of return} \\ \text{on initial investment}\end{array} = \frac{\$14{,}000 - \$8{,}400}{\$42{,}000} = \underline{\underline{0.13}} \text{ (rounded)}$$

3. The investment varies between $42,000 and $0 over the five-year period. The average is [($42,000 + $0)/2] = $21,000.

$$\begin{array}{c}\text{Accounting rate of return} \\ \text{on average investment}\end{array} = \frac{\$14{,}000 - \$8{,}400}{\$21{,}000} = \underline{\underline{0.27}} \text{ (rounded)}$$

4. Factor = $42,000/$14,000 = 3.00

For $n = 5$, the closest table factor (2.9906) corresponds to a discount rate of 20 percent. This is the project's IRR.

(*Note:* Even though cash flows normally occur throughout the year, for computational purposes most discounting models assume they occur at the end of each period.)

5.

Present value of cash inflows @ 16% ($14,000 × 3.2743)	$45,840
Initial investment	−42,000
Net present value	$3,840

b)

	Year 1	*Year 2*	*Year 3*	*Year 4*	*Year 5*
Income taxes on operating cash inflows ($14,000 × 0.40)	$ 5,600	$ 5,600	$ 5,600	$ 5,600	$ 5,600
Less: Depreciation tax shield*	−2,520	−3,696	−3,528	−3,528	−3,528
Cash outflow for income taxes	$ 3,080	$ 1,904	$ 2,072	$ 2,072	$ 2,072
Operating cash inflow	$14,000	$14,000	$14,000	$14,000	$14,000
Less: cash outflow for income taxes	−3,080	−1,904	−2,072	−2,072	−2,072
After-tax cash inflows	$10,920	$12,096	$11,928	$11,928	$11,928

* Calculation of depreciation tax shield:

Year	*Cost (1)*	*ACRS rate (2)*	*ACRS deduction (Cost × ACRS rate) (3) = (1) × (2)*	*Tax rate (4)*	*Tax shield (ACRS deduction × Tax rate) (3) × (4)*
1	$42,000	0.15	$6,300	0.40	$2,520
2	42,000	0.22	9,240	0.40	3,696
3	42,000	0.21	8,820	0.40	3,528
4	42,000	0.21	8,820	0.40	3,528
5	42,000	0.21	8,820	0.40	3,528

c) 1. Calculation of cumulative cash inflows:

Year	*Cash inflows*	*Cumulative cash inflows*
1	$10,920	$10,920
2	12,096	23,016
3	11,928	34,944
4	11,928	46,872

$$\text{Payback period} = 3 + \frac{\$42{,}000 - \$34{,}944}{\$46{,}872 - \$34{,}944} = \underline{\underline{3.59 \text{ years}}}$$

2. First trial: Net present value at 12 percent discount rate:

Year	*Cash inflows*	*Present value factor*	*Present value of cash inflows*
1	$10,920	0.8929	$ 9,750
2	12,096	0.7972	9,643
3	11,928	0.7118	8,490
4	11,928	0.6355	7,580
5	11,928	0.5674	6,768
			$42,231
Initial investment			−42,000
Net present value			$ 231

Second trial: Net present value at 14 percent discount rate:

Year	*Cash inflows*	*Present value factor*	*Present value of cash inflows*
1	$10,920	0.8772	$ 9,579
2	12,096	0.7695	9,308
3	11,928	0.6750	8,051
4	11,928	0.5921	7,063
5	11,928	0.5194	6,195
			$40,196
Initial investment			−42,000
Net present value			$(1,804)

IRR is approximately 12 percent.

3. Net present value at 16 percent discount rate:

Year	*Cash inflows*	*Present value factor*	*Present value of cash inflows*
1	$10,920	0.8621	$ 9,414
2	12,096	0.7432	8,990
3	11,928	0.6407	7,642
4	11,928	0.5523	6,588
5	11,928	0.4761	5,679
			$38,313
Initial investment			−42,000
Net present value			$(3,687)

17 Capital Budgeting II

INTRODUCTION
INCREMENTAL ANALYSIS
MUTUALLY EXCLUSIVE INVESTMENTS
CAPITAL RATIONING
INVESTMENT AND FINANCING DECISIONS
LEASE-PURCHASE DECISIONS
UNCERTAINTY OR RISK
SUMMARY

INTRODUCTION

THE BASIC ELEMENTS OF CAPITAL BUDGETING WERE EXAMINED IN CHAPTER 16. We discussed the importance of capital budgeting, its relationship to strategic planning and yearly budgeting, the characteristics of several project evaluation models, the development of cash flow predictions, and the need for postselection review. Because the discounting models consider profitability and the timing of cash flows, we concluded they were superior to the payback and accounting rate-of-return models. Discounting models do, however, require the specification of time value of money to be used as a cutoff or discount rate. We noted that for-profit organizations may use their weighted-average cost of capital as the time value of money if a set of stringent criteria are met.

This chapter builds on the framework developed in Chapter 16. The purpose of this chapter is to present a number of specialized but important topics pertaining to the nature of proposed investments, the availability and source of investment financing, and risk. Because discounting models are better investment guides than nondiscounting models, they are used exclusively in this chapter.

INCREMENTAL ANALYSIS

The investment proposals discussed in Chapter 16 dealt exclusively with new projects that were to be accepted or rejected in their entirety. The relevant revenues and costs included the incremental cash inflows and outflows associated with the project. In this chapter we apply the same type of analysis to the evaluation of cost reduction proposals and the determination of optimal investment size.

Cost Reduction Proposals

Undertaking a new project or extending the life of an old project results in incremental cash inflows as well as incremental cash outflows. Investment proposals are also frequently made for **cost reduction proposals,** that is, projects that do not call for incremental cash inflows but instead reduce cash outflows associated with current activities. Because cost reduction proposals do not result in additional cash receipts, the initial investment must be compared with subsequent cash savings.

Example 17–1 The Scheiner Shoe Company owns a fully depreciated machine that has no salvage value. Because of careful maintenance it has a remaining useful life of five years with yearly operating costs of $20,000. Management is considering the acquisition of a new machine to perform the same task. The new machine costs $18,000, has a five-year life, and has no salvage value. Yearly operating costs of the new machine will be $13,000. For tax purposes, Scheiner uses the Accelerated Cost Recovery System (ACRS). The machine is five-year qualifying property. ACRS rates (see Exhibit 16–6) for five-year property are: Year 1, 15 percent; Year 2, 22 percent; Year 3, 21 percent; Year 4, 21 percent; and Year 5, 21 percent. The income tax rate is 40 percent and Scheiner's cost of capital is 14 percent. Ignore the investment tax credit.

As determined in Exhibit 17–1, the net present value (NPV) of this cost reduction proposal is $1,288. It appears that it should be accepted. However, this conclusion assumes only two feasible alternatives: (1) continue operations with the current machine, and (2) continue operations with the new machine. This assumption is correct if the activity must be performed (for example, if the organization is a governmental agency that must provide the product or service or if the organization has a contract to provide the product or service). In this case, the revenues, if any, are fixed and the objective of the analysis is to minimize costs.

For-profit organizations usually have three alternatives:

1. Continue operations with the current machine
2. Continue operations with the new machine
3. Discontinue operations

In most situations the third alternative is not considered unless the accounting system provides a warning signal, such as low earnings or negative operating cash flows. If there is doubt as to whether an operation should be continued, a complete analysis of all predicted cash receipts and disbursements should be made. Only in this way will the firm avoid throwing good money after bad.

Example 17–2 Assume that the expected cash inflows associated with production using either machine in Example 17–1 are $18,000 a year. A present value analysis of the alternatives to continue operations with the current machine or to continue operations with the new machine is presented in Exhibit 17–2.

The analysis in Exhibit 17–2 shows that the net present value of operating with the current machine is $(4,120) and the NPV of operating with the new machine is $(2,832). Because the NPV of operating with either machine is negative, Scheiner should, if possible, discontinue production. Note that the NPV of the cost reduction proposal in Exhibit 17–1 was $1,288; the difference in the NPVs of the two machines found in Exhibit 17–2 is also $1,288 ($4,120 − $2,832).

EXHIBIT 17–1 **Net Present Value of a Cost Reduction Proposal**

	Year 1	2	3	4	5
Cash savings:					
Operating costs of current machine	$ 20,000	$ 20,000	$ 20,000	$ 20,000	$ 20,000
Operating costs of new machine	−13,000	−13,000	−13,000	−13,000	−13,000
Cost savings before income taxes	$ 7,000	$ 7,000	$ 7,000	$ 7,000	$ 7,000
Additional income taxes*	− 1,720	− 1,216	− 1,288	− 1,288	− 1,288
Cash savings after income taxes	$ 5,280	$ 5,784	$ 5,712	$ 5,712	$ 5,712
Present value of $1 @ $r = 0.14$	×0.8772	×0.7695	×0.6750	×0.5921	×0.5194
Present value	$ 4,632	$ 4,451	$ 3,856	$ 3,382	$ 2,967
Total present value of cost savings					$ 19,288
Less: Initial investment					−18,000
Net present value					$ 1,288

* Computation of additional taxes:

	Year 1	2	3	4	5
Additional taxes on cost savings before income taxes @ 0.40	$ 2,800	$ 2,800	$ 2,800	$ 2,800	$ 2,800
Less: Tax shield from additional depreciation†	−1,080	−1,584	−1,512	−1,512	−1,512
Increase in income taxes	$ 1,720	$ 1,216	$ 1,288	$ 1,288	$ 1,288

† Computation of depreciation tax shield:

Year	Cost of new machine (1)	ACRS rate (2)	ACRS deduction (3) = (1) × (2)	Depreciation on old machine (4)	Increase in depreciation (5) = (3) − (4)	Tax rate (6)	Tax shield (5) × (6)
1	$18,000	0.15	$2,700	$0	$2,700	0.40	$1,080
2	18,000	0.22	3,960	0	3,960	0.40	1,584
3	18,000	0.21	3,780	0	3,780	0.40	1,512
4	18,000	0.21	3,780	0	3,780	0.40	1,512
5	18,000	0.21	3,780	0	3,780	0.40	1,512

Although either type of analysis may be used for evaluating cost reduction proposals, the authors prefer the one in Exhibit 17–1 because it emphasizes the differences in cash flows that result from using the two machines if discontinuing operations is not a feasible alternative.

We can also evaluate cost reduction proposals by calculating the present value of life-cycle costs. An investment's **life-cycle costs** consist of all costs associated with a project, including the initial investment and the after-tax costs of operation and maintenance.

Assume that the new machine in Example 17–1 has lower operating costs because it uses less electricity and requires fewer repairs and less maintenance

EXHIBIT 17–2 Present Value Analysis of Operating With Current and New Machine

(a) Continue operations with current machine

	Year				
	1	*2*	*3*	*4*	*5*
Cash inflows from operations	$ 18,000	$ 18,000	$ 18,000	$ 18,000	$ 18,000
Cash outflows for operations	−20,000	−20,000	−20,000	−20,000	−20,000
Net cash inflows (outflows) before income taxes	$ (2,000)	$ (2,000)	$ (2,000)	$ (2,000)	$ (2,000)
Income tax savings @ 0.40*	800	800	800	800	800
Net cash inflows (outflows) after income taxes	$ (1,200)	$ (1,200)	$ (1,200)	$ (1,200)	$ (1,200)
Present value of $1 @ $r = 0.14$	×0.8772	×0.7695	×0.6750	×0.5921	×0.5194
Present value of net cash outflows	$ (1,053)	$ (923)	$ (810)	$ (711)	$ (623)
Total present value of net cash outflows					$ (4,120)

* Income tax savings:

	Year				
	1	*2*	*3*	*4*	*5*
Taxes saved from net cash outflows @ 0.40	$ 800	$ 800	$ 800	$ 800	$ 800
Less: Depreciation tax shield	− 0	− 0	− 0	− 0	− 0
Income tax savings	$ 800	$ 800	$ 800	$ 800	$ 800

(b) Continue operations with new machine

	Year				
	1	*2*	*3*	*4*	*5*
Cash inflows from operations	$ 18,000	$ 18,000	$ 18,000	$ 18,000	$ 18,000
Cash outflows for operations	−13,000	−13,000	−13,000	−13,000	−13,000
Net cash inflows (outflows) before income taxes	$ 5,000	$ 5,000	$ 5,000	$ 5,000	$ 5,000
Income taxes @ 0.40*	− 920	− 416	− 488	− 488	− 488
Net cash inflows (outflows) after income taxes	$ 4,080	$ 4,584	$ 4,512	$ 4,512	$ 4,512
Present value of $1 @ $r = 0.14$	×0.8772	×0.7695	×0.6750	×0.5921	×0.5194
Present value of net cash inflows	$ 3,579	$ 3,527	$ 3,046	$ 2,672	$ 2,344
Total present value of net cash inflows					$ 15,168
Less: Initial Investment					−18,000
Present value of investment					$ (2,832)

* Computation of income taxes:

(Continued)

EXHIBIT 17–2 *(Continued)*

	Year 1	2	3	4	5
Taxes on net cash inflows @ 0.40	$ 2,000	$ 2,000	$ 2,000	$ 2,000	$ 2,000
Less: Depreciation tax shield†	− 1,080	− 1,584	− 1,512	− 1,512	− 1,512
Additional income taxes	$ 920	$ 416	$ 488	$ 488	$ 488

† Computation of depreciation tax shield:

Year	*Cost (1)*	*ACRS rate (2)*	*ACRS deduction (3) = (1) × (2)*	*Tax rate (4)*	*Tax shield (3) × (4)*
1	$18,000	0.15	$2,700	0.40	$1,080
2	18,000	0.22	3,960	0.40	1,584
3	18,000	0.21	3,780	0.40	1,512
4	18,000	0.21	3,780	0.40	1,512
5	18,000	0.21	3,780	0.40	1,512

than the current machine. The life-cycle costs of the current machine consist of its after-tax cost of repairs and electricity over the remaining useful life. The life-cycle costs of the new machine consist of its initial investment plus its after-tax costs of repairs and electricity less its depreciation tax shield over its useful life. A present value analysis of these costs is shown in Exhibit 17–3.

As shown in Exhibit 17–3, the present value of life-cycle costs is lower for the new machine than for the current machine. This agrees with our previous conclusion that the new machine should be used if production is to continue. The difference in the present value of the life-cycle costs between the two machines is $1,287 ($41,198 − $39,911). This amount differs from the NPV of $1,288 found in Exhibit 17–1 because of rounding.

Life-cycle costs are important for individuals as well as organizations. If an individual is evaluating the costs of a new heating and air-conditioning system for his or her home, the present value of all costs over the life of the system are relevant to the decision. If different systems are available (for example, a heat pump or a gas furnace with electric air conditioning), the life-cycle costs of the alternatives are likely to differ.

Variable Investment Size

We can also use incremental analysis if the size of a proposed investment can vary. Stores, ships, hospitals, and factories can usually be constructed in various sizes. For these projects, management must (1) determine whether to accept or reject the investment proposal and (2) select the optimal investment size for acceptable investments. The key to determining the optimal investment size is to use the profit-maximizing rule of economics. Profits are maximized at that point where marginal revenues equal marginal costs.[1] When applied to the problem

[1] Assuming marginal revenue exceeds marginal cost prior to this point. See Exhibit 15–8 and footnote 4 in Chapter 15.

at hand, this rule is modified to state that profits are maximized at the point where the incremental present value of subsequent net cash inflows equals the incremental investment.

Consider the situation presented in Exhibit 17–4. The first column presents the alternative investment sizes for a particular project. The second column presents the corresponding present value of subsequent net cash inflows. Because the discount rate is an imputed opportunity cost, a manager might be tempted to conclude that the optimal investment is $120,000, the point at which the project's net present value is zero. The additional analyses in columns 4, 5, and 6 reveal that this is not the case. The optimal investment size is $70,000. Beyond $70,000 the incremental investments have negative net present values. Increasing the investment size by $10,000, from $70,000 to $80,000, increases the incremental present value of subsequent cash flows by only $8,000. The net present value of this incremental investment is $(2,000).

EXHIBIT 17–3 Present Value Analysis of Life-Cycle Costs

(a) Current machine

Year	Cash outflows (1)	Tax savings @ 0.4 (2)	Depreciation tax shield (3)	After-tax cash outflows (4) = (1) − (2) − (3)	Present value factor (5)	Present value (4) × (5)
1	$20,000	$8,000	$0	$12,000	0.8772	$10,526
2	20,000	8,000	0	12,000	0.7695	9,234
3	20,000	8,000	0	12,000	0.6750	8,100
4	20,000	8,000	0	12,000	0.5921	7,105
5	20,000	8,000	0	12,000	0.5194	6,233
Total present value of after-tax costs						$41,198

(b) New machine

Year	Cash outflows (1)	Tax savings @ 0.4 (2)	Depreciation tax shield* (3)	After-tax cash outflows (4) = (1) − (2) − (3)	Present value factor (5)	Present value (4) × (5)
0	$18,000	$ 0	$ 0	$18,000	1.0000	$18,000
1	13,000	5,200	1,080	6,720	0.8772	5,895
2	13,000	5,200	1,584	6,216	0.7695	4,783
3	13,000	5,200	1,512	6,288	0.6750	4,244
4	13,000	5,200	1,512	6,288	0.5921	3,723
5	13,000	5,200	1,512	6,288	0.5194	3,266
Total present value of after-tax costs						$39,911

* See Exhibit 17–2 for computations.

EXHIBIT 17–4 **Net Present Value Analysis With Investment Size as a Variable**

1	2	3	4	5	6
Size of initial investment	*Present value of subsequent net cash inflows*	*Net present value of investment*	*Incremental investment*	*Incremental present value of subsequent net cash inflows*	*Net present value of incremental investment*
$ 40,000	$ 60,000	$20,000	$40,000	$60,000	$20,000
50,000	75,000	25,000	10,000	15,000	5,000
60,000	87,000	27,000	10,000	12,000	2,000
70,000*	97,000*	27,000*	10,000*	10,000*	0*
80,000	105,000	25,000	10,000	8,000	(2,000)
90,000	110,000	20,000	10,000	5,000	(5,000)
100,000	114,000	14,000	10,000	4,000	(6,000)
110,000	118,000	8,000	10,000	4,000	(6,000)
120,000	120,000	0	10,000	2,000	(8,000)

* Optimal.

MUTUALLY EXCLUSIVE INVESTMENTS

With the exception of projects that have multiple internal rates of return, the net present value and internal rate of return models lead to identical accept or reject decisions when used to evaluate independent projects. This is not always the case when the projects are mutually exclusive or when capital rationing exists. We consider mutually exclusive projects next and capital rationing later in this chapter.

Two investments are **mutually exclusive** if the acceptance of one automatically causes the rejection of the other (for example, two alternative uses of a single plot of land). The key problem in evaluating mutually exclusive investments is to select the better of two (or more) investment proposals when all proposals satisfy the organization's minimum investment criteria. Consider, for example, the problem faced by a local department store that is evaluating the desirability of purchasing a delivery truck. Several makes and styles are available. An independent analysis of each indicates that an investment in any one is acceptable. However, only one truck is needed. Unfortunately, if these mutually exclusive investments were ranked on the basis of their net present values and their internal rates of return, there could be a conflict.

The conditions that lead to different rankings when using net present value and internal rate of return models are

1. The initial investments of the projects differ
2. The expected lives of the projects differ
3. The timing and amount of the predicted cash flows differ

Initial Investment

Assume that an organization with a cost of capital of 12 percent must select one of the two mutually exclusive projects presented in Exhibit 17–5. The IRR of both projects exceeds the cutoff rate and the net present value of both projects is positive at the discount rate. If they were independent, both would be accepted. As mutually exclusive projects, the IRR model ranks Project A first and the NPV model ranks Project B first. In this case, if the true opportunity cost of investment capital is 12 percent, Project B should be selected to maximize the total net present value of the organization. The selection of Project A would leave $180,000 available for investment elsewhere. Assuming this money could earn a return of only 12 percent, its net present value would be zero and the total net present value of this alternative would be less than the net present value of B:

Alternative: Invest in A

	Initial investment	*Annual net cash inflows*
Project A	$100,000	$ 40,000
Remainder	180,000	59,261*
Total annual net cash inflows		$ 99,261
Present value factor for annuity @ 0.12, $n = 4$		× 3.0374
Present value of net cash inflows		$301,495
Initial investment		−280,000
Net present value		$ 21,495

* ($180,000 ÷ 3.0374)

Alternative: Invest in B

	Initial investment	*Annual net cash inflows*
Project B	$280,000	$100,000
Present value factor for annuity @ 0.12, $n = 4$		× 3.0374
Present value of net cash inflows		$303,740
Initial investment		−280,000
Net present value		$ 23,740

EXHIBIT 17–5 Alternative Rankings of Mutually Exclusive Investments of Differing Size

Project	*Initial investment*	*Subsequent net cash flows*
A	$100,000	$ 40,000/year for 4 years
B	280,000	100,000/year for 4 years

	Internal rate of return		*Net present value @ $r = 0.12$*	
Project	*Rate*	*Rank*	Amount	Rank
A	0.22	1	$21,495	2
B	0.16	2	23,740	1

Investment Life

Assume that an organization with a cost of capital of 12 percent must select one of the two mutually exclusive investments presented in Exhibit 17–6. Again, as independent projects, both are acceptable using either model. As mutually exclusive investments, the IRR model ranks Project C first, whereas the NPV model ranks Project D first.

The difference in rankings between the two models is caused by the models' reinvestment rate assumptions. The IRR model assumes cash flows are reinvested at the project's internal rate of return and the NPV model assumes cash flows are reinvested at the discount rate. Thus the relative desirability of Projects C and D depends on what rate of return the subsequent cash flows can earn. If the opportunity cost of invested capital remains at 12 percent throughout the life of both projects, Project D should be selected. The selection of Project C would provide $120,000 for other investments at the end of Year 1. If these investments can earn a return of only 12 percent, their net present value is zero and the total net present value of Project D exceeds the net present value of Project C.

Timing and Amount of Cash Flows

Assume that an organization with a cost of capital of 12 percent must select one of the two mutually exclusive projects presented in Exhibit 17–7. Again, as independent projects, both are acceptable using either the IRR or NPV models. As mutually exclusive investments, however, the IRR model ranks Project E first, whereas the NPV model ranks Project F first.

The difference in rankings for these two projects is caused by the reinvestment rate assumption just discussed. Since Project E has the larger cash inflows in its early years, the IRR model assumes these will be reinvested at a 20 percent rate, whereas the NPV model assumes they will only earn 12 percent. Because Project F has lower cash flows in the early years, the reinvestment rate assumption is that there are fewer future dollars. As shown for projects with different lives, Project F should be selected if the opportunity cost of invested capital remains at 12 percent.

EXHIBIT 17–6 Alternative Rankings of Mutually Exclusive Investments of Differing Lives

		Subsequent net cash flows			
Project	*Initial investment*	*Year 1*	*Year 2*	*Year 3*	*Year 4*
C	$100,000	$120,000	$ 0	$ 0	$ 0
D	100,000	0	50,000	50,000	50,000

	Internal rate of return		*Net present value @ r = 0.12*	
Project	*Amount*	*Rank*	*Amount*	*Rank*
C	0.20	1	$7,148	2
D	0.14	2	7,225	1

EXHIBIT 17–7 Alternative Rankings of Mututally Exclusive Investments of Differing Timing and Amounts of Cash Flows

		Subsequent net cash flows		
Project	*Initial investment*	*Year 1*	*Year 2*	*Year 3*
E	$100,000	$80,000	$40,000	$10,000
F	100,000	10,000	50,000	90,000

	Internal rate of return		Net present value @ r = 0.12	
Project	*Amount*	*Rank*	*Amount*	*Rank*
E	0.20	1	$10,438	2
F	0.18	2	12,851	1

The existence of a limited pool of investment funds complicates the analysis of mutually exclusive projects. It would be necessary to give formal consideration to subsequent investment opportunities. Unfortunately this may not be possible.

CAPITAL RATIONING

Capital rationing occurs when the total funds required for investment proposals meeting the organization's investment criteria exceed the total funds available for investment. Theoretically capital rationing should not occur. If the organization cannot obtain sufficient financing to fund all acceptable projects at the discount or cutoff rate it is using, the rate is too low. In practice, capital rationing is caused by arbitrary administrative decisions and/or the transaction's cost of obtaining additional financing in time to increase the current capital budget.

The problems caused by capital rationing are similar to those encountered in evaluating mutually exclusive investments. Management must select the best proposals from a set that satisfies the organization's minimum investment criteria. There are at least three ways of making the selections:

1. Ranking the projects using some criterion and selecting acceptable projects from the top until funds are exhausted
2. Trial and error
3. Mathematical programming

Ranking

The most frequently discussed project-ranking criteria are internal rate of return and present value index. The **present value index**, sometimes called **profitability index** or **excess present value index**, is the present value of a project's net cash inflows or savings divided by the initial investment. In equation form,

$$PVI = \frac{\sum_{i=1}^{n} \frac{S_i}{(1+r)^i}}{P} \qquad (17\text{–}1)$$

where

PVI = Present value index
S_i = Predicted cash inflow (or savings) in time period i
r = Minimum required discount rate
i = Time period when cash flow occurs
n = Life of the investment
P = Initial investment

When the PVI is used to evaluate investment proposals, acceptable projects have a present value index greater than or equal to one. The present value index of the cost reduction proposal discussed in Example 17–1 is 1.072 ($19,288 ÷ $18,000). The present value index is used in place of net present value when ranking projects to improve the comparability of projects of varying size.

Example 17–3

Holston Incorporated has a maximum of $400,000 available for investment in new capital projects during 19x0. However, the capital-budgeting committee has identified six proposals, requiring total initial investments of $782,000, that exceed Holston's minimum internal rate of return criterion of 12 percent. These projects are described in Exhibit 17–8.

If the projects are ranked and accepted on the basis of their internal rate of return, the results are as shown in Exhibit 17–9(a). Note that Project B must be rejected even though its internal rate of return is greater than that of Project D which is accepted. Projects E, A, and C have consumed available funds to the point where the investment funds required for Project B are not available. Accordingly, B is passed over in favor of Project D. The $68,000 remaining in the capital budget is assumed to be invested at its opportunity cost of 12 percent. The final net present value, when the selection is made on the basis of IRR, is $59,782.

If the projects are ranked and accepted on the basis of their present value index, the results are as shown in Exhibit 17–9(b). Once again, Project B is rejected because of insufficient funds at the time it comes up for consideration. The final net present value, when the selection is made on the basis of PVI, is $67,304.

EXHIBIT 17–8 Description of Investment Proposals Competing for Limited Funds

	Project					
	A	B	C	D	E	F
Initial investment	$(60,000)	$(250,000)	$(150,000)	$(72,000)	$(50,000)	$(200,000)
Subsequent annual net cash flows	$ 39,000	$ 50,000	$ 37,500	$ 12,000	$ 25,000	$ 30,000
Life in years	2	11	8	14	3	19
Net present value @ r = 0.12	$ 5,914	$ 46,885	$ 36,285	$ 7,538	$ 10,045	$ 20,974
Present value index	1.0986	1.1875	1.2419	1.1047	1.2009	1.1048
Internal rate of return	0.20	0.16	0.18	0.14	0.24	0.14

EXHIBIT 17–9 Final Ranking and Net Present Value of Accepted Projects

(a) Ranking on the basis of internal rate of return

Project	*IRR*	*Investment*	*Total investment*	*NPV*
E	0.24	$ 50,000	$ 50,000	$10,045
A	0.20	60,000	110,000	5,914
C	0.18	150,000	260,000	36,285
D*	0.14	72,000	332,000	7,538
Balance	0.12	68,000	400,000	0
			Total net present value	$59,782

(b) Ranking on the basis of present value index

Project	*PVI*	*Investment*	*Total investment*	*NPV*
C	1.2419	150,000	$150,000	$36,285
E	1.2009	50,000	200,000	10,045
F†	1.1048	200,000	400,000	20,974
			Total net present value	$67,304

* Projects B and F are rejected because they require too large an investment.
† Project B is rejected because it requires too large an investment.

The differences between the IRR and PVI rankings are attributed to the previously discussed reinvestment rate assumptions of both the internal rate of return and net present value models. The IRR ranking favors short-lived projects with high internal rates of return (such as E and A) over long-lived projects with lower internal rates of return (such as F). If reinvestments are to take place at the discount or cutoff rate, the PVI ranking is superior. However, this assumption is questionable if capital rationing continues in the future. Neither IRR or PVI rankings consider investment size. Indeed, the PVI is computed to eliminate the effect of project size on the rankings that would occur if NPV were used to rank the proposals.

Trial and Error

Because neither the IRR nor PVI ranking criteria considers investment size, they both can lead to nonoptimal results. If an organization's objective is to maximize investors' wealth, the projects that are selected for investment should maximize the organization's net present value. For the relatively simple situation presented here, the set of projects that maximize net present value is easy to determine. Projects B and C require a total investment of $400,000, and their total net present value is $83,170 ($46,885 + $36,285). Unfortunately the trial-and-error approach rapidly becomes unwieldy as the number of combinations of attractive projects increases.

We have assumed that each project in Exhibit 17–8 is indivisible; that is, each project must be accepted or rejected in its entirety. If fractional investments in projects are allowed and the rate of return from fractional investments is the same as that for the entire project, ranking by present value index leads to optimal results. See Exhibit 17–10. Unfortunately fractional investments with these characteristics occur infrequently.

Mathematical Programming

Professor Weingartner has suggested the use of linear or integer programming to select projects under conditions of capital rationing.[2] If fractional investments are permitted, we can use the following linear programming model to determine the optimal selection of projects in the one-period case.

Maximize:

$$\sum_{j=1}^{n} b_j x_j \qquad (17\text{–}2)$$

Subject to:

$$\sum_{j=1}^{n} c_j x_j \leq C \qquad (17\text{–}3)$$

$$0 \leq x_j \leq 1 \qquad (17\text{–}4)$$

where

n = Number of projects available
b_j = Net present value of project j
x_j = Portion of project j accepted
c_j = Initial investment for project j as a whole
C = Budget limit

The situation presented in Example 17–3 would be formulated as follows:

Maximize:

$$5{,}914A + 46{,}885B + 36{,}285C + 7{,}538D + 10{,}045E + 20{,}974F$$

Subject to:

(1)	60,000A +	250,000B +	150,000C +	72,000D +	50,000E +	200,000F	≤	400,000
(2)	A						≤	1
(3)		B					≤	1
(4)			C				≤	1
(5)				D			≤	1
(6)					E		≤	1
(7)						F	≤	1
(8)	A						≥	0
(9)		B					≥	0
(10)			C				≥	0
(11)				D			≥	0
(12)					E		≥	0
(13)						F	≥	0

[2] H. Martin Weingartner, *Mathematical Programming and the Analysis of Capital Budgeting Problems* (Englewood Cliffs, N.J.: Prentice-Hall, 1963).

EXHIBIT 17–10 Final Ranking and Net Present Value of Accepted Projects When Fractional Investments Are Permitted

(a) Ranking on the basis of internal rate of return

Project	*IRR*	*Portion*	*Investment*	*Total investment*	*NPV*
E	0.24	1.00	$ 50,000	$ 50,000	$10,045
A	0.20	1.00	60,000	110,000	5,914
C	0.18	1.00	150,000	260,000	36,285
B	0.16	0.56	140,000	400,000	26,256
				Total net present value	$78,500

(b) Ranking on the basis of present value index

Project	*PVI*	*Portion*	*Investment*	*Total investment*	*NPV*
C	1.2419	1.00	150,000	$150,000	$36,285
E	1.2009	1.00	50,000	200,000	10,045
B	1.1875	0.80	200,000	400,000	37,508
				Total net present value	$83,838

The final selection of investments would be as indicated in Exhibit 17–10(b). The total net present value is $83,838.

If fractional investments were not permitted, we could make the optimal selection using integer programming. Although a discussion of integer programming is beyond the scope of this book, its use would result in the selection of projects B and C. The use of mathematical programming also provides shadow price information that is useful in evaluating the marginal effect of changes in constraints on the value of the objective function.[3]

INVESTMENT AND FINANCING DECISIONS

In evaluating investment proposals it is important to separate the investment and financing decisions. If this is not done, management may accept projects that do not meet the organization's minimum investment criteria or they may reject projects that exceed the minimum criteria.

Using the following example, Professors Ferrara, Thies, and Dirsmith illustrate how an unacceptable investment opportunity can appear to be acceptable if the investment and financing decisions are mixed together.[4]

---

[3] For a further discussion of this topic, see the previously cited work by Weingartner, or the book by Osteryoung referenced at the end of this chapter.

[4] William L. Ferrara, James B. Thies, and Mark W. Dirsmith, *The Lease-Purchase Decision* (New York: National Association of Accountants, 1980): pp. 41–42.

Example 17–4 Consider the following investment proposal:

Initial investment in facilities	$330,000
Useful life	10 years
Salvage value	$ 0
Net after-tax cash inflows:	
Years 1–5	$ 70,000
Years 6–10	$ 50,000
Minimum required after-tax rate of return	0.15

Using a 15 percent discount rate, the project is unacceptable because it has a net present value of $(12,010):

Years	*Net cash inflows*	*Present value factors* r = *0.15*	*Present value*
1–5	$70,000	3.352	$234,640
6–10	50,000	1.667*	83,350
Total present value of future cash flows			$317,990
Less: Initial investment			−330,000
Net present value			$ (12,010)

* (Present value of annuity, n = 10, r = 0.15) − (Present value of annuity, n = 5, r = 0.15) = 5.019 − 3.352 = 1.667.

To understand how this investment can appear to be acceptable, assume that the seller of the facilities will let us pay for the investment in three equal payments of $120,000, one at Time 0 and the others at the ends of Years 1 and 2. The net present value might then be determined as follows:

	Years	*Net cash flows*	*Present value factors* r = *0.15*	*Present value*
Present value of cash inflows:				
	1–5	$ 70,000	3.352	$234,640
	6–10	50,000	1.667	83,350
				$317,990
Less: Present value of cash outflows:				
	0	120,000	1.000	$120,000
	1	120,000	0.870	104,400
	2	120,000	0.756	90,720
				−315,120
Net present value				$ 2,870

With a positive net present value of $2,870, the investment appears acceptable. However, this analysis mixes the investment and financing decisions, which should not be done. The reason for the increase in net present value is that $210,000 ($330,000 − $120,000) of the initial investment is being financed at an interest rate that is less than the minimum required rate of return. With two

$120,000 payments, one each at the ends of Years 1 and 2, the interest rate implicit in financing $210,000 is approximately 10 percent:

$$\text{Annuity factor} = \frac{\$210{,}000}{\$120{,}000} = \underline{\underline{1.75}}$$

For $n = 2$, the closest value in Table F corresponds to $r = \underline{\underline{0.10}}$.

The calculation that resulted in a positive net present value is erroneous because the 10 percent interest rate on the loan was compared with the 15 percent minimum required rate of return. The correct comparison is between the interest rate on the loan and other sources of financing. If funds could be borrowed from a bank at a rate less than 10 percent (for example, 8 percent), this alternative is preferable to financing the purchase from the seller.

Professors Ferrara, Thies, and Dirsmith drew the following conclusions from their analysis:

1. Do not combine investment decisions with financing decisions.
2. Financing decisions should be based on alternative costs of borrowing, whether they be implicit or explicit.
3. Investment decisions should treat the cost of facilities as if they were all paid at the beginning of Year 1, that is, Year 0. Any other assumption would violate the preceding (first) conclusion.[5]

LEASE-PURCHASE DECISIONS

Once management has determined that an investment is acceptable, it should then consider how to acquire the needed plant and equipment. Two alternatives that are often available are purchase or lease. In a leasing situation, the individual or organization owning the property is called the **lessor**, and the individual or organization acquiring use of the property is called the **lessee.**

Leasing may be more attractive than purchasing for several reasons. The interest rate inherent in the lease may be lower than that available elsewhere, or alternative sources of financing may not be available. The lessor may also provide maintenance services of superior quality and/or lower cost due to economies of scale. If technology is changing rapidly, leasing may be preferred to avoid a long-term commitment to a particular asset. Finally, some companies, as a matter of policy, do not sell their equipment. Hence the only way of obtaining it is with a lease.

Income taxes are often crucial in deciding whether to lease or purchase plant and equipment. If a leasing arrangement does not meet certain criteria, it is treated as a purchase for income tax purposes.[6] If this occurs, the lessee records the leased property as an asset, the lease obligation as a liability, and deducts

---

[5] Ferrara, Thies, and Dirsmith, p. 43.

[6] The criteria for capitalizing leases for income tax purposes are not clearly defined in the regulations. Although the concepts are similar to those used in financial accounting, there are also differences that may cause a lease to be treated as a purchase in financial accounting and a lease for income taxes and vice versa.

depreciation and interest in calculating taxable income. The lease payment is not deductible in determining taxable income because the transaction is treated as a purchase.

If the lease is treated as a lease for tax purposes, the lessee is allowed to deduct the lease payment in calculating taxable income. The income taxes are thereby reduced by the amount of the tax shield provided by the payment.

Various types of analyses have been proposed to determine whether a lease or a purchase is better. One type of analysis is to compute the present value of the future cash outflows under the two alternatives and select the alternative with the lower present value. The discount rate used for this type of analysis is the after-tax borrowing rate.[7]

Example 17–5

Eastlake Company has accepted a proposal requiring an investment in equipment. Although the equipment has an expected useful life of eight years, Eastlake plans to use the equipment for only five years. The equipment has a purchase price of \$700,000 and a salvage value at the end of five years of \$200,000. The equipment is five-year qualifying property for ACRS depreciation and Eastlake will take the full 10 percent investment tax credit if the equipment is purchased. Eastlake can borrow money from a bank at an 8 percent after-tax cost.

The equipment can also be acquired by leasing. Under this alternative, equal annual lease payments of \$110,000 will be made at the beginning of each year.

Assume that the lease qualifies as a lease for tax purposes and that Eastlake's income tax rate is 40 percent.

To determine which alternative is better, we should compare the present values of the future cash flows under each alternative. The cash flows associated with purchasing are the purchase price, investment tax credit, depreciation tax shield, and salvage value. The cash flows associated with leasing are the lease payments and the tax shield related to the lease payment. Note that since the lease payments are made at the beginning of each year, they are prepaid and the deduction for income taxes will not occur until the end of the year. For example, the first lease payment is made at the beginning of Year 1 (that is, Time 0), but the deduction for tax purposes does not occur until the tax return for Year 1 is filed (that is, the end of Year 1). The expected cash flows are shown in Exhibit 17–11.

When the cash flows under the two alternatives are discounted at the 8 percent rate, the present value of leasing (\$298,646) is less than the present value of purchasing (\$337,799). Since we are dealing with cash outflows, the objective is to minimize present values. Hence Eastlake should lease the equipment unless there are nonfinancial reasons for purchasing.

The lease versus purchase decision is one that management should consider carefully. Because of the tax implications, the advice of a tax accountant may be needed to assure that a lease will be treated as a lease rather than as a purchase for tax purposes.

---

[7] This analysis and the following example are based on Ferrara, Thies, and Dirsmith, Chapter 6. See their study if you are interested in other ways of analyzing the lease-purchase decision.

EXHIBIT 17–11 Present Value of Purchase and Lease Alternatives

(a) Purchase alternative

Cash flows	Year 0	1	2	3	4	5
Purchase	$(700,000)					
Investment tax credit	70,000					
Depreciation tax shield*		$39,900	$58,520	$55,860	$55,860	$ 55,860
Salvage value						200,000
Income taxes on gain†						(80,000)
Total	$(630,000)	$39,900	$58,520	$55,860	$55,860	$175,860
Present value of $1 @ 0.08	× 1.0000	×0.9259	×0.8573	×0.7938	×0.7350	×0.6806
Present value of cash flows	$(630,000)	$36,943	$50,169	$44,342	$41,057	$119,690
Total present value of cash flows						$(337,799)

* Computation of depreciation tax shield:

Year	Cost − 50% investment tax credit (1)	ACRS rate (2)	ACRS deduction (3) = (1) × (2)	Tax rate (4)	Depreciation tax shield (3) × (4)
1	$665,000	0.15	$ 99,750	0.40	$39,900
2	665,000	0.22	146,300	0.40	58,520
3	665,000	0.21	139,650	0.40	55,860
4	665,000	0.21	139,650	0.40	55,860
5	665,000	0.21	139,650	0.40	55,860

† Computation of income taxes on gain:

Initial investment		$700,000
Less:		
Accumulated depreciation	$665,000	
50 percent of investment tax credit	35,000	−700,000
Basis at end of life		$ 0
Salvage value		200,000
Gain on sale at end of life		$ 200,000
Income tax rate		× 0.40
Taxes on gain		$ 80,000

(b) Lease alternative

Cash flows	Year 0	1	2	3	4	5
Lease payment	$(110,000)	$(110,000)	$(110,000)	$(110,000)	$(110,000)	$ 0
Tax shield at 0.40		44,000	44,000	44,000	44,000	44,000
Total	$(110,000)	$ (66,000)	$ (66,000)	$ (66,000)	$ (66,000)	$ 44,000
Present value of $1 @ 0.08	× 1.0000	× 0.9259	× 0.8573	× 0.7938	× 0.7350	× 0.6806
Present value of cash flows	$(110,000)	$ (61,109)	$ (56,582)	$ (52,391)	$ (48,510)	$ 29,946
Total present value of cash flows						$(298,646)

UNCERTAINTY OR RISK

The previous analyses have, for the most part, assumed that the cash flows associated with a proposed project are known with certainty. Because this is seldom the case, much of the capital-budgeting literature deals with the evaluation of risk or uncertainty.[8]

According to the capital-budgeting literature, the risk associated with a proposed project can be evaluated from three viewpoints:

1. The individual project
2. The firm's portfolio of projects
3. The firm's shareholders

If a single project would constitute a significant portion of the organization's activities and the organization's investors are not diversified,[9] risk analysis should be performed from the perspective of individual projects. Techniques such as sensitivity analysis, probability trees, and simulation are used for this purpose. These techniques are applied to uncertainty in short-range planning in the appendix to Chapter 8. Because their extension to capital budgeting is straightforward, they are not discussed here. (See the finance books and references at the end of this chapter.)

If an organization with nondiversified investors is large enough to undertake several projects, risk analysis should be performed from the perspective of the firm's portfolio of projects. In this context, each project is evaluated in terms of its impact on the firm's portfolio. By itself, a project may be quite risky; however, when it is added to a portfolio of projects, it may actually reduce the overall risk of the portfolio. This happens if the expected returns from the project have a low correlation with the expected returns of other projects in the portfolio. For example, an organization that produces typewriters may be able to reduce its overall risk by expanding into word processing equipment. By producing typewriters only, the organization's earnings are likely to decrease over time as people switch from typewriters to word processing equipment. By diversifying into word processing equipment, earnings may become more stable, thereby reducing the organization's overall risk.

In recent years several financial theorists have argued that capital expenditure proposals should be evaluated from the viewpoint of diversified investors in the firm. The theorists view such people as indirect investors in a widely diversified portfolio of projects. The investors are not interested in the risk associated with specific projects, nor are they interested in the project's impact on the risk of specific firms. Rather, they are interested in how the risk of a proposed project relates to the market portfolio of all projects undertaken by all firms. In this context, they emphasize the relationship between the expected returns from the project and the expected returns from the market portfolio of all projects. This relationship is identified as **systematic risk**. According to the capital asset pricing

---

[8] As previously indicated, the words "risk" and "uncertainty" are used synonymously in this text. See footnote 7 in Chapter 16.

[9] A nondiversified investor has a significant portion of his or her funds invested in the securities of a single firm or industry.

model, the evaluation of systematic risk leads to the development of a discount rate for each type of project a firm undertakes. If the project's expected net present value is positive at this discount rate, the project should be accepted.

We present these approaches to evaluating risk in capital budgeting to alert you to their potential significance. A thorough discussion of this topic is beyond the scope of a cost accounting textbook.[10]

Decision Trees

One response to the risks associated with a project is to delay a complete commitment to it at the outset and make a series of sequential decisions as the project progresses. To analyze these decisions, we can construct probability trees for each alternative action at each decision point. The action whose corresponding probability tree has the highest net present value is preferred once a decision point is reached. The path to each decision point is affected by previous decisions and the actual results. A complete diagram of these sequential investment decision points, the probability trees associated with each decision, and the paths to each decision point is called a **decision tree**.

Example 17–6

An employee of the Allegheny Development Company has discovered a potentially marketable product. Management must decide whether or not to invest in the further development of this product. There is a 40 percent probability the development will succeed and a 60 percent probability it will fail. If it fails, Allegheny will have lost funds with a net present value of $100,000. If the development is successful, Allegheny will build a plant to manufacture it. However, management must then determine the plant size. Given successful product development, the possible outcomes of building large and small plants are presented as follows:

Net present value payoff table

Action	*High Demand* Pr = *0.70*	*Low Demand* Pr = *0.30*
Large plant	$800,000	$200,000
Small plant	$500,000	$500,000

A decision tree for the Allegheny Development Company's investment proposal is presented in Exhibit 17–12. The two decision points are represented by squares and the origin of each probability tree is represented by a circle. The analysis proceeds by working backward from the final outcomes through each of the decision points. We assume that the optimal decision is always made.

Allegheny's second decision, if development is successful, is to build either a large or a small plant. A probability tree analysis of each alternative indicates that the larger plant should be built if we reach the second decision point.

[10] For an introduction to risk and capital budgeting, see Thomas E. Copeland, and J. Fred Weston, *Financial Theory and Corporate Policy*, 2nd ed. (Reading, Mass.: Addison-Wesley, 1983); James C. Van Horne, *Financial Management and Policy*, 6th ed. (Englewood Cliffs, N.J.: Prentice-Hall, 1983); and Jerome Osteryoung, *Capital Budgeting: Long-Term Asset Selection*, 2nd ed. (Columbus, Ohio: Grid, 1978).

EXHIBIT 17–12 Decision Tree for Evaluating Sequential Decisions

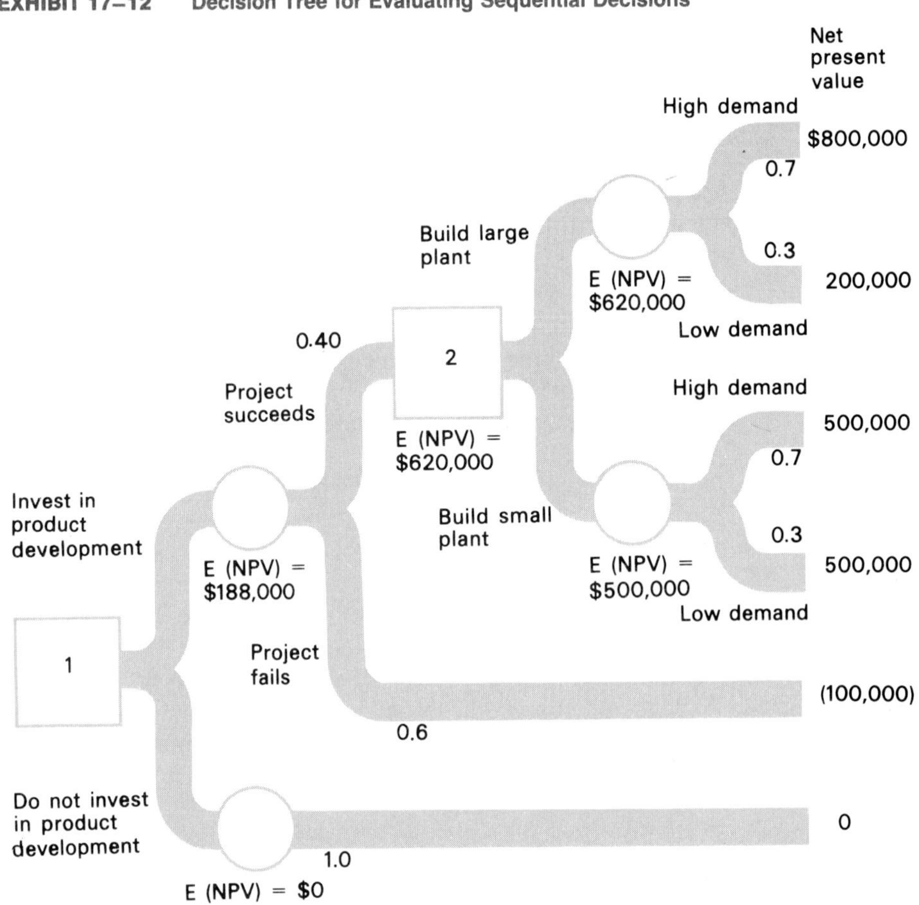

Accordingly, the net present value of building the large plant is used as the value of the project at the second decision point. Proceeding backward, we find the net present value of investing in product development to be $188,000. It is concluded that the project is desirable.

SUMMARY

This chapter has built on the material in Chapter 16 to present a number of specialized but important topics pertaining to the nature of proposed investments, the availability and sources of investment financing, and project risk. In particular, we examined:

- The use of incremental analysis for evaluating cost reduction proposals and determining optimal investment size.
- The use of NPV and IRR models for evaluating mutually exclusive investments.

- The use of ranking, trial and error, and programming techniques for allocating investment funds when capital rationing exists.
- The need to separate investment and financing decisions.
- The use of decision trees in evaluating risky projects.

When risky projects are evaluated from the point of view of nondiversified investors, sensitivity analysis, probability trees, and simulation are useful. When projects are evaluated from the point of view of diversified investors, different procedures may be more appropriate. These procedures are discussed in finance books.

KEY TERMS

Capital rationing
Cost reduction proposals
Decision tree
Excess present value index
Lessee
Lessor
Life-cycle costs
Mutually exclusive (investments)
Present value index
Profitability index
Systematic risk

SELECTED REFERENCES

Bierman, Harold J., Jr., and Seymour Smidt, *The Capital Budgeting Decision,* 6th ed., New York: The Macmillian Company, 1984.

Copeland, Thomas E., and J. Fred Weston, *Financial Theory and Corporate Policy,* 2nd ed., Reading, Mass.: Addison-Wesley, 1983.

Dyckman, Thomas R., and James C. Kinard, "The Discounted Cash Flow Investment Decision Model with Accounting Income Constraints," *Decision Sciences* **4,** No. 3 (July 1973): 301–313.

Ferrara, William L., James B. Thies, and Mark W. Dirsmith, *The Lease-Purchase Decision,* New York: National Association of Accountants, 1980.

Hertz, David B., "Risk Analysis in Capital Investment," *Harvard Business Review* **42,** No. 1 (January-February 1964): 95–106.

——, "Investment Policies That Pay Off," *Harvard Business Review* **46,** No. 1 (January-February 1968): 96–108.

House, William C., Jr., *N.A.A. Research Monograph No. 3, Sensitivity Analysis in Making Capital Investment Decisions,* New York: National Association of Accountants, 1968.

Keane, Simon, "The Internal Rate of Return and the Reinvestment Fallacy," *Abacus* **15,** No. 1 (June 1979): 48–55.

Osteryoung, Jerome, *Capital Budgeting: Long-Term Asset Selection,* 2nd ed. Columbus, Ohio; Grid, 1978.

Robichek, Alexander A., Donald G. Ogilvie, and John D. Roach, "Capital Budgeting: A Pragmatic Approach," *Financial Executive* **37,** No. 4 (April 1969): 26–38.

Rubinstein, Mark E., "A Mean-Variance Synthesis of Corporate Financial Theory," *The Journal of Finance* **38,** No. 1 (March 1973): 167–181.

Sharpe, William F., *Portfolio Theory and Capital Markets,* New York: McGraw-Hill, 1970.

Singhvi, Surendra S., and Robert J. Lambrix, "Investment Versus Financing Decisions," *Management Accounting* **65,** No. 9 (March 1984): 54–56.

Spiller, Earl A., Jr., "Capital Expenditure Analysis: An Incident Process Case," *Accounting Review* **56,** No. 1 (January 1981): 158–165.

Van Horne, James C., *Financial Management and Policy,* 6th ed., Englewood Cliffs, N.J.: Prentice-Hall, 1983.

Weingartner, H. Martin, *Mathematical Programming and the Analysis of Capital Budgeting Problems,* Englewood Cliffs, N.J.: Prentice-Hall, 1963.

REVIEW QUESTIONS

17–1 In what ways do cost reduction proposals differ from proposals to extend the life of an old project or undertake a new one?

17–2 Under what circumstances may an organization be "throwing good money after bad" when it accepts a cost reduction proposal?

17–3 What rule of economics assists in determining a project's optimal size?

17–4 Why do the NPV and IRR models sometimes provide different rankings when they are used to evaluate mutually exclusive investments?

17–5 In the absence of capital rationing, which of these models (NPV or IRR) is preferred for evaluating mutually exclusive investments? Why?

17–6 What is capital rationing? What conditions are likely to lead to its existence?

17–7 Define or describe "present value index."

17–8 Given the need for capital rationing, what common fault of the IRR and the PVI models may lead to nonoptimal results when they are used to rank indivisible investments?

17–9 Explain why investment and financing decisions should be separated.

17–10 What is a decision tree? How does a decision tree differ from a probability tree?

REVIEW PROBLEM

Cost Reduction Proposal

Baxter Manufacturing Company is evaluating a proposal to replace a machine used in production with a new, more efficient machine. The current machine was acquired in early January 19x1 for $120,000. For tax purposes, it is being depreciated using the straight-line method over its eight-year useful life with no salvage value. A full year's depreciation was taken in 19x1. Yearly operating costs excluding depreciation are $40,000.

The new machine costs $150,000. It has a five-year life with no salvage value. Yearly operating costs excluding depreciation would be $20,000. For tax purposes, Baxter will use ACRS depreciation for the new machine. The machine is five-year qualifying property.

If the new machine is aquired, it will be placed in service in January 19x4. The current machine will be sold for $40,000 at that time. Baxter pays income taxes at a 40 percent rate and has a cost of capital of 16 percent. Ignore the investment tax credit.

REQUIREMENTS

a) Determine the after-tax cash savings for each year if the new machine is acquired.

b) Determine the initial investment if the new machine is acquired.

c) Determine the net present value of the cost reduction proposal. Should the new machine be acquired?

The solution to this problem is found at the end of the Chapter 17 problems and exercises.

EXERCISES

17–1 Cost Reduction Proposal

The management of Southern Fabrics is considering the advisability of installing a computer to control the production process. The computer would reduce production costs by $0.06 per square yard during its estimated useful life of five years. It would cost $1,000,000 installed and have an estimated removal cost of $100,000 at the end of its useful life. Management anticipates a stable sales and production volume of 8,000,000 square yards during each of the next five years.

REQUIREMENT

Evaluate the desirability of purchasing the computer given a discount rate of 10 percent and an income tax rate of 40 percent. Use ACRS depreciation for tax purposes, and ignore the investment tax credit. The property is five-year qualifying property for ACRS calculations.

17–2 Cost Reduction Proposal

Consider the following data for a cost reduction proposal:

Initial investment	$500,000
Useful life	5 years
Salvage value	$ 50,000
Expected annual production	35,000 units
Variable cost savings per unit of output:	
Direct materials	$ 0
Direct labor	2
Factory overhead	2
Total variable cost savings per unit	$ 4
Fixed cost savings per year (all currently require a cash outflow)	$20,000

ACRS depreciation will be used for tax purposes, and the property is five-year qualifying property.

REQUIREMENT

Evaluate the desirability of making the investment using a discount rate of 14 percent and an income tax rate of 40 percent. Ignore the investment tax credit.

17–3 Evaluating Life-Cycle Costs

Marsha Gibson is considering the purchase of a new automobile. She will use the automobile for personal purposes for five years and has narrowed her choice to two alternatives, Model X and Model Y. The following data relate to each alternative:

	Model X	*Model Y*
Cost	$12,000	$14,000
Estimated value at end of 5 years	3,000	4,000
Estimated maintenance cost per year:		
Year 1	$ 100	$ 100
Year 2	100	200
Year 3	500	300
Year 4	300	300
Year 5	300	300
Estimated insurance cost per year:		
Year 1	$ 300	$ 350
Year 2	250	300
Year 3	200	250
Year 4	150	200
Year 5	150	200
Estimated gasoline cost per year	$ 350	$ 350

REQUIREMENT

Determine the present value of the life-cycle costs of each model using a discount rate of 12 percent. Assume that cash flows for maintenance and gasoline occur at the end of each year and that cash flows for insurance occur at the beginning of each year. Which model should Ms. Gibson select if her decision is based solely on costs?

17–4 Evaluating Life-Cycle Costs

Terry Brown is considering the purchase of a new water heater for his home. Either a gas or electric water heater can be acquired. The following cost data have been estimated for each type:

	Electric	*Gas*
Cost	$ 300	$ 350
Operating cost per year	$ 80	$ 50
Life	10 years	10 years

REQUIREMENT

Determine the present value of the life-cycle costs of each type of water heater using a discount rate of 10 percent. Assume that cash flows occur at the end of each year.

17–5 Mutually Exclusive Investments

Presented is information pertaining to three mutually exclusive investment proposals:

Project	*Initial investment*	*Life (in years)*	*End of year cash inflow*
A	$200,000	4	$ 80,000
B	200,000	9	50,000
C	980,000	9	200,000

REQUIREMENTS

a) Rank these three projects according to their internal rate of return, net present value, and present value index. Assume a time value of money of 10 percent.

b) Explain the difference in rankings.

c) If unlimited funds are available at 10 percent, which project should be selected?

17–6 Mutually Exclusive Investments

Presented is information pertaining to three mutually exclusive investment proposals:

Project	*Initial investment*	*Life (in years)*	*End of year cash inflow*
X	$ 50,000	5	$16,000
Y	50,000	10	10,500
Z	250,000	10	48,000

Assume the company has a 12 percent time value of money.

REQUIREMENTS

a) Rank these three projects according to their internal rate of return, net present value, and present value index.

b) Explain the difference in rankings.

c) If unlimited funds are available at 12 percent, which project should be selected?

17–7 Evaluating Mutually Exclusive Investments

Presented are four sets of mutually exclusive investment proposals:

Set	*Project*	*Investment*	*Life (in years)*	*End of year cash inflow*
1	A	$40,000	4	$16,000
	B	40,000	8	10,000
2	C	$60,000	5	$20,000
	D	60,000	14	12,000
3	E	$40,000	8	$10,000
	F	60,000	8	15,000
4	G	$60,000	5	$20,000
	H	80,000	5	25,000

REQUIREMENTS

a) Rank the proposals in each set in accordance with their internal rate of return and net present value. Assume a 14 percent time value of money.

b) Explain why the results of each set of rankings are similar or dissimilar.

17–8 Capital Rationing

A company with a 12 percent time value of money and limited investment funds is evaluating the desirability of several investment proposals:

Project	*Initial investment*	*Life (in years)*	*End of year cash inflow*
A	$60,000	2	$37,520
B	40,000	5	13,200
C	40,000	3	20,000
D	20,000	9	4,000
E	60,000	10	13,200

REQUIREMENTS

a) Rank the projects according to their internal rate of return, net present value, and present value index.

b) Explain the cause of any difference in rankings.

c) Which projects should be selected if $80,000 is available for investment?

d) Which projects should be selected if $100,000 is available for investment?

17–9 Capital Rationing

A company with a 14 percent time value of money and limited investment funds is evaluating the desirability of the following investment proposals:

Project	*Initial investment*	*Life (in years)*	*End of year cash inflow*
A	$30,000	2	$20,000
B	20,000	7	4,900
C	20,000	4	8,300
D	10,000	10	2,400

REQUIREMENTS

a) Rank the projects according to their internal rate of return, net present value, and present value index.

b) Which projects should be selected if $40,000 is available for investment?

c) Which projects should be selected if $50,000 is available for investment?

17–10 Optimal Investment Size

The Smith Manufacturing Company is considering a proposal in which investment size is a variable. Relevant data are as follows:

Size of initial investment	*Present value of subsequent net cash flows*
$ 80,000	$ 85,000
100,000	120,000
120,000	150,000
140,000	175,000
160,000	195,000
180,000	205,000
200,000	210,000
220,000	215,000

REQUIREMENT

Determine the optimal investment size.

17–11 Lease or Purchase

Clayton Corr has decided to acquire a new automobile for personal use. He has determined the one he wants and is now trying to decide whether he should lease or buy it. He expects to use the automobile for five years regardless of the financing method. For simplicity in the analysis, Corr is assuming that payments under either alternative occur on an annual rather than a monthly basis. The following data relate to the alternatives:

Lease alternative:	
Annual payments	$ 4,800
Buy alternative:	
Cost	$15,000
Down payment required	3,000
Expected resale value at end of 5 years	4,000

If the automobile is purchased, Corr can obtain a loan from a bank and repay the principal in five equal end-of-year installments of $2,400. Interest at 12 percent on the unpaid balance will also be payable at the end of each year. Payments on the lease are due at the beginning of each year.

Assume all operating costs are the same under either alternative. Ignore income taxes.

REQUIREMENT

Using a 12 percent time value of money, determine whether the lease or buy alternative is more attractive.

17–12 Lease or Purchase

BRI Company has evaluated an investment proposal for a new machine and determined that it meets their investment criteria. Now management is trying to determine whether the machine should be leased or purchased. If purchased, the machine will require an initial investment of $30,000. It has a useful life of five years and an expected salvage value of $5,000 at the end of its useful life. If purchased, the machine qualifies for five-year ACRS depreciation for tax purposes and BRI will take the full 10 percent investment tax credit.

Funds for purchasing can be obtained from a local bank at a 13 percent interest rate. The principal will be repaid in five equal end-of-year payments, and interest on the unpaid balance will also be due at the end of each year.

If the machine is leased, BRI will make annual lease payments of $7,500 at the beginning of each year.

BRI is subject to a 40 percent income tax rate.

REQUIREMENT

Determine the present value of the lease and purchase alternatives using the after-tax cost of debt (rounded to the nearest percentage) as the discount rate. Which alternative is more attractive?

PROBLEMS

17–13 Cost Reduction Proposal

The Cracker Chemical Company currently discharges liquid wastes into the Morrisville Municipal Sewer System. However, the Morrisville city government has informed Cracker Chemical that a surcharge of $5 per thousand cubic liters will soon be imposed for the discharge of this effluent. This has prompted management to evaluate the desirability of treating its own liquid waste.

A proposed system consists of three major elements. The first is a 7,500 cubic liter retention basin that permits unusual discharge to be held and treated before going through the downstream system. The second is a continuous self-cleaning rotary filter where solids are removed. The third is an automated neutralization process where materials are added to control the alkalinity-acidity range.

The system is designed to process 500,000 cubic liters a day. However, company officials estimate that only about 200,000 cubic liters of liquid waste would be processed in a workday. The company operates 300 days a year.

The initial investment in the system would be $500,000 and annual operating costs are estimated to be about $180,000. The system has an estimated useful life of ten years and a salvage value of $50,000.

For computational purposes assume that all cash flows occur at the end of each year. Ignore income taxes.

REQUIREMENTS

a) Determine the project's net present value at a discount rate of 18 percent.

b) Determine the project's internal rate of return.

c) Determine the project's accounting rate of return on average investment.

17–14 Pricing an Investment That Reduces Costs

Wardl Industries is a manufacturer of standard and custom-designed bottling equipment. Early in December 19x3, Lyan Company asked Wardl to quote a price for a custom-designed bottling machine to be delivered on April 1, 19x4. Lyan intends to make a decision on the purchase of such a machine by January 1 so Wardl would have the entire first quarter of 19x4 to build the equipment.

Wardl's standard pricing policy for custom-designed equipment is 50 percent markup on full cost. Lyan's specifications for the equipment have been reviewed by Wardl's Engineering and Cost Accounting Departments, and they made the following estimates for direct materials and direct labor:

Direct materials	$256,000
Direct labor (11,000 DLH × $15)	165,000

Factory overhead is applied on the basis of direct-labor hours. Wardl normally plans to run its plant 15,000 direct-labor hours per month and assigns overhead on the basis of 180,000 direct-labor hours per year. The overhead application rate for 19x4 of $9.00 per direct-labor hour is based on the following budgeted factory overhead costs for 19x4:

Variable factory overhead	$ 972,000
Fixed factory overhead	648,000
Total factory overhead	$1,620,000

The Wardl production schedule calls for 12,000 direct-labor hours per month during the first quarter. If Wardl is awarded the contract for the Lyan equipment, production of one of its standard products would have to be reduced. This is necessary because production levels can only be increased to 15,000 direct-labor hours each month on short notice. Furthermore, Wardl's employees are unwilling to work overtime.

Sales of the standard product equal to the reduced production would be lost, but there would be no permanent loss of future sales or customers. The standard product whose production schedule would be reduced has a unit sales price of $12,000 and the following cost structure:

Direct materials	$2,500
Direct labor (250 DLH × $15)	3,750
Factory overhead (250 DLH × $9)	2,250
Total cost	$8,500

Lyan needs the custom-designed equipment to increase its bottle-making capacity so that it will not have to buy bottles from an outside supplier. Lyan Company requires 5,000,000 bottles annually. Its present equipment has a maximum capacity of 4,500,000 bottles with variable manufacturing costs of $0.15 per bottle. Thus Lyan has had to purchase 500,000 from a supplier at $0.40 each. The new equipment would allow Lyan to manufacture its entire annual demand for bottles at a variable cost of $0.14 per bottle.

Wardl estimates that Lyan's annual bottle demand will continue to be 5,000,000 bottles over the next five years, the estimated economic life of the special-purpose equipment. Wardl further estimates that Lyan has an after-tax cost of capital of 14 percent and is subject to a 40 percent marginal income tax rate, the same rates as Wardl.

REQUIREMENTS

a) Wardl Industries plans to submit a bid to Lyan Company for the manufacture of the special-purpose bottling equipment.

1. Calculate the bid that Wardl would submit if it follows its standard pricing policy for special-purpose equipment.
2. Calculate the minimum bid that Wardl would be willing to submit on the Lyan equipment that would result in the same profits as planned for the first quarter of 19x4.

b) Wardl Industries wants to estimate the maximum price Lyan Company would be willing to pay for the special-purpose bottling equipment.

1. Calculate the present value of the after-tax savings in directly traceable cash outlays that Lyan could expect to realize from the new special-purpose bottling equipment.
2. Identify the other factors that Wardl would have to incorporate in its estimate of the maximum price that Lyan would be willing to pay for the equipment.
3. Describe how the cost savings from part (b)(1) and the other factors from part (b)(2) would be combined to calculate the estimate of the maximum price that Lyan would be willing to pay for the equipment. (CMA Adapted)

17–15 Cost Reduction Proposal

The WRL Company makes cookies for its chain of snack food stores. On January 2, 19x1, WRL Company purchased a special cookie cutting machine; this machine has been used for three years. WRL Company is considering the purchase of a newer, more efficient machine. If purchased, the new machine would be acquired on January 2, 19x4. WRL Company expects to sell 300,000 dozen cookies in each of the next five years. The selling price of the cookies is expected to average $0.50 per dozen.

WRL Company has two options: continue to operate the old machine, or sell the old machine and purchase the new machine. No trade-in was offered by the seller of the new machine. To help decide which option is more desirable, the following information has been assembled:

	Old machine	*New machine*
Original cost of machine at acquisition	$90,000	$120,000
Salvage value at the end of useful life for depreciation purposes	$10,000	$ 0
Useful life from date of acquisition	8 years	5 years
Expected annual cash operating expenses:		
Variable cost per dozen	$ 0.20	$ 0.14
Total fixed costs	$15,000	$14,000
Depreciation method used for tax purposes	Straight-line	ACRS
Estimated cash value of machines:		
January 2, 19x4	$40,000	$120,000
December 31, 19x8	$ 7,000	$ 20,000

WRL Company is subject to an overall income tax rate of 40 percent. Assume that all operating revenues and expenses occur at the end of the year. Assume that any gain or loss on the sale of machinery is treated as an ordinary tax item and will affect the taxes paid by WRL Company at the end of the year in which it occurred. Ignore the investment tax credit.

REQUIREMENTS

a) Use the net present value method to determine whether WRL Company should retain the old machine or acquire the new machine. WRL has a 16 percent time value of money.

b) Without being influenced by your answer to part (a), assume that the quantitative differences are so slight between the two alternatives that WRL Company is indifferent to the two proposals. Identify and discuss the nonquantitative factors that are important to this decision that WRL Company should consider.

c) Identify and discuss the advantages and disadvantages of using discounted cash flow techniques (for example, the net present value method) for capital investment decisions. (CMA Adapted)

17–16 Cost Reduction Proposal

A firm is considering the replacement of two of its printing presses. These presses were bought five years ago for $35,000 each and have a remaining useful life of five years. The firm does not expect to realize any return from scrapping the old printing presses in five years, but if they are sold now, the firm would receive $2,000 per press. The old machines are being depreciated over their ten-year life using the straight-line method with no salvage value.

One new press is expected to replace the two old ones. The new press may be purchased for $55,000 and is expected to increase sales by $8,000 per year and to economize on operating costs. For each of the old presses maintenance costs are $5,000 per year. If the new press is purchased, maintenance costs will be $7,500 per year. Each printing press requires one operator at a cost of $14,000 per year. ACRS depreciation will be taken on the new press for tax purposes over five years. The salvage value of the new press is estimated to be $1,500 five years from now.

The firm uses an 18 percent after-tax discount rate to evaluate similar projects. The firm's income tax rate is 40 percent. Ignore the investment tax credit.

REQUIREMENT

Based on the net present value approach should the old printing presses be replaced? (CGA Adapted)

17–17 Timesharing as a Cost Reduction Proposal

John and May Boyd and their two children rent a beach-front condominium for a two-week vacation each summer. The condo rents for $950 per week. This year, on their way to the beach, the family visited Mayfield Mountain, a new timesharing resort. After a ''free'' three day and two night stay, a sales representative encouraged the Boyd's to become interval owners of a mountain-side condominium. The sales representative explained:

> If you invest today you can be assured of tomorrow's vacations in this luxury resort. Each unit costs over $150,000; however, with timesharing you have a right to use the unit, and Mayfield Mountain's other vacation facilities, for two weeks each year for less than what it costs you to stay at the beach. Here is how it works over a ten-year period:

Cost of renting:	
$950 per week × 2 weeks × 10 years	$19,000
Cost of timesharing:	
Initial investment	$14,000
Initial closing costs	75
Maintenance fees ($160 per week × 2 weeks × 10 years)	3,200
	$17,275
Advantage of timesharing	$ 1,725

> The maintenance fees are paid each year. They include the costs of utilities, property taxes, maintenance, and replacement of worn-out furniture and appliances.
>
> Incidentally, the advantage of timesharing is really more than $1,725. With timesharing you know that the initial $14,075 will buy your share of the property. There will be no additional investments. However, the rent is likely to go up. We did not incorporate this inflation into our analysis. Furthermore, you own an interest in the unit until you sell it or deed it to your children. Hence the advantages of timesharing will continue to accumulate beyond ten years.

REQUIREMENTS

a) Evaluate the sales representative's analysis. Does timesharing have an advantage of $1,725 over a ten-year period? Why or why not?

b) Given a time value of money of 12 percent, determine the net present value of the renting and the timesharing alternatives over a ten-year period. Assume rent and maintenance fees are paid at the start of each year.

c) John and May must pay for their vacations in after-tax dollars. They file a joint return and their marginal tax rate is 40 percent. Given a time value of money of 12 percent,

   1. Determine the investment required to pay the rent on the beach-front condominium for the next ten years,

   2. Determine the total investment required to purchase the timesharing unit and pay the maintenance fees for the next ten years.

   Assume rent and maintenance fees are paid at the start of each year.

d) What conclusions do you draw from the analyses in parts (b) and (c)?

17–18 Mutually Exclusive Investments

To meet expanding consumer demand, the Jackson Power Co. has determined that it must expand its yearly electric generating capacity by 15 billion kwh. The required capacity can be provided by constructing two coal-fired steam plants or one nuclear plant.

Presented is construction and other cost information about each alternative:

	Two steam plants (total)	*Nuclear plant*
Initial investment	$700,000,000	$950,000,000
Yearly operating costs (excluding depreciation):		
Operations	$180,000,000	$100,000,000
Maintenance	$ 50,000,000	$ 30,000,000
Transmission	$ 70,000,000	$ 60,000,000
Life	40 years	40 years
Cost to dismantle plant at end of useful life	$ 10,000,000	$300,000,000

REQUIREMENT

Determine the present value *of all cash outflows* associated with *each* alternative. Assume a time value of money of 10 percent. Ignore taxes. The appropriate present value factors are 9.7791 and 0.0221.

17–19 Mathematical Programming

For the situation presented in Exercise 17–8, formulate the objective function and constraints necessary to maximize net present value when a maximum of $120,000 is available for investment. Assume fractional investments are permitted.

17–20 Linear Programming for Multiple Investment Criteria[11]

Presented is selected information pertaining to five investment proposals currently being evaluated by Consolidated Industries:

	Project				
	A	*B*	*C*	*D*	*E*
Initial investment (000)	$100	$300	$200	$300	$200
First year's accounting income	$15,000	$(20,000)	$ 30,000	$ 25,000	$25,000
First year's cash flow	$40,000	$ 40,000	$130,000	$100,000	$65,000
Internal rate of return	30.4%	45.6%	13.5%	24.2%	22.2%
Net present value (000) @ $r = 0.12$	$42.941	$432.208	$ 3.769	$ 87.095	$55.574

[11] Adapted from "Capital Budgeting: A Pragmatic Approach," by Alexander A. Robichek, Donald G. Ogilvie, and John D. Roach, *Financial Executive* **39,** No. 4 (April 1969): 26–38, with permission.

All five projects satisfy Consolidated's minimum investment criterion, a rate of return of 12 percent. However, Consolidated is operating under a number of constraints:

- Only $640,000 is available for capital expenditures.
- These funds must be invested in such a way that they will provide an accounting income of at least $60,000 and a cash inflow of at least $170,000 during their first year.

REQUIREMENTS

a) Formulate the objective function and constraints Consolidated Industries should use to maximize the average internal rate of return of selected projects. Assume that fractional investments are permitted.

b) Formulate the objective function and constraints Consolidated Industries should use to maximize the net present value of selected projects. Assume that fractional investments are permitted.

c) If you have computer facilities, determine the value of the objective function and the optimal solution for parts (a) and (b).

d) What is the probable cause of any differences in the optimal solution?

17–21 Lease vs. Buy: No Taxes

Mr. Raven, President of Fly By Nite Airlines, was disappointed as he reviewed the controller's present value analysis of an investment proposal that would double the airline's passenger carrying capacity:

Annual operating cash receipts	$10,000,000
Annual operating cash disbursements	−8,000,000
Net cash flows	$ 2,000,000
Present value of an annuity of $1 in arrears, $n = 10$, $r = 0.20$	× 4.1925
Present value	$ 8,385,000
Initial investment, cost of planes	−9,000,000
Net present value	$ (615,000)

Because he wanted to be the chief executive of a major airline, he proceeded to contact Leasing International. The latter agreed to lease the planes to Fly By Nite in exchange for ten equal payments of $1.8 million at the end of each year. The terms of the lease specified that Fly By Nite would perform all maintenance and pay all property taxes and insurance.

REQUIREMENTS

a) Determine the present value of the lease payments using a discount rate of 20 percent. Is this amount less than the present value of the net cash flows? If so, should the planes be leased?

b) Assuming Fly By Nite's weighted-average cost of capital is 20 percent, what is likely to happen to common stock prices if the lease is accepted?

17–22 Lease vs. Purchase: Income Taxes

LeToy Company produces a wide variety of children's toys, most of which are manufactured from stamped parts. The Production Department recommended that a new stamping machine be acquired. The Production Department further recommended that the company only consider using the new stamping machine for five years. Top management has concurred with the recommendation and has assigned Ann Mitchum of the Budget and Planning Department to supervise the acquisition and to analyze the alternative financing available.

After careful analysis and review, Mitchum has narrowed the financing of the project to two alternatives. The first alternative is a lease agreement with the manufacturer of the stamping machine. The manufacturer is willing to lease the equipment to LeToy for five years even though it has an economic useful life of ten years. The lease agreement calls for LeToy to make annual payments of $62,000 at the beginning of each year. The manufacturer (lessor) retains the title to the machine, and there is no purchase option at the end of five years. Any investment tax credit is claimed by the lessor and does not flow through to LeToy (lessee). This agreement would be considered a lease by the Internal Revenue Service.

The second alternative would be for LeToy to purchase the equipment outright from the manufacturer for $240,000. LeToy can claim an investment tax credit of $24,000 if it purchases the equipment. Preliminary discussions with LeToy's bank indicate that the firm would be able to finance the asset acquisition with a 13 percent loan. The principal would be repaid in five equal end-of-year payments and interest on the unpaid balance would also be due at the end of each year.

If purchased, LeToy would depreciate the equipment over five years using the ACRS method for tax purposes. The market value of the equipment at the end of five years would be $45,000.

All maintenance, property taxes, and insurance are the same under both alternatives and are paid by LeToy. LeToy requires an after-tax return of 18 percent for investment decisions and is subject to a 40 percent corporate income tax rate on both operating income and capital gains and losses.

REQUIREMENTS

a) Calculate the relevant present value cost of the leasing alternative for LeToy Company.

b) Calculate the relevant present value of the purchase alternative for LeToy Company.

(CMA Adapted)

17–23 Lease or Purchase

Madisons, Inc., has decided to acquire a new piece of equipment. It may do so by an outright cash purchase of $25,000 or by a leasing alternative of $6,000 per year for five years. Other relevant information follows:

Estimated useful life	5 years
Estimated salvage value if purchased	$3,000
Annual cost of maintenance contract to be acquired with either lease or purchase	$ 500

The full purchase price of $25,000 could be borrowed from a bank at 10 percent annual interest and repaid in one payment at the end of the fifth year.

ADDITIONAL INFORMATION

- Assume a 40 percent income tax rate and use ACRS depreciation for tax purposes. The equipment qualifies for a five-year write-off, and if the equipment is purchased, the full 10 percent investment tax credit will be taken.
- Interest on the bank loan would be paid at the end of each year.
- The yearly lease rental would be paid at the beginning of each year.
- Assume that annual maintenance costs occur at the end of each year.

REQUIREMENT

Should Madisons purchase or lease the equipment? (CPA Adapted)

17–24 Sensitivity Analysis of an Investment Proposal

The Bristol Light Company is evaluating an investment proposal that has the following characteristics:

Initial investment:	
Fixed assets	$180,000
Working capital	$ 60,000
Project life	5 years
End of life recovery:	
Fixed assets	$ 30,000
Working capital	$ 60,000
Annual operations:	
Unit sales	6,000
Unit selling price	$30
Unit variable costs	$10
Annual fixed cost (excluding depreciation)	$ 10,000

ADDITIONAL INFORMATION

- The income tax rate is 40 percent.
- Ignore the investment tax credit.
- The appropriate time value of money is 14 percent.
- For computations in this problem, use straight-line depreciation and assume that a full year's depreciation is taken during the first year.

REQUIREMENTS

a) Determine the project's net present value.

b) Determine the minimum yearly sales required to provide a 14 percent return on initial investment.

c) If the unit selling price is reduced to $15, how many units must be sold each year to earn a 14 percent rate of return?

d) *Describe* the manner in which the use of ACRS depreciation for tax purposes would affect the answers to parts (a), (b), and (c). No additional computations are required.

17–25 Uncertain Sales Estimates

Hi-Tech Toy Company designs and manufactures toys. Past experience indicates that the product life-cycle of a toy is three years. Promotional advertising produces large sales in the early years, but there is a substantial sales decline in the final year of a toy's life.

Consumer demand for new toys placed on the market tends to fall into three classes. About 30 percent of the new toys sell well above expectations, 60 percent sell as anticipated, and 10 percent have poor consumer acceptance.

A new toy has been developed. The following sales projections were made by carefully evaluating consumer demand for the new toy:

Consumer demand for new toy	*Probability of occurring*	*Estimated sales in*		
		Year 1	*Year 2*	*Year 3*
Above average	30%	$1,200,000	$2,500,000	$600,000
Average	60	700,000	1,700,000	400,000
Below average	10	200,000	900,000	150,000

Variable costs are estimated at 30 percent of the selling price. Special machinery must be purchased at a cost of $860,000 and will be installed in an unused portion of the factory (which Hi-Tech has unsuccessfully been trying to rent to someone for several years at $50,000 per year and has no prospects for future use). Fixed cash expenses (excluding depreciation) are predicted to be $50,000 per year on the new toy. The new machinery is five-year qualifying property for ACRS depreciation. However, it has an estimated salvage value of $110,000 at the end of the three-year life-cycle of the toy and will be sold at that time. Advertising and promotion expenses will total $100,000 the first year, $150,000 the second year, and $50,000 the third year. These expenses will be deducted as incurred for income tax purposes.

Hi-Tech's management believes that state and federal income taxes will total 40 percent of income in the foreseeable future. Ignore the investment tax credit.

REQUIREMENTS

a) Prepare a schedule computing the expected sales of this new toy in each of the three years, taking into account the probability of above average, average, and below average sales occurring.

b) Assume that the expected sales computed in part (a) are $900,000 in the first year, $1,800,000 in the second year, and $410,000 in the third year. Prepare a schedule of net cash flows from sales of the new toy for each of the years involved and from disposition of the machinery.

c) Assuming a minimum desired rate of return of 10 percent, prepare a schedule of the present value of the net cash flows calculated in part (b). Assume that the cash flows occur at the end of each year. (CPA Adapted)

17–26 Decision Trees

The Swiss Cheese Company is evaluating the desirability of introducing a new cheese spread for sale to the general public. Three alternative actions are available at this time:

1. Introduce nationally
2. Introduce regionally and then decide whether to go national
3. Do not introduce

If the product is introduced nationally, there is an equal probability of a high or low demand. The high demand would result in a very attractive net present value of $900,000, whereas the low demand would result in a negative net present value of $200,000.

Alternatively, the product may be introduced in a representative region. If the demand for the product in the region is low, the product will be discontinued. The net present value of this sequence of events is $(30,000). If the regional demand is high and Swiss Cheese elects to stay regional, the project will have a net present value of $100,000. If the regional demand is high and Swiss Cheese elects to go national, they will be faced with one of the following results:

	National demand	
	High	*Low*
Net present value	$600,000	$(120,000)

The lower net present values of these outcomes (when compared with the values expected from a "go national" campaign) result from certain inefficiencies and a delay in generating cash inflows.

There is an 80 percent probability that national demand will be high if regional demand is high, and a 50 percent probability that regional demand will be high.

REQUIREMENT

Determine the optimal action.

SOLUTION TO REVIEW PROBLEM

a)

	Year				
	19x4	*19x5*	*19x6*	*19x7*	*19x8*
Operating costs of current machine	$40,000	$40,000	$40,000	$40,000	$40,000
Operating costs of new machine	−20,000	−20,000	−20,000	−20,000	−20,000
Cost savings before income taxes	$20,000	$20,000	$20,000	$20,000	$20,000
Additional income taxes*	−5,000	−800	−1,400	−1,400	−1,400
Cash savings after taxes	$15,000	$19,200	$18,600	$18,600	$18,600

* Computation of additional income taxes:

	Year				
	19x4	*19x5*	*19x6*	*19x7*	*19x8*
Additional taxes on cost savings before income taxes @ 0.40	$ 8,000	$ 8,000	$ 8,000	$ 8,000	$ 8,000
Less: Tax shield from additional depreciation†	−3,000	−7,200	−6,600	−6,600	−6,600
	$ 5,000	$ 800	$ 1,400	$ 1,400	$ 1,400

† Computation of tax shield from additional depreciation:

Year	*Cost of new machine (1)*	*ACRS rate (2)*	*ACRS deduction on new machine (3) = (1) × (2)*	*Straight-line depreciation on current machine (4)*	*Increase in depreciation (5) = (3) − (4)*	*Tax rate (6)*	*Tax shield (5) × (6)*
19x4	$150,000	0.15	$22,500	$15,000	$ 7,500		$3,000
19x5	150,000	0.22	33,000	15,000	18,000	0.40	7,200
19x6	150,000	0.21	31,500	15,000	16,500	0.40	6,600
19x7	150,000	0.21	31,500	15,000	16,500	0.40	6,600
19x8	150,000	0.21	31,500	15,000	16,500	0.40	6,600

b)

Cost of new machine		$150,000
Less: Proceeds from sale of current machine	$40,000	
Tax shield from loss on sale of current machine*	14,000	−54,000
Initial investment		$ 96,000

* Computation of tax shield from loss on sale of current machine:

Cost of machine	$120,000
Less: Accumulated depreciation ($15,000 × 3 years)	−45,000
Book value of machine	$ 75,000
Sales price of machine	−40,000
Loss on sale of machine	$ 35,000
Tax rate	× 0.40
Tax shield from loss	$ 14,000

c)

Year	*After-tax cost savings*	*Present value of $1 @ 0.16*	*Present value*
19x4	$15,000	0.8621	$ 12,932
19x5	19,200	0.7432	14,269
19x6	18,600	0.6407	11,917
19x7	18,600	0.5523	10,273
19x8	18,600	0.4761	8,855
Total present value of cost savings			$ 58,246
Less: Initial investment			−96,000
Net present value			$(37,754)

The new machine should not be acquired since the cost reduction proposal has a negative net present value.

18 Inventory Planning and Control Systems

INTRODUCTION
PURPOSE OF INVENTORY MODELS
INVENTORY COSTS
ECONOMIC ORDER QUANTITY (EOQ)
RELEVANT COSTS
ASSUMPTIONS UNDERLYING EOQ MODEL
ACCURACY OF COST PREDICTIONS
REORDER POINT (ROP)
OTHER APPROACHES TO INVENTORY PLANNING AND CONTROL
SUMMARY
APPENDIX: PLANNING AND CONTROL WITH PERT

INTRODUCTION

BECAUSE OF THE COST ACCOUNTANT'S KNOWLEDGE OF COST BEHAVIOR, THE accounting data base, and firm-wide planning and control systems, he or she frequently assists in the development, implementation, and operation of specialized planning and control models. In these activities, the cost accountant usually works with people whose specialty is operations research or production. Although experts in model development, these people are not likely to succeed fully in their efforts without the cost accountant's help. If a model is to be used for a single, special decision, the cost accountant assists by supplying relevant cost data. If the model is to be used repetitively, the cost accountant assists in developing procedures for supplying relevant cost data on a continuous basis. If relevant data cannot be developed or if its development is prohibitively expensive, the model may have to be modified. Here considerable interaction occurs between the cost accountant and the model-development specialists. Following development and implementation, the cost accountant frequently signals the need to adjust operations, control procedures, or the model.

Although the cost accountant's training in model development is limited, he or she should have a general understanding of the information needs of planning and control models. The purpose of this chapter is to present the basic elements of a particular planning and control model that all cost accountants should be familiar with and to illustrate the problems encountered in supplying relevant cost data for use in specialized models. We will focus on the economic order quantity model as a framework for illustrating and analyzing the problems encountered in using an inventory planning and control model.

PURPOSE OF INVENTORY MODELS

Inventory management is an extremely important but difficult task. Inventories are necessary to maintain smooth operations and to satisfy customers' needs. Most organizations have substantial investments in a large number of inventory items. A small retail store may have hundreds of inventory items. A large manufacturing firm may have tens of thousands of inventory items. Even service organizations, such as hospitals, are likely to have thousands of inventory items. Because of the tremendous detail involved in separately reviewing each item, inventory decisions must be based either on the judgment of clerks or on formal policies established by management.

Numerous inventory planning and control models have been developed to aid management in establishing inventory policies. These models often suggest the quantity of inventory that should be ordered at one time and when orders should be placed. The objective of inventory planning and control models is to maintain adequate inventory levels at minimum inventory costs.

INVENTORY COSTS

Total annual inventory costs include the total cost of purchases, ordering inventory, and carrying inventory. In equation form:

$$\begin{matrix}\text{Total} \\ \text{inventory} \\ \text{costs}\end{matrix} = \begin{matrix}\text{Total} \\ \text{cost of} \\ \text{purchases}\end{matrix} + \begin{matrix}\text{Total} \\ \text{ordering} \\ \text{costs}\end{matrix} + \begin{matrix}\text{Total} \\ \text{carrying} \\ \text{costs}\end{matrix} \qquad (18\text{–}1)$$

The total cost of purchases is equal to the number of units purchased during the year multiplied by the unit purchase price. On an annual basis, the total cost of purchases varies directly with the number of units purchased. **Ordering costs** are costs incurred in placing and receiving orders for inventory. Some ordering costs are fixed; others are variable. On an annual basis, the total variable ordering costs vary directly with the number of orders placed. **Carrying costs** are costs incurred to hold items in inventory. They also include fixed and variable components. On an annual basis, the total variable carrying costs vary directly with the average inventory investment.

Inventory planning and control models attempt to minimize total annual inventory costs. These models usually specify:

1. The **economic order quantity** (EOQ)—the quantity of inventory that should be ordered at one time to minimize total annual ordering and carrying costs.
2. The **reorder point** (ROP)—the inventory level at which an order for additional inventory should be placed.

Only costs that vary in total for the year with variations in the order quantity and reorder point are relevant in making order quantity and reorder point decisions. In the basic inventory models, the only relevant costs are the variable ordering costs and the variable carrying costs. Costs that are assumed not to vary with the order quantity and reorder point include the total cost of purchases, the fixed ordering costs, and the fixed carrying costs. Although the adjective "variable" will not be used in describing costs in the balance of this chapter, keep in mind that the costs used in the analysis, unless stated otherwise, are variable costs. The impact of changes in the unit purchase price, fixed ordering costs, and fixed carrying costs are discussed after the basic economic order quantity and reorder point models are introduced.

ECONOMIC ORDER QUANTITY (EOQ)

The quantity of inventory ordered at one time affects inventory ordering and carrying costs. If a few large orders are placed, annual ordering costs will be low, but annual carrying costs will be high. Conversely, if many small orders are placed, annual ordering costs will be high, but annual carrying costs will be low. For an order quantity of Q units and annual usage of A units, A/Q orders are required each year. The annual ordering costs are:

$$\text{Annual ordering costs} = \left(\frac{A}{Q}\right)P \tag{18–2}$$

where

A = Annual use (demand) in units
Q = Order quantity in units
P = Cost of placing an order

Assuming that usage is even throughout the year and that Q units are received just as the old inventory is depleted, inventory will vary between Q and zero units. The average inventory is $Q/2$. The annual carrying costs are:

$$\text{Annual carrying costs} = \left(\frac{Q}{2}\right)H \tag{18–3}$$

where H = Annual cost of carrying one unit in inventory for one year.

By adding the ordering costs and carrying costs in Eqs. 18–2 and 18–3, the total annual cost, T, of ordering and carrying an inventory item is:

$$T = \left(\frac{A}{Q}\right)P + \left(\frac{Q}{2}\right)H \tag{18–4}$$

Because such important carrying costs as insurance, personal property taxes, and the cost of invested capital vary with the dollar value of inventory, the annual carrying cost of one unit is often expressed as a function of the unit cost:

$$H = Ci \tag{18–5}$$

where

C = Unit cost
i = Annual cost of carrying one unit in inventory for one year, expressed as a percentage of inventory cost

By substituting Eq. 18–5 in Eq. 18–4, the total annual cost, T, of ordering and carrying an inventory item is:

$$T = \left(\frac{A}{Q}\right)P + \left(\frac{Q}{2}\right)Ci \tag{18–6}$$

Example 18–1

Good Department Stores sell 3,000 units of a particular item evenly throughout the year. The item costs \$10 per unit, ordering costs are \$30 per order, and annual carrying costs are 20 percent of average inventory cost. Good currently places four orders for 750 units each year.

Good's inventory policy results in the sawtooth inventory pattern illustrated in Exhibit 18–1. Upon receipt of an order, there are 750 units in stock. Subsequently inventory declines until it reaches zero. At that time, the next order is received. On average, Good has 375 (750 ÷ 2) units in stock. The total annual ordering and carrying cost of this inventory policy is $870:

Annual ordering costs [(3,000 ÷ 750) × $30]	$120
Annual carrying costs [(750 ÷ 2) × ($10 × 0.20)]	750
Total	$870

The total annual ordering and carrying costs of several alternative inventory order quantities are computed in Exhibit 18–2(a) and illustrated in Exhibit 18–2(b). Note that total costs are minimized at that order quantity where annual ordering and carrying costs are equal. Because this is always the case, a formula for the order quantity that minimizes the sum of these costs is developed by setting them equal to each other and solving for Q:

Carrying costs = Ordering costs

$$\left(\frac{Q}{2}\right)Ci = \left(\frac{A}{Q}\right)P$$

multiplying each side of the equation by Q:

$$\left(\frac{Q^2}{2}\right)Ci = AP$$

dividing each side of the equation by Ci and multiplying by 2:

$$Q^2 = \frac{2AP}{Ci}$$

solving for Q:

$$Q^* = \sqrt{\frac{2AP}{Ci}} \qquad (18\text{–}7)$$

EXHIBIT 18–1 **Basic Sawtooth Inventory Pattern**

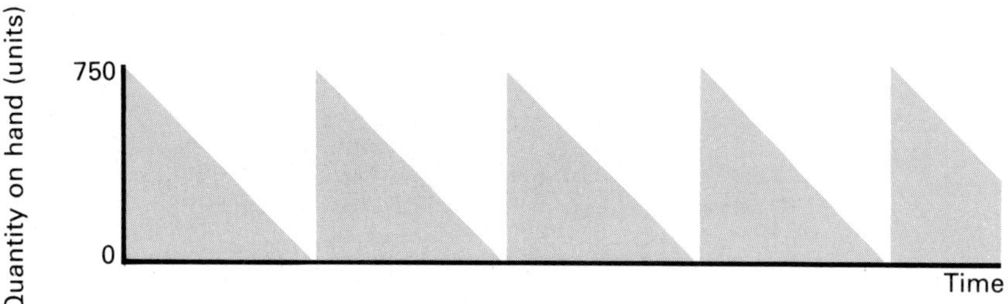

An asterisk is added to the Q in Eq. 18–7 to indicate this is the optimal or "economic" order quantity.[1] In words Eq. 18–7 is expressed as follows:

$$\text{Economic order quantity} = \sqrt{\frac{2 \times \text{Annual use in units} \times \text{Variable cost of placing an order}}{\text{Unit cost} \times \text{Annual carrying cost as a percent of inventory cost}}}$$

Good Department Stores' economic order quantity for Example 18–1 is 300 units:

$$Q^* = \sqrt{\frac{(2 \times 3{,}000 \times \$30)}{(\$10 \times 0.20)}} = \underline{\underline{300}} \text{ units}$$

Eq. 18–7 may also be used to determine the economic lot size (ELS) for manufacturing operations. The **economic lot size** is the optimal size of a production run that minimizes the total annual ordering, setup, and carrying costs for manufactured goods. When determining the economic lot size, P includes the costs that do not vary with the size of a production run but vary in total for the year with the number of production runs. Examples of such costs include clerical costs and setup costs. C represents unit variable manufacturing costs such as direct materials, direct labor, and variable factory overhead.

RELEVANT COSTS

Estimates of annual use (demand) in units, annual carrying costs per unit, and the variable cost of placing an order are required to use the EOQ formula. Although information on the annual demand for finished goods or merchandise inventory is available in the sales forecast prepared by marketing personnel and information on the annual use of raw materials is available in the purchases budget,[2] cost information may not be available in the form needed by the EOQ model.

---

[1] The economic order quantity formula may also be found by taking the first derivative of the total cost function with respect to Q, setting it equal to zero, and solving for Q:

$$T = \left(\frac{A}{Q}\right)P + \left(\frac{Q}{2}\right)Ci$$

$$\frac{d}{dQ} = -\frac{AP}{Q^2} + \frac{Ci}{2}$$

$$\frac{Ci}{2} - \frac{AP}{Q^2} = 0$$

$$Q^* = \sqrt{\frac{2AP}{Ci}}$$

The calculus approach shows why the purchase cost of inventory is not relevant in EOQ decisions. The first derivative of CA, the annual purchase cost, with respect to Q is zero.

[2] Sales forecasts and purchases budgets were considered in Chapter 10. However, the Chapter 10 discussion of the timing of materials purchases did not consider the EOQ. Accordingly, that discussion is subject to modification.

EXHIBIT 18–2 **Total Annual Ordering and Carrying Costs of Alternative Order Quantities**

(a) Computed

Annual use	3,000	3,000	3,000	3,000	3,000	3,000
Order quantity	50	100	300	750	1,000	1,500
Number of orders	60	30	10	4	3	2
Average inventory	25	50	150	375	500	750
Costs:						
Ordering (number of orders × $30)	$1,800	$ 900	$300	$120	$ 90	$ 60
Carrying (average inventory × $10 × 0.20)	50	100	300	750	1,000	1,500
Total	$1,850	$1,000	$600	$870	$1,090	$1,560
			Minimum			

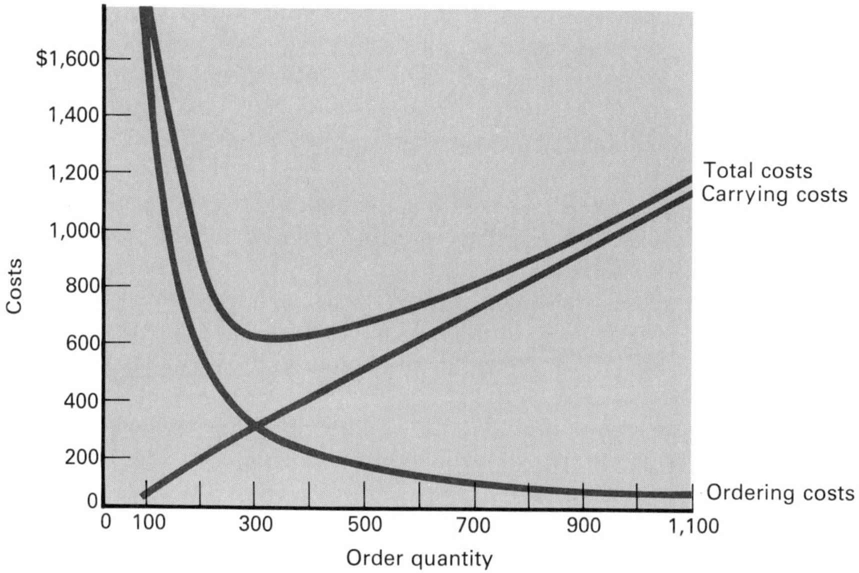

Unit Cost

When materials are purchased from outside suppliers, the unit invoice price less any early payment discounts is used as the unit cost in the EOQ model. A major complication occurs if the supplier offers volume discounts. In this case, there is a potential interaction between the EOQ and the invoice price (that is, C is a function of Q and Q^* is a function of C). Because volume discounts tend to follow an erratic step function, a single formula cannot be developed to incorporate them into the determination of Q^*. Consequently a trial-and-error approach may be necessary.

Example 18–2

Assume Good Department Stores purchase 2,000 units of a particular product annually. Ordering costs are $9 per order and annual carrying costs are $10 per unit regardless of the purchase price. The purchase price, however, depends on the size of the order. The following unit prices are available:

Order size	*Purchase price*
0–99	$5.00
100–199	4.80
200 or more	4.60

Using Eq. 18–7, the economic order quantity is 60 units:

$$Q^* = \sqrt{\frac{(2 \times 2{,}000 \times \$9)}{\$10}} = \underline{\underline{60}} \text{ units}$$

If Good places orders for 60 units each, the annual ordering costs are $300 [(2,000 units ÷ 60 units per order) × $9] and the annual inventory carrying costs are $300 [(60 units per order ÷ 2) × $10]. Although an order quantity of 60 units minimizes the total annual ordering and carrying costs, it may not minimize total annual inventory costs because of quantity discounts available if orders are placed in larger lot sizes. If the order size is 60, the cost per unit is $5.00 and the total purchases cost is $10,000 (2,000 units × $5.00). Adding this cost to the ordering and carrying costs gives total annual inventory costs of $10,600 ($300 + $300 + $10,000).

Because the $5.00 purchase price is not the lowest price available, a trial-and-error approach is used to determine if the EOQ gives the lowest total annual inventory cost. The total annual inventory cost using the EOQ solution should be compared with the total annual inventory costs at higher order quantities where breaks occur in the purchase price. For Example 18–2, breaks occur at 100 and 200 units. Exhibit 18–3 shows the computation of total annual costs at these levels.

For the data in Example 18–2, Exhibit 18–3 shows that total annual inventory costs are minimized at an order size of 100 units. With this order size, total costs are $10,280, which is $320 ($10,600 − $10,280) less than total costs using the EOQ. At 200 units, the total costs are $10,290. Even though this is less than total annual costs using the EOQ, it is $10 more than total annual costs with an order

EXHIBIT 18–3 Economic Order Quantity With Volume Discounts

Annual use	2,000	2,000	2,000
Order quantity	60	100	200
Number of orders	33.33	20	10
Average inventory	30	50	100
Purchase cost per unit	$5.00	$4.80	$4.60
Total annual inventory costs:			
Ordering (number of orders × $9)	$ 300	$ 180	$ 90
Carrying (average inventory × $10)	300	500	1,000
Purchases (annual use × cost per unit)	10,000	9,600	9,200
Total	$10,600	$10,280	$10,290

size of 100 units. Hence, to minimize total inventory costs, orders should be placed for 100 units.

The basic rule when volume discounts are available is as follows:

1. Calculate the EOQ.
2. If the EOQ is not in the minimum purchase price range, compare the total annual inventory cost of the EOQ size with the total annual inventory costs of higher order quantities at price breaks and select the order size with the lowest total annual inventory costs.

The optimal quantity will always be found at a price break whenever a quantity discount causes the optimal order quantity to be greater than the quantity suggested by the EOQ model. To verify that this is true, calculate the total annual inventory costs for Good if orders are placed in sizes other than 100 units. For example, if the order size is 110 units, the total annual inventory cost is $10,313.64:

Cost of ordering [(2,000/110) × $9]	$ 163.64
Cost of carrying [(110/2) × $10]	550.00
Purchases (2,000 × $4.80)	9,600.00
Total	$10,313.64

Although this is less than the total annual inventory cost at the EOQ, it is $33.64 ($10,313.64 − $10,280.00) higher than the total cost when the order size is 100 units.

If the purchaser pays transportation costs on purchased goods, such costs should be included in *C*, the unit cost. Nonmanufacturing organizations may classify these costs as a period expense in external reports, but this practice is followed as a matter of expediency. Transportation-in is part of the cost of inventory. If such costs are subject to volume discounts, a trial-and-error approach to the determination of Q^* is again required.

Carrying Costs

Carrying costs are affected by such factors as insurance, personal property taxes, variable storage costs, deterioration, and obsolescence. Fixed costs such as depreciation and property taxes on storage facilities are not relevant to the calculation of carrying costs for the EOQ model because they are incurred regardless of the order quantity. Most EOQ models ignore limitations on storage capacity. If fixed cash flows can be reduced by disposing of some current capacity or if additional capacity is necessary to hold Q^* units, further analysis is required. Increasing or decreasing capacity is a capital-budgeting decision, a topic discussed in Chapters 16 and 17.

Because the money invested in inventory could be invested elsewhere, carrying costs should also include an imputed opportunity cost on the investment in average inventory. The interest rate on borrowed money is frequently used as the imputed opportunity cost rate. However, the rate of return that management wants to earn on inventory investments is a better choice. The issues involved in determining this rate are beyond the scope of this book. One alternative is to use the cost of capital (discussed in Chapter 16). Because opportunity costs are not recorded in the accounting records, total *recorded* carrying costs will be less than the total carrying costs at the economic order quantity.

Ordering Costs

Ordering costs include the costs of processing the requisition for goods (prepared in the storeroom and sent to the Purchasing Department), the purchase order (prepared in the Purchasing Department and sent to the vendor), the receiving report (prepared by the Receiving Department with copies sent to the Purchasing and Accounts Payable Departments), the voucher (prepared by the Accounts Payable Department and sent to the Treasurer's Office), and the payment check (prepared by the Treasurer's Office). A troublesome aspect of these costs is that their major component, salaries, is likely to follow a step function. In large organizations, where the total volume of orders makes the steps narrow relative to the total number of orders, salaries may be treated as a variable cost. See Exhibit 18–4(a). This is not the case for small organizations. Here a small change in the total number of orders processed may result in a relatively large shift in total ordering costs. See Exhibit 18–4(b). In this case, it may be desirable to order quantities larger than Q^* because the reduction in fixed ordering costs more than offsets the increase in carrying costs. Again this analysis must be conducted outside the EOQ model.

ASSUMPTIONS UNDERLYING EOQ MODEL

The economic order quantity model just presented is the classical one found in the production literature. Although it provides a useful framework for analyzing order quantity problems, it is subject to a number of limiting assumptions. Among

EXHIBIT 18–4 Order Costs in Large and Small Organizations (The steps represent personnel costs; the upward slope represents additional order processing costs.)

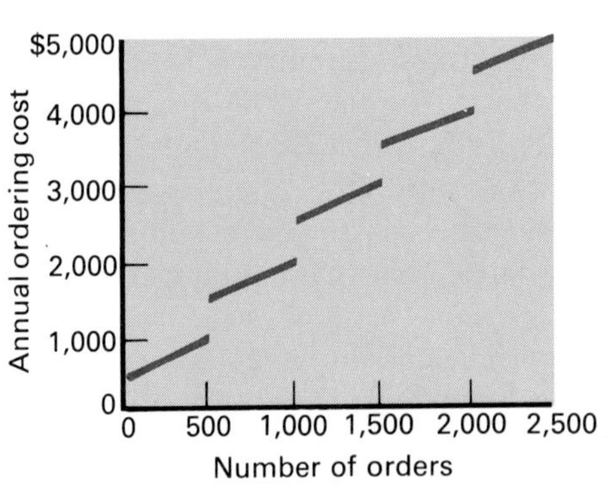

VC = $1
FC = $500/500 orders

(a) Large organizations

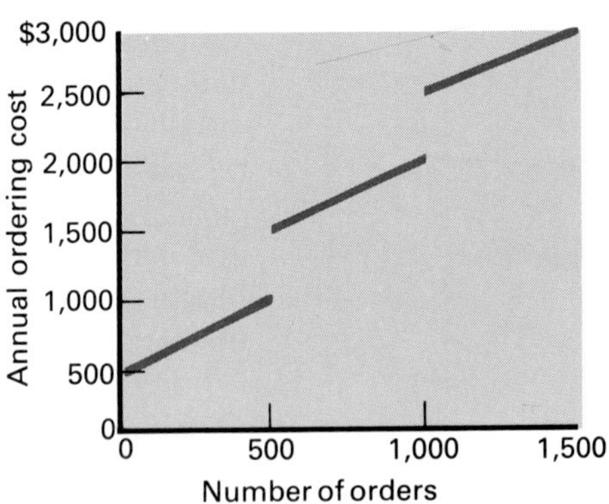

VC = $1
FC = $500/500 orders

(b) Small organizations

the more important are the following:

1. *Procurement or production is in batches.* The model is applicable to purchases and to determining lot sizes in a job shop. It is not directly applicable to continuous production.
2. *All ordering and carrying costs are known.* We have already discussed some of the problems of determining relevant costs. The impact of errors in cost prediction is discussed in the next section of this chapter.
3. *Stockouts are not permitted.* The model does not foresee the possibility of intentional stockouts (inventory shortages) and hence does not include a balancing of stockout costs against the cost of carrying inventory.
4. *Demand rate is constant and known.* The assumption of constant, or uniform, demand is reflected in the constant downward slope in Exhibit 18–1. If demand were not constant, the slope would be irregular.
5. *Lead time is certain.* The basic model assumes that the time required to receive an order once it is placed is constant and known in advance. Uncertainty in demand and lead time is discussed later in this chapter.

ACCURACY OF COST PREDICTIONS

The difficulty of obtaining accurate cost predictions for specialized decision models should be readily apparent from the previous discussion. Because of the effort and cost involved in cost estimation and prediction, the accountant and model developer should determine how sensitive the model is to errors and what effect such errors could have on the organization. If the potential effect of error is large, a high degree of accuracy is required. Fortunately the EOQ model is relatively insensitive to prediction errors. Even with large prediction errors, an organization may substantially benefit from the EOQ model.

The effect of 50 percent error rates in predicting P or i on the total annual ordering and carrying costs of Good Department Stores in Example 18–1 is computed in Exhibit 18–5. The largest effect is an opportunity loss of $36.50. This compares quite favorably with the costs that are incurred when the order quantity varies from the quantity specified by the EOQ model. See Exhibit

EXHIBIT 18–5 Effect of Fifty Percent Prediction Errors on Order Quantity and Actual Costs

Error	P = $15	P = $45	i = 0.10	i = 0.30	None
Resulting order quantity	212	367	424	245	300
Number of orders	14.15	8.17	7.08	12.24	10.00
Average inventory	106.0	183.5	212.0	122.5	150.0
Actual costs:					
Ordering (number of orders × $30)	$424.50	$254.10	$212.40	$367.20	$300.00
Carrying (average inventory × $10 × $0.20)	212.00	367.00	424.00	245.00	300.00
Total	$636.50	$621.10	$636.40	$612.20	$600.00
Opportunity loss	$ 36.50	$ 21.10	$ 36.40	$ 12.20	$ 0

18–2(a). Even with large prediction errors, the EOQ model gives results that are "in the ballpark." The same results might not be obtained by human judgment. For example, with Good's current policy of placing four orders for 750 units each, the total annual ordering and carrying costs are \$870 as computed in Example 18–1. As shown in Exhibit 18–5, prediction errors of 50 percent do not cause the total costs to approach this current cost.

REORDER POINT (ROP)

Because inventories cannot be ordered and received instantly, orders for additional inventories are placed before current stocks are depleted. The reorder point must consider both the lead time required to replenish stocks after an order is placed and inventory demand during the lead time.

ROP with Certainty

Assuming demand takes place evenly throughout a year containing n work days, the daily demand is:

$$\text{Daily demand} = \frac{A}{n} \tag{18–8}$$

If the lead time required to fill an order is always L days, the reorder point in units, R, is:

$$R = L\left(\frac{A}{n}\right) \tag{18–9}$$

An order for Q^* additional unit is placed when inventory declines to R units.

Example 18–3

Assuming a work year of 250 days and a lead time of 10 work days, the reorder point for an inventory item with an annual demand of 3,000 units is 120 units:

$$R = 10\left(\frac{3{,}000}{250}\right) = \underline{\underline{120}} \text{ units}$$

Occasionally R will be greater than Q^*. This may happen if the lead time is long and/or the order quantity is small. In this case, one or more orders will always be outstanding and previously ordered goods that have not yet arrived must be included in reorder computations. For Example 18–3, an order would be placed when units on hand plus units on order equal 120.

ROP With Uncertainty

The previous discussion assumed equal daily demand and a constant lead time. Unfortunately these asumptions are unrealistic. Because of variations in lead time and daily demand, it is desirable to maintain an inventory cushion to prevent "stockouts" (no inventory) and the resulting loss of sales or disruption of production. Such cushions are called **safety stocks.** Exhibit 18–6 illustrates the possible effect of variations in lead time demand on inventory with and without safety stocks.

Safety stocks increase the reorder point by the number of units kept as the cushion. Eq. 18–9 is modified as follows to include the safety stocks:

$$R = L\left(\frac{A}{n}\right) + S \tag{18–10}$$

where

R = Reorder point in units
L = Lead time in days
A = Annual demand in units
n = Number of working days in a year
S = Safety stock in units

Because safety stocks act as a base inventory layer, they increase the average inventory level (by S units) and annual carrying costs (by $S \times Ci$ dollars). Annual carrying costs are increased from the amount computed in Eq. 18–3; they are now:

$$\text{Annual carrying costs} = \left[\left(\frac{Q}{2}\right) + S\right]Ci \tag{18–11}$$

EXHIBIT 18–6 Effect of Variation in Lead Time and Lead-Time Demand on Inventories

(a) Without safety stocks

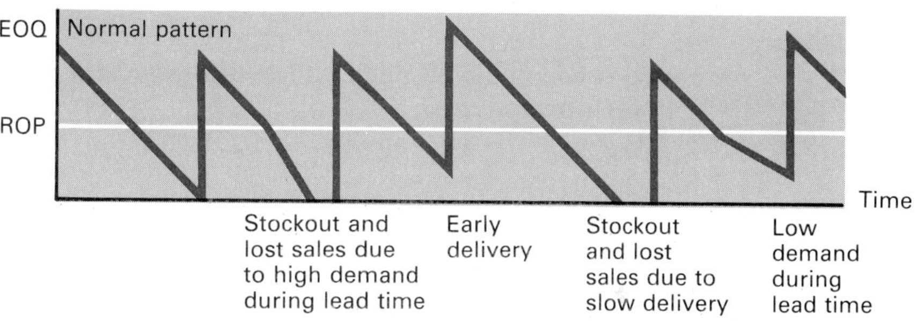

(b) With safety stocks

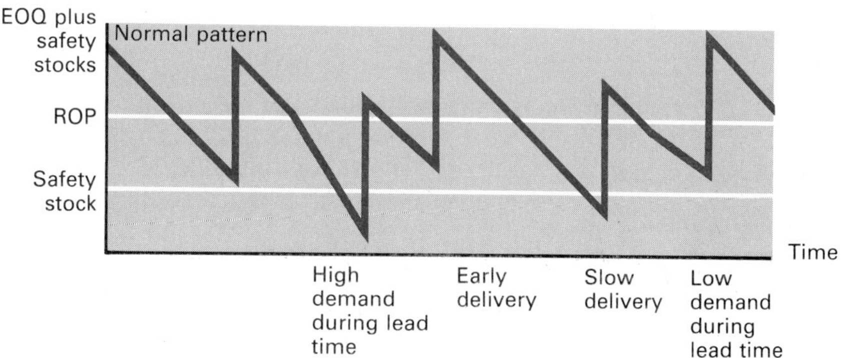

Decisions about safety stocks are made independently of EOQ decisions because the cost of carrying safety stock is not affected by the order quantity. In determining safety-stock levels, management may:

1. Specify an arbitrary amount based on judgment or rules of thumb, such as setting safety stocks equal to 20 percent of expected demand.
2. Specify an inventory service level, such as maintaining sufficient safety stocks to reduce the probability of lead-time stockouts to 10 percent.
3. Attempt to minimize the total annual costs of stockouts and carrying safety stocks.

Before inventory service levels can be specified, a probability distribution of lead-time demand must be developed. Although such a distribution may be based on actual observations of demand and lead time, companies frequently assume that lead-time demand follows such theoretical probability distributions as the "normal," "exponential," or "Poisson."[3] This procedure is acceptable if the actual and theoretical distributions are similar.

Example 18–4

The management of Good Department Stores believes the lead-time demand for one of their products is normally distributed with a mean of 120 units and a standard deviation of 20 units. They want to establish a reorder point that will reduce the probability of a stockout during each lead time to 5 percent. The problem is to find R so that

$$Pr\ (\text{lead-time demand} \geq R) \leq 0.05$$

From the table for the area under a normal curve (Table A in Appendix B of this book), the z-value that leaves 5 percent of the distribution *in a single tail* is 1.65. Accordingly,

$$Pr\ (\text{lead-time demand} \geq 120 + 1.65(20)) \leq 0.05$$

The reorder point is 153 units [120 + 1.65(20)]. The safety stock is the excess of R over the expected lead-time demand. For Example 18–4, the safety stock is 33 units (153 − 120).

If it is possible to estimate stockout costs and the probability of stockouts at various safety stock levels, safety stocks can be set at the level that minimizes the total annual cost of stockouts and carrying safety stocks.

Example 18–5

In the absence of safety stocks, the Hodges Company has set the reorder point for an inventory item at 250 units. Management anticipates placing an average of 10 orders per year for this item. Stockout costs are estimated to be $100 per occurrence regardless of the total amount of the inventory shortage. Annual carrying costs are $5 per unit. Inventory records reveal the following about safety

---

[3] National Association of Accountants, *N.A.A. Research Report 40: Techniques in Inventory Management* (New York: National Association of Accountants, 1964) p. 68.

EXHIBIT 18–7 Computation of Total Expected Safety Stock and Stockout Costs

Safety stock costs						Stockout costs								
Units of safety stock		*Unit carrying cost per year*		*Total annual carrying cost*	*Cost per stockout*		*Probability of stockout*		*Annual orders*		*Expected annual stockout cost*	*Expected total cost*
0	×	$5	=	$ 0	$100	×	0.50	×	10	=	$500	$500
5	×	$5	=	$ 25	$100	×	0.40	×	10	=	$400	$425
10	×	$5	=	$ 50	$100	×	0.35	×	10	=	$350	$400
15	×	$5	=	$ 75	$100	×	0.31	×	10	=	$310	$385
20	×	$5	=	$100	$100	×	0.29	×	10	=	$290	$390

stock levels and the probability of a stockout:

Units of safety stock	*Probability of a stockout on each reorder*
0	0.50
5	0.40
10	0.35
15	0.31
20	0.29

The cost-minimizing safety stock is 15 units. See Exhibit 18–7. Hodges should increase the reorder point to 265 (250 + 15) units.

Although minimizing the total annual cost of stockouts and carrying safety stocks is theoretically appealing, stockout costs are very difficult to estimate. In a merchandising establishment, stockout costs include the extra cost of processing back orders and the opportunity cost of lost sales. Although the opportunity cost of lost sales is frequently specified as the selling price less the invoice price, opportunity costs are considerably greater if dissatisfied customers subsequently patronize other establishments. The stockout costs of manufacturing organizations are even more difficult to estimate. They might include the opportunity cost of lost sales (perhaps reduced by the contribution margin of other products produced during the stockout period), the cost of idle time, and any costs of expediting production after materials are received.[4]

Signaling Need for Reorders

Once the economic order quantity and the reorder point are determined, some system must be established for signaling the need to place an order. Three frequently mentioned alternatives are:

1. Perpetual inventory systems
2. Two-bin inventory systems
3. Constant order cycles

[4] For a further discussion of inventory models, consult an operations research textbook.

A **perpetual inventory system** is an inventory recordkeeping system that keeps track of the exact number of units in stock at all times. Under a perpetual inventory system, a reorder is signaled when the records indicate the reorder point has been reached. Until recent years, perpetual inventory records were kept only for critical or costly inventory items. However, advances in computer technology now make it easier for manufacturing and retail establishments to maintain records on a perpetual basis. As a result, this method is displacing some uses of two-bin inventory systems and constant order cycles.

Because of the cost of maintaining perpetual inventory records, some organizations use a "two-bin" system to signal the need to reorder. A **two-bin inventory system** is an inventory reorder point system in which units of each inventory item are divided into two groups (or placed in two bins) in order to provide a reorder signal. As soon as the first group (or bin) is depleted, an order is placed. The quantity in the second group (or bin) protects against a stockout during the replenishment period.

A **constant order cycle** is an inventory reorder system in which inventory ordering is made on the basis of a preestablished time schedule. Constant order cycles make it possible to smooth the flow of order processing and combine orders sent to individual suppliers. This may result in reduced order-processing costs and in volume discounts on purchasing and transportation. However, constant order cycles require larger safety stocks than perpetual or two-bin systems. The safety stock must provide protection from variations in lead-time demand and from variations in demand during the period between inventory reviews.

OTHER APPROACHES TO INVENTORY PLANNING AND CONTROL

The economic order quantity model is an approach to inventory planning and control that minimizes the total cost of inventory when the ordering and carrying costs are given. However, if the ordering and/or carrying costs can be reduced, the total costs can also be reduced. Other approaches to inventory planning and control have been developed to reduce these costs.

A-B-C Approach

The **A-B-C approach** to inventory management uses several different methods to make inventory reordering decisions within the same organization. The A-B-C approach is based on the premise that in most inventories a small percentage of the items accounts for a large percentage of the annual dollar usage. Conversely, a large percentage of the inventory items accounts for a small percentage of the annual dollar usage. Recognition of this situation has led to the division of inventory into two or more classifications.

Example 18–6

A company with over 20,000 inventory items found that 10 percent of them accounted for over 77 percent of total sales volume. Another 20 percent of the items accounted for 17 percent of usage, and 70 percent of the items accounted for just over 5 percent of usage. The company divided the items into three inventory categories (A, B, and C) and applied different inventory-management techniques to each.[5]

One possible way of implementing the A-B-C approach is to use the EOQ models, safety stocks based on balancing of carrying and stockout costs, and perpetual inventory records for the A items. The B items might be controlled with EOQ models, safety stocks based on service levels, and two-bin systems. Finally, C items might be placed on a constant order cycle with sufficient safety stocks to prevent depletion. When the A-B-C approach is used, the division of inventories into two or more categories is a matter of judgment.

Just-in-Time Scheduling

Another approach to inventory planning and control that has received attention in recent years is the just-in-time (sometimes called Kanban) approach, which has been used extensively by Japanese industry. The **just-in-time approach** to inventory planning is based on the premise that inventory is a waste and materials and parts should be available only at the time they are needed for use. Under the just-in-time approach, production takes place in small lot sizes to reduce the quantity of finished goods inventory on hand. This requires a system that permits rapid changeover between product lines in the manufacturing facility or the availability of extra machines to produce for immediate needs. In terms of the traditional EOQ model, rapid changeover capability and extra machines both reduce start-up costs.

Material Requirements Planning

Material Requirements Planning (MRP) is an approach to inventory planning used by manufacturing organizations to determine when raw materials must be purchased and components or subassemblies manufactured. The EOQ and reorder point may be determined from past usage of a material or component, but MRP is future oriented because it is based on a master production schedule. The **master production schedule** shows when the units should be produced to meet budgeted sales after taking capacity constraints into account.

Once the master production schedule has been developed, it is analyzed to determine the requirements for materials, components, and subassemblies. Lead times are taken into account to determine when the materials must be ordered and components and subassemblies started in production. Lead times include process time, setup time, and slack time. Process time is the time required to process the batch or order the material. Setup time is the time required to setup or change over all the resources required for production. Slack time is built into the process for resolving scheduling conflicts, assuring that all materials and parts are available, movement of materials, and unexpected events.

Once the requirements for materials, components, and subassemblies are determined, they are compared with any inventory on hand to determine the additional units needed for production. Order quantity and lot size rules are then

---

[5] *N.A.A. Research Report 40,* pp. 6–7.

used to determine the quantity of materials to order and the size of the production run. The result is a schedule showing the requirements for all materials, components, and subassemblies used in production.

Material Requirements Planning is a critical part of a system known as Manufacturing Resource Planning (MRP II). **Manufacturing Resource Planning** is a data base system used to plan and schedule production and materials. The major tool used to implement MRP II is the computer. Using a computer for planning lets management coordinate all activities from production to distribution. It also lets managers analyze "what if" type questions to predict the impact of alternative plans on future operations.

After studying both Kanban and MRP II systems, William Goddard reached two conclusions about the pros and cons of each system:

> Kanban can succeed only where the user produces highly repetitive products. MRP II, however, works equally well for highly engineered one-of-a-kind environments, make-to-stock products, and finished-to-order products.
>
> MRP II has better tools than Kanban, but these tools are more costly. It is very important for a company to properly evaluate not only the costs, but what the paybacks will be. Unless the general manager and his staff can visualize a sizable return, they will not invest enough of their time and energy to ensure that the company will become a successful user.[6]

SUMMARY

The planning and control of inventories requires a determination of how much and when to order and the implementation of a procedure for signaling the need to order. Economic order quantity models have been developed to minimize the total cost of ordering and carrying inventory. Reorder point models have been developed to ensure that replenishments arrive before stockouts occur. Although sophisticated approaches to the establishment of safety stocks attempt to minimize the total costs of carrying safety stocks and of stockouts, safety stocks are more likely to be based on desired service levels or judgment. Finally, the need to order is signaled by perpetual inventory records, the depletion of the first of two bins of stock, or periodic review. Other approaches to planning and controlling inventory include the A-B-C approach, Material Requirements Planning, and the just-in-time approach.

The cost accountant's role in establishing economic order quantities and reorder points is representative of the tasks he or she performs in the development and implementation of specialized models. The cost accountant must provide relevant cost data. The development of such data requires an analysis of cost behavior. It may also involve the adjustment of historical costs to provide better predictions of future costs and the estimation of several types of opportunity costs that do not appear in accounting records. Because of the cost and uncertain nature of cost predictions, it is advisable to determine the sensitivity of the model to prediction errors and the potential effect on the organization of such errors. The economic order quantity is relatively insensitive to cost prediction errors.

---

[6] Walter E. Goddard, "Kanban Versus MRP II—Which is Best for You?" *Modern Materials Handling* **37** (November 5, 1982): p. 40.

APPENDIX Planning and Control with PERT

PERT (Program Evaluation and Review Technique) is a method of project planning and control applicable to any complex project that consists of a number of activities, including activities whose initiation depends on the completion of other activities. Originally developed by the U.S. Navy to plan and control the Polaris missile project, PERT has been used to plan and control such diverse activities as the design and/or production of automobiles, bridges, homes, machine tools, roads, ships, and weapons systems. It has also been used in budgeting, the installation of automatic data processing systems, and the development of audit programs.[7]

PERT/TIME

The basic element of PERT is a network of the interrelationships between all major activities required to complete a project. The development of this network forces planners to identify all activities that make up a project and to identify those activities that must be completed before each subsequent activity begins. Such a list, for a hypothetical project, is presented in the first two columns of Exhibit 18–8. Once the list is completed, each *activity* is represented in a network by an *arrow* such as the following for Activity A:

The initiation and completion of each activity is called an **event.** *Events* are represented by *nodes* or small circles.

A complete PERT network for the activities listed in Exhibit 18–8 is presented in Exhibit 18–9(a). Needless to say, the development of PERT networks requires much forethought and work. Inconsistencies in sequencing become glaringly obvious when illustrated in network form. The elimination of these problems before work starts is a major benefit of PERT. Very complex projects may have several levels of networks. For example, Activity A may contain so many subactivities that another network is developed for it alone.

Once the PERT network is developed, we try to estimate the normal time required to complete each activity and the project as a whole. **Normal time** is the average expected time to complete an activity under normal, efficient operating conditions. We can estimate the normal times by asking the person in charge of each activity to supply three time estimates:

1. t_o = *An optimistic time estimate,* indicating the shortest possible time required to complete the activity.
2. t_m = A *modal time estimate,* indicating the most likely time required to complete the activity.
3. t_p = A *pessimistic time estimate,* indicating the longest possible time required to complete the activity.

These time estimates are assumed to represent the extreme values and mode of a beta distribution. We compute the expected time required to complete an activity, t_e, by using the following formula:

$$t_e = \frac{t_o + 4t_m + t_p}{6} \qquad (18\text{–}12)$$

[7] See Peter H. Burger, "PERT and the Auditor," *Accounting Review* **39,** No. 1 (January 1964): 103–120; and Don T. De Coster, "The Budget Director and PERT," *Business Budgeting* **13,** No. 2 (March 1964): 13–17.

EXHIBIT 18–8 List of Activity and Time Requirements

List of activities		*Time estimates (weeks)*			
Activity	*Required to start*	*Optimistic (t_o)*	*Most likely (t_m)*	*Pessimistic (t_p)*	*Expected* (t_e)*
A	B, C	2	5	14	6
C	F	3	5	7	5
B	D, E	1	2	3	2
F	I	3	5	13	6
E	H	1	2	15	4
D	G	2	2	2	2
G	None	2	3	4	3
H	None	2	4	6	4
I	None	2	2	8	3

$$^*t_e = \frac{t_o + 4t_m + t_p}{6}$$

Times for each activity are indicated in the four columns on the right of Exhibit 18–8. We place the expected times to complete each activity on the PERT network as in Exhibit 18–9(b). We also assign a number to each of the events in Exhibit 18–9(b). Although the assignment usually works backwards from the last event (completion of the project), it sometimes proceeds forward from the first event. There is no required order for the assignment of numbers within the network.

Our next step is to determine the expected time required to complete the project as a whole. The project completion time is equal to the total time required to complete all activities on the longest path through the network. To determine this path, we first work forward through the network indicating the earliest possible time, T_E, each event can take place. This is done in Exhibit 18–9(c). The total time required to complete this project is

EXHIBIT 18–9 Development of PERT Network and Critical Path

(a) Developing the network of activities

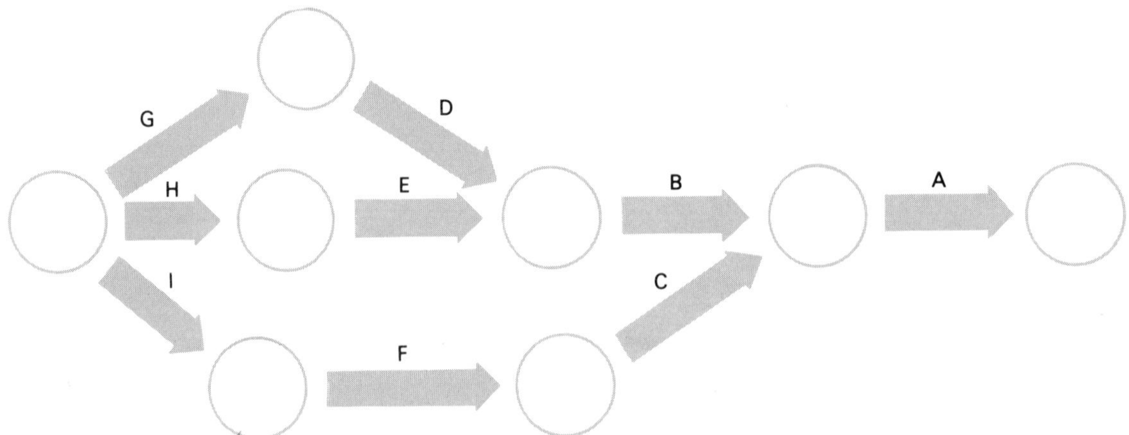

EXHIBIT 18–9 *(Continued)*

(b) Specifying completion times and labeling events

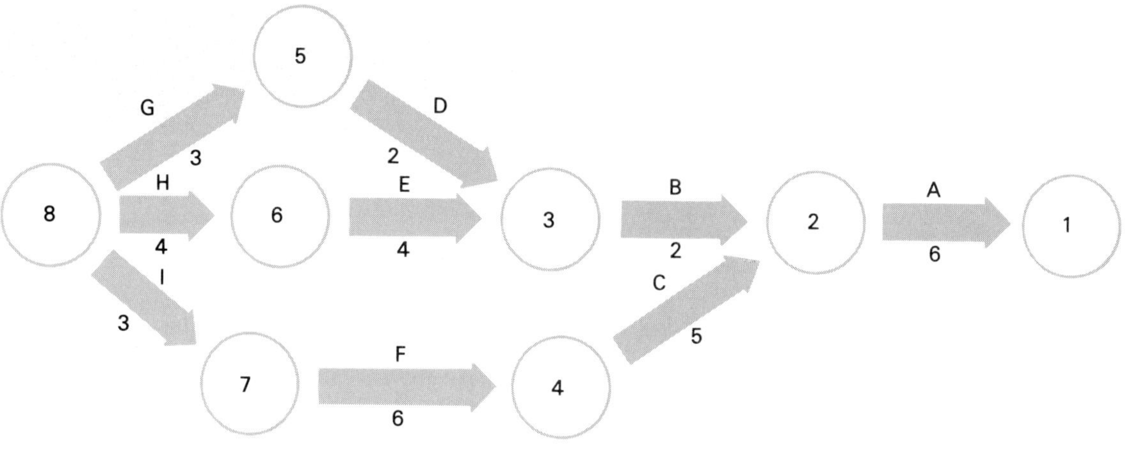

(c) Determining the critical path

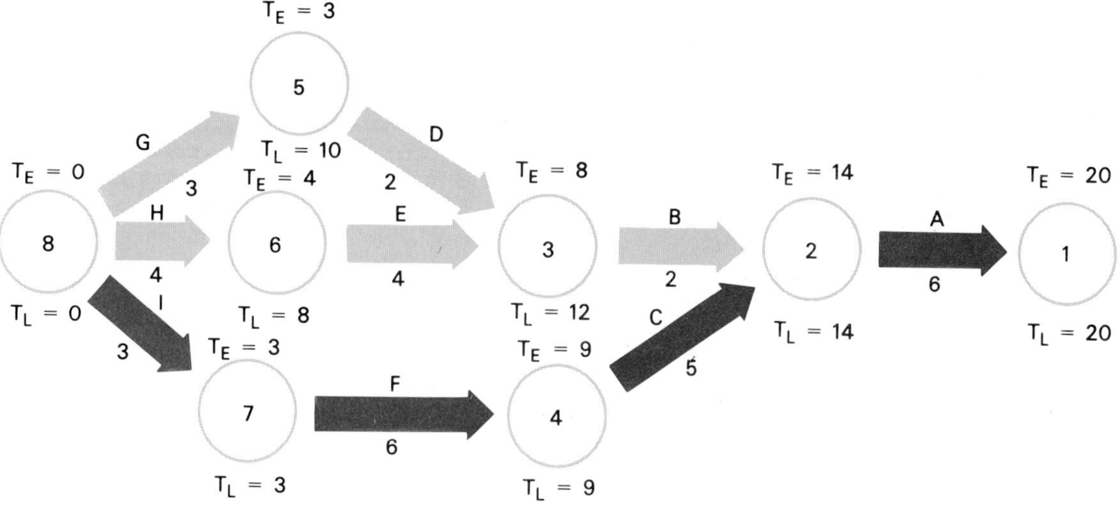

20 weeks. Next we determine the latest time each event can occur without delaying the project, T_L. To do this,we set T_L for the last event equal to T_E and work backwards through the network. The path for events where the earliest and latest starting times are equal is called the **critical path.** Any delay in activities on the critical path causes a delay in the completion of the project. This path is indicated by a heavy line in Exhibit 18–9(c). The amount of time by which an activity or series of activities can be delayed without becoming part of the critical path is called **slack.**

If the critical path contains a large number of activities, the completion time for the project as a whole will follow a normal distribution with a mean equal to T_E for the last event and a standard deviation equal to:

$$\sigma_{TE} = \sqrt{\sum_i \frac{1}{36}(t_{pi} - t_{oi})^2} \qquad (18\text{–}13)$$

where i = An activity on the critical path.

Assuming the critical path in Exhibit 18–9 contains a large number of activities (obviously it does not), σ_{TE} is 2.9 weeks:

$$\sigma_{TE} = \sqrt{\frac{1}{36}(14-2)^2 + \frac{1}{36}(7-3)^2 + \frac{1}{36}(13-3)^2 + \frac{1}{36}(8-2)^2}$$

$$\sigma_{TE} = \underline{\underline{2.9}} \text{ weeks}$$

Using this information, we can determine the probability of completing the project during a specific period with the aid of tables for the normal distribution. For example, with an expected completion time of 20 weeks and a standard deviation of 2.9 weeks, the probability of completing the project in 24 weeks or less is found with the aid of Appendix Table A.

$$z = \frac{24 - 20}{2.9} = 1.38$$

Twenty-four weeks is 1.38 standard deviations from 20 weeks. In Table A, 8.38 percent of the area under the normal curve is beyond $z = +1.38$. Hence the probability of completing the project in 24 weeks or less is 0.9162 (1.0000 − 0.0838).

PERT/COST

PERT/Cost is a frequently used extension of PERT. **PERT/Cost** is a PERT network that includes the expected cost of each activity. It requires the person (or persons) responsible for each activity to develop cost predictions associated with completing an activity in the normal time. These costs are known as **normal costs.** Once these costs are determined, the predicted cost of the project as a whole is determined by summing the normal cost of each activity. The cost accountant is likely to become involved in the development of these predictions. Again, all of the problems of cost behavior and relevance are present.

PERT/COST RESOURCE ALLOCATION SUPPLEMENT

PERT/Cost resource allocation supplement is a technique used to determine which activities in a PERT network should be shortened to reduce the total time required to complete the project. If a project cannot be completed in the required timeframe, it may be necessary to expedite it. When this is done, the people responsible for critical-path activities are requested to provide estimates of crash times and crash costs. The **crash time** is the shortest possible time in which an activity can be completed. The **crash cost** is the cost associated with completing an activity in the shortest possible time. The crash times and costs are then compared to the previously developed predictions of normal times and normal costs to determine the cost of "buying time" on the critical path. If there is a linear relationship between time and cost, the cost of buying one unit of time for an activity is:

$$\text{Cost of one unit of time} = \frac{\text{Crash cost} - \text{Normal cost}}{\text{Normal time} - \text{Crash time}} \qquad (18\text{–}14)$$

EXHIBIT 18–10 Time and Cost Predictions for Normal and Crash Programs

	Time required		*Cost*	
Activity	*Normal program*	*Crash program*	*Normal program*	*Crash program*
A	6	4	$ 6,000	$8,000
B	2	1½	2,000	2,500
C	5	4	6,000	7,500
D	2	1	1,500	2,250
E	4	3	4,000	5,000
F	6	5	5,000	6,500
G	3	2½	3,000	4,000
H	4	3½	3,500	4,000
I	3	1½	4,000	8,500
Total normal program cost			$35,000	

Using the expected times in Exhibit 18–8 for the normal times, time and cost predictions for the normal program and a crash program are shown in Exhibit 18–10. Recall that the critical path includes Activities A-C-F-I, and the total time to complete the project is 20 weeks given the normal program. In this case the total cost is $35,000 as shown in the fourth column of Exhibit 18–10.

If the manager of the project believes that 20 weeks is too long, he or she can reduce the total time by incurring additional costs to do some of the activities on the critical path on a crash basis. Only the activities on the critical path should be considered in determining which activities to speed up (or crash) because the activities that are not on the critical path already have slack time. The activity that should be crashed first is the one with the lowest cost per period of time. The weeks by which the normal program can be shortened by the crash program, the incremental cost of the crash program, and the incremental cost per week for the activities on the critical path are shown in Exhibit 18–11.

The data in column 4 of Exhibit 18–11 show that Activity A can be shortened with the lowest incremental cost per unit of time. Buying time for Activity A costs $1,000 per week compared with $1,500 for Activities C and F and $3,000 for Activity I. If Activity A is done on a crash basis, the total project time is cut by two weeks and the expected completion time is now 18 weeks with a total cost of $37,000. If the manager wants to reduce the completion time further, he or she could do so by putting more activities on a crash basis. Since the critical path still includes Activities A-C-F-I, either of Activities C

EXHIBIT 18–11 Incremental Time and Costs of Crash Program for Critical-Path Activities

Activity	*Weeks shortened*	*Incremental cost of crash program*	*Incremental cost per week*
A	2	$2,000	$1,000
C	1	1,500	1,500
F	1	1,500	1,500
I	1½	4,500	3,000

and F should be crashed because they each have an a incremental crash cost of $1,500 per week. Two more weeks could be cut from the expected completion time if both of these activities are done on a crash basis. This would increase total costs by $3,000 to $40,000.

Two comments regarding this PERT/Cost resource allocation supplement analysis are in order: (1) time cannot be reduced below the crash time; and (2) if sufficient time is purchased on the critical path, another sequence of activities may become critical. For example, in Exhibit 18–9(c), if five weeks are purchased from Activities A-C-F-I, the critical path will shift to Activities A-B-E-H from A-C-F-I.

PERT FOR TIME AND COST CONTROL

Having established the plans for the times and costs of each activity, we now need to develop information to compare plans with actual results. These comparisons should be made frequently in order to identify time and cost problems before they get out of hand. When necessary, activities are rescheduled and resources are reallocated. The cost accountant plays a vital role in these control activities. An information system must be set up that accumulates actual time and cost data by project and activity. Because work may occur simultaneously in several different departments or areas of responsibility, the system is much more complex than the simple job-cost system discussed in Chapter 3. There, a job-cost sheet accompanied a job through one or more departments. Here, information must be collected from several different departments or responsibility areas simultaneously working on the job. This requires some central job control center.

PROBLEM AREAS

Despite its usefulness as a planning and control technique, PERT is not without its problems. The beta distribution assumption may be incorrect. While management concentrates its efforts on the original critical path, delays can cause another path to become critical. In fact, as the number of paths in the project increases, a definite downward bias creeps into the estimated project completion time because of the increased probability of a critical-path shift. The use of a normal probability distribution in determining project completion time probabilities is limited by the assumption that the project's completion time is normally distributed.[8] Finally, there are the normal problems of estimating and predicting costs, recordkeeping, and performance evaluation.

[8] Simulation may be used to overcome the problems caused by the probability of a critical-path shift and the normal distribution assumption.

KEY TERMS

- A-B-C approach
- Carrying costs
- Constant order cycle
- Economic lot size
- Economic order quantity
- Just-in-time approach
- Manufacturing Resource Planning
- Master production schedule
- Material Requirements Planning
- Ordering costs
- Perpetual inventory system
- Reorder point
- Safety stocks
- Two-bin inventory system

APPENDIX KEY TERMS

Crash cost
Crash time
Critical path
Event
Normal cost
Normal time
PERT/Cost
PERT/Cost resource allocation supplement
Program Evaluation and Review Technique (PERT)
Slack

SELECTED REFERENCES

Bowers, Billy B., "Product Costing in the MRP Environment," *Management Accounting* **64,** No. 6 (December 1982): 24–27.

Bunch, Robert G., "The Effect of Payment Terms on Economic Order Quantity Determination," *Management Accounting* **48,** No. 5 (January 1967): 53–63.

Burger, Peter H. "PERT and the Auditor," *Accounting Review* **39,** No. 1 (January 1964): 103–120.

Cohen, Morris A., and Robert Halperin, "Optimal Inventory Order Policy for a Firm Using the LIFO Inventory Costing Method," *Journal of Accounting Research* **18,** No. 2 (Autumn 1980): 375–389.

Constantinides, George M., Yuji Ijiri, and Robert A. Leitch, "Stochastic Cost-Volume-Profit Analysis with a Linear Demand Function," *Decision Sciences* **12,** No. 3 (July 1981): 417–427.

Das, Chandrasekhar, "A Unified Approach to the Price-Break Economic Order Quantity (EOQ) Problem," *Decision Sciences* **15,** No. 3 (Summer 1984): 350–358.

Davenport, Frederick J., "Financial Management Through MRP," *Management Accounting* **63,** No. 12 (June 1982): 26–29.

DeCoster, Don T., "The Budget Director and PERT," *Business Budgeting* **13,** No. 2 (March 1964): 13–17.

Elikai, Fara, and Shane Moriarity, "Variance Analysis with PERT/COST," *Accounting Review* **57,** No. 1 (January 1982): 161–170.

Goodard, Walter E., "Kanban Versus MRP II—Which is Best for You?" *Modern Materials Handling* **37,** No. 3 (November 5, 1982): 40–48.

Kaplan, Robert S., "Measuring Manufacturing Performance: A New Challenge for Managerial Accounting Research," *Accounting Review* **58,** No. 4 (October 1983): 686–705.

Kimes, James D., "Are You Really Managing Your Inventory?" *Management Accounting* **65,** No. 8 (February 1984): 70–73.

Kuzdrall, Paul J., and Robert R. Britney, "Total Setup Lot Sizing With Quantity Discounts," *Decision Sciences* **13,** No. 1 (January 1982): 101–112.

Morse, Wayne J., and James H. Scheiner, "Cost Minimization, Return on Investment, Residual Income: Alternative Criterion for Inventory Models," *Accounting and Business Research* **9,** No. 36 (Autumn 1979): 320–324.

Rubin, Paul A., David M. Dilts, and Beth A. Barron, "Economic Order Quantities with Quantity Discounts: Grandma Does It Best," *Decision Sciences* **14,** No. 2 (April 1983): 270–281.

Seglund, Ragnor, and Santiago Ibarreche, "Just-in-Time: The Accounting Implications," *Management Accounting* **66,** No. 2 (August 1984): 43–45.

REVIEW QUESTIONS

18–1 What purpose is served by inventories?
18–2 What is the objective of inventory-control models?
18–3 What types of inventory costs are irrelevant in determining the economic order quantity?
18–4 What costs are balanced in determining the economic order quantity?
18–5 What changes are made in the EOQ formula when it is used to determine economic lot sizes in manufacturing operations?
18–6 Mention several individual costs that should be included in the determination of unit carrying costs. Are all of these costs recorded in the accounting records?
18–7 What assumptions underlie the use of the EOQ formula?
18–8 How is the reorder point determined when demand and lead time are certain?
18–9 Mention two causes of stockouts.
18–10 Identify three approaches to the establishment of safety stocks.
18–11 Why is it difficult to establish safety stocks that minimize the total annual cost of stockouts and holding safety stocks?
18–12 Mention three possible ways of signaling the need for reorders. Which of them requires larger safety stocks? Why?
18–13 Identify and describe three approaches other than the EOQ to inventory management?
18–14 In general, what is the role of the cost accountant in the development and implementation of specialized planning and control models?

REVIEW PROBLEM

Economic Order Quantity, Reorder Point, and Safety Stocks

Walker Company normally uses 5,000 units of a raw material annually. In the past, Walker has placed five orders for 1,000 units each year. This policy has resulted in annual ordering costs of $250 and annual carrying costs of $1,000. Walker has 250 work days per year.

REQUIREMENTS

a) Determine the ordering cost per order and the annual carrying cost per unit.

b) Determine the economic order quantity.

c) Assuming Walker does not maintain safety stocks, determine the annual cost savings obtainable through the use of the economic order quantity.

d) Assuming Walker does not maintain safety stocks and the lead time is 20 work days, determine the reorder point.

e) Assuming Walker desires a safety stock equal to 10 days usage and the lead time is 20 work days, determine the units of safety stock required and the reorder point.

f) What are the annual carrying costs associated with the policy in part (e)?

The solution to this problem is found at the end of the Chapter 18 problems and exercises.

EXERCISES

18–1 Impact of Order Quantity on Costs

Faced with a cash shortage the management of Brown Manufacturing Company ordered a 50 percent reduction in all manufacturing lot sizes. The lot sizes have previously been determined with the use of an EOQ model.

REQUIREMENT

Use the words "increase," "decrease," or "no change" to indicate the impact of management's decision on each of the following:

1. Total annual inventory carrying costs
2. Prime cost per unit
3. Full absorption cost per unit
4. Total annual setup costs
5. Setup costs per lot
6. Total of annual inventory carrying and annual manufacturing costs

18–2 Economic Order Quantity

Barclay Company sells 20,000 pocket calculators evenly throughout the year. The cost of carrying one unit in inventory for one year is $4 and the ordering cost is $64 per order.

REQUIREMENTS

a) Determine the economic order quantity.

b) Determine the annual cost of ordering and the annual cost of carrying inventory associated with the EOQ. (CPA Adapted)

18–3 Economic Order Quantity

The Aron Company requires 40,000 units of Product Q for the year. The units will be required evenly throughout the year. It costs $60 to place an order. It costs $10 to carry a unit in inventory for one year.

REQUIREMENTS

a) Determine the economic order quantity.

b) Determine the annual carrying and ordering costs associated with the EOQ. (CPA Adapted)

18–4 Determining Inventory Costs and EOQ

Goldsticker, Inc., uses 20,000 units of Component X each year. In the past, Goldsticker placed five orders for 4,000 units. This policy resulted in annual ordering and carrying costs of $400 and $10,000, respectively, for Component X.

REQUIREMENTS

a) Determine the ordering cost per order and the carrying cost per unit of Component X.

b) Determine the economic order quantity.

c) Determine the yearly cost savings obtainable through the use of economic order quantities assuming Goldsticker does not maintain safety stocks.

18–5 Determining Inventory Costs and EOQ

Matsum Corporation uses 10,000 pounds of Material Y per year. In the past, Matsum has placed four orders for 2,500 lbs. This policy has resulted in annual ordering costs of $200 and annual carrying costs of $5,000.

REQUIREMENT

Assuming Matsum does not maintain safety stocks, determine the annual cost savings obtainable through the use of economic order quantities.

18–6 Impact of Quantity Discounts on EOQ

All units of a particular item cost $50 each when purchased in quantities of less than 40 units and $45 each when purchased in quantities greater than or equal to 40 units. Transportation-in costs an additional $2 per unit regardless of the order quantity. Variable ordering costs are $9 per order and variable carrying costs equal $2 per unit per year.

REQUIREMENT

Determine the optimal order quantity for this unit assuming an annual demand of 100 units.

18–7 Impact of Quantity Discounts on EOQ

The Elmridge Company currently purchases a particular item in 10 unit lots. Elmridge's annual use of this item is 500 units. Ordering costs are $10 per order. Carrying costs are $4 per unit per year.

REQUIREMENTS

a) Determine the total annual ordering and carrying costs associated with Elmridge's current order size.

b) Determine the economic order quantity for this item.

c) Assume the supplier has recently instituted purchase discounts as follows:

Order size	*Unit discount*
0–9	none (price is $40)
10–19	$0.50
20–49	1.00
50–74	1.50
75–124	2.00
125–up	3.00

Determine the optimal order size. Round calculations to the nearest dollar.

18–8 Reorder Point

The following information is available for Material Y:

Annual use	20,000 units
Working days per year	250
Lead time in working days	30

Material Y is used evenly throughout the year.

REQUIREMENT

Determine the reorder point in units.

18–9 Reorder Point With Safety Stocks

The following information is available for Material B:

Annual use	10,000 units
Working days per year	250
Safety stock in units	400
Normal lead time in working days	30

Material B is used evenly throughout the year.

REQUIREMENT

Determine the reorder point in units. (CPA Adapted)

18–10 Determining Reorder Point and Safety Stock Level

The following information is available for Material A:

Annual use	7,200 units
Working days per year	240
Normal lead time in working days	20
Maximum lead time in working days	45

Material A is used evenly throughout the year.

REQUIREMENT

Determine the reorder point and safety stock necessary to avoid the possibility of a shortage of Material A. (CPA Adapted)

18–11 Minimizing Total Safety Stock and Stockout Costs

The Wood County Supply Depot wants to determine the cost-minimizing safety stock for Part No. 7800. Each stockout will cost $160 and the cost of carrying each unit of safety stock is $4 per year. Part No. 7800 is ordered four times per year.

The probabilities of running out of safety stock at possible safety stock levels are as follows:

Units of safety stock	*Probability of stockout*
5	0.45
10	0.20
20	0.10
30	0.05

REQUIREMENT

Determine the number of units of safety stock that will result in the lowest annual cost.

18–12 Minimizing Total Safety Stock and Stockout Costs

The Beckley Company wishes to determine the cost-minimizing level of safety stock for Product D. The following information is available:

Stockout cost	$120 per occurrence
Carrying cost of safety stock	$ 3 per unit per year
Number of purchase orders	5 per year

The available options open to Beckley are as follows:

Units of safety stock	*Probability of running out of safety stock*
10	50%
20	40%
30	30%
40	20%
50	10%
55	5%

REQUIREMENT

Determine the number of units of safety stock that will result in the lowest annual cost. (CPA Adapted)

PROBLEMS

18–13 Economic Lot Size: Alternative Production Procedures

The Echo Valley Machine Shop manufactures replacement parts for a well-known brand of hand tools. A particular part has a monthly demand of 5,000 units. It can be manufactured on any of three machines as follows:

Machine	*Set-up costs*	*Variable costs per unit*	*Maximum production per setup*
Engine lathe	$ 200	$2.00	500
Turret lathe	800	1.00	2,000
Automatic lathe	1,800	0.50	8,000

Monthly holding and storage costs are $2 per finished unit.

REQUIREMENTS

a) Determine the economic lot size for each machine.

b) Which machine should be used to minimize total monthly inventory costs?

18–14 After-Tax Effect of EOQ Model

Ace Manufacturing uses 8,100 units of Y each year. The differential costs of holding one unit of Y for one year, expressed as a prortion of unit cost, are:

Insurance	0.01
Storage	0.05
Personal property taxes	0.01
Deterioration	0.02
Total	0.09

Each unit of Y costs $400. Variable ordering costs are $50 per order. The income tax rate is 50 percent and the after-tax opportunity cost of inventory investments amounts to 8 percent. Ace currently places one order for 8,100 units each year.

REQUIREMENTS

a) Determine the economic order quantity.

b) Determine the after-tax effect on net income of the use of the economic order quantity.

18–15 EOQ, ROP, and Shelf Life

The Harrison Memorial Hospital Pharmacy places orders for a particular inventory item in lot sizes of 800 units. Additional information about this inventory item is as follows:

Annual demand	12,000 units
Ordering cost	$15 per order
Unit purchase cost	$20 per unit

Inventory carrying costs are estimated to be 20 percent of average inventory investment.

REQUIREMENTS

a) Determine the optimal order quantity for this inventory item.

b) Determine the total annual ordering and carrying costs associated with the current order quantity and the one determined in part (a).

c) Assuming that the pharmacy is open 300 days per year, that average daily demand for this inventory item is constant, and that the lead time required to fill an order is five working days, determine the optimal reorder point in units.

d) The shelf life of this item is limited. Assuming that shelf life is based on the number of days it may be used *after* it is placed in inventory, determine the optimal lot size under each of the following circumstances. (Assume a 300-day year.)

1. Shelf life = 5 days.
2. Shelf life = 50 days.

18–16 Determining EOQ, ROP, and Cost Savings

The Astro Chemical Company operates 250 days a year. Each day Astro uses 80 barrels of a volatile chemical. Because of the chemical's unstable nature, annual storage costs are $15 per barrel. Fortunately the supplier of this chemical is very dependable and no "safety" stocks are required. The lead time required to receive an order is three work days. Variable order-processing costs are $9.60 per order.

REQUIREMENTS

a) Determine the economic order quantity and the reorder point in units.

b) Assuming that on the first day of the work year Astro receives a shipment of 400 barrels, develop a sawtooth diagram to illustrate the operation of the inventory policy developed in part (a) over a 16-day period. (*Hint:* Use a dashed line to represent total inventory ordered and on hand.)

c) Assume Astro is considering the desirability of renting a completely automated order-processing and payment system. This system would increase yearly fixed costs by $1,500 per inventory item and reduce the variable ordering costs to $0.93 per order.

   1. Determine the maximum benefit of renting the system for one year.
   2. Evaluate this system from the point of view of the supplier.

18–17 Determining EOQ, ROP, and Safety Stocks

SaPane Company is a regional distributor of automobile window glass. With the introduction of new subcompact cars and the expected high level of consumer demand, management recognizes a need to determine the total inventory cost associated with maintaining an optimal supply of replacement windshields for the new subcompact cars introduced by major manufacturers. SaPane is expecting a daily demand for 36 windshields. The purchase price of each windshield is $50.

Other costs associated with ordering and maintaining an inventory of these windshields are as follows:

- The historical ordering costs incurred in the Purchase Order Department for placing and processing orders are as follows:

Year	*Orders placed and processed*	*Total ordering costs*
19x3	20	$12,300
19x4	55	12,475
19x5	100	12,700

  Management expects the ordering costs to increase 16 percent in 19x6 over the amounts and rates experienced in these years.

- The windshield manufacturer charges SaPane a $75 shipping fee per order.
- A clerk in the Receiving Department receives, inspects, and secures the windshields as they arrive from the manufacturer. This activity requires 8 hours per order received. This clerk has no other responsibilities and is paid at the rate of $9 per hour. Related variable overhead costs in this department are applied at the rate of $2.50 per hour.
- Additional warehouse space will have to be rented to store the new windshields. Space can be rented as needed in a public warehouse at an estimated cost of $2,500 per year plus $5.35 per windshield.
- Breakage cost is estimated to be 6 percent of the average inventory value.
- Taxes and insurance on the inventory are $1.15 per windshield.
- The desired before-tax rate of return on the investment in inventory is 21 percent of the purchase price.

Six working days are required from the time the order is placed with the manufacturer until it is received. SaPane uses a 300-day work year when making economic order quantity computations.

REQUIREMENTS

a) Calculate the following values for SaPane Company for 19x6.
   1. The value for ordering cost that should be used in the EOQ formula
   2. The value for carrying costs that should be used in the EOQ formula
   3. The economic order quantity
   4. The minimum annual relevant cost at the economic order quantity point
   5. The reorder point in units

b) Without being influenced by your answer to part (a), assume the economic c der quantity is 400 units, the carrying cost is $28 per unit, and the stockout cost is $720 per stockout. SaPane wants to determine the proper level of safety stock in order to minimize its relevant costs. Using the following probability schedule, determine the proper amount of safety stock.

Units of safety stock	*Probability of stockout on each reorder*
0	0.25
60	0.12
120	0.05
180	0.02

(CMA Adapted)

18–18 Estimating Costs for Use in Inventory Models

The Corbin Furniture Company manufactures several types of occasional furniture in lots of varying sizes. The controller has recently returned from an executive development program where he learned that inventory models might be profitably employed to determine optimal lot sizes. These models require information about annual demand, setup costs, per-unit variable costs, and the opportunity cost of funds invested in inventory.

The controller decided to test such a model on inventory item 10-15X1. He quickly determined the annual demand to be 100 units and the treasurer told him that Corbin's before-tax opportunity cost of funds was 25 percent. From his own records he knew that the materials cost was $60 per unit and that variable overhead was 80 percent of direct-labor costs. That left him with the problem of determining direct-labor costs.

After an extensive analysis of job-cost sheets, he accumulated the following information on batch size and direct-labor costs:

Batch number	*Batch size (units)*	*Direct-labor cost*
1	35	$ 800
2	55	1,000
3	50	900
4	26	700
5	20	600
6	25	650
7	45	1,050
8	40	700
9	28	700
10	57	1,200
11	38	1,000
12	60	1,400

REQUIREMENTS

a) Use the high-low method of cost estimation to determine the "fixed" labor cost per batch and variable labor cost per unit.

b) Develop an equation that represents the total out-of-pocket costs associated with each batch.

c) Determine the economic lot size using the results of parts (a) and (b) and the given information.

d) Using either a scatter diagram or a computer program for the least-squares method, estimate the "fixed" and variable labor costs associated with each batch.

e) Using the results of part (d), develop an equation that represents the total out-of-pocket costs associated with each batch.

f) Determine the economic lot size using the results of parts (d) and (e) and the given information.

g) Assuming the answer to part (f) is correct, determine the cost of prediction error of using the economic order quantity developed in part (c).

18–19 Inventory Requirements of Small and Large Firms

The Elastic Dollar Discount Store and Mom and Dad's Appliance Shop are located on opposite sides of a busy street. Both stores sell auto cassette decks. They incur identical costs to order and carry the cassette decks ($20 per order and $2 per unit per year), charge identical prices, and base purchases on economic order quantity models. Last year, Elastic Dollar sold 1,125 auto cassette decks, whereas Mom and Dad's sold 125. Ms. Well, the owner of Mom and Dad's, was pleased until she learned that Elastic Dollar's return on money invested in cassette decks was considerably larger than Mom and Dad's.

REQUIREMENT

Given the existence of identical selling prices and purchase costs, what factor(s) is (are) responsible for Elastic Dollar's higher return on inventory investments? Ignore safety stocks in any computations.

18–20 Minimizing Total Safety Stock and Stockout Costs

For a single inventory cycle, total stockout and carrying costs are minimized at the critical probability of carrying excess inventory, P^*, that equalizes the expected cost of carrying one additional unit throughout the cycle and the expected cost of being one unit short during the cycle. Let:

Y = Cost of carrying one additional unit through the inventory cycle
Z = Cost of being one unit short during the inventory cycle

REQUIREMENTS

a) Develop a formula to determine P^* from Y and Z.

b) Each Sunday, the Main Street News Stand purchases copies of a New York newspaper for \$0.80 and sells them for \$2.00. Papers unsold at the end of the day are worthless. Historical data pertaining to Sunday's newspaper are as follows:

Demand for papers	*Frequency*
140	24
150	36
160	20
170	10
180	8
190	2

How many copies should the Main Street News Stand stock?

18–21 Safety Stocks to Provide a Service Level

The Normal Supply Company sells 40,000 units of part RX600 each year. The annual carrying cost per unit of this part is \$8. Normal's variable costs of placing an order total \$25. Based on an analysis of delivery times and daily demand, management has determined that lead-time demand is normally distributed with a mean of 1,000 units and a standard deviation of 200 units.

REQUIREMENTS

a) Determine the economic order quantity and the reorder point ignoring safety stock requirements.

b) What is the probability of a stockout during each lead time if no safety stocks are maintained?

c) Determine the reorder point and safety stock levels that would reduce the probability of a stockout during each lead time to:

1. 20 percent
2. 10 percent
3. 5 percent
4. 1 percent

d) Indicate the annual safety stock carrying costs required to provide the service levels indicated in part (c).

18–22 PERT: Critical and Slack-Path Analysis (Appendix)

A recently prepared staff report recommends changes in certain operating procedures. Implementation of the recommendations is being considered. The process of implementation would require review by a number of departments according to the following estimated network. (All times are shown in days.)

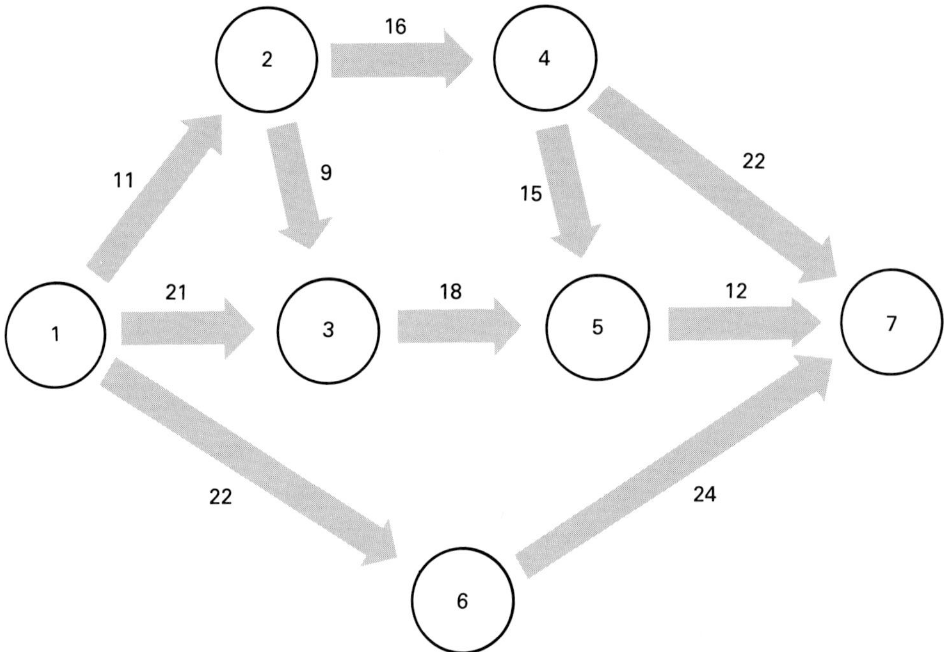

REQUIREMENTS

a) Identify the critical path.

b) For each activity, specify the earliest time it can begin, the earliest time it can be completed, and the slack time. (CIA Adapted)

18–23 Developing a PERT Network and Determining Critical Path (Appendix)

International Industries Limited (IIL) is considering the desirability of building a new manufacturing facility. Before approving the project, management has requested an estimate of the time required between granting approval and full-scale production. The following information is available about the activities necessary before the new facility attains full operating capacity.

Activity	*Immediately preceding activity*	t_e *(months)*
Install equipment	Build plant, ship equipment	2
Train workers	Hire workers	1
Ship equipment	Order and build equipment	3
Order and build equipment	Finalize plans	3
Hire workers	Relocate management personnel	4
Build plant	Finalize plans	10
Relocate management personnel	Finalize plans	2
Start-up phase	Install equipment, train workers	3
Finalize plans	None	3

Full operating capacity is attained after the start-up phase.

REQUIREMENTS

a) Develop a PERT network for the listed activities. (*Hint:* Start with the last activity and work backwards.)

b) Determine the estimated time required to attain full operating capacity. Clearly identify the critical path.

18–24 Developing a PERT Network and Determining Critical Path (Appendix)

The Dryfus Company specializes in large construction projects. The company management regularly employs the Program Evaluation and Review Technique (PERT) in planning and coordinating its construction projects. The following schedule of separable activities and their expected completion times have been developed for an office building that Dryfus Company is to construct.

	Activity description	*Predecessor activity*	*Expected activity completion time (in weeks)*
a.	Excavation	—	2
b.	Foundation	a	3
c.	Underground utilities	a	7
d.	Rough plumbing	b	4
e.	Framing	b	5
f.	Roofing	e	3
g.	Electrical work	f	3
h.	Interior walls	d, g	4
i.	Finish plumbing	h	2
j.	Exterior finishing	f	6
k.	Landscaping	c, i, j	2

REQUIREMENTS

a) Develop a PERT network for the activities listed.

b) Determine the estimated time required to complete the office building. Clearly identify the critical path. (CMA Adapted)

18–25 Discussion of a PERT Application (Appendix)

The Capital City Construction Company has just been awarded a \$1.5 million contract to resurface the main runway at Triangle Airport. Tentative plans call for closing the airport during the final 12 days of the project, October 1 through October 12. Because this will cause considerable inconvenience to passengers and a loss of revenue to area businesses, the airport authority has included in the contract a clause offering a $10,000-a-day bonus for every day the project is completed before October 16. However, a $10,000-a-day penalty will be assessed for every day the airport is closed beyond October 16. Because of the scheduled visit of a VIP, the airport cannot be closed before October 1.

REQUIREMENTS

a) Develop an equation to represent total project revenues.

b) How might PERT/Time and the PERT/Cost resource allocation supplement assist the Capital City Construction Company to obtain maximum profits on this project?

18–26 Analyzing a PERT Network for Critical Path and Slack

Whitson Company has just ordered a new computer for its financial information system. The present computer is fully utilized and no longer adequate for all the financial applications Whitson would like to implement. The present financial system applications must all be modified before they can be run on the new computer. Additionally, new applications that Whitson would like to have developed and implemented have been identified and ranked according to priority.

Sally Rose, Manager of Data Processing, is responsible for implementing the new computer system. Rose listed the specific activities that had to be completed and determined the estimated time to complete each activity. In addition, she prepared a network diagram to aid in the coordination of the activities. The network diagram and the activity list are as follows:

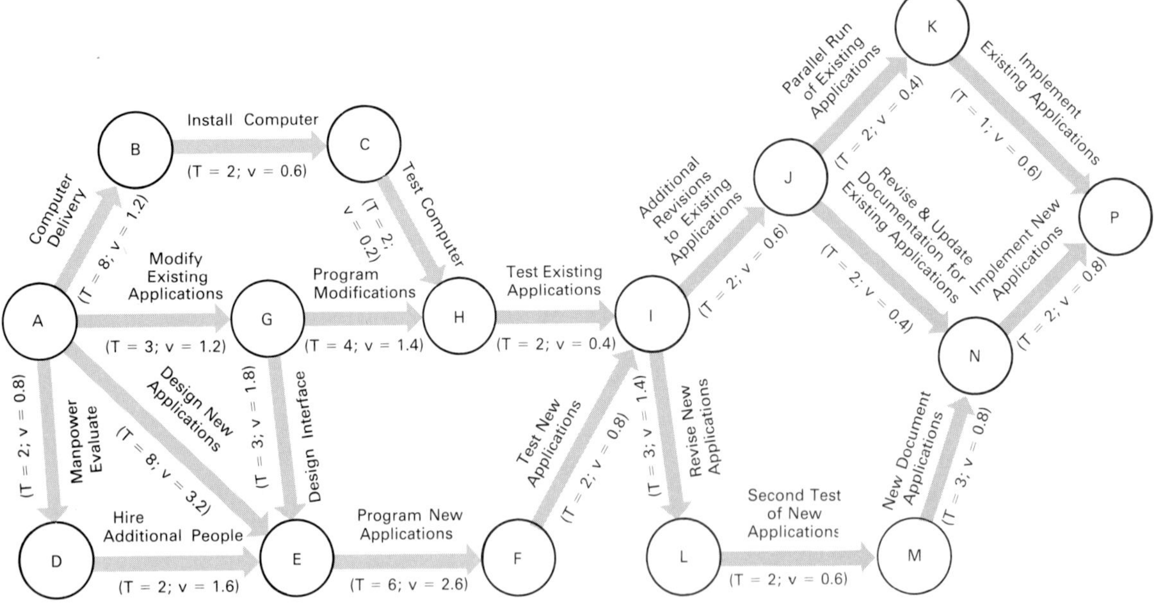

Activity	*Description of activity*	*Expected time required to complete (in weeks)*	*Variance in expected time (in weeks)*
AB	Wait for delivery of computer from manufacturer.	8	1.2
BC	Install computer.	2	0.6
CH	Perform general test of computer.	2	0.2
AD	Complete an evaluation of manpower requirements.	2	0.8
DE	Hire additional programmers and operators.	2	1.6
AG	Design modifications to existing applications.	3	1.2
GH	Program modifications to existing applications.	4	1.4
HI	Test modified applications on new computer.	2	0.4
IJ	Revise existing applications as needed.	2	0.6
JN	Revise and update documentation for existing applications as modified.	2	0.4
JK	Run existing applications in parallel on new and old computers.	2	0.4
KP	Implement existing applications as modified on the new computer.	1	0.6
AE	Design new applications.	8	3.2
GE	Design interface between existing and new applications.	3	1.8
EF	Program new applications.	6	2.6
FI	Test new applications on new computer.	2	0.8
IL	Revise new applications as needed.	3	1.4
LM	Conduct second test of new applications on new computer.	2	0.6
MN	Prepare documentation for the new applications.	3	0.8
NP	Implement new applications on the new computer.	2	0.8

REQUIREMENTS

a) Determine the number of weeks that will be required to fully implement Whitson Company's financial information system (that is, both existing and new applications) on its new computer and identify the activities that are critical to completing the project.

b) Whitson Company's top management would like to reduce the time necessary to begin operation of the entire system.

1. Which activities should Sally Rose attempt to reduce in order to implement the system sooner? Explain your answer.
2. Discuss how Sally Rose might proceed to reduce the time of these activities.

c) The General Accounting Manager would like the existing financial information system applications to be modified and operational in 22 weeks.

1. Determine the number of weeks that will be required to modify the existing financial information system applications and make them operational.
2. What is the probability of implementing the existing financial information system applications within 22 weeks? (CMA Adapted)

18–27 Developing a PERT Network and Estimating Completion Time With Uncertainty (Appendix)

Presented is information pertaining to the activities required to complete a project.

Activity	*Immediately preceding activity*	*Time estimates (in days)* Optimistic	Most likely	Pessimistic
A	None	4	5	12
B	A	4	6	14
C	A	2	5	14
D	B	8	9	13
E	C	1	2	15
F	D,E	2	5	8

REQUIREMENTS

a) Calculate the expected completion time of each activity.

b) Develop a PERT network for the project.

c) Identify the activities on the critical path and indicate the expected time required to complete the project.

d) What is the probability of completing the project within 25 days?

e) Mention several factors that limit the analyses performed in parts (a) through (d).

18–28 PERT/Cost Resource Allocation Supplement (Appendix) (This problem is a continuation of Problem 18–27.)

Assume that management wants to reduce the expected time to complete the project (discussed in Problem 18–27) to 24 days. Estimates of the normal cost, crash cost, and crash time of each activity are as follows:

Activity	*Normal cost*	*Crash time*	*Crash cost*
A	$1,000	4 days	$1,200
B	1,800	3	2,600
C	900	4.5	1,250
D	2,000	5.5	4,000
E	1,250	3	1,380
F	1,200	4	1,350

REQUIREMENTS

a) How should the project be changed to reduce the expected completion time to 24 days? (*Hint:* Normal time = t_e.)

b) What additional problems would be incurred if it became necessary to reduce the expected completion time to 17 days? 15 days?

18–29 PERT/Cost Resource Allocation Supplement (Appendix)

The Tipton Company acquires retail hardware stores that are having difficulties or have recently gone out of business. Generally the interior of stores can be used with little additional cost or effort. Tipton usually stocks the store with its own brands of merchandise, hires new employees, and modifies the building exterior to match the company's standard store exterior.

The company has experienced difficulty in getting the stores opened on schedule. The person responsible for store openings in the past had many years experience in the retail business and managed the opening process on an ad hoc basis. The new manager for store openings has less retail experience but has used network analysis to organize and control store openings for a previous employer.

The new manager for store openings has suggested that network analysis be applied to the new Fox Village store. The network diagram and accompanying schedule that follow have been prepared for the Fox Village store. The schedule describes the activities, the estimated normal times of each activity, and the normal cost of each activity required to open the store. The schedule also presents the crash time for those activities that can be accomplished in a shorter time period and the related additional cost required to achieve the crash time. The sales manager estimates that the Fox Village store should produce a contribution to corporate profits of about $2,000 per week.

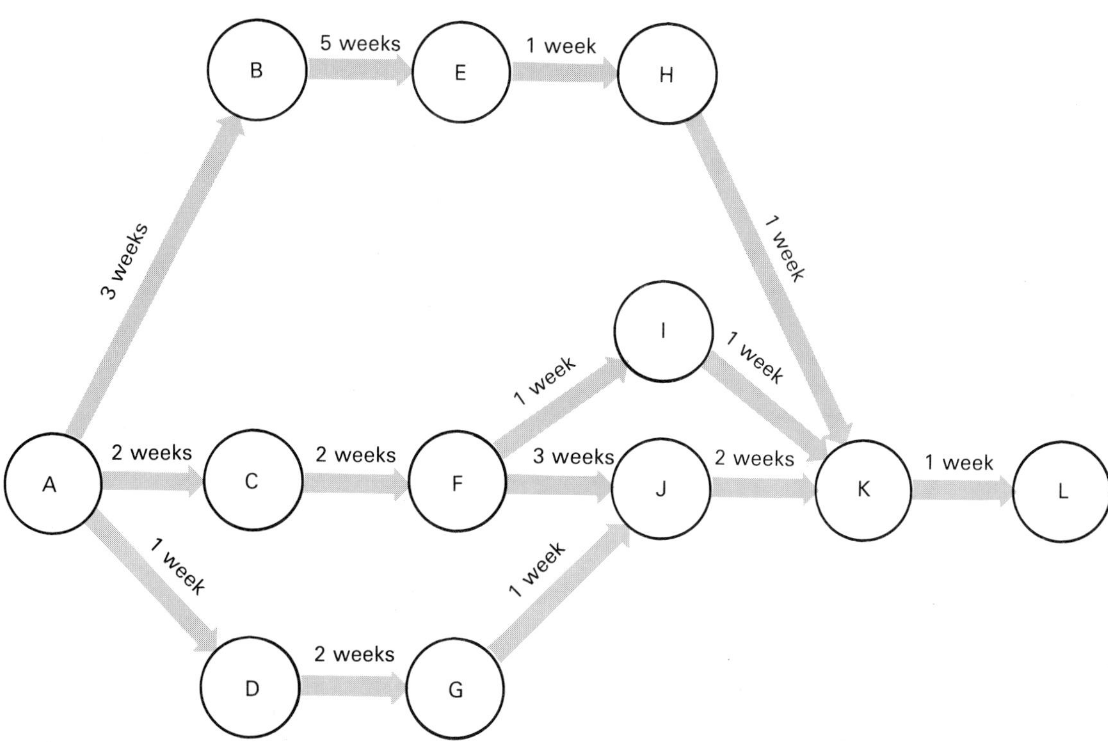

Activity	*Description of activity*	*Normal time (in weeks)*	*Crash time (in weeks)*	*Normal cost*	*Incremental cost to achieve crash time*
AB	Design exterior.	3	1	$ 5,000	$4,500
AC	Determine inventory needs.	2	NC	500	0
AD	Develop staffing plan.	1	NC	500	0
BE	Do exterior structural work.	5	3	27,000	3,500
EH	Paint exterior.	1	NC	4,000	0
HK	Install exterior signs.	1	NC	15,000	0
CF	Order inventory.	2	NC	1,500	0
FI	Develop special prices for opening.	1	NC	2,000	0
IK	Advertise opening and special prices.	1	NC	8,000	0
FJ	Receive inventory.	3	2	4,000	2,000
DG	Acquire staff.	2	1	3,000	1,000
GJ	Train staff.	1	NC	5,000	0
JK	Stock shelves.	2	1	3,500	1,500
KL	Make final preparations for grand opening.	1	NC	6,000	0

NC = No change in time is possible.

REQUIREMENTS

a) Determine the normal critical path for the opening of the Fox Village store and identify:

1. Those activities on the critical path
2. The length in weeks required to open the store
3. The normal costs to be incurred in opening the store

b) What is the minimum time in which the Fox Village store could be opened and what are the costs incurred to achieve this earlier opening? Support your answer with an appropriate explanation and calculations.

c) Should Tipton Company proceed with the normal schedule or should it attempt a crash program? Explain your answer. (CMA Adapted)

18–30 Developing Network and Using PERT/Cost Resource Allocation Supplement (Appendix)

Presented is information pertaining to the activities required to complete a project.

		Normal		*Crash*	
Activity	*Immediately preceding activity*	*Time (in days)*	*Cost*	*Time (in days)*	*Cost*
A	None	5	$1,200	3	$2,000
B	A	4	1,600	3	2,800
C	A	8	2,000	5	3,800
D	A	3	1,600	2	2,800
E	B	3	1,200	2	1,600
F	D	4	1,200	2	1,600
G	C,E,F	5	1,600	4	2,100

REQUIREMENTS

a) Develop a PERT network for the project. Be sure to clearly identify the critical path and T_E and T_L for each event.

b) How should the project be changed if the project must be completed in 13 days?

c) What is the total normal cost for the project as it is developed in part (a) and the total crash cost of the project as presented in part (b)?

d) What factors may limit the usefulness of the analysis performed in parts (a) through (c)?

SOLUTION TO REVIEW PROBLEM

a) Ordering costs per order = $250 ÷ 5 = $50.00

Annual carrying costs per unit = $1,000 ÷ (1,000/2) = $2.00

b) $Q^* = \sqrt{\dfrac{2 \times 5{,}000 \times \$50}{\$2}} = 500$ units

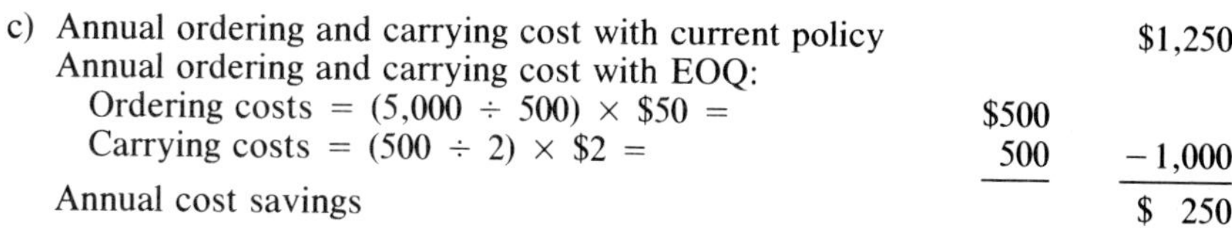

c)

Annual ordering and carrying cost with current policy		$1,250
Annual ordering and carrying cost with EOQ:		
Ordering costs = (5,000 ÷ 500) × $50 =	$500	
Carrying costs = (500 ÷ 2) × $2 =	500	– 1,000
Annual cost savings		$ 250

d) Reorder point = 20 × (5,000 ÷ 250) = 400 units

e) Safety stock required = 10 × (5,000 ÷ 250) = 200 units

Reorder point with safety stock = 400 + 200 = 600 units

Because the reorder point with safety stocks exceeds the economic order quantity of 500 units, Walker would reorder when the units on hand plus the units on order equal 600 units.

f) Annual carrying costs = [(500 ÷ 2) + 200] × $2 = $900

19 Quality Control and Variance Investigation

INTRODUCTION
SOURCES OF VARIANCES
DECISION SIGNIFICANCE OF VARIANCES
THE DECISION TO INVESTIGATE
RESPONSIBILITY FOR VARIANCES
QUALITY COSTS
SUMMARY
APPENDIX: ESTIMATING THE PROBABILITY A PROCESS IS IN CONTROL

INTRODUCTION

PERFORMANCE REPORTS AND ACCOUNTING VARIANCES ARE INTENDED TO alert management to the existence of potential problems and opportunities. Occasionally materials price variances are self-explanatory, but most variances are not. To determine the cause of variances, additional investigation is required. This investigation may be as simple as asking a machine operator "What happened?" or as complex as stopping an assembly line or shutting down a power plant for inspection by highly trained personnel.

In recent years, managers of American companies have become increasingly concerned with product quality as they try to compete with high-quality, low-priced imports. Increasingly, managers have come to realize that the old adage "You get what you pay for" does not always apply to quality. This is especially true when recognition is given to the costs of warranty repairs, legal liability, and product recalls, as well as the opportunity cost of lost sales. Many managers now believe higher quality products give companies a better competitive position and that improved quality leads to higher productivity and lower unit costs. For these reasons, quality control has become an important issue in American companies.

The purposes of this chapter are to classify cost variances on the basis of their underlying cause, introduce basic concepts involved in quality control, examine alternative criteria used in making the decision to investigate a variance, and identify the types of costs incurred because of poor quality. In this chapter variance investigation is developed for first-line management and operating personnel rather than for top-level management. This shift in emphasis is desirable for a number of reasons. First, monthly performance reports are not timely enough to obtain the maximum control benefits of variance investigation. Second, monthly reports are highly aggregated, reflecting the net result of many favorable and unfavorable events. Finally, monthly reports are stated in terms of dollars, whereas the underlying activities they summarize, and operating personnel control on a continuous basis, are stated in nondollar measures.

SOURCES OF VARIANCES

Four possible sources[1] of production variances are:

1. Random fluctuations in efficient operations
2. Measurement errors in accumulating production data
3. Inappropriate standards
4. Operating errors

Random Fluctuations

Although an aura of precision surrounds the use of standards, a reality of imprecision clouds their development. Standards are point estimates, but the expected values used in developing them have a probability distribution. Indeed, variability is inherent in all production processes. Random fluctuations in materials usage and labor or machine hours occur under efficient operating conditions. They are expected and can be reduced only by changing the product or production process. They are accepted because management believes the costs of reducing the variability exceed the benefits of reduction.

Example 19–1

When properly adjusted, the Natural Spring Water Company's bottle-washing machine breaks 2 to 4 percent of the bottles it cleans. The standard allowance for breakage is set at the expected value of 3 percent. Breakage could be reduced to 1 percent by purchasing a new machine. However, a special study indicates that the cost of such a machine exceeds any potential benefits.

Variance investigation costs money and no benefits are derived if the investigation concludes that no changes in activities or standards are required. In making the decision to investigate, consideration should be given to costs, possible benefits, and the probability that the variance is merely a random fluctuation. If the variance is due to random variability in the process, an investigation should not be made because there has been no change in the process. For example, Natural Spring Water Company probably would not investigate a washing machine breakage rate of 3.2 percent. Although this is an unfavorable deviation from the 3 percent standard, it is well within the normal range of 2 to 4 percent.

Measurement Errors

Improper assignment of materials, labor, or machine time may cause variances. The assignment of incorrect quantities of materials to jobs is an example of a measurement error. Such "errors" may average out to standard during the month, but they are sources of variances in reports developed for short time periods. Variance investigation may reveal that production is under control, but recordkeeping needs improvement. Perhaps a greater danger is the concealment of nonrandom variances by the improper assignment of materials and time. When this happens, variances cannot signal a real need to adjust plans and/or operations.

---

[1] The outline used in this section is based on Joel S. Demski, *Information Analysis* (Reading, Mass.: Addison-Wesley, 1972), Chapter 6. However, Demski mentions five sources of production variances. These authors' list includes two of Demski's sources, prediction errors and model errors, under the caption, "inappropriate standards."

Inappropriate Standards

Even if operations are efficient, variances will occur if the standards are inappropriate for the product or production process. Three possible causes of inappropriate standards are:

1. The use of tight standards
2. The use of a wrong model to develop standards
3. The use of wrong data in the model

Tight Standards If standards are intentionally set above expected levels of productivity, unfavorable variances should occur. Under these circumstances, the decision to investigate should be based on a comparison of results with expectations rather than on a comparison of results with standards.

Wrong Model Variances may also result if the wrong model is used to develop standards. For example, labor standards based on an analysis of a prior period's experience will result in a series of favorable efficiency variances if the production process follows the learning-curve phenomenon.

Wrong Data Variances occur if the data used in developing standards contain measurement errors or were based on process conditions that no longer exist. Failure to include changes in costs or in the production process in a multiproduct linear programming model is an example of not adjusting to changed conditions.

Operating Errors

Variances can result from a failure to follow prescribed procedures. Operating errors are favorable if the actual procedures are more efficient than the prescribed procedures; they are unfavorable if the actual procedures are less efficient than the prescribed procedures. Both favorable and unfavorable operating errors deserve investigation. Management may wish to study favorable variances due to operating errors to improve operations in the future and to ensure that company policies were not violated in achieving the favorable variances. Management certainly wants to avoid conditions that lead to unfavorable variances whenever possible.

DECISION SIGNIFICANCE OF VARIANCES

The decision significance of a variance depends on its source. Assuming that standards are based on efficient operating conditions and that management is aware of the variability inherent in the current production process, the variance may have one of the following:

1. No decision significance
2. Planning significance
3. Control significance

No Decision Significance

Variances resulting from random fluctuations inherent in the current production process have no decision significance. Knowledge of a random fluctuation will not result in a reassessment of the organizations's plans or an attempt to alleviate its cause. Management does not want to spend time and money investigating random fluctuations because their cause, the current production process, is already known.

Planning Significance

Variances resulting from inappropriate standards have planning significance. Such variances should be investigated and once their cause is determined, appropriate adjustments should be made in standards and plans. Changes in product mix, production volume, and/or production procedures may be necessary.

In Appendix A to Chapter 15, linear programming was used to determine the optimal production mix and volume of multiproduct firms. A change in objective function or constraint coefficients may result in changes in the optimal production mix and volume. Accordingly, if it is determined that the coefficients are wrong, the model's solution should be reevaluated. When indifference ranges are developed for the original solution, additional analysis may not be necessary if the new coefficients are within the original indifference range.

Example 19–2

In Example 15–26, the standard cost of raw materials for Product C was \$5 and the linear programming indifference range was $-\infty$ to $+\$6.50$. An increase in the cost of raw materials to \$6 will not change the optimal solution. However, standards should be changed to reflect the increased materials' cost, and management may wish to reevaluate the acceptability of the current profit plan.

Variances caused by favorable operating errors may also have planning significance. If an employee develops a more efficient way of accomplishing a task, management will want to incorporate this efficiency into the organization's plans and standards.

Control Significance

Variances caused by measurement errors and unfavorable operating errors have control significance. These variances should also be investigated and appropriate actions taken to alleviate their cause. Possible causes include equipment failure, machine out of adjustment, a decline in raw materials quality, poor workmanship, and poor recordkeeping. The latter two may, in turn, be caused by lack of supervision, lack of proper training, inexperience, lack of motivation, deterioration in working conditions, excessive workloads, and even sabotage. Favorable variances resulting from unethical or illegal actions, or actions that violate company policies also have control significance. Action should be taken to ensure that company policies are followed and that employees and managers act in an ethical and legal manner.

THE DECISION TO INVESTIGATE

Once management is aware of the inherent variability of a production process, variances caused by random fluctuations in the process have no decision significance and should not be investigated because variance investigation is a costly activity. To avoid excessive investigation of random fluctuations, three types of variance investigation criteria have been developed:

1. Arbitrary criteria based on "materiality"

2. Criteria based on statistical significance
3. Criteria based on expected costs

Materiality

Sometimes either professional judgment or accepted practice is used to set investigation criteria at some percentage of standard. The rule might call for the investigation of all variances greater than 5 percent of standard. Inherent in this criteria is the assumption that variances of 5 percent or less are caused by random fluctuations, whereas variances greater than 5 percent are caused by nonrandom factors. This may or may not be the case.

Example 19–3

The Natural Spring Water Company's standards call for 64 ounces of water in each bottle. A sample of filled bottles discloses that the water contained in the bottles averages 65 ounces. If a 5 percent materiality criterion were used, management would not investigate the cause of this variance because the 1-ounce variance (65 ounces − 64 ounces) is less than the allowed 3.2-ounce variance (0.05 × 64 ounces).

Materiality criteria may be established by considering the resources available for variance investigation. If management has only enough time or money to investigate 10 percent of all variances, they may investigate the largest 10 percent of the variances for a day. This criterion may result in large variances being investigated some days and smaller ones on other days because the variances included in the 10 percent depend on the size of all variances.

The problem with using criteria based on materiality is that it is difficult, if not impossible, to distinguish between variances due to random fluctuations and those due to the process being out of control. Without some knowledge of the production process, management may investigate a variance when it is simply a random fluctuation or fail to investigate a variance when it is caused by the process being out of control. Investigation based on statistical significance overcomes this limitation of materiality criteria.

Statistical Significance

Investigation criteria based on statistical significance compare actual results with previous results obtained *under efficient operating conditions*. If the probability of obtaining a variance as large as or larger than the actual one is small, the variance is investigated. Note that the criteria used to evaluate performance must be developed from observations of efficient production under normal operating conditions. When actual results are within statistical limits, the operation is said to be under **statistical process control** (SPC). That is, the variances follow a normal distribution and are presumably due to random fluctuations that are an inherent part of the production process.

Statistical process control can be used for both attributes and variables data. **Attributes data** refer to measurements used to classify a situation into one of two or more categories such as (1) number of defects per unit of output or (2) conforming and nonconforming products. **Variables data** refer to continuous measurements taken on a physical characteristic such as weight, length, or thickness. A complete discussion of SPC is beyond the scope of this text, but the following discussion will introduce concepts involved in applying SPC to variables data.[2]

SPC is based on control charts. A **control chart** is a graphic illustration of data taken from a process. The chart includes a central line showing the average of the process and upper and lower control limits based on probabilities derived from statistical theory. Our primary focus in this section is on the development of control charts based on efficient operating conditions.

Control charts are used in SPC because a process that is in statistical control has certain characteristics related to variability and location. **Variability** or dispersion refers to the spread of the distribution and is measured in terms of the process standard deviation. **Location** refers to the average of the distribution. The process mean ($\overline{X}$, pronounced X-bar) is a measure of location. If the distribution follows a normal curve, we can derive the characteristics of the distribution using statistical theory.

In statistical process control, $\overline{X}$ and R control charts are used for variables data. Based on samples taken from the population, **$\overline{X}$ charts** show the average values of the variable being measured within each sample and ***R* charts** show ranges of the data within each sample. R charts are used to estimate the process variability. Both $\overline{X}$ and R control charts are needed to determine if a process is in control.

***R* Charts** The first step in using statistical process control is to develop an R chart to determine if the process is in control with respect to variability. If the range within individual samples is too large, the process is unstable, and hence the sample data do not come from a process operating under efficient conditions. Developing an R chart requires taking samples from the process and determining the range of the individual observations in each sample.

Example 19–4 As the first step in using SPC, the Natural Spring Water Company has taken 30 samples of five bottles each and measured the weight of the water in each bottle. The weights of the water in the first sample of five bottles consisted of the following:

Item number	*Weight (in ounces)*
1	65.0
2	66.5
3	64.8
4	63.6
5	65.7

The **range** (R) of a sample is the difference between the highest measurement and the lowest measurement. For this sample, the range is 2.9 ounces (66.5 − 63.6). Exhibit 19–1 shows data and R values for the 30 samples.

[2] For further information on statistical process control see Eugene L. Grant, and Richard S. Leavenworth, *Statistical Quality Control,* 5th ed. (New York: McGraw-Hill, 1980).

We can plot the data in Exhibit 19–1 on a graph to form an R chart. See Exhibit 19–2. The central line on an R chart is the mean of the R values, $\overline{R}$ (pronounced R-bar). $\overline{R}$ is calculated by dividing the sum of the ranges for all samples by the number of samples. In equation form,

$$\overline{R} = \frac{\Sigma R_i}{k} \tag{19–1}$$

where

$\overline{R}$ = Mean of R values
R_i = Range for sample i
k = Number of samples

Using Eq. 19–1, the central line on the R chart is 2.58 ounces (77.4 ÷ 30).

EXHIBIT 19–1 Weight of Water for 30 Samples of $n = 5$

Sample number	Observation 1	2	3	4	5	R	$\overline{X}$
1	65.0	66.5	64.8	63.6	65.7	2.9	65.12
2	66.4	64.0	64.7	62.9	64.4	3.5	64.48
3	64.3	63.5	66.0	63.8	65.1	2.5	64.54
4	63.4	65.3	65.0	63.0	66.1	3.1	64.56
5	67.0	65.2	64.1	64.9	65.6	2.9	65.36
6	63.6	63.8	65.0	65.9	64.6	2.3	64.58
7	66.8	63.6	63.5	64.5	67.3	3.8	65.14
8	64.2	64.1	65.0	66.4	66.3	2.3	65.20
9	65.3	64.1	66.4	65.0	64.6	2.3	65.08
10	65.1	64.4	65.3	64.1	63.8	1.5	64.54
11	65.3	65.1	64.7	64.6	64.2	1.1	64.78
12	65.0	65.6	64.1	66.5	64.5	2.4	65.14
13	68.0	65.9	63.1	64.8	64.1	4.9	65.18
14	63.8	65.3	65.8	65.2	65.8	2.0	65.18
15	66.3	66.3	65.7	64.5	64.1	2.2	65.38
16	66.4	65.0	65.3	64.1	64.7	2.3	65.10
17	63.8	63.7	65.9	66.7	63.4	3.3	64.70
18	64.3	64.8	64.3	65.7	65.9	1.6	65.00
19	66.8	65.3	66.8	65.1	65.0	1.8	65.80
20	65.4	66.0	64.6	67.8	65.4	3.2	65.84
21	63.9	66.1	64.8	67.6	65.3	3.7	65.54
22	67.3	64.5	67.0	67.5	65.7	3.0	66.40
23	65.4	65.4	64.4	64.8	62.8	2.6	64.56
24	64.6	65.4	65.0	64.8	62.7	2.7	64.50
25	66.0	64.4	65.0	65.2	65.0	1.6	65.12
26	66.1	64.6	67.0	66.4	66.4	2.4	66.10
27	67.0	63.7	64.7	65.1	62.8	4.2	64.66
28	65.0	65.1	64.5	65.1	65.1	0.6	64.96
29	64.1	63.9	64.7	65.0	65.0	1.1	64.54
30	63.8	66.5	62.9	65.0	65.8	3.6	64.80
						77.4	1,951.88

EXHIBIT 19–2 ***R* Chart**

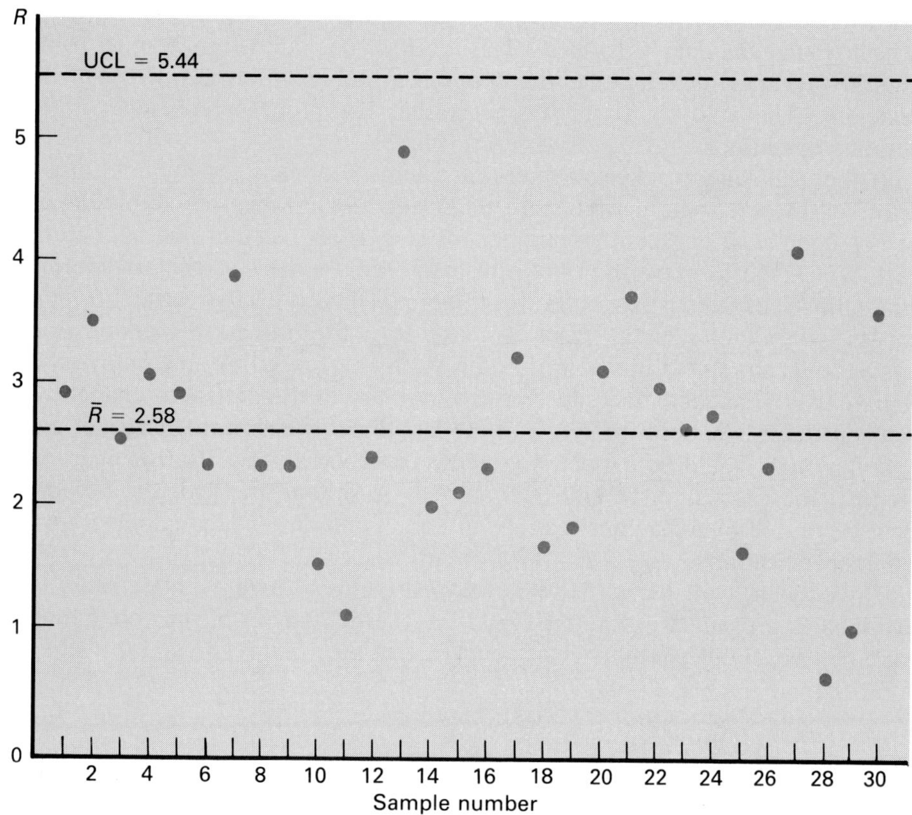

We can easily establish the upper and lower control limits for R by using published tables developed by statisticians for this purpose. Exhibit 19–3 gives the factors for three standard deviation (3-sigma) control limits for R based on a normal distribution. To use this table, first we find the line for the number of observations in each subgroup (sample) and read across to find the upper and lower control limit factors for the R chart. For the data in Exhibit 19–1, the subgroup (sample) size is 5. The factor for the lower control limit is 0, and the factor for the upper control limit is 2.11. These factors are multiplied by $\overline{R}$ to obtain the control limits. For these data:

$$\text{Upper control limit} = D_4\overline{R} = 2.11 \times 2.58 = \underline{\underline{5.44}}$$

$$\text{Lower control limit}^3 = D_3\overline{R} = 0 \times 2.58 = \underline{\underline{0.00}}$$

Because the control limits on the R chart are based on the normal distribution, approximately 99.73 percent of all sample ranges will fall within the 3-sigma

[3] To be technically correct, there is no lower control limit in this case. Since the lower limit for a 3-sigma R chart turns out to be less than 0 where $n \leq 6$, a lower limit does not exist in these cases.

control limits if the underlying population is normally distributed. If an R value falls outside the control limits, the process is out of control with respect to variability. For the data in Exhibit 19–1, the R values fall within 3-sigma control limits giving no indication that the process is out of control with respect to variability. The analysis so far suggests that the process represents normal operating conditions.

If the samples are taken in time-order sequence, runs tests should also be performed to determine if trends are occurring in the range of sample data. A **run** is a number of consecutive points above or below a center line on a control chart. We can perform two types of runs tests. We use one runs test to determine if the number of runs is less than would be expected if all the variability in the process is random. If an R chart fails this test, the process dispersion is not constant over time. The unstable variability may be caused by an employee who often adjusts a machine and causes the variability in the output to change with each adjustment. We use the second runs test to determine if the length of a run is greater than would be expected given random variability. If an R chart fails this test, the process dispersion has shifted. A shift in the process variability might be caused by a machine that is worn and is no longer producing within the design specifications.

Once again, statisticians have developed tables to help evaluate runs. One such table is presented in Exhibit 19–4. To test the number of runs on a control chart, first we count the number of points above the central line and the number

EXHIBIT 19–3 Table of Factors for 3-Sigma Control Limits

Number of observations in subgroup	*Factor for $\overline{X}$ chart*	*Factors for R chart*	
		Lower control limit	*Upper control limit*
n	A_2	D_3	D_4
2	1.88	0	3.27
3	1.02	0	2.57
4	0.73	0	2.28
5	0.58	0	2.11
6	0.48	0	2.00
7	0.42	0.08	1.92
8	0.37	0.14	1.86
9	0.34	0.18	1.82
10	0.31	0.22	1.78

Upper control limit for $\overline{X} = \overline{\overline{X}} + A_2\overline{R}$
Lower control limit for $\overline{X} = \overline{\overline{X}} - A_2\overline{R}$

Upper control limit for $R = D_4\overline{R}$
Lower control limit for $R = D_3\overline{R}$

Abridged from Eugene L. Grant and Richard S. Leavenworth, *Statistical Quality Control*, 5th ed. (New York: McGraw-Hill Book Company, 1980), Table C, p. 631. Reproduced by permission of the publisher.

EXHIBIT 19–4 Critical Values for Runs Tests

(a) Critical values for total number of runs about a center line

$r \setminus s$	6	7	8	9	10	11	12	13	14	15	16	17	18	19	20
6	3														
7	4	4													
8	4	4	5												
9	4	5	5	6											
10	5	5	6	6	6										
11	5	5	6	6	7	7									
12	5	6	6	7	7	8	8								
13	5	6	6	7	8	8	9	9							
14	5	6	7	7	8	8	9	9	10						
15	6	6	7	8	8	9	9	10	10	11					
16	6	6	7	8	8	9	10	10	11	11	11				
17	6	7	7	8	9	9	10	10	11	11	12	12			
18	6	7	8	8	9	10	10	11	11	12	12	13	13		
19	6	7	8	8	9	10	10	11	12	12	13	13	14	14	
20	6	7	8	9	9	10	11	11	12	12	13	13	14	14	15

Adapted from Frieda S. Swed, and C. Eisenhart, "Tables for Testing Randomness of Grouping in a Sequence of Alternatives," *Annals of Mathematical Statistics,* Vol. XIV (1943), pp. 71–86, with permission.

(b) Critical values for lengths of runs on either side of the median

Total number of points (k)	*Length of run*
10	5
20	7
30	8
40	9
50	10

Adapted from Frederick Mosteller, "Note on an Application of Runs to Quality Control Charts," *Annals of Mathematical Statistics,* Vol. XII (1941), p. 232, with permission.

of points below the central line. For the data in Exhibit 19–2, 14 points are above and 16 points are below the central line. Let s equal the smaller of these two counts and r equal the larger. The critical value is found in Exhibit 19–4(a). For $s = 14$ and $r = 16$, the critical value is 11. We then compare this value with the number of actual runs on the chart.

The number of actual runs can be determined by counting the groups of consecutive points above and below the central line[4] or by connecting the points on the control charts and adding one to the number of times the line crosses the central line. This latter procedure is illustrated in Exhibit 19–5(a). For these data, the line connecting the R values crosses the central line 14 times and the number of runs is, therefore, 15 (14 + 1). Because this number exceeds the critical value (that is, 15 > 11), the chart passes this test.

[4] If any of the R values fall on the central line, those points should be thrown either above or below the central line to increase the number of runs if possible.

EXHIBIT 19–5 ***R* Chart Illustrating Runs**

(a) Number of Runs

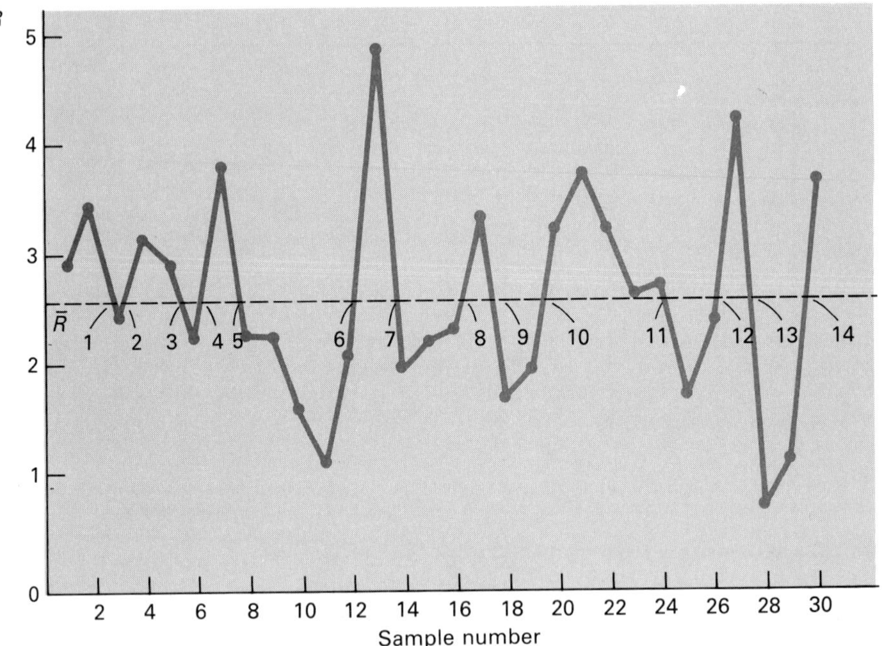

(b) Lengths of Runs

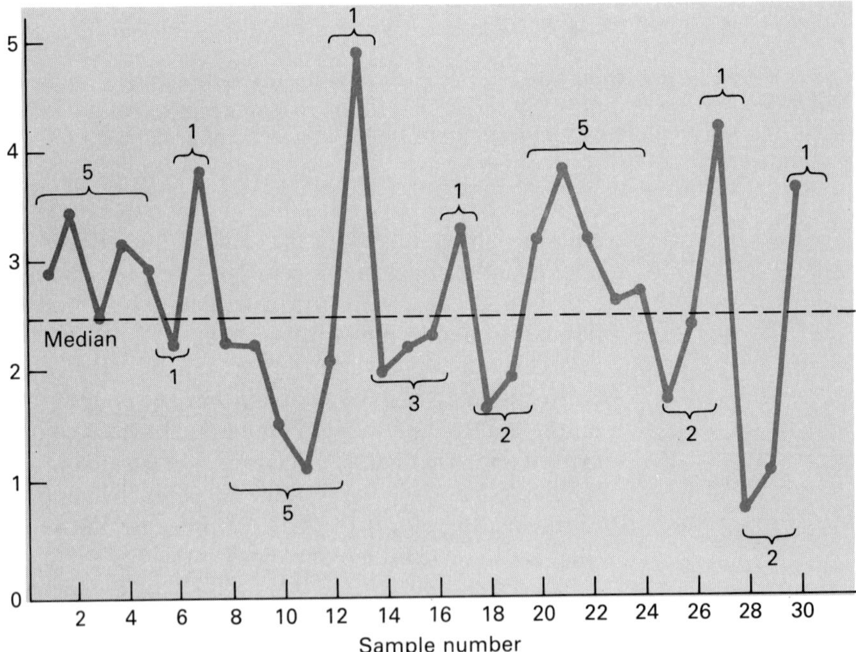

To test for the lengths of runs, the longest run on either side of the median line is determined[5] and compared to a critical value. Note that the central line in this test is based on the median and not the average. The median is the midpoint of the values if they are arrayed from lowest to highest. Since there are 30 R values in Exhibit 19–2, the median is the average of the 15th and 16th arrayed values or 2.45 [(2.4 + 2.5)/2]. Counting the lengths of the runs on either side of this line gives a longest run of 5. See Exhibit 19–5(b). The critical value for this test is found in Exhibit 19–4(b), where k is the number of points on the chart. With $k = 30$, the critical value is 8. Because the longest run is less than the critical value (that is, $5 < 8$), the R chart passes this runs test.

Since the R chart has no values outside the control limits and passes both runs tests, we have no evidence that the fluctuations in the data are due to nonrandom occurrences. The data in Exhibit 19–1 still appear to represent normal operations. *If management wants the random variability reduced, they will have to change the process. The employees cannot reduce this variability because it is inherent in the production operations.*

$\overline{X}$ Charts Once we have determined that a process is in control with respect to variability, we can develop an $\overline{X}$ chart. The $\overline{X}$ chart is a plot of the average value, $\overline{X}$, of each sample and is used to determine if the process is in control with respect to the average. The average for each sample is the sum of the measurements in the sample divided by the number of units in the sample.

Example 19–5 For the data in Example 19–4, the average value for the sample is 65.12 ounces. [(65.0 + 66.5 + 64.8 + 63.6 + 65.7)/5].

The average for each sample taken by the Natural Spring Water Company is shown in Exhibit 19–1. These data are plotted on an $\overline{X}$ chart in Exhibit 19–6.

The central line, $\overline{\overline{X}}$ (pronounced X-double bar), on an $\overline{X}$ chart is the overall average of all the observations. We calculate it by dividing the sum of the $\overline{X}$ values by the number of samples. In equation form,

$$\overline{\overline{X}} = \frac{\Sigma \overline{X}_i}{k} \tag{19–2}$$

where

$\overline{\overline{X}}$ = Central line on an $\overline{X}$ chart
$\overline{X}_i$ = Average value for sample i
k = Number of samples

For the data in Exhibit 19–1, $\overline{\overline{X}}$ is 65.06 ounces (1,951.88 ÷ 30). Thus the central line on the $\overline{X}$ chart is at 65.06 ounces.

We can easily establish the upper and lower control limits for $\overline{X}$ using the factors for $\overline{X}$ charts shown in Exhibit 19–3. When $n = 5$, the factor, A_2, for 3-sigma control limits on an $\overline{X}$ chart is 0.58. The upper control limit is calculated

---

[5] If any of the R values fall on the median line, those points should be thrown either above or below the median line to decrease the length of the run if possible.

EXHIBIT 19–6 $\overline{X}$ Chart

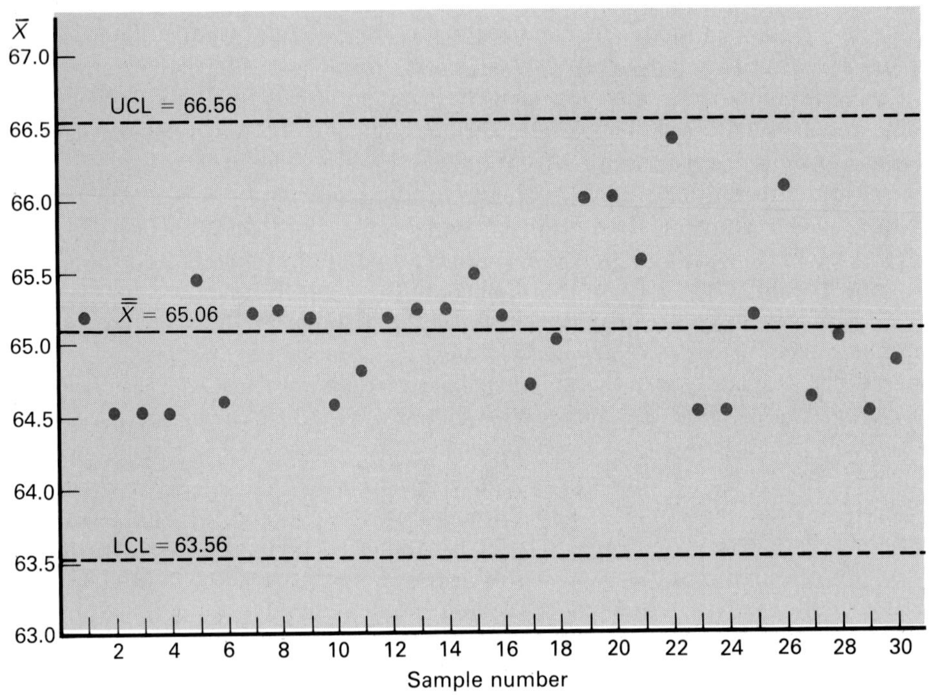

as $\overline{\overline{X}} + A_2\overline{R}$ and the lower control limit is $\overline{\overline{X}} - A_2\overline{R}$. For the data of the Natural Spring Water Company, the upper control limit on the $\overline{X}$ chart is 66.56 [65.06 + (0.58 × 2.58)] and the lower control limit is 63.56 [65.06 − (0.58 × 2.58)]. These control limits are shown on the $\overline{X}$ chart in Exhibit 19–6.

As Exhibit 19–6 shows, all the $\overline{X}$'s for the 30 samples of bottled water fall within the control limits. If the samples are in time-order sequence, we should also perform runs tests on the $\overline{X}$ chart to determine if there is a trend in the process average or if it has shifted. These runs tests are identical to those used for the *R* chart and you can verify that the $\overline{X}$ chart in Exhibit 19–6 passes both runs tests. Thus the process is in control with respect to the average of the process as well as variability. If any of the $\overline{X}$'s were outside the control limits or the chart failed a runs test, the process would have been out of control with respect to the average of the process. When this occurs, an investigation is needed to determine what caused the out-of-control point.

An investigation of out-of-control points may reveal that they are due to either employee or management controllable factors. For example, an employee who continually adjusts a machine may cause a point to be out of control because the process average is constantly changing. An example where management may be responsible for out-of-control points is purchasing materials that have different characteristics causing the output to vary. Regardless of who is responsible, if the cause can be determined, that point should be eliminated and new control limits developed.

These control charts for the Natural Spring Water Company appear to represent operations under normal conditions. Consequently they can be used as a starting point for maintaining statistical process control. As more samples are taken over time, the additional R and $\overline{X}$ values are plotted on the charts. As long as the range and average stay within the control limits and runs above and below the control limits do not occur, the process is in statistical process control and the variances do not need to be investigated because they are due to random fluctuations. If a point falls above or below the control limits or an excessively long run occurs, the process has gone out of control and an investigation is needed. Exhibit 19–7 is an $\overline{X}$ chart showing a process where the average is drifting higher as successive samples are taken. This indicates a need to investigate the process to determine what is causing the average to drift higher.

Control Charts for Unknown Distributions The published tables giving factors for $\overline{X}$ and R control charts assume the underlying population is normally distributed. If the underlying population is not normally distributed, it may be necessary to develop control limits on the basis of Chebyshev's inequality. For more information on this subject, you can consult any book on statistical process control.

An important, but seldom addressed, question in the establishment of control limits is the number of samples on which they should be based. Professors Grant and Leavenworth note:

> On statistical grounds it is desirable that control limits be based on at least 25 subgroups. Moreover, experience indicates that the first few subgroups obtained when a control chart is initiated may not be representative of what is measured later; the mere act of taking and recording measurements is sometimes responsible for a change in the pattern of variation.

EXHIBIT 19–7 **$\overline{X}$ Chart With Trend in Average**

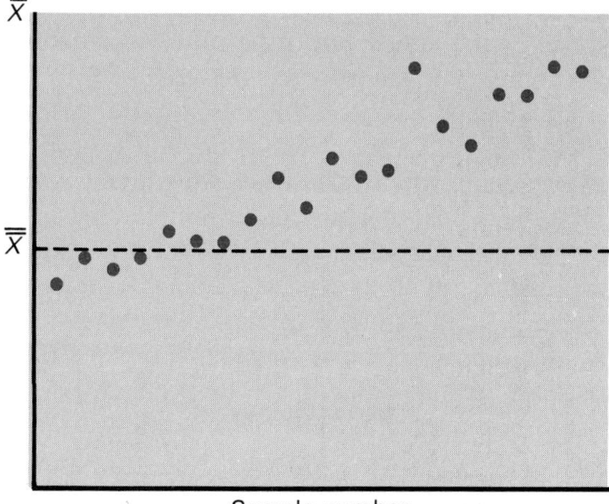

> For these reasons, if 25 subgroups can be obtained in a short time, it is desirable to wait for 25 or more subgroups; this would be true, for example, where a new subgroup was measured every hour.
>
> However, where subgroups are obtained slowly there is a natural desire on the part of those who initiated the control charts to draw some conclusions from them within a reasonable time. This impatience for an answer frequently leads to the policy of making preliminary calculations of control limits from the first 8 or 10 subgroups, with subsequent modification of limits as more subgroups are obtained.[6]

Expected Costs

Despite the apparent precision of statistical control charts, some people must select $\overline{X}$ and R control limits on the basis of either professional judgment or accepted practice. The establishment of these limits is not usually based on a formal analysis of expected costs, although it is possible to include them in the analysis. The relevant cost data used in deciding whether to investigate a variance include the cost of investigation, the cost of correcting a process that is out of control, and the cost savings of correcting a process that is out of control.

Although the development of investigation criteria based on expected costs is relatively new and the criteria themselves have limited applications at this time, the concepts underlying these criteria provide a framework for analyzing the impact of cost on the variance investigation decision. It seems likely that investigation criteria based on expected costs will find their greatest application in controlling operations that are performed on a continuous basis by some automatic process.

Example 19–6

The Natural Spring Water Company's bottle-washing machine is fully automated. An operator turns it "on" and "off" and maintenance personnel inspect and adjust it each evening.

When the machine is properly adjusted, it breaks an average of 3 percent of the bottles it cleans. When it is out of adjustment, the breakage rate averages 5 percent.

Each day at noon the production supervisor determines the morning breakage rate and decides whether or not additional maintenance is required before bottle washing resumes in the afternoon. If the supervisor determines that maintenance is necessary, the machine is inspected at a cost of \$60. If it is out of adjustment, the cost of adjusting it is an additional \$40. Because the machine processes 200,000 bottles every afternoon and each bottle costs \$0.07, the cost of not correcting the machine when it is out of adjustment is \$280 [200,000 × (0.05 − 0.03) × \$0.07)]. This cost information is summarized in Exhibit 19–8.

Assume that on a particular day, after having completed the calculation of the morning breakage rate, the supervisor believes there is a 60 percent probability that the machine is in adjustment. In making the decision to inspect (investigate) the machine, the supervisor must consider the expected cost of inspection, the expected cost of adjustment to correct the process if it is out of control, and the expected cost of not inspecting. The general rule is to investigate if the expected

[6] Grant and Leavenworth, p. 123.

EXHIBIT 19–8 Expected Costs

	State of nature	
Action	*In control*	*Out of control*
Investigate	\$60	\$100 (\$60 + \$40)
Do not investigate	0	\$280

cost of not investigating is greater than the expected cost of investigation and correction. The following equation expresses this rule:

$$\text{Investigate if} \quad L(1 - P) > I + C(1 - P) \tag{19–3}$$

where

L = Excess operating costs if out of control
P = Probability that process is in control
$1 - P$ = Probability that process is out of control
I = Cost of inspection
C = Cost of correction if out of control

For Example 19–6,

Expected cost of not inspecting = \$280(1 − 0.6) = \$112

Expected cost of inspection and correction = \$60 + \$40(1 − 0.6) = \$76

Since the expected cost of not inspecting exceeds the expected cost of inspection and correction, the bottle-washing machine should be inspected.

The critical probability (that the process is in control), P^*, at which the expected costs of investigation and correction are equal to the expected costs of not investigating, may be determined by substituting P^* for P in Eq. 19–3 and solving for P^*:

$$L(1 - P^*) = I + C(1 - P^*)$$

$$P^* = 1 - \frac{I}{L - C} \tag{19–4}$$

where P^* = Critical probability that the process is in control.

Once the critical probability is calculated, the supervisor need only compare the evaluation of the probability that the process is in control, P, with the critical probability, P^*. If $P > P^*$, the decision is to not inspect. If $P < P^*$, the decision is to inspect the process. For Example 19–6, the critical probability is 0.75:

$$P^* = 1 - \frac{\$60}{\$280 - \$40} = 0.75$$

Since $P < P^*$ (that is, $0.60 < 0.75$), the bottle-washing machine should be inspected. This agrees with our previous conclusion using expected costs in the analysis.

Unfortunately P (the probability that a process is in control) must be based partially on professional judgment. Control charts do not indicate the probability that a process is in control. They indicate only the probability of obtaining a value as large as or larger than the actual result when the process is in control. This information may help a decision maker estimate P, but it does not determine P. A Bayesian approach to determining P is discussed in the appendix to this chapter.

RESPONSIBILITY FOR VARIANCES

As noted in the discussion of statistical process control, variability is an inherent part of all production processes. If both $\overline{X}$ and R charts are in control, there is no evidence that the variability in the process is due to nonrandom fluctuations. The only way to improve an in-control process is to change it either by narrowing the degree of dispersion or by shifting the process average. These changes can only be made by management because employees are not responsible for, nor capable of, changing the process.

Example 19–7

As noted in Example 19–1, the breakage rate for Natural Spring Water Company's bottle-washing machine averages 3 percent and fluctuates between 2 and 4 percent. If the average rate or the variability of the breakage rate is to be reduced, management must change the process to accomplish the reduction.

If either the $\overline{X}$ or R charts have points outside the control limits, the process is out of control. The reasons for the nonrandom variation are called **special** or **assignable causes.** When nonrandom variation occurs, employees may be responsible for the variance. Possible employee causes include out of adjustment machines, failure to understand what is required on the job, and lack of training in proper operating procedures. Management may also be responsible for nonrandom variation. This might occur if they purchase different grades of materials or refuse to maintain machines in proper operating condition. Note that measurement errors may also cause out-of-control points on a control chart.

If managers are to use SPC in maintaining quality control, it is imperative that they understand the differences between random and special causes of variation in a process. Employees should not be held responsible for random variations because the system itself is causing the variability. Only management actions can reduce variances due to random fluctuations in a process.

QUALITY COSTS

Although statistical process control provides a method for determining when a process is out of control, it does not help management evaluate the costs of maintaining quality or producing nonconforming products. To evaluate and analyze these costs, we need a quality cost program. The basic objective of such a program is to improve the profits of the organization. Since top management is accustomed to data expressed in dollars, a quality cost program should provide reports that show the types and dollar amounts of quality costs.

Types of Quality Costs

Quality costs are costs incurred because poor product quality may or does exist. Thus quality costs are divided into two types:

1. Costs incurred because nonconforming products may exist.
2. Costs incurred because nonconforming products do exist.

The first type is incurred to ensure that products conform to engineering specifications. The second type is incurred because products are produced that do not confom to specifications. Note that these are costs associated with quality of conformance, not quality of design.

Quality of conformance refers to the degree to which a product meets its design specifications. **Quality of design** refers to the quality characteristics that are engineered into and purported to exist in a product. For example, a Cadillac and a Chevrolet automobile may be used for the same function, transportation, but their design qualities are different. However, each should conform to its own specifications. The degree to which the final product meets its specifications is quality of conformance.

Costs incurred because nonconforming products may exist are divided into two categories: prevention and appraisal. **Prevention costs** are the costs of planning, implementing, and maintaining the quality control system. These costs include quality engineering, training of quality control personnel, writing procedures for inspecting and testing, pilot studies, and systems development. **Appraisal costs** are the costs incurred in determining the degree to which raw materials and products conform to design specifications. These costs include incoming material inspection, maintaining the accuracy of test equipment, product quality audits, and field testing.

The costs incurred when nonconforming products are produced are divided into two categories of failure costs: internal failure and external failure. **Internal failure costs** are costs incurred because products, components, and/or materials fail to meet quality requirements, causing losses within the plant. These costs include scrap, repair, rework, downtime, and yield losses. **External failure costs** are costs incurred when products fail to meet design specifications after shipment to customers. These costs include costs for handling complaints, warranty charges, allowances for nonconforming products, repairs of nonconforming products, and lost customer goodwill.

Quality costs are incurred in many different departments within an organization and most accounting systems are not designed to accumulate or report the costs by quality cost category. In addition, some types of quality costs such as lost customer goodwill are not even recorded by the accounting system. For these reasons, many companies do not know how large their quality costs are or in what areas they can be reduced.

If a company is to have a quality cost program, it must first identify the costs incurred in each of the four categories. These costs then need to be collected and reported to management in a quality cost report. An example of a quality cost report is presented in Exhibit 19–9. If a series of quality cost reports over time is prepared, management can then analyze these data to determine where their quality costs are being incurred and how they can be reduced.

EXHIBIT 19–9 Quality Cost Report

	Current month's cost	*Percent of total*
Prevention costs:		
Quality planning	$ 3,000	1.5%
Quality engineering	5,000	2.5
Quality training	1,000	0.5
Quality management	2,000	1.0
Total prevention	$ 11,000	5.5
Appraisal costs:		
Laboratory acceptance testing	$ 4,000	2.0
Inspection and testing of products	10,000	5.0
Product quality audits	4,000	2.0
Maintenance and calibration of test equipment	7,000	3.5
Field performance testing	6,000	3.0
Total appraisal	31,000	15.5
Internal failure costs:		
Scrap	$ 15,000	7.5
Rework and repair	30,000	15.0
Reinspection and retest	5,000	2.5
Downtime	8,000	4.0
Total internal failure	58,000	29.0
External failure costs:		
Complaints	$ 10,000	5.0
Warranty replacement	50,000	25.0
Out of warranty repairs	20,000	10.0
Allowances for nonconforming products	15,000	7.5
Returned products processing	5,000	2.5
Total external failure	100,000	50.0
Total quality costs	$200,000	100.0

The data in Exhibit 19–9 show that a major portion of the quality costs are failure costs. These failure costs can probably be reduced if more money is spent on prevention and appraisal. The amount of the reduction in total quality costs (and the increase in profits) depends on the cost/benefit tradeoff that occurs from spending more on prevention and appraisal activities.

Example 19–8

For 19x5, the Natural Spring Water Company had failure costs of $100,000. Management has determined that failure costs can be reduced by spending more money on prevention and appraisal activities. If spending $20,000 on prevention and appraisal reduces the failure costs by $50,000, a favorable cost/benefit tradeoff exists and the profits of the company will increase by $30,000 ($50,000 − $20,000).

To determine whether a favorable cost/benefit tradeoff occurs from spending more on prevention and appraisal, we need to understand the behavior of quality costs. This behavior is referred to as the economics of quality costs.

Economics of Quality Costs

As a general rule, failure costs increase as the percentage of nonconforming items increase. For example, more costs will be incurred for repairs and rework of nonconforming items, customer complaints, and lost customer goodwill as the percentage of nonconforming items increase. To reduce these costs, more money must be spent on prevention and appraisal activities. Thus a tradeoff exists between the types of quality costs. This tradeoff is illustrated in Exhibit 19–10.

As shown in Exhibit 19–10, total quality costs are at a minimum at Point A. This point represents the optimal level and occurs where the lines representing the two types of quality costs intersect. If a company is operating to the right of Point A, total quality costs can be reduced by spending more money on prevention and appraisal to reduce the percentage of nonconforming items. The Natural Spring Water Company was operating in this area in Example 19–8.

Determining the optimal level of quality costs for an organization may be impossible for several reasons. First, some failure costs such as the cost of lost customer goodwill may not be available and impossible to obtain. This means the reported failure costs may be understated. If all failure costs were included, the failure cost line in Exhibit 19–10 would be steeper and the optimal level of nonconforming items less than shown on the graph. Under these circumstances, reducing the percentage of nonconforming items would further reduce the total costs.

A second reason we may not be able to determine the optimal level of quality costs is that the graph represents quality costs at a specific point in time. However, quality cost relationships change over time and the optimal level at one point may not be the optimal level at another point. For these reasons, we should use

EXHIBIT 19–10 **Economics of Quality Costs**

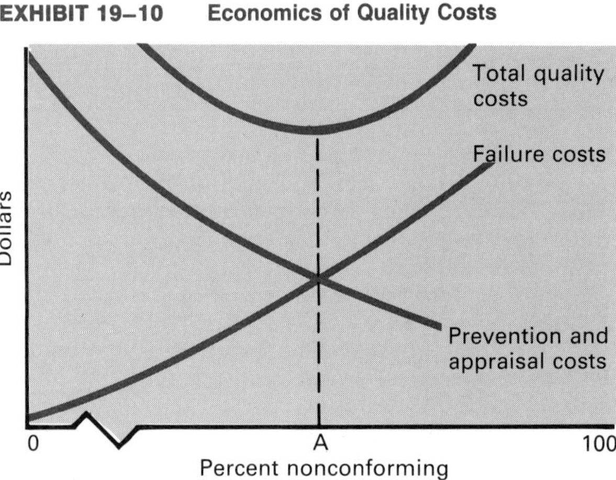

the graph as an aid in understanding quality costs and not as a guide to specific actions. We should evaluate each quality improvement project on its own merits by considering the costs and benefits of the proposed action.

SUMMARY

Maintaining quality in an organization requires a system for identifying and evaluating variances and analyzing quality costs. Although variance analyses based on cost accounting data alert management to the existence of potential problems and opportunities, they seldom identify their specific source. Additional investigation is required. The investigation of a variance may reveal that it was caused by a random fluctuation, a measurement error, inappropriate standards, or an operating error.

Because the investigation of random fluctuations in a process does not provide useful information, decision rules are formulated to avoid triggering an investigation. These decision rules may be based on some materiality criteria, involve the use of statistical process control, or use cost minimization rules. In the final analysis, all variance-investigation rules rely on professional judgment. However, control charts and cost minimization rules give explicit recognition to the variation that is inherent in all production processes.

The investigation of a variance may conclude that it was a random fluctuation and of no decision significance. Alternatively, the investigation may conclude that the variance has planning or control significance. A variance that results in a revision of standards and plans has planning significance. A variance that results in the adjustment of inefficient production or recordkeeping has control significance.

Although variance investigation criteria such as statistical process control provide data for operating personnel to use in evaluating if a process is out of control, an organization's management may be more interested in quality cost data. These data consist of prevention, appraisal, internal failure, and external failure costs. A tradeoff exists between these types of costs, and an understanding of this tradeoff can help management reduce their total quality costs and improve their profit performance.

APPENDIX
Estimating the Probability a Process Is in Control

To make the decision to investigate variances on the basis of expected costs, we must know the probability that a process is in control. We cannot obtain this probability directly from sampling. Sample results do not indicate the probability that a process is in control; they indicate only the probability of obtaining a variance as large as or larger than the actual result when the process is in control. However, this information may help a decision maker estimate the probability a process is in control when it is combined with prior beliefs regarding this probability.

Bayes' Theorem is a systematic procedure for revising probabilities. It can be used to combine prior (subjective) probabilities regarding the in- or out-of-control state of a process with actual sample results in order to calculate a revised probability that a process is in control. This revised probability can then be used to compute the expected costs of investigating and the expected costs of not investigating.

Bayes' Theorem for the revision of probabilities is:

$$P = \frac{P(\theta_1)\,P(x \mid \theta_1)}{P(\theta_1)\,P(x \mid \theta_1) + P(\theta_2)\,P(x \mid \theta_2)} \tag{19–5}$$

where

P = Posterior (revised) probability that the process is in control
$P(\theta_1)$ = Prior probability that the process is in control
$P(x \mid \theta_1)$ = Probability of sample result x, given that the process is in control
$P(\theta_2)$ = $(1 - P(\theta_1))$, prior probability that the process is out of control
$P(x \mid \theta_2)$ = Probability of sample result x, given that the process is out of control

Use of Bayes' Theorem assumes the existence of an in-control probability distribution and a single out-of-control probability distribution. Although we can obtain information on the in-control distribution from historical data, the assumption of a single probability distribution for the out-of-control state is a major limitation of the Bayesian approach as presented here. Information on the prior probability that the process is in control may reflect a supervisor's professional judgment before any sample data are obtained. It may also be based on historical data. For example, in 100 random inspections, the process was in control 90 percent of the time.

Example 19–9

The Natural Spring Water Company has developed the probability distributions presented in Exhibit 19–11 for the bottle-washing machine's in-control and out-of-control states. They have also determined, on the basis of prior experience, that there is a 70 percent probability that the machine is in control at any given noon hour. On a particular day, the morning breakage rate was 3.5 percent.

Using the information in Exhibit 19–11, the 70 percent prior probability that the machine is in control, and the actual morning 3.5 percent breakage rate, the posterior probability that the process is in control is 0.82:

$$P = \frac{(0.7)(0.2)}{(0.7)(0.2) + (0.3)(0.1)} = \underline{\underline{0.82}}$$

If the critical probability, P^*, for the decision to investigate is 0.75, there would be no investigation.

If the morning breakage rate were 4 percent, the posterior probability would be 0.58:

$$P = \frac{(0.7)(0.15)}{(0.7)(0.15) + (0.3)(0.25)} = \underline{\underline{0.58}}$$

and the process would be investigated.

EXHIBIT 19–11 Probability Distribution of Breakage

In control: θ_1		*Out of control: θ_2*	
Percent breakage	*Probability $P(x \mid \theta_1)$*	*Percent breakage*	*Probability $P(x \mid \theta_2)$*
4	0.15	6.5	0.10
3.5	0.20	6	0.25
3	0.30	5	0.30
2.5	0.20	4	0.25
2	0.15	3.5	0.10

EXHIBIT 19–12 Probability Distributions of Breakage

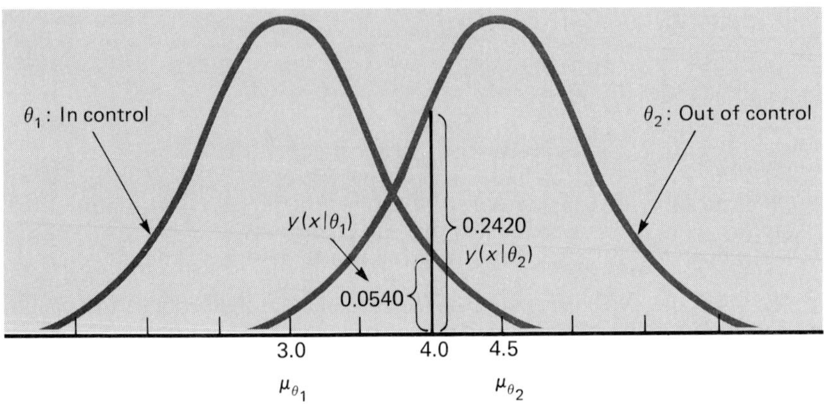

Because this analysis was based on a complete enumeration of all possible outcomes, it can be used when the underlying probability distributions for θ_1 and θ_2 are not normal. When the underlying distributions are normal, appropriate values for the ordinates of the normal curve, $y(x \mid \theta_1)$ and $y(x \mid \theta_2)$, are substituted in Eq. 19–5 for $P(x \mid \theta_1)$ and $P(x \mid \theta_2)$.[7] Ordinate values of the standard normal curve are presented in Table B of Appendix B to this book.

Assume the following distributions have been developed for the bottle-washing machine:

	In control: θ_1	*Out of control:* θ_2
μ_θ (percent breakage)	3.0	4.5
σ_θ (percent breakage)	0.5	0.5

A breakage rate of 4 percent is observed. This is two standard deviations from the mean of θ_1 and one standard deviation from the mean of θ_2. In Table B of Appendix B ordinate values for one and two standard deviations are 0.2420 and 0.0540, respectively. This information is illustrated in Exhibit 19–12.

With a 70 percent prior probability of the machine being in control, the posterior probability of the machine being in control is 0.34:

$$P = \frac{(0.7)(0.0540)}{(0.7)(0.0540) + (0.3)(0.2420)} = \underline{\underline{0.34}}$$

(*Note:* Do not compare this result with the 0.58 probability developed in Example 19–9 because the probabilities are based on different distributions.)

---

[7] We consider only the special case in which σ_{θ_1} and σ_{θ_2} are equal. When they are not equal Eq. 19–5 is modified as follows:

$$P = \frac{P(\theta_1)(1/\sigma_{\theta_1})\, y(x \mid \theta_1)}{P(\theta_1)(1/\sigma_{\theta_1})\, y(x \mid \theta_1) + P(\theta_2)(1/\sigma_{\theta_2})\, y(x \mid \theta_2)}$$

where $y(x \mid \theta_1)$ and $y(x \mid \theta_2)$ refer to the values of the probability density function of the normal curve. For a complete discussion of the more general case, see Robert Capettini, and Dennis Collins, "The Investigation of Deviations from Standard Costs in the Presence of Unequal State Variances," *Journal of Business, Finance, and Accounting* **5**, No. 4 (Winter 1978): 335–352.

KEY TERMS

Appraisal costs
Assignable cause (of variance)
Attributes data
Control chart
External failure costs
Internal failure costs
Location
Prevention costs
Quality of conformance
Quality costs
Quality of design
R charts
Range
Run
Special cause (of variance)
Statistical process control
Variability
Variables data
$\overline{X}$ charts

SELECTED REFERENCES

Buckman, A. G., and Bruce L. Miller, "Optimal Investigation of a Multiple Cost Processes System" *Journal of Accounting Research* **20,** No. 1 (Spring 1982): 28–41.

Capanella, Jack, and Frank J. Corcoran, "Principles of Quality Costs," *Quality Progress* **16,** No. 4 (April 1983): 16–22.

Capettini, Robert, and Dennis Collins, "The Investigation of Deviations from Standard Costs in the Presence of Unequal State Variances," *Journal of Business, Finance, and Accounting* **5,** No. 4 (Winter 1978): 335–352.

Clark, John, "Costing for Quality at Celanese," *Management Accounting* **66,** No. 9 (March 1985): 42–46.

Crosby, Philip B., *Quality is Free,* New York: New American Library, 1979.

Demski, Joel S., *Information Analysis,* Reading, Mass.: Addison-Wesley, 1972.

Dittman, David, and Prem Prakash, "Cost Variance Investigation: Markovian Control Versus Optimal Control," *Accounting Review* **54,** No. 2 (April 1979): 358–373.

Grant, Eugene L., and Richard S. Leavenworth, *Statistical Quality Control,* 5th ed., New York: McGraw-Hill, 1980.

Jacobs, Fredric H., "An Evaluation of the Effectiveness of Some Cost Variance Investigation Models," *Journal of Accounting Research* **16,** No. 1 (Spring 1978): 190–203.

_____, "When and How to Use Statistical Cost Variance Investigation Techniques," *Cost and Management* **57,** No. 1 (January-February 1983): 26–32.

Kaplan, Robert S., "The Significance and Investigation of Cost Variances: Survey and Extensions," *Journal of Accounting Research* **13,** No. 2 (Autumn 1975): 311–337.

Lundvall, Daniel M., "Quality Costs," in *Quality Control Handbook,* 3rd ed., eds. J. M. Juran, Frank M. Gryna, Jr., and R. S. Bingham, Jr. New York: McGraw-Hill, 1974.

Morse, Wayne J., "Measuring Quality Costs," *Cost and Management* **57,** No. 4 (July-August 1983): 16–20.

Onsi, Mohamed, "Quantitative Models for Accounting Control," *Accounting Review* **42,** No. 2 (April 1967): 321–330.

Quality Cost Committee, *Quality Costs—What and How,* 2nd ed., Milwaukee: American Society for Quality Control, 1971.

Roth, Harold P., and Wayne J. Morse, "Let's Help Measure and Report Quality Costs," *Management Accounting* **65,** No. 2 (August 1983): 50–53.

Zannetos, Zenon S., "Standard Costs as a First Step to Probabilistic Control: A Theoretical Justification, an Extension and Implications," *Accounting Review* **39,** No. 2 (April 1964): 296–304.

Zebda, Awni, "The Investigation of Cost Variances: A Fuzzy Set Theory Approach," *Decision Sciences* **15,** No. 3 (Summer 1984): 359–388.

REVIEW QUESTIONS

19–1 Identify four possible sources of production variances.

19–2 What is meant by the "planning significance" of variances?

19–3 What is meant by the "control significance" of variances?

19–4 Mention three types of variance investigation criteria.

19–5 What is "statistical process control"?

19–6 How is the central line on $\overline{X}$ and R control charts determined?

19–7 How are control limits established on an R chart?

19–8 How are control limits established on an $\overline{X}$ chart?

19–9 What assumption is inherent in the use of published tables of control chart factors?

19–10 What important dimension of the decision to investigate is not included in statistical control chart criteria?

19–11 How may the expected costs of investigation and the expected costs of not investigating be incorporated into an investigation-decision rule?

19–12 How can control charts help distinguish between random and special (assignable) causes of variation?

19–13 Who is responsible for variances due to special (assignable) causes?

19–14 Identify four categories of quality costs.

19–15 What tradeoff exists between the types of quality costs?

REVIEW PROBLEM

R and $\overline{X}$ Control Charts

To implement statistical process control on the length of a product, Franklin Company has taken 20 samples of 5 products each and recorded the length in millimeters. The data for the 20 samples in time-order sequence are as follows:

	Observation						
Sample	*1*	*2*	*3*	*4*	*5*	$\overline{X}_i$	R_i
1	10.0	9.8	9.7	9.9	10.3	9.94	0.6
2	10.2	10.4	10.0	9.9	9.8	10.06	0.6
3	10.0	10.1	10.2	10.1	10.1	10.10	0.2
4	9.6	10.0	10.1	10.2	10.2	10.02	0.6
5	10.5	10.3	9.7	10.1	9.9	10.10	0.8
6	10.2	10.0	10.1	9.9	9.6	9.96	0.6
7	9.9	10.0	10.2	10.1	10.1	10.06	0.3
8	10.4	9.7	9.8	10.0	10.0	9.98	0.7
9	10.3	9.5	9.6	9.8	10.0	9.84	0.8
10	10.1	10.1	10.2	9.9	10.0	10.06	0.3

Sample	Observation 1	2	3	4	5	$\overline{X}_i$	R_i
11	10.3	9.8	10.0	10.1	9.9	10.02	0.5
12	9.9	10.2	10.1	9.8	10.0	10.00	0.4
13	10.0	10.4	10.2	9.8	9.8	10.04	0.6
14	9.9	10.0	10.0	10.4	10.2	10.10	0.5
15	10.1	9.9	9.7	9.9	10.0	9.92	0.4
16	10.0	10.2	10.5	9.8	9.9	10.08	0.7
17	9.5	9.6	10.2	10.0	9.8	9.82	0.7
18	10.0	9.9	10.3	10.5	10.0	10.14	0.6
19	9.6	9.7	10.1	10.2	10.0	9.92	0.6
20	10.1	10.0	10.0	9.8	10.2	10.02	0.4
					Total	200.18	10.9

Assume the lengths of the parts are normally distributed.

REQUIREMENTS

a) Plot the R and $\overline{X}$ values for each sample on control charts.

b) Determine the central line and upper and lower control limits for the R chart.

c) Determine if the process is in control with respect to variability.

d) Determine the central line and upper and lower control limits for the $\overline{X}$ chart.

e) Determine if the process is in control with respect to average.

The solution to this problem is found at the end of the Chapter 19 problems and exercises.

EXERCISES

19–1 Decision Signifiance of Variances

Indicate whether each of the following sources of deviations from standards is of planning significance, of control significance, or of no decision significance:

a) Materials price variance resulted from purchasing in small lots.

b) An operator was "lulled to sleep by the din of a stamping machine."

c) A door-to-door salesperson had to change clothes after meeting an unfriendly dog.

d) Employees received an across-the-board increase in wages.

e) An increase in machine downtime related to age of equipment.

f) A delivery truck ran out of gas (there was no equipment failure).

g) A fan belt broke on a delivery truck (the fan belt had passed a recent inspection).

h) An excessive increase in retail inventories of Company X goods was observed by a representative of Company X.

i) A systematic increase in favorable efficiency variances was noticed.

19–2 Variance Investigation With Materiality Criterion: Attributes Data

In the manufacture of rubber gaskets for automobile windows, various nonconformities such as cracks and blemishes occur. During the past, approximately 20 out of every 500 gaskets manufactured could not be sold because of these cracks and blemishes. During a recent period, a sample of 200 gaskets was inspected and 9 were rejected for these nonconformities.

REQUIREMENTS

a) Determine the percentage of nonconforming items in the sample of 200. How does this percentage compare with the historical percentage?

b) If management uses a 5 percent materiality criterion for investigating variances, should the variance be investigated?

c) If management uses a 10 percent materiality criterion for investigating variances, should the variance be investigated?

19–3 Variance Investigation With Materiality Criterion: Variables Data

In the manufacture of automobile windshields, the glass must meet certain specifications. The specification for the thickness of the glass calls for an average thickness of 0.3 inches. During a particular day, a sample of 20 windshields was taken and the thickness of the glass measured. The average thickness of the glass for the 20 windshields was 0.28 inches.

REQUIREMENTS

a) Determine the variance of the sample mean from the specification.

b) If management uses a 10 percent materiality criterion for investigating variances, should the variance be investigated?

c) If management uses a 5 percent materiality criterion for investigating variances, should the variance be investigated?

19–4 Determining Mean and Range for Samples

Windslow Company selects samples of a particular part periodically and measures their weight in grams. The results of measuring five parts in each of three samples are as follows:

	Sample		
Item number	*1*	*2*	*3*
1	168	171	168
2	165	167	167
3	170	162	169
4	175	175	170
5	164	176	171

REQUIREMENTS

a) Determine the mean, $\overline{X}$, for each of the three samples.

b) Determine the range, R, for each of the three samples.

c) Determine the average of the R's, $\overline{R}$, for the samples.

d) Determine the average of the $\overline{X}$'s, $\overline{\overline{X}}$, for the samples.

19–5 Determining Mean and Range for Samples

R & M Company selects samples of a particular part and measures their length in inches. The results of measuring eight parts in each of four samples are as follows:

	Sample			
Item number	*1*	*2*	*3*	*4*
1	8.50	8.54	8.57	8.54
2	8.48	8.52	8.52	8.53
3	8.45	8.50	8.50	8.50
4	8.50	8.53	8.51	8.49
5	8.51	8.57	8.49	8.52
6	8.50	8.58	8.54	8.50
7	8.53	8.54	8.52	8.51
8	8.49	8.53	8.50	8.52

REQUIREMENTS

a) Determine the mean, $\overline{X}$, for each of the samples.

b) Determine the range, R, for each of the samples.

c) Determine the average of the $\overline{X}$'s, $\overline{\overline{X}}$, for the samples.

d) Determine the average of the R's, $\overline{R}$, for the samples.

19–6 Determining Values for Central Line and Control Limits

Dayton Company produces thermostats for controlling heating and air-conditioning systems. To test the accuracy of the devices, samples of five thermostats are selected periodically and the temperature at which the device operated recorded. The following data were recorded during a recent week when 30 samples were taken. The data are for the actual temperature that activated the thermostat when it was set at 68 degrees.

$$\Sigma\overline{X} = 2{,}025$$
$$\Sigma R = 36$$

REQUIREMENTS

a) Determine the value for the central line on an R chart.

b) Determine the values for the control limits on an R chart.

c) Determine the value for the central line on an $\overline{X}$ chart.

d) Determine the values for the control limits on an $\overline{X}$ chart.

19–7 Determining Values for Central Line and Control Limits

Putnam Company produces detergent for dishwashers. The detergent is packaged in 35-ounce boxes using automated equipment. Samples of six boxes each are periodically selected from the production process and the weights of the contents measured. After 20 samples were taken, the sum of the $\overline{X}$ values from the 20 samples is 715 and the sum of the R values from the 20 samples is 28.

REQUIREMENTS

a) Determine the value for the central line on an R chart.

b) Determine the values for the control limits on an R chart.

c) Determine the value for the central line on an $\overline{X}$ chart.

d) Determine the values for the control limits on an $\overline{X}$ chart.

19–8 Investigation Based on Expected Costs

The cost of investigation is \$2,000; the cost of correction if the process is out of control is \$1,000; the excess operating costs if an out-of-control process is not corrected are \$10,000.

REQUIREMENTS

a) If the probability the process is in control is 0.8, should the process be investigated? Show computations.

b) If the probability the process is in control is 0.6, should the process be investigated? Show computations.

19–9 Investigation Based on Expected Costs

The cost of investigating a variance is \$600. If the process is out of control, the cost of correction is \$400. If the process is out of control and it is not corrected, the excess operating costs are \$3,000.

REQUIREMENTS

a) If the probability the process is in control is 0.6, should the process be investigated? Show computations.

b) If the probability the process is in control is 0.8, should the process be investigated? Show computations.

19–10 Determining and Evaluating P^*

For each of the following independent cases, determine the critical probability, P^*, at which the expected costs of investigation and correction are equal to the expected costs of not investigating. Also indicate for each case if a process should be investigated when the probability that it is in control is 0.5.

Case	*Cost of investigation* I	*Cost of correction if out of control* C	*Excess operating costs if out of control* L
1	\$ 10	\$ 70	\$100
2	40	100	500
3	75	100	250
4	80	200	300
5	100	800	700

19–11 Classifying Quality Costs

Classify each of the following quality costs as a prevention cost, appraisal cost, internal failure cost, or external failure cost:

a) Quality engineering

b) Rework

c) Scrap

d) Lost customer goodwill

e) In-warranty repairs

f) Laboratory acceptance testing

g) Quality training

h) Calibration of test equipment

i) Reinspection and retest

j) In-process inspection

19–12 Classifying Quality Costs

During January 19x6, Madden Company incurred the following quality costs:

Cost of scrap	$20,000
Warranty costs	8,000
Quality engineering	2,500
Inspection of finished products	10,000
Out-of-warranty repairs and replacement	6,000
Rework	12,000
Materials inspection	7,000
Quality training	2,000
Product testing	3,000
Downtime	5,000

REQUIREMENTS

a) Determine the total costs incurred in each of the following categories:

1. Prevention
2. Appraisal
3. Internal failure
4. External failure

b) Which of the costs in part (a) were incurred because quality problems *may* exist?

c) Which of the costs in part (a) were incurred because quality problems *do* exist?

PROBLEMS

19–13 Cost Patterns and Variance Analysis

The Clark Company has a contract with a labor union that guarantees a minimum wage of $500 per month to each direct-labor employee having at least 12 years of service. One hundred employees currently qualify for coverage. All direct-labor employees are paid $5.00 per hour.

The direct-labor budget for 19x0 was based on the annual usage of 400,000 hours of direct labor at \$5, or a total of \$2,000,000. Of this amount, \$50,000 [100 employees × \$500] per month (or \$600,000 for the year) was regarded as fixed. Thus the budget for any given month was determined by the formula \$50,000 + \$3.50 (direct-labor hours worked).

Data on performance for the first three months of 19x0 follow:

	January	*February*	*March*
Direct-labor hours worked	22,000	32,000	42,000
Direct labor costs budgeted	\$127,000	\$162,000	\$197,000
Direct-labor costs incurred	110,000	160,000	210,000
Variance	17,000F	2,000F	13,000U

The factory manager was perplexed by the results, which showed favorable variances when production was low and unfavorable variances when production was high, because he believed his control over labor costs was consistently good.

REQUIREMENTS

a) Why did the variances arise? Explain and illustrate, using amounts and diagrams as necessary.

b) Does this direct-labor budget provide a basis for controlling direct-labor costs? Explain, indicating changes that might be made to improve control over direct-labor cost and to facilitate performance evaluation of direct-labor employees.

(CPA Adapted)

19–14 Cost Patterns and Variance Analysis

Old Dominion Manufacturing Company contains two production processes that operate in a single production department. A simple and a multiple regression analysis of total overhead and direct-labor hours reveals the following relationships:

$$T = \$2{,}000 + \$21.875X_0$$
$$T = \$2{,}000 + \$5X_1 + \$50X_2$$

where

X_0 = Total department direct-labor hours
X_1 = Process A direct-labor hours
X_2 = Process B direct-labor hours

During a recent accounting period actual results were as follows:

Process	*Direct-labor hours*
A	400
B	350
Department total	750
Total overhead =	\$21,100

REQUIREMENTS

a) Using the rate developed by simple regression analysis, determine the production department's overhead spending variance (three-way analysis).

b) Using the rates developed by multiple regression analysis, determine the production department's overhead spending variance (three-way analysis).

c) What is the primary source of the variance computed in part (a)? What are the behavioral implications of the analysis contained in part (a)?

19–15 *R* and $\overline{X}$ Control Charts

The Special Foods Corporation produces low-calorie and low-sodium foods for sale to people on diets. One of the products is a cereal called "Corn Crispies." Standards call for 400 grams of cereal in each box. To maintain control of the process, the company has decided to implement statistical process control on the weight of the cereal. Twenty samples of five boxes each were taken and the contents of each box weighed. The data for the first 20 samples in time-order sequence are as follows:

	Observation (weight in grams)				
Sample	*1*	*2*	*3*	*4*	*5*
1	402	403	400	398	397
2	401	404	405	399	400
3	400	398	395	401	405
4	397	395	396	399	400
5	401	402	400	395	400
6	396	398	397	399	400
7	394	400	401	400	399
8	398	404	406	402	401
9	402	402	397	399	400
10	398	401	403	402	402
11	400	400	398	399	400
12	403	396	400	401	401
13	399	394	396	397	398
14	400	401	400	399	401
15	404	400	402	399	399
16	399	401	401	406	403
17	400	397	398	400	399
18	402	401	400	400	401
19	396	402	401	399	400
20	402	403	400	400	402

Assume the weights are normally distributed.

REQUIREMENTS

a) Determine $\overline{X}$ and R for each of the samples.

b) Plot the $\overline{X}$ and R values for each sample on control charts.

c) Determine if the process is in control with respect to variability.

d) If the process is in control with respect to variability, determine if the process is in control with respect to average.

19–16 *R* and $\overline{X}$ Control Charts

The Magic Muffler Shop uses statistical process control to keep track of variances in muffler installation times. Based on past experience, management has determined that installation times are normally distributed with an average of 30 minutes. The range of installation times in samples of size five averages 14 minutes.

Data for the most recent eight samples of five installation times each are as follows:

	Observation						
Sample	*1*	*2*	*3*	*4*	*5*	$\overline{X}_i$	R_i
1	20	24	25	20	36	25	16
2	37	35	35	19	39	33	20
3	27	19	26	36	27	27	17
4	23	22	25	24	31	25	9
5	35	37	26	38	39	35	13
6	21	39	33	27	30	30	18
7	36	39	35	38	42	38	7
8	25	23	27	35	25	27	12

REQUIREMENTS

a) Using the average time of 30 minutes and the average range of 14, establish the central line and upper and lower control limits on *R* and $\overline{X}$ charts.

b) Plot *R* and $\overline{X}$ for the eight samples on control charts. Is there evidence that the process is out of control?

c) If the variability in the installation times is to be reduced, who should be responsible for making the necessary changes?

19–17 *R* and $\overline{X}$ Control Charts

The High Tech Bank is an aggressive, efficient southwestern bank with several branches. After the branches close in the evening, all checks received by all branches are sent to the Operations Department for processing. The first step in processing is to translate the dollar amount of each check into machine-readable marks. Five encoding-machine operators accomplish this task at speeds of up to 2,000 checks per hour. To improve operations, High Tech wants to establish control charts for hourly check processing. They have obtained the following data from eight randomly selected hours:

	Checks encoded per hour (000) by operator						
Sample hour	*1*	*2*	*3*	*4*	*5*	$\overline{X}_i$	R_i
1	1.40	1.40	1.30	1.30	1.60	1.40	0.3
2	1.60	1.55	1.75	1.25	1.85	1.60	0.6
3	1.40	1.35	1.45	1.30	1.50	1.40	0.2
4	1.30	1.35	1.35	1.15	1.35	1.30	0.2
5	1.50	1.50	1.40	1.35	1.75	1.50	0.4
6	1.40	1.40	1.50	1.20	1.50	1.40	0.3
7	1.30	1.25	1.35	1.20	1.40	1.30	0.2
8	1.30	1.30	1.30	1.25	1.35	1.30	0.1

REQUIREMENTS

a) Develop control charts for R and $\overline{X}$.

b) Verify that the sample data used in developing these charts are within the control limits.

c) What action should be taken if any sample values used in developing the charts fall outside the control limits?

d) Does a review of the sample data reveal any consistent differences between individual operators? How might the control charts be modified to recognize these differences?

19–18 Determining Percentage of Products Not Meeting Specifications

Maxwell Manufacturing Company produces a part that is currently sold to two different users, X Company and Y Company. The length of the part has been in statistical control with a process average (μ) of 100.0 millimeters (mm) and a standard deviation (σ) of 2 mm. X Company's specifications require that the length of the parts be between 95 mm and 105 mm (100 $\pm$ 5 mm) and Y Company's specifications require that the length of the parts be between 94 and 102 mm (98 $\pm$ 4 mm). Assume that the lengths of the parts are normally distributed.

REQUIREMENTS

a) Determine the percentage of products that do not meet X Company's specifications. (*Hint:* Use Table A in Appendix B for the area under the normal curve to determine the proportion of products falling outside the specification limits.)

b) Determine the percentage of products that do not meet Y Company's specifications.

c) It has been suggested that the process average be adjusted to 99 mm. What will be the effect of this shift on the percentage of products out of specifications if the process variability remains the same?

19–19 Nonconforming Products: Variables Data

Turner Manufacturing Company is interested in maintaining statistical control over the weight of a product. Samples of nine parts each are taken periodically and the average of the $\overline{X}$'s is 600 grams and the standard deviation of the $\overline{X}$'s is 6 grams. The process standard deviation is estimated from the standard deviation of the $\overline{X}$'s using the following equation:

$$\hat{\sigma}_x = \hat{\sigma}_{\bar{x}}\sqrt{n}$$

$$\hat{\sigma}_x = 6 \times \sqrt{9} = 6 \times 3 = \underline{\underline{18}}$$

REQUIREMENTS

a) Determine the percentage of products with a weight greater than or equal to 620 grams. (*Hint:* Use Table A in Appendix B for the area under the normal curve to determine the proportion of products with lengths greater than or equal to 620 grams.)

b) Determine the percentage of products with a weight less than or equal to 570 grams.

c) Assume Turner has set specifications for the product of 600 ± 20 grams. That is, any parts weighing less than 580 grams (600 − 20) or more than 620 grams (600 + 20) must be reprocessed before they can be sold. What percentage of the products do not meet the specifications?

d) If Turner desires to have 98 percent of the parts fall within the specification limits in part (c), what type of change must be made in the process? Who should be responsible for this change?

19–20 Determining P^* When Inspection and Correction Are Combined

In some processes, inspection and correction are equivalent. When this is so, the critical probability is based on an analysis of the cost of inspection, I, and the excess operating costs if the process is out of control, L.

REQUIREMENTS

a) For the situation just described, develop an equation for determining the critical probability, P^*.

b) Use the equation developed in part (a) to find P^* when L = \$600 and I = \$120.

19–21 Daily Decision Rules Based on Critical Probabilities

The Eastwick Production Company is highly automated. To ensure efficient operations, the assembly line is always adjusted at the end of each five-day work week. Additionally, the line is monitored on a daily basis, and any special adjustments that might be necessary are made after regular working hours.

ADDITIONAL INFORMATION

- Daily production costs fluctuate around \$20,000 when the assembly line is in adjustment and around \$24,000 when the assembly line is out of adjustment.
- Past experience indicates that if the line is out of adjustment, it will remain out of adjustment until the necessary adjustments are made.
- Special inspections, to determine the exact cause of substandard production, cost \$3,600.
- If special adjustments are deemed necessary, a special crew must be paid double time to work the "graveyard" (third) shift. These adjustment costs total \$4,000. If special adjustments are made, the assembly line will remain in adjustment for the rest of the week.

REQUIREMENT

Formulate decision rules for each work day, based on the probability the line is in adjustment, to help management determine when to adjust the assembly line.

19–22 The Case of the Favorable Price Variance

A particular production process has the following standard (allowed) cost per unit produced:

Direct materials:	
Component A	$ 12.00
Other	30.00
Direct labor	60.00
Variable overhead	42.00
Fixed overhead	30.00
Total standard cost	$174.00

A 100 percent inspection is made at the end of the production process. A defect rate of 5 percent of units completed is expected due to quality problems with Component A. It is not currently feasible to inspect Component A prior to completion of the product. Because of the 5 percent failure rate, a standard cost of $183.16 ($174 ÷ 0.95) is used to cost the good units in external financial statements.

During a recent week, the purchasing agent was able to purchase 1,100 units of Component A from a new supplier who offered a lower price and immediate delivery. All 1,100 units of Component A were used during the week to produce 1,100 units of final product. Of these 1,100 units, 1,023 were good and 77 were nonconforming due to defects in Component A.

At the end of the week, the accounting department made the following variance computations:

Materials price variance:

1,100 ($9 − $12) =	$3,300 Favorable

Spoilage variance:

Actual production	1,100
Standard production (1,023 ÷ 0.95)	−1,077
Excess production	23
Standard cost	× $ 174
Spoilage variance	$4,002 Unfavorable

Although the purchasing agent was quite pleased, the production supervisor was very unhappy with these results.

REQUIREMENTS

a) Assume that the company has excess production capacity and that no sales were lost due to the excess spoilage. Determine the incremental cost to the company of the purchasing agent's actions.

b) Assume that the company is operating at capacity and that it could have sold more good units if it were able to produce them. Determine the incremental cost to the company of the purchasing agent's actions. Each good unit has a selling price of $200. Assume that there are no variable selling costs.

19–23 The Case of the Hidden Quality Costs

The World's Best Beer at one time purchased coiled aluminum from an outside supplier. They then produced aluminum cans from the coil and placed their brew in the cans. Because of the volume of their operations, World's Best purchased an aluminum fabricating mill. They now produce their own aluminum coil from aluminum ingots. The operation consists of four steps:

1. The ingots are scalped to remove impurities and ensure a smooth, even surface.
2. The ingots are heated to facilitate the rolling operation.
3. The ingots are hot rolled to the thickness of aluminum plate and the ends of each plate are sheared.
4. The plate is cold rolled and coiled and the sides are sheared.

This operation results in a considerable amount of scrap. A typical 25,000-pound ingot produces 20,000 pounds of aluminum coil. Scrap losses are detailed as follows:

1. Scalping results in a 4 percent loss. Hence, for each 25,000-pound ingot that enters the scalping operation, a 24,000-pound scalped ingot emerges.
2. There is no loss in the heating operation. However, the hot rolling and end shearing operation produces an additional 12.5 percent loss. Hence, for each 24,000-pound scalped and heated ingot that enters the operation, a 21,000-pound plate emerges.
3. The cold rolling and side shearing operation produces a final 4.762 percent loss. Hence, for each 21,000-pound plate that enters the operation, a 20,000-pound coil emerges.

The costs assigned to a 20,000-pound coil are as follows:

Cost element	*Scalping*	*Heating*	*Hot roll*	*Cold roll & coil*
Direct materials	$30,000	$31,000	$32,100	$36,500
Direct labor	100	100	400	200
Variable overhead	400	600	2,000	1,500
Fixed overhead	500	400	2,000	1,800
Total	$31,000	$32,100	$36,500	$40,000

Last week, thirty 25,000-pound ingots yielded 580,000 pounds of aluminum coil. One entire coil was scrapped due to an improper adjustment on the coiler. Management requested an immediate explanation noting that World's Best must have higher quality standards for it to remain profitable.

REQUIREMENTS

a) Using World's Best Beer's accounting data, what cost was assigned to the scraped coil?

b) How much scrap cost is included in the cost of a typical coil?

c) For last week, determine the cost of management controllable scrap and the cost of employee controllable scrap.

d) Is it appropriate to include fixed costs in the computations? Why or why not?

19–24 Estimating *P*: A Bayesian Approach (Appendix)

A large check-sorting machine can sort 1,000,000 checks per hour. When properly adjusted, it has the following probability distribution for missorts and rejects:

In control: θ_1

Error rate	*Probability*
0.0010	0.2
0.0008	0.3
0.0005	0.3
0.0003	0.2

When out of adjustment, the machine's missort and rejection rate distribution is:

Out of control: θ_2

Error rate	*Probability*
0.0020	0.1
0.0015	0.4
0.0010	0.4
0.0008	0.1

Before any sample data are observed, there is an 80 percent probability the machine is properly adjusted.

At the end of operations on a recent day, the machine's error rate was 0.0010.

REQUIREMENT

Determine the probability that the machine is out of adjustment.

19–25 Prior Probabilities in Estimating *P* (Appendix)

"This Bayesian approach to estimating *P* is a good idea, but perhaps we can improve it if we eliminate $P(\theta_1)$ and $P(\theta_2)$. That leaves:

$$P = \frac{P(x \mid \theta_1)}{P(x \mid \theta_1) + P(x \mid \theta_2)}$$

Because these values all depend on sample results, subjectivity is completely eliminated from the determination of *P*."

REQUIREMENT

Comment.

19–26 Sequential Revisions of Prior Probabilities (Appendix)
The following distribution of error rates exists for a certain process:

In control: θ_1		*Out of control:* θ_2	
Error rate	*Probability*	*Error rate*	*Probability*
0.07	0.1	0.09	0.1
0.06	0.2	0.08	0.2
0.05	0.4	0.07	0.3
0.03	0.2	0.06	0.3
0.02	0.1	0.05	0.1

Before any sample results are obtained, the prior probability that the process is in control is 0.8. The critical probability for the decision to investigate is 0.5.

REQUIREMENTS

a) Should an investigation be made if a sample reveals an error rate of 0.07?

b) Accept the result of requirement (a) as the revised prior probability. Should an investigation be made if the next sample revealed an error rate of 0.06?

19–27 The Decision to Correct: A Bayesian Approach (Appendix)
Bayesian Jones (a sudent at a northeastern university) has just purchased a new Centurion from Bostville Motors. Before departing on a 4,700-kilometer trip to Los Angeles, Bayesian must decide whether to have his car tuned at a cost of $40. Because it is new, he believes there is a 90 percent probability that the car is properly tuned. However, because gasoline costs $1.20 per liter, Bayesian decides to obtain some additional information.

While speaking with another Centurion owner he learns that, when properly tuned, a Centurion obtains the following kilometers per liter of gasoline:

μ_{θ_1} = 100 kilometers per liter
σ_{θ_1} = 20 kilometers per liter

When out of tune, the Centurion is a gas guzzler:

μ_{θ_2} = 50 kilometers per liter
σ_{θ_2} = 20 kilometers per liter

Faced with these facts, Bayesian Jones departed on a test drive.

REQUIREMENTS

a) Determine the critical probability at which the cost of tuning the car is equal to the excess operating costs of a 4,700-kilometer trip. (*Hint:* Because there are no costs of inspection, it is necessary to first develop an appropriate formula for P^*.)

b) On the test trip, Bayesian's Centurion averages 80 kilometers per liter. Should he have the Centurion tuned? Ordinate values for 1 and 1.5 standard deviations are 0.2420 and 0.1295, respectively.

SOLUTION TO REVIEW PROBLEM

a) R chart and $\overline{X}$ chart

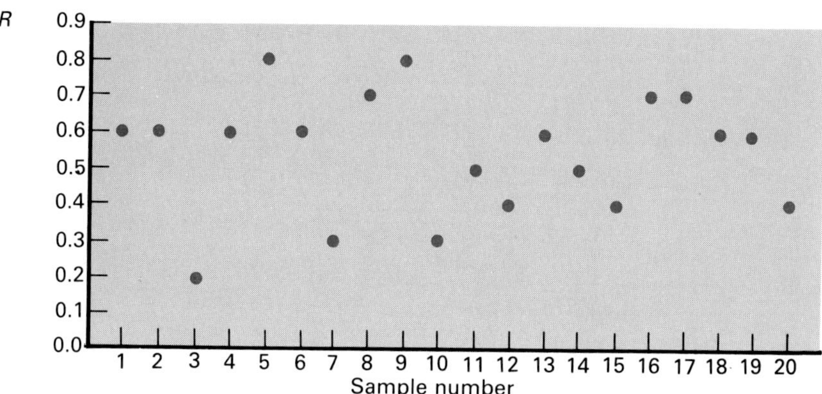

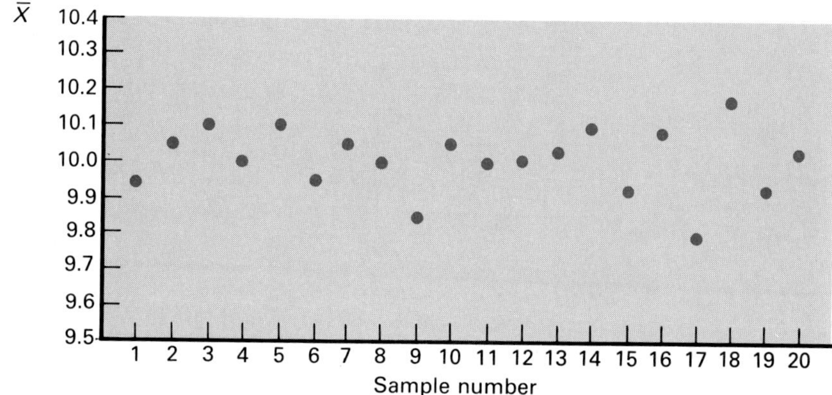

b) $\overline{R} = 10.9 \div 20 = \underline{\underline{0.545}}$

$\text{UCL}_R = D_4\overline{R} = 2.11 \times 0.545 = \underline{\underline{1.15}}$

$\text{LCL}_R = D_3\overline{R} = \text{None}$

c) All R values are within the control limits.

Number of runs test:
$s = 8$, $r = 12$, critical value $= 6$
Actual number of runs $= 9$

Chart passes the number of runs test.

Length of runs test:
Critical value $= 7$
Longest run on either side of the median (0.6) $= 3$*

Chart passes the length of runs test.

Since all points fall within the control limits and the R chart passes the runs tests, the process is in control with respect to variability.

* Note that the R values equal to the median of 0.6 are thrown either above or below the median to decrease the length of a run. The longest run of 3 is from samples 10 to 12.

d) $\overline{\overline{X}} = 200.18 \div 20 = \underline{\underline{10.009}}$

$UCL_{\overline{X}} = \overline{\overline{X}} + A_2\overline{R} = 10.009 + (0.58 \times 0.545) = \underline{\underline{10.325}}$

$LCL_{\overline{X}} = \overline{\overline{X}} - A_2\overline{R} = 10.009 - (0.58 \times 0.545) = \underline{\underline{9.693}}$

e) All $\overline{X}$ values are within the control limits.

Number of runs test:
$s = 8$, $r = 12$, critical value = 6
Actual number of runs = 14
$\overline{X}$ chart passes the number of runs test.

Length of runs test:
Critical value = 7
Longest run on either side of the median (10.02) = 2
$\overline{X}$ chart passes the length of runs tests.

Since all $\overline{X}$ values are within the control limits and the chart passes both runs tests, the process is in control with respect to average.

20 Special Considerations in Payroll Accounting

INTRODUCTION
THE GENERAL TREATMENT OF LABOR COSTS
PAYROLL AND LABOR DISTRIBUTION ACCOUNTING
PAYROLL PROCEDURES
PAYROLL ACCOUNTING PROBLEMS
SUMMARY

INTRODUCTION

TO MORE CLEARLY FOCUS ON OTHER IMPORTANT ISSUES, WE HAVE ASSUMED throughout most of this book that all production employees' salaries and wages are payable directly to them. In reality, the determination of payroll liabilities is complicated by deductions from the earnings of employees paid to third parties on behalf of employees, such as federal income taxes deducted and paid to the Internal Revenue Service. Additional complications arise from employee **fringe benefits** paid by the employer for the benefit of employees, but not reflected in employees' earnings statements. Examples include retirement benefits and health insurance. The number and dollar amount of these deductions and fringe benefits make accounting for them complex and important. Additionally, when it comes to their paychecks, the individual employees are auditors who demand the highest level of accuracy. Almost nothing is more apt to lead employees to question the accuracy of the accounting system, and the budgeting and performance evaluation information related to it, than errors in their paychecks.

The purpose of this chapter is to examine important factors that complicate the determination of payroll liabilities and costs, and the distribution of labor costs. We begin the chapter with a brief overview of the general treatment of labor costs. Next we examine the most significant factors affecting payroll accounting and labor costing. Then we discuss and illustrate payroll procedures and payroll accounting problems. A comprehensive illustration concludes the chapter.

THE GENERAL TREATMENT OF LABOR COSTS

The general treatment of various labor costs is summarized in Exhibit 20–1. **Gross earnings** are the stated earnings of employees computed as a specified amount per hour, week, month, or other unit of time. In the case of production employees, gross earnings are often based on hours on the job, as evidenced by time cards or similar records, multiplied by the wage rate. That portion of gross earnings paid for time spent working on specific products, as evidenced by work

EXHIBIT 20–1 General Treatment of Various Labor Costs

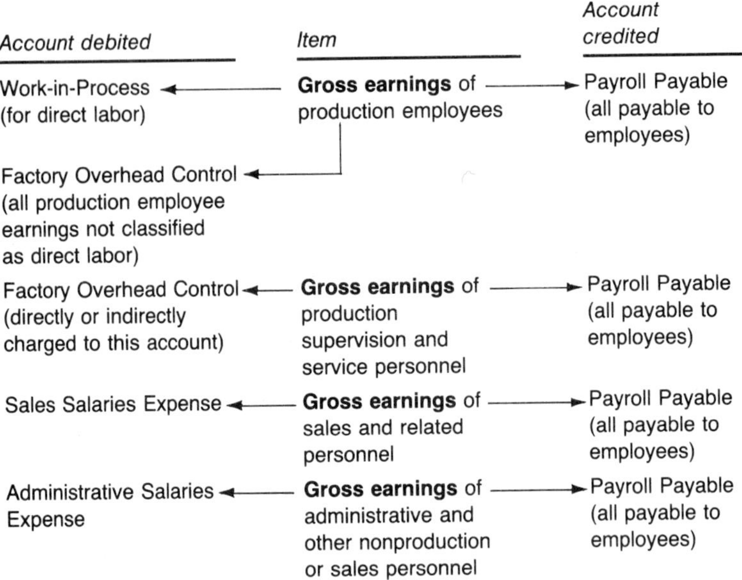

tickets or similar records, is identified as **direct labor** and assigned to Work-in-Process. Any difference between the gross earnings of production employees, credited to Payroll Payable, and direct-labor costs, charged to Work-in-Process, is assigned to Factory Overhead Control. Possible causes of such a difference include overtime premiums, shift differentials, idle time, and time spent on production-related tasks such as receiving instructions, maintenance, and cleaning.

The salaries and wages paid to production supervisors and other personnel whose primary function is to facilitate or support production departments are also credited to Payroll Payable and, ultimately, debited to Factory Overhead Control before being assigned to products.

For financial reporting purposes, the salaries and wages of sales, administrative, and other nonproduction personnel are credited to Payroll Payable and debited to an expense account such as Sales Salaries Expense or Administrative Salaries Expense. These earnings are treated as period costs because the efforts of sales and administrative personnel do not produce a tangible product intended for sale. Nevertheless, for management purposes, we often want to trace sales and administrative costs to nonmanufacturing services or activities. An advertising firm, for example, might assign costs to jobs just as a manufacturing firm would, even though the advertising firm does not produce a physical product and all salaries and wages are treated as period costs for external reporting. This job-cost information might be used for cost-plus billing or to determine the profitability of individual jobs. In this situation, the firm would maintain separate accounting records for internal and external purposes.

PAYROLL AND LABOR DISTRIBUTION ACCOUNTING

Two categories of factors require us to modify the general treatment of labor costs:

1. Those required by law, such as income taxes, social security taxes, unemployment taxes, and compensation insurance.
2. Those that result from voluntary agreements between employer and employee, such as pension plans and vacation pay.

Some of these items are deducted from the gross earnings of employees and reduce the salaries and wages distributable to them. Other items, paid by the employer as additional labor costs, increase total labor costs above the amount of employees' gross earnings. After all deductions are made from gross earnings, the remainder is payable directly to employees. The deductions from gross earnings are payable to third parties. The employer's total labor costs are computed by adding all additional labor costs to gross earnings. The computation of the payroll payable to employees and the employer's total labor costs is illustrated in Exhibit 20–2.

Federal Income Taxes

Employers are required by law to withhold federal income taxes from each employee's gross earnings. The amount withheld depends on the employee's gross earnings, marital status, and the number of exemptions the employee claims on a withholding certificate (called a **W-4 form**) that each employee must complete prior to being paid. The employee can claim exemptions for himself or herself, for each of the employee's dependents, and for other circumstances specified by the tax code. Based on the employee's gross pay, marital status, and exemptions, the federal income taxes to be withheld are determined by consulting tax rate tables prepared by the Internal Revenue Service.

States and cities that have income taxes typically have similar withholding (and remitting) procedures. Because of this similarity, state income tax withholdings are omitted from textbook illustrations and discussions, permitting a clearer focus on underlying concepts.

Federal Insurance Contribution Act

The Federal Insurance Contributions Act (FICA) requires all but a limited number of exempt government employees *and* employers to pay **FICA taxes** for government-sponsored retirement benefits, life insurance, and medical insurance. These

EXHIBIT 20–2 Computation of Payroll Payable to Employees and Total Labor Costs

Gross earnings	*Gross earnings*
less deductions:	*plus additional labor costs:*
Federal income taxes	Employer FICA taxes
State income taxes	Federal unemployment taxes
Employee FICA taxes	State unemployment taxes
Union dues	Compensation insurance
Insurance purchased by employee	Pension plan
Charitable contributions	Vacation pay
= Payroll payable to employees	= Total labor cost

benefits are officially known as Old Age and Survivors Insurance, Medicare, and Medicaid. However, FICA taxes and the related benefits are often referred to as "**Social Security.**" Employers are required by law to withhold FICA taxes from each employee's gross earnings. What's more, employers are subject to additional FICA taxes. FICA tax rates and FICA taxable earnings are subject to frequent change. In 1985 the FICA tax rate for employees was 7.05 percent and employers paid an additional 7.05 percent in FICA taxes. The FICA tax rate is currently scheduled to be 7.51 percent for both employees and employers in 1988. Not all earnings of all employees are subject to FICA taxes. The Social Security laws currently specify that the earnings subject to FICA taxes change automatically, starting from a maximum of $39,600 in 1985 and increasing in subsequent years as average wage levels increase. For consistency and simplicity, textbook examples, exercises, and problems assume employees and employers pay identical FICA taxes at a rate of 7.51 percent on the first $40,000 of each employee's annual earnings. Using a rate of 7.51 percent and maximum FICA taxable earnings of $40,000, employee, employer, and total FICA taxes for several representative annual gross earnings are as follows:

Gross earnings	*Earnings subject to FICA taxes*	*Employee's FICA taxes*	*Employer's FICA taxes*	*Total FICA taxes*
$10,000	$10,000	$ 751.00	$ 751.00	$1,502.00
20,000	20,000	1,502.00	1,502.00	3,004.00
40,000	40,000	3,004.00	3,004.00	6,008.00
45,000	40,000	3,004.00	3,004.00	6,008.00
60,000	40,000	3,004.00	3,004.00	6,008.00

If an employee earns more than $40,000 a year, only the first $40,000 of gross earnings are subject to FICA taxes. An employee who has annual gross earnings of more than $40,000 and who works for two or more employers during a single year, may have more than $3,004 in FICA taxes withheld. If this happens, the employee may claim a refund for these excess withholdings when filing his or her tax return, or the employee may use these excess withholdings to pay any income taxes due.

Although the employee and the employer pay FICA taxes, the FICA taxes paid by the employer are not included in the determination of gross earnings. Consequently, gross earnings understate the employer's total labor costs. Because the computation of FICA-taxable earnings starts over on January 1 of each year, an employer's additional labor costs for FICA taxes will normally be higher in the earlier (than in the later) portion of the year. Likewise, the **net pay** (gross earnings less deductions) of employees earning more than the taxable base will be lower in the earlier (than in the later) portion of the year.

Both federal income tax witholdings and FICA taxes must be remitted to the Internal Revenue Service. The statutory timing for these remittances depends on the total liability for employee withholdings and employer contributions. Large employers may be required to remit taxes as soon as three business days after a payroll is issued. In any event, withholdings must be remitted no later than the end of the month following each calendar quarter. For example, withholdings for the first quarter (January, February, and March) must be remitted by April 30.

Employers must provide each employee and the Internal Revenue Service with an annual statement (called a **W-2 form**) indicating the employee's gross earnings, income taxes, and FICA taxes withheld for the calendar year. The W-2 form must be delivered to the employee by January 31 of the following year, or within 30 days of the employee's last paycheck, if the employee is not employed on December 31. The employee must file a copy of the W-2 form with his or her income tax return.

Unemployment Taxes

Employers must also pay federal and state **unemployment taxes.** The proceeds are used to provide income to persons who are temporarily unemployed. No portion of these taxes is withheld from an employee's gross earnings. As this book goes to press, unemployment taxes are paid on the first $7,000 earned each year by each employee; however, the unemployment tax base is subject to change. Because unemployment tax rates vary with an organization's labor turnover experience and location, *a federal rate of 0.8 percent and a state rate of 2.7 percent are used in all examples and assignment materials in this text.* It is also assumed that unemployment taxes for a calendar quarter are remitted to the Internal Revenue Service and the appropriate State Unemployment Commission by the end of the month following the calendar quarter. Like FICA taxes, unemployment taxes cause an organization's total labor bill to exceed the gross earnings of employees; and, because unemployment taxes are also levied on a limited wage base starting on January 1 of each year, they also cause total labor costs to be higher in the earlier portions of the year than in the later portions of the year.

Compensation Insurance

To provide income to employees who are unable to work due to a job-related illness or injury, employers must carry some form of **compensation insurance.** This insurance may be obtained from the state in which the employer is located or from a private insurance company. If obtained from a state, the premium is stated as a percentage of gross earnings. To simplify textbook illustrations and assignment material, we will assume that compensation insurance is purchased from a private company as part of a larger package. Consequently, compensation insurance does not appear as a separate item in examples or assignments.

Voluntary Items Affecting Labor Costs

Income tax withholdings, FICA taxes, unemployment insurance, and compensation insurance are required by law. Organizations also provide a number of additional employee fringe benefits that are not legally mandated, including such items as: life insurance, health insurance, sick leave, sabbatical leave, tuition payments for the employee or employee's dependents, free or subsidized parking, subsidized cafeterias, free or subsidized recreational facilities, pension plans, and vacation pay, to name just a few. Although the cost of many of these items is shared between the employee and the employer, to the extent that they are provided by the employer, they result in the incurrence of additional labor costs. We will briefly consider pension plans and vacation pay as representative of the many types of voluntary fringe benefits that produce additional labor costs.

Pension Plans A **pension** is a sum of money paid a former employee as a retirement benefit. With the exception of certain government employees who do not participate in FICA (social security), pensions supplement FICA retirement benefits. Organizations enter into pension plan agreements to provide pensions to employees after they retire. In the past many organizations, especially units of government, had **unfunded pension plans,** in which monies were not set aside for future retirement benefits. Instead, pension payments were made directly to retired employees by the former employer. Today almost all nongovernment organizations have **funded pension plans,** in which monies for future pension payments are set aside on a regular basis, usually to a pension fund administered by an independent financial institution. Pension benefits are then paid out of the pension fund by the pension plan administrator.

The primary advantage of a funded pension plan is the security it offers employees. A funded pension plan also tends to result in the employer making pension fund expenditures during the periods benefiting from employees' efforts.

Although there are a number of variations in the operation of funded pension plans, we will assume that the employer contributes a fixed percentage of each employee's earnings to a plan administered by a financial institution such as a bank or an insurance company.[1] Regardless of the variability in plan funding, the employer's pension fund costs should be recognized in periods prior to the employee's retirement, when the employee is earning the right to receive future pension payments.

Vacation Pay **Vacation pay** refers to wages paid employees for vacation or holiday periods when they are not working. Because employees earn the right to paid vacations and holidays by working, vacation pay is an additional labor cost incurred during periods employees are working. The effect of vacation pay is to raise total labor costs above the amount represented by gross earnings for work periods. A vacation pay liability should be recognized as the right to receive vacation pay accrues. The vacation pay liability is discharged when payments are made to vacationing employees.

Assume an employee works 40 hours a week, 50 weeks per year, and has 2 weeks of paid vacation each year. If the employee is not entitled to any other fringe benefits, the effect of the paid vacation is to increase labor costs by 4 percent (2 weeks vacation ÷ 50 weeks of work). An amount equal to 4 percent of gross payroll should be credited to the liability account, Accrued Vacation Pay, and debited to an appropriate account such as Factory Overhead Control

---

[1] This type of a plan is called a defined contribution plan. Under a *defined contribution plan,* the employer's payments are fixed. However, actual benefits may vary depending on changes in the proceeds from and the market value of securities in the pension fund portfolio. Under a *defined benefit plan,* the benefits to a retired employee are fixed. However, the employer's contribution will vary depending on the proceeds from and the market value of securities in the pension fund portfolio.

or Administrative Salaries Expense. If the employee earns $10 per hour, the weekly accrual will be $16 (40 hours × $10 per hour × 0.04). After 50 weeks the total accrual will be $800, an amount sufficient for 2 weeks of paid vacation.

If employees receive fringe benefits in addition to vacation pay, the cost of these fringe benefits should also be assigned to periods employees are working, rather than to vacation periods. Assume that an employee earns $500 per week and has 2 weeks of paid vacation each year, and that the employer contributes an amount equal to 10 percent of gross earnings to a funded pension plan. The vacation pay accrual is 4 percent of total labor costs:

$$\frac{\text{Labor cost of vacation periods}}{\text{Labor cost of nonvacation periods}} = \frac{\$500 \times 1.10 \times 2}{\$500 \times 1.10 \times 50} = \underline{\underline{0.04}}$$

However, when the vacation pay accrual is stated as a percentage of gross earnings, rather than total labor costs, it will be larger than 4 percent:

$$\frac{\text{Labor cost of vacation periods}}{\text{Gross earnings of nonvacation periods}} = \frac{\$500 \times 1.10 \times 2}{\$500 \times 50} = \underline{\underline{0.044}}$$

If the employer also has to pay FICA taxes of 7.51 percent on the vacation pay, the accrual should be 4.7 percent of gross earnings:

$$\frac{\text{Labor cost of vacation periods}}{\text{Gross earnings of nonvacation periods}} = \frac{\$500 \times 1.1751 \times 2}{\$500 \times 50} = \underline{\underline{0.047}}$$

We assume that vacation earnings are paid in addition to all other annual wages. Regardless of when the employee goes on vacation, if he or she earns more in a year than the base earnings for FICA or unemployment tax purposes, the cost of these taxes is not regarded as a cost of vacation pay. If, however, an employee earns less than the base earnings for FICA or unemployment taxes, the cost of these taxes is regarded as a cost of vacation pay. An employee earning $500 per week earns a total of $25,000 for 50 work weeks ($500 × 50). The vacation pay is subject to FICA taxes, which have an earnings base of $40,000; however, the vacation pay is not subject to unemployment taxes, which have an earnings base of $7,000.

PAYROLL PROCEDURES

In prior chapters, payroll required only two basic journal entries, one to record the liability for gross earnings and assign labor costs to appropriate accounts, and a second to record payment of gross earnings. Now that we have deductions from gross earnings and additional labor costs paid by the employer, we must modify these payroll and labor costing procedures. We use three basic journal entries:

1. Record the liabilities for and the distribution of gross earnings.
2. Record the liabilities for and the distribution of additional labor costs.
3. Record the payment of labor-related liabilities.

The general form of the first and second entries is presented in Exhibit 20–3.

EXHIBIT 20–3 **Recording Gross Earnings and Additional Labor Costs**

Account debited	*Item*	*Accounts credited*
Work-in-Process ← (for direct labor) Factory Overhead Control ← (all production employee earnings not classified as direct labor)	**Gross earnings** of production employees →	Income Tax Withholdings Payable FICA Taxes Payable Other Deductions Payable Payroll Payable
Factory Overhead Control ←	**Additional labor costs** for production employees →	FICA Taxes Payable Federal Unemployment Taxes Payable State Unemployment Taxes Payable Pension Fund Liability Accrued Vacation Pay Other Fringe Benefit Liabilities
Factory Overhead Control ← (directly or indirectly charged to this account)	**Gross earnings** of production supervision and service personnel →	Income Tax Withholdings Payable FICA Taxes Payable Other Deductions Payable Payroll Payable
Factory Overhead Control ← (directly or indirectly charged to this account)	**Additional labor costs** of production supervision and service personnel →	FICA Taxes Payable Federal Unemployment Taxes Payable State Unemployment Taxes Payable Pension Fund Liability Accrued Vacation Pay Other Fringe Benefit Liabilities
Sales Salaries Expense ← (or similar account)	**Gross earnings** of sales and related personnel →	Income Tax Withholdings Payable FICA Taxes Payable Other Deductions Payable Payroll Payable
Sales Salaries Expense ← (or similar account)	**Additional labor costs** of sales and related personnel →	FICA Taxes Payable Federal Unemployment Taxes Payable State Unemployment Taxes Payable Pension Fund Liability Accrued Vacation Pay Other Fringe Benefit Liabilities
Administrative Salaries Expense ←	**Gross earnings** of administrative and other nonproduction or sales personnel →	Income Tax Withholdings Payable FICA Taxes Payable Other Deductions Payable Payroll Payable
Administrative Salaries Expense ←	**Additional labor costs** of administrative and other nonproduction or sales personnel →	FICA Taxes Payable Federal Unemployment Taxes Payable State Unemployment Taxes Payable Pension Fund Liability Accrued Vacation Pay Other Fringe Benefit Liabilities

Comparing Exhibits 20–1 and 20–3, note that the account Payroll Payable is no longer credited for the gross earnings of employees. In other chapters, Payroll Payable represented the total liability for gross earnings. In this chapter, the total liability for gross earnings is broken down into separate liabilities for each of the deductions from gross earnings, and for the net amount payable directly to employees. Only this net amount is credited to Payroll Payable. In most manufacturing organizations, the additional labor costs for production employees are assigned to Factory Overhead Control. An additional entry would be made in a subsidiary account to indicate the nature of the expense, for example, Production Employees' State Unemployment Taxes. For simplicity, we assume that the additional labor costs of other employees are assigned to the same control account as their gross earnings. In the case of indirect labor, an appropriate entry would also be made in a subsidiary ledger, for example, Production Supervisors' State Unemployment Taxes, which might be a subsidiary account to Factory Overhead Control. The additional labor costs of other personnel would also be recorded in appropriate subsidiary accounts, or in an account that indicates both the category of the employee and the nature of the expense, for example, Administrative Employees' State Unemployment Taxes.

Example 20–1

The Tulip Company pays and records all labor costs on the last day of each month. The following data are taken from the Tulip Company's payroll records for the month of November 19x0:

Direct labor	$50,000
Other production salaries and wages	30,000
Administrative salaries and wages	10,000
Gross earnings	$90,000

ADDITIONAL INFORMATION

- All payroll, except $5,000 of administrative salaries, is subject to FICA taxes at a rate of 7.51 percent.
- Only $20,000 of production salaries and wages are subject to federal and state unemployment taxes at rates of 0.8 and 2.7 percent, respectively. None of the other payroll is subject to unemployment taxes.
- Federal income taxes withheld from all gross earnings amounted to $28,000.
- Tulip contributes an amount equal to 10 percent of employee gross earnings to a funded pension plan.
- All employees are entitled to a paid vacation each year. The accrual for vacation pay averages 6 percent of gross earnings.
- Tulip has one production department and no service departments.

We now present summary journal entries, with supporting computations for November's payroll and related costs. We could have prepared the three entries for each type of employee (production, production supervision and service, and administrative); however, to save space, we used compound entries.

1. Record the liabilities for and the distribution of gross earnings:

Account	Debit	Credit
Work-in-Process	50,000.00	
Factory Overhead Control	30,000.00	
Administrative Salaries Expense	10,000.00	
Income Tax Withholdings Payable		28,000.00
FICA Taxes Payable [($90,000 − $5,000) × 0.0751]		6,383.50
Payroll Payable		55,616.50

2. Record the liability for and the distribution of additional labor costs (be sure to follow the supporting computations below the journal entry):

Account	Debit	Credit
Factory Overhead Control	19,508.00	
Administrative Salaries Expense	1,975.50	
FICA Taxes Payable		6,383.50
Federal Unemployment Taxes Payable		160.00
State Unemployment Taxes Payable		540.00
Pension Fund Liability		9,000.00
Accrued Vacation Pay		5,400.00

	Factory overhead control	*Admin. salaries expense*	*Total*
FICA taxes:			
($80,000 × 0.0751)	$ 6,008.00		$ 6,383.50
($5,000 × 0.0751)		$ 375.50	
Federal unemployment taxes:			
($20,000 × 0.008)	160.00		160.00
State unemployment taxes:			
($20,000 × 0.027)	540.00		540.00
Pension:			
($80,000 × 0.10)	8,000.00		9,000.00
($10,000 × 0.10)		1,000.00	
Vacation pay:			
($80,000 × 0.06)	4,800.00		5,400.00
($10,000 × 0.06)		600.00	
Total	$19,508.00	$1,975.50	$21,483.50

3. Record the payment of labor-related liabilities:

Account	Debit	Credit
Payroll Payable	55,616.50	
Income Tax Withholdings Payable	28,000.00	
FICA Taxes Payable	12,767.00	
Federal Unemployment Taxes Payable	160.00	
State Unemployment Taxes Payable	540.00	
Pension Fund Liability	9,000.00	
Accrued Vacation Pay	5,400.00	
Cash		111,483.50

The third journal entry represents the summary of a number of disbursements that would take place at various points in time. The most immediate disbursement would be for the payroll, whereas the disbursement for accrued vacation pay might not take place for a year. The details pertaining to the timing of payroll disbursements are illustrated in a more comprehensive example later in this chapter.

PAYROLL ACCOUNTING PROBLEMS

A number of issues make payroll accounting problematical and deserve special attention, including the magnitude of the additional labor costs, the volume of payroll transactions, and the timing of payroll disbursements. Each is considered in the sections that follow.

Magnitude of Additional Labor Costs

Most manufacturing organizations assign the additional labor costs paid for the benefit of production employees to Factory Overhead Control. This procedure was appropriate when these additional costs were a small portion of both direct labor and of factory overhead. In 1957 employee fringe benefits averaged 15 percent of gross earnings. However, a recent U.S. Chamber of Commerce survey found that employee fringe benefits now range between 18 and 65 percent of gross earnings, with an average of 37 percent of gross earnings. The following example of typical fringe benefits for an employee earning $20,000 per year illustrates how rapidly they build up:

Payroll fringe benefit:	*Percent of Gross Earnings*
Employer's FICA taxes	0.0751
State unemployment taxes [0.027 × ($7,000/$20,000)]	0.0095
Federal unemployment taxes [0.008 × ($7,000/$20,000)]	0.0028
Pension plan	0.1000
Vacation pay (4 weeks vacation including holidays ÷ 48 work weeks)	0.0833
Medical, dental, and life insurance	0.0500
Other (parking, recreation, cafeteria, employee facilities, time off for jury duty)	0.0400
Total	0.3607

The magnitude of employee fringe benefits has led some employers to prefer paying current employees overtime premiums on a regular basis, rather than hiring additional employees, during periods of economic expansion. This is because many fringe benefits (for example, insurance) are set at a fixed amount per employee per year regardless of the number of hours worked, and many other fringe benefits (for example, FICA taxes) are set at a percentage of some maximum base earnings. Once the fixed benefits have been incurred and the maximum base earnings have been paid, overtime premiums of 50 percent or more can be less costly than paying additional fringe benefits.

The magnitude of production employees' fringe benefits can lead to errors in product costing when these costs are assigned to Factory Overhead Control. This can happen under one of two circumstances:

1. In the absence of fringe benefits, factory overhead would be applied on the basis of something other than direct labor; however, the presence of fringe benefits makes total factory overhead correlate most highly with direct labor, which is used for overhead application. Under these circumstances, the nonlabor costs in factory overhead are not applied on the best basis.
2. Although employee fringe benefits are a large portion of factory overhead and are best applied on the basis of direct labor, another basis (for example, machine hours) that is best for other overhead costs, is used. Under these circumstances, the labor costs in factory overhead are not applied on the best basis.

Only when employee fringe benefits are a small portion of labor costs and factory overhead, or when other, nonemployment-related overhead costs are best applied using a labor basis, is it acceptable to follow the traditional procedure of placing all employee fringe benefits in Factory Overhead Control.

An alternative procedure of accounting for production employees' fringe benefits, illustrated in Exhibit 20–4, is to assign these costs to a separate cost pool, such as an account titled Production Employee Fringe Benefits. The costs accumulated in this pool would be assigned to products using some labor-related basis such as direct-labor dollars or direct-labor hours. The fringe benefits earned by production supervisors and other indirect laborers would still be placed in Factory Overhead Control, which would be assigned on whatever basis is deemed most appropriate.

Although many organizations have changed to this or a similar procedure for applying fringe benefit costs, most have not. The reasons for not changing include inertia, satisfaction with current procedures, a lack of knowledge of alternatives, and the cost of modifying the current accounting system. Unfortunately, failing to modify a firm's accounting system as circumstances change makes the system less relevant to management and results in the accountants, who supervise the system and fail to argue for a desirable change, seem out of touch with reality and in a world of their own.

Volume of Payroll Transactions

The need to prepare payroll checks and records in a timely, accurate, and cost-effective manner has led large organizations to use automated payroll accounting procedures. Indeed, payroll accounting was one of the first widespread applications of mainframe computers. Today payroll accounting software is widely available for personal computers.

EXHIBIT 20–4 A Preferred Treatment of Gross Earnings and Additional Labor Costs of Production Employees

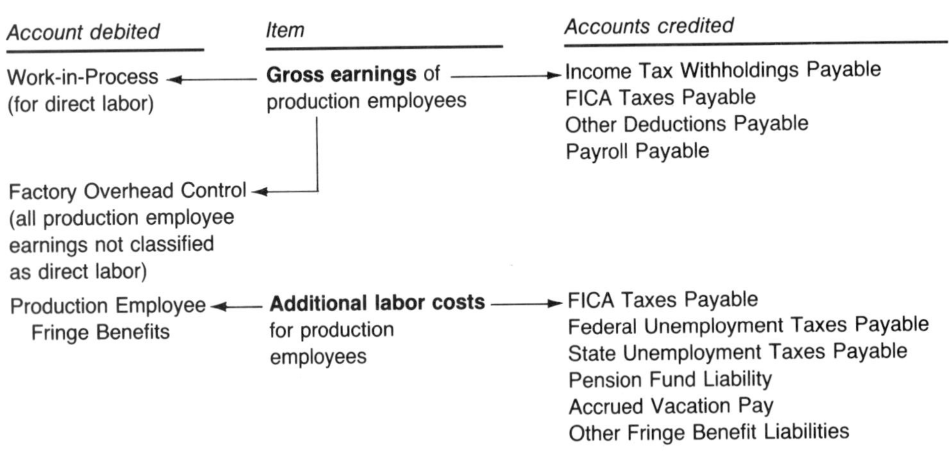

Payroll accounting is complicated by seemingly endless detail in two areas:

1. The determination of payroll and payroll-related liabilities
2. The distribution of payroll costs

To determine payroll and related liabilities, employers must keep detailed records of the gross earnings, the deductions from gross earnings, and the net pay of each employee as well as the additional labor costs paid for the benefit of each employee. This must be done for each pay period and on a cumulative basis for each quarter and year. In developing these records, employers must consider each employee's wage rate, regular and overtime hours worked, tax exemptions claimed by the employee, income tax withholdings appropriate for the employee's gross earnings, FICA taxes (and whether or not the employee has passed the maximum FICA earnings base), federal and state unemployment insurance (and whether or not the employee has passed the maximum unemployment insurance earnings base), pension plan agreements, vacation pay agreements, voluntary deductions from the employee's gross earnings, and other voluntary fringe benefits paid by the employer. Employers must keep these records in detail for each employee and for each third party who is to receive disbursements for the benefit of employees. For example, employers must disclose the federal income taxes withheld from gross earnings both in the records maintained for each employee and in the records filed with the Internal Revenue Service.

Payroll Procedures Are Highly Automated Exhibit 20–5 summarizes the determination of payroll liabilities and the records necessary for payroll accounting. The **payroll master file** contains information on each employee's pay rate, federal, state, and local tax exemptions, and voluntary deductions. **Employee earnings records** contain year-to-date information on each employee's earnings and deductions. These records may also contain information about each employee's accumulated fringe benefits for vacation pay, sick leave, pension, and other items.

The **time cards** and related records contain information about the number of hours, days, or weeks an employee has worked during a specific pay period. Each employee's gross earnings is computed by multiplying the time worked by the appropriate rate, or rates if overtime is involved, per unit of time.

The employer's payroll accounting system must maintain files of the liabilities paid and payable to each third party for the benefit of each employee. One such file might indicate the federal income tax withholdings paid and payable to the Internal Revenue Service for the benefit of each employee. Another file might indicate the total pension fund liabilities paid and payable for each employee. Yet a third file might indicate the total vacation pay earned by each employee and the remaining vacation pay liability for each employee.

The information in the earnings records and the files for liabilities to third parties are periodically updated. Most of the information needed for this updating is taken from the payroll master file and the time records. Processing this information yields a payroll register and information about the additional labor

EXHIBIT 20–5 Determining Payroll Liabilities and Sorting Records for Each Payee

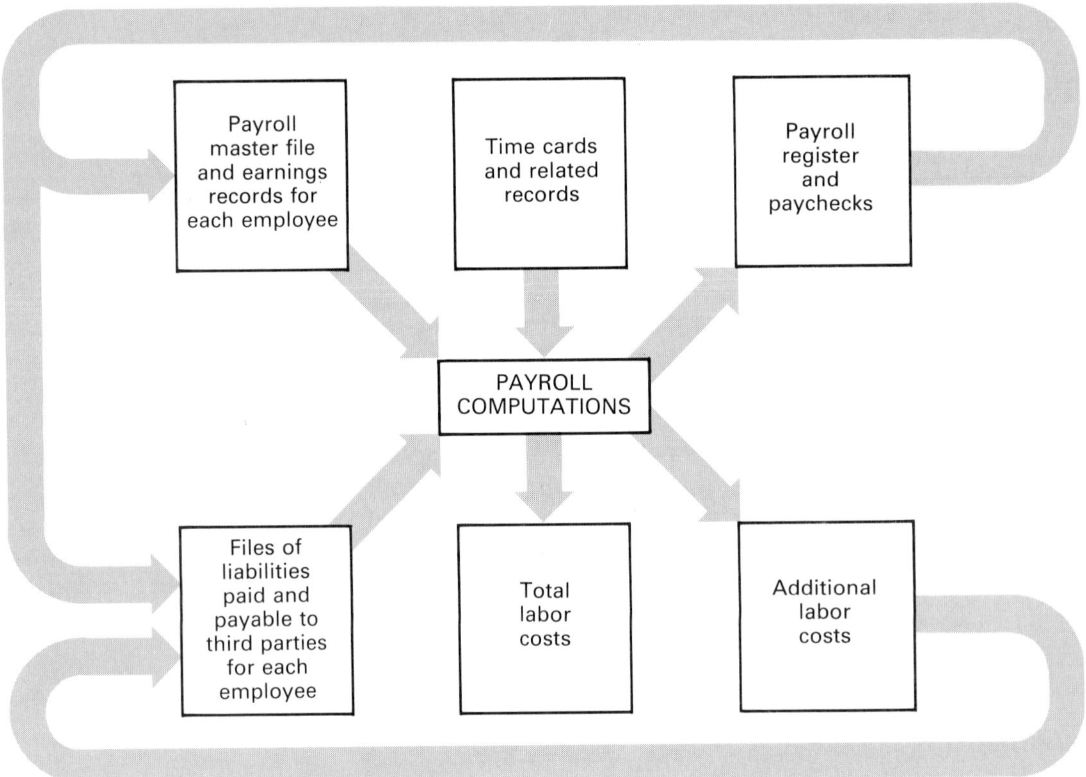

costs to be paid by the employer. The **payroll register** details the gross earnings, deductions from gross earnings, and payroll payable to each employee and in total for the current payroll period. The payroll register is used to update the employee earnings records as well as some of the files pertaining to third-party liabilities. It also serves as the basis for the credits in the first set of payroll journal entries. Because payroll payable is paid soon after its determination, the information in the payroll register for a particular pay period can serve as the subsidiary ledger for Payroll Payable.

A Separate Payroll Checking Account Is Often Used Employees' paychecks can be prepared at the same time as the payroll register. If this is done, Cash will be credited and Payroll Payable will be debited as soon as the checks are issued. Many organizations maintain a separate checking account for payroll. An amount equal to the payroll payable is drawn on the organization's main checking account and placed in the payroll checking account each pay period. The use of a separate payroll checking account facilitates bookkeeping efficiency by segregating this high-volume area. The payroll register can also serve as the payroll check register, with any balance in the payroll checking account equaling the outstanding checks.

The additional labor cost information produced by the payroll computations is used to update the files of liabilities paid and payable to third parties. It also serves as the basis for the credits in the second set of payroll journal entries.

After payroll liabilities are determined and records for each employee are sorted, total labor costs must be distributed. The distribution of total labor costs is represented by the debits in the first and second payroll journal entries. The box labeled "total labor costs" in Exhibit 20–5 is further detailed in Exhibit 20–6. Here the total labor costs are assigned to the appropriate production, service, selling, and administrative accounts. As discussed previously, these allocations depend on each employee's departmental assignment, whether or not direct-labor

EXHIBIT 20–6 Distribution of Total Labor Costs

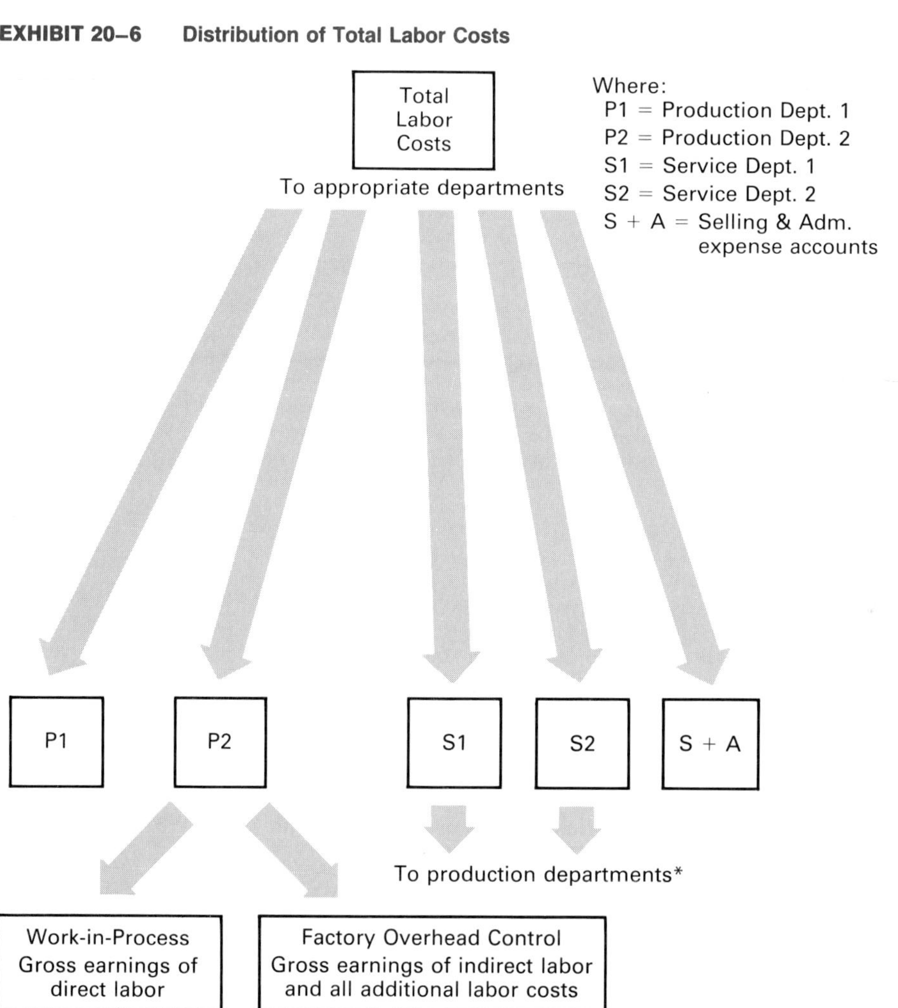

* Procedures for allocating service departments costs to production departments are discussed in Chapter 6.

costs are involved, and whether or not the labor costs being distributed are gross earnings or additional labor costs.

Internal Control Is Important Internal control procedures for payroll are especially important in organizations with many employees. There are many stories of unscrupulous supervisors, paymasters, bookkeepers, or computer operators putting extra employees on the books and pocketing the fictitious employee's paycheck, or giving themselves an unauthorized raise. As a minimum, the duties of determining the payroll, distributing the paychecks, and reconciling the payroll checking account should be separated. The paymaster or whoever distributes the paychecks should know the employees personally or demand identification. Internal auditors should periodically verify that all persons on the payroll do, in fact, work for the organization. Procedures must also be developed to verify pay periods and pay rates. Employees should be paid by check rather than in cash. If employees are paid in cash, they should sign a pay stub indicating the amount of cash received. The total of the signed pay stubs should equal the cash set aside for payroll payable.

Transaction Dates and Comprehensive Illustration

A number of timing problems related to the accrual and payment of payroll liabilities further complicate payroll accounting. These problems are illustrated with a comprehensive example of payroll accounting. The example also demonstrates the need to keep track of accumulated FICA earnings and unemployment tax earnings. Because the setting is that of a merchandising rather than a manufacturing firm, all payroll costs are period costs.

Example 20–2

The Badger Gift Shop began operations on March 22, 19x5. Each of the store's five employees is paid $32 per day. Badger does not have a pension plan or paid vacations.

ADDITIONAL INFORMATION

- Employees are paid on Tuesday for the previous week's (Monday–Friday only) work.
- All payroll costs are assigned to the account Salaries and Wages Expense.
- Federal income taxes withheld from each employee's paycheck average 20 percent of gross earnings.
- FICA taxes of 7.51 percent of gross earnings are to be paid by each employee and by Badger on the first $40,000 of each employee's annual gross earnings.
- State and federal unemployment taxes of 2.7 percent and 0.8 percent are to be paid by Badger on the first $7,000 earned by each employee.
- Income taxes, FICA taxes, and unemployment taxes for each calendar quarter are remitted to the appropriate agency on the last day of the month following the quarter. *Only amounts pertaining to wages actually paid during the quarter are remitted. Any end-of-quarter accrual pertaining to unpaid wages is not to be remitted until after the following quarter.*
- Badger accrues unpaid expenses and recognizes all previously unrecorded liabilities at the end of each month.

o Calendars for March and April of 19x5 are:

March

S	M	T	W	T	F	S
	1	2	3	4	5	6
7	8	9	10	11	12	13
14	15	16	17	18	19	20
21	22	23	24	25	26	27
28	29	30	31			

April

S	M	T	W	T	F	S
				1	2	3
4	5	6	7	8	9	10
11	12	13	14	15	16	17
18	19	20	21	22	23	24
25	26	27	28	29	30	

All journal entries required on March 30, March 31, April 6, April 13, and April 30 are presented in the paragraphs that follow. These dates are selected to illustrate the timing issues involved in payroll accounting. Try to develop the appropriate entries on your own as an exercise before you study the solution. Note that the entries can be classified into one of three categories: (1) recording the liability for and the distribution of gross earnings; (2) recording the liability for and the distribution of additional labor costs; and (3) recording the payment of labor-related liabilities.

On *March 30* Badger must record all liabilities and expenses pertaining to the previous week's payroll as well as the payment of the payroll payable. None of the other liabilities will be paid until April 30, the end of the month following the first calendar quarter. Because employees earn $32 per day, it will take 218.75 work days ($7,000 ÷ $32) before the unemployment tax base is reached. Consequently unemployment taxes and FICA taxes must be paid on all March and April earnings.

Salaries and Wages Expense ($32 × 5 employees × 5 days)	800.00	
Income Tax Withholdings Payable ($800 × 0.20)		160.00
FICA Taxes Payable ($800 × 0.0751)		60.08
Payroll Payable		579.92
Salaries and Wages Expense	88.08	
FICA Taxes Payable		60.08
Federal Unemployment Taxes Payable ($800 × 0.008)		6.40
State Unemployment Taxes Payable ($800 × 0.027)		21.60
Payroll Payable	579.92	
Cash		579.92

On *March 31* Badger must accrue the payroll liabilities and the payroll expense for the last three days of March prior to preparing March 31 financial statements. If Badger did not prepare financial statements as of March 31, these accruals would not be needed.

Salaries and Wages Expense ($32 × 5 employees × 3 days)	480.00	
Income Tax Withholdings Payable ($480 × 0.20)		96.00
FICA Taxes Payable ($480 × 0.0751)		36.05
Payroll Payable		347.95

Salaries and Wages Expense	52.85	
FICA Taxes Payable		36.05
Federal Unemployment Taxes Payable ($480 × 0.008)		3.84
State Unemployment Taxes Payable ($480 × 0.027)		12.96

On *April 6,* assuming that Badger does not reverse the March 31 payroll accrual, Badger must record the additional payroll liabilities and expenses for April 1 and 2 and record the payment of the payroll payable.

Salaries and Wages Expense ($32 × 5 employees × 2 days)	320.00	
Income Tax Withholdings Payable ($320 × 0.20)		64.00
FICA Taxes Payable ($320 × 0.0751)		24.03
Payroll Payable		231.97
Salaries and Wages Expense	75.20	
FICA Taxes Payable		64.00
Federal Unemployment Taxes Payable ($320 × 0.008)		2.56
State Unemployment Taxes Payable ($320 × 0.027)		8.64
Payroll Payable ($347.95 + $231.97)	579.92	
Cash		579.92

The *April 13* journal entries are identical to the March 30 entries; Badger must record all liabilities and expenses pertaining to the previous week's payroll as well as the payment of the payroll payable.

Salaries and Wages Expense ($32 × 5 employees × 5 days)	800.00	
Income Tax Withholdings Payable ($800 × 0.20)		160.00
FICA Taxes Payable ($800 × 0.0751)		60.08
Payroll Payable		579.92
Salaries and Wages Expense	88.08	
FICA Taxes Payable		60.08
Federal Unemployment Taxes Payable ($800 × 0.008)		6.40
State Unemployment Taxes Payable ($800 × 0.027)		21.60
Payroll Payable	579.92	
Cash		579.92

On *April 20* and *April 27* Badger would make payroll entries identical to those made on April 13.

April 30 falls on a Friday, and the weekly payroll will not be paid until the following Tuesday; consequently Badger must accrue five days' payroll expenses and liabilities on this date. April 30 is also the last day of the month following the first calendar quarter. By this date Badger must remit all payroll tax liabilities pertaining to wages actually paid during the previous quarter.

Salaries and Wages Expense ($32 × 5 employees × 5 days)	800.00	
Income Tax Withholdings Payable ($800 × 0.20)		160.00
FICA Taxes Payable ($800 × 0.0751)		60.08
Payroll Payable		579.92
Salaries and Wages Expense	88.08	
FICA Taxes Payable		60.08
Federal Unemployment Taxes Payable ($800 × 0.008)		6.40
State Unemployment Taxes Payable ($800 × 0.027)		21.60
Income Tax Withholdings Payable	160.00	
FICA Taxes Payable	120.16	
Federal Unemployment Taxes Payable	6.40	
State Unemployment Taxes Payable	21.60	
Cash		308.16

Only taxes pertaining to wages actually paid during the first quarter are remitted in this example, and the only wages paid during the first quarter were paid on March 30. If Badger had a larger payroll, the firm might be required to make earlier remittances to government agencies.

SUMMARY

Two categories of factors require us to modify the general treatment of labor costs: (1) those required by law, for example, income taxes, FICA taxes, unemployment taxes, and compensation insurance; and (2) those that result from voluntary agreements between employer and employee, for example, pension plans and vacation pay. Some of these items are deductions from the gross earnings of employees and reduce the earnings distributable to them. Other items, paid by the employer for the benefit of employees, increase total labor costs above the amount of employees' gross earnings.

Three types of journal entries are required for payroll accounting: (1) entries to record the liability for and the distribution of gross payroll; (2) entries to record the liabilities for and the distribution of additional labor costs; and (3) entries to record the payment of labor-related liabilities. The preparation of these entries is complicated by a number of factors, including the magnitude of additional labor costs, the volume of payroll transactions, and the timing of payroll disbursements.

Because of their magnitude, the fringe benefits of production employees should be assigned to a separate labor cost pool such as Production Employee Fringe Benefits, rather than to Factory Overhead Control. Because of the volume of payroll transactions, payroll accounting procedures have become highly automated, and many organizations have implemented a variety of internal controls to safeguard the assets used to pay employees.

KEY TERMS

Compensation insurance
Direct labor
Employee earnings records
FICA taxes
Fringe benefits
Funded pension plans
Gross earnings
Net pay
Payroll master file
Payroll register
Pension
Social Security
Time cards
Unemployment taxes
Unfunded pension plans
Vacation pay
W-2 form
W-4 form

REVIEW QUESTIONS

20–1 Explain how the portion of production employees' gross earnings assigned to Factory Overhead Control is determined.

20–2 Why are the salaries and wages of sales or administrative personnel treated as period costs? Why might it be desirable to assign the costs of nonproduction personnel to jobs or services?

20–3 Starting with gross earnings, how is payroll payable to employees calculated?

20–4 Starting with gross earnings, how is an organization's total labor cost determined?

20–5 Identify three factors that affect the federal income taxes withheld from an employee's gross earnings.

20–6 Indicate whether the employee, the employer, or both bear the cost of the following taxes that are based on an employee's gross earnings: income taxes, FICA taxes, unemployment taxes.

20–7 Why may FICA and unemployment taxes be higher in the earlier than in the later part of a year?

20–8 Mention several voluntary items affecting labor costs.

20–9 Why are funded pension plans preferred to unfunded pension plans?

20–10 To what periods should pension fund costs and vacation pay costs be assigned?

20–11 Identify the three basic payroll journal entries.

20–12 Under what circumstances can the assignment of production employees' fringe benefits to Factory Overhead Control be undesirable?

20–13 What is the preferred treatment of production employees' fringe benefits when these costs are a significant portion of total overhead?

20–14 Why do many organizations maintain a separate checking account for payroll? When such an account is used, what does any balance in the payroll checking account represent?

20–15 Describe some basic procedures that should be followed to help control payroll funds.

EXERCISES

20–1 Determining FICA and Unemployment Taxes

Assume that a FICA tax rate of 7.51 percent is applied to the first $40,000 earned each year by each employee, and federal and state unemployment tax rates of 0.8 percent and 2.7 percent, respectively, are applied to the first $7,000 earned each year by each employee.

REQUIREMENT

Determine the total FICA taxes and the total unemployment taxes paid by the employee and/or the employer for employees with the following annual gross earnings:

1. $5,000
2. $10,000
3. $20,000
4. $40,000
5. $80,000

20–2 Determining FICA and Unemployment Taxes

Assume that a FICA tax rate of 7.51 percent is applied to the first $40,000 earned each year by each employee, and federal and state unemployment tax rates of 0.8 percent and 2.7 percent, respectively, are applied to the first $7,000 earned each year by each employee.

REQUIREMENT

Determine the total FICA taxes and the total unemployment taxes paid by the employee and/or the employer for employees with the following annual gross earnings:

1. $4,000
2. $8,000
3. $16,000
4. $32,000
5. $64,000

20–3 Net Pay Computations: Payroll Register

The Wolfe County Highway Department employs four persons, one of whom receives a salary of $500 per week. Information from their 19y1 payroll records is as follows:

Name	*Earnings to date*	*Pay rate*	*Hours this week*	*Federal income tax withheld this week*
W. Pack	$20,500	$500 per week	45	$50
T. Backa	7,000	$4 per hour	48	38
S. Timer	1,000	$4 per hour	20	10
S. Patch	15,000	$8 per hour	40	45

ADDITIONAL INFORMATION

- The basic work week is 40 hours. Hourly employees are paid a 50 percent premium for overtime.
- All employees have their employer deduct $5 per week toward the purchase of Wolfe County Highway Bonds.
- A FICA tax rate of 7.51 percent is applied to the first $40,000 earned each year by each employee.

REQUIREMENT

Set up and fill in a payroll register similar to the following one. Be sure to total each column.

	Earnings			*Deductions*			
Name	*Regular wages*	*Overtime premium*	*Gross*	*Income tax*	*FICA*	*Bonds*	*Net pay*

20–4 Net Pay Computations: Payroll Register

Payroll information for the Fast Gas Service Center follows:

Name	*Pay rate*	*Hours this week*	*Income tax withholding rate*
H. Chew	$4 per hour	15	0.07
M. Green	4 per hour	40	0.10
F. Nelson	6 per hour	50	0.20
T. Ward	4 per hour	20	0.08
P. Zuman	4 per hour	45	0.15

ADDITIONAL INFORMATION

- The basic work week is 40 hours. Employees are paid a 50 percent premium for overtime.
- All employees are members of the Service Station Attendants' Union and have their employer deduct a "buck-a-week" ($1) for union dues.
- All wages are subject to a FICA tax rate of 7.51 percent.

REQUIREMENT

Set up and fill in a payroll register similar to the one presented in Exercise 20–3, changing the caption "Bonds" to "Dues." Be sure to total each column.

20–5 Determining Payroll Payable and Total Labor Costs

The Lake View Hotel employs 57 people, including one general manager, six supervisors, and 50 service staff. Employees, who are paid weekly throughout each 52-week year, receive four weeks of paid vacation per year. Lake View contributes an amount equal to 5 percent of employee gross earnings to a pension plan. Information about employee wage rates is as follows:

Employee classification	*Weekly gross earnings*
Manager	$1,152
Supervisor	750
Service staff	400

ADDITIONAL INFORMATION

- All employees purchase health insurance through their employer for $15 per week.
- All service staff employees have union dues of $2 per week deducted from their gross earnings and paid to their union.
- Federal income tax withholdings average 30 percent of the manager's salary, 25 percent of supervisors' salaries, and 15 percent of service staff salaries.
- A FICA tax rate of 7.51 percent is applied to the first $40,000 earned each year by each employee.
- Federal unemployment taxes of 0.8 percent and state unemployment taxes of 2.7 percent are paid on the first $7,000 earned each year by each employee.

REQUIREMENTS

a) Determine the payroll payable for the seventh week of 19x7.

b) Determine the total labor cost for the seventh week of 19x7.

c) Determine the total labor cost for the forty-sixth week of 19x7.

20–6 Determining Payroll Payable and Total Labor Costs

The Downtown Health Club began operations on June 1, 19x2, with 15 employees whose gross earnings are $1,800 each per month. Employees receive one month of paid vacation per year and the Downtown Health Club contributes an amount equal to 7.5 percent of employee gross earnings to a pension plan.

ADDITIONAL INFORMATION

- A FICA tax rate of 7.51 percent is applied to the first $40,000 earned each year by each employee.
- Federal unemployment taxes of 0.8 percent and state unemployment taxes of 2.7 percent are paid on the first $7,000 earned each year by each employee.
- Federal income tax withholdings average 18 percent of gross earnings.

REQUIREMENTS

a) Determine the August 19x2 payroll payable to employees.

b) Determine the August 19x2 total labor cost. Be sure to consider the total cost of vacations in any vacation pay accrual.

c) Determine the September 19x2 total labor cost.

20–7 Effective Average Hourly Wage Rate

Sally Jones works 40 hours a week, 48 weeks a year, for a total of 1,920 hours per year. Her base pay is $10 per hour. Jones is entitled to the following fringe benefits, which are paid entirely by her employer, the Classic Print Company:

- Four weeks of paid vacation.
- FICA taxes are applied at a rate of 7.51 percent of gross earnings on the first $40,000 earned each year.
- Federal unemployment taxes are applied at a rate of 0.8 percent of gross earnings on the first $7,000 earned each year.
- State unemployment taxes are applied at a rate of 2.7 percent of gross earnings on the first $7,000 earned each year.
- Health insurance costing $12 per week.
- Pension plan contributions equal to 10 percent of gross earnings.
- Free parking. An average of 500 employees park in the employee parking lot each day. Annual costs of maintenance, taxes, insurance, and depreciation on the lot total $10,000.

REQUIREMENT

Determine Jones' effective average hourly wage rate per hour of work.

20–8 Marginal Analysis of Overtime Versus Hiring
(This is a continuation of Exercise 20–7.)

The Classic Print Company employs several employees in the same wage category as Sally Jones. Because of an increase in sales, the Classic Print Company projects the need for 1,500 additional work hours in this wage category during the coming year. The additional labor hours can be provided by spreading overtime over the employees in Sally Jones' category or by hiring one additional full-time employee (1,920 hours). A union contract prohibits part-time employment.

ADDITIONAL INFORMATION

- Employees are paid a 50 percent wage premium for overtime.
- No pension plan contributions are made for overtime hours.
- The employee parking lot has excess capacity.
- New employees are immediately entitled to all fringe benefits.

REQUIREMENT

Prepare an analysis to help management determine whether Classic Print should use overtime or hire an additional employee.

20–9 Effective Average Hourly Wage Rate

John Davis works 36 hours a week, 47 weeks a year, for a total of 1,692 hours per year. His base pay is $8 per hour. Davis is entitled to the following fringe benefits, which are paid entirely by his employer, the Silicon Valley Chip Company:

- Five weeks of paid vacation.
- FICA taxes are applied at a rate of 7.51 percent of gross earnings on the first $40,000 earned each year.
- Federal unemployment taxes are applied at a rate of 0.8 percent of gross earnings on the first $7,000 earned each year.
- State unemployment taxes are applied at a rate of 2.7 percent of gross earnings on the first $7,000 earned each year.
- Health insurance costing $20 per week.
- Pension plan contributions equal to 10 percent of gross earnings.
- Free use of employee parking, recreational, and dining facilities. These facilities serve the Silicon Valley Chip Company's 1,500 employees on a nondiscriminatory basis. Annual costs of owning and operating these facilities are $2,400,000.

REQUIREMENT

Determine Davis' effective average hourly wage rate.

20–10 Marginal Analysis of Overtime Versus Hiring (This is a continuation of Exercise 20–9.)

The Silicon Valley Chip Company employs several employees in the same wage category as John Davis. Because of an increase in sales, Silicon Valley Chip Company projects the need for 1,600 additional work hours in this category during the coming year. The 1,600 additional hours can be provided by spreading overtime over the employees in John Davis' work category or by hiring an additional full-time employee (1,692 hours). A union contract prohibits part-time employment.

ADDITIONAL INFORMATION

- Employees are paid a 50 percent wage premium for overtime.
- No pension plan contributions are made for overtime hours.
- The employee parking, recreational, and dining facilities have excess capacity. The variable costs of serving one additional employee are $1,200 per year.
- New employees are immediately entitled to all fringe benefits.

REQUIREMENT

Prepare an analysis to help management determine whether the Silicon Valley Chip Company should use overtime or hire an additional employee.

PROBLEMS

20–11 Nonmanufacturing Payroll Accounting: Basic Journal Entries

The following data were taken from the Slagle Company's payroll records for the month of October 19x5:

Administrative salaries	$10,000
Sales salaries	50,000
Total payroll	$60,000

ADDITIONAL INFORMATION

- o Slagle does not provide any fringe benefits to employees.
- o All payroll, except $4,000 of administrative salaries, is subject to FICA taxes of 7.51 percent.
- o Only $2,000 of sales salaries are subject to federal and state unemployment taxes of 0.8 percent and 2.7 percent, respectively.
- o Federal income tax withheld from all salaries amounted to $21,000.

REQUIREMENTS

Prepare journal entries for the following:

a) Recording liabilities for and distribution of gross earnings.

b) Recording liabilities for and distribution of additional labor costs.

c) Recording payment of all payroll-related liabilities.

20–12 Nonmanufacturing Payroll Accounting: Basic Journal Entries

The following data were taken from the Happy-Time Pizza Club's payroll records for the month of April 19y3.

Administrative salaries	$ 4,000
Dining room employees' wages	2,000
Kitchen employees' wages	5,000
Maintenance employees' wages	1,500
Total payroll	$12,500

ADDITIONAL INFORMATION

- o The Happy-Time Pizza Club provides only legally required fringe benefits.
- o All payroll is subject to FICA taxes of 7.51 percent.
- o All payroll except administrative salaries is subject to federal and state unemployment taxes of 0.8 percent and 2.7 percent, respectively.
- o Federal income tax withheld from salaries and wages amounted to $2,750.

REQUIREMENTS

Prepare journal entries for the following:

a) Recording the liabilities for and the distribution of gross earnings.

b) Recording the liabilities for and distribution of additional labor costs.

c) Recording payment of all payroll-related liabilities.

20–13 Manufacturing Payroll Accounting: Basic Journal Entries

The Canton Company pays and records all labor costs on the last day of each month. The following data are taken from the Canton Company's payroll records for January 19x1:

Direct labor	$25,000
Other production salaries and wages	15,000
Administrative salaries and wages	5,000
Gross earnings	$45,000

ADDITIONAL INFORMATION

- All payroll, except $3,000 of administrative salaries, is subject to FICA taxes at a rate of 7.51 percent.
- Only $10,000 of production salaries and wages are subject to federal and state unemployment taxes at rates of 0.8 percent and 2.7 percent, respectively.
- Federal income taxes withheld from all gross earnings amounted to $14,000.
- All employees are entitled to a paid vacation each year. The accrual for vacation pay averages 5.5 percent of gross earnings.
- Canton contributes an amount equal to 10 percent of gross payroll to a funded pension plan.
- Canton has one production department and no service departments.

REQUIREMENTS

Prepare summary journal entries, with supporting computations, for January's payroll. Include entries for the following:

a) Recording the liabilities for and the distribution of gross earnings.

b) Recording the liabilities for and the distribution of additional labor costs.

c) Recording the payment of all labor-related liabilities except vacation pay.

20–14 Manufacturing Payroll Accounting: Basic Journal Entries

The following data were taken from the Golden Hills Mining Company's payroll records for June 19x0:

Administrative salaries	$10,000
Sales salaries	2,000
Production salaries and wages	50,000

ADDITIONAL INFORMATION

- Direct labor chargeable to Work-in-Process amounted to $40,000.
- All payroll is subject to FICA taxes at a rate of 7.51 percent.
- Only $10,000 of production salaries and wages are subject to federal and state unemployment taxes at rates of 0.8 percent and 2.7 percent, respectively.
- Federal income tax withheld from all salaries amounted to $28,000.

- All employees are entitled to a paid vacation each year. The accrual for vacation pay averages 8 percent of gross payroll.
- Golden Hills has a defined contribution pension plan. Contributions by the employer equal 10 percent of gross payroll.
- Forty production workers are members of a union and pay dues of $10 per month. Golden Hills deducts these dues from employees' gross wages and forwards them to the union.

REQUIREMENTS

Prepare the journal entries for the following:

a) Recording liabilities for and distribution of gross earnings.

b) Recording liabilities for and distribution of additional labor costs.

c) Recording the payment of all labor-related liabilities except accrued vacation pay.

20–15 Nonmanufacturing Payroll Journal Entries

The Adirondack Gift Shop started operations on March 22, 19x5. Each of the store's five employees is paid $20 per day. Federal income taxes withheld from each employee's salary average $2 per day. Adirondack does not have a pension plan or paid vacations.

ADDITIONAL INFORMATION

- Employees are paid on Tuesday for the previous week's (Monday–Friday only) work.
- FICA taxes are applied at a rate of 7.51 percent of gross earnings on the first $40,000 earned each year.
- Federal unemployment taxes are applied at a rate of 0.8 percent of gross earnings on the first $7,000 earned each year.
- State unemployment taxes are applied at a rate of 2.7 percent of gross earnings on the first $7,000 earned each year.
- Income taxes, FICA taxes, and unemployment taxes for each calendar quarter are remitted to the appropriate agency on the last day of the month following the quarter. Only amounts pertaining to wages actually paid during the quarter are remitted. *Any end-of-quarter accrual pertaining to unpaid wages need not be remitted until after the following quarter.*
- Adirondack accrues unpaid expenses and recognizes all previously unrecorded liabilities at the end of each month.
- Calendars for March and April of 19x5 are:

March

S	M	T	W	T	F	S
	1	2	3	4	5	6
7	8	9	10	11	12	13
14	15	16	17	18	19	20
21	22	23	24	25	26	27
28	29	30	31			

April

S	M	T	W	T	F	S
				1	2	3
4	5	6	7	8	9	10
11	12	13	14	15	16	17
18	19	20	21	22	23	24
25	26	27	28	29	30	

REQUIREMENT

Prepare *all* journal entries required on these dates: March 30, March 31, April 6, April 13, and April 30.

20–16 Manufacturing Payroll Journal Entries[2]

Speedway Enterprises started operations on March 7, 19y9. One hundred employees are on the payroll. A five-day, forty-hour week is normal for the employees. Information from the payroll files includes the following:

Department	*Number of employees*	*Individual pay rate*	*Federal income tax withholding rate*
Administration	5	$1,000 per week	25%
Sales	15	400 per week	20%
Production	80	50 per day	15%

ADDITIONAL INFORMATION

- Employees are paid on Tuesday for the previous week's (Monday–Friday only) work.
- Speedway does not have a pension plan or paid vacations.
- Income taxes, FICA taxes, and so on for each calendar quarter are remitted to the appropriate agency on the last day of the month following the quarter. Only amounts pertaining to wages actually paid during the quarter are remitted. *Any end-of-quarter accruals pertaining to unpaid wages are not remitted until after the following quarter.*
- Speedway accrues unpaid expenses and recognizes all previously unrecorded liabilities at the end of each month.
- Production employee fringe benefits are assigned to Factory Overhead Control.
- Rates for taxes are as follows:

FICA	7.51% of the first $40,000
Federal unemployment	0.8% of the first $7,000
State unemployment	2.7% of the first $7,000

- Calendars for March and April of 19y9 are as follows:

March

S	M	T	W	T	F	S
		1	2	3	4	5
6	7	8	9	10	11	12
13	14	15	16	17	18	19
20	21	22	23	24	25	26
27	28	29	30	31		

April

S	M	T	W	T	F	S
					1	2
3	4	5	6	7	8	9
10	11	12	13	14	15	16
17	18	19	20	21	22	23
24	25	26	27	28	29	30

---

[2] Adapted from a problem prepared by Professor James Brown.

REQUIREMENTS

Prepare journal entries, when appropriate, for March 29, March 31, April 5, April 26, and April 30, for the following:

a) Recording liabilities for and distribution of gross payroll.

b) Recording liabilities for and distribution of additional labor costs.

c) Recording payment of labor-related liabilities.

20–17 Normal Job-Order Costing and Payroll Accounting: Journal Entries On Monday morning, 2/7/x7, the Tupper Company had one job in process. The costs assigned to it were:

	Job 211
Direct materials	$ 800
Direct labor	400
Factory overhead	400
Production employee fringe benefits	100
Total	$1,700

During the week starting 2/7/x7 the following transactions took place:

- Raw materials costing $2,000 were purchased on account.
- Jobs 212 and 213 were started and the following costs were assigned to them:

	Job 212	*Job 213*
Direct materials	$1,000	$300
Direct labor	600	100

- Additional costs assigned to Job 211 include direct-labor costs of $400.
- Gross earnings of production employees for the week amounted to $2,000. Of this amount, $300 was deducted for federal income taxes.
- Biweekly gross earnings of the production supervisor were recorded. They totaled $1,000. Of this amount, $200 was deducted for federal income taxes.
- January's manufacturing utilities bill was received and recorded. It amounted to $900.
- Miscellaneous factory overhead costs of $150 were recorded.
- Jobs 211 and 212 were transferred to finished goods inventory.

ADDITIONAL INFORMATION

- Tupper uses a normal cost system.
- The cost of production employee fringe benefits is assigned to a separate account and applied on the basis of direct-labor dollars.
- Other overhead costs are applied on the basis of direct materials.

- All earnings are subject to a FICA tax rate of 7.51 percent.
- All earnings are subject to federal and state unemployment taxes. The federal rate is 0.8 percent. The state rate is 2.7 percent.
- All employees are entitled to a paid vacation and sick leave each year. The accrual for vacation pay and sick leave averages 15 percent of gross payroll.

REQUIREMENT

Prepare all journal entries affecting inventory accounts, Factory Overhead Control, and Production Employee Fringe Benefits for the week of 2/7/x7. Do not prepare entries for the payment of any liabilities.

20–18 Normal Process Costing and Payroll Accounting: Journal Entries

The Ozone Company's April 1, 19y3, work-in-process inventory contained 1,000 units that were complete as to materials and three-quarters complete as to conversion. Costs in process on April 1 were as follows:

Direct materials		$10,000
Conversion:		
Direct labor	$7,500	
Factory overhead	3,000	
Production employee fringe benefits	1,500	12,000
Total		$22,000

Factory overhead is applied at the rate of $5 per machine hour and production employee fringe benefits are applied at 20 percent of direct labor. During April the following events occurred:

- 12,000 units were started and 10,000 units were completed.
- Materials costing $150,000 were purchased on account.
- Materials costing $120,000 were placed in process.
- Gross earnings of production employees amounted to $107,500. Of this amount, $20,000 was deducted for income taxes.
- Gross earnings of production supervisors amounted to $6,000. Of this amount, $2,000 was deducted for income taxes.
- Miscellaneous factory overhead costs amounted to $41,000.
- 8,600 machine hours were used.
- The April 30 ending inventory contained 3,000 units that were complete as to materials and one-half complete as to conversion.

ADDITIONAL INFORMATION

- Ozone uses weighted-average process costing.
- All earnings are subject to a FICA tax rate of 7.51 percent.
- All earnings are subject to federal and state unemployment taxes. The federal rate is 0.8 percent. The state rate is 2.7 percent.

- Ozone contributes an amount equal to 8 percent of gross earnings to a pension plan.
- All employees are entitled to a paid vacation each year. The accrual for vacation pay averages 15 percent of gross payroll.

REQUIREMENTS

a) Prepare a cost of production report for April.

b) Prepare all journal entries affecting inventory accounts, Factory Overhead Control, and Production Employee Fringe Benefits. Do not prepare entries for the payment of any liabilities.

21 Transfer Pricing

INTRODUCTION
CORPORATE VIEWPOINT
ECONOMICS OF TRANSFER PRICING
DETERMINING TRANSFER PRICES
TRANSFER-PRICING PRACTICES
THE TRANSFER-PRICING PROBLEM
INTERNATIONAL TRANSFER PRICING
ACCOUNTING ENTRIES
SUMMARY

INTRODUCTION

RESPONSIBILITY ACCOUNTING FOR DECENTRALIZED UNITS ORGANIZED AS profit and investment centers was considered in Chapters 12 and 13. Performance measures for these units included profits, return on investment, and residual income. In discussing these measures, we noted that measurement problems exist in calculating the performance measure and that the choice of a performance measure can cause behavioral problems. Another problem in evaluating the performance of profit and investment centers occurs when goods are transferred within a company between these units. Because the amount recorded for the intracompany transfer is recorded as a sale by one unit and a purchase by another unit, the amount charged affects the performance measures of both units. A **transfer price** is the exchange value assigned a product or service that one unit of an organization provides or offers another unit of the same organization.

The purpose of this chapter is to consider the economics of transfer pricing, methods used for determining the amount to be recorded for intracompany transfers, and the transfer-pricing problem. Transfer pricing is not a new topic. The costs assigned to goods transferred between production departments and the costs assigned for services provided by service departments are both transfer prices. The distinguishing feature of the transfer prices discussed in this chapter is that they are assigned to products or services transferred between investment or profit centers.

A major goal of transfer pricing is to enable divisions that exchange goods or services to act as quasi-independent businesses. A good transfer price also helps us evaluate the performance of the decentralized units. Under ideal circumstances, the transfer price will promote congruence between the goals of divisions and the organization as a whole. Transfer-pricing problems occur because a single transfer price may not accomplish all these objectives. Because profit and investment centers are evaluated as independent units, their managers may use transfer prices that are not in the best interest of the organization as a whole. They do this to maximize their individual performance measures. As noted in Chapter 13, one of the reasons for creating decentralized units is to promote local decision making. If corporate management is aware of problems caused by transfer prices and dictates the price to be used for intracompany transfers, they have reduced divisional autonomy and diminished the reason for creating the decentralized units.

CORPORATE VIEWPOINT

Before discussing the economics of transfer pricing and the advantages and disadvantages of various transfer-pricing techniques, we present two examples to orient you to the profit-maximizing viewpoint of the organization as a whole. This perspective was introduced in Chapter 2 and elaborated on in Chapters 8 and 15. Briefly, it involves a consideration of the revenues, differential costs, and opportunity costs of alternative actions.

Example 21–1

Division A, which is operating at 60 percent of capacity, manufactures two products, X_1 and X_2. Product X_1 is sold outside the organization for \$42. Product X_2 is sold to Division B at a transfer price of \$44. The costs of Division A associated with these two products are:

	Product	
	X_1	X_2
Direct materials	\$10	\$15
Direct labor	10	10
Variable factory overhead	10	10
Fixed factory overhead	5	5
Variable selling	2	0
Total	\$37	\$40

Division B has just received an offer from another company to supply them with a product similar to X_2 at a price of \$38 per unit.

From the viewpoint of the corporation, this is merely a make-or-buy decision. The relevant costs are the differential costs of the alternative actions. If the fixed manufacturing costs of Division A cannot be reduced, the relevant costs are:

Make (\$15 + \$10 + \$10)	\$35
Buy	\$38

The advantage of making is \$3 per unit (\$38 − \$35).

From the viewpoint of Division B, this is a cost-minimization decision (buy from the source that charges the lowest price). If Division A does not lower its price, Division B's costs are minimized and profits are maximized by purchasing outside.

From the viewpoint of Division A, this is a decision to accept (lower price) or reject (do not lower price) a special order. Although a sale at \$38 provides a \$3 contribution towards fixed costs and profits, Division A might elect not to lower its price. If central management forced Division A to lower the price of X_2, divisional autonomy would be reduced just as it would be reduced if central management forced Division B to buy X_2 at $44. Furthermore, there is no reason for central management to even be aware of this situation in a large multidivisional corporation.

Example 21–2

Assume the situation is as given in Example 21–1 except that Division A is operating at capacity and can sell all of Product X_1 it can produce. Both products use equal amounts of Division A's limited capacity and there is a 1-to-1 tradeoff between the production of X_1 and X_2.

Even though the corporation still regards this as a make-or-buy decision, the costs of making have changed. They now include an outlay and an opportunity cost. The outlay costs total $35 (see Example 21–1). The opportunity cost is the net benefits forgone if the limited capacity of Division A is used to produce X_2:

Selling price of X_1	$42
Differential costs of X_1 ($10 + $10 + $10 + $2)	−32
Opportunity cost of making X_2	$10

Accordingly, the relevant costs of the make-or-buy decision are:

Make ($35 + $10)	$45
Buy	$38

In this case, Product X_2 should be purchased from the outside supplier. If there were no outside supplier, the relevant cost of manufacturing X_2 would still be $45. This is another way of saying that X_2 should not be produced and processed further in Division B unless the resultant revenues cover all outlay costs (including the $35 in Division A) and provide a contribution of at least $10. From the corporation's viewpoint, the relevant costs in a make-or-buy decision are the external price, the outlay costs of manufacture, and the opportunity cost of manufacture. The opportunity cost is zero if there is excess capacity.

ECONOMICS OF TRANSFER PRICING

To understand the transfer-pricing problem, we must consider the economics of transfer pricing from the viewpoint of the organization and from that of the individual divisions. The economics of transfer pricing are based on the premise that profits are maximized at the volume where marginal revenue equals marginal cost. **Marginal revenue** is the increment to total revenue received when one additional unit is sold. **Marginal cost** is the increment to total cost incurred in the production and sale of one additional unit. We will examine the economics of transfer pricing when (1) a competitive intermediate market exists for the product and (2) no intermediate market exists for the product. The **intermediate market** refers to the market for the product that is transferred from one unit of an organization to another unit of the same organization.

Competitive Intermediate Market

Assume a corporation contains two manufacturing divisions, S and D. Division S manufactures Product S. Product S may be sold in a perfectly competitive market at price P_S or transferred to Division D for further processing into Product D. Because a perfectly competitive intermediate market exists, Division S will never sell Product S in the intermediate market or to Division D for less than P_S. Similarly, Division D will never pay more than P_S for Product S. From the viewpoint of the company and Division S, the production of S should continue until the marginal cost of S, MC_S, equals the marginal revenue of S, P_S. Similarly, the production of D should continue until the marginal cost of D, MC_D, equals the marginal revenue of D. For purposes of this illustration, let the marginal revenues of Product D less the additional marginal cost incurred to process Product S into Product D equal the **net marginal revenue** of Product D, NMR_D. Accordingly, the production of D should continue until NMR_D equals P_S.

We can use a graph to illustrate how NMR_D is calculated. NMR_D is developed by subtracting the additional marginal cost of completing the intermediate product in Division D (additional MC_D) from the MR of the final product as follows:

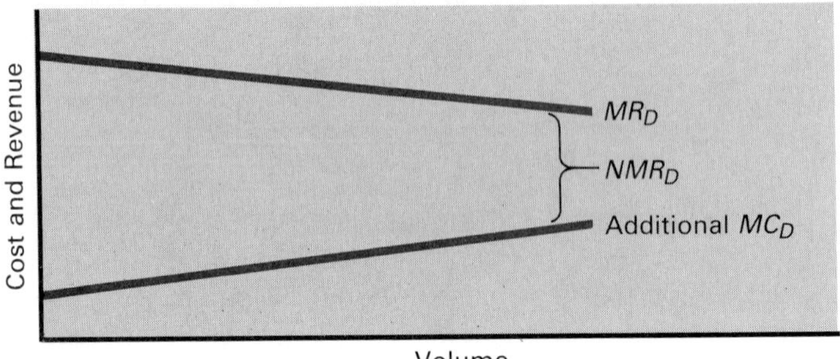

The basic set of facts in the preceding illustration is used under three slightly different assumptions in Exhibit 21–1. In Exhibit 21–1(a), MC_S and NMR_D just happen to intersect at P_S. Because the market for the intermediate product is perfectly competitive, the appropriate transfer price is P_S. The profits of the corporation are represented by the dark-shaded area between lines NMR_D and MC_S to the left of the production volume. This dark-shaded area above line P_S represents the profits of Division D because it shows the NMR_D minus the cost of the intermediate product. The dark-shaded area below line P_S represents the profits of Division S because it shows the revenues from the sale of Product S less the costs of producing S. Note that regardless of whether a transfer or an outside sale and purchase is made, the profits of both divisions and the firm remain unchanged.

In Exhibit 21–1(b), MC_S equals P_S at a volume in excess of that where NMR_D equals P_S. Accordingly, Division S should engage in some outside sales. Again, since this is a perfectly competitive market, the appropriate transfer price is P_S and the profits of the corporation are represented by the dark-shaded area. The dark-shaded area above line P_S represents the profits of Division D. The dark-shaded area below line P_S represents the profits of Division S.

EXHIBIT 21–1 Perfectly Competitive Market for Intermediate Product

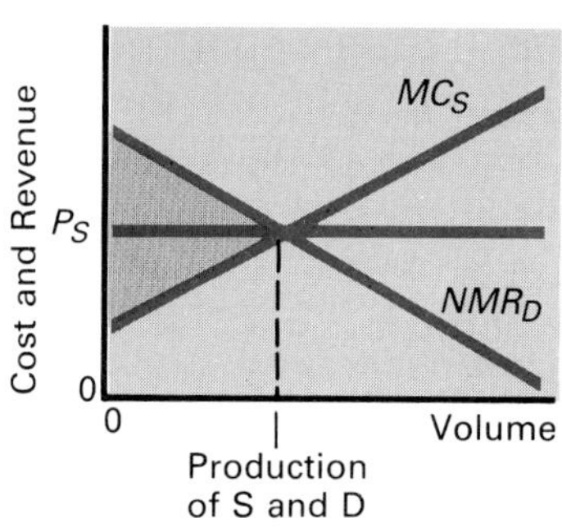

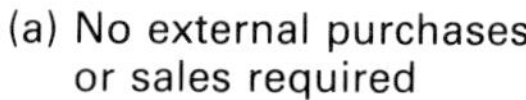
(a) No external purchases or sales required

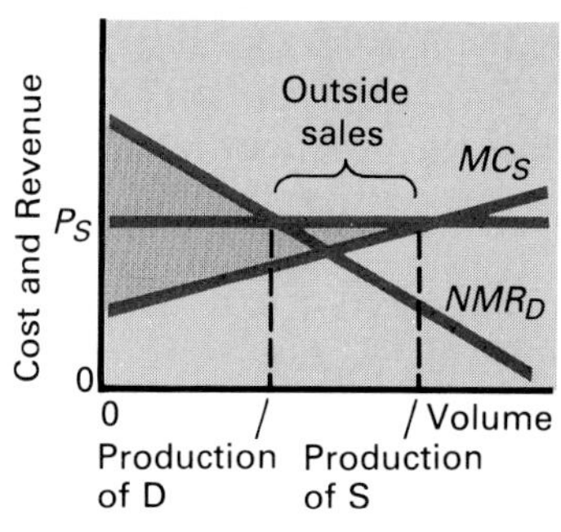

(b) Some external sales of intermediate product

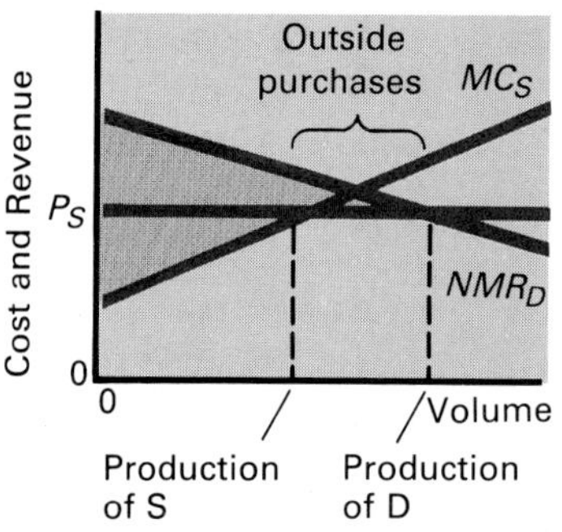

(c) Some external purchases of intermediate product

In Exhibit 21–1(c), NMR_D equals P_S at a volume in excess of that where MC_S equals P_S. Accordingly, Division D should engage in some outside purchases. The appropriate transfer price remains at P_S, and the profits of the corporation are represented by the dark-shaded area. The dark-shaded area above line P_S represents the profits of Division D. The dark-shaded area below line P_S represents the profits of Division S.

As the graphs in Exhibit 21–1 show, if a perfectly competitive market for the intermediate product exists, the transfer price should be the market price. Both supplying and purchasing divisions will then act in a manner that maximizes the profits of the organization as a whole.

No Intermediate Market

In the absence of an intermediate market, Division S is the only source of Product S and Division D is the only user of Product S. Accordingly, all production of S is intended for further processing into D and the profit-maximizing production of Products S and D occurs at that volume where NMR_D equals MC_S. This situation is represented in Exhibit 21–2(a). The corporation's profits are represented by the dark-shaded area. The transfer price, P_S, that leads both divisions to act in a manner that maximizes corporate profits is the marginal cost of Product S at that volume where NMR_D equals MC_S. With P_S as the transfer price, the dark-shaded area above line P_S represents the profits of Division D, and the dark-shaded area below line P_S represents the profits of Division S.

If the transfer price is increased, Division D will reduce production because NMR_D will equal P_S at a lower volume. Conversely, if the transfer price is lowered, Division S will reduce production because P_S will equal MC_S at a lower volume. In both cases total corporate profits will be reduced. Unfortunately the profits of Divisions S or D may be increased.

Consider the situation presented in Exhibit 21–2(b) where Division S has increased the transfer price to P_S^* Since NMR_D now equals the transfer price at a lower volume than in Exhibit 21–2(a), Division D will demand fewer units than it would have at the lower transfer price, P_S. Total corporate profits are still represented by the dark-shaded area in Exhibit 21–2(b). Profits of Division D are represented by the dark-shaded area above line P_S^*, and profits of Division S are represented by the dark-shaded area below line P_S^*. Although the total corporate profits and the profits of Division D are lower in Exhibit 21–2(b) than in Exhibit 21–2(a), increasing the transfer price has increased the profits of Division S.

The situation in Exhibit 21–2(b) occurs because NMR_D is the *average* rather than the *marginal* revenue curve of Division S. The marginal revenue curve of Division S is identified as MR_S in Exhibit 21–2(b). This did not happen when there was a competitive market for the intermediate product because both the average and marginal revenue curves of Division S equaled P_S. Here we have an example of the transfer-pricing problem. Division S acting in its own best interest as an independent unit increases the selling price of Product S to maximize its profits. The result is a decline in total corporate profits.

As another example, consider the case of constant marginal costs in Exhibit 21–3 where the marginal cost of producing S is the same at all levels of output. From the viewpoint of the company, the transfer price, P_S, should be set at MC_S, as shown in Exhibit 21–3(a). Total company profits are shown by the dark-shaded area, and all of these profits are attributable to Division D. Division S would report zero profits or a loss equal to any fixed costs it might have because its revenues just equal its variable costs. In an attempt to obtain a positive profit or recover fixed costs, Division S may attempt to raise the transfer price of Product S to P_S^* as shown in Exhibit 21–3(b). If this occurs, profits of Division D are represented by the dark-shaded area above line P_S^*, and profits of Division S are represented by the dark-shaded area below line P_S^*. Although this improves Divison S's profit situation, it reduces the profits of the company as a whole because Division D will purchase S only until NMR_D equals P_S^*.

EXHIBIT 21–2 **No Market for Intermediate Product**

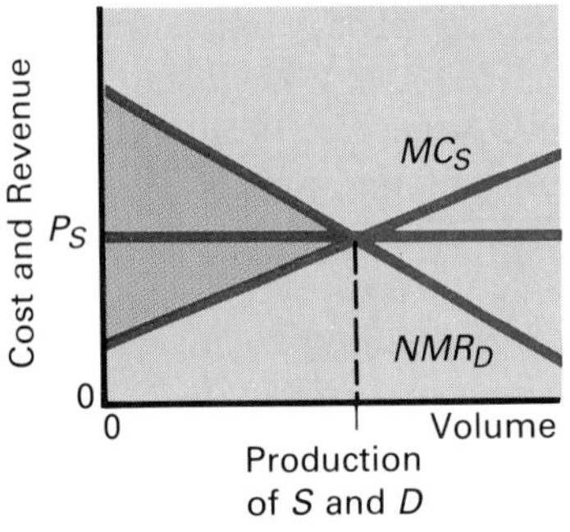

(a) Profit maximizing solution for corporation

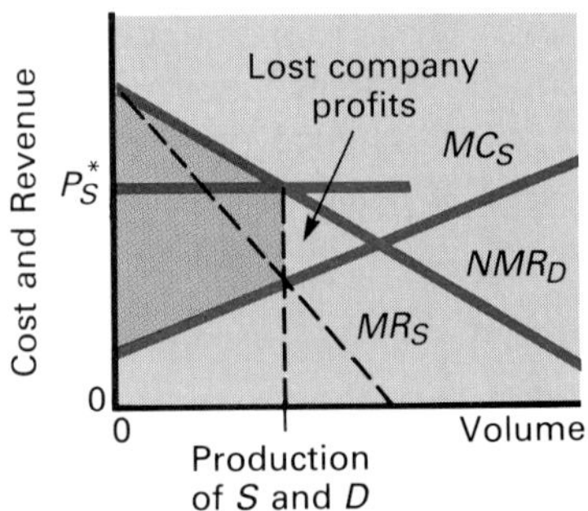

(b) Profit if transfer price is increased to P_S^*

EXHIBIT 21–3 The Case of Constant Marginal Costs

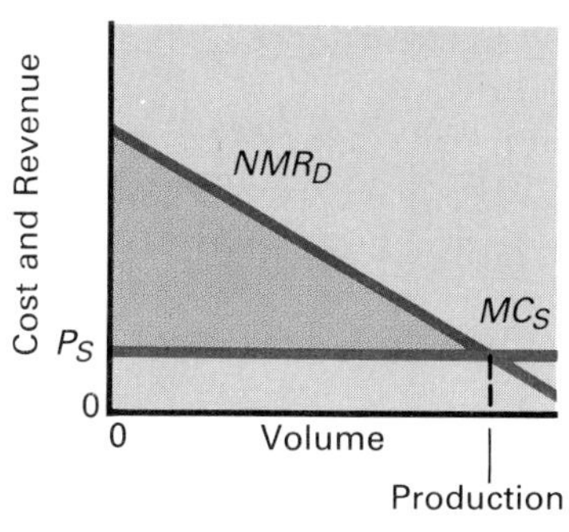

(a) Profit maximizing solution for company

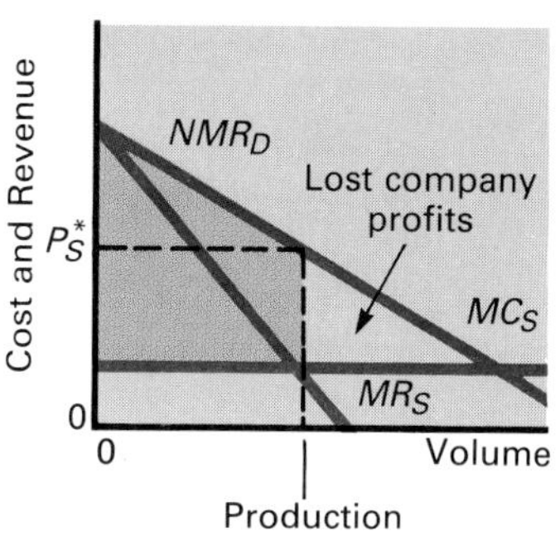

(b) Profit if transfer price is increased to P_S^*

DETERMINING TRANSFER PRICES

Having examined relevant costs from the viewpoint of the corporation and the economics of transfer pricing from the viewpoint of the corporation and individual divisions, we are ready to consider several widely discussed transfer prices. Transfer prices are sometimes set based on market price, variable costs, variable cost plus opportunity cost, full cost or full cost plus, or negotiated prices.

Market Price

When there is an existing market with established prices for an intermediate product and the actions of the company will not affect prices, market prices are ideal transfer prices. If divisions are free to buy and sell outside the firm, the use of market prices preserves divisional autonomy and leads divisions to act in a manner that maximizes corporate profits.[1] (See Exhibit 21–1.)

When substantial selling expenses are associated with outside sales, many firms specify the transfer price as market price less selling expenses. The internal sale allegedly does not require the incurrence of order-getting and order-filling costs.

Variable Cost

If there is excess capacity in the supplying division, establishing a transfer price at variable cost[2] leads the purchasing division to act in a manner that is optimal from the corporation's viewpoint (see Exhibit 21–3(a)). The purchasing division has the corporation's variable costs as its own variable cost as it faces the final market. Unfortunately, establishing the transfer price at variable cost causes the supplying division to report zero profits or a loss equal to any fixed costs. If

[1] Professor Goetz presents an interesting example of a situation in which the use of market prices does not lead to optimal performance. This occurs because of product indivisibilities and the inability of profit centers to buy and sell outside the firm. See Billy E. Goetz, "Transfer Pricing: An Exercise in Relevancy and Goal Congruence," *Accounting Review* **42,** No. 3 (July 1967): 435–440.

[2] Recall that variable costs tend to approximate marginal costs in the relevant range.

excess capacity does not exist (see Example 21–2), establishing a transfer price at variable cost may not lead to the optimal action.

Variable Cost Plus Opportunity Cost

From the viewpoint of the corporation, the optimal transfer price is variable cost plus any opportunity cost. Because all relevant costs are included in the transfer price, the purchasing division is led to act in an optimal manner regardless of whether or not excess capacity exists.

With excess capacity in the supplying division, the transfer price is the variable cost per unit. Without excess capacity, the transfer price is set at the sum of the variable and opportunity costs. Following this rule in Example 21–1, where Division A has excess capacity, the transfer price of Product X_2 would be set at X_2's variable cost of \$35 per unit. At this transfer price, Division B would buy X_2 internally rather than externally at \$38 per unit. In Example 21–2, where Division A is operating at capacity, the transfer price per unit would be set at \$45, the sum of X_2's variable and opportunity costs (\$35 + \$10). At this transfer price, Division B would buy X_2 externally for \$38. In both situations Division B has acted in accordance with the profit-maximizing viewpoint of the organization as a whole.

There are two problems with this profit-maximizing rule. First, when the supplying division has excess capacity, establishing the transfer price at variable cost causes the supplying division to report zero profits or a loss equal to any fixed costs. Second, when the supplying division produces several products, determining opportunity costs is difficult.

Some researchers have suggested using linear programming models to determine opportunity costs and establish transfer prices in multiple-product firms. However, the use of such models seems to negate the need for decentralization. To develop the model, central management must obtain substantial information from each division. After evaluating the output of the model, central management dictates the transfer price that will lead each division to act in an optimal manner. Clearly this reduces divisional autonomy. Of more concern is the fact that the model's output also specifies the quantities each division should produce; central management knows what each division should do. It would appear that if such a situation exists, there is little need for decentralized decision making.

Full Cost or Full Cost Plus

Full cost eliminates the supplying division's loss on the intermediate product, and full cost plus provides the supplying division with a contribution toward unallocated costs and profits. Although "full cost plus" transfer prices may not maximize company profits, they are widely used. Their popularity stems from several factors, including ease of implementation, justifiability, and perceived fairness. Once everyone agrees on full cost plus pricing rules, internal disputes are minimized.

In full cost plus transfer pricing, "cost" should refer to standard cost rather than actual cost. This prevents the supplying division from passing on the cost of inefficient operations, and it allows the buying division to know its cost in advance of purchase.

Negotiated Prices

Negotiated transfer prices, like market-based transfer prices, are believed to preserve divisional autonomy. Negotiated transfer prices are established through meetings between the supplying and purchasing divisions. Individual transfer prices may lead to some suboptimal decisions, but this is regarded as a small price to pay for other benefits of decentralization. When negotiated transfer prices are used, some corporations establish arbitrary procedures to help settle disputes between divisions. However, the existence of an arbitrator with any real or perceived authority reduces divisional autonomy.

Other Transfer Prices

Some researchers[3] have also suggested the use of dual transfer prices to avoid problems caused by divisions acting in their own self-interest. Using dual prices, each division's profit on a product would equal the total company profit. Divisions would then continue production until corporate marginal revenue equaled corporate marginal cost.

Professor Solomons[4] has suggested that when transfers are significant or potentially significant and no competitive market exists for the intermediate product, the supplying division's costs should be transferred in two parts: first, a cost per unit, and second, an annual lump-sum charge for fixed costs. This supplies the receiving division with more complete cost information about the intermediate product. It is similar to the dual-rate method of service department cost allocation discussed in Chapter 6.

TRANSFER-PRICING PRACTICES

Surveys of transfer-pricing techniques show that market price, adjusted market price, standard full cost plus markup, and negotiated price are the most commonly used transfer prices. One survey by Professor Yunker[5] of transfer-pricing techniques in multinational corporations found that market price, standard full cost plus markup, negotiated price (cost plus negotiated markup), and adjusted market price (market price less selling costs) were the most frequently used transfer prices. Another survey by Professors Benke and Edwards[6] found adjusted market price to be the most popular transfer price. Benke and Edwards defined adjusted market price as market price less selling and bad debt expenses that are avoided by selling internally.

Professors Benke and Edwards also found that some companies use more than one transfer-pricing technique. A primary technique was used for the majority of internal sales, but a secondary technique was used whenever the primary one was deemed inappropriate. For example, market price may be used for those products that are sold externally, whereas another transfer price may be used for those products that have no outside market.

---

[3] Joshua Ronen, and George McKinney, III, "Transfer Pricing for Divisional Autonomy," *Journal of Accounting Research* **8,** No. 1 (Spring 1970): 99–112.

[4] David Solomons, *Divisional Performance: Measurement and Control* (Homewood, Ill.: Irwin, 1965): 200–203.

[5] Penelope J. Yunker, *Transfer Pricing and Performance Evaluation in Multinational Corporations* (New York: Praeger, 1982).

[6] Ralph L. Benke, Jr., and James Don Edwards, *Transfer Pricing: Techniques and Uses* (New York: National Association of Accountants, 1980).

THE TRANSFER-PRICING PROBLEM

A transfer-pricing problem exists when divisions, acting in their own best interest, set transfer prices or make decisions based on transfer prices that are not in the best interest of the organization as a whole. The seriousness of the transfer-pricing problem depends on the extent to which the affairs of divisions are intertwined. When intermediate products have established markets and divisions are free to buy and sell outside the firm, the use of market prices avoids the transfer-pricing problem. A potential transfer-pricing problem exists when divisions exchange goods or service for which there is no established market.

Example 21–3

Divisions A and B of Perkins, Inc., are organized as profit centers. Division A produces an intermediate product, which is transferred to Division B for completion and sale. No outside market exists for the intermediate product. Fixed costs of Division A are $10,000 per month, and variable costs are $30 per unit. Division B has fixed costs of $20,000 per month and variable costs of $10 per unit.

The final product is sold in an imperfectly competitive market. The following revenues occur at various monthly volumes:

Units	*Revenues*
1,000	$ 90,000
2,000	160,000
3,000	210,000
4,000	240,000

Division B is currently producing and selling 2,000 units of the final product each month. To produce these units, Division B acquires the intermediate product from Division A at a transfer price of $50 per unit for a total cost of $100,000 (2,000 × $50).

At a $50 transfer price, management of Division B is maximizing profits by producing and selling 2,000 units. (See Exhibit 21–4.) If Division B produced and sold any other quantity, its profits would be less than they are currently.

Although Division B's profits are maximized at 2,000 units when the transfer price is $50, profits of the organization are not maximized at that level. For the organization as a whole, profits are maximized at a volume of 3,000 units. (See Exhibit 21–5.) The current company profit of $50,000 per month is $10,000 less than the maximum the company could earn at a volume of 3,000 units.

EXHIBIT 21–4 Division B's Profits With Transfer Price of $50

Units	*Cost of units acquired from A*	*Additional costs in B*	*Total costs*	*Revenues*	*Profit (loss)*
1,000	$ 50,000	$30,000	$ 80,000	$ 90,000	$10,000
2,000	100,000	40,000	140,000	160,000	20,000
3,000	150,000	50,000	200,000	210,000	10,000
4,000	200,000	60,000	260,000	240,000	(20,000)

EXHIBIT 21–5 Profits for Organization as a Whole

Units	*Division A costs*	*Division B costs*	*Total costs*	*Revenues*	*Profits*
1,000	$ 40,000	$30,000	$ 70,000	$ 90,000	$20,000
2,000	70,000	40,000	110,000	160,000	50,000
3,000	100,000	50,000	150,000	210,000	60,000
4,000	130,000	60,000	190,000	240,000	50,000

The problem is to determine a transfer price that will motivate the manager of Division B to acquire 3,000 units per month from Division A. Apparently a transfer price of $50 is too high because the manager of Division B is acquiring only 2,000 units at that price. The transfer price that will maximize Division B's profits at 3,000 units is $30, the unit variable cost of Division A. (See Exhibit 21–6.)

Although the profits for the organization are maximized when the transfer price is $30 per unit, a problem exists if the performance of the divisions is evaluated using profits. With a transfer price of $30 per unit, Division A will show a loss of $10,000 and Division B will show a profit of $70,000:

	Division A	*Division B*
Sales:		
External	0	$210,000
Internal ($30 × 3,000)	$ 90,000	0
Total	$ 90,000	$210,000
Costs:		
Direct division costs:		
A [$10,000 + $30(3,000)]	$100,000	0
B [$20,000 + $10(3,000)]	0	$ 50,000
Transfer from A	0	90,000
Total costs	– 100,000	– 140,000
Profits (loss)	$(10,000)	$ 70,000

With a $10,000 loss, the manager of Division A will try to increase the transfer price. As we have seen, however, increasing the transfer price will cause the manager of Division B to decrease production so that profits for the organization

EXHIBIT 21–6 Division B's Profits With Transfer Price of $30

Units	*Cost of units acquired from A*	*Additional costs in B*	*Total costs*	*Revenues*	*Profit (loss)*
1,000	$ 30,000	$30,000	$ 60,000	$ 90,000	$30,000
2,000	60,000	40,000	100,000	160,000	60,000
3,000	90,000	50,000	140,000	210,000	70,000
4,000	120,000	60,000	180,000	240,000	60,000

as a whole are not maximized. In this case, the operations of Divisions A and B are intertwined to such an extent that the transfer price results in decisions that are not optimal from the organization's viewpoint.

Suboptimization may be tolerated on some products to obtain the benefits of decentralization, but we reach a point where the transfer-pricing problem becomes so severe that cost and revenue centers should be used in place of investment or profit centers. We cannot develop an operating rule to identify this point, but we can point out specific examples. Perhaps the most obvious is that of a single-product firm that attempts to operate its manufacturing and marketing activities as separate profit or investment centers. The affairs of these two divisions cannot be disentangled, and any attempt to do so will reduce the profits of the entire business. Perkins, Inc., is an example of an organization whose transfer-pricing problem is so severe that the divisions should not be organized as profit centers.

INTERNATIONAL TRANSFER PRICING

In recent years there has been a tremendous growth in multinational enterprises that own or control the operations of subsidiaries in two or more countries. In establishing transfer prices between divisions that operate in different countries, multinational enterprises consider many factors, including:

- Performance evaluation
- Motivation of division managers
- Minimization of income taxes
- Import duties
- Risks of inflation and exchange rate fluctuations
- Transfers of funds across national boundaries[7]

We have already discussed the issues related to performance evaluation and motivation, and these issues are as important to multinational enterprises as they are to domestic organizations. However, other issues, such as minimization of income taxes and import duties are sometimes so important in international transfer pricing that the issues of performance evaluation and motivation are considered secondary. If all the issues cannot be resolved using one transfer price, the organization must decide which issues are the most important. This may lead to arbitrary transfer prices that are not based on any of the methods previously discussed.

The minimization of income taxes is often one of the most important issues in international transfer pricing. In the absence of governmental regulations, multinational enterprises may reduce their tax payments, at least temporarily, by establishing a transfer price that will move profits from high-tax to low-tax countries.

---

[7] For an expanded discussion of the issues in international transfer pricing, see Benke and Edwards, Chapter 6.

Example 21–4 Commonwealth Industries has divisions in Countries G and H. The division in Country H manufactures an intermediate product at a cost of £60 (60 pounds) per unit. The product is shipped to Country G where it is completed at a cost of £10 per unit and sold for £100 per unit. The income tax rates in Countries G and H are 50 percent and 10 percent, respectively.

We will consider only two of the many transfer prices Commonwealth could set for the intermediate product, a low transfer price of £60 and a high transfer price of £90. We will also assume that no other expenses are associated with the product. The low transfer price results in all the product's profit being taxed at 50 percent in Country G. The high transfer price results in all the product's profit being taxed at 10 percent in Country H. The impact of these alternative transfer prices on company taxes and after-tax profits is illustrated in Exhibit 21–7. In the absence of other considerations, Commonwealth would set the transfer price at £90. This results in all the profits being taxed at the lower Country H rate.

If the objective of international transfer prices is to minimize taxes, the financial data reported by foreign divisions may not be useful in evaluating their performance. When this occurs, an organization may maintain one set of records for tax purposes and another set for performance evaluation purposes. This practice, however, may cause problems if the taxing authorities believe that the transfer price used for tax purposes does not reflect economic reality.

To prevent multinational enterprises from arbitrarily shifting income from one country to another, in many countries the ability to select tax-minimization

EXHIBIT 21–7 Impact of Transfer Price on Income Taxes

LOW TRANSFER PRICE: £60

	Country G division		*Country H division*		*Elimination**	*Combined*
Sales	£100		£60		£60	£100
Cost of goods sold	−70	(£60 + £10)	−60		(60)	−70
Income before taxes	£ 30		£ 0			£ 30
Income taxes	−15	(50 percent)	−0			−15
Net income	£ 15		£ 0			£ 15

HIGH TRANSFER PRICE: £90

	Country G division		*Country H division*		*Eliminations**	*Combined*
Sales	£100		£90		£90	£100
Cost of goods sold	−100	(£90 + £10)	−60		(90)	−70
Income before taxes	£ 0		£30			£ 30
Income taxes	−0		−3	(10 percent)		−3
Net income	£ 0		£27			£ 27

* Intracompany transactions are eliminated in developing combined income statements.

transfer prices is restricted by regulations similar to Section 482 of the U.S. Internal Revenue Code:

> In any case of two or more organizations, trades, or businesses . . . owned or controlled directly or indirectly by the same interests, the Secretary may distribute, apportion, or allocate gross income, deductions, credits, or allowances between or among such organizations, trades, or business, if he determines that such distribution, apportionment, or allocation is necessary in order to prevent evasion of taxes or clearly to reflect the income of any of such organizations, trades, or businesses.

The enforcement of regulations such as Section 482 is partially responsible for the extensive use of "full cost plus" international transfer pricing.[8]

ACCOUNTING ENTRIES

The accounting entries involved in transfer pricing are similar to those for parent and subsidiary corporations. Each division may record entries as a completely independent entity, but intracompany sales, cost of goods sold, and inventory profits must be eliminated (as in Exhibit 21–7) when corporate financial statements are prepared. For a more thorough discussion, consult any advanced accounting textbook.

SUMMARY

When divisions engage in intracompany transactions, appropriate transfer prices must be established. From the organization's viewpoint, the optimal transfer price is variable cost plus an opportunity cost. If a competitive market exists for the intermediate product, this optimal transfer price will equal the market price. In other situations it may be necessary to accept suboptimal results and use cost-plus or negotiated prices to preserve divisional autonomy.

A transfer-pricing problem exists when divisions, acting in their own best interests, set transfer prices or make decisions based on transfer prices that are not in the best interest of the organization as a whole. The existence of a severe transfer pricing problem is evidence that the affairs of two or more divisions are so intertwined that they should not function as investment or profit centers.

---

[8] In another survey, Professors Tang, Walter, and Raymond found that full cost (actual or standard) plus an allowance for profit is the most frequently used international transfer price of U.S. and Japanese firms. See Roger Y. W. Tang, C. K. Walter, and Robert H. Raymond, "Transfer Pricing—Japanese vs. American Style," *Management Accounting* **60,** No. 7 (January 1979): 12–16.

KEY TERMS

Intermediate market
Marginal cost
Marginal revenue
Net marginal revenue
Transfer price

SELECTED REFERENCES

Abdel-Khalek, A. Rashad, and Edward J. Lusk, "Transfer Pricing—A Synthesis," *Accounting Review* **49,** No. 1 (January 1974): 8–23.

Benke, Ralph L., Jr., and James Don Edwards, *Transfer Pricing: Techniques and Uses,* New York: National Association of Accountants, 1980.

Coburn, David L., Joseph K. Ellis, III, and Duane R. Milano, "Dilemmas in MNC Transfer Pricing," *Management Accounting* **63,** No. 5 (November 1981): 53–58, 69.

Goetz, Billy E., "Transfer Pricing: An Exercise in Relevancy and Goal Congruence," *Accounting Review* **42,** No. 3 (July 1967): 435–440.

Hershleifer, Jack, "On the Economics of Transfer Pricing," *Journal of Business* **29,** No. 3 (July 1956): 172–184.

_____, "Economics of the Divisionalized Firm," *Journal of Business* **30,** No. 2 (April 1957): 96–108.

Lococo, Lawrence J., "Selecting the Right Transfer Pricing Model," *Management Accounting* **64,** No. 9 (March 1983): 42–45.

Mays, Robert L., Jr., "Divisional Performance Measurement and Transfer Prices," *Management Accounting* **63,** No. 10 (April 1982): 20–24.

Merville, Larry J., and J. William Petty, "Transfer Pricing for the Multinational Firm," *Accounting Review* **53,** No. 4 (October 1978): 935–951.

Solomons, David, *Divisional Performance: Measurement and Control,* Homewood, Ill.: Irwin, 1965.

Stone, Willard E., "Legal Implications of Intracompany Pricing," *Accounting Review* **36,** No. 1 (January 1964): 38–42.

Tang, Roger Y. W., C. K. Walter, and Robert H. Raymond, "Transfer Pricing—Japanese vs. American Style," *Management Accounting* **60,** No. 7 (January 1979): 12–16.

Watson, David J. H., and John V. Baumler, "Transfer Pricing: A Behavioral Context," *Accounting Review* **50,** No. 3 (July 1975): 466–474.

Yunker, Penelope J., *Transfer Pricing and Performance Evaluation in Multinational Corporations,* New York: Praeger, 1982.

REVIEW QUESTIONS

21–1 What is a transfer price? How are transfer prices entered on the books of the supplier and receiver?

21–2 What basic premise underlies the economics of transfer pricing?

21–3 If a division faces a perfectly competitive market for its product, how should an intracompany transfer price be determined?

21–4 From the viewpoint of the corporation, is there any general transfer-pricing rule that will lead to the maximization of corporate profits?

21–5 Under what circumstances will the short-run interest of the supplying division's management be injured by the implementation of this rule?

21–6 List several methods that are used for determining transfer prices.

21–7 Why are competitive market prices ideal transfer prices?

21–8 Why does the use of linear programming models to establish transfer prices negate the need for decentralization?

21–9 Describe the transfer-pricing problem and indicate the circumstances under which it is most likely to occur.

21–10 Can the transfer-pricing problem be so severe that a business should not decentralize? Why?

21–11 What issues are involved in international transfer pricing that are not encountered in domestic transfer pricing?

21–12 How might transfer prices help a multinational corporation reduce its income tax payments?

21–13 How do government regulations affect the transfer prices that multinational organizations establish?

REVIEW PROBLEM

Determining Various Transfer Prices and Divisional Profits

The Rienhart Corporation has decentralized its operations by forming Divisions A and B. Division A manufactures a product that can be sold outside the firm for $20 per unit or transferred to Division B for further processing. If the product is sold to outsiders, Rienhart incurs selling costs of $1 per unit. Division A's standard costs of producing 10,000 units of the product annually are as follows:

Direct materials	$ 40,000
Direct labor	30,000
Variable factory overhead	30,000
Fixed factory overhead	60,000
Total	$160,000

In a typical year, Division A sells 70 percent of the product to outsiders and transfers 30 percent to Division B for further processing. For the units of the product transferred internally, Division B incurs the following standard costs annually in converting the intermediate product into the final product:

Direct labor	$20,000
Variable factory overhead	15,000
Fixed factory overhead	25,000
Total	$60,000

The final product is sold for $45 and Division B incurs selling costs of $2 for each unit sold.

REQUIREMENTS

a) Determine the transfer price for the intermediate product using the following bases:

1. Market value
2. Market value less selling cost
3. Standard variable cost
4. Standard full cost

b) Determine the profits for each division using each transfer price in part (a).

c) If Division A has excess capacity, which transfer price should be used from the viewpoint of the corporation? Why?

d) If Division A has no excess capacity, which transfer price should be used from the viewpoint of the corporation? Why?

The solution to this problem is found at the end of the Chapter 21 problems and exercises.

EXERCISES

21–1 Determining Production Volume and Transfer Price: Perfect Competition

Division A of McIntire Company produces Product A, which can be transferred to Division B of McIntire or sold to outsiders in a perfectly competitive market for $250 per unit. The total and marginal costs associated with possible production levels of Product A are as follows:

Number of units	*Total costs*	*Marginal cost per unit*
100	$ 50,000	$200
200	65,000	150
300	77,500	125
400	87,500	100
500	100,000	125
600	115,000	150
700	132,500	175
800	155,000	225
900	182,500	275
1,000	215,000	325

REQUIREMENTS

a) Calculate the profits of Division A associated with each level of production if Product A is sold to outsiders.

b) What level of production will maximize Division A's profits?

c) What transfer price should be used for units of Product A that are transferred to Division B? Why?

21–2 Determining Production Volume and Transfer Price: Imperfect Competition

Division X of Robeson Corporation produces Product X, which can be transferred to Division Y for further processing into Product Y or sold to outsiders in an imperfectly competitive market. The following annual revenue and cost data are available for various levels of production and sales if all Product X production is sold to outsiders.

Number of units	*Total costs (000)*	*Marginal cost per unit*	*Total revenues (000)*	*Marginal revenue per unit*
1,000	$ 2,200	$1,200	$ 2,000	$2,000
2,000	3,200	1,000	3,800	1,800
3,000	4,000	800	5,400	1,600
4,000	4,700	700	6,800	1,400
5,000	5,300	600	8,000	1,200
6,000	6,000	700	9,000	1,000
7,000	6,900	900	9,800	800
8,000	8,000	1,100	10,400	600
9,000	9,400	1,400	10,800	400
10,000	11,000	1,600	11,000	200

REQUIREMENTS

a) Determine the number of units that will maximize Division X's profits if Product X is sold to outsiders.

b) Determine the profits of Division X if it produces and sells the number of units determined in part (a). What will profits be if Division X produces and sells 1,000 fewer units? If Division X produces and sells 1,000 more units?

c) Assume Division X is producing and selling Product X to outsiders at the level that maximizes divisional profits. If excess capacity exists, what price should Division X charge for units transferred to Division Y?

21–3 Determining Various Transfer Prices

Tyler Corporation produces solar-powered calculators and solar cells used in the manufacture of these calculators. The operations of the company are decentralized into two divisions, a Solar Cell Division and a Calculator Division. During 19x7, the Solar Cell Division produced 500,000 solar cells and incurred the following costs:

Variable costs	$250,000
Fixed costs	$300,000

During 19x7, 100,000 solar cells were transferred to the calculator division and the other 400,000 cells were sold outside the company. The outside sales produced revenues totaling $600,000.

REQUIREMENTS

Determine the transfer price for the solar cells in 19x7 using the following bases:

a) Market price

b) Variable cost

c) Variable cost plus a 10 percent markup

d) Full cost

21–4 Determining Various Transfer Prices

The Micro Division of Watson Corporation produces chips that are used in the manufacture of video games. The standard costs of producing 100,000 chips annually are as follows:

Direct materials	$ 50,000
Direct labor	100,000
Variable factory overhead	100,000
Fixed factory overhead	200,000
Total	$450,000

The chips can be sold outside the firm for $6 per unit if the company incurs selling expenses of $0.50 per unit. The chips can also be used by the Game Division of Watson Corporation in their manufacturing operations.

REQUIREMENTS

Assume the Game Division wants to acquire chips from the Micro Division. Determine the transfer price for the chips if it is based on:

a) Market price
b) Market price less variable selling costs
c) Standard variable manufacturing cost
d) Standard variable manufacturing cost plus a 20 percent markup
e) Standard full manufacturing cost

21–5 Make or Buy in a Transfer Pricing Situation

Mar Company has two decentralized divisions, X and Y. In recent years Division X has purchased 1,000 units of a product annually from Division Y at $75 per unit. Because Division Y plans to raise the price to $100 per unit, Division X wants to purchase these units from outside suppliers for $75 per unit. Division Y's costs are as follows:

Variable costs	$70 per unit
Fixed costs	$15,000 per year

If Division X buys from an outside supplier, the facilities Division Y uses to manufacture these units would remain idle.

REQUIREMENT

From the viewpoint of the company as a whole, should Division X purchase from Division Y at $100 per unit or from outside at $75 per unit? Why?

(CPA Adapted)

21–6 Transfer Prices and Make or Buy Decision

Mississippi Corporation has split its operations into two divisions, A and B. One of the products of Division A, Product X, is sold to Division B for further processing. Division B is currently being charged $50 per unit for Product X. Since Division B has recently learned that it can acquire Product X from an external supplier for $45 per unit, the manager of Division B wants Division A to reduce the transfer price to this amount.

Division A incurs the following costs to produce Product X at an annual volume of 20,000 units:

Total variable costs	$500,000
Total fixed costs	$400,000

REQUIREMENTS

a) Determine Division A's profits from the sale of Product X to Division B at a price of $50.

b) Assume Division A cannot sell Product X outside the firm and the fixed costs cannot be reduced if production of Product X is discontinued. From the organization's viewpoint, should Division B purchase the product from the external supplier? Why?

c) Assume Division A cannot sell Product X outside the firm, but fixed costs can be reduced by $200,000 if production of Product X is discontinued. From the organization's viewpoint, should Division B purchase the product from the external supplier? Why?

21–7 Make or Buy with and without Capacity Constraints

Divisional Enterprises has two independent profit centers, A and B. Division A manufactures a product with variable costs of $50 that can be sold outside the company for $100 or processed further in Division B. For each of the following situations, indicate whether B should buy outside or inside in order to maximize company profits. Fill in each of the spaces with the words "Inside," "Outside," or "Either" to indicate B's source of supply.

*Cost to buy**	*A has excess capacity*	*A does not have excess capacity†*
$40		
$90		
$100		
$110		

* Any differences between buying and selling price are due to long-term contracted arrangements.
† When A does not have excess capacity, the product can be shipped to B only by reducing outside sales.

21–8 Make or Buy with Capacity Constraints

Kecks, Inc., has two independent divisions, X and Y. Division X manufactures a product with variable costs of $200 per unit that can be sold outside the firm in a perfectly competitive market for $300 per unit. This same product is also used in the manufacturing process of Division Y. Currently Division Y uses 10,000 units of this product annually and has a long-term contract with an external supplier to acquire this amount at $210 per unit.

REQUIREMENTS

a) Assuming Division X has no excess capacity, should Division Y purchase from Division X or the external supplier in order to maximize company profits? Why?

b) Repeat part (a) assuming the long-term contract is for $320 per unit instead of $210 per unit.

21–9 Transfer Pricing and Profit Center Performance

Ajax Division of Carlyle Corporation produces electric motors, 20 percent of which are sold to Bradley Division of Carlyle and the remainder to outside customers. Carlyle treats its divisions as profit centers and allows division managers to choose their sources of sale and supply. Corporate policy requires that all interdivisional sales and purchases be recorded at variable cost as a transfer price. Ajax Division's estimated sales and standard cost data for the year ending December 31, 19x2, based on their full capacity of 100,000 units are as follows:

Ajax Division
Budgeted Segmented Income Statement
For the Year Ending December 31, 19x2

		Bradley		*Outsiders*
Sales		$ 900,000		$8,000,000
Costs:				
Variable	$900,000		$3,600,000	
Fixed	300,000	−1,200,000	1,200,000	−4,800,000
Profits		$(300,000)		$3,200,000
Unit sales		20,000		80,000

Ajax has an opportunity to sell an additional 20,000 units per year to an outside customer at a price of $75 per unit. Bradley can purchase its requirements from an outside supplier at a price of $85 per unit.

REQUIREMENTS

a) Assuming that Ajax Division wants to maximize its profits, should Ajax take on the new customer and drop its sales to Bradley for 19x2? Why?

b) Determine the change in the 19x2 profits of the company as a whole if Ajax Division takes on the new customer and Bradley must purchase from the outside supplier.

c) Assume, instead, that Carlyle permits the division managers to negotiate the transfer price for 19x2. The managers agreed on a tentative transfer price of $75 per unit, to be reduced based on an equal sharing of the additional profits to Ajax, resulting from the sale to Bradley of 20,000 motors at $75 per unit. Determine the actual transfer price for 19x2. (CPA Adapted)

21–10 Transfer Pricing and Performance Evaluation

National Appliance Corporation has decentralized its operations by creating a Motor Division and an Appliance Division. During 19x5, the Motor Division produced 50,000 motors and transferred 10,000 of these to the Appliance Division using a transfer price of $50 per unit. The results of operations for 19x5 were as follows:

National Appliance Company
Divisional Income Statements
For the Year Ended December 31, 19x5

		Motor Division		*Appliance Division*
Sales:				
To outsiders		$2,400,000		$5,000,000
To Appliance Division		500,000		
Total		$2,900,000		$5,000,000
Costs:				
Variable	$1,400,000		$2,300,000*	
Fixed	1,000,000	−2,400,000	2,000,000	−4,300,000
Profits		$ 500,000		$ 700,000

* Includes $500,000 for purchases of motors from the Motor Division.

The division managers are currently negotiating the 19x6 transfer price for motors and would like to know the impact various transfer prices would have had on their division's 19x5 performance.

REQUIREMENTS

a) Determine the 19x5 profits of each division if the transfer price had been based on market value.

b) Determine the 19x5 profits of each division if the transfer price had been based on the Motor Division's variable cost.

21–11 International Transfer Pricing and Tax Minimization

Multinational Corporation has divisions located in Countries A and B. The division in Country A produces a product with variable costs of $50 per unit and fixed costs of $200,000 per year. During 19x3, 10,000 units were produced with 80 percent sold to outsiders at $100 per unit and 20 percent transferred to the division in Country B for further processing. The division in Country B incurs additional processing costs of $10 per unit and fixed costs of $15,000 per year. The final product is sold in Country B for $125 per unit. Profits are taxed at a 30 percent rate in Country A and at a 20 percent rate in Country B.

REQUIREMENTS

a) Determine the income taxes that Multinational Corporation would pay to Countries A and B using each of the following transfer prices:

1. Market value
2. Full cost
3. Variable cost

b) If divisional performance is evaluated using after-tax income, which transfer price in part (a) would the manager of the division in Country A prefer?

c) If divisional performance is evaluated using after-tax income, which transfer price in part (a) would the manager of the division in Country B prefer?

d) Assuming there are no legal problems with using any of the transfer prices in part (a), from the company's viewpoint which transfer price is preferred?

21–12 International Transfer Pricing and Tax Minimization

Transworld Corporation is decentralized geographically. Division X is located in Country X and produces a product that can be sold to outside customers for $300 per unit. The product produced by Division X can also be processed further by Division Y (located in Country Y) and sold for $500 per unit of final product. Division X incurs the following costs in producing 5,000 units of Product X annually:

Variable manufacturing costs	$120 per unit
Fixed manufacturing costs	$500,000 per year

Division X usually sells 3,000 units of Product X to outside customers in Country X annually and incurs selling costs of $30 per unit sold. The remaining 2,000 units of Product X are transferred to Division Y for further processing. No selling costs are incurred on the units transferred to Division Y.

Division Y incurs the following additional costs in processing Product X into the final product:

Variable manufacturing costs	$100 per unit
Fixed manufacturing costs	$50,000 per year

Division Y also incurs selling expenses on the final product of $40 per unit.

Profits of Division X are taxed at a 15 percent rate in Country X, and profits of Division Y are taxed at a 40 percent rate in Country Y.

REQUIREMENTS

a) Determine the income taxes Transworld Corporation would pay to Countries X and Y using each of the following transfer prices:

1. Market value
2. Market value less selling costs avoided on transfers to Division Y
3. Variable manufacturing cost
4. Full manufacturing cost

b) Assuming there are no legal problems with using any of the transfer prices in part (a), which transfer price would Transworld Corporation prefer? Why?

PROBLEMS

21–13 Transfer Pricing and Divisional Performance Evaluation

The Ajax Division of Gunnco, operating at capacity, has been asked by the Defco Division of Gunnco Corporation to supply it with electrical fitting No. 1726. Ajax sells this part to its regular customers for $15.00 each. Defco, which is operating at 50 percent capacity, is willing to pay $10.00 for each fitting. Defco will put the fitting into a brake unit it manufactures on a cost-plus basis for a commercial airplane manufacturer.

Ajax has a variable cost of producing fitting No. 1726 of $8.50. The cost of the brake unit being built by Defco is as follows:

Purchased parts—outside vendors	$45.00
Ajax fitting—No. 1726	10.00
Other variable costs	28.00
Fixed overhead and administration	16.00
Total	$99.00

Defco believes the price concession is necessary to get the job.

The company uses return on investment and dollar profits in performance measurement.

REQUIREMENTS

a) If you were Ajax's division controller, would you recommend that Ajax supply fitting No. 1726 to Defco? (Ignore any income tax issues.) Why or why not?

b) Would it be to the short-run economic advantage of Gunnco Corporation for the Ajax Division to supply the Defco Division with fitting No. 1726? (Ignore any income tax issues.) Explain your answer.

c) Discuss the organization and manager behavior difficulties, if any, inherent in this situation. As the Gunnco controller, what would you advise the Gunnco Corporation president do in this situation? (CMA Adapted)

21–14 Part Acquisition: Corporate Viewpoint

The Dodd Tool Company comprises three divisions, A, B, and C. In manufacturing an industrial drill press, Division C uses a motor assembly produced by Division B. Because of an increase in sales volume, Division C wants to purchase additional motor assemblies from B at the current transfer price of $102. Although B's variable production costs for this part are only $80, Division B is reluctant to supply additional units because the division is operating at capacity and would incur an opportunity cost of $27 per unit since the motor assemblies sell outside the firm for $107 each.

Two outside suppliers, the Apex Fitting Company and the Burns Machine Shop, have offered to supply the required assemblies at the following prices:

Apex	$105 per unit
Burns	$110 per unit

Just as the manager of Division C was to sign with Apex, she received a call from the manager of Division A who urged her to sign with Burns. Division A, which manufactures electric motors, is operating at 60 percent of capacity. The Burns Machine Shop purchases electric motors from Division A. If Division C purchases motor assemblies from Burns, Burns will purchase the motors used in those assemblies from Division A at a price of $50 each. The variable cost of each motor is $35.

REQUIREMENTS

a) Assuming Division B manufactures its own motors, determine the optimal action from the viewpoint of the corporation.

b) Assuming Division B purchases motors from Division A at a price of $50 each, determine the optimal action from the viewpoint of the corporation.

c) Determine the optimal action for the situations in parts (a) and (b) if Division B has excess capacity.

21–15 Part Acquisition: Corporate Viewpoint

The Cobble Manufacturing Company comprises three divisions, X, Y, and Z. In manufacturing electric drills for home workshops, Division Z uses a motor assembly that it currently acquired from Gates Company for $15 per unit. Because of an increase in sales volume, Division Z wants to purchase additional motor assemblies.

The manufacturing facilities of Division Y can be used to produce the motor assemblies needed by Division Z. However, Division Y is currently operating at capacity producing motor assemblies for household appliances such as food processors. Division Y sells these motor assemblies to outsiders for $25 per unit and incurs variable costs of $15 per unit and fixed costs of $200,000 per year. The operating capacity of Division Y is 100,000 motor assemblies annually. The motor assemblies produced by Division Y can be modified easily without additional cost for use by Division Z. The manager of Division Y, however, insists on a transfer price of $25 per unit for any motor assemblies sold to Division Z.

Since the transfer price offered by Division Y exceeds the current cost of the assemblies used by Division Z, the manager of Division Z is reluctant to accept this offer. Two other offers have also been received. Gates Company has offered to supply the additional motor assemblies for $17 per unit. Gates is charging $2 over the $15 current price because Gates is currently operating at capacity and would have to invest in additional equipment to produce more assemblies. Another producer of assemblies, Stein Company, has offered to supply the required assemblies to Division Z for $21 per unit.

The manager of Division Z has just received a memo from the manager of Division X urging him to accept the offer from Stein. Division X, which produces electric motors, is operating at 50 percent of capacity. Stein purchases their electric motors from Division X. If Division Z purchases motor assemblies from Stein, Stein will purchase the motors used in those assemblies from Division X at a price of $12 each. The variable cost of each motor is $9.

REQUIREMENTS

a) Assuming Division Y manufactures its own motors, determine the optimal action from the viewpoint of the corporation.

b) Assuming Division Y purchases motors from Division X at a price of $12 each, determine the optimal action from the viewpoint of the corporation.

c) Determine the optimal action for the situations in parts (a) and (b) if Division Y has excess capacity.

21–16 Divisionalization and Transfer Pricing

A. R. Oma, Inc., manufactures a line of men's perfumes and after-shave lotions. The manufacturing process is basically a series of mixing operations with the addition of certain aromatic and coloring ingredients; the finished product is packaged in a company-produced glass bottle and packed in cases containing six bottles.

A. R. Oma thinks that the sale of its product is heavily influenced by the appearance and appeal of the bottle and therefore has devoted considerable managerial effort to the production of bottles. This has resulted in the development of certain unique production processes in which management takes considerable pride.

The two areas (that is, perfume production and bottle manufacture) have evolved over the years in an almost independent manner; in fact, a rivalry has developed between management personnel as to "which division is the more important" to A. R. Oma. This attitude is probably intensified because the bottle-manufacturing plant was purchased intact ten years ago and no real interchange of management personnel or ideas (except at the top corporate level) has taken place.

Since the acquisition, all bottle production has been absorbed by the Perfume Division. Each area is considered a separate profit center and evaluated as such. As the new corporate controller, you are responsible for the definition of a proper transfer price to use in crediting the Bottle Division and debiting the Perfume Division.

At your request, the Bottle Division general manager has asked certain other bottle manufacturers to quote a price for the quantity and sizes of bottles demanded by the Perfume Division. These competitive prices are:

Volume	*Total price*	*Price per case*
2,000,000 eq. cases*	$ 4,000,000	$2.00
4,000,000	7,000,000	1.75
6,000,000	10,000,000	1.67

* An "equivalent case" represents six bottles each.

A cost analysis of the internal bottle plant indicates that they can produce bottles at these costs:

Volume	*Total cost*	*Cost per case*
2,000,000 eq. cases	$3,200,000	$1.60
4,000,000	5,200,000	1.30
6,000,000	7,200,000	1.20

(Your cost analysts point out that these costs represent fixed costs of $1,200,000 and variable costs of $1.00 per equivalent case.)

These figures have given rise to considerable corporate discussion as to the proper value to use in the transfer of bottles to the Perfume Division. This interest is heightened because a significant portion of a division manager's income is an incentive bonus based on divisional profit.

The Perfume Division has the following costs in addition to bottle costs:

Volume	*Total cost*	*Cost per case*
2,000,000 cases	$16,400,000	$8.20
4,000,000	32,400,000	8.10
6,000,000	48,400,000	8.07

After considerable analysis, the Marketing Research Department has furnished you with the following price-demand relationship for the finished product:

Sales volume	*Total sales revenue*	*Sales price per case*
2,000,000 cases	$25,000,000	$12.50
4,000,000	45,600,000	11.40
6,000,000	63,900,000	10.65

REQUIREMENTS

a) The A. R. Oma Company has used market-based transfer prices in the past. Using the current market prices and costs, and assuming a volume of 6,000,000 cases, calculate the income for:
   1. The Bottle Division
   2. The Perfume Division
   3. The corporation

b) Is this production and sales level the most profitable volume for:
   1. The Bottle Division?
   2. The Perfume Division?
   3. The corporation?

   Explain your answer.

c) What is likely to happen to corporate profits if the Perfume Division is free to set its own sales volume, and if market-based transfer prices are used?

d) The A. R. Oma Company uses the profit center concept for divisional operations.
   1. Define a "profit center."
   2. Under what conditions should a profit center be established?
   3. Should the two divisions of the A. R. Oma Company be organized as profit centers?

(CMA Adapted)

21–17 Transfer Pricing: Propriety of Profit Centers

Based on past experiences, the following monthly cost and revenue data are available for Capettini, Inc.

FIRM AS A WHOLE

Total production and sales	*Total costs*	*Incremental cost*	*Unit selling price*	*Total revenue*	*Incremental revenue*	*Profit*
1,000	$40,000	$40,000	$50	$ 50,000	$50,000	$10,000
2,000	60,000	20,000	40	80,000	30,000	20,000
3,000	69,000	9,000	30	90,000	10,000	21,000
4,000	79,000	10,000	25	100,000	10,000	21,000
5,000	91,000	12,000	20	100,000	0	9,000

DEPARTMENT P (PRODUCTION)

Total production	*Total costs*	*Incremental costs*
1,000	$35,000	$35,000
2,000	50,000	15,000
3,000	54,000	4,000
4,000	59,000	5,000
5,000	66,000	7,000

DEPARTMENT S (SALES & DISTRIBUTION)

Total sales	*Total costs*	*Incremental costs*
1,000	$ 5,000	$5,000
2,000	10,000	5,000
3,000	15,000	5,000
4,000	20,000	5,000
5,000	25,000	5,000

In the past, Departments P and S have operated as cost centers. However, the assistant controller (recently returned from an executive development program) has suggested that changing P and S to profit centers will result in higher profits because the managers of P and S will be more profit-conscious. To make the profit center idea work, the manager of P will "sell" his production to the manager of S at a price the manager of P sets at the start of each month. Once this transfer price is set, it cannot be changed until the start of the following month and P must supply all units ordered by S during the month at this price. Managers' profit results will be evaluated monthly.

REQUIREMENTS

a) Briefly state the criteria that the manager of Department S should use in determining the number of units to purchase from P.

b) Prepare a schedule that indicates the net marginal revenue (incremental revenues less incremental costs) of Department S at each sales volume. Beside this schedule indicate the number of units S will purchase from P at each of the following transfer prices: $45, $25, and $5. Assume transfers can be made only in 1,000-unit increments and that all units are transferred at the same price.

c) For each set of transfer prices and Department S demand in part (b), determine the profits of Department P.

d) Which of the three transfer prices mentioned in parts (b) and (c) will the manager of Department P select?

e) Determine the resulting monthly incomes of each department and the firm as a whole. Assume there are no fixed costs.

f) Evaluate the propriety of establishing profit centers in this organization.

21–18 Transfer Pricing: Propriety of Profit Centers

The production and sales departments of Dally Corporation are currently organized as cost centers. Their monthly costs at various levels of production and sales are as follows:

Units produced and sold	*Production department costs*	*Sales department costs*
1,000	$ 60,000	$ 30,000
2,000	115,000	55,000
3,000	165,000	75,000
4,000	200,000	100,000
5,000	240,000	130,000

Monthly revenues from the sale of the product are:

Units sold	*Revenues*
1,000	$150,000
2,000	275,000
3,000	375,000
4,000	450,000
5,000	500,000

Sales occur only in 1,000-unit increments.

Management of Dally Corporation is thinking about changing the production and sales departments to profit centers and evaluating them as such on a monthly basis. You have been asked to evaluate the desirability of converting the production and sales departments to profit centers.

REQUIREMENTS

a) Prepare a schedule that indicates the net marginal revenue (incremental revenues less incremental costs) of the sales department at each sales volume.

b) Determine the number of units the sales department would purchase from the production department at each of the following transfer prices: $90, $70, and $45. Assume that transfers can be made only in 1,000-unit increments and that all units are transferred at the same price.

c) For each set of transfer prices and units purchased by the sales department in part (b), determine the profits of the production department. Which of the transfer prices will the manager of the production department prefer?

d) Assuming administrative costs are fixed and total $100,000 per month, what level of production and sales will maximize profits for the corporation? What are the profits at this level?

e) Evaluate the propriety of establishing profit centers in this organization.

21–19 Transfer Pricing With Opportunity Cost

PortCo Products is a divisionalized furniture manufacturer. The divisions are autonomous segments with each division being responsible for its own sales, costs of operations, working capital management, and equipment acquisition. Each division serves a different market in the furniture industry. Because the markets and products of the divisions are so different, there have never been any transfers between divisions.

The Commercial Division manufactures equipment and furniture that is purchased by the restaurant industry. The division plans to introduce a new line of counter and chair units that feature a cushioned seat for the counter chairs. John Kline, the Division Manager, has discussed the manufacturing of the cushioned seat with Russ Fiegel of the Office Division. They both believe a cushioned seat currently made by the Office Division for use on its deluxe office stool could be modified for use on the new counter chair. Consequently Kline has asked Russ Fiegel for a price for 100-unit lots of the cushioned seat. The following conversation took place about the price to be charged for the cushioned seats.

Fiegel: "John, we can make the necessary modifications to the cushioned seat easily. The raw materials used in your seats are slightly different and should cost about 10 percent more than those used in our deluxe office stool. However, the labor time should be the same because the seat fabrication operation is basically the same. I would price the seat at our regular rate—full cost plus 30 percent markup."

Kline: "That's higher than I expected, Russ. I was thinking that a good price would be your variable manufacturing costs. After all, your capacity costs will be incurred regardless of this job."

Fiegel: "John, I'm at capacity. By making the cushioned seats for you, I'll have to cut my production of deluxe office stools. Of course, I can increase my production of economy office stools. The labor time freed by not having to fabricate the frame or assemble the deluxe stool can be shifted to the frame fabrication and assembly of the economy office stool. Fortunately I can switch my labor force between these two models of stools without any loss of efficiency. As you know, overtime is not a feasible alternative in our community. I'd like to sell it to you at variable cost, but I have excess demand for both products. I don't mind changing my product mix to the economy model if I get a good return on the seats I make for you. Here are my standard costs for the two stools and a schedule of my factory overhead." [See the standard costs and overhead schedule following the conversation.]

Kline: "I guess I see your point, Russ, but I don't want to price myself out of the market. Maybe we should talk to Corporate to see if they can give us any guidance."

PortCo Products
Office Division
Standard Costs and Prices

	Deluxe office stool		*Economy office stool*
Direct materials:			
Framing	$ 8.15		$ 9.76
Cushioned seat:			
Padding	2.40		
Vinyl	4.00		
Molded seat (purchased)			6.00
Direct labor:			
Frame fabrication (0.5 × $7.50 per DLH)	3.75	(0.5 × $7.50 per DLH)	3.75
Cushion fabrication (0.5 × $7.50 per DLH)	3.75		
Assembly* (0.5 × $7.50 per DLH)	3.75	(0.3 × $7.50 per DLH)	2.25
Factory overhead (1.5 DLH × $12.80 per DLH)	19.20	(0.8 DLH × $12.80 per DLH)	10.24
Total standard cost	$45.00		$32.00
Selling price (30 percent markup)	$58.50		$41.60

*Attaching seats to frames and attaching rubber feet.

PortCo Products
Office Division
Factory Overhead Budget

Overhead item	*Nature*	*Amount*
Supplies	Variable—at current market prices	$ 420,000
Indirect labor	Variable	375,000
Supervision	Nonvariable	250,000
Power	Use varies with activity; rates are fixed	180,000
Heat, air, and light	Nonvariable—light is fixed regardless of production, whereas heat and air conditioning vary with fuel charges	140,000
Property taxes and insurance	Nonvariable—any change in amounts or rates is independent of production	200,000
Depreciation	Fixed dollar total	1,700,000
Employee benefits	20 percent of supervision, direct and indirect labor	575,000
	Total overhead	$3,840,000
	Capacity in DLH	300,000
	Overhead rate per DLH	$12.80

REQUIREMENTS

a) John Kline and Russ Fiegel did ask PortCo corporate management for guidance on an appropriate transfer price. Corporate management suggested they consider using a transfer price based on variable manufacturing costs plus opportunity cost. Calculate a transfer price for the cushioned seat based on variable manufacturing cost plus opportunity cost.

b) Which transfer price system—full cost, variable manufacturing cost, or variable manufacturing cost plus opportunity cost—would be best as the underlying concept for an intracompany transfer price policy? Explain your answer. (CMA Adapted)

21–20 Transfer Pricing with Constant Marginal Costs: Calculus

Division A manufactures an intermediate product that does not have a market. This product is processed further in Division B and then sold at a price that is a function of the total volume of sales.

The costs associated with this product in Division A include fixed costs of \$50,000 per year and variable costs of \$10 per unit. The additional selling and manufacturing costs incurred in Division B include fixed costs of \$75,000 per year and variable costs of \$50 per unit.

The price function for the final product is:

$$P = 100 - 0.001X$$

where

P = Unit selling price
X = Total sales volume of the final product

REQUIREMENTS

a) From the viewpoint of the company determine:

1. The optimal annual sales volume and selling price for this product.
2. The annual contribution of the product to profits and other joint expenses.

b) Determine the unit transfer price that will lead Division B to produce and sell the optimal number of units.

c) What impact will the preceding transfer price have on the operating results of Division A?

d) Assuming that Division A has the freedom to set the transfer price and that Division B has the freedom to select the production and sales volume of the final product, determine what will happen if Division A sets the transfer price at \$25 per unit.

21–21 Optimal Production Volume and Transfer Pricing: Calculus

The production and marketing departments of Ringside Corporation are organized as profit centers. However, all units manufactured by the Production Department are transferred to the Marketing Department for sale. The Production Department's annual cost function is represented by the following equation:

$$TC(P) = 50{,}000 + 10X + 0.005X^2$$

where

$TC(P)$ = Total manufacturing costs
X = Number of units manufactured

The Marketing Department's annual cost function is:

$$TC(M) = 20{,}000 + 6X$$

where

$TC(M)$ = Total marketing costs
X = Number of units sold

The revenue function for the product sold by the Marketing Department is as follows:

$$TR = 100X - 0.002X^2$$

where

TR = Total revenues
X = Number of units sold

Administrative costs are all fixed and total $100,000 annually. Ringside has a policy of carrying no inventories.

REQUIREMENTS

a) Determine the marginal revenues and marginal costs from the company's viewpoint.
b) Determine the optimal production and sales volume for the company. What are the profits at this volume? (*Hint:* Profits are maximized at the point where marginal revenues equal marginal costs.)
c) Determine the transfer price that will motivate the Production Department to produce the optimal volume in part (b).
d) Determine the profits of each department using the optimal volume in part (b) and transfer price in part (c).
e) How might the manager of the Marketing Department react to the distribution of profits between the two divisions found in part (d)? What is he or she likely to do to try to improve the department's profits?
f) Should Ringside's Production and Marketing Departments be evaluated as profit centers? If not, how might their performance be evaluated?

21–22 Allocating Production Between Sales of Intermediate and Final Product

Presented is information about the costs and revenues of a particular intermediate and final product.

Production		*Intermediate product*		*Final product*	
Units	*Total costs*	*Unit sales*	*Total revenue*	*Sales*	*Net marginal revenue*
5	$ 50	5	$175	5	$200
10	100	10	350	10	200
15	150	15	525	15	200
20	200	20	665	20	150
25	250	25	775	25	150
30	350	30	825	30	150
35	450	35	875	35	100
40	550	40	900	40	100
45	700	45	925	45	100
50	850	50	950	50	50

REQUIREMENT

Determine the number of units to be sold in the intermediate market and the number of units to be processed further into the final product. (*Hint:* Profits are maximized at the point where marginal revenues equal marginal costs. In determining what to do with each batch of production, compare the marginal revenues from each alternative action.)

21–23 Transfer Pricing: Different Buying and Selling Prices for the Intermediate Product

If there is an existing market with established prices for intermediate products and the market is of such a size that the actions of the company will not affect prices, market prices are ideal transfer prices.

The textbook examples assume identical buying and selling prices for intermediate products. Because of transportation costs, it is likely that these prices will differ. For example, the buying division might have to pay the market price plus transportation costs, whereas the selling division would receive the market price less transportation costs.

Assuming a constant market price for an intermediate product, Professor J. R. Gould[9] has analyzed three cases in which the selling and buying prices of the intermediate product are not equal:

1. $P_B > P_S > P$
2. $P > P_B > P_S$
3. $P_B > P > P_S$

where

P_B = Price to buy (market price plus transportation costs)
P_S = Price to sell (market price less transportation costs)
P = Dollar value at which the internal marginal costs for the intermediate product (MC_S) equal the net marginal revenue from the sale of the final product (NMR_D)

[9] J. R. Gould, "Internal Pricing in Firms When There Are Costs of Using an Outside Market," *Journal of Business* (January 1964): pp. 61–67.

Diagrams for each case follow.

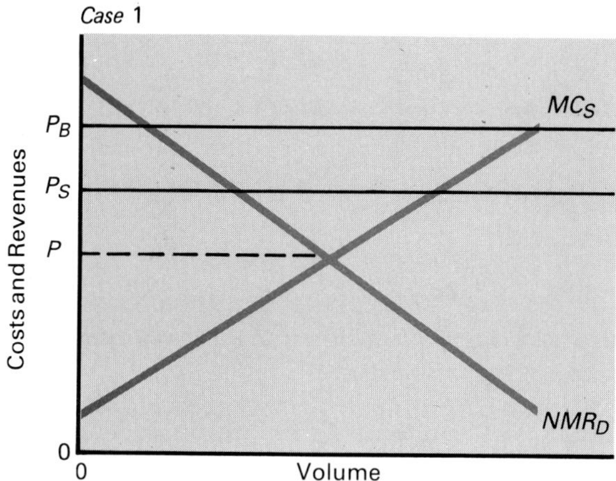

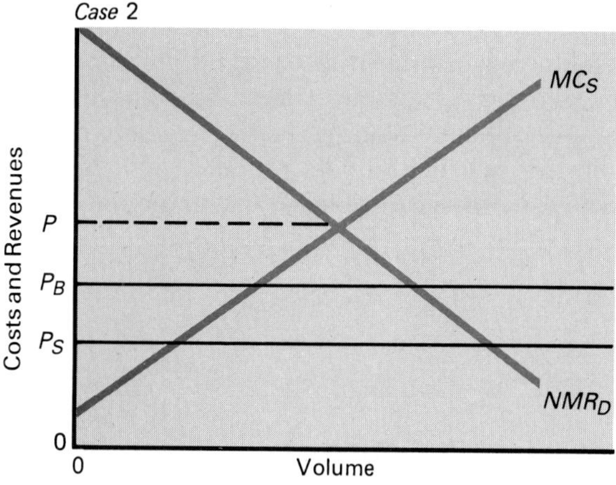

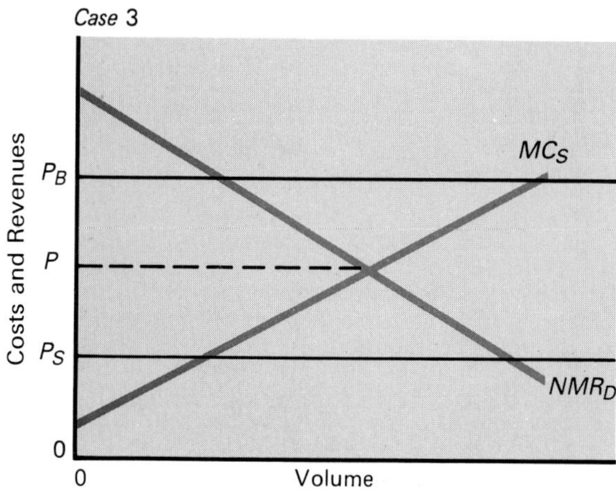

REQUIREMENTS

Assuming a profit-maximizing firm, identify on each diagram:

a) The effective net marginal revenue curve for the intermediate product

b) The effective net marginal cost curve for the intermediate product

c) The amount of any outside purchases of the intermediate product

d) The amount of any outside sales of the intermediate product

e) The optimal transfer price

21–24 Transfer Pricing: Declining Marginal Revenues for Intermediate Product (Sell or Process Further)

The textbook examples assume that when a market exists for an intermediate product it is of such a size that the actions of the company will not affect prices. This is not always the case.

Assume that the intermediate product cannot be purchased externally and that the demand curve for the intermediate product is negatively sloped. Increasing volumes can be sold only by lowering the selling price.

In the following diagram the dashed lines represent the demand and the marginal revenue curves for the intermediate product, the solid lines represent the marginal cost of manufacturing the intermediate product and the net marginal revenue from the sale of the final product, and the dotted line illustrates the effect of adding the marginal revenue curve for the intermediate product to the net marginal revenue curve for the final product.

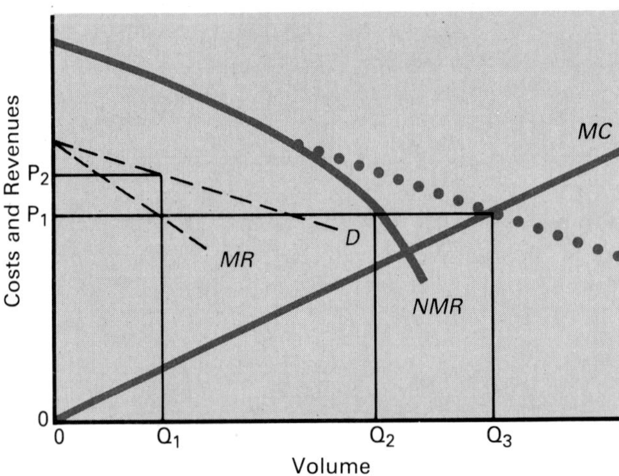

REQUIREMENTS

On the diagram clearly indicate:

a) The number of units to be sold in the intermediate market

b) The number of units to be processed further into the final product

c) The selling price of the intermediate product

d) The transfer price that will lead to optimal production of the intermediate product and sale of the final product

21–25 International Transfer Pricing and Performance Evaluation Magnum Aerospace (Canada) is a wholly-owned subsidiary of Magnum Aerospace Inc., a U.S.-based multinational corporation. The Canadian Division was set up over 20 years ago as a means of satisfying a Canadian content requirement for a large government aircraft contract. Since that time, the Canadian Division has managed to aggressively market itself as the foremost Canadian supplier of aircraft engines. By 19x1, the Canadian Division was involved in assembling components to build aircraft engines and provide replacement parts throughout Canada. The major opportunity facing the division in the foreseeable future is winning an engine bid on the new fighter aircraft program for which the government is inviting tenders.

Most of the major components used in the engines assembled and sold by Magnum Aerospace (Canada) were purchased from the Aircraft Engine Division of the parent firm, located in the United States. The Canadian government charged a duty of 22.5 percent of the invoice price on all components shipped across the border from the United States. Other components were either manufactured in-house or purchased from local suppliers.

One of the most critical components transferred to the Canadian Division from the Aircraft Engine Division was a special control unit that regulates the thrust generated by the engine. This unit has long been regarded as one of the major technological advantages associated with Magnum Aerospace engines. The units have to be manufactured within very precise specifications and tolerances because the engine is expected to meet rigorous performance standards. As a result, the control units require specialized equipment, processes, and technical skills to build. The contribution of the control unit to the reliability and longevity of Magnum Aerospace engines has helped the unit to secure a ready market as a replacement part in the engines of competing manufacturers.

In late 19x1, Magnum Aerospace (Canada) submitted its plan for 19x2 to the parent company. In the plan, the Canadian Division indicated that it expected to use an estimated $2,250,000 in control units. Historically, the Division purchased between $900,000 and $3,600,000 in control units from the Aircraft Engine Division. However, for 19x2, Magnum Aerospace (Canada) proposed that the control units be purchased from a large British firm rather than from the Aircraft Engine Division of the parent. In the plan, the Canadian Division reported that it could save as much as $600,000 from this purchase as a result of the reduced purchase price and a lower duty charged on goods entering the country from Britain. The cost savings had been calculated on the basis of a quotation on the control units that the Canadian Division had received from the British supplier. The Canadian Division manager pointed out the distinct pricing advantage that Magnum Aerospace (Canada) could have over the competition with respect to the upcoming Canadian government fighter plane program.

When informed of this proposal, the management of Aircraft Engine Division expressed strong opposition. They argued that such an arrangement would be detrimental to the long-run interest of Magnum Aerospace. For the British company to fulfill the contract, the Component Division, which actually manufactured the control unit, would have to send the relevant blueprints and production process sheets to the British firm. With this knowledge, the British firm could easily manufacture similar control units and capture the large replacement market throughout Europe. In addition, the Aircaft Engine Division argued that the price quoted by the British firm for the control units was a distress price and not a legitimate market price for such a component. As the cost data in Exhibit 1 revealed, the Component Division, as the largest maker of these units, could not manufacture the units at a cost equal to the quoted selling price of the British offer. The Aircraft Engine Division went so far as to accuse the British firm of either dumping, or trying to buy the blueprints and production process. They were very much opposed to allowing the Canadian Division to source the control units via an external supplier.

MAGNUM AEROSPACE INC.

The parent company, Magnum Aerospace Inc., was a large decentralized multinational corporation with business interests in the aerospace industry as well as in consumer goods and computer services. In the aerospace sector, the firm was organized into product line divisions (such as the Aircraft Engine Division) and manufacturing divisions (such as the Component Division). The product line divisions were responsible for assembling and selling their products throughout the continental United States. For performance evaluation purposes, each product line division was regarded as a profit center and held responsible for earning a satisfactory profit on their activities. Because of the nature of the product lines, there was very little interaction among the product line divisions. Nevertheless, all transactions between divisions of Magnum Aerospace were expected to be conducted on an arm's length basis. The manufacturing divisions were responsible for designing, engineering, and manufacturing items that would be assembled by the product divisions. The manufacturing divisions were generally characterized by large amounts of investment in plant and equipment. To ensure that these assets were profitably utilized, the manufacturing divisions were classified as investment centers for performance evaluation purposes. Because of the high level of interdivisional activity between the manufacturing divisions and the product divisions, it was necessary to establish a clear transfer price system. As a result, all goods would be transferred between the divisions at market price, where applicable, or at a price negotiated between the two divisions.

Several years ago, an arrangement regarding the manufacture of the previously mentioned control units was arrived at between the Component Division and the Aircraft Engine Division. According to the agreement, the Component Division would invest, build, and operate a plant devoted solely to the manufacture of the control unit. The entire output from the plant would be sold to the Aircraft Engine Division. In exchange, the Aircraft Engine Division agreed to absorb all underapplied fixed factory overhead and engineering costs incurred within the control unit plant and to cover the full costs of control unit production plus a guaranteed 10 percent return, after taxes, on the full investment in the plant.

Over the years, the transfer price of the control units had been set in the following manner. The Aircraft Engine Division would estimate its annual requirements for control units. The Component Division would estimate the total production and factory costs needed to manufacture the estimated output. From this information, a transfer price per unit would be established and used for the period. At the end of the year a book adjustment would be made between the divisions to account for any over- or underapplication of fixed factory costs and return on investment.

THE CURRENT CONFLICT

As a result of the arrangement between the Component Division and the Aircraft Engine Division, Magnum Aerospace (Canada) was required to purchase all of its control units from the Aircraft Engine Division. The Canadian Division was treated at arm's length, just like any other customer, by the Aircraft Engine Division. Over the years, the Canadian Division has generally purchased as much as 10 percent of the control units produced by the plant.

Recently some dissatisfaction with respect to this arrangement had been expressed by the management of Magnum Aerospace (Canada). They felt that the Canadian Division, being an integral part of the organization, should have access to the control units directly from the plant rather than through the Aircraft Engine Division. They argued that the current price, plus the 22.5 percent duty that they had to pay made them less competitive in the Canadian market. As a profit center, the Canadian Division found it very difficult to achieve their targets when saddled with the huge duty charge on the components. In addition, the Canadian Division's management felt they should be able to exercise more autonomy regarding issues such as sourcing, product pricing, and sales mix. They pointed out that the major hope they have for a decent year in 19x2 lay with successfully winning a bid on the government's F-18 fighter program. The savings associated with the British firm's offer on the control unit would give Magnum Aerospace (Canada) a cost edge as well as a healthy margin for meeting their profit target.

Exhibit 1
Projected Cost of Control Unit Requirements for Magnum Aerospace (Canada)

		Aircraft Engine sourcing		*British firm sourcing*
Invoice price to Magnum Aerospace (Canada)		$2,071,043		$1,728,264
Duty charges	(22.5%)	– 465,985	(10%)	– 172,826
Total paid by Magnum Aerospace (Canada)		$2,537,028		$1,901,090

(continued)

Cost Structure:	
Direct material	$ 907,042
Direct labor	126,564
Factory overhead-variable	201,007
Factory overhead-fixed*	473,868
Direct engineering cost*	121,632
Packing costs	83,370
Return on investment to the Component Division*	157,560
Total	$2,071,043

* Over- or underallocation on these items is charged to the Aircraft Engine Division at the end of the period.

REQUIREMENTS

a) Which offer is most beneficial to the parent company? The Canadian Division? Why?

b) Given the existing transfer price system for the control units, what types of action might the managers of

1. The Canadian Division
2. The Aircraft Engine Division
3. The Component Division

undertake to score on their performance evaluation criteria?

c) Should the parent company allow the Canadian Division to select the supplier for the control units? Why?

d) Should any changes be made in the system with respect to the handling of the control units? Support your answer with clear examples relating to the issue at hand. (CGA Adapted)

SOLUTION TO REVIEW PROBLEM

a)

1. Market value = $20 per unit
2. Market value less selling costs = $20 − $1 = $19 per unit
3. Standard variable cost = $\dfrac{\$40{,}000 + \$30{,}000 + \$30{,}000}{10{,}000}$ = $10 per unit
4. Standard full cost = $\dfrac{\$160{,}000}{10{,}000}$ = $16 per unit

b)

1. Transfer price = $20

		Division A		*Division B*
Sales:				
To outsiders	(7,000 × $20)	$140,000	(3,000 × $45)	$135,000
To Division B	(3,000 × $20)	60,000		
Total		$200,000		$135,000
Costs:				
Product from Division A			(3,000 × $20)	$ 60,000
Division manufacturing		$160,000		60,000
Selling	(7,000 × $1)	7,000	(3,000 × $2)	6,000
Total		−167,000		−126,000
Profits		$ 33,000		$ 9,000

2. Transfer price = $19

		Division A		Division B
Sales:				
To outsiders	(7,000 × $20)	$140,000	(3,000 × $45)	$135,000
To Division B	(3,000 × $19)	57,000		
Total		$197,000		$135,000
Costs:				
Product from Division A			(3,000 × $19)	$ 57,000
Division manufacturing		$160,000		60,000
Selling	(7,000 × $1)	7,000	(3,000 × $2)	6,000
Total		− 167,000		− 123,000
Profits		$ 30,000		$ 12,000

3. Transfer price = $10

		Division A		Division B
Sales:				
To outsiders	(7,000 × $20)	$140,000	(3,000 × $45)	$135,000
To Division B	(3,000 × $10)	30,000		
Total		$170,000		$135,000
Costs:				
Product from Division A			(3,000 × $10)	$ 30,000
Division manufacturing		$160,000		60,000
Selling	(7,000 × $1)	7,000	(3,000 × $2)	6,000
Total		− 167,000		− 96,000
Profits		$ 3,000		$ 39,000

4. Transfer price = $16

		Division A		Division B
Sales:				
To outsiders	(7,000 × $20)	$140,000	(3,000 × $45)	$135,000
To Division B	(3,000 × $16)	48,000		
Total		$188,000		$135,000
Costs:				
Product from Division A			(3,000 × $16)	$ 48,000
Division manufacturing		$160,000		60,000
Selling	(7,000 × $1)	7,000	(3,000 × $2)	6,000
Total		− 167,000		− 114,000
Profits		$ 21,000		$ 21,000

c) If Division A has excess capacity, a transfer price based on standard variable cost of $10 would be optimal from the viewpoint of the corporation. This price would motivate the manager of Division B to acquire additional units of the intermediate product from Division A until the net marginal revenue of B equals the marginal cost of A.

d) If Division A has no excess capacity, a transfer price based on market value less selling cost of the intermediate product would be optimal from the viewpoint of the corporation. This price reflects the opportunity cost to the corporation of processing a unit of the intermediate product further rather than selling it externally.

APPENDIX A An Introduction to the Time Value of Money

When asked if they would rather have \$100 today or Jones's I.O.U. for \$100 one year hence, rational decision makers respond they would rather have \$100 today. There are two reasons for this: first, the time value of money, and second, risk. A dollar today is worth more than a dollar tomorrow or at some other future time. Having a dollar today provides flexibility. It may be spent, buried, or invested in a number of projects. If invested in a savings account, it will amount to more than one dollar at some future time because of the effect of interest. The interest paid by a bank, or borrower, for the use of money is analogous to the rent paid for the use of land, buildings, or equipment. Furthermore, we live in an uncertain world and, for a variety of reasons, the possibility exists that Jones will not pay his debts as they come due.

FUTURE AMOUNT

If we deposited \$100 in an insured savings account, the future amount of money we will have in the account depends on four factors: the interest rate, the time period, whether interest is simple or compound, and, if compound, the frequency of compounding.

Example A–1

Assume a local bank pays interest at 6 percent compounded annually. In two years a deposit of \$100 will amount to \$112.36:

Principal	\$100.00
Interest for the first year (\$100.00 × 0.06)	6.00
Amount at the end of the first year	\$106.00
Interest for the second year (\$106.00 × 0.06)	6.36
Amount at the end of the second year	\$112.36

This is an example of compound interest because the second year's interest is based on the principal plus accumulated interest from the first year. In effect, interest is paid on interest. **Compound interest** is computed on the original investment and all subsequent interest earnings that remain on deposit. **Simple interest** is only computed on the original investment regardless of whether or not interest is left on deposit. Under simple interest, a \$100 deposit that earns interest at the rate of 6 percent per year will amount to \$112.00 in two years. Each year's interest is \$6. Differences in the growth of principal plus interest under simple and compound interest are illustrated in Exhibit A–1. Unless specified otherwise, all situations in this appendix involve compound interest.

The computations for Example A–1 can also be presented as:

$$\$100\,(1 + 0.06)(1 + 0.06) = \underline{\underline{\$112.36}}$$

or

$$\$100(1 + 0.06)^2 = \underline{\underline{\$112.36}}$$

This leads to the following formula for the computation of a future amount:

$$S = P(1 + r)^n \qquad \text{(A–1)}$$

EXHIBIT A–1 Future Amounts Under Simple and Compound Interest (Principal = \$100, Interest Rate = 0.06)

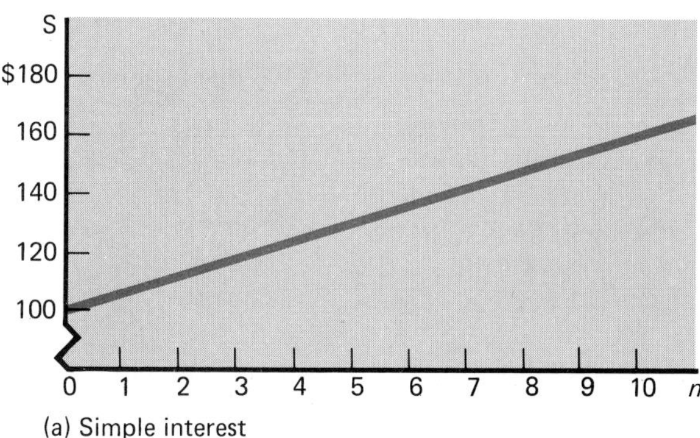

(a) Simple interest

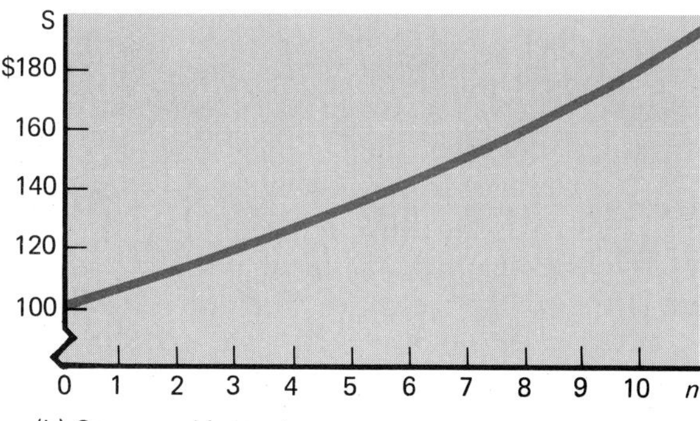

(b) Compound interest

where

S = Future amount
P = Present amount
r = Interest rate
n = Number of periods

Eq. A–1 states that if P dollars are invested for n periods with interest compounded each period at r percent, the investment will amount to S dollars.

When n is large, Eq. A–1 has computational advantages over the approach in Example A–1 for computing S. To further simplify computations, standard tables for the future amount of \$1 are readily available. See Table D in Appendix B. Using Table D, we need only select the factor that corresponds to n and r, and multiply the factor by the number of multiples of \$1 contained in P. With $n = 2$ and $r = 0.06$, the future amount of \$1 in Table D is \$1.1236 and the future amount of \$100 is \$112.36:

$$S = \$100\,(1.1236) = \underline{\underline{\$112.36}}$$

Besides the interest rate, the number of periods, and whether interest is compound or simple, the frequency of compounding also affects the growth of principal plus interest. With interest stated as an annual rate and compounding occurring several times per year, we cannot directly use the annual interest rate or the number of years the money is left on deposit in Eq. A–1 or Table D. We modify them as follows:

$$r = \frac{\text{Annual interest rate}}{\text{Number of times interest is compounded each year}}$$

$$n = \begin{pmatrix}\text{Number of years principal}\\ \text{and interest remain}\\ \text{on deposit}\end{pmatrix} \times \begin{pmatrix}\text{Number of times}\\ \text{interest is}\\ \text{compounded each year}\end{pmatrix}$$

Example A–2

A \$1,000, five-year note bears interest at an annual rate of 12 percent. Interest is compounded semiannually. Principal and interest are to be paid in one lump sum at the end of five years:

$$r = 0.12 \div 2 = \underline{\underline{0.06}}$$
$$n = 5 \times 2 = \underline{\underline{10}}$$

In Table D the factor for the future amount of \$1 with $r = 0.06$ and $n = 10$ is 1.7909. Multiplying this factor by the number of multiples of \$1 in the note, the maturity value of the note is \$1,790.90.

$$S = \$1{,}000(1.7909) = \underline{\underline{\$1{,}790.90}}$$

If interest were compounded annually rather than semiannually, we would go to Table D to find the factor for the future amount of \$1 with $r = 0.12$ and $n = 5$. It is 1.7623, and the future amount of \$1,000 would be \$1,762.30 (1.7623 × \$1,000). From the investor's viewpoint, there is an advantage to more frequent compounding of interest. For Example A–2, this advantage is \$28.60 (\$1,790.90 − \$1,762.30).

PRESENT VALUE

In many situations we wish to determine the present worth (value) of a series of future cash flows.

Example A–3

Assume Campbell is a solid citizen with a steady job who always pays her debts on time. She offers you her noninterest-bearing note for $2,000 due three years from today. Assuming a time value of money of 10 percent, how much would you pay for the note?

In this case, S, r, and n are known and we wish to find the present value P. In Eq. A–1,

$$S = P(1 + r)^n$$

Solving for P:

$$P = \frac{S}{(1 + r)^n} \qquad \text{(A–2)}$$

The value of P in Eq. A–2 is the present value of S dollars to be received in n periods, discounted at interest rate r each period. For Example A–3,

$$P = \frac{\$2{,}000}{(1 + 0.1)^3} = \underline{\underline{\$1{,}502.63}}$$

To simplify computations, Table E in Appendix B contains factors for the present value of $1 for various combinations of r and n. Using Table E the present value factor for $1 to be received at the end of three periods discounted at 10 percent is 0.7513. Therefore, the present value of $2,000 to be received at the end of three periods discounted at 10 percent is $1,502.60 ($2,000 × 0.7513). The three-cent difference between this answer and the solution computed using Eq. A–2 is due to rounding in the development of table factors.

Eq. A–2 and/or Table E can also be used to find the present value of a series of cash flows. Such a series is represented as:

$$P = \frac{S_1}{(1 + r)^1} + \frac{S_2}{(1 + r)^2} + \cdots + \frac{S_i}{(1 + r)^i} + \cdots + \frac{S_n}{(1 + r)^n} \qquad \text{(A–3)}$$

where

S_i = Cash flow of period i
n = Number of periods when last cash flow occurs

Example A–4

Assuming a time value of money of 10 percent, determine the present value of a $1,000, 8 percent bond maturing in three years and paying interest *at the end of each year.*

Note the distinction between the face rate of interest on the bond and the time value of money. With an 8 percent face rate of interest the annual interest payment is $80 ($1,000 × 0.08). Because the time value of money is greater than the face rate of interest, the present value of this bond, $950.244, is less than $1,000. As an exercise, verify the bond's present value and then check your computations with those in Exhibit A–2.

EXHIBIT A–2 **Computation of Present Value**

	Time 0	Year 1	Year 2	Year 3	Total receipts
Interest receipts		$ 80	$ 80	$ 80	$ 240
Principal receipts				1,000	1,000
Total receipts		$ 80	$ 80	$1,080	$1,240
Present value factor @ 10% (Table E)		× 0.9091	× 0.8264	× 0.7513	
	$ 72.728 ← (Year 1)				
	66.112 ← (Year 2)				
	811.404 ← (Year 3)				
Present value	$950.244				

PRESENT VALUE OF AN ANNUITY IN ARREARS

The concept of an annuity is frequently used to simplify present value computations. An **annuity** is a series of *consecutive* and *equal* cash flows. An annuity is said to be an **annuity in arrears** when the cash flows occur at the end of each period. An annuity is identified as an **annuity due** or an **annuity in advance** when the cash flows occur at the start of each period. Most annuities considered in this text are annuities in arrears.

The formula for the present value of an annuity in arrears is:

$$P = S\left(\frac{1}{r}\left(1 - \frac{1}{(1+r)^n}\right)\right) \tag{A–4}$$

Fortunately tables for the present value of an annuity of $1 in arrears for various combinations of r and n are readily available. See Table F in Appendix B. Except for the cumulative impact of rounding, the factors in Table F could be derived by summing the factors in Table E. Consider an annuity in arrears of $1 per period for three periods with $r = 0.10$. In Table F the present value of this annuity is $2.4869. Summing the appropriate factors in Table E, we can determine the present value to be $2.4868:

n	*Present value of $1 @ 10% (Table E)*
1	$0.9091
2	0.8264
3	0.7513
Total	$2.4868

To see how the use of annuity tables can simplify computations, consider the cash flows in Example A–4. They can be broken down into two parts: an annuity of $80 per period for three periods and a single receipt of $1,000 at the end of three periods. We can use Tables E and F to compute the solution as follows:

Present value of interest, $n = 3$, $r = 0.10$ (Table F)	
$80 × 2.4869 =	$198.952
Present value of principal, $n = 3$, $r = 0.10$ (Table E)	
$1,000 × 0.7513 =	751.300
Present value	$950.252

Although the computational savings are minimal in this example, the advantage of using annuity tables increases with the number of periods involved in the annuity.

DEFERRED ANNUITIES

A decision maker occasionally encounters a **deferred annuity** in which an annuity will not begin for two or more periods. Deferred annuities are frequently encountered with pensions and leases. They are also encountered in capital expenditure situations when it takes several periods to get operations started.

Example A–5

Find the present value of an annuity in arrears of $1,000 per year for three years when the first payment is to be received at the end of five years. The time value of money is 12 percent. The following diagram should help you understand this situation:

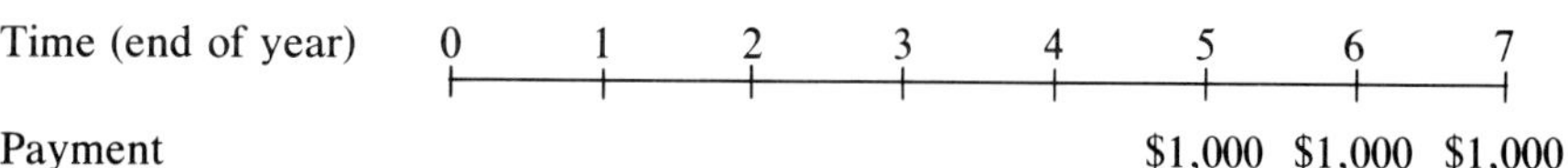

We want to find the present value (value at time zero) of the three $1,000 cash flows. There are at least three ways of doing this.

First, we can use Table E to independently compute the present value of each cash flow.

	Time 0	Year 5	Year 6	Year 7
Cash flow		$1,000	$1,000	$1,000
Present value factor @ 12% (Table E)		× 0.5674	× 0.5066	× 0.4523
	$ 567.40 ←	(Year 5)		
	506.60 ←		(Year 6)	
	452.30 ←			(Year 7)
Present value	$1,526.30			

Second, we can use Table F to compute the present value of the annuity as of Time 4 and then use Table E to compute the present value of this amount as of Time 0. Note that the end of year 4 is the start of year 5.

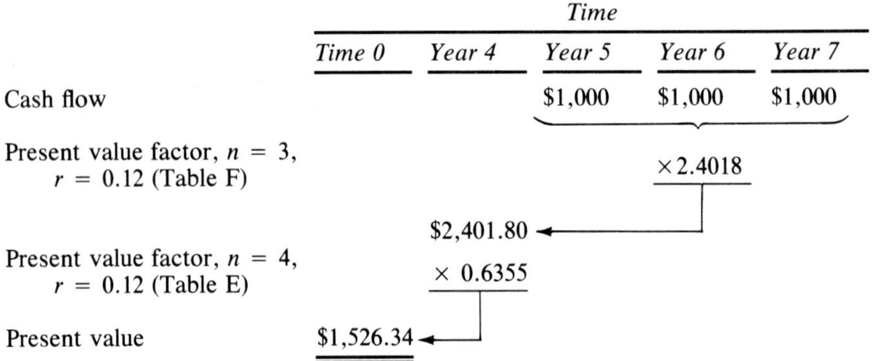

Time
Time 0
Year 4
Year 5
Year 6
Year 7
Cash flow
$1,000
$1,000
$1,000
Present value factor, n = 3, r = 0.12 (Table F)
×2.4018
$2,401.80
Present value factor, n = 4, r = 0.12 (Table E)
× 0.6355
Present value
$1,526.34

Third, using Table F, we can subtract the factor for $n = 4$, $r = 0.12$ from the factor for $n = 7$, $r = 0.12$, and then multiply the difference by \$1,000.

Present value factor, $n = 7$, $r = 0.12$ (Table F)	4.5638
Present value factor, $n = 4$, $r = 0.12$ (Table F)	−3.0374
Present value of a deferred annuity of \$1	1.5264
Annual amount of annuity	× \$1,000
Present value	\$1,526.40

If the annuity were for seven periods, its present value would be \$4,563.80 (4.5638 × \$1,000). However, this includes the present value of four cash receipts that did not occur (3.0374 × \$1,000 = \$3,037.40). Subtracting the present value of the receipts that did not occur leaves the present value of the deferred annuity (\$4,563.80 − \$3,037.40 = \$1,526.40).

Of the three procedures, the third is preferred because of its simplicity. Note, however, that there are many alternative ways of arriving at the correct solution to present value problems. Also note the importance of keeping track of the time periods with which you are dealing.

FINDING AN INTEREST RATE

Occasionally a decision maker encounters situations in which the present value and the future cash flows are known, and the time value of money that equates them must be found.

Example A–6

In exchange for a loan of \$2,800 today, Mr. Jones promises to pay \$1,000 at the end of each of the next four years. Determine the interest rate that is implicit in this loan. This situation is illustrated as follows:

	Time 0	Year 1	Year 2	Year 3	Year 4
Cash flow		\$1,000	\$1,000	\$1,000	\$1,000
Present value factor $n = 4$, $r = X$ (Table F)			× factor		
Present value	\$2,800 ←				

The immediate problem is to find the present value factor that equates the present value with the future cash flows. Once this factor is found, we can enter the annuity table at the appropriate value of n and go across the corresponding row until the closest table factor is found. The corresponding value of r is the time value of money that equates the present value and the future cash flows.

If:

$$\begin{pmatrix}\text{Present}\\ \text{value of}\\ \text{annuity}\end{pmatrix} = \begin{pmatrix}\text{Amount of}\\ \text{periodic}\\ \text{cash flows}\end{pmatrix} \times \begin{pmatrix}\text{Factor for the present}\\ \text{value of the annuity of \$1}\\ \text{for } n \text{ periods at } r\end{pmatrix}$$

then:

$$\text{Factor} = \frac{\text{Present value of annuity}}{\text{Amount of periodic cash flows}}$$

For Example A–6, the factor is 2.8:

$$\text{Factor} = \frac{\$2{,}800}{\$1{,}000} = \underline{\underline{2.8}}$$

For $n = 4$, the closest factor in Table F is 2.7982. The corresponding time value of money is 16 percent. In this textbook, interpolations are not performed for factors that are not listed in the appropriate table. In practice, very detailed tables, calculators with built-in present value functions, or computer routines are used to determine the time value of money.

APPENDIX B Tables

TABLE A Areas Under the Normal Curve

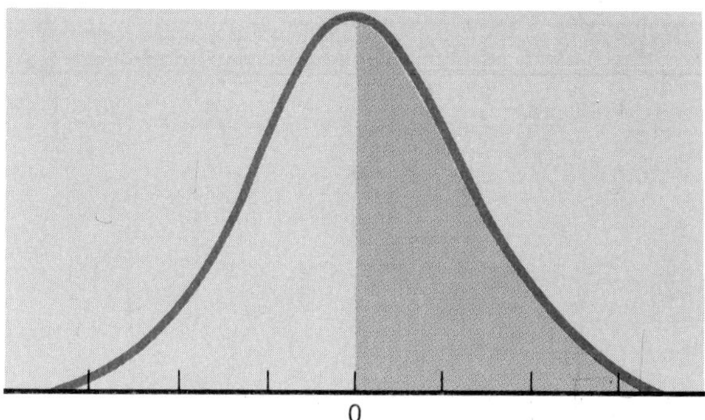

$$z = \frac{x - \mu}{\sigma}$$

where z is the normal deviate.

Example: The table shows that
$p(z \geq 1) = 0.1587$.

z	0.00	0.01	0.02	0.03	0.04	0.05	0.06	0.07	0.08	0.09
0.0	0.5000	0.4960	0.4920	0.4880	0.4840	0.4801	0.4761	0.4721	0.4681	0.4641
0.1	0.4602	0.4562	0.4522	0.4483	0.4443	0.4404	0.4364	0.4325	0.4286	0.4247
0.2	0.4207	0.4168	0.4129	0.4090	0.4052	0.4013	0.3974	0.3936	0.3897	0.3859
0.3	0.3821	0.3783	0.3745	0.3707	0.3669	0.3632	0.3594	0.3557	0.3520	0.3483
0.4	0.3446	0.3409	0.3372	0.3336	0.3300	0.3264	0.3228	0.3192	0.3156	0.3121
0.5	0.3085	0.3050	0.3015	0.2981	0.2946	0.2912	0.2877	0.2843	0.2810	0.2776
0.6	0.2743	0.2709	0.2676	0.2643	0.2611	0.2578	0.2546	0.2514	0.2483	0.2451
0.7	0.2420	0.2389	0.2358	0.2327	0.2296	0.2266	0.2236	0.2206	0.2177	0.2148
0.8	0.2119	0.2090	0.2061	0.2033	0.2005	0.1977	0.1949	0.1922	0.1894	0.1867
0.9	0.1841	0.1814	0.1788	0.1762	0.1736	0.1711	0.1683	0.1660	0.1635	0.1611
1.0	0.1587	0.1562	0.1539	0.1515	0.1492	0.1469	0.1446	0.1423	0.1401	0.1379
1.1	0.1357	0.1335	0.1314	0.1292	0.1271	0.1251	0.1230	0.1210	0.1190	0.1170
1.2	0.1151	0.1131	0.1112	0.1093	0.1075	0.1056	0.1038	0.1020	0.1003	0.0985
1.3	0.0968	0.0951	0.0934	0.0918	0.0901	0.0885	0.0869	0.0853	0.0838	0.0823
1.4	0.0808	0.0793	0.0778	0.0764	0.0749	0.0735	0.0721	0.0708	0.0694	0.0681
1.5	0.0668	0.0655	0.0643	0.0630	0.0618	0.0606	0.0594	0.0582	0.0571	0.0559
1.6	0.0548	0.0537	0.0526	0.0516	0.0505	0.0495	0.0485	0.0475	0.0465	0.0455
1.7	0.0446	0.0436	0.0427	0.0418	0.0409	0.0401	0.0392	0.0384	0.0375	0.0367
1.8	0.0359	0.0351	0.0344	0.0336	0.0329	0.0322	0.0314	0.0307	0.0301	0.0294
1.9	0.0287	0.0281	0.0274	0.0268	0.0262	0.0256	0.0250	0.0244	0.0239	0.0233
2.0	0.0228	0.0222	0.0217	0.0212	0.0207	0.0202	0.0197	0.0192	0.0188	0.0183
2.1	0.0179	0.0174	0.0170	0.0166	0.0162	0.0158	0.0154	0.0150	0.0146	0.0143
2.2	0.0139	0.0136	0.0132	0.0129	0.0125	0.0122	0.0119	0.0116	0.0113	0.0110
2.3	0.0107	0.0104	0.0102	0.0099	0.0096	0.0094	0.0091	0.0089	0.0087	0.0084
2.4	0.0082	0.0080	0.0078	0.0075	0.0073	0.0071	0.0069	0.0068	0.0066	0.0064
2.5	0.0062	0.0060	0.0059	0.0057	0.0055	0.0054	0.0052	0.0051	0.0049	0.0048
2.6	0.0047	0.0045	0.0044	0.0043	0.0041	0.0040	0.0039	0.0038	0.0037	0.0036
2.7	0.0035	0.0034	0.0033	0.0032	0.0031	0.0030	0.0029	0.0028	0.0027	0.0026
2.8	0.0026	0.0025	0.0024	0.0023	0.0023	0.0022	0.0021	0.0021	0.0020	0.0019
2.9	0.0019	0.0018	0.0018	0.0017	0.0016	0.0016	0.0015	0.0015	0.0014	0.0014
3.0	0.00135	0.0013	0.0013	0.0012	0.0012	0.0011	0.0011	0.0011	0.0010	0.0010
4.0	0.00003									

The values for the areas under the normal curve in Table A are taken from *CRC Handbook of Tables for Mathematics,* Revised 4th edition, © CRC Press, Inc., 1975. Used by permission of CRC Press, Inc.

TABLE B Ordinate Values for the Normal Curve

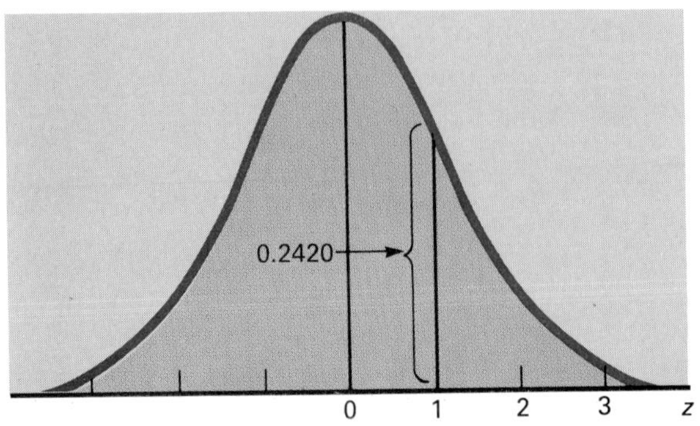

$$z = \frac{x - \mu}{\sigma}$$

where x is the normal deviate.

Example: The table shows that the ordinate, y, at $z = 1$ is 0.2420

z	0.00	0.01	0.02	0.03	0.04	0.05	0.06	0.07	0.08	0.09
0.0	0.3989	0.3989	0.3989	0.3988	0.3986	0.3984	0.3982	0.3980	0.3977	0.3973
0.1	0.3970	0.3965	0.3961	0.3956	0.3951	0.3945	0.3939	0.3932	0.3925	0.3918
0.2	0.3910	0.3902	0.3894	0.3885	0.3876	0.3867	0.3857	0.3847	0.3836	0.3825
0.3	0.3814	0.3802	0.3790	0.3778	0.3765	0.3752	0.3739	0.3725	0.3712	0.3697
0.4	0.3683	0.3668	0.3653	0.3637	0.3621	0.3605	0.3589	0.3572	0.3555	0.3538
0.5	0.3521	0.3503	0.3485	0.3467	0.3448	0.3429	0.3410	0.3391	0.3372	0.3352
0.6	0.3332	0.3312	0.3292	0.3271	0.3251	0.3230	0.3209	0.3187	0.3166	0.3144
0.7	0.3123	0.3101	0.3079	0.3056	0.3034	0.3011	0.2989	0.2966	0.2943	0.2920
0.8	0.2897	0.2874	0.2850	0.2827	0.2803	0.2780	0.2756	0.2732	0.2709	0.2685
0.9	0.2661	0.2637	0.2613	0.2589	0.2565	0.2541	0.2516	0.2492	0.2468	0.2444
1.0	0.2420	0.2396	0.2371	0.2347	0.2323	0.2299	0.2275	0.2251	0.2227	0.2203
1.1	0.2179	0.2155	0.2131	0.2107	0.2083	0.2059	0.2036	0.2012	0.1989	0.1965
1.2	0.1942	0.1919	0.1895	0.1872	0.1849	0.1826	0.1804	0.1781	0.1758	0.1736
1.3	0.1714	0.1691	0.1669	0.1647	0.1626	0.1604	0.1582	0.1561	0.1539	0.1518
1.4	0.1497	0.1476	0.1456	0.1435	0.1415	0.1394	0.1374	0.1354	0.1334	0.1315
1.5	0.1295	0.1276	0.1257	0.1238	0.1219	0.1200	0.1182	0.1163	0.1145	0.1127
1.6	0.1109	0.1092	0.1074	0.1057	0.1040	0.1023	0.1006	0.0989	0.0973	0.0957
1.7	0.0940	0.0925	0.0909	0.0893	0.0878	0.0863	0.0848	0.0833	0.0818	0.0804
1.8	0.0790	0.0775	0.0761	0.0748	0.0734	0.0721	0.0707	0.0694	0.0681	0.0669
1.9	0.0656	0.0644	0.0632	0.0620	0.0608	0.0596	0.0584	0.0573	0.0562	0.0551
2.0	0.0540	0.0529	0.0519	0.0508	0.0498	0.0488	0.0478	0.0468	0.0459	0.0449
2.1	0.0440	0.0431	0.0422	0.0413	0.0404	0.0396	0.0387	0.0379	0.0371	0.0363
2.2	0.0355	0.0347	0.0339	0.0332	0.0325	0.0317	0.0310	0.0303	0.0297	0.0290
2.3	0.0283	0.0277	0.0270	0.0264	0.0258	0.0252	0.0246	0.0241	0.0235	0.0229
2.4	0.0224	0.0219	0.0213	0.0208	0.0203	0.0198	0.0194	0.0189	0.0184	0.0180
2.5	0.0175	0.0171	0.0167	0.0163	0.0158	0.0154	0.0151	0.0147	0.0143	0.0139
2.6	0.0136	0.0132	0.0129	0.0126	0.0122	0.0119	0.0116	0.0113	0.0110	0.0107
2.7	0.0104	0.0101	0.0099	0.0096	0.0093	0.0091	0.0088	0.0086	0.0084	0.0081
2.8	0.0079	0.0077	0.0075	0.0073	0.0071	0.0069	0.0067	0.0065	0.0063	0.0061
2.9	0.0060	0.0058	0.0056	0.0055	0.0053	0.0051	0.0050	0.0048	0.0047	0.0046
3.0	0.0044	0.0043	0.0042	0.0040	0.0039	0.0038	0.0037	0.0036	0.0035	0.0034
4.0	0.0001									

Tabled values are computed as $y = \frac{1}{\sqrt{2\pi}} e^{-(1/2)z^2}$

TABLE C Critical Points for the *t*-Distribution

Example: The table shows that $p(z \geq 1.886) = 0.10$ for 2 degrees of freedom.

d.f.	0.10	0.05	0.025	0.01	0.005
1	3.078	6.314	12.706	31.821	63.657
2	1.886	2.920	4.303	6.965	9.925
3	1.638	2.353	3.182	4.541	5.841
4	1.533	2.132	2.776	3.747	4.604
5	1.476	2.015	2.571	3.365	4.032
6	1.440	1.943	2.447	3.143	3.707
7	1.415	1.895	2.365	2.998	3.499
8	1.397	1.860	2.306	2.896	3.355
9	1.383	1.833	2.262	2.821	3.250
10	1.372	1.812	2.228	2.764	3.169
11	1.363	1.796	2.201	2.718	3.106
12	1.356	1.782	2.179	2.681	3.055
13	1.350	1.771	2.160	2.650	3.012
14	1.345	1.761	2.145	2.624	2.977
15	1.341	1.753	2.131	2.602	2.947
16	1.337	1.746	2.120	2.583	2.921
17	1.333	1.740	2.110	2.567	2.898
18	1.330	1.734	2.101	2.552	2.878
19	1.328	1.729	2.093	2.539	2.861
20	1.325	1.725	2.086	2.528	2.845
21	1.323	1.721	2.080	2.518	2.831
22	1.321	1.717	2.074	2.508	2.819
23	1.319	1.714	2.069	2.500	2.807
24	1.318	1.711	2.064	2.492	2.797
25	1.316	1.708	2.060	2.485	2.787
26	1.315	1.706	2.056	2.479	2.779
27	1.314	1.703	2.052	2.473	2.771
28	1.313	1.701	2.048	2.467	2.763
29	1.311	1.699	2.045	2.462	2.756
30	1.310	1.697	2.042	2.457	2.750
40	1.303	1.684	2.021	2.423	2.704
60	1.296	1.671	2.000	2.390	2.660
120	1.289	1.658	1.980	2.358	2.617
∞	1.282	1.645	1.960	2.326	2.576

The values of the *t*-distribution in Table C are taken from Table III of Fisher and Yates: *Statistical Tables for Biological, Agricultural, and Medical Research,* published by Longman Group Ltd., London (previously published by Oliver & Boyd, Edinburgh), by permission of the authors and publishers.

TABLE D* **Amount of $1**

$S = 1\,(1 + r)^n$

Periods n	Time value of money 0.06	0.08	0.10	0.12	0.14	0.16	0.18	0.20	0.22	0.24
1	1.0600	1.0800	1.1000	1.1200	1.1400	1.1600	1.1800	1.2000	1.2200	1.2400
2	1.1236	1.1664	1.2100	1.2544	1.2996	1.3456	1.3924	1.4400	1.4884	1.5376
3	1.1910	1.2597	1.3310	1.4049	1.4815	1.5609	1.6430	1.7280	1.8158	1.9066
4	1.2625	1.3605	1.4641	1.5735	1.6890	1.8106	1.9388	2.0736	2.2153	2.3642
5	1.3382	1.4693	1.6105	1.7623	1.9254	2.1003	2.2878	2.4883	2.7027	2.9316
6	1.4185	1.5869	1.7716	1.9738	2.1950	2.4364	2.6996	2.9860	3.2973	3.6352
7	1.5036	1.7138	1.9487	2.2107	2.5023	2.8262	3.1855	3.5832	4.0227	4.5077
8	1.5939	1.8509	2.1436	2.4760	2.8526	3.2784	3.7589	4.2998	4.9077	5.5895
9	1.6895	1.9990	2.3579	2.7730	3.2519	3.8030	4.4355	5.1598	5.9874	6.9310
10	1.7909	2.1589	2.5937	3.1058	3.7072	4.4114	5.2338	6.1917	7.3046	8.5944
11	1.8983	2.3316	2.8531	3.4785	4.2262	5.1173	6.1759	7.4301	8.9117	10.6571
12	2.0122	2.5182	3.1384	3.8960	4.8179	5.9360	7.2876	8.9161	10.8722	13.2148
13	2.1329	2.7196	3.4523	4.3635	5.4924	6.8858	8.5994	10.6993	13.2641	16.3863
14	2.2609	2.9372	3.7975	4.8871	6.2613	7.9875	10.1473	12.8392	16.1822	20.3191
15	2.3966	3.1722	4.1772	5.4736	7.1379	9.2655	11.9738	15.4070	19.7423	25.1956
16	2.5404	3.4259	4.5950	6.1304	8.1373	10.7480	14.1290	18.4884	24.0856	31.2426
17	2.6928	3.7000	5.0545	6.8660	9.2765	12.4677	16.6723	22.1861	29.3844	38.7408
18	2.8543	3.9960	5.5599	7.6900	10.5752	14.4625	19.6733	26.6233	35.8490	48.0386
19	3.0256	4.3157	6.1159	8.6128	12.0557	16.7765	23.2145	31.9480	43.7357	59.5679
20	3.2071	4.6609	6.7275	9.6463	13.7435	19.4608	27.3931	38.3376	53.3576	73.8643
21	3.3996	5.0338	7.4002	10.8038	15.6676	22.5745	32.3238	46.0051	65.0963	91.5915
22	3.6035	5.4365	8.1403	12.1003	17.8610	26.1864	38.1421	55.2061	79.4175	113.573
23	3.8197	5.8715	8.9543	13.5523	20.3616	30.3762	45.0076	66.2474	96.8893	140.831
24	4.0489	6.3412	9.8497	15.1786	23.2122	35.2364	53.1090	79.4968	118.205	174.631
25	4.2919	6.8485	10.8347	17.0001	26.4619	40.8742	62.6686	95.3962	144.210	216.542
26	4.5494	7.3964	11.9182	19.0401	30.1666	47.4141	73.9490	114.475	175.936	268.512
27	4.8223	7.9881	13.1100	21.3249	34.3899	55.0004	87.2598	137.371	214.642	332.955
28	5.1117	8.6271	14.4210	23.8839	39.2045	63.8004	102.967	164.845	261.864	412.864
29	5.4184	9.3173	15.8631	26.7499	44.6931	74.0085	121.501	197.814	319.474	511.951
30	5.7435	10.0627	17.4494	29.9599	50.9501	85.8499	143.371	237.376	389.758	634.820

* For an introduction to the use of this table, see Appendix A.

TABLE E* **Present Value of $1**

$$P = \frac{1}{(1 + r)^n}$$

Periods n	0.02	0.04	0.06	0.08	0.10	0.12	0.14	0.16	0.18	0.20	0.22	0.24
	Time value of money											
1	0.9804	0.9615	0.9434	0.9259	0.9091	0.8929	0.8772	0.8621	0.8475	0.8333	0.8197	0.8065
2	0.9612	0.9246	0.8900	0.8573	0.8264	0.7972	0.7695	0.7432	0.7182	0.6944	0.6719	0.6504
3	0.9423	0.8890	0.8396	0.7938	0.7513	0.7118	0.6750	0.6407	0.6086	0.5787	0.5507	0.5245
4	0.9238	0.8548	0.7921	0.7350	0.6830	0.6355	0.5921	0.5523	0.5158	0.4823	0.4514	0.4230
5	0.9057	0.8219	0.7473	0.6806	0.6209	0.5674	0.5194	0.4761	0.4371	0.4019	0.3700	0.3411
6	0.8880	0.7903	0.7050	0.6302	0.5645	0.5066	0.4556	0.4104	0.3704	0.3349	0.3033	0.2751
7	0.8706	0.7599	0.6651	0.5835	0.5132	0.4523	0.3996	0.3538	0.3139	0.2791	0.2486	0.2218
8	0.8535	0.7307	0.6274	0.5403	0.4665	0.4039	0.3506	0.3050	0.2660	0.2326	0.2038	0.1789
9	0.8368	0.7026	0.5919	0.5002	0.4241	0.3606	0.3075	0.2630	0.2255	0.1938	0.1670	0.1443
10	0.8203	0.6756	0.5584	0.4632	0.3855	0.3220	0.2697	0.2267	0.1911	0.1615	0.1369	0.1164
11	0.8043	0.6496	0.5268	0.4289	0.3505	0.2875	0.2366	0.1954	0.1619	0.1346	0.1122	0.0938
12	0.7885	0.6246	0.4970	0.3971	0.3186	0.2567	0.2076	0.1685	0.1372	0.1122	0.0920	0.0757
13	0.7730	0.6006	0.4688	0.3677	0.2897	0.2292	0.1821	0.1452	0.1163	0.0935	0.0754	0.0610
14	0.7579	0.5775	0.4423	0.3405	0.2633	0.2046	0.1597	0.1252	0.0985	0.0779	0.0618	0.0492
15	0.7430	0.5553	0.4173	0.3152	0.2394	0.1827	0.1401	0.1079	0.0835	0.0649	0.0507	0.0397
16	0.7284	0.5339	0.3936	0.2919	0.2176	0.1631	0.1229	0.0930	0.0708	0.0541	0.0415	0.0320
17	0.7142	0.5134	0.3714	0.2703	0.1978	0.1456	0.1078	0.0802	0.0600	0.0451	0.0340	0.0258
18	0.7002	0.4936	0.3503	0.2502	0.1799	0.1300	0.0946	0.0691	0.0508	0.0376	0.0279	0.0208
19	0.6864	0.4746	0.3305	0.2317	0.1635	0.1161	0.0829	0.0596	0.0431	0.0313	0.0229	0.0168
20	0.6730	0.4564	0.3118	0.2145	0.1486	0.1037	0.0728	0.0513	0.0365	0.0261	0.0187	0.0135
21	0.6598	0.4388	0.2941	0.1986	0.1351	0.0925	0.0638	0.0443	0.0309	0.0217	0.0154	0.0109
22	0.6468	0.4219	0.2775	0.1839	0.1228	0.0826	0.0560	0.0382	0.0262	0.0181	0.0126	0.0088
23	0.6341	0.4057	0.2618	0.1703	0.1117	0.0738	0.0491	0.0329	0.0222	0.0151	0.0103	0.0071
24	0.6217	0.3901	0.2470	0.1577	0.1015	0.0659	0.0431	0.0284	0.0188	0.0125	0.0084	0.0057
25	0.6095	0.3751	0.2330	0.1460	0.0923	0.0588	0.0378	0.0245	0.0159	0.0105	0.0069	0.0046
26	0.5976	0.3607	0.2198	0.1352	0.0839	0.0525	0.0331	0.0211	0.0135	0.0087	0.0057	0.0037
27	0.5859	0.3468	0.2073	0.1252	0.0763	0.0469	0.0291	0.0182	0.0115	0.0073	0.0046	0.0030
28	0.5744	0.3335	0.1956	0.1159	0.0693	0.0419	0.0255	0.0157	0.0097	0.0061	0.0038	0.0024
29	0.5631	0.3206	0.1845	0.1073	0.0630	0.0374	0.0224	0.0135	0.0082	0.0050	0.0031	0.0019
30	0.5520	0.3083	0.1741	0.0994	0.0573	0.0334	0.0196	0.0116	0.0070	0.0042	0.0026	0.0015

* For an introduction to the use of this table, see Appendix A.

TABLE F* Present Value of $1 in Arrears†

$$P = \sum_{i=1}^{n} \left(\frac{1}{(1+r)^n} \right) = \frac{1}{r} \left(1 - \frac{1}{(1+r)^n} \right)$$

Periods	*Time value of money*											
n	0.02	0.04	0.06	0.08	0.10	0.12	0.14	0.16	0.18	0.20	0.22	0.24
1	0.9804	0.9615	0.9434	0.9259	0.9091	0.8929	0.8772	0.8621	0.8475	0.8333	0.8197	0.8065
2	1.9416	1.8861	1.8334	1.7833	1.7355	1.6901	1.6467	1.6052	1.5656	1.5278	1.4915	1.4568
3	2.8839	2.7750	2.6731	2.5771	2.4869	2.4018	2.3216	2.2459	2.1743	2.1065	2.0422	1.9813
4	3.8077	3.6299	3.4651	3.3121	3.1699	3.0374	2.9137	2.7982	2.6901	2.5887	2.4936	2.4043
5	4.7134	4.4518	4.2124	3.9927	3.7908	3.6048	3.4331	3.2743	3.1272	2.9906	2.8636	2.7454
6	5.6014	5.2422	4.9173	4.6229	4.3553	4.1114	3.8887	3.6847	3.4976	3.3255	3.1669	3.0205
7	6.4720	6.0020	5.5824	5.2064	4.8684	4.5638	4.2883	4.0386	3.8115	3.6046	3.4155	3.2423
8	7.3255	6.7328	6.2098	5.7466	5.3349	4.9676	4.6389	4.3436	4.0776	3.8372	3.6193	3.4212
9	8.1622	7.4353	6.8017	6.2469	5.7590	5.3283	4.9464	4.6065	4.3030	4.0310	3.7863	3.5655
10	8.9828	8.1108	7.3601	6.7101	6.1446	5.6502	5.2161	4.8332	4.4941	4.1925	3.9232	3.6819
11	9.7868	8.7604	7.8869	7.1390	6.4951	5.9377	5.4527	5.0286	4.6560	4.3271	4.0354	3.7757
12	10.5753	9.3851	8.3839	7.5361	6.8137	6.1944	5.6603	5.1971	4.7932	4.4392	4.1274	3.8514
13	11.3485	9.9856	8.8527	7.9038	7.1034	6.4236	5.8424	5.3423	4.9095	4.5327	4.2028	3.9124
14	12.1063	10.5632	9.2950	8.2442	7.3667	6.6282	6.0021	5.4675	5.0081	4.6106	4.2646	3.9616
15	12.8493	11.1184	9.7123	8.5595	7.6061	6.8109	6.1422	5.5755	5.0916	4.6755	4.3152	4.0013
16	13.5778	11.6523	10.1059	8.8514	7.8237	6.9740	6.2651	5.6685	5.1624	4.7296	4.3567	4.0333
17	14.2918	12.1657	10.4773	9.1216	8.0216	7.1196	6.3729	5.7487	5.2223	4.7746	4.3908	4.0591
18	14.9921	12.6593	10.8276	9.3719	8.2014	7.2497	6.4674	5.8178	5.2732	4.8122	4.4187	4.0799
19	15.6784	13.1339	11.1581	9.6036	8.3649	7.3658	6.5504	5.8775	5.3162	4.8435	4.4415	4.0967
20	16.3515	13.5903	11.4699	9.8182	8.5136	7.4694	6.6231	5.9288	5.3527	4.8696	4.4603	4.1103
21	17.0112	14.0292	11.7641	10.0168	8.6487	7.5620	6.6870	5.9731	5.3837	4.8913	4.4756	4.1212
22	17.6580	14.4511	12.0416	10.2007	8.7715	7.6446	6.7429	6.0113	5.4099	4.9094	4.4882	4.1300
23	18.2922	14.8568	12.3034	10.3711	8.8832	7.7184	6.7921	6.0442	5.4321	4.9245	4.4985	4.1371
24	18.9139	15.2470	12.5504	10.5288	8.9847	7.7843	6.8351	6.0726	5.4509	4.9371	4.5070	4.1428
25	19.5234	15.6221	12.7834	10.6748	9.0770	7.8431	6.8729	6.0971	5.4669	4.9476	4.5139	4.1474
26	20.1210	15.9828	13.0032	10.8100	9.1609	7.8957	6.9061	6.1182	5.4804	4.9563	4.5196	4.1511
27	20.7069	16.3296	13.2105	10.9352	9.2372	7.9425	6.9352	6.1364	5.4919	4.9636	4.5243	4.1541
28	21.2813	16.6631	13.4062	11.0511	9.3066	7.9844	6.9607	6.1520	5.5016	4.9697	4.5281	4.1566
29	21.8444	16.9837	13.5907	11.1584	9.3696	8.0218	6.9830	6.1655	5.5098	4.9747	4.5312	4.1585
30	22.3964	17.2920	13.7648	11.2578	9.4269	8.0552	7.0027	6.1772	5.5168	4.9789	4.5338	4.1601

* For an introduction to the use of this table, see Appendix A.

† The present value of an annuity of $1 in advance may be determined by entering the table for $n - 1$ periods and adding 1 to the corresponding factor in the table.

Glossary

A-B-C approach (to inventory management) An approach to inventory management in which several different methods are used to make inventory reordering decisions within the same organization.

Abnormal spoilage Spoilage that is not expected to occur under efficient operating conditions.

Absorption costing A type of product costing in which all manufacturing costs, including direct materials, direct labor, variable factory overhead, and fixed factory overhead, are assigned to products.

Accelerated Cost Recovery System (ACRS) A provision of the United States Tax Code providing for the rapid depreciation of assets in the determination of taxable income.

Account classification method (of cost estimation) A method of cost estimation that uses the cost accountant's professional judgment to analyze costs recorded in each account and determine whether they are fixed, variable, or mixed costs.

Accounting A specialized information system used to provide economic information concerning the past, current, or expected future activities of an organization.

Accounting rate of return The average annual increase in net income that results from acceptance of a project divided by either the initial investment or the average investment in the project.

Actual cost system A cost system in which actual direct materials, actual direct labor, and actual factory overhead are assigned to products.

Actual factory overhead rate An overhead rate determined after the end of the period as actual factory overhead for the period divided by actual units of activity for the period.

Agency costs Additional costs the organization incurs because local managers maximize their utility at the expense of the organization as a whole.

Agency relationship A relationship that exists when one party hires another party to perform a service.

Agency theory A structured attempt to explain the actions of agents.

Agent The employee in an agency relationship.

Annuity A series of equal and consecutive cash flows.

Annuity due An annuity with cash flows occurring at the start of each period.

Annuity in advance (See *Annuity due*.)

Annuity in arrears An annuity with cash flows occurring at the end of each period.

Appraisal costs Costs incurred to determine the degree of conformance of raw materials and products to design specifications.

Assignable causes (in statistical process control) (See *Special causes*.)

Attributes data (in statistical process control) Measurements used to classify a situation into one of two or more categories.

Augmented matrix A matrix divided into two parts by a vertical line. The left half contains a matrix that is to be inverted and the right half contains an identity matrix.

Authoritative approach to budgeting An approach to budgeting whereby top management develops the final budget without consulting employees at lower management levels.

Autocorrelation A condition that exists when the estimating error at time *t* is affected by the value of a previous observation.

Autocratic approach to budgeting (See *Authoritative approach to budgeting*.)

Average annual activity The activity level required to satisfy customer demand over a number of years.

Bail-out factor The time required to recover the initial investment in a project from any source.

Binding constraint In linear programming, a constraint that has an impact on the optimal solution.

Break-even point The unit or dollar sales volume at which total revenues equal total costs.

Budget A formal plan of action expressed in monetary terms.

Budget variance The difference between the actual and budgeted costs of a discretionary cost center.

Budgetary control A type of accounting control whereby actual and budgeted costs are compared.

Budgetary slack Slack in a budget resulting from the intentional understating of expected sales or overstating of expected costs.

Budgeted income statement A forecast of sales revenue, expenses, and income for the budget period.

By-products In distinguishing between major products and by-products, by-products have low relative sales value.

Capacity costs Fixed costs incurred to provide the current level of manufacturing facilities. (Also see *Committed fixed costs*.)

Capital budgeting The identification of potentially desirable investments, their subsequent evaluation, and the selection of investments that meet certain criteria.

Capital-budgeting policies Organizational rules specifying procedures to be followed to obtain approval for capital expenditure proposals.

Capital rationing A situation that occurs when the total funds required for investment proposals meeting the organization's investment criteria exceed the total funds available for investment.

Carrying costs Costs incurred to hold items in inventory.

Cash break-even point The unit or dollar sales volume at which operating cash receipts equal operating cash disbursements.

Cash budget A detailed listing of budgeted cash receipts and disbursements.

Central tendency (measure of) A summary statistic indicating the location of the center of a distribution.

Chief financial executive A single executive position combining the responsibilities of the controller and the treasurer.

Coefficient of determination A measure of the proportion of the total variation in the dependent variable explained by the regression.

Coefficients matrix A matrix containing the coefficients of unknown variables.

Committed fixed costs Fixed costs required to maintain the current production or service capacity.

Common costs Costs incurred for the benefit of two or more cost objectives.

Common segment costs Costs related to more than one segment of a business and not directly identified with the operations of a particular segment.

Compensation insurance Insurance purchased by employers to provide income to employees who are unable to work due to a job-related illness or injury.

Completed contract method of accounting An accounting procedure used for external reporting whereby all income and expenses related to a contract are recognized on completion of the contract.

Compound interest depreciation A residual amount calculated by subtracting imputed interest on net book value at the beginning of each year from the predicted operating cash inflows for that year.

Conditional loss (See *Cost of prediction error*.)

Conditional probability The probability of the occurrence of an event given that another event has occurred.

Constant dollars Dollars of uniform purchasing power.

Constant order cycle An inventory reorder system in which inventory ordering is made on the basis of a preestablished time schedule.

Consultative approach to budgeting An approach to budgeting whereby management develops the final budget after consulting employees about important aspects of current operations and their projections for the future. The final budget is set without the formal agreement of employees.

Contribution income statement An income statement in which costs are classified by behavior. Variable manufacturing costs and variable selling and administrative costs are grouped together, as are fixed manufacturing and fixed selling and administrative costs.

Contribution margin The difference between revenues and variable costs, it indicates the amount of money available to cover fixed costs and provide a profit.

Contribution margin percent The portion of each sales dollar that goes toward covering fixed costs and profits.

Contribution margin ratio (See *Contribution margin percent.*)

Control chart (in statistical process control) A graphic illustration of data taken from a process.

Controller An organization's chief accountant.

Corporate administrative costs The costs of operating a central headquarters and maintaining the corporation as a separate entity.

Corporate service costs The costs of providing services to divisions.

Correlation coefficient A standardized measure of the relationship between two variables.

Cost A measure of economic sacrifice.

Cost accounting That portion of accounting concerned with the accumulation, assignment, and analysis of production and activity cost data to provide information for external reporting, internal planning and control of ongoing operations, and special decisions.

Cost Accounting Standards Board An agent of the U.S. Congress that between 1970 and 1980 issued 19 cost accounting standards. The purpose of the standards was to narrow the cost accounting options available in estimating, accumulating, and reporting the costs of defense contracts.

Cost accounting system A set of procedures for accumulating costs and assigning them to cost objectives.

Cost avoidance concept A concept of inventory valuation, according to which ending inventories have value only to the extent that they avert the necessity of incurring costs in the future.

Cost center An organizational unit whose management is financially responsible only for its costs.

Cost element method of prorating Bases the prorating on the percentage of the cost element (direct materials, direct labor, or overhead) in each affected account.

Cost objectives Objects, such as jobs or products, to which costs are assigned.

Cost of capital (See *Weighted-average cost of capital.*)

Cost of goods manufactured Total costs assigned to products completed during a given period.

Cost of prediction error The difference between the payoff of the best action and the payoff of the chosen action.

Cost of production report A summary of the unit and cost data of a department in a process cost system.

Cost pool A group of related costs that are allocated together to cost objectives.

Cost reduction proposals Capital expenditure proposals for projects that do not involve incremental cash inflows but instead reduce cash outflows associated with current activities.

Cost structure The relationship that exists between an organization's fixed and variable costs.

Cost-volume-profit analysis A technique used to analyze the impact of changes in volume on costs, revenues, and profits.

Cost-volume-profit graph A graph illustrating revenues, costs, and profits or losses at various sales volumes.

Crash cost In PERT, the cost associated with completing an activity in the shortest possible time.

Crash time In PERT, the shortest possible time in which an activity can be completed.

Critical path In PERT, the path(s) for events where the earliest and the latest starting times are equal. Any delay of an event on this path will delay the completion of the project.

Cross-sectional analysis An analysis of observations taken during a single period at a number of facilities.

Current manufacturing costs The total additions to Work-in-Process during a given period.

Customer margin The contribution each class of customer makes toward covering common costs and providing for a profit.

Cutoff rate (See *Discount rate.*)

Debt (after-tax cost of) The effective interest rate multiplied by one minus the tax rate.

Decision tree A complete diagram of sequential investment decision points, the probabilities associated with each decision, and the paths to each decision point.

Defective units (See *Spoiled units*.)

Deferred annuity An annuity that does not begin for two or more periods.

Degrees of freedom The number of observations in a sample minus the number of previously computed statistics used in computing the statistic of interest.

Democratic approach to budgeting (See *Participative approach to budgeting*.)

Departmental overhead rate Total departmental overhead divided by total units of activity in the department.

Dependent variable A variable whose changes are explained by changes in one or more independent variables.

Depreciation tax shield The reduction in taxes that results from depreciation.

Differential analysis The determination of the difference between the cash flows of competing actions.

Direct costing (See *Variable costing*.)

Direct departmental costs Departmental costs that are not allocated from a cost pool.

Direct labor Wages paid production employees for the time they actually spend working on a particular product or process.

Direct-labor ticket A record used to determine the time an employee spends working on a job.

Direct materials Cost of the primary raw materials converted into finished goods.

Direct method (of service dept. cost allocation) Gives no recognition to services provided other service departments. The costs of each department are allocated directly to production departments on the basis of the relative portion of services rendered.

Direct product costs Direct materials and direct labor.

Direct segment costs Costs that are immediately identified with the operations of a specific segment of a business.

Discount rate In capital budgeting, the minimum rate of return required for a project to be acceptable.

Discretionary cost center A cost center that does not have clearly defined relationships between effort and accomplishment.

Discretionary fixed costs Fixed costs not required to maintain current production or service capacity in the near terms. These costs are set at a fixed amount each year at management's discretion.

Dispersion (measure of) A summary statistic indicating the spread of a distribution.

Division A quasi-independent segment of an organization.

Dual rate methods (of service dept. cost allocation) Methods of cost allocation that distinguish between fixed and variable service department costs and allocate them on separate bases.

Dummy variable An independent variable that takes on the value of one or zero depending on whether or not some specified condition exists.

Economic lot size The optimal size production run that minimizes the total annual clerical, setup, and carrying costs for manufactured goods.

Economic order quantity The quantity of inventory that should be ordered at one time to minimize total annual inventory ordering and carrying costs.

Effective budget A budget with a high probability of successful implementation that will move the organization toward its long-run goals.

Employee earnings records A file containing year-to-date information on each employee's earnings and deductions.

Engineering method (of cost estimation) A method of cost estimation based on determining the costs that should be incurred if product specifications are met.

Equity capital (cost of) The discount rate that equates all future cash dividends paid to common shareholders with the current market price of common stock.

Equivalent unit The amount of direct materials, direct labor, or factory overhead required to produce one unit of finished product.

Equivalent units in process Units completed plus equivalent units in the ending inventory.

Equivalent units manufactured A measure of the amount of work performed during the period. Often computed as the equivalent units in process during the period minus the equivalent units in the beginning inventory.

Event The initiation or completion of an activity in a PERT network, represented by a node or small circle.

Ex post standards Standards developed after production takes place and based on prices in effect at the time production took place.

Excess present value index (See *Present value index.*)

Expected activity for the coming year Planned activity for the coming year. It is developed giving full recognition to machine capabilities, the need for repairs and maintenance, nonworking hours, and production requirements for current sales and desired inventory changes.

Expected payoff with perfect information The sum of the products of the payoffs of the best action for each event and the probability of that event.

Expected value The weighted average of the possible cash flows associated with decision alternatives.

Expected value of perfect information The difference between the expected payoff with perfect information and the expected payoff of the best action given current information. It is the maximum amount a manager would be willing to pay for additional information.

Expected value of sample information The difference between the expected payoff with imperfect information and the expected payoff of the best action using only current information.

External failure costs Costs incurred when it is determined that products fail to meet design specifications after they are delivered to customers.

Factory overhead All manufacturing costs other than direct materials and direct labor.

FICA taxes Taxes paid by the employee and employer for government-sponsored retirement benefits, life insurance, and medical insurance.

Final cost objective A cost objective from which costs are not reassigned to other cost objectives.

Financial accounting That portion of accounting concerned with the development and use of general-purpose financial statements intended for the primary use of persons external to the organization.

Fixed cost A cost that does not respond to changes in the volume of activity within a given period. Total fixed costs do not increase as the volume of activity increases within a given period.

Fixed overhead budget variance The difference between actual and budgeted fixed factory overhead.

Fixed overhead volume variance The difference between budgeted fixed factory overhead and the fixed factory overhead costs assigned to products.

Flexible budget A budget based on cost-volume relationships and drawn up for the actual level of production. It is used to determine what costs should be at the actual level of production.

Frequency distribution A bar graph showing the number of observations in each group.

Fringe benefits A type of employee compensation paid by the employer but not reflected in employee earnings statements.

Full cost In this book, full cost includes direct materials, direct labor, factory overhead, distribution costs, and selling and administrative costs. The use of this term is sometimes restricted to manufacturing costs.

Functional income statement An income statement in which costs are classified according to function such as manufacturing or selling and administrative. Variable and fixed costs are included within each category.

Funded pension plan A pension plan in which monies for future pension payments are set aside on a regular basis, usually to a pension fund administered by an independent financial institution. Pension benefits are paid out of the pension fund by the plan administrator.

Graphic analysis A form of linear programming used to determine the optimal product mix in situations involving only two products.

Gross earnings The stated earnings of employees computed as a specified amount per hour, week, month, or other unit of time.

Heteroscedasticity A condition that exists when the distribution of the dependent variable is not the same at all values of the independent variable.

High-low method (of cost estimation) A method of cost estimation that uses data from two observations, the observations containing the highest and lowest activity, to estimate fixed and variable costs.

Historical cost The original cost of an asset recorded in the accounting records.

Homoscedasticity A condition that exists when the distribution of the dependent variable is the same at all values of the independent variable.

Hurdle rate (See *Discount rate.*)

Identity matrix A square matrix that contains ones along the upper-left to lower-right diagonal and zeros everywhere else.

Idle time Nonproductive time caused by a lack of work.

Imputed opportunity cost The interest that could be earned if the cash invested in one activity were invested in another.

Independent variable A variable used to explain changes in a dependent variable.

Indifference range In linear programming, the range that specifies the upper and lower limits between which a parameter can vary without changing the optimal solution.

Indirect costs Costs allocated to a cost objective from a cost pool.

Indirect departmental costs Costs allocated to departments from service department cost pools.

Indirect materials Low-cost materials that are difficult to associate with specific units of product.

Indirect product costs Factory overhead.

Indirect segment costs (See *Common segment costs.*)

Initial investment Expenditures associated with the acquisition of new property and the preparation of the property for use.

Intermediate cost objective A cost objective to which costs are allocated and from which costs are reallocated to other cost objectives.

Intermediate market A market for a product that is transferred from one unit of an organization to another unit of the same organization.

Internal failure costs Costs incurred because products, components, or materials fail to meet quality requirements, causing losses within the plant.

Internal rate of return The discount rate that equates the present value of a project's estimated net cash inflows with the initial investment.

Investment center An organizational unit whose management is financially responsible for the relationship between the unit's profits and total assets.

Investment tax credit A provision of the United States Tax Code providing for a reduction of income taxes in the year of acquisition of qualifying personal property.

Investment turnover A performance measure, computed as sales divided by investment.

Isoprofit line In graphic analysis, a line showing mixes of two products that yield identical profits.

Job-cost sheet A record used to accumulate costs for a specific job.

Job-order cost system A cost system in which costs are assigned to specifically identifiable batches of goods or to a specifically identifiable project.

Joint costs Costs incurred prior to the split-off point.

Joint probability The probability of the joint occurrence of two events.

Joint products Two or more products simultaneously produced from a single set of inputs.

Just-in-time (approach to inventory planning) An approach to inventory planning based on the premise that inventory is a waste and materials and parts should only be available at the time they are needed for use.

Kanban (approach to inventory planning) (See *Just-in-time (approach to inventory planning).)*

Labor efficiency variance The impact on costs of deviations between the actual and the allowed use of direct labor when the labor rate is held constant at standard.

Labor mix variance The impact on labor costs of deviations between the actual and the standard mix of direct labor.

Labor rate variance The impact on costs of changes in the labor rate when the quantity of direct labor is held constant at actual.

Labor yield variance The impact on labor costs of deviations between the actual and the total standard labor hours allowed for the work done.

Learning curve phenomenon A condition that exists when unit or average unit costs decline in a systematic manner as cumulative production increases.

Least-squares criterion A mathematical criterion specifying that the sum of the squared vertical differences between observed data and a line representing an equation developed using regression analysis be minimized.

Lessee The individual or organization acquiring leased property.

Lessor The individual or organization owning leased property.

Life-cycle costs All costs associated with a project, including the initial investment and the after-tax costs of operation and maintenance.

Line managers Managers who can trace their authority and responsibility directly to production activities, sales activities, or both.

Linear algebra method (of service dept. cost allocation) A series of equations recognizing the services each department receives from other departments is formulated and solved with the aid of matrix algebra. Gives complete recognition to reciprocal services.

Linear programming An optimization model used to assist managers in making decisions under constrained conditions when linear relationships can be assumed.

Linear regression A method of cost estimation in which the mathematical criterion of least squares is used to fit an equation for a straight line through a number of observations of activity and cost.

Location (in statistical process control) The average of a distribution.

Long-range planning Within the framework of the organization's strategic plan, an activity that is concerned with identifying and selecting major courses of action that will achieve the strategic plan.

Longitudinal analysis An analysis of observations taken over a period of time at a single facility.

Major products In distinguishing between major products and by-products, major products have high relative total sales value.

Management accounting That portion of accounting concerned with providing special-purpose financial statements and reports to managers and other persons within the organization.

Management by exception An approach to management whereby management directs attention to only those activities that are not proceeding according to plan.

Manufacturing Resource Planning A data base system used to plan and schedule production and materials.

Manufacturing cost budget A detailed forecast of the materials, labor, and overhead costs that should be incurred by the production department in producing the number of units called for in the production budget.

Manufacturing supplies (See *Indirect materials*).

Margin of safety The excess of actual or budgeted sales over break-even sales.

Marginal cost The increment in total cost required to produce and sell one additional unit.

Marginal revenue The increment in total revenue received when one additional unit is sold.

Master budget The organization's formal plan of action for the coming year, encompassing all areas of responsibility within the organization.

Master production schedule A schedule indicating when units should be produced to meet budgeted sales after taking capacity constraints into account.

Matching concept A financial accounting concept stating that when the relationship between costs and revenues is clear, costs incurred to generate future revenues should not be expensed until the revenues are recognized.

Material Requirements Planning An approach to inventory planning used by manufacturing organizations to determine when raw materials must be purchased and components or subassemblies manufactured.

Materials mix variance The impact on materials costs of deviations between the actual and the standard mix.

Materials price variance The impact on costs of changes in the price of direct materials when the quantity of direct materials is held constant.

Materials quantity variance The impact of deviations between the actual and the allowed use of direct materials when the price of direct materials is held constant at standard.

Materials requisition record A record used to record the transfer of direct materials costs from Stores Control to Work-in-Process.

Materials yield variance The impact on materials costs of deviations from the total standard materials allowed for the work done.

Matrix An array of numbers.

Mean A measure of central tendency. The average value computed by summing the values of all observations and dividing by the number of observations.

Median A measure of central tendency. The value of the observation that splits the observations, when they are arrayed highest to lowest, into two equal groups.

Mixed costs Contain a fixed and a variable cost element. They are positive, like fixed costs, when volume is zero, and they increase in a linear fashion, like variable costs, as volume increases.

Mode A measure of central tendency. The most frequent value.

Model A simplified representation of a real-world phenomenon.

Multicollinearity A condition that exists when two independent variables are highly correlated with each other.

Multinational companies Organizations that have divisions or subsidiaries in two or more countries.

Multiple linear regression A type of linear regression in which there are two or more independent variables.

Mutually exclusive investments Competing investment proposals where the acceptance of one automatically causes the rejection of the other.

Net book value Historical cost less accumulated depreciation and other valuation adjustments recorded in the accounting records.

Net marginal revenue Similar to net realizable value, marginal revenue less marginal costs to complete and sell.

Net pay The amount of pay actually received by an employee during a pay period in the form of cash. It is computed as gross earnings less deductions.

Net present value The present value of a project's net cash inflows less the amount of the initial investment.

Net realizable value Selling price less costs to complete and sell.

Net sales value (See *Net realizable value*.)

Nominal dollars Dollars that have not been adjusted for changes in purchasing power.

Nonbinding constraint In linear programming, a constraint that does not have an impact on the optimal solution.

Normal annual activity (See *Average annual activity*.)

Normal cost In PERT, the cost associated with completing an activity in the normal time.

Normal cost system A cost system in which actual direct materials and actual direct labor are assigned to products. Factory overhead is assigned to products using a predetermined overhead rate established before the start of the period.

Normal spoilage Spoilage that is expected to occur under efficient operating conditions.

Normal time In PERT, the average expected time to complete an activity under normal, efficient operating conditions.

Objective function In linear programming, the function that is to be maximized or minimized.

Operations scheduling An approach to planning used within the framework of an organization's master budget. It deals with the weekly, daily, or hourly assignment of salespeople to potential customers, assignment of jobs to specific workers, and procurement of resources.

Opportunity cost The expected net cash inflow that could be obtained if the resources used in a proposed action were used in the most desirable other alternative action.

Opportunity loss The net disadvantage of the potential action when compared to the best available alternative.

Order filling costs Costs incurred to place ordered goods in the possession of purchasers.

Order getting costs Costs incurred to obtain a sales order.

Ordering costs Costs incurred in placing and receiving orders for inventory.

Out-of-pocket costs (See *Outlay costs*.)

Outlay costs Costs that require future expenditures of cash or other resources.

Overtime premium Bonus wages in excess of the regular hourly rate paid to production employees who work more than the regular number of hours.

Participative approach to budgeting An approach to budgeting whereby all levels of management actively participate in the development of the master budget and the budgeting process continues until everyone formally accepts the budget.

Payback period The time required to recover the initial investment in a project from operational sources.

Payback reciprocal A project's annual net cash inflows divided by the initial investment.

Payoff table A table used to enumerate the alternative actions management may take and the possible monetary outcomes of each.

Payroll master file A file containing information on each employee's pay rate; federal, state, and local tax exemptions; and voluntary deductions.

Payroll register A record detailing each employee's gross earnings, deductions from gross earnings, and net earnings for the current pay period and for the year to date.

Pension A sum of money paid a former employee as a retirement benefit.

Performance report A comparison of actual and budgeted data.

Period costs Expired costs not necessary for production.

Perpetual inventory system An inventory recordkeeping system that keeps track of the exact number of units in stock at all times.

Perquisite Something of value obtained from an employer in addition to monetary compensation.

Personal property Includes most tangible property other than buildings and land.

PERT (See *Program Evaluation and Review Technique.*)

PERT/Cost A PERT network that includes expected costs for each activity.

PERT/Cost Resource Allocation Supplement A technique used to determine which activities in a PERT network should be shortened to reduce the total time required to complete the project.

Plant-wide overhead rate Total plant-wide overhead divided by units of activity in the factory.

Post audit (of capital expenditures) A review of the performance of a project comparing predictions with actual results.

Practical capacity The maximum level of activity possible, allowing for routine repairs and maintenance, nonworking hours, and plant shutdowns for vacations.

Predetermined overhead rate Predicted factory overhead for the year divided by predicted units of activity for the year.

Preferred stock (cost of) The discount rate that equates all future cash dividends paid to preferred shareholders with the current market price of preferred stock.

Present value index The present value of a project's net cash inflows or savings divided by the initial investment.

Prevention costs The costs of planning, implementing, and maintaining the quality control system.

Price index A standardized measure of the amount of money needed to purchase a standardized package of goods and services.

Pricing decisions The setting of specific prices for specific products or services.

Pricing policies Statements on management's attitudes toward pricing products and services.

Prime product costs Direct materials and direct labor.

Principal The employer in an agency relationship.

Probability tree A diagram showing the possible values of the independent and dependent variables and the joint probabilities of each outcome.

Process A standardized operation, or a series of standardized operations, used in the continuous production of units of a homogeneous product.

Process cost system A system used to assign costs to units of a homogeneous product as the units pass through one or more production processes.

Product costing The assignment of costs to inventories as they are converted from raw materials to finished goods.

Product costs Costs assigned to inventory accounts as products are produced.

Product margin The contribution each product makes toward covering common costs and providing for a profit.

Production budget A budget indicating the number of units of final product that must be produced to meet budgeted sales and ending inventory requirements.

Production departments Departments where the primary activities of a manufacturing plant, converting raw materials into finished goods, take place.

Profit center An organizational unit whose management is financially responsible for the difference between the unit's revenues and costs.

Profit-volume graph A graph illustrating profits or losses for various sales volumes.

Profitability index (See *Present value index.*)

Program Evaluation and Review Technique (PERT) A method of project planning and control applicable to any complex project that consists of a number of activities, including activities whose initiation depends on the completion of other activities.

Program results review A systematic evaluation of a program to determine if it is accomplishing its objectives.

Prorate To distribute proportionately.

Purchases budget A budget indicating the raw materials that must be acquired to meet production needs and ending inventory requirements. Usually stated in terms of units and dollars.

Pure labor efficiency variance (See *Labor yield variance.*)

Pure sales volume variance The impact on the contribution margin of deviations between the actual and the budgeted unit sales.

Quality costs Costs incurred because poor product quality may or does exist.

Quality of conformance A measure of the degree to which a product meets its design specifications.

Quality of design The quality characteristics engineered into and purported to exist in a product.

R charts (in statistical process control) A graph illustrating the range of data within each sample. Used to estimate process variability.

Range (of a sample) In statistical process control, the difference between the highest and lowest measurement.

Ratchet principle An approach to setting standards whereby an increase in performance becomes the new standard.

Rate of return (See *Internal rate of return* and *Return on investment.*)

Raw materials inventory record A record used to keep track of inventory levels and costs for a specific raw material.

Real property Includes buildings and land.

Relevant costs Costs that differ between competing alternative actions.

Relevant range The range of observations within which a linear cost function is a good approximation of the economists' curvilinear cost function.

Reorder point The inventory level at which an order for additional inventory should be placed.

Residual income Income minus a charge for invested capital.

Responsibility accounting The structuring of performance reports addressed to individual members of an organization in a manner that emphasizes the factors they can control.

Responsibility center An organizational unit for which a performance report is prepared.

Return on investment A measure of the relationship between income and investment.

Revenue center An organizational unit whose management is financially responsible for the unit's revenues.

Rework Work performed on defective or spoiled units to bring such units into conformance with quality standards.

Risk A situation in which possible outcomes and their probabilities can be specified in advance.

Robinson-Patman Act A United States law prohibiting discrimination in prices charged purchasers of commodities of like grade and quantity where the effect might be to lessen competition.

Run (in statistical process control) A number of consecutive points above or below a center line on a control chart.

Safety stock An inventory cushion maintained to prevent stockouts and the resulting loss of sales or disruption of production.

Sales budget A forecast of planned unit and dollars sales for the budget period.

Sales mix variance The impact on the budgeted contribution margin of deviations between the actual and the budgeted mix of total units actually sold.

Sales price variance The impact on the contribution margin of a change in selling price, given the actual sales volume.

Sales volume variance The impact on the contribution margin of a change in the sales volume, assuming no changes in the selling price or variable costs.

Scalar A matrix containing a single number.

Scatter diagram method (of cost estimation) A method of cost estimation in which observations of cost and activity are plotted on graph paper and professional judgment is used to draw a cost-estimating line with an equal number of observations on either side.

Scrap Left over bits and pieces of raw materials.

Segment margin The contribution a segment of a business makes toward covering common costs and providing for a profit.

Segment reports Income statements that show operating results for portions or segments of a business.

Self-service The service a service department provides itself.

Selling and administrative expense budget A detailed forecast of planned selling and administrative expenses for the budget period.

Semivariable costs (See *Mixed costs.*)

Sensitivity analysis The study of the responsiveness of a model's dependent variable to changes in one or more of the model's independent variables.

Service costing The assignment of costs to units of service.

Service departments Departments that facilitate the operation of production departments.

Shadow price (of a resource) In linear programming, the amount by which total contribution will change if there is a one unit change in an available resource.

Simple linear regression A type of linear regression in which there is only one independent variable.

Single rate methods (of service department cost allocation) Methods that do not distinguish between fixed and variable service department costs, but rather allocate them together using some common basis.

Slack In PERT, the amount of time by which an activity or series of activities can be delayed without becoming part of the critical path.

Social security taxes (See *FICA taxes.*)

Special causes (in statistical process control) The reason for a nonrandom variation.

Split-off point The point at which joint products become separately identifiable.

Spoiled units Units that do not meet quality standards and must be junked, sold as seconds, or reworked.

Staff managers Managers who cannot trace their authority and responsibility directly to production or sales activities.

Standard cost center A cost center that has clearly defined relationships between effort and accomplishment.

Standard costs Allowable costs per unit of work performed. May be viewed as a budget for one unit.

Standard deviation A measure of dispersion. The square root of the variance.

Standard error of the coefficient A measure of how accurate the estimated value of a coefficient is as an estimator of the true value of the coefficient.

Standard error of the estimate A measure of the dispersion of observations of the dependent variable around an equation.

Standard normal distribution A theoretical probability distribution having a mean of zero and a standard deviation of one.

Statement of cost of goods manufactured A financial summary of the activity in the Work-in-Process inventory account.

Statement of cost of goods manufactured and sold A financial summary of the activity in Work-in-Process and Finished Goods Inventory accounts.

States of nature Possible events or outcomes that can occur for an alternative.

Statistical process control A condition said to exist when actual results are within statistical limits.

Step costs Costs that are constant within a range of activity, but different between ranges of activity.

Step-down method (of service dept. cost allocation) (See *Step method.*)

Step method (of service dept. cost allocation) Gives some recognition of services provided other service departments. An order of allocation is established and costs are allocated to other departments served, except that once a department's costs are allocated, no costs are reallocated to it.

Stochastic simulation The repeated random assignment of values to a model's independent variables and the subsequent computation of the value(s) of the model's dependent variable(s).

Strategic planning The broadest and most pervasive type of planning, it deals with such fundamental issues as the long-run goals and characteristics of the organization.

Subsidiary (See *Division.*)

Sunk costs Historical costs that result from past decisions over which management no longer has control.

Systematic risk A factor accounting for the relationship between the expected returns from a project and the expected returns from the market portfolio of all projects.

***t*-distribution** A theoretical probability distribution, similar in shape to the standard normal distribution except that its dispersion varies with the size of the sample and the resulting degrees of freedom.

***T*-statistic** The number of standard errors of the estimate that the estimated value of the coefficient is from zero.

Territory margin The contribution a territory makes toward covering common costs and providing for a profit.

Theoretical capacity The maximum level of activity possible if production took place at maximum speed, with 100 percent efficiency, without interruptions.

Theory X A view of motivation that assumes work is inherently distasteful and people avoid work, lack creativity, and must be motivated to work by economic rewards.

Theory Y A view of motivation that assumes work is natural, people are creative, and people are motivated to work by a variety of needs.

Time-adjusted rate of return (See *Internal rate of return.*)

Time cards Contain information about the number of hours, days, or weeks an employee has worked during a specific pay period.

Total cost method of prorating Bases the prorating on the percentage of total cost in each affected account.

Total costs in process Costs in Work-in-Process at the beginning of the period plus current manufacturing costs.

Total sales variance The impact of variations in the selling price and sales volume on the contribution margin.

Transfer price The exchange value assigned a product or service that one unit of an organization provides or offers another unit of the same organization.

Treasurer The officer responsible for money management and who serves as the custodian of the organization's funds.

Two-bin inventory system An inventory reorder point system in which units of inventory are divided into two groups in order to provide a reorder signal.

Uncertainty Sometimes defined as a situation in which possible outcomes and/or their probabilities cannot be specified in advance. (Also see *Risk*.)

Unemployment taxes Federal and state taxes paid by employers. Proceeds are used to provide income to persons who are temporarily unemployed.

Unfunded pension plan A pension plan in which monies are not set aside for future retirement benefits. Instead, pension payments are made directly to retired employees by their former employer.

Unit contribution margin The difference between the unit selling price and the unit variable costs.

Utility theory A systematic attempt to explain a manager's decision preferences under conditions involving risk.

Vacation pay Wages paid employees for vacation or holiday periods when employees are not working.

Variability (in statistical process control) The spread of a distribution measured in terms of the process standard deviation.

Variable cost A cost that changes in direct proportion to changes in the volume of activity.

Variable costing A type of product costing in which only variable manufacturing costs are assigned to products. All other costs, including fixed factory overhead, variable selling and administrative, and fixed selling and administrative, are treated as period costs.

Variable overhead efficiency variance The difference between the standard variable overhead costs for the actual labor hours (or other activity base) and the standard variable overhead cost for the allowed labor hours (or other activity base).

Variable overhead spending variance The difference between actual variable overhead costs and the variable overhead allowed for the actual labor hours (or other activity base).

Variables data (in statistical process control) Continuous measurements taken on physical characteristics such as weight, length, or thickness.

Variance A measure of dispersion. Computed as the average squared deviations of individual observations from the population mean.

Vector A matrix that has only a single row or column.

Vector of knowns A column vector containing the known values.

Vector of unknowns A column vector containing variables whose currently unknown amounts are to be determined by matrix algebra.

W-4 form A form completed by each employee on which the employee indicates the number of exemptions claimed and marital status for the purpose of withholding federal income taxes.

Waste A by-product of a production process that has no value. The disposal of waste may result in the incurrence of additional costs.

Weighted-average cost of capital A measure of the after-tax cost of debt, preferred stock, and common equity to the organization.

Work-in-process Materials in the process of being transformed into finished goods.

X-bar chart (in statistical process control) A plot of the average value of each sample, used to determine if the process is in control with respect to the average.

Index

A-B-C approach (to inventory planning and control), defined, 812–813
Abnormal spoilage, defined, 120, 598
Absorption costing
  arguments in favor of, 356
  budgets (use in), 393–394
  cause of underapplied or overapplied overhead, 349–352
  compared with variable costing, 343–348, 353, 360
  conflict with cost-volume-profit model, 341
  defined, 343
  functional classification of costs, 341
  income statement format, 345, 346, 348, 353
  planned overapplied and underapplied overhead, 352, 397–398
  reconciliation with variable costing, 344–348, 353
Accelerated Cost Recovery System, 721
Account activity, 11–12
Account classification method (of cost estimation), defined, 230
Account interrelationships, 11–12
Accounting
  cost, compared to management, 4
  defined, 1
  financial, 2
  financial, compared to management, 1–3
  management, 2
  management, compared to financial, 1–3
  model of the firm, 2–3
Accounting rate of return
  computation, 708–709
  defined, 708
Actual cost system
  contrasted with normal, 61–62, 68–69
  described, 61–68
  limitations, 65–68
  process costing, 104–107
Actual factory overhead rate, defined, 62
Agency costs, defined, 563
Agency problem, discussed, 563
Agency relationship, defined, 563
Agency theory
  as explanation for actions of divisional managers, 563–564
  defined, 563
Agent, defined, 563
Aircraft industry, use of learning curves, 263
Annuity
  defined, 958
  present value of, 958–960
Annuity due, defined, 958
Annuity in advance, defined, 959
Annuity in arrears, defined, 958
Anthony, R. N., 55, 56n
Appraisal costs, defined, 857
Assignable cause (of variance), 856
Attributes data, defined, 844
Augmented matrix, defined, 204
Authoritative approach to budgeting, defined, 390
Autocorrelation, defined, 262
Autocratic approach to budgeting; *see* Authoritative approach to budgeting
Average annual activity, defined, 354
Average cost
  defined, 23
  illustrated, 24
  See also Learning curve
Avoidable cost; *see* Outlay cost

Bail-out factor, defined, 707
Baker, K. R., 646n
Bartley, J. W., 730, 731n
BASIC, computer program for matrix inversion, 205
Bayes' Theorem, 653, 860, 861
Behavioral considerations
  of agency theory, 563–564
  in budgeting, 389–394
  in controller's office, 9
  in decentralization, 547–548
  of direct-labor tickets, 60
  in performance evaluation, 449–450, 507–508, 556–559, 560

Behavioral considerations *(continued)*
in record keeping, 60
in transfer pricing, 913–914, 922–924
Benke, R. L., 921, 921n, 924n
Beta distribution, use in PERT, 815, 820
Break-even point, defined, 292
Brown, J., 909n
Budget
defined, 6, 387
reconciliation of budgeted and actual income, 513–514, 519
Budget variance; *see* Variance(s)
Budgetary control, defined, 509
Budgetary slack, defined, 392
Budgeted changes in retained earnings, illustrated, 400
Budgeted contribution income statement, illustrated, 409
Budgeted income statement
defined, 399
illustrated, 400
Budgeted statement of financial position, illustrated, 403
Budgeting
approaches to, 390–391
behavioral considerations, 389–394
building blocks, 393–394
effective budget, defined, 391
requirement for, 391–392
feasibility and acceptability, 404
flexible budget, based on cost-volume-profit relationships, 455
defined, 455
use in performance evaluation, 455–456
goals and subgoals, 391–392
master budget, approaches, 390–391
assembly, 394–403
defined, 387
objectives, 389–390
nonmanufacturing organizations, 402–403
objectives of, 389–390
overhead, 397–398
performance evaluation and, 392, 449–451
planning levels, long-range planning, 389
master budget, 389
operations scheduling, 389
strategic planning, 388
predetermined allocation rates for service departments, 197–198
reconciliation of budgeted and actual income, 513–514
role of controller, 8, 389
use of computers, 404–410
use of standard costs, 393–394
Burden, 29n
Burger, P. H., 815n
By-products, defined, 157
By-products and scrap
distinguished from joint products, 157
miscellaneous income, 157–158
net realizable value, 158–159

Calculus, 25n, 289n, 657n, 802n
Capacity costs, defined, 20, 231
See also Fixed costs
Capettini, R., 646n, 862n
Capital asset pricing model, 776–777
Capital budgeting
capital rationing, occurrence of, 767
ranking investments, 767–769
selection by mathematical programming, 770–771
selection by trial and error, 769–770
cash-flow estimation, depreciation as a tax shield, 721–723
disinvestment, 723–725
impact of price-level changes, 726–729
initial investment, 719–720
investment tax credit, 719–720
operations, 720–722
committee, 705
cost reduction proposals, 758–762
defined, 704
investment and financing decisions, 771–773
lease-purchase decisions, 773–775
mutually exclusive investments, 764–766
policies, 704–705
price-level changes and undervalued assets (impact of), 556–558
relationship to long-range and strategic planning, 389, 704–705
subsequent control and performance evaluation, 725
uncertainty, approaches to, 776–778
variable investment size, 762–763
See also Cost of capital
Capital-budgeting models
accounting rate of return, computation, 708–709
defined, 708
relationship to performance measures, 709
adjusting for inflation, 729–732
bail-out factor, 707
benefits of using, 705
impact of changing prices on, 726–732
internal rate of return, compared to net present value, 714, 764–767
compared to payback and accounting rate of return, 713
computation, 710–712
defined, 710
payback reciprocal as an approximation, 712–713
problem of multiple rates, 713
problem with mutually exclusive investments, 764–767
ranking investments with, 764–767
reinvestment rate assumption, 766
net present value, compared to internal rate of return, 714, 764–767
computation, 712, 714
defined, 714
mutually exclusive investments, 764–767
present value index, 767–768
reinvestment rate assumption, 766
payback period, bail-out factor, 707
computation, 707
criticisms of, 707–708
defined, 706
payback reciprocal as an approximation of internal rate of return, 712–713

Capital rationing, defined, 767
Carrying costs
  defined, 799
  inventory planning and control models, 805–806
Cash break-even point, defined, 302
Cash budget
  defined, 400
  illustrated, 401, 410
Cash management, 400
Causality, problem of determining, 245
Central tendency
  defined, 246
  statistical measures of, 246–248
Chebyshev's inequality, 853
Chief financial executive, defined, 9
Chief financial officer, 9
Coefficient of correlation; *see* Correlation coefficient
Coefficient of determination
  defined, 256
  equation for computing, 257
Coefficients matrix
  defined, 204
  illustrated, 203–204
Collins, D., 862n
Committed fixed costs, defined, 20
Common costs
  in performance reports, 507n
  problem, 507
Common segment costs, defined, 357
Compensation insurance, defined, 885
Completed contract method of accounting, 198n
Compound interest, defined, 955
Compound interest depreciation
  computation, 733–734
  use in measuring investment performance, 562, 733–734
Conditional loss, defined, 650
Conditional probability, defined, 652
Constant dollars, defined, 729
Consultative approach to budgeting, defined, 390
Contribution income statement
  defined, 341
  illustrated, 342
  illustrated for segment, 359
  use for segment reporting, 357–360
Contribution margin
  average unit, 305–306
  defined, 341
  unit, defined, 291
Contribution margin percent, defined, 292
Contribution margin ratio; *see* Contribution margin percent
Control account, 29, 58, 59, 181
Control chart
  defined, 845
  illustrated, 847, 850, 852, 853
Controllable costs, 450, 466–467
Controller
  authority, 7–8
  defined, 7
  divisional, 547
  duties, 8
  required knowledge, 9
  role in budgeting, 8, 389
  role in internal auditing, 8–9
  role in special decisions, 8
Conversion costs, defined, 30
Copeland, T. E., 777n
Corr, A. V., 656n
Correlation, 61
Correlation coefficient
  defined, 244, 255
  equation for computing, 255
Cost
  defined, 3
  distinguished from expense, 27n
Cost accounting
  basic premise, 5
  defined, 3, 19
  development, 4
  relationship to financial accounting, 3–4
  relationship to management accounting, 4
Cost Accounting Standards Board, 198–200, 662
Cost accounting system, defined, 19
Cost allocation
  departmental overhead rates, 76, 103, 182
  direct and indirect departmental costs, 181–196
  hierarchy of bases, 200
  need, 28
  nonmanufacturing costs, 198
  plant-wide overhead rate, 75–76, 103
  plant-wide rate, 182
  purposes, 182–183
  service departments, basis of cost allocation, 184–185
    cost per unit of service, 197
    predetermined allocation rates, 197–198
    problems, 183–184
    self-service ignored, 184
    techniques, 185–197
  uses, 183
  See also By-products and scrap; Joint products; Overhead
Cost avoidance concept, 356–357
Cost behavior
  average cost, 23–24
  differences between economic and accounting, 24–26
  fixed, 20–21
  mixed (semivariable), 21–22
  patterns, 19–24
  step, 22
  total cost, 22–23
  variable, 20
Cost center, defined, 453
Cost element method of prorating, defined, 73, 608
Cost estimation
  adjusting data for price changes, 241–243
  causality, 245
  cost-volume-profit (use), 290
  cross-sectional analysis, 239
  data requirements and limitations, 240–243
  dummy variables, 239
  historical cost use, 229
  learning curves, 265–266
  longitudinal analysis, 239
  methods, account classification, 230–231
    engineering methods, 230
    high-low, 232–234
    multiple linear regression, 237–239
    scatter diagram, 234
    simple linear regression, 235–237
  selection of activity base, 244
  selection of equation, 244–245
  statistical considerations, 244–245
Cost objectives, defined, 77, 180
Cost of capital
  after-tax cost of debt, computation, 717
  defined, 717

Cost of capital *(continued)*
computation, 716–718
cost of equity capital, computation, 718
defined, 718
cost of preferred stock, computation, 717–718
defined, 717
rationale underlying use, 716–717
use in capital budgeting, 716–717
use in inventory models, 805
weighted-average, computation, 718
defined, 716
reflects expectations about inflation, 730
Cost of goods manufactured, defined, 31
Cost of prediction error, defined, 650
Cost of production report
defined, 103
described, 106
illustrated, 107, 109, 111, 114, 116, 119, 121
Cost or market, lower of, 150n, 157n
Cost per equivalent good unit manufactured, described, 118
Cost per equivalent unit, described, 105–106
Cost per equivalent unit in process
compared with cost per equivalent unit manufactured, 110
described, 108
Cost per equivalent unit manufactured
compared with cost per equivalent unit in process, 110
described, 110
Cost pool
defined, 77, 180
homogeneous, defined, 199–200
test for determining number, 182
Cost prediction
role of controller, 8
use of historical costs, 3, 35
Cost reduction proposals, defined, 758
Cost-volume-profit
accounting models, 289–290
analysis of uncertainty, 308–317
assumptions, 300–302, 340–341
basic relationships, 290–300
basis of special decisions, 643–644
break-even point, defined, 292
cash break-even point, defined, 302
conflict with absorption costing, 301, 340
cost structure, 299–300
data, 290
economic models, 289
graph, 294–296, 300, 301
income taxes, 303
margin of safety, defined, 296
multiple products, 304–307
product mix decisions, 307–308
profit planning, 297–299
profit-volume graph, described, 295–296
relationship to variable costing, 341, 356
Cost-volume-profit graph, defined, 294
Crash cost (in PERT), defined, 818
Crash time (in PERT), defined, 818
Critical path (in PERT), defined, 817
Critical probability, 855
Cross-sectional analysis, defined, 239
Current manufacturing costs, defined, 31
Customer margin, defined, 358
Cutoff rate, defined, 716

Debt, after-tax cost of, defined, 717
Decentralization
advantages, 547–548
problems, 548
See also Division
Decision making, costs and, 35–37
Decision to investigate; *see* Variance(s)
Decision tree
defined, 776
illustrated, 778
DeCoster, D. T., 815n
Defective units; *see* Spoiled units
Deferred annuity
defined, 959
present value, 959–960
Defined benefit plan, described, 886n
Defined contribution plan, described, 886n
Degrees of freedom, defined, 249
Democratic approach to budgeting; *see* Participative approach to budgeting
Demski, J. S., 841n
Denominator activity levels, alternative bases for applying fixed overhead, 354–355
Department
cost, 183–196
overhead rates, 76
predetermined allocation rates, 197–198
Department of Defense, 56
Departmental overhead rates
cost pools required, 182
defined, 74
in process costing, 103
Dependent variable, defined, 230
Depreciation tax shield
cost reduction proposals, 759–760
defined, 721
Differential analysis
defined, 36
use in making special decisions, 643–647
Differential cost, 644
Direct costing; *see* Variable costing
Direct departmental costs, defined, 182
Direct labor
defined, 29, 882
discussed, 59–60
Direct-labor ticket, defined, 59
Direct materials
defined, 29
discussed, 58–59
Direct method (of service department cost allocation)
defined, 186
illustrated, 187–188, 196
Direct product costs, defined, 30
Direct segment costs
defined, 357–358
illustrated, 57
Dirsmith, M. W., 771, 771n, 773, 773n, 774n
Discount rate, defined, 713
Discretionary cost center
defined, 453, 508–509
performance reports, 508–509
Discretionary fixed costs, defined, 20, 508

Dispersion
defined, 246
statistical measures of, 249–250
Division
advantages of decentralization, 547–548
agency relationship, 563–564
controller, 547
defined, 545
investment center, 545
investment decision, price-level changes and undervalued assets, 556–558
organization structure, 545–547
performance evaluation, allocated indirect costs, 559–560
defining investment, 551–552
depreciation methods, 560–562
interest expense, 559
leased assets, 558
measuring investment, 552–554
multinational companies, 562
price level changes and undervalued assets, 554–556
problems in measuring, 551–562
reasons for allocating indirect costs, 560
residual income, 551
return on investment, 548–551
unrecorded assets, 558–559
problems associated with decentralization, 548
See also Transfer price
Dollar value LIFO, 112
Dual rate methods (of service department cost allocation), defined, 194
Dummy variable, defined, 239
Durban, 262n

Economic considerations in selecting optimal investment size, 762–763
Economic cost behavior, 24–26
Economic cost-volume-profit model, 289, 658
Economic lot size, defined, 802
Economic order quantity
computations, 800–802
defined, 799
volume discounts, 803–805
Economic pricing models, 656–659
Economic Recovery Tax Act, 719
Economics of quality costs, 859–860
Economics of transfer pricing, 915–918
Edwards, J. D., 921, 921n, 924n
Eisenhart, C., 849
Employee earnings records, defined, 893
Engineering, 5
Engineering methods (of cost estimation), defined, 230
Equal variance, 262
Equity capital, cost of, defined, 718
Equivalent good units, described, 117–118
Equivalent units in process, defined, 108
Equivalent units manufactured, defined, 110
Exception reports, 450
Excess present value index; *see* Present value index
Expected activity for the coming year, defined, 354
Expected payoff with perfect information, defined, 650
Expected value, defined, 648
Expected value of perfect information, defined, 651
Expected value of sample information, defined, 655
Expense, distinguished from cost, 27n
Exponential distribution, use in safety stock models, 810
Ex post standards, defined, 474–475
External failure costs, defined, 857

Factory overhead
defined, 29
See also Overhead
Farragher, E. J., 715, 715n
Federal Insurance Contributions Act, 883
Federal Trade Commission, 5, 662
Ferrara, W. L., 771, 771n, 773, 773n, 774n
FICA taxes, described, 883
FIFO process costing, 109–112
Final cost objective, defined, 182
Financial accounting, defined, 2
Finished goods, described, 4
First derivative, rule for finding, 25
Fixed costs
absorption costing treatment, 343
committed, 20
defined, 20
discretionary, 20
illustrated, 21
negative, 233
variable costing treatment, 343
Fixed overhead variances; *see* Variance(s)
Flexible budget
defined, 455
use in performance evaluation, 455–456
Fremgen, J. M., 183, 183n, 356, 357n, 559n, 560
Frequency distribution, 246–247
Fringe benefits, defined, 881
F-statistic, 257n
Full cost, defined, 198
Full-cost markup, 660–661
Full-cost performance reports, 469–470
Functional income statement
defined, 341
illustrated, 342
illustrated for segment, 359
Funded pension plans, defined, 886
Future amount, 954–956

General Accounting Office, 198
Generally accepted accounting principles, 2, 72–73, 150n, 343, 593
Goals, in budgeting, 388, 391–392
Goddard, W. E., 814, 814n
Goetz, B. E., 919n
Gould, J. R., 946n
Grant, E. L., 845n, 848, 853, 854n
Graphic analysis, described, 663
Gross earnings, defined, 881

Heteroscedasticity, defined, 262
High-low method (of cost estimation), defined, 232
Hillman, D. A., 471, 471n
Historical cost
as investment measure, 552–558
defined, 553
sunk cost, 35
use of data, 3, 35–37
Homogeneous products, 102
Homoscedasticity, defined, 262
Horngren, C. T., 357, 357n, 378n

Hospital, 5, 198
Hurdle rate, defined, 716

Identity matrix, defined, 201
Idle time, defined, 59
Imputed opportunity cost, defined, 37
Incremental cost, use in capital budgeting, 758–762
Independent variable, defined, 230
Indifference range, defined, 668
Indirect costs, defined, 182
Indirect departmental costs, defined, 182
Indirect materials, defined, 29
Indirect product costs, defined, 30
Indirect segment costs; *see* Common segment costs
Inflation
  adjusting capital budgeting models for, 729–732
  adjusting historical costs for, 241–243
  impact on capital budgeting models, 726–732
  investment decisions, impact on, 556–558
  performance evaluation, impact on, 554–556
Information
  benefits of, 648
  cost and value of, 229, 854–856
  cost of, 648
Information acquisition decisions
  conditional loss, 649–650
  described, 648–656
  expected payoff with perfect information, 650–651
  expected value, 649
  expected value of perfect information, 651
  expected value of sample information, 655–656
  payoff table, 648–649
  revising probabilities using sample information, 651–655
Initial investment, defined, 719
Input-mix decisions, 647
Integer programming, use in capital-budgeting decisions, 770, 771
Interest
  compound, defined, 955
  compound distinguished from simple, 954–956
  simple, defined, 955
Intermediate cost objective, defined, 182
Intermediate market, defined, 915
Internal auditing, role of controller, 8–9
Internal control
  procedures for payroll, 896
  spoiled units, 115
Internal failure costs, defined, 857
Internal rate of return, defined, 710
Internal Revenue Code, 926
Internal Revenue Service, 5, 881, 883–885, 893
Inventories
  in manufacturing organizations, 4–5
  in retail organizations, 4, 26–28
Inventory planning and control
  accuracy of cost predictions, 807
  approaches, A-B-C approach, 812–813
    comparison of Kanban and MRP II, 814
    economic order quantity, 800–802
    just-in-time approach, 813
    Materials Requirements Planning, 813–814
  assumptions of EOQ model, 806–807
  purpose of inventory models, 798–799
  relevant costs, carrying, 805–806
    ordering, 806
    stockout, 808–811
    unit, 803–805
    variable, 799
  reorder point models, certainty, 808
    uncertainty, 808–810
  reorder systems, constant order cycle, 812
    perpetual inventory system, 812
    two-bin inventory system, 811–812
  safety stocks, 808–810
Investment center
  defined, 453, 548
  See also Division
Investment decision
  price-level changes and undervalued assets, impact of, 556–558
  See also Capital budgeting
Investment performance, impact of depreciation methods on measures of, 732–734
Investment tax credit, defined, 719
Investment turnover, defined, 549
Isoprofit line, defined, 664

Jaedicke, R. K., 310, 310n
Jensen, R., 646n
Job-cost sheet
  defined, 57
  illustrated, 57
  major projects, 820
Job-order cost system, defined, 56
Job-order costing
  actual, 61–68
  basic elements, 56–61
  compared to process costing, 102–103
  cost objective, 181
  journal entries, 65
  normal, 68–74
  standard cost systems, 607–608
Joint costs, defined, 147
Joint probability, defined, 652
Joint products
  costing, journal entries, 153, 156
    lower of cost or market rule, 150n
    multiple split-off points, 153–154
    net realizable value, 151–157
    physical measures, 149–150
    sales value, 150–151
    sales value for intermediate products, 154–157
    use of standards, 613
  defined, 147
  distinguished from by-products and scrap, 157
  special decisions, sell or process further, 159–160
    total production decisions, 160–161
  split-off point, defined, 147
  See also By-products and scrap
Just-in-time approach (to inventory planning and control), defined, 813

Kanban approach (to inventory planning and control); *see* Just-in-time approach
Kaplan, R. S., 646n
Kim, S. H., 715, 715n

Labor variances; *see* Variance(s)
Learning curve
  cost patterns, 263
  cost-volume-profit analysis, 300–301
  estimating costs, 265–266
  estimating percentage, 265
  illustrated, 264
  model, 263–264
Learning curve analysis, 263–266
Learning curve phenomenon, defined, 263
Lease-purchase decisions, 773–775
Least-squares criterion, defined, 235
Leavenworth, R. S., 845n, 848, 853, 854n
Lessee, defined, 773
Lessor, defined, 773
Liao, S. S., 183, 183n, 559n, 560
Life-cycle costs, defined, 760
LIFO, 112
Likert, R., 559n
Line managers, defined, 7
Linear algebra method (of service department cost allocation)
  defined, 191
  illustrated, 191–194
  use of percentages, 186n
Linear programming
  binding constraint, defined, 665
  capital-budgeting decisions, use in, 770–771
  defined, 663
  dual solution, 666
  feasible region, 664–665
  graphic analysis, 663–665
  income taxes, 671
  indifference range, 668–669
  infeasible region, 664–665
  isoprofit line, defined, 664
  materials mix decision, use in, 472, 474–475
  minimization, 472n
  multiple constraints and multiple products, 669
  nonbinding constraint, defined, 665
  objective function, described, 664
  opportunity costs, 666
  optimal solution, 664–665
  product mix decisions, use in, 662–671
  role of cost accountant, 670–671
  sensitivity analysis, 667–668
  shadow price, 666–667
  simplex method, 666–667
  single constraint, 663
  transfer pricing, 920
Linear regression, defined, 235
Location (in control charts), defined, 845
Longitudinal analysis, defined, 239
Long-range planning, defined, 389

Major products, defined, 157
Make or buy, 644–645, 914–915
Management accounting, defined, 2
Management by exception, defined, 390
Manes R. P., 646n
Manufacturing burden, 29n
Manufacturing cost budget
  as basis for performance evaluation, 454–455
  defined, 397
  illustrated, 397–398, 408
Manufacturing overhead
  defined, 29n
  See also Factory overhead
Manufacturing Resource Planning, defined, 814
Margin of safety, defined, 296
Margin percent on sales, 549n
Margin cost, defined, 24, 915
Marginal revenue, defined, 915
Marketing contribution, described, 505–506
Marketing costs, controllable, 504
Marketing performance reports
  compared with manufacturing performance reports, 504–507
  illustrated, 506, 515
Master budget
  defined, 387
  nonmanufacturing organizations, 402–403
Master production schedule, defined, 813
Matching concept, defined, 27
Matching costs and production, 240
Materials inventory record
  defined, 58
  illustrated, 57
Materials Requirements Planning, defined, 813
Materials requisition record
  defined, 58
  illustrated, 57
Materials variances; *see* Variance(s)
Matrix, defined, 200
Matric algebra
  basic elements, 200–205
  use in cost allocation, 192–193
McKinney, G., 921n
Mean, defined, 246
Median, defined, 246
Medicaid, 884
Medicare, 190n, 884
Miles, R. E., 450, 450n
Miller, E. L., 562n
Mix variance; *see* Variance(s)
Mixed costs
  defined, 21
  illustrated, 21
Mode, defined, 246
Model
  accounting model of the firm, 2–3
  defined, 3, 313
  role of cost accountant in model implementation, 670–671, 798
  wrong model and variances, 842
Monte Carlo simulation, 314
Morse, W. J., 304n
Mosteller, F., 849
Multicollinearity, defined, 263
Multinational companies, defined, 562
Multiple departments, cost flow, 112–113
Multiple linear regression, defined, 235
Multiple products, in cost-volume-profit analysis, 304–307
Municipal government, 402
Mutually exclusive investments, described, 764

Nager, 262n
National Association of Accountants, 183, 551n, 810n, 813n
Net book value
  as investment measure, 552–558, 560–562
  defined, 552
Net marginal revenue, defined, 916
Net pay, defined, 884
Net present value
  defined, 714
  See also Capital-budgeting models
Net realizable value, defined, 122, 151

Net sales value, defined, 151
Nominal dollars, defined, 729
Nonchargeable time, accounting for, 59–60
Nonmanufacturing costs, allocation of, 198–200, 559–560
Nonsymetric distribution, illustrated, 248
Normal annual activity; *see* Average annual activity
Normal cost (in PERT), defined, 818
Normal cost system
  contrasted with actual, 61–62, 68–69
  defined, 62
  described, 68–74
  external reporting requirements, 72–74
  overhead problems in cost estimation, 240
  predetermined overhead rate, 69–71, 197, 349–352, 354–355
  process costing, 108–109
  separately accounting for spoilage, 603
  treatment of overapplied and underapplied overhead, 71–74
Normal distribution
  ordinate values, 862
  use in safety stock models, 810
Normal distribution and tables, use of, 250–253
Normal distribution of variances, 262
Normal spoilage, defined, 120, 598
Normal time (in PERT), defined, 815

Objective function (in linear programming), described, 664
Objectives of book, 9–10
Objectivity, 2
Ogilvie, D. G., 791n
Operations scheduling, defined, 389
Opportunity cost
  defined, 36
  in economic models, 24n
  inventory models, 805
  linear programming, 666
  safety stock models, 811
  and special decisions, 36–37
  transfer pricing, 915, 920
Opportunity loss, defined, 37
Optimal solution (in linear programming), 664–665
Order-filling costs, defined, 504
Order-getting costs, defined, 504
Ordering costs
  defined, 799
  inventory planning and control models, 806
Organization chart
  centralized, 7, 452
  controller's department, 8
  decentralized, 545–547
Osteryoung, J., 771n, 777n
Out-of-pocket costs, defined, 35
Outlay costs, defined, 35
Outlier observation, 234, 236
Overhead
  absorption costing treatment, 343
  basis of application, 61, 75–76, 891–892
  control accounts, 349, 465–466
  cost pool, 77, 180–181
  departmental overhead rates, 76, 103, 180–181, 197
  factory overhead, defined, 29
  fixed overhead rate, 349–350
  labor taxes and fringe benefits, 889–890
  overapplied and underapplied, 71–74, 349–352
  planned overapplied and underapplied, 352
  plant-wide rate, 75–76, 103, 180
  predetermined overhead rate, 62, 69–71, 102, 589
  problems in cost estimation, 240
  product cost, 29–30
  product costing problem, 61
  prorating, 73–74
  spoilage costs, 120
  variable costing treatment, 343
  variable overhead rate, 349
  See also Cost allocation; Variance(s)
Overhead variances; *see* Variance(s)
Overtime premiums, accounting for, 60

Parametric linear programming, 669n
Park, S. H., 646n
Participative approach to budgeting, defined, 390–391
Payback period, defined, 706
Payback reciprocal, defined, 712
Payoff table
  defined, 648–649
  illustrated, 649, 777
  information acquisition decision, 648–649
Payroll accounting
  compensation insurance, 885
  computers, use of, 892
  employee earnings records, 893
  factors affecting, 883
  federal income taxes, 883
  Federal Insurance Contributions Act, 883–885
  internal control, 896
  payroll master file, 893
  payroll register, 894
  pension plans, 886
  problems, magnitude of additional labor costs, 891–892
    volume of payroll transactions, 893–896
  procedures, 887–890
  separate checking account, use of, 894–896
  time cards, use of, 893
  unemployment taxes, 885
  vacation pay, 886–887
  voluntary items affecting labor costs, 885–887
Payroll master file, defined, 893
Payroll register, defined, 894
Pension, defined, 886
Performance evaluation
  behaviorally sound, 449–450, 507–508
  budget as a basis, 392
  dicretionary cost centers, 508–509
  flexible budget, use of, 455–456
  inflation, impact on, 554–556
  marketing, 505–507
  multinational organizations, 562
  nonmonetary data, 470, 507–508
  problem of unrecorded assets, 558–559
  responsibility accounting, controllable and noncontrollable costs, 450, 466–467, 504–505
    defined, 451
    manufacturing, 454–456
  responsibility centers, 453–454, 503, 545
  transfer pricing problem, 913–914, 922–924

Performance evaluation *(continued)*
See also Division; Performance reports; Variance(s)
Performance reports
characteristics, accurate, 451
behaviorally sound, 449–450
cost effective, 451
relevant, 450
timely, 450–451
corporate structure, 451–454, 467–469
defined, 6
discretionary cost centers, 508–509
full cost, 469–470
manufacturing, based on flexible budget, 455–456
full cost performance reports, 469–470
illustrated, 469
service departments costs, 469
marketing, compared with manufacturing, 504–507
illustrated, 506, 515
some problems, 505–507
use of variable cost of goods sold, 504
special decisions, use in, 507
See also Performance evaluation; Variance(s)
Period costs
allocated for pricing, 198–200
compared to product costs, 28
defined, 28
under absorption and variable costing, 343
Perpetual inventory system, defined, 811
Perquisite, defined, 563
Personal property, qualifying for investment tax credit, 719
PERT
crash cost, 818
crash time, 818
critical path, 817
defined, 815
job planning and control, use in, 725
network, illustrated, 816–817
normal cost, 818
normal time, 816
PERT/Cost, 818
PERT/Cost resource allocation supplement, 818–820
PERT/Time, 815–818
problem areas, 820
slack, 817
time and cost control, use in, 820
Piece rate system, described, 60
Planning and control, 5–6
See also Budgeting; Cost-volume-profit; Division; Performance evaluation; Variance(s)
Planning levels, 388–389
Plant-wide overhead rate
defined, 74
with multiple departments, 74–76
with service departments, 180, 182
Poisson distribution, use in safety stock models, 810
Posey, I. A., 95n, 142n, 304n, 420n
Post audit, defined, 732
Practical capacity, defined, 354
Predetermined overhead rate
defined, 62
development of, 69–71
Preferred stock, cost of, defined, 717
Present value, 957–960
Present value index, defined, 767
Present value of an annuity in arrears, 958–959
Prevention costs, defined, 857
Price index, defined, 243
Price-level changes
adjusting data in cost estimation for, 241–243
capital budgeting models, impact on, 726–732
investment decisions, impact on, 556–558
performance evaluation, impact on, 554–556
Pricing
absorption costing facilitates, 356
cost-based approaches, 659–660
cost-plus, 660–661
decisions, 656
economic approaches, 656–659
joint cost allocation and, 150
justification and legal forces, 55–56, 198, 662
policies, 656
role of costs, 198, 661–662
variable costing facilitates, 356
See also Transfer pricing
Prime product costs, defined, 30
Principal (in agency relationship), defined, 563
Probability tree
defined, 312
illustrated, 313
Process, defined, 103
Process costing
basic concepts, 102–106
compared to job-order costing, 102–103
equivalent units, 104–105
FIFO, 109–112
journal entries, 105, 108, 113–114, 117, 118, 120, 123
LIFO, 112
production report, cost of, described, 106
spoilage, 115–123
alternative treatments, 115–120, 598–607
disposal value, 122–123, 604–607
rework, 607
subsequent departments, 112–114
weighted average, 108–109
Process costing system, defined, 103
Product costing
compared to service costing, 33–35
concepts, 26–35
defined, 19
Product costs
compared to period costs, 28
conversion costs, 30
defined, 28
direct costs, 30
direct labor, 29
direct materials, 29
errors caused by magnitude of employees' fringe benefits, 891–892
factory overhead, 29
indirect costs, 30
prime costs, 30
Product line decisions, 507
Product margin, defined, 358
Product-mix decisions, 646, 662–671
Production budget
defined, 396
illustrated, 397, 407
Production departments, defined, 180

Profitability index; *see* Present value index
Profit center, defined, 453, 504
Profit planning, cost-volume-profit, 297–299
Profit-volume graph, described 295–296
Program results review, defined, 509
Prorate, defined, 73, 608
Prorating
  cost element method, 73–74, 609–610
  objective, 73, 593–594, 608
  reversal of, 612
  theoretically correct method, 609–610
  total cost method, 73–74, 610–611
Purchases budget, defined, 398
  illustrated for manufacturing firm, 398, 408
Purely competitive market, decribed, 657
Pyle, W. C., 559n

Quadratic loss function, 236
Quality costs
  defined, 857
  economics of, 859–860
  objective of measuring, 856
  report, illustrated, 858
  types of, 857–859
Quality of conformance, defined, 857
Quality of design, defined, 857

R; *see* Correlation coefficient
R charts
  defined, 845
  illustrated, 847, 850
Range (of sample), defined, 845
Rao, Kailas, J., 172n
Rappaport, A., 697n, 745n
Ratchet principle, defined, 392
Rate of return; *see* Capital-budgeting models, internal rate of return
Raw materials, described, 4
Rayburn, G., 661, 661n
Raymond, R. H., 926n
Real property, defined, 719
Regression analysis
  statistical assumptions, 262–263
  use in cost estimation, 235–239
Relevant costs
  defined, 36
  in inventory models, 799, 802–806
  in linear programming, 670–671
  in performance reports, 450
  See also Opportunity cost
Relevant range
  cost estimates, 25, 26, 240
  cost-volume-profit, 289, 301
  defined, 26
Reorder point, defined, 799
Residual income, defined, 551
Responsibility accounting
  basic tenet, 562
  comparison of marketing and manufacturing reports, 504
  defined, 451, 503
Responsibility center(s)
  defined, 453, 503
  evaluated as investment centers, 545
  types of, 453–454
Return on investment
  defined, 548, 659, 732
  performance measure, 548–551
  pricing decisions, 659
Revenue center, defined, 453, 503
Rework, defined, 607
Risk
  defined, 309n
  systematic, 776
Roach, J. D., 791n
Robichek, A. A., 310, 310n, 791n
Robinson-Patman Act, 662
Ronen, J., 921n
R-squared; *see* Coefficient of determination
Run (in control charts), defined, 848

Safety stocks, defined, 809
Salamon, G. L., 646n
Salary, defined, 20n
Sales
  forecast in budgeting, 396
  volume estimates, 290, 656–659
Sales budget
  defined, 396
  illustrated, 407
Sales variances; *see* Variance(s)
Scalar, defined, 203
Scatter diagram method (of cost estimation), defined, 234
Scrap
  defined, 157
  See also By-products and scrap
Securities and Exchange Commission, 2
Segment decisions, 646
Segment margin, defined, 359
Segment reports, defined, 357
Self-service, defined, 184
Selling and administrative expense budget
  defined, 398
  illustrated, 399, 409
Semivariable costs
  defined, 21
  See also Mixed costs
Sensitivity analysis
  in budgeting, 404
  defined, 309–310, 667
  in inventory models, 807
  in linear programming, 667–668
Service costing
  compared to product costing, 33–35
  defined, 33
Service department decisions, 645–646
Service departments
  cost allocation in performance reports, 469
  defined, 180
  predetermined allocation rates, 197–198
  self-service, 184
Shadow price, defined, 667
Shank, J. K., 193n
Simple interest, defined, 955
Simple linear regression, defined, 235
Simplex method, 666–667
Simulation, 313
Single rate methods (of service department cost allocation), defined, 194
Slack, in budgets, 392
Slack (in PERT), defined, 817
Social Security; *see* Federal Insurance Contributions Act
Solomons, D., 551n, 921, 921n
Sorter, G. H., 357, 357n, 378n
Special cause (of variance), 856
Special decisions
  role of controller, 8
  use of cost data, 6
  use of performance reports, 507

Special order, 6, 644, 914–915
Split-off point, defined, 147
Spoilage
  abnormal, defined, 120, 598
  alternative treatments, 115–120, 598–607
  disposal value, 122–123, 604–607
  normal, defined, 120, 598
  rework costs, 607
Spoiled units, defined, 115, 598
Staff managers, defined, 7
Standard cost(s)
  as basic building block in budgeting, 393
  compared to actual and normal, 589–590
  defined, 392, 588
  development of, 393–394
  in financial statements, 593
  motivating standard, 394
  as subgoal, 391–392
  systems, characteristics, 589–594
    cost flows, described, 590–593
    cost flows, illustrated, 591–592
    disposition of variances, 593–594
    inventory valuation, 589–590
    job-order costing, 607–608
    joint products, 613
    journal entries, 590–593, 597, 603, 606, 607
    not required for variance analysis, 588
    process costing with spoilage, 598–607
    process costing without spoilage, 594–597
    rework, 607
  tight standards, 394
  uses, 394, 588
  See also Variance(s)
Standard cost center, defined, 453
Standard deviation, defined, 249
Standard error of the coefficient
  defined, 261
  equation for computing, 261
Standard error of the estimate
  defined, 259
  equation for computing, 259
Standard normal distribution, defined, 250
Standards, ex post, 474–475
State Unemployment Commission, 885
Statement of cost of goods manufactured
  defined, 31
  discussed, 30–33
  illustrated, 33
Statement of cost of goods manufactured and sold
  defined, 31
  illustrated, 34
States of nature, defined, 648
Statistical analysis, of uncertainty, 310–312
Statistical assumptions in regression analysis, 262–263
Statistical concepts, 246–254
Statistical considerations in regression analysis, 254–261
Statistical process control
  control charts for unknown distributions, 853
  control limits for *R* charts, 847–848
  control limits for *X*-bar charts, 851–852
  defined, 844
  out-of-control points, reasons for, 852–853
  R charts, 845–851
  runs tests for *R* charts, 848–851
  runs tests for *X*-bar charts, 852
  X-bar charts, 851–853
Step costs
  cost-volume-profit, 301
  defined, 22
  illustrated, 21
  variable costs as an approximation, 22–23
Step method (of service department cost allocation)
  defined, 188
  illustrated, 188–191
Step-down method (of service department cost allocation); *see* Step method
Sticky costs, described, 262
Stochastic simulation
  defined, 313
  illustrated, 314–315
  PERT, use in, 820n
Stockout, 808–811
Strategic planning, defined, 388
Subsidiary account, 29, 58, 59, 181
Subsidiary ledger, 29, 58–59, 181
Successive allocation method (of service department cost allocation), 194
Sundry accounts, described, 105n
Sunk costs, defined, 35
Swalm, R. O., 315, 316n
Swed, Frieda S., 849
Symmetric distribution, illustrated, 247
Systematic risk, defined, 776

Tang, R. Y. W., 926n
Target profit, 659–660
Tax Equity and Fiscal Responsibility Act, 719
Taxes
  absorption costing acceptable, 356
  cost of capital, 716–717
  depreciation as a tax shield, 721–723, 759–760
  federal income taxes withheld, 883
  FICA, 883–885
  historical cost, 35
  impact on break-even point, 303
  impact on cash break-even point, 303–304
  impact on cost behavior, 303
  international transfer pricing, 924–926
  investment tax credit, 719–720
  lease-purchase decisions, 773–774
  loss carrybacks and carryforwards, 303n
  role of controller, 8
  unemployment, 885
  variable costing not acceptable, 356
Taylor, R. E., 646n
t-distribution, defined, 253
t-distribution and tables, use of, 253–254
Technology, problem in cost estimation, 241
Territory margin, defined, 358
Theil, 262n
Theoretical capacity, defined, 354
Theory X, 390
Theory Y, 391
Thies, J. B., 771, 771n, 773, 773n, 774n
Time adjusted rate of return; *see* Capital-budgeting models, internal rate of return

Time cards, described, 893
Time-series analysis, 239
Time value of money
  annuity, 958–959
  compound interest, 954–956
  concept, 954
  deferred annuity, 959–960
  finding an interest rate, 960–961
  future amount, 954–956
  present value, 957–960
  simple interest, 954–955
Total cost
  behavior, 22–23
  economic models, 24–26
  equation, 23
  illustrated, 22, 24, 25
Total cost method (of prorating variances), defined, 73, 608
Total costs in process, defined, 108
Transfer price
  accounting entries, 926
  alternative transfer prices, full cost or full cost plus, 920
    market price, 919
    negotiated prices, 921
    other, 921
    variable cost, 919–920
    variable cost plus opportunity cost, 920
  corporate viewpoint, 914–915
  defined, 913
  economics of, 915–918
  international, 924–926
  practices, 921
  problem, 913, 918, 922–924
Transferred-in costs, 112–114
Treasurer, defined, 9
T-statistic, defined, 261
Two-bin inventory system, defined, 811–812

U.S. Chamber of Commerce, 891
U.S. Congress, 198, 719
U.S. Navy, 815
U.S. price commission, 56
Uncertainty
  approaches to analysis, capital asset pricing model, 776–777
    decision trees, 777–778
    probability trees, 312–313, 776–778
    sensitivity analysis, 309–310, 776
    statistical analysis, 310–312
    stochastic simulation, 313–315, 776
  budgeting, 394, 404
  capital budgeting, 776–778
  cost-volume-profit, 308–315
  defined, 309n
  inventory planning and control, 808–811
  linear programming, 667–669
  utility, 315–317
  See also Variance(s), decision to investigate
Unemployment taxes, described, 885
Unequal variance, 262
Unfunded pension plans, defined, 886
Unit contribution margin, defined, 291
Utility, 315–317
Utility theory, defined, 315

Vacation pay, accounting for, 886–887
VanHorne, J. C., 777n
Variability (in control charts), defined, 845
Variable cost
  approximation of step costs, 22–23
  compared with marginal cost, 25–26
  defined, 20
  illustrated, 21, 22
Variable costing
  arguments in favor of, 356–357
  behavioral classification of costs, 345
  compared with absorption costing, 343–348, 360
  controversy, 356–357
  defined, 343
  income statement format, 345, 346, 348, 353
  performance reports, 510–514, 515
  reconciliation with absorption costing, 344–348
  relationship to cost-volume-profit models, 341
Variable overhead variances; *see* Variance(s)
Variable-cost markup, 660–661
Variables data, defined, 844
Variance(s)
  abnormal spoilage, 599–603
  administration, 512
  classification as favorable or unfavorable, 455, 505n
  decision significance, control, 843
    none, 842–843
    planning, 843
  decision to investigate, estimating probability process is in control, 860–862
    expected costs criterion, 854–856
    materiality criterion, 844
    statistical significance criterion, 844–854
  discretionary cost center budget, 509
  disposition, adjustment to Cost of Goods Sold, 72, 593
    criteria, 71–74, 593–594
    interim financial statements, 71, 593
    prorating, cost-element method, 73–74, 609–610
    prorating, theoretically correct method, 609–610
    prorating, total cost method, 73–74, 610–611
    subsequent periods, 612
  distribution costs, 510
  fixed overhead, budget, 462–463
    volume, 463–464
  flexible budgets, use of, 455–456
  labor, efficiency, 460–461
    mix, 475
    pure efficiency, 475
    rate, 460–461
    total, 460–461
    yield, 475
  materials, joint price-quantity, 458–459
    mix, 473–475
    price, 456–460
    pure price, 457–459
    pure quantity, 458–459
    quantity, 457–460
    timing, 459–460
    total, 456–460, 472–474
    yield, 473–475
  overhead, four-way, 464–465
    three-way, 464–466
    two-way, 464, 466
    See also fixed overhead and variable overhead
  responsibility for, 856
  sales, based on budgeted variable costing income, 510

Variance(s) *(continued)*
sales contribution variances distinguished from revenue variances, 519–520
sales of a single product, sales price, 511–514
sales volume, 511–514
total, 510–514
sales of multiple products, pure sales volume, 515–518
sales mix, 515–518
sales price, 517
sales revenue variance, defined, 503
sources, inappropriate standards, 842
measurement errors, 841
operating errors, 842
random fluctuations, 841
variable overhead, efficiency, 461–462
spending, 461–462
total, 461–462
volume, appendix to flexible budget, 463–464
based on standards, 463–466
Variance (statistical), defined, 249
Vector (in matrix algebra), defined, 201
Vector of knowns
defined, 204
illustrated, 204
Vector of unknowns
defined, 204
illustrated, 204–205
Vergin, R. C., 450, 450n
Vice-president of finance, 9
Volume variance; *see* Variance(s)

W-2 form, defined, 885
W-4 form, defined, 883
Wage-price guidelines, 56
Wages, defined, 20n
Walter, C. K., 926n
Waste, defined, 157
Watson, 262n
Weighted average process costing, 108–109
Weighted-average cost of capital
defined, 716
See also Cost of capital
Weingartner, H. M., 770, 770n, 771n
Weston, J. F., 777n
Williamson, R. W., 648n
Wolk, H. I., 471, 471n
Work-in-process, defined, 4

X-bar charts
defined, 845
illustrated, 852, 853

Yield variance, 473–475
Yunker, P. J., 921n

z-distribution; *see* Normal distribution
Zimmerman, J. L., 507n, 564n